The Papers of Dwight David Eisenhower

THE PAPERS OF DWIGHT DAVID EISENHOWER

THE PRESIDENCY: KEEPING THE PEACE
XXI

EDITORS

LOUIS GALAMBOS   DAUN VAN EE

EXECUTIVE EDITOR
ELIZABETH S. HUGHES

ASSOCIATE EDITORS
JANET R. BRUGGER   ROBIN D. COBLENTZ
JILL A. FRIEDMAN

ASSISTANT EDITOR
NANCY KAY BERLAGE

THE JOHNS HOPKINS UNIVERSITY PRESS

BALTIMORE AND LONDON

This book has been brought to publication with the generous assistance of the National Endowment for the Humanities, the National Historical Publications and Records Commission, the Eisenhower World Affairs Institute, and the France-Merrick Foundation.

The Johns Hopkins University Press, 2715 North Charles Street,
Baltimore Maryland 21218-4363
www.press.jhu.edu

All illustrations in this volume are from the
Dwight D. Eisenhower Library, Abilene,
Kansas, unless indicated otherwise.

Library of Congress Cataloging-in-Publication Data

Eisenhower, Dwight D. (Dwight David), 1890–1969.
The papers of Dwight D. Eisenhower.

Vol. 6 edited by A. D. Chandler and L Galambos;
v. 7– , by L. Galambos.
Includes bibliographies and index.
Contents: v. 1–5. The war years.—[etc.]—
v. 10–11. Columbia University.—v. 12–13. NATO and the
Campaign of 1952.
1. World War, 1939–1945—United States.   2. World War,
1939–1945—Campaigns.   3. United States—Politics and
government—1953–1961.   4. Presidents—United States—
Election—1952.   5. Eisenhower, Dwight D. (Dwight David),
1890–1969.   6. Presidents—United States—Archives.
I. Chandler, Alfred Dupont, ed.   II. Galambos, Louis, ed.
III. United States. President (1953–1961 : Eisenhower)
IV. Title.
E742.5.E37   1970   973.921′092′4[B]   65-027672
ISBN 0-8018-1078-7 (v. 1–5)
ISBN 0-8018-2061-8 (v. 6–9)
ISBN 0-8018-2720-5 (v. 10–11)
ISBN 0-8018-3726-x (v. 12–13)
ISBN 0-8018-4752-4 (v. 14–17)
ISBN 0-8018-6638-3 (v. 18)
ISBN 0-8018-6684-7 (v. 19)
ISBN 0-8018-6699-5 (v. 20)
ISBN 0-8018-6718-5 (v. 21)

We dedicate these four concluding volumes of *The Papers of Dwight David Eisenhower* to the Board of Advisors of the Eisenhower Papers and to the Board of Trustees of the Johns Hopkins University, who together made it possible for us to complete this grand project.

Contents

The Papers of Dwight David Eisenhower

The Presidency: Keeping the Peace

Ending an Era

AUGUST 1960 TO JANUARY 1961

23

"To keep the Free World free"

To Harold Macmillan   *August 8, 1960*
Cable. Secret

Dear Harold:[1] Since my return from Denver I have discussed more
fully your letter concerning the Cuban problem which Chris kindly
acknowledged for me at my request.[2] It is indeed most gratifying
and reassuring that we are in general agreement in our analysis and
estimate that the Castro regime is fully committed to a course in-
imical to our mutual interests in the area and that the only hope
for an improvement in the situation must lie in its replacement.[3]

As you have so accurately pictured, the great majority of the liberal middle-class elements in Cuba, which were primarily responsible for Castro's accession to power, have now withdrawn their support and many have fled the country to engage in open opposition
to the Castro regime. From these very people who are the most
knowledgeable as to the internal political situation we have received
the unanimous view that the Castro regime's police control and
Communist terror tactics have thoroughly intimidated the politically
articulate Cubans, and that left undisturbed, the regime will increase
its domination to the point that internal opposition is unlikely ever
to attain sufficient strength and resolution to overthrow Castro.
Scarcely a day passes that opposition leaders do not stress to us their
view that with the clear promise of support from the U.S.S.R. and
Red China, time is now working for Castro. In the short run I doubt
that this is true; Castro's open bid for a satellite role has had the effect of thoroughly alarming most of the Governments in this Hemisphere and, hopefully, has disposed many of them to support pressures and efforts to bring about a change of regime in Cuba. Yet
their foundations too often rest uneasily on outmoded societies ripe
for change, and to make such changes in an evolutionary manner
is the responsibility of any wise government. Should Castro manage
to survive for another year or more, these nations run the risk of
being overtaken by revolution with conditions such as those now existing in Cuba. This kind of change, when it brings Communism in
its wake, is intolerable from the standpoint of our national interest
and that of the liberal democratic Christian tradition which we all
share.[4]

You ask quite understandably how we really mean to achieve our
aim of unseating Castro and replacing him by a more suitable
regime. Depending somewhat on the results of the forthcoming
Council of Foreign Ministers in San Jose, Costa Rica on August sixteenth, we expect to move ahead with further economic measures

designed to bring pressure on the Cuban economy. To be sure, this will cause some Cubans to rally to Castro's support, but the great mass of Cubans, who were completely apathetic toward Castro and Bastista before January first, 1959, are still chiefly concerned with their own individual well-being.[5] We are now receiving more and more reports of a return to that earlier apathy on the part of the *campesinos*, particularly as they discover that most of the promises have been empty ones and that often they are worse off than before.[6]

Moreover, although relatively poor and accustomed to hardship by our standards, by Latin American standards Cubans have had one of the highest levels of living in the area and far higher than comparable classes in the Middle and Far East.[7] A recently returned long-time resident among the country people remarked, "The average Cuban sugar worker wants to receive his earnings in cash and go to the store, buy a white *guayabera*,[8] white shoes, a bottle of rum and go to a dance; not be paid in script redeemable at a government (people's) store where only work clothing and rice and beans are to be had and a lecture by the Government official is the only entertainment offered." I do not underestimate the strength of the fanatic minority still dedicated to Castro nor conceive of any broad support for the abandonment of all of the measures taken by his regime. On the other hand, we have ample evidence to suggest that even among the masses there is as of now no deep unquestioning commitment to his revolution. Moreover, the Government's virulent anti-United States campaign until now has had singularly little effect despite its control and utilization of all the public information media in the country.

The recent spontaneous gesture of protest by the Congregation at the Cathedral in Habana which shouted "Cuba, Yes; Communism, No" has been followed by a pastoral letter read on August 7 in all the Catholic churches on the island in which the communist influence now evident in the present Cuban regime is strongly condemned.[9] Reports of growing opposition among students to the seizure of the University of Habana by a Communist-led minority is another hopeful sign.[10] We must emphasize that the world struggle is not Communism against capitalism; it is dictatorship against freedom. The Cuban development is one manifestation of this truth.[11]

We are steadily intensifying our counter-propaganda efforts in the other countries of the Hemisphere. We shall emphasize to the OAS and to the UN whenever the occasion may arise the extent to which communism has assumed control in Cuba. We shall seek and use every possible opportunity short of outright intervention which might bring pressure to bear on Castro. In line with this latter point we have sought informally by various means not only to discourage

To Harold Macmillan   *August 1, 1960*
Cable. Secret

Dear Harold:[1] Thank you for your letter of July 22 which further re-
assures me of our common understanding of the several problems
which we have been discussing.[2] With particular reference to our
joint consultations with de Gaulle, I have finally settled on a further
reply to his letter of June 10, which I am assured reflects Selwyn
Lloyd's comments to Chris Herter and your views as reported during the close consultation with your Embassy here. I will be sending
my letter out within the next several days, but am enclosing an advance copy for you.[3]

I have also just received from your Embassy the draft of your own
letter to de Gaulle and believe that it is very good. One point, however, troubles me somewhat. I would hope that you would agree to
deleting the last sentence in the first paragraph, or perhaps changing it to reflect the fact that we both have the same attitude on strategic questions. I wonder if you might not also like to note in the second sentence of the same paragraph that you had felt free to seek
my views in as much as de Gaulle told you he had sent me a copy
of his letter to you.[4]

With warm personal regard, *As ever*

[1] State Department officials sent this message to the American embassy in London
for delivery to Prime Minister Macmillan.
[2] Responding to Eisenhower's message regarding U.S. policy toward Cuba (see no.
1582), Macmillan had characterized Castro as "the very Devil." Cuba's position—"sitting right at your doorstep"—made the strategic implications even more important
than economic considerations, Macmillan had written.
[3] For background on tripartite consultations among British, French, and U.S. officials, and de Gaulle's June 10 letter, see no. 1572. "Our people are fixing up with
yours the right kind of line," Macmillan had written. "It seems to me that what we
must do is neither to disappoint the French nor lead them up the garden path. We
want broad strategic discussions but we do not want to upset NATO. This is a delicate but not impossible balance." Eisenhower had suggested to Secretary Herter that
the reply to de Gaulle might include the possibility of tripartite discussions of NATO
problems. After seeing a draft reply, however, British Foreign Secretary Lloyd had
insisted that the suggestion be removed (Telephone conversation, Eisenhower and
Herter, July 1, 1960, Herter Papers, Telephone Conversations; and State, *Foreign Relations, 1958–1960*, vol. VII, pt. 2, *Western Europe*, p. 398). For Eisenhower's reply to
de Gaulle see the following document.
[4] Macmillan would send Eisenhower the final version of his response to de Gaulle.
"You will see," he wrote "that this takes account of the points you made." The last
sentence of the first paragraph would read: "I have not sent you a full answer sooner,
since you told me you had sent a copy of your letter to President Eisenhower and I
thought it was only sensible to find out what he thought about the strategic aspect

1598   *EM, AWF, International Series*

To Charles André Joseph Marie de Gaulle
Cable. Secret   *August 2, 1960*

Dear General de Gaulle:[1] I am replying further to your letter of June 10, to which I had sent a preliminary comment on June 18, regarding the more effective organization of our tripartite consultations.[2]

I think we are now in agreement with regard to the method of our consultation in the political field, and our designated representatives should accordingly begin during the summer to plan for the next regular occasion for a tripartite Foreign Ministers' meeting, which would normally occur in New York during the early fall at the time of the opening of the United Nations General Assembly. Should an emergency arise in the interim, our Foreign Ministers might conceivably need to meet earlier. With regard to tripartite political consultations at the highest level, it is my own concept, with which I know you agree, that these occasional meetings play an important role in the organization of our work and the conduct of our business.

Passing to the question of strategic cooperation which you raise in your letter, I believe that there are means of arranging tripartite military discussions here which would meet the concerns which you mention.[3] During some of our previous tripartite talks in 1959, military representatives participated. Discussions were held on African questions in the State Department at which high-ranking military officers of the three countries were present. At that time, the French representative, Ambassador Alphand, who was accompanied by General Gelee, asked for separate military talks.[4] Subsequently, it is my understanding, we agreed to holding such separate talks among our military representatives. However, this offer was not followed up subsequently by our partners, and hence I assume the basis then envisaged did not meet your desire. Accordingly, I now suggest a somewhat different approach in the effort to meet your point of view.

I remain ready to hear from you your more precise ideas as to when tripartite conversations on military and strategic questions might profitably be held. I think we should not contemplate formal combined staff planning but I am prepared to have our military representatives engage in talks on subjects of interest to you in various parts of the world, primarily outside the NATO area. I will wait to hear from you on this point at your convenience.

With regard to who would participate in these talks, I would assume that, as was envisaged in the past, these talks would take place here, and I would designate a high-ranking officer. This would not be our Representative on the Standing Group. However, I can understand that you would wish to designate your senior officer in Washington, who is, I understand, your Standing Group Representative.[5] I have no objection to this on the understanding that he would be acting in a national capacity, and we would not be thus interfering with the work of a NATO mechanism.

I have informed Prime Minister Macmillan of my views on this subject, and believe that we can coordinate satisfactorily our thoughts so that tripartite consultations in the military field soon occur.[6]

I would also like to point out, in this general connection, my own view that the soundest basis for developing between us a close European military cooperation, lies in the perfecting of a viable NATO, and that we should take all possible steps to this end. I believe this is a matter of capital importance to us all, and I would greatly appreciate your comments on this particular point.

I shall look forward to hearing from you and take this opportunity to repeat that I, for my part, am prepared to have our military experts enter into discussions with your representatives and our British friends at your mutual convenience on military and strategic questions.[7]

With warm personal regard, *Sincerely*

[1] State Department officials drafted this message to General de Gaulle. After Defense Secretary Gates approved the draft, Eisenhower sent it to the American embassy in Paris for delivery to the French president (State, *Foreign Relations, 1958–1960*, vol. VII, pt. 2, *Western Europe*, p. 398).

[2] For background see the preceding document. Eisenhower's June 18 letter is no. 1565.

[3] De Gaulle's June 10 letter had warned that the absence of strategic cooperation "would detract greatly from the importance of political cooperation." He recommended that the military representatives to NATO's Standing Group should hold tripartite strategic discussions outside the group's regular deliberations (State, *Foreign Relations, 1958–1960*, vol. VII, pt. 2, *Western Europe*, p. 386). Eisenhower had asked Secretary Herter if there weren't "some way we could really get outside of this standing group into a real tripartite discussion of strategic and military questions in return for which De Gaulle would get on with NATO." Herter had replied that France was basically interested in nuclear weapons and that "there was danger of a real break in this whole picture" (Telephone conversation, Eisenhower and Herter, July 1, 1960, Herter Papers, Telephone Conversations).

[4] The talks had taken place in Washington on April 16–21, 1959. Hervé Alphand was the French ambassador to the United States; Max Gelée was the French representa-

tive to the NATO Standing Group until July 1960 (see State, *Foreign Relations, 1958–1960*, vol. XIV, *Africa*, pp. 44–53; see also *ibid.*, vol. VII, pt. 2, *Western Europe*, p. 193).
[5] General Clark L. Ruffner, former commander of the Third Army, was the U.S. representative to the Standing Group.
[6] See the preceding document.
[7] For developments see no. 1610.

1599   *EM, AWF, International Series: Ghana*

To Kwame Nkrumah   *August 2, 1960*
Cable. Secret

As Ambassador Halm has doubtless reported to you, the State Department has been keeping in touch with African Ambassadors here on the rapidly changing situation in the Congo.[1] We are agreed that this situation is unique and that, while it presents grave dangers to world peace, it is also a great challenge to statesmanship and an opportunity for the UN in general and the African states in particular. If this challenge can be successfully met I feel that the world may be able to enter on a new stage of interdependence and healthy development.[2]

We are also agreed that the immediate problem is the speedy resolution of the Belgian troop and Katanga questions.[3] I am convinced that SYG Hammarskjold, though hampered by strong conflicting pressures and passions, is doing his best to carry out his SC mandate. In this effort the US is backing and supporting him to the hilt, not only because we believe that the SC resolution is the right one, but also because we feel that if the UN were unsuccessful or discredited in the Congo, the results for world peace and cooperation would be disastrously tragic.

Important as are these immediate problems, I believe we should start looking beyond them to the situation which will exist after they are solved. The Congo will, I fear, have almost no trained experienced personnel to administer the country and operate the economy. This puts the Congo, it seems to us, in a position unique amongst all newly independent countries. It will be forced for a period of a few years at least, to entrust the country's essential services to outsiders. In this situation it seems vital to me that the Congo be effectively protected against conflicting power politics or other pressures which could not but have an unfortunate effect on its healthy, harmonious and independent development. Our first thought was that this protection might be provided by means of a contract between the UN and the Congolese Government under which the former would be the exclusive agent for the supply of administrative, technical and financial assistance to the latter. As Secretary Herter told Prime Minister Lumumba last week, the US is prepared to contribute its fair share to this common effort.[4]

In these circumstances Secretary Herter and I would greatly appreciate the benefit of an exchange of views with you. I am therefore asking my Ambassador to the Congo, The Honorable Clare H. Timberlake, to stop at Accra to see you, probably on August 5.[5] He has been back in Washington on consultation for a few days during which Secretary Herter and I have discussed the Congo situation with him fully.[6] He has my full confidence and I hope you will be able to see him and share with him quite frankly your thoughts on this urgent problem.

[1] William Q. M. Halm, ambassador from Ghana to the United States.

[2] Intertribal conflict and military rebellion had broken out in the Republic of Congo, formerly the Belgian Congo, a few days after gaining its independence on June 30, 1960. Without the permission of the Congolese government, Belgium had deployed troops to protect its remaining white citizens; this action violated an as yet unratified treaty made by the two countries on the eve of independence. In response, the Congolese government had appealed to the United Nations for military aid to help restore order to the region, and the Security Council had agreed. On July 14 the Security Council had passed a resolution authorizing Secretary General Hammarskjöld to organize military and technical assistance and asking the Belgian troops to withdraw from the Congo (Telephone conversations, Eisenhower and Herter, July 12, 13, Aug. 8, 9, and Hagerty and Herter, July 20, Herter Papers, Telephone Conversations). For background see Eisenhower, *Waging Peace*, pp. 571–76; see also *Public Papers of the Presidents: Eisenhower, 1960–61*, pp. 635–36, 679, 683; Ernest W. Lefever, *The Crisis in the Congo: A United Nations Force in Action* (Washington, D.C., 1965), esp. pp. 1–45; Rajeshwar Dayal, *Mission for Hammarskjold: The Congo Crisis* (Princeton, 1976), pp. 1–47.

[3] Katanga Province had declared itself independent from the Congo Republic on July 11. With large copper and uranium mines, it was the wealthiest of the Congo's provinces and retained substantial Belgian investments. Katanga's new president had requested the presence of the Belgian military while refusing U.N. troops right of entry. The Congolese government accused Belgium of masterminding the secession. For developments see no. 1611.

[4] On July 27, 1960, Herter and other officials had met with Congo's Prime Minister Patrice Lumumba. A former postal clerk, Lumumba had emerged as the leader of the militant faction of the Congo's nationalist movement. The Administration viewed him as an unstable, pro-Soviet force in the increasingly conflicted Congolese government. Lumumba had come to the United States to solicit technical assistance and economic aid and had threatened to turn elsewhere if the United Nations did not persuade Belgium to remove its troops (State, *Foreign Relations, 1958–1960*, vol. XIV, *Africa*, pp. 351–66, 368).

[5] Timberlake (A.B. University of Michigan 1929), the new U.S. Ambassador to the Congo, would meet August 6 with Nkrumah, an anti-colonialist whom the Administration viewed as an ally of Lumumba. Although Nkrumah would agree that the United Nations should handle all technical and financial assistance to the Congo, he would write Eisenhower that any attempt to detach Katanga from the Congo state, a development that some Africans felt the United States supported, would have "di-

sastrous consequences" for African opinion and the balance of world political forces (Aug. 5, 1960, AWF/I: Ghana; State, *Foreign Relations, 1958–1960*, vol. XIV, *Africa*, pp. 390–92). For developments see no. 1605.

[6] Timberlake had attended the National Security Council meeting on August 1, along with Eisenhower and the Secretary of State (NSC meeting minutes, AWF/NSC).

1600 *EM, AWF, International Series:*
Macmillan

To HAROLD MACMILLAN *August 4, 1960*
Cable. Top secret

Dear Harold:[1] Many thanks for your helpful message of July 30 with further regard to POLARIS.[2]

I am delighted that you have been able to reconsider the matter of facilities in Scottish waters and that your people feel they can work out some suitable position in the Clyde area.

I fully understand your problem in presenting this project in such a way as to get the fullest public support for it in your country. I therefore agree with your suggestion that our people should proceed immediately to discuss the matter here in Washington, and I am asking that either Chris Herter or Under Secretary Merchant get together with Harold Caccia at an early date for further detailed conversations on this important subject.[3]

With warm regard, *As ever*

[1] State Department officials cabled this message to the American embassy in London for delivery to Prime Minister Macmillan.

[2] For background see no. 1584. Macmillan had told Eisenhower that his Cabinet had discussed the Polaris issue further and that they had agreed to reconsider the U.S. request for berthing facilities in the Clyde River. "They fully realize the importance of this project to the strength of the West, and for the peace and security of the world." In order to gain the fullest possible public support, Macmillan said, the question of operational control of the missile submarines had to be addressed. He understood Eisenhower's difficulties with his original proposal regarding dual control (see no. 1584) but hoped they could work out a suitable plan that could relieve the anxieties of the British people (Macmillan to Eisenhower, July 30, 1960, PREM 11/2940).

[3] For developments see no. 1686.

To Robert McGowan Littlejohn   *August 4, 1960*
Personal

Dear John: With further reference to your letter regarding General McNamara, I find that the date of his retirement, under existing conditions, would be in July of 1962 (rather than June 1, 1961 as you state in your letter).[1]

I am well aware of the competence and reputation of General McNamara. The problem, as you know, is that there is a limit to the number of Lieutenant Generals allowed by law. I can only say that I shall keep the matter very much in mind.

While I am always glad to see you and George, nothing could be gained by meeting to discuss this particular problem.[2] I repeat that I have high admiration for General McNamara; the problem is something entirely removed from his qualifications.[3]

With warm regard, *As ever*

[1] Major General Littlejohn had spent most of his career in the Quartermaster Corps. He had been with Eisenhower in the Philippines and in 1942 became Quartermaster for the European Theater of Operations (ETO). He headed the War Assets Administration in 1946–1947, before retiring with a disability (for background see Chandler, *War Years*, no. 385; Galambos, *Chief of Staff*, no. 941; Galambos, *NATO and the Campaign of 1952*, no. 735; and Galambos and van Ee, *The Middle Way*, no. 123). Littlejohn had written on July 23 that Quartermaster General Andrew Thomas McNamara would be forced to retire from active duty on June 1 unless promoted or given a change of assignment. Littlejohn praised McNamara's record as Quartermaster General and said his retirement would be a "tragedy to the Army, to the Nation and to National Defence." On July 25 the President had promised to look into the matter. After checking with the Army, Eisenhower learned that although McNamara would complete the normal four-year tour in June 1961, he would not have to retire until July 1962, when he would have completed 35 years of service and five years as a permanent Major General.

[2] Littlejohn had suggested that he and Major General George Anthony Horkan (USA, ret.) meet with the President. Horkan was chairman of the U.S. Committee on Purchases of Blind-Made Products. He had served as Chief Quartermaster of the European command before he became Quartermaster General in 1951 (for background see Galambos, *NATO and the Campaign of 1952*, no. 226, and Galambos and van Ee, *The Middle Way*, no. 642). All correspondence is in the same file as the document.

[3] At the time of his retirement in 1964 McNamara would be promoted to the rank of Lieutenant General.

To Arthur Sherwood Flemming   *August 5, 1960*

Dear Arthur: Much as I *like* your comments concerning my talk before the Republican National Convention, I cannot hope that it made such an impact as you suggest.[1] But even if it approached the heights you suggest, I am more than gratified. I am particularly pleased because I worked so hard on it in an effort to express as clearly as possible my basic philosophy and, in so doing, to try to convince the listening audience of the necessity for continuing the policies and programs for which the Republican Party stands.[2] If in some measure I succeeded, I am more than repaid for any effort on my part.

New subject: Monday afternoon I saw Dr. Jules Stein and Dr. Sydney Farber.[3] I think you know that one of Dr. Stein's primary interests is research in the field of prevention of blindness. I asked the gentlemen to come to see you to present their case—and some time after I am back in Washington I should like to talk to you further about the matter.[4]

With warm regard, and again my thanks, *As ever*

[1] HEW Secretary Flemming's letter is not in EM. On Eisenhower's address to the Republican National Convention see no. 1592; see also *Public Papers of the Presidents: Eisenhower, 1960–61*, pp. 589–601.

[2] Eisenhower had said that the delegates had come to the Convention "with a unity of basic conviction and philosophy unprecedented in the nation's political history. This is because the purposes and ideals for which your Party has striven, have commanded your loyal cooperation and the respect of the public. And under them our people have realized great gains."

[3] Jules Stein (M.D. Rush Medical College 1921) was chairman of the board of the Music Corporation of America, which he had founded in 1924. Trained as an ophthalmologist, Stein had created (1959) an organization entitled Research to Prevent Blindness, Incorporated. Sidney Farber (M.D. Harvard 1927), Professor of Pathology at the Harvard Medical School, was also chairman of the Division of Laboratories and Research of the Children's Medical Center in Boston and the founder and Scientific Director of the Children's Cancer Research Foundation.

[4] Stein and Farber would meet with Eisenhower in Newport on August 1, 1960, to ask for the President's help in getting congressional support for an increase of $250 million in medical research funding by the National Institutes of Health (NIH) (see Gosden to Whitman, July 20, 1960, and other documents in same file as document; see also *Congressional Quarterly Almanac*, vol. XVI, *1960*, pp. 383–86). On August 6 Stein and Farber would report in a letter to the President that they had met with Flemming and that he had given "fresh consideration" to an increased level of spending that would represent "not only an amount which can be spent wisely, but also the amount which, when joined with the constantly increasing private efforts, will form the foundation for a medical research program of a size commensurate with the magnitude of the problem" (same file as document). On August 26 Congress would pass a $4.35 billion appropriation bill to finance the Labor and the Health,

Education and Welfare Departments for the next fiscal year. The total amount was $334,135,950 over the President's initial budget request, with most of the increase coming in additional funding for NIH and hospital construction (see *New York Times*, Aug. 26, 27, 1960).

1603   *EM, WHCF, Official File 147-C*

To Edgar Newton Eisenhower   *August 6, 1960*
Personal

Dear Ed: I shall of course be delighted to have you use a set of my clubs in your match with the British jurists. I have several different sets and you can decide when you arrive in Washington which seems best for you. I expect to be there the latter part of the month, but if I am not, Bob Schulz can see that you are fully equipped.[1]

With regard to federal versus state rights, I shall pass along to Dick Nixon your comments. I wonder, however, if you know about the urgent and practical efforts we have been making over these past seven years to return to the states "the rights which the federal government has usurped."[2] One of the greatest obstacles we have encountered has been the reluctance of the governors to take back the authority and responsibility which the Administration believes are really [theirs]. In this effort there is included the proposal that certain special tax revenues should be [returned to the states].[3]

As I say, governors themselves are reluctant to take on these responsibilities because of the problem created when the federal government stops, for example, taxing certain telephone usage, [or] having to try to get their state legislatures to raise an equivalent amount of taxes themselves. *This they do not like to do.*

In other words, I agree with your theory, but it is not always so easy to apply.

With warm regard, *As ever*

[1] Edgar had written on August 2 (same file as document) that he had been invited to play golf with British golfers who would attend the American Bar Association convention in Washington, D.C., at the end of August. He did not wish to bring clubs across the country for just two games, and thought that since Eisenhower's hands were of similar size, the President's "grips would come closer to fitting me than any I could find otherwise." Colonel Robert L. Schulz was the President's military aide.
[2] The President's brother had written that he was "happy about the Republican nominees," and hoped that "Nixon will give some consideration to the constitutional differences in the rights and privileges of the federal government and the respective states." He was convinced that "anyone advocating a return to the states of the rights which the federal government has usurped, will win enthusiastic support from a great many people who might otherwise remain home on election day."

[3] The remainder of this sentence is missing from the text in our source. In 1957 Eisenhower had created a Joint Federal-State Action Committee, composed of governors and federal executive branch officials, and had charged them with finding a way to transfer specific functions and revenue sources from the federal to the state governments. The committee, which dissolved itself in April 1960, admitted it had failed in its mission, having agreed only to proposals shifting to the states federal programs involving vocational education and sewage plant construction, along with a portion of the ten percent excise tax on local telephone service (*Congressional Quarterly Almanac*, vol. XVI, *1960*, p. 366).

1604   *EM, WHCF,*
                                        President's Personal File 171

To WILLIAM EDWARD ROBINSON   *August 6, 1960*

Dear Bill: Just a line to thank you for your letter of the third. I am heartened by the report you give of at least some disaffection among the Southern Democrats.[1]

I am sorry you could not make it this weekend, but I realize the invitation was very late and I quite understand. And I am grateful to you for giving me so much of your time earlier.[2]

With warm regard, *As ever*

P.S. I'll see what I can do about that Eisenhower Exchange Fellowship dinner, but at this point my fall schedule is most uncertain.[3]

[1] Coca-Cola President Robinson's August 3, 1960, letter is in the same file as the document. He had described what he called "almost universal revulsion" caused by the Democratic Convention in Los Angeles. He believed that despite the entrenched opposition among third and fourth generation southerners to voting Republican, "This time many will cross the line for the first time, but I'm afraid most of them will stay away from the polls in great numbers."

[2] Robinson had visited with the President in Newport twice in July (see no. 1590). The President had returned to Newport on August 1, 1960, following his trips to Denver and to the Republican National Convention in Chicago.

[3] For background see no. 118. Robinson had reiterated an invitation to the Eisenhower Exchange Fellowships trustees dinner in September. "As I understand it, you will not be expected to prepare a speech for the occasion, so that it should be a relaxed and heartwarming evening in connection with a project I'm sure is dear to your heart." The President would find it possible to address the Eisenhower Exchange Fellowships trustees on September 26 in Philadelphia. He would emphasize the connection between a sound economy and American leadership of the free world (*New York Times*, Sept. 27, 1960).

To Kwame Nkrumah   *August 7, 1960*

Dear Mr. President:[1] It has given me great pleasure to receive your letter of July twenty-sixth concerning the Volta River project.[2] The United States Government has followed your endeavors in this regard with sympathetic interest, and the Under Secretary of State, Mr. Douglas Dillon, has given this matter his personal attention. Last year, you will recall, Mr. Dillon suggested to Ambassador Chapman that you request the cooperation of the International Bank for Reconstruction and Development in reviewing the Volta River project in the light of your country's development plans and that the Bank be looked to as the focal point for mobilizing international financing.[3] The Under Secretary did so with the confidence that you would receive sound and objective economic advice, and I understand that the Bank has submitted a report to your Government.[4] Especially in view of your report on the developments which have taken place since then, I quite understand your desire to proceed with the more tangible aspects of this project as soon as possible.[5]

I agree with you that it is now desirable to pursue negotiations with the Bank and the aluminum companies here in Washington.[6] In the absence of Mr. Dillon, I have requested the Acting Assistant Secretary of State for Economic Affairs, Mr. Edwin M. Martin,[7] to follow these discussions as closely as possible. The Secretary of State and the Deputy Under Secretary for Political Affairs, Mr. Raymond Hare, as well as Assistant Secretary of the Treasury Grady Upton, will also be discussing the Volta project with your Finance Minister, Mr. Gbedemah, next week.[8] These officials and others in the United States Government will be pleased to cooperate with him in his efforts to conclude arrangements so that construction may proceed with a minimum of delay.[9]

With this letter I send you my warmest personal regards and my very best wishes for the progress of your country and its people.[10] *Sincerely*

---

[1] The State Department drafted this letter, and cabled the text to the U.S. embassy in Accra for delivery to the Ghanian president.

[2] For background see nos. 440 and 510. Nkrumah had written Eisenhower that plans for the Volta River hydro-electric power scheme had reached a critical stage (AWF/I: Ghana). Nkrumah had sent a similar letter to the prime ministers of Canada and Britain. British and Canadian investors had promoted the hydro-electric project in order to take advantage of Ghana's extensive bauxite mines for aluminum production; after Ghana had won its independence, however, their interest had waned. U.S. investors were now negotiating to carry forward the project.

[3] Daniel Ahmling Chapman (B.A. Oxford 1936) was Ghana's ambassador to the United States and permanent representative to the United Nations. For background

on the discussions see State, *Foreign Relations, 1958–1960,* vol. XIV, *Africa,* p. 657.

[4] The International Bank for Reconstruction and Development (IBRD, the World Bank) had sent the Ghanaian government reports, requested by Nkrumah, on the economy of Ghana and on the Volta River Project (Nkrumah to Eisenhower, July 26, 1960, AWF/I: Ghana).

[5] Negotiations on the financing of the power project had gone forward, Nkrumah had reported, since Eisenhower's last letter on the subject (no. 510). A consortium, the Volta Aluminum Company (Valco), planned to participate in the power operation and to erect a smelter plant in Ghana. The Kaiser Engineering Company, in co-operation with the U.S. government, had completed an assessment of the project, and a London accounting firm was currently reviewing its findings. Ghanian officials had also discussed financing with representatives from the IBRD, and they had completed a preliminary round of negotiations with Valco (Nkrumah to Eisenhower, July 26, 1960, AWF/I: Ghana).

[6] The IBRD had agreed to loan half the capital needed to build the power and dam project if Ghana worked out a satisfactory contract with Valco. Nkrumah felt, however, that Ghana's projected contribution would heavily tax his country's limited resources and hoped that Valco would contract for power at a higher price; he also wanted better loan terms: a lower rate of interest and a longer repayment period. Nkrumah hoped the U.S. government might help negotiate a more satisfactory agreement at the discussions scheduled to resume at the IBRD in Washington on August 8 and wanted the financial arrangements concluded before September, as preliminary work had already begun on the dam. Whether or not a satisfactory sales agreement was made with Valco before then, he said, Ghana must continue with its plans and trust that its "friends abroad" would assist in "bringing the entire integrated project into operation" (Nkrumah to Eisenhower, July 26, 1960, AWF/I: Ghana).

[7] Edwin McCammon Martin (A.B. Northwestern 1929) was the Minister for Economic Affairs at the American embassy in London and the alternate U.S. Permanent Representative to NATO; he was also Department Chief of United States Regional Organizations.

[8] Thomas Graydon Upton (A.B. Harvard 1931) also served as a director for several U.S. government-supported international loan agencies, including the Loan Development Fund and the IBRD. For background on Hare see no. 54, and on Gbedemah see no. 440.

[9] Herter had told Eisenhower that this letter, while not committing to "any specific course of action," was intended to be "friendly and responsive" to Nkrumah's specific request that the President intervene in the negotiations with the IBRD. He also said that the State Department was considering how to conclude these negotiations and that the Development Loan Fund and the Export-Import Bank might become involved (Herter to Eisenhower, Aug. 5, 1960, AWF/I: Ghana).

[10] The following week Nkrumah would again urge Eisenhower to exert his personal influence to help conclude a satisfactory agreement (Nkrumah to Eisenhower, Aug. 8, 1960, *ibid.*). Informed of the message on August 10, the President would immediately authorize Secretary of State Herter to tell Nkrumah that the United States was attempting to put together a program satisfactory to all parties involved (John Eisenhower, Memorandum for Record, Aug. 10, 1960, *ibid.*; Telephone conversation, Eisenhower and Herter, Aug. 10, 1960, Herter Papers, Telephone Conversations). For further developments see Nkrumah to Eisenhower, August 26; Dillon to Eisenhower, September 16, and Eisenhower to Nkrumah, September 19, 1960, all in AWF/I: Ghana; State, *Foreign Relations, 1958–1960,* vol. XIV, *Africa,* pp. 658–63; and no. 1707; for a contemporary's viewpoint see Geoffrey Bing, *An Account of Kwame Nkrumah's Ghana from 1950 to 1966* (Worcester and London, 1968), pp. 392–95, 444–45.

To Henry Robinson Luce   *August 8, 1960*
Personal and confidential

Dear Harry: Your editorial of August eighth on the essentiality of a sound dollar is magnificent.[1] I hope that you can repeat the same theme many times in different keys over the coming three months.

Your editorial of August first, to which you had already called my attention, is from my viewpoint most pleasing.[2] I am more than flattered by your complimentary personal references but, of course I recognize that the assistance of able and dedicated associates was largely responsible for the kind of things you have said.

I plead guilty to the general charge that many people have felt I have been too easy a boss.[3] Respecting this there are one or two things that you might like to think over. (I do not mean to defend, merely to explain).

Except for my first two years as President, during which I enjoyed the benefit of a very skimpy majority in the Congress, I have had to deal with a Congress controlled by the opposition and whose partisan antagonism to the Executive Branch has often been blatantly displayed. The hope of doing something constructive for the nation, in spite of this kind of opposition, has required the use of methods calculated to attract cooperation, even though a natural impulse would have been to lash out at partisan charges and publicity-seeking demagogues.

Another point—the government of the United States has become too big, too complex, and too pervasive in its influence on all our lives for one individual to pretend to direct the details of its important and critical programming. Competent assistants are mandatory; without them the Executive Branch would bog down. To command the loyalties and dedication and best efforts of capable and outstanding individuals requires patience, understanding, a readiness to delegate, and an acceptance of responsibility for any honest errors—real or apparent—those associates and subordinates might make. Such loyalty from such people cannot be won by shifting responsibility, whining, scolding or demagoguery. Principal subordinates must have confidence that they and their positions are widely respected, and the chief must do his part in assuring that this is so.

Of course I could have been more assertive in making and announcing decisions and initiating programs. I can only say that I adopted and used those methods and manners that seemed to me most effective. (I should add that one of my problems has been to control my temper—a temper that I have had to battle all my life!)

Finally, there is the matter of maintaining a respectable image of

American life before the world! Among the qualities that the American government must exhibit is dignity. In turn the principal governmental spokesman must strive to display it. In war and in peace I've had no respect for the desk-pounder, and have despised the loud and slick talker. If my own ideas and practices in this matter have sprung from weakness, I do not know. But they were and are deliberate or, rather, natural to me. They are not accidental.[4] *As ever*

[1] In the August 8 issue of *Life* Magazine, Luce had praised the Republican economic record, saying that "the natural expansion of a stable dollar economy benefits more people than a feverish, artificial, inflationary expansion." He charged that the Democratic platform promising "cheaper money and looser credit policies than the Republicans," would, in combination with "their expansive attitude toward the federal budget," "make inflation a cancerous danger again." See also Ann Mari May, "President Eisenhower, Economic Policy, and the 1960 Presidential Election," *Journal of Economic History*, 50, no. 2 (June 1990), pp. 417–27.

[2] The August 1, 1960, editorial in *Life* had stated that "The Eisenhower era made possible the much greater achievements of the people." Luce believed that Eisenhower had made his priority in taking office the healing of the "wounds of 20 years of highly partisan government and chronic emergency. It was his genius to give the latent unity and goodwill of the American people a chance to recover and grow. He has been the least 'divisive' of modern Presidents—and the most widely beloved." He praised the President for modernizing and strengthening the American military posture and for winning the "guardianship of world peace," while facing down Communist threats of war in the Taiwan Straits and Berlin.

[3] Luce had written that there was some "substance to the charge that Ike has rather reigned than ruled. He has tended to assume, as you can in the Army but not in the White House, that an order once given is self-executing; a certain lack of follow-through has marred some of his best intentions, notably the rejuvenation of the Republican party. He has been an easy boss."

[4] Luce would respond on August 17 (same file as document). He termed Eisenhower's August 8th letter "one of the most interesting that any President ever wrote" and suggested that "sometime in the next year or two you should write an article for *Life* on The Presidency. This suggestion is just something you might file in your mental notebook for consideration at the proper time."

1608   *EM, AWF, Name Series*

TO CARTER L. BURGESS   *August 8, 1960*
Personal

Dear Carter: I have your message and fully understand the reasons that have dictated your decision to decline accepting the position as head of the National Citizens for Nixon group. I knew, of course, that it would mean sacrifice on your part, but I was hopeful that you might find conditions such as would permit you to undertake the task over these next three months.[1]

Of course I most deeply appreciate your consideration of the matter, and I am particularly touched by your offer to be of the maximum service you possibly can in view of your necessary preoccupations in this business world. I have read this part of your memorandum to the Vice President and he told me that he is not only grateful for your offer but expects to take full advantage of it.[2]

With warm personal regard, *Cordially*

[1] President of American Machine and Foundry Corporation since 1958, Burgess (B.A. Virginia Military Institute) had served as Assistant Secretary for Manpower and Personnel in the Department of Defense from 1954 to 1957. In a longhand note Burgess had written that never before had he "given a matter as much intense consideration as I have the question you posed to me" (n.d., AWF/N). He had declined the post, however, because his "stockholders, employees and customers would wonder how I could now take on full time partisan and public political duties away from my job at the company." On the Nixon-Lodge Volunteer Clubs see Ambrose, *Nixon*, vol. I, *The Education of a Politician, 1913–1963*, p. 561.

[2] Burgess had written that he had long been convinced of the "need to elect Mr. Nixon to the Presidency" and had told the Vice-President of the "need to continue the work for peace and prosperity which you have so ably led and fostered these past eight years and before." He volunteered to work for Nixon "in our community and in our travels," to contribute funds, and, "if needed and desired, to be available over weekends in the Vice President's headquarters office to assist his staff in the endless endeavors between now and election." Burgess added that he had not yet communicated with Nixon because he wanted to tell Eisenhower of his reasons first.

1609   *EM, WHCF, Official File 101-0*

To ELMER HESS   *August 8, 1960*
Personal

Dear Elmer: Of course I have no objection to your taking the action, on your personal responsibility, that you suggest in your letter of August second.[1]

The only two cases of which I have any knowledge that were treated in this way were those of Colonel Keller and Colonel Kimbrough. In each case the individual was highly competent in his own specialty.[2] I know of no case where such action has been taken as a recognition of past service, even though that service has been characterized by great loyalty and dedication.

In any event, I repeat that I have no objection whatsoever to your taking the action you propose.[3]

With warm regard, *Sincerely*

[1] Hess (M.D. University of Pennsylvania 1911), a urologist, had served in the U.S. Army Corps during World War I, and as president of the American Medical Associ-

ation from 1955–1956. He had sought Eisenhower's permission to request Congress to appoint Major General Howard McCrumb Snyder as a consultant for life to the Surgeon General of the United States Army (same file as document). He wrote that such a step would be "a nice recognition of Howard's devotion to you, as your physician."

[2] Keller may have been Lieutenant Colonel William S. Keller. Colonel James Claude Kimbrough (M.D. Vanderbilt University 1916) was a urologist who had served at Sternberg General Hospital in the Philippines 1937–1938. During World War II he was chief of professional services in the European Theater of Operations. Since 1946 Kimbrough had been chief of urology service at Walter Reed Army Hospital.

[3] There is no further correspondence on this subject in EM. On May 1, 1961, Snyder would be awarded the Legion of Merit. He would be cited for outstanding service as special medical assistant to the Supreme Allied Commander in Europe from 1951 through 1952, and as senior medical officer for the White House throughout the Eisenhower Administrations (*New York Times*, May 2, 1961).

1610   *EM, AWF, Ann Whitman Diary Series*

MEMORANDUM FOR FILES   *August 10, 1960*
Secret

I have talked to the Secretary of State about General de Gaulle's letter of yesterday, received here by cable.[1] Neither of us understands exactly what de Gaulle is getting at. But we note that the copy of the de Gaulle message has been sent to Prime Minister Macmillan. State Department is drafting a message to Macmillan (which I shall have possibly by the end of the week) through which the British and ourselves may reach some common understanding of the problems posed by de Gaulle and develop our own ideas concerning them.[2] General de Gaulle has been referring to this "tripartite world strategy" for many months. In talking to me, he has always been so hazy in propounding his theories that apparently I have never been able to respond adequately. He speaks of "our West", but he names only our three countries. I am sure he does not mean to ignore Germany, Italy, the Low Countries, the Scandinavian countries, or Turkey and Greece. However, his thinking on this whole matter seemed to show his readiness to set up our three nations as the controlling groupment of NATO.

He does voice his old complaint about the overwhelming influence of the United States in the NATO complex. I once told him that the United States had no ambition to carry the heavy responsibilities that had been force[d] upon it in NATO. It has there the equivalent of six divisions, a large fleet, and an extensive air force, supported by a great logistic system. At least in the early days the Europeans insisted upon an American commander because geographical remoteness would tend to make that commander impartial as between the conflicting claims of the European countries and, secondly, because in that combination of naval, air, ground and supply strength we are the largest contributor.

The General's complaint about our nuclear selfishness is something that the Executive Department cannot help. In lieu of bilateral agreements of this kind, we have argued for a joint stock pile to be available for the defense of Western Europe.

Apparently the General thinks we should carry all these burdens, but abdicate any control over the deployment of the forces, even though another part of his argument is the right of France to control all of its own forces for its own defense.[3]

---

[1] For background on tripartite negotiations between the United States, Great Britain, and France see no. 1598. In response to Eisenhower's earlier letter (see *ibid.*), de Gaulle had stated that consultations among the three foreign ministers at the time of the United Nations General Assembly meetings in September "must be held without fail." He believed, however, that Eisenhower's plan for a possible meeting of the heads of the three governments was "too restrictive to bring about joint action by our West and to render our alliance more truly effective." De Gaulle also blamed the current crisis in the Congo (see no. 1599) in part on a lack of harmony among the three Western countries. Something was "gravely defective" in the alliance, he said; it had "no political solidarity" in the face of the world's "seething dangers." NATO, he maintained, reserved to the United States the power to conduct atomic war in Europe and effectively deprived France of the responsibility of defending herself. He wanted the leaders of the United States, Great Britain, and France to reorganize the alliance to cope with world problems. He asked Eisenhower to meet with him and Prime Minister Macmillan in September (De Gaulle to Eisenhower, Aug. 9, 1960, AWF/I: de Gaulle; see also State, *Foreign Relations, 1958–1960*, vol. VII, pt. 2, *Western Europe*, pp. 400–401).

Eisenhower had told Secretary Herter that what de Gaulle really wanted was "a triumvirate." The President and the Secretary agreed to "go slow" in responding and to ask Macmillan about his reaction to de Gaulle's letter (*ibid.*, pp. 402–5). In a brief response Eisenhower would tell the French president that he would study the important questions he had raised, and that he would soon be writing "at some length" (Eisenhower to de Gaulle, Aug. 12, 1960, AWF/I: de Gaulle).

[2] Instead of drafting a letter to Macmillan, State Department officials, accompanied by the U.S. ambassador to Great Britain, would meet with the British leader in London on August 17 to discuss de Gaulle's letter. Macmillan would suggest that if Eisenhower was opposed to a meeting with de Gaulle in September, he should "play it soft" and merely point out some of the difficulties involved. The President might suggest that their foreign ministers discuss these topics before a meeting of the three leaders. Macmillan would also note de Gaulle's desire to have France become a nuclear power and his belief that national armies must remain under national command. Some of the difficulties in dealing with the French leader, Macmillan said, were "based at least partly on a misunderstanding on his part as to how NATO really works." He thought Eisenhower might ask de Gaulle to circulate his views in advance of the foreign ministers meeting on September 23 (State, *Foreign Relations, 1958–1960*, vol. VII, pt. 2, *Western Europe*, pp. 408–11; see also Macmillan to Eisenhower, Aug. 13, 1960, *ibid.*; Telephone conversation, Herter and Whitman, Aug. 12, 1960, Herter Papers, Telephone Conversations; and Macmillan, *Pointing the Way*, pp. 248–49).

[3] For developments see no. 1632.

To Sékou Touré   *August 15, 1960*

Dear Mr. President: Thank you for your telegram of August seventh outlining the views of your Government on the troubled Congo situation which has caused us all such concern.[1]

The United States Government and people fully share your desire to see the problems of the Congo settled as rapidly as possible. As you know, we have been requested on several occasions to assist the Government of the Republic of the Congo unilaterally. I believe very strongly, however, that the present crisis in the Congo can be surmounted only through the united efforts of all countries which believe in human freedom and justice, with these efforts coordinated through the United Nations under the effective leadership of Secretary General Dag Hammarskjold.[2] The United States is proud of its role in responding to the appeal from the Secretary General and I am especially gratified that among the troops flown by American planes was the entire Guinean contingent.[3]

I believe that the August ninth resolution in the Security Council will prove to be a great step toward calming the situation in the Congo as a whole.[4] As you know, this resolution called upon the Government of Belgium for the immediate withdrawal of Belgian troops from Katanga under "speedy modalities to be determined by the Secretary General." The United States voted for this resolution as it has for the others on the same problem, and will continue to support the United Nations effort to the limit of its ability.

In view of your prominent position in Africa, it would be a great contribution to peace if you were able to use your influence to encourage the fullest possible support for the United Nations effort in the Congo.[5]

I deeply appreciate your warm expression of friendship which is wholeheartedly reciprocated by the United States Government and me personally. *Sincerely*

---

[1] Touré, the President of Guinea, had written urging the United States to take vigorous action to ensure that all Belgian troops were rapidly removed from the Congo, including Katanga, the province that had seceded shortly after independence. His appeal, he said, was "a cry of alarm from Africa, humiliated and under attack by its enemies" (Touré to Eisenhower, AWF/I: Guinea). For background see no. 1599; State, *Foreign Relations, 1958–1960*, vol. XIV, *Africa*, pp. 395, 411–12; Lefever, *Crisis in the Congo*, esp. pp. 1–45; Dayal, *Mission for Hammarskjold*, pp. 1–47.

[2] Declining to act unilaterally, the United States had provided food supplies, logistical support, and financial backing for the U.N.'s peacekeeping mission (see State, *Foreign Relations, 1958–1960*, vol. XIV, *Africa*, pp. 294–96, 298).

[3] The United States had airlifted the majority of the U.N. troops from various African

nations to the Congo (see, for example, Wilcox to Cargo, July 19, 1960, AWF/I: Macmillan).

[4] Although the United Nations had already passed two resolutions calling for the removal of Belgian troops from the Congo, the August ninth resolution had asked specifically for Belgium's withdrawal from Katanga. It also declared that the admission of U.N. troops into Katanga was necessary (*New York Times*, Aug. 9, 1960). U.N. forces would enter the province a few days later, but the full withdrawal of Belgian troops would be delayed.

[5] Secretary of State Herter had suggested that Eisenhower send this message to Touré to "stress personally with him the need to support the United Nations in Congo" (Herter to Eisenhower, Aug. 13, 1960, AWF/I: Guinea; Eisenhower's changes to the State Department draft of this paragraph are in *ibid.*). For developments see no. 1714.

1612

EM, WHCF, *Confidential File: Eisenhower Administration*

To STANLEY HOFLUND HIGH   *August 15, 1960*
Personal and confidential

Dear Stanley: I was so impressed with the memorandum that you prepared for your editors, a copy of which you recently sent Ann, that at Cabinet this morning I took the great liberty of distributing the document, on a personal and confidential basis, to all who were present.[1] It seems to me to present our foreign policy efforts of the last eight years so accurately and so effectively that I felt it would be of help to those people, most of whom were in the room, who will be charged with the major portion of the job of "selling" those efforts to the American people in the political campaign this fall. I trust you do not disapprove of my action, and I congratulate you not only on a fine document (it goes without saying, a highly gratifying one, too) but also on the skill with which you presented your arguments.[2]

Thank you very much.

With warm regard, *As ever*

[1] High, the senior editor of *Reader's Digest*, had sent Presidential Secretary Ann Whitman a copy of his assessment of Eisenhower's foreign policy, an article that he hoped to publish before the upcoming elections. He had proposed that the President was not "out of date" as some Washington journalists had claimed, but was instead the author of a new policy that was "more promising than anything proposed by his critics." The cornerstone, he thought, was Eisenhower's attempt to develop "people-to-people understanding" by visiting other countries and by welcoming numerous heads of state to the United States. "Given time," this approach "might develop strength enough to deter even the maddest warmonger." Its success, he concluded, had already caused "something approaching panic" among the "Kremlin Reds." High had suggested to his editors that a factual article that was not "overtly partisan," might

wield "momentous influence" on a campaign in which foreign policy issues were likely to be crucial (Memo from Stanley High, July 21, 1960; Gardner to Whitman, Aug. 10, 1960; and Whitman to Gardner, Aug. 16, 1960, all in same file as document). [2] High would write that he was pleased that Eisenhower had distributed his memorandum (High to Eisenhower, Aug. 17, 1960, *ibid.*). He would later tell Ann Whitman that the article would not be published but that he would be flattered if anyone at the White House could use his ideas (Telephone conversation, Whitman to High, Sept. 20, 1960, *ibid.*).

1613   *EM, AWF, Name Series*

To CHARLES VINCENT MCADAM, SR.   *August 15, 1960*
Personal

Dear Charlie: It was nice to have your letter of August eleventh.[1]

Quite naturally, I am ready to see you any time you might run down here either for an evening or for some office appointment during the day.

My own feeling, at the moment, is that I would not be as much interested in contributing a series of short articles, with considerable frequency, as I would be in writing three or four longer pieces in the course of a year—in the meantime possibly working on the text of a book.[2]

Of course I do not know the range of the work in which your syndicate engages; but no matter whether or not you and I find that we could dovetail our ideas in this connection, I would enjoy an opportunity to talk to you about everything from peanuts to politics.

Should you want to come down any time soon give Mrs. Whitman a ring and we can arrange it.[3]

Please remember me warmly to Peg and, of course, all the best to yourself.[4] *As ever*

[1] McAdam's letter is in AWF/N. He had reminded the President of their discussion regarding the possibility of publishing with the McNaught Syndicate after January 1961 (see no. 1418). For Eisenhower's responses to earlier invitations to write after the end of his presidency see nos. 1424 and 1430.
[2] McAdam had suggested they discuss the idea during a round of golf.
[3] On September 8 the President and McAdam would dine at the White House (off-the-record); on September 17 Eisenhower would play golf with McAdam at the Gettysburg Country Club. For developments on Eisenhower's decision to publish his memoirs see nos. 1624 and 1650.
[4] McAdam's wife was the former Marguerite Wimby.

To BERNARD MANNES BARUCH   *August 15, 1960*

Dear Bernie: Any ninetieth birthday would rate a special salute—and
when a man has served his country and his fellow citizens as well
and faithfully as have you, that salute has more than a special meaning. I know you have the admiration and respect and affection of
uncounted numbers of our citizens, as you have long had mine.[1]

There is a great deal of talk these days about the superior capabilities and values of youth.[2] But I think that the vim, vigor and vi-
tality of youth must always be salted and seasoned with the wisdom
of experience and the tolerance of maturity. When such wisdom is
combined in an individual, as it is in you, with an eagerness for the
new and an enthusiasm for the future, then a mere ninety simply
becomes the occasion for a new look into the future of the country
we love so much.

So—a Happy Birthday! My warmest felicitations and personal regard are yours. *As ever*

[1] The President's longstanding friend and adviser would turn ninety on August 19
(*New York Times*, Nov. 4, 1960). Baruch had chaired the War Industries Board during
World War I and had advised several American presidents (for further background
see *Eisenhower Papers*, vols. I–XVII).
[2] On July 13 forty-three-year-old John F. Kennedy had won the Democratic presidential nomination (see no. 1616 and *New York Times*, July 14, 1960). See also no.
1646.

1615   *EM, AWF, Dulles-Herter Series*

To CLARENCE DOUGLAS DILLON   *August 17, 1960*

Dear Dillon:[1] Herewith a letter written by Harold S. Geneen, President of the International Telephone and Telegraph Corporation, to
General Summerfield. Its purport is to urge some kind of action on
the part of government to guarantee private investments abroad.[2]

This matter has been discussed from time to time in various White
House meetings, in some of which Foster Dulles was a participant.
He and I always agreed that there was little that could be done in
this respect.

I should like to have a short analysis of the whole situation and the
State Department's views concerning changes in attitude or policy.[3]

With your reply, will you please return this letter, which I must
turn back to General Summerfield. *Sincerely*

[1] Secretary of State Herter was in Costa Rica attending meetings of the Organization of American States.

[2] Harold Sydney Geneen (B.S. New York University 1934), president and chief executive officer of IT&T since 1959, was formerly executive vice-president of the Raytheon Manufacturing Company. In March he and Eisenhower had discussed the effect of Cuba's seizure of American business properties on the security of U.S. private enterprise around the world. "We have now reached, in my opinion, a critical void in which some basic statement of policy and leadership needs urgently to be announced," Geneen had written. "American business must know what its government intends to do to help, what the government intends to do to encourage continued investment abroad, and what the government will do to protect such investment" (Geneen to Summerfield, Aug. 12, 1960, AWF/D; for background on the appropriation of American properties in Cuba see no. 1370; see also *New York Times*, Jan. 11, Feb. 24, Mar. 5, Nov. 22, 1959).

[3] Dillon would reply with a statement for possible inclusion in a response to Geneen. The statement, he told Eisenhower, took note of American reliance on "recognized principles of international law for the protection of American investors overseas" and declared that the United States would continue to take "every action consistent with international law and the public interest" to secure the rights of investors. The statement itself, however, admitted that new investments would receive far greater protection than existing investments. Although he had arranged to meet with Geneen to hear his suggestions, Dillon would not recommend any policy changes or new legislation on the subject (Dillon to Eisenhower, Aug. 24, 1960, AWF/D-H; see also *New York Times*, Oct. 13, 1960). There is no further correspondence on this subject in AWF.

1616   *EM, AWF, Name Series*

To Percy Walter Thompson   *August 17, 1960*
Personal and confidential

Dear Perc: Thank you very much for your letter. My only piece of family news is that Susie had her tonsils out yesterday morning. This afternoon John and I went to visit her in the hospital and she is sitting up in bed, drawing pictures, reading books about horses, and opening her fan mail. I think she is feeling very important—anyway the doctors say she is doing splendidly.[1]

I particularly noticed your observation in the last major paragraph of your letter, "To some, neither Presidential candidate is acceptable (Mr. Nixon is not because of his NAACP affiliation)." I checked this afternoon to find out what was the basis of any such belief. I learned that in 1946, when Mr. Nixon was a freshman Congressman, a local California chapter of the NAACP made him an honorary member. However, I am assured that he is not now a member of the organization in any capacity whatsoever.[2]

On the other side of the slate the reports I have from the South are extremely unfavorable to both members of the Democratic ticket. I am told that many people there consider that Senator John-son has betrayed them, while Mr. Kennedy they believe to be a com-plete "radical."[3]

At the very least Mr. Nixon has been a moderate in his political philosophy. He has consistently argued that education and under-standing are much more important than rigidly conceived laws in bringing about improvement in the racial situation.[4] For myself I be-lieve that everybody should be protected in his right to vote and to this extent I have advocated laws. Moreover, I insisted upon the re-sponsibility of enforcing the properly issued orders of the Federal courts.[5] In these two ideas I think that Mr. Nixon and I are com-pletely agreed and it is for these reasons that I do not think it quite fair to say that he has any affiliation with the NAACP.

Give my love to Bea and of course all the best to yourself. I hope you have a grand success in your race for Secretary of State.[6]

With warm regard, *As ever*

[1] Thompson, Barbara Eisenhower's father, was running as Republican candidate for Florida Secretary of State. He had written on August 15, 1960 (AWF/N) with com-ments on the Republican Convention (see no. 1593).

[2] Thompson was concerned that while many voters in the South were prepared to support the Republican ticket on the national level, Nixon's rumored affiliation with the NAACP was hurting the party's chances. Nixon had admitted that he was an hon-orary member of the NAACP and that he supported the organization's goal of equal-ity (Ambrose, *Nixon*, vol. I, *The Education of a Politician, 1913–1963*, p. 414). Eisen-hower's secretary, Ann Whitman, had queried Nixon's secretary, Rose Woods, about Nixon's relationship with the NAACP. Woods had responded with the information the President passed on in this letter to Thompson (Ann Whitman memorandum, n.d., AWF/N).

[3] On Johnson's introduction of civil rights legislation in the Senate see no. 1078. On Kennedy's civil rights record see Lawson, *Black Ballots*, pp. 250–56.

[4] See Ambrose, *Nixon*, vol. I, *The Education of a Politician, 1913–1963*, pp. 537–38.

[5] See, for example, no. 374.

[6] On Thompson's loss in November see no. 1710.

1617   *EM, WHCF, Official File 3-K*

TO LLOYD BURNS MAGRUDER   *August 17, 1960*

Dear Colonel Magruder: It was nice to hear from you. As far as the bill for retired military personnel is concerned, I have gone to extraor-dinary lengths to get the deadlock on this issue broken in the Sen-ate, both by direct and indirect conversations with the principal par-ties involved. Thus far they seem to be adamant against moving for reasons that I cannot understand. But I would think that those individuals would become increasingly sensitive to this issue before the session ends. I very much hope we shall get the results we want.[1]

I need not add that I am personally most appreciative of your comments concerning what I have been trying to do these past years. The commendation of my West Point friends is always particularly heart-warming.[2]

With personal regard, *Sincerely*

[1] Magruder (USMA 1905) and Eisenhower had met in Washington while Magruder served in the War Department's G-4 (logistics) section 1931–1935. He had written August 14 (same file as document) to thank Eisenhower for his renewed efforts to "right the wrong perpetrated by the Pay Act of 1 June 1958 against the already retired personnel of the Armed Forces." For background see no. 1570.

In his budget message for FY 1962 Eisenhower had requested legislation that would increase retirement pay by restoring the traditional formula that had long been used to calculate it (*Public Papers of the Presidents: Eisenhower, 1960–61*, p. 956; see also Memorandum of Conference, May 19, 1959, AWF/D). There had been no action taken on repeated proposals to equalize pay until May 1960, when the House passed H.R. 11318 and refered it to the Senate. Congress would, however, pass no bill on this issue during that session (*Congressional Record*, 86th Cong., 2d sess., 1960, 106, pt. 8:10192–98).

[2] "You have been a President of whom our Alma Mater can be proud," Magruder wrote.

1618   *EM, WHCF, Official File 116-PP*

To Nils Myklebost   *August 17, 1960*

Dear Nils: Thank you for taking the trouble to write to me from Norway.[1] You were thoughtful to tell me of your approval of my conduct in Paris and to send me your good wishes for the months left in my Presidency.[2]

I am indeed sorry that you are sometimes embarrassed by the fact that you are American born; I would hope that you can, secretly at least, take some pride in this same circumstance. At any rate I am glad you are usually able to keep your temper even when the going seems rough.[3]

One thing I can promise you; we in the United States will do everything possible to keep the Free World free and help those less fortunate than we are to win their rights to liberty.[4]

With best wishes, *Sincerely*

[1] Nils was the twelve-year-old son of Tor Myklebost, chief of the Norwegian Foreign Office's Press Section. The boy's mother was an American and he was born in the United States during his father's tour of duty as press attaché at the Norwegian em-

bassy in Washington. Following established routine, his letter to the President (May 21) had been forwarded to the State Department and then back to the American embassy in Norway. The ambassador thought Eisenhower would enjoy reading it for the "forthright, boyish way" Myklebost had expressed himself (Willis to John S. D. Eisenhower, July 19, 1960). Several drafts of a reply, including one containing the President's handwritten emendations, and all related correspondence are in the same file as the document.

[2] The boy had said that he had read the newspaper articles about the collapse of the Paris summit in May (see no. 1538). He told Eisenhower not to worry about Khrushchev, whom he described as a "big liar." He also commended the President for keeping his temper.

[3] The young man had said that he had a hard time keeping his temper when the boys in his class teased him because he was American. But, he added, he really thought they envied him.

[4] Myklebost had hoped "that the USA will continue to protect us all in the free world."

1619   *EM, WHCF, Official File 108*

To Edward H. Teller   *August 19, 1960*
Personal

Dear Dr. Teller: Early this morning, I had opportunity to read the final article of your series on atomic affairs.[1] This note is to let you know how strongly I agree with the basic principle you expounded in the article—the need to substitute openness for secrecy in our handling of technical nuclear information.[2]

With best wishes, *Sincerely*

[1] The series of articles, which grew out of conversations between nuclear physicist Teller and the science editor of the *Houston Post*, had appeared in the *New York Herald Tribune*. "If we want disarmament," Teller had said, "we must accept complete openness," which was needed for "a justified trust" among nations. Although military operations should still be kept secret, there were "extremely strong arguments for complete freedom of technical information." He proposed a complete reexamination that would "lead to an orderly liquidation of all technical secrets." Teller believed that such openness would produce a favorable response from the Soviets (*New York Herald Tribune*, Aug. 19, 1960).

[2] Teller was "deeply honored" that Eisenhower had read his article. "Even more," he would write, "I am encouraged by your kind words of agreement on the necessity of establishing an open world" (Teller to Eisenhower, Sept. 6, 1960, same file as document).

To Henry Cabot Lodge   *August 19, 1960*

Dear Cabot: In the past seven and a half years the United Nations has indeed, as you say, grown greatly in influence and as an agency for the preservation of peace. This has not been so because of any one nation or any one man. But the United States has sought to nurture that growth. As her Representative you have applied extraordinary talents of firmness, perseverance, and imagination to pressing in that forum our aims of peace with freedom and justice.[1]

For your services in this cause and to the United States you have, I am sure, the gratitude of all the American people—especially, perhaps, groups of our citizens most recently of foreign origin. In behalf of all Americans and for my own part, I thank you.[2]

I accept your resignation as the Representative of the United States to the United Nations and to the Security Council, effective, as you wish, September third. The deep regret I feel at contemplating your leaving your United Nations post is mitigated by the knowledge that you do so only to offer yourself to the nation in an elective post of high responsibility and opportunity for service. In this effort you have, as you know, my heartiest endorsement. The country could ill afford in these times to lose the service of a man of your abilities.[3]

With warm regard, *As ever*

[1] On August 17 Lodge had submitted his resignation as the United States Ambassador to the United Nations, and as the U.S. Representative to the Security Council, in order to campaign actively as the Republican vice-presidential nominee (same file as document). For background on Lodge's July 28 nomination see no. 1593 and *New York Times,* July 29, 1960. The United Nations had grown in size, influence and "indispensability," Lodge wrote. He attributed the growth to strong and steady American help made possible by Eisenhower's policies.
[2] Lodge had thanked the President for the experience of serving as an ambassador and a cabinet member. For background on Lodge's appointment see Galambos, *NATO and the Campaign of 1952,* no. 1040.
[3] For developments see nos. 1695, 1700, and 1701.

1621   *EM, AWF, Administration Series*

To Ezra Taft Benson   *August 22, 1960*
Personal

Dear Ezra: I have read your "Brief Report on Europe and Middle East Trade Trip."[1] Since this report is not addressed specifically to any individual or office, I am somewhat uncertain as to its eventual use; however, I am sure you have given a copy to the State Department, probably inviting it to the particular attention of Secretary Dillon. Additionally, I believe that copies should go to Mr. Nixon and to any others in government whom you believe should be, or might be, interested.

I like the report and I think there is one point that you should take up urgently with the State Department. It is that of supplying ten to fifteen thousand tons of seed wheat to Jordan, through a third country.[2]

*   *   *   *   *

Likewise, I read the folder of clippings from newspapers which defend the principles of the farm program that we have been proposing over the last seven and a half years. I am all for improvements on any proposals we have heretofore put forward—so long as they are indeed improvements. Moreover, I think we must give to our candidates, both national and others, the same privilege that we extended to the Democratic majority in Congress over the past months. We established certain guide lines and promised that I would approve any bill sent to me which did not violate the limits established. In other words, to this extent we cannot complain if someone produces a program which in its specifics differed with others that we have projected in the past—so long as the proposals do in fact observe the guide lines.[3]

I was gratified to note among the clippings that notice has been taken of my re-affirmation of support for you and your conduct of the Agriculture Department.[4]

With warm regard, *As ever*

---

[1] Secretary of Agriculture Benson had headed a delegation to Belgium, West Germany, the Netherlands, France, Egypt, Jordan and Israel, the latest in a series of agricultural trade and market development trips. He and his colleagues had examined possibilities for market development in the Middle East and had gathered information on the potential impact of European Economic Community proposals on U.S. farmers (Brief Report on Europe and Middle East Trip of Secretary of Agriculture Ezra Taft Benson, July 30–August 18, 1960, AWF/A).

[2] Benson had reported that the United Arab Republic (the union of Egypt and Jordan) was facing problems of limited crop acreage and a rapidly growing population. A three-year drought had compounded matters, especially in Jordan. The Agriculture Department had recommended that the amount of grain Jordan received from the United States under Title II of P.L. 480 be increased (*ibid.*; for background on the Agricultural Trade Development and Assistance Act of 1954 see no. 24; on Title II, which provided for famine and urgent relief programs to "friendly" nations, see Peterson, *Agricultural Exports, Farm Income, and the Eisenhower Administration*, pp. 42–43). Jordan urgently needed wheat for seeding as the planting season was due to begin in September, Benson explained, but it had to be obtained through a third country to supply the correct variety. The full amount of the recommended increase

awaited approval from the International Commodity Association. Jordan's Prime Minister, according to the report, had expressed "strong opposition to Communism" and "would not even accept emergency wheat from Russia." In reply to Eisenhower's letter Benson would merely say that Jordan's request for seed wheat was "already under consideration" (Aug. 23, 1960, AWF/A).

[3] Benson had sent a collection of editorials that decried what the authors viewed as a deprecatory attitude shown toward his agricultural policies by presidential candidates Richard M. Nixon and John F. Kennedy (the editorials as well as several others that Benson would send Eisenhower on Sept. 15, are in AWF/I). Earlier in the summer Nixon had suggested ideas for improving the farm program, and Benson had publicly stated that he thought that New York governor Nelson A. Rockefeller stood a better chance of winning the election than Nixon. Speculation had spread about the rift between Nixon and Benson, and some Republicans felt the Secretary was a liability to the campaign (*New York Times,* June 21, July 24, 1960; Benson, *Crossfire,* pp. 538–40; for background see nos. 1411 and 1263.

[4] The President had defended Benson at a news conference held a few days earlier on August 24, 1960 (*Public Papers of the Presidents: Eisenhower, 1960–61,* pp. 650–51). Benson would tell Eisenhower that he had planned additional trade trips abroad; he would schedule them around his campaign activities for which, he said, there was "widespread demand" (Benson to Eisenhower, Sept. 9, 1960, AWF/A).

1622   *EM, AWF, Dulles-Herter Series*

To Clarence Douglas Dillon   *August 22, 1960*

Memorandum for the Acting Secretary of State:[1] Secretary Benson called me to say that he had received word through the Agriculture Minister of Egypt that Nasser would very much like to make a visit to this country.[2]

Secretary Benson was quite impressed with what he saw and heard during his recent trip to that country and personally endorses an invitation to President Nasser.

I would want the matter to be studied very carefully before committing myself.[3]

[1] Under Secretary Dillon was in charge of the State Department while Secretary Herter was attending meetings of the foreign ministers of the Organization of American States in San José, Costa Rica.

[2] For background see the preceding document. Agriculture Secretary Ezra Taft Benson had recently returned from an eighteen-day trade development and goodwill mission to Western Europe and the Middle East (see Benson, *Cross Fire,* pp. 534–38; and *New York Times,* July 31, Aug. 10, 19, 1960; see also Telephone conversation, Eisenhower and Benson, Aug. 19, 1960, AWF/D).

[3] For developments see no. 1628.

To Felix Edgar Wormser   *August 22, 1960*
Personal

Dear Felix: In answering your former letter, I contented myself with
sending you a memorandum from the Treasury Department—this
because of my obvious inability to become an expert in this highly
complicated matter.[1]

In late 1952, when I was President-elect, I had many recommendations from individuals both in this country and abroad to do
something about our monetary system. Many wanted the price of
gold to be raised (this was from foreigners). Others wanted us to establish immediately gold convertibility. I realized that this was not a
subject on which I could develop a proper answer, and I directed
inquiries either directly or indirectly to a number of individuals who
were considered as more or less expert. I recall that I got an indirect report from Allan Sproul, who was then President of the Federal Reserve Bank of New York. I had another from George Whitney of Morgan's. I got a memorandum from Bernie Baruch and
from others whose names I do not now recall.[2]

The consensus of domestic advisers was to let the matter alone.
Individuals, on whose judgment I am compelled to depend and with
whom I have been closely associated over the past eight years, have
taken the same general line.

You make one observation in your letter that differs from my understanding of the situation.[3] You say, "To be sure the foreigner can
exchange his paper dollars for gold, but the American citizen cannot." It is my understanding that central banks that hold dollar reserves may have the right to demand gold, but I am informed that
the private citizen cannot.

Finally, I have always had the greatest confidence in Bob Anderson and his Under Secretary Julian Baird. I should like to set up for
you an appointment to come down and talk to one or both of these
men. I do not say that there would be a complete meeting of minds,
but I do assure you that they both have no other purpose than to
advance the interests of the United States.[4]

With warm regard, *As ever*

[1] Wormser had written (August 2, 1960) to suggest that the Administration restore
the rights of citizens to redeem paper currency for gold. "Failure to correct this serious error may plague us in the campaign," he wrote, "for it implies that we Republicans have acquiesced in the action of the New Deal in removing the power of
the purse from the people and transferring it to Washington." Eisenhower had responded on August 6: "The question you raise in your letter of the second of August
has been endlessly discussed by me and my associates. I can only say that I shall speak
to Dick Nixon and Bob Anderson once more about it."

On August 12 Anderson had provided the President with a memorandum on the subject, which Eisenhower had forwarded to Wormser (Eisenhower to Wormser, Aug. 15, 1960). Anderson had said that "Establishment of full redeemability of dollars into gold within the United States today is neither feasible nor desirable." Confidence in the U.S. monetary system could be achieved not by internal gold convertibility but by the "continued application of sound and tested fiscal, monetary, and debt management policies." Anderson added that he believed it important that the American gold stock remain centralized and that its use should be "limited to providing a reserve for our own monetary system and to performing its essential role in international trade and finance."

[2] See Galambos and van Ee, *The Middle Way*, nos. 265 and 341. Sproul would serve as president of the Federal Reserve Bank of New York until 1956; Whitney, chairman of the advisory council of Morgan Guaranty Trust, had served as chairman of the board of J. P. Morgan until November 1955.

[3] On August 19, 1960, Wormser had written the President that he found Anderson's memorandum, "rather amazing." "The Treasury cannot convince me," he wrote, "that an irredeemable paper dollar is better than one redeemable in gold."

[4] Wormser would write Eisenhower on September 6, 1960, that although he had had a "delightful discussion" with Anderson, they were "still miles apart, as you surmised we might be." Wormser believed that his major differences with Anderson lay in the area of the "moral issues involved, especially the impairment of an important property right and the lack of integrity in a currency that is irredeemable in gold." Anderson, however, feared "chaos would ensue" if redeemability were restored and was worried that the United States might experience a "serious deflation on returning to gold." Wormser concluded: "I have faith that moral and economic laws are more powerful than governments. They will ultimately decide the gold question." All correspondence is in the same file as the document.

1624   *EM, AWF, Name Series*

To DOUGLAS MCCRAE BLACK   *August 22, 1960*
Personal

Dear Doug: Thank you very much for your note. I am most happy that you found your trip to the Argentine so interesting and informative.[1]

Then, of course, I am deeply interested in Bob Jones' book. I knew he had been working on it and I am looking forward to reading it as quickly as I can get hold of a copy. You are more than generous to promise to send me an early one.[2]

*   *   *   *   *

One of these days I think you and I might want to get together for a talk—that is, if you are still interested in possible future writings of mine. When you were here before we talked about the possibility of you and Ben Hibbs getting together. By no means am I certain that this would be a workable arrangement but *if there were* to be some cooperative enterprise between you and somebody else, I would think this particular one as satisfactory as any other.[3]

Although I have a feeling that aside from a book project, I might want occasionally to write an article on a topic then current, it is entirely possible that you would feel it better to be my sole contact with the publishing world—and we could come to some agreement that would allow you to offer these to any periodical of your own choosing.[4]

My difficulty in reaching a clear impression of exactly how I want to work after January twentieth stems from several causes:

(*a*). I am now very busy and it seems as if a hundred important people are trying to get me to do something entirely new—all different.[5]

(*b*). I will not know until sometime about the end of next January what my actual retired status is to be.[6]

(*c*). When I get to the end of my term, it is likely that I shall want to take a rather prolonged period of rest and recreation—something on the order of two or three months.[7] Should I do so, I think is important that I plan to get some competent help on the job who could be browsing through my records (which I think are in very good shape) with a view to helping me to search out the basic character of the book. By this I mean should it have any tinge of an autobiography; should it be a mere narrative of the decisions and programming and efforts of the past eight years, with reasons for them, or should it tend to be more an analytical and philosophical approach to events, trends and personalities that I have encountered, with a view of reaching conclusions that might be, in my own opinion worth while. (Or should it be something of a combination of these?)

If someone like this were going through my records during the early weeks and would be ready to discuss such points with me, I would not have to feel that the earlier period had been wasted.

In any event, as I say, one of these days we should, if you are interested, have another talk about these things.[8]

With warm regard, *As ever*

---

[1] Doubleday and Company President Black had written August 19 (AWF/N). He had been a member of a delegation representing the President at ceremonies honoring the one hundred fiftieth anniversary of the independence of Argentina (see Weeks to Eisenhower, June 2, 1960, and Eisenhower to Weeks, June 7, 1960, both in WHCF/OF 160, and *New York Times*, May 18, 1960).

[2] Black had said that in September Doubleday would publish Robert Tyre ("Bobby") Jones, Jr.'s, *Golf is My Game*.

[3] Eisenhower had discussed his presidential memoirs with Black at an hour-long

White House meeting on March 21 (Ann Whitman memorandum, AWF/AWD). Ben Hibbs, a Kansas native and former director of the Curtis Publishing Company, had edited the *Saturday Evening Post* since 1942. Eisenhower had met Hibbs in 1947, when he had suggested that Eisenhower publish his memoirs in the *Saturday Evening Post* (for background see Galambos, *Chief of Staff*, nos. 1775, 1923, and 1945).

[4] At a meeting on September 19 the President would ask Hibbs to discuss Eisenhower's writing plans with Black (Ann Whitman memorandum, Sept. 19, 1960, and Telephone conversation, Eisenhower and Black, Sept. 19, 1960, both in AWF/AWD; see also Ambrose, *Eisenhower*, vol. II, *The President*, p. 611, and *New York Times*, Mar. 28, 1961).

[5] For examples of some of the offers received by the President see nos. 1437 and 1639.

[6] On March 14, 1961, by special act of Congress, Eisenhower would regain the five-star rank he had resigned in 1952. The bill would entitle him to a $25,000 presidential pension and to $50,000 for office expenses and salaries for three military aides. He would not be paid the compensation due a General of the Army (see *Congressional Quarterly Almanac*, vol. XVI, *1961*, p. 82; *New York Times*, Mar. 4, 8, 15, 1961; and Ambrose, *Eisenhower* vol. II, *The President*, p. 611).

[7] On February 7, 1961, the Eisenhowers would travel by train to Palm Springs, California. They would return to Gettysburg on April 17 (*New York Times*, Feb. 7, Apr. 18, 1961).

[8] Eisenhower and Black would meet on August 29 (Ann Whitman memorandum, AWF/AWD). For developments see no. 1636.

1625   *EM, AWF, Name Series*

To Mamie Doud Eisenhower   *August 22, 1960*

Memorandum: Republicans are having a closed circuit television dinner on September 29th. Its purpose is to raise money for the campaign.

I rather think that I may have to go to Boston for a quick trip, to make a speech that evening—leaving here in the late afternoon and returning the following morning.[1]

Chairman Morton hopes that you will attend the Washington dinner.[2] He further submits a request that you, during a contrived break in the proceedings, make an appearance with these words:

"I have never made a political speech. This is my first. It is very short and factual.

"I am going to vote for Pat and Dick on November eighth."

They think this would be a ten-strike, particularly because it would be natural for you to include Pat in your statement. They want to emphasize the difference between the wives of the two candidates as potential First Ladies.[3]

I send you this in memorandum form because I have been forgetting it for the past three days when I am home.[4]

¹ The President would not fly to Boston. Instead, he would address 2,000 diners at the Conrad Hilton Hotel in Chicago, where he would call the Nixon-Lodge ticket the best hope for continued sound government and the team best qualified to carry on his fight for peace with justice. The message would be carried to 38,000 Republicans in thirty-six U.S. cities (*Public Papers of the Presidents: Eisenhower, 1960*, pp. 734–37, and *New York Times*, Sept. 30, 1960).
² This was U.S. Senator Thruston Ballard Morton of Kentucky, Chairman of the Republican National Committee.
³ Senator Kennedy was married to the former Jacqueline Lee Bouvier.
⁴ As it turned out, the First Lady would not make the speech. Her mother, Mrs. Elivera Carlson Doud, would pass away on September 28, and Mrs. Eisenhower would be in Denver, Colorado, seeing to the funeral arrangements. The following day the President would attend the funeral in Denver (Eisenhower, *Waging Peace*, p. 586, and *New York Times*, Sept. 30, 1960).

1626   *EM, President's Personal File 858*

To CHARLES ABRAHAM HALLECK   *August 25, 1960*
Personal

Dear Charlie: Until I was brought to the platform last evening to unveil the portrait of Everett Dirksen, I had been given no inkling of the complete composition of the party nor of my expected part in it.¹ Naturally, since I was requested to unveil the portrait of my friend, I talked in an informal vein about my association with him since he had become the minority leader of the Senate.² Knowing nothing of the details of the remainder of the program, it did not occur to me that by addressing my remarks entirely to Everett's function, it may have seemed that I was slighting your own vital part in our cooperative efforts during these past years.

Nothing could have been further from my mind than to be guilty of such a seeming neglect. I think that it is scarcely necessary for me to tell you how appreciative I am of your friendship and how much I admire you capabilities as our leader in the House. Ever since we became co-workers—back in early 1953—I have always felt the need of your invaluable assistance and have been deeply grateful for it.³ *Devotedly*

¹ The President had attended a private dinner given by Representative Everett McKinley Dirksen of Illinois. The function was one of a series of farewell dinners scheduled by the Senate and House leaders (*New York Times*, Aug. 25, 1960).
² Dirksen had been a strong Taft supporter before the 1952 Republican National convention. Following Eisenhower's election, Dirksen had generally supported the Administration's program on foreign affairs, and Eisenhower had endorsed Dirksen in the 1956 Senate election (Galambos and van Ee, *The Middle Way*, no. 1592). After Dirksen became the Republican leader in January 1959, he and the President had

met frequently at the White House (Neil MacNeil, *Dirksen: Portrait of a Public Man* [New York, 1970], pp. 133–51, and Edward L. Schapsmeier and Frederick H. Schapsmeier, *Dirksen of Illinois: Senatorial Statesman* [Urbana, Ill., 1985], p. 116).

[3] Halleck, House minority leader since 1959, had also backed Taft in the 1952 presidential campaign. The President had previously acknowledged Halleck's support and cooperation; see Galambos and van Ee, *The Middle Way*, nos. 23 and 1542.

Later this day Eisenhower would see Halleck and Dirksen at an off-the-record meeting in the White House (Ann Whitman memorandum, Aug. 25, 1960, AWF/AWD).

1627   *EM, AWF, International Series:*
                                                                    Macmillan

TO HAROLD MACMILLAN   *August 26, 1960*
Cable. Secret

Dear Harold: The questions raised in your letter of August 11 were so important that I wanted you to hear our views first hand.[1] McCone and Merchant have reported to me on their conversations with you and your people and it appears that a good mutual understanding was reached.[2] In the present situation here, it would have been folly to seek Congressional approval at this time for our fallback position on the safeguarding of nuclear detonations in our seismic research program. This problem is one to which we shall have to return and on which we shall then need to consult further with you.

Now that there is a recess in the Geneva negotiations, we shall be working closely with you in the planning for the resumption of negotiations on September twenty-seventh. The gap between us and the Soviets on many crucial issues is a very wide one but we shall bend our best efforts to making sure that our positions are sound, and to persuading the Soviets to take reasonable positions which might make possible further progress.[3]

With warm personal regard, *As ever*

[1] For background on the U.S. proposal regarding the seismic research program see no. 1581; see also NSC meeting minutes, August 16, 1960, AWF/NSC. On August 2 the Soviet Union had rejected the proposal to contribute to a pool of nuclear devices for research. Soviet officials reiterated their earlier demands for limitations on any detonations made by the United States or Great Britain for research purposes (State, *Documents on Disarmament, 1960*, pp. 185–87). Macmillan had written that although the Russians had not accepted the proposal, he thought that "their rejection of it was made in a way which might have been a good deal worse, and indicated that . . . they would be ready for reciprocal safeguards to be applied to their own devices if ever they should conduct nuclear explosions for research." He hoped that Eisenhower would present his second proposal, involving an offer by

the United States to open its seismic research devices for inspection by Britain and the Soviet Union (see no. 1581), before the current congressional session ended (Macmillan to Eisenhower, Aug. 11, 1960, PREM 11/3584; see also Telephone conversation, Eisenhower and Herter, Aug. 12, 1960, Herter Papers, Telephone Conversations).

[2] On August 15, before leaving for London, Atomic Energy Commission Chairman John A. McCone had told Eisenhower that the fall-back position, which would allow Soviet inspection of U.S. nuclear devices used in the research program, "would cause a great deal of trouble in the Congress." Eisenhower had instructed McCone to tell Macmillan that the political problems regarding the matter made it impossible to present the proposal at that time but that he did not want to be placed in the position of breaking up the Geneva negotiations. He also told McCone that he would accept any treaty reducing military weapons if there were "a proper quid pro quo" and if adequate inspections were included (Goodpaster, Memorandum of Conference, Aug. 19, 1960, AWF/D).

McCone and Under Secretary of State for Political Affairs Livingston T. Merchant had reported to Eisenhower that the British had pressed them "very hard" for a statement of U.S. intentions regarding unilateral seismic experiments. They had wanted a commitment that the United States would not proceed during the remainder of Eisenhower's term in office. McCone and Merchant had told Macmillan that the United States would take "no precipitous action" and would resume negotiations at the end of the five-week recess in the Geneva talks. The British and U.S. officials had agreed that during the recess they would summarize "very strictly" the issues separating the East from the West and would discuss possible solutions (Goodpaster, Memorandum of Conference, Aug. 23, 1960, *ibid.*).

[3] Upon resumption of the Geneva talks, the U.S. representative would propose a moratorium on tests below the 4.75 megaton threshold, effective for the period that remained of the two-year seismic research program plus a three-month period to review research results. The Soviet Union labeled the proposal "ambiguous and imprecise" and called for a moratorium of from four to five years. Disarmament discussions would be held in the First Committee of the United Nations from October 13 to December 20. The Soviet Union, however, would not consider a further resolution of the differences that remained between the East and West until a new administration took office (State, *Documents on Disarmament, 1960*, pp. 251–53, 277–87, 297–375).

1628   *EM, AWF, Dulles-Herter Series*

To CLARENCE DOUGLAS DILLON   *August 26, 1960*
Confidential

Memorandum for the Acting Secretary of State: I have read your memorandum of August twenty-fifth concerning the interest of President Nasser in visiting the United States and agree with your conclusion, particularly in the light of your comment concerning our relations with Israel.[1] I do want to point out, however, that Ben-Gurion visited the United States not too long ago, even though, as I remember, his visit was "informal."[2]

[1] For background see no. 1622. The principal advantage to a visit by the United Arab Republic's President Gamal Abdul Nasser, Dillon wrote, would be the opportunity for him to gain a "more sympathetic understanding" of U.S. policies and problems, which in turn might help him see the United States "in a more favorable light" and "realize clearly our sincere desire for friendship with the Arabs." Among the disadvantages were a possible negative reaction in Congress, an adverse effect on U.S. relations with Jordan, Israel, and Iran, and a rise in Nasser's prestige in the Middle East and Africa. Nasser's continued denunciations of U.S. actions and policies had prompted State Department officials to advise against an invitation to the Egyptian leader "now or in the immediate future" (Dillon to Eisenhower, Aug. 25, 1960, AWF/D-H).

[2] Eisenhower had met with Israeli Prime Minister David Ben Gurion at the White House on March 10. He would meet with Nasser in New York on September 26 while the United Nations General Assembly was in session (see the Chronology; see also Telephone conversation, Goodpaster and Herter, Sept. 14, 1960, Herter Papers, Telephone Conversations; Memorandum, [Sept. 1960], AWF/AWD; Goodpaster, Memorandum of Conference, Sept. 28, 1960, AWF/D; Eisenhower, *Waging Peace*, pp. 584–85; and *New York Times*, Mar. 11, Sept. 27, 1960).

1629   *EM, AWF, DDE Diaries Series*

To John Moors Cabot   *August 26, 1960*

Dear John:[1] Several times during recent weeks I have had occasion to wonder how the development of the new capital of Brasilia is progressing. In particular, I have wondered how it is working out as a capital, and whether it is beginning to realize for Brazil some of the advantages it was intended to achieve, as for example the opening up of the interior and "vitalization" of Brazil's economy.

When you have a moment, I will be grateful for a brief informal report of your impressions on this matter.[2]

With warm regard, *Sincerely*

[1] Cabot (A.B. Harvard 1923) had been with the U.S. Foreign Service since 1926. Formerly U.S. Ambassador to Colombia, he had become Ambassador to Brazil in July 1959. Eisenhower had visited Brasilia in February during his Latin American goodwill tour (see nos. 1403 and 1452).

[2] Cabot would report that the move to the new city of Brasilia, built from scratch with futuristic architecture, had slowed since its inauguration as the capital in April 1960. The government still had operations in the old capitol of Rio de Janeiro and was not functioning efficiently: the Brazilian Congress even found it difficult to muster a quorum. Constant construction, the lack of diversions, the high cost of housing, and the disorganization of public utilities made living conditions difficult. The frenetic pace of industrialization and road-building into the interior had led to inflation and taxpayers' discontent.

Nevertheless, Brazilians remained intensely proud of their new capital, he thought, and they had retained their interest in the endeavor. Plans for moving the U.S. foreign office from Rio were proceeding, and the move would be undertaken in stages through the upcoming year. In short, Brasilia was suffering "inevitable growing pains," but Cabot was confident that this "glittering new city" would continue to rise "with a dignity worthy of our great sister republic of South America" (Cabot to Eisenhower, Aug. 31, 1960, AWF/I: Brazil; for background see *New York Times*, Apr. 22, 1960, and Alexander, *Juscelino Kubitschek and the Development of Brazil*, pp. 213–35).

1630   *EM, WHCF, Official File 3-C*

To Ward Murphy Canaday   *August 27, 1960*
Personal

Dear Ward: I cannot agree more with you with regard to your irritation at the information carried in the press about the Discoverer XIV. For almost eight years I have battled against such leaks and this one—as with the others—I had investigated.[1] The report is that the information was that the material was "leaked and promoted" by the manufacturer. However, I do not dismiss the possibility that some of the Air Force people involved also talked too much.[2]

If you could give me a formula as to how to correct such a situation, I would be more than grateful! At any rate, I assure you that I regret the matter just as much as you do and that I have all these years done everything I can to prevent such occurrences. *Sincerely*

[1] Canaday, president of the Overland Corporation and Director of the Fund for Peaceful Atomic Development, had written on August 22, 1960, to voice his *"great* concern over the information divulged in apparently official news releases." He was especially upset with the description in the August 19 *New York Times* of the instruments, carried in the satellite nose cone, that were designed to enable surveillance satellites to provide information on terrain and enemy missile firings. The information, Canaday thought, had been supplied by the Air Force. Canaday had forwarded his note to Presidential Secretary Ann Whitman, adding that he hoped it was not "an intrusion" (Canaday to Whitman, Aug. 22, 1960). Whitman had queried Andrew Goodpaster, "How answer this one?" (Whitman to Goodpaster, n.d.). See Watson, *Into the Missile Age, 1956–1960*, pp. 383–90.

[2] Goodpaster had responded to Whitman on August 26 that this type of "free, boastful information is unnecessary and unwise." At the President's direction he had looked into the matter and had found no official announcements on the subject. "The report is that this was leaked and 'promoted' by the manufacturer. However, I suspect that some of the Air Force people involved also talked too much." Goodpaster added that he encouraged Canaday to offer any suggestion "as to how this situation could be corrected, without shooting the violators or breaching the 'freedom of the press.'" All correspondence is in the same file as the document.

To Clifford Roberts   *August 27, 1960*
Personal

Dear Cliff: Ann reported to me yesterday the success you have had to date with your money raising campaign for VOLUNTEERS FOR NIXON.[1] I think you should be highly gratified by the response you have had.

I am delighted to send to you the contribution I had been planning to turn in to the Nixon-Lodge campaign effort. A check for $500 is enclosed.[2]

I know it is not necessary to add that I am personally grateful for this latest in a long series of chores you have undertaken to assure the continuance of moderate government—nonetheless, thank you!

With warm regard, *As ever*

[1] The President had written Roberts on August 17, 1960, regarding Roberts's efforts on behalf of the Volunteers. Eisenhower had seen Roberts's August 15 letter to Presidential Secretary Ann Whitman and its enclosure, asking for contributions to the Volunteers for Nixon. The President was "particularly interested to learn of the response" Roberts would receive because the people named on his list were "the group that should be anxious to see that moderate government continues in this country." On August 18 Roberts had reported to Whitman that he had received twenty responses to his letters, with eighteen contributions. The donations ranged from $50 to $3,000, with an average of about $1,000. On August 25 Roberts would tell Whitman that about forty checks had come in, a figure which he found "remarkable," since many people were away in August. See also no. 1608, and *New York Times*, August 22, 1960.

[2] Roberts had wondered whether Eisenhower would consider making a contribution through him to the Volunteers for Nixon. Whitman reported that Roberts intended this to be "neither a request or a suggestion." In a memorandum to Roberts on August 27 Whitman had reported that Eisenhower had asked her to use her own checking account but had "no objection to listing his name" among contributors to the fund. For developments see no. 1655. All correspondence is in AWF/N, Roberts Corr.

To Charles André Joseph Marie de Gaulle
Secret   *August 30, 1960*

Dear General De Gaulle:[1] As I promised in my recent brief note, I have now given serious study to your letter of August ninth.[2] I would first like to respond to your suggestion that we meet with Prime Minister Macmillan in September. In this connection I recall our conversations of last May in which we agreed that, in addition to other forms of tripartite consultations, meetings of the three of us would be of great value in world politics.[3] I continue to hold to this thought. I believe that in this case we must give careful thought to what public presentation we could make so as not, on the one hand, to use the Berlin situation as an excuse and thus run the danger of provoking the Russians nor, on the other, to offend our allies and thus weaken our common defense posture.

With regard to the time of such a meeting, I have myself already scheduled numerous public engagements as well as receptions for foreign visitors during the next three months. I would in consequence find it difficult to arrange for another meeting with you in the near future. I would like to suggest, therefore, that we agree in principle to our meeting at a time and place mutually agreeable but that we suspend any final decisions until after our Foreign Ministers have met on September twenty-third.[4] To make their meeting a more meaningful one it should be prepared as thoroughly as possible through the means we have previously agreed to. It would also seem advantageous to exchange papers in advance of this meeting. In this connection I recall that at Rambouillet you said that you would put your thoughts on NATO into memorandum form for Mr. Macmillan and me.[5] This paper would be a valuable document for the discussion of our Foreign Ministers, who I hope will consider thoroughly the matters raised in your letter.

As I have indicated, it would be more convenient to me and probably more satisfactory all around if the meeting involving the three of us were held later in the year. I have been giving serious consideration to a trip to the United Kingdom some time before the year end to see old wartime friends from Britain and across the Channel. This might provide a suitable occasion for a meeting of the two of us with Mr. Macmillan.

Before our ministers meet in September I believe that I should address myself to some of the thoughts set forth in your letter of August ninth, and I am doing so in the friendly and forthright spirit which characterized your letter. As we have each said in the past, a frank exchange of views is essential among friends and allies.

I agree completely as to the desirability of making the Atlantic Alliance more efficient. I have always considered the Alliance a keystone of American policy. In the whole history of NATO, the U.S. did not try to push itself into a place of prominence. Instead it has responded to requests from others with understanding and in a spirit of allied helpfulness. This belief and faith in NATO is shared by the U.S. Congress, both major political parties, and the vast majority of the American people. It has provided the basis for an historic shift in the attitude of the American people towards Europe.

Twenty years ago it would have been impossible to secure the approval of the American people to a long-term involvement on the European continent of thousands of American soldiers and a good part of America's defenses. Today, there is no real opposition to the continuation of that American presence in Europe as a part of the free world's defenses. This attitude on the part of the American people results from their view that our European partners in NATO share with us a common desire to ensure the effective defense of the Atlantic area. If the American people, however, should come to feel that their European allies no longer share this common desire, I must very frankly say that the historic shift in American policy could again reverse itself. Our people might be no longer willing to continue their long-term involvement in the defense of Europe and pressures could mount for a complete return of American troops, with increasing dependence on a strategy in which our defenses center in the United States. I should emphasize that I am not describing here a policy change which I would advocate. I am only setting forth what I believe could be an inevitable trend in the United States.

Another point deserves to be made. Our essential alliances are not confined to the European continent or NATO alone. The U.S. has defensive arrangements with forty-three nations throughout the world. Some of these, such as that with Spain which provides us with essential bases for nuclear air strikes, are bilateral; others are multilateral. In some of these latter France is present; in others, it is not. France, similarly, has its own international relationships and alliances, of which the Community is the latest example.

For us this system of alliances provides a great measure of strength; it serves to make more effective the deterrent. At the same time alliances give members a feeling of confidence, knowing both that unified defenses provide a greater strength for all and that the very existence of special ties give them greater international status. We recognize that there are imperfections and have sought to improve the contacts and liaisons between the various multilateral organizations. Much more can be done in this field but only with the willing acquiescence of the members.

Just as the way in which the U.S. views the world has changed in the post-war era, so has the viewpoint of the smaller and medium-sized powers. They are no longer content to let larger countries speak for them or seek to control in any way their destinies. Each instead seeks to have his voice and views considered, both in bilateral relationships and in international instances. Given the facts of the situation today I must confess that I cannot see how the three of us can so organize, as you suggest, a "real political and military cooperation" if that cooperation implies lessening or subordinating of America's close working relationship with other nations and other alliances or if it implies a reorganization of NATO whose effect would be to remove American forces from Europe.

Once again you have stressed your opposition to the system of integration in NATO which you categorize as unacceptable to France today. I frankly must confess that I cannot understand completely your reasoning. It seems to me that to return to a prewar system of alliances, that is to say, a coalition of powers whose military efforts are not closely joined together, would diminish greatly the effectiveness of a Western alliance. The revolution in military strategy and military technology makes it more, not less, essential that nations integrate their military efforts. National forces fulfilling national missions each on its own soil could well result in a completely ineffective defense force. As I have said before any such policy would compel the return of American troops to this hemisphere. Aside from the strictly military advantages of an integrated alliance over the prewar system, there is the much greater deterrent effect an integrated force creates. When an alliance's military forces are welded into an effective unit, any potential aggressor knows that his aggression must of necessity automatically and simultaneously be met not only by the resistance of his intended victim, but by the united effort of that country's allies as well.

At the time it took place I regretted profoundly the withdrawal of the French naval units from the NATO forces in the Mediterranean.[6] This action did not, of course, diminish the defense forces of the alliance in the Mediterranean although it did make more difficult the coordination of their efforts in the case of war. It did create, however, a major breach in the NATO wall of solidarity. Other actions by France in the field of air defense and nuclear storage have, I am afraid, blocked efforts to strengthen the NATO structure while no serious attempt has been made by France to explain to us or to other NATO countries its ideas on how the alliance could be made more effective. It seems to me that the French Government which has both privately and publicly said that NATO must be revised or reformed, should provide NATO and the NATO members with concrete ideas on how that reform should be effected. Otherwise, does not the continual stress on the supposed inadequacies of NATO merely weaken it further?

In your letter you cited the Congo as an example of a problem concerning which you believe we should have acted more in unison.[7] The differences which we have had as for instance in past Security Council votes, have not been the result of any lack of consultation with one another. I have, in fact, been struck by the frequency and fullness of the consultations that have taken place among our representatives on virtually a daily basis in Paris, here in Washington, and in Brussels as well. I am enclosing a copy of the record of these consultations over the past weeks, which has been prepared for me here.[8] If despite this process our positions remained somewhat apart, I doubt that any more formal or elaborate tripartite arrangements at whatever level could have altered this. I cannot believe that our differences were in large measure responsible for the disorder and anarchy in that country. It seems to me that our differences followed, and did not precede the Congo disorders. It is true that our attitude toward the role the United Nations should play has been different and that France may hesitate to rely upon the UN, but I believe it is a fact that in our consultations on the Congo, France did not present alternatives to a resort to the UN.

Given the speed at which events have moved, I believe our consultation on the Congo has been full and I regret to learn that you believe we are out of step. I know that our basic objectives for the Congo are identical. I hope that our governments can continue their discussions on African matters for this reason and that the French Government will make substantive suggestions capable of being implemented by us and acceptable to the peoples concerned.

I must confess, my dear General, that I cannot quite understand the basic philosophy of France today. On one hand, France rejects the concept of close union needed to make effective the alliance's defensive forces, stating that such action takes from France the essential attribute of national identity. At the same time France proposes a close union of itself, the UK and the U.S. to work out common plans and policies with all the implications of the veto and of imposition of decisions on others which this suggestion holds. These two proposals appear to me incompatible. Additionally, I am sure our NATO partners would find them unacceptable.

The role which France would want to play in a special tripartite relationship is also unclear to me. Do you envisage France speaking in this forum for the other continental members of the alliance? Do you believe that it would be wise to diminish the close relationship of my government with that of Chancellor Adenauer, a relationship which has since the war served to draw the Federal Republic firmly to the West? These questions puzzle me.

I am basically uninformed as to your thinking on the mechanism for intra-European consultation. I believe the United States has a legitimate interest in the form and in the purpose of this mechanism, given the possible effect on the NATO alliance of the creation of another consultative mechanism.

This letter has perhaps been over-long but I believe that it contains some of our apprehensions and some indication of our reserves. I hope you will feel free to answer frankly and fully the questions I have posed in the same feeling of close friendship which I have for you and for France. As you know, I have always attached the greatest importance to our meetings and to our correspondence. I know that you will agree with me that a candid exchange of views can make more fruitful our future discussions and those of our Foreign Ministers.

I am taking the liberty of sending a copy of this letter to Prime Minister Macmillan in view of the fact that you sent to him a copy of your letter to me.[9]

With warm personal regard, *Your good friend*

[1] On August 24 a copy of this message, drafted by State Department officials, was sent to Secretary Herter, then attending OAS meetings in San José, Costa Rica. Two days later another copy was sent to Prime Minister Macmillan through the American embassy in London. The U.S. ambassador was instructed to "report urgently" any comments Macmillan might have (Dillon to Eisenhower, Aug. 24, 1960, AWF/I: de Gaulle; and Eisenhower to de Gaulle, Aug. 26, 1960, AWF/I: Macmillan).
[2] For background on de Gaulle's letter and Eisenhower's interim response see no. 1610.
[3] On the Paris meetings see State, *Foreign Relations, 1958–1960*, vol. VII, pt. 2, *Western Europe*, pp. 360–65.
[4] The foreign ministers of the United States, France, and Great Britain would meet on September 21–22, following the opening of the United Nations General Assembly (see *ibid.*, p. 419).
[5] The President had met with de Gaulle on September 13–14, 1959 (see no. 1309).
[6] For background see nos. 1112 and 1318.
[7] On the situation in the Congo see no. 1599.
[8] See "Meetings with French on the Congo Crisis," AWF/I: Macmillan. This document listed eighteen separate meetings held between June 1 and August 18.
[9] Macmillan would write Eisenhower on August 27 that he was delighted with the first three paragraphs of the reply to de Gaulle. He was especially gratified at the third paragraph relating to a December visit to Great Britain. "With regard to the arguments set out in the main part of your letter," Macmillan added, "it seems to me that you are quite right in sending a full expression of your point of view, if only in the hope that it will draw something a little more concrete out of the General" (AWF/I: Macmillan; see also Macmillan to Eisenhower, Sept. 2, 1960, *ibid.*). For developments see nos. 1642 and 1665.

1633   *EM, AWF, DDE Diaries Series*

To Harold Edward Stassen   *August 30, 1960*

Dear Harold: Thank you very much for your letter of August twenty-sixth. I assume that it is intended as a memorandum of information rather than as any official invitation.[1]

If a number of leaders in the several activities that you mention should want to pay this kind of compliment to Mamie and me, I should, in principle, be delighted to accept. However, I do not believe it is possible for us to fix, at this time, a definite date for such a ceremony. It is possible that we shall want to leave this city on January twentieth for an extended trip to the South.[2] Moreover, Pennsylvania weather promises to be much more salubrious in the late spring than it does in mid-winter.

In any event, if and when the committee that you speak of is formed, I shall be glad to see them at any time after the election that may suit the convenience both of the committee and myself.[3] It would be understood, of course, that if any important group or groupments would prefer to abstain from such a ceremony, then the whole matter, without prejudice, would best be dropped.

As far as the place is concerned, I can think of none better than the square in Gettysburg.[4]

Thank you very much for your thoughtfulness.

With warm regard, *As ever*

[1] Stassen had written on August 26 (AWF/D) of plans underway for a "Welcome Home" to the President and Mrs. Eisenhower by the people of Pennsylvania upon the conclusion of Eisenhower's second term. The final plans would be in accordance with the President's ideas, he said, and nothing would be decided until Eisenhower was consulted personally.

[2] The President would spend February 1–3 hunting at former Treasury Secretary Humphrey's Milestone Plantation in Thomasville, Georgia. On February 7 the Eisenhowers would board a train for a six-week vacation in Palm Springs, California (see *New York Times*, Feb. 1, 3, 1961, and no. 1624).

[3] Current plans, Stassen wrote, called for the chairman to be a "citizen-cultural leader" such as the president of Pennsylvania State College. Participation would include senior elected officials of both parties, professionals, school children, and representatives of labor, management, and farming.

[4] On January 21, 1961, the Eisenhowers would be welcomed by 2,000 people in the Gettysburg town square. Later they would attend a dinner given by 200 civic leaders at the Hotel Gettysburg. On April 17 the State of Pennsylvania would officially welcome the Eisenhowers (see Susan Eisenhower, *Mrs. Ike*, pp. 303–6, and *New York Times*, Jan. 22, Apr. 18, 1961).

1634   *EM, AWF, International Series:*
                                                                    Malaya

To Tunku Abdul Rahman Putra   *August 31, 1960*

Dear Mr. Prime Minister: I have read with much interest your letter of August 9, 1960, explaining the motivation for the Government of the Federation of Malaya's recent decision prohibiting the import of all goods of South African origin with effect from the first of August, and inquiring whether the United States, for its part, would consider the possibility of taking some positive action to demonstrate objection to the present trends in South African policy.[1]

This Government has, of course, been following developments in South Africa very closely and has indeed taken particular note of the steps taken by the Federation of Malaya and other countries in reaction to the policies pursued by the South African Government. The position of the United States Government on the apartheid question is, I believe, clear and unequivocal as demonstrated by the statements of United States officials at the United Nations and in Washington and by our support of the resolutions on the apartheid item in the 13th and 14th General Assemblies. In addition, the Government of the people of the United States, as you know, is actively engaged in the complex process of eliminating racial discrimination in this country.[2] We take pride in the steady progress that is being made. We congratulate you and the Malayan Government on the leadership you are providing for the development of a unified Malayan nation, with full respect for the rights and opportunities of all elements of your multi-racial society.

While the influence of world public opinion through the medium of the United Nations and other international organizations cannot be expected in every case to produce quickly those changes deemed desirable in human societies, the forum of international organizations still affords us, I believe, the most desirable approach to the resolution of such complex social problems as racial discrimination which are, in fact, world-wide and not limited to one or two nations. Thus, while the United States fully understands the motivation for Malaya's policy of boycotting South African goods, I must state frankly that it is unlikely that the United States could adopt such a policy.

The foregoing discussion is necessarily a brief resume of the United States views on this difficult problem which has so many ramifications.

I look forward very much to seeing you here in October, when we shall have the opportunity to discuss various matters of mutual interest.[3] In the meanwhile, I wish to thank you again for your thoughtfulness in writing to me about this subject. *Sincerely*

---

[1] Rahman had written Eisenhower of his government's conviction that action was necessary to induce South Africa to change its racial policies. Violence against South Africa's Negro population was increasing, and the policy of strict racial separation known as apartheid prevented normal diplomatic relations involving officials from Asian and African countries. He had suggested to the South African foreign minister that his government gradually begin to enfranchise Africans in order to avert disaster. Rahman had asked Eisenhower "to consider whether it would not

be in the interest of the future of the human race for your country to give to the world and South Africa some positive indication of your objection to the present dangerous trends in South African policy." He had also offered to host a conference to discuss what course of action countries might take against the policy (Rahman to Eisenhower, Aug. 9, 1960, AWF/I: Malaya; see also *New York Times*, Aug. 1 and 22, 1960).

[2] The question of apartheid in South Africa had been part of the agenda of every regular General Assembly since 1952. In the 13th General Assembly (1958) the United States and sixty-nine other nations had voted for a resolution reaffirming the value of equality before the law of all persons regardless of race and noting that discrimination was inconsistent with the human rights provisions of the Charter of the United Nations. The 14th General Assembly (1959) resolution had directly condemned South Africa's racial policies; for the complete text of U.N. General Assembly Resolution 1248 (XIII), see U.N. doc. A/4090, and for the text of U.N. General Assembly Resolution 1375 (XIV), see U.N. doc. A/4354, as cited in State, *Foreign Relations, 1958–1960*, vol. II, *United Nations and General International Matters*, pp. 160–61, 288–90.

[3] Eisenhower would meet with Rahman on October 25, 1960 (see Memorandum of Conversation, Oct. 26, 1960, and additional documents in AWF/I: Malaya).

1635   *EM, AWF, DDE Diaries Series*

ELWOOD RICHARD QUESADA   *September 1, 1960*

Dear Pete: If I only had a proper medal for you?[1]

[1] Eisenhower had added this note by hand at the bottom of a memorandum from FAA chief Quesada (Sept. 1, 1960, AWF/D), who had written that he had recently inventoried the number of "Deputies" in the Federal Aviation Agency. Finding 335, an "abuse too obvious to dwell upon," Quesada had reduced the number to eight. He had then discovered 625 "Assistants," "many of whom were former 'Deputies.'" He eliminated 345. Ending "this undesirable and unnecessary 'layering of supervision' will result in an annual saving of $838,500," he wrote. See Robert Burkhardt, *The Federal Aviation Administration* (New York, 1967); and Rochester, *Takeoff at Mid-Century*.

1636   *EM, AWF, DDE Diaries Series*

TO DOUGLAS MCCRAE BLACK   *September 2, 1960*
Personal

Dear Doug: Thank you very much for your note about John.[1] Frankly, I believe that he might like to talk over with you the possibility that you mention. As you know, he has always been interested in writing and teaching and even if he did not want to talk definitively at this moment, I am quite sure he would like to discuss it in principle. Again, my gratitude for notifying me in advance.[2]

I hope that I shall get to see you and Ken at least briefly while you are here next Wednesday with John.[3]

In the meantime, give my love to Maudie, and all the best to yourself. *As ever*

[1] Black's note about Colonel John S. D. Eisenhower is not in EM.

[2] Black probably had suggested that Colonel Eisenhower outline and research his father's presidential memoirs (John S. D. Eisenhower, *Strictly Personal*, pp. 304–5, and *New York Times*, Mar. 28, 1961; see also Telephone conversation, Eisenhower and Black, Sept. 14, 1960, AWF/AWD). For background on Eisenhower's decision to have Doubleday and Company, Inc., publish his memoirs see no. 1624.

[3] On September 7 the President, Black, Kenneth Dale McCormick, editor-in-chief of Doubleday since 1942, and John Eisenhower would meet (off-the-record) at the White House. For developments see no. 1650.

1637   *EM, AWF, Name Series*

To WILLIAM EDWARD ROBINSON   *September 2, 1960*

Dear Bill: Today two things came to my attention that probably I should have known long before. Certainly if I had been aware of them, I should have tried in some measure to thank you, Bob, and the entire Coca Cola organization.[1]

First, I find that you supplied, free of charge, cokes for all the staff who were with me at Newport this summer.[2] Secondly, I discover that you also gave the White House enough cokes for the thousands of people that attended the British Bar Association-American Bar Association garden party last Monday. (If I had known what was involved, I might have curbed my last minute invitation to any member of the American contingent to walk in the gates!).[3] Be that as it may, you and your associates contributed immeasurably to making the affair pleasant and, I hope, successful.

My personal indebtedness to you is already so great that it defies any expression of gratitude. But I did want to tell you that I am deeply appreciative of the kindness of the Coca Cola organization in the hospitality it enables me to offer to guests and to workers in the vineyard.

Of course, what baffles me most is that you do all these things so quietly—but that is characteristic.

Thank you.

With warm regard, *As ever*[4]

[1] Robinson and Robert Winship Woodruff were the chairman of the board and chairman of the executive committee and director of the Coca-Cola Company, respectively.
[2] The President had vacationed in Newport, Rhode Island, July 7–August 7 (see nos. 1590 and 1596).
[3] Leading judges and lawyers of the British Commonwealth had joined members of the American Bar Association at their annual assembly in Washington (see no. 1603). Addressing the assembly session the afternoon of August 29, the President had appealed for removal of limits on the United States' adherence to the International Court of Justice. At the end of his remarks Eisenhower explained that invitations to the White House garden party had at first been limited due to the ABA officers' anxiety over space. "All are welcome," he said, "and I shall expect you this evening . . ." (see *Public Papers of the Presidents, Eisenhower, 1960–61*, pp. 663–66, and *New York Times*, Aug. 30, 1960).
[4] The President had added a handwritten postscript: "When you do such things give me some advance notice—at least I could produce a *feeble* commercial. D."

1638   *EM, AWF, Administration Series*

To Charles Douglas Jackson   *September 5, 1960*
Personal

Dear C. D.: I am quite ready to stand in whatever breach Mr. Khrushchev can create by the lies, distortions and deceit that he will use at the United Nations.[1] The first thing to do of course is to try to determine the character of the breach and what are the things that will most effectively show him up for the liar that he is.

By no means should you think that this subject has been overlooked by me, by the State Department, or, while he was at the U.N., by Cabot Lodge.[2] Long before Mr. Khrushchev ever announced his plan to come to New York we were considering such a possibility. (In fact while you speak of the "firming up" of his appearance, I still would want to know that he is at least in the air and know something about his ETA before I could accept his statement as fact).[3] Put it this way: without attempting to guess exactly what the man will try to do, we are attempting to keep prepared and if we believe that there is something effective we can do to place our case properly before the world and refute the false charges of the Soviets, through a speech at the United Nations, I will be ready, at a time of our own choosing, to make such a talk.[4]

Many thanks for your letter. It was thoughtful of you to give me your ideas on this subject.

With warm regard, *As ever*

[1] Jackson had written Eisenhower regarding the upcoming session of the United Nations General Assembly and Soviet Premier Khrushchev's decision to attend. The

presence of Khrushchev and the heads of other Communist states, Jackson had written, would subject the United States to a "propaganda barrage of incredible concentration and ferocity." Eisenhower was the only man in the country who could "effectively stand up, be listened to, and believed," he said. It was a moment for "incisiveness, boldness, and virile action." Jackson had sent Eisenhower the draft of a speech for presentation at the United Nations; the message, he said, would show Khrushchev that there was no "moratorium on U.S. decision making until the next President is inaugurated" (Jackson to Eisenhower, Sept. 2, 1960, AWF/A; see also "Draft Speech by the President Before the 15th General Assembly of the United Nations" [Aug. 19, 1960], AWF/A, Jackson Corr.; Jackson to Whitman, Sept. 2, 9, 1960; Whitman to Jackson, Sept. 12, 1960, both in AWF/A).

[2] Ambassador Lodge had resigned his position at the United Nations on September 3 to campaign actively as the Republican vice-presidential nominee (see no. 1620).
[3] On September 1 Khrushchev had made the announcement that he would head the Soviet delegation to the United Nations (see State, *Foreign Relations, 1958–1960*, vol. II, *United Nations and General International Matters*, p. 305; and Eisenhower, *Waging Peace*, pp. 576–77; see also *New York Times*, Sept. 2, 1960).
[4] In an address on September 22 that was probably less strident than Jackson had suggested, Eisenhower would strongly support the activities of the United Nations, particularly with regard to the newly-formed African nations (see *Public Papers of the Presidents: Eisenhower, 1960–61*, pp. 707–20; see also Ann Whitman memorandums, Sept. 12, 15, 19, 22, 1960, AWF/AWD; Goodpaster, Memorandums of Conference, Sept. 14, 19, 1960, AWF/D; Telephone conversation, Herter and Goodpaster, Sept. 8, 1960, Herter Papers, Telephone Conversations; and Eisenhower, *Waging Peace*, pp. 578–81).

1639   *EM, AWF, DDE Diaries Series*

To Aksel Nielsen   *September 5, 1960*

Dear Aks: I do not see how I can possibly accept membership on the Board of any commercial company.[1] I have had a number of suggestions of this kind, but have come to the conclusion that it would not be in keeping with the course I set for myself a good many years ago.[2]

Quite naturally I am complimented that the Board members of United would think I could contribute anything to their deliberations, and certainly—if I were going on any industrial or transportation or financial body—I could think of no finer one than United. Won't you please express my appreciation to those who were responsible for the suggestion?

With warm regard, *As ever*

[1] Nielsen had written that at the September 1 United Airlines board meeting the members had proposed to elect Eisenhower to the board on January 22 (Sept. 2, 1960, AWF/N). Nielsen said that there might be "a dozen reasons why" the President would want to decline the offer, but he thought there were also many reasons

to accept. First, he said, they were "a real swell bunch of fellows," and second, United Airlines was preeminent in the industry. It would also serve Eisenhower's transportation needs, Nielsen said, because directors were entitled to use United's executive plane whenever they wanted it.

[2] On this same day the President had replied in similar fashion to Vernon Bigelow Stouffer, chairman of the Stouffer Corporation and also a member of the United Airlines Board of Directors (AWF/D).

1640   *EM, AWF, International Series: Argentina*

To Arturo Frondizi   *September 7, 1960*
Confidential

Dear Mr. President and Esteemed Friend: I have given your recent letter and accompanying memorandum the prompt attention which I promised in my initial message.[1]

Your views command particular respect in my eyes and in the councils of this Government, and in this instance they have provided a major point of reference for me and for my advisors in our continuing review of what the United States should be accomplishing by its efforts in support of the hemispheric objectives which our two Governments share.[2] We in the United States seek peace and freedom and progress for all the world, with resources which, although large, are not limitless; and I think that the very range of our endeavors tends at times to distort the assessment of what we have achieved and of what may perhaps be left undone.

The courage with which you and your Government have faced the economic problems which beset your country, Mr. President, has been impressive. We know that, notwithstanding short-range political disadvantages, your essential economic decisions have been made with a determination to have Argentina help itself to the greatest degree possible. The evidences of this quality in your Government have been influential in the shaping of the policies of my Government, which have been and continue to be directed toward close and productive cooperation with your Government. To the fullest extent feasible, the United States Government will continue to support the inter-related programs of financial stabilization and economic development which are embodied in your Government's forward-looking policies.[3]

In order to define Argentina's requirements and to evaluate prospective projects, it would appear appropriate for discussions to be held promptly between those officials of our two Governments most directly concerned with this matter. The Under Secretary of State, Mr. C. Douglas Dillon, is now in Bogota at the meeting of the Committee of 21 and, if you agree, this may provide an opportunity for your representative to discuss this subject with him.[4] This could be useful in preparing for further discussions which we would be pleased to have with your Minister of Economy, Eng. Alvaro C. Alsogaray, if he visits Washington in late September, as I understand he is scheduled to do in connection with meetings of the governing bodies of the International Monetary Fund and the International Bank for Reconstruction and Development.[5] This would not preclude, of course, the presentation by your Government of detailed proposals through any other official channels.

Imbued with the purpose of responding to the needs of our friends in this hemisphere for continuing social development, the United States has now embarked, as you know, on a new program of financial cooperation in that vital field.[6] I assume, Mr. President, that your Government has also been giving consideration to ways in which we might be of appropriate assistance in this regard.

I think that you will also be interested to learn that my Secretary of Agriculture, Mr. Ezra T. Benson, is planning to travel in South America during October, and I hope that he will have an opportunity during this trip to exchange views with you respecting United States policies and measures affecting agricultural commodities and their marketing.[7] Since there is full recognition here of the crucial importance of earnings from agricultural exports to Argentine recovery efforts, I am particularly desirous of eliminating misunderstandings and misinterpretations in this field.

Please be assured, Mr. President, that there is complete realization within this Government of the importance of your Government's current economic program and of the necessity that it be carried to a successful conclusion.[8]

With warm personal regard, *Sincerely*

[1] On the Argentine President's correspondence see Frondizi to Eisenhower, August 9, 1960; Eisenhower to Frondizi, August 16, 1960, AWF/I: Argentina. The State Department had drafted this reply (Herter to Eisenhower, Sept. 2, 1960, *ibid.*).
[2] Frondizi had written to resume the "frank discussions" started during Eisenhower's December 1959 visit to Argentina (see no. 1383). Frondizi had undertaken similar discussions with various leaders during his June trip to Europe, where he had emphasized the "absolute necessity for the highly developed countries to step up their collaboration in the development of the underdeveloped nations if all the peoples of the free world wish to preserve the way of life common to all of them." The Argentinian President feared repercussions if his austere economic reforms failed to spur the Argentine economy. During the current world crisis, he had reflected, underdeveloped countries and former colonies, many increasingly nationalistic, were choosing either western-style development or revolution leading to dictatorship. Argentina had chosen a "Western way of life," but the United States had failed to provide enough assistance to ensure her success. Frondizi had complained that Argentina could not afford the slow and bureaucratic procedures of the international credit agencies. His country needed aid immediately to create employment and to

finance highway, housing, and power projects; without such aid he would fail in his "program of stabilization, despite the immense sacrifices laid upon the entire Nation, and the social and political results will be unpredictable." Frondizi's accompanying memorandum outlined Argentina's most pressing economic problems and needs. For background see State, *Foreign Relations, 1958–1960*, vol. V, *American Republics*, pp. 628–37.

[3] President Eisenhower had told Dillon and General Goodpaster that the Argentine President's letter was "rather emotional in tone" and that Frondizi saw his own problem clearly but did not "appreciate the difficulties we undergo regarding our aid programs and trade restrictions." He thought that Frondizi should be told that "we are somewhat astonished that the situation appears as bad to him as he indicated." He also asked Dillon to provide the Argentinians with "scientific evidence regarding the unsatisfactory sanitary status of the meat they wished to export to the United States" (Memorandum of Conference with the President, Aug. 18, 1960, AWF/D).

Herter had advised the President not to take issue with Frondizi's unfavorable comments as the tone of this letter was meant to be "friendly and affirmative." The State Department had expected the Argentine government to request additional financial assistance, he had explained, and steps were being taken to correct Frondizi's misunderstanding about U.S. aid efforts and procedures. The United States wanted Frondizi's economic program to succeed, he continued, and there was interagency agreement to provide further assistance in the field of highway construction (Memorandum for the President, Sept. 2, 1960, *ibid.*).

[4] The Committee of 21 meeting in Bogotá, Colombia, Sept. 5–13, 1960 (for background see no. 1580).

[5] Engineer Alvaro C. Alsogaray, educated at the Argentine Military Academy and future Ambassador to the United States, would meet with Dillon and other officials on September 28, 1960, in Washington. Alsogaray would report that his government and the Development Loan Fund and Export-Import Bank were working out an agreement on highway construction aid. They would also discuss possible funding for a housing program. The United States wanted to cooperate, the Under Secretary would say, but it did not make loans unless requested and would need more details before making any commitments (State, *Foreign Relations, 1958–1960*, vol. V, *American Republics*, pp. 643–46).

[6] For background on the Social Progress Trust Fund see no. 1532 and 1580; on the Argentinians' critical reaction to U.S. aid plans see *New York Times*, September 5, 1960.

[7] Frondizi had complained about the obstacles involved in exporting agricultural products to the United States (Frondizi to Eisenhower, Aug. 9, 1960, AWF/I: Argentina). Benson would meet with Frondizi on October 29, during his fifteen-day trip to South America. He would report that the United States was prepared to import Argentine beef and to hold consultations on agricultural trade problems (*New York Times*, Oct. 30, 1960).

[8] On October 25 the United States would announce a new Development Loan Fund program for housing and highway construction in Argentina (*New York Times*, Oct. 26, 1960).

To WILLIAM J. HOPKINS   *September 8, 1960*

Memorandum for the Executive Clerk's Permanent White House File: For the benefit of my successors I wish to make this record of my objections to S. J. Res. 170, 86th Congress, even though, as explained below, it finally received my approval, albeit reluctantly.[1]

The joint resolution creates a United States Citizens Commission on NATO which is to meet with similar citizens commissions from other NATO countries "to explore means by which greater cooperation and unity of purpose may be developed to the end that democratic freedom may be promoted by economic and political means." By express provision, the Commission has no authority to speak for or to represent the United States Government. Its members are to be appointed by the President of the Senate and the Speaker of the House of Representatives and $300,000 is authorized to be appropriated to the Department of State for Commission purposes.

This legislation in its original form was a concurrent resolution not requiring the approval of the President. It established no Commission, no appropriation was authorized and, although not specific on the question of appointment, it was implicit that United States representatives would in some manner be selected by the Congress. The State Department more than a year ago, after bringing the matter to my attention, had indicated to the Congress that there was no objection to such a concurrent resolution, provided specifically that the United States representatives were designated by the Legislative Branch.[2]

The measure presented to me, however, was a joint resolution requiring my approval and further involving the Executive Branch by authorizing an appropriation to the Department of State for the funding of the Commission.

Through inadvertence these changes in the form and substance of the legislation were never discussed with me and the Department of State supported the measure in its new form. I ultimately concluded that I should approve the measure rather than vitiate the efforts of a number of people, all working in good faith and for a good cause.

My objection to the legislation is one of principle and can be simply stated: If the Executive Branch is to handle the finances of such a commission and if the President is to approve the legislation creating the Commission, then appointments to the Commission should be made by the President. Only in such form would the measure fully accord with the historic separation of powers doctrine and the Executive's Constitutional responsibility for the conduct of the nation's foreign relations.

[1] For background on the joint resolution see *Congressional Quarterly Almanac*, Vol. XVI, *1960*, pp. 348–49. On September 6 Eisenhower had discussed his objections to the resolution with Secretary Herter. On the following day he told Herter that he had decided to sign the bill "mindful that the Congress *had* passed it and not believing it worth a veto." He decided, however, to file this memorandum reflecting his views (Goodpaster, Memorandum of Conference, Sept. 7, 1960; and McPhee to Whitman, Sept. 9, 1960; both in AWF/D).

[2] Herter had reminded Eisenhower that they had discussed the legislation "in its broadest outline" during the President's visit to London in August 1959 (McPhee to Whitman, Sept. 9, 1960, *ibid.*; on the visit see no. 1303; and State, *Foreign Relations, 1958–1960*, vol. VII, pt. 2, *Western Europe*, pp. 849–58).

1642
EM, AWF, International Series:
Macmillan

To Harold Macmillan
Cable. Secret

September 8, 1960

Dear Harold: I have received your two recent notes, and thank you for them.

Within recent days, I have heard several reports that General de Gaulle continues to deplore the failure, as he sees it, of our three countries to intervene together in the Congo crisis and lay down a pattern of behavior to be followed by the Congolese. I am sure you must be as puzzled as I am to see how this last purpose could have been achieved.

It will be interesting to learn what his reaction is to the long letter I sent him recently.[1]

With warm regard, *As ever*

[1] Eisenhower was probably referring to Macmillan's brief letters of August 27 and September 2, 1960 (both in AWF/I: Macmillan), voicing his approval of the President's response to Charles de Gaulle's letter of August 9, 1960. The French president had criticized Western lack of unity over the crisis in the Congo; he was also critical of the U.N.'s reliance on African rather than U.S. and British troops (State, *Foreign Relations, 1958–1960*, vol. XIV, *Africa*, p. 406). Eisenhower had sent the Prime Minister a draft and final copy of his August 30 letter to de Gaulle (no. 1632; see also nos. 1598 and 1610). In his reply Macmillan would write Eisenhower that he also did not see how "we could have organized the Congo as de Gaulle suggests," and he added that they must continue to support the United Nations as "the best chance of keeping the Russians out" (Sept. 9, 1960, AWF/I: Macmillan). For background see nos. 1599 and 1611; Alistair Horne, *Harold Macmillan*, 2 vols. (New York, 1988–89), vol. 2 (1989), pp. 206–8, and Macmillan, *Pointing the Way*, pp. 246–47. For developments see no. 1714.

To John Gedroice Powers *September 8, 1960*
Personal and confidential

Dear Mr. Powers: Since our talk of a few weeks ago I have been thinking over the possible character of my future activities.[1] Your letter
presents a number of intriguing suggestions; but I have come to a
decision that will make it impossible, I think, for me to take advantage of the opportunities you outline.[2]

When I wrote a book in 1948 it was published by Doubleday Company, whose President, Douglas Black, became my warm friend.[3]
There are one or two other individuals in the publishing world with
whom I would like, as a matter of sentiment, to be connected—
again because of past experiences and friendships.

I am not formally committed to this course of action; but my past
connection with these several friends has been so satisfactory that I
must tell you in all frankness that I plan, once I have laid down the
duties of this office, to confer with them with a view to establishing
the contacts of which I speak.[4]

I have explained this situation to you so that you will see that I
mean no disrespect either to the sincerity or the attractiveness of
your own suggestions.

While I would find most interesting any future conversation with
you, as I did our earlier one, I thought it only fair to make my position perfectly clear.[5]

With best wishes, *Sincerely*

[1] Powers (A.B. Princeton 1938; LL.B. Harvard 1941) had been president of Prentice-
Hall, Inc., since 1954. He had practiced law for two years before becoming the general counsel for the book publishing firm and in 1947 was promoted to editor-in-
chief and vice-president and director. The President had met with Powers on July 7
at the White House.

[2] Powers had written on August 26 (AWF/N) that Eisenhower's background of successful administration in the Armed Forces, the government and education would
provide "the basis for a broad publishing association." He suggested that the President could write about topics of his own choosing and could, in addition, plan and
direct a complete publishing program using other authors, in areas in which he had
unique experience. Powers had also invited Eisenhower to join in policy making for
all divisions of Prentice-Hall and its subsidiaries as a general advisor or as a member
or honorary chairman of the Board of Directors.

[3] On December 30, 1947, Eisenhower and Black had agreed informally to publish
the General's memoirs of World War II. The book was published in 1948 as *Crusade
in Europe* (see Eisenhower, *At Ease*, pp. 323–29; Galambos, *Chief of Staff*, no. 1977;
and no. 1636 in these volumes).

[4] For background on Eisenhower's decision to publish his memoirs with Doubleday
and Company, Inc., see no. 1624. For developments see no. 1650.

[5] The President would not meet with Powers again before January 20.

TO MIGUEL YDÍGORAS FUENTES   *September 12, 1960*

Great and Good Friend: I wish again to express my appreciation for
your friendly letter of August twenty-third delivered personally into
my hands by your Ambassador, Carlos Alejos.[1] I am indeed pleased
to renew the personal exchange of views I first enjoyed with you during your visit to Washington in February, 1958.[2] Your frank and comprehensive comments on the present situation in Guatemala have
been studied with interest and sympathy by officials of this government.[3]

   Your letter further confirms my conviction that the countries in
this Hemisphere face, individually and collectively, a very definite
threat to our democratic way of life and to our American system that
requires our constant vigilance and resolute action. From the very
inception of our independence we in the Americas have recognized
that we share a common destiny and that a threat from without to
any one of us is a threat to all of us. This firm belief and our determination to uphold it was overwhelmingly confirmed at San Jose
just a few days ago. Your timely efforts in alerting others to the most
recent threat to the American system merit special commendation.[4]

   I have noted with particular satisfaction your account of your efforts to provide the benefits of economic and social justice to the
Guatemalan people without sacrificing democratic freedoms and
practices. This is particularly important since it describes exactly that
which distinguishes our system from the doctrine some now are
seeking to impose in this Hemisphere. This insidious doctrine proposes that our peoples must relinquish their personal freedom and
their individuality in order to achieve the material progress we seek.
In response to this challenge, our representatives at the meeting of
the Committee of Twenty-One in Bogota have proposed that the
forces of domestic action and of international cooperation working
hand in hand can achieve the economic and social advancement of
our people without sacrificing the fundamental human rights and
freedoms which we have achieved and preserved at great costs. As
an immediate demonstration and as tangible evidence of our sincere devotion to this objective I recommended, and the Congress
of the United States approved, the authorization of $500 million for
this purpose.[5]

   It would indeed be a tragedy for us all and a great triumph for
Communism if your country having once freed itself of the Communist yoke should again find that yoke reimposed.[6] You may be
sure that the needs of Guatemala, both for the immediate and for

the long term, will be given prompt and sympathetic attention by my Government, which has responded willingly in the past to Guatemalan needs. As you know, just a few days ago approval was given of a total of $9.6 million in loans and credits by the Export Import Bank and by the Development Loan Fund.[7] Active consideration is being given to other loan requests already filed with our leading institutions.

Regarding your current situation, I suggest that through your Ambassador here in Washington you provide the specific details of the needs for special assistance referred to in your letter to me. Ambassador Alejos has shown himself to be a most energetic and conscientious representative of your government and he is already well acquainted with those officials charged with the responsibility of handling such requests and the procedures involved.[8]

Again, I would like to assure you of my sympathy and of my deep concern over the enormous difficulties you are facing so resolutely. I extend to you my cordial best wishes for your personal health and happiness, together with my wish for the continued prosperity and peace with justice of the Guatemalan people.[9]

With assurances of my highest esteem, *Sincerely*

[1] Eisenhower had met with Guatemala's Ambassador Alejos on September 1. After reading Ydígoras's letter about Guatemala's serious economic and political difficulties (AWF/I: Guatemala), Eisenhower had told the ambassador that he would consult with the State Department and send a more substantive reply soon. Eisenhower had also remarked that the United States was interested in doing all it could to cope with Castro and Communism and that he appreciated Guatemala's efforts to do the same (Memorandum of Conversation, Sept. 1, 1960; see also Herter to Eisenhower, Aug. 31, and Eisenhower's interim reply of Aug. 31, all in *ibid.*).
  The State Department drafted this reply to the President.
[2] Eisenhower had met with Ydígoras in Washington on February 25, 1958 (President's daily appointments).
[3] Ydígoras had stated that Guatemala's general economy had continued to deteriorate as coffee prices fell, creating a dire fiscal crisis, even after his government had reformed the economy on an austerity basis (for background see no. 981). Communist and pro-Castro forces had taken advantage of the situation, he said, and were attempting to overthrow his government. Ydígoras had asked for an additional $20 million in aid from the United States in order to carry out reforms and stem Communist influence. He had offered to provide a detailed request either through Guatemala's ambassador in Washington or by a special mission (Ydígoras to Eisenhower, Aug. 23, 1960, Herter to Eisenhower, Sept. 10, 1960, both in AWF/I: Guatemala). Eisenhower had asked Herter to have the State Department prepare a reply to Ydígoras's "terrific exposition" of the attempt to make Guatemala a "Communist beachhead" (Telephone conversation, Eisenhower and Herter, Sept. 10, 1960, Herter Papers, Telephone Conversations; for previous discussions of Communist penetration see no. 404).
[4] The sixth and seventh meetings of the Consultation of the American Foreign Ministers had been held consecutively at San José, Costa Rica, August 16–30 (State, *Foreign Relations, 1958–1960*, vol. V, *American Republics*, p. 638). Eisenhower was referring to Guatemala's presentation of its problems with Cuba before the Inter-

American Peace Committee (see State, *Foreign Relations, 1958–1960*, vol. V, *American Republics*, Supplemental Microfiche GT-31, n. 3). At the conclusion of the conference the delegates had signed the Declaration of San José, which condemned extracontinental intervention in the hemisphere (*New York Times*, Aug. 29 and 30, 1960; see also Rabe, *Eisenhower and Latin America*, pp. 165–66).

⁵ The Committee of 21 had met in Bogotá, Columbia, September 5–13, 1960. The delegates had passed the Act of Bogotá, which cited Latin America's need for social and economic reforms. U.S. officials had begun to implement the program at the conference even though Congress had not yet given final authorization for what came to be known as the Social Progress Trust Fund (P.L. 86-735). See *Congressional Quarterly Almanac*, vol. XVI, *1960*, pp. 216–18; on the fund see no. 1580, and for additional background see Rabe, *Eisenhower and Latin America*, pp. 141–44, 165–66.

⁶ On communism's influence among Guatemala's political rulers in the decade between 1944 and 1954 see Galambos and van Ee, *The Middle Way*, no. 870.

⁷ See State, *Foreign Relations, 1958–1960*, vol. V, *American Republics*, Supplemental Microfiche, GT-31, n. 2, and on further loan negotiations see *ibid.*, GT-30.

⁸ Ambassador Alejos would meet with the President on November 3, 1960, to discuss Guatemala's need for budgetary support and for highway construction loans. Eisenhower would respond that general budgetary support might set a precedent for continuing requests and that he preferred to help with specific development loans (Memorandum of Conversation, Nov. 3, 1960, AWF/I: Guatemala).

⁹ For later developments in Guatemala's political situation see the additional correspondence in AWF/I: Guatemala, and Eisenhower, *Waging Peace*, p. 613.

1645   *EM, AWF, Dulles-Herter Series*

To Wilber Marion Brucker   *September 12, 1960*
Secret

Dear Mr. Secretary: It is my desire that there should be clarification of the relationship between the Chief of the United States Diplomatic Mission in Panama¹ and the Governor of the Panama Canal Zone² in matters affecting the relations between the United States and the Republic of Panama or any other nation.

I therefore direct that in the exercise of his functions, the Governor of the Canal Zone shall consult with the Chief of the United States Diplomatic Mission in the Republic of Panama on all matters which may have foreign affairs implications, and with respect to such matters shall be guided by the foreign policy considerations set forth by the Chief of the United States Diplomatic Mission in the Republic of Panama. In the event of their failure to agree with respect to any proposed action to which the Chief of the United States Diplomatic Mission in the Republic of Panama shall object for reasons of foreign policy, such action shall be deferred pending a mutual decision thereon by the Secretary of the Army and the Secretary of State.³

I would appreciate it if you would issue appropriate instructions to the Governor of the Panama Canal Zone.

I am sending a copy of this letter to the Secretary of State for his information.[4] *Sincerely*

---

[1] Joseph S. Farland (B.A. West Virginia University 1936) had been appointed U.S. Ambassador to Panama in June 1960 (*New York Times*, June 25, 1960). Formerly the U.S. Ambassador to the Dominican Republic, he had also practiced law, served as an agent with the F.B.I., and was president of the Farland Fuel Corporation.

[2] Major General William Arnold Carter (USMA 1930) had been sworn in as the new governor in July, despite the fact that the State Department had wanted a civilian rather than a military appointment (John S.D. Eisenhower, Memorandum of Conference, Sept. 1, 1960, AWF/D).

[3] On September 1, 1960, Eisenhower had met with Secretary of the Army Brucker, Secretary of State Herter, and Livingston Merchant, Under Secretary of State for Political Affairs. The State Department and Department of the Army had agreed that similar restraints should apply to the Commander in Chief of the Caribbean (*ibid.*).

Hoping to improve relations with Panama, Eisenhower would publicly announce (Sept. 17) that the Panamanian flag would be flown in the Canal Zone (*New York Times*, Sept. 18, 1960; see also Ann Whitman memorandum, Aug. 9, 1960, AWF/AWD). For background see nos. 1355, 1380, and 1443; LaFeber, *The Panama Canal*, pp. 128–29; and Michael L. Conniff, *Panama and the United States: The Forced Alliance* [Athens and London, 1992], p. 113).

[4] The State Department had drafted these letters for the President (Herter to Eisenhower, Sept. 8, 1960, AWF/D-H).

1646

EM, AWF, DDE Diaries Series

To GABRIEL HAUGE   September 12, 1960
Personal

Dear Gabe: I think your suggestion about the growth of the tree has a real application if used in the proper context.[1] However, we primarily consider a tree's development as a very slow growth—in other words, as a result of the passage of time. I believe that between the ages of the two candidates there is slightly less than four years. Consequently the sentence when used has to be clearly directed toward capacity based on experience.

It was good to see you the other day. I hope that you will not fail to send to me, whenever convenient, your impressions of the progress we are making.[2]

With warm regard, *As ever*

---

[1] Eisenhower had met with Hauge for thirty-five minutes on September 8, 1960. On September 9 Hauge had telephoned Ann Whitman (Ann Whitman memorandum, n.d., AWF/D) to add to his conversation with Eisenhower about the best way to dra-

matize Democratic presidential nominee Kennedy's lack of experience. Hauge had suggested the President could use the phrase: "You can't build a tree; it has to grow." [2] There is no further correspondence with Hauge on this subject in AWF.

1647

EM, AWF, International Series: Japan

To Hayato Ikeda

September 14, 1960

Dear Mr. Prime Minister:[1] I deeply appreciate the warm sentiment for the United States expressed in your personal letter to me which Foreign Minister Kosaka handed to Secretary Herter.[2]

The American people share with the vast majority of Japanese the earnest wish for lasting American-Japanese friendship. Let me assure you that the American people fully understand the circumstances which led to the request by your government to postpone my visit to Japan. I share the regret, which you were kind enough to express, that the planned visit could not be carried out at that moment.[3] But I assure you that the ties that link Japan and the United States are much too strong to be impaired by such momentary developments.

Rather than dwelling unnecessarily on events of the past, I would prefer to stress my great confidence in the future of relations between our two countries. The partnership existing between Japan and the United States today is built on a solid foundation of common interest, mutual confidence, and mutual trust. I am certain that we can look forward with assurance to even closer ties between our two countries in the coming years. I trust, too, that at some future time I may have an opportunity to accept your cordial invitation.[4] *Sincerely*

[1] Ikeda, former Minister of Trade and Industry, had been elected prime minister of Japan on July 18. On the following day he had announced his Cabinet, which included Zantaro Kosaka as Foreign Minister (see State, *Foreign Relations, 1958–1960,* vol. XVIII, *Japan; Korea,* pp. 376–86). A copy of this message, with Eisenhower's handwritten emendations on the State Department draft, is in AWF/I: Japan. The text of this letter was cabled to the American embassy in Tokyo for delivery to Ikeda.

[2] The prime minister had expressed "profound regrets" to Eisenhower that the Japanese government was "compelled" to cancel his scheduled visit to Japan in June; he had also conveyed his gratitude for the President's sympathetic understanding of the decision (Ikeda to Eisenhower, Sept. 9, 1960, AWF/I: Japan; for background on the trip cancellation see nos. 1564 and 1568; on Kosaka's meetings with Secretary Herter and other State Department officials see State, *Foreign Relations, 1958–1960,* vol. XVIII, *Japan; Korea,* pp. 398–403).

[3] Eisenhower had added the preceding sentence to the State Department draft.

[4] At a White House dinner honoring the Crown Prince and Princess of Japan on September 27, Crown Prince Akihito would present Eisenhower with the Collar of the

Supreme Order of the Chrysanthemum (see Eisenhower to Akihito, Sept. 28, 1960, AWF/I: Japan and AWF/D).

1648   *EM, AWF, DDE Diaries Series*

To RICHARD MILHOUS NIXON   *September 14, 1960*
Telegram

Dear Dick: Just now Dr. Walsh was in my office. He told me what an excellent job you did in your talks at the launching of the HOPE and the City Plaza in San Francisco yesterday.[1] I am delighted to have such an enthusiastic first hand report. I hear, too, that you have had excellent receptions all along your tour and that you as usual handled everything with your customary skill.[2] With warm regard to Pat and my friends who are with you and all the best to yourself, of course. Keep up the good work! *As ever*

[1] William Bertalan Walsh (B.S. St. Johns 1940; M.D. Georgetown 1943) was president of Project HOPE, an international nonprofit organization dedicated to health education, health policy research and medical humanitarian assistance. On September 13, 1960, in San Francisco, Vice-President Nixon had dedicated the S.S. *HOPE*, a reconditioned hospital ship which on the following day would set sail for the Far East as part of a joint private-government project to educate local doctors and to create goodwill abroad.
[2] On Nixon's campaign tour see *New York Times*, September 14, 1960. See also no. 1661.

1649   *EM, AWF, Name Series*

To DAVID M. BLUM   *September 14, 1960*
Personal and confidential

Dear Mr. Blum: Through the papers I am reminded that I made a blunder when I expressed myself as not exactly certain as to what office you were seeking in your campaign.[1] I am truly sorry that I made a comment that might have in any way offended you.

My only excuse is that I was not only talking in an informal and extemporaneous fashion, but was trying to introduce some bit of levity in the meeting, which I thought might be getting just a bit too serious. In any event, to make some amends for my blunder, in addition to my apology which I hereby submit, I am sending a small donation to the Treasurer of your campaign.[2]

With best wishes to you and Mrs. Blum for success in your campaign, and with the hope that I may see you here in Congress before I leave this office next January.³ *Sincerely*

¹ During remarks made at the opening of the Republican campaign at the Baltimore, Maryland, airport on September 12, 1960, Eisenhower had quipped: "And I might mention that right behind me here is a little boy carrying a unique sign. It says: 'I am for Nixon, I am for Lodge, I am for Blum.' I am not exactly sure who Mr. Blum is, but down at the bottom the sign says: 'I am for the Orioles.' So I think this particular crowd at least could, by adoption of Dick and Cabot into their teams, possibly bring some luck." See *New York Times*, September 13, 1960, and *Public Papers of the Presidents: Eisenhower, 1960–61*, pp. 694–96. Blum was the Republican candidate for Congress from the Maryland Seventh District (Baltimore City).
² A note at the bottom of this letter indicated that a "personal check of Ann C. Whitman, payable to David E. Shay, Campaign Manager for David M. Blum," was enclosed.
³ Incumbent Democrat Samuel Nathaniel Friedel would defeat Blum in his bid for Congress.

1650   *EM, AWF,*
                                                    Ann Whitman Diary Series

MEMORANDUM FOR THE FILES   *September 14, 1960*
Personal and confidential

The President called Douglas Black, of Doubleday and Company, to report on a conversation he had had on Thursday evening, the 8th, with Charles McAdam of the McNaught Syndicate and to ask Mr. Black to get in touch with Mr. McAdam.¹

The President told Mr. Black that Mr. McAdam had talked to him about whatever he might consider writing for newspaper publication after January 20th of next year. The President told Mr. McAdam that he had "signed up" with Mr. Black; that he was not particularly interested in writing for newspapers; that his principal connection with the publishing world would be Mr. Black.

Mr. McAdam wanted the President to make a commitment that anything the President should write that was intended for newspaper use would be given to Mr. McAdam on an option basis for handling it. Mr. McAdam implied that he could produce greater revenues than any other newspaper syndicate could for such an activity.²

The President told Mr. McAdam that he would tell Mr. Black of their conversation (as he has now done).

The President suggested to Mr. Black that he talk to Mr. McAdam (both of them are good personal friends of the President and know each other) and tell Mr. McAdam of his feeling that the President certainly would have no objection to permitting Mr. Black to work out an arrangement with Mr. McAdam, if newspaper publication became a matter of moment and if such an arrangement was agreeable to all concerned.[3]

---

[1] Eisenhower dictated this memorandum to Presidential Secretary Ann Whitman; see Telephone conversation, Eisenhower and Black, September 14, 1960, AWF/AWD. For background on the President's decision to publish his memoirs with Doubleday and Company see no. 1624. On the meeting with McAdam see no. 1613.
[2] Eisenhower had received similar requests by other newspaper publishers (see nos. 1430 and 1624, and Eisenhower to Nielsen, Sept. 19, 1960, AWF/N).
[3] Black had agreed to get in touch with McAdam. For developments see no. 1737.

1651   *EM, AWF, DDE Diaries Series*

To WILBER MARION BRUCKER   *September 19, 1960*

Dear Wilber: Mrs. Eisenhower and I take quite an interest in the Distaff project.[1] This noon, meeting with some of the leaders to have our pictures taken with them, we learned that the ticket sales for a charity show to support the project are going very badly indeed.[2]

I know that you are interested in this project also, and it occurs to me that you might suggest that all officers of the Army in Washington might examine the matter and determine whether they would like to help make this show a success, regardless of their intentions of contributing funds directly.[3]

With warm regard, *Sincerely*
P.S. Don't bother to reply.

---

[1] The Army Distaff Foundation, Inc., had been created by the Army Wives Council in January 1959 to provide a home for the widows of Army officers. By November the nonprofit, charitable corporation had acquired land, obtained approved architectural plans, and had contracted with a builder. At that time they had begun an appeal to raise $750,000 for construction (see Mrs. Davis to Mrs. Eisenhower, June 19, 1959, WHO/SO: Army, and Dahlquist to Persons, Nov. 27, 1959, WHCF/PPF 47, Army Distaff Foundation). On August 11 the President had attended a reception at the Army and Navy Club with guests who were gathered for the Army Distaff Foundation Dinner.
[2] The President and Mrs. Eisenhower had received the representatives of the Army Distaff Foundation at the White House (Ann Whitman memorandum, Sept. 19, 1960, AWF/AWD). To raise funds for the proposed residence hall the foundation was sponsoring the American premiere of "I Aim at the Stars" on September 28. On August 15 the chairman of the benefit committee had asked the Eisenhowers for permission to place their names at the head of the select list of patrons (Decker to Dwight and Mamie Eisenhower, WHO/SO: Army). On the film see *New York Times*, September 20, 1960.

[3] Construction of Distaff Hall, located on a fourteen-acre tract overlooking the Rock Creek Park in northwest Washington, D.C., would be underway by November (Army Distaff Hall Newsletter, vol. I, no. 9, Nov. 30, 1960, WHO/SO: Army). For developments see no. 1728.

1652   *EM, AWF, International Series: Macmillan*

To Harold Macmillan   *September 20, 1960*
Cable. Secret

Dear Harold:[1] I am most appreciative of your understanding letter of September 15. I have thought over the important questions you raise and discussed them at some length with Chris and Lord Home yesterday.[2]

As you say it is difficult to determine specific tactics until we see how Khrushchev proposes to act and also until we are able to assess the atmosphere at the General Assembly. I am convinced that it is essential for our two delegations to concert closely and to be prepared to move very quickly. Although it seems preferable to defer any public announcement or firm decision on timing for the moment, I now believe your attendance at the General Assembly would be a real service to the West. I am impressed also by the desirability, in the meantime, of having some outstanding Western leader answer Khrushchev and his satellites relatively early in the proceedings. Mr. Menzies would be superb in such a role and I hope you might be able to persuade him to attend, preferably at an early date. I realize the problems you would face should Khrushchev request a meeting with you in New York. His behavior in New York may prove the best guide to your answer.[3]

With warm regard, *As ever*

[1] A State Department draft of this letter is in AWF/M: G (see Dillon to Eisenhower, Sept. 19, 1960, *ibid.*).

[2] Prime Minister Macmillan had agreed with Eisenhower's decision to attend the U.N. General Assembly soon after the session opened (for background see no. 1638). Macmillan had issued a statement the previous evening saying that he would decide "in the light of the developing situation" whether to travel to New York and take part in the discussions. His decision, he told Eisenhower, would be determined by how Khrushchev proposed "to play the hand" and what his Commonwealth colleagues decided. He had asked Eisenhower for his recommendations in the event that Khrushchev asked him for a private meeting (Macmillan to Eisenhower, Sept. 15, 1960, State Department Files, Presidential Correspondence).

Alexander Frederick Douglas-Home, leader of the House of Lords and former Secretary of State for Commonwealth Relations, had succeeded Selwyn Lloyd as foreign minister in July. Eisenhower had told Lord Home that he had originally planned to address the General Assembly after Khrushchev had departed but since indications were that the Soviet leader might stay until Christmas, he had decided to speak first "to set the atmosphere." The three men also discussed control of nuclear weapons, relations between the Soviet Union and Communist China, and the situations in Berlin and the Congo (Goodpaster, Memorandum of Conference, Sept. 19, 1960, AWF/D).

[3] After discussions with his Cabinet, Macmillan would tell Eisenhower that he had decided to attend the meetings. He also wrote that he would do his best to persuade Australian Prime Minister Robert Menzies to attend as well. Macmillan would leave on September 25 and meet with Eisenhower two days later; he would meet with Khrushchev on October 2 and 4. Menzies would address the General Assembly on October 5 (Macmillan to Eisenhower, Sept. 22, 23, 1960, AWF/I: Macmillan; State, *Foreign Relations, 1958–1960*, vol. II, *United Nations and General International Matters*, pp. 361–62; Macmillan, *Pointing the Way*, pp. 275–81; *New York Times*, Oct. 6, 1960).

1653   *EM, AWF, International Series:*
                                                                 Iran

To Mohammad Reza Pahlavi   *September 20, 1960*
Secret

Your Imperial Majesty:[1] Thank you very much for your letter of March thirtieth with its reaffirmation of your continuing determination to maintain the freedom and independence of Iran.[2] I appreciate the heavy pressures to which you are being subjected and your resistance to them continues to arouse my profound admiration and respect.

I have followed with interest through the telegrams of Ambassador Wailes your courageous and dignified handling of the latest approach made to Your Majesty by the Chairman of the Council of Ministers of the USSR.[3] You clearly recognized the true nature of that melange of diplomatic, economic, and military threats and blandishments, and met it with dignity and determination. I and my countrymen are confident that you will meet future similar beguilements with equal acumen and dexterity.

I wish to repeat my previous assurances that Iran does not stand alone in its struggle to preserve its integrity, freedom, and independence. The United States, along with other friendly countries, will continue its support to Iran as a worthy and hard-pressed member of the community of the Free World.

It is sometimes said that during the period of national election campaigns the United States is vacillating and incapable of decisive action. Nothing could be further from the truth. The fact that an election will soon take place in this country will not weaken the determination of our government and people to take any actions necessary to assist free nations in responding to threats of communist aggression wherever they may occur. The next President of the United States, whoever he may be, will, I am confident, be as determined as I to maintain the steady course of our resistance to communist imperialism. This determination finds its reality in the basic belief of the American people that peoples such as yours must look for their future to common endeavor in and for freedom.

In the general area of defense, in your last letter you expressed the somewhat gloomy opinion that the Iranian armed forces could not be expected to participate effectively in any future conflict. Information available to me indicates that your forces would be an effective and hard-fighting element in the defense of the CENTO area, and that their capability will be enhanced as new weapons and equipment can be supplied and your forces are trained in their use. The F-86 Sidewinder weapons system has demonstrated in combat its ability to match any comparable system of potential enemies, and I note with gratification that your first SS-10 and SS-11 weapons are expected to be operational early in 1961.[4] But arms and numbers of men are relatively meaningless if morale and fighting spirit are lacking. I am confident that Iran's military forces today and in the future will play as brave and gallant a role in any conflict as have the heroes of Iran's long history.

You also mentioned that the project for strengthening Iran's existing military forces, which was an outgrowth of our correspondence in 1958, is not being implemented as rapidly as had been planned. I assure you that it continues to be our desire that Iran possess modern and efficient armed forces. Although we have not been able to keep pace with the time scale originally envisaged, our people, as you know, are working closely with yours in this field, and I hope and believe that our mutual goal of improved Iranian military forces will be achieved. In this connection, I repeat that you may depend on the sympathetic and prompt consideration by the United States, within its available means, of Iran's needs for economic assistance as they may develop.

I would like you to know that we in Washington were greatly impressed by the ability, the determination, and the common sense of officials of your government who have visited the United States recently to discuss financial and economic problems now confronting Iran.[5] We are further impressed by the vigor with which Your Majesty's government has begun measures to check the calamities which inflation and balance of payments problems can bring. We in this country are particularly conscious that the genuine defensive strength of any nation can be no greater than the economic base upon which it rests, and consequently, we strive constantly to assure a proper balance between defense needs and the demands for economic growth. Insofar as we are able, our efforts will be designed to enable you to do likewise.

In another field, I note with pleasure that since your letter was written Iran's relations with Iraq have improved measurably owing to Your Majesty's wise, judicious, and patient attitude toward that troubled country. While the situation in Afghanistan is troubling in the sense of that country's heavy dependence upon the USSR for military and economic assistance, we have no reason to believe that the Afghan government has abandoned its often expressed determination to preserve its independence and integrity. With regard to the recent furor over the nature of Iran's relations with Israel, you must have noted that this subject evoked little interest at the recent Arab conference in Beirut.[6]

I have greatly enjoyed the close friendship which we have developed over the years. It is something which I will always treasure. I am confident that my successor, whoever he may be, will strive to establish with you the same cordial relationship based upon candor in the exchange of ideas and that he will appreciate as much as I the wise leadership which you are giving your great country.

In closing let me express my confidence that Iran will, under your guidance, continue to enjoy the blessings of Almighty God in independence and prosperity.[7]

With warm regard, *Sincerely*

---

[1] This message, drafted by State Department officials, was sent by cable to the American embassy in Tehran for delivery to the Shah (see Herter to Eisenhower, Sept. 19, 1960, AWF/I: Iran).

[2] In response to Eisenhower's letter of March 12 (see no. 1455), the Shah had reiterated his concern regarding relations with Iraq and Afghanistan and had expressed his disappointment over U.S. reluctance to supply him with all the military equipment he had requested. Although higher oil revenues would enable Iran to increase its total land forces, the Shah had also reminded Eisenhower that the military improvement program established between the two countries in 1958 had not been completed. U.S. Ambassador to Iran Edward T. Wailes had suggested that although at some future date U.S. plans for the modernization of Iranian armed forces should be conveyed to the Shah, an immediate reply was not necessary. Secretary Herter and Defense Department officials had recommended postponing an answer pending a study of a five-year plan for military assistance to Iran (Pahlavi to Eisenhower, Aug. 4, 1960, WHO/OSS: International, Iran; see also State, *Foreign Relations, 1958–1960*, vol. XII, *Near East Region; Iraq; Iran; Arabian Peninsula*, pp. 674, 700–701; see also no. 779; and Herter to Eisenhower, Apr. 21, 1960, AWF/I: Iran).

[3] On July 19 the Soviet Union had told the Shah that normal relations between the two countries could not exist if there were foreign bases on Iranian soil. The Soviets had urged a Soviet-Iranian agreement prohibiting the use of military bases in either country by third parties. This agreement, according to the Soviets, would lead to better relations and increased economic aid for irrigation projects and electrical plants in Iran (State, *Foreign Relations, 1958–1960*, vol. XII, *Near East Region; Iraq; Iran; Arabian Peninsula*, pp. 690–91; see also NSC meeting minutes, July 28, Sept. 15,

1960, AWF/NSC; see also Synopsis of State and Intelligence Material Reported to the President, Aug. 10, 30, Sept. 13, 1960, AWF/D).

[4] The Sidewinder was a guided air-to-air missile that could home onto the infrared emissions from jet engine tailpipes; it could be used with F-86 Sabrejet aircraft. The SS-10 and the SS-11 were anti-tank missiles.

[5] Between June 23 and July 1 an Iranian delegation had met with State and Commerce Department officials regarding economic stabilization measures. Secretary Herter had called the meetings a "significant step forward" and had praised the Iranians for their "constructive attitudes" (State, *Foreign Relations, 1958–1960,* vol. XII, *Near East Region; Iraq; Iran; Arabian Peninsula,* pp. 679–80).

[6] On August 21 the foreign ministers of nine Arab League countries had begun meetings in Beirut on issues regarding Palestine and inter-Arab relations (*New York Times,* Aug. 22, 29, 1960).

[7] The Shah would thank Eisenhower for the "unswerving support" of the United States in Iran's resistance to Communist pressures. He would, however, reiterate his concern for Iran's military weakness in the face of the Soviet Union, which, he wrote, was "armed to the teeth with the most modern weapons and missiles." He wished to continue his friendly relationship with Eisenhower after he left office and asked that the President plan a future visit to Iran (Palhavi to Eisenhower, Oct. 3, 1960, AWF/I: Iran; see also Herter to Eisenhower, Oct. 27, 1960; and Eisenhower to Palhavi, Oct. 28, 1960, both in *ibid.*).

1654   *EM, AWF, Administration Series:*
                                                      William P. Rogers Corr.

WILLIAM PIERCE ROGERS   *September 20, 1960*

Seems to me we should be able to do something about this.[1]

[1] Eisenhower had handwritten this comment to the Attorney General on a staff memorandum dated September 14, 1960 (AWF/D). The memorandum indicated that the Justice Department would announce that crime had reached a new high in 1959 and was continuing to rise. Juvenile crimes had doubled since 1948 and were increasing at a rate over twice as fast as the juvenile population. At Eisenhower's request Presidential Secretary Ann Whitman had sent this note to Rogers (Whitman to Rogers, Sept. 20, 1960, AWF/A). There is no written reply in AWF. For Eisenhower's concern over juvenile delinquency see nos. 1172 and 1595, and *Public Papers of the Presidents: Eisenhower, 1960–61,* pp. 313–17. For additional correspondence on the subject see Cope to Eisenhower, October 4, and Eisenhower to Cope, October 6, 1960, both in WHCF/OF 85-B.

To Aksel Nielsen   *September 20, 1960*

Dear Aks: Next week there will be in Denver a man that I am certain you will want to meet and that I know you will like. He is Charles Rhyne, formerly president of the American Bar Association (its youngest president, I believe) and now Chairman of the Volunteers for Nixon-Lodge.[1] He is interested in many of the same things as you are, and extremely personable and likeable.

I took the liberty of asking him to call you (incidentally he is a North Carolina Democrat!)—and this note is merely to alert you to that fact.[2]

Ann tells me that you won't be in Washington until the tenth; I shall see you at the dinner for the King and Queen of Denmark and, I hope, for a more leisurely chat.[3] But at the moment I am inundated with all the appointments the State Department wants me to make, particularly in connection with influx of Prime Ministers and such to the United Nations, and feel that I have no time at all of my own.[4]

With warm regard, *As ever*

[1] Charles Sylvanus Rhyne (LL.B. George Washington University 1937) had been among the ninety-six guests at the President's stag dinner for the National Volunteers for Nixon-Lodge Committee on September 19 (Ann Whitman memorandum, Sept. 19, 1960, AWF/AWD; on the committee, an organization directed to Independents and Democrats, see no. 1631). Nixon had named Rhyne, who practiced law in Washington, D.C., as chairman of the committee on August 21 (*New York Times*, Aug. 22, 1960). Rhyne had been president of the American Bar Foundation from 1957 to 1958 and had lectured on aviation law at George Washington University from 1948 to 1953. He had written several books about aviation law and had edited and written numerous articles for legal publications.
[2] Rhyne was born in Charlotte, North Carolina, and was a former vice-president of the Duke University Alumni Association.
[3] King Frederik IX and Queen Ingrid would visit Washington, D.C., October 11–14. As Presidential Secretary Ann Whitman had indicated, the Eisenhowers would host a dinner for the King and Queen on the evening of their arrival (see Ann Whitman memorandum, Oct. 11, 1960, AWF/AWD, and *New York Times*, Oct. 12, 1960).
[4] On the upcoming United Nations General Assembly meeting in New York City see nos. 1634 and 1660.

To Arleigh Albert Burke   *September 21, 1960*

Dear Arleigh: Nate Twining tells me that the staff organization setup at SAC headquarters is working beautifully.[1] He attributed it to the fact that each Chief of Staff had selected outstanding personnel for this duty and that each officer involved had been instructed to make the thing work.

While this is exactly the kind of thing I expect from you, I want you to know that I am grateful that this operation is off to a good start. Thanks very much.[2] *Sincerely*

[1] Eisenhower was referring to the new Joint Strategic Target Planning Staff (JSTPS), which had been charged with developing a strategic target list and a single integrated operational plan for the first strike of a nuclear attack. The JSTPS would be responsible for committing specific weapons systems to various targets in case of war. Chief of Naval Operations Burke had initially opposed interservice coordination of strategic planning, and the Joint Chiefs of Staff and the Secretary of Defense had debated the subject over the past several months. On August 11 Eisenhower had discussed the plans with Burke, Secretary of Defense Gates, and General Nathan Farragut Twining, Chairman of the JCS.

Burke had objected to placing the new multi-service planning body under the direction of the Commander in Chief, Strategic Air Command (CINCSAC) at Offut Air Force Base in Nebraska. During the heated discussion, Twining had predicted that the Navy would try to sabotage the plan if it was approved on a trial basis. Eisenhower had stated that "too much emotion was being displayed" over this aspect of strategic planning, and that it was not a "good way to respond to serious military problems, nor did it speak too well of the ability of good men to get together and work out solutions in the nation's interest." Eisenhower had generally supported Gates and had directed that any "initial strike must be worked out in detail to make sure that all blows were struck simultaneously" (see Goodpaster, Memorandum of Conference, Aug. 11, 1969, AWF/D; for background see *Strategic Air Command: People, Aircraft, and Missiles*, ed. by Norman Polmar [Annapolis, 1979], p. 67; Watson, *Into the Missile Age*, pp. 485–95, and Peter J. Roman, *Eisenhower and the Missile Gap* [Ithaca, NY, 1995], pp. 98–103). Eisenhower also sent a similar letter to General Thomas D. White, Air Force Chief of Staff (Sept. 21, 1960, same file as document).
[2] Burke would agree that the JSTPS was "off to a good start" and say that "everyone concerned was doing their very best to make the thing work" (Burke to Eisenhower, Sept. 26, 1960, same file as document).

1657   *EM, AWF, International Series: Mali*

To Modibo Keita   *September 23, 1960*

Dear Mr. President:[1] Thank you for your telegram of August twenty-fifth and your letter of August thirtieth, as well as your telegram of September twenty-second, announcing the proclamation of the Republic of Mali. I deeply appreciate the confidence you have shown in bringing these matters to my attention, and I have read with great interest the documents which you forwarded.[2]

As Ambassador Yost informed you, the United States has delayed taking any action on the crisis in the Mali Federation in the hope that the two member States would be able to reconcile their differences.[3] Since both members have now declared their separate existence, I have decided to announce United States recognition of the Republic of Mali. After careful consideration of Ambassador Yost's report and the reports of our posts in Bamako and Dakar, I have also come to the conclusion that it would serve no useful purpose to delay further United States recognition of Senegal.

I assure you that this action in no way indicates any less sympathy for you or for the Government and people of the Republic of Mali. As you know, the United States was the first country after France to set up a Consulate at Bamako, and now that our Embassy in Mali has been established in Bamako, I confidently expect the cordial relations existing between our two countries to become even closer. Pending the arrival of an Ambassador in Bamako, Mr. John Gunther Dean has been designated Charge D'Affaires ad interim.[4]

I shall follow with considerable interest developments in your country and assure you that the United States earnestly wishes to cooperate with you in the future development of the Republic of Mali.[5]
Sincerely

[1] State Department officials drafted this message, which was sent by cable to the American consulate in Bamako, in the West African country of Mali, for delivery to President Keita.

[2] The Federation of Mali, an autonomous state created by the union of the Soudanese Republic and Senegal, had come into existence in April 1959 and had achieved independence, within the French Community, on June 20, 1960 (see Eisenhower to Keita, June 20, 1960, AWF/I: Mali). After a military *coup d'etat* on August 20, Senegal had seceded from the federation. Subsequently both countries had become independent, Senegal remaining within the French Community and the Soudanese Republic becoming the Republic of Mali (State, *Foreign Relations, 1958–1960*, vol. XIV, *Africa*, pp. 55–56, 72–73, 117–18, 130, 213, 220, 226–27).

In his first and second messages Keita had described the coup and the subsequent move of the federal government of Mali from Dakar to Bamako. He had reminded Eisenhower of the recognition granted to the federation after it had declared independence in June and asked that no recognition be granted to the "unconstitutional secession" of the state of Senegal. Eisenhower had also received a message from Senegalese prime minister Mamadou Dia announcing the country's withdrawal from the Federation of Mali and asking for recognition. State Department officials had recommended against immediate presidential replies pending negotiations between the two countries in Paris (Keita to Eisenhower, Aug. 25, 30, 1960; Dia to Eisenhower, Aug. 20, 1960; see also Calhoun to Goodpaster, Aug. 23, 25, Sept. 2, 1960; all in AWF/I: Mali).

After the Soudanese government had adopted the name of the Republic of Mali and had withdrawn the powers previously granted to the federation, Acting Secretary Dillon had recommended that Eisenhower recognize both countries. On this same day Eisenhower would send a message, drafted by State Department officials, to Senegalese President Leopold Sedar Sanghor extending recognition (Keita to Eisenhower, Sept. 22, 1960; Dillon to Eisenhower, Sept. 23, 1960; and Stoessel to Goodpaster, Sept. 13, 1960; all in AWF/I: Mali; and Stoessel to Goodpaster, Sept. 23, 1960; Eisenhower to Sanghor, Sept. 23, 1960; both in AWF/I: Senegal).

³ Charles Woodruff Yost was U.S. Ambassador to Morocco.

⁴ John Gunther Dean (B.S. Harvard 1947) had held several diplomatic positions with the Economic Cooperation Administration. He had been the political officer in the American embassy in Laos and U.S. Consul to Togo.

⁵ Fearing Soviet influence, Eisenhower would authorize an aid package to Mali totaling $2.3 million. He would discuss U.S.-Senagalese relations with Prime Minister Dia in December (Herter to Eisenhower, Dec. 8, 1960, AWF/I: Senegal; Telephone conversation, Herter and Eisenhower, Dec. 9, 1960, Herter Papers, Telephone Conversations; and State, *Foreign Relations, 1958–1960*, vol. XIV, *Africa*, pp. 236–38, 245–49).

1658   *EM, AWF, Administration Series:*
Atomic Energy Commission

To John Alex McCone   *September 28, 1960*

Memorandum for Chairman McCone: The matter of the Dutch nuclear submarine, which has been up for attention several times previously, has been raised with me again.¹

I personally have felt that we should give the necessary technical cooperation and assistance to make it possible for them to build this submarine. In fact, the latest information that had been given to me, which I approved, seemed to provide a method of doing this, and I understood the project would go forward without further delay.

If there is anything holding this up, will you please let me know what it is.²

¹ In December 1957 the United States had offered to help its NATO allies in the construction of nuclear submarines. The offer, which provoked interest from France, Italy, and the Netherlands, had alarmed some members of Congress, who contended that the Administration was attempting to turn over atomic secrets without a formal agreement. In May 1960 a tentative compromise had been agreed to by the Atomic Energy Commission and the State and Defense Departments. Under terms of the agreement the United States would provide the Netherlands with designs and technical assistance to build the submarine hull and the non-nuclear part of the propulsion machinery; technical assistance on building the atomic power plant would be postponed until a later time (see *New York Times*, May 15, 1960).

² In June the Joint Congressional Committee on Atomic Energy had held a secret committee meeting to hear testimony from AEC Chairman McCone and other members of the Administration on efforts to supply atomic submarine secrets to the Netherlands. A majority of the committee members opposed the proposal and feared that atomic submarine secrets might fall into Soviet hands. According to the *New York Times*, the Committee's opposition meant that there was no possibility that any plan would be approved in 1960 (see *New York Times*, June 10, 1960). The Dutch would withdraw their request for an atomic submarine as Eisenhower's term was drawing to a close (State, *Foreign Relations, 1958–1960*, vol. VII, pt. 1, *Western European Integration and Security; Canada*, pp. 634–35, 656–57).

To Christian Archibald Herter   September 28, 1960
Personal

Memorandum for the Secretary of State: Quite occasionally there are
brought to me reports, by visitors to foreign lands, to the effect that
some of our Ambassadors are not performing up to the standard
that we should expect. Sometimes a complaint alleges indifference,
sometime arrogance, and other times a degree of ignorance.[1]

In any event, I should like to have you, once more, have studied
the idea of developing a kind of an inspectional system that could
keep you and me well informed of our diplomatic activities. Foster
and I discussed a number of times having "Ambassadors at Large"
but for one reason or another, the idea was always abandoned.[2] I
wonder whether we could not find it possible to require each of the
men we appoint as regional Assistant Secretaries of State to make
an annual pilgrimage so as to determine for himself, through direct
observation and conversations with knowledgeable people in several
capitals, just exactly how we are getting along.

This is something I should like to talk to you about at your convenience.[3]

[1] Eisenhower had received a memorandum on the preceding day from Clarence
B. Randall, Chairman of the President's Council on Foreign Economic Policy. Randall had recently returned from Europe where he had represented the United
States at the opening of the tariff conferences in Geneva. He had also visited the
American embassies in The Hague, Brussels, Paris, and London to discuss economic matters with the ambassadors and their economic staffs. Randall had warned
Eisenhower of "a severe bias" by the British against Under Secretary of State Douglas Dillon's perceived favoritism toward France and the Common Market (see no.
1415). Randall had told his British colleagues that Dillon was an able, dedicated
public servant and was not Anglophobic. Randall also noted that Ambassador W.
Walton Butterworth, U.S. Representative to the Economic Community, the Coal
and Steel Community, and to the European Atomic Agency (Euratom) was "universally regarded as hostile to Great Britain" and "a menace." Randall recommended replacing him with someone else. In addition Randall also reported that
an administrative assistant to Secretary Dillon had been "indiscreet" in expressing
his attitudes and had been "throwing his weight around a little too much" (Randall to Eisenhower, Sept. 27, 1960, AWF/I: D-H; see also Eisenhower to Herter,
Sept. 30, 1960, *ibid.*).
[2] For discussions between Eisenhower and former Secretary of State John Foster
Dulles regarding the issue of ambassadors-at-large see Galambos and van Ee, *The
Middle Way*, nos. 376, 1183; see also no. 1516 in these volumes.
[3] Eisenhower and Under Secretary Dillon would discuss the need for two ambassadors-
at-large able to visit every embassy semi-annually. Eisenhower would tell Dillon that
he thought that "the State Department had not kept up with the times and had preferred to remain as much as possible with the old systems." No one in authority, he
said, had ever seen all of the ambassadors at work. The State Department had tentatively agreed to the establishment, in 1961, of a three-man panel of consultants,

Dillon would reply (John S.D. Eisenhower, Memorandum of Conference, Oct. 5, 1960, AWF/D).

1660   *EM, AWF, Dulles-Herter*

To Clarence Douglas Dillon   *September 28, 1960*

Memorandum for the Acting Secretary of State: The Commissioner of Police of New York City has several times taken up with me the possibility of the Federal government defraying part of the cost of protecting, during this unusual session of the General Assembly of the United Nations, the principal figures visiting there.[1] The actual situation is this, as given to me by the Commissioner:

The Commissioner has felt it necessary to mobilize all of the personnel and equipment available to the City. This means that for a period of weeks, he has had to go to a seven day week, with hours ranging from twelve to eighteen. He has been forced to refuse all applications for leave and to cancel others.

The only way that the Commissioner has of making up for the overtime put in by the entire Police Force is to give, after the closing of the Assembly, an equivalent time off to all involved. According to his statements this will leave the City stripped of proper police protection for a very considerable period. He reports that he could make up for the daily overtime, but this means, he feels, that it would be highly dangerous to the safety of the City if he should attempt to make up the time required by the two days additional duty per week which had been performed by the Force in this period.

He thinks that as a matter of equity, the Federal government should pay at least two-sevenths of the additional time put in by the Police Force during the period for this particular purpose. He states also that it would do no good to wait until the next session of the Congress because he will have to begin, immediately after the end of the Assembly, to provide furloughs in such quantity that the police duty will be inadequately performed. He hopes that some kind of contingency or emergency fund can be used.

While I personally doubt that there is any way of determining exactly what the proper share of the Federal government's obligation might be in this situation, I do think that there is considerable merit in Commissioner Kennedy's argument.

Would you please let me have your comments?[2]

¹ For background on the Fifteenth Session of the United Nations General Assembly see nos. 1638 and 1652. In addition to leaders from the Western and non-aligned nations and the Soviet bloc countries, representatives from the newly-independent African nations were attending the session. Three days before the Assembly's opening Dillon had asked Eisenhower for a statement appealing for "calm and reasonable conduct" by all individuals during the session, at a time when New York would be faced "with an enormous security problem" (State, *Foreign Relations, 1958–1960*, vol. II, *United Nations and General International Matters*, pp. 306–8, 314–22, 327–28, 341–42; *Public Papers of the Presidents: Eisenhower, 1960–61*, p. 702).

Stephen Patrick Kennedy (LL.B. New York University 1950) had been a member of the New York Police Department since 1929 and commissioner since 1955. On September 22, facing increased public pressure regarding the safety of the delegates, Kennedy had requested "public support" from the State Department. At that time Dillon had stated that he thought Kennedy was "entitled to it" considering his cooperation with all their requests. Kennedy had met with Eisenhower on September 26 in New York City (*ibid.*, pp. 345–46; and *New York Times*, Sept. 16, 23, 1960).

² After Cuban leader Fidel Castro left New York City on this same day, Kennedy would relax some of the restrictions he had placed on the police force (*New York Times*, Sept. 29, 1960). For developments see no. 1671.

24

"We missed by such a narrow margin"

To Richard Milhous Nixon   *October 1, 1960*
Personal and confidential

Dear Dick: The following is for your personal and confidential information, and I request that it be seen by no other individual except, of course, your own private secretary.

I rather think that your appearance at the closed circuit dinner on September 29th may mark the beginning of an upsurge in general enthusiasm for our national ticket. I thought, and I know many others who felt the same, that you rang the bell.[1]

Over past weeks there have come to me directly and indirectly expressions of hope that our campaign might produce more "zip" and that it should be more hardhitting—not necessarily in terms of personal attack but in urgent support of our own plans, programs and candidates.

There is one situation in Illinois that bothers me very much. While I was in Chicago I heard repeated criticisms of Governor Stratton and the expression of a lot of unhappiness among Republican leaders concerning him.[2] Such comments would usually end up with the statement "Nixon will carry the State, but the Governor is down the drain."

On this I should like to make two observations. As we all know, the presence on any slate of a candidate who is very weak will invariably damage, to some extent, the whole ticket. Consequently we must try to find ways of giving him a boost.

Second, the criticisms of Governor Stratton—whom I have always considered my good personal friend—were invariably accompanied by the comment, "He has been a very good, even outstanding, Governor, but he has offended all Republican leaders in the State." This has been because of sins of omission and of commission, according to my informants.

The sin of omission is that of failing to consult Republican leaders on matters of projected programs and plans. According to reports the Governor runs a one-man show and is very secretive. Moreover, he acts like a little Napoleon. This infuriates some of the leaders, whose personal support is therefore lukewarm or entirely lacking.

In one instance the publisher of a series of country newspapers said that he intended, as always, to support the Republican ticket, except that, in this instance, he was going to support the Democratic candidate for Governor.[3] This, I told him, would not fail to weaken the whole ticket, and I therefore hoped he could find some way to change his mind.

My own feeling about this situation is that it *should be easy* to correct, particularly because of the Governor's reputation for efficiency. I should think that if the Governor would merely arrange to meet for an hour or even a half hour weekly with some of the principal leaders to discuss with them his ideas and programs, that much of this difficulty would be cleared up.

Our Senatorial candidate seems to be a very smart man, and I gave him this report in part, with the expressed hope that he might find some way of making the above-mentioned point with the Governor, in such a way as not to offend the latter.[4]

The sin of commission to which I refer—again merely repeating comments made to me—was the appointment of Jim Kemper as the National Committeeman against the objections of such Republican stalwarts as Ed Ryerson and Doug Stuart.[5] There is no use here of repeating the tenor of their complaints about this particular individual. Moreover, I don't see how anything of a corrective nature could be undertaken at this time.

Nevertheless, I am sure that the whole affair could be measurably improved if the Governor could find some way of making friendly overtures to the disgruntled individuals, and particularly of taking them into his confidence.

My thought is that in your position as our Presidential nominee, and without disclosing the source of your information, you might be able to have a heart to heart talk with Stratton. Possibly Morton could be able to do something along a similar line, if you should so suggest.[6] The matter is so delicate and must be kept so secret that I shall speak to no one except you concerning it.[7]

With all the best, *As ever*

---

[1] In his speech to a Republican fund-raising dinner in Boston, Vice-President Nixon had accused his Democratic opponents of wanting "to return America to the mess we left behind eight years ago" (*New York Times*, Sept. 30, 1960).

[2] On Eisenhower's trip to Chicago see no. 1592. William Grant Stratton (A.B. University of Arizona 1934) had served as governor of Illinois since 1953. He had previously served as Illinois Republican Congressman from 1941–1943, and from 1947–1949.

[3] Otto Kerner, a former Cook County judge and United States District Attorney, was running as the Democratic candidate for governor of Illinois.

[4] The Illinois Republican candidate for the Senate was Samuel W. Witwer, a Chicago lawyer and leading Methodist layman. Witwer was making his first run for public office.

[5] In July, James Scott Kemper, treasurer of the Republican National Committee from 1944–1949, had been elected Republican national committeeman from Illinois. Kemper was a Chicago insurance executive and former U.S. Ambassador to Brazil (*New York Times*, July 7, 1960). Edward Larned Ryerson (Ph.B. Yale 1908) was director of the Inland Steel Company. Robert Douglas Stuart, president and chairman of the board of Quaker Oats, had served as U.S. Ambassador to Canada from 1953 to 1956.

⁶ Thruston B. Morton, U.S. Senator from Kentucky, had been Chairman of the Republican National Committee since 1959.

⁷ There is no further correspondence in AWF relating to this matter. Stratton would be defeated in the November election (see *New York Times*, Nov. 9, 1960).

1662

EM, AWF, International Series: Nehru

To Jawaharlal Nehru

October 2, 1960

Dear Prime Minister: I have received your letter of September twenty-ninth, informing me of your intention to submit to the current session of the General Assembly a resolution calling for a meeting between the Chairman of the Council of Ministers of the USSR and myself.¹ I assure you again that I share the concern expressed in this communication over the present state of international relations, and I understand and sympathize with the motives which led you to propose this step.

As President of the United States I have sought on every occasion to explore to the full any possibility for the resolution of outstanding international questions by negotiation.

Following the refusal last May of the Soviet Government to participate in the long-awaited Summit Conference which was to deal with certain of these questions, especially disarmament and problems arising out of the war, the President of France, the Prime Minister of the United Kingdom and I issued a declaration which stated: "They remain unshaken in their conviction that all outstanding international questions should not be settled by threat or the use of force but by peaceful means through negotiation. They themselves remain ready to take part in such negotiations at any suitable time in the future." Speaking for the United States this statement still holds good.²

I have at no time utilized any threats whatsoever with reference to any international question. This is, I am sure you will agree, a matter of historical record.

On the other hand, the Soviet Union, far from following a comparable policy of restraint, appears to have undertaken with deliberate intent a policy of increasing tension throughout the world and in particular of damaging relations with the United States.

Instead of avoiding threats of the use of force, the Soviet Government has threatened rocket retaliation against many members of the United Nations including the United States on the pretext of contrived and imaginary intentions on the part of these countries. While these threats have necessarily only strengthened our resolve to maintain our readiness to deter and, if necessary, to resist any aggression, they have nevertheless caused uneasiness throughout the world.

The Soviet Government has refused any thought of an impartial international body to investigate the shooting down on July first of an aircraft of the United States Air Force, and is still holding incommunicado two members of its crew.[3]

The Soviets have unilaterally disrupted the ten-nation disarmament talks in Geneva with full knowledge that the Western Powers there represented were about to submit new proposals which took into account those made earlier by the Soviet Union.[4]

I believe that a comparison of the international behavior of the participants of the Paris Meeting since its collapse demonstrates where the responsibility lies for the increase of international tension and the failure to make any progress in the solution of outstanding problems.

I reiterate what I said in my speech before the General Assembly on September twenty-second:[5] "The United States is always ready to undertake serious negotiations with the Soviet Union and other interested countries on any unresolved international question, and especially in the field of disarmament." I also pointed out that there are needs for great constructive action, for which I have made proposals to the General Assembly, that are primary in their importance to the peace and progress of major areas of the world. However, the chief problems in the world today are not due to differences between the Soviet Union and the United States alone, and therefore are not possible of solution on a bilateral basis.

The questions which are disrupting the world at the present time are of immediate and vital concern to other nations as well. The importance of these matters is such as to go beyond personal or official relations between any two individuals, and I have many times personally pledged myself, regardless of every kind of personal consideration, to meet with anyone at any time if there is any serious promise of productive results. There is nothing in the words or actions of the Government of the Soviet Union which gives me any reason to believe that the meeting you suggest would hold any such promise. I would not wish to participate in a mere gesture which in present circumstances might convey a thoroughly misleading and unfortunate impression to the peoples of the world.

If the Soviet Union seriously desires a reduction in tensions it can readily pave the way for useful negotiations by actions in the United Nations and elsewhere. If Soviet representatives should wish to discuss concrete measures to reduce tensions, my representatives, including the Secretary of State, are always available for this purpose. Should such exploratory discussions reveal that the Soviet Union is prepared to return to the path of peaceful negotiation with some prospect of fruitful results, then I personally would be prepared to meet and negotiate with the representative of the Soviet Government and with the heads of other governments as their interests were involved.[6] *Sincerely*

[1] Indian Prime Minister Nehru's letter was signed by the presidents of Ghana, Yugoslavia, Indonesia, and the United Arab Republic (all in AWF/I; the draft resolution is in AWF/I: Ghana). Eisenhower had told Secretary of State Herter that he thought Khrushchev had "stirred up" the five nations and that the resolution was "so illogical" that it had to have been "contrived." Nehru's participation with the other four neutral nations had particularly irritated him, Eisenhower said. Eisenhower told Herter that he was opposed to recognizing the five leaders as a neutral bloc. "Each one is important enough to answer individually," he said, "but their act in submitting the resolution together is one of effrontery." He told Herter that he had worked on the State Department draft of the reply to make it "more convincing" and "tougher." The most important consideration, Eisenhower said, was to make sure the resolution did not pass. Eisenhower had also discussed the reply with Prime Minister Macmillan, who agreed that the West had to rescue the neutral nations from the "foolish position" in which they had placed themselves (Goodpaster, Memorandums of Conference, Oct. 1, 5, 6, 1960, AWF/D; see also State, *Foreign Relations, 1958–1960*, vol. II, *United Nations and General International Matters*, pp. 370–71, 380; and Eisenhower, *Waging Peace*, pp. 586–88).

A State Department draft of this response with Eisenhower's handwritten emendations is in AWF/D. Identical letters were sent to the leaders of the other four countries (see AWF/I).

[2] On the failed Summit Conference see no. 1538.

[3] On the downed plane see no. 1583.

[4] See no. 1577.

[5] See *Public Papers of the Presidents: Eisenhower, 1960–61*, pp. 707–20; see also no. 1638.

[6] On October 5 Under Secretary of State Dillon would tell Eisenhower that Japan and Argentina had offered to sponsor an "innocuous" alternative resolution that would be acceptable to the United States. He would not have objected if the original resolution had read "two governments," Eisenhower said; he objected to mentioning two individuals by name (John S. D. Eisenhower, Memorandum of Conference, Oct. 5, 1960, AWF/D). In a meeting on October 6 Eisenhower would tell Indonesian President Sukarno that he "had no quarrel" with the intent of the resolution, but "he did not see what good could be achieved by such a meeting" (Goodpaster, Memorandum of Conference, Oct. 6, 1960, *ibid.*).

The General Assembly would eliminate references to the U.S. and Soviet leaders from the resolution, but Nehru and the the other sponsors would withdraw it on October 5 (State, *Foreign Relations, 1958–1960*, vol. II, *United Nations and General International Matters*, p. 399).

To Milton Stover Eisenhower   *October 2, 1960*

Dear Milton: Mamie Moore has just told me that she is going to enter Mary Washington College at Fredericksburg, if accepted. Obviously we don't need to bother our heads any more about this.[1]

I do hope you are improving. It must be difficult to hold on to any shred of good disposition under such circumstances.[2] *As ever*

[1] Miss Moore was the daughter of the First Lady's sister, Mabel Moore. The President and his brother had been in contact about her college prospects (Ann Whitman memorandum, Sept. 19, 1960, AWF/AWD). On Eisenhower's relationship with his goddaughter see no. 1595.

[2] Milton Eisenhower had suffered a back injury in mid-September (Milton Eisenhower to Eisenhower, Oct. 18, 1960, WHCF/OF 103-A-2). For developments see no. 1692.

To Hussein ibn Talal   *October 4, 1960*

Your Majesty: This morning, Secretary Herter called me to tell me of his talk with you. I was gratified to know of the good discussion that you had with him, and I deeply appreciate your kindness in sending your good wishes to me.[1]

At the same time, I want to express my warm congratulations for the forthright manner in which you upheld free world principles in the General Assembly yesterday.[2] Coming at a time when attempts are being made to effect its destruction, your emphasis on the vital importance of the United Nations as the only hope of peace and freedom for humanity was indeed timely. To you and to your country, I extend the sincere best wishes of my countrymen and myself.[3]

With assurances of my high esteem and respect, *Sincerely*

[1] Herter had told Eisenhower that Jordan's King Hussein had made a "very courageous speech" on the preceding day. His attacks on communism and on the United Arab Republic's President Nasser had led some observers to suggest that he had "sounded his own death knell" (Telephone conversation, Eisenhower and Herter, Oct. 4, 1960, AWF/D).

[2] Hussein had accused the Soviet Union of seeking "to destroy the United Nations, to hamper its deliberations, to block its decisions and, by rowdy tactics and petulant walk-outs, to demean the reputation of the Security Council and the General Assembly" (*New York Times*, Oct. 4, 1960).

[3] At a meeting with the Jordanian leader at the White House on October 7 Eisenhower would repeat his congratulations. Hussein would later write that he had been

"deeply moved" by the "friendliness and understanding" demonstrated by the American people, and he would thank Eisenhower for his words of encouragement and congratulations (Goodpaster, Memorandum of Conference, Oct. 11, 1960, AWF/D; and Hussein to Eisenhower, Oct. 7, 1960, AWF/I: Jordan).

1665   *EM, AWF, International Series: Adenauer*

To Konrad Adenauer   *October 5, 1960*
Cable. Secret

Dear Mr. Chancellor: General Norstad and Ambassador Dowling have reported to me on their recent conversations with you. I understand from them that you expect to have a full discussion this week with Debré and Couve de Murville on General de Gaulle's views on nuclear matters as well as on NATO and on European integration. I thought it might be useful for you to have some of my thoughts on these matters before your meeting with the French.[1]

On nuclear matters, I have been much impressed with the strong feeling of various European leaders, including yourself and M. Spaak, that the European countries should have an increased role in the nuclear aspect of NATO's defenses. We are considering, under my personal direction, the possibility of a multilateral, NATO-wide means for dealing with the problem.[2]

On NATO matters generally, I want to say first that I have been most impressed by the strong statements you have recently made in support of NATO.[3] As for your meeting with the French, you are of course aware that there is a very wide divergence between myself and General de Gaulle on several basic points. I have pointed out these differences directly to General de Gaulle, and our representative in NATO has made them clear to the Council.[4] In brief, I feel strongly the importance of integration in the light of modern military technology and strategy. The U.S. has assigned its own forces to NATO on the assumption that they would participate in an integrated defense system for the area. There would be little justification for their continued presence if there were no integrated system.

Although it is clear that my views on how NATO's defenses are to be organized differ from those of de Gaulle, I should add that we have, on the other hand, recently made limited progress with the French on certain specific NATO defense problems. They have agreed to the concept of integrated air defense in Europe, although insisting on special arrangements for most of French territory.[5] The French have also recently signed a NATO Atomic Stockpile agreement with us for their NATO-committed forces in Germany. It is noteworthy that the French have accepted in this agreement the same provisions for U.S. custody and SACEUR control as in our agreement with you and with other countries.[6]

I am heartened by the feeling that your views and mine are very close on these NATO defense matters, and I was most interested to learn from Ambassador Dowling that you intend to speak very forthrightly to Debré and Couve on these questions.

With respect to the political functions of NATO, I have serious reservations about a proposal that suggests the U.S., the U.K. and France as a mechanism for preserving order in other areas of the world, because of the danger that any such structure might take on overtones of a "directorate".[7] If that should come about, important interests of other NATO countries would be ignored and opposition in other areas of the world would surely occur.

Similarly dangerous to NATO, in my view, would be any Six Nation bloc within NATO, in which separate national states, not moving toward the goal of European unity, acted on political and military matters properly dealt with in NATO.[8]

As a constructive step for improving the political cohesion of the West, I feel that NATO consultation, covering all areas of the world, should be further developed and strengthened. The U.S. has itself sought to make maximum use of the NATO Council for this purpose, and we certainly intend to continue this effort in view of the obvious need to achieve the maximum harmonization of Free World policies in the light of the world-wide Communist threat. It appears to us that the study of means for improving the Alliance is a subject best considered in the discussions of long-range planning in NATO. We ourselves expect to contribute some ideas, and it might be useful to suggest to the French that they also make use of this forum.

Finally, I would like to comment on General de Gaulle's views on the future development of the Six Country movement.[9] I know that in this field also your views and mine have long been very close indeed. We both regard the Six Country integration movement as of very basic importance to the future of our world. A Europe moving toward real unity will strengthen and reinforce the NATO Alliance as a whole. I think we would both be prepared to support any steps designed to further progress toward the concept of true integration embodied in the Rome treaties. Quite frankly, however, I am not aware of the exact nature of de Gaulle's proposals in this field. If his proposals clearly will contribute to achieving the goals of integration, then I believe they are deserving of the support of other members of the Six. If, on the other hand, they would be likely to weaken the integration concept, a serious question would arise. While the U.S. has a deep interest, it is not of course directly involved in the discussions of de Gaulle's proposals; this is primarily a matter which the other Five must work out with France. You yourself obviously are in a most influential position in respect to these developments. Perhaps if you and others of the Six were to put up to de Gaulle specific proposals which will unmistakably contribute to further progress toward genuine integration, de Gaulle's intentions in this field might well become clearer.

I mean for this letter to confine itself to those matters that may have a direct bearing on your talk with Debré and Couve de Murville. There are, of course, many other subjects, especially affecting Berlin, which are much on my mind these days.[10]

With warm personal regard, *Sincerely*

[1] On September 12 Lauris Norstad, Supreme Allied Commander, Europe, had reported to Eisenhower on his September 9 visit with Adenauer. Walter C. Dowling, former U.S. Ambassador to Korea and U.S. Ambassador to the Federal Republic of Germany since December 1959, had met with Adenauer on September 30 (see State, *Foreign Relations, 1958–1960*, vol. IX, *Berlin Crisis 1959–1960; Germany; Austria*, p. 598; and *ibid.*, vol. VII, pt. 1, *Western European Integration and Security; Canada*, pp. 628– 32). Michael Debré was the French Prime Minister; Maurice Couve de Murville was Foreign Minister. State Department officials had sent this message to the American embassy in Bonn with instructions to deliver it to Adenauer at the earliest opportunity before the Debré visit. Fearing that Adenauer might tell Debré that he had received this special letter from the President, Ambassador Dowling was to warn the German leader that this was a personal communication from Eisenhower and that he should "treat it accordingly in his talks with the French."

[2] Eisenhower had discussed the creation of an integrated nuclear strike force with Paul Henri Spaak, Secretary General of NATO, on the preceding day (*ibid.*, pp. 638– 44). The U.S. State and Defense Departments were attempting to formulate plans for a multilateral NATO nuclear strike force. At this time the internal debate had centered on proposals for using medium-range Polaris missiles, to be launched from submarines manned by international crews drawn from the NATO member nations (Watson, *Into the Missile Age*, pp. 550–61).

[3] Adenauer had stated that he wanted some reforms in the NATO structure but wanted them based on a greater integration of the alliance's military capabilities (*New York Times*, Oct. 3, 1960).

[4] See no. 1632; and Goodpaster, Memorandum of Conference, Sept. 28, 1960, AWF/D. W. Randolph Burgess was U.S. Chief of Mission to NATO.

[5] For background on the issue of air defense see no. 1404. On September 12 Norstad and Debré had reached a settlement, and the North Atlantic Council had approved the basic principles of an integrated air defense on September 28 (State, *Foreign Relations, 1958–1960*, vol. VII, pt. 1, *Western European Integration and Security; Canada*, p. 640).

[6] For background on the NATO atomic stockpile system see no. 1454. On September 23 arrangements had been completed for the agreement, which, according to press reports, called for NATO-wide nuclear weapons and joint exercises for units possessing a nuclear capability. Acceptance of the offer of nuclear weapons for its NATO forces in West Germany did not, however, change French opposition to the stockpiling of nuclear warheads on their soil (*New York Times*, Sept. 6, 24, 1960).

[7] For background on tripartite consultations see no. 1632.

[8] For background on the six nations of the European Economic Community and the Rome treaties see nos. 753 and 1415.

[9] In July de Gaulle had proposed a plan for a council of the six EEC nations that would lead to a political as well as an economic union of Western Europe. The organization would have a permanent secretariat in Paris, four separate standing committees dealing with the political, economic, cultural, and defense policies of the members, and an assembly consisting of representatives of the parliaments of the six nations (State, *Foreign Relations, 1958–1960*, vol. VII, pt. 1, *Western European Integration and Security; Canada*, pp. 294–301; see also Synopsis of State and Intelligence Material Reported to the President, Aug. 10, 1960, AWF/D).

[10] For background on the Berlin situation see no. 1325. In July Soviet Premier Khrushchev had alluded to a date when the Soviet Union might sign a separate peace treaty with the German Democratic Republic, and in August, after a series of actions designed to restrict the activities of West German liaison missions, East Germany had issued an order that temporarily closed East Berlin to West German citizens (State, *Foreign Relations, 1958–1960*, vol. IX, *Berlin Crisis 1959–1960; Germany; Austria*, pp. 552–63, 570–75, 593–600; NSC meeting minutes, Sept. 21, 1960, AWF/NSC; and State, *Documents on Germany 1945–1985*, pp. 715–17). For developments see no. 1687.

1666   *EM, AWF, Name Series*

To EDGAR NEWTON EISENHOWER   *October 5, 1960*
Personal

Dear Ed: I read the pamphlet written by Charles W. Briggs, a banker from St. Paul. In its general theme the piece is admirable, even though long-winded. There are certain passages that, in my opinion, are not only eloquent but persuasive.[1]

Since the man's purpose seems to be that solely of informing the public rather than that of influencing political bodies at the moment, I suppose that his treatise, with its many generalities, is about as effective as any paper of a similar nature could be. I do object to his apparent assumption that he has just discovered the obvious truths that he deals with and apparently believes that no one else has been fighting against the trend toward paternalistic government. He should, I think, analyze some of the fights of the past eight years and give his judgment concerning them so as to identify the people who, by and large, agree with his point of view and those who are definitely on the other side.

I believe that education of the public has got to carried on incessantly on a most positive basis and in simple terms. Examples should be used that are not only clear-cut and irrefutable, but that clearly exemplify the evil that we should be trying to eliminate. Just shouting about the matter is not enough. Preachers, writers, poets and ordinary people have been inveighing against sin, the devil and human misconduct for a good many millennia. Seemingly they have not made much progress.

Related to the argument—but noting another angle—is a clipping I enclose from the *United States News and World Report*, a magazine that most times seems quite responsible and intelligently written. If the example of Sweden should ever be applied throughout the world, there is a lesson in it for us. It should be read more for that lesson rather than for the historical interest we might have in Sweden.[2] The lesson is that people, by and large, seem to want to shift responsibility, both for their own individual problems and public activities, to the shoulders of someone else—for proof you only have to go back to Roman history.

One last thought: We bleat plaintively about freedom—yet only 60 per cent of the eligible voters in the United States actually voted in 1956. (If some "sucker" government wants to take care of this, we seem to think that this looks like a very beautiful existence.)

For myself the whole business makes me as mad as I can get. *As ever*

---

[1] Charles William Briggs was an attorney in St. Paul, Minnesota. Edgar Eisenhower described the pamphlet, entitled "A Return to Candor in Politics" (St. Paul, 1960), as "an economic and spiritual approach to the affairs of government today" (Sept. 22, 1960, AWF/N). The pamphlet is not in EM; the President's thank-you note is in *ibid*.

[2] The President sent a brief paragraph reporting that recent elections in Sweden had kept the ruling Socialist party in power. Voters had resoundingly defeated conservatives' campaign to lower taxes and reduce the benefits and social services provided by the state (*U.S. News and World Report*, Oct. 3, 1960, p. 80). For Eisenhower's previous criticisms of socialism in Sweden see no. 1462.

1667   *EM, AWF, DDE Diaries Series*

To GORDON GRAY   *October 5, 1960*

Dear Mr. Gray: I am sure that you know how strongly I feel that all mechanisms of Government should continue to function vigorously throughout the remainder of the months of this Administration.[1] I have had occasion to make my views known to the members of the National Security Council in meetings of that body.

You also know the importance I attach to the work of the Operations Coordinating Board which has responsibilities in operations coordination in many ways as important as the policy advisory function performed by the Council itself with the assistance of the Planning Board. I have often pointed out that my own attendance at NSC meetings is a duty which, while self-imposed, is nevertheless mandatory. I expect other members to attend except in those rare instances when some other obligation is overriding.

The same consideration should apply, for example, to attendance at meetings of the OCB, which of course concerns itself with responsibilities delegated by the President, and to the Planning Board.[2] I trust that you will make it clear to all involved that there should be no tendency to minimize the importance of attendance during this period when the end of this Administration is approaching. *Sincerely*

[1] Gray, Special Assistant to the President for National Security Affairs, was responsible for planning NSC meetings (see no. 1578; for developments see no. 1773).
[2] The Operations Coordinating Board (OCB) oversaw implementation of national security policy (see no. 1273 and Galambos and van Ee, *The Middle Way*, no. 2158). Membership on the board included the Under Secretary of State, Deputy Secretary of Defense, Director of Central Intelligence, Director of the U.S. Information Agency, Director of the International Cooperation Administration, and representatives of the President. Occasionally it also included representatives of other agencies assigned responsibilities by the President for implementation of national security policies. The Planning Board formulated policy recommendations to be considered by the NSC and was composed of the Special Assistant to the President for National Security Affairs and representatives at the assistant secretary rank appointed by the President (see Greenstein, *The Hidden-Hand Presidency*, pp. 124–37).

1668   *EM, WHCF,*
                                                    President's Personal File 194

To Kevin Coyle McCann   *October 6, 1960*

Dear Kevin: Even as I gird myself for the shock of finding myself seventy years of age, I am reminded that you, too, are to celebrate (if such a word can properly be used these days) your own birthday anniversary soon.[1] I assure you by means of this note of my felicitations and, of course, my good wishes always.

All of this reminds me that I never formally thanked you for working on the original draft of the Catholic Charities speech.[2] You know me well enough to realize that I am an inveterate rewrite man and I realize that the final version was considerably changed.[3] That fact does not at all diminish my gratitude to you for your help.

With affectionate regard to Ruth—and a Happy Birthday to yourself.[4] *As ever*

[1] Eisenhower's birthday was October 14. McCann was born October 11, 1904.
[2] The President had spoken at the dinner of the National Conference of Catholic Charities in the grand ballroom of the Statler Hilton Hotel in New York City on September 26. The occasion had marked the fiftieth anniversary of the organization. In addition to praising Catholic Charities as an exemplary model of American volunteerism and generosity, Eisenhower addressed the need for continued private char-

ity and its value in maintaining the nation's spiritual heritage (see *Public Papers of the Presidents: Eisenhower, 1960–61*, pp. 728–32, and *New York Times*, Sept. 27, 1960).
[3] On the President's editing see, for example, nos. 526 and 1182.
[4] McCann's wife was the former Ruth Potter.

1669   *EM, AWF, International Series: Germany*

To Konrad Adenauer   *October 7, 1960*
Personal and confidential

Dear Mr. Chancellor: I am writing to you on a personal and confidential basis not only as my good friend of long standing but also as the leader of a nation whose economic and financial power has grown to great dimensions in the community of free nations. With that power has come an equal responsibility for the success of free nations and our free economies in a critical and rapidly evolving era of the world's history. Upon us both rest great responsibilities that, I think, our two governments should consider together.

In the financial and economic sphere, no less than in the political and strategic sphere, mutual understanding and cooperation between Europe and the United States are vital.

In the United States, we recognized this when in 1948, we established the Marshall Plan.[1] Despite impending elections, inflationary pressures, and heavy demands upon our resources from our own people, we gave a priority to the pressing need to restore Europe to economic and financial health and strength. We diverted goods to Europe and provided from our budget the means which Europe lacked to finance these goods.

After the Marshall Plan came the need for military assistance to fend off the Communist threat and the need to give aid to less-developed countries. At that time, I myself testified before our Congress, as Commander of the NATO Forces, that the need for military assistance would be temporary.[2] Ever since, the American people have hoped that the burden of our foreign expenditures, economic and military, would eventually be lifted or at least substantially reduced by the cooperation of other nations.

Today the situation has substantially changed. The success of the Marshall Plan has led to the full recovery of Europe. The United States is now paying out to foreign countries more than we receive from our sales to them. This means that certain surplus countries, and notably the Federal Republic of Germany, are accumulating short-term dollar claims on the United States on a large scale. We meanwhile have lost, in the course of two and a half years, substantial amounts of gold while at the same time additional short-term dollar holdings have accumulated in other industrial countries. I believe that this burden upon our balance of payments should be reduced in a very substantial degree during the forthcoming year.

The Federal Republic is now the country which most nearly approaches the international financial and economic situation of the United States in 1948. It is consistently taking in from other countries far more than it is paying out. A continuation of this situation would stimulate demands for trade restrictions and threaten the future of economic development in the free world.

I have great admiration for the statesmanship which you have displayed in leading the Federal Republic to unparalleled internal economic revival and in promoting the constructive advance of the European Continent. I now ask you to give your personal attention to the wider area of your nation's financial and economic relations with the United States on the one hand and the developing countries on the other.

The broad courses of action are clear. Long-term financing from Germany is needed for development in the less-developed areas. A way should be found also to finance the dollar cost of defense which now falls on the United States. Finally, a larger market is needed in Germany for the goods of the United States and of the developing countries.

Action along these lines would conform to economic reality. Moreover, it is essential to maintain the political strength of the free world. And insofar as aid to less-developed countries is concerned, it commends itself both as a moral act and one in the self-interest of every industrialized nation.

Failure to make prompt, decisive and substantial progress in these directions may well set in motion cumulative events of a serious disruptive character, deleterious to world trade and prejudicial to the position and prestige of both our countries as leaders of the free world. Once set in motion these disruptive forces would be difficult to restrain. In my view, the next year is an important one in this respect.

I am sure that you will appreciate the strength of my conviction in this regard, but naturally I can set forth in this letter only the outline of the problem. Many technical and detailed considerations need to be discussed between our two governments. For such discussions with your staff, Cabinet, and, if you so desire, yourself, I suggest that I send to Bonn Secretary Anderson and Under Secretary Dillon of my Cabinet at a time that may be convenient to your government and to my two representatives. The two representatives I suggest have already had the opportunity to discuss these problems with Minister Erhard and President Blessing.[3]

With warm regard, *Sincerely*

[1] On the European Recovery Program (Marshall Plan) see Galambos, *Chief of Staff*, nos. 1482 and 2023.

[2] Eisenhower testified before the Senate and House Foreign Relations and Armed Services Committees on February 1 and 2, 1951 (see Galambos, *NATO and the Campaign of 1952*, no. 51).

[3] Ludwig Erhard, former Bavarian Minister of Economics and member of the Bundestag, was vice-chancellor and minister of economic affairs of the Federal Republic. Karl Blessing was president of the Bundesbank. Adenauer would agree that West Germany should "follow the path" of the Marshall Plan and make a "considerable contribution" to the aid of underdeveloped countries. He told Eisenhower that his government had started preparatory work on the issue and that he would personally participate in talks with U.S. representatives at any time (Adenauer to Eisenhower, Oct. 20, 1960, AWF/I: Germany). For developments see no. 1716.

1670   *EM, AWF, DDE Diaries Series*

To Ralph Emerson McGill   *October 7, 1960*
Personal and confidential

Dear Ralph:[1] I have so often found myself in enthusiastic agreement with the articles that you syndicate over the country that I hope you will not find it amiss for me to express some disagreement with one of your commentaries which was labeled, "Which Way Conservatism?"[2]

You say that American conservatism creates an image of the "safe deposit vault, not growth and the long-view consideration of new ideas and needs."[3]

I think that the issues of conservatism in its several degrees cannot be analyzed or accurately definite unless they are viewed in a broader economic and political area, including what we so loosely call "liberalism."

Indeed, over the years one of the matters that has bothered me very considerably is what the self-proclaimed liberal means by that term—and the same goes for the conservative.

In 1949, during a period when, as a result of a letter that I had written and which had been highly publicized in 1948, I thought I had attained a complete confidence that I was forever removed from active political effort.[4] On September 3, of that year, I gave a speech in St. Louis on what I called "The Middle Road." You have possibly never even heard of that effort, but so far as I am concerned it still represents the heart of my philosophy toward the proper responsibilities of government and its relationships with the individual.[5]

The people who nowadays proclaim themselves liberals either directly or indirectly support centralization of power in Washington.

This is the very antithesis of what Jefferson believed and taught, yet we think of Jefferson as a liberal. You mentioned Goldwater. Regardless of my complete disagreement with some of his beliefs, he does follow Jefferson in his championship of the authority of the several sub-divisions of government—that is, "States' Rights."

Another thing that I find the self-styled liberals proclaiming is that the budget in our country is of no importance whatsoever when compared to some of our other internal needs. The argument is over-simplified by saying "The conservatives think more of a dollar than they do of a human life or of a child's education or proper care for the aged."

Now let's see where this argument ends up if we follow it with a reasonable amount of common sense.

The American dollar is today the principal medium of exchange in most portions of the world. We are the principal banker for the free world.

Manifestly, the countries that have considerable holdings of our dollars are completely happy with holding these dollars as long as they are confident in their soundness. But when they believe that we ourselves may be guilty of actions that may bring about the debasement of that dollar, uneasiness develops.

This statement needs no proving; anyone who has talked with the financial authorities of the world's principal countries knows it to be the next thing to gospel.

---

[1] Eisenhower had dictated but would not complete this letter. He would decide not to send it to McGill, long-time editor of *The Atlanta Constitution*, because, according to a note on the text, he "did not have time enough to get [it] in proper shape."

[2] The article (n.d., AWF/D) had characterized Senator Barry Goldwater as "the best illustration of what was wrong with American conservatism." American conservatism, McGill charged, was static, limited, and lacking in innovation.

[3] McGill had said that America could not conserve her interests by locking them up. The "Goldwaters of now and our past" had, in effect, retreated from creativity and declared that the way to be prepared for the future was "to stand pat with what we have, and maybe even conduct a strategic retreat here and there."

[4] In his letter of January 22, 1948, to Leonard V. Finder, a New Hampshire newspaper publisher, Eisenhower had disavowed any intention of becoming a presidential candidate in the 1948 elections (see no. 1381; see also Galambos, *Chief of Staff*, no. 1998).

[5] Eisenhower had delivered the speech on September 5 (see Galambos, *Columbia University*, no. 532; for additional references to the speech see nos. 1207 and 1381 in these volumes).

To Clarence Douglas Dillon   *October 8, 1960*

Dear Douglas: I have your report on the request of the Police Department of New York City that the Federal government accept some responsibility for the protection of delegates to the United Nations General Assembly in that city.[1]

While I was in New York City, I discussed with Commissioner Kennedy the relief that might be accorded by the Congress; he replied that this would do them no good for the simple reason that he would have to make up the time at a later date out of his personnel, and therefore the city would be woefully unprotected.[2]

---

[1] For background see no. 1660. Dillon had agreed that, "if legally possible," the government should share in the extra costs incurred by the police department. "The circumstances are unprecedented and of an emergency nature," he replied, "and deserve our sympathetic assistance." The suggestion had been made to draw on funds allocated for mutual security, but Dillon rejected that proposal because he thought that such expenditures would be "clearly far from any intent of the Congress." He was unaware of any available funds from other government agencies, but he agreed to pursue the issue with the Bureau of the Budget. He suggested that Eisenhower consult with New York City Police Commissioner Stephen Kennedy and the mayor of New York City to determine the expenses involved. He also suggested that any payment be preceded "by full Congressional consultation and concurrence," that legislation be considered to cover similar situations in the future, and that New York authorities include provisions in their own budgets for such contingencies (Dillon to Eisenhower, Oct. 6, 1960, AWF/D-H).

[2] Commissioner Kennedy would give Eisenhower an accounting of the department's costs on November 3, during a presidential campaign visit to New York. In December State Department officials would announce the decision to recommend an appropriation of $2.9 million in the next budget as reimbursement for New York's expenses (*New York Times*, Oct. 15, 17, Nov. 4, Dec. 3, 10, 1960).

1672   *EM, WHCF,*
                                        President's Personal File 1727

To Louis Morton Hacker   *October 9, 1960*
Personal

Dear Louis: In today's book review section of the NEW YORK TIMES, I noticed your name as the reviewer of a book entitled "The Question of Government Spending."[1] This accident reminded me that it has been a long—too long—time since I have seen you or, indeed, heard from you. I do hope that you are well, active, and enjoying life.

Over and above the impulse to renew contact with you, I wanted also to record my approval of your review.[2] As I understand Mr. Bator's argument, he seems to be one of those over-educated people who feels a responsibility for controlling the American economy and for changing the entire American system.

I applaud what you had to say about his book!

With warm regard, *Sincerely*

[1] Hacker, an economic historian, had been a professor and administrator at Columbia University when Eisenhower was its president (for background see no. 587). Hacker's review of Francis Michel Bator's work, *The Question of Government Spending: Public Needs and Private Worth* (Cambridge, Mass., 1959), had been published in *The New York Times Book Review*, October 6, 1960. Bator was an associate professor of economics at the Massachusetts Institute of Technology, where he had also received his B.S. (1949) and Ph.D. An advocate of using government spending to boost economic growth, Bator would later serve in various advisory positions in the Kennedy and Johnson administrations.

[2] Hacker had observed that few people were as yet "convinced that standards of living will continue to rise, because of increases in productivity, when resources and investments are diverted from private producer goods to public consumer goods." He concluded that Bator had not "proven his case in economic terms" but that his book was nonetheless an important contribution to economic knowledge.

1673   *EM, WHCF, Official File 85-B*

To Helen Rogers Reid   *October 10, 1960*

Dear Helen: Thank you so much for your note of the sixth.[1]

As for a further appearance of mine before the United Nations General Assembly, I have by no means a closed mind on the subject. With the departure of most of the headliners from the scene, I most sincerely hope that the Assembly will settle down to the serious work at hand, and I do not, at the moment, think I can add anything to the deliberations.[2]

With affectionate regard, *As ever*

[1] For background on the Fifteenth Session of the United Nations General Assembly and Eisenhower's speech on September 22 see no. 1638. Reid was former president and chairman of the board of the *New York Herald Tribune;* her letter is not in EM.

[2] Among the heads of nations attending the General Assembly session, Cuban leader Castro had left New York on September 28; British Prime Minister Macmillan on October 5. Soviet Premier Khrushchev would leave on October 13. For future deliberations see no. 1730.

To Leo A. McPherson   *October 11, 1960*
Personal

Dear Mr. McPherson: I regret that you drew any inference from my
television talk of last evening that I was accusing anybody of adopt-
ing the Karl Marx type of thinking. In answer to a question which
included the term "little people", I strenuously objected to the implication that any of us should regard any group of citizens in our
country as being down-trodden, poverty-stricken victims of those
possessing great wealth. I did point out that Karl Marx described
the workmen of his day in these terms. I said that this kind of thinking had no application in our country whatsoever because our workmen had now become part of our great "middle class" and this was
the group against which Karl Marx employed his most bitter invec-
tive.[1]

But, I repeat, I never accused anyone—and I would never accuse
anyone whether or not I was in any partisan contest—of being a
"follower of Karl Marx."[2] *Sincerely*

[1] The previous evening NBC television had broadcast live a question and answer session between the President and a panel of ten women (*New York Times*, Oct. 11, 1960).
The Volunteers for Nixon-Lodge, an adjunct of the Republican National Committee, had sponsored the program. McPherson, a voter from Columbus, Ohio, had sent
the White House a telegram about one of Eisenhower's answers. He complained
that, "As a democrat who voted for you," he resented Eisenhower's implication that
Democrats were followers of Marxist philosophy (Oct. 11, 1960, WHCF/OF 138-C-
4-E). The President had referred to Karl Marx, the founder of modern communism,
in response to a question about the idea that since "the little man and common man
can't take care of himself," "the government has to take care of him." Eisenhower
had criticized "fuzzy thinking" by opponents of capitalism whose theories were no
longer applicable today: "Marx was always talking about a degraded vassal beaten
down by his bosses. The workman today is not that vassal. He's one of the middle
class and Marx hated the middle class." "The working man today is a citizen like you
and me," the President added, and was an "important individual." Eisenhower himself "knew something about labor" because he had worked eighty-four hours every
week before going to West Point and said he "liked it" (*New York Times*, Oct. 11, 1960).

After receiving this reply, McPherson would apologize to the President, writing
that Eisenhower's entire career was evidence that he "would not deliberately resort
to unfair political tactics." He said that he had complained because he was sensitive
to past Republican charges that Democrats were soft on communism. He admitted
that he should instead have stated more clearly his opinion that "the name of Karl
Marx should not be mentioned in an American Presidential Campaign." McPherson
also thanked the President for his service to the nation, telling him that he held the
respect of his countrymen "despite party affiliation" (McPherson to Eisenhower, Oct.
14, 1960, WHCF/OF 138-C-4-E).

[2] During the program Eisenhower had also challenged criticisms of his Administration made by presidential candidate John F. Kennedy, and he had defended his
record on civil rights. While there had been allegations that the program was re-

hearsed (*New York Times*, Oct. 11, 1960; see also Ann Whitman memorandum, Oct. 10, 1960, AWF/AWD), the Republicans claimed otherwise.

1675   *EM, AWF, DDE Diaries Series*

To JOHN AND PRISCILLA WILSON   *October 11, 1960*

Dear Mr. and Mrs. Wilson: Over the years I have so often, in terms of admiration, respect and affection, publicly referred to Dick Nixon that it never occurred to me in the television panel performance last evening that I had failed to make sufficiently emphatic my opinions about him.[1] I enclose an excerpt from a talk that I made about him over television about two weeks ago.[2]

In any event, I shall try to make this point more definite at some future opportunity—but before election day.[3]

Thank you for calling the matter to my attention. *Sincerely*

[1] On October 10, 1960, the Wilsons of New York City had sent a telegram to the President congratulating him on his televised interview with Republican women—his first appearance on a national television network in support of the Republican presidential ticket (see no. 1674; and *New York Times*, Oct. 11, 1960). They said Eisenhower's commendation of vice-presidential nominee Henry Cabot Lodge's character was "strong," and they described his tribute to Nixon's experience as "well portrayed." They were, however, worried that he "did not make any comment relative to Nixon's character or that you liked repeat liked Nixon." Praising Eisenhower as "the most honest forthright and personable President we have known in almost a century's time," they argued that "a personal I like Nixon as a person endorsement" was essential (WHCF/OF 138-C-4-E).

[2] Eisenhower had enclosed a copy of remarks he had made during a closed-circuit television broadcast from Chicago on September 29 (see no. 1625). Eisenhower had praised Nixon's "vast richness of experience in domestic affairs, foreign relations, and person-to-person diplomacy." He called the Vice-President's counsel "invaluable" and termed Nixon "a man possessed of the character, patience, and sound judgment so essential for effective leadership in the troubled world of tomorrow" (WHCF/OF 138-C-4-E).

[3] For developments see no. 1679.

1676   *EM, AWF, DDE Diaries Series*

To DALE MORGAN   *October 13, 1960*

Dear Dale: I could not possibly neglect to answer your letter, even though my reply must necessarily be short. The knowledge that you,

Philip and your dad—and other members of your family—so clearly understand the consequences for America of this coming election and your readiness to give your full time to working for what you believe right is nothing less than heart-warming to me.[1]

If I only knew how to inspire the same kind of work and dedication in the hearts and minds of all others who believe with us that we must have responsibility in government, integrity in our fiscal affairs, and experience and firmness, as well as a conciliatory attitude in our foreign affairs, to get into this fight up to their necks, it would certainly be won. I think irresponsible promises, blandishments and just sheer habit are working so much against us that we need a fighting army for the sake of our country.

To you and to all working with you my best wishes and warmest regard.[2] *Affectionately*

[1] Dale Morgan, an old family friend from Savannah, was Headquarters Chairman of the Georgians For Nixon organization of Chatham County, Georgia (see Galambos, *NATO and the Campaign of 1952*, no. 469). She was the daughter of Major General Henry Benton Sayler, a long-time friend of Eisenhower (see Galambos, *Chief of Staff*, no. 704). Both Sayler and her husband, G. Philip Morgan, were leaders in the organization. Morgan had told Eisenhower about her local campaign efforts in support of Nixon. Although she was neglecting her family responsibilities, she said, this campaign was the "most important thing" in their lives and she and her husband "agreed that that was the way it has to be." She asked Eisenhower not to bother answering her letter (Morgan to Eisenhower, Oct. 8, 1960).

[2] Morgan would reply that this was the most thrilling and inspiring letter she had ever received. She would describe additional campaign activities, noting that Marjorie Merriweather Post May, the noted philanthropist and heiress to the Postum Cereal Company (see Galambos and van Ee, *The Middle Way*, no. 576, and Galambos, *Columbia University*, no. 414), had sent her a $500 contribution for the Nixon campaign. Morgan would also explain that she had refused all requests to ask Eisenhower for favors and would not "infringe" on their friendship. She had heard, however, that people from Savannah were writing Eisenhower "using the Sayler and Morgan names" without her family's permission (Oct. 23, 1960). Presidential Secretary Ann Whitman would write Morgan that the President had seen her second letter and had asked her to again express his gratitude for her efforts (Oct. 26, 1960). All correspondence is in WHCF/OF 138-C-4 Republican Presidential Campaign.

1677

EM, AWF, International Series:
Macmillan

TO HAROLD MACMILLAN   *October 14, 1960*
Cable. Confidential

Dear Harold: I appreciated your letter of October seventh and am gratified that you found your arrangements and your reception in

New York agreeable. For me, as always, it was a keen personal pleasure to see you again, and I think our talks were highly useful.[1]

Your coming to New York, along with Mr. Menzies and Mr. Diefenbaker, was a strong contribution to the solid front which the West presented to Mr. Khrushchev's attacks. Your speech before the General Assembly made a strong impression on the people of this country.[2]

Yesterday I received your touching note of October twelfth sending greetings on my birthday.[3] Since this is the date, I must say that I don't feel much older. While in some ways I will be glad to set down the burdens of this office on January twentieth next, I will miss the great satisfaction I have had from our close relationship which will of course lose its official nature. I look forward to future meetings—at times, I trust, under somewhat more relaxed conditions. In the meantime, I will keep the possibility of getting together in December very much in mind.[4]

With warm regard, *As ever*

[1] For background on Macmillan's decision to attend the United Nations General Assembly see no. 1652. Eisenhower had met with Macmillan on September 27 in New York and on October 2 in Washington (see Goodpaster, Memorandums of Conference, Sept. 28, Oct. 6, 1960, AWF/D; see also Seip to Goodpaster, Sept. 26, 1960, AWF/I: Macmillan).

[2] Macmillan had addressed the General Assembly on September 29; Canadian Prime Minister Diefenbaker on September 26; and Australian Prime Minister Menzies on October 5 (see *New York Times*, Sept. 27, Oct. 6, 1960). Soviet Premier Khrushchev had attempted to interrupt Macmillan's speech by removing his shoe and banging it on the desk in front of him (Macmillan, *Pointing the Way*, pp. 275–79). In his October 7 letter Macmillan had written that the Western heads of government had made an effective response to the Soviets and that the West was "ahead on points." He also told the President that he thought Khrushchev's "dramatic method" was effective at first but had "begun to bore the so-called uncommitted countries" (Macmillan to Eisenhower, Oct. 7, 1960, PREM 11/2981; see also Eisenhower to Nash, Oct. 4, 31, 1960; and Nash to Eisenhower, Sept. 30, Oct. 10, 1960, AWF/I: New Zealand).

[3] Macmillan had noted that his birthday message was "rather sad" because it was the last of its kind that he would be able to send Eisenhower while he occupied "the greatest position in the world" (Macmillan to Eisenhower, Oct. 12, 1960, AWF/I: Macmillan).

[4] Eisenhower would not visit Great Britain in December.

1678   *EM, AWF, Administration Series*

To Richard Milhous Nixon   *October 14, 1960*
Straight wire

Despite the fact that I had to miss your broadcast last evening because of an engagement with the King and Queen of Denmark,[1]

I have heard so many glowing reports of your performance that I hasten to send a word of congratulations.[2] Keep up the good work. Please tell Pat, too, how much I appreciated her comments on the panel show I did with the ladies (incidentally, a charming and most intelligent group).[3] We are all following your progress with the greatest interest. *Warm personal regard*

[1] The President and Mrs. Eisenhower had attended a performance by the Royal Danish Ballet at Loew's Capitol Theater with King Frederik IX and Queen Ingrid, who had been visiting Washington for several days (see no. 1655).

[2] The third in a series of debates between presidential candidates Richard M. Nixon and John F. Kennedy had been televised nationally on October 13 (*New York Times*, Oct. 14; Ambrose, *Nixon*, vol. I, *The Education of a Politician, 1913–1963*, pp. 581–83; see also no. 1683). The President had telephoned the Vice-President on this day and, according to his secretary Ann Whitman, had recommended that Nixon try to leave the impression that he was giving thoughtful consideration to panelists' questions. Eisenhower had also suggested that Nixon drop the issue of the United States' role in defending the Quemoy-Matsu islands from Chinese Communist forces, a controversy which had come to dominate the debates (Memorandum of Conversation, Oct. 14, 1960, AWF/AWD; for background see nos. 838 and 895).

[3] On Eisenhower's televised question and answer session with a group of Republican women see no. 1674. The Vice-President's wife was Patricia Ryan Nixon.

1679

EM, WHCF,
President's Personal File 442

To Lionel Hastings Ismay

October 14, 1960

Dear Pug: At noon today there was delivered to me the beautifully bound copy of your memoirs (to which I have looked forward with anticipation and even some impatience.[1] I am deeply grateful to you, and profoundly touched by the inscription you placed in the volume.

And just now a telephone call from Al Gruenther's office informs me that you and Kathleen are cutting short your visit to this country and returning early next week to England. I am distressed to hear this, particularly since the reason given me is your health.[2] Mamie and I had hoped, as I am sure you know, to have you join us at dinner at the White House on the twenty-fifth, the first evening after my return from a trip (billed as non-political, but don't take that too seriously!) through the West and briefly touching in Mexico. There were many things I wanted to talk to you about, but of course I understand why, if you are not feeling up to par, you want to get home.[3]

I hope that you will soon be feeling better and I even dare look forward to another opportunity to see you—perhaps even before the end of my term or, should that not be possible, if Mamie and I take an extended trip your way some time after January twentieth.[4]

Do take care of yourself. Thank you once again for your book—and thank you, too, for setting the record straight, as I know you have done in it.[5]

With affectionate regard, *As ever*

[1] The President and Ismay first had discussed the memoirs in January 1959 (see no. 1012).

[2] Ismay had been suffering from recurring bouts of pneumonia (for background see nos. 1012 and 1409).

[3] On the dinner see Eisenhower to Gruenther, October 3, 1960, AWF/A, and Eisenhower to Ismay, October 16, 1960, same file as document. Missing the dinner had been a "bitter disappointment," Ismay would reply on November 4 (AWF/D). On October 17 Eisenhower would begin his trip to Detroit, Michigan; Richfield, Minnesota; Abilene, Kansas; Palm Springs and San Francisco, California; Del Rio, Texas; Ciudad Acuña, Mexico; and Houston, Texas; he would deliver a series of speeches endorsing Nixon and Lodge (on the Republican nominees see no. 1593).

[4] Ismay would write on November 4 that his health was steadily improving (AWF/D).

[5] For background on the reaction of Eisenhower and Ismay to the publication of Field Marshal Montgomery's memoir see no. 1012. For developments see no. 1697.

1680   *EM, AWF, Gettysburg Series*

TO JOHN WESLEY HANES, SR.   *October 14, 1960*

Dear Johnnie: For once in my life and despite the fact that I know of my reputation for occasional garrulity, I am at a loss for words to express my gratitude for such a welcome gift as you are making to me.[1] "Ben Tullock Primrose 4th" has a pedigree so outstanding as to put her automatically, in the Blue Ribbon class, and of course the fact that you have arranged with Ted Ryan to breed her to "Maximilian" adds a high degree of anticipation to a gift that is already almost overwhelming.[2]

Though my words are feeble, I do send you a "Thank you" that is deeply felt. One day you will have to come to Gettysburg to see the heifer and to give us an opportunity to talk, to our hearts content, of Angus and cabbages and perhaps even kings.[3]

With warm regard, *Sincerely*

[1] Eisenhower had discussed his Aberdeen Angus herd with New York corporate executive Hanes at a White House stag dinner in July 1957 (see no. 228). At that time Hanes had offered to breed an animal especially for the President. On October 11 he wrote of his success and enclosed the pedigree of the Angus calf.

Presidential Secretary Ann Whitman may have drafted this letter. In the bottom margin of Hanes's letter Eisenhower had written: "Nice letter—This is indeed something!! Keep copy of pedigree & send original to Nevins."

[2] Hanes had explained that breeding Eisenhower's new acquisition to the highly-regarded international champion Maximilian might well result in a calf with "one of the most unique pedigrees in the entire Angus breed." Theodore Ryan owned Mole's Hill Farm in Sharon, Connecticut. Maximilian was an international grand champion. The President's herdsman would later agree that the calf had the finest pedigree possible (Nevins to Whitman, Oct. 16, 1960; see also Whitman to Nevins, Oct. 13, 1960).

[3] The President would not meet with Hanes before leaving office. The reference is to a Lewis Carroll poem in *Through the Looking Glass* (1872). All correspondence is in AWF/Gettysburg.

1681   *EM, AWF, International Series: Tunisia*

To Habib Bourguiba   *October 15, 1960*
Confidential

Dear Mr. President: Thank you for bringing to my attention, in the letter brought to me by Ambassador Bourguiba on October third, your feeling that the assistance we have been furnishing your country is insufficient to enable you and your courageous people to achieve the economic goals which you have set for yourselves.[1] I had assumed that the $20 million in Special Assistance, plus the substantial Development Loan Fund loans and very large wheat shipments which we have provided over the last twelve months, combined with the spirit and industry of your people and the large supplemental expenditures by your own government, were sufficient to ensure a major degree of progress toward those goals.[2] If this is not so, I agree that we both must take another look at the problem and see what can be done to enable Tunisia to succeed.

I asked Under Secretary Dillon to give close personal attention to your problem as soon as I received your message, and he advises me that the first step both of our governments might find useful would be a review at a relatively high level of the nature and dimensions of the problems you face and the most effective means by which they may be met.[3] If you agree, our people will be available to meet with yours in Tunis whenever you desire.

I realize planning takes time even with the very best intentions on both sides. In order that the planning required will not be unduly hurried, and in order to insure that the current progress of your country is not slowed down, I am instructing Ambassador Walmsley to make available immediately to your government $10 million in cash out of the $20 million we had planned to provide in Fiscal Year 1961. If, after the planners have arrived at relatively firm conclusions, it seems that more economic assistance will be required, I will do my best to meet the situation insofar as it is possible to do so.[4]

We shall, of course, continue to make available sufficient wheat and other surplus commodities to enable you to continue your present work relief and child feeding programs. I also understand our Development Loan Fund has under active consideration a loan request for your agricultural development bank which I hope can be agreed upon soon.

Before closing, Mr. President, permit me to take this opportunity to thank you and your country's excellent Ambassador, Mongi Slim, for the leadership you have displayed both in the work of the United Nations and in other councils outside of that organization.[5] I know it is the hope of both of us that some way be found towards a lasting peace, and I also know both of us believe the United Nations, as presently operated, is the best forum so far devised in which our objective might be obtained. By continuing to offer your country's wise counsel, especially in helping younger African nations to understand the differences between the Free World and the Communist Bloc both as to their goals and as to the means used to attain them, you will have performed a great service for all humanity.

I am quite certain the experts of our two countries will be able to arrive at mutually satisfactory conclusions regarding the economic problems of Tunisia and how they can be best solved.[6] If for any reason it appears to you that sufficient progress is not being made in the next few weeks, do not hesitate to write me again.

With warm regard, *Sincerely*

---

[1] Eisenhower had met with Habib Bourguiba, Jr., Tunisia's ambassador to France and President Bourguiba's son, and with Tunisia's ambassador to the United States on October 3, 1960 (State, *Foreign Relations, 1958–1960,* vol. XIII, *Arab-Israeli Dispute; United Arab Republic; North Africa,* pp. 902–3). President Bourguiba had written that Tunisia's "very existence" depended upon his country's "unceasing struggle against underdevelopment." Facing "the permanent presence of a mass of 300,000 people without employment or resources," and a seriously depleted treasury, he had taken advantage of Eisenhower's request that he should write the President directly "whenever an important problem made it necessary to resort to such a procedure."

[2] Bourguiba had asked for additional U.S. aid to finance his government's economic development and public works programs. Tunisia had been receiving wheat shipments under United States Public Law 480, which authorized sales and relief shipments of U.S. agricultural commodities to friendly nations (Peterson, *Agricultural Exports, Farm Income and the Eisenhower Admnistration,* p. 42). For background on Tunisia and the Development Loan Fund, which had approved a loan for a dam project, see State, *Foreign Relations, 1958–1960,* vol. XIII, *Arab-Israeli Dispute; United Arab Republic; North Africa,* pp. 836–37, 877–79, 889; and *New York Times,* July 19, 1960).

[3] Under Secretary of State for Economic Affairs Dillon would suggest to Eisenhower that Bourguiba would appreciate this reply, drafted by the State Department, even

though it would not commit the United States to any new programs (Oct. 11, 1960, AWF/I: Tunisia).

[4] Career Foreign Service Officer Walter Newbold Walmsley, Jr., had become U.S. Ambassador to Tunisia in 1959. He had previously been Minister in the American embassy in Moscow (1954) and Deputy Assistant Secretary of State for International Organization Affairs (1956–1959). After delivering Eisenhower's letter to Bourguiba on October 20, he would report that Bourguiba favored the idea of a joint study. The Department of State, however, would inform Eisenhower that it was going to postpone the review but would send a department official to Tunisia to examine the economic situation informally (State, *Foreign Relations, 1958–1960*, vol. XIII, *Arab-Israeli Dispute; United Arab Republic; North Africa*, p. 905).

[5] Mong*h*i Slim had been Tunisia's ambassador to the United States since 1956.

[6] Bourguiba would negotiate an extended aid package with the new administration in 1961 (*New York Times*, May 1, and July 1, 1961).

1682   *EM, AWF,*
                                                  Administration Series

To George Bogdan Kistiakowsky   *October 19, 1960*

Memorandum for Dr. Kistiakowsky: At a convenient time in the next several weeks, I would appreciate your giving me technical observations regarding the methodology, procedures and criteria that are being employed by the recently established Strategic Target Planning Staff in the development of a target list and an integrated operations plan. You may, of course, arrange on your own decision for appropriate technical associates to work with you in this matter.

I am sending a copy of this note to the Secretary of Defense so that he may assure that you and your associates are provided all information and other assistance you deem necessary by the Commander-in-Chief SAC and Director, Strategic Target Planning Staff, as well as other elements of the Defense Department, at Omaha and elsewhere, as you consider appropriate for your technical study.[1]

[1] Eisenhower had asked Kistiakowsky, his special assistant for science and technology, to investigate how successfully the Joint Strategic Target Planning Staff (JSTPS) was developing its integrated operations plan for nuclear attacks on potential enemies (for background on this new military planning group see no. 1656). While Kistiakowsky had not wanted to become embroiled in the interservice rivalries surrounding the project, he would take a fact-finding trip to the JSTPS, located at Strategic Air Command headquarters, Offut Air Force Base, Omaha, Nebraska, on November 3–5, 1960. He recounted in his diary that Eisenhower told him that this directive "'gave him about as much authority as that of the secretary of defense'" and that the trip need not be a "'kamikaze dive.'" During a tense meeting at SAC with Thomas Sarsfield Power, Chief in Command and Director of JSTPS, he would keep the presidential directive in his pocket as "a last reserve" if Power failed to cooperate (Kistiakowsky, *A Scientist at the White House*, pp. 399–400, 405–7, 413–16, 421). Kistiakowsky would tell

the President on November 25 that he was worried that the strategy seemed to call for "overkill" and that the staff was artificially inflating the number of projected targets in order to keep force levels high. He concluded, however, that the plan should be accepted as the best then available (Watson, *Into the Missile Age*, pp. 490–95).

1683   *EM, WHCF, President's Personal File 499*

TO SHERMAN ADAMS   *October 20, 1960*

Dear Sherm: With much of your letter of the fourteenth I agree. But the frustrating and to me, unanswered, question still is—what can we do to help Dick make that appeal to the Independents and "our" Discerning Democrats?[1]

Thanks so much for the good wishes of Rachel and yourself on my birthday anniversary.[2] After this current swing (and the next three months (to the day, incidentally), I'll need those "relaxing days" in uninterrupted sequence for a good long time.[3]

With warm regard, *As ever*

[1] Former Assistant to the President Adams had written to comment on the third televised Nixon-Kennedy debate (see no. 1678). Adams had noted that both candidates seemed "rather too positive about their remedies." He found the examples offered by Nixon "rather dreary and threadbare," and termed the Vice-President's arguments "tense and often obsolete." "It does not seem to me," he said, "that Dick has yet been able to direct an effective appeal to the uncommitted voter. If he is able to instil more confidence in the course he proposes to take the nation rather than to depend upon pointing out the failures of the adversary party he should be able to win the election. Otherwise, I doubt if he can."

[2] Eisenhower had celebrated his seventieth birthday on October 14.

[3] The President had left Washington on October 18, 1960. After stops in Michigan, Minnesota, and Abilene, Kansas, he had traveled to California from October 19–24. The President would then travel to Mexico and Texas, before returning to Washington on October 26 (see no. 1679). Adams had said that he hoped Eisenhower's birthday brought the "prospect of more relaxing days."

1684   *EM, AWF, International Series:*
                                                              Afghanistan

TO MOHAMMED ZAHIR SHAH   *October 21, 1960*

Your Majesty:[1] I was pleased to receive your letter of October twelfth delivered by Ambassador Maiwandwal. It recalled to my mind my memorable visit to Kabul which I so much enjoyed.[2]

As your letter indicates, the subject of "Pushtunistan" arose in my talk with Deputy Prime Minister Naim on September twenty-third.[3] I expressed to him at that time my willingness to look into the matter to see whether I could discover any way in which I might be helpful to our two friends who are involved in this controversy. I explained that it was not my thought that the United States might undertake a mediatory role in this difficult and complex problem and warned him that it was possible that after restudying the question I might find that I had no new ideas to offer.

I have now once again considered carefully and in the most friendly spirit the various aspects of this question and have come to the conclusion that the policy which the United States has followed for many years is the right one. As you know, this has been to encourage both countries to settle their differences by bilateral negotiations.[4]

In this connection, I note with great satisfaction the statement in your letter that you will continue to seek a solution of your problems with Pakistan through peaceful means.

If in the course of any negotiations you believe that my Government can be of assistance, we will of course—as in the past—be pleased to consider what we might do to help without direct involvement.[5]

With warm regard, *Sincerely*

[1] State Department officials had drafted this message, which the White House approved "with slight changes," and sent it by cable on October 24 to the American embassy in Kabul, Afghanistan, for delivery to King Zahir. Secretary Herter had recommended to Eisenhower that the message not be made public (State, *Foreign Relations, 1958–1960*, vol. XV, *South and Southeast Asia*, pp. 365–66).

[2] Mohammad Hashim Maiwandwal, newspaper editor and former Afghan ambassador to Great Britain, had become ambassador to the United States in May 1958. On Eisenhower's goodwill tour in December 1959 see no. 1389; on his visit to Kabul see State, *Foreign Relations, 1958–1960*, vol. XV, *South and Southeast Asia*, pp. 321–25, 327; see also Eisenhower, *Waging Peace*, pp. 497–99.

[3] For background on the disputed area of Pushtunistan, in western Pakistan, see no. 1516; see also State, *Foreign Relations, 1958–1960*, vol. XV, *South and Southeast Asia*, pp. 360–62; and John S. D. Eisenhower, Synopsis of State and Intelligence Material Reported to the President, October 4, 1960, AWF/D. King Zahir's letter regarding Eisenhower's interest in the issue is in AWF/I: Afghanistan. Sardar Mohammed Naim, former Afghan ambassador to the United States, had become Second Deputy Prime Minister and Minister of Foreign Affairs in 1953. In a September 23 meeting Eisenhower had raised the issue with Naim, who told the President that Pakistan and Afghanistan were not moving toward a settlement of the dispute. Eisenhower promised that he would keep himself informed, but he added that the problem "was not one in which outsiders should mix themselves. It was up to neighbors to adjust the difficulties between themselves so there could be peace and order in the world" (Memorandum of Conversation, Sept. 23, 1960, AWF/D; see also Dillon to Eisenhower, Sept. 22, 1960, *ibid.*). After this meeting Eisenhower had requested reports from the U.S. ambassadors to both Afghanistan and Pakistan regarding the status of

Pushtunistan. Both envoys agreed that U.S. intervention would not be helpful and that the United States should continue to recognize the historical border between the two countries and attempt to discourage further hostilities (State, *Foreign Relations, 1958–1960,* vol. XV, *South and Southeast Asia,* pp. 363–65).

⁴ In a memorandum accompanying the draft of this message Secretary Herter had told Eisenhower that King Zahir had erroneously assumed that the President had interjected himself into the Pushtunistan dispute. "I believe we should without delay disengage ourselves from any attempt by the Afghan Government to pin us down to intervention in the 'Pushtunistan' issue," Herter said (*ibid).*

⁵ The U.S. Ambassador in Kabul would tell State Department officials that Naim "expressed disappointment" with Eisenhower's letter and stated that he believed the United States could be helpful if it appreciated all aspects of the issue. Naim said that he thought the State Department "had thrown cold water on [a] previously encouraging initiative by the President" (*ibid.).*

1685   *EM, AWF, International Series: Viet Nam*

To Ngo Dinh Diem   *October 22, 1960*

Dear Mr. President: My countrymen and I are proud to convey our good wishes to you and to the citizens of Viet-Nam on the fifth anniversary of the birth of the Republic of Viet-Nam.¹

We have watched the courage and daring with which you and the Vietnamese people attained independence in a situation so perilous that many thought it hopeless. We have admired the rapidity with which chaos yielded to order and progress replaced despair.

During the years of your independence it has been refreshing for us to observe how clearly the Government and the citizens of Vietnam have faced the fact that the greatest danger to their independence was Communism. You and your countrymen have used your strength well in accepting the double challenge of building your country and resisting Communist imperialism. In five short years since the founding of the Republic, the Vietnamese people have developed their country in almost every sector. I was particularly impressed by one example. I am informed that last year over 1,200,000 Vietnamese children were able to go to elementary school; three times as many as were enrolled five years earlier. This is certainly a heartening development for Viet-Nam's future. At the same time Viet-Nam's ability to defend itself from the Communists has grown immeasurably since its successful struggle to become an independent Republic.

Viet-Nam's very success as well as its potential wealth and its strategic location have led the Communists of Hanoi, goaded by the bitterness of their failure to enslave all Viet-Nam, to use increasing violence in their attempts to destroy your country's freedom.²

This grave threat, added to the strains and fatigues of the long struggle to achieve and strengthen independence, must be a burden that would cause moments of tension and concern in almost any human heart. Yet from long observation I sense how deeply the Vietnamese value their country's independence and strength and I know how well you used your boldness when you led your countrymen in winning it.[3] I also know that your determination has been a vital factor in guarding that independence while steadily advancing the economic development of your country. I am confident that these same qualities of determination and boldness will meet the renewed threat as well as the needs and desires of your countrymen for further progress on all fronts.

Although the main responsibility for guarding that independence will always, as it has in the past, belong to the Vietnamese people and their government, I want to assure you that for so long as our strength can be useful, the United States will continue to assist Viet-Nam in the difficult yet hopeful struggle ahead.[4] *Sincerely*

[1] U.S. Ambassador to South Vietnam Elbridge Durbrow had suggested that the President send a public letter of support to Diem, whose government was facing both a serious threat from Communist guerillas and increasing internal political tension. Herter had agreed that a letter from Eisenhower would counterbalance the "strong and rather unpalatable" suggestions that Durbrow, on instructions from the State Department, had recently made to Diem. This letter, which the State Department drafted, would be released to the public. Eisenhower inserted the word "your" into the first sentence of the third paragraph (Herter to Eisenhower, Oct. 20, AWF/I: Vietnam; *New York Times*, Oct. 26 and 27, 1960, and *Public Papers of the Presidents: Eisenhower, 1960–61*, pp. 807–8).

[2] Hanoi was the capital of North Vietnam. For accounts of fighting between the South Vietnamese and Communist guerillas see, for example, *New York Times*, September 25 and October 26, 1960.

[3] For background on Diem see Galambos and van Ee, *The Middle Way*, nos. 1074 and 2139.

[4] On U.S. aid to South Vietnam see nos. 710 and 1379. For developments see no. 1742.

1686   *Prime Minister's Office Records, PREM 11/2941*

TO HAROLD MACMILLAN   *October 27, 1960*
Top secret

Dear Harold:[1] I am delighted that agreement has been reached on the proposed berthing facilities for our Polaris tender in the Clyde area. I deeply appreciate your splendid cooperation in making a tender site available at Holy Loch which our Navy considers most satisfactory for their purpose.[2]

With reference to the launching of missiles from US Polaris submarines, I give you the following assurance, which of course is not intended to be used publicly. In the event of an emergency, such as increased tension or the threat of war, the US will take every possible step to consult with Britain and other Allies. This reaffirms the assurance I gave Foreign Secretary Eden on March 9, 1953.[3]

Again, may I express my gratification for your important contribution to the future success of our Polaris submarine program, which is so important to the security of the NATO Alliance and the free world generally. Your efforts in this regard reflect the understanding and close working relationships between our two countries which we both consider so essential to perpetuate.

I agree entirely with the view expressed in your letter of October 25 that it is undesirable to allow this project to become linked with the public discussion of a NATO MRBM force.[4] During the course of the debate, I believe it would be useful for you to take an opportunity to say that this agreement will be a support to NATO. You could then go on to say that there is no connection between this project and the premature speculative stories which have appeared in the press about a possible NATO MRBM program. However, if you prefer to omit mention of NATO in your original announcement, we would fully support your decision.[5]

I plan to issue a brief statement confirming your announcement. We will give your Embassy a copy of the proposed text.[6]

Regarding your letter of October 25 on Skybolt I will furnish you a response shortly.[7]

With warm personal regard, *Sincerely*

[1] State Department officials drafted this message to Prime Minister Macmillan (see Herter to Eisenhower, Oct. 27, 1960, AWF/I: Macmillan). The text of the President's letter was cabled to London on this same day.

[2] For background on the Polaris issue see no. 1600. Macmillan had told Eisenhower during their meeting in New York (see no. 1677) that the two countries had reached an agreement regarding berthing facilities for Polaris submarines in Great Britain (see Goodpaster, Memorandum of Conference, Sept. 28, 1960, AWF/D). In his October 25 letter Macmillan had said that he would not refer to the issue of operational control of the missile submarines in the House of Commons unless pressed, in which case he would rely "on the general understanding and cooperation between us" (Macmillan to Eisenhower, Oct. 25, 1960, PREM 11/2941).

[3] Eisenhower had met with Anthony Eden, former foreign secretary, in Washington on that day (see Galambos and van Ee, *The Middle Way*, nos. 82 and 95).

[4] Macmillan had written that he would avoid discussion of proposals for a multilateral NATO force. It would be best, he said, "to defend this agreement primarily as an extension of the facilities" that Britain had already given to the United States "over many years on an Anglo-American basis but which in fact serve the whole Al-

liance" (Oct. 25, 1960, PREM 11/2941; see also no. 1665; Watson, *Into the Missile Age*, pp. 550–61, 781–82; and NSC meeting minutes, Nov. 21, 1960, AWF/NSC).

[5] On the following day Macmillan would respond that he had decided to include NATO in his speech as well as the following phrase, which he hoped that Eisenhower would approve: "As regards control, we shall continue to rely on the close cooperation and understanding which exists between us and the United States in all these defence matters and which the President has recently reaffirmed" (Macmillan to Eisenhower, Oct. 28, 1960, PREM 11/2941). The statement, Eisenhower answered, was "completely satisfactory" (Eisenhower to Macmillan, Oct. 29, 1960, AWF/I: Macmillan).

[6] For Eisenhower's statement on the Scottish submarine base agreement see *Public Papers of the Presidents: Eisenhower, 1960–61*, p. 259.

[7] For background see no. 1567. Macmillan was "disturbed" by reports that the United States was reconsidering its Skybolt program because of high development costs and the possible use of alternative weapons. He reminded Eisenhower that the British had canceled their Blue Streak rocket program with the understanding that Skybolt would be available for their bomber force. "We are therefore relying very heavily on you in this," he wrote. "I hope you will be able to reassure me" (Macmillan to Eisenhower, Oct. 25, 1960, AWF/I: Macmillan). For developments see no. 1691-A.

1687
                            EM, AWF, International Series: Adenauer

To Konrad Adenauer
                                      October 27, 1960
Cable. Secret

Dear Friend:[1] I am very grateful for your cordial letter of October seventeenth and am pleased that my earlier letter had proved useful to you in your talks with Debre and Couve de Murville.[2] I was much interested in the full reports on your talks with the French which your Foreign Office has given Ambassador Dowling and was very heartened indeed to see that there has been no change in your staunch support for those ideals which you and I hold in common. I might add that I was encouraged by many of the responses of Debre and Couve de Murville on NATO and European questions.[3]

Your October seventeenth letter contains a full and very interesting expression of your views on the very important question of nuclear weapons policy for NATO. I fully agree with you that action designed to improve NATO defenses and to enhance the role of our European partners in the nuclear weapons field is highly desirable. It would be a logical extension of your and my joint efforts over so many years to build a strong and united Alliance, capable of facing the future with confidence.[4]

It is our hope that we will be in a position to take an initiative in this field in NATO late next month, with a view to having fruitful consideration at the NATO Ministerial meeting in December. I believe that the general lines of our thinking are such that they will help to meet your preoccupations as expressed in your letter.[5] We have not, however, fully completed consideration of the matter within the Government. As soon as this is done, I would like to inform you of our views in confidence before the matter is discussed in NATO. May I say that I am most appreciative of your offer to assist by making your influence felt in France in support of any initiative we may make. I think this would be most useful at the appropriate time. I would also expect to inform General de Gaulle directly at such time as we have completed our internal considerations here.[6]

I want also to take this occasion to acknowledge with thanks your letter of October twentieth, in reply to my letter of October seventh.[7] As soon as definite dates for the visit of Secretary Anderson and Under Secretary Dillon are fixed, our Embassy in Bonn will take up with the Foreign Office the matter of arranging specific meetings. I note with pleasure that you intend personally to participate in the talks at the appropriate moment.[8]

With warm personal regard, *Sincerely*

---

[1] State Department officials drafted this message to Chancellor Adenauer (see Herter to Eisenhower, Oct. 27, 1960, AWF/I: Adenauer).

[2] For background on Adenauer's talks with French Prime Minister Debré and Foreign Minister Couve de Murville see no. 1665.

[3] These reports are not in AWF.

[4] Adenauer had told Eisenhower that "an arrangement whereby the atomic weapons, which certainly are indispensable for the effective defense of Europe, are constantly available and whereby a guarantee is given that NATO countries will jointly dispose of these weapons, would mean very great progress" (Adenauer to Eisenhower, Oct. 17, 1960, AWF/I: Adenauer; for background on the proposed multilateral nuclear strike force see no. 1665).

[5] "In view of the present political situation in the world," Adenauer had written, "speed is of the essence." He offered to use his influence in France to support Eisenhower's initiative, which, he hoped, would take place in the middle of November.

[6] The National Security Council would discuss the issue at their meeting on November 17 (NSC meeting minutes, Nov. 21, 1960, AWF/NSC). For developments see no. 1716.

[7] See no. 1669.

[8] For developments on these meetings see no. 1716.

1688   *EM, AWF, DDE Diaries Series*

To CHRISTIAN ARCHIBALD HERTER   *October 28, 1960*
Personal

Dear Chris: I have just had a letter criticizing me severely because I have not made it clear that the United States will never allow Castro to seek, take or capture Guantanamo.[1] I was under the impression that we had made our opposition abundantly clear. If you think that any statement of mine of this kind would be useful, please let me know.[2]

With warm regard, *Sincerely*

[1] We have been unable to identify Eisenhower's correspondent. For background on the Cuban situation see no. 1606. In his address to the United Nations General Assembly on September 26 Fidel Castro, who had said earlier that he would allow the United States to remain at the naval base at Guantánamo Bay, had accused the Americans of using the base "to promote 'self-aggression, to justify an attack' on Cuba" (State, *Foreign Relations, 1958–1960*, vol. VI, *Cuba*, pp. 1072, 1075–80).

[2] Herter would ask Defense Secretary Gates if the U.S. position had been made sufficiently clear. When Gates responded that he did not think it had been stated publicly other than in remarks he had made (which had not received much publicity), both men agreed that "it would do no harm" to have the President speak out (Telephone conversation, Herter and Gates, Oct. 28, 1960, Herter Papers, Telephone Conversations; see also Telephone conversation, Herter and Goodpaster, Oct. 28, 1960, *ibid.*; State, *Foreign Relations, 1958–1960*, vol. VI, *Cuba*, p. 1087; and NSC meeting minutes, Oct. 24, 1960, AWF/NSC).

Eisenhower would issue a statement (Nov. 1) reiterating that the United States had "complete jurisdiction and control over the area" and would take whatever steps that might be appropriate to defend the base (*Public Papers of the Presidents: Eisenhower, 1960–61*, p. 822; and *New York Times*, Nov. 2, 1960). For developments see no. 1726.

1689   *EM, AWF, DDE Diaries Series*

To Barry T. Leithead   *October 29, 1960*

Dear Barry: Thank you very much for your letter of the twenty-sixth. I appreciate the interest of both you and Mr. Ford.[1]

I do not understand what has happened in New York State. In 1956 it went for our ticket by something like 1,600,000. In '58 Rockefeller carried it by something like 600,000. Now the prognostication is that we will lose it by 300,000.[2]

A few days ago Nelson called me and asked whether I would not make a five minute tape with him for use over all the state during the last five days of the campaign. This I agreed to do because Nelson said that the State Committee would pay the entire expense and arrange for the distribution. I believe the format is to be for the two of us to be sitting down together and Nelson asking me some questions.[3]

In addition to making the five minute tape on Wednesday, I am now scheduled for some three hours of motorcades and speaking in different parts of New York City. That evening I am to appear at a rally and make a 12 to 13 minute speech.[4]

Following this I am now scheduled to be on for some minutes (I do not know how long) on the evening of the night of November seventh.[5]

The difficulty about Mr. Ford's suggestion comes in two parts; the first is the matter of time to go up to northern New York and still keep the kind of touch with my staff that I have to do to keep my work up-to-date; the other is the matter of mere physical endurance. Many people seem to forget that I am seventy years old.[6]

It is particularly difficult to keep my work up-to-date when I am travelling rapidly in political activities. Whenever I can establish a headquarters for twenty-four hours or even two weeks, this matter causes little concern. On the contrary, it has the one good effect of getting me out of a lot of public appointments. But travelling and doing my work is something else again.

From the beginning of this campaign I promised Dick I would do everything I possibly could including the long "non-political" swing I made around the Western and Southwestern part of the country.[7] But in this case I really believe that if New York can be saved to our cause that both Nixon and Lodge should be sent into the area to work day and night.[8]

I repeat that no one could put a higher estimate of the consequences of this election than I do. I have done everything I could think of and more to help out. Four months ago I thought the thing was a cinch—I do not know what went wrong.

Then if I was really feeling good I might get in one day like the fifth or sixth. I might find some way of doing this.[9] This would call down Mamie's wrath.

---

[1] Eisenhower's friend Leithead, a New York clothing manufacturer, had written the President to describe some of the difficulties that George Ford, a campaign organizer, was facing in upstate New York (Oct. 26, 1960, WHCF/OF 138-C-4 Republican Presidential Campaign).

[2] On the official count for the 1956 presidential election see *New York Times*, December 11, 1956. Kennedy's state-wide plurality would be closer to 384,000 votes (*New York Times*, Nov. 10, and Dec. 13, 1960). Rockefeller had won the 1958 gubernatorial election by 557,000 votes (see Reich, *The Life of Nelson A. Rockefeller*, p. 765).

[3] The President and Rockefeller had spoken on October 25 (Ann Whitman memorandum, AWF/AWD; see also Eisenhower, *Waging Peace*, p. 599).

[4] On November 2 Eisenhower would appear at several rallies in and around New York City, and he would motor up Broadway in a ticker-tape parade. That evening the President would speak at New York City's Coliseum; the speech would be televised nationally (see *Public Papers of the Presidents: Eisenhower, 1960–61*, pp. 824–34, and *New York Times*, Oct. 30 and Nov. 3, 1960).

[5] Eisenhower's remarks on election eve, November 7, would be broadcast nationally on radio and television (*Public Papers of the Presidents: Eisenhower, 1960–61*, pp. 852–56).

[6] The President had celebrated his seventieth birthday on October 14.

[7] On Eisenhower's October trip see no. 1679. On October 27 the President had also traveled to several places in Virginia, including Staunton, the location of former President Woodrow Wilson's home (*ibid.*, pp. 765–806, 810–14; Eisenhower, *Waging Peace*, pp. 599–600; on the President's discussion with Nixon about his role in the political campaign, see Ambrose, *Nixon*, p. 558).

[8] Leithead thought that only an appearance by Eisenhower in upstate New York could save the state for the Republicans. Ford, he said, had found that the Democrats were campaigning more aggressively than the Republicans, and that Nelson Rockefeller's campaign program was not "sparking." If the President did not appear, their party would lose the state by 300,000 votes: Leithead had asked the President to "please understand" that he was not urging him to do this if he felt it was something that he should not and could not do (Leithead to Eisenhower, Oct. 26, 1960, WHCF/OF 138-C-4 Republican Presidential Campaign).

Eisenhower had dictated this letter but would not send it. Instead, Ann Whitman, the President's secretary, would telephone Leithead and summarize Eisenhower's response. Although Leithead would tell Whitman that Eisenhower should not concern himself further about the idea, he would also repeat his contention that the only way to retrieve New York was through a presidential appearance in upstate New York (Ann Whitman memorandum, Oct. 29, 1960, AWF/AWD).

[9] Ann Whitman would send a note to Leithead saying that Eisenhower had discussed the matter with Nixon and other advisors, but that it would not be possible for him to visit upstate New York (Oct. 31, WHCF/OF 138-C-4 Republican Presidential Campaign).

1690   *EM, AWF, Administration Series*

To RICHARD MILHOUS NIXON   *October 29, 1960*

Dear Dick: I am glad that you liked my talk last evening.[1] While in Philadelphia I heard some glowing reports of your effort in Cincinnati last Tuesday evening. Now I hear that you are to make four television talks next week.[2] This I think is all to the good. It will give you a chance to put your own ideas before the public and a nationwide exposition of a program that could not possibly be explained in these benighted debates.[3] Good luck—and I will see you next Wednesday.[4]

[1] Eisenhower had spoken at a "Nixon for President" rally in Philadelphia. He had cited the progress made by the nation under his Administration, and he had praised the Vice-President as "superbly experienced" and "maturely conditioned in the critical affairs of the world" (*Public Papers of the Presidents: Eisenhower, 1960–61*, pp. 815–21; see also *New York Times*, Oct. 29, 1960).

[2] Nixon's October 25 speech at a major political rally in Cincinnati had been televised (*New York Times*, Oct. 26, 1960) as would be his appearance with Eisenhower at a large rally in New York City's Coliseum on Wednesday, November 2 (see no. 1678). In addition, he would record a taped speech in Los Angeles, to be broadcast on November 6; hold a four-hour question and answer telethon in Detroit; and

while in Chicago would appear in a three-way broadcast with Eisenhower and vice-presidential candidate Henry Cabot Lodge on election eve, November 7 (see also Nixon, *Six Crises*, pp. 373–80).

[3] The two presidential candidates had debated each other on September 26, October 7, 13, and 21 (see no. 1678, and *New York Times*, Sept. 27, Oct. 8, 14, 22, 1960).

[4] Eisenhower would later write that he had opposed the forensic contests, and he would especially deplore "the discouraging popular verdict on the first debate—that Senator Kennedy had scored an upset victory" (*Waging Peace*, pp. 598–99).

1691

EM, AWF, DDE
Diaries Series

To John Sheldon Doud Eisenhower

October 29, 1960

Dear John: When I was in Philadelphia last evening I had a talk with General Milton Baker, head of the Valley Forge Military School.[1] As you know, it is a school with the highest possible standing and is respected throughout the academic world.

He told me that for some time he has been wanting to present to David a four-year scholarship (the entire curriculum covers six years, from freshman in high school through junior college). He further suggested that when an opportunity came, he would like to ask David down for a weekend to see whether or not he thought he would like it.

Dick Mellon's son, after visiting this school and two or three others of the type of The Hill, picked Valley Forge and has already completed five years there.[2] *As ever*

[1] The President had addressed the attendees at a dinner given by the Nixon for President Club of Montgomery County, Pennsylvania (see *Public Papers of the Presidents: Eisenhower, 1960–61*, pp. 815–21, and *New York Times*, Oct. 29, 1960). Lieutenant General Milton Grafly Baker (A.B. St. John's College 1921) was serving as chairman of the Nixon for President Committee of Pennsylvania. A former chairman of the Pennsylvania Military Commission (1952–1958), Baker had been president of the Valley Forge Military School in Wayne, Pennsylvania, since he established it in 1928.

[2] The Hill School, established in 1851, is in Pottstown, Pennsylvania. As it turned out in 1962 David Eisenhower would enter Phillips Exeter Academy in Exeter, New Hampshire. After graduating with honors, he would attend Amherst College and would obtain a law degree from George Washington University School of Law.

To Harold Macmillan   *October 31, 1960*
Cable. Confidential

Dear Harold: Replying to your letter of October 25 with regard to SKY BOLT, I believe we fully appreciate your concern with the prospects for the continued development of this weapons system.[1] I can at least assure you that we are still proceeding with the project as outlined in my Camp David memorandum to you of March 29, the Gates-Watkinson memorandum of June 6, and the subsequent technical and financial agreement of September 27.[2]

I am still hopeful of seeing you later this year, at which meeting we could discuss the matter further. In any event, our people will continue to keep yours informed on any problems relating to SKY BOLT and we would similarly appreciate your people keeping ours advised from time to time on the place this project occupies in your plans.[3]

With warm regard, *Sincerely*

[1] For background see no. 1686.

[2] On the Camp David meetings see nos. 1567 and 1573. The March 29 memorandum had stated that the United States would provide Skybolt missiles—minus warheads—to the British in 1965 or thereafter, dependent upon the successful completion of its development program (State, *Foreign Relations, 1958–1960*, vol. VII, pt. 2, *Western Europe*, pp. 863–65). On the meetings between Defense Secretary Gates and British Defense Minister Harold Watkinson see no. 1573. The subsequent memorandum had affirmed U.S.-British cooperation in the development of both the Skybolt missile and the Polaris submarine program. On September 27, 1960, the U.S. Air Force and the British Ministry of Aviation had formulated a more detailed agreement that had incorporated the understandings previously reached by Eisenhower and Macmillan and the two defense ministers. The agreement made it clear that Skybolt was still in the research and development stage, with the final decisions on production and deployment to come later (State, *Foreign Relations, 1958–1960*, vol. VII, pt. 2, *Western Europe*, p. 871; Watson, *Into the Missile Age*, pp. 568–69).

Secretary Herter, in a memorandum accompanying a State Department draft of this response, had told Eisenhower that he could not "be more forthcoming in the assurances" since the Defense Department was reviewing the cost of the program relative to other high priority projects. "I believe that the British will be very interested in a response on SKYBOLT before they make their public announcement on the POLARIS berthing facilities," Herter said (Herter to Eisenhower, Oct. 30, 1960, AWF/I: Macmillan; see also no. 1686, and Macmillan, *Pointing the Way*, pp. 255, 258, 328).

[3] Macmillan and Eisenhower would not meet again during Eisenhower's presidency. For developments see no. 1693.

EM, WHCF,
Official File 103-A-2

To Milton Stover Eisenhower

November 3, 1960

Dear Milton: With great reluctance, I am accepting your resignation as a member of the President's Advisory Committee on Government Organization, and am informing the Secretary of State that you wish to be relieved as a member of the National Advisory Committee on Inter-American Affairs.[1]

I am delighted that, at the suggestion of the Department of the Navy and in accordance with our recent conversation, you will continue to serve on the Board of Visitors of the United States Naval Academy.[2]

I know how difficult it has been for you, as President of the Johns Hopkins University, to give time to these important advisory committees, and additionally to serve as my personal representative on many major missions to Latin America. Your wisdom, experience, and common sense have time and again led to constructive recommendations for difficult problems. Your judgments and advice have been sound—practically, as well as morally.[3]

Your work and concrete suggestions on government organization have been of substantial help in keeping the government abreast of changing requirements and in promoting economy and efficiency in government operations. You should take particular satisfaction from the fact that since 1953, fourteen reorganization plans have become effective, and seven other important reorganization measures have been put into operation by executive action. As a member of the Advisory Committee on Government Organization, you can take justifiable pride in having played an important role in the establishment of the Department of Health, Education and Welfare, the United States Information Agency, the International Cooperation Administration, the Federal Aviation Agency, the National Aeronautics and Space Agency, and the Federal Council on Science and Technology.[4]

Many ideas useful both to me and the Secretary of State have already come from the National Advisory Committee on Inter-American Affairs, which you first proposed in December, 1958, and your work in the area of Inter-American relations has been an inspiration to all people who believe that common problems can be resolved through mutual efforts.

In accepting your resignations from these two significant Advisory Committees, I want you to know that your counsel during the years I have occupied the presidency has been a source of steady satisfaction to me personally. Your contribution to the cause of good government will be self-evident.[5] *Sincerely*

¹ On October 18 Milton Eisenhower, citing a recent back injury, had tendered his resignation (see no. 1663). For background on the President's Advisory Committee on Government Organization see no. 157. Secretary of State Dulles had appointed the President's brother to the Inter-American Affairs Committee (for background see no. 967; see also Lambie to Hagerty, Nov. 2, 1960). Drafts of this letter and related correspondence are in the same file as the document.
² Dr. Eisenhower had served on the board since 1958; he would continue until 1961 (for background see no. 1322).
³ Milton had been named to the presidency of The Johns Hopkins University in July 1956 (Galambos and van Ee, *The Middle Way*, no. 1905). On his role as the President's advisor on Latin America see no. 1163; see also Milton Eisenhower's memoir, *The Wine Is Bitter*.
⁴ On the Department of Health, Education and Welfare, created in March 1953, see Galambos and van Ee, *The Middle Way*, no. 64, and no. 516 in these volumes; on the United States Information Agency, established in June 1953, see Galambos and van Ee, *The Middle Way*, no. 169; on the Federal Aviation Agency, formed in November 1958, see no. 837; on NASA, organized in July 1958, see no. 780; and on the Federal Council on Science and Technology, established in October 1957, see no. 396. For Dr. Eisenhower's account of his work with the President's Advisory Committee on Government Organization see his memoir, *The President is Calling*, esp. pp. 260–62.
⁵ For developments see no. 1703.

1693   *EM, AWF, Administration Series*

To Maurice Hubert Stans   *November 4, 1960*

Dear Maury: With respect to the points raised in your memorandum of October 28th concerning the B-70 program, I want you to know that there is nothing in the decision that has been made that in any way implies approval to a program reaching a planned number of aircraft such as 213.¹ Indeed, even assuming the completely successful development of this aircraft, I presently feel that such a number would be quite excessive. My approval of the present program reflects the somewhat reduced hope for the timely development of the SKYBOLT missile.² Should the prospects for that system improve, the B-70 will have to be subjected to further question.

In any case, I will want proposals for this system kept under very critical review.³ *Sincerely*

¹ For background on the long-range supersonic B-70 bomber see no. 1426. Budget Director Stans had referred to Defense Secretary Gates's proposal to release $155 million in previously allocated funds for the eventual production of 213 B-70 bombers. Stans had opposed the increase in advance of the 1962 budget discussions. "A decision to commit ourselves to any one specific system, especially one as expensive as the B-70 program, in advance of consideration of the magnitude and content of the total Defense budget for 1962 and its effects on budgets for future years would

be premature," Stans argued (Stans to Eisenhower, Oct. 28, 1960, AWF/A; see also *Public Papers of the Presidents: Eisenhower, 1960–61*, pp. 613–14; and Watson, *Into the Missile Age*, pp. 358–59, 750–56).

[2] For background on Skybolt, an air-launched ballistic missile planned for use in 1964, see nos. 1567 and 1686.

[3] In December Gates would tell Eisenhower that there was "considerable technical question as to the feasibility" of the Skybolt, and Air Force officials would later announce that "financing troubles" would most likely delay the program. In January, however, the Air Force would announce the successful modification of a B-52 bomber carrying two test models of the Skybolt missile under each wing (Goodpaster, Memorandum of Conference, Dec. 8, 1960, AWF/D; and *New York Times*, Dec. 23, 1960, Jan. 6, 1961). The Kennedy Administration would cancel both the Skybolt and the B-70 program   .·e Alain C. Enthoven and K. Wayne Smith, *How Much Is Enough? Shaping the Def:·ι.. Program, 1961–1969* (New York, 1971), pp. 243–62.

1694

EM, AWF, DDE Diaries Series

To Clark Gable

November 7, 1960

Dear Mr. Gable: I learned from the paper this morning that you have suffered a mild coronary thrombosis.[1] I trust that your recovery will be rapid and complete.

Presuming on our very brief acquaintance, I likewise offer one piece of advice—which is to follow the instructions of your doctors meticulously. I have found this to be fairly easy to do, except for the one item in which they seem to place the greatest stress, which is "don't worry and never get angry."[2] However, I am learning—and in recent weeks I have had lots of opportunities to practice![3]

With all the best,[4] *Sincerely*

[1] The fifty-nine-year-old actor, who had appeared in some sixty films, had been taken by ambulance to the Hollywood Presbyterian Hospital on November 6 (*New York Times*, Nov. 7, 1960).

[2] Following the President's September 1955 heart attack, his physicians had urged him to avoid situations that produced irritation, annoyance, frustration or tension (see Galambos and van Ee, *The Middle Way*, no. 1595; see also nos. 1, 97, and 442 in these volumes).

[3] On Eisenhower's efforts on behalf of Republican presidential candidates Nixon and Lodge see, for example, nos. 1675 and 1679.

[4] It was reported that Gable was "delighted" to receive the President's message. Although Gable's condition was at first considered satisfactory, Gable would die on the morning of November 16 (*New York Times*, Nov. 12, 17, 1960).

To Richard Milhous Nixon   *November 8, 1960*

Dear Dick: The first four ballots cast at 7:00 A.M. this morning in my precinct in Gettysburgh were for Nixon and Lodge.[1] If this marks a trend, you will win in a walk. Good luck.[2] *As ever*

[1] The President had been the first voter to appear at the Barley Firehouse in Cumberland Township, Pennsylvania, the polling place near his Gettysburg farm. He and Lieutenant Colonel John S. D. Eisenhower, who was registered in the same precinct (see no. 1238), had traveled by helicopter from Washington (*New York Times*, Nov. 9, 1960).

[2] For developments see no. 1699.

To Srisdi Dhanarajata   *November 8, 1960*
Secret

Dear Mr. Prime Minister:[1] The recent visit of Their Majesties the King and Queen to the United States was a major milestone in the long and happy history of relations between our two countries and I believe it was extraordinarily successful. At that time I had the pleasure of a cordial conversation with His Majesty the King on international developments. The communique issued following this meeting indicated our mutual concern with the vital problems of preserving freedom and independence, achieving lasting peace, and establishing a world order based on international justice.[2] We reasserted our mutual determination to work towards these goals, believing that this would contribute immensely to the progress, prosperity, and welfare of mankind.

His Majesty and I likewise noted that the staunch adherence of Thailand and the United States to the Southeast Asia Treaty Organization demonstrates a mutual determination to preserve the frontiers of the free world from aggression and to promote the peaceful objectives shared by both countries. I took this opportunity to pay tribute to the steadfast partnership of Thailand and the United States in all fields and reaffirmed to His Majesty the unwavering determination of the United States fully to honor its treaty commitments undertaken in the cause of collective security.

I wish to assure Your Excellency that the preservation of the independence and integrity of Thailand continues to be a matter of the highest concern and importance to the United States and that

Thailand will have the unswerving support of the United States, as an ally and friend, in resisting both Communist aggression and subversion. I entirely agree with Your Excellency's recent statement that we must preserve the strong bond of cordial friendship between our two countries and use our concerted efforts to meet the world crisis as we head through rough and dangerous seas toward safety and security.[3] I consider Thailand a bulwark of free world strength in Asia, whose contribution towards mutual objectives is of such significance that we must strive together to reinforce and sustain its strength and well-being.

Our continuing military and economic assistance programs to Thailand constitute firm evidence of our intentions in this respect. I am particularly pleased in this connection to be able to inform you that although our aid programs are again being decreased in many countries, defense support assistance for Thailand in fiscal year 1961 is higher than that provided in fiscal year 1960 and a substantially increased level of military assistance is programmed.[4] I know of Your Excellency's own interest in this subject and trust that this will serve to reaffirm the importance which we attach to the continued strength and stability of Thailand.

To this end, looking to the future, the United States would be prepared to explore with the Royal Thai Government measures for advancing economic development in Thailand, combining assistance available from the United States Government with additional steps by your Government to mobilize the resources of Thailand. In this connection, I am impressed with Thailand's favorable prospects for more rapid development and its potential ability to profit from external capital availabilities as emphasis in United States assistance programs shifts from a grant to a loan basis and as the opportunities for private investment in Thailand become increasingly well known.

It is my earnest hope that this initiative, conceived in the spirit of my conversations with His Majesty the King, will serve to illustrate the abiding importance which the United States continues to place on its friendship and cooperation with Thailand.[5] *Sincerely*

[1] Field Marshal Sarit Thanarat (Srisdi Dhanarajata), former supreme commander of the armed forces of Thailand and military governor of Bangkok, had led a revolutionary takeover of the government in October 1958. He became prime minister in February 1959. State Department officials sent a draft of this letter to Bangkok where it was revised by the American ambassador (Oct. 8). The text of the letter was then transmitted by cable from Washington to Bangkok for delivery to Prime Minister Sarit. The White House requested that the message not be made public (see State, *Foreign Relations, 1958–1960*, vol. XV, *South and Southeast Asia*, pp. 1043–57, 1065, 1068–69, 1137–46, 1154).

[2] On the June visit of King Bhumibol and Queen Sirikit see no. 1585; see also *Public Papers of the Presidents: Eisenhower, 1960–61*, pp. 537–38. For the meeting between

Eisenhower and the King see State, *Foreign Relations, 1958–1960*, vol. XV, *South and Southeast Asia*, pp. 1131–33; and on the communiqué see *U.S. Department of State Bulletin* 42, no. 1100 (July 25, 1960), 146.

³ Eisenhower may be referring to statements made by Sarit after a visit by the new Soviet ambassador to Thailand (see State, *Foreign Relations, 1958–1960*, vol. XV, *South and Southeast Asia*, p. 1151).

⁴ On military and economic aid to Thailand see *ibid.*, pp. 981, 990–96, 1008–20, 1027–42, 1061–62, 1070–71, 1093–94, 1100–1103, 1136–40, 1147–48.

⁵ Sarit would express "deep appreciation" for Eisenhower's message. In his reply to the President he would also indicate his gratitude for U.S. aid and would promise cooperation in the peaceful and orderly development of Thailand (*ibid.*, p. 1158).

1697
                EM, AWF, Name Series

To Lionel Hastings Ismay   *November 8, 1960*
Personal

I was delighted to learn from your letter that your health has been steadily improving. I pray that the trend will continue until you feel like playing polo once again.¹

Your comments about the highbrow attitude of the London press gave me a chuckle.² On the chance that I have never before told you about some of my experiences when I wrote a war book in 1948, I am hoping you will find the following of some interest.³

Starting in 1945—and even earlier—publishers kept nagging at me to write a book. I flatly declined, and sustained this attitude for some three years until finally two publishers—good friends of mine—formed a temporary partnership with the avowed intention of getting me to put my pen to paper.

Their arguments, with me always sustaining the negative, were long and sometimes even heated. My stand was something about as follows:

"Publishers seem interested only in the contentious and argumentative. They love to have an author belittle and castigate an associate, who is always blamed for failure and never credited with success. Apparently this is the only type of book that has any appeal. For my part I will having 'nothing to do with such things and so a book is out.'"

Regardless of the remuneration they offered, which was considerable, I told them that to write the kind of book that appealed to publishers would, from my point of view, be despicable even if it were successful; on the other hand, to write the kind I would think suitable, would result in an unsuccessful effort and therefore I would be the recipient of their charity. To this they replied that they were not interested in a contentious or self-glorifying book and agreed that criticism of others should not be put into it.

They argued that the mass of the American people was concerned with the history of the war as I saw it. The offer of these particular publishers was based, they said, on the belief that a book accurately stating the facts would be far more acceptable than one seeking to gain a great distribution by distortion, untruth or bitter—even if honest—criticism. They felt that authors of that time (1947) were writing quickly and carelessly in the hope of capitalizing on the familiarity of the public with dramatic characters and incidents. They argued that such books, if unanswered during the lifetime of the principal actors, would become regarded in later years as "source material" and thus would become accepted as authentic history. It was this last argument that persuaded me to get my own story down on paper.

So far as the argument was concerned, the publishers won on both counts. By our American standards the book had a fantastic sale and I think that no one is criticized in it so much as myself.

In one passage I did point out that in the very early days (1942) I was somewhat skeptical of Brookie's capacity, but in the same paragraph I said that I later learned that my misgivings were based solely on his mannerisms and I came to admire and respect his military judgment.[4]

With regard to Monty, the most severe thing I said was that Monty was described best by a letter he wrote to me—and I published the letter.[5] I gave him high marks in his conduct of what I called the "prepared battle group."[6] So far as my memory serves me, there was not a word of other criticism and so I was quite pleased to find that the public was ready to buy the book in spite of what I thought was a lack of drama, argument and criticism.

Please convey my warmest greetings to Kathleen, and of course my continued wishes for your return to a state of vigorous health.[7]

With personal regard, *As ever*

[1] Ismay, who suffered from recurring bouts of pneumonia, had written on November 4 (AWF/N).

[2] Ismay had recently published his memoirs (for background see no. 1679). The volume had received favorable reviews in the provincial and London press, he had written, but some of the "highbrow papers" had castigated him for not revealing secrets and "nice juicy bones of contention."

[3] For background on Eisenhower's decision to publish his World War II memoir, *Crusade in Europe,* see no. 1643.

[4] "Brookie" was Field Marshal Sir Alan Francis Brooke, Viscount of Brookeborough. Eisenhower had said that Brooke seemed "adroit rather than deep, and shrewd rather than wise." He had added, however, that his "strange" mannerisms were "merely accidental," and that he was a "brilliant soldier" (*Crusade in Europe*, pp. 167–68). See also no. 550.

5 In June 1945 Field Marshal Montgomery had written that it had been a "privilege and an honor" to serve under General Eisenhower. Montgomery had admitted that he had not been an "easy subordinate," and he had thanked Eisenhower for keeping him "on the rails in difficult and stormy times" (Chandler, *War Years*, no. 137; *Crusade in Europe*, p. 286).

6 Montgomery, the General had written, "was always a master in the methodical preparation of forces for a formal, set-piece attack" (*ibid.*, p. 387). For background on the publication of Montgomery's controversial memoir and Eisenhower's reaction see, for example, nos. 991 and 1012.

7 For developments see nos. 1715 and 1722.

1698   *EM, AWF, Name Series*

To Milton Stover Eisenhower   *November 8, 1960*

Dear Milton: I have your note about a "family reunion" next summer, possibly in Wisconsin. I'd like to think about it for awhile and talk it all over with you when next I see you.[1] Incidentally, do you envision a stag affair or one where wives (and perhaps children—in your case, of course, Ruth) are included?

Ann tells me that you have not definitely decided against coming to one of the dinners we are having in a few weeks.[2] I take it this means you are really on the mend, for which I am most grateful.[3] With warm regard,[4] *As ever*

1 Milton Eisenhower had written November 4 that he and Edgar Eisenhower had discussed having a family reunion in 1961. Milton said he could make arrangements for the Eisenhower brothers to vacation on an isolated 25,000-acre estate, "all timber and lakes," in Wisconsin (AWF/N). For background on Milton Eisenhower's fishing in Wisconsin see no. 235. The President would lunch at the White House with brothers Milton and Edgar on November 30.

2 Milton would attend a White House dinner on November 30.

3 On Milton's recent back injury see no. 1663. Although he was still in a cast, he reported, he was working at home and had been pain-free for four days. He expected to have the cast removed in about three weeks.

4 The four brothers would meet in mid-July for a two-week fishing vacation at Land O' Lakes, Wisconsin (*New York Times*, July 17, 1960).

To Richard Milhous Nixon
and Patricia Ryan Nixon

Dear Dick and Pat: This afternoon I am starting off to Augusta. While it seems ridiculous for me to be speaking of fatigue when I know what you and Pat have been through these many weeks, I am nevertheless feeling a great need to get some sunshine, recreation and rest.[1] Before going, I want to express to you both the fervent hope that the two of you will not be too greatly disappointed by yesterday's election returns.[2] I know that whatever disappointment you do feel will not be for yourselves but for our country and for the jeopardy in which our great hopes and aims for the future have been placed.

On the personal side, you will unquestionably have a happier life during these next four years, especially because of your closer contact with your two beautiful daughters. Of course I have no indication of what your future plans may be—possibly you do not know yourselves. But wherever you go or whatever activities in which you may be engaged, you will have my best wishes.[3]

I assure you that my official confidence in you, Dick, has not been shaken for a moment, and of course all four of you may be certain that the affection that Mamie and I feel for you will never grow less.[4]

With warm regard, *As ever*

[1] Eisenhower would travel to Augusta, Georgia, for a two-week vacation beginning on November 9.

[2] On November 8 Senator John F. Kennedy had defeated Vice-President Richard M. Nixon for the presidency; see *New York Times*, November 9, 1960. See also Eisenhower, *Waging Peace*, pp. 597–602; and Nixon, *Six Crises*, pp. 374–426. In a telephone call on this same day, Nixon had told the President: "You were magnificent, as far as I am concerned." Eisenhower had urged the Vice-President to take a "good rest" and had added, "We can be proud of these last eight years" (Ann Whitman memorandum, Nov. 9, 1960, AWF/D). In a separate telephone conversation with Milton Eisenhower, however, the President would say that at first he had felt as though the "work of eight years was down the drain" (Ann Whitman memorandum, Nov. 10, 1960, AWF/D).

[3] See Ambrose, *Nixon*, pp. 626–49.

[4] On that same day Eisenhower had also telegraphed Henry Cabot Lodge, congratulating him on "a magnificent campaign in the finest tradition of a great American family" (WHCF/OF 138-A). Eisenhower had also sent congratulatory wires to John F. Kennedy and Lyndon Johnson (*ibid.*).

EM, AWF,
Administration Series

To Arthur Sherwood Flemming   *November 9, 1960*

Dear Arthur: Thanks very much for your note of the, it now seems, fateful day of yesterday.[1] Whether or not I managed to contribute anything of a positive nature to the campaign I do not know, but at the very least I personally want to take a measure of gratification in your comments.

But to Dick, and to those of you who travelled the long and weary miles with him, belongs the major part of the credit for a job well done.[2] I regret exceedingly, as I know you do, that we missed by such a narrow margin, but I still take pride in the numbers of Independents and Democrats that Dick and Cabot, and the programs and policies in which we believe, attracted.[3]

With warm regard, *As ever*

[1] Secretary of Health, Education, and Welfare Flemming had written Eisenhower on November 8 (AWF/A) to let him know of his admiration and appreciation for the way in which the President had participated in the campaign: "I feel that you have said the right thing in the right way, and I am confident that it has influenced a great many voters." See also *New York Times*, November 9, 1960.

[2] On Flemming's campaign efforts for Nixon see, for example, *New York Times*, September 16, 1960.

[3] Although Senator John F. Kennedy had defeated the Vice-President in electoral votes by a count of 303 to 219, the popular vote was very close. Eisenhower would later note: "A switch of fewer than 12,000 votes in five states would have reversed the result" (*Waging Peace*, p. 601). See Theodore C. Sorenson, "Election of 1960," in *History of American Presidential Elections, 1789–1968*, Arthur Schlesinger, ed., 4 vols. (New York, 1971), vol. IV, *1940–1968*, pp. 3449–69.

EM, AWF,
Administration Series

To Nelson Aldrich Rockefeller   *November 9, 1960*

Dear Nelson: With the race so close and the defeat so recent, it is hard to appraise the errors we made. But I did everything I could think of—and I am confident you did too—to bring about the victory for Dick and Cabot that we all so much wanted for the good of our country.[1]

Thanks for your note of the seventh and, once again, thanks for the official hospitality you extended to me the other day in New York.[2]

With warm regard, *As ever*

[1] See no. 1699; see also Sorenson, "Election of 1960," pp. 3449–69; and *New York Times*, November 9, 1960.

[2] Governor Rockefeller's letter (AWF/A), which he had written after talking to New York Republican campaign chairmen, had expressed election-eve optimism: "Enthusiasm is running high and there is confidence in victory on all sides." Democratic presidential candidate John F. Kennedy had, however, carried New York.

Eisenhower had campaigned in New York on November 2, 1960. Rockefeller had joined the President at campaign functions on Long Island, in Westchester, and in New York City (see *New York Times*, Nov. 3, 1960).

1702   *EM, WHCF, Official File 138-A-1*

To Miriam D. Bryngelson   *November 10, 1960*
Personal

Dear Mrs. Bryngelson: Thank you for your letter. I am most appreciative of your complimentary references to me and of the confidence that your note implies.[1]

As we know, every President is sworn to uphold the Constitution of the United States. As of now, the Constitution provides for the "Electoral College" method of electing a President. For an individual, even the President, to interfere with this procedure would be unconstitutional and therefore unthinkable.[2]

On the other hand, there are many people who, believing that the popular vote should be controlling in a national election, have been urging a Constitutional amendment to provide that in each state the electoral delegation be selected according to the popular vote cast for each candidate. This should make effective the idea expressed in your letter.[3]

Incidentally, I agree that an amendment such as this would be desirable.

With best wishes, *Sincerely*

[1] Mrs. O. W. Bryngelson of Augusta, Georgia, had written on November 9 (same file as document) about her disappointment with the results of the presidential election. She thought, incorrectly, that the majority of the popular vote had been for Nixon, even though Kennedy had won the election. "Can't something right now be done about this? Can't you now as President rule that the popular vote wins—not the electoral vote?" she wrote. "There MUST be some way whereby the *majority* of the people can have whom they want, and thus make this a truly democratic nation."

[2] See also no. 1703.

[3] There is no record of such an amendment having been introduced in Congress in 1960. In the elections of 1824, 1876, and 1888, the presidential candidates who received the most popular votes had later been defeated in the Electoral College.

To Milton Stover Eisenhower   *November 10, 1960*

Dear Milton: I have read and re-read your letter of October 18th, which accompanied your resignations from the various Committees to which you had been appointed.[1] Needless to say, I find your comments most interesting.

I am delighted that you plan to do some writing on the governmental activities in which you have been most intimately engaged during these past eight years.[2] Our nation, as a whole, needs much better information than it now has of the workings of our government. For example, I send you a thermofax copy of a letter I received this morning from a good lady in Augusta. She is deadly serious and means well. But her knowledge of the powers and limitations of the Presidency is something less than perfect.[3]

As you know, I will be doing some writing of my own, but even if we should be, at times, dealing with the same subjects—as we unquestionably will—it will not hurt at all to have some iteration and reiteration in the kind of effort that we are both contemplating.[4]

With warm regard, *As ever*

[1] See no. 1692. Milton Eisenhower's five-page letter outlining his observations on the work of the President's Advisory Committee on Government Organization, the National Advisory Committee on Inter-American Affairs, and the Naval Academy Board of Visitors is in AWF/N. He had complained that Congress had thwarted the Eisenhower Administration's efforts to restructure the federal government. He had also maintained that only "the President and principal Executive officers" had "the intimate knowledge and experience on which to base wise reorganization." Members of Congress could not "be well informed in this technical area" and were "too often motivated by political considerations."

[2] As a member of the National Advisory Committee on Inter-American Affairs, Dr. Eisenhower had considered it his greatest privilege to serve as the President's Personal Representative in carrying out special missions in seventeen of the twenty Latin American countries. These missions had addressed long-standing problems: "For a hundred years the United States maintained a patronizing attitude toward Latin America, and was even sometimes guilty of imperialism." The Administration's efforts, Milton Eisenhower concluded, had helped improve matters. Democratic institutions had been established, dictators had been "ousted," and relations with many of the countries were "better than ever before." He intended to supplement his official reports on United States-Latin American relations with magazine articles or a book on the subject. In 1963 he would publish *The Wine is Bitter: The United States and Latin America* (New York).

[3] See the preceding document.

[4] On Eisenhower's decisions to publish his memoirs with Doubleday and Company and to write articles for the *Saturday Evening Post* see no. 1737.

EM, WHCF, Confidential File:
                                                Trade Agreements and Tariffs

To Wilton Burton Persons   *November 12, 1960*

Dear Jerry: The attached letter is returned, approved. However, will
you please tell State that the supplementary document should be
corrected so as to eliminate any specific references to National Security Council papers.[1]

My approval was based on information from Mr. Areeda to the effect that there is every reasonable assumption that Poland will meet
her dollar obligations to us promptly and fully.[2] *As ever*

[1] On November 9 Phillip E. Areeda (LL.B. Harvard 1954), Assistant Special Counsel
to the President, had sent Eisenhower a memorandum with a recommendation from
Secretary Herter that the President restore most-favored nation status to imports
from Poland. Eisenhower had approved this step in the National Security Council in
1958, contingent upon the settlement of outstanding claims against Poland. The President had also asked the State Department in September 1960 to inform Poland that
he was waiting for "a propitious moment to take the step"; Herter had subsequently
told Polish officials that the United States would take action by November 15. Areeda
had enclosed a draft letter to Treasury Secretary Anderson that would accomplish
the restoration. At the bottom of the memorandum Eisenhower had written that he
had two questions. One regarded the citation of NSC papers in the letter to Anderson; the other question involved Poland's outstanding financial obligations to the
United States (Areeda to Eisenhower, Nov. 9, 1960, same file as document). Areeda
had agreed that the citation of NSC papers "item and verse" was "certainly improper,"
and he promised to contact Secretary Herter about the matter. Areeda had added
that there was no reason to believe that the Poles would not honor their agreements
insofar as financial obligations were concerned (Ann Whitman memorandum, Nov.
10, 1960, AWF/D; see also Goodpaster to Areeda, Nov. 14, 1960, same file as document).
[2] On November 16 the White House would release the letter from Eisenhower to Anderson restoring most-favored nation status to Polish imports, effective on December 16 (see *U.S. Department of State Bulletin* 42, no. 1119 [December 5, 1960], 863–
64). Areeda would write that the State Department had "undertaken to mend its ways"
regarding the mention of NSC documents, and it had "revised the offending pages
in all of its file copies" (Areeda memorandum, Dec. 6, 1960, same file as document).

1705   *EM, AWF, International Series:*
                                                      Central African Republic

To Michel Gallin-Douathe   *November 14, 1960*

Dear Mr. Ambassador: I have learned with deep regret that so soon
after our friendly meeting on November third you were the victim
of a most unfortunate incident on your way back to New York.[1]

I want you to know how sincerely I deplore this incident. I assure you that this Government has endeavored to eliminate the causes of such occurrences in this country, and that our efforts will continue toward this end.

As I told you and your colleagues on October sixteenth and as I had the opportunity to tell you personally on November third, the United States attaches great importance to the friendship of the African people.[2] I hope that you will judge this regrettable incident, which reflects the attitude of only a minority of the citizens of this country, in its proper perspective. *Sincerely*

[1] Gallin-Douathe, ambassador to the United States from the newly independent state of the Central African Republic, had presented his credentials to Eisenhower on November 3. On his way back to New York, shortly after the ceremony, the diplomat had been refused service in a restaurant near Baltimore. Although he seemed to have taken the encounter "quietly and objectively," Secretary Herter told Eisenhower, the "incident had left an unfortunate impression" on Gallin-Douathe, coming so soon after meeting the President. A State Department report of the incident quoted the ambassador as saying "that although he felt disappointed, he had had enough experience of the world to understand that things like this happened in the United States and that they were the actions of individuals and not a reflection of government policy." He also stated that he would not make the incident public nor would he inform his government since he did not wish to see relations between his country and the United States begin "in such an unfortunate fashion." Herter had suggested that Eisenhower express his regret to the ambassador and had enclosed a State Department draft of this message, which was delivered to Gallin-Douathe through the U.S. delegation at the United Nations (Herter to Eisenhower, Nov. 11, 1960, AWF/I: Central African Republic; see also *Report on the Incident Involving Ambassador Gallin-Douathe of the Central African Republic, ibid.*).

[2] Eisenhower is probably referring to remarks he made in Washington on October 14 to the heads of U.N. delegations from the new African nations and Cyprus (see *Public Papers of the Presidents: Eisenhower, 1960–61*, pp. 760–63).

1706

EM, AWF, Name Series

To Aksel Nielsen

November 15, 1960

Dear Aks: Thanks for your note of the 9th: apparently everything is moving along to your satisfaction with regard to the Columbine investment—I am delighted.[1]

Colorado was one of the brighter spots in the entire election picture.[2] I sent Peter Dominick a note of congratulations and, of course, I was highly pleased that Gordon Allott was returned to the Senate.[3]

Joel is down here with us.[4] Mamie is fine, except for the fact that she has a tooth that is bothering her and must eventually come out.[5]

All join in warm regard to you. *As ever*

[1] Nielsen had been overseeing the President's real estate investments near the Columbine Country Club in Denver (for background see no. 1070). He reported that the land had been purchased and arrangements had been made for city water and planning and zoning had been approved (AWF/N). See also Eisenhower to Nielsen, November 14, 1960, AWF/N.

[2] Vice-President Nixon had won Colorado's six electoral votes in the recent presidential election. The Republicans had also taken two of Colorado's seats in the House of Representatives and had retained a seat in the Senate (see nos. 1699 and 1700, and *New York Times*, Nov. 9, 1960).

[3] Peter Hoyt Dominick (A.B. Yale 1937; J.D. Yale 1940) had been elected to represent Colorado's second district in the House of Representatives (*New York Times*, Nov. 11, 1960). He had practiced law in New York and Colorado since 1940 and had served as a member of the House of Representatives in the Colorado General Assembly since 1955. Gordon Llewellyn Allott had been Republican Senator from Colorado since 1955.

[4] Joel Carlson was Mrs. Eisenhower's maternal uncle. The Eisenhowers had traveled to Augusta, Georgia, on November 9. The President would return to the White House on November 23.

[5] The First Lady would return to Washington, D.C., to have the tooth extracted on November 19 (*New York Times*, Nov. 22, 1960).

1707

EM, AWF, International Series: Ghana

To Kwame Nkrumah

November 17, 1960

Dear Mr. President: I have your letter, delivered by the Embassy of Ghana to the State Department on October 22, 1960, giving a status report on your power rate negotiations with Kaiser International, representing the Volta Aluminum Company, and an explanation of the difference in views which has arisen between Kaiser Engineers and the World Bank on the advisability of extending the transmission system throughout Ghana in the immediate future.[1]

It is my understanding that, fortunately, construction of the expanded transmission system does not need to begin as soon as the dam and power plant, since these latter take somewhat longer to build. It is also my understanding that there is no disagreement about the need for building the transmission system. The issue arises, rather, over when the demand for power will justify its construction. I feel sure that well before construction need start, in order to have it ready when power will be ready for delivery, facts will be available which will permit full agreement on the issue now in dispute.[2]

In recognition of the great importance of this project to the future of Ghana and in confidence that appropriate financing arrangements can be made for the construction of the additional transmission lines when they are needed, I have instructed the Secretary of State to follow the matter with the closest of attention.[3] *Sincerely*

[1] For background see no. 1605. Nkrumah's letter to Eisenhower about the funding negotiations regarding the Volta River hydroelectric project is in AWF/I: Ghana. Nkrumah was concerned that the rate that the Volta Aluminum Company (VALCO) had offered to pay for power would not offset the large cash deficits Ghana expected in the early years of the project. To close the gap, the Ghanians argued that construction of a full transmission system, beyond the main project of the dam and smelter, would be the most economical solution, although it would initially require extra loans. A full transmission system, Nkrumah claimed, would extend service to mining companies and private consumers in Southern Ghana, improving the standard of living and encouraging the development of local industries. Nkrumah asked Eisenhower for his assurances of U.S. aid, which they had discussed previously during Nkrumah's visit to the United Nations meeting in New York City in September (see State, *Foreign Relations of the United States, 1958–1960*, vol. XIV, *Africa*, pp. 661–68).

[2] Herter had explained to Eisenhower that the State Department and the World Bank were not yet convinced that the full transmission system was the best option. This letter, drafted by the State Department, would leave the door open for future consideration of this option without delaying the beginning of the main project of building the dam and smelter (Herter to Eisenhower, Nov. 14, 1960, AWF/I: Ghana).

[3] The Kennedy administration, concerned about Nkrumah's relations with the Soviet Union, would continue the debate on the loan commitments. In December 1961 the United States would agree to fund the project through various agencies. Plans would be drawn to construct electric facilities in the south of Ghana (*New York Times*, Dec. 16, 1961).

1708   *EM, AWF, Administration Series*

To FREDERICK HENRY MUELLER   *November 18, 1960*

Dear Fritz: This refers to my previous letter to you concerning the participation by the United States in the New York World's Fair. I wonder if you could not advance the date of the report you are to make to me, after consultation with the appropriate Federal agencies, to, say, December fifteenth. I believe it would be helpful if we could have your recommendations by that time.[1]

With warm regard, *As ever*

[1] On November 12 (AWF/A) the President had asked Secretary of Commerce Mueller to consult with a number of federal agencies about federal participation in the fair and to submit a report not later than January 1. The report is not in AWF.

The New York World's Fair Corporation had been organized in August 1959, and Eisenhower had approved a recommendation that the United States host a world's fair in New York City (U.S. Congress, House, *New York's World Fair, 1964–65*, 86th Cong., 2d sess., 1960, H. Rept. 86-2111, pp. 1–4).

In his annual budget message to the Congress on January 16, Eisenhower would say that at his request Mueller was developing plans in anticipation of authorizing legislation for federal participation in the New York World's Fair, which was scheduled to open in spring 1964 (*Public Papers of the Presidents: Eisenhower, 1960–61*, p. 984).

In August 1961 the House would pass H.R. 7763, which authorized President Kennedy to plan for U.S. participation in the fair and directed him to report to Congress by January 15, 1962 (*Congressional Quarterly Almanac*, vol. XVII, *1961*, p. 380). The New York World's Fair would open on April 22, 1964 (*New York Times*, Apr. 23, 1964).

1709

EM, WHCF,
President's Personal File 833

To Winston Spencer Churchill

November 18, 1960

[*Dear Winston:*] Just as I was about to dictate a note of felicitations on your eighty-sixth birthday anniversary, hoping I could time it properly to arrive in London on the 30th, I was informed that you had suffered the accident about which I cabled you.[1] I was heartened by your reply, and I do hope that by the time your birthday comes around, you will once again be up and about.[2]

But the main purpose of this letter is to salute you proudly, both on the personal basis and because of all you have done in your wonderfully long and brilliant career for the good of the people of the world.[3] Incidentally, I have just finished Pug's book; I am delighted at the accolade of praise I find there for you, sentiments in which I heartily join.[4]

Do take the best possible care of yourself and have a Happy Birthday!

With affectionate regard to Clemmie and to yourself, in which Mamie joins,[5] [*As ever*]

[1] On November 15 the former Prime Minister had fallen and broken a small bone in his back (*London Times*, Nov. 17, 18, 1960, and *New York Times*, Nov. 17, 18, 1960). Eisenhower had cabled him on November 16.

[2] Churchill had replied that he had been thinking about the President and would write to him soon (Nov. 17, 1960).

[3] See no. 1012; see also *Public Papers of the Presidents: Eisenhower, 1959*, p. 29).

[4] See nos. 1679 and 1697 for background on *The Memoirs of General Lord Ismay*. Ismay had conveyed his devotion to the Prime Minister throughout the volume. He had also discussed the Eisenhower-Churchill relationship (see, *ibid.*, pp. 112–17, 259).

[5] On December 2 Churchill would say he was progressing well and that he wished Eisenhower a happy and peaceful future. He also said he did not need to tell the President of the "high regard and affection" in which he held him (see also *New York Times*, Nov. 27, 1960). For developments see no. 1721. All correspondence is in AWF/ I: Churchill.

1710

EM, WHCF,
President's Personal File 1428

TO PERCY WALTER THOMPSON

November 19, 1960

Dear Perc: As things turned out, the results of the election were not quite the sweeping "national disaster" you (and I, too) thought the day afterwards.[1] But I am distressed that your own campaign was not successful; I would have been highly gratified had you managed to buck the Democratic machinery in your State—and I know it would have been a good thing for the people of Florida.[2] But so do such things go.
With warm regard, *As ever*

[1] On November 9 (same file as document) Colonel Thompson, Colonel John S. D. Eisenhower's father-in-law, had written to thank the President for remembering his birthday, a day he referred to as "something of a national disaster." On the November 8 Republican defeat see nos. 1700 and 1701.
[2] Thompson had been the Republican candidate for Florida's Secretary of State. He had expressed appreciation for Eisenhower's support during his campaign (for background see no. 1616).

1711

EM, WHCF, Official File 138-C-4

TO GEORGE LLOYD MURPHY

November 20, 1960

Dear George: Your letter of the eleventh, which has just managed to reach me, seemingly implies a farewell and an abdication on your part from the political scene. Neither premise do I countenance for a moment.[1]
As for the election: I know how disappointed you are, and I must say that the lugubrious post mortem discussions here at the Augusta National have in the main agreed with your own verdict as to *why*. I, too, felt like I had been hit in the solar plexus with a ball bat, especially in the first few days.[2] But now my normal optimism has taken command and *if* we can get all factions of the Republican Party working together, I have every hope that 1964 will be a different story.[3] So don't turn in your suit—the Party needs you very much.
And on the personal side: Mrs. Eisenhower and I are tentatively planning to be in the desert area for some considerable time after January 20th, and we shall, of course, look forward to seeing you and your bride.[4] I do hope that you will shake off that "incipient influenza" (and don't let the Chamber of Commerce of Palm Springs

know about *that*), and that you will be your normal, ebullient self the next time I see you.[5]

Meantime, my personal and deep gratitude for the dedicated and tireless efforts you made on behalf of the things in which we both believe.

With warm regard, *As ever*

[1] Hollywood actor Murphy had been the national honorary chairman of the Celebrities Committee for Nixon-Lodge. His letter (same file as document) had been mailed to the White House and then forwarded to Augusta, Georgia, where the President had been vacationing since November 9 (see no. 1706). Murphy said he had enjoyed twenty years as a "volunteer in the political vineyards" and planned to write of some of his more "humorous and peculiar experiences."

[2] For background on the defeat of Vice-President Richard M. Nixon by Senator John F. Kennedy see nos. 1700 and 1701. Murphy had criticized Nixon's campaign advisers for not incorporating Eisenhower's "valuable assistance from the very outset." He also felt that had Eisenhower been consulted on the matter of the Nixon-Kennedy debates, "a different decision might have been taken" (on the debates see nos. 1678 and 1690). On the discussions with friends at Augusta see Slater, *The Ike I Knew*, p. 230.

[3] In 1964 Democratic President and former Senator Lyndon B. Johnson would defeat Republican Senator Barry M. Goldwater (see John Bartlow Martin, "Election of 1964," in Schlesinger, *History of American Presidential Elections*, pp. 3565–3704).

[4] On February 6 the Eisenhowers would travel to Palm Springs, California, where they would remain until April 22 (see *New York Times*, Feb. 7–Apr. 22, 1961). Murphy's wife was the former Juliette Henkel.

[5] Murphy said he had contracted "incipient influenza and pneumonia" as a result of his campaign efforts in New York, Los Angeles, and Palm Springs.

1712   *EM, AWF, DDE Diaries Series*

To ARTHUR J. MORRIS   *November 21, 1960*
Personal

Dear Mr. Morris: As my secretary wired you, I am leaving Augusta early tomorrow morning for an overnight stay in Albany, Georgia, and returning directly from there to Washington, a circumstance that precludes the possibility of my meeting with you here.[1]

I have read with interest the talk that you recently gave before the Consumer Bankers Association.[2] I agree with your assessment of the Communist danger and the method by which it works. I also agree that too many in the free world are seemingly indifferent to this danger. The flexibility of the free world defense must be as great as the many-sided character of the Communist attack. No single type of defense can possibly be effective. In its broadest sense education is possibly the most effective tool in the whole arsenal of free world defense. However, I must point out that we cannot depend merely on "university" training. Uneducated people must learn to walk before they run. Incidentally, there are in the whole of the Congo now only sixteen individuals who have had a college education.[3]

Another factor in the problem is that our own particular form of economy and government could not possibly be adapted to every single nation of the world—at least without decades of education and indoctrination. Our nation started out as a thinly-populated region containing vast resources. The pioneering stock was sturdy, adventurous and passionately dedicated to freedom. Moreover, among the population there was a sprinkling of educated leaders, such as those among the clergy and others in the merchant and governmental classes.

In these modern days people of the underdeveloped countries live in conditions that contrast sharply with those of our own beginnings, particularly in Asia where the regions are crowded and the per capita resources meagre indeed.

The point is that we must not expect our own particular brand of representative government to be adopted in every detail by the underdeveloped countries, and we can scarcely expect that education can make any appreciable and immediate improvement in the situation. Yet the problem is an immediate one.

By no means do I decry your idea. What I am trying to say, though hastily and inadequately, is that our defense must be both broad and deep—and it must be alert.

People who are starving are not at the moment interested in the difference between forms of governments. They are interested in promises, even though better informed people may know that such promises are completely false. They are interested in some immediate material help, even though others may know that help may be proffered as a means of attaining domination over the recipient nation.

It is my conviction that education, including vocational as well as academic training, world wide publicity service, technical skill, capital loans, and the maintenance of a free world economic and military strength that will deny the Communist penetration through force of arms, are all necessary.

Such a university as you propose would of course be most useful in building an understanding of all these factors to such students as were qualified to attend and were able to do so. This would be a great step forward.

All of this represents, as I say, my immediate and hasty reaction to your proposal. Since my term of office is so near the expiration date, I am not certain whether, under the circumstances and in view of this letter, you still would want to talk to me. I have a feeling you would be better advised to pursue your suggestion with someone who will be able to be more helpful than I can possibly be. I do not, however, preclude the possibility of such an appointment, if you still want to see me. In that event, I suggest you call my office some time after my return to Washington.[4]

With best wishes, *Sincerely*

[1] Eisenhower would hunt quail at the plantation of Nettie and William Alton Jones on November 23 before returning to Washington that evening (*New York Times*, Nov. 23, 1960).
[2] Arthur J. Morris (University of Virginia 1899) had practiced law before developing the "Morris Plan" system of banking (see Galambos, *Columbia University*, no. 192). He was a member of the Consumers Bankers Association, which had been founded in 1919. We have been unable to locate a copy of Morris's speech.
[3] For background on the Congo crisis see nos. 1599 and 1611.
[4] There is no reply in AWF. Eisenhower would not meet with Morris before he left Washington in January 1961.

1713   *EM, AWF, Administration Series*

To John Hay Whitney   *November 24, 1960*
Personal

Dear Jock: I am quite sure that your four years' service in your vital post has done much to strengthen the basic friendship between the governments of Great Britain and the United States and, indeed, our two peoples. Your presence in London has always given me a feeling of great confidence that our affairs there would prosper.[1]

I cannot tell you how delighted I am that you are going to give close personal attention to the HERALD TRIBUNE.[2] As I have often told you, there is, among the criteria by which I judge the soundness and integrity of any newspaper, one to which I attach great importance. That rule is "The news columns belong to the public; the editorial pages to the paper itself." I can and do get annoyed by what I consider to be stupid editorials—but as long as no attempt is made to write editorials in news stories, I invariably give such a paper my respect, even if that gift is sometimes grudgingly made.

I think that some newspapers have cheapened themselves too much by their indiscriminate use of columnists; to my mind the practice involves an abdication of responsibility. Some papers, notably the TIMES, while boasting that they do not employ columnists, have given their entire paper over to columnists. Almost every news item is published under a particular by-line and such persons are given, obviously, a high degree of latitude in expressing their personal "opinions." This I deplore.[3]

Incidentally, and in this connection, I have a gripe this morning against the HERALD TRIBUNE. It contained a story by a man that I have never before heard of—Gaston Coblentz. He wrote a piece about Anderson's visit to Bonn on the Balance of Payments problem. I enclose the clipping. This seems to me to be reporting at its worst.[4]

Happily, I rarely find such examples in the HERALD TRIBUNE. In any event, despite such people as Lippman, Alsop and this fellow Coblentz, I remain loyal to the paper.[5]

I had a very enjoyable visit with Walter Thayer at Augusta. In him I think you have one of the finest associates any one could find. I congratulate you on your wisdom in that particular selection and this I do "without equivocation or any intention to evade."[6]

This is Thanksgiving Day. I came back from Georgia last evening after a day and a half shooting with Pete at Blue Springs Plantation. The first day I was really hot. But the second day an attack of bursitis seemed to me to have caught up with me completely and for the first two hours I could not even hit the ground, much less a bird. After a noonday rainstorm, we got a couple more hours of shooting and then I did very much better.[7]

The men at Pete's plantation report an unusually large number of birds this year.

Give my warm greetings and affectionate regard to your Betsey, and, of course, all the best to yourself.[8] *As ever*

[1] The President had appointed Whitney as U.S. Ambassador to Great Britain in 1956 (see Galambos and van Ee, *The Middle Way*, no. 1662). Whitney had tendered his resignation on November 18 (AWF/A). Eisenhower's confidence in him, Whitney wrote, had always been his "mainstay."

[2] Whitney had acquired the *New York Herald Tribune* in 1958 (see no. 825). He was looking forward, he said, to having the paper "keep the soundest sort of spotlight turned on Washington" in order to promote effective policies. On the state of the *New York Herald Tribune* upon Whitney's return to the United States see Kahn, *Jock*, pp. 271–73.

[3] For more on Eisenhower's distaste for certain types of journalists see no. 1528.

[4] Gaston Coblentz (B.A. Harvard 1939) had been a foreign correspondent for the *New York Herald Tribune* since 1946. During World War II he served as a major in the U.S. Army Air Force. In 1963 he would leave the newspaper to become a partner in the stockbrokerage firm Mitchell Hutchins and Company, Inc. Coblentz had criticized Secretary of the Treasury Robert B. Anderson's mission to West Germany; it offered, he said, a guide to conducting unsuccessful negotiations with an allied nation. Coblentz had accused Anderson, who had been trying to negotiate a solution to the gold-outflow problem (see no. 1669), of mishandling the negotiations and exhibiting insensitivity toward the Germans. For developments see no. 1724.

[5] The President was referring to Walter Lippmann and Joseph Wright Alsop, Jr. (see also no. 680).

[6] Eisenhower had played eighteen holes of golf with Walter Nelson Thayer (A.B. Colgate College 1931; LL.B. Yale 1935) on November 16. Thayer had been counsel for the Citizens for Eisenhower-Nixon in 1952. In 1955 he had joined J. H. Whitney and

Company as a managing partner. He also had advised Whitney on his purchase of the *New York Herald Tribune*.

[7] Following his vacation in Augusta, Georgia (Nov. 9–22), the President had joined a quail hunt on the estate of William Alton ("Pete") Jones in Albany, Georgia (see no. 1718).

[8] Whitney would thank Eisenhower for the "generous" letter accepting his resignation (Jan. 4, AWF/A).

1714   *EM, AWF, International Series: Guinea*

To Sékou Touré   *November 25, 1960*
Cable. Unclassified

Dear Mr. President: Your cable of November 20, 1960, I regret to say, reflects a serious misunderstanding of the policy of the United States Government in support of African freedom. I am prompted, therefore, to recall to you that the United States has been in the forefront of those nations who have favored emancipation of all peoples, including Africans, in accordance with the purposes and principles of the Charter of the United Nations.[1] The record of our actions over many years in support of African emancipation is open for all to see.

With specific reference to the Republic of the Congo, the United States warmly welcomed its independence. We have recognized and upheld its unity and territorial integrity through United Nations actions. We have refrained from unilateral intervention in its internal affairs.[2] Although considerable partisanship has been demonstrated by some states, our support for the recognition by the United Nations of M. Kasavubu as Chief of State, a constitutional position which is universally accepted and recognized in the recent report of the U.N., is not a question of partisanship but an attempt to strengthen one of the essential foundations of stable and effective government in that unhappy country.[3] This, I believe, is in strict conformity with the interests of the Congolese Government and people. As you are aware, a large number of African states have taken a similar stand. In view of the support by most countries for the United Nations role in the Congo and the fact that United Nations success is vital for the welfare of the Congolese, I sincerely hope that you will give full support to the United Nations effort there.[4] *Sincerely*

[1] Guinean President Touré had accused the United States of partisanship in the Congo crisis (see nos. 1599 and 1611). He had requested that the U.S. government cease supporting "the enemies of African emancipation" who were "employing every possible means against the legitimate government of the Congo to attack the unity and territorial integrity of the Congolese government." Touré's reference was both

to Belgium, which had deployed forces in the Congo without permission, and to forces opposed to Patrice Lumumba, the recently-ousted Prime Minister who was bidding for the leadership of Congo's central government. Guinea and several other African states supported Lumumba, who had opposed the United Nations peacekeeping mission in the Congo and had solicited support from the Soviet Bloc. Touré's cable is in AWF/I: Guinea, and *Public Papers of the Presidents: Eisenhower, 1960–61*, pp. 867–68; see also *New York Times*, November 27, 1960.

[2] See no. 1611 for background.

[3] Joseph Kasavubu was President of the Congo Republic. A leader in his country's movement for independence, he had been elected in May 1960 (*New York Times*, Mar. 25, 1969). In the chaos following independence, however, various rival factions had emerged to compete for control of the government. In early September the Chief of Staff of the Congo forces had arrested Lumumba and on November 22 the General Assembly of the United Nations had seated a delegation led by Kasavubu, accepting him as the legitimate head of state. Civil War in the Congo would continue after Eisenhower left office, and Lumumba would later be killed, while allegedly attempting to escape imprisonment (see Synopsis of State and Intelligence Material Reported to the President, December 28, 1960, AWF/D; Eisenhower, *Waging Peace*, pp. 574–76, and for background see Lefever, *Crisis in the Congo*, pp. 38–43).

[4] Touré had threatened that if the United States continued to show partisanship, Guinea would refuse to continue working with the United Nations and would take "any position in African affairs consistent with Congolese interests" (Touré to Eisenhower, Nov. 20, 1960, AWF/I: Guinea).

1715   *EM, AWF, Name Series*

To Lionel Hastings Ismay   *November 25, 1960*

Dear Pug: I have been fascinated by your book—so much so that I am writing to you a letter that has grown into a volume. Its only purpose is to search out, with you, whether or not during the course of our association in the war we failed to keep each other, in any detail, as completely informed as we should have. As you know, no other experience lives in my memory so warmly and with such a sense of satisfaction as my association with the Prime Minister and you and a good many other British leaders of the war.[1]

So this letter I am writing is not in any way to argue a point with you; it is really meant to be one long question mark respecting points that leave me just a little puzzled.

Assuming that you are again strong enough to be bored by such matters, I shall send the letter on in a week or so.[2]

With affectionate regard to Kathleen, and of course, all the best to yourself,[3] *As ever*

[1] For background on Ismay's recently published memoir see no. 1679.

[2] Ismay had been recovering from pneumonia (see *ibid.*). Eisenhower's lengthy letter to him is no. 1722.

[3] Ismay would reply on December 2 that he awaited the President's longer letter with the "keenest anticipation." He said he did not know if he could answer all of Eisenhower's questions because he did not keep a personal diary and had left his official records in the office when he left the job. He also was not present at all of the official meetings between Eisenhower and Churchill. Churchill, he added, was "rather naughty" about not telling him what had transpired and did not share written communications unless they were in complete accord with his own arguments.

1716   *EM, AWF, International Series: Adenauer*

To Konrad Adenauer   *November 26, 1960*
Cable. Secret

Dear Friend:[1] I was gratified to receive your letter of November 24, 1960 and to hear that you welcome our intention to make proposals for increasing NATO's nuclear role a subject of discussion at the December Ministerial Meeting.[2] Under Secretary Dillon has given you the general outline of our thinking. We are proceeding with urgent consultations within the American Government and with appropriate members of the legislative branch, to ensure that our proposals will be as definitive as possible. Depending on the outcome of these consultations, we are planning to present our views to the Permanent NATO Council next week so that there will be time for consideration of the matter before the Ministerial meeting.[3]

I have given thought to your feeling that I should take part personally in the December NATO Meeting which you indicate should be held at the level of Heads of Governments. While I can appreciate the force of your observations regarding the continuing need that NATO evidence its solidarity and sense of direction, I do not believe that this necessarily requires a meeting of the kind you suggest.[4] For my part, I should for various reasons find it difficult to go to Paris in December. I am certain that our Foreign Ministers will be able, in discussing the important subjects which appear on their agenda, to give that leadership an impetus which we all agree is a continuing necessity for NATO.

I am glad that you consider the talks which Secretary Anderson and Under Secretary Dillon recently had in Bonn to have been generally successful. I am awaiting Secretary Anderson's report upon his return, and we will undoubtedly be communicating with your Government further on these matters through diplomatic channels.[5]

With renewed gratitude and warm personal regard, *Sincerely*

[1] State Department officials drafted this message, which was sent to the American embassy in Bonn for delivery to Chancellor Adenauer.

² For background see 1687.

³ In a November 17 meeting the National Security Council had discussed nuclear requirements for NATO and had agreed that the United States would make a commitment to maintain nuclear weapons for approved NATO military plans. The council also discussed NATO stockpile arrangements, a proposal for a multilateral medium-range ballistic missile force (see no. 1686), and the deployment of Polaris submarines (NSC meeting minutes, Nov. 17, Dec. 1, 1960, AWF/NSC; see also Watson, *Into the Missile Age*, pp. 558–61).

⁴ Adenauer had written that a heads of government meeting in December had become "practically a tradition" and that if such a meeting were not held, the Soviet government would regard it "as a sign of weakness" and would believe that the alliance "was shaky or even disunited" (Adenauer to Eisenhower, Nov. 24, 1960, AWF/I: Adenauer). Eisenhower had told Secretary Herter that in spite of Adenauer's opinion, there was little left for him to do at the meeting (Telephone conversation, Eisenhower and Herter, Nov. 25, 1960, Herter Papers, Telephone Conversations).

⁵ For background see no. 1687. The talks, Adenauer had written, were "somewhat complicated" but had "proceeded harmoniously and led to agreement." In their meeting two days later, Secretaries Anderson and Dillon would tell Eisenhower that they had informed Adenauer that the U.S. support costs in Germany accounted for a $4 billion deficit in the annual balance of payments. According to Anderson, Adenauer had not understood the problem "at all well, in spite of repeated explanations." In subsequent meetings, however, German representatives had offered to make $200 million in additional purchases of American products in connection with their foreign aid program for the coming year. The Germans also offered to buy $250 million worth of military equipment in the United States (Goodpaster, Memorandum of Conference, Dec. 1, 1960, AWF/D; see also John S. D. Eisenhower, Memorandum of Conference, Nov. 30, 1960, *ibid.*; and Eisenhower, *Waging Peace*, pp. 604–7). For developments see no. 1723.

1717   *EM, AWF, DDE Diaries Series*

To Earl H. Blaik   *November 26, 1960*

Dear Red: George Allen has just called me to give me the sad news about Victor.¹ He has always been a good personal friend but even long before I met him, he was the soul of kindness and thoughtfulness toward my wife, during the years that I was absent in World War II.²

George tells me that Mrs. Emanuel is so ill that it would be futile for me to attempt to send her a note of condolence.³ But I did want you to know, as one of Victor's closest friends, of our sense of grief and loss in his passing.⁴

I know that he has one son in Britain, but I think I have never met any close relative of his. I would appreciate it if, on my behalf, you would find it possible to convey to him or to any other persons in his family, the sentiments I have so feebly expressed in this letter.⁵

With warm personal regard, *Sincerely*

[1] Victor Emanuel, board chairman of the Avco Manufacturing Company, had passed away on this same date (see also no. 1517).

[2] For background on the friendship see Galambos, *Chief of Staff*, no. 1488.

[3] Dorothy Emanuel had been ill for several years (see no. 557).

[4] Following his retirement as football coach at the United States Military Academy, Blaik had become vice-president and a management committee member at Avco Manufacturing Company (see no. 1014).

[5] In addition to his widow, Emanuel was survived by two sons, Albert II and Barton (see also no. 557).

1718   *EM, AWF, Name Series*

To William Alton Jones   *November 28, 1960*

Dear Pete: Over the weekend I started to brag to someone about the pistol you had given me—and suddenly discovered that I had left it behind at Blue Springs Plantation.[1] Next time you come by this way, be sure to bring it along (or better still, make a special trip and we'll get up a bridge game or something).[2] After all, you remember how competent I was with that pistol![3]

I rather hastily wrote Nettie to thank her for my latest enjoyment of the extraordinary hospitality that the Jones family dispenses.[4] About all I can say to you is that I am permanently, lastingly and greatly in your debt. I hope you don't mind; I rather like the situation.

With warm regard, *As ever*

[1] The Eisenhowers had spent the Thanksgiving holiday weekend at the White House (see the Chronology for a list of their guests). The President had visited Jones at Blue Springs Plantation in Albany, Georgia, November 22–23 (see no. 1713).

[2] Jones would lunch with the President at the White House on January 17.

[3] For Eisenhower's account of the quail hunt on Jones's estate see no. 1713.

[4] Eisenhower had written that he was "very susceptible" to the Joneses' "kind of 'spoiling'" (Nov. 25, 1960; see also Jones to Eisenhower, Nov. 10, 1960, both in AWF/N).

25

Farewells and Warnings

TO ROBERT BERNERD ANDERSON   *December 1, 1960*

Memorandum for the Secretary of the Treasury. Copy: The Attorney General: This morning I was visited by a man named Lewis Rosenstiel, President of Schenley Industries, Inc.[1] The motive behind the visit was, he frankly (and refreshingly) admitted, mercenary, but the ideas he expressed, he thinks, are likewise important to the government.

By and large he argues that there is a very great volume of illicit liquor manufacturing in this country, a process that not only robs Federal and State governments of enormous revenues, but creates great health dangers to the population. He gave me a number of statistics of various kinds in his effort to substantiate this statement, and to me his statistical presentation seemed impressive.[2]

Another phase of the same question involves what he feels to be an excessive allowance of liquor that can properly be carried back by returning visitors to this country without tax. He believes that the $500 allowance for each returning visitor is possibly too large, but he is more interested in the amounts brought home of such items as liquor, perfume, furs and jewelry. He thinks that the government, both State and Federal, is being deprived of a great many millions of revenues and, of course, both the illicit manufacturer and the unjustified imports create very bad competition for his particular company.[3]

There is one difference between his argument and that normally brought to me by corporate heads in this country. In the usual case I am asked to support a higher tariff. His primary argument is that we should block up loop holes in the revenue collection, particularly when they involve tax evasion.

He believes that the internal revenue forces should be strengthened and that there should be a coordinated State and Federal effort to stamp out illicit distilling.

I informed him that I would communicate with you and the Attorney General on the matter and that if either of you should like to call on him for statistics or information bearing on these questions, you should notify him. Incidentally, he says there is a wealth of this kind of information available.

Please let me know informally what, if any, action you might take in the matter.[4]

[1] Lewis Solon Rosenstiel had founded Schenley Industries, which made alcoholic beverages, after the repeal of prohibition in 1933. He had served as chairman of the board since 1934, and as president since 1948. Eisenhower had met with Rosenstiel for twelve minutes that morning.
[2] See, for example, *New York Times,* January 12, February 20, 1960.

³ See Richard McGowan, *Government Regulation of the Alcohol Industry: The Search for Revenue and the Common Good*, (Westport, Conn., 1997), pp. 48–54, 113–36.
⁴ There is no further correspondence on this issue in AWF.

1720   *EM, AWF, DDE Diaries Series*

To EDWARD HAROLD LITCHFIELD   *December 1, 1960*
Personal and confidential

Dear Dr. Litchfield: After discussing with you a possible future connection between me and the University of Pittsburgh, I began to search both my memory and my records to determine what commitments, definite or conditional, I had already made for the years ahead.¹ I am speaking only of those that touch upon educational institutions.

First of all, I have been, since 1952, a Trustee Emeritus of Columbia University.² This circumstance would not of itself create any interference with plans involving another university, but it happens that there are now operative at Columbia a special activity in the founding of which I had a personal part, and in which I am deeply interested. So I shall, I am sure, want to take occasional advantage of the fact that I am privileged to attend the Trustees' meetings of Columbia University, even though I shall not have any other function at the University.³

Another circumstance that has some bearing on this problem is that some years ago I agreed with the President of Gettysburg College that should I take up a permanent residence in that area, I would accept his invitation to establish my office in one of the college buildings. As you can see, my acceptance of their invitation automatically creates for me a definite interest in that institution.⁴

More important than these two is, however, an understanding that has long existed between my brother and me—I refer to the brother who is President of Johns Hopkins University. That understanding was if ever I should be freed of all official duties and the Trustees of Johns Hopkins would feel an inclination to invite me to become one of their members, I would be glad to accept. Should that desire be expressed I would obviously not only feel obligated to accept, but frankly I would want to do so because it would be a great privilege for me to serve in some capacity under my brother's chairmanship, he having so long and selflessly supported me, often in a very active role, in the problems facing me during the eight years just past.⁵

Then, of course, beyond the circumstances I have just described is the further fact that I have intentions of devoting most of my time to the study of and writing about governmental and international matters that I conceive can be of great interest to our nation.[6]

I give you these details so as to make certain of your understanding that I do not lightly decline the privilege you extend to me of serving as one of your Trustees at Pittsburgh. The prospect you outlined had many appealing features and I am complimented that you should have considered me in such a connection.

I am sending this letter for your eyes only, so as to eliminate any chance I might appear unappreciative of your courtesy, or disregardful of the fact that your suggestion to me was made on an informal and exploratory basis. *Sincerely*

[1] Eisenhower had met with University of Pittsburgh Chancellor Litchfield at the White House on August 16.

[2] On Eisenhower's acceptance of his election as president and trustee emeritus of Columbia University see Galambos, *NATO and the Campaign of 1952*, no. 1005.

[3] Among the organizations the President had established at Columbia were the American Assembly (see no. 172), the Institute of War and Peace Studies (see no. 995), and the New York School of Social Work (see no. 381).

[4] On the Gettysburg College offices see nos. 544, 1242, and 1437.

[5] On January 9 the President would accept an offer to become a trustee of the Johns Hopkins University. He would attend an all-day meeting, his first, on May 16 (*New York Times*, May 10, 16, 1961). On his appreciation for the support of his brother Milton see, for example, nos. 1399 and 1692.

[6] For background on Eisenhower's decision to publish his memoirs see nos. 1643 and 1650.

1721

EM, AWF, International Series:
Churchill

To Winston Spencer Churchill   *December 1, 1960*

[*Dear Winston:*] When Joyce Hall told me today that he was to see you some time next week, I could not resist the opportunity to send you a little note merely to say how delighted I am by the reports we have received of your progress in recovering from the accident that felled you temporarily.[1]

You can, I am sure, well understand my disappointment at the result of our recent election.[2] At present I am trying to arrange for an orderly transfer of the official business of government to the incoming Administration.[3] We have often discussed the virtues and disadvantages of the political systems of your country and mine;

about all I can say is that I now have some new and personal arguments to add (all of which I shall some time hope to tell you).

Give my affectionate regard to Clemmie and, of course, all the best to yourself. *As ever*

[1] Greeting card manufacturer Joyce Clyde Hall had visited the President at the White House. Churchill had broken a small bone in his back as a result of a fall at his home on November 15 (see no. 1709, and *New York Times*, Nov. 27, 1960). Hall, who had promoted a U.S. exhibition of Churchill's paintings in 1957 (see no. 86), may have been planning his trip to England in order to arrange to have the former Prime Minister's paintings featured on greeting cards (*New York Times*, Oct. 28, 1961).

[2] Democratic Senator John F. Kennedy had defeated Vice-President Richard M. Nixon on November 8 (see nos. 1699 and 1700).

[3] On December 6 Eisenhower would meet with President-elect Kennedy to discuss the transfer of responsibilities. Eisenhower's memorandum on the meeting is no. 1724. See also Eisenhower, *Waging Peace*, p. 603.

1722

To LIONEL HASTINGS ISMAY
Personal

EM, AWF, Name Series

December 3, 1960

Dear Pug: I am fascinated by your book. Indeed, I have become something of a local promoter for your volume, and am missing no chance to tell my friends that they owe it to themselves to read such an accurate, behind the scenes, account concerning much of the thinking, planning and incidents of World war II.[1]

As you know so well, I have held a great admiration, respect and affection for Winston. Possibly, had I been as close to him as you were during all the eventful period of World War II, my sentiments toward him would be even more emphatically expressed. In any event, you leave no doubt as to where he ranks in your estimation, and I must say that I am delighted to know that you do hold such strong and favorable convictions about your old Chief.[2]

In what follows I give you some comments for yourself, only. I have some interest in an attempt to fill up what seemed to be a few gaps in the perfection of our mutual understandings of those days, but have no intention of criticizing anyone, on either side, or of arguing the correctness of any decisions concerning which we might have some slight differences of opinion. Whenever these suggestions involved me and my own headquarters, it is not quite accurate to describe them as a British versus American conference. There were many highly competent and respected British officers on my own staff, and I consulted with them as frequently and as intimately as I did with the American members.[3]

Concerning many of the events and operations in which, in our different capacities, we were involved, I have learned better what you, and your associates, were then thinking. For the first time I learned something of your and their impressions as to what *we*, on our side, were thinking. Of course, in such cases you report fact as to yourselves, deductions as to us. Even so I find that my own understanding of these situations, viewed from the opposite angle, is not often or generally different from yours.[4]

I believe your account of the differing viewpoints concerning SLEDGEHAMMER is completely representative of the thinking on both sides. Of course, in this case, many of our people, *looking backward*, still believe that we would have been better off had we undertaken that operation in late 1942 in view of the fact that Hitler was so busy on the Eastern front.[5] *I do not share this view* and have often publicly stated that I think the alternative, TORCH, provided us with many later advantages, not the least of which was the training opportunity, through which both sides learned how Allied commands could and should work effectively.[6]

*   *   *   *   *

You and I agree, even if others may not do so, that the only reasonable ground for argument concerning ANVIL, renamed DRAGOON, was the posing of political against largely military objectives. This I tried to make perfectly clear in my own book. In our intimate discussions in the summer of 1944, I told Winston that I thought he was probably right as to the political problem, but he paid no attention to my urging that he take the subject to President Roosevelt and his political advisers rather than to come to me as an individual who was necessarily required to make decisions on the *military basis only*. But from your book I now understand that he *had already*, before talking to me, made strong representations to President Roosevelt, without success.[7]

*   *   *   *   *

At another point, when you begin the description of OVERLORD planning, you say something to the effect that Montgomery was the one who insisted that the planned attack was on a too narrow front.[8]

Shortly before I left the African Theatre—but after I had been informed that I was to be commander of OVERLORD—I learned that Montgomery was to be my British ground commander, even though I had told the Prime Minister, who earlier had said I could have my choice between Alexander and Montgomery, that I should prefer to have Alexander.[9]

Montgomery came to see me in Algiers before he departed for Britain. It happened that I had, some time previously, seen the outlined Cossack Plan. It was brought to me by a General Chambers of the American Army even before I had been named the Commander Designate of OVERLORD. I told Chambers that it was none of my business to pass judgment upon a plan that would presumably be executed by someone else. Nevertheless, I considered that, while the plan apparently made the best possible use of the materiel that could be made available by the proposed target date, the concept involved a plan too weak in numbers and frontage, if there were contemplated a heavy and rapid buildup with the purpose of smashing through the defending front at an early date. I had Beedle Smith come in with me during this examination and we decided, off the cuff, that a five division attack was far more desirable.[10]

Holding this opinion in the back of my mind, I told Monty when he called upon me, prior to his departure for Britain, that I desired him first of all to give my convictions to the planners in London, with the further opinion that in order to achieve the strength I believed necessary, we should accept a delay of a month. You relate this incident as if Monty was the author of the idea. Insofar as I know, he had never seen the outlined plan made by Freddie Morgan before he and I met in Algiers and discussed the matter.[11]

*   *   *   *   *

Then at another place, you talk about the "narrow front" as opposed to the "broad front" plan for invading Germany.[12] This was an expression that came into a great deal of popular usage through the writings of newspaper people who either had differing views from my own concerning the best way to conduct our invasion, or from reporters who had, at this stage of the war, set themselves up as arm-chair strategists of a very high type. Actually Humfrey Gale and Freddie de Guingand, both men of great competence, agreed with my own supply officers that the lines of communication *north of the Ruhr* could not support more than some thirty to thirty-five divisions for any penetration into Germany.[13]

This matter came in for a considerable argument in early September when Montgomery first made the suggestion that if I would give him all the supplies available in the Theatre, he would go on and take Berlin, while the other Allied divisions in France should remain on the defensive. I went to Brussels to confer with Montgomery, taking with me Gale and Tedder. That was the time when the so-called "pencil thrust" really came into our vocabulary. We were unanimous in our convictions that this scheme was impractical—in fact, slightly hair-brained. However, I did promise him *all the support* in the way of supplies and forces that he could *possibly use if he would and could, as a preliminary, seize a bridgehead over the Rhine and hold it.* This, in his usual methodical fashion, he started to plan. I assigned to him our fine Airborne Corps and 500 tons of supplies a day (which was all he requested). As you know, the attempt miserably failed, with the loss of almost the whole of the British Airborne Division. Incidentally, this was the operation in which Montgomery put into effect his concept of "carpet dropping of airborne troops." My staff opposed it, but because he was the commander in the field, I approved. No matter what later opportunities may have come up, certainly at that moment he proved that the pencil thrust to Berlin was impractical.[14]

Of course, back in the early planning stage there had been much argument about the possibility of concentrating, when the time came, on a single crossing of the Rhine.[15] The conviction that I personally held throughout the campaign was that, by the time we had actually gotten to the place that we were ready to make a penetration to the German heartland, we would have more troops in hand than could possibly be used on one single line of communications.

We had always contemplated the use of the Northern Route and assumed that we would have to make there a real power crossing.[16] But in the meantime, as we began systematically and with overwhelming success to defeat and capture the German forces west of the Rhine, my orders to the troops consistently called for commanders to be alert toward any unforeseen opportunity to cross that obstacle. As you know, two such opportunities were found, one at Remagen, which took place, I think, on the 7th of March, and the other at Mannheim, about the 22nd or 23rd. Both of these antedated the initiation of the so-called main threat on the north of the Ruhr.[17]

To make sure of success of the northern operations, I assigned the entire American 9th Army to Monty and gave him very considerable assistance from the airborne forces.[18]

To have refused to employ the remainder of our armies would have been, in my humble opinion, a great mistake. We had an opportunity for a great double envelopment of the very considerable German forces on the Ruhr front, and each of our own attacking forces was of such power—and incidentally our air superiority was so great—that no Hitler force could possibly endanger either. Indeed, to have tried to use them all in one column would have been an unwarranted *dispersion in depth* and would have compelled many of our forces to lie idle when they could have been more profitably employed defeating what was left of the German Army and in pushing on to the Elbe.

In spite of the fact that I know of no American commander who, because of his earlier experience with Montgomery, had any confidence in that individual's strategic concepts (even though they admitted that in certain types of battles he was a master tactician) I persisted in keeping, up to the capture of the Ruhr, the left strong, by assigning to it the maximum American forces that the supply lines and logistic arrangements could accommodate.[19]

General Brooke in particular was more than fearful of attacking both through Frankfurt and through the line north of the Ruhr. By March twenty-fourth, with both penetrations going well, he expressed himself differently.[20] I think the calculations of the effect of the Frankfurt attack were proved accurate by the results. That column not only pushed through, ready to join hands with Montgomery when he made his expected advance on the north, but actually had to turn part of its forces backward (northwest) in the northern sector so as to make certain there would be no escape of Germans in the Ruhr pocket.

Foreseeing these developments, my staff and I calculated that our most speedy and rapid advance after the envelopment of the Ruhr, would be through the central part of Germany, rather than along the northern coast. Terrain-wise the coastal area provided the worst route open at that season. But as quickly as this plan was known, I came under criticism from General Brooke because now he seemed to think that the front would be too narrow. He was very anxious for Montgomery to push along the northern coast and wanted me to reassign the Ninth U. S. Army to Montgomery. This I would not do until we had once split into two the German forces and area.[21] However, after we crossed the Rhine, I again offered Ridgway's Airborne Corps to Montgomery to help him along. He declined to accept it until some days later when he requested it to make a thrust toward Lubeck, thus keeping the Russians out of Denmark.[22]

The whole point of this rather lengthy dissertation is that the terms "broad front" and "narrow front" mean now and meant then nothing, unless they were applied to specific cases and specific circumstances.[23]

Further to this "Montgomery" plan, backward looking as to "what might have been" rarely adds much to understanding. The practice began long ago—when it is reported that after Hannibal's refusal to assault Rome one of his lieutenants is quoted as saying "Hannibal, you know how to win victories, but not how to use one."[24]

$$*\quad*\quad*\quad*\quad*$$

I think none of us should forget that in the winter months of February and March of 1944, when all of us were working so hard planning OVERLORD, the Prime Minister himself more than once expressed his great misgivings about the cross Channel operations. You will recall his talking of the "Channel tides running red with Allied blood" and the "Beaches choked with the bodies of the flower of American and British manhood." At that time he talked in terms of two years for bringing the war to a successful conclusion, and two or three times he said to Bradley, Smith and me that if the Allied operations were successful, by Christmas, in capturing his beautiful and beloved Paris, then he would proclaim to the world that this was the most successful and brilliant military operation of all times.[25] It seems to me that these arguments about narrow and broad fronts and the operational plans developed, should be studied in connection with the knowledge we then had, with the growing strength of our own forces and the waning strength of the enemy, and in light of the knowledge that after all, it was *only eleven months from the day we landed until Jodl signed the surrender terms.*[26]

*   *   *   *   *

Your book discusses one other point that likewise attracted my special attention. As I understand it, you believe that the British authorities during '43 and '44 attributed American hesitancy to go along with certain projects in the Mediterranean to American fear that the British were attempting to weaken, delay, or even abandon OVERLORD.[27]

I suppose that any such British belief would not have applied to the proposal for capturing Dodecanese. Respecting that proposal, you will recall that we were then very busy with our own affairs in the Central Mediterranean. The opposition of my own headquarters to the project was not in any sense the result of a conflict between British and American views; it was the result of the consolidated thinking (the Navy possibly excepted) in my own headquarters.[28] We felt that if we detached the strength for any such operation we would become acutely embarrassed.

Respecting other proposals made by the British, even before we had captured Sicily, I think there are some grounds for your conclusion. I do not recall whether or not you personally came to Algiers in June of 1943, along with the Prime Minister, General Brooke and General Marshall. But I remember one specific incident during the period we were in Algiers that bears upon the point.

One afternoon Brooke and I took a walk and he gave me, in specific terms, his concept of our most appropriate line of operations against Hitler. In brief, he stated that he believed it was a very grave error for the Western Allies to attempt to invade Northern Europe with major land forces and he believed that a very costly stalemate, or even worse, could ensue. He argued that with our superior naval strength and our growing air superiority, we should continue to batter Germany, but so far as land operations were concerned, content ourselves with "nibbling around the edges."

He thought we should knock Italy out of the war (which could not easily be reinforced by Germany) and that, in addition, we should make raids along the Western European coast all the way up to Norway, upsetting the Germans, and forcing them to keep their troops in place, but never, ourselves, paying the cost of heavy operations. Later, I learned that General Marshall had gained the impression that other British officials held a similar "concept"; though as I remember he did not tell me he gained it from General Brooke.[29]

I believe that there was a period during the summer of '43 and through the following winter that the Americans, while realizing that the British would go through with any previous commitment, including OVERLORD, nevertheless felt that the British hope was to avoid any attack on the continent itself until, to use an expression of General Brooke's, "German morale had cracked."[30]

On the other hand, I certainly never detected any slacking off in preparations for OVERLORD, by the British or by ourselves. I was personally so confident that we could launch OVERLORD strongly and promptly in the spring of 1944 that I bet Montgomery five pounds that we would end the war by Christmas of that year. I lost the bet; but there were two factors which I did not take into account. The first of these was the late date of the assault across the Channel, and second, was that I did not conceive that Hitler would continue fighting after we had once lined up the Allied Armies on the banks of the Rhine.[31]

Of course I possibly was always prejudiced in favor of OVERLORD because you may remember that it was I, personally, who first presented the basis of the OVERLORD plan to General Marshall early in 1942. Shortly afterward, he was sent by the President to London to get British agreement to that particular operation.[32]

And, as I said earlier in this volume, I think results show that both the British and ourselves put maximum effort into the operation.

*   *   *   *   *

Right here I decided that I have written enough. After all I merely wanted to say that in my estimation you have written the outstanding book of World War II Memories. Congratulations—and I hope that a million people get to read it.[33]

With warm regard

[1] A draft of this letter containing Eisenhower's extensive handwritten emendations is in AWF/D. For background on Ismay's recently published World War II memoir see nos. 1679 and 1697.

[2] On the President's esteem for the former Prime Minister see no. 1709. Ismay would reply on December 30 (AWF/N) that some of his friends thought he had been "rather too extravagant" in praising Churchill. It was deliberate, Ismay wrote, because Churchill was "the only man in Britain who was absolutely indispensable and irre-

placeable for the first three years of the war. . . . Anyway, if I could have found any more superlatives to apply to Winston I would gladly have used them."

[3] Ismay's memoir had reported that British and American members of General Eisenhower's staff had worked together "as harmoniously as though they had always served under the same flag" (Ismay, *Memoirs*, p. 263). In March 1943 General Eisenhower had written he did not allow, "ever, an expression to be used in this Headquarters in my presence that even insinuates a British vs. American problem exists. . . . The job of winning this war is difficult, even with all of us pulling together as one complete team" (Chandler, *War Years*, no. 899). The General's memoir, *Crusade in Europe*, contained the same thought: "In the organization, operation, and composition of my staff we proceeded as though all its members belonged to a single nation" (p. 76).

[4] Ismay recalled that at the outset of the meetings of the Combined Chiefs of Staff both sides gave the impression that they would cling obstinately to their own ideas and there was little hope of reaching agreement. The British knew exactly what they wanted; the Americans felt at a disadvantage in not having agreed upon plans to put forward (Ismay, *Memoirs*, pp. 285–86). See also n. 27 below.

[5] The British were strongly opposed to SLEDGEHAMMER, a codename for a limited-objective attack across the Channel designed to take advantage of a collapse in German morale or to be a "sacrifice" operation to aid the hard-pressed Soviets. The operation was canceled in July 1942 (see Ismay, *Memoirs*, p. 259; and Chandler, *War Years*, nos. 386 and 387).

[6] The first Allied combined offensive, Operation TORCH—the invasion of North Africa—began on November 8, 1942 (see Chandler, *War Years*, no. 445; see also Eisenhower, *Crusade in Europe*, p. 71). Ismay would reply that he believed "that TORCH was a far better bet than SLEDGEHAMMER."

[7] ANVIL (later renamed DRAGOON), the invasion of southern France, took place in August 1944. See Ismay, *Memoirs*, pp. 342, 363–64, and Eisenhower, *Crusade in Europe*, pp. 283–84. Ismay would reply that Churchill had been "badgering" Roosevelt about the operation on both military and political grounds before the end of June 1944.

[8] According to Ismay (*Memoirs*, pp. 344–45), Field Marshal Montgomery had insisted on doubling the frontage of the attack when planning the Allied invasion of France.

[9] In his own account, Eisenhower explained that he had preferred Alexander, whom he admired and with whom he had already worked closely (see Eisenhower, *Crusade in Europe*, p. 211). Ismay would reply that he had not known about Eisenhower's preference.

[10] Brigadier General William E. Chambers was an American staff officer for COSSAC (Chief of Staff to the Supreme Allied Commander [Designate] and his invasion planning staff). Brigadier General Walter Bedell ("Beedle") Smith was Eisenhower's chief of staff. On the meeting and the plan see Chandler, *War Years*, no. 1473, and Eisenhower, *Crusade in Europe*, p. 217.

[11] For Ismay's recollection see his *Memoirs*, p. 344. General Frederick Edgworth Morgan (COSSAC) had sent the outline to Eisenhower in Algiers in late 1943. In early January Montgomery had left for London as the General's deputy. Ismay would reply (Dec. 30) that Montgomery had pressed for strengthening of the initial assault in January 1944, but he did not say at the time that Eisenhower had instructed him to do so.

[12] Following the successful drive to the Seine in late August 1944, one of the great controversies of the war began to emerge—the question of a broad-front approach to Germany versus a single thrust (see Chandler, *War Years*, no. 1909; Ismay, *Memoirs*, p. 385; Eisenhower, *Crusade in Europe*, p. 306).

[13] Lieutenant General Humfrey Gale had been among Eisenhower's principal logistic officers at SHAEF. Major General Francis Wilfred de Guingand had been Montgomery's chief of staff (see Chandler, *War Years*, no. 1473).

[14] On the conference in Brussels, attended by Eisenhower, Gale, and Marshal of the Royal Air Force Lord Arthur William Tedder, and on Eisenhower's view of Montgomery's plan to capture Berlin see Chandler, *War Years*, no. 1945, and no. 1012 in these volumes.

[15] See Chandler, *War Years*, no. 2254, and Eisenhower, *Crusade in Europe*, pp. 225–28.

[16] See Chandler, *War Years*, no. 2254.

[17] On the First Army's capture of the railway bridge at Remagen see Chandler, *War Years*, no. 2319; on the establishment of a bridgehead across the Rhine at Mannheim see *ibid.*, nos. 2321 and 2348. See also Eisenhower, *Crusade in Europe*, pp. 378, 384, 394.

[18] See Chandler, *War Years*, no. 2374.

[19] See *ibid.*, no. 2381, and no. 1697 in these volumes.

[20] On the meeting between General Eisenhower and General Alan Francis Brooke see *ibid.*, no. 2355. See also no. 550 in these volumes.

[21] See Chandler, *War Years*, no. 2373, and Eisenhower, *Crusade in Europe*, pp. 371–72.

[22] See Chandler, *War Years*, nos. 2418, 2440, 2452, and 2471.

[23] Ismay would agree with Eisenhower. By using the terms he had merely tried to point out that "a very acrimonious battle under that title took place between the American and British Chiefs of Staff after they had become good friends and did not impair their friendship or determination to co-operate with each other."

[24] Ismay had written (*Memoirs*, p. 385) that the British had supported Montgomery's proposal for an immediate advance on Berlin by way of the Ruhr. He would reply that he tried to say "much the same thing" in his memoir.

The quote is attributed to Maharbal, commander of Hannibal's cavalry. Following a brilliant victory over the Romans at Cannae, Maharbal had urged Hannibal to march on Rome immediately. Hannibal declined (see J. F. Lazenby, *Hannibal's War: A Military History of the Second Punic War* [Warminster, England, 1978], p. 85; and Serge Lancel, *Hannibal* [Oxford, 1998], p. 109).

[25] See no. 1709. On British misgivings, often voiced by Churchill, see *Crusade in Europe*, pp. 70, 194, and 243.

[26] On the German surrender effected by Field Marshal Alfred Gustav Jodl on May 7, 1945, see Chandler, *War Years*, nos. 2498 and 2499.

[27] See Ismay, *Memoirs*, pp. 286–87, 296–97.

[28] On the British assault on the Dodecanese Islands in September 1943 see Chandler, *War Years*, no. 1289.

[29] See Eisenhower, *Crusade in Europe*, pp. 167–68. Ismay would reply that Churchill had steeled himself to take the plunge in 1943 and "thereafter he never wavered." But he continued to "search for opportunities to 'nibble round the edges.'" Brooke and the General Staff held the same view as Churchill, Ismay wrote. The British realized that the "coup de grace" had to take place in Europe, but they wanted to wait until the Germans "were on their last legs."

[30] See Eisenhower, *Crusade in Europe*, p. 70.

[31] See David Eisenhower, *Eisenhower: At War, 1943–45* (New York, 1986), p. 556, and Irving, *The War Between the Generals*, p. 338. Ismay had not known about the wager, he replied. He had bet 10 pounds on the "more optimistic forecast that the war would be over within a hundred days of the date on which we broke out of our bridgehead. Had the attempt on Hitler's life on 21st July succeeded," he said, "I might have won my money with a good deal of time to spare."

[32] See Eisenhower, *Crusade in Europe*, p. 45; Stephen E. Ambrose, *The Supreme Commander: The War Years of General Dwight D. Eisenhower* (New York, 1970), pp. 30–35; and Chandler, *War Years*, nos. 1 and 161.

[33] On January 4 (AWF/N) Eisenhower would thank Ismay for providing a "clearer understanding" of his book and of "what actually happened."

To Konrad Adenauer   *December 5, 1960*
Cable. Secret

Dear Friend:[1] I appreciate very much the sentiments expressed in your letter of November 29, 1960. As much as I would have liked to see you and other old NATO associates in Paris again, this will unfortunately not be possible.[2]

I am still hopeful that, as indicated in my earlier letter, we will be able very soon now to present to the NATO Council our views on the NATO nuclear question.[3]

The news of your illness has been distressing to me and I hope that your recovery will be both rapid and complete.[4]

With renewed gratitude and warm personal regard, *Sincerely*

[1] State Department officials drafted this message, which was transmitted to the American embassy in Bonn for delivery to Chancellor Adenauer (see Dillon to Eisenhower, Dec. 2, 1960, AWF/I: Adenauer).

[2] For background see no. 1716. Adenauer had hoped that Eisenhower would attend the NATO ministerial meeting so that the participants could express to him "their heartfelt thanks" for all he had done for the organization (Adenauer to Eisenhower, Nov. 29, 1960, AWF/I: Adenauer).

[3] Secretary of State Herter would present the U.S. recommendations to the ministerial session of the North Atlantic Council on December 17. He would suggest a special multilateral force to operate mid-range ballistic missiles with "multilateral ownership, financing and control, [that] would include mixed manning to the extent considered operationally feasible by SACEUR" (see nos. 1665 and 1686). As an initial step, Herter told the council, the United States would commit to NATO five Polaris submarines that would operate under existing procedures. Decisions on requirements for a medium-range ballistic missile program beyond 1964 should be considered only after NATO long-range planning had been completed and the possibilities of the new weapons had been considered (State, *Foreign Relations, 1958–1960*, vol. VII, pt. 1, *Western European Integration and Security; Canada*, pp. 674–83). For developments see no. 1733.

[4] Adenauer had been confined to his home with a cold and tonsillitis and had canceled previously planned trips to London and Paris (*New York Times*, Dec. 3, 5, 16, 1960).

1724   *EM, AWF, Ann Whitman Diary Series*

Diary   *December 6, 1960*
Confidential

Account of my December 6th, 1960 meeting with President-elect Kennedy:
1. I arranged for an informal military parade in front of the White

House to receive the President-elect. I met him on the north portico of the mansion.[1]

We immediately started talks in my office.

2. It quickly became apparent that any single meeting, no matter of what length, could do little more than hit the high spots in the problem of transferring Federal control from one Administration to another.

The agenda suggested in advance by Senator Kennedy (copy attached) had as its first three items: Berlin, the Far East and Cuba. He had previously been briefed by Allen Dulles a number of times and had some familiarity with the details of these three subjects. Even so, there was no point in trying to go deeply into the details of these subjects because a full morning could be easily devoted to the possibilities, both adverse and favorable, that lie before us. Three short memoranda on these subjects are attached.[2]

3. The Senator was interested in the National Security setup and its operations. He suggested also that I give him any ideas I might have about improving the Pentagon operation.

I explained to him in detail the purpose and work habits of the Security Council, together with its two principal supporting agencies—the Planning Board and the Operations Coordinating Board. I said that the National Security Council had become the most important weekly meeting of the government; that we normally worked from an agenda, but that any member could present his frank opinion on any subject, even on those that were not on the formal agenda. I made clear to him that conferences in the White House are not conducted as Committee meetings in the Legislative Branch. There is no voting by members and each group has one purpose only—to advise the President on the facts of particular problems and to make to him such recommendations as each member may deem applicable. I described how "splits" in Planning Board papers were handled.

He, obviously, could not be expected to understand the operations of the Security Council from one short briefing, and I urged him to appoint, as soon as he possibly could, an individual that he would want to take over the duties, after January 20, of Gordon Gray. I stated that if he would do this, Mr. Gray would make it his business to acquaint such an individual in detail with the operations of the National Security Council and with the general content of the files.[3]

Regarding the Pentagon setup, the Senator mentioned a report he had just received from the so-called Symington Committee. From the papers I had learned something about the report and while I consider it so useless as to be ridiculous, I was careful to say nothing about the report as such.[4]

I did urge him to avoid any reorganization *until he himself could become well acquainted with the problem.* (Incidentally, I made this same suggestion with respect to the White House staff, the National Security Council, and the Pentagon). I told him that improvements could undoubtedly be made in the Pentagon and the command organization, but I also made it clear that the present organization and the improved functioning of the establishment had, during the past eight years, been brought about by patient study and long and drawn out negotiations with the Congress and the Armed Services.[5] Much has been said about "streamlining" such an organization in the belief that too many advisers and assistants are impeding the making of wise and prompt decisions. I think that something along this line might possibly be done, but in a mechanism such as the Defense establishment, which spends something on the order of 42 billion dollars a year. I pointed out that the Secretary of Defense should be fortified with the finest military and civilian advisers he could get. I pointed out the value of our scientific experts and their counsel. The importance of scientific research is illustrated by the amount of money devoted to the designing, development and testing of any weapons, without placing a single one of them in the operational inventory. (Incidentally, this figure is 6½ billion dollars. Another 23½ billion dollars goes to pay for maintenance of personnel and equipment.) This emphasized, I told him, the need for earnest study and thinking before making radical changes.

4. I spent some time explaining the difference between the functions of the White House staff as an immediate supporting body to the President on the one hand, and the relations between the President and his Cabinet officers. These, both individually and collectively, are always in contact with the President on any important problem affecting one or more.

I told him that without a personal staff all the detailed problems that would arise, even after major policies had been approved, would come directly to the attention of the President—and all of this without any coordination among Departments.

I told him the divisions within the White House were the Military Aides on the one hand and the civilian staff on the other. This civilian staff comprehends a legal section, an economic section, a liaison section and a secretarial section. The records section is a somewhat separated organism, because it is not only manned and headed by civil service personnel, but is the only permanent body in the White House.

The Senator seemed to be a bit amazed when I told him about the great numbers of people that operate in the Signal Corps, Transportation and Evacuation activities, all under the Military Aides. I also described the functions of Camp David.

Within the civilian side, many minor problems arise at the staff level among the different Departments. To expect each Department head to take up each of these with the President or to hold special Cabinet meetings would be undesirable and indeed in the long run impossible. Consequently this coordination is achieved by the President's personal staff, operating under its chief, a man whom I have given the title "The Assistant to the President."[6]

Aside from certain responsibilities of the President touching upon the Regulatory Commissions, there are ten statutory Departments, each headed by a Cabinet officer and, in addition to these, we have the Bureau of the Budget, the Atomic Energy Commission, the Office of Civil and Defense Mobilization, the Council of Economic Advisers, the General Services Administration, the Federal Aviation Agency, and the Veterans Administration.

In addition we have the Central Intelligence Agency, the Civil Service Commission and the United States Information Agency. The Assistant to the President, the Director of the Bureau of the Budget, and the Director of the Office of Civil and Defense Mobilization have been accorded Cabinet rank, as has the President's Representative to the United Nations.[7]

With all these agencies officially and directly subordinate to the President only, and with every problem engaging the attention of any agency normally affecting others, it is easy to see that there is a vast volume of staff coordination required. All of this is done by the President's personal staff.

I said nothing to him about the ceremonies, making of engagements, confidential correspondence, and many other activities which of course are handled normally by the President directly with the responsible individual.

5. Senator Kennedy wanted to get my personal thinking about Macmillan, De Gaulle and Adenauer. I gave him my opinions concerning these people as I have formed them over many years of association with them. I told him that I did not believe that my own comments would mean too much. I did venture the opinion that if he would take the trouble to meet them and talk with them individually and collectively, he would be impressed by their ability and their integrity, even though there would be many instances where he would disagree with their stated opinions.

6. I voluntarily brought up the question of NATO and our ballistic missile proposal to that organization.[8] I told him that De Gaulle has created a number of difficulties in the operation of NATO.[9] I gave Senator Kennedy my opinion that it was the most important alliance to which we belong, one whose maintenance and strength was vital to our own security and prosperity.

In this context I brought up the subject of dealing more closely with our allies in the matter of atomic weapons. I told him that our hands were somewhat tied because the *Joint Committee of Congress dealing with atomic matters was formed and is operating under a law that was written at a time when we had a true monopoly of atomic manufacture.*[10] Today the international club is growing and I think it is worse than silly to allow America's interests and responsibilities in this field to be handled by a Committee whose principal purpose is to stand watch over the *operations* of the Atomic Energy Commission—which is an operative and *not* a policy making organization. I told him that our relations with the Congress on this subject should be handled through the Foreign Relations Committees and the Defense Committees in both Houses. Frankly, I see no need for the continuance of the Joint Committee on Atomic Energy.

7. I talked to the Senator for some twenty minutes on the present situation and the Balance of Payments and foreign confidence in the dollar, and the way that confidence is affected by the balance or imbalance of budgets. I attach a copy of a short memorandum on the matter, but after I had talked to him Secretary Anderson gave him a much longer briefing on the whole matter, lasting some forty-five minutes.[11] I pray that he understands it. Certainly his attitude was that of a serious, earnest seeker for information and the implication was that he will give full consideration to the facts and suggestions we presented.

Partly because of the outflow of gold caused by the great deployments we have abroad, but also because of other reasons, including my conviction that America is carrying far more than her share of free world defense, I told him that I was going to warn the NATO community of the U.S.'s intention of redeploying some of its troops from Europe unless other arrangements could, at the very least, stop this drain on our gold. I told him that I informed him of this so he would not be surprised, and the decision was made and the announcement would be made in such a way as to leave him a free hand in reversing this policy if he so chooses.[12] I told him that while I believe thoroughly that the European nations, all of which have been so vastly strengthened by the billions we poured out through the Marshall Plan and since, were reaching a level of productivity that is for them unprecedented, they still seem to be unwilling to pick up what seemed to us to be their fair share of the defense burden. This government has pointed out to them often that we have taken the responsibility for the creation and maintenance of the free world's deterrent. We provide a vast portion of the navies and most of the bombing force in the free world. And we think that the European nations and Canada should be prepared to maintain a much larger proportion of the ground defense formations.[13]

8. On the personal side, Senator Kennedy asked me whether I

would be prepared, upon call from him, to serve the country in such areas and in such manner as may seem appropriate. I told him that, of course, the answer was obvious, but I did say that I thought I had the right, after many long years of service and in view of my age, to suggest that if he should request anything from me, it should be normally in terms of conferences and consultations on subjects on which I have had some experience, rather than errands which might necessitate frequent and lengthy travel. While I did not exclude the possibility of making some trip for some extraordinary reason, I did say that in the main I would like to have this restriction on my understanding.

9. Senator Kennedy was very much concerned with the activities of General Goodpaster, and said he would like to hold Goodpaster for two months into the new Administration. I told him that I thought a better solution would be for him to appoint a man right now who could take Goodpaster's post (the duties of which I detailed at some length) and allow Goodpaster to leave with the rest of us on January 20th. He said he would be handicapped unless he had Goodpaster for a month or two, really favoring the second. Of course I had to say that he would soon be the Commander-in-Chief and he could *order* General Goodpaster to do anything, and those duties would be efficiently performed; but I told him, also, of Goodpaster's great desire to go to active line duty and that a particular spot was being held for him. I asked the Senator if he would assure me that that spot would be held.

(That evening I called General Decker and told him the details of this conversation and asked him, as a personal favor to me, to make it his business to protect Goodpaster's future to this extent. He said there would be no trouble about this).[14]

Later in the conversation with the three Secretaries, Senator Kennedy repeated this promise, and I think there should be no difficulty in fulfilling it.[15]

10. Finally, I told the Senator that this hurried description of his many functions and duties would possibly be confusing, but if he should like to come back at any time all he had to do was give my secretary a ring and we would set up an appointment promptly.[16]

[1] For background on the November 6 election see no. 1700. Senator John F. Kennedy had gone unaccompanied to the three-hour meeting, which had begun at 9:00 A.M.; for more on the briefing see Eisenhower, *Waging Peace*, p. 603; Ambrose, *Eisenhower*, vol. II, *The President*, pp. 606–8; Theodore C. Sorenson, *Kennedy* (New York, 1965), pp. 231–33; Arthur M. Schlesinger, Jr., *A Thousand Days: John F. Kennedy in the White House* (Cambridge, Mass., 1965), pp. 126, 160–61, 163.

[2] These memorandums are in AWF/AWD.

[3] Kennedy would appoint McGeorge Bundy (A.B. Yale 1940), a Republican, as his national security adviser. Bundy was a former political analyst for the Council of For-

eign Relations and Professor of Government and Dean of Faculty of Arts and Sciences at Harvard University.

⁴ A six-man committee of civilian experts, headed by Senator Stuart Symington (Dem., Missouri), had proposed a reorganization of the Defense Department that would centralize all defense powers under the Secretary of Defense and abolish the separate departments of the armed services (*New York Times*, Dec. 6, 1960).

⁵ On Defense Department reorganization see Galambos and van Ee, *The Middle Way*, nos. 207 and 693; and nos. 630 and 802 in these volumes.

⁶ Wilton B. ("Jerry") Persons had succeeded Sherman Adams as Assistant to the President in October 1958.

⁷ Maurice H. Stans was Budget Director; Leo A. Hoegh was the Director of the Office of Civil and Defense Mobilization; and James J. Wadsworth was U.S. Ambassador to the United Nations.

⁸ See nos. 1665 and 1723.

⁹ See nos. 1318 and 1687.

¹⁰ Eisenhower is referring to the Atomic Energy Act of 1946 (see Galambos, *Chief of Staff*, no. 920). On the Atomic Energy Act of 1954 and its subsequent amendments see Galambos and van Ee, *The Middle Way*, nos. 298 and 612; and nos. 628 and 718 in these volumes.

¹¹ For more on this issue see Goodpaster, Memorandum of Conference, Nov. 14, 1960, AWF/D.

¹² On December 16 Secretary Herter would report to the NATO ministers that redeployment of some U.S. forces would be necessary unless the balance of payments problem were solved. Eisenhower, who had taken a direct hand in shaping Herter's talk, would also mention NATO troop redeployment in his Annual Budget Message to the Congress (State, *Foreign Relations, 1958–1960*, vol. VII, pt. 1, *Western European Integration and Security; Canada*, pp. 680–81; Telephone conversation, Eisenhower and Herter, Dec. 9, 1960, Herter Papers, Telephone Conversations; and *Public Papers of the Presidents: Eisenhower, 1960–61*, p. 958).

¹³ See no. 1669.

¹⁴ George Henry Decker, former Commander-in-Chief, United Nations Command, was Army Chief of Staff.

¹⁵ Immediately after his meeting with the President, Kennedy had met with Secretaries Herter, Gates, and Anderson. Goodpaster would remain with the Kennedy administration until April 1961 and would then be assigned to active line duty (see no. 1735).

¹⁶ Kennedy would meet again with Eisenhower on January 19, the day before his inauguration, to review the world situation (*New York Times*, Jan. 20, 1961; see also Fred L. Greenstein and Richard H. Immerman, "What Did Eisenhower Tell Kennedy about Indochina? The Politics of Misperception," *Journal of American History*, 79, no. 2 [1992], pp. 568–87).

1725   *EM, WHCF, Office File 3-R*

To Sterling Morton   *December 6, 1960*

Dear Mr. Morton: Thank you for your note of commendation regarding the action I recently took because of the difficulties our government is experiencing because of the unfavorable Balance of Payments situation.[1] I am sure you understand that as a soldier for over forty years, I have no desire to work a hardship upon the personnel stationed overseas. But some steps *had* to be taken—and taken immediately.[2]

With best wishes, *Sincerely*

[1] For background see nos. 1713 and 1724. In an attempt to close the deficit gap in the balance of payments, Eisenhower had ordered (Nov. 16) a mandatory reduction in the number of dependents of military personnel stationed abroad from the current level of 484,000 to 200,000. Morton, chairman of the board and a director of the Morton Salt Company of Chicago (see Galambos, *NATO and the Campaign of 1952*, no. 292), had congratulated Eisenhower on the decision. A well-seasoned traveler, Morton had found that the dependents of military and civilian men overseas caused "ill-will" towards the United States. Servicemen, he observed, usually got along very well, "but the customs, costumes and manners of the dependents are often most irritating to foreigners." He had suggested filling homeward-bound planes and ships to capacity in order to speed the reduction (Morton to Eisenhower, Nov. 30, 1960, same file as document).

In his directive, Eisenhower had also requested that the Defense and the State Departments, the Central Intelligence Agency, and the International Cooperation Administration reduce their overseas staffs wherever possible. In addition, the President had asked all federal agencies to cut their foreign spending. With these and several other thrift measures, he hoped to save $1 billion dollars overall in expenditures (U.S., *Federal Register*, vol. 25, pp. 12221–23; *Congressional Quarterly Almanac*, vol. XVI, *1960*, pp. 709–12; *New York Times*, Nov. 17, 1960).

[2] For developments see no. 1729.

1726   *EM, AWF, Dulles-Herter Series*

To CHRISTIAN ARCHIBALD HERTER   *December 7, 1960*
Top secret

Memorandum for the Secretary of State: This refers to the memorandum on Cuba sent to me under date of December 2, 1960 by Doug Dillon.[1]

I approve the suggestions regarding the reorganization of the government's program with respect to that country, except that I think Mr. Willauer should have a position directly subordinate to the Secretary of State for so long as Cuba remains a critical problem in our foreign relations. There should be no doubt as to the authority of the Special Assistant in the State Department (Mr. Willauer) to coordinate covert and overt activities, nor as to his responsibility for conveying policy guidance to the operating agencies. In their broad outline, these policies will, of course, be subject to the approval of higher authority.[2]

¹ For background on the Cuban situation see no. 1606. Acting Secretary Dillon's memorandum referred a November 29 meeting Eisenhower had held with Administration officials regarding the coordination of U.S. policies toward Cuba. The President had expressed his unhappiness regarding the worsening situation in that country and had questioned whether things were "beginning to get out of hand." Emphasizing that he did not want to turn over the government to a new administration "in the midst of a developing emergency," he had recommended the appointment of a "coordinating chief," who would be responsible for all overt and covert actions regarding Cuba, someone who could answer his questions directly (Gordon Gray, Memorandum of Meeting with the President, Dec. 5, 1960, WHO/OSANSA, Special Assistants, Presidential Meetings with the President).

Dillon had written that the 5412 Group (Special Group), a subcommittee established by NSC 5412/1 to review covert action proposals, had agreed that U.S. moves regarding Cuba "must be completely geared into each other." The group had recommended that a senior official in both the State Department and the CIA work together "in the closest intimacy," devoting their full time to the problem. Dillon had recommended Whiting Willauer, U.S. Ambassador to Costa Rica; CIA Director Allen Dulles had recommended C. Tracy Barnes, CIA Special Assistant for Paramilitary and Psychological Operations. Dillon had also told Eisenhower that the Special Group wanted to "continue and intensify" its supervision of covert operations (Dillon to Eisenhower, Dec. 2, 1960, AWF/D-H; see also State, *Foreign Relations, 1958–1960,* vol. VI, *Cuba,* pp. 789, 850–51, 861–63, 1126; and William M. Leary, ed., *The Central Intelligence Agency: History and Documents* [University, Ala., 1984], p. 63).

² On December 8 the 5412 Group would discuss plans for an amphibious landing on the Cuban coast, to be preceded by air strikes launched from Nicaragua. The purpose of the operation was to seize a limited portion of Cuban territory and establish a visible presence—an action that would draw dissidents in Cuba to the landing force and precipitate a general uprising. Ambassador Willauer would later report that final judgment regarding the success of such a plan would have to be made "almost at the last minute" after determining Castro's capabilities and the strength of internal opposition. He further stated that final operations under the plan should not proceed "unless the U.S. Government were prepared to do everything else needed overtly or covertly . . . in order to guarantee success" (Willauer to Merchant, Jan. 18, 1960, WHO/OSANSA: Special Assistants (Presidential), Meetings with the President; and State, *Foreign Relations, 1958–1960,* vol. VI, *Cuba,* p. 1175).

On January 3 Eisenhower would announce that after "a long series of harassments, baseless accusations, and vilifications" he was ending diplomatic and consular relations with Cuba. There was, he said, "a limit to what the United States in self-respect can endure" (*Public Papers of the Presidents: Eisenhower, 1960–61,* p. 891). For more on the issue see no. 1771.

1727   *EM, AWF, International Series:*
                                                        Pakistan

To Mohammad Ayub Khan   *December 7, 1960*

Dear Mr. President: Word has reached me through Mr. A. Ogden Pierrot, Jr. that you are planning to convert the greens on the golf course at Rawalpindi from sand to grass, and that you are experiencing some difficulty in locating the plant materials best suited to the climate and soil.[1]

We have developed, in the southern part of our country, a product known as "Tifgreen" (a type of Bermuda grass), which our Department of Agriculture feels is ideal for your purpose. Accordingly I am taking the liberty of sending you enough nursery stock to develop a culture which, in the course of a year, should provide enough grass for eighteen greens. I hope you will accept this small gift as a token of my appreciation of the cordial hospitality you accorded to me and my party on our visit a year ago.[2]

To assist and advise in the care and propagation of the Tifgreen stock, I would like to offer the services of Mr. S. P. Swenson, who is in Pakistan with an International Cooperation Administration agricultural mission. Furthermore, I am told that Dr. Zafar Alam, Principal of the Punjab Agricultural College in Lyallpur, West Pakistan, is an expert in such matters.[3]

I certainly hope that you will find the grass satisfactory for your use.[4]

With warm regard, *Sincerely*

[1] A. Ogden Pierrot, Jr., an export director with Bell Helicopter Company in Washington, D.C., was working in the U.S. embassy in Pakistan (see Pierrot to Ramsey, Sept. 20, 1960, AWF/I: Pakistan).
[2] Pierrot had reported that 10 to 12 square yards of the hybrid turf Bermuda grass would suffice (see the related correspondence in AWF/I: Pakistan). On the President's visit to Pakistan in December 1959 see no. 1359.
[3] Stanley Prescott Swenson (Ph.D. University of Minnesota 1936) of Washington State University, had been on special assignment as the head of a party from Washington State participating in the Inter-College Exchange Program with the University of Punjab, Lahore, Pakistan, since 1958. Alam was a native Pakistani who had a good reputation with U.S. agricultural scientists.
[4] Kahn's reply is not in AWF.

1728

To WILLIAM ALTON JONES

EM, AWF, Name Series

December 8, 1960

Dear Pete: While I know Mamie will write you immediately concerning your gift to the Army Distaff Foundation, I thought perhaps— as a third person—I could tell you how really thrilled she was by your wonderfully (but characteristically) generous contribution. I think she feels that you and she, together, are responsible for every brick and every stone. And, because her heart is so much in the cause, she will have lasting satisfaction, as I hope you will, in the good your gift will do.[1]

Once again, my gratitude to you is limitless.

With personal regard, *As ever*

P.S. I had fun reading my non-invitation to your Christmas Party; if I had a calender I should be tempted to put down the 1961 date *now.*[2]

[1] The First Lady was honorary president of the Women's Advisory Committee of the Army Distaff Foundation. For background on the foundation and on Army Distaff Hall, a residence for Army widows, see no. 1651. When completed, the building would have 716 rooms, including 300 living facilities, a chapel, a dining room, an infirmary, and hobby and social rooms. It would be completed and ready for occupancy on January 17, 1962 (telephone conversation, General Benedict, Executive Director, Army Distaff Foundation, June 5, 2000).
[2] We have been unable to find Jones's invitation in EM.

1729   *EM, AWF, Administration Series*

To ROBERT BERNERD ANDERSON   *December 9, 1960*
Personal

Dear Bob: I think our people need a little bit more information on the factual details of the outflow of gold.[1] This morning my paper says that Goldwater was wildly cheered by fifteen hundred businessmen at the Waldorf when he made the assertion to the effect that American policies for the last fifteen years have been completely wrong and the further assertion that it was time America was acting like a world leader and should stop grovelling on its knees before little second rate countries. He particularly attacked foreign economic aid and said that America had immediately to change its policies in this regard.[2]

What I think we should do is to provide some kind of an accurate estimate of the causes of the gold outflow—for example, under such titles as

Tourism
The $500 exemption for free entry
Troops stationed in foreign countries, including unnecessary personnel
Economic Aid
The Development Fund
The Inter-American Bank
Foreign Private investment
Miscellaneous

I believe if a statement of this kind were made either in a speech or even as a matter of just a Treasury release, it might be helpful.[3] I am not in the slightest bit disturbed by Goldwater's presentation. He is trying to parlay woeful ignorance into political popularity. But I was disturbed by the story that fifteen hundred of his listeners obviously approved of his uninformed views.

With warm regard, *As ever*

[1] For background see nos. 930, 1040, 1669, and 1725. See also Eisenhower, *Waging Peace*, pp. 604–7; Saulnier, *Constructive Years*, pp. 119–22, and Morgan, *Eisenhower versus 'The Spenders,'* p. 174. By the end of 1960 the drain on American gold reserves had reached crisis proportions, and the price of gold on the London market soared. As rumors spread that the dollar would be devalued by the new administration, speculators exchanged more and more dollars for gold in foreign markets. The President had discussed with his advisors various options to redress the deficit in the U.S. balance of payments. These measures included redeploying troops from Europe back to the United States and reducing the number of dependents overseas in order to cut expenditures abroad; Eisenhower had also suggested substituting uranium and plutonium for gold as a medium of exchange (Goodpaster, Memorandum of conference with the President, Nov. 9, 1960, AWF/D). In January the President would issue an order barring Americans from foreign ownership of gold (Anderson to Eisenhower, Jan. 13, 1961, AWF/AWD; *New York Times*, Jan. 15, 1961). For developments see no. 1732.

[2] The Senator from Arizona had spoken at a meeting of the National Association of Manufacturers held at the Waldorf Astoria Hotel in New York City on December 8. Goldwater had suggested restrictions on the amount of money tourists could take out of the country as a means of halting the gold drain. He had also recommended that Congress curtail foreign economic aid because the United States had received nothing of great value in return (Anderson to Eisenhower, Jan. 13, 1961, AWF/AWD; *New York Times*, Dec. 9, 1960).

[3] Eisenhower had addressed the issue during his news conference on November 16, 1960. He had outlined the factors contributing to the gold outflow and had explained the reasons why the Administration was taking steps to limit the number of overseas military dependents (*Public Papers of the Presidents: Eisenhower, 1960–61*, pp. 861–66). The Treasury Department would release its own year-end statement on the gold drain on January 5, 1960 (*New York Times*, Jan. 6, 1960).

1730   *EM, AWF, International Series:*
                                                                          Macmillan

To HAROLD MACMILLAN   *December 10, 1960*
Cable. Secret

Dear Harold: As a result of the review which I mentioned in my message yesterday, you will be glad to know that our final decision, though a most difficult one, is to abstain on the Afro-Asian resolution on Colonialism.[1] We are instructing our representative to make a statement explaining our vote, which will make clear that while the wording of certain paragraphs makes it impossible for us to vote in favor of the resolution, we do support the general principles the sponsors had in mind.[2]

With warm regard, *As ever*

[1] Early in November forty-two African and Asian nations had presented to the United Nations General Assembly a resolution calling for the end of colonialism. The resolution had been offered after Soviet Premier Khrushchev had demanded immediate independence for all remaining colonies (State, *Foreign Relations, 1958–1960*, vol. II, *United Nations and General International Matters*, pp. 430–32, 433–35, 447, 450–51). As a vote neared on December 8, Secretary Herter had informed Eisenhower that although much of the language was objectionable, concern for public reaction throughout the world and especially relations with the new and emerging African states had persuaded him that the U.S. delegation should support the proposal. Although Eisenhower leaned toward abstention, he agreed to support the resolution but asked that U.N. Ambassador Wadsworth publicly explain the decision "paragraph by paragraph so there will be no misunderstanding of our meaning" (Herter to Goodpaster, Dec. 8, 1960, AWF/D-H; and Telephone conversations, Eisenhower and Herter, Dec. 8, 1960, Herter Papers, Telephone Conversations).

Macmillan had written that he was "very shocked" to hear that Eisenhower supported the resolution and asked that the President reconsider. "This vote on behalf of the American people, if it is given, will have a most discouraging effect upon all our people here and overseas who are working so hard for progress," Macmillan said. "Do let us stand together, at least on a decision to abstain, and thus dissociate ourselves from a resolution which has no connection with reality" (Macmillan to Eisenhower, Dec. 9, 1960, AWF/I: Macmillan). After receiving Macmillan's message, Eisenhower had told Herter that considering the stand taken by America's "strongest ally," he thought they should abstain from voting. He asked Herter to cable Macmillan saying that they were restudying the issue and that he would hear further from them (Telephone conversations, Dec. 9, 1960, Herter Papers, Telephone Conversations).

[2] Wadsworth would tell Herter that he was "shocked and disheartened" by the last minute reversal of instructions that changed the U.S. position from support to abstention. He and the other members of the delegation believed that the decision would weaken the record of the United States regarding colonialism. Macmillan, on the other hand, would tell Eisenhower that he was sure that the decision was correct. "It will be a great help to us," he wrote, "and I am most grateful" (Macmillan to Eisenhower, Dec. 12, 1960, AWF/I: Macmillan). The resolution was passed on December 14 with the United States, Great Britain, and France abstaining (State, *Foreign Relations, 1958–1960*, vol. II, *United Nations and General International Matters*, pp. 458, 460–61; *New York Times*, Dec. 15, 1960).

1731

EM, WHCF,
President's Personal File 269

To Frances Payne Bolton

December 14, 1960

Dear Frances: Thank you very much for your provocative letter of December tenth. You pose in it questions about which I have pondered for a good many number of months, even years. I have posed them to myself and wondered exactly how I could answer them.[1]

So far I have come to one conclusion only. The answers cannot be given quickly. They cannot come without profound contemplation and through profound study. It is because these questions do demand the best thinking of which each of us is capable and their expression in the clearest possible terminology, that I have set for myself a writing task during the months to come, the basic purpose of which will be to try to get hold of answers that may have some validity and appeal.[2]

More than this I cannot say at this time. But I do want to quote to you one sentence from your own letter—"certainly we have little to offer if we seek only personal gain . . ."[3] This sentence should constantly be held as a maxim before every individual, so that each could truly dedicate himself to the good of the whole and not merely to the satisfaction of personal ambition. Indeed, I think of personal ambition as something like the tempering of steel. If there is too little, the steel softens and becomes useless; if too much, it becomes brittle and breaks.

In any event, I shall keep your letter to remind me to get back to work at times when, with my inherent laziness, my inclination might be to forget it because of the difficulty of the task.

With affectionate regard, *As ever*

[1] Mrs. Bolton, a Republican Representative from Ohio's twenty-second congressional district, served on the House Committee on Foreign Affairs. In 1940 she had been elected to the 76th Congress to fill the vacancy caused by the death of her husband, Chester Castle Bolton, and had served in the House ever since. Representative Bolton had written that since Americans were entering "very dangerous days," the Republican party should do some fundamental thinking in order to take consistent, far-reaching action. She had turned to the President for an outline of the basic principles of the American dream and of a Republican strategy to build a leadership capable of bringing about unity and peace (same file as document).

[2] On Eisenhower's decision to publish his memoirs see nos. 1643 and 1650.

[3] Bolton had inquired about the meaning of America, and the goals that Americans should strive to achieve. She added, "Certainly we have little to offer if we seek only personal gain of which you and I have seen all too much."

1732   *EM, AWF, Administration Series*

To Clarence Douglas Dillon   *December 15, 1960*
Personal

Dear Doug: I have just come from two days in the hospital where I have been taking my annual physical.[1] Upon reaching my office I encountered a piece of gossip which apparently has achieved some circulation and which purported to say that I was definitely in favor of your accepting the post of Secretary of the Treasury, if it should be definitely offered. As you know, this is not correct and should anyone ask you a specific question on the matter, I would hope that you would make this clear. We did, of course, talk over the pros and cons of the tentative invitation and you laid out some of the conflicting considerations that would necessarily affect your decision.[2]

Obviously, it is no part of my responsibility to try, unduly, to influence you, but I do want to make it clear that on balance I am against the proposal.

Even if you could have, in advance, a solid guarantee that you would be the sole authority in determining upon matters that fall within the scope of Treasury responsibility, it is inconceivable to me that any President would, in practice, retain only nominal control over these important operations. But without such unbreakable guarantee, you would become a scapegoat of the radicals.

You and I are both dedicated to the prevention of debasement of our currency through any cause, domestic or foreign. I can think of no one who could do this better than you, provided you were working with a President who agreed with you in this philosophy and if you were sturdily supported by him in any recommendations you might make to the Congress, and in your activities in financing and refinancing governmental operations. Because I do not see how you can anticipate this in an atmosphere that resembles anything like that suggested during the recent political campaign, I repeat that, for whatever my opinion is worth, I would not favor your acceptance.[3]

I send this note only because of the gossip that came to my ears, which reported that I had given you a contrary view. Soo—all this is just to clear the atmosphere.

With warm personal regard, *As ever*

P.S.: I shall hope to have an early report on your trip.[4]

---

[1] Eisenhower had entered Walter Reed Hospital on the evening of December 13 and left the morning of December 15, 1960 (President's daily appointments).

[2] Eisenhower had spoken with Dillon as well as Vice-President Nixon about the President-elect's intention of appointing Dillon as the new Secretary of the Treasury (Telephone Conversation, Nixon and Eisenhower, Nov. 14; Eisenhower and Dillon, Dec. 8, 1960, AWF/N). The President would meet with Dillon on the morning of December 16, 1960, to discuss the offer (President's daily appointments).

[3] Although Eisenhower expressed disapproval of the prospective appointment (see *Waging Peace*, p. 603), he had previously told Dillon that if he assumed the post he might be able to alleviate the current gold drain difficulties (see no. 1729). If Dillon were offered the position, Eisenhower said, he should accept "at once and do everything in his power to protect our currency." The President added that he "would take it himself," if Kennedy were to offer him the job (Goodpaster, Memorandum of Conversation, Nov. 28, 1960, AWF/D). When Dillon called to notify Eisenhower

that he had accepted the post, the President told him that "it may work out for the good of the country" (Telephone Conversation, Dillon and Eisenhower, Dec. [16], 1960, AWF/D). For developments see no. 1759.

[4] Eisenhower wrote an additional postscript by hand: "I tried to give you this on the phone—but I do not know the hour of your arrival from Paris."

1733   *EM, AWF, Dulles-Herter Series*

To Christian Archibald Herter   *December 15, 1960*
Secret

Dear Chris:[1] Thanks for your message concerning the NATO discussions. By now you know that the revised sentence you propose is quite acceptable to me.[2]

I share your reaction to the breach of security in the press story concerning the raising of the redeployment issue, and I hope you will make the most intensive possible effort to find its source on your return, since there must have been no more than a handful of people who knew of the proposed addition during the time we had the phrasing "material redeployment" under consideration.[3]

I hope the meetings go well and that you will extend my best wishes to our NATO friends.[4]

With warm personal regard, *As ever*

[1] This message was sent by cable to the American embassy in Paris for delivery to the Secretary of State, who was attending the NATO Ministerial Meeting.

[2] For background on the NATO meeting and Secretary Herter's statement regarding long-range plans for NATO see no. 1723. Herter had told Eisenhower that he had discussed his statement regarding the possible redeployment of U.S. troops with Treasury Secretary Anderson and other State and Defense Department officials. The group had recommended the insertion of a sentence that read: "In fact some redeployment may become a necessity unless our balance of payments can be brought into a more reasonable equilibrium." Herter had asked Eisenhower to authorize the insertion of this sentence, and the President had approved the change both by cable (Dec. 14) and by telephone (Herter to Eisenhower, Dec. 14, 1960, AWF/D-H; and State, *Foreign Relations, 1958–1960*, vol. VII, pt. 2, *Western Europe*, p. 681).

[3] Herter had written that he was "horrified" by a story in the *New York Times* reporting that he was prepared to tell the NATO members that the United States might have to consider a "material redeployment" of its troops in Europe. He had told Eisenhower that the story had heightened his anxiety regarding certain sections of the State Department. For discussions regarding redeployment see John S. D. Eisenhower, Memorandum of Conference, Nov. 30, 1960; and Goodpaster, Memorandum of Conference, Dec. 8, 1960, both in AWF/D.

[4] For developments see NSC meeting minutes, Dec. 23, 1960, AWF/NSC; and no. 1739.

To George O. Strecker   *December 15, 1960*

Dear George: Many thanks for your letter. A long time ago I was told by one of the permanent staff members here at the White House that the last few months of any Administration would be relatively calm. Such has certainly not been my own situation (and I hear from all of my top associates much the same story).[1] I do plan some sort of a "report" on my stewardship, but whether it will take the form of a television address before January twentieth or a published document after that time, I cannot yet say.[2]

I know that "retirement" presents problems for many.[3] Because of your great interest in the political scene, is there not some way you can utilize your time and talents to the benefit of the Republican Party in Illinois? I should think you might find such an effort stimulating and satisfying.

At any rate, Mamie joins me in best wishes to you and Frances for a fine holiday season, and in warm personal regard. *Sincerely*

[1] We have been unable to identify Strecker, of Lake Forest, Illinois; he had written on December 12 (same file as document). On the President's campaign activities during the recent presidential election see, for example, nos. 1648 and 1689.

[2] Strecker had presumed that Eisenhower was busy preparing messages before relinquishing the presidency. On January 17 the President would deliver his Farewell Address to the American People on radio and television. Acknowledging the threat of communism and the importance of keeping the peace, Eisenhower would state that the conjunction of an immense military establishment and a large arms industry was new in the American experience. The total economic, political, and spiritual influence was "felt in every city, every State house, every office of the Federal government." Americans, he said, had to understand the "grave implications" of this phenomenon: "In the councils of government, we must guard against the acquisition of unwarranted influence, whether sought or unsought, by the military-industrial complex. The potential for the disastrous rise of misplaced power exists and will persist" (*Public Papers of the Presidents: Eisenhower, 1960–61*, pp. 1034–40, and *New York Times*, Jan. 18, 1961).

[3] Strecker had complained that retirement had become "wearisome." It was "an age problem," he wrote, that some people handled more graciously than others.

1735   *EM, AWF, DDE Diaries Series*

To John Fitzgerald Kennedy   *December 16, 1960*

Dear Senator Kennedy: I have now heard from both Secretary Gates and General Decker regarding your desire to retain General Goodpaster temporarily after your Inauguration. They have arranged, as you asked, for him to stay on in your office for a period ending sometime in February or March, the exact date to be determined later.[1] At the same time, they have taken steps to see that, as we agreed, when he ends his service here he will be sent to the same assignment that is now planned for him.[2]

With best wishes, *Sincerely*

[1] On December 6 the President had noted his lengthy discussion with President-elect Kennedy regarding the retention of Goodpaster (see no. 1724).

[2] Kennedy would promise Eisenhower to release Goodpaster (Dec. 21, 1960, AWF/D). For Goodpaster's remarks on the resiliency of the U.S. government during the transition from the structured Eisenhower approach to the less formal Kennedy administration see Kenneth W. Thompson, ed., *Papers on Presidential Transitions and Foreign Policy*, vol. V, *Reflections of Five Public Officials* (Lanham, Md., 1987), pp. 15–34.

In April 1961 Goodpaster would leave Kennedy's service to command the Army's Eighth Infantry Division in Germany. He would return to the United States in December 1962 to serve as assistant to the chairman of the Joint Chiefs of Staff. He would become director of the Joint Staff in 1967, and in 1969 he would assume the duties of Supreme Allied Commander, U.S. Forces, Europe, until he retired in 1974. Three years later he would be called out of retirement to serve as the Superintendent of the United States Military Academy.

1736   *EM, AWF, DDE Diaries Series*

TO JOHN FITZGERALD KENNEDY   *December 19, 1960*
Personal

Dear Senator Kennedy: I regret that it did not occur to me, earlier, to offer you as President-elect one facility that might be of some possible use, namely the use of a governmental plane. Knowing something about the problems of the Secret Service and their work in providing for the safety of the President-elect and his family, I think it possible that the use of such a plane, during this interregnum, might be of real utility to you.

Should the idea appeal to you, I shall be glad to issue the necessary directions upon receipt of a telephone call. On the other hand, should you decide otherwise, I would hope that the existence of this suggestion and this letter itself might be held confidential. For this reason I have marked the letter personal.[1]

With best wishes, *Sincerely*

[1] President-elect Kennedy would thank the President for the offer on December 21 (AWF/D). He would use the same plane he had used during his campaign, he explained, and did not plan to travel extensively before January 20.

To Douglas McCrae Black   *December 19, 1960*
Personal

Dear Doug: Enclosed is a copy of a personal letter I have sent to Harry Luce. As you know, he is a good friend of mine and so I have tried to explain to him my future plans.[1] In the letter you will note that I have said nothing about your arrangements with Ben Hibbs. In the event that Harry should talk to you, I do not mind your informing him about the arrangement with Ben; but since I am most hopeful of keeping the business arrangements of this kind in your hands, I think it would be proper for you to say that this is a matter for your decision.[2]

With warm personal regard, *As ever*

---

[1] On Eisenhower's decision to publish his memoirs with Black's Doubleday and Company see nos. 1624 and 1650. On December 17 the President had replied to Time Life publisher Luce's December 14 letter regarding a book on Eisenhower's Administration (both letters are in Eisenhower Post-Presidential Papers, Principal File). Eisenhower had explained that his decision to work with another publisher did not "imply any lack of interest in you and your great publishing enterprise." The President added that he feared he might have decided as he had because he was "a very lazy man." He was hoping to spend the early months of 1961 leading "a vegetable's life" and therefore had chosen to leave all publishing decisions to someone else. For background on Luce's interest in publishing the President's memoirs in *Life* magazine see nos. 1418 and 1424.

[2] Benjamin Hibbs was the editor of the *Saturday Evening Post.* In September Eisenhower had asked Black and Hibbs to discuss publishing his memoirs with Doubleday and Company and writing articles in the *Saturday Evening Post* (see no. 1624). See also Luce to Eisenhower, Dec. 21, 1960, and Whitman to Black, Dec. 21, 1960, both in WHCF/PPF 951. For developments see no. 1751.

To Spyros Panagiotes Skouras   *December 19, 1960*

Dear Spyros: I cannot tell you how grateful I am for your suggestion that you build at the Gettysburg farm a Preview Room for the showing of films.[1]

If we are to go further with the idea, I think we shall have to have a meeting, because I would have to decide on such things as location and so on. I am not certain that there exists now a room in which the project could be carried out. In any event it would be nice to talk to you about it. If you would call either Mrs. Whitman or Mr. Stephens, a date could be easily set up.[2]

Of course if the whole installation should become one demanding a major effort, we would, I think, have to reconsider the matter.[3]

Thank you again for the thoughtfulness of your generous suggestion.

With best wishes to you and yours for a fine holiday season, and with warm personal regard, *Sincerely*

[1] Twentieth Century Fox President Skouras had made the offer in a letter of December 13 (AWF/A). He said he wanted to provide the President with this form of "richly deserved" relaxation so that he could "continue to enjoy the pleasure of viewing our films, as well as those of other companies throughout the world."

[2] The President would meet with Skouras at the White House on December 27 and again on January 13.

[3] The room would not be built, and the Eisenhowers would view films shown from a reel-to-reel projector on a portable screen at their home in Gettysburg (Communication from Carol Hegeman, National Park Service, July 14, 2000, EP).

1739   *EM, AWF, International Series:*
                                                        Canada

To John George Diefenbaker   *December 21, 1960*
Cable. Confidential

Dear John: Thank you for your message of December 14 reiterating your interest in the holding of an early NATO Heads of Government meeting.[1]

In making our preparations for the NATO Ministerial Meeting we had in mind your interest in holding an early Heads of Government meeting, and took special note of your statements of November 24 and December 7 on the subject.[2] We agree with you that the important task of long-range planning on which the Alliance is embarked would be one of the chief topics at such a meeting. We concluded, however, that while the Ministerial Meeting in Paris would see us well launched on this task of planning, it will still be some time before we are in a position to take Government decisions on the planners' work. Therefore we believe that the question of convening a Heads of Government meeting should be held open pending further progress on these long-range studies.

I can assure you, however, that your strong interest in this matter will be kept in mind, and that Secretary Herter, in the talks which he will be having in the coming weeks with Secretary-designate Rusk, will bring your views to the attention of the Secretary-designate.[3]

With warm regard, *Sincerely*

¹ The American ambassador to Canada had delivered Diefenbaker's message to Eisenhower on December 14. State Department officials, who drafted this reply, had requested that the ambassador inform Diefenbaker that this was "privileged correspondence and not for public release." Diefenbaker had told Eisenhower that problems relating to the nuclear policy of NATO had reinforced his desire for a meeting of the heads of government. Diefenbaker also stated that the Canadian Secretary of State for External Affairs would make the suggestion at the NATO ministerial meeting opening in Paris on December 16 (Diefenbaker to Eisenhower, Dec. 14, 1960, AWF/I: Canada; see also State, *Foreign Relations, 1958–1960*, vol. VII, pt. 1, *Western European Integration and Security; Canada*, pp. 802–3; on the NATO meetings see no. 1723).
² These statements are not further identified.
³ Dean Rusk (B.A. Davidson College 1931; M.A. St. Johns College; Oxford 1934), a former associate professor of government and dean of faculty at Mills College, had served as Special Assistant to the Secretary of War and as head of the Secretary of State's Office of United Nations Affairs. He had left his position as Assistant Secretary of State for Far Eastern Affairs in 1952 to head the Rockefellar Foundation. President-elect Kennedy had announced his selection as Secretary of State on December 12.

1740   *EM, AWF, International Series:*
                                                              Pakistan

To Mohammad Ayub Khan   *December 22, 1960*
Cable. Confidential

Dear Mr. President: Thank you for your letter of November 29, 1960, delivered by your Ambassador on December 16.¹ I appreciate your thoughtfulness in sharing your views with me, and am glad to have observations on Algerian developments which reflect your broad outlook and your active interest in working for world peace.²

Your apprehensions concerning the danger of Communist infiltration in North Africa are indeed justified.³ I share your appreciation of the difficulties faced by President de Gaulle in his courageous efforts to find a solution mutually acceptable to the peoples of France and of Algeria. I am keenly aware of Pakistan's common ties with France and the free world, and with the people of Algeria, and am gratified by your desire to encourage a settlement satisfactory to both.⁴

As you know, my Government, with its basic interest in the right of self-determination and its long association with the Republic of France as an ally, watches with deep interest and sympathy all efforts to settle the issue peacefully. At the moment, President de Gaulle is making a valiant effort to achieve a just solution and is, I believe, well aware of the interest and good wishes of his friends. I am of the opinion that the course now being followed by President de Gaulle is the most promising of any taken up to the present time.[5] I question whether chances of success will be enhanced by an offer of good offices, but will keep in mind the helpful and penetrating observations you have been good enough to convey.[6] I read President de Gaulle's speech of December 20 with great interest and trust that you will agree with my conclusion that it holds out real hope for a lasting settlement.[7] If you agree, I believe that your so informing him privately would give him considerable encouragement in the present situation.

Thank you again for sharing your views on a topic to which I am giving my closest attention.

With warm regard, *Sincerely*

[1] The Pakistani President's November 29, 1960, letter to Eisenhower is in WHCF/ OF 181-A. Aziz Ahmed, Pakistan's ambassador to the United States (1959–1963), had been educated at Punjab and Cambridge universities. He would later serve as the secretary-general of the Ministry of Foreign Affairs.

[2] For background on the Algerian rebellion see no. 1525. Khan had told Eisenhower that he felt the conflict between Algeria and France had worsened since April 1959, when he had offered to help negotiate a peace settlement. The Communist influence in Africa would expand, he feared, if the conflict continued.

[3] Kahn had written that the Soviet and Chinese Communists had offered aid to Algerian nationalists. He warned the President that if the Algerian nationalists succumbed to Communist propaganda, a situation similar to that which had developed in Southeast Asia might arise, allowing the Communists to establish a firm foothold in Africa. The Communist countries, he said, would "only be too glad to exploit the situation to their advantage and to the loss of the free world."

[4] Although Khan appreciated the efforts of de Gaulle to work out a settlement, he thought that a policy of self-determination was "possibly the only means of resolving the issue peacefully." Pakistan, he wrote, was allied with France and the free world through SEATO, but it also shared common bonds of religion with Algeria.

[5] For background see State, *Foreign Relations, 1958–1960*, vol. XIII, *Arab-Israeli Dispute; United Arab Republic; North Africa*, pp. 687–711). That summer de Gaulle had unsuccessfully attempted to negotiate a settlement with representatives of the Algerian national front. While the French President promoted a policy of Algerian self-determination in the hope that Algeria would remain formally linked with France, neither proponents of complete independence nor those who desired full Algerian integration with France favored his proposals. De Gaulle, however, would hold secret negotiations with liberationists through the end of 1960 even as violent conflict between various opposing factions continued (*Algeria: A Country Study*, edited by Harold D. Nelson [Washington, D.C., 1986], 4th edition, pp. 65–77).

[6] Khan had asked Eisenhower to use his "good offices and influence" to press the French government for early settlement of the issue (Khan to Eisenhower, Nov. 29, 1960, WHCF/OF 181-A Algeria).

[7] In his speech de Gaulle had invited the leaders of the Algerian rebellion to negotiate peace and self-determination. He had appealed to French voters to support his policy in an upcoming referendum, which would, if passed, provide Algeria with provisional autonomy in preparation for ultimate self-determination (*New York Times*, Dec. 21, 1960). In January 1961 French voters would approve de Gaulle's proposals (*Algeria: A Country Study*, pp. 65–67). Algeria would gain its independence in 1962.

To Charles Erwin Wilson

Dear Charlie: I can well understand that the editorial from Barron's Financial Weekly, which you were kind enough to send me, pleased you; it does me, too, of course, and gratified me highly that one publication, at least, appreciates the results of our efforts in the Defense Department these past eight years.[1]

To the best of my knowledge, I have not met Mr. McNamara, but I trust Henry Ford's ability to spot good men,[2] and I am hopeful that he will continue the Defense policies started by you and carried on by Neil McElroy and Tom Gates.[3]

With best wishes for the holiday season to you and Jessie, and warm personal regard, *As ever*

[1] Former Secretary of Defense Wilson had sent a copy of "Salute to the Pentagon," the lead article of the December 10, 1960, edition of *Barron's National Business and Financial Weekly* (Wilson to Eisenhower, Dec. 20, 1960, same file as document). The article maintained that the Eisenhower Administration was providing incoming Secretary of Defense, Robert Strange McNamara, appointed on December 13, with armed forces and a defense establishment that were "second to none." *Barron's* concluded that although Eisenhower had inherited a "faulty strategy" and an "obsolete military force" from his predecessor, Wilson and his "able" successors had built and maintained a powerful military establishment that was efficient, effective, and technologically advanced. "In the past eight years each branch of the service successfully has undergone a change more sweeping and profound than anything in military annals."
[2] McNamara (A.B. University of California 1937) was president of the Ford Motor Company; Henry Ford II was its chief executive officer. Wilson had also sent Eisenhower a copy of the congratulatory telegram he had cabled MacNamara. He told the President that although he did not know McNamara well, his friends had spoken highly of him.
[3] Neil H. McElroy had been Secretary of Defense (1957–1959) and was currently chairman of the board of Procter & Gamble; Thomas S. Gates, Jr., had become Secretary of Defense in 1959.

To Christian Archibald Herter

Memorandum for the Secretary of State: There are a number of factual questions to which I should like to have brief written answers before January 20th.[1] In each case I should like a statistical answer rather than a dissertation on the subject. The first series are similar in character and pertain to those nations which have become independent since 1945. The factual data I should like to have is:

1. The date of each nation's independence.
2. Its exact political relationship to its mother country before independence.
3. The official name of the country and its capital.
4. The name of its current Prime Minister or responsible executive in the nation.
5. Population.
6. Principal product.
7. The amount and kind of aid we have extended to the nation since its founding.
8. Do we consider the head of government really and truly neutral, Western-oriented, or the opposite?[2]

*   *   *   *   *

B. I should like to have the statistics on and the amount of aid we have extended since January of 1953 to each of the Latin American countries.
1. Under what auspices was this aid extended—i.e., ICA, IMF, Ex-Im Bank, DLF, American Bank, World Bank? (I understand that under the recent five hundred million dollar authorization for social development, we have not yet extended any aid because of lack of appropriations).[3]
2. In the case of the South American countries I should like also to know the name of the chief executive officer as of the beginning of 1961.

*   *   *   *   *

C. I should like to talk to you about the possibility of providing me with a short final report from the State Department on its operations. I think that that part of it that is covered by Foster Dulles' term of office could be done in very brief fashion, but would, of course, refer to such matters as the Korean Armistice, the Geneva Accord on Viet Nam, the Formosa Doctrine, the Aswan Dam and Suez Canal difficulty, the Mid East Resolution, the Lebanon incident, the settlement of the early Iran difficulty with the expulsion of Mossadegh, the settlement of the Trieste matter, and an account of the Guatemala action of some years ago, so far as such a report would not violate basic security.[4]

*   *   *   *   *

D. Respecting your own tenure of office, I would hope that you could give me a fairly good account of our principal preoccupations, including our relationship to and support of the United Nations. I would be grateful if you can have your staff prepare such a paper and while for my personal use accuracy is absolutely essential, I would not expect any extraordinary amplification of detail. The document of which I am thinking would be something of an aide memoire. *As ever,*

[1] In response to the President's request, Herter would send Eisenhower three extensive reports entitled, "Information on Newly-Independent Countries," "Aid Extended to Latin American Countries and Names of Chief Executive Officers," and "Highlights in United States Foreign Policy 1953–1960" (Herter to Eisenhower, Jan. 15, 1961, AWF/Misc.: Miscellaneous-Future Reference).

[2] Herter would note that in regards to this item that it would be misleading to attempt to categorize the political orientation of the heads of government of newly-independent countries without elaborate qualification: for example, some leaders were antagonistic to their former colonizer, but were friendly to the United States; other leaders were oriented to the West, but their countries were not; still others professed neutrality, yet opportunistically accepted aid from both the West and the Communist bloc while seemingly favoring the Soviets. A few leaders, he said, were "truly neutral." Herter would offer to furnish a more detailed account of any individual leader at Eisenhower's request (*ibid.*).

[3] See no. 1644. The report on aid to Latin American countries would state that Congress had authorized $500 million for what came to be known as the Social Progress Trust Fund on September 8, 1960, and it was planned that the President's Budget for 1962 would request a supplemental appropriation for 1961 of $500 million in anticipation of the program (Herter to Eisenhower, Jan. 15, 1960, "Aid Extended to Latin American Countries and Names of Chief Executive Officers, Enclosure 2b, AWF/Misc.: Miscellaneous-Future Reference).

[4] On the Korean Armistice see Galambos and van Ee, *The Middle Way,* no. 345; on the Geneva Accords see no. 985; on the Formosa Doctrine see no. 1265; on the Aswan Dam and Suez Crisis see no. 1932, and on the Middle East Resolution (Eisenhower Doctrine) see no. 2155; on the Iran situation see no. 282; on the Trieste settlement see nos. 1060 and 1128; on the Guatemala coup see no. 965, all in *ibid.*; and on the Lebanon incident see no. 770 in this volume.

1743   *Gruenther Papers*

To Alfred Maximilian Gruenther   *December 26, 1960*

Dear Al: This note is addressed *only* to a score of my intimate friends.[1]

During my entire life, until I came back from World War II as something of a VIP, I was known by my contemporaries as "Ike."

Whether or not the deep friendships I enjoy have had their beginnings in the ante or post-war period, I now demand, *as my right,* that you, starting January 21, 1961, address me by that nickname. No longer do I propose to be excluded from the privileges that other friends enjoy.[2]

With warm regard, *As ever*

[1] See, for example, Slater, *The Ike I Knew,* p. 235.
[2] With this letter Presidential Secretary Ann Whitman would enclose a personal note,

wishing General Gruenther a successful 1961 and asking him to "watch over the President, please."

1744 *EM, AWF, Administration Series*

To WILLIAM PIERCE ROGERS *December 28, 1960*

Dear Bill: I appreciated very much the clarity with which you expounded for ⸱ your opinion on the unconstitutionality of the legislation that pɪ⸱. .ibits the Inspector General of the ICA to be paid except on condition that the President would turn over to the Congressional Committees every report, no matter of what character, submitted to him by that Agency.[1]

This incident impels me to ask you for a possibly less formal, but nevertheless accurate, statement as to your opinion of the constitutionality of laws which vest Executive powers in the independent Regulatory Commissions, whose members are not subject to removal by the President except for neglect of duty or malfeasance in office. As I understand it, Regulatory Commissions are supposed to be extensions of the Congressional function, but it seems to me that they get into the matter of Executive decisions frequently and therefore I should like to have your opinion on the matter. Of course, there are unquestionably precedents for such a study and I would be quite happy to have merely the opinion of some former Attorney General in the event that you agreed with it.

The same question arises respecting the so-called "Atomic Energy Act." In this case the Commission has certain authority to prevent the President from taking action that he may think necessary. If this statement is correct, then is the constitutionality of this provision of that Act also called into question?[2]

Again I request that you make your statement as informal and as brief as possible, consistent with accuracy. *As ever*

[1] On December 22, 1960, Attorney General William P. Rogers had written to advise Eisenhower regarding the President's authority to issue directives to the Secretary of State and the Secretary of the Treasury authorizing them to make available mutual security program funds for the expenses of the Office of the Inspector General and Comptroller (WHCF/OF 99-E). The question had arisen due to efforts by Virginia Congressman Porter Hardy, Jr. (Dem.), Chairman of the House Foreign Operations and Monetary Affairs Subcommittee of the Committee on Government Operations, to block funding for the International Cooperation Agency unless certain documents relating to foreign aid programs were made available to the Committee (see Hardy to Eisenhower, Oct. 17, 1960, *ibid.,* and State, *Foreign Relations, 1958–1960,* vol. IV, *Foreign Economic Policy,* pp. 547–48). On December 23, 1960, Eisenhower would issue a statement forbidding disclosure to Congress of certain documents relating to aid

to South American countries (see *Public Papers of the Presidents: Eisenhower, 1960–61*, pp. 881–83).
² Eisenhower may have been referring to the exchange of atomic energy information with foreign countries (see, for example, no. 1659). Rogers would reply that although many problems in this "complex" legal field were unresolved, the courts seemed to believe that a president retained substantial control—including the power to remove officials—over independent regulatory commissions if the functions at issue involved the exercise of executive authority, as opposed to quasi-judicial and quasi-legislative powers. Thus a president could, for example, remove a member of the Atomic Energy Commission if he refused to follow his directions in a matter involving "programs of international cooperation, both peaceful and military" (Rogers to Eisenhower, Jan. 13, 1961, Eisenhower Post-Presidential Papers, Principal File).

1745

EM, WHCF,
President's Personal File 1853

To LIVINGSTON TALLMADGE MERCHANT   *December 28, 1960*
Personal

Dear Livie: After writing the attached,¹ it occurred to me that you might be interested in one of the last conversations that I had with the late Foster Dulles. The subject under discussion was the logical successor to Foster as Secretary of State.

The obvious choice was, of course, Chris Herter. But the matter of his physical ability to carry on the task raised some grave questions in my mind. Three other individuals were thought of as possibilities. They were Secretary Anderson, Under Secretary Dillon and yourself.

While the reports from Johns Hopkins on Secretary Herter's physical condition came in with sufficient promptitude that I was never called upon to make a selection, I did want you to know that both of us felt that you, a career officer in the State Department, deserved just as much consideration as any other individual.²

I tell you this story only to give a specific illustration of the respect and admiration in which I have held you for years. *As ever*

¹ The day before, Eisenhower had written acknowledging Merchant's forthcoming resignation as Under Secretary of State for Political Affairs; Merchant had notified him that he would submit the formal letter to the President-elect on January 20, 1961 (Eisenhower to Merchant, Dec. 27, 1960, and Merchant to Eisenhower, Dec. 23, 1960, both in same file as document). Merchant had told Eisenhower that it had been an honor and privilege to serve under him, and that he would always remember the President's "many acts of consideration and thoughtfulness."
² See nos. 1137 and 1139 and Eisenhower, *Waging Peace*, p. 359.

To THOMAS KEITH GLENNAN   *December 29, 1960*

Dear Keith: Under your leadership, the National Aeronautics and Space Administration, since its inception on October 1, 1958, has compiled a record of achievement of which every American can be justly proud.[1] Therefore, while accepting your resignation as Administrator of NASA, effective January 20, 1961, I wish to express my thanks for the great contribution you have made.[2]

Our Nation's non-military aeronautical and space activities are vastly expanding human knowledge of phenomena in the atmosphere and outer space and applying this knowledge for the benefit of all mankind. The progress that is being made is striking testimony to your ability to quickly bring together an effective and dedicated staff, to plan an imaginative program of space exploration, and to implement this plan with vigor and determination.

In little more than two years NASA has successfully launched meteorological satellites, such as Tiros I and Tiros II, that promise to revolutionize methods of weather forecasting;[3] demonstrated the feasibility of satellites for global communications by the successful launching of Echo I;[4] produced an enormous amount of valuable scientific data, such as the discovery of the Van Allen Radiation Belts;[5] successfully launched deep-space probes that have established the greatest range over which man has tracked, and made gratifying progress toward the goal of manned space flights.[6]

Because of the organization and program you have helped to create, Americans can look forward to a remarkable future in space exploration. It is hard to realize—yet inexorably true—that the near future will hold such wonders as the orbital flight of an astronaut, the landing of instruments on the moon, the launching of the giant Saturn, and the reconnaissance of Mars and Venus by unmanned vehicles.[7]

As you return to private life, you carry with you my appreciation, respect, and friendship. I wish you a long, happy, and healthy future.

With warm regard, *As ever*

[1] See no. 780.
[2] Glennan had written on December 28, 1960, resigning as Administrator of NASA effective January 20, 1961, and describing the activities of NASA since its inception in 1958 (AWF/A). Eisenhower had also received letters of resignation from the Director of the Office of Civil and Defense Mobilization, Leo Hoegh (Dec. 28, 1960, AWF/A); Postmaster General, Arthur E. Summerfield (Dec. 27, 1960, AWF/A); the Administrator of Veterans Affairs, Sumner G. Whittier (n.d., AWF/A); and Secretary of Commerce Frederick H. Mueller (Dec. 30, 1960, AWF/A).
[3] On the launch of the 270-pound weather forecasting satellite Tiros I see *New York*

Times, April 2, 1960; on Tiros II see *ibid.*, November 23, 1960; see also Glennan, *The Birth of NASA*, pp. 109–12.

[4] Echo I, an inflatable satellite for global communications was launched on August 12, 1960 (see no. 780; see also *New York Times*, Aug. 13, 1960, and Glennan, *The Birth of NASA*, pp. 204–5).

[5] Van Allen radiation belts, doughnut-shaped zones of highly energetic charged particles trapped at high altitudes in the magnetic field of the Earth, were named for James Alfred Van Allen, the American physicist who discovered them in 1958.

[6] Within NASA, the Space Task Group had been placed in charge of the manned space flight program, Project Mercury, in November 1958 (see Watson, *Into the Missile Age*, pp. 398–400).

[7] The first Saturn rocket would be launched in January 1964 (see *New York Times*, Jan. 30, 1964). The Saturn would eventually be used to land men on the moon, an endeavor whose wisdom Eisenhower doubted; see NSC meeting minutes, December 21, 1960, AWF/NSC; Glennan, *The Birth of NASA*, pp. 292, 308, 312–17; Sylvia Doughty Fries, *NASA Engineers and the Age of Apollo* (Washington, D.C., 1992); and McDougall, *The Heavens and the Earth*, pp. 301–24.

1747   ·   *EM, AWF, DDE Diaries Series*

To Urbanus Edmund Baughman   *December 29, 1960*

Dear Chief Baughman: Before I leave office I want to express to you the personal gratitude that Mrs. Eisenhower and I feel, as do John and Barbara, for the splendid service all members of the White House Detail of the United States Secret Service have given us these past eight years.[1] Without the help of Jim Rowley and his assistants, we could not, of course, possibly have performed our official duties or, indeed, enjoyed any degree of private life.[2]

We are especially indebted to you for the efficiency with which you have supervised and directed the many activities of the White House Detail having to do with the protection and safety of the entire family, including most particularly our grandchildren.[3]

With warm personal regard, *Sincerely*

[1] On the President's esteem for the United States Secret Service Chief and his department see no. 711.

[2] On this same day Eisenhower would write a second letter to Baughman, again expressing appreciation for the services of James J. Rowley, Head of the White House detail, and for Rowley's principal subordinates, and the agent who served as Eisenhower's personal bodyguard. On December 30 the President would thank each of the men directly and would write a third letter to Baughman acknowledging the unique tasks performed by his personal bodyguard. All correspondence is in AWF/D.

[3] In 1953 four Secret Service agents were assigned to protect the Eisenhower grandchildren. By 1961 the "diaper detail" had grown to almost a dozen men (see John S. D. Eisenhower, *Strictly Personal*, pp. 170–72; Galambos and van Ee, *The Middle Way*, no. 246; no. 121 in these volumes; and Susan Eisenhower, *Mrs. Ike*, pp. 291–92).

To William Alton Jones

Dear Pete: The teacher at the Indian school in South Dakota—whose story you already know—came in today with two pupils (together with some of the Indian boys who were in the East visiting the home of a chaplain at the school). The two girls, as you know, made this visit to the Eastern seaboard by reason of your generosity. I have had them photographed and if the picture turns out well, I shall send you a copy to remind you of the great appeal we found in the teacher's request for help on behalf of her students.[1]

I am counting on seeing you the weekend of the seventh. If Mamie's "house settling instincts" force me to go to Gettysburg as one of her assistants during that weekend, I think we could still work out a little bridge and, if the weather will only moderate, do a little skeet shooting.[2]

Incidentally, I stopped for a few minutes at the farm the other day and in one of the pastures I counted eleven pheasant walking around in the snow—also a covey of quail.[3]

With warm regard, *As ever*

[1] The President and Jones had been in Augusta, Georgia, when they learned of Virginia L. Horger's October 15 letter to Eisenhower requesting help in obtaining travel assistance for two of her students. Horger, who taught twelve-year-old girls at St. Elizabeth's School for Indian Boys and Girls in the Standing Rock Indian Reservation in Wakpala, South Dakota, had wanted to take the girls to her parents' home in Virginia for the Christmas holiday. The Under Secretary of the Interior, feeling that Horger's letter had "sufficient appeal" and was "so obviously sincere" that Eisenhower might want to sign a reply personally, had forwarded it to the White House (see Bennett to Goodpaster, and draft reply, Nov. 8, 1960). "A week in a warm home where love and the Christmas spirit dominate might do more good than years of merely talking about what and why they should learn," the teacher wrote. "I weep when I think of sending them to their huts where it is impossible to understand and appreciate Christmas as it should be." On November 17 Presidential Secretary Ann Whitman had written Horger that the President's friends had offered to help. The following day Eisenhower had signed, but did not send, a staff-drafted letter that explained that although he had been impressed by her work, no governmental agency could appropriately help her. Although Jones had offered to provide the girls' round trip airfare, Horger had decided to drive East in an effort to reduce costs. Jones then provided return transportation to South Dakota. The President contributed $50 to the project (see Whitman to Horger, Nov. 17, 28, 1960, and Whitman to Akins, Nov. 18, 20, 1960; Horger to Whitman, Nov. 21, 1960; and Whitman to Jones, Nov. 28, 1960).

On December 29 Eisenhower would meet with Horger and the members of her party in the White House. The teacher would thank the President on January 3. All papers are in the same file as the document.

[2] The Eisenhowers would spend January 4 in Gettysburg preparing for the move to their farm following President-elect Kennedy's inauguration (see no. 1633). On January 7 the President would fly to Fort Gordon, Georgia, to bid farewell to the Army

and receive his last review as President. He would spend the remainder of the weekend playing golf in Augusta. Jones would not accompany him (see *New York Times*, Jan. 5, 8, 1961, and Slater, *The Ike I Knew*, pp. 239–41).

[3] See Galambos and van Ee, *The Middle Way*, no. 1885.

1749

EM, AWF, International Series:
Macmillan

To HAROLD MACMILLAN   *December 31, 1960*
Cable. Secret

Dear Harold:[1] Your cable on the Laotian situation puzzles me because of your statement that we have been following diverging lines of effort. Certainly we agree with you that Phouma should resign, and it has been my understanding that some representatives of your government were undertaking to bring this about.[2]

At the same time we have been bringing to bear all the influence we can muster to get parliamentary approval of Boun Oum's claim to recognition as the head of the constitutional government. He has seemed resistant.[3]

Conversations with the State Department confirm that my understanding, as indicated above, is also theirs.

So far as the question of the International Commission is concerned, I have understood that Boun Oum and his associates have been firmly, up until this moment, opposed to its return to Laos.[4] In any event, it would be difficult for me to see how the International Commission could be helpful to us and to our side before Boun Oum's position had been certified as legal by his Parliament.

This morning it appears quite likely that this whole matter has been overtaken by events. Fragmentary reports are to the effect that the North Vietminh are invading Laos to help the Pathet Lao and that Chinese troops may have been parachuted into the area. These reports, if true, put the whole matter on a much more urgent basis than heretofore. For my part I cannot see any course other than supporting the King and Boun Oum and their government with every immediately available resource, in the meantime continuing efforts to make clear the legitimacy of the Boun Oum position.

I heartily agree with all you say about the need for unity, and you know how earnest have been my efforts to achieve it in all our relations. Indeed a vital factor in my decision in the troublesome question of voting for or abstention in the matter of the Asia-African resolution was that in such a welter of conflicting considerations the need for us standing together was of the utmost importance.[5]

I feel that all of us who see the dangers in a Laotian invasion should immediately make our intentions to oppose the move clear to each other and before the world and each of us move rapidly to do his part so that our essential unity cannot be questioned.[6]

Happy New Year! *With warm regard*

[1] Several drafts of this message, with Eisenhower's handwritten emendations, are in AWF/I: Macmillan.

[2] For background on the tangled Laotian situation see no. 1320. Although the conflict in northern Laos had remained fairly quiet during the last part of 1959, political antagonisms between the Laotian King and its prime minister had resulted in a government takeover (Dec. 30) by the Royal Laotian Army. Attempts to unify the various anti-communist factions had failed, and another coup in August 1960 had resulted in the installation of Souvanna Phouma, a neutralist leader and former prime minister, as the new prime minister. Pro-Western Boun Oum, a pretender to the throne of the Kingdom of Southern Laos, became Secretary of State for National Defense. General Phoumi Nosavan, a leader in the December 1959 coup, had immediately asked for U.S. aid in overthrowing the new government. The American ambassador to Laos had recommended that the U.S. accept Souvanna Phouma as prime minister and work toward a reconciliation with Phoumi. The CIA, the Joint Chiefs of Staff, and the Defense Department, however, all viewed Souvanna Phouma as a Communist sympathizer and opposed the ambassador's proposal.

In September Boun Oum and Phoumi Nosavan began a revolt against the Souvanna Phouma government, and by December Souvanna had been forced to flee to Cambodia. The factions began fighting for control of Vientiane, the governmental capital, and American personnel were evacuated from the embassy compound. In an attempt to stabilize the situation the King had appointed Boun Oum as head of a provisional government—one that the United States could support.

On this last day of 1960 State and Defense Department officials had reported to Eisenhower that forces from North Vietnam, supplied by airdrops from the Soviet Union, were moving into Laos, while two columns of Pathet Lao insurgents were converging on Vientiane, threatening to cut the country in half. Eisenhower stated that although he needed more information before authorizing military intervention, it might soon be time to employ the Seventh Fleet and its force of Marines against the Communists. The most important considerations, he said, were to pressure the Laotian parliament to legitimize the Boun Oum government and to solidify allied support for the U.S. position. "If war is necessary, we will do so with our allies or unilaterally, since we cannot sit by and see Laos go down without a fight" (State, *Foreign Relations, 1958–1960*, vol. XVI, *East Asia-Pacific Region; Cambodia; Laos*, pp. 708–1029, *passim*, and Microfiche Supplement; Synopses of State and Intelligence Material Reported to the President, July–Dec., 1960, AWF/D; NSC meeting minutes, Mar. 17, July 21, Aug. 16, 25, Sept. 12, 15, 21, Oct. 6, 18, 24, Nov. 2, 8, Dec. 8, 21, 29, 1960, AWF/NSC; *U.S. Department of State Bulletin* 43, no. 1109 [September 26, 1960], 499; see also Herter to Eisenhower, Dec. 8, 1960, AWF/D-H; Telephone conversation, Eisenhower and Herter, Nov. 21, 1960, Herter Papers, Telephone Conversations; Eisenhower, *Waging Peace*, pp. 607–10; Macmillan, *Pointing the Way*, pp. 329–33; and Bernard B. Fall, *Anatomy of a Crisis: The Laotian Crisis of 1960–1961* [Garden City, N.Y., 1969]).

Macmillan had written that he was "disturbed" that for the first time in many years U.S.-British policies "although of the same strategic purpose," had been "a little divergent on tactics." He supported proposals meant to persuade Souvanna Phouma to resign and to convince Boun Oum to seek parliamentary sanction for his gov-

ernment. The first step, he said, was "to get established a proper legitimate government" (Macmillan to Eisenhower, Dec. 30, 1960, AWF/I: Macmillan).

[3] Eisenhower had originally added the sentence, "He has seemed stubbornly reluctant" but changed it in a subsequent draft. He had also eliminated a sentence he
had previously included: "Incidentally, we have had some indication that his reluctance is based upon a doubt that Parliament would endorse him."

[4] The International Commission for the Supervision and Control of the Armistice in
Laos (ICC), composed of Canada, Poland, and India, had been established as a re-
sult of the 1954 Geneva Accords (see Galambos and van Ee, *The Middle Way*, no. 873).
With the establishment of a Laotian coalition government in 1956, the power of the
ICC had been greatly reduced and its mission was terminated in July 1958 (State,
Foreign Relations, 1955–1957, vol. XXI, *East Asian Security; Cambodia; Laos*, pp. 577–
78, 860–61, 1045; State, *Foreign Relations, 1958–1960*, vol. XVI, *East Asia-Pacific Region; Cambodia; Laos*, pp. 475–76).

[5] On the Asian-African resolution see no. 1730.

[6] For developments see no. 1752.

1750   *EM, AWF, DDE Diaries Series*

TO EARL MARVIN PRICE   *December 31, 1960*
Personal

Dear Earl: Thank you for your letter—it was nice to hear from you
again.[1]

Of course I have made mistakes, many of them. But I have tried
always to do what I thought at the time was in the national good.
And, I might add, I think the middle-of-the-road is still the only constructive policy for dealing with human concerns of vast proportions. Balance in the whole is far more important than pressure in
any part.[2]

Happy New Year. *As ever*

[1] Eisenhower's West Point classmate owned Earl M. Price and Company, an office
supplies firm, in Bakersfield, California (for further background see Chandler, *War
Years*, no. 2059). He had written that he and his family had felt as proud of Eisenhower's "beautiful sense of modesty" as they had of his many successes (Dec. 27,
WHCF/PPF 175).

[2] Price had criticized the President for having been "a wee bit too careful not to rock
the boat," and added that he thought Eisenhower had taken the middle of the road
when an "audacious rightward turn would have been better."

To CHARLES DOUGLAS JACKSON   *December 31, 1960*
Personal

Dear C.D.: I, too enjoyed greatly our chat the other day.[1]

It was something of a jolt to me to find, in your letter of the 28th, a suggestion of personal disappointment in the event that I should do any magazine writing for any publication other than LIFE. It had not occurred to me that any such project could really have a personal angle, based upon a friendship that I have long valued.[2]

Doug Black has, of course, been one of my close friends since 1947, when he undertook the publication of a book I wrote.[3] It has been only natural therefore that over the years he has from time to time suggested the interest of Doubleday in any post-governmental writing I might do. He was always quite well aware of the fact that other book publishers occasionally made similar suggestions. However, he never put his own proposals in any urgent tones; rather he put them on the basis of "we are here if you would like to talk to us."

In casual conversations I told him of my boyhood devotion to the SATURDAY EVENING POST. I was a steady reader of it during all my youthful years. Consequently, when there arose in conversation the possibility of my doing anything—outside the book area—it was only natural that I should think and talk a little about that publication.

In 1948 Mr. Black decided the best combination for publishing "Crusade" would be a Doubleday-Herald Tribune Syndicate. This time I think he felt that a combination of book-weekly magazine would be better. Indeed, I informed him that I would not write directly for any newspaper.

Some time back there finally began to be a series of suggestions made to me, but to all I replied that I was not ready to make any specific agreement or sign anything on the dotted line.[4] For example, Harry Luce suggested the matter a year or so ago and very recently let me know that his interest in it had not flagged.[5] In the meantime, I told Doug Black to explore in preliminary fashion such arrangements as would seem desirable to him. During the course of this time I talked to Mr. Hibbs, and received from a number of publishing concerns expressions of interest, some in general, others in specific terms.[6] Being preoccupied with official matters and recoiling from any prospect of involving myself in "looking for the best bargain" and getting somewhat sick of the whole business, I finally told Black I would conform to any informal arrangements that he might deem satisfactory. Naturally I would and have not signed any official document, but am personally committed as indicated.

In putting all these facts before you (at least as I know them), I have two reasons:

(*a*) to assure you that it never occurred to me that any friend of mine could have such a deep personal interest in any writing I might do that I ran the risk of hurting his feelings because of failure to confer with him;

(*b*) that just as in 1948, I wanted to avoid any involvement in a commercial competition for any writing I might produce.

As I told you the other day, it is my impression that the Doubleday-Saturday Evening Post combination has reached the point of a clear, even though informal understanding—to exist as along as both sides are completely happy with the venture.[7] *As ever*

P.S. Happy New Year

[1] The President had met with former Special Assistant Jackson on December 27. On Jackson's departure from the White House in 1954 see Galambos and van Ee, *The Middle Way*, no. 663.

[2] Eisenhower had decided to publish his memoirs with Doubleday and Company and contribute articles to the *Saturday Evening Post*; see nos. 1624 and 1650. Jackson had become publisher of *Life* magazine in April (see no. 1513).

[3] Eisenhower is referring to his World War II memoir, *Crusade in Europe* (see no. 1643).

[4] See, for example, nos. 1418 and 1643.

[5] See nos. 1424 and 1737.

[6] Hibbs was editor of the *Saturday Evening Post* (see no. 1624).

[7] The President's choice of Doubleday would be announced on March 27 (*New York Times*, Mar. 28, 1961). In 1963 the first volume of Eisenhower's memoirs, *Mandate for Change*, would be published. The second volume, *Waging Peace*, would appear in 1965. Although the *Saturday Evening Post* would not publish Eisenhower's presidential memoirs in serial form, it would print an article by the ex-President in May 1961. The *New York Times* would publish excerpts from the first volume of Eisenhower's memoirs in 1963.

1752
EM, AWF, International Series:
de Gaulle

TO CHARLES ANDRÉ JOSEPH MARIE DE GAULLE
Cable. Secret   *January 2, 1961*

Dear General de Gaulle:[1] The dangerously worsening situation in Laos leads me to write you.[2] The evidence is indisputable that the Soviets are conducting a massive air lift in support of the Pathet Lao and others in rebellion against the King of Laos. There is also growing evidence of substantial intervention of indeterminate proportion from North Viet-Nam.[3] It is not my purpose to raise with you the legal niceties of the status of the Boun Oum government which, as you know, we have been urging to complete the final steps of applicable constitutional process.[4] What I do want to tell you is that we take most seriously this evidence of an effort by the Soviet bloc to bring the Kingdom of Laos under its domination and control. The United States takes very seriously its obligation under the SEATO Treaty as we assume you and the other parties do likewise.[5] It seems to me that this is a time when we should make clear to the other side that, whereas from time to time we may differ on tactics and methods, we are nevertheless at one and resolute in the face of any Sino-Soviet threat. I hope we can make this unity clear to the world.[6]

In closing let me say again how I admire your statesmanship and wisdom and courage in dealing with the terribly difficult problem of Algeria. We were proud to be of some assistance to you during the course of the debate in the United Nations General Assembly.[7] My thoughts are with you and my hopes that your leadership will prosper.

With warm personal regard, *Sincerely*

[1] State Department officials drafted this message to French President de Gaulle. A copy was sent to British Prime Minister Macmillan (see Herter to Eisenhower, Jan. 2, 1961, AWF/I: de Gaulle).

[2] For background on the situation in Laos see no. 1749.

[3] On this day Eisenhower had discussed with State and Defense Department officials the JCS and CIA reports that the planned offensive of the Boun Oum government forces against the Pathet Lao and other Laotian Communist forces had broken down and that the Soviet Union and North Vietnam were supplying the insurgents (U.S. Department of State, *Foreign Relations of the United States, 1961–1963*, 24 vols., Washington, D.C., 1988–, vol. XXIV, *Laos Crisis* [1994], pp. 1–4; and Goodpaster, Memorandum of Conference, Jan. 2, 1961, AWF/D).

[4] According to Secretary Herter the King of Laos, Savang Vatthana, had called a meeting in Vientiane of the Laotian assembly, purportedly to recognize the Boun Oum government (State, *Foreign Relations, 1961–1963*, vol. XXIV, *Laos Crisis* [1994], p. 1).

[5] For background on the Southeast Asia Treaty Organization see Galambos and van Ee, *The Middle Way*, no. 974. Although Laos had not signed the treaty, the signatories (the United States, the United Kingdom, France, Australia, New Zealand, the Philippines, and Thailand) had pledged to protect Laotian territory against aggression.

[6] On this day Eisenhower had stated that he was "very impatient" with the French on the Laos issue and had added: "The French: The older I get the more disgusted with them I am—not the French people but their governments. De Gaulle is as bad as any of the previous ones" (State, *Foreign Relations, 1961–1963*, vol. XXIV, *Laos Crisis*, p. 2).

[7] For background on the Algerian situation see no. 1740. The United States had abstained from a vote on a resolution recognizing United Nations responsibility in the promotion of Algerian independence. France had boycotted the two-week debate on the resolution, maintaining that the United Nations had no jurisdiction in France's internal affairs (State, *Foreign Relations, 1958–1960*, vol. XIII, *Arab-Israeli Dispute; United Arab Republic; North Africa*, pp. 709–18; *New York Times*, Dec. 20, 1960).

Although de Gaulle would agree that the situation was "fraught with danger for the future of Laos," he avoided a direct answer to Eisenhower's request for a display of Western unity. He blamed the disintegration of the Laotian government and the subsequent hostilities on the lack of a "precise and firm agreement" among the Western powers. De Gaulle added that he had appreciated American support in the United Nations during the debate on Algeria, which had "made clear the great necessity for concerted action on the part of our Governments" (de Gaulle to Eisenhower, Jan. 5, 1961, AWF/I: de Gaulle; and Stoessel to Goodpaster, Jan. 18, 1961, *ibid.*). For developments see no. 1756.

1753   *EM, AWF, Administration Series*

To Sherman Adams   *January 2, 1961*

Dear Sherm: Unfortunately I never had a chance to inspect the little Bavarian Church that intrigued you so much when you visited there some years ago. Actually my effort for this year's Christmas card was inspired by a picture post card that I picked up there.[1]

From someone visiting my office a few days ago, I heard that your book was to be published within the next month. If it is indeed true that your own work on it is finished, I can well imagine what a relief it is. I know you have had a tough job and I am sure it was a well worth while one. Naturally I am going to have a lively interest in reading it.[2]

I trust that you have enough New Hampshire snow this winter so that you and Rachel can indulge your passion for taking the slopes at breakneck speed. I am quite ready to follow your example in a trout stream, but I will be ——— if I am ever going to put on a ski that, in any event, looks to me more like a weapon of war than an item of sport.[3]

Give my love to Rachel and, of course, again a Happy New Year to you both. *As ever*

P.S.: I trust that the prognostications in your final paragraph will come true. At the very least, I am complimented that you believe so.[4]

---

[1] Former Assistant to the President Adams had written on December 26 that the church shown in Eisenhower's Christmas painting was in Ramsau, near Berchtesgaden. He had visited the site for more than an hour, he said, and it was one of the most enjoyable days he could remember. The President had often sent reproductions of his paintings as Christmas greetings during his Administration (see, for example, Galambos and van Ee, *The Middle Way*, nos. 1186 and 1617).

[2] For background on Adams's memoir see nos. 964 and 977. The book would be published as *Firsthand Report: The Story of the Eisenhower Administration* (New York, 1961).

[3] Since his resignation in 1958 Adams had managed a ski resort in New Hampshire. On the President's retirement later this month see no. 1633.

Adams had predicted that Eisenhower's accomplishments in "this great world transition" would "loom larger with the years."

1754   *EM, AWF, Name Series*

TO HOWARD McCRUM SNYDER, SR.   *January 2, 1961*

Dear Howard: I am grateful for your New Year's letter with the generous sentiments you so beautifully express.[1]

It goes without saying that so long as possible it would be a great comfort and convenience to Mamie and me for you to be in a position where we could confer with you on our health problems, which seem to recur more frequently than they did in our younger years. Whether or not we can make arrangements that would permit you to render this kind of service, of which we have been so appreciative, I do want you to know of my gratitude for your offer.[2] It would be fine if I knew of some way of whisking you and Alice around to my favorite shooting, golfing and fishing places.[3]

Again, Happy New Year, and warm regard, *As ever*

[1] Snyder had written December 31 to express the gratitude he felt as a result his "privileged association" with the President (AWF/N).
[2] Eisenhower's personal physician said: "It is hoped that an office can be established that will make it possible for me to keep astride the advances in medicine, and that I will be always available for service to you should you need or wish it." See also Eisenhower's final report to the Secretary of the Army on Snyder's professional and personal qualifications (Jan. 20, WHCF/OF 101-O). In May Snyder would be awarded the Legion of Merit (see no. 1609).
[3] Snyder had accompanied the President on many vacations (see, for example, *New York Times,* Jan. 17, May 27, 1960). Snyder's wife was the former Alice Elizabeth Concklin.

1755   *EM, AWF, DDE Diaries Series*

TO HELEN N. HARRIS   *January 2, 1961*
Telegram

Please assure all the signers and endorsers of the message that I received this morning that it is a bright spot in a day that is darkened by Laos, packing and snow that prohibits a journey to a golf course.[1] Mamie and I send to all of you our very best wishes for a Happy New Year, a message that is in this instance endorsed by Ann Whitman, Jim Hagerty, Howard Snyder, Moaney and Delores.[2]

[1] Mrs. Harris was the secretary at the Augusta National Golf Club. The New Year's greeting that she, members of the staff at Augusta, and several of the Eisenhowers' friends had sent on December 31 is in WHCF/PPF 31-A. The Eisenhowers would relocate to their Gettysburg home on January 20 (see no. 1633). On the worsening situation in Laos see no. 1752.
[2] These were Presidential Secretary Ann Whitman, Press Secretary James C. Hagerty, and Presidential Physician Howard M. Snyder. Sergeant John A. Moaney and his wife Delores were the Eisenhowers' personal aides.

1756   *EM, AWF, International Series: Nehru*

To Jawaharlal Nehru   *January 3, 1961*
Cable. Secret

Dear Prime Minister:[1] A new and tragic chapter in the brief history of Laos as an independent nation has begun with the continuing air delivery of sizeable quantities of munitions and military supplies by the Soviet Union to Pathet Lao rebel forces and by substantially increased assistance to those forces, in both materiel and personnel, from north Viet-Nam.[2] I am deeply troubled by the renewal of fratricidal warfare in this small and weak but strategically important Kingdom, whose only "offense" is geographical: it lies in the path of Communist expansionist intent in Asia, and is perhaps the most vulnerable spot on the entire periphery of the communist-controlled Eurasian land mass.

Concerned as I am by this renewed crisis in Laos, and knowing that you greatly share in that concern, I am moved to write to you in utmost frankness about my views of developments there, about the objectives of our efforts there, and about what are *not* our objectives. I know that there may be little if anything new to you in the facts I shall present, but I want very much to let you know my thinking on their implications for all of us.

Our policy with respect to Laos is consistent with our policy elsewhere in the world. We hope Laos, like other nations, will have an opportunity to develop in peace and freedom its fullest potential. It is obvious that Laos cannot be a threat to any of its neighbors—least of all to its two militarily strong communist neighbors.[3] It is equally obvious that our presence in Laos is no threat to anyone. We have no military bases there, and seek none. We do not seek to have Laos join SEATO or any other alliance.

We have no quarrel whatsoever with a neutral policy for Laos, so long as the Lao Government desires it. We do, however, have our own grave reservations as to the threat to Laos caused by bringing into the Government communist-indoctrinated elements having the support of, and very probably under the guidance and direction of, outside communist powers, who also have the direct support of armed dissident elements within the country who are supplied and led from the outside. This, we believe, might well prove as disastrous to Laos as it has to other erstwhile independent nations. The conditions which now confront us result from the fact that the Pathet Lao have never observed the spirit and intent of the Vientiane accords of 1957, which attempted to absorb these Pathet Lao elements into the national life of Laos.[4] There is ample evidence that the Neo Lao Hak Zat did not function as a political party only. It served as a vehicle for the communists' enhanced political potential while retaining the military potential of the Pathet Lao forces.[5] This military potential was later greatly expanded. Throughout the life of this struggling new nation nothing has posed any threat to it except communist-directed efforts to take it over. Efforts to attain this objective have gone on through the years, and a major source of their support has finally been most dramatically revealed through large-scale and continuing Soviet air drops to the rebels.

Our efforts in Laos have always been in support of the King and his Government. We supported Souvanna Phouma during the time he headed the Government, even though the lessons of Lao history over several years caused us to doubt the wisdom of many of his actions, and we felt certain that he would never be able to negotiate successfully a settlement with the communists short of virtually complete capitulation. We carried out our aid to Laos in accordance with his wishes and with his express permission. Even during extremely critical days we ceased, on November 30, all military supply under the existing military assistance agreements, in accordance with his wishes; we did not resume such support until the newly established government requested resumption on December 16.[6]

I am mindful of the fact that our respective Governments have not always advocated the same approach, perhaps due to our somewhat varying assessment of the predatory nature of the communist threat, but we have constantly worked for the same goal—the continued independence of Laos. I am sure you will agree that a communist bloc victory in the present hostilities would be a matter of grave concern to both our countries. It would, of course, extend the eastern prong of the pincers with which the Sino-Soviet bloc would like to envelop the Subcontinent, and would bring the security of the rest of the free Southeast Asian countries, four of whom border on Laos, into serious question.[7]

Since the USSR, for one reason or another, is providing strong military support for a drive to bring Laos under communist rule, this may be a new indication of their objectives: they may provide direct support for the Peiping regime's military pressure on other countries bordering on territory under its control. I find it impossible to reconcile the present actions of the USSR and their Chinese Communist and North Vietnamese partners in Laos with the professed desire of the USSR for a peaceful world. If Mr. Khrushchev sincerely believes in "peaceful co-existence" he will withdraw USSR military assistance now being extended to communist-directed forces in Laos, and will exercise whatever influence he may possess to restrain his two partners.

We believe that the problem in Laos merits multinational attention. We would support an international control program which gave promise of insuring the security of Laos. I very much appreciated the interest evidenced by your Government's approach to us in connection with the ICC.[8] Our consistent policy has been to respect the position of the Lao Government on this question and we have outlined to you some of our reservations based on past performance in its areas of responsibility—due chiefly to communist-imposed restrictions on its functions and the blocking and delaying tactics of the Polish members.[9] I do not have a closed mind on this subject, however, and expect that our two governments will remain in consultation as to the advisability of some sort of ICC action.

Events may move rapidly in the next few days. It is impossible to say now just what the Lao situation will require.

I hope that we will keep in close touch concerning this situation, which is of such obvious concern to both of us. I hope you will let me have the benefit of your ideas. President-elect Kennedy is being provided with full information so that he can follow developments closely.[10]

With warm regard, *Sincerely*

[1] This message was drafted by State Department officials. Secretary Herter had told Eisenhower that a personal communication to the Indian prime minister regarding U.S. objectives in Laos "could be extremely helpful" (Herter to Eisenhower, Jan. 3, 1961, AWF/I: Nehru).

[2] For background on the situation in Laos see no. 1749.

[3] The reference is to Communist China and North Vietnam.

[4] In August 1957 the Laotian government had reached an agreement with the Pathet Lao insurgents that called for ending the hostilities, holding further elections, and forming a united government (for background see State, *Foreign Relations, 1955–1957*, vol. XXI, *East Asian Security; Cambodia; Laos*, pp. 906–8, 912–22).

[5] The reference was to the political arm of the Pathet Lao.

[6] See State, *Foreign Relations, 1958–1960*, vol. XVI, *East Asia-Pacific Region; Cambodia; Laos*, pp. 978–82, 1012–13.

[7] Burma, Cambodia, South Vietnam, and Thailand shared a common border with Laos.

[8] On the International Control Commission, made up of representatives from Canada, India, and Poland, see no. 1749. India, the Soviet Union, and all of the Communist bloc countries had proposed and supported the reactivation of the commission (State, *Foreign Relations, 1958–1960*, vol. XVI, *East Asia-Pacific Region; Cambodia;*

Laos, p. 1026; see also State, *Foreign Relations, 1961–1963*, vol. XXIV, *Laos Crisis*, pp. 4–5).

[9] In his January 11 response Nehru would blame the Laotian conflict on the deactivation of the ICC. "There was no check," he wrote, "to the ambitions of the rival groups which were often encouraged and aided by outside agencies." Arms were being supplied to both sides in the conflict, he maintained, and he recommended that the commission be reestablished to deal with the problem (Nehru to Eisenhower, Jan. 11, 1961, AWF/I: Nehru).

State Department officials would find Nehru's response "curt, captious and unforthcoming." "Its coolness (as contrasted to the warmth and detailed nature of the President's letter), its failure to address itself to most of the substance of the letter, and its equation of the 'two sides' in Laos, approaches being insulting." No written response would be forthcoming; the department would instead instruct the American ambassador to speak personally with Nehru. "This would put our point of view on the record and, more importantly, require Nehru to speak to our views rather than to ignore them as he did in the written exchange" (Merchant to Herter, Jan. 13, 1961, AWF/I: Nehru).

[10] Eisenhower and Kennedy, with their top advisors, would discuss the Laotian situation on January 19 (see State, *Foreign Relations, 1961–1963*, vol. XXIV, *Laos Crisis*, pp. 19–20). For developments see no. 1775.

1757   *EM, AWF, Name Series*

To ROBERT WINSHIP WOODRUFF   *January 3, 1961*
Top Secret. Personal.
Confidential. Eyes only

Dear Bob: I wonder whether you share my feeling of amazement—coupled in my case with some sadness—to witness what I think of as a constant deterioration in the tone of Ralph McGill's writings. I always thought of him as one of the ablest and keenest newspaper men that I had known. He has a great sensitivity to trends and tides, and has always seemed courageous enough to buck them when they were not the ones that he particularly wanted to ride. Naturally there have been times where I have disagreed with him—and in such cases he had his say and I had none. Nevertheless I have continued over the years to like and respect his work.[1]

Now it seems to me that he has sold himself on a naive belief that we have a new genius in our midst who is incapable of making any mistakes and therefore deserving of no criticism whatsoever. It appears as if he has almost adopted a cult, surrendering completely his own critical ability and his power of analysis.[2] He has spoken in glowing terms of Soapy Williams[3] (I assume you have your own judgment on that appointment) and he has hailed the assembly of brains with which the President-elect is to be surrounded.[4] I think he is possibly correct in his high opinion of Rusk. Everything I have heard about that individual seems good.[5] But when you have a menagerie in the State Department comprising one individual who is no less than a crackpot, another noted for his indecisiveness, and still another of demonstrated stupidity, and, finally, one famous only for his ability to break the treasury of a great state, it is very difficult for me to share Ralph's high opinion—either political, economic or social—of such a group.[6]

It would be interesting to know whether Ralph would like to be a Chairman of a Board in which he had the new Secretary of Labor, the Secretary of Agriculture and the Attorney General. At least he could call them three of a kind—so defined by their common lack of experience or anything that would enhance the confidence of the American people in their future operations.[7]

The two or three fine individuals soon to be appointed, serve to emphasize the need for more.

I do not want you to think that I could not go on for two or three hours in expressing my complete lack of enthusiasm for the majority of the recent appointments. My sole purpose was to grieve a bit over a change that I believe I see in an individual for whom I had the greatest admiration and to wonder whether you perceive anything of the same trend.

Please give my best to Miss Nell; I had a lovely note from her (as I did from you) the other day; both I deeply treasure.[8]

With all the best to yourself, and looking forward to shooting with you later in the month, even if I have to do so left handed,[9] *As ever*

P.S. Thanks for the article on "The Quail Hunter." I might add that he is also always very profane when the dog breaks the point.[10]

---

[1] On Eisenhower's opinion of editor and publisher McGill see no. 1670. Since the November presidential election, McGill had regularly praised the incoming Kennedy administration in his front-page, daily column in the *Atlanta Constitution*.

[2] The source of Eisenhower's irritation is not difficult to locate. McGill had criticized the Eisenhower Administration for its lack of "boldness and innovation," adding that it tended to "wait until the fat was in the fire before trying to prevent its being placed there again." Kennedy, in contrast, was likely to be a "strong President," who would "use the powers of his office," and would "move boldly to rally public opinion behind him so as to bring Congress along. . ." (*Atlanta Constitution*, Dec. 5, 9, 1960).

[3] Eisenhower was referring to Gerhard Mennen Williams, Governor of Michigan from 1948–1960, whose family had been involved in the manufacture of toiletries. Kennedy had announced Williams's appointment as Assistant Secretary of State for African Affairs on December 1, 1960 (*New York Times*, Dec. 2, 1960).

[4] See *Atlanta Constitution*, Dec. 22, 1960.

[5] Kennedy had announced the appointment of Dean Rusk as Secretary of State on December 12, 1960 (*New York Times*, Dec. 13, 1960). Eisenhower had served with Rusk in the War Department after World War II (see Galambos, *Chief of Staff*, no. 1421; see also Thomas J. Schoenbaum, *Waging Peace and War: Dean Rusk in the Truman, Kennedy, and Johnson Years* [New York, 1988], pp. 263–89). Praising the appointment, McGill had argued that a presidentially directed foreign policy, which he expected

from the new administration, would be an improvement over Dulles's reign during the Eisenhower years. Whereas Dulles had "irritated even those who respected him," the Kennedy staff was "better prepared to meet the demands of the sixties. It is not cast in the mould of the old style European diplomat" (*Atlanta Constitution*, Dec. 16, 1960).

[6] In addition to Rusk and Williams, Kennedy's appointments to the State Department included Chester Bowles as Under Secretary, George W. Ball as Under Secretary for Economic Affairs, Adlai Stevenson as Ambassador to the United Nations, and W. Averell Harriman as roving ambassador-at-large.

[7] Kennedy had appointed Arthur J. Goldberg as his Secretary of Labor, and Orville L. Freeman as his Secretary of Agriculture. He had named his brother, Robert F. Kennedy, as Attorney General.

[8] Eisenhower was referring to Woodruff's wife, Nell Hodgson Woodruff.

[9] Eisenhower had suffered from bursitis during his vacation in Georgia; see no. 1713.

[10] "What is a Quail Hunter?" by Charles Dickey lauded the "magical" qualities of the men who came "in assorted sizes" but shared the same creed: "To enjoy every second of every minute of every hour of every hunting trip—and to violently protest when the sun sinks beneath the horizon and it gets too dark to hunt."

1758   *EM, AWF, DDE Diaries Series*

To ROBERT MONTGOMERY   *January 3, 1961*

Dear Bob: My letter of July 3, 1958, which you have just returned to me, used incorrectly the expression "literary or dramatic rights to a story of my life." This expression seems broader in its implications than the arrangement that you and I had in view when we discussed the matter some time earlier.[1] In view of the probability that I may be, later this year, doing some writing myself, it would seem that a letter conveying to you certain rights and privileges as I described them in my recalled letter might also mean that any articles or book that I might produce would be subject to this same understanding.[2] Consequently I am rewriting the original letter in an effort to describe more accurately what rights and opportunities I tried to offer; namely those involving the possible future presentation by moving pictures, the theatre or television of phases of my life. I dispatch the new letter along with this.[3]

With warm regard, *Sincerely*

[1] The letter is no. 766.

[2] On the President's decision to publish his memoirs see no. 1624.

[3] In the revised version Eisenhower would grant advance permission to Montgomery to undertake motion picture, theater or television projects. He would not give Montgomery permission to publish written documents based upon the President's writings or papers. Montgomery would, however, be able to inspect Eisenhower's personal papers and documents, as well as papers in the possession of the Eisenhower family. To produce or release any project of this kind, the President said, would re-

quire his cooperation and consent, or that of his surviving heirs—specifically Mrs. Eisenhower or Colonel John S. D. Eisenhower (Eisenhower to Montgomery, Jan. 3, 1961, AWF/D).

As it turned out, Montgomery would serve as one of Eisenhower's advisers with the television networks. In the fall of 1961 the former President would give two CBS television interviews about his Administration (*New York Times*, Oct. 13, and Nov. 24, 1961). Eisenhower would terminate the business arrangement with Montgomery in February 1964 (see the correspondence and related material in Eisenhower Post-Presidential Papers, Principal File).

1759   *EM, AWF, Administration Series*

TO CLARENCE DOUGLAS DILLON   *January 4, 1961*

Dear Doug: I agree with your conclusion that, in view of the new responsibilities you will soon assume, I should, as I now do, accept your resignation as Under Secretary of State, to be effective today, as you have requested. Even though there are still important matters devolving upon your office during the next two weeks, the future advantages of your having the time to work closely with Secretary Anderson in preparing for the orderly turnover of responsibility of the Treasury Department, can scarcely be overemphasized.[1]

In an earlier letter I have tried to express to you my deep appreciation of the great contributions you have made, both as the United States Ambassador to France, and later as our Under Secretary of State for Economic Affairs, to the solution of many difficult international situations.[2]

Respecting the appointment to the new post you are now to occupy, there are of course always some difficulties to be overcome when any highly placed officer of one Administration is called upon to serve immediately thereafter in one controlled by a different political party. But, I want to express the hope and equal confidence that, with your continued and urgent support of the sound fiscal and financial policies in which you so much believe, success in your new post will have a vital and favorable effect upon our nation and the free world.[3]

You are undertaking one of the most difficult tasks of the Government. It is filled with many responsibilities and challenges. The capacity of each of the free nations to meet its domestic needs and to sustain an appropriate portion of the common defense for an indefinite period requires the maintenance of a strong national and international financial structure. I know that you will dedicate your best efforts to that end.

You may be sure of my continued interest in the operations of the Treasury Department, and I look forward to a personal performance on your part fully as brilliant as that which has characterized your service of the past eight years.

Again, my thanks—and to you and your charming family I send my warm personal regard. *As ever*

₁ Dillon had tendered his resignation on December 21, effective at Eisenhower's convenience, in order to prepare for his duties as the new administration's Secretary of the Treasury. He told Eisenhower that he deeply appreciated the opportunity to have served under his "inspiring leadership."

[2] See no. 1732.

[3] On December 31 Eisenhower's longtime friend Clifford Roberts had called Eisenhower at the behest of their old associate Clarence Dillon, the Under Secretary's father (for background see Galambos and van Ee, *The Middle Way*, no. 34). The elder Dillon was upset by speculation that the appointment had caused a rift between Eisenhower and his son. Eisenhower told Roberts that he had recommended that Dillon should not accept the appointment unless Kennedy agreed to give him a free hand in presenting his policies to Congress. The President had also said that even though he had urged Dillon to decline the offer, he "had no right to pressure" Dillon. The President had promised Roberts that he would give Dillon a vote of confidence in his letter accepting Dillon's resignation. This letter would be released to the public (*New York Times*, Dec. 17, 1960, and Jan. 5, 1961). For background on Dillon's appointment see C. Douglas Dillon, "The Kennedy Presidency: The Economic Dimension," in *Portraits of American Presidents*, edited by Kenneth W. Thompson, 11 vols. (Lanham, Md., 1982–98), vol. IV, *The Kennedy Presidency: Seventeen Intimate Perspectives of John F. Kennedy* (1985), pp. 128–31.

1760   *EM, AWF, Administration Series*

To THOMAS SOVEREIGN GATES   *January 4, 1961*

Dear Tom: Many thanks for your note of December thirtieth and the copy of the Bolte Committee Report on officer personnel practices that it enclosed.[1]

It is obvious that the group has carried out a thorough and searching study, and has put forward specific, concrete proposals. This is exactly the type of thing I had in mind in my past discussions with you of just such a project. The Committee has made a major contribution in this difficult, important field—which cannot fail to have enduring value as a landmark for future policy and action.[2]

To you and Mr. Finucane, I extend earnest thanks for leadership in this whole endeavor. Through you, I send to the members of the Committee and to all others associated in the work sincere appreciation of their fine contribution.[3]

With warm regard, *Sincerely*

[1] Defense Secretary Gates had presented Eisenhower with the published report of the Department of Defense Ad Hoc Committee to Study and Revise the Officer Personnel Act of 1947 (Washington, 1960). Gates's letter and a copy of the report are in AWF/A. General Charles Lawrence Bolte (B.S. Armour Institute of Technology 1917) had chaired the committee. During World War II Bolte had served as Commander of the 34th Infantry Division. Following the war he served as the Director of the Plans and Operations Division, General Staff, Commanding General of the 7th U.S. Army in Germany, and Vice Chief of Staff. He had retired in 1955.

[2] The work represented five months of study by a committee of distinguished retired admirals and generals from all four services. The report, which Gates thought "might well be a decisive step toward more effective teamwork," covered the entire field of career management for officer personnel of the Armed Services on active duty. The committee believed "that all officers on active duty, whether Regular or not, should be treated with equality in their personal career patterns except insofar as their tenure requires differences in the management of their careers." Their recommendations called for equitable guidelines for promotions and for the discharge of officers who had been passed over for advancement after having completed specified years of service. Selection boards with uniform standards and procedures were to be established and most restrictions on procurement of Regular officers, except for graduates of the three military academies, were to be lifted. The committee also recommended that Congress establish a mandatory retirement age of 62, except for a small number of lieutenant generals, generals, vice admirals and admirals.

[3] Charles C. Finucane was Assistant Secretary of Defense for Manpower, Personnel and Reserve. No action would be taken on the Bolte Committee report during Eisenhower's Administration.

1761   *EM, AWF, Name Series*

To Clarence Francis   *January 4, 1961*
Personal

Dear Clare: Much as I would like to do anything that might be helpful to you in your present position, I simply cannot agree to anything that could have commercial value for any industrial firm.[1] I have been forced to decline many suggestions, most of them involving glittering offers of directorships with no duties, on the grounds that I have never allowed my name or picture to be used for any purpose that has any advertising value, except for charitable purposes.[2]

Nevertheless, I thank you very much for your thought and quite understand that you meant it in the most kindly way. But I am committed to adhering to a policy, the violation of which would cause me difficulty and embarrassment in the future.

With warm regard, *As ever*

[1] In a letter written on December 30 and addressed to Presidential Secretary Ann Whitman, Francis had offered to give the President a Studebaker car of his choice

(AWF/N). In exchange, the chairman of the board of Studebaker-Packard wrote, he desired a photograph of the Eisenhowers and their grandchildren in the car to be used in an advertisement.

[2] See, for example, no. 1639.

1762   *EM, AWF, DDE Diaries Series*

To Samuel Taliaferro Rayburn   *January 5, 1961*

Dear Mr. Sam: For the last time, as President, I wish you a happy and gratifying birthday, a sentiment in which Mamie wholeheartedly joins. Few Americans can point to such a richness of friends and to respect so universally felt, as you can on this anniversary. With a multitude of others I salute you as a distinguished public servant and devoted American.[1]

I add this more personal comment—that over these eight difficult but inspiring years your personal friendship and selflessness in cooperating in those things involving the vital welfare of our country have meant a very great deal to me. I know the new Administration will likewise draw liberally on your wisdom and character.[2] In that fact I find an abiding satisfaction.

May it be His will that you have many more birthdays, for our country's sake as well as for your friends.[3]

With warm personal regard, *Sincerely*

[1] Rayburn would celebrate his seventy-ninth birthday on January 6 (*New York Times*, Jan. 7, 1961). At its opening on January 3, the Eighty-seventh Congress had elected Rayburn as Speaker of the House for the tenth time.

[2] For background on the President's admiration for the Texas Democrat see no. 782. Democratic President-elect John F. Kennedy would be inaugurated on January 20 (see no. 1782 and *New York Times*, Jan. 21, 1961).

[3] Rayburn would reply on January 6 that he was grateful to have the respect of a man of Eisenhower's "high type and character" (AWF/D). The congressman would not complete his twenty-fifth term in the House of Representatives; he would die on November 16 (*New York Times*, Jan. 4, Nov. 17, 1961).

To Tunku Abdul Rahman Putra al-Haj   *January 6, 1961*
Secret

Dear Prime Minister: Thank you for your recent letter concerning your efforts to prevent further deterioration of the situation with respect to West New Guinea.[1] As you are aware, the United States shares your grave concern over this situation. We are most sympathetic with your continued efforts to reduce tension in the area.[2]

This Government will give careful and thorough consideration to your thoughtful suggestion that a United Nations commission be sent to West New Guinea.[3] There appear to be some difficult questions as to how such a commission would be constituted and what its terms of reference would be. Consequently, I am instructing Ambassador Byington to discuss this matter with you in the near future.[4] In the meantime, and having in mind the complexities involved, I believe it would be useful if representatives of the Department of State explored with your Ambassador in Washington some of the practical implications. If you are agreeable, I will request the Department of State to arrange for such a meeting.[5]

I am particularly glad that you are persisting in your attempt to seek an amelioration of the difficulties that have arisen over West New Guinea, and I wish you well in this endeavor.[6] *Sincerely*

---

[1] The letter from the Prime Minister of Malaya is in AWF/I. Relations between Indonesia and the Netherlands had deteriorated as a result of their dispute over ownership of West New Guinea. The Netherlands opposed Indonesian control but had promised the island a degree of self-determination. In August 1960 Indonesia had severed all diplomatic ties with the Netherlands and had accused the Dutch of reinforcing their military installations in West New Guinea. Rahman was concerned that Indonesia was preparing to use the military against the Netherlands to enforce its claim of ownership. President of Indonesia Achmed Sukarno had stated, Rahman said, that "before the cock crows next year Irian Barat [West New Guinea] would become part of Indonesia provided that the Indonesians were united." Rahman had heard that Indonesia's minister of national security and chief of staff was planning a visit to the Soviet Union to obtain arms and equipment, which in fact proved to be the case (*New York Times,* Jan. 8, 1961). For background see no. 662; State, *Foreign Relations, 1958–1960,* vol. XVII, *Indonesia,* pp. 551–70; and *New York Times,* August 17, 1960, and January 8, 1961.

[2] Meeting with Eisenhower and the Secretary of State in Washington in October 1960, Rahman had asked for support of his proposals for settlement of the dispute, which he had offered to help mediate. On December 6, however, Rahman had rescinded his offer, citing lack of cooperation from Indonesian officials (*New York Times,* Oct. 27 and Dec. 7, 1960).

[3] Rahman had complained that neither the Netherlands nor Indonesia were "serious" about reaching a settlement. Although he could "fully appreciate" the Netherlands' intention to follow a policy of self-determination for West New Guinea, the in-

habitants were not in a position to assume control of their country. The prime minister had suggested that the Netherlands government invite a U.N. fact-finding commission to visit West New Guinea and agree to abide by its recommendations. He had already sent a message to the Netherlands government, he told Eisenhower, and would welcome United States' assistance in persuading the Dutch to agree.

The Netherlands had already announced in November 1960 that it was willing to subject its policies to the scrutiny and judgment of the United Nations. On January 4, 1961, the Netherlands government had offered to let the United Nations investigate Indonesian assertions that the Dutch were preparing to attack Indonesia (*New York Times*, Nov. 3, 25, 1960, and Jan. 5, 1961).

[4] Homer Morris Byington (A.B. Yale 1930) had become U.S. Ambassador to Malaya in 1959, after serving as Minister Plenipotentiary at the American embassy in Madrid, Spain (1954–1959). He had been with the U.S. Foreign Service since 1930.

[5] The Secretary of State would suggest that Eisenhower's reply, drafted by the State Department, should be transmitted through the American embassy in Malaya and that instructions concerning further discussions with the Prime Minister should be sent later (Herter to Eisenhower, Jan. 4, 1961, AWF/I: Malaya).

[6] Rahman had said Malaya would do all it could to ease the situation, although tension was increasing. He predicted that unless some action was taken immediately by the Dutch, trouble would break out with disastrous consequences. This dispute would continue after the end of Eisenhower's Administration.

1764   *EM, AWF, Administration Series*

To Thomas Sovereign Gates   *January 6, 1961*

Dear Tom: On the successful discharge of the duties that you have borne, the safety of our nation has vitally depended. In accepting your resignation as Secretary of Defense, effective January 20, 1961, I assure you of my deep appreciation and admiration of the distinguished contribution you have made in carrying out this task.[1]

Today the United States has a military strength second to none, with the greatest striking power in our history. At the same time, provision has been made to see that this pre-eminence can be sustained in future years. In the building and maintaining of this deterrent power, the work of you and your splendid team of associates has been outstanding. But you have not only seen that our armed forces are well designed, fit and ready for their tasks; you have shown a keen understanding that we maintain these forces for purposes that are entirely peaceful—to preserve security, justice and freedom.[2]

In each of the offices you have held in this Administration, your service has been marked by fairness and open-mindedness in approaching your problems, as well as hard work and willingness to consider all points of view, coupled with decisiveness and good judgment. You have stood like a rock for honest judgments and responsible military programs against the unsound and spurious, from whatever quarter advanced.

I add one personal note. For a President, there is a special cause for gratitude when he can feel certain, always, of the unfailing loyal and able support of his chief lieutenants, as I do of yours.

I hope you will take with you, as your term of service ends, the satisfaction of a difficult, vital job always superbly done.[3]

My very best wishes to you and your family now and in the future, and my warm regard, *As ever*

---

[1] Gates's resignation letter, dated January 4, 1961, is in AWF/A. He had also sent a summary review of the activities of the Department of Defense for the years 1953–1960. Gates had told the President that his association with him had been uniquely rewarding. He thanked Eisenhower for his "selfless understanding and personal support," saying that the President had contributed to the nation's strong defense posture. The White House would release the summary and the texts of both letters (*New York Times*, Jan. 8 and 16, 1961).

[2] See no. 1741.

[3] Gates had served as Under Secretary of the Navy, 1953–1957; Secretary of the Navy, 1957–1959; Deputy Secretary of Defense, 1959, and as Secretary of Defense, 1959–1961. On January 18 Eisenhower would award Gates the Medal of Freedom for his contributions to national security (*New York Times*, Jan. 19, 1960). Gates would become President of New York's Guaranty Trust Company after the Administration's term ended. In 1976 President Gerald R. Ford would appoint Gates to lead the U.S. liaison mission to China.

1765   *EM, AWF, DDE Diaries Series*

To Katherine Boyce Tupper Brown Marshall
January 6, 1961

Dear Mrs. Marshall: This morning I was trying to send you, belatedly, a New Year's bouquet, but found that you were living in Pinehurst. I trust that the weather is fair and that your winter sojourn will be very pleasant.[1]

In a few days I leave this office and hope to spend about three months doing absolutely nothing. I have made no engagements and have even refused to consider any such until after June thirtieth.

While this is in the nature of a "goodbye" letter from me as President, I do want you to know that if I can be of any service to you at any time in the future, I would deem it an honor to have any such suggestion. Even though I shall be on the vacational period for the next few months, any letter addressed to me at Gettysburg, Pennsylvania, will find its way to me sooner or later. And I shall hope, of course, to be in touch with you from time to time in my new capacity as private citizen!²

With best wishes for your continued good health and, of course, the hope that 1961 will be kind to you.³ *Affectionately*

¹ General George C. Marshall's widow had been spending the winter at their home in Pinehurst, North Carolina (Communication from Sharon Ritenour Stevens, Virginia Military Institute, Aug. 3, 2000, EP).

² On January 23 the President would travel to Albany and Thomasville, Georgia, for hunting and quail shooting. On February 7 he and Mrs. Eisenhower would travel to Palm Springs, California, where they would remain until mid-April (*New York Times*, Jan. 24–Apr. 18, 1961).

³ Mrs. Marshall would thank Eisenhower for his "gracious and wonderful" New Year's greeting. She would add: "In this Republican town my stock has gone 'way up'" as a result of the President's demonstrated affection for her (undated, WHCF/PPF 182).

1766   *EM, AWF, Name Series*

To James Campbell Hagerty   *January 9, 1961*

Dear Jim: I accept, of course, your resignation as Press Secretary to the President, to be effective as of January twentieth.¹

You are much too generous in your letter in your references to my role as "teacher" in the affairs of government. I feel rather that you and I and other members of the Administration have worked together—and, I think, effectively—to do what we felt was right for the nation's good.²

In your important role, you have been invaluable to me. You have striven tirelessly to present to the public, through the various news media, an accurate and objective report of the activities of the President and of the White House. You have handled major news stories with understanding and intelligence. Your great knowledge of the technical aspects of the distribution of news has enabled the people of the country to get the broadest and most comprehensive coverage of events that has ever been possible, and you have, I know, won the plaudits of the Press Corps in so doing.

As you go into private life, you carry with you my best wishes for your success and happiness.³

With warm regard to you and to Marge.⁴ *As ever*

¹ Hagerty's resignation letter, dated January 6, 1961, is in AWF/N.

² Describing Eisenhower as his "constant teacher in the affairs of government," Hagerty hoped that he had absorbed to some degree "the great wisdom, forbearance, and understanding" that had always guided Eisenhower's actions as President of the United States (*ibid.*).

[3] Hagerty would join the American Broadcasting Corporation after the Administration's term ended. He would remain with ABC until his retirement in 1975.
[4] Marjorie Lucas Hagerty was the Press Secretary's wife.

1767   *EM, WHCF, Official File 99-G-1*

To Bal F. Swan   *January 10, 1961*
Personal

Dear Bal: There is no recommendation in the State of the Union message to the effect that there should be further taxation on Savings and Loan Associations and Mutual Savings Banks. I simply do not know how such an idea could possibly have originated.[1]

With warm regard, *Sincerely*

[1] Swan owned a ranch on the South Platte River near Denver. Eisenhower had been fishing there on July 29 (see no. 1596; for background on Swan see Galambos and van Ee, *The Middle Way*, no. 386). On January 5 (same file as document) Swan had written that he had heard rumors about the tax increases. Further taxing the savings and loans and mutual savings banks, he wrote, would harm an industry that has the responsibility of increasing the pace of housing activity.

For the President's Annual Message to the Congress on the State of the Union, transmitted January 12 to the House and on January 13 to the Senate, see *Public Papers of the Presidents: Eisenhower, 1960–61*, pp. 913–31.

1768   *EM, AWF, Administration Series*

To Barry Morris Goldwater   *January 10, 1961*

Dear Barry: Just a note to confirm our breakfast conversation to the effect that I shall be happy to speak at the May first Recognition Dinner for Republican Congressmen and Senators, about which I have your January second letter.[1] I must repeat that while I have consistently declined to consider any invitation for a public appearance during the first half of 1961, yet I feel that in view of your expressed desire for me to speak at that meeting, the occasion would be for me not only a personal privilege but a duty that I owe to my associates in our Party. Consequently, barring unforeseen circumstances, you can count on my presence.[2]

With warm regard, *Sincerely*

[1] Eisenhower, who had met with Goldwater on the day previous (President's daily appointments), had agreed to a request from the Arizona Senator. Goldwater was Chair-

man of the Republican Senatorial Campaign Committee; William Edward Miller, Chairman of the Republican Congressional Committee, had joined in making the request (Goldwater and Miller to Eisenhower, Jan. 2, 1961, AWF/A). The two men had told Eisenhower that every incumbent Republican senator had been reelected and two new Republican senators and twenty-one new Republican congressional representatives had won election. This victory, they suggested, could be repeated in 1962 with good organization, determination, and a strong financial position; they thought a recognition dinner would help to raise campaign contributions.

On this day Eisenhower would also write Miller that he had accepted the invitation (AWF/A: Goldwater Corr.). Miller, a congressmen from New York (B.A. Notre Dame 1935), would become Chairman of the Republican National Committee in 1961 and vice-presidential candidate in 1964. After World War II he had assisted the prosecution at the Nuremberg War Trials. In thanking the President, Miller would write that he and Goldwater believed that the only chance for rehabilitation of the party was complete unity within Republican ranks. If Republicans did not succeed in the congressional elections of 1962, the "presidential nomination might not mean much to anyone." Eisenhower, he said, was the only person loved and respected by all groups within the party, and only he could provide the leadership required to unify the Republicans (Miller to Eisenhower, Jan. 16, 1961, AWF/A: Goldwater Corr.).

[2] At the $100-plate fundraiser held on June 2, 1961, Eisenhower would discuss the "immoral" deficit spending of the Kennedy administration (*New York Times*, June 2, 1961).

1769   *EM, AWF, Dulles-Herter Series*

To Christian Archibald Herter   *January 11, 1961*

Dear Chris: As Secretary of State for nearly two years, and for the two years just preceding as Under Secretary, you have made a distinguished contribution, for which the people of our country have cause for deep gratitude.[1] As I accept your resignation, concluding your official service in this vital and important field as of January twentieth, I pay tribute to both your ability and devotion.[2]

Never have you lost sight of our main goals. First, of course, we have sought to stay at peace, and this we have done. I know you find deep satisfaction in this, just as I do.

Notwithstanding the periods of crisis and peril the years have brought—and will continue to bring—we have demonstrated our will for peace, while safeguarding security and furthering justice and freedom. Collective security arrangements have been maintained and strengthened, preserving free peoples against Communist encroachment and oppression. We have worked hard and long to bring under control the threat of nuclear war, through proposals for safeguarded international control measures, and patient and persistent negotiation to this end. We have sought to advance the use of the atom for peace. We have ranged our influence on the side of human dignity, and national and individual freedom and sought to achieve greater mutual understanding between the United States and other nations. We have helped other countries in the course of self-development through our mutual security programs and efforts. Despite all provocation and hostility, we have avoided being drawn away from our constructive efforts into a mere sterile struggle with the Communist bloc.

For the years that lie ahead, bound to be marked by grave and complex problems but bearing bright promise of progress, I know we both believe that the nation's best hope lies in continued pursuit of these objectives, and we both pray that our country may continue to march successfully toward them.

For your steady hand and wise counsel throughout our service together, and for the privilege I have had of working with you in close association, I am deeply grateful.

You have my best wishes for happy years ahead for yourself and your family.

With warm regard, *Sincerely*

---

[1] Herter had become Secretary of State on April 22, 1959, as a result of the illness and subsequent death of John Foster Dulles (see no. 1139).

[2] In his resignation letter Herter had told Eisenhower that the opportunity to serve under the President's leadership had been "an inspiring privilege." He had enclosed a summary of accomplishments effected during his and Dulles's terms in office (Herter to Eisenhower, Jan. 6, 1961, AWF/D-H).

1770   *EM, AWF, DDE Diaries Series*

To Paul Gray Hoffman   *January 11, 1961*

Dear Paul: I cannot leave the Presidency without giving to you some expression of my gratitude for the friendship and the help, both official and unofficial, that you have given to me so generously during the years. Beyond this, your record of public service is so impressive as to command the respect of any thinking American.[1]

I recall the time when you, a Republican, were called upon by a Democratic President to be the Administrator of the Marshall Plan, devised to restore the industrial capacity of Europe, broken by the war.[2] The present productivity of Europe is proof of the wisdom and energy with which you executed that Plan, and my admiration for your performance is enhanced by the fact that you carried it out in less time and with far less money than had been originally projected.

In another instance, your wisdom might be questioned, but not your energy and dedication, in your determination that I should stand for the Presidency. I have somewhat less than normal reason to congratulate you about this particular incident. I remember, of course, the intensive salesmanship that you used on me in the days when you felt I should become the Republican candidate, and I shall never forget your subsequent and tireless work as head of the Citizens for Eisenhower movement, in the fall of 1952.[3] Of course I pray that, in this, you have not been disappointed. But, the kind of work in which I have been engaged for these eight years will finally be evaluated by history; you and I do not have to worry ourselves too much about it.

Finally, I come to your work in the United Nations, especially in your Administration of the Special Fund. I have learned much about it both from you and from others, and again I not only applaud your achievements, but I sincerely hope that you will be permitted to carry on the work. I cannot believe that anyone else would be so well fitted for it.[4]

With my warm greetings to Dorothy and, of course, all the best to yourself, *As ever*

[1] Hoffman, former chairman of the board of the Studebaker-Packard Corporation, had been an administrator of the Economic Cooperation Administration, a member of the U.S. delegation to the United Nations, president of the Ford Foundation, member of the Business Advisory Council of the Department of Commerce, and a trustee and board member of many colleges, universities, and corporations. Since 1959 he had been the Managing Director of the United Nations Special Fund for Under-Developed Countries (see also Galambos and van Ee, *The Middle Way*, no. 61).

[2] For more on the Marshall Plan see Galambos, *Chief of Staff*, no. 1482.

[3] See Galambos, *NATO and the Campaign of 1952*, nos. 410 and 740.

[4] For Hoffman's activities with the fund in 1960 see *New York Times*, March 16, May 26, November 1, 1960. He would remain in the position until 1966.

1771   *EM, AWF, Name Series*

To William Douglas Pawley   *January 11, 1961*

Dear Bill: I am returning to you the original letter you sent to me from your friend in Cuba.[1] In these waning days of the Administration, about all I could do was to send it along to the two Agencies most concerned (which I have done). I took care, of course, to remove all identifying material.[2]

With warm regard, *As ever*

[1] For background on the Cuban situation see no. 1726; see also State, *Foreign Relations, 1958–1960*, vol. VI, *Cuba*, pp. 1164–74, 1178–86. An unidentified Cuban had

told Under Secretary for Latin American Affairs Pawley that the government had nationalized 80 percent of the economy and 90 percent of the land. His country had become part of the international Communist system, with Russian ships delivering large quantities of weapons and ammunition. Cuba was now also a center for the dissemination of Communist propaganda and advice on waging guerrilla campaigns against other Latin American governments. Pawley's friend had asked for "rapid and strong action" and had suggested that the United States occupy Cuba (AWF/N).

On December 28 Pawley had reported to Eisenhower that the presidents of Argentina and Peru had taken strong anti-Castro stands. Many Latin American governments, however, believed that since Castroism had made great inroads among the poorer people, they would be overthrown if they took similar action. Eisenhower later stressed the importance of Latin American support for any actions taken against Castro's regime, and indicated that the United States should perhaps recognize the anti-Castro front as the Cuban government (Goodpaster, Memorandum of Conference, Jan. 6, 1961, AWF/D; see also State, *Foreign Relations, 1958–1960*, vol. VI, *Cuba*, pp. 1188–89).

[2] CIA Director Allen Dulles would generally concur with the appraisal given in the memorandum. He would, however, note that the analysis had tapered off and had ended inconclusively. "For this, however, I can hardly blame the writer as no one has found any easy solution" (Goodpaster to Allen Dulles, and Allen Dulles to Goodpaster, Jan. 12, 1961, both in AWF/N).

1772

EM, AWF, International Series:
Formosa (China)

To Chiang Kai-shek

Personal and confidential

January 12, 1961

Dear Mr. President: I have read with profound appreciation the kind sentiments which you have expressed in your letter of December fourteenth regarding my work and United States assistance to the Republic of China during the past eight years.[1] The close and fruitful relations that have existed between our two countries during this period have been a source of great gratification to me. As I made clear during my visit to Taiwan last June, I have been deeply impressed by the fortitude with which the Republic of China, under your dedicated leadership, has resisted Communist aggressive threats and pressures and by the energy and skill with which your Government has moved to promote the economic and social development of Taiwan.[2] I am proud that the United States through its military and economic assistance programs has been able to help the Republic of China develop its military and economic strength.[3]

I am pleased to know that discussions between representatives of our two countries have continued in Taiwan in pursuance of conversations in June and my reply to certain points raised by you at that time which was conveyed to you by Ambassador Drumright in

August. In this connection I am glad to tell you that, after careful consideration of your request for the delivery of several C-130 or other transport planes, I have authorized the delivery to your Government of one C-130B at this time.[4] You will appreciate, I am sure, that in view of the large number of countries which look to the United States for military equipment, as well as the requirements of our own armed forces, it is difficult to make immediately available to your Government more than one of these aircraft. However, if in the light of your experience with this aircraft it should become apparent that another of the same type could be effectively utilized, I am confident that the United States Government would give serious consideration to a further request from you.

In closing, I wish to reiterate my deep admiration for a staunch and courageous ally and my hope that the friendly ties that unite the Chinese and American peoples and the solidarity of our two countries will be strengthened even further in the future.

With the Season's Greetings, *Sincerely*

[1] Chiang's letter is reprinted in State, *Foreign Relations, 1958–1960*, vol. XIX, *China*, pp. 747–49.

[2] See no. 1571.

[3] See Burton I. Kaufman, "Eisenhower's Foreign Economic Policy with Respect to East Asia," in *The Great Powers in East Asia 1953–1960*, Warren I. Cohen and Akira Iriye, eds. (New York, 1990), pp. 104–20.

[4] On December 22 Secretary of State Herter had sent the President an initial draft reply to Chiang's letter, expressing regret that it was not possible to grant his request due to the "complex and lengthy nature of the aid-scheduling process" (Herter to Eisenhower, Dec. 22, 1960, AWF/I: Formosa [China]). On January 4, however, Herter had sent Eisenhower a revised draft reply. The Secretary of State noted that the Bureau of Far Eastern Affairs and other government agencies had altered their opinions and now recommended supplying a large-capacity transport aircraft to the Republic of China. The President signed this second draft and sent his reply to Taipei by telegram on this same day.

1773   *EM, AWF, Administration Series*

To Gordon Gray   *January 13, 1961*

Dear Gordon: In accepting your resignation as my Special Assistant for National Security Affairs, effective January 20, 1961, as you request, I thank you not only for your outstanding service in this and earlier assignments, but also for your clear and thoughtful observations concerning the National Security Council.[1]

You have been almost uniquely in position to know its value to me and to the vital work of assuring our country's security now and in the future. The Council itself has admirably fulfilled its function of advice and counsel at the top echelon of government, with thorough, searching and far-ranging debate and deliberation upon the great issues of U.S. national security. In addition, the Council has, as you say, served as the "capstone of mechanisms for assisting you in the formulation of policy and in assuring the timely and effective implementation of policy decisions taken by you." I am especially grateful for your report because somehow, despite our previous efforts, our people have not received an accurate and valid appreciation of the National Security Council's effectiveness—in which you and your predecessors, as well as your staff, have had such an important part.[2]

But my appreciation to you does not stop with your current contributions to the work of the National Security Council, nor even with your previous distinguished service in prior positions. Over the whole wide range of security affairs, it has been a great help to me to have had, as one of my closest associates, a man of your wise understanding, integrity and dedication to our nation's interests. I deem myself, and our country, indeed fortunate.

To you and your fine family I extend my best wishes for happy and rewarding future years.

With warm regard, *Sincerely*

[1] Gray had submitted his resignation to Eisenhower on this day and had included a laudatory history of the NSC, its planning board, and the Operations Coordinating Board under Eisenhower's Administration (see Gray to Eisenhower, Jan. 13, 1961, AWF/A). Before taking office as Eisenhower's Special Assistant for National Security Affairs in July 1958, Gray had served as Assistant Secretary of Defense and Director of the Office of Defense Mobilization.

[2] An earlier draft of this letter had contained this sentence: "Such an appreciation is all the more necessary at a time when this structure is bound to be reviewed and reevaluated." The sentence was deleted before the President signed this letter. Some prominent Democrats had expressed criticism of the NSC's organization and operations (see nos. 1211 and 1724). President Kennedy would make substantial changes in the NSC's structure and procedures; see Prados, *Keepers of the Keys*, pp. 92–103.

1774   *EM, AWF, Name Series*

To Lionel Hastings Ismay   *January 13, 1961*

Never shall I tire of seeing your handwriting—and I hope that you will find it possible to be in touch with me even more frequently than has been possible these past eight years.[1]

You are characteristically understanding of the emotions that crowd my mind these days. I appreciate beyond words your comments concerning what I have tried earnestly to do. The verdict on my efforts will of course be left to history, and I don't have to worry about it now—but it is wonderful to know of your approval.[2]

With affectionate regard to you and to your Lady.

[1] Ismay had apologized for writing frequently, but said it was the President's own fault for being so kind to him (Jan. 6, 1961, AWF/N). For their recent correspondence see, for example, nos. 1697 and 1722.

[2] Noting that the President was coming to the end of a chapter Ismay had written that when Eisenhower left the White House there was "bound to be a pang." The sadness, however, would soon give way to "a sense of well justified pride and richly deserved relief." He commended the President's leadership and ability to keep the confidence and affection of the American people. He had no doubt of what the verdict of history would be.

1775

EM, AWF, International Series:
Cambodia

To Samdech Preah Norodom Sihanouk Upayvareach
Confidential   *January 16, 1961*

Dear Prince Sihanouk:[1] I understand the concern expressed in your letter of January 1, 1961 over recent developments in Laos, and I fully share your distress over the tragic trend of events there.[2]

American officials have been in close touch with representatives of other interested countries, including your distinguished Ambassador at Washington, in a continuing effort to find a means of resolving the crisis.[3] Mindful of the urgent need to seek restoration of peace and to avoid any widening of the conflict, we have been giving careful thought to various proposals for a peaceful settlement. I believe our efforts to find a workable, peaceful solution are an important aspect of our intention to support the independence and territorial integrity of Laos by all possible means.

Your suggestion for convoking an international conference of interested countries again shows to me clearly the constructive spirit in which you approach this problem.[4] We are giving it serious study along with other proposals for international action, including your earlier plan for neutralization of Cambodia and Laos, which was discussed in some detail between representatives of our countries in New York and Washington.[5] American officials were impressed by the plan and offered suggestions and cooperation. Although events have moved rapidly in Laos since September, I believe we should not lose sight of certain elements in this earlier proposal when considering the more recent suggestions. I have in mind that your proposal for specific steps went further than merely defining desirable goals; it incisively directed attention to the problem of devising practicable means of achieving these goals. In my opinion, the steps you outlined then still provide valuable guidance.

Our study of these various proposals is not yet completed nor, I believe, has the Royal Government of Laos yet definitively stated a position in this regard. Nevertheless, I assure you that my concept of the objectives to which any action should be directed corresponds closely to the thoughts expressed in your letter, namely that peace should be restored and the Lao people should be able to choose the political way of life it prefers, free of outside intervention aimed at compromising the independence and integrity of the Kingdom. Unfortunately, long and bitter experience has forced us to face the fact that we cannot rely merely on the promises, even the most solemn promises, of powers bent on expansion. In the case of Laos, I believe we cannot presume to gamble the freedom of the Lao people on the promises of Communist regimes which by repeated intervention there have demonstrated their intent to subjugate the Kingdom to alien domination. This brings us to the most difficult problem: how can reliable assurance be obtained that outside intervention, in all its insidious forms, will in fact be stopped? A realistic answer to this question is, I believe, the crux of the matter. Should you have any further thoughts on means of obtaining such assurance, I know they would be most helpful in view of your demonstrated knowledge, experience and understanding. I believe our Governments should continue to consult each other on this question.

Your comments regarding the economic burden placed on Cambodia by the influx of the refugees from Laos have prompted me to ask Ambassador Trimble to ascertain whether the United States can usefully make a contribution to the emergency relief of these individuals.

I should like again to thank you for your thoughtful message of December 30, and reiterate the satisfaction afforded me by our correspondence and especially by our personal meetings. I have always admired your insight, your devotion to the welfare of the Cambodian people and your dedication to the cause of world peace.[6]

With warm regard

---

[1] State Department officials drafted this letter to the Cambodian Chief of State.

[2] For background on the Laotian crisis see no. 1749. For recent confrontations between the forces of the Boun Oum government, which had been legalized by the Laotian parliament on January 3, and Communist rebel groups see Synopsis of State and Intelligence Material Reported to the President, Jan. 4, 9, 1961, AWF/D; and State, *Foreign Relations, 1961–1963*, vol. XXIV, *Laos Crisis*, pp. 5–11.

Sihanouk had commented on the Laotian refugees, whose numbers when added to those from South Vietnam had compromised the country's five-year plan for economic development. He had called for a conference of the signatories of the 1954 Geneva Accords and the countries that had participated in the International Commission for the Supervision and Control of Laos. The proposed conference, he wrote, should also include the United States (which had not signed the 1954 pact) and those countries sharing a common border with Laos (Sihanouk to Eisenhower, Jan. 1, 1961, AWF/I: Cambodia).

[3] See nos. 1749 and 1752. Nong Kimny, a member of the Cambodian administration since 1932 and former chief of the King's Cabinet, was the Cambodian ambassador to the United States.

[4] Secretary Herter had told Eisenhower that he believed that Sihanouk was "genuinely concerned" with the effect on his country of the Laotian conflict, and he did not think they should reject the proposal outright (Herter to Eisenhower, Jan. 13, 1961, AWF/I: Cambodia).

[5] Sihanouk had proposed a "neutralized belt," consisting of Cambodia and Laos, to be supervised by a commission of neutral countries that would assure nonintervention. Herter had told Eisenhower that although the proposal "did not coincide fully with U.S. views, it reflected a more realistic appreciation of the practical problems involved" (*ibid.*).

[6] State and Defense Department officials from the Eisenhower Administration would meet with their counterparts in the incoming administration on this day to discuss the Laotian conflict. Eisenhower would meet with President-elect Kennedy on the same subject on January 19 (see State, *Foreign Relations, 1961–1963*, vol. XXIV, *Laos Crisis*, pp. 12–25).

1776

*AWF, International Series:
Nepal*

To Mahendra Bir Bikram Shah Deva   *January 16, 1961*
Cable. Confidential

Your Majesty: Thank you very much for your letter of December 22, 1960, in which you are good enough to describe conditions which prompted you to dispense with parliamentary government.[1]

As you know, I shall return to private life in the very near future. I shall, however, continue to follow with lively interest the progress of friendly relations between our countries, and the development of the body politic in Nepal. As a citizen of a nation which has, I believe, demonstrated the many advantages of a broadly-based representative government, I am gratified to know that in your proclamation of December 26 you announced your determination to further the consolidation of the foundations of democracy. I shall therefore watch with profound interest the steps taken to evolve a stable, democratic system of government in Nepal.[2]

I can assure you that I share your hope that friendly relations between our countries will continue to grow closer and stronger; and I sincerely hope you will share your thoughts and aspirations with my successor.

With all good wishes for your good health, and with warm regard, *Sincerely*

[1] King Mahendra's letter is not in EM. On December 15 the King had dissolved the cabinet and suspended the parliament of Nepal. He had told the American ambassador that he had taken the step on his own responsibility with no outside influence because he believed the leaders "were guilty of corruption and of aiding and abetting Communism." He reaffirmed his belief in democracy and expressed his desire to continue friendly relations with all countries, including the United States. He added that he intended to appoint a Council of State, which would form a new government to run Nepal until the country was ready for a parliamentary rule (NSC meeting minutes, Dec. 21, 1960, AWF/NSC; and State, *Foreign Relations, 1958–1960*, vol. XV, *South and Southeast Asia*, pp. 612–14).

[2] On December 26 King Mahendra had appointed himself chairman of a new council of ministers. He had announced that "he was determined to save Nepal 'from corrupt practices and insure smooth working and resuscitation of the democratic system in times to come.'" On January 6 he had stated that he would "try to instill a 'new awareness' in the people through a system of 'guided democracy'" (*New York Times*, Dec. 27, 1960, Jan. 6, 1961).

1777   *EM, AWF, DDE Diaries Series*

To JOSEPH HOWARD McCONNELL   *January 16, 1961*

Dear Joe: For almost eight years I have lived in ignorance of the identity of the individuals who so thoughtfully and kindly provided the means by which was built the house at Augusta, now known as Mamie's Cabin.[1] But now that my tour in the Presidency is ending, Cliff has agreed to give me the names of the donors so that I might, even after this long delay, express, in some measure, the gratitude my wife and I feel to each of you.[2]

The house has enabled Mamie and me, when in Augusta, to entertain good friends in a family atmosphere and, when we so chose, to live in complete privacy. The consideration of the group in assuring that the house would be available to us through our lifetime, rather than merely during my service as President, doubles its value to us, particularly on the sentimental side.

I shall hope, at some future time, to have an opportunity to thank you more intimately and personally. But I did not want to leave this office without making a written record of my gratitude. Incidentally, you will find along with this letter a picture of Mamie and me standing in front of the Cabin.

Cliff has informed me that he is trying to arrange one weekend in the late spring when we might gather at Augusta for a real get-together. I am asking him to delay making any firm plans until I can straighten out my affairs as I undertake the job of living as a private citizen. This I have not done in half a century. But I will let him know the prospects as soon as I can.[3]

With warm regard, *As ever*

[1] For background on the house, overlooking the fairways at Augusta National Golf Course, see Galambos and van Ee, *The Middle Way*, no. 480.
[2] Cliff Roberts was chairman of the executive committee at Augusta. The President would write thank-you letters to all fifty-six people named on Roberts's list (the list is in AWF/D).
[3] Eisenhower would spend the weekend of May 4–7 at Augusta (*New York Times*, May 5, 1961).

1778   *EW, WHCF, Confidential File: CAB*

To WHITNEY GILLILAND   *January 18, 1961*

Memorandum for the Chairman, Civil Aeronautics Board:[1] After considerable deliberation I have concluded that the recommendations of the Civil Aeronautics Board in the *Trans-Pacific Route Case, Docket 7723 et al.*, should, with minor exceptions set forth at the end of this memorandum, be disapproved.[2]

When I requested in February 1959 that this proceeding be undertaken by the Board, I sincerely hoped that it would be possible at the conclusion of the case to provide greater competition among United States flag carriers in the Pacific.[3]

The study made by the Board is excellent. Much evidence is set forth in support of the Board's recommendations for additional United States flag service on major routes to the Orient. My decision not to approve the Board's principal recommendations is predicated solely on considerations of foreign policy, a responsibility that is mine and which the Board, of course, does not share.

My review of the record in this case persuades me that our foreign relations would be adversely affected were we at this time to add second carriers on our major routes to the Orient. Duplication of service on major routes presently served by a single carrier means inevitably—as history shows—that greater United States flag capacity would be offered. This result is made all the more certain by the advent in recent months of jet service which in and of itself means greater capacity because much larger and much faster aircraft are involved.

Greatly increased capacity—always of considerable concern to other nations engaged in international commercial aviation—should not in my judgment be approved unless traffic forecasts for the routes in question plainly show that the additional capacity can be absorbed without engendering a legitimate fear abroad that United States flag carriers will collect so much of the traffic as to make service on the route by a foreign carrier economically untenable or marginal at best. The evidence in the case at hand, including particularly the traffic forecasts does not establish the circumstances I have described. It is reasonable, therefore, to predict that approval of the Board's major recommendations in this case would unsettle our international relations—particularly with Japan which would be faced with an additional United States carrier on all but one of the now existing four routes from the United States to Tokyo.

For these reasons I have concluded that the Board's major recommendations should be disapproved, but I recommend to the Board that within the next several years it update the evidence in this case and again consider the addition of second United States flag carriers on major routes to the Orient.

The Board in the Mainland-Hawaii part of this case has concluded that another airline—until now a carrier engaged solely in service on the North American continent—should be authorized to provide service between San Francisco and Los Angeles and Honolulu. Due to the advent of Hawaii as a State, the President, under the law, no longer has jurisdiction over service between the Mainland and Hawaii. It would be my hope, however, that the Board would reconsider its decision to authorize additional service between the Mainland and Hawaii by a carrier which heretofore has not been engaged in service over the Pacific. At some future time it may be deemed advisable from every standpoint to add a second United States carrier on the California-Hawaii-Tokyo route. The carrier selected—which would presumably be a carrier customarily engaged in international commercial aviation in the Pacific—should also be authorized to carry local traffic between the Mainland and Hawaii. To do otherwise would be to handicap such a second carrier in terms of its ability to compete with the carrier now serving this route to the Orient, a carrier which already has full traffic rights between the Mainland and Hawaii and which is thus able materially to support its overall route to the Orient.[4]

Those of the Board's recommendations that I do approve are (a) the renewal for an indefinite period of Northwest Airlines' authority to serve Okinawa, Korea, Taiwan, Hong Kong, and the Philippines; (b) the renewal for an indefinite period of Pan American World Airways' authority to serve Japan, Viet Nam, Singapore, Sumatra, Java, Federation of Malaya, Thailand, Burma, and points within

India and Pakistan lying north of the twentieth parallel; (c) the amendment of Pan American's certificate to redesignate Australia as an intermediate point and adding Java as a new intermediate point on its South Pacific route; (d) the renewal and amendment of South Pacific Airlines' certificate as recommended by the Board; (e) the amendment of Trans World Airlines' certificate as recommended by the Board; (f) the Board's denial of applications.[5]

[1] Eisenhower had appointed Whitney Gillilland Chairman of the Civil Aeronautics Board in April 1960 (*New York Times*, Apr. 22, 1960); Gillilland had been serving on the Board since the previous November. Before assuming his post on the CAB, he had served as Chairman of the Foreign Claims Settlement Commission. He had also been elected president of the Federal Bar Association in September 1959.

[2] For background see nos. 224, 315, and 573. The Civil Aeronautics Board had recommended that operation of parallel routes by Pan American and Northwest Airlines between the United States and Tokyo and other Far Eastern points was justified by present and potential passenger and freight traffic in the area (*New York Times*, Jan. 20, 1961).

[3] See Eisenhower to Durfee, February 18, 1959, WHCF/OF 62.

[4] The CAB had awarded Western Airlines a route between Los Angeles and San Francisco and Hawaii. Pan American Airlines had held a monopoly on this route up to this point. Eisenhower was presumably referring to Northwest Airlines as the second carrier then operating between California and Hawaii. The Board would comply with the President's request.

[5] The issues raised by Eisenhower would not be resolved during his Administration. In March the CAB would meet to consider reopening discussion of Pacific air routes (see *New York Times*, Mar. 12, 1961; see also Bender and Altschul, *The Chosen Instrument*, pp. 515–17).

1779   *EM, WHCF, President's Personal File 1940*

TO DAPHNE MOANEY   *January 18, 1961*

Dear Daphne: As one of my last letters from the White House I am, as I promised, replying to the questions you brought to me on behalf of the History Class of Montclair High School.[1]

Won't you please convey to all your classmates my greetings and best wishes for the future? *Sincerely*

Answers to questions submitted by the
History Class, Montclair High School

1. We have, it seems to me, two major—but indivisible—national purposes. One is to make sure that all the people of our country are enabled to live in freedom and in justice and in equality, under a progressive, but not a stifling, form of government. The other national purpose is the achievement of a just and durable peace in the world, in which all peoples may

be enabled to choose and sustain the kind of government that is best suited to their individual needs and aspirations.[2]

2. From the beginning of our Republic, there has been, domestically, a continuing struggle between those who believe in the continuation of progressive, responsible government with authority properly allocated to its several echelons, on the one hand, and, on the other, those who believe that strong, centralized political control of all governmental functions is best for our people and for the nation's economy. That struggle has been with me every day of the past eight years; it has manifested itself in every problem presented to me. Possibly the most difficult foreign problem was the Middle East situation in 1957.[3]

3. I shall always be ready to serve my country in any way that may seem appropriate.[4]

4. In the political or any other field, as long as I am able, I shall continue to fight for the principles and policies for which I believe.[5]

5. Mrs. Eisenhower looks forward, as do I, to a more private life than has been possible these past eight—indeed, these past twenty years.[6]

6. *Except in the most unusual circumstances,* I believe that no man should serve in the Presidency more than eight years. Aside from the obvious risks in permitting any individual to develop such a political machine, no one man should normally be expected, or allowed, indefinitely, to make the appropriate decisions in all the vital questions affecting our Nation. Because of our position in the world and our particular form of government, greater responsibility and heavier burdens devolve upon the President than upon any other officer in the world. Because of this, the factor of age can become important in selecting a president; a man should be neither immature on the one hand, or too much advanced in age on the other.[7]

7. I am going to enjoy the freedom that belongs to every private citizen.[8]

8. I regret that the Senators have moved. But I suspect that the new ball club that will be established in Washington will have at least one avid rooter in the Gettysburg area.[9]

9. The answer to question number nine is still classified as TOP SECRET.[10]

---

[1] Daphne Moaney was the daughter of the President's personal aide John A. Moaney. Eisenhower had met with the Moaney family on October 31 (see the Chronology for the names of the family members).

[2] Students from Daphne's school in Montclair, New Jersey, had asked Eisenhower to give his views on the "National Purpose" (see Daphne Moaney to Eisenhower, Oct. 28, 1960). See also Whitman to Daphne Moaney, November 13, 1960.

³ The second question was: "What do you think has been the most challenging incident that has presented its self [*sic*] during your term of office?"
⁴ The class wanted to know if Eisenhower would be willing to take special assignments
given him by President Kennedy.
⁵ This question concerned the President's plans regarding his involvement in party
politics.
⁶ Eisenhower had been asked about Mamie's feelings concerning the end of his public career.
⁷ The question was: "Considering your popularity, would you have been willing, if
the Constitution allowed it, to run again?"
⁸ The students had asked what Eisenhower was going to do after leaving the White
House.
⁹ This question concerned the President's thoughts about the departure of the Washington Senators baseball club to Minnesota, an event that had occurred after the
end of the 1960 baseball season. The new Washington Senators club, an expansion
franchise, would begin its first season in April 1961 (see Leonard Koppett, *Koppett's
Concise History of Major League Baseball* [Philadelphia, 1998], pp. 278—79).
¹⁰ The students wanted to know the score of the President's "best game of golf in the
last 8 years." All correspondence is in the same file as the document.

1780   *EM, AWF, International Series:*
                                                              Netherlands

TO JAN EDUARD DE QUAY   *January 19, 1961*
Cable. Confidential

*Dear Mr. Prime Minister:*¹ Thank you for your letter of January 6, 1961
concerning civil aviation matters which have recently been discussed
between our two countries.²

At the time that Foreign Minister Luns and I discussed the matter of a West Coast route for KLM, I indicated that the United States
would take another look at this sensitive question to see if some resolution could be achieved.³ However, during the examination of this
question, it became evident to us that other developments of tran-
scending importance were involved. Under the circumstances it was
found impossible to open negotiations with the Netherlands on these
civil aviation matters.

I deeply regret that we were unable to achieve a solution, especially because of the importance which I know you attach to this
matter. I have the highest personal regard for the Dutch people and
I hope you will appreciate the difficulties which made necessary the
decision not to undertake negotiations on your request. *Sincerely*

¹ State Department officials drafted this message, which was sent to the American
ambassador at The Hague for delivery to the Dutch Prime Minister. Secretary Herter
had recommended that the text should not be released to the media (Stoessel to

Goodpaster, Jan. 13, 1961; and Herter to Eisenhower, Jan. 18, 1961, both in AWF/I: Netherlands). De Quay, a former professor of business administration, had been minister of war in 1945. He had become prime minister in May 1959.

[2] De Quay's letter is in AWF/I: Netherlands. For background on Dutch interest in a west coast route for the Dutch airline KLM see no. 61. In January 1960 the two countries had met in Washington to discuss Dutch landing rights in Los Angeles. On February 3 the State Department had denied the Dutch request, explaining that KLM Airways had not offered anything in exchange; the decision had led to widespread indignation in the Netherlands. In April the Dutch government had told the United States that it would not acquiesce in the decision (*New York Times,* Jan. 7, 26, Feb. 5, 10, 12, Apr. 23, 1960).

[3] Joseph M. A. H. Luns had met with Eisenhower on October 7. According to Herter, the subsequent U.S. decision to cancel further talks was based on "the balance of payments problem and certain collateral steps taken by the United States in this regard." The Netherlands government was deeply disappointed over the U.S. decision not to reactivate civil air consultations, de Quay had written, and he did not believe that the decision was unavoidable due to the U.S. balance of payments problem. He had asked that the United States reconsider its decision and resume negotiations at an early date (de Quay to Eisenhower, Jan. 6, 1961, AWF/I: Netherlands). The CAB would deny West-Coast landing rights to KLM until 1962; see Straszheim, *The International Airline Industry,* pp. 13, 40.

1781   *EM, WHCF, Official File 5-F*

To John Edgar Hoover   *January 19, 1961*

Dear Edgar: But the "voice" of the FBI is an important one to me, both officially and personally! And to the rest of the country, too.

I am grateful for your letter. I admire the splendid performance of the whole organization which you head. And I have been impressed by and grateful for the prompt and thoughtful responses I have always had from you to any query of mine.

I repeat that my admiration of the work of the FBI is great. And I wish there were about a thousand J. Edgar Hoovers in key spots in the government![1]

With warm regard, *As ever*

[1] Hoover's letter is not in EM. Hoover had become the first director of the Federal Bureau of Investigation in 1924. He would remain in the position until his death in 1972.

To Richard Milhous Nixon   *January 19, 1961*

Dear Dick: I am replying to your letter of January fifteenth, not in the sense that in doing so I am putting a period to our long and satisfying association and friendship, but rather to thank you for the generosity of the sentiments you expressed.[1]

As you know, I am not an individual that accepts defeat easily. When I have to recognize a major setback, my sole reaction is to redouble effort in order to recover lost ground. In the November eighth election we, the Republican Party, endured such a setback. It was, however, not so much a blow to the convictions, policies and principles that we espouse as it was to our effort to awaken the American people to the importance of the issues raised and the advantage to the country of following Republican counsel.[2]

This conviction and this feeling will, I think, be expressed more and more emphatically and effectively as all of us in the Party, and those who, outside the Party, agree with us in the main, put our hands to the wheel and get the wagon rolling down to the wire in the fall of 1962.[3]

With such thoughts in mind I am sure that you and I will find many reasons, in addition to the personal, to confer together from time to time. I believe we not only should, but will want to keep our contacts on a fairly frequent basis.

On the more personal side, it has been a great satisfaction to Mamie and me to have the support and friendship of you and Pat during these eight years.[4] I have always felt a complete confidence in your ability and capacity for taking on the Presidency at any instant and, as you will recall, I have never, since 1953, allowed us to be found in any position where any single accident could take us both out of the current scene.[5] The passage of the years has taken me out, so far as active participation is concerned, but the future can still bring to you a real culmination in your service to the country.[6]

With affectionate regard to you and Pat, *As ever*

---

[1] Nixon had expressed gratitude for Eisenhower's leadership and for the privilege of serving as Vice-President. He had written: "Never in this nation's history has one man in public life owed so much to another as I owe to you."

[2] On the election of President-elect Democratic Senator John F. Kennedy and the Republican defeat in Congress (see nos. 1699 and 1700). On January 20 Eisenhower and Nixon would attend the inaugural ceremonies (*New York Times*, Jan. 21, 1961).

[3] On this same day Nixon would announce that he would join a Los Angeles law firm and would devote a substantial amount of time to efforts to build up the Republican party in California (*New York Times*, Jan. 18, 20, 21, 1961). In 1962 Eisenhower would urge Nixon to seek the California Republican gubernatorial nomination.

Nixon would win the nomination, but lose the election (see Ambrose, *Nixon*, vol. I, *The Education of a Politician, 1913–1963*, pp. 650–74, and Nixon, *Memoirs*, pp. 292–305).

[4] The Vice-President had written that he and Mrs. Nixon had appreciated the Eisenhowers' many gestures of friendship. For background on the Eisenhowers' relationship with the Nixons see, for example, nos. 476 and 1678.

[5] On Eisenhower's concern for an orderly transfer of power to the Vice-President in the case of presidential disability see no. 566.

[6] In 1968 General Eisenhower would endorse Nixon for the Republican presidential nomination. Nixon would win the election and would be re-elected in 1972. In August 1974 he would resign while the House Judiciary Committee considered impeachment proceedings. Eisenhower would remain active as an elder statesman until his death on March 28, 1969 (see Stephen E. Ambrose, *Nixon*, vol. III, *Ruin and Recovery, 1973–1990* [New York, 1991], pp. 422–45; John S. D. Eisenhower, *Strictly Personal*, pp. 328–37; Nixon, *Memoirs*, vol. II, pp. 647–55; and *New York Times*, Jan. 21, 1961, July 19, Oct. 28, 1968, Jan. 21, Mar. 29, 1969).

Outside the White House the First Lady with Arthur S. Flemming in connection with the Federal Service Campaign for National Health.

The President watches as Arnold Palmer tees off at the Gettysburg Country Club, September 9, 1960. At left is T. Richard Sleichter, the golf pro at the club.

The President poses with Cliff Roberts (*far right*) and professional golfers Ben Hogan (*left*) and Byron Nelson (*near right*) at the Augusta National Golf Club.

Eisenhower's painting of the "Old Barn."

Eisenhower greets President-elect John F. Kennedy at the White House, December 6, 1960.

Eisenhower meets with President-elect John F. Kennedy in the Oval Office, December 6, 1960.

Eisenhower meets with members of the Science Advisory Committee at the White House, December 19, 1960. Attending were John Bardeen, George Beadle, David Beckler, Detlev Bronk, Harvey Brooks, James Fisk, James Illian, George Kistiakowsky, Robert Loeb, Donald Nornig, Wolfgang Panofsky, Emanual Piore, I. I. Rabi, Glenn Seaborg, John Tukey, Alvin Weinberg, Jerome Wiesner, and Walter Zinn.

4

But each possible action must be weighed in the light of a larger

consideration: The need to maintain balance -- balance between the private

and the public economy, balance in the distribution of influence and power,

balance between the needs of the moment and the long-time welfare of the

nation.

I am satisfied that our people generally, as well as our government,

have done reasonably well in this regard in the face of constant stress and

threat, but I recognize that there are dangers. I mention only two, as

examples.

IV

Everyone recognizes that a major element in keeping the peace is

our military establishment. Our arms must be mighty, ready for instant

action, so that no potential aggressor may be tempted to risk destruction.

Our permanent military organization

that known by any of my predecessors in pea

fighting men of World War II or Korea.

Until the latest of our world conflicts

armaments industry. American makers of p

as required, make swords as well.

Now we can no longer risk emergenc

So we have created a permanent armaments

And we have three and a half million men an

defense activities. We annually spend on mil

income of all United States corporations.

5

This conjunction of an immense military establishment and a large

arms industry is new in the American experience. The total influence --

economic, political, even spiritual -- is felt in every city, every State

house, every office of the Federal government. We recognize the imperative

need for this development. Yet we must not fail to comprehend its grave

implications. Our toil, resources and livelihood are all involved; so is the

very structure of our society.

In the councils of government, we must guard against the acquisition

of unwarranted influence by the military-industrial complex. The potential

for the disastrous rise of misplaced power exists and will persist.

We must never let the weight of this combination endanger our

liberties or democratic processes. We should take nothing for granted.

Only an alert and knowledgeable citizenry can compel the proper meshing

of the huge industrial and military machinery of defense with our peaceful

methods and goals, so that security and liberty may prosper together.

Closely akin to, and largely responsible for the sweeping changes

in our industrial-military posture, has been the technological revolution

during recent decades.

In this revolution, research has become central; it also becomes

more formalized, complex, and costly. A steadily increasing share is

conducted for, by, or at the direction of, the Federal government.

Eisenhower's handwritten changes to his farewell address, warning of the dangers of the military-industrial complex, January 9, 1961.

Eisenhower finds time for painting during retirement at his farm
in Gettysburg, July 1966.

Eisenhower checks his brushes as he prepares to paint. Painting of Abraham
Lincoln in the background; on the easel, "The Fisherman."

Mamie and Dwight Eisenhower enjoy retirement on the porch at their farm in Gettysburg, 1966.

Bibliography:
Note on Primary Sources

The documents that appear in these volumes, as selected Eisenhower items or as sources for the information that appears in the annotations, have for the most part come from the extraordinarily rich collections housed in the Dwight D. Eisenhower Presidential Library in Abilene, Kansas. Most were culled from the Eisenhower Manuscripts, cited as EM in these volumes. The "Bibliography: Note on Primary Sources" in volume XVII of our series, which covers Eisenhower's First Administration, contains a description of EM's constituent files and a key to the abbreviations we use for them.

The smaller and richer of the two EM collections is the Ann Whitman File (Eisenhower's Papers as President), which we abbreviate as AWF. The most important collections in AWF are the DDE Diaries Series (AWF/D); the Dulles-Herter Series (AWF/D-H); the International Series (AWF/I); the International Meetings Series (AWF/IM); the NSC Series (AWF/NSC); the Administration Series (AWF/A); the Cabinet Series (AWF/Cabinet); the Legislative Meetings Series (AWF/LM); the Ann Whitman Diary Series (AWF/AWD); the Name Series (AWF/N); the Gettysburg Series (AWF/Gettysburg); and the Miscellaneous Series (AWF/Misc., an odd assortment of subject files covering unrelated topics). A separate group, the Microfilm Series (AWF/M), is not yet open to researchers and should not be confused with the commercially filmed series of the Ann Whitman File. The AWF Microfilm series comprises images from Ann Whitman's files as they were photographed in the White House periodically between 1955 and 1960. Among the relevant subsections of AWF/M are the Official Files (AWF/M: OF); the Personal Files

(AWF/M: Pers); the Geographic Files (AWF/M: G); and the Administrative and Personal Files (AWF/M: AP).

Far larger than the Ann Whitman File is the vast collection of Eisenhower's records as President, the White House Central Files (WHCF). This group includes the Confidential File (WHCF/CF), the Official File (WHCF/OF), the President's Personal File (WHCF/PPF), the General File (WHCF/GF), and the Alphabetical File (WHCF/Alpha). WHCF/OF and WHCF/PPF are especially rich sources for letters written to and by Eisenhower.

As was the case for volumes XIV–XVII, a number of collateral collections in Abilene also help to fill out the historical record of the Second Administration. Foremost among these are the papers of John Foster Dulles and Christian A. Herter, Eisenhower's Secretaries of State. The portion of the Dulles Papers most useful to us was the White House Memoranda Series, which includes general correspondence files and records of Dulles's meetings with Eisenhower. Other valuable sections contain memorandums of Dulles's telephone conversations as well as separate chronological and subject series. The Herter Papers also contains a rich series containing records of Herter's telephone conversations with the President.

The records of the White House Office, also in the Eisenhower Presidential Library, were maintained by some of Eisenhower's closest assistants: Andrew J. Goodpaster, L. Arthur Minnich, Robert Cutler, Gordon Gray, and Dillon Anderson. These files, which are valuable for foreign, domestic, and national security matters, include the records of the Office of the Special Assistant for National Security Affairs (WHO/OSANSA) and those of the Office of the Staff Secretary (WHO/OSS). Other documents relating to national security came from the files of the Joint Chiefs of Staff—the "CCS" file—found in Record Group 218 in the National Archives. Also in the National Archives is a relatively small collection that we cite as "State Department Files, Presidential Correspondence" (Record Group 59).

Given the difficulty of locating declassified copies of Eisenhower's important correspondence with British Prime Minister Harold Macmillan, we were fortunate to obtain access to an additional source of material for this last set of volumes. The Public Record Office in Kew, England, has released most of the letters and cables exchanged between the two Western leaders. Most of the documents that we used were located in record class PREM 11, which contains correspondence and papers from the Prime Minister's Office generated or received from 1951 until 1964. Each subject file in this record class is designated with a particular number, which we provide in our document headings and annotations.

There are extensive finding aids available to most of the collections listed in this note and in the note that appears in volume XVII. Interested researchers should contact the custodians of the manuscripts for information on security classification, donor-imposed restrictions, and copyright regulations.

Daun van Ee

Bibliography:
Secondary Sources Cited

Abrams, Herbert L. "Shielding the President from the Constitution: Disability and the 25th Amendment." *Presidential Studies Quarterly*. Vol. XXIII, no. 3 (Summer 1993).

Abramson, Rudy. *Spanning the Century: The Life of W. Averell Harriman, 1891–1986*. New York, 1992.

Acheson, Dean. *Present at the Creation: My Years in the State Department*. New York, 1969.

Adams, Sherman. *Firsthand Report: The Story of the Eisenhower Administration*. New York, 1961.

Adenauer, Konrad. *Memoirs 1945–1953*. Chicago, 1966.

Alexander, Robert J. *Juscelino Kubitschek and the Development of Brazil*. Athens, Ohio, 1991.

Allen, Craig. *Eisenhower and the Mass Media: Peace, Prosperity, & Prime-Time TV*. Chapel Hill, 1993.

Allen, George Edward. *Presidents Who Have Known Me*. New York, 1960. Reprint.

Alteras, Isaac. *Eisenhower and Israel*. Gainesville, Fla., 1993.

Ambrose, Stephen E. *Duty, Honor, Country: A History of West Point*. Baltimore, 1966.

———. *The Supreme Commander: The War Years of General Dwight D. Eisenhower*. New York, 1970.

———. *Eisenhower*. 2 vols. New York, 1983–84. Vol. I, *Soldier, General of the Army, President Elect, 1890–1952* (1983); vol. II, *The President* (1984).

———. *Nixon*. 3 vols. New York, 1987–91. Vol. I, *The Education of a Politician, 1913–1963* (1987); vol. III, *Ruin and Recovery, 1973–1990* (1991).

American Meat Institute. *Meat: Reference Book of the Industry*. Chicago, 1941.

Anderson, Totton J. "The 1958 Election in California." *Western Political Quarterly*, vol. XII, no. 1, pt. 2 (March 1959).

Arnold, Peri E. *Making the Managerial Presidency: Comprehensive Reorganization Planning, 1905–1980*. Princeton, 1986.

Ashton, Nigel John. *Eisenhower, Macmillan and the Problem of Nasser: Anglo-American Relations and Arab Nationalism*. London, 1996.

"The Automobile Dealer Franchise Act: A 'New Departure' in Federal Legislation?" *Northwestern University Law Review*. Vol. 52 (May–June 1957).

Baker, James T. *Eric Hoffer.* Boston, 1982.

Barnard, John. *Walter Reuther and the Rise of the Auto Workers.* Boston, 1983.

Barrett, William. *What is Existentialism?* New York, 1964.

Bartley, Ernest R. *The Tidelands Oil Controversy: A Legal and Historical Analysis.* Austin, 1953.

Baruch, Bernard M. *Baruch: My Own Story.* New York, 1957.

Bass, Harold F. "The President and the National Party Organization." In *Presidents and Their Parties,* edited by Robert Harmel. New York, 1984.

Bates, Daisy. *The Long Shadow of Little Rock: A Memoir.* New York, 1962.

Bator, Francis Michel. *The Question of Government Spending: Public Needs and Private Worth.* Cambridge, Mass., 1959.

Beals, Melba Pattillo. *Warriors Don't Cry.* New York, 1994.

Beard, Edmund. *Developing the ICBM.* New York, 1976.

Bender, Marilyn, and Altschul, Selig. *The Chosen Instrument.* New York, 1981.

Benedict, Michael Les. *A Compromise of Principle: Congressional Republicans and Reconstruction 1863–1869.* New York, 1974.

Benson, Ezra Taft. *Freedom to Farm.* New York, 1960.

——. *Cross Fire: The Eight Years with Eisenhower.* New York, 1962.

Berg, A. Scott. *Goldwyn: A Biography.* New York, 1989.

Berkowitz, Edward D. *America's Welfare State from Roosevelt to Reagan.* Baltimore, 1991.

——, and McQuaid, Kim. *Creating the Welfare State: The Political Economy of 20th-Century Reform.* 4th edition. Lawrence, Kans., 1992.

Berman, Daniel M. *A Bill Becomes A Law: Congress Enacts Civil Rights Legislation.* New York, 1966.

Bernstein, Richard J. *John Dewey.* New York, 1966.

Berry, Jeffrey M. *Feeding Hungry People: Rulemaking in the Food Stamp Program.* New Brunswick, N.J., 1984.

Beschloss, Michael R. *Mayday: Eisenhower, Khrushchev, and the U-2 Affair.* New York, 1986.

Best, Gary Dean. *Herbert Hoover: The Postpresidential Years 1933–1964.* 2 vols. Stanford, 1983. Vol. II, *1946–1964.*

Bing, Geoffrey. *An Account of Kwame Nkrumah's Ghana from 1950 to 1966.* Worcester and London, 1968.

Bissell, Richard M., Jr. *Reflections of a Cold Warrior: From Yalta to the Bay of Pigs.* New Haven, 1996.

Bohi, Douglas R., and Russell, Milton. *Limiting Oil Imports: An Economic History and Analysis.* Baltimore, 1978.

Bohlen, Charles E. *Witness to History 1929–1969.* New York, 1973.

Bone, Hugh H. "The 1958 Election in Washington." *Western Political Quarterly,* vol. XII, no. 1, pt. 2 (March 1959).

Bonsal, Philip. *Cuba, Castro, and the United States.* Pittsburgh, 1971.

Borklund, C. W. *The Department of Defense.* New York, 1968.

Botti, Timothy J. *Ace in the Hole: Why the United States Did Not Use Nuclear Weapons in the Cold War, 1945 to 1965.* Westport, Conn., 1996.

Bragin, Charles. *Dime Novels: Bibliography 1860–1928.* Brooklyn, N.Y., 1938.

Brands, H. W., Jr. *Cold Warriors: Eisenhower's Generation and American Foreign Policy.* New York, 1988.

Bright, Charles D. *The Jet Makers: The Aerospace Industry from 1945 to 1972.* Lawrence, Kans., 1978.

Brownell, Herbert. *Hearings Before the House Judiciary Special Subcommittee on Study of Presidential Inability.* 85th Congress. 1st. sess., April 1, 1957.

———, with John P. Burke. *Advising Ike: The Memoirs of Attorney General Herbert Brownell.* Lawrence, Kans., 1993.

Bryant, Sir Arthur. *The Turn of the Tide: A History of the War Years Based on the Diaries of Field-Marshal Lord Alanbrooke, Chief of the Imperial General Staff.* Garden City, N.Y., 1957.

———. *Triumph in the West: A History of the War Years Based on the Diaries of Field-Marshal Lord Alanbrooke, Chief of the Imperial General Staff.* Garden City, N.Y., 1959.

Burk, Robert Frederick. *The Eisenhower Administration and Black Civil Rights.* Knoxville, Tenn., 1984.

Burkhardt, Robert. *The Federal Aviation Administration.* New York, 1967.

Burnett, William Riley. *Bitter Ground.* New York, 1958.

Burns, Arthur F. *Prosperity Without Inflation.* New York, 1957.

Burr, William. "Avoiding the Slippery Slope: The Eisenhower Administration and the Berlin Crisis, November 1958–January 1959." *Diplomatic History* 18, no. 2 (1994).

Butcher, Harry C. *My Three Years with Eisenhower: The Personal Diary of Captain Harry C. Butcher, USNR.* New York, 1946.

Canada, Department of Fisheries and Fisheries Research Board. *The Commercial Fisheries of Canada.* Ottawa, 1957.

"Can Our High Schools Do the Job?" *Carnegie Corporation of New York Quarterly* 6, no. 2 (April 1958).

Carper, Edith T. "Lobbying and the Natural Gas Bill." In *Case Studies in American Government,* edited by Edwin A. Bock and Alan K. Campbell. Englewood Cliffs, N.J., 1962.

Carr, Charles C. *ALCOA: An American Enterprise.* New York, 1952.

Castiglioga, Frank. *France and the United States: The Cold Alliance Since World War II.* New York, 1992.

Chang, Gordon H. *Friends and Enemies: The United States, China and the Soviet Union, 1948–1972.* Stanford, 1990.

Cheape, Charles W. *Walter Carpenter at Du Pont and General Motors.* Baltimore, 1995.

Chester, Edward W. *United States Oil Policy and Diplomacy: A Twentieth-Century Overview.* Westport, Conn., 1983.

Christensen, Thomas J. *Useful Adversaries: Grand Strategy, Domestic Mobilization, and Sino-American Conflict, 1947–1958.* Princeton, 1996.

Christie, W. J. *A Study of Freshwater Fishery Regulation Based on North American Experience.* Food and Agriculture Organization of the United Nations. Fisheries Technical Paper No. 180. Rome, 1978.

Churchill, Winston S. *A History of the English Speaking Peoples.* 4 vols. London, 1956–58. Vol. III, *The Age of Revolution* (1957).

———. *Second World War: Memoirs of the Second World War.* Boston, 1959.

Clifford, A. Jerome. *The Independence of the Federal Reserve System.* Philadelphia, 1965.

Clowse, Barbara Barskdale. *Brainpower for the Cold War: The Sputnik Crisis and National Defense Education Act of 1958.* Westport, Conn., 1981.

Cochrane, Willard W., and Ryan, Mary E. *American Farm Policy, 1948–1973.* Minneapolis, 1976.

Coit, Margaret L. *Mr. Baruch.* Boston, 1957.

Cole, Alice C.; Goldberg, Alfred; Tucker, Samuel A.; and Winnacker, Rudolph A., eds. *The Department of Defense: Documents on Establishment and Organization, 1944–1978.* Washington, D.C., 1979.

Collier, Ken. "Eisenhower and Congress: The Autopilot Presidency." *Presidential Studies Quarterly* 24, no. 2 (1994).

Collins, James. *The Existentialists: A Critical Study*. Chicago, 1952.

Committee for the White House Conference on Education. *Report to the President*. Washington, D.C., 1956.

Conant, James Bryant. *My Several Lives: Memoirs of a Social Inventor*. New York, 1970.

Conference of Foreign Ministers. *Foreign Ministers Meeting, May–August, 1959, Geneva*. Washington, D.C., 1959.

Conger, Mary. "The Farmer's Side of the Case." *Saturday Evening Post*, April 9, 1960.

Conniff, Michael L. *Panama and the United States: The Forced Alliance*. Athens and London, 1992.

Considine, Robert Bernard. *MacArthur the Magnificent*. Philadelphia, 1942.

———. *Thirty Seconds over Tokyo*. New York, 1943.

Cordier, Andrew Wellington; Foote, Wilder; and Harrelson, Max, eds., *Public Papers of the Secretaries-General of the United Nations*. 8 vols. New York and London, 1969–77. Vol. IV, *Dag Hammarskjöld, 1958–1960*, edited by Andrew Wellington Cordier and Wilder Foote (1974).

Cray, Ed. *General of the Army: George C. Marshall, Soldier and Statesman*. New York, 1990.

Crouch, Winston W.; Bollens, John C.; and Scott, Stanley. *California Government and Politics*. 6th ed. Englewood Cliffs, N.J., 1977.

Cumming, Robert Denoon. *Starting Point: An Introduction to the Dialectic of Existence*. Chicago and London, 1979.

Cutler, John Levi. "Gilbert Patten and his Frank Merriwell Saga." *Maine Bulletin* 36, no. 10. University of Maine Studies, 2d ser., no. 31 (May 1934).

Dann, Uriel. *King Hussein and the Challenge of Arab Radicalism: Jordan, 1955–1967*. New York, 1989.

Davis, James W. *The President as Party Leader*. New York, 1992.

Davis, Kenneth S. *The Eisenhower College Collection: The Paintings of Dwight D. Eisenhower*. Los Angeles, 1972.

Dayal, Rajeshwar. *Mission for Hammarskjöld: The Congo Crisis*. Princeton, 1976.

Dedman, Martin J. *The Origins and Development of the European Union 1945–95*. London and New York, 1996.

De Gaulle, Charles. *The War Memoirs of Charles de Gaulle*. 3 vols. New York, 1955–60. Vol. I, *The Call to Honour, 1940–1942*, translated by Jonathan Griffin (1955); vol. II, *Unity, 1942–1944*, translated by Richard Howard (1959); vol. III, *Salvation, 1944–1946*, translated by Richard Howard (1960).

———. *Memoirs of Hope: Renewal and Endeavor*. New York, 1971.

———. *Letters, Notes et Carnets, Juin 1940–Juillet 1941*. Librairie Plon, 1980.

"De Gaulle: The Risks, the Rewards." *Life*, June 2, 1958.

Diamond, William. *Development Banks*. Baltimore, 1957.

Dillon, C. Douglas. "The Kennedy Presidency: the Economic Dimension." In *Portraits of American Presidents*, edited by Kenneth W. Thompson. 11 vols. Lanham, Md., 1982–98. Vol. IV, *The Kennedy Presidency: Seventeen Intimate Perspectives of John F. Kennedy* (1985).

Disraeli, Benjamin. *Lothair*. New York, 1870.

Divine, Robert A. *Blowing on the Wind: The Nuclear Test Ban Debate 1954–1960*. New York, 1978.

———. *The Sputnik Challenge*. New York and Oxford, 1993.

Donald, David Herbert. *Lincoln*. New York, 1995.

Donovan, Robert J. *Eisenhower: The Inside Story*. New York, 1956.

———. *Conflict and Crisis: The Presidency of Harry S. Truman, 1945–1948*. New York, 1977.

———. *Confidential Secretary: Ann Whitman's 20 Years with Eisenhower and Rockefeller*. New York, 1988.

Dooley, Thomas A. *The Night They Burned the Mountain*. New York, 1960.

Dulles, Eleanor Lansing. *John Foster Dulles: The Last Year*. New York, 1963.

Dulles, John Foster. "Our Policies Toward Communism in China." *U.S. Department of State Bulletin* 37, no. 942 (July 15, 1957).

———. "The Challenge of Change: The Basic Philosophy, the Rationale, Which Underlies U.S. Foreign Policy." *U.S. Department of State Bulletin* 38, no. 991 (June 23, 1958).

———. *The Spiritual Legacy of John Foster Dulles: Selections from his Articles and Addresses*, edited by Henry P. Van Dusen. Philadelphia, 1960.

Duncan, David Douglas. *The Kremlin*. Greenwich, Conn., 1960.

Dykhuizen, George. *The Life and Mind of John Dewey*. Carbondale and Edwardsville, Ill., 1973.

Eban, Abba Solomon. *Abba Eban: An Autobiography*. New York, 1977.

Eckes, Alfred E., Jr. *The United States and the Global Struggle for Minerals*. Austin, 1979.

Edgerton, Russell. *Sub-Cabinet Politics and Policy Commitment: The Birth of the Development Loan Fund*. Syracuse, 1970.

Eisenhower, David. *Eisenhower: At War, 1943–45*. New York, 1986.

Eisenhower, Dwight D. *Crusade in Europe*. Garden City, N.Y., 1948.

———. "Open Letter to America's Students." *Reader's Digest* (October 1948). And *Thirtieth Anniversary Reader's Digest Reader* (1951).

———. *The White House Years: Mandate for Change, 1953–1956*. Garden City, N.Y., 1963.

———. *The White House Years: Waging Peace, 1956–1961*. Garden City, N.Y., 1965.

———. *At Ease: Stories I Tell to Friends*. Garden City, N.Y., 1967.

———. *The Papers of Dwight David Eisenhower*. Baltimore, 1970–2001. Vols. I–V, *The War Years*, edited by Alfred D. Chandler, Jr. (1970); vol. VI, *Occupation, 1945*, edited by Alfred D. Chandler, Jr., and Louis Galambos (1978); vols. VII–IX, *The Chief of Staff*, edited by Louis Galambos (1978); vols. X–XI, *Columbia University*, edited by Louis Galambos (1983); vols. XII–XIII, *NATO and the Campaign of 1952*, edited by Louis Galambos (1989); vols. XIV–XVII, *The Presidency: The Middle Way*, edited by Louis Galambos and Daun van Ee (1996).

Eisenhower, John S. D. *Strictly Personal*. Garden City, N.Y., 1974.

———. *Intervention! The United States and the Mexican Revolution 1913–1917*. New York, 1993.

Eisenhower, Milton S. *The Wine Is Bitter*. New York, 1963.

———. *The President Is Calling*. New York, 1974.

Eisenhower, Susan. *Mrs. Ike: Memories and Reflections on the Life of Mamie Eisenhower*. New York, 1996.

Elder, Donald C. *Out from Behind the Eight-Ball: A History of Project Echo*. AAS History Series, edited by R. Cargill Hall. 17 vols. to date. San Diego, Calif., 1977–95. Vol. 16 (1995).

Emme, Eugene M., ed. *The History of Rocket Technology: Essays on Research, Development, and Utility*. Detroit, 1964.

Enthoven, Alain C., and Smith, K. Wayne. *How Much Is Enough? Shaping the Defense Program, 1961–1969*. New York, 1971.

Ewald, William Bragg, Jr. *Eisenhower the President: Crucial Days: 1951–1960*. Englewood Cliffs, N.J., 1981.

Fall, Bernard B. *Anatomy of a Crisis: The Laotian Crisis of 1960–1961*. Garden City, N.Y., 1969.

Faubus, Orval Eugene. *Down From the Hills*. Little Rock, Ark., 1980.

Ferling, John E. *The First of Men: A Life of George Washington*. Knoxville, Tenn., 1988.

Ferrell, Robert H. *Peace in Their Time: The Origins of the Kellogg-Briand Pact*. New Haven, 1952.

———. *Ill-Advised: Presidential Health and Public Trust*. Columbia, Missouri, 1992.

———. *Harry S. Truman, A Life*. Columbia, Missouri, and London, 1994.

Fisher, James T. *Dr. America: The Lives of Thomas A. Dooley, 1927–1961*. Amherst, 1997.

Fligstein, Neil. *The Transformation of Corporate Control*. Cambridge, Mass., 1990.

Freeman, Douglas Southall. *Lee's Lieutenants: A Study in Command*. New York, 1942–44.

———. *George W. ~ gton: A Biography*. 7 vols. New York, 1948–57. Vol. V, *Victory with the Help of France* ~ airfield, N.J., 1981; vol. VII, *First in Peace* by Carroll, John Alexander and Ashworth, Mary Wells (1957).

Freidel, Frank, and Pencak, William, eds. *The White House: The First Two Hundred Years*. Boston, 1994.

Frier, David. *Conflict of Interest in the Eisenhower Administration*. Baltimore, 1970.

Fries, Sylvia Doughty. *NASA Engineers and the Age of Apollo*. Washington, D.C., 1992.

Funk, Arthur L. *Charles de Gaulle: The Crucial Years*. Norman, Okla., 1959.

Gaitskell, Hugh. "Disengagement: Why? How?" *Foreign Affairs* 36, no. 4 (1958).

Galambos, Louis, and Milobsky, David. "Organizing and Reorganizing the World Bank, 1946–1972: A Comparative Perspective." In *Business History Review* 69 (Summer 1995).

Gallick, Edward C. *Competition in the Natural Gas Pipeline Industry: An Economic Policy Analysis*. Westport, Conn., 1993.

Gallup, George H. *The Gallup Poll: Public Opinion 1935–1971*. 3 vols. New York, 1972. Vol. III, *1959–1971*.

Gardner, Paul F. *Shared Hopes, Separate Fears: Fifty Years of U.S.-Indonesian Relations*. Boulder, Colo., 1997.

Garside, Grenville. "The Jackson Subcommittee on National Security." In *Staying the Course: Henry M. Jackson and National Security*, edited by Dorothy Fosdick. Seattle, 1987.

Gavin, James M. *War and Peace in the Space Age*. New York, 1958.

Geelhoed, E. Bruce. *Charles E. Wilson and Controversy at the Pentagon, 1953 to 1957*. Detroit, 1979.

Gellman, Irvin F. *The Contender: Richard Nixon: The Congress Years, 1946–1952*. New York, 1999.

Gendzier, Irene L. *Notes from the Minefield: United States Intervention in Lebanon and the Middle East 1945–1958*. New York, 1997.

Gibney, Frank. "The Deeper Problem in Education: It is to Dig Out Educationists' Debris and Rediscover Learning's True Nature." *Life*, March 31, 1958.

Glennan, T. Keith. *The Birth of NASA: The Diary of T. Keith Glennan*, edited by J. D. Hunley. Washington, D.C., 1993.

Godbey, John C. "Unitarian Universalist Association." In *Encyclopedia of Religion*, vol. 15, edited by Mircea Eliade. New York, 1987.

Goodpaster, Andrew Jackson. "Presidential Transitions and Foreign Policy: Eisenhower and Kennedy." In *Presidential Transitions and Foreign Policy*. Vol. V. *Reflections of Five Public Officials*, edited by Kenneth W. Thompson. Lanham, Md., 1986.

Gordon, H. Scott. "The Eisenhower Administration: The Doctrine of Shared Responsibility. In *Exhortation and Controls: The Search for a Wage-Price Policy 1945–1971*, edited by Craufurd C. Goodwin. Washington, D.C., 1975.

Gottschalk, Stephen. "Christian Science." In *Encyclopedia of Religion*. Vol. 3, edited by Mircea Eliade. New York, 1987.

Gould, Lewis L. *The Presidency of William McKinley*. Lawrence, Kans., 1980.

Greene, John Robert. *The Crusade: The Presidential Election of 1952*. Lanham, Md., 1985.

Greenstein, Fred I. *The Hidden-Hand Presidency: Eisenhower as Leader*. New York, 1982.

————, and Immerman, Richard H. "What Did Eisenhower Tell Kennedy about Indochina? The Politics of Misperception." *The Journal of American History* 79, no. 2 (1992).

Griffith, Robert W. "Dwight D. Eisenhower and the Corporate Commonwealth." *American Historical Review* 87, no. 1 (1982).

————, ed. *Ike's Letters to a Friend, 1941–1958*. Lawrence, Kans., 1984.

Groueff, Stephane. *Manhattan Project: The Untold Story of the Making of the Atomic Bomb*. Boston, 1967.

Groves, Leslie M. *Now It Can Be Told: The Story of the Manhattan Project*. New York, 1983.

Hacker, Louis Morton. *The World of Andrew Carnegie: 1965–1901*. Philadelphia, 1968.

Haddow, Robert H. *Pavilions of Plenty: Exhibiting American Culture Abroad in the 1950s*. Washington, D.C., 1997.

Hagerty, James C. *The Diary of James C. Hagerty: Eisenhower in Mid-Course, 1954–1955*, edited by Robert H. Ferrell. Bloomington, Ind., 1983.

Halberstam, David. *The Fifties*. New York, 1993.

Halperin, Morton H., ed. *Sino-Soviet Relations and Arms Control*. Cambridge, Mass., 1967.

Hamby, Alonzo L. *Man of the People: A Life of Harry S. Truman*. New York, 1995.

Hawley, Ellis W. *Herbert Hoover and the Historians*. West Branch, Iowa, 1989.

Heckscher, August. *Woodrow Wilson*. New York, 1991.

Hershberg, James G. *James B. Conant: Harvard to Hiroshima and the Making of the Nuclear Age*. New York, 1993.

Hewlett, Richard J. and Holl, Jack M. *Atoms for Peace and War 1953–1961*. Berkeley, 1989.

Hickman, Bert G. *Growth and Stability of the Postwar Economy*. Washington, D.C., 1960.

Hill, Jim Dan. "Mighty Both the Sword and Pencil." *Saturday Review of Literature* 71 (November 1958).

Hinton, Harold. *China's Turbulent Quest*. Bloomington, Ind., 1972.

Hittle, J. D. *The Military Staff: Its History and Development*. Harrisburg, Penn., 1961.

Hoffer, Eric. *The True Believer: Thoughts on the Nature of Mass Movements*. New York, 1951.

Hoffman, Steven A. *India and the China Crisis*. Berkeley, 1990.

Hogan, J. Michael. *The Panama Canal in American Politics*. Carbondale, Ill., 1986.

Holland, Matthew F. *America and Egypt: From Roosevelt to Eisenhower*. Westport, Conn., 1996.

Holt, Daniel D., and Leyerzapf, James W. *Eisenhower: The Prewar Diaries and Selected Papers, 1905–1941*. Baltimore, 1998.

Horne, Alistair. *Harold Macmillan*. 2 vols. New York, 1988–89. Vol. 2 (1989).

Howard, Michael. *Disengagement in Europe*. London, 1958.

Hsü, Immanuel C. Y. *The Rise of Modern China*. New York and Oxford, 1990.

Huckaby, Elizabeth. *Crisis at Central High, Little Rock, 1957–58*. Baton Rouge, 1980.

Hughes, Emmet John. *America the Vincible*. Garden City, N.Y., 1959.

————. *The Ordeal of Power: A Political Memoir of the Eisenhower Years*. New York, 1963.

Humphrey, George M. *The Basic Papers of George M. Humphrey as Secretary of the Treasury, 1953–1957*, edited by Nathaniel R. Howard. Cleveland, 1965.

Hurd, Charles. *U.S. Mail: The Story of the United States Postal Service*. New York, 1960.

Hyman, Harold M. *A More Perfect Union: The Impact of the Civil War and Reconstruction on the Constitution*. Boston, 1975.

"If You're Still Wondering About Fall-Out Danger." *U.S. News & World Report,* June 21, 1957.

Immerman, Richard H. *John Foster Dulles: Piety, Pragmatism, and Power in U.S. Foreign Policy.* Wilmington, Del., 1999.

Irving, David. *The War Between the Generals.* New York, 1981.

Ismay, Hastings Lionel. *The Memoirs of General Lord Ismay.* New York, 1960.

Jackson, Richard L. *The Non-Aligned, The UN, and the Superpowers.* New York, 1983.

James, D. Clayton. *The Years of MacArthur.* 3 vols. Boston, 1970–85. Vol. I, *1880–1941* (1970).

Jameson, John R. *Big Bend National Park: The Formative Years.* El Paso, 1980.

Jewkes, John. *The Sources of Invention.* London and New York, 1958.

Johnson, Chalmers A. *MITI and the Japanese Miracle: The Growth of Industrial Policy, 1925–1975.* Stanford, Calif., 1982.

Johnson, R. W. "Sekou Touré and the Guinean Revolution." In *African Nationalism and Independence,* edited by Timothy K. Welliver. New York, 1993.

Jones, Howard Palfrey. *Indonesia: The Possible Dream.* New York, 1971.

Jones, Robert Tyre (Bobby), Jr. *Golf Is My Game.* Garden City, N.Y., 1960.

Jones, Vincent C. *Manhattan: The Army and the Atomic Bomb.* Special Studies. U.S. Army in World War II. Washington, D.C., 1985.

Jónsson, Hannes. *Friends in Conflict: The Anglo-Icelandic Cod Wars and the Law of the Sea.* London, 1982.

Kahin, Audrey R., and Kahin, George McT. *Subversion as Foreign Policy: The Secret Eisenhower and Dulles Debacle in Indonesia.* New York, 1995.

Kahn, E. J., Jr. *Jock: The Life and Times of John Hay Whitney.* Garden City, N.Y., 1981.

Katcher, Leo. *Earl Warren: A Political Biography.* New York, 1967.

Kaufman, Burton I. *Trade and Aid: Eisenhower's Foreign Economic Policy, 1953–1961.* Baltimore, 1982.

———. "Eisenhower's Foreign Economic Policy with Respect to East Asia." In *The Great Powers in East Asia, 1953–1960,* edited by Warren I. Cohen and Akira Iriye. New York, 1990.

Kemenes, Egon. "The Hungarian Economy, 1945–1969." In *Modern Hungary: Readings from The New Hungarian Quarterly,* edited by Denis Sinor. Bloomington, Ind., 1977.

Kent, Frank Richardson. *The Great Game of Politics: An Effort to Present the Elementary Facts about Politics, Politicians, and Political Machines, Candidates and Their Ways, For the Benefit of the Average Citizen.* Garden City, N.Y., 1926.

Kettl, Donald F. *Leadership at the Fed.* New Haven, 1986.

Khrushchev, Nikita S. *Khrushchev Remembers: The Last Testament.* Translated and edited by Strobe Talbott. Boston, 1974.

Killian, James R., Jr. *Sputnik, Scientists, and Eisenhower: A Memoir of the First Special Assistant to the President for Science and Technology.* Cambridge, Mass., 1977.

Kim, Quee-Young. *The Fall of Syngman Rhee.* Berkeley, Calif., 1983.

Kingseed, Cole C. *Eisenhower and the Suez Crisis of 1956.* Baton Rouge and London, 1995.

Kistiakowski, George Bogdan. *A Scientist at the White House: The Private Diary of President Eisenhower's Special Assistant for Science and Technology.* Cambridge, Mass., 1976.

Kluger, Richard. *The Paper: The Life and Death of the New York Herald Tribune.* New York, 1986.

Kocher, Paul H. *California's Old Missions: The Story of the Founding of the 21 Franciscan Missions in Spanish Alta California 1769–1823.* Chicago, 1976.

Koppett, Leonard. *Koppett's Concise History of Major League Baseball*. Philadelphia, 1998.

Kornitzer, Bela. *The Great American Heritage: The Story of the Five Eisenhower Brothers*. New York, 1955.

Kovaleff, Theodore Philip. *Business and Government During the Eisenhower Administration*. Athens, Ohio, 1980.

Kraft, Joseph. "Ike *vs.* Nixon." *Esquire*, April 1960.

Kraske, Jochen; with Becker, William H.; Diamond, William; and Galambos, Louis. *Bankers with a Mission: The Presidents of the World Bank, 1946–91*. New York, 1996.

Kunz, Diane B. *The Economic Diplomacy of the Suez Crisis*. Chapel Hill, 1991.

LaFantasie, Glenn. "Monty and Ike Take Gettysburg." *MHQ: The Quarterly Journal of Military History*, vol. 8 (Autumn 1995).

LaFeber, Walter. *The Panama Canal: The Crisis in Historical Perspective*. New York, 1978.

Lancel, Serge. *Hannibal*. Oxford, 1998.

Larson, Arthur. *Eisenhower: The President Nobody Knew*. New York, 1968.

Lasby, Clarence G. *Eisenhower's Heart Attack*. Lawrence, Kans., 1997.

Lawrence, David. "The President and His Day's Work." *The Century Magazine* (March 1917).

——. "America Must Advertise." *Saturday Evening Post*, April 13, 1918.

——. "The Presidency is Too Big for One Man." *U.S. News & World Report*, October 7, 1955.

——. "'Modern Republicans' and 'Modern Democrats.'" *U.S. News & World Report*, April 5, 1957.

——. "Peoples Above Governments." *U.S. News & World Report*, April 19, 1957.

——. "The Need for Cabinet Government." *U.S. News & World Report*, November 22, 1957.

——. "There's a Gap in the Olympics." *Washington Evening Star*, February 26, 1960.

Lawson, Steven F. *Black Ballots: Voting Rights in the South, 1944–1969*. New York, 1976.

Lazenby, J. F. *Hannibal's War: A Military History of the Second Punic War*. Warminster, England, 1978.

Leary, William M., ed. *The Central Intelligence Agency: History and Documents*. University, Ala., 1984.

Lee, R. Alton. *Eisenhower & Landrum-Griffin: A Study in Labor-Management Politics*. Lexington, Ky., 1990.

Lefever, Ernest W. ed. *Arms and Arms Control: A Symposium*. New York, 1962.

——. *The Crisis in the Congo: A United Nations Force in Action*. Washington, D.C., 1965.

Lehman, Kenneth. "Revolutions and Attributions: Making Sense of Eisenhower Administration Policies in Bolivia and Guatemala." *Diplomatic History* 21, no. 2 (1997).

Leonard, Thomas M. *Panama, the Canal and the United States*. Claremont, Calif., 1993.

Levine, Alan J. *The Missile and Space Race*. Westport, Conn., 1994.

Lincoln, Abraham. *The Complete Works of Abraham Lincoln*, edited by John G. Nicolay and John Hay. 12 vols. c.1905.

Little, Douglas. "His Finest Hour?: Eisenhower, Lebanon, and the 1958 Middle East Crisis." *Diplomatic History* 20, no. 1 (1996).

Lodge, Henry Cabot. *The Storm Has Many Eyes*. New York, 1973.

Lovell, John P. *Neither Athens Nor Sparta? The American Service Academies in Transition*. Bloomington, Ind., 1979.

Lowenthal, David. "The Social Background of West Indian Federation." In *The West Indies Federation*, edited by David Lowenthal. New York, 1961.

Lubell, Samuel. *The Future of American Politics*. New York, 1952.

Luce, Henry R. "Our Great Hope: Peace Is the Work of Justice." *American Bar Association Journal* 43 (1957).

Lyons, Gene M., and Morton, Louis. *Schools for Strategy: Education and Research in National Security Affairs.* New York, 1965.

Macaulay, Stewart. *Law and the Balance of Power: The Automobile Manufacturers and Their Dealers.* New York, 1966.

McCallum, John. *Six Roads from Abilene: Some Personal Recollections of Edgar Eisenhower.* Seattle, 1960.

McCracken, Harold. *The Charles M. Russell Book: The Life and Work of the Cowboy Artist.* Garden City, N.Y., 1957.

McCullough, David. *Truman.* New York, 1992.

McDougall, Walter A. *The Heavens and the Earth: A Political History of the Space Age.* New York, 1985.

McFarland, John W., Graves, Pleasant, and Graves, Audrey, eds. *Lives from Plutarch.* New York, 1972.

MacFarquhar, Roderick. *The Origins of the Cultural Revolution.* 2 vols. New York, 1974–1983. Vol. II, *The Great Leap Forward* (1983).

McGill, Ralph. "The Meaning of Lincoln Today: Idea of a National Dialogue a Critical One Then and Now." *Vital Speeches of the Day* 26, no. 11 (1960).

McGowan, Richard. *Government Regulation of the Alcohol Industry: The Search for Revenue and the Common Good.* Westport, Conn., 1997.

Macmillan, Harold. *Riding the Storm, 1956–1959.* London, 1971.

———. *Pointing the Way, 1959–1961.* London, 1972.

McNeil, Alex. *Total Television: The Comprehensive Guide to Programming from 1948 to the Present.* 4th ed., New York, 1996.

MacNeil, Neil, and Metz, Harold W. *The Hoover Report: 1953–1955.* New York, 1956.

———. *Dirksen: Portrait of a Public Man.* New York, 1970.

McPherson, Edward, ed. *The Political History of the United States of America during the Period of Reconstruction.* 1875. Reprint: New York, 1969.

Mansbridge, Jane L. *Why We Lost the ERA.* Chicago, 1986.

Marshall, Michael W. *Ocean Traders.* New York, 1990.

Martin, Curtis. "The 1958 Election in Colorado." *Western Political Quarterly,* vol. XII, no. 1, pt. 2 (March 1959).

Martin, John Bartlow. "Election of 1964." In *History of American Presidential Elections, 1789–1968,* edited by Arthur M. Schlesinger. 4 vols. New York, 1971. Vol. IV, *1940–1968.*

———. *Adlai Stevenson and the World: The Life of Adlai E. Stevenson.* New York, 1977.

Martin, Joseph William, Jr. *My First Fifty Years in Politics,* as told to Robert J. Donovan. New York, 1960.

Mason, Edward S. and Asher, Robert E. *The World Bank Since Bretton Woods: The Origins, Policies, Operations, and Impact of the International Bank for Reconstruction and Development.* Washington, D.C., 1973.

Mathews, Donald G., and de Hart, Jane Sherron. *Sex, Gender, and the Politics of ERA: A State and the Nation.* New York, 1990.

Maxwell, Neville. *India's China War.* New York, 1970.

May, Ann Mari. "President Eisenhower, Economic Policy, and the 1960 Presidential Election." *Journal of Economic History* 50, no. 2 (June 1990).

May, Madeleine. "Overheard at the Fair." *Atlantic Monthly* 202, (August 1958).

Mead, Frank S. *Handbook of Denominations in the United States,* revised by Samuel S. Hill. Nashville, 1985.

Medaris, John B. *Countdown for Decision.* New York, 1960.

Mencken, Henry Louis. *A Carnival of Buncombe,* edited by Malcom C. Moos. Baltimore, 1956.

Miles, Wyndham. "The Polaris." In *The History of Rocket Technology,* edited by Eugene M. Emme. Detroit, 1964.

Miller, Lawrence. *Truman: The Rise to Power.* New York, 1986.

Milobsky, David. *Leadership and Competition: Technological Innovation and Organizational Change at the U.S. Department of Defense, 1955–1968.* Ann Arbor, Michigan, University Microfilms International, 1996.

Minami, Ryōshin. *The Economic Development of Japan: A Quantitative Study.* New York, 1994.

Mollenhoff, Clark R. *The Pentagon: Politics, Profits and Plunder.* New York, 1967.

Montgomery, Bernard Law. *The Memoirs of Field-Marshal Montgomery The Viscount of Alamein, K.G.* Cleveland and New York, 1958.

Montgomery, Gayle B., and Johnson, James W. *One Step from the White House: The Rise and Fall of Senator William F. Knowland.* Berkeley and Los Angeles, 1998.

Moore, William W. *Fighting for Life: The Story of the American Heart Association 1911–1975.* Dallas, 1983.

Moran, Lord Charles. *Churchill: Taken from the Diaries of Lord Moran.* Boston, 1966.

Morgan, Iwan W. *Eisenhower versus 'The Spenders': The Eisenhower Administration, the Democrats and the Budget, 1953–60.* London, 1990.

Morris, Joe Alex. *Nelson Rockefeller: A Biography.* New York, 1960.

Morris, Roger. *Richard Milhous Nixon: The Rise of An American Politician.* New York, 1990.

Morrow, E. Frederic. *Black Man in the White House.* New York, 1963.

Morrow, John H. *First American Ambassador to Guinea.* New Brunswick, N. J., 1968.

Murphy, Paul L. *The Constitution in Crisis Times, 1918–1969.* New York, 1972.

Murphy, Robert D. *Diplomat Among Warriors.* Garden City, N.Y., 1964.

Nash, Gerald D. *United States Oil Policy 1890–1964.* Westport, Conn., 1968.

National Archives and Records Service. *United States Government Organization Manual 1957–1958.* Washington, D.C. Revised June 1, 1957.

Nelson, Harold D., ed. *Algeria: A Country Study.* 4th ed. Washington, D.C., 1986.

Netboy, Anthony. *The Salmon: A Vanishing Species?* Boston, 1968.

———. *The Salmon: Their Fight for Survival.* Boston, 1974.

Neu, Charles E. "The Rise of the National Security Bureaucracy." In *The New American State,* edited by Louis Galambos. Baltimore, 1987.

Neustadt, Richard E. *Presidential Power: The Politics of Leadership.* New York, 1976.

Nevins, Arthur S. *Gettysburg's Five-Star Farmer.* New York, 1977.

Nixon, Richard Milhous. *Six Crises.* New York, 1962.

———. *RN: The Memoirs of Richard Nixon.* 2 vols. New York, 1978. Vol. I.

Nkrumah, Kwame. *Ghana: The Autobiography of Kwame Nkrumah.* New York, 1957.

Noble, George Bernard. *Christian A. Herter.* In *American Secretaries of State and their Diplomacy.* 20 vols. New York, 1927–85. Vol. 18. New York, 1970.

Obosu-Mensah, Kwaku. *Ghana's Volta Resettlement Scheme: The Long-term Consequences of Post-colonial State Planning.* San Francisco, 1996.

Oehser, Paul H. *The Smithsonian Institution.* New York, 1970.

Office of the Secretary of Defense. *History of the Office of the Secretary of Defense,* edited by Alfred Goldberg. 3 vols. to date. Washington, D.C., 1984–1997. Vol. I, *The Formative Years, 1947–1950,* by Steven L. Reardon (1984); vol. IV, *Into the Missile Age, 1956–1960* by Robert J. Watson (1997). See also Watson, Robert J.

Overstreet, Harry A., and Overstreet, Bonaro W. *What We Must Know About Communism.* New York, 1958.

Paarlberg, Don. *American Farm Policy: A Case Study of Centralized Decision-Making.* New York, 1964.

"Panama Reassured on Titular Sovereignty in Canal Zone." *U.S. Department of State Bulletin* 41, no. 1068 (Dec. 14, 1959).

Parmet, Herbert S. *Eisenhower and the American Crusades.* New York, 1972.

Patterson, James T. *Mr. Republican: A Biography of Robert A. Taft.* Boston, 1972.

Paul, Oglesby. *Take Heart: The Life and Prescription for Living of Dr. Paul Dudley White.* Boston, 1986.

Peck, Merton J. *Competition in the Aluminum Industry 1945–1958.* Cambridge, Mass., 1961.

Pegram, Dudley F. *Transportation: Economics and Public Policy.* Homewood, Ill., 1968.

Perret, Geoffrey. *Eisenhower.* New York, 1999.

Peskin, Allan. *Garfield.* Kent, Ohio, 1978.

Peterson, Trudy Huskamp. *Agricultural Exports, Farm Income, and the Eisenhower Administration.* Lincoln, Neb., 1979.

Pfau, Richard. *No Sacrifice Too Great: The Life of Lewis L. Strauss.* Charlottesville, 1984.

Pogue, Forrest C. *George C. Marshall.* 4 vols., New York, 1963–87. Vol. IV, *Statesman, 1945–1959* (1987).

Pollack, Jack Harrison. *Earl Warren: The Judge Who Changed America.* Englewood Cliffs, N.J., 1979.

Pollock, John. *Billy Graham: Evangelist to the World and Authorized Biography of the Decisive Years.* New York, 1979.

Polmar, Norman, ed. *Strategic Air Command: People, Aircraft, and Missiles.* Annapolis, 1979.

Porter, Kirk H., and Johnson, Donald Bruce, comps. *National Party Platforms, 1840–1968.* Urbana, Ill., 1970.

Powell, Richard Pitts. *Pioneer Go Home.* New York, 1959.

Prados, John. *Keepers of the Keys: A History of the National Security Council from Truman to Bush.* New York, 1991.

President's Commission on Veterans' Pensions. *Veterans' Benefits in the United States: Findings and Recommendations.* Washington, D.C., 1956.

President's Council on Youth Fitness. "Action for Youth Fitness." Washington, D.C., 1958.

Preston, Richard A.; Wise, Sydney F.; and Werner, Herman O. *Men In Arms: A History of Warfare and Its Interrelationships with Western Society.* New York, 1962.

Pruden, Caroline. *Conditional Partners: Eisenhower, the United Nations, and the Search for a Permanent Peace.* Baton Rouge, 1998.

Public Papers of the Presidents of the United States: Dwight D. Eisenhower, January 1 to December 31, 1955. Washington, D.C., 1959.

Public Papers of the Presidents of the United States: Dwight D. Eisenhower, January 1 to December 31, 1956. Washington, D.C., 1958.

Public Papers of the Presidents of the United States: Dwight D. Eisenhower, January 1 to December 31, 1957. Washington, D.C., 1958.

Public Papers of the Presidents of the United States: Dwight D. Eisenhower, January 1 to December 31, 1958. Washington, D.C., 1959.

Public Papers of the Presidents of the United States: Dwight D. Eisenhower, January 1 to December 31, 1959. Washington, D.C., 1960.

Public Papers of the Presidents of the United States: Dwight D. Eisenhower, January 1, 1960, to January 20, 1961. Washington, D.C., 1961.

Quirk, Robert E. *Fidel Castro.* New York, 1993.

Rabe, Stephen G. *Eisenhower and Latin America: The Foreign Policy of Anticommunism.* Chapel Hill, 1988.

Rabi, I. I. *My Life and Times as a Physicist.* Claremont, Calif., 1960.

Raucher, Alan R. *Paul G. Hoffman: Architect of Foreign Aid.* Lexington, Ky., 1985.

Reardon, Steven L. *The Formative Years, 1947–1950.* Washington, D.C., 1984.

Reddaway, John. *Burdened With Cyprus: The British Connection.* London, 1986.

Reich, Cary. *The Life of Nelson A. Rockefeller: Worlds to Conquer 1908–1958.* New York, 1996.

Reichard, Gary W. *The Reaffirmation of Republicanism: Eisenhower and the Eighty-Third Congress.* Knoxville, Tenn., 1975.

Reinhard, David W. *The Republican Right Since 1945.* Lexington, Ky., 1983.

Rice, Lester. "Light Club Big Hitter." *National Golfer* (December 1957).

Richardson, James L. *Germany and the Atlantic Alliance: The Interaction of Strategy and Politics.* Cambridge, Mass., 1966.

Ridgely-Nevitt, Cedric. *American Steamships on the Atlantic.* Newark, Del., London and Toronto, 1981.

Ries, John C. *The Management of Defense: Organization and Control of the U.S. Armed Services.* Baltimore, 1964.

Rigden, John S. *Rabi: Scientist and Citizen.* New York, 1987.

Rochester, Stuart I. *Takeoff at Mid-Century: Federal Civil Aviation Policy in the Eisenhower Years 1953–1961.* Washington, D.C., 1976.

Roman, Peter J. *Eisenhower and the Missile Gap.* Ithaca, N.Y., 1995.

Rostow, W. W. *Eisenhower, Kennedy, and Foreign Aid.* Austin, Tex., 1985.

Royal Institute of International Affairs. *Documents on International Affairs 1957,* edited by Nobel Frankland. London, 1960.

———. *Documents on International Affairs 1958,* edited by Gillian King. London, 1962.

———. *Documents on International Affairs 1959,* edited by Gillian King. London, 1963.

Royal Ministry of Foreign Affairs. *The Cyprus Question: Discussion at the North Atlantic Treaty Organisation, September–October 1958.* Athens, 1958.

Ruddy, T. Michael. *The Cautious Diplomat: Charles E. Bohlen and the Soviet Union, 1929–1969.* Kent, Ohio, 1986.

Russell, Fred. *Bury Me in an Old Press Box: Good Times and Life of a Sportswriter.* New York, 1957.

"Salute to the Pentagon: Mr. McNamara Inherits an Armed Force Second to None." *Barron's,* December 19, 1960.

Sanders, M. Elizabeth. *The Regulation of Natural Gas: Policy and Politics, 1938.* Philadelphia, 1981.

SarDesai, D. R. *Southeast Asia Past & Present.* 4th ed. Boulder, Col., 1997.

Saulnier, Raymond J. *Constructive Years: The U.S. Economy Under Eisenhower.* Lanham, Md. 1991.

Schapsmeier, Edward L., and Schapsmeier, Frederick H. *Dirksen of Illinois: Senatorial Statesman.* Urbana, Ill., 1985.

Schlesinger, Arthur M., Jr. *A Thousand Days: John F. Kennedy in the White House.* Cambridge, Mass., 1965.

Schoenbaum, Thomas J. *Waging Peace and War: Dean Rusk in the Truman, Kennedy, and Johnson Years.* New York, 1988.

Serrin, William. *The Company and the Union.* New York, 1973.

Shaffer, Edward H. *The Oil Import Program of the United States.* London, 1968.

———. *Canada's Oil and the American Empire.* Edmonton, Alberta, 1983.

Sihanouk, Norodom. *My War with the CIA: The Memoirs of Prince Norodom Sihanouk*, as related to Wilfred Burchett. New York, 1973.

Sills, David L. *The Volunteers: Means and Ends in a National Organization*. Glencoe, Ill., 1957.

Slater, Ellis D. *The Ike I Knew*. Baltimore, 1980.

Sloan, John W. *Eisenhower and the Management of Prosperity*. Lawrence, Kans., 1991.

Smith, Adam. *An Inquiry into the Nature and Causes of the Wealth of Nations*. London, 1776.

Smith, Earl E. T. *The Fourth Floor: An Account of the Castro Communist Revolution*. New York, 1962.

Smith, George David. *From Monopoly to Competition: The Transformation of Alcoa, 1888–1986*. Cambridge, 1988.

Smith, Merriman. *A President's Odyssey*. New York, 1961.

Smith, Richard Norton. *Thomas E. Dewey and His Times*. New York, 1982.

Smith, Roger M. *Cambodia's Foreign Policy*. Ithaca, N.Y., 1969.

Sokolofsky, Homer E. *Kansas Governors*. Lawrence, Kans., 1990.

Sorenson, Theodore C. *Kennedy*. New York, 1965.

———. "Election of 1960." In *History of American Presidential Elections, 1789–1968*, edited by Arthur M. Schlesinger, Jr. 4 vols. New York, 1971. Vol. IV, *1940–1968*.

Spaak, Paul-Henri. *The Continuing Battle: Memoirs of a European 1936–1966*. Boston, 1971.

Spector, Ronald H. *Advice and Support: The Early Years 1941–1960*. In *The United States Army in Vietnam*, edited by David F. Trask. Washington, D.C., 1985.

Stalin, J. V. *Works*. 13 vols. Moscow, 1952–1955. Vol. 1, *1901–1907* (1952).

Stampp, Kenneth M. *The Era of Reconstruction, 1865–1877*. New York, 1966.

Stans, Maurice Hubert. "Must We Delude Ourselves in Disaster?" *Reader's Digest* (July 1959).

Steiner, George. "A Better Way to Deal with China." *Harper's* (June 1957).

Stevenson, Jordan & Harrison. *Monthly Digest of Business Conditions and Probabilities* (October 1958).

Stoetzer, O. Carlos. *The Organization of American States*. 2d edition. Westport, Conn., 1969.

Stone, Richard D. *The Interstate Commerce Commission and the Railroad Industry: A History of Regulatory Policy*. New York, 1991.

Stover, John F. *American Railroads*. Chicago, 1961.

Straszheim, Mahlon R. *The International Airline Industry*. Washington, D.C., 1969.

Strauss, Lewis L. *Men and Decisions*. New York, 1962.

Sulzberger, Cyrus Leo. "Logic, Love and American Understanding of China." *New York Times*, May 29, 1957.

———. "Why We Are Losing Out in Propaganda." *New York Times*, January 15, 1958.

———. *What's Wrong with U.S. Foreign Policy?* New York, 1959.

———. *The Last of the Giants*. New York, 1970.

Suri, Jeremi. "America's Search for a Technological Solution to the Arms Race: The Surprise Attack Conference of 1958 and a Challenge for 'Eisenhower Revisionists.'" *Diplomatic History* 21, no. 3 (1997).

Tananbaum, Duane. *The Bricker Amendment Controversy: A Test of Eisenhower's Political Leadership*. Ithaca, 1988.

Taylor, Maxwell D. *Swords and Plowshares*. New York, 1972.

Terraine, John, ed. *The Life and Times of Lord Mountbatten*. London, 1969.

Tiedemann, Arthur E. "Big Business and Politics in Prewar Japan." In *Dilemmas of Growth in Prewar Japan*, edited by James William Morley. Princeton, 1971.

Tiffany, Paul A. *The Decline of American Steel: How Management, Labor, and Government Went Wrong.* New York, 1988.

Tomson, William J. *Khrushchev: A Political Life.* Oxford, 1995.

Truman, Margaret. *Harry S. Truman.* New York, 1974.

Tuch, Hans N., and Schmidt, G. Lewis, eds. *Ike and USIA: A Commemorative Symposium.* Washington, D.C., 1991.

Tugwell, Franklin. *The Politics of Oil in Venezuela.* Stanford, 1975.

Ulam, Adam B. *Stalin: The Man and His Era.* Boston, 1989.

United Nations. *Security Council Documents, 1957: Twelfth year, Plenary Meetings. United Nations Security Council: Verbatim Record of the 797th Plenary Meeting, Oct. 27, 1957. S/PV.797. Microfiche.*

————. *Yearbook of the United Nations, 1946–1947.* New York, 1947.

————. *Yearbook of the United Nations, 1948–1949.* New York, 1950.

————. *Yearbook of the United Nations, 1950.* New York, 1951.

————. *Yearbook of the United Nations, 1957.* New York, 1958.

————. *Yearbook of the United Nations, 1960.* New York, 1961.

————. *Yearbook of the United Nations, 1994.* New York, 1995.

United States Atomic Energy Commission. *Twenty-fourth Semiannual Report of the Atomic Energy Commission, July 1958.* Washington, D.C., 1958.

United States Atomic Energy Commission. *Twenty-fifth Semiannual Report of the Atomic Energy Commission, January 1959.* Washington, D.C., 1959.

United States. Department of Defense. *Ad Hoc Committee to Study and Revise the Officer Personnel Act of 1947.* Report. Washington, D.C., 1960. The Bolte Report.

United States Government Organization Manual, 1957–1958. Washington, D.C., revised June 1, 1957.

"United States Participates in Economic Talks at Paris." *U.S. Department of State Bulletin* 42, no. 1075 (February 1, 1960).

"The U.N. as a Peace Mechanism." *U.S. Department of State Bulletin* 41, no. 1959 (October 12, 1959).

U.S. Commission On Organization of the Executive Branch of the Government, *Final Report to the Congress.* Washington, D.C., 1955.

U.S. Congress. House. Committee on Armed Services. *Authorizing the Exchange of Land Between the United States and Puerto Rico.* 83d Cong., 2d sess., 1954. H. Rept. 1335.

U.S. Congress. House. Committee on Foreign Affairs. *New York World's Fair, 1964–65.* 86th Cong., 2d sess., 1960. H. Rept. 86-2111.

U.S. Congress. House. Committee on Foreign Affairs. Subcommittee on Europe. *Hearings on Poland Aid Program and Eastern Europe.* 85th Cong., 1st sess., 1957.

U.S. Congress. House. Committee on Interstate and Foreign Commerce. "Natural Gas Act: Regulation of Producers' Prices." *Committee Hearings.* Senate Library, vol. 1605. 85th Cong., 1st sess., 1957.

U.S. Congress. House. Committee on the Judiciary. *An Analysis of Replies to a Questionnaire and Testimony at a Hearing on Presidential Inability.* 85th Cong., 1st sess., March 26, 1957.

U.S. Congress. House. Committee on Judiciary. Subcommittee on Antitrust. *Automobile Dealer Franchises.* 84th Cong., 2d sess., July 2, 1956.

U.S. Congress. House. *International Travel: A Report on the Barriers to International Travel and Ways and Means of Promoting and Developing, Encouraging, and Facilitating Such Travel.* A Message from the President of the United States. 85th Cong., 2d sess. *Mis-*

cellaneous House Documents, House Doc. 381. Fiche 4, no. 12142. V. 46, n. 348, 372, 381, 449. Washington, D.C., 1958.

U.S. Congress. Senate. Committee on Armed Services. *Providing for the Exchange of Certain Lands in Puerto Rico.* 87th Cong., 2d sess., 1962. S. Rept. 1913.

U.S. Congress. Senate. Committee on Armed Services. *Providing for Exchange Between the United States and the Commonwealth of Puerto Rico of Certain Lands and Interest.* 83d Cong., 1st sess., 1953. S. Rept. 163.

U.S. Congress. Senate. Committee on Foreign Relations. "Ambassadorial Appointments." *Committee Hearings.* Vol. 1275.2. 85th Cong., 1st sess., 1957.

U.S. Congress. Senate. Committee on Foreign Relations. "The Nomination of Maxwell Henry Gluck to be Ambassador to Ceylon." *Committee Hearings.* Vol. 1275.2. 85th Cong., 1st sess., 1957.

U.S. Congress. Senate. Committee on Foreign Relations. Subcommittee on State Department Organization and Public Affairs. *United States Aid in Vietnam.* 86th Cong., 2d sess., 1960.

U.S. Congress. Senate. *Committee Hearings,* 85th Cong. Vol. 1220, 1957.

U.S. Congress. Senate. Committee on Rules and Administration. *Study of the Effectiveness of Governmental Organization and Procedure in the Contest with World Communism.* S. Res. 115. S. Rept. No. 302. 86th Cong., 1st sess., 1959.

U.S. Congress. Senate. Subcommittee of the Committee on Appropriations. *Treasury and Post Office Departments Appropriations, 1958: Hearings on H.R. 4897.* 85th Cong., 1st sess., 1957.

U.S. Department of State. *American Foreign Policy; Current Documents, 1957.* Washington, D.C., 1961.

————. *American Foreign Policy; Current Documents, 1958.* Washington, D.C., 1962.

————. *American Foreign Policy; Current Documents, 1959.* Washington, D.C., 1963.

————. *American Foreign Policy; Current Documents, 1960.* Washington, D.C., 1964. Washington, D.C.

————. *Documents on Disarmament, 1945–1959.* 2 vols. Washington, D.C., 1960. Vol. II, *1957–1959.*

————. *Documents on Disarmament, 1960.* Washington, D.C., 1961.

————. *Documents on Germany, 1944–1985.* Washington, D.C., 1985.

————. *Foreign Relations of the United States, 1950.* 7 vols. Washington, D.C., 1976–81. Vol. V, *The Near East, South Asia, and Africa* (1978).

————. *Foreign Relations of the United States, 1952–1954.* 16 vols. Washington, D.C., 1979–89. Vol. XIV, *China and Japan,* 2 pts. (1985).

————. *Foreign Relations of the United States, 1955–1957.* 27 vols. Washington, D.C., 1985–92. Vol. I, *Vietnam* (1985); vol. III, *China* (1986); vol. IV, *Western European Security and Integration* (1986); vol. V, *Austrian State Treaty; Summit and Foreign Ministers Meetings, 1955* (1988); vol. VI, *American Republics: Multilateral; Mexico; Caribbean* (1987); vol. VII, *American Republics: Central and South America* (1987); vol. VIII, *South Asia* (1987); vol. IX, *Foreign Economic Policy; Foreign Information Program* (1987); vol. X, *Foreign Aid and Economic Defense Policy* (1989); vol. XI, *United Nations and General International Matters* (1988); vol. XII, *Near East Region; Iran; Iraq* (1991); vol. XIII, *Near East: Jordan-Yemen* (1988); vol. XIV, *Arab-Israeli Dispute 1955* (1989); vol. XV, *Arab-Israeli Dispute January 1–July 26, 1956* (1989); vol. XVI, *Suez Crisis July 26–December 31, 1956* (1990); vol. XVII, *Arab-Israeli Dispute, 1957* (1990); vol. XVIII, *Africa* (1989); vol. XIX, *National Security Policy* (1990); vol. XX, *Regulation of Armaments; Atomic Energy* (1990); vol. XXII, *Southeast Asia* (1989); vol. XXIII, 2 vols. *Japan,* pt. 1 (1991); *Korea,* pt. 2 (1993); vol.

XXIV, *Soviet Union; Eastern Mediterranean* (1989); vol. XXV, *Eastern Europe* (1990); vol. XXVI, *Central and Southeastern Europe* (1992); vol. XXVII, *Western Europe and Canada* (1992).

———. *Foreign Relations of the United States, 1958–1960.* 19 vols. Washington, D.C., 1986–94. Vol. I, *Vietnam* (1986); vol. II, *United Nations and General International Matters* (1991); vol. III, *National Security Policy; Arms Control and Disarmament* (1996); vol. IV, *Foreign Economic Policy* (1992); vol. V, *American Republics* (1991); vol. VI, *Cuba* (1991); vol. VII, pt. 1, *Western European Integration and Security; Canada* (1993); pt. 2, *Western Europe* (1993); vol. VIII, *Berlin Crisis 1958–1959* (1993); vol. IX, *Berlin Crisis 1959–1960; Germany; Austria* (1993); vol. X, pt. 1, *Eastern Europe Region; Soviet Union; Cyprus* (1993); pt. 2, *Eastern Europe; Finland; Greece; Turkey* (1993); vol. XI, *Lebanon and Jordan* (1992); vol. XII, *Near East Region; Iraq; Iran; Arabian Peninsula* (1993); vol. XIII, *Arab-Israeli Dispute; United Arab Republic; North Africa* (1992); vol. XIV, *Africa* (1992); vol. XV, *South and Southeast Asia* (1992); vol. XVI. *East Asia–Pacific Region; Cambodia; Laos* (1992); vol. XVII, Indonesia (1994); vol. XVIII, *Japan; Korea* (1994); vol. XIX, *China* (1996); vols. XVII/XVIII, *Indonesia; Japan; Korea*, Microfiche Supplement no. 462.

———. *Foreign Relations of the United States, 1961–1963.* 24 vols. Washington, D.C., 1988–. Vol. XXIV, *Laos Crisis* (1994).

U.S., Joint Chiefs of Staff. *The History of the Joint Chiefs of Staff.* 6 vols. to date. Wilmington, Del., 1979–; Washington, D.C., 1986. Vol. V. *The Joint Chiefs of Staff and National Policy, 1953–1954*, by Robert J. Watson (1986). Vol. VI. *The Joint Chiefs of Staff and National Policy, 1955–1956*, by Kenneth W. Condit (1992).

U.S., Office of the Secretary of Defense. *History of the Office of the Secretary of Defense*, edited by Alfred Goldberg. 3 vols. to date. Washington, D.C., 1984–1997. Vol. IV. *Into the Missile Age, 1956–1960*, by Robert J. Watson (1997).

U.S. Lincoln Sesquicentennial Commission. *Abraham Lincoln Sesquicentennial 1959–1960.* Washington, D.C., 1960.

U.S. Postal Service. *Postage Stamps of the United States.* Washington, D.C., 1970.

U.S. President. *Economic Report of the President, 1958.* Washington, D.C., 1958.

Vandenberg, Arthur H., Jr. *The Private Papers of Senator Vandenberg.* Boston, 1952.

van Ee, Daun. "From the New Look to Flexible Response." In *Against All Enemies: Interpretations of American Military History from Colonial Times to the Present*, edited by Kenneth J. Hagan and William R. Roberts. Westport, Conn., 1986.

Vietor, Richard H. K. *Energy Policy in America since 1945: A Study of Business-Government Relations.* Cambridge, 1984.

Voltaire. "La Beguele." In *The Oxford Dictionary of Phrase, Saying, and Quotation*, edited by Elizabeth Knowles. Oxford and New York, 1997.

von Braun, Wernher. "The Redstone, Jupiter, and Juno." In *The History of Rocket Technology*, edited by Eugene M. Emme. Detroit, 1964.

Wall, Irwin M. "The United States, Algeria, and the Fall of the Fourth French Republic." *Diplomatic History* 18, no. 4 (1994).

Walters, Vernon A. *Silent Missions.* New York, 1978.

Washburn, Abbott. "Why Did President Eisenhower Put So Much Faith in People-to-People Contacts?" *People* (Summer 1990).

Washburn, Wilcomb E., comp. *The American Indian and the United States: A Documentary History.* 4 vols. New York, 1973. Vol. III.

———. *Red Man's Land/White Man's Law: A Study of the Past and Present Status of the American Indian.* New York, 1971.

Washington, George. *Basic Writings of George Washington*, edited by Saxe Commins. New York, 1948.

Watson, Robert J. *Into the Missile Age: 1956–1960*. Washington, D.C., 1997.

Weeks, Edward. "The Peripatetic Reviewer." *Atlantic Monthly* 202 (July 1958).

Weigley, Russell F. *The American Way of War: A History of United States Military Strategy and Policy*. Bloomington, Ind., and London, 1977.

Weiss, Roger J. "The Automobile Dealer Franchise Act of 1956—An Evaluation." *Cornell Law Quarterly*, vol. 48 (1962–63).

Welter, Rush. *Popular Education and Democratic Thought in America*. New York, 1962.

White, Theodore H. *The Making of the President 1960*. New York, 1967.

White, William S. *The Taft Story*. New York, 1954.

Wiley, Bell Irvin, and Milhollen, Hirst Dillon. *They Who Fought Here*. New York, 1959.

Wilhelm, Peter. *The Nobel Prize*. Stockholm and London, 1983.

Wilson, Woodrow. *The Papers of Woodrow Wilson*, edited by Arthur S. Link. 69 vols. Princeton, N.J., 1966–94. Vol. 63, *September 4–November 5, 1919* (1990).

Wind, Herbert Warren. "The Masters." In *The Spectacle of Sport from Sports Illustrated*, edited by Norton Wood. Englewood Cliffs, N.J., 1957.

Wriston, Henry Merritt. *Prepare for Peace!* New York, 1941.

———. "Leadership: Individualists vs. Security." *Wall Street Journal*, June 1, 1960.

Yergin, Daniel. *The Prize: The Epic Quest for Oil, Money and Power*. New York, 1991.

Glossary

AAU	Association of American Universities
ABA	American Bar Association
ADA	Americans for Democratic Action
AEC	Atomic Energy Commission
AFBF	American Farm Bureau Federation
AF of L	American Federation of Labor
ALCOA	Aluminum Company of America
ANP	Aircraft Nuclear Propulsion project
ANVIL	Code name for invasion of the south of France in August 1944
ANZUS	Australia, New Zealand, United States
AP	Associated Press
AQUATONE	Code name for U-2 flights over Soviet Union
ARPA	Advanced Research Projects Agency
ASNE	American Society of Newspaper Editors
Atlas	Liquid-fuel intercontinental ballistic missile program
AT&T	American Telephone and Telegraph Company
AWF	Ann Whitman File (Eisenhower's presidential papers)
BAC	Business Advisory Council
BBC	British Broadcasting Corporation
Blue Streak	Intermediate-range liquid-fuel British ballistic missile
BOAC	British Overseas Airways Corporation
CAA	Civil Aeronautics Administration
CAB	Civil Aeronautics Board
CASTLE	Hydrogen bomb tests at Bikini Atoll, Pacific, March–April 1954

CEA	Council of Economic Advisors
CED	Committee for Economic Development
CENTO	Central European Treaty Organization
CHINCOM	China Committee of the Paris Consultative Group (meets in Paris, May 7, 1957)
CIA	Central Intelligence Agency
CIGS	Chief of the Imperial General Staff
CINCARIB	Commander in Chief, Caribbean
CINCSAC	Commander in Chief, Strategic Air Command
CIO	Congress of Industrial Organizations
Common Market	European Economic Community
Corporal	Mobile, surface to surface, liquid-fuel guided missile, with nuclear warhead capability
COSSAC	Chief of Staff to the Supreme Allied Commander
DAT	French Territorial Air Defense
Discoverer XIV	United States Air Force prototype recoverable satellite program. Discoverer XIV was launched August 19, 1960, the capsule recovered in the air
DLF	Development Loan Fund
DM	Deutschemark
DRAGOON	New code name for ANVIL, the 1944 invasion of southern France
Echo I	United States passive communications satellite, launched August 12, 1960
EDC	European Defense Community
EEC	European Economic Community
EFTA	European Free Trade Association (Outer Seven)
EM	Eisenhower Manuscripts
EOKA	National Organization of Cyprus Fighters; Greek Cypriot liberation movement in Cyprus
EURATOM	European Atomic Agency
Explorer I	Earth satellite
FAA	Federal Aviation Agency
FCDA	Federal Civil Defense Administration
F-86	Jet fighter plane, carrying a Sidewinder weapons system
FHA	Federal Housing Administration
FOA	Foreign Operations Administration
FPC	Federal Power Commission
GATT	General Agreement on Tariffs and Trade
GNP	Gross National Product

GOP	Grand Old Party (Republican party)
GSA	General Services Administration
HARDTACK	Thermonuclear experiments at Bikini and Enewetok atolls in the northern Pacific Marshall Islands, May 1958
Honest John	Surface-to-surface, free flight, solid propellant rocket with nuclear warhead capability
HOPE	Health Opportunity for People Everywhere
HUSKY	Code name for Allied invasion of Sicily in July 1943
IADB	Inter-American Development Bank
IAEA	International Atomic Energy Agency
IAM	International Association of Machinists
IBM	International Business Machines
ICA	International Cooperation Administration
ICBM	Intercontinental Ballistic Missile
ICC	Interstate Commerce Commission
ICC	International Commission for the Supervision and Control of the Armistice in Laos
IDA	International Development Association
ILO	International Labor Organization
IMF	International Monetary Fund
IMG	Informational Media Guaranty program
INS	Immigration and Naturalization Service
IRBM	Intermediate Range Ballistic Missile
IRS	Internal Revenue Service
JCAE	Joint Committee on Atomic Energy
JCS	Joint Chiefs of Staff
JSTPS	Joint Strategic Target Planning Staff
Jupiter	Liquid propellant, one-stage intermediate range ballistic missile equipped with a nuclear warhead
MAAG	Military Assistance Advisory Group
MARKET-GARDEN	Code name for airborne operation to establish a bridgehead across the Rhine in the Netherlands in September 1944: Operation MARKET involved seizure of bridges in the Nijmegen-Arnhem area; Operation GARDEN was to open a corridor from Eindhoven northward toward Germany
Matador	Subsonic, surface-to-surface, guided tactical missile, equipped with a nuclear warhead
MEDICO	Medical International Corporation
Mercury	*See* Project Mercury

MRBM	Mid-range ballistic missile with a range in the interval 500–3,000 nautical miles
MSA	Mutual Security Administration
NAACP	National Association for the Advancement of Colored People
NASA	National Aeronautics and Space Agency
NATO	North Atlantic Treaty Organization
Navaho	Ramjet-powered Mach 3 cruise missile launched by rocket booster
NHPC	National Historical Publications Commission
NIH	National Institutes of Health
Nike Ajax	Mobile or fixed-site, surface-to-air guided missile designed to intercept manned bombers and airbreathing missiles
NLRB	National Labor Relations Board
NPC	National Petroleum Council
NS	Nuclear Ship
NSC	National Security Council
NYA	National Youth Administration
OAS	Organization of American States
OASI	Old Age and Survivors Insurance program
OCB	Operations Coordinating Board
ODM	Office of Defense Mobilization
OECD	Organization for Economic Cooperation and Development
OEEC	Organization for European Economic Cooperation
OSS	Office of Strategic Services
Outer Seven	*See* European Free Trade Association
OVERLORD	Code name for the Allied invasion of Northwest Europe in the spring, 1944
Pemex	Petróleos Mexicanos, the Mexican oil company
PHS	Public Health Service
POL	Petroleum, Oil, Lubricants
Polaris	Submarine-launched solid-fuel ballistic missile, equipped with a nuclear warhead
Project Mercury	NASA's manned satellite program
PWA	Public Works Administration
RCA	Radio Corporation of America
Reclama	Request to authority to reconsider its decision or its proposed action
Redstone	First U.S. large ballistic missile

REDWING	Pacific test series that included the first air drop of a hydrogen bomb, May 1956
Regulus	Surface-to-surface, jet powered-guided missile, equipped with a nuclear warhead
REA	Rural Electrification Administration
ROK	Republic of Korea
SAC	Strategic Air Command
SACEUR	Supreme Allied Commander, Europe
SACLANT	Supreme Allied Commander, Atlantic
Saturn	Large space-vehicle launching booster
SEATO	Southeast Asia Treaty Organization
SEC	Securities and Exchange Commission
SHAPE	Supreme Headquarters Allied Powers, Europe
Sidewinder	Air-to-air rocket with non-nuclear warhead
SIOP	Single Integrated Operations Plan for nuclear warfare
Skybolt	Air-launched ballistic missile, designed to be compatible with British aircraft
Sky Hawk	U.S.-Canada projected air defense exercise
Sky Shield	U.S.-Canada projected air defense exercise
SLEDGEHAMMER	Code name for a limited-objective attack across the Channel in 1942 designed either to take advantage of a crack in German morale or as a "sacrifice" operation to aid the Russians
Snark	Subsonic turbojet-powered cruise missile
SSN	Nuclear powered submarine
SS-10 and SS-11	Anti-tank missiles
Talos	Shipborne, surface-to-air missile, equipped with solid-propellant rocket/ramjet engine, and nuclear or nonnuclear warhead
Tartar	Shipborne, surface-to-air missile equipped with solid propellant rocket engine and nonnuclear warhead
Terrier	Surface-to-air missile equipped with a solid fuel rocket motor
Thor	Liquid propellant, one stage, rocket-powered intermediate range ballistic missile equipped with a nuclear warhead
Tiros I and II	Television Infrared Observation Satellite. Code name for meteorological satellite series equipped with television cameras to scan earth's weather conditions; launched April 1 and November 23, 1960, respectively

Titan	Surface-to-surface ballistic missile program
TORCH	Code name for Allied invasion of North and Northwest Africa on November 8, 1942
Triton	The U.S. Navy's nuclear-powered radar-picket submarine
UAR	United Arab Republic
UAW	United Automobile Workers of America
UGF	United Givers Fund
U.N.E.F.	United Nations Emergency Force
UNGA	United Nations General Assembly
UP	United Press
USGA	United States Golf Association
USIA	United States Information Agency
USO	United Service Organizations
U-2	Secret spy plane designed to penetrate Soviet air defenses at high altitudes
VA	Veterans Administration
Valco	Volta Aluminum Company
Van Allen Belt	A belt of intense radiation in the magnetosphere composed of energetic charged particles trapped by the earth's magnetic field; discovered by physicist James Alfred Van Allen in 1958.
VOA	Voice of America
WEU	Western European Union
WHCF	White House Central Files
WPA	Work Projects Administration; also Works Progress Administration

Chronology

1957

January   20   Washington. Takes Oath of Office.

21   Washington. Morning appointments with S. Adams; State Senator and Mrs. Jones (New Jersey). Poses for photographs with Vice-President and Mrs. Nixon, Senator Sparkman, and Congressman Martin. To Capitol with Senator Bridges and Mrs. Eisenhower. Witnesses swearing-in of Vice-President Nixon. Takes Oath of Office. Attends luncheon in the Supreme Court Room with Vice-President and Mrs. Nixon and Mrs. Eisenhower. Departs for White House and watches Inaugural Parade from reviewing stand. To National Guard Armory with Major and Mrs. J. S. D. Eisenhower, General and Mrs. Snyder, and Mrs. Eisenhower. Attends Inaugural parties at Statler Hotel, Mayflower Hotel, and Sheraton Park Hotel.

22   Washington. Morning appointments with Raymond J. "Steve" Saulnier and B. M. Shanley; RNC members; Governor and Mrs. Clyde and daughter (Utah), and S. Adams; A. F. Burns; Fitzsimons Army Hospital staff; General Persons and J. C. Hagerty; E. J. Hughes. Swims.

23   Washington. Morning appointments with General Persons; Legislative Leaders; Senator Bridges and I. J. Martin; S. Adams; Secretary Dulles, S. Adams,

General Persons, J. C. Hagerty, B. N. Harlow, Budget Director Brundage, and M. Snyder; J. C. Hagerty and M. Snyder; news briefing; news conference. Afternoon appointments with Secretary Seaton and S. Adams; S. Adams; Captains Beach and Aurand. Swims.

24   Washington. Morning appointments with General Goodpaster; Ambassador Lodge (to Spain); General Cutler. National Security Council session followed by appointments with General Clark; General Cutler; W. J. Hopkins; S. Adams; M. Snyder; S. Adams. Hosts reception with Mrs. Eisenhower for Diplomatic Corps and State Department Officials.

25   Washington. Morning appointments with S. W. Richardson; C. A. Herter; A. W. Dulles, Dr. Herbert Scoville, Arthur C. Lundahl, and General Goodpaster; General Persons and B. N. Harlow; General Goodpaster; B. M. Shanley; S. Adams, G. D. Morgan, and K. B. McCann; G. D. Morgan; General Goodpaster; B. M. Shanley. To Gettysburg farm with General Gruenther and G. E. Allen. Inspects farm. To Camp David, Maryland, with General Gruenther and G. E. Allen.

26   Camp David, Maryland. To Gettysburg farm with General Gruenther and G. E. Allen. Visits G. E. Allen's farm and returns to Camp David.

27   Camp David, Maryland. To White House with Mrs. Eisenhower.

28   Washington. Morning appointments with G. D. Morgan; M. Snyder; General Cutler; General Goodpaster; H. Hoover, Jr.; Thad Hutcheson, Congressman Alger, and General Persons; Senators Flanders and Sparkman, Brook Hayes, and S. Adams; cartoonists Gib Crockett and Jim Berryman; Congressman Curtis, Attorney General Brownell, and S. Adams (off the record); Attorney General Brownell. Off-the-record appointments with Harold E. Stassen; R. L. Biggers. Afternoon appointments with W. J. Hopkins; General Persons.

29   Washington. Morning appointments with General Goodpaster; Legislative Leaders; Senator Bridges; S. Adams; B. M. Shanley; S. Adams; General Persons;

Delmar H. Nucker (High Commissioner, Pacific Islands) and Jack Anderson; General Goodpaster; Secretary Wilson; Junior Achievement representatives, Lancaster County. Attends luncheon of Republican senators at Capitol. Afternoon appointments with Generals Persons and Goodpaster; Secretary Dulles, H. Hoover, Jr., W. M. Rountree, and General Goodpaster; M. B. Folsom and Dr. Harold C. Hunt; Secretary Dulles; S. Adams. Hosts dinner with Mrs. Eisenhower for Supreme Court Justices.

30   Washington. Morning appointments with W. J. Hopkins; S. Adams; B. M. Shanley; General Cutler and J. S. Lay; A. B. Kline and G. M. Hauge; G. D. Morgan; General Goodpaster; news briefing; news conference. Late morning appointments with General Persons and Colonel Schulz; M. J. McCaffree. To MATS terminal with B. M. Shanley, General Goodpaster, and Colonel Schulz to greet King Saud ibn Abd al-Aziz (Saudi Arabia). Afternoon appointments with B. M. Shanley; royal family of Saudi Arabia, Secretary Dulles, H. Hoover, Jr., W. M. Rountree, and Ambassadors Richards (to Middle East) and George Wadsworth (to Saudi Arabia); King Saud and interpreter. Hosts stag dinner in honor of King Saud.

February 1   Washington. Morning appointments with Captain Beach; W. J. Hopkins; B. M. Shanley; B. N. Harlow; Reserve Officers Association members; S. Adams and G. M. Hauge. Cabinet meeting, followed by appointments with Attorney General Brownell; B. M. Shanley; General Goodpaster; Generals Norstad and Goodpaster; General Goodpaster. Lunch. Afternoon appointments with General Goodpaster; R. B. Anderson; Secretary Dulles; W. M. Rountree and Secretary Dulles; King Saud and interpreter; royal family of Saudi Arabia, Secretary Dulles, H. Hoover, Jr., C. A. Herter, Ambassador Richards, W. M. Rountree, and William A. Staltsfus (Recorder, State Department); Secretary Dulles and C. A. Herter; Generals Goodpaster and Snyder. Attends dinner honoring King Saud at Mayflower Hotel.

2   Washington. To MATS terminal with Colonel Schulz. Boards *Columbine* en route to Augusta, Georgia, with

Generals Snyder and Goodpaster, Secretary and Mrs. Wilson, and M. Snyder. Greeted at Bush Field, Augusta, by Major General Phillip Gallager, Jerome Franklin, and C. Roberts; Boy Scout troop. To Augusta National Golf Club for golf with C. Roberts, W. E. Robinson, and E. B. Dudley. Dinner at Augusta National Golf Club with Generals Snyder and Goodpaster, W. E. Robinson, and C. Roberts.

3   Augusta, Georgia. Morning golf game with W. E. Robinson, B. T. Leithead, E. B. Dudley. Returns to Washington aboard *Columbine*.

4   Washington. Morning appointments with General Goodpaster; Generals Persons and Goodpaster, and B. N. Harlow. Appointments with National Guard Association members, B. N. Harlow, and Generals Persons and Goodpaster. Appointment on Highway Program with Secretary Weeks, John A. Volpe, Bertram D. Tallamy, and Louis S. Rothschild. Late morning appointments with Ambassador Raymond A. Hare (to Egypt); Senator Goldwater; D. MacArthur; General Cutler; G. D. Morgan; General Goodpaster. To Shoreham Hotel with M. Kestnbaum for Citizens Committee for the Hoover Report luncheon. Presents award to H. Hoover, Sr., for his work on the Hoover Commission. Afternoon appointments with S. Adams; W. J. Hopkins. Hosts dinner with Mrs. Eisenhower in honor of Vice-President Nixon and Cabinet members.

5   Washington. Morning appointments with General Persons and I. J. Martin; General Goodpaster; Legislative Leaders; General Cutler and J. S. Lay; Secretary Weeks and H. C. McClellan; American Retail Federation representatives; H. Hoover, Jr.; Prince Amir Abdul Ilah (Iraq), Ambassador Mousa Al-Shabandar (from Iraq), W. M. Rountree, and W. T. Buchanan; General Goodpaster. Hosts for Crusade for Freedom luncheon. Afternoon appointments with H. E. Stassen; Dr. M. S. Eisenhower; G. D. Morgan; S. Adams. To Statler Hotel for Coast and Geodetic Survey Sesquicentennial Dinner.

6   Washington. Morning appointments with General Goodpaster; Secretary Brucker, Generals Taylor, Persons, and Goodpaster, and B. N. Harlow; Am-

bassador Henry J. Taylor (to Switzerland); news briefing. News conference, followed by appointments with Dr. Charles Malik (Minister of Foreign Affairs, Lebanon), Ambassador Victor A. Khouri (from Lebanon), and Fraser Wilkins (Director, Office of Near Eastern Affairs); General Goodpaster; Water Pollution Control Advisory Board; S. Adams; District of Columbia Auditorium Commission. Lunch. Appears in Red Cross film. Afternoon appointments with S. Adams; H. M. Alcorn; Franz Etzel (Vice-President, European Coal and Steel Community), Louis Armand (President, French Railroad System), Francesco Giordani (President, Italian Research Council), Max Kohnstamm (Chief of Staff, European Coal and Steel Community), Admiral Strauss, Ambassador Butterworth (European Coal and Steel Community), Gerard Smith, General Goodpaster, and G. M. Hauge; M. Snyder. Swims.

7   Washington. Morning appointments with General Goodpaster and W. J. Hopkins; General Twining; M. D. Sprague and R. B. Robertson; National Security Council session; Secretary Dulles; J. B. Hollister; Boy Scouts of America representatives regarding Boy Scout Week; Postmaster General Summerfield and J. Z. Anderson; W. J. Hopkins; S. Adams. Lunch. Appointments with Ambassador Taft (to Ireland); General Curtis. Entertains at White House reception with Mrs. Eisenhower.

8   Washington. Morning appointments with Captain Beach; W. J. Hopkins; General Goodpaster; G. D. Morgan; General Cutler; S. Adams; General Persons; Attorney General Brownell; S. Adams. Cabinet meeting. Late morning appointment with Secretary Dulles, W. M. Rountree, and General Goodpaster; King Saud and interpreter; Saudi Arabian officials, King Saud, Secretary Dulles, W. M. Rountree, Ambassador Wadsworth, and W. A. Staltsfus; Secretary Dulles; M. J. McCaffree. To MATS terminal with Mrs. Eisenhower en route to Thomasville, Georgia. Arrives at Spence Air Force Base, Moultrie, Georgia. To Milestone Plantation, near Thomasville, Georgia.

9   Thomasville, Georgia. Hunting.

10   Thomasville, Georgia. Attends services at First Presbyterian Church. To Sinkolo Plantation to inspect Angus cattle. Returns to Milestone Plantation.

11   Thomasville, Georgia. Quail hunting.

12   Thomasville, Georgia. To Glen Arven Country Club. Golf with John Walters (golf pro), J. C. Hagerty, and G. E. Allen. Quail hunting with Secretary Humphrey, G. E. Allen, General Snyder, and Ambassador Whitney (to Great Britain). Dinner with E. Doud, General Snyder, Mr. and Mrs. G. E. Allen, and Secretary and Mrs. Humphrey. Bridge with G. E. Allen, Ambassador Whitney, W. E. Robinson.

13   Thomasville, Georgia. Quail hunting. Luncheon at Mitchell Lodge. Turkey shoot at Greenwood farms. Returns to Milestone Plantation. Evening appointment with General Goodpaster.

14   Thomasville, Georgia. To Glen Arven Country Club for golf with Ambassador Whitney, W. E. Robinson, and G. E. Allen. To Swift farms for quail hunting. Dinner with Secretary and Mrs. Humphrey, General Snyder, Mr. and Mrs. G. E. Allen, W. E. Robinson, and Ambassador Whitney. Bridge with Ambassador Whitney, G. E. Allen, and W. E. Robinson.

15   Thomasville, Georgia. To Spring Hill Plantation for turkey shoot. Returns to Milestone Plantation for bridge with Secretary Humphrey, G. E. Allen, and W. E. Robinson. Dinner with E. Doud, General Snyder, Mr. and Mrs. G. E. Allen, Secretary and Mrs. Humphrey, and W. E. Robinson. Bridge with Secretary Humphrey, G. E. Allen, and W. E. Robinson. Late evening appointments with Secretary Dulles and Ambassador Lodge; General Snyder and Dr. Frank Miller.

16   Thomasville, Georgia. Appointments with General Snyder and Dr. Miller; Secretary Dulles and Ambassador Lodge. Bridge with Secretary Humphrey, G. E. Allen, and W. E. Robinson. Dinner with Secretary and Mrs. Humphrey, Mr. and Mrs. G. E. Allen, E. Doud, W. E. Robinson, and General Snyder. Bridge with Secretary Humphrey, G. E. Allen, and W. E. Robinson.

17 Thomasville, Georgia. Visits Holly Hill Plantation. Afternoon bridge with Secretary Humphrey, G. E. Allen, and W. E. Robinson. Evening bridge with G. E. Allen, William Slater, and Secretary Humphrey.

18 Thomasville, Georgia. Bridge with G. E. Allen, W. Slater, and Secretary Humphrey. Dinner with Secretary and Mrs. Humphrey, Mr. and Mrs. G. E. Allen, and W. Slater. Bridge with W. Slater, G. E. Allen, and Secretary Humphrey.

19 Thomasville, Georgia. To Spence Air Force Base with Mrs. Eisenhower. Boards *Columbine* for Washington. Arrives at MATS terminal and proceeds to White House. Appointments with General Goodpaster; B. M. Shanley; Secretary Dulles, General Persons, and J. C. Hagerty; Ambassador Lodge; Robert Hill; B. N. Harlow; J. W. Barba.

20 Washington. Morning appointments with S. Adams and J. C. Hagerty; Secretary Dulles; bipartisan Legislative Leaders. Late morning appointments with Senator Johnson; Secretary Dulles and J. C. Hagerty; Ambassador Lodge; Ambassador John M. Allison (to Indonesia); General Cutler; J. C. Hagerty; General Persons. Lunch. Attends swearing-in ceremony of Postmaster General Summerfield for second term. Afternoon appointment with Secretary Dulles. Delivers nationwide radio and television broadcast on Middle East situation.

21 Washington. Morning appointments with S. Adams; National Security Council session; A. Larson; Ambassador Whitney; W. J. Hopkins; M. J. McCaffree; S. Adams. Lunch, followed by appointments with Attorney General Brownell; S. Adams; General Goodpaster; J. C. Hagerty; General Goodpaster; G. M. Hauge and R. J. Saulnier. To Walter Reed Hospital for x-rays.

22 Washington. Morning appointments with W. J. Hopkins; General Goodpaster and J. C. Hagerty; Secretary Dulles; General Goodpaster.

23 Washington. Morning appointments with S. Adams and General Goodpaster; General Goodpaster; J. C. Hagerty; B. M. Shanley.

24 [Page missing.]

25 Washington. Morning appointments with J. C. Hagerty; General Cutler; W. J. Hopkins; Lessing J. Rosenwald (President, American Council of Judaism) (off the record). Presents Guggenheim International Award to Ben Nicholson. Late morning appointment with Secretary Dulles and C. B. Elbrick. To Health, Education, and Welfare building with J. C. Hagerty to deliver "Voice of America" speech. Lunch. Off-the-record evening appointment with Dr. Isadore Ravdin and Generals Snyder and Cutler.

26 Washington. Morning appointments with General Goodpaster; General Persons and I. J. Martin; Legislative Leaders. Late morning appointments with J. Z. Anderson; B. M. Shanley; Governor Anderson, Senators Curtis and Hruska, Mayor Rosenblatt (Omaha, Nebraska), and J. Z. Anderson regarding drought in Nebraska; General Goodpaster; Prime Minister Mollet, Foreign Minister Pineau, Ambassador Alphand (from France), Louis Joxe (Secretary General, French Ministry of Foreign Affairs), Secretary Dulles, H. Phleger, W. M. Rountree, and Colonel Walters (interpreter); S. Adams. Hosts luncheon in honor of Prime Minister Mollet. Appointments with Prime Minister Mollet and French officials; Ambassador Houghton (to France) and Secretary Dulles; S. Adams; J. C. Hagerty; General Goodpaster and W. J. Hopkins.

27 Washington. Morning appointments with S. Adams; W. J. Hopkins; Major Florence Judd (nurse, Walter Reed Hospital); S. Adams. Poses for photographs for Federal Service Campaign for National Health Agencies and Federal Joint Crusade. Off-the-record appointment with S. Adams, Attorney General Brownell, R. B. Anderson, and A. S. Flemming. Late morning appointments with William D. Kerr (Partner, Bacon, Whipple, and Co.); W. E. Kerr and investment bankers; J. W. Barba; Vice-President Nixon; Mr. and Mrs. O. R. Reid. Greets delegates to 1957 *New York Herald Tribune* high school forum. Appointments with Prime Minister Mollet and French officials; Prime Minister Mollet. Lunch. Afternoon

appointments with E. Frederic Morrow and S. Adams (off the record); Budget Director Brundage; Cabinet meeting; Secretary Humphrey; H. M. Alcorn, Joseph Bachelder, General Persons, T. E. Stephens, and H. Pyle (off the record).

28 Washington. Morning appointments with Generals Cutler and Goodpaster and Admiral Strauss; P. Young; Erich Ollenhauer (Head, German Social Democratic Party), Ambassador Heinz L. Krekeler (from Germany), Fritz Heine (Public Relations Director, Social Democratic Party), C. B. Elbrick, and Nora M. Lejins (interpreter, State Department); Prime Minister Mollet, Foreign Minister Pineau, and Secretary Dulles; National Security Council session; W. J. Hopkins; Robert Fogan and Ralph Lucier (off the record). To Pentagon for luncheon in honor of A. S. Flemming and G. Gray. Witnesses swearing-in of M. D. Sprague as Assistant Secretary of Defense and Robert Dechert as General Counsel, Department of Defense. Afternoon appointment with B. M. Shanley. Dinner at White House with Mrs. Eisenhower honoring Congressman Sam Rayburn.

March 1 Washington. Morning appointments with W. J. Hopkins; General Cutler; General Goodpaster; General Persons; J. Z. Anderson; Citizen Advisers on Mutual Security Program. Late morning appointments with B. F. Fairless; B. M. Shanley; General Goodpaster; Ambassador Najib-Ullah (from Afghanistan) and W. T. Buchanan; Attorney General Brownell and S. E. Sobeloff; Secretary Dulles, Attorney General Brownell, S. E. Sobeloff, J. L. Rankin, H. Phleger, and E. A. McCabe regarding off-shore rights; Secretary Dulles; Secretary Dulles and H. E. Stassen; Secretary Wilson and General Goodpaster; General Goodpaster; K. S. Adams (Chairman of the Board, Phillips Petroleum). Lunch. Afternoon appointment with B. M. Shanley.

2 Washington. Morning off-the-record appointment with Attorney General Brownell and Judge Charles E. Whittaker (of Missouri). Other morning appointments with Judge Whittaker; Attorney General Brownell and Judge Whittaker; Attorney General

Brownell and W. P. Rogers; Budget Director Brundage, I. J. Martin, and Generals Persons and Goodpaster. Late morning appointments with General Persons; Jesus A. Villamer (off the record); P. G. Hoffman (off the record); General Goodpaster.

3 [Page missing.]

4 Washington. Morning appointments with W. J. Hopkins; J. C. Hagerty and General Goodpaster; General Persons; International Development Advisory Board; T. S. Voorhees; General Curtis; Attorney General Brownell and General Persons; W. W. Aldrich. Greets 4-H Club achievement winners. Lunch. Afternoon appointments with General Goodpaster; Secretary Wilson, R. J. Cordiner, Budget Director Brundage, Colonel Randall, Admiral Fechteler, Generals Persons, Goodpaster, and Maddux, and B. N. Harlow; J. C. Hagerty.

5 Washington. Morning appointments with General Goodpaster and Colonel Schulz; B. M. Shanley; General Persons and I. J. Martin; W. J. Hopkins; General Goodpaster; Legislative Leaders; Secretary Wilson, A. Larson, and L. A. Minnich; Belgian officials; General Cutler; H. Roemer McPhee; G. D. Morgan; A. S. Flemming and General Goodpaster. Lunch. Afternoon appointments with H. Pyle; Secretary Humphrey, Budget Director Brundage, R. J. Saulnier, A. M. Cole, Percy Rappaport (Assistant Director, Bureau of the Budget), Generals Burgess and Persons, G. M. Hauge, and I. J. Martin (off the record); Secretary Humphrey; General Bragdon. Hosts state reception with Mrs. Eisenhower.

6 Washington. Morning appointments with Captain Aurand; General Goodpaster; J. C. Hagerty; G. D. Morgan; General Persons. National Security Council session. Late morning appointments with Secretary Dulles, Ambassador Richards, and General Goodpaster; General Persons; B. N. Harlow; G. D. Morgan. Accepts staff car from World War II African Campaign for Abilene Foundation. Afternoon appointments with Colonel William H. Baumer (Assistant to President, Johnson and Johnson Co.) and B. M. Shanley; Joyce Hall and Dr. Franklin Murphy (Chancellor, University of Kansas).

7   Washington. Morning appointments with B. M. Shanley; J. C. Hagerty; Heinrich von Brentano (Minister of Foreign Affairs, Germany), Ambassador Krekeler, C. A. Herter, C. B. Elbrick, N. M. Lejins, General Goodpaster, and W. T. Buchanan; Budget Director Brundage and General Persons; J. C. Hagerty; Generals Goodpaster and Persons, J. C. Hagerty, G. D. Morgan, I. J. Martin, B. N. Harlow, G. M. Hauge, and H. Pyle; news briefing; news conference. Late morning appointments with Secretary Folsom; Bertha S. Adkins (Assistant Chairman, RNC); General Persons; Charles Ritz (Paris Hotel) and Colonel Schulz. Attends reception honoring L. W. Hall with General Persons and B. M. Shanley.

8   Washington. Morning appointments with G. D. Morgan; J. C. Hagerty; Attorney General Brownell and G. D. Morgan. Receives inauguration flag from J. George Stewart and Arthur E. Cook (Capitol Architects). Late morning appointments with General Goodpaster; General Cutler; G. D. Morgan; J. W. Barba; Ambassador van Roijen (from Netherlands); Eisenhower Exchange Fellows executive committee; G. D. Morgan; Secretary Mitchell. Afternoon appointments with B. M. Shanley; General Goodpaster; J. C. Hagerty; General Persons and J. C. Hagerty; C. A. Herter, C. D. Dillon, W. M. Rountree, H. Phleger and General Goodpaster.

9   Washington. Morning appointments with General Goodpaster; General Persons and G. D. Morgan; J. C. Hagerty; G. M. Hauge; W. J. Hopkins; Senator Wiley, Wilson C. Hefner (Administrative Assistant, Senator Wiley), and General Persons; General Persons; Dr. Frederick Brown Harris (Senate Chaplin); General Persons and J. C. Hagerty. Signs Joint Resolution to promote peace and stability in the Middle East. Late morning appointment with Senator H. A. Smith and General Persons.

10   Washington. To National Presbyterian Church with Mrs. Eisenhower.

11   Washington. Morning appointments with Ambassador Dantes Bellegarde (from Haiti) and Edmund S. Glenn (State Department interpreter); Captain Aurand; J. C. Hagerty; General Persons; S. Adams

and Budget Director Brundage. Afternoon appointment with General Persons. Cabinet meeting. Late afternoon appointments with RNC Executive Committee; H. Darby; Senators Knowland and Johnson and Congressmen Martin and Rayburn.

12 Washington. Morning appointments with General Persons; Legislative Leaders; G. D. Morgan; Ambassador Ernani de Amaral Peixote (from Brazil), Roy R. Rubottom (Acting Assistant Secretary of State, Inter-American Affairs); General Cutler; B. M. Shanley; J. C. Hagerty. Off-the-record appointment with R. B. Anderson, S. Adams, A. S. Flemming, and G. D. Morgan. Ambassador Mariane Puga Vega (from Chile) presents his credentials. Afternoon appointment with H. Darby. To Walter Reed Hospital for examination. Returns to office for appointment with S. Adams. Attends dinner at Supreme Court with Mrs. Eisenhower.

13 Washington. Morning appointments with W. J. Hopkins; Captain Aurand; J. C. Hagerty; C. A. Herter, J. C. Hagerty, and General Goodpaster; G. M. Hauge; news briefing; news conference. Late morning appointments with Captain Aurand; National Manpower Council; C. A. Herter and H. E. Stassen; General Goodpaster; S. Adams. Practices golf, followed by appointments with S. Adams, G. D. Morgan, and I. J. Martin; General Gruenther and Andre de Staercke (Belgium Permanent Representative to NATO) (off the record).

14 Washington. Morning appointments with General Goodpaster; W. J. Hopkins; B. N. Harlow and Generals Persons and Goodpaster; J. B. Hollister. National Security Council session. Appointments with U.S. Ambassador Conant (to Germany, retiring); Fred Lazarus (off the record); S. Adams, C. B. Randall, B. N. Harlow, and General Goodpaster; General Goodpaster; G. D. Morgan; S. Adams. Afternoon appointments with S. Adams; W. J. Hopkins; S. Adams and General Goodpaster; General Goodpaster. Witnesses swearing-in of G. Gray as Director, Office of Defense Mobilization. Late afternoon appointments with A. S. Flemming; General Taylor; General Goodpaster. To MATS terminal en route to

Norfolk, Virginia. Arrives at Norfolk Naval Air Station and motors to SACLANT Headquarters. Poses for photographs. Meets with Admirals Wright and Eaton and Vice Admirals Smith, Wellborn, and Goldthwaite; members of NATO staff. Receives NATO flags from Admiral Wright. To pier and boards U.S.S. *Canberra.*

15   Aboard U.S.S. *Canberra,* en route to Bermuda. Breakfast meeting with General Snyder, Captain Aurand, and J. C. Hagerty. Luncheon with Captains Aurand and Mauro (Commanding Officer, U.S.S. *Canberra*), Commander Norton, General Snyder, and J. C. Hagerty. Dinner with General Snyder, J. C. Hagerty, and Commander Norton.

16   Aboard U.S.S. *Canberra,* en route to Bermuda. Observes demonstration on starboard deck. Luncheon with General Snyder, Captain Aurand, and J. C. Hagerty. Practices golf. Dinner with General Snyder, J. C. Hagerty, Captain Aurand, and Lieutenants Crandall and Coiner. Views movie "Three Coins in a Fountain."

17   Aboard U.S.S. *Canberra,* en route to Bermuda. Poses for photographs and attends church services on deck. Guest of the crew for lunch. Afternoon appointment with General Goodpaster, Captain Aurand, and J. C. Hagerty. Sunbathes and practices golf. Hosts dinner for U.S.S. *Canberra* officers, General Snyder, Captain Aurand, and J. C. Hagerty.

18   Aboard U.S.S. *Canberra,* en route to Bermuda. Views movies of Terrier Missiles. Appointments with Commanders Norton, Hubbard, and Stecher. Practices golf. Fishing with Captain Aurand. Practices golf. Attends Happy Hour Show with General Snyder, Captain Aurand, and J. C. Hagerty.

19   Aboard U.S.S. *Canberra,* en route to Bermuda. Tours deck with Captain Mauro and observes air demonstration. Dinner with U.S.S. *Canberra* officers. Views movies in cabin.

20   Aboard U.S.S. *Canberra,* en route to Bermuda. Poses for photographs on deck, followed by departure ceremony. Boards presidential barge for Hamilton, Bermuda. Arrives at Albuoy Point and greets Prime

Minister Macmillan. To Mid Ocean Club with Prime Minister Macmillan. Appointments with Secretary Dulles, General Goodpaster, Andrew Berding, and William Macomber; Secretary Dulles, General Goodpaster, Ambassador Whitney, W. M. Rountree, and C. B. Elbrick. Inspects White House staff quarters with Prime Minister Macmillan. Dinner with Secretary Dulles, Selwyn Lloyd (British Foreign Affairs Secretary), and Prime Minister Macmillan.

21   Hamilton, Bermuda. Morning appointments with General Goodpaster; Secretary Dulles. Attends morning session with Prime Minister Macmillan, British, and U.S. officials. Hosts luncheon for Prime Minister Macmillan. Poses for photographs. Afternoon session with Prime Minister Macmillan, British, and U.S. officials. Appointment with Ambassador Whitney. Dinner with Secretary Dulles, H. Phleger, General Snyder, Colonel Draper, and Captain Aurand.

22   Hamilton, Bermuda. Morning appointments with Captain Aurand; General Goodpaster; Secretary Dulles and General Goodpaster; General Goodpaster; Captain Aurand; J. C. Hagerty. Practices golf. Appointments with Prime Minister Macmillan; General Goodpaster. Lunch with Secretaries Dulles and Quarles, R. B. Robertson, Admiral Strauss, Robert Murphy, Benson E. L. Timmons, and General Goodpaster. Appointments with luncheon party and Prime Minister Macmillan, S. Lloyd, Patrick Deane, and Norman Brooke; Prime Minister Macmillan, S. Lloyd, Secretary Dulles, General Goodpaster, and Patrick Deane. Afternoon session with Prime Minister Macmillan and British and U.S. officials. Appointment with Captain Aurand. Attends dinner hosted by Governor General Woodall with Prime Minister Macmillan and British and U.S. officials.

23   Hamilton, Bermuda. Morning appointments with General Goodpaster; Secretary Dulles; J. C. Hagerty; General Goodpaster; Secretary Dulles; General Goodpaster; Prime Minister Macmillan. Observes changing of guard at Mid Ocean Club. Hosts luncheon in honor of Prime Minister Macmillan. Afternoon appointments with staff members.

Evening appointments with Ambassador Whitney; Prime Minister Macmillan, S. Lloyd, Admiral Strauss, Secretary Dulles, and G. Smith. Dinner with Prime Minister Macmillan, S. Lloyd, and Secretary Dulles. Appointment with General Goodpaster and Norman Brooke.

24   Hamilton, Bermuda. To Kindley Air Force Base with Prime Minister Macmillan, Colonel Draper. Returns to Washington.

25   Washington. Morning appointments with W. J. Hopkins; S. Adams; B. M. Shanley and G. D. Morgan; Vice-President Nixon. Presents Young American Medal for Bravery to Edmund Lawrence Zernach (Lawrenceville, Indiana) and Young American Medal for Service to William A. Steiger (Oshkosh, Wisconsin). Secretary Thomas says goodbye. Appointment on foreign economic policy with Secretaries Dulles and Wilson, C. A. Herter, M. D. Sprague, J. B. Hollister, S. Adams, B. N. Harlow, and Generals Goodpaster and Persons, followed by appointments with General Persons; Secretary Dulles. Afternoon appointments with B. M. Shanley; S. Adams; Budget Director Brundage, S. Adams, General Persons, G. D. Morgan, B. N. Harlow, and I. J. Martin; Danny Thomas (television star); Attorney General Brownell; Secretary Dulles and grandson; bipartisan Legislative Leaders; Secretary Dulles.

26   Washington. Morning appointments with W. E. Robinson; General Persons, G. D. Morgan, I. J. Martin, and S. Adams; Legislative Leaders.

27   Washington. Morning appointment with B. M. Shanley; news briefing; news conference. Late morning appointments with Mrs. Peter Gibson (President, National Federation of Republican Women) and H. Pyle; G. D. Morgan; General Goodpaster. Makes film for Committee on Employment of the Physically Handicapped.

28   Washington. Morning appointments with S. Adams and B. M. Shanley; W. J. Hopkins; General Persons; B. M. Shanley; Secretary Dulles; National Security Council session; Secretary Humphrey; Senator Pot-

ter and American Battle Monuments Commission; General Persons. Appointment with Vietnamese officials Ngo Dinh Nhu (brother and Adviser of President), Ambassador Tran Van Chuong (from Vietnam), E. S. Glenn, William J. Sebald (Deputy Assistant Secretary of State, Far Eastern Affairs), W. T. Buchanan, followed by appointments with G. D. Morgan; S. Adams. Lunch. Afternoon appointments with Captain Aurand; Lord Tedder (Marshal, Royal Air Force); S. Adams; J. C. Hagerty; W. J. Hopkins; G. M. Hauge.

29 Washington. Morning appointments with Ambassador Lodge; S. Adams; G. Gray and General Goodpaster; Cabinet meeting; Attorney General Brownell; bipartisan Legislative Leaders; G. D. Morgan. Receives Sword of Hope from Joyce Dezeller (cured cancer victim) on behalf of 1957 Cancer Crusade. Late morning appointments with General Goodpaster and W. J. Hopkins; James R. Killian (Science Advisory Committee); Office of Defense Mobilization, Science Advisory Committee; S. Adams. Greets National Photographers Association in Rose Garden. To Gettysburg farm with Colonel Tkach. Inspects farm with General Nevins. Dinner with Mrs. Eisenhower, Mr. and Mrs. G. E. Allen, General and Mrs. Nevins, and Colonel Tkach.

30 Gettysburg. Observes new filly with G. E. Allen. Tours Eisenhower farm and Allen farm with G. E. Allen, General Nevins, Colonel Tkach, R. S. Hartley (herdsman), and W. A. Jones. Walks to duck pond with G. E. Allen and W. A. Jones. Dinner with Mrs. Eisenhower, General and Mrs. Gruenther, Mr. and Mrs. G. E. Allen, and W. A. Jones.

31 Gettysburg. Practices golf with G. E. Allen. To White House with Mrs. Eisenhower.

April 1 Washington. Appointments with H. Phleger; Lieutenant General Aurand (father, Captain Aurand); W. J. Hopkins; Ambassador Houghton; S. Adams; Secretary Benson and G. D. Morgan; J. S. Lay and General Goodpaster; A. Nielsen. Attends swearing-in of Thomas S. Gates as Secretary of the Navy. Afternoon appointments with A. W. Dulles and General Goodpaster (off the record), followed by appointments with S. Adams; J. C. Hagerty and General Goodpaster; J. C. Hagerty; A. Nielsen; General Persons; S. Adams; C. A. Herter, Budget Director Brundage, S. Adams, Generals Goodpaster and Persons, and B. N. Harlow to discuss mutual aid.

2   Washington. Morning appointments with General Persons and I. J. Martin; G. D. Morgan and General Goodpaster; Budget Director Brundage; Legislative Leaders; H. Pyle; U.S. Ambassador Bruce (to Germany); G. D. Morgan; S. Adams. Addresses guests at 13th Annual Advertising Council Conference. Appointments with Stanley High (off the record); G. D. Morgan; General Goodpaster; S. Adams; Secretary Dulles; Secretary Dulles, R. B. Robertson, Admiral Radford, M. D. Sprague, W. J. McNeil, B. E. L. Timmons, R. Murphy, U.S. Ambassador Bruce, and General Goodpaster; Secretary Dulles; S. Adams and G. M. Hauge. Practices golf.

3   Washington. Morning appointments with General Persons and I. J. Martin; J. C. Hagerty; Secretary Dulles, Reverend Eugene Carson Blake (President, National Council of Churches of Christ), Reverend Roswell P. Barnes (Associate Secretary General), Dr. Kenneth L. Maxwell (Department of International Affairs), and G. M. Hauge; S. Adams, J. C. Hagerty, I. J. Martin, H. Pyle, G. M. Hauge, Generals Persons and Goodpaster, G. D. Morgan, and B. N. Harlow; news briefing; news conference. Attends performance of the Dartmouth Glee Club in conference room. Receives Pan American Society Gold Insigne. To Statler Hotel with Mrs. Eisenhower to deliver address at Fifth Annual Republican Women's National Conference. Golf at Burning Tree Country Club with General Snyder and G. E. Allen.

4   Washington. Morning appointments with Postmaster General Summerfield; S. Adams; General Goodpaster and W. J. Hopkins; National Security Council session; H. Ford; I. J. Martin; H. Ford. Lunch. Afternoon appointments with S. Adams; Secretary Dulles, C. A. Herter, and General Goodpaster about the Middle East situation; Harry D. Anheler (Secret Service, retired), Benjamin Adamowski (State's Attorney, Illinois), J. Rowley; General Goodpaster;

B. M. Shanley; S. Adams. Off-the-record appointment with Budget Director Brundage, A. M. Cole, S. Adams regarding urban renewal. Greets National Education Association Centennial Celebration Banquet participants at Sheraton Park Hotel.

5 Washington. Morning appointments with Budget Director Brundage, A. R. Jones, and S. Adams (off the record); S. Adams; Attorney General Brownell; Cabinet meeting; A. Larson and S. Adams; B. M. Shanley; General Cutler. To Gettysburg farm with Mrs. Eisenhower and Colonel Tkach. Tours farm.

6 Gettysburg. To hog farm, Feaster farm, and new house with Chief West. Inspects cattle with G. E. Allen. To Sears Roebuck Farm Products store in Chambersburg, Pennsylvania, with E. Doud and G. E. Allen. Dinner with Mrs. Eisenhower, General and Mrs. Gruenther, Mr. and Mrs. G. E. Allen, and E. Doud.

7 Gettysburg. Inspects farm with General Nevins. Hunts at Redding farm and duck pond and inspects school house and Feaster farm with General Gruenther and G. E. Allen. Practices golf with G. E. Allen and General Gruenther. Walks with G. E. Allen. Views Masters Golf Match on television. To White House with Mrs. Eisenhower and Colonel Tkach.

8 Washington. Morning appointments with J. W. Barba; General Persons. Appointments with Hawaii Statehood Commission; Council of Mayors; G. Gray and General Goodpaster. Off-the-record appointments with Margaret L. Coit (author, writing about B. M. Baruch); General Cutler; Frederick M. Dearborn and Generals Cutler and Goodpaster. Lunch. Afternoon appointments with W. J. Hopkins; General Goodpaster.

9 Washington. Morning appointments with Secretary Humphrey, General Persons, and I. J. Martin; Legislative Leaders; Senator Knowland and General Persons; General Robert M. Littlejohn (retired); General Curtis; B. M. Shanley; Ambassador Fletcher Warren (to Turkey); H. Pyle; J. C. Hagerty; General Goodpaster. Lunch. To General Snyder's office. Practices golf.

10   Washington. Morning appointments with General Persons; G. D. Morgan; Frank J. Donahue, W. A. Ruschmeyer, and Colonel Schulz (off the record); General Goodpaster; news briefing; news conference. Late morning appointments with Dr. M. S. Eisenhower; Alberto Gainza Paz (Editor and Publisher, *La Prensa*, Argentina), R. R. Rubottom, and J. C. Hagerty; Senator Blakely; J. C. Hagerty; Mahesh Chandra (Publisher, *The Statesman*, India) and J. C. Hagerty. To Burning Tree Country Club for golf with Congressman Halleck and J. E. McClure. Evening appointments with General Goodpaster; S. Adams.

11   Washington. Morning appointments with H. Hoover, Jr.; W. J. Hopkins; Polish American leaders. National Security Council session. Late morning appointments with Secretary Wilson; L. M. Pexton; General Cutler; U.S. Ambassador Frederick M. Alger (to Belgium, retiring); General Goodpaster; G. M. Hauge; Ambassador Arnold D. P. Heeney (from Canada) and S. Adams (off the record); General Goodpaster; General Persons. Luncheon with Emergency Agency appointees. Afternoon appointments with S. Adams; General Persons; Congressmen Bow and Taber and General Persons (off the record); B. M. Shanley. Receives baseball tickets from Calvin R. Griffith. Practices golf on the south lawn.

12   Washington. Morning appointments with W. J. Hopkins; Postmaster General Summerfield; Secretary Wilson and General Goodpaster; Cabinet meeting; G. D. Morgan; G. M. Hauge; General Goodpaster. Plants black walnut tree from Illinois. Returns to office with Mrs. Eisenhower and Susan E. Eisenhower and visits with Mr. and Mrs. Norman L. McLaren (San Francisco, California). Sends telephone message to Republican Regional Conference, Omaha, Nebraska. Late morning appointments with A. F. Burns; S. Adams. To Gettysburg with Colonel Tkach. To farm. Inspects horse barn.

13   Gettysburg. Inspects trees on front lawn. Feeds horses and visits dollhouse with S. Eisenhower. Visits Brannon farm with G. E. Allen. Tours new school

house with Mrs. Eisenhower, E. Doud, and Major and Mrs. J. S. D. Eisenhower and family. Visits Feaster farm.

14   Gettysburg. Attends Presbyterian Church of Gettysburg with Mrs. Eisenhower. Returns to farm. To White House.

15   Washington. Morning appointments with S. Adams; A. Nielsen; General Goodpaster; Senator Malone and General Persons; J. B. Hollister; G. M. Hauge. Lunch. To Griffith Stadium with S. Adams and A. Nielsen for baseball game. Throws out two balls. Off-the-record stag dinner at White House.

16   Washington. Morning appointments with J. C. Hagerty; General Persons, G. M. Hauge, and I. J. Martin; Secretary Humphrey and S. Adams; Legislative Leaders; Secretary Humphrey; S. Adams; Senator Allott and I. J. Martin; W. J. Hopkins. Meeting regarding small business conference on technical and distribution research. Late morning appointments with C. A. Herter, General Goodpaster, and C. D. Dillon; C. A. Herter, S. Adams, and G. M. Hauge; Mr. and Mrs. E. N. Eisenhower. Lunch. Afternoon appointments with Attorney General Brownell; S. Adams; J. C. Hagerty; M. J. McCaffree; B. M. Shanley. Practices golf on south lawn. Returns to office for appointments with General Persons; J. C. Hagerty.

17   Washington. Morning appointments with General Patrick J. Hurley (retired); S. Adams; Lyndon Teachers College baseball team; Ambassador Henry de Torrente (from Switzerland); J. C. Hagerty; S. Adams; news briefing; news conference. Greets New Jersey Girl Scouts and Congresswoman Dwyer. Appointments with Advisory Commission on Presidential Office Space; Secretary Wilson, S. Adams, Budget Director Brundage, and B. N. Harlow; G. D. Morgan and General Goodpaster. Lunch. Afternoon appointments with W. J. Hopkins; R. B. Robertson; National Security Council session; Secretary Humphrey; General Goodpaster. Off-the-record stag dinner.

18   Washington. Morning appointments with S. Adams; General Goodpaster; U. E. Baughman (Chief, Se-

cret Service); Secretary Benson; J. C. Hagerty; General Goodpaster; W. J. Hopkins; B. M. Shanley. Eye doctor. Late morning appointments with M. J. McCaffree; S. Adams. Greets Harris Ellsworth, Christopher Phillips, and Fred Lawton after their swearing-in as Civil Service Commissioners, followed by appointments with B. M. Shanley; General Goodpaster. Sits for sculptor. To MATS terminal en route to Augusta, Georgia. To Augusta National Golf Club for golf with C. Roberts, W. E. Robinson, and R. W. Woodruff. To Club House for tea. Visits with W. E. Robinson, C. Roberts, Mr. and Mrs. R. W. Woodruff, and General Snyder.

19   Augusta, Georgia. Practices golf. Fishes in lake. Plays golf with C. J. Schoo and E. B. Dudley. Visits with C. W. Jones, W. A. Jones, E. D. Slater, W. E. Robinson, Mr. and Mrs. C. J. Schoo, Mr. and Mrs. R. W. Woodruff, and General and Mrs. Snyder. Dinner with W. A. Jones, C. W. Jones, E. D. Slater, W. E. Robinson, and Secretary and Mrs. Humphrey.

20   Augusta, Georgia. Golf with W. A. Jones, C. W. Jones, and E. B. Dudley. Fishes. Dinner with Mrs. Eisenhower, Secretary and Mrs. Humphrey, General and Mrs. Snyder, and Mr. and Mrs. R. W. Woodruff.

21   Augusta, Georgia. Attends Easter services at Reid Memorial Presbyterian Church with Mrs. Eisenhower and Secretary and Mrs. Humphrey. Golf with R. W. Woodruff, W. A. Jones, and C. W. Jones. Visits with Colonels Draper and Thomas, and Major Leland Straugh.

22   Augusta, Georgia. Practices golf. Sits in sun with Secretary Humphrey. Practices driving golf balls with E. B. Dudley. Plays golf with C. Roberts, Albert Bradley (Executive Vice-President, General Motors), and E. B. Dudley.

23   Augusta, Georgia. Appointments with H. E. Stassen and General Goodpaster; General Goodpaster. Practices golf with Secretary Humphrey. Golf with J. Roberts, J. Franklin, and E. B. Dudley.

24   Augusta, Georgia. Sits in sun. Golf with B. T. Leithead, E. B. Dudley, and Elbert Peabody. Fishes.

25   Augusta, Georgia. Appointments with Secretary Mitchell, George C. Lodge (Director of Information, U.S. Department of Labor), J. C. Hagerty; Secretary Mitchell. Practices putting. Golf with R. W. Woodruff, E. B. Dudley, C. J. Schoo. Visits R. T. Jones with C. Roberts and R. W. Woodruff. Bridge with R. W. Woodruff, W. E. Robinson, C. Roberts, and B. T. Leithead.

26   Augusta, Georgia. Golf with C. Roberts, E. B. Dudley, W. E. Robinson, and General Henry B. Saylor. Dinner with C. Roberts, Douglas Casey, and W. A. Jones.

27   Augusta, Georgia. Golf with Doyle Dewitt, John D. Ames (President, United States Golf Association), and E. B. Dudley.

28   Augusta, Georgia. Attends Reid Memorial Presbyterian Church with J. C. Hagerty. Golf with T. R. "Dick" Garlington, C. Roberts, and E. B. Dudley. Fishes.

29   Augusta, Georgia. Golf with C. Roberts, E. B. Dudley, and E. D. Slater. Fishes with J. Roberts.

30   Augusta, Georgia. Golf with E. B. Dudley, Gene Stout, and C. Roberts. Returns to Washington, D.C. Appointment with Secretary Dulles, C. A. Herter, and W. S. Robertson aboard the *Columbine*. Evening appointments with General Goodpaster; W. J. Hopkins; General Goodpaster; S. Adams; Colonel Schulz; General Goodpaster.

May   1   Washington. Morning appointments with S. Adams; B. N. Harlow and I. J. Martin; G. D. Morgan; Legislative Leaders; S. Adams; General Cutler and J. S. Lay; S. Adams. Attends swearing-in of D. A. Quarles as Deputy Secretary of Defense and James H. Douglas as Secretary of the Air Force. Appointment with Mrs. J. G. Lee (President, National Council, League of Women Voters), B. M. Shanley, and J. C. Hagerty. Receives National Council, League of Women Voters in Rose Garden. Afternoon appointments with C. B. Luce; Secretary Humphrey, S. Adams, Budget Director Brundage, and M. Kestnbaum (off the record); Secretary Humphrey; Secretary Folsom; S. Adams; General Arthur E. Stoddard (President,

Union Pacific Railroad); J. C. Hagerty and Captain Aurand. Practices golf on south lawn.

2   Washington. Morning appointments with J. C. Hagerty; W. J. Hopkins; B. M. Shanley; B. M. Shanley and Captain Aurand; General Goodpaster. Attends swearing-in of A. Wheaton as Associate Press Secretary, followed by appointments with General Goodpaster; S. Adams; General Goodpaster; National Security Council session. Receives poppy from Carl W. Zeller (President, American Legion Auxiliary). Off-the-record appointment with Admiral Strauss, C. A. Herter, S. Adams, B. N. Harlow, Ambassador Wadsworth, and General Goodpaster. Lunch. To Burning Tree Country Club with Colonel Tkach. Golf with Congressmen Arends and Halleck and Colonel Belshe.

3   Washington. Morning appointments with J. C. Hagerty; Secretary Wilson and General Goodpaster; S. Adams; Governor Furcolo, Charles Mahoney (Secretary to Governor Furcolo), and S. Adams. Cabinet meeting, followed by appointments with Ambassador Lodge; S. Adams; Admiral Strauss, G. Smith, and General Goodpaster; Ambassador Wadsworth; S. Adams; Senators Knowland and Hickenlooper; B. M. Shanley and M. M. Rabb; General Goodpaster; S. Adams. Lunch. Sends telephone message to Third Regional Republican Conference in Salt Lake City, Utah. Afternoon appointments with S. Adams; General Goodpaster; G. M. Hauge. To MATS terminal with Colonel Tkach en route to Gettysburg. Fishes at Little Fishing Lodge. Visits with General and Mrs. Nevins, General Gruenther, and Mr. and Mrs. G. E. Allen.

4   Gettysburg. To Gettysburg Country Club for golf with G. E. Allen, General Nevins, and Richard "Dick" Sleichter (golf pro). Poses for photographs for farm magazine. Tours Allen farm, hog farm, and Feaster farm with General Gruenther and G. E. Allen.

5   Gettysburg. Tours duck pond with G. E. Allen.

6   Washington. Morning appointments with G. D. Morgan; W. J. Hopkins; General Goodpaster; Gen-

eral Cutler; B. M. Shanley; A. W. Dulles, C. A. Herter, D. A. Quarles, Generals Goodpaster, Twining, and Cabell, and Richard Bissell (off the record); S. Adams; Generals Curtis and Quesada and S. Adams; Ambassador Sebald (to Australia); G. M. Hauge. Receives scroll from Dwight D. Eisenhower Class of Alpha Phi Omega. Receives Genevieve Farris (Goodwill Worker of the Year). Lunch. Afternoon appointments with Colonel Draper; Admiral Strauss and General Goodpaster; David A. Morse (Director, International Labor Organization); T. E. Stephens. Practices golf on south lawn. Hosts stag dinner at White House.

7 Washington. Morning appointments with S. Adams; Louis A. Johnson; Michael A. Stepovich (off the record) and Secretary Seaton; Ambassador Adolfo A. Vicchi (from Argentina, retiring), Victor Purse, and R. R. Rubottom; Attorney General Brownell; G. M. Hauge; U.S. Ambassador Francis H. Russell (to New Zealand); S. Adams. Receives Alaskan delegation to discuss statehood. Hosts luncheon for Presidential Representatives to Inter-American Commission. Poses for photographs with luncheon guests. Afternoon appointments with General Goodpaster and Colonel Draper; Secretary Dulles and C. A. Herter; S. Adams. Practices golf on south lawn.

8 Washington. Morning appointments with S. Adams, General Persons, B. N. Harlow, and I. J. Martin; Legislative Leaders; news briefing; news conference. Appointments with Howard Rusk (Chairman, Health Resources Advisory Committee, Office of Defense Mobilization); S. Adams; M. J. McCaffree. To MATS terminal to meet President Ngo Dinh Diem (Republic of Vietnam) with B. M. Shanley, General Goodpaster, and Colonel Tkach. Poses for photographs. Lunch. To Burning Tree Country Club with General Snyder for golf with Colonel Belshe. Hosts State Dinner with Mrs. Eisenhower in honor of President Diem.

9 Washington. Morning appointments with W. J. Hopkins; General Goodpaster; Secretary Dulles; Secretary Dulles and Ambassador Richards; S. Adams and I. J. Martin; Secretary Dulles, C. A. Herter, J. B. Hol-

lister, M. D. Sprague, D. A. Quarles, and B. N. Harlow; bipartisan Legislative Leaders. Late morning appointments with S. Adams; Secretaries Wilson and Weeks, S. Adams, General Curtis, and J. Z. Anderson; Secretary Wilson; B. M. Shanley; President Diem, Secretary Dulles, W. S. Robertson, Ambassador Tran Van Chuong, U.S. Ambassador Eldridge Durbrow (to Vietnam), Nguyen Huu Chau (Interior Secretary of State, Vietnam), Charles Segewich (interpreter); Secretary Dulles; G. D. Morgan; B. M. Shanley. Lunch. Afternoon appointments with J. C. Hagerty; B. M. Shanley; S. Adams; B. M. Shanley; G. D. Morgan. Practices golf on south lawn. Evening appointment with Congressman Martin.

10　Washington. Morning appointments with J. C. Hagerty; General Goodpaster; W. J. Hopkins; S. Adams; G. M. Hauge. National Security Council session. Cabinet meeting. Sends telephone message to Republican Regional Meeting, Louisville, Kentucky. Receives Centennial Emblem from American Institute of Architects leaders. Lunch. Afternoon appointments with Reverend Billy Graham; J. C. Hagerty; Admiral Strauss and General Goodpaster. To Burning Tree Country Club for golf with Major J. S. D. Eisenhower and Colonel Belshe. To Vietnam Embassy with Mrs. Eisenhower for dinner in their honor by President Diem.

11　Washington. Morning appointments with J. C. Hagerty; General Goodpaster; W. J. Hopkins. To MATS terminal en route to Gettysburg with Field Marshal Montgomery. To Gettysburg Battlefield. To Feaster farm with Field Marshal Montgomery, Generals Snyder and Nevins, Mr. and Mrs. Heckitt, and G. E. Allen. To Redding farm, Feaster farm, and back to Eisenhower farm with Field Marshal Montgomery, G. E. Allen, and General Snyder.

12　Gettysburg. To Gettysburg Museum with Field Marshal Montgomery, G. E. Allen, and General Snyder. Greets J. C. Hagerty, Mr. and Mrs. George Rosensteel, and Joseph Rosensteel (Chief Historian, Gettysburg National Museum). Tours battlefield. Attends services at Presbyterian Church of Gettysburg with Mrs. Eisenhower and Field Marshal Montgomery. To Battle of Gettysburg diorama. To Allen farm to inspect horses with Field Marshal Montgomery and General Snyder. Fishes at Aker farm. Inspects Camp David and returns to Gettysburg farm.

13 Gettysburg. Walks around farm and visits Feaster farm with Field Marshal Montgomery. Returns to Feaster farm with General Nevins. To Gettysburg Country Club for golf with G. E. Allen and Colonel Moore. Returns to Washington, D.C. with Mrs. Eisenhower and E. Doud.

14 Washington. Morning appointments with Dr. M. S. Eisenhower; B. M. Shanley; General Cutler; General Persons and I. J. Martin; G. M. Hauge; Legislative Leaders; S. Adams and Budget Director Brundage; B. M. Shanley; G. M. Hauge. Receives final committee report of President's Committee for Hungarian Refugee Relief, followed by appointments with J. C. Hagerty; G. Gray; J. Clifford Folger. Lunch. Afternoon appointments with General Goodpaster; Richard Mahar (General Chairman, Interfaith Committee), Joe E. Brown, Jackie Robinson, and M. M. Rabb; G. M. Hauge. Practices golf on south lawn. Hosts stag dinner.

15 Washington. Morning appointments with B. M. Shanley; G. D. Morgan; G. M. Hauge; Admiral Strauss and General Goodpaster; Secretary Humphrey; Secretary Humphrey, David W. Kendall and S. Adams; news briefing; news conference. Appointments with National Monument Commission; S. Adams and M. Kestnbaum; H. Hoover, Sr.; General Goodpaster; Major J. S. D. Eisenhower; S. Adams and J. C. Hagerty. Lunch. To Burning Tree Country Club for golf with Major J. S. D. Eisenhower, J. C. Hagerty, and Colonel Belshe.

16 Washington. Morning appointments with S. Adams; M. J. McCaffree; W. J. Hopkins; G. D. Morgan; General Goodpaster; S. Adams and H. Pyle. National Security Council session. Special meeting with National Security Council, Department of State, Department of Defense, and Atomic Energy Commission representatives. Late morning appointments with Secretary Dulles; S. Adams; G. M. Hauge; Cap-

tain Aurand; Dr. Milton Katz (Director, International Legal Studies, Harvard University Law School). Lunch. Afternoon appointments with S. Adams; Owen R. Cheatham (President, Georgia-Pacific Plywood Co.) and S. Adams (off the record); Secretary Humphrey; B. M. Shanley; J. C. Hagerty. Visits General Smith at Walter Reed Hospital.

17   Washington. Greets Yale University, class of 1908. Morning appointments with General Goodpaster; Henry R. Luce; J. C. Hagerty; Ambassador Norman Robertson (from Canada) and H. Charles Spruks (Acting Chief of Protocol); J. C. Hagerty; Ambassador Taylor; W. J. Hopkins; S. Adams; S. P. Skouras; Secretary Dulles; General Goodpaster. Sends telephone message to Republican Regional Conference in Cincinnati, Ohio. Lunch with Major J. S. D. Eisenhower. To MATS terminal en route to Gettysburg with General Snyder. To Gettysburg Country Club for golf with G. E. Allen.

18   Gettysburg. To Gettysburg Country Club with G. E. Allen and D. David Eisenhower II for golf with G. E. Allen. Shoots at skeet range. Tours Feaster farm and surrounding farms with G. E. Allen. Practices golf. Watches movie "Guys and Dolls" with Mrs. Eisenhower, Colonel Tkach, and Mr. and Mrs. G. E. Allen.

19   Gettysburg. To Feaster farm and Allen farm to inspect horses with G. E. Allen and grandchildren. Feeds horses at Eisenhower farm with grandchildren. To school house with Major and Mrs. J. S. D. Eisenhower. To Washington with Mrs. Eisenhower and E. Doud.

20   Washington. Morning appointments with General Goodpaster; J. C. Hagerty; S. Adams and General Persons; J. C. Hagerty; Secretary Wilson and General Goodpaster; Generals Cutler and Goodpaster; Richard K. Mellon (Pittsburgh, Pennsylvania); General Goodpaster. Receives People-to-People poster from John W. Hanes, Jr. and Edward Lipscomb (Chairmen, People-to-People). Delivers address at annual American Red Cross Convention at Constitution Hall. Poses for photographs. Afternoon appointments with Larry Richey and B. M. Shanley; B. N. Harlow and Major J. S. D. Eisenhower; E. J.

Hughes; S. Adams. To Sheraton Park Hotel with Mrs. Eisenhower for dinner hosted by Postmaster General and Mrs. Summerfield.

21   Washington. Morning appointments with W. J. Hopkins; Philip Areeda; J. C. Hagerty; General Persons and J. C. Hagerty; Legislative Leaders; Mr. and Mrs. David Maxwell (President, American Bar Association); Ambassador Charles E. Bohlen (to Phillippines); H. M. Alcorn, T. E. Stephens, S. Adams, and H. Pyle. Lunch. Receives the Bradley Commission Report. Delivers radio and television speech, "The Need for Mutual Security in Waging Peace."

22   Washington. Morning appointments with R. J. Saulnier; Generals Goodpaster and Cutler and J. S. Lay; J. C. Hagerty. Receives report from Peter Grimm (Director, U.S. Operations Mission under I.C.A.). News briefing; news conference, followed by appointments with General Persons and J. C. Hagerty; A. Larson and S. Adams; I. J. Martin; Senator Bricker and I. J. Martin; General Goodpaster. To Burning Tree Country Club for golf with Major J. S. D. Eisenhower, Colonel Belshe, and William Flenniken. Off-the-record evening appointment with Dr. M. S. Eisenhower.

23   Washington. Morning appointments with S. Adams and General Persons; S. Adams and P. E. Areeda; B. M. Shanley; Secretary Seaton, Felix E. Wormser (Assistant Secretary of the Interior), General Persons, G. D. Morgan, G. M. Hauge, J. Z. Anderson, and Budget Director Brundage; Congressman McConnell. National Security Council session. Presents awards at Departmental Auditorium to national essay contest winners of the President's Committee on the Employment of the Physically Handicapped and to Hugh Deffner (Handicapped American of the Year). Hosts luncheon for Howell G. Crim (retiring White House Chief Usher). Afternoon appointments with Captain Aurand; G. D. Morgan; W. J. Hopkins; General Goodpaster; Attorney General Brownell; General Persons; Dillon Anderson; General Persons.

24   Washington. Morning appointments with General Persons; General Goodpaster; J. C. Hagerty; Gen-

eral Goodpaster; S. Adams. Cabinet meeting. Sends telephone message to Republican Regional Conference, Trenton, New Jersey. Late morning appointments with Secretary Humphrey; Budget Director Brundage, A. R. Jones, and Generals Persons and Goodpaster; S. Adams. Lunch. Afternoon appointments with General Goodpaster; B. M. Shanley; G. D. Morgan; J. C. Hagerty. Practices golf on south lawn. Tours Jones Point on Navy pleasure boat *Barbara Anne* with Mrs. Eisenhower and Major and Mrs. J. S. D. Eisenhower and family.

25 Washington. Morning appointment with General Goodpaster, followed by meeting to discuss disarmament. To Burning Tree Country Club for golf with General Parks, Colonel Belshe, and G. E. Allen.

26 Washington. To MATS terminal with Major J. S. D. Eisenhower and General Snyder en route to Gettysburg. Greets Chancellor Adenauer, W. T. Buchanan, Hans Weber (interpreter), Hans Zonds, and George Velk. Inspects barn with Major J. S. D. Eisenhower, General Snyder, and Chancellor Adenauer. Lunch. Inspects Angus cattle and poses for photographs with Chancellor Adenauer at Feaster farm. To Gettysburg Air Park with Chancellor Adenauer and H. Weber. Returns to Washington with Chancellor.

27 Washington. Morning appointments with M. J. McCaffree; W. J. Hopkins; B. M. Shanley. Receives photograph from Barbara Jean Bossus (Dairy Princess) of Holstein heifer, a gift for Gettysburg farm. National Security Council session. Attends swearing-in of F. M. Dearborn as Special Assistant, Security Operations Coordination, followed by appointments with Dr. Henry Wriston (Director, American Assembly); S. Adams; B. M. Shanley. Hosts luncheon in honor of Chancellor Adenauer. Afternoon appointments with General and Mrs. Clay; Secretary Humphrey; Ambassador Alphand; Postmaster General Summerfield; Post Office Advisory Committee; G. D. Morgan; General Persons; B. M. Shanley; J. C. Hagerty; General Persons; S. Adams. Off-the-record appointment with Vice-President Nixon, S. Adams, General Persons, and Congressmen Martin, Hal-

leck, Arends, Allen, Simpson, Holt, Brown, Keating, Derounian, Laird, and Michel.

28   Washington. Morning appointments with General Persons and I. J. Martin; Legislative Leaders. Receives West Point Yearbook from cadets. Late morning appointments with Frank Jorgensen (San Francisco, California); R. B. Anderson (off the record); Secretary Humphrey (off the record); F. Jorgensen; Chancellor Adenauer and German and U.S. officials; S. Adams. Meeting to discuss Girard case with Secretaries Dulles and Wilson, W. S. Robertson, G. D. Morgan, Generals Goodpaster, Persons, Randall, and Jones, R. Dechert, and M. D. Sprague. Afternoon appointments with A. Larson; General Goodpaster; J. C. Hagerty. Practices golf on south lawn. Appointment with S. Adams. Hosts stag dinner.

29   Washington. Morning appointments General Persons; W. J. Hopkins; G. D. Morgan; C. A. Herter, D. A. Quarles, Attorney General Brownell, G. Gray, A. W. Dulles, Budget Director Brundage, J. E. Hoover, G. C. McConnaughey, Generals Persons and Cutler, J. S. Lay, and A. M. Washburn (off the record); S. Adams; Congressman Coudert; S. Adams; Ambassador Frances Willis (to Norway); G. M. Hauge; B. M. Shanley; Secretary Mitchell; General Persons; C. S. Thomas and H. M. Alcorn. Receives Mary Field Schwarz and Eugene Guy Bizzell, Teachers of the Year. Lunch. To Burning Tree Country Club for golf with E. B. Dudley, Max Elben, and Colonel Belshe. Appointment with General Goodpaster. Hosts stag dinner.

30   Washington. No official appointments.

31   Washington. Morning appointments with General Goodpaster; W. J. Hopkins; General Persons; G. D. Morgan; General Persons. To Burning Tree Country Club for golf with G. E. Allen, W. E. Robinson, and J. E. McClure.

June   1   Washington. Morning appointments with General Goodpaster; G. D. Morgan; S. Adams. To Burning Tree Country Club for golf with W. E. Robinson, G. E. Allen, and J. E. McClure.

2   Washington. Attends services at National Presbyterian Church with Mrs. Eisenhower.

3   Washington. Morning appointments with General Persons and J. C. Hagerty; J. C. Hagerty; General Persons; General Persons and Senators Carlson, Dirksen, and O'Mahoney; Ambassador Manuel de Moya Alonza (from Dominican Republic) and W. T. Buchanan; General Persons. Poses with Congressman Dellay for photographs. Late morning appointments with Ambassador Llewellyn E. Thompson (to U.S.S.R.); Budget Director Brundage, General Goodpaster, and M. M. Rabb. Cabinet meeting. To Old House Office Building with General Persons and J. C. Hagerty for box lunch with Republican congressional members. Afternoon appointments with J. C. Hagerty; General Goodpaster; B. M. Shanley; General Cutler; A. Nielsen; B. M. Shanley; Generals Goodpaster and Persons and B. N. Harlow. Off-the-record appointments with Secretary Humphrey, Charles White, Arthur Homer, and Avery Adams; Senators Johnson and Knowland, Congressmen Rayburn and Martin, General Persons, and B. N. Harlow.

4   Washington. Morning appointments with General Goodpaster; W. J. Hopkins; S. Adams and General Goodpaster; S. Adams, Generals Goodpaster and Persons, B. N. Harlow, and I. J. Martin; Legislative Leaders; S. Adams; B. M. Shanley; Ambassador Koichiro Asakai (from Japan) and W. T. Buchanan; H. M. Alcorn, B. S. Adkins, Senator Schoeppel, Congressman Simpson, and H. Pyle reported on regional republican conferences; Secretary Wilson, S. Adams, and General Persons; A. Larson; S. Adams; G. D. Morgan; W. J. Hopkins. To Burning Tree Country Club with General Snyder for golf with J. Black, G. E. Allen, and Monty Moncrief. Appointment with Secretary Dulles.

5   Washington. Off-the-record appointment with D. A. Quarles. Receives Naval Academy yearbook, followed by appointments with Dr. Reginald Smart and General Snyder; Boris Timshenko (landscape artist); B. M. Shanley and General Goodpaster; news briefing; news conference. Greets General Marshall

at guest house, followed by appointments with S. Adams; editors from India (off the record); Ambassador Houghton; General Goodpaster. Swims. Lunch. Afternoon appointments with S. Adams; U.S. Ambassador Ellsworth Bunker (to India); Reverend Earbon Anderson; A. Larson and S. Adams; Vice Admiral Edmund T. Wooldridge (Commandant, National War College), General Robert P. Hollis (Commandant, Industrial College of the Armed Forces), and Colonel F. O. Hartel; G. M. Hauge; General Cutler and G. D. Morgan; G. D. Morgan; S. Adams; W. J. Hopkins. Off-the-record evening appointment with Secretary Humphrey and U.S. Steel representatives Roger Blough, Joseph Block, and Clifford Hood.

6   Washington. To MATS terminal en route to U.S. Naval Auxiliary Air Station, Mayport, Florida. Boards U.S.S. *Saratoga.* Lunch in presidential dining room with Secretaries Humphrey, Gates, Dulles, and Wilson, A. Larson, Budget Director Brundage, M. Kestnbaum, General Snyder, and Captain Aurand. Appointment with General Goodpaster. Meets at Flag Plot with Captain Aurand, Secretaries Dulles, Wilson, and Gates, A. Larson, Budget Director Brundage, G. Gray, General Snyder, J. C. Hagerty, and Admirals Strauss, Burke, Pirie, and Wright. Meets Commander "Duke" Windsor (broke jet speed record, 1956). Observes training exercises. Greets Commander Small (son, West Point classmate). Dinner with Secretaries Dulles, Humphrey, and Wilson, Admiral Burke, G. Gray, General Persons, G. M. Hauge, Major J. S. D. Eisenhower, and Captain Moore. Observes night launchings. To Combat information Center for Aircraft Early Warning briefing. Evening appointments with Secretary Dulles; Generals Goodpaster and Snyder and Captain Sidney Brody; Major J. S. D. Eisenhower; General Goodpaster.

7   Aboard U.S.S. *Saratoga.* Morning appointments with Captain Aurand; J. C. Hagerty, Generals Snyder and Goodpaster, and Captain Aurand. Breakfast with Admiral Wright, Secretaries Dulles, Humphrey, and Wilson, Captains Paul Stahl, Draper Kauffman, and Crittenberger, and Colonel Draper. Meets with Sec-

retaries Wilson, Humphrey, and Gates. Witnesses launchings at Flag Plot. Late morning appointments with A. Larson; Secretary Dulles; Major J. S. D. Eisenhower; J. C. Hagerty; Admiral Strauss. Addresses officers and crew members of U.S.S. *Saratoga.* Meets with Secretary Wilson and J. C. Hagerty. Lunch with Commander Rowney, Secretaries Gates, Wilson, and Humphrey, Admirals Wright and Pirie, Captain Aurand, and Generals Cutler and Goodpaster. Appointment with General Cutler. Disembarks and boards *Columbine* en route to MATS terminal. To Sheraton Park Hotel with Mrs. Eisenhower for National Committee of the Republican Party Campaign Conference.

8 Washington. Morning appointments with General Persons; General Goodpaster and W. J. Hopkins; General Persons; General Goodpaster and Captain Aurand; General Goodpaster and J. C. Hagerty. To Burning Tree Country Club for golf with Dan Kimball, Clyde Lucas, and Colonel Belshe.

9 Washington. Attends services National Presbyterian Church. To American University with J. C. Hagerty for ground-breaking ceremonies at School of International Service. Delivers address and receives honorary degree.

10 Washington. Appointments canceled because of sickness.

11 Washington. Photographs taken in office. Appointments with General Goodpaster; General Persons and I. J. Martin; G. D. Morgan; B. M. Shanley.

12 Washington. Hosts breakfast for Republican congressmen. Morning appointments with B. M. Shanley; J. C. Hagerty, and Ed Morgan and daughter; General Persons; General Goodpaster; U.S. Ambassador Young (to The Netherlands); General Goodpaster; Dr. Aubrey A. Anduze (Legislature President, Virgin Islands), Senator Lugo, and John B. Merwin (Senator at Large); Generals Cutler and Goodpaster; General Persons. Receives various church groups.

13 Washington. Morning appointments with W. J. Hopkins; General Bragdon; J. Z. Anderson; General

Goodpaster; H. M. Alcorn, and I. Lee Potter (Special Assistant, Republican Party of the South). National Security Council session. Late morning appointments with Generals Persons and Goodpaster and J. Z. Anderson; U.S. Ambassador Scott McLeod (to Ireland); Daniel C. Gainey (Owatonna, Minnesota) and B. M. Shanley; G. D. Morgan; General Goodpaster; General Persons. Lunch. Afternoon appointments with W. J. Hopkins; General Persons; B. M. Shanley; J. C. Hagerty; General Persons; General Goodpaster. Off-the-record evening appointment with Vice-President Nixon, H. M. Alcorn, General Persons and Republican senators.

14   Washington. Hosts breakfast for Republican congressmen. Poses for photographs with congressmen in north portico. Morning appointments with General Persons and B. N. Harlow; B. M. Shanley; H. Ellsworth; L. A. Minnich; Reverends John L. Sheridan (President, Mount St. Mary's College) and William Culhane (Assistant to Sheridan), Senator Beall, and John C. Ahlers (Executive Secretary, Senator Beall). Late morning appointments with Captain Aurand; B. N. Harlow; Secretary Folsom; C. B. Randall, John H. Stambough, and B. M. Shanley. Receives Committee for National Trade Policy, followed by appointments with B. M. Shanley and J. C. Hagerty; G. M. Hauge; W. J. Hopkins; L. A. Minnich. Lunch. To Burning Tree Country Club for golf with Frank L. Pace (General Dynamics) and Douglas R. Christie. Returns to office for appointment with L. A. Minnich.

15   Washington. Morning appointments with B. N. Harlow; General Cutler and J. C. Hagerty; L. A. Minnich; Young Republican National Federation officers, J. C. Hagerty, and L. A. Minnich. To Little Hunting Creek Lodge (Catoctin, Maryland) with General Snyder and G. E. Allen for fishing.

16   Washington. No official appointments.

17   Washington. Morning appointments with W. J. Hopkins; G. D. Morgan; General Persons and J. C. Hagerty; Cabinet meeting; Secretary Dulles; R. B. Anderson (off the record); R. B. Anderson and Robert Craft (off the record); Dominick L. Strada

(National Commander, AMVETS), Thomas Burke (President, National Service Foundation), and Earle D. Chesney. Receives AMVETS scholarship winners, followed by appointments with U.S. Ambassador John Morrs Cabot (to Colombia); Judge Phillips. Lunch. Afternoon appointments with W. J. Hopkins; L. A. Minnich; S. Adams; Emma Michie and family (off the record); Ernest R. "Tex" Lee and family, Richard Miller, Thomas Schlass, Robert Schlass, and George Miller; Allan Shivers (off the record); Senator Mundt. Receives winners of Alexander Hamilton Scholarship. Late afternoon appointments with Attorney General Brownell and General Persons; G. D. Morgan; S. Adams, General Persons, and Republican senators.

18   Washington. Morning appointments with B. M. Shanley and H. Pyle; General Persons, B. N. Harlow, and I. J. Martin; Legislative Leaders; Senator Knowland and General Persons; Secretary Benson. Greets delegates to National 4-H Club Conference. Late morning appointments with Hazel H. Abel (former senator, Lincoln, Nebraska); G. D. Morgan; T. E. Stephens; Secretary Benson; S. Adams. Greets National Association of Television and Radio Farm Directors. Lunch. Afternoon appointments with J. C. Hagerty; Secretary Dulles, D. A. Quarles, D. MacArthur, Admiral Radford, W. S. Robertson, M. D. Sprague, J. C. Hagerty, and General Goodpaster; A. S. Flemming, Nelson A. Rockefeller, Budget Director Brundage, Arthur Kimball, Don Price, S. Adams, and General Goodpaster; A. S. Flemming; General Goodpaster; B. M. Shanley; General Persons; B. M. Shanley; General Persons. Hosts stag dinner.

19   Washington. Morning appointments with W. J. Hopkins; General Goodpaster; Senator Humphrey and General Persons; news briefing; news conference. Late morning appointments with S. Adams; B. N. Harlow; Secretary Dulles and G. Smith; Secretary Dulles. Appointment with Prime Minister Kishi (Japan), Japanese officials, Secretary Dulles, D. MacArthur, W. S. Robertson, and J. Owen Zurhellen (interpreter). Hosts stag luncheon in honor of Prime Minister Kishi. To Burning Tree Country Club for

golf with Prime Minister Kishi, Takizo Matsumoto, and Senator Bush.

20 Washington. Morning appointments with W. J. Hopkins; B. M. Shanley and H. Pyle; G. Gray and S. Adams (off the record); Eugene C. Pulliam (Central Newspapers, Inc.) (off the record); National Security Council session. Late morning appointments with Budget Director Brundage, A. R. Jones, and General Goodpaster; General Goodpaster; Attorney General Brownell, G. D. Morgan, and Lloyd Wright (Chairman, Commission on Government Security). Lunch. Afternoon appointments with S. Adams; G. D. Morgan; Secretary Weeks. To Constitution Hall with Mrs. Eisenhower for Young Republican National Federation program, "Young America's Tribute to the President."

21 Washington. Hosts breakfast for Republican congressmen. Morning appointments with General Persons; G. Gray (off the record); S. Adams and J. C. Hagerty; Cabinet meeting; J. C. Hagerty; W. J. Hopkins; B. M. Shanley; G. D. Morgan. Appointments with Prime Minister Kishi, Japanese officials, Secretary Dulles, D. MacArthur, W. S. Robertson, J. O. Zurhellen, A. Berding, and General Goodpaster; Secretary Dulles and G. Smith; General Goodpaster. Lunch. Afternoon appointment with B. N. Harlow and General Goodpaster. To MATS terminal en route to Gettysburg. To Gettysburg Country Club for golf with G. E. Allen.

22 Gettysburg. To Gettysburg Country Club for golf with G. E. Allen and General Nevins. Inspects farm with General Nevins and G. E. Allen. Shoots skeet with General Nevins and G. E. Allen. Watches movie with Mrs. Eisenhower, General and Mrs. Snyder, and General and Mrs. Nevins.

23 Gettysburg. Takes pictures of farm. Practices golf with G. E. Allen. Returns to Washington.

24 Washington. Morning appointments with W. J. Hopkins; General Goodpaster; Secretary Benson; Ernest O. Lawrence, Mark M. Mills, Dr. Edward Teller (University of California, Berkeley, Radiation Labo-

ratory), Admiral Strauss, and General Goodpaster on atomic test progress; Admiral Strauss; G. M. Hauge; U.S. Ambassador Earl E. T. Smith (to Cuba); B. M. Shanley; General Goodpaster; General Curtis; Major Robert N. Barger (Civil Air Patrol), General Walter R. Ages (Commander, Civil Air Patrol), and General Curtis; General Curtis; General Goodpaster; R. J. Saulnier; J. C. Hagerty; Attorney General Brownell and S. Adams (off the record); General Goodpaster. Lunch. Afternoon appointment with General Persons. To MATS terminal en route to Williamsburg, Virginia, for Governor's Conference. Dinner. Delivers address at Governor's Conference. Visits at Williamsburg Inn with S. Adams and J. C. Hagerty; Governor and Mrs. Stanley, Mr. and Mrs. Tom Stanley, Jr., Mr. and Mrs. David Stanley, and Mrs. Hugh Chatham.

25   Williamsburg. To Langley Air Force Base en route to MATS terminal. Appointment with Vice-President William R. Tolbert (Liberia) and Ambassador George A. Padmore (Liberia). Witnesses swearing-in of General Quesada as Special Assistant, followed by appointments with S. Adams; J. C. Hagerty; Senator Watkins and General Persons; A. Larson; Senator Saltonstall, D. A. Quarles, General Persons, and B. N. Harlow; K. C. Royall. Lunch. To Burning Tree Country Club for golf with K. C. Royall, Budget Director Brundage, and Colonel Belshe. Evening appointment with W. J. Hopkins.

26   Washington. Hosts breakfast for Republican congressmen. Morning appointments with General Persons; U.S. Ambassador Horace A. Hildreth (to Pakistan); R. J. Saulnier and G. M. Hauge; news briefing; news conference. Receives Indonesian Parliamentary Delegation, followed by appointments with S. Adams; Senator Cooper; General Persons; General Goodpaster; G. D. Morgan. Lunch. Afternoon appointments with General Goodpaster; Secretary Dulles; National Security Council session; Admiral Strauss, Secretary Wilson, D. A. Quarles, Budget Director Brundage, General Goodpaster, and B. N. Harlow; Admiral Strauss; General Persons; General Goodpaster. Off-the-record appoint-

ment with General Persons and Senators Knowland, Dirksen, Thye, Williams, Purtell, Mundt, Beall, Goldwater, and Barrett.

27 Washington. Makes film for International Geophysical Year. Morning appointments with B. M. Shanley; General Persons, G. D. Morgan, and I. J. Martin; Legislative Leaders; Congressmen Murray and Rees and I. J. Anderson; Dr. Detlev W. Bronk (President, National Academy of Sciences), Dr. Alan T. Waterman (Director, National Science Foundation), and G. M. Hauge; G. M. Hauge and Generals Randall and Goodpaster. Receives Student National Education Association, followed by appointments with Congressman Kearns and photographer; S. Adams and General Persons; S. Adams, General Persons, G. D. Morgan, J. Z. Anderson, and R. E. Merriam; S. Adams. Hosts luncheon for Republican governors and former governors. Visits Captain Edward E. Hazlett at Bethesda Naval Medical Center. Afternoon appointments with G. M. Hauge; W. J. Hopkins; General Goodpaster; General Persons; G. D. Morgan; J. C. Hagerty; General Persons and Republican senators (off the record).

28 Washington. Hosts breakfast for Republican congressmen. Cabinet meeting. Appointments with U.S. Ambassador Lodge; Colonel Draper. Attends Islamic Center dedication ceremonies with Mrs. Eisenhower. Appointments with General Goodpaster; General Persons; G. D. Morgan; J. C. Hagerty and General Goodpaster. To Gettysburg. Plays golf at Gettysburg Country Club. Walks around farm with Mrs. Eisenhower.

29 Gettysburg. To Gettysburg Country Club for golf with Generals Heaton and Nevins. Inspects cattle at Feaster farm with General and Mrs. Heaton. Skeet shooting. Inspects school house and Allen farm. Returns to skeet range with General Heaton. Views movie "The Beau James" with Mrs. Eisenhower, General and Mrs. Heaton and General and Mrs. Nevins.

30 Gettysburg. Practices golf with General Heaton. Inspects school house. Attends 94th anniversary celebration of Battle of Gettysburg at Gettysburg High

School Auditorium with Mrs. Eisenhower, General and Mrs. Heaton, and Colonel Tkach. Views "Hell's Crossroads" with Mrs. Eisenhower, General and Mrs. Heaton and General and Mrs. Nevins.

July   1   Gettysburg. Takes photographs of farm with General Heaton. To Gettysburg Country Club for golf with Generals Heaton and Nevins. Inspects patio and barbecue pit under construction. Practices skeet shooting with General Heaton and Sergeant Moaney. Takes photographs with Mrs. Eisenhower, General and Mrs. Heaton, General and Mrs. Nevins, and Colonel Tkach. Signs four bills brought by G. D. Morgan and Wayne Hawks.

        2   Washington. Morning appointments with W. J. Hopkins; General Persons and I. J. Martin; Legislative Leaders; V. E. Peterson and S. Adams; Rena C. Ridenour (Chief, Correspondence Section, retiring); Charles B. Shuman (President, American Farm Bureau Federation) and J. Z. Anderson; B. M. Shanley; G. D. Morgan and H. R. McPhee; General Cutler, F. M. Dearborn, and J. S. Lay. Lunch. Afternoon appointments with W. J. Hopkins; Ralph Reed (American Express Co.); Alfred Redpath (Trustee, Columbia University); General Persons; Robert Montgomery and Andrew Wyeth; General Goodpaster; S. Adams. Practices golf on south lawn. Hosts stag dinner.

        3   Washington. Morning appointments with S. Adams; Admiral Strauss, John F. Floberg, John S. Graham, and Harold Vance; G. Gray; news briefing; news conference. Late morning appointments with J. C. Hagerty; B. M. Shanley; Bishop Hanns Lilje (President, Lutheran World Federation, Germany), Ambassador Krekeler, Paul C. Empie (Executive Director, National Lutheran Council), and G. M. Hauge; G. D. Morgan; General Persons. Lunch. Afternoon appointments with Attorney General Brownell and S. Adams; General Goodpaster. National Security Council session. Late afternoon appointments with Secretary Wilson, D. A. Quarles, and General Goodpaster; A. W. Dulles; Secretary Humphrey and R. B. Anderson; General Goodpaster; G. D. Morgan; J. C. Hagerty, General

Goodpaster, Captain Aurand, and Colonel Draper; S. Adams. To MATS terminal with General Snyder and J. Rowley en route to Gettysburg. Walks around garden with Mrs. Eisenhower. Inspects skeet range, cattle, and duck pond.

4   Gettysburg. To Gettysburg Country Club for golf with General Nevins. Walks to barn and inspects patio and barbecue pit. Rides his horse "Sporty Miss."

5   Gettysburg. Visits R. S. Hartley at Brannon farm. Inspects school house being remodeled by Major J. S. D. Eisenhower with Mr. and Mrs. W. A. Jones. To Gettysburg Country Club for golf with General Nevins, W. A. Jones, and G. E. Allen.

6   Gettysburg. To Gettysburg Country Club for golf with General Nevins, W. A. Jones, and G. E. Allen. Receives nut tree from Northern Nut Growers Association and poses for photographs. To Brannon farm for photographs with 1956 champion steer. Meets with Chesapeake and Ohio Railroad Co. representatives. Receives C & O Railroad lantern. Poses for photographs with bulls Black Brutus and Ankonia 3551, R. S. Hartley, and James Coyner (American Angus Association). To southeast pasture for photographs with James Coyner and cattle. Poses for photograph with H. Purdy and cattle. Returns to Brannon farm for photographs with H. Purdy and Black Brutus.

7   Gettysburg. Inspects cattle at Feaster farm with General Nevins, W. A. Jones, and G. E. Allen.

8   Gettysburg. Returns to Washington. Morning appointments with W. J. Hopkins; General Persons; B. M. Shanley; R. J. Saulnier; U.S. Ambassador James M. Langley (to Pakistan); J. C Hagerty; Attorney General Brownell, S. Adams, and G. D. Morgan; General Persons and B. N. Harlow; Admiral Strauss, Budget Director Brundage, and General Goodpaster; Generals Cutler and Goodpaster; B. M. Shanley. Off-the-record lunch meeting with Generals Gruenther and Smith. Afternoon appointments with Major J. S. D. Eisenhower; B. M. Shanley; J. C. Hagerty. Poses for photograph with White House Police Force, followed by appointments with Gen-

eral Persons; B. M . Shanley; R. B. Anderson, Secretary Humphrey, Budget Director Brundage, A. M. Cole, R. J. Saulnier, S. Adams, G. M. Hauge, I. J. Martin, and Generals Persons and Burgess; Budget Director Brundage; S. Adams; General Persons.

9   Washington. Morning appointments with General Persons and I. J. Martin; S. Adams; Legislative Leaders; Senator Knowland. Receives representatives from League of Women Voters, District of Columbia, Home Rule Committee, and District government officers to discuss District of Columbia Home Rule. Late morning appointments with U.S. Ambassador Hill (to Mexico) and family; R. L. Biggers (off the record); J. C. Hagerty; Secretary Dulles and W. M. Rountree; Virgil Pinkley (*Los Angeles Mirror*) and C. Roberts (off the record); R. B. Anderson and S. Adams; General Goodpaster. Lunch. To Burning Tree Country Club for golf with C. Roberts, E. D. Slater, and F. F. Gosden. Hosts stag dinner.

10   Washington. Morning appointments with W. J. Hopkins; General Persons; G. D. Morgan; B. M. Shanley; Senator Russell and General Persons; S. Adams; General Clark; S. Adams; Secretary Wilson, D. A. Quarles, and Generals Randall and Goodpaster; S. Adams; Secretary Wilson. Receives new official army flag from Secretary Brucker and General Taylor. Late morning appointments with G. Gray; General Goodpaster; S. Adams. Hosts stag luncheon in honor of Prime Minister Huseyn Shaheed Suhrawardy (Pakistan). Afternoon appointments with Vice-President Nixon; C. B. Randall; U.S. Marshal Joseph Job (New Jersey), Assemblyman Charles Krause (New Jersey), and B. M. Shanley; Colonel Draper and Major Joseph E. Barrett; General Goodpaster. Practices golf on south lawn. Evening appointment with G. D. Morgan.

11   Washington. Morning appointments with T. E. Stephens; A. Burton Mason; National Security Council session; Secretary Dulles; G. Gray, General Cutler, and J. S. Lay; Malcolm Forbes (Republican gubernatorial candidate, New Jersey) and family, H. M. Alcorn, L. Richard Guylay, B. M. Shanley, and Sheriff Neil G. Duffie (Essex County, New Jersey);

Secretary Dulles and W. M. Rountree; Prime Minister Suhrawardy, Secretary Dulles, and Ambassador Mohammed Ali (Pakistan); Secretary Dulles; J. C. Hagerty; G. D. Morgan; General Goodpaster. Lunch. To Burning Tree Country Club for golf with Congressmen Westland, Halleck, and Bates. Hosts off-the-record stag dinner.

12   Washington. Off-the-record breakfast with Senator Knowland. Morning appointments with Secretary Weeks; G. D. Morgan. Cabinet meeting. Late morning appointments with Secretary Dulles and W. M. Rountree; John M. Ashbrook and Jerrie Kent (Young Republican National Federation); S. Adams; General Goodpaster; Prime Minister Suhrawardy, Secretary Dulles, W. M. Rountree, Ambassador Mohammed Ali (Pakistan), Ambassador Langley, M. S. A. Baig (Secretary, Ministry of Foreign Affairs and Commonwealth Relations, Pakistan), Akhter Husain (Secretary, Ministry of Defense, Pakistan), Syed Amjad Ali (Minister of Finance, Pakistan), Begum Akhtar Sulaiman (Prime Minister's daughter), Syud Ahmed (press attaché, Pakistan Embassy); S. Ahmed and J. C. Hagerty; General Goodpaster and Captain Aurand; S. Adams; General Persons. Lunch. Afternoon appointment with General Goodpaster. Boards helicopter en route to Camp David, Maryland. Inspects "Apple" (bomb shelter) with Mrs. Eisenhower and grandchildren. Practices golf. Views movie, "Big Land" with Mrs. Eisenhower and grandchildren.

13   Camp David, Maryland. To Gettysburg farm with General Snyder and grandchildren. Inspects Tea House. To Gettysburg Country Club for golf with G. E. Allen and General Nevins. To Feaster farm with General Nevins and G. E. Allen to inspect cattle with R. S. Hartley. To skeet range with G. E. Allen and General Nevins. Inspects vegetable garden with G. E. Allen and General Nevins. Practices golf with D. D. Eisenhower II. Views "Cinderella" with Mrs. Eisenhower and grandchildren.

14   Gettysburg. Walks to Tea House. Inspects lawn with Chief West and Eugene Clapsaddle (Gettysburg Nurseries). Tours Feaster and Redding farms with Mrs. G. E. Allen. Walks to Tea House with Colonel

Tkach, G. E. Allen, and Chief West. Practices golf with D. D. Eisenhower II. Views movie "Duel in Durango" with Mrs. Eisenhower, grandchildren, Rose Woods, and Sergeant and Mrs. Moaney.

15   Gettysburg. To Highpoint, Virginia, for briefing with J. C. Hagerty, General Goodpaster, Bradley Patterson, Albert Toner, Captain Aurand, and Colonels Schulz and Draper. Inspects Univac. Poses for photographs and returns to Washington. Appointments with S. Adams; Attorney General Brownell; General Persons and I. J. Martin; General Goodpaster. Lunch. Afternoon appointments with W. J. Hopkins; Secretary Wilson; S. Adams; Secretary Seaton.

16   Washington. Morning appointments with Colonel Schulz; S. Adams, General Persons, and I. J. Martin; G. D. Morgan; Legislative Leaders; General Persons. Receives cabinet of silver from Peter Roberts (Conservative M. P. and Master Cutler, Sheffield, England) for work on Anglo-American relations during the war. Late morning appointments with Science Advisory Group about defense issues and civilians; General Cutler; U. S. Ambassador Joseph S. Farland (to Dominican Republic); C. B. Randall; S. Adams. Lunch. To Burning Tree Country Club for golf with Congressmen Halleck, Haskell, and May. To Pentagon with Mrs. Eisenhower for dinner hosted by Secretary and Mrs. Wilson.

17   Washington. Morning appointments with Major J. S. D. Eisenhower; B. M. Shanley; General Persons; S. Adams; B. M. Shanley; G. D. Morgan; Michael McKeogh (President's driver during war); U.S. Ambassador Jacob D. Beam (to Poland). Receives saddle from Colonel and Mrs. George Cheschier (Louisville, Kentucky); news briefing; news conference. Late morning appointments with R. B. Anderson and Secretary Humphrey; General Taylor. Lunch. Afternoon appointments with General Goodpaster and Major J. S. D. Eisenhower. To Burning Tree Country Club for golf with G. E. Allen.

18   Washington. Morning appointments with S. Adams and W. J. Hopkins; General Goodpaster; J. A. McCone; Secretary Dulles; Budget Director Brundage; General Cutler. National Security Council session.

Appointments with A. W. Dulles and General Cutler (off the record); General Persons. Greets American Field Service students on White House grounds. Lunch. Afternoon appointments with A. Nielsen and Major J. S. D. Eisenhower; Governors Stratton and Dwinell and S. Adams; R. B. Anderson and Secretary Humphrey; B. M. Shanley; S. Adams; G. D. Morgan; General Goodpaster. Practices golf on south lawn. To residence of Major J. S. D. Eisenhower.

19   Washington. Morning appointments with General Goodpaster and Major J. S. D. Eisenhower; Congressman McConnell; S. Adams; Albert C. Jacobs (President, Trinity College) and Major J. S. D. Eisenhower; M. M. Rabb; General Persons; Charles H. Shepherd (White House carpenter, retiring) and B. M. Shanley. Witnesses swearing-in of Leo A. Hoegh as Civil Defense Administrator. Late morning appointments with J. C. Hagerty and Captain Aurand; I. J. Martin; R. B. Anderson and Secretary Humphrey; Cabinet meeting; S. Adams and General Persons; General Goodpaster and Major J. S. D. Eisenhower. Lunch. Afternoon appointments with General Snyder, Colonel Schulz, and Major J. S. D. Eisenhower; General Goodpaster. To MATS terminal en route to Gettysburg. To Gettysburg Country Club for golf with General Nevins. Visits Major and Mrs. J. S. D. Eisenhower. Barbecues birthday dinner for General Nevins, Mrs. Nevins, J. S. D. Eisenhower and family and guests.

20   Gettysburg. To Gettysburg Country Club for golf with Major J. S. D. Eisenhower and General Nevins. Watches grandchildren ride horses in north pasture with Mrs. Eisenhower and Major and Mrs. J. S. D. Eisenhower. To Feaster farm with Major J. S. D. Eisenhower to meet with R. S. Hartley. Visits home of Major J. S. D. Eisenhower with Mrs. Eisenhower.

21   Gettysburg. Attends services with Mrs. Eisenhower at Presbyterian Church of Gettysburg.

22   Gettysburg. Returns to Washington. Morning appointments with S. Adams and General Persons; General Goodpaster and Major J. S. D. Eisenhower; W. J. Hopkins; Major J. S. D. Eisenhower; B. M.

Shanley; R. J. Saulnier; U.S. Ambassador Maxwell H. Gluck (to Ceylon). Poses for photographs with Milton W. Glenn (congressional candidate) and son. Late morning appointments with Robert Hatcher (Chairman, Democrats for Eisenhower); General Bragdon and Major J. S. D. Eisenhower; Captain Aurand; S. Adams, Generals Gruenther and Persons, G. D. Morgan, I. J. Martin, J. Z. Anderson, E. D. Chesney, and H. R. McPhee; S. Adams. Lunch. Afternoon appointments with B. M. Shanley; Secretary Dulles; General Persons; Secretary Folsom, Congressman McConnell, S. Adams, and General Persons; Congressmen Tabor and Ford, Budget Director Brundage, S. Adams, General Persons, P. Rappaport, and J. Harold Stewart (Bureau of the Budget); General Goodpaster and Major J. S. D. Eisenhower; S. Adams and J. C. Hagerty; General Persons and J. C. Hagerty; General Persons; Major J. S. D. Eisenhower.

23   Washington. Morning appointments with G. D. Morgan; General Persons and I. J. Martin; J. Z. Anderson; Legislative Leaders; Major J. S. D. Eisenhower; S. Adams. Receives World Council for Welfare of the Blind, followed by appointments with Ambassador Pote Sarasin (from Thailand); General Goodpaster; Generals Lemnitzer (Vice Chief of Staff, Army) and Goodpaster and Major J. S. D. Eisenhower. Lunch. Afternoon appointments with Congressman Osmers and B. M. Shanley; S. Adams; J. C. Hagerty; S. Adams. Hosts off-the-record stag dinner.

24   Washington. Morning appointments with W. J. Hopkins; S. Adams; Postmaster General Summerfield; S. Adams, General Persons, J. C. Hagerty, and I. J. Martin; L. M. Pexton; Major J. S. D. Eisenhower. Cabinet meeting. Late morning appointments with Generals Goodpaster and Cutler and J. S. Lay; G. D. Morgan; Secretary Seaton and William F. Quinn (future Governor of Hawaii); S. Adams and General Persons; Major J. S. D. Eisenhower. To Burning Tree Country Club for golf with J. C. Hagerty, J. Black, and Major J. S. D. Eisenhower. Hosts off-the-record stag dinner.

25　Washington. Morning appointments with General Goodpaster and Major J. S. D. Eisenhower; Secretary Dulles, D. A. Quarles, Admirals Strauss and Radford, Generals Twining, Starbird, Cutler, Loper, and Goodpaster, and Major J. S. D. Eisenhower (off the record); National Security Council session; G. Gray; W. P. Rogers and General Persons. Greets Boys Nation delegates studying government, followed by appointments with Senator Revercomb and General Persons; U.S. Ambassador Peterson (to Denmark). Lunch. Afternoon appointments with General Goodpaster; D. A. Quarles, Secretary Weeks, R. B. Anderson, G. Gray, A. S. Flemming, W. P. Rogers, G. D. Morgan, J. Z. Anderson, and Loftus Becker (Legal Counsel, Department of State) about oil (off the record); G. D. Morgan; Major J. S. D. Eisenhower. Practices golf on south lawn. Late afternoon appointment with General Persons.

26　Washington. Breakfast meeting with Senator Knowland. Morning appointments with Generals Norstad and Goodpaster; General Goodpaster; Generals Emerson C. Itschner (Chief, Army Engineers) and Goodpaster; G. M. Hauge. Receives sterling silver baseball replica from C. R. Griffith and Walter B. Geroud (President, A. G. Spaulding Co.). Late morning appointments with Generals Goodpaster and Cutler and J. S. Lay; U.S. Ambassador White (to Sweden). Receives courtesy call from His Royal Highness Sardar Shah Mahmud (Afghanistan), Ambassador Najib-Ullah (from Afghanistan), and V. Purse, followed by appointments with Senator H. A. Smith and General Persons; G. D. Morgan; I. J. Martin and Major J. S. D. Eisenhower; Major J. S. D. Eisenhower; General Persons; C. A. Herter. Lunch. To Burning Tree Country Club for golf with G. E. Allen and W. E. Robinson. Off-the-record appointment with C. A. Herter and General Goodpaster.

27　Washington. Morning appointments with General Goodpaster and Major J. S. D. Eisenhower; J. C. Hagerty. To Burning Tree Country Club for golf with W. E. Robinson, G. E. Allen, and James E. Lemon.

28　Washington. Attends services at National Presbyterian Church.

29   Washington. Morning appointments with B. M. Shanley; Major J. S. D. Eisenhower; General Persons; G. Gray; General Lane and Colonel Alvin C. Welling; U.S. Ambassador Walter P. McConaughy (to Burma); Friends of the Land representatives. Witnesses swearing-in of Robert B. Anderson as Secretary of the Treasury, followed by appointments with Senator Knowland; Secretary Weeks, Secretary Seaton, G. Gray, G. D. Morgan, D. Anderson, and General Persons (off the record); Secretary Seaton; J. C. Hagerty. Lunch. Attends ceremony for signing of Instrument of Ratification of the Statute of the International Atomic Energy Agency, followed by appointments with Senator Hickenlooper; General Bragdon; General Persons. Practices golf on south lawn.

30   Washington. Morning appointments with B. M. Shanley; W. J. Hopkins; General Persons, C. D. Dillon, and I. J. Martin; G. D. Morgan; Legislative Leaders; General Persons; Dr. Louis H. Evans; General Persons, G. D. Morgan, and J. C. Hagerty; L. A. Minnich; B. M. Shanley; Secretary Folsom and General Persons (off the record); General Persons. Lunch. To Burning Tree Country Club for golf with G. E. Allen. Afternoon appointment with C. A. Herter. Greets Jerry Lewis. Attends baseball game at Griffith Stadium.

31   Washington. Morning appointments with Major J. S. D. Eisenhower; General Persons; Attorney General W. P. Rogers (acting); General Persons; J. C. Hagerty; news briefing; news conference; Senator Capehart and S. Adams; General Cutler and J. S. Lay; S. Adams; Major J. S. D. Eisenhower; General Persons. Lunch. Afternoon appointments with General Persons; W. T. Faricy, Daniel Loomis (President, Association of American Railroads), and S. Adams; General Persons; Senator Case and General Persons (off the record); Major J. S. D. Eisenhower; General Persons. Swims.

August   1   Washington. Morning appointment with H. M. Alcorn and General Persons. Greets administrative assistants to Republican senators, followed by appointments with J. C. Hagerty and General Persons;

Major J. S. D. Eisenhower; National Security Council session; Secretary Wilson. Receives delegates to Girls Nation in rose garden. Late morning appointments with S. Adams and J. C. Hagerty; Secretary Wilson; S. Adams and J. C. Hagerty. Listens to All-American Male Chorus (Central City, Colorado), followed by appointments with General Persons; Major J. S. D. Eisenhower. Swims. Lunch. To Burning Tree Country Club for golf with G. E. Allen. Evening appointments with General Persons; Major J. S. D. Eisenhower. Dinner at home of Major J. S. D. Eisenhower.

2   Washington. Morning appointments with J. C. Hagerty; Budget Director Brundage; Major J. S. D. Eisenhower; Secretary Weeks and G. D. Morgan; J. B. L. Lawrence; Senator Potter; Cabinet meeting; Admiral Strauss; J. C. Hagerty; Ambassador Yousef Haikal (from Jordan) and V. Purse; Secretary Wilson and Major J. S. D. Eisenhower; Dr. Frederick Fink (former football player); W. J. Hopkins; S. Adams; G. D. Morgan. Lunch. Afternoon appointments with B. M. Shanley; Major J. S. D. Eisenhower; B. M. Shanley; General Persons; Major J. S. D. Eisenhower. Practices golf on south lawn.

3   Washington. Breakfast meeting with Senator Knowland. Morning appointments with Major J. S. D. Eisenhower; G. D. Morgan. To Burning Tree Country Club for golf with J. E. McClure, Carlson Lyman, and Carlton Smith. Meets Mrs. Eisenhower at MATS terminal. Evening appointment with Secretary Dulles.

4   Washington. Attends services at National Presbyterian Church with Dr. M. S. Eisenhower.

5   Washington. Morning appointments with J. C. Hagerty; G. D. Morgan; General Snyder; General Persons; Major J. S. D. Eisenhower; Ambassador Mauricio Luis Yadarola (from Argentina); J. C. Hagerty; G. M. Hauge and R. J. Saulnier; Major J. S. D. Eisenhower; Congressman Miller and Sergeant Moaney; S. Adams; B. M. Shanley. Receives visiting British Parliament members. Lunch. Afternoon appointments with W. J. Hopkins; Major J. S. D. Eisenhower; General Cutler and Major J. S. D. Eisenhower;

B. M. Shanley and Major J. S. D. Eisenhower; J. C. Hagerty; Secretary Dulles and J. C. Hagerty. Practices golf on south lawn.

6 Washington. Morning appointments with Major J. S. D. Eisenhower; B. M. Shanley; W. J. Hopkins; General Persons, S. Adams, and I. J. Martin; B. N. Harlow; Legislative Leaders. Late morning appointments with Vice-President Nixon; Malcolm Muir (President and Editor-in-Chief, *Newsweek*); D. A. Quarles, Admirals Strauss, Radford, and Parker, Generals Loper, Twining, and Starbird, and Major J. S. D. Eisenhower; Generals Taylor and Persons (off the record); W. P. Rogers, M. D. Sprague, S. Adams, and Secretary Wilson; Secretary Wilson. Off-the-record lunch with Ambassador Whitney, followed by afternoon appointments with Major J. S. D. Eisenhower; B. M. Shanley; Major J. S. D. Eisenhower; S. Adams. Practices golf on south lawn. Visits Mrs. Eisenhower at Walter Reed Hospital.

7 Washington. Morning appointments with W. J. Hopkins; B. M. Shanley; General Persons; General Persons and B. N. Harlow; B. M. Shanley; J. B. Hollister and B. N. Harlow; Senator Morton, Congressman Ayes, and E. A. McCabe (off the record); S. Adams, J. C. Hagerty, General Persons, G. D. Morgan, I. J. Martin, G. M. Hauge, A. Wheaton, and Major J. S. D. Eisenhower; news conference. Late morning appointments with Secretary Dulles and Colonel Lincoln; G. D. Morgan; B. M. Shanley; Major J. S. D. Eisenhower. Lunch. Afternoon appointments with G. M. Humphrey; General Persons; Major J. S. D. Eisenhower; M. M. Rabb; B. M. Shanley. Practices golf on south lawn. Visits Mrs. Eisenhower at Walter Reed Hospital.

8 Washington. Morning appointments with General Persons; Major J. S. D. Eisenhower; General Persons and G. D. Morgan. Greets secretaries of Republican congressional members and poses for photographs. National Security Council session. Presents Distinguished Service Medal to Admiral Radford (retiring). Late morning appointments with Vice-President Nixon; Major J. S. D. Eisenhower. Lunch. To Burning Tree Country Club for golf with Major

J. S. D. Eisenhower. Visits Mrs. Eisenhower at Walter Reed Hospital.

9   Washington. Breakfast meeting with Senator Knowland. Morning appointments with W. J. Hopkins; Major J. S. D. Eisenhower; Dr. Elson (off the record); Secretary Anderson, F. C. Scribner, and S. Adams; S. Adams; Secretaries Dulles and Anderson, General Cutler, G. Smith, and Major J. S. D. Eisenhower; Secretary Dulles, General Persons, and B. N. Harlow; G. M. Hauge and national Lutheran church leaders. Presents photographs of Aberdeen Angus cattle to Ambassador Melas (from Greece). Late morning appointments with Ambassador Melas, B. M. Shanley, and V. Purse; G. M. Hauge; B. M. Shanley. Lunch. Afternoon appointments with S. Adams and Major J. S. D. Eisenhower; Secretary Weeks; Admiral Strauss, General Cutler, G. Smith, and Major J. S. D. Eisenhower; General Cutler and Major J. S. D. Eisenhower; W. J. Hopkins; G. D. Morgan; S. Adams. Practices golf on south lawn, followed by evening appointment with Major J. S. D. Eisenhower. Visits Mrs. Eisenhower at Walter Reed Hospital.

10 Washington. Morning appointment with Major J. S. D. Eisenhower. To Burning Tree Country Club for golf with Generals Parks and Heaton and G. E. Allen. Dinner with Mrs. Eisenhower at Walter Reed Hospital.

11 Washington. Attends services at National Presbyterian Church. Visits Mrs. Eisenhower at Walter Reed Hospital.

12 Washington. Morning appointments with B. M. Shanley; R. J. Saulnier; General Persons; G. Gray and L. A. Minnich; General Bragdon; Secretaries Wilson and Gates, Admiral Albert G. Mumma (Navy Bureau of Ships), Budget Director Brundage, and Major J. S. D. Eisenhower to discuss shipbuilding program; Secretaries Wilson and Brucker, W. M. Holaday (Special Assistant, Secretary of Defense, Guided Missiles), Admiral Radford, D. A. Quarles, Generals Lemnitzer and Daley, and Major J. S. D. Eisenhower; Admiral Radford; B. M. Shanley; General Persons and B. N. Harlow. Visits Mrs. Eisenhower at Walter Reed Hospital. Afternoon ap-

pointments with General Persons; S. Adams; Budget Director Brundage; Major J. S. D. Eisenhower; B. M. Shanley; General Persons. Swims. Evening appointments with J. B. Hollister, C. A. Herter, Admiral Radford, and B. N. Harlow (off the record); Senators Johnson, Knowland, Saltonstall, and Hayden, Congressmen Martin, Rayburn, Cannon, Taber, Passman, and Wigglesworth, J. B. Hollister, C. A. Herter, Admiral Radford, and B. N. Harlow to discuss foreign aid bill (off the record).

13   Washington. Morning appointments with General Persons, G. D. Morgan, and I. J. Martin; S. Adams; Legislative Leaders; Senators Knowland and Saltonstall; Senator Saltonstall; General Persons; S. Adams; General Persons; Secretary Mitchell; J. C. Hagerty; B. M. Shanley; G. D. Morgan; Major J. S. D. Eisenhower. To Burning Tree Country Club for golf with J. C. Hagerty and Colonel Belshe. To Walter Reed Hospital for x-rays and dinner with Mrs. Eisenhower.

14   Washington. Morning appointments with Major J. S. D. Eisenhower; W. J. Hopkins; S. Adams and General Persons; Secretary Weeks; General Persons; Senator Holland (off the record); General Persons; G. D. Morgan; S. Adams; B. M. Shanley; General Persons; Senator Payne. Off-the-record appointments with Congressman Halleck and General Persons; C. A. Herter. Lunch with General Gruenther (off the record). Afternoon appointments with Major J. S. D. Eisenhower; G. D. Morgan; J. C. Hagerty and B. N. Harlow; J. C. Hagerty. News conference on mutual security legislation, followed by appointments with G. D. Morgan; B. M. Shanley; Postmaster General Summerfield; S. Adams. Practices golf on south lawn. To Walter Reed Hospital to visit Generals Terry and Lang, Mrs. Eisenhower, Mrs. D. A. Quarles, and General and Mrs. Lasher.

15   Washington. Morning appointments with B. M. Shanley; Major J. S. D. Eisenhower; S. Adams, General Persons, J. C. Hagerty, and B. N. Harlow; Congressman Scrivner (off the record); S. Adams; N. H. McElroy (designated Secretary of Defense); Dr.

William Y. Elliott (Harvard University); J. C. Hagerty; General Henry B. Sayler; G. D. Morgan. Attends swearing-in of General Twining as Chairman, Joint Chiefs of Staff. Late morning appointments with Major J. S. D. Eisenhower; S. Adams. Lunch. Afternoon appointments with Major J. S. D. Eisenhower; B. M. Shanley; Captain Aurand; R. W. Woodruff (off the record); General Persons; Major J. S. D. Eisenhower; S. Adams; Major J. S. D. Eisenhower. Practices golf on south lawn. To Walter Reed Hospital with Major J. S. D. Eisenhower for dinner with Mrs. Eisenhower.

16   Washington. Morning appointments with General Persons; S. Adams; Congressman Fulton and B. N. Harlow; Secretary Wilson, General Randall, and Major J. S. D. Eisenhower; Mary V. Downey, Senator Bush, and E. A. McCabe regarding Downey's son imprisoned in China (off the record); G. Gray; G. D. Morgan; W. J. Hopkins; General Persons. Lunch. Afternoon appointment with Major J. S. D Eisenhower. Visits Mrs. Eisenhower at Walter Reed Hospital with Major J. S. D. Eisenhower and family. Late afternoon appointment with S. Adams and General Persons. Practices golf on south lawn.

17   Washington. Breakfast meeting with Congressman Martin. Morning appointment with Major J. S. D. Eisenhower. To Burning Tree Country Club for golf with Colonel Belshe, Major J. S. D. Eisenhower, and G. E. Allen. To Walter Reed Hospital for dinner with Mrs. Eisenhower.

18   Washington. Visits Mrs. Eisenhower at Walter Reed Hospital with Major and Mrs. J. S. D. Eisenhower and family. Lunch with Mrs. Eisenhower.

19   Washington. Breakfast with Congressman Rayburn. Morning appointments with S. Adams and G. D. Morgan; B. M. Shanley; Dr. Harry J. Reed (Coordinator, Rural Development Program) and T. D. Morse; U.S. Ambassador Matthews (to Austria); D. A. Quarles; General Persons; W. J. Hopkins. Lunch. Afternoon appointments with B. M. Shanley; Carter Burgess; Major J. S. D. Eisenhower; General Goodpaster; Postmaster General Summerfield; Postmaster General Summerfield and E. O. Sessions (off the

record); General Persons; J. C. Hagerty. Practices golf on south lawn. To Walter Reed Hospital with Major J. S. D. Eisenhower for dinner with Mrs. Eisenhower.

20 Washington. Morning appointments with C. A. Herter, O. Hatfield Chilson, S. Adams, General Persons, G. D. Morgan, and I. J. Martin; Legislative Leaders; S. Adams. Poses for photograph with Congressman Tewes and for *Life* Magazine, followed by appointments with General Persons; Senator H. A. Smith and General Persons. Lunch. To Burning Tree Country Club for golf with Bob Hope, J. Black, Colonel Belshe. Visits Mrs. Eisenhower and Mrs. Wilson at Walter Reed Hospital.

21 Washington. Morning appointments with General Persons and G. D. Morgan; Secretary Benson; General Persons; General Goodpaster and W. J. Hopkins; news briefing; news conference. Late morning appointments with J. C. Hagerty and B. M. Shanley; G. D. Morgan and J. C. Hagerty; Secretary Dulles; J. C. Hagerty; General Goodpaster; S. Adams. Lunch. Afternoon appointments with S. Adams and B. M. Shanley; G. M. Hauge; General Persons; General Goodpaster; Secretary Dulles, Generals Twining and Goodpaster, Major J. S. D. Eisenhower, and W. M. Rountree (off the record); G. D. Morgan. To Walter Reed Hospital for dinner with Mrs. Eisenhower. Visits Mrs. Wilson.

22 Washington. Breakfast with Senator Knowland. Morning appointments with S. Adams; Lewis K. Gough (Co-Chairman, Veterans Committee, People-to-People Program) and E. D. Chesney (off the record). National Security Council session. Late morning appointments with Secretary Dulles, Generals Twining and Goodpaster, Loy W. Henderson, and W. M. Rountree (off the record); Major J. S. D. Eisenhower; S. Adams and G. D. Morgan; G. D. Morgan. Lunch. To Burning Tree Country Club for golf with Congressmen Arends, Halleck, and Budge. To Walter Reed Hospital for dinner with Mrs. Eisenhower. Visits Congressmen Cole and Hess.

23 Washington. Morning appointments with S. Adams; B. M. Shanley; R. Bissell and Generals Cabell, Twin-

ing, and Goodpaster (off the record). Cabinet meeting. Late morning appointments with Secretary Dulles; Secretary Anderson and General Persons; General Persons; Senator Knowland and General Persons; P. G. Hoffman (off the record); General Goodpaster; General Cutler and J. S. Lay; S. Adams; General Goodpaster. Lunch. Afternoon appointments with S. Adams, G. D. Morgan, and Budget Director Brundage; J. C. Hagerty; Budget Director Brundage, John S. Patterson, S. Adams, and G. D. Morgan; Generals Goodpaster and Persons and B. N. Harlow; General Goodpaster; G. D. Morgan; I. J. Martin. Practices golf on south lawn. Late afternoon appointment with General Goodpaster. To Walter Reed Hospital for dinner with Mrs. Eisenhower.

24   Washington. To MATS terminal en route to Gettysburg. To Gettysburg Country Club for golf with Major J. S. D. Eisenhower, General Nevins, and R. Sleichter. Tours farm with Dr. M. S. Eisenhower, Ruth Eakin Eisenhower, and General Nevins. To skeet range. Walks to duck pond and back with Chief West. To Major J. S. D. Eisenhower's residence with Dr. M. S. Eisenhower and R. E. Eisenhower for dinner.

25   Gettysburg.

26   Washington. Breakfast meeting with Senator Johnson. Morning appointments with General Persons; J. C. Hagerty; General Goodpaster; Admiral Cato Glover (off the record); W. J. Hopkins; Secretary Anderson, Julian B. Baird (President, First National Bank, Minnesota), and General Burgess (off the record); S. Adams; G. D. Morgan; Secretary Dulles; Secretary Dulles, Generals Goodpaster, Persons, Twining, and Cabell, and W. M. Rountree (off the record). Lunch. Afternoon appointments with S. Adams and H. Pyle; Budget Director Brundage; General Persons and B. N. Harlow. Practices golf on south lawn. Off-the-record appointments with Senator Russell; Secretary Dulles, Generals Twining and Cabell, and W. M. Rountree. To Walter Reed Hospital for dinner with Mrs. Eisenhower.

27   Washington. Morning appointments with T. E. Stephens; General Persons and I. J. Martin; Leg-

islative Leaders; Congressman Halleck; G. D. Morgan; T. E. Stephens; Major J. S. D. Eisenhower. Poses for photographs with Little World Series Baseball Championship Team (Monterey, Mexico). Lunch. To Burning Tree Country Club for golf with K. C. Royall, Vernon Johnson, Colonel Belshe. Visits Mrs. Eisenhower at Walter Reed Hospital.

28   Washington. Morning appointments with J. C. Hagerty; General Goodpaster; G. D. Morgan; S. Adams; B. N. Harlow and General Goodpaster; S. Adams and General Goodpaster; W. J. Hopkins; Secretary Dulles, Major J. S. D. Eisenhower, G. Smith, W. M. Rountree, and J. C. Hagerty; Postmaster General Summerfield; W. J. Hopkins. Lunch. Afternoon appointments with Major J. S. D. Eisenhower; J. C. Hagerty; G. D. Morgan. Practices golf on south lawn. Appointments with Secretary Wilson, A. Larson, Conger Reynolds (U.S.I.A.), and S. Adams; General Goodpaster. To Walter Reed Hospital with Major J. S. D. Eisenhower for dinner with Mrs. Eisenhower.

29   Washington. Breakfast meeting with Senator Knowland. Morning appointments with W. J. Hopkins; T. E. Stephens; S. Adams; J. C. Hagerty; J. Z. Anderson; G. D. Morgan; G. D. Morgan and B. N. Harlow; T. E. Stephens; General Persons; Governor Quinn; General Goodpaster. Lunch. To Burning Tree Country Club for golf with Ambassador Whitney, J. E. McClure, and R. Clark. Visits Mrs. Eisenhower and Colonel George Adamson (former aide to the late General Pershing) at Walter Reed Hospital.

30   Washington. Records off-the-record announcement in broadcast room. Morning appointments with J. C. Hagerty; T. E. Stephens; Attorney General Brownell; S. Adams; J. C. Hagerty. To Post Office Building to address guests at Magsaysay stamp ceremony. Late morning appointments with Secretary Dulles; S. Adams; G. D. Morgan. Lunch. Afternoon appointments with T. E. Stephens; Secretary Dulles, H. E. Stassen, and G. Smith; General Goodpaster; J. C. Hagerty. To Walter Reed Hospital. Departs Walter Reed Hospital with Mrs. Eisenhower. Late after-

noon appointments with General Goodpaster; Vice-President Nixon; W. J. Hopkins; G. D. Morgan; Dr. M. S. Eisenhower.

31   Washington. Morning appointments with J. C. Hagerty; T. E. Stephens. To Burning Tree Country Club for golf with General Twining, S. Adams, and Colonel Belshe.

September 1   Washington. Attends services at National Presbyterian Church. Visits Colonel and Mrs. Schulz in Alexandria, Virginia. Visits Colonel and Mrs. Moore at their farm in Hillsboro, Virginia. Inspects cattle and horses.

2   Washington. Morning appointments with General Goodpaster; General Gruenther and grandchildren; G. D. Morgan and General Goodpaster; G. M. Hauge. Lunch. Afternoon appointments with Secretary Dulles. Practices golf on south lawn.

3   Washington. Morning appointments with W. J. Hopkins; General Goodpaster; A. R. Jones; S. Adams; General Persons and B. N. Harlow; J. C. Hagerty; J. C. Hagerty, S. Adams, Generals Goodpaster and Persons, G. D. Morgan, H. Pyle, B. N. Harlow, and A. Wheaton; news conference. Late morning appointments with S. Adams; T. E. Stephens; General Cutler and J. S. Lay; Mr. and Mrs. David O. McKay (President, Mormon Church); S. Adams; General Goodpaster; Attorney General Brownell and Warren Olney. Lunch. Afternoon appointments with T. E. Stephens; S. Adams; H. M. Alcorn and T. E. Stephens; J. Z. Anderson; General Goodpaster; T. E. Stephens; Secretary Dulles, Vice-President Nixon, and General Persons (off the record).

4   Washington. Morning appointments with J. C. Hagerty; G. D. Morgan; General Persons and B. N. Harlow; W. J. Hopkins; General Goodpaster. To MATS terminal with Mrs. Eisenhower. Boards *Columbine* en route to Newport, Rhode Island. Arrives at Quonset Point Naval Air and receives silver bowl from the people of Rhode Island. Boards *Barbara Anne* and sails to Constellation Pier. Greeted by Admiral and Mrs. Crommelin and Lieutenant Tell. Sails to Newport. Gives brief speech at Old Colony

House. Receives silver bowl and ladle, silver tray, and mounted lobster. To naval base.

5   Newport. Walks to the base headquarters. Sails to Fort Adams dock aboard *Barbara Anne*. To Newport Country Club for golf with Howard G. Cushing (President, Newport Country Club), Norman Palmer (Newport Country Club Pro), and J. C. Hagerty. Sails to Constellation Pier. Motors to Summer White House. Inspects grounds and garden. To office.

6   Newport. Meets with Mayor and Mrs. Peterson (Minneapolis). Poses for photographs with Petersons. Sails to Fort Adams dock aboard *Barbara Anne*. To Newport Country Club for golf with H. G. Cushing, N. Palmer, and J. C. Hagerty. Returns to Summer White House. Walks to office. Tours grounds with Mrs. Eisenhower.

7   Newport. Airborne for Washington, D.C. for morning appointments with W. J. Hopkins; Attorney General Brownell, General Persons, G. D. Morgan, and J. C. Hagerty; Attorney General Brownell; Secretary Dulles, L. W. Henderson, Generals Twining, Cutler, Goodpaster, Cabell, and Whisenand, and D. A. Quarles, and W. M. Rountree (off the record); Secretary Dulles and W. M. Rountree; J. C. Hagerty; Colonel Schulz; G. D. Morgan. Lunch. Afternoon appointments with Ambassador Sat Hayri Urguplu (from Turkey); J. C. Hagerty; Generals Cabell and Goodpaster (off the record). Motors to Dr. M. S. Eisenhower's home in Baltimore, Maryland, with Major and Mrs. J. S. D. Eisenhower for R. E. Eisenhower's debutante party. To Friendship International Airport (Baltimore, Maryland) en route to Quonset Point, Rhode Island. Poses for photographs with Admiral Crommelin at naval base and at Summer White House.

8   Newport. To office. Attends service with J. C. Hagerty and Captain Aurand at base chapel. Poses for photographs with Chaplain Robert E. Jenkins and four girl scouts. To Newport Country Club for golf with J. C. Hagerty, N. Palmer, and Commander James Dowdell. To Summer White House. Receives General and Mrs. Snyder, W. E. Robinson, and Captain Aurand.

9   Newport. Poses for photographs and signs Civil Rights Bill. To Newport Country Club for golf with J. C. Hagerty, W. E. Robinson, H. G. Cushing, and N. Palmer. Tours Newport with Mrs. Eisenhower and W. E. Robinson.

10   Newport. Appointment and photographs with Rhode Island Republican leaders. To Newport Country Club for golf with W. E. Robinson, N. Palmer, and J. C. Hagerty. Plays bridge with H. G. Cushing, Harold Vanderbilt, and W. E. Robinson.

11   Newport. Signs Immigration Bill and poses for photographs. Appointment and photographs with Secretary Benson. To Newport Country Club for golf with H. G. Cushing, W. E. Robinson, and N. Palmer. Views movie "Three Ten to Yuma" with Mrs. Eisenhower, General and Mrs. Snyder, and W. E. Robinson.

12   Newport. To Newport Country Club for golf with H. G. Cushing, W. E. Robinson, and N. Palmer. Appointment with General Goodpaster. Fishes with Sergeant Moaney.

13   Newport. Appointment with George Morrison (Chairman, General Baking Company). To Newport Country Club for golf with J. C. Hagerty, H. G. Cushing, and N. Palmer. Meets Mrs. Kennedy. Visits H. G. Cushing. To Price's Neck Landing. Checks lobster pots with Mr. and Mrs. H. G. Cushing and Mr. and Mrs. John Pratt.

14   Newport. Appointment with Attorney General Brownell; Governor Faubus; S. Adams, Congressman Hays, and J. C. Hagerty; Attorney General Brownell. Poses for photographs with Governor Faubus. Late morning appointments with Attorney General Brownell; W. Hawks; S. Adams and G. D. Morgan; Captain Aurand; J. C. Hagerty. Lunch. To Newport Country Club for golf with W. E. Robinson, H. G. Cushing, and N. Palmer. Views movie "The Proud Ones" with W. E. Robinson.

15   Newport. Attends services at First Presbyterian Church. Poses for photographs. Visits with Colonel and Mrs. Isaac Gill and W. E. Robinson.

16   Newport. Appointments with General Cutler and W. Sullivan. To Newport Country Club for golf with H. G. Cushing, W. E. Robinson, N. Palmer, and J. C. Hagerty. Views movie "Badlands of Montana."

17   Newport. Morning appointment with Budget Director Brundage. To Newport Country Club for golf with H. G. Cushing, J. C. Hagerty, and N. Palmer. Afternoon appointment with Paul Begley (Chief Navy Photographer). Fishes with J. C. Hagerty and Sergeant Moaney in Millvale. Views movie "St. Joan" with Mrs. Eisenhower.

18   Newport. Appointments with foreign officers attending Naval War College. To Newport Country Club for golf with H. G. Cushing, N. Palmer, and J. C. Hagerty. Barbeques with Mrs. Eisenhower and Captain Miller.

19   Newport. To Newport Country Club for golf with H. G. Cushing, Congresswoman Dwyer, and N. Palmer. Sails around naval base and Newport with General and Mrs. Snyder, Captain Aurand, Captain Miller, M. J. McCaffree, Lieutenant Gerald H. Weyrauch, Mrs. J. C. Daniels, and Admiral Crommelin aboard *Barbara Anne*. Fishes with General Snyder and Sergeant Moaney in Millvale.

20   Newport. Appointments with Lewis Calvani and Theodore C. Jarrett (Newport Chamber of Commerce); Admiral Hewitt. To Newport Country Club for golf with N. Palmer, local golf pros Gary Letiecq, Robert Fitta, Robert Dalessio, and William McGuinnes. Afternoon appointment with J. C. Hagerty. Plays bridge with W. E. Robinson, G. E. Allen, and E. D. Slater.

21   Newport. To Newport Country Club for golf with E. D. Slater, G. E. Allen, and H. G. Cushing. Plays bridge with E. D. Slater, G. E. Allen, and W. E. Robinson.

22   Newport. Appointments with J. C. Hagerty; Captain Aurand. Attends services at Chapel by the Sea. To Newport Country Club for golf with W. E. Robinson, E. D. Slater, G. E. Allen, and N. Palmer. Dinner with Mrs. Eisenhower, G. E. Allen, E. D. Slater,

and W. E. Robinson. Bridge with G. E. Allen, E. D. Slater, and W. E. Robinson.

23   Newport. Airborne for Washington. To Sheraton Park Hotel for annual meeting of Board of Governors of the International Bank for Reconstruction and Development, International Monetary Fund, and International Finance Corporation. Greets meeting leaders and addresses group. Witnesses swearing-in ceremony for Rocco C. Siciliano as Special Assistant to the President, Personnel Management. National Security Council session. Late morning appointments with Secretary Dulles and W. M. Rountree; Prince Faisal (Saudi Arabia), Ambassador Abdullah (from Saudi Arabia), Secretary Dulles, W. M. Rountree, Camille Nowfel (interpreter, State Department), and Ahmed Abd Al-Jaffar (interpreter); Secretary Dulles; Attorney General Brownell. To Statler Hotel. Addresses guests at President's Conference on Technical and Distribution Research for the Benefit of Small Business. To MATS terminal en route to Newport, Rhode Island. Views movie "Song of the South" with Mrs. Eisenhower, Mrs. Snyder, Captain Miller, and Lieutenant Weyrauch.

24   Newport. Airborne for Washington. Delivers nationwide television and radio address concerning school integration in Little Rock, Arkansas.

25   Washington. To MATS terminal en route to Newport. To Newport Country Club for golf with Captain George R. Muse, J. C. Hagerty, and N. Palmer. Greets Mildred Pickett (mother, N. Palmer) and poses for photographs.

26   Newport. Appointment with H. Ford II. To Newport Country Club for golf with H. Ford II, H. G. Cushing, and N. Palmer. Poses for photographs. Tours submarine *Seawolf* and greets crew. Receives tie clasp and photograph of *Seawolf*. Appointment with C. Roberts and Lieutenant Weyrauch. Visits with Mr. and Mrs. H. G. Cushing.

27   Newport. Appointment with T. E. Stephens. To Newport Country Club for golf with C. Roberts, H. G. Cushing, J. C. Hagerty, and N. Palmer. Hosts tea party with Mrs. Eisenhower for King Leopold III

(Belgian ex-Chief of State), Princess Liliane (Belgium), Admiral and Mrs. Crommelin, Admiral and Mrs. Rice, Admiral and Mrs. Ingersoll, and Mrs. John C. Daniel. Poses for photographs with Mrs. Eisenhower, King Leopold, and Princess Liliane. Meets with General and Mrs. Snyder and T. E. Stephens. Views movie "Canyon River" with Mrs. Eisenhower and Captain Miller.

28 Newport. Meets with Captain William F. Amsden; Admiral Ingersoll and Captain Aurand; T. E. Stephens. To Newport Country Club for golf with H. G. Cushing, J. C. Hagerty, and N. Palmer. Greets nuns from the St. Augustine Convent and Salve Regina College. Dinner and bridge with General Gruenther, G. E. Allen, and E. D. Slater.

29 Newport. Lunch with General Gruenther, G. E. Allen, and E. D. Slater. To Newport Country Club for golf with G. E. Allen, E. D. Slater, and J. C. Hagerty. Greets Mrs. Jack Allen (wife of caddie) and family; John F. Phelan (Newport City Solicitor) and children. Presents "Mr. President" golf ball to Jerry Martlane (caddie). Meets with Mr. and Mrs. Howard Wilson Brooks.

30 Newport. Appointment with Admiral Crommelin. To Newport Country Club for golf with J. C. Hagerty, H. G. Cushing, and N. Palmer. Greets Newport Police Department; Mr. and Mrs. Thomas Rando and family, and Mrs. Ranee Farrell. News conference. Greets Albert "Bud" Fisher (Manager of Hazards Beach). Boards *Columbine* en route to Washington. Appointments with Generals Taylor, Wheeler, and Goodpaster, Secretary Brucker, and J. C. Hagerty (off the record); General Cutler.

October 1 Washington. Morning appointments with General Goodpaster; T. E. Stephens; Secretary Anderson; Attorney General Brownell; S. Adams; A. Larson; Secretary Dulles; R. J. Saulnier; J. C. Hagerty, H. Pyle, and G. D. Morgan. Lunch. Afternoon appointments with Attorney General Brownell, S. Adams, and J. C. Hagerty; Attorney General Brownell and J. C. Hagerty; Attorney General Brownell, S. Adams, and J. C. Hagerty; Governors Clement, Collins, Hodges, and McKeldin, S. Adams, H. Pyle, J. C. Hagerty, and

Frank Bane; Attorney General Brownell; G. M. Humphrey, T. E. Stephens, S. Adams, J. C. Hagerty, and Attorney General Brownell; S. Adams, J. C. Hagerty, and Attorney General Brownell. Practices golf on south lawn. Visits home of Secretary and Mrs. Dulles with Mrs. Eisenhower.

2   Washington. Morning appointment with S. Adams. Observes National Day of Prayer at National Presbyterian Church. Appointments with T. E. Stephens; National Security Council session; General Goodpaster; General Burgess; J. C. Hagerty. Lunch. To Burning Tree Country Club for golf with Vice-President Nixon and Colonel Belshe.

3   Washington. Appointments with B. M. Shanley; General Cutler; S. Adams; S. Adams and T. E. Stephens; news briefing; news conference; Mrs. Saylor; Postmaster General Summerfield; General Goodpaster. Lunch. To Burning Tree Country Club for golf with W. C. Gilliam, Tom Beavers, and Colonel Belshe.

4   Washington. Appointments with T. E. Stephens; General Goodpaster; S. Adams; General Cutler and J. S. Lay. Airborne for Gettysburg. To Gettysburg Country Club for golf with G. E. Allen. Examines livestock at Feaster farm.

5   Gettysburg. To Gettysburg Country Club for golf with Mrs. G. E. Allen. Visits with Major and Mrs. J. S. D. Eisenhower and children, General and Mrs. Nevins, and Mr. and Mrs. G. E. Allen.

6   Gettysburg. Visits with Mrs. Eisenhower and Major and Mrs. J. S. D. Eisenhower and children.

7   Gettysburg. Inspects cattle at Feaster farm. Airborne for Washington. Appointments with T. E. Stephens; J. C. Hagerty; T. E. Stephens; S. Adams. Practices golf.

8   Washington. Appointments with General Goodpaster; W. J. Hopkins; S. Adams; S. Adams and General Goodpaster; D. A. Quarles, Dr. Waterman, W. M. Holaday, Dr. John P. Hagen, S. Adams, Generals Persons, Cutler, and Goodpaster, and H. Pyle, and B. N. Harlow; S. Adams, General Goodpaster, and

J. C. Hagerty; Senator H. A. Smith and General Persons; J. C. Hagerty; T. T. Krishna-Machari (Finance Minister, India), Ambassador Mehta (from India), and W. M. Rountree; Secretary Wilson and Generals Goodpaster and Randall; Brian Robertson and Ambassador Caccia (from Britain). Lunch. Afternoon appointments with Secretary Benson, S. Adams, P. E. Areeda, and D. Paarlberg (off the record); Secretary Benson; S. Adams; J. C. Hagerty; Dr. Bronk, S. Adams, J. C. Hagerty, and General Goodpaster (off the record); Generals Persons and Goodpaster. Practices golf on south lawn.

9   Washington. Appointments with T. E. Stephens; General Goodpaster. Witnesses swearing-in of N. McElroy as Defense Secretary. Presents Medal of Freedom to C. E. Wilson. Appointments with Secretary McElroy, Admiral Burke, and Generals Twinning, Taylor, White, Pate, Cutler, and Goodpaster; General Cutler; General Bragdon; Colonel Schulz; J. C. Hagerty; General Goodpaster; J. C. Hagerty; news briefing; news conference; General Caffey; Budget Director Brundage, M. H. Stans, and S. Adams (off the record). Records broadcast. To Burning Tree Country Club for golf with Colonel Belshe and Generals Parks and Irvine.

10   Washington. Breakfast meeting with Komla Gbedemah (Finance Minister, Ghana). Appointments with Ambassador Gomez (from Colombia) and W. T. Buchanan; National Security Council session; General Cutler; A. Larson; Henry Heald (President, Ford Foundation), Donald David (Vice-President, Ford Foundation), C. A. Herter, A. W. Dulles, and A. Larson (off the record); C. A. Herter and A. W. Dulles (off the record); General Goodpaster. Off-the-record luncheon with President's Advisory Committee on Government Organization. Afternoon appointments with Vice-President Nixon (off the record); B. N. Harlow and General Goodpaster; General Goodpaster; H. R. McPhee; A. Wheaton; General Persons; T. E. Stephens. Practices golf.

11   Washington. Appointments with S. Adams and General Goodpaster; General Persons; T. E. Stephens; Secretary McElroy, W. M. Holaday, and Generals

Persons and Goodpaster; General Goodpaster; Cabinet meeting; General Cutler; NATO Naval Chaplains; Pennsylvania Livestock Expedition representatives; W. J. Hopkins; General Goodpaster. Lunch. Practices golf on south lawn. Afternoon appointment with T. E. Stephens. Attends football game at Griffith Stadium.

12   Washington. Breakfast meeting with Senator Knowland. Records message for fundraising dinner. To Fort Meade for golf with Generals Heaton and Parks and Colonel Belshe.

13   Washington. Attends services with Mrs. Eisenhower at National Presbyterian Church. Visits Major and Mrs. J. S. D. Eisenhower.

14   Washington. Appointments with General Persons; General Goodpaster; B. M. Shanley; J. C. Hagerty; Ambassador Thanat Khoman (from Thailand); Governor Luis Muñoz-Marin (Puerto Rico); Secretary Anderson, R. J. Saulnier, W. M. Martin, and P. E. Areeda; R. J. Saulnier; Secretary McElroy and General Goodpaster; Prime Minister Manuel Cisneros (Peru), Ambassador Berckemeyer (from Peru), Ambassador Achilles (to Peru), and R. R. Rubottom; Ambassador Achilles; J. C. Hagerty and Generals Persons and Goodpaster. Off-the-record appointments with Attorney General Brownell, Secretary Brucker, W. P. Rogers, Generals Persons, Taylor, Wheeler, and Goodpaster, and Colonel George M. Seignious; Attorney General Brownell; Secretary Mitchell. Receives birthday cake from Republicans. Practices golf.

15   Washington. Appointments with T. E. Stephens; General Goodpaster; Carson G. Frailey (President, National Symphony Orchestra Association) and Howard Mitchell (Conductor, National Symphony); Ambassador Castillo (from Honduras); T. E. Stephens; Ambassador Rahman (from Malaya). Receives Bible from Bible Society groups. Appointments with Dr. Elson and J. C. Hagerty; Secretary Folsom; Science Advisory Committee; Secretary Dulles. Lunch. To Burning Tree Country Club for golf with Generals Parks and Quesada and W. P. Rogers.

16   Washington. Appointments with M. Snyder, F. M. Dearborn, J. C. Hagerty, and Generals Cutler, Persons, and Goodpaster (off the record); General Cutler; Ambassador Briggs (to Brazil); J. C. Hagerty; S. Adams; Ambassador Allen and S. Adams; Budget Director Brundage; T. E. Stephens and J. C. Hagerty; S. Adams. Delivers address at Inter-American Press Association. To Burning Tree Country Club for golf with Ambassador Whitney and General Parks. Dentist appointment.

17   Washington. Appointments with Colonel Schulz; General Goodpaster; S. Adams; H. R. McPhee; Secretary Dulles and S. Adams; National Security Council session; S. Adams. Greets Queen Elizabeth and Prince Philip (England). Hosts luncheon for Queen Elizabeth and Prince Philip. Appointments with S. Adams and P. E. Areeda; Prime Minister John G. Diefenbaker (Canada), Ambassador Robertson (from Canada), and Secretary Dulles. Hosts state dinner and reception in honor of Queen Elizabeth and Prince Philip.

18   Washington. Breakfast meeting with Ambassador Lodge (off the record). Appointments with Ambassador Lodge (off the record); J. C. Hagerty; N. A. Rockefeller (off the record). Presents National Geographic Society Medal to Prince Philip; Cabinet meeting. Lunch. Afternoon appointments with S. Adams; S. Adams and P. E. Areeda; S. Adams; S. Adams and A. Larson; General Goodpaster; Secretary Dulles (off the record). Practices golf on south lawn.

19   Washington. Breakfast with Congressman Halleck (off the record). Appointments with J. C. Hagerty; S. Adams; U.S. Ambassador Byington (to Malaya); General Cutler and J. S. Lay; S. Adams. Lunch. To Burning Tree Country Club for golf with Generals Twining and Quesada and Colonel Belshe. Attends dinner at British Embassy with Mrs. Eisenhower hosted by Queen Elizabeth and Prince Philip.

20   Washington. Presents Lord Carleton Papers to Queen Elizabeth. Attends War Memorial dedication services at Washington Cathedral. Attends services at National Presbyterian Church.

21 Washington. Appointments with S. Adams; Lala Durga Das (*Hindustan Times*), Ambassador Mehta, and A. H. Douglas (off the record); Attorney General Brownell and S. Adams (off the record); J. C. Hagerty; M. A. Linton, A. Cheate, and C. Boels; International Congress of Actuaries delegates; A. W. Dulles and J. C. Hagerty; B. M. Shanley; R. J. Saulnier; S. Adams. Lunch. Afternoon appointments with C. S. Thomas and T. E. Stephens; A. B. Mason; S. Adams. Practices golf. Meets with Supreme Court justices and officers.

22 Washington. Appointments with W. J. Hopkins; S. Adams; J. C. Hagerty; A. Larson; General Goodpaster; S. Adams; Secretary Dulles, C. A. Herter, Ambassador Whitney, J. W. Jones, L. T. Merchant, J. C. Hagerty, and General Goodpaster; G. M. Humphrey (off the record). Airborne for New York. Appointments with New York Republican candidates; A. F. Burns; E. N. Eisenhower; B. M. Baruch; G. E. Allen; Ben Zukerman (tailor); Dr. M. S. Eisenhower; R. Montgomery; Robert Gray; Mr. and Mrs. H. Phleger and Mr. and Mrs. H. Flanigan; Mr. and Mrs. R. W. Woodruff; General Cutler; C. Hilton and J. Binns. Addresses guests at National Fund for Medical Education dinner. Attends play, "My Fair Lady."

23 New York. Airborne for Washington. Appointments with H. R. McPhee; Secretary Folsom and J. A. Perkins; Giovanni Malagodi (Secretary General, Italian Liberal Party), Ambassador Manlio Brosio (from Italy), and General Goodpaster; Preston Hotchkis and T. E. Stephens; S. Adams; B. N. Harlow and General Goodpaster; Freemason members; Secretaries McElroy and Anderson, Budget Director Brundage, and Generals Cutler and Goodpaster; General Goodpaster. Practices golf. Hosts informal dinner for Secretary Dulles, Prime Minister Macmillan, and S. Lloyd.

24 Washington. Off-the-record appointments with J. R. Killian, General Cutler, and S. Adams; Board of Consultants, Foreign Intelligence Activities; Edward L. Ryerson. National Security Council session, followed by appointments with Secretary McElroy and General Goodpaster; Secretary Dulles, L. T. Mer-

chant, and G. Smith; General Goodpaster. Lunch. Afternoon appointments with S. Adams; G. M. Hauge. Delivers address at Atoms for Peace ceremony. Appointments with U.S. Ambassador Whitney; General Persons; General Goodpaster. Hosts informal dinner for Prime Minister Macmillan.

25   Washington. Appointments with S. Adams; J. C. Hagerty; General Persons; G. Gray and General Goodpaster; H. M. Alcorn; Foreign Service Council; Paul Heymans and Howard S. Cullman; General Goodpaster; H. R. Luce; R. E. Samuel, R. H. Mulready, and T. E. Stephens. Luncheon. Afternoon appointments with Prime Minister Macmillan, S. Lloyd, Paul-Henri Spaak (Minister, Foreign Affairs, Belgium), Secretary Dulles, and C. B. Elbrick (off the record); Secretary Dulles, A. W. Dulles, D. A. Quarles, Admiral Strauss, Dr. Scoville, and Generals Loper and Goodpaster. Hosts meeting of British and American officials. Appointment with Secretary Dulles, Prime Minister Macmillan, and S. Lloyd. Practices golf.

26   Washington. Appointments with E. J. Hughes (off the record); George W. Perkins (Permanent U.S. NATO Representative, retiring); U.S. Ambassador Kemper (to Brazil, former) and General Goodpaster; Secretary Seaton, Channing Walker, and T. E. Stephens; B. M. Shanley. Attends Army-Navy football game at Annapolis. Meets with Maryland Roads Commission.

27   Washington. Celebrates Theodore Roosevelt Centennial at Grace Reformed Church.

28   Washington. Appointments with J. C. Hagerty; General Goodpaster. Witnesses swearing-in of A. Larson as Special Assistant to the President. Appointments with S. Adams, A. Larson, G. M. Hauge, and General Goodpaster; S. Adams and A. Larson; John M. Budinger; Generals Norstad and Goodpaster; Secretary Dulles; S. Adams; General Goodpaster; S. Adams.

29   Washington. Appointments with S. Adams and J. C. Hagerty; J. C. Hagerty; General Goodpaster; W. J. Hopkins; Generals Goodpaster and Cutler, Dr.

Isidor I. Rabi, G. Gray, and Admiral Strauss; Admiral Strauss and General Goodpaster; H. R. McPhee; John E. Gleason (Commander, American Legion), William F. Hauck (Director, American Legion), and E. D. Chesney; S. Adams and J. C. Hagerty; S. P. Skouras. To Burning Tree Country Club for golf with General Parks, C. Evans, and Colonel Belshe.

30 Washington. Appointments with Secretary McElroy, and Generals Randall, Cutler, and Goodpaster; news briefing; news conference; Federal Home Loan Bank and District Bank boards; General Goodpaster; Senator Saltonstall and General Persons. Lunch. S. Adams; Budget Director Brundage, Admiral Strauss, General Goodpaster, and Secretary Anderson; S. Adams and R. K. Gray. Practices golf.

31 Washington. Morning appointments with S. Adams; General Goodpaster; Atomic Energy Commission; Secretary Dulles; National Security Council session; General Goodpaster; S. Adams; S. Adams and Senator H. A. Smith; T. E. Dewey. Lunch. Afternoon appointments with G. D. Morgan; Secretary Weeks and S. Adams; Secretary Weeks; General Twining (off the record); Attorney General Brownell (off the record); General Goodpaster. Practices golf. Appointment with Secretary Seaton, S. Adams, and General Persons.

November 1 Washington. Morning appointments with S. Adams; K. B. McCann; W. J. Hopkins; General Goodpaster; Budget Director Brundage; Secretary Dulles; Cabinet meeting; Secretary Dulles; Secretary Folsom; Dewey Long; S. Adams; J. A. McCone; S. Adams, G. D. Morgan, and H. R. McPhee. Airborne for West Point. Attends football games. Attends dinner for Class of 1915.

2 West Point. Tours West Point campus. Attends Class of 1915 gift ceremony. Watches football game. Airborne for Washington.

3 Washington. No official appointments.

4 Washington. Off-the-record breakfast meeting with N. A. Rockefeller, Budget Director Brundage, A. S. Flemming, and General Goodpaster. Appointments with J. R. Killian, S. Adams, and General Cut-

ler (off the record); G. Gray, Generals Cutler and Goodpaster, and Security Resources Panel (off the record); General Cutler; H. J. Johnson and D. Metzger (off the record); B. M. Shanley; S. Adams; General Kenneth Strong (personal friend) and A. W. Dulles; S. Adams and A. Larson; T. E. Stephens. Lunch. Afternoon appointments with Budget Director Brundage, R. C. Siciliano, and S. Adams; H. E. Stassen (off the record); S. Adams and A. Larson. Practices golf. Hosts stag dinner.

5   Washington. Appointments with T. E. Stephens; General Persons; S. Adams and A. Larson; General Goodpaster; M. J. McCaffree; Secretary Dulles; Cabinet meeting; General Carl Spaatz (personal friend); U.S. Ambassador James W. Riddleberger (to Yugoslavia); Governor Knight, Mr. Stears, and S. Adams; W. J. Hopkins; General Goodpaster. To Burning Tree Country Club for golf with Generals Twining and Quesada, and J. E. McClure. Appointment with A. Larson.

6   Washington. Appointments with General Cutler; A. Larson; S. Adams; R. J. Saulnier; A. Larson; Generals Cutler and Goodpaster; Security Resources Panel; Secretary Weeks and G. Gray (off the record). Receives painting and animal feed from Eric B. Lomax. Appointments with G. D. Morgan; B. S. Adkins and R. K. Gray. Lunch. Afternoon appointments with A. Larson; S. Adams; W. J. Hopkins; Secretary Folsom, J. A. Perkins, E. L. Richardson, L. G. Derthick, S. Adams, and General Persons; Senator Johnson (off the record); General Persons; Barbara Anne Eisenhower and friend; S. Adams; Attorney General Brownell. Practices golf. Appointment with S. Adams and A. Larson.

7   Washington. Breakfast meeting with L. W. Douglas. Appointments with S. Adams; National Security Council session; Secretary Dulles, A. W. Dulles, and General Goodpaster (off the record); Secretary Dulles; G. D. Morgan; Jockey Club members; Dean Frank J. Welch and S. Adams (off the record); A. Larson; S. Adams. Practices golf. Swims. Delivers television and radio address on "Science and Security."

8   Washington. Breakfast meeting with Senator Bridges. Appointments with S. Adams; Cabinet meeting; Secretary McElroy. Witnesses swearing-in of Attorney General Rogers. Appointment with Ambassador Lodge. Attends FBI National Academy graduation exercises. Attends luncheon in honor of Attorney General Rogers. Airborne for Germantown, Maryland. Dedicates new Atomic Energy Commission building. Airborne for Washington. Appointments with General Cutler; S. Adams; General Persons; S. Adams; A. Larson; S. Adams.

9   Washington. Appointments with General Persons; Senator Ellender and General Persons; S. Adams and G. M. Hauge; General Goodpaster; S. Adams; Colonel Amado Martelinio; G. D. Morgan; General Goodpaster; R. K. Gray. To Burning Tree Country Club for golf with Major J. S. D. Eisenhower and Colonel Belshe.

10 Washington. Attends services with D. D. Eisenhower II at National Presbyterian Church. Physical examination at Walter Reed Hospital. Dinner with Dr. T. W. Mattingly and Generals Heaton and Snyder.

11 Washington. X-rays at Walter Reed Hospital. Addresses guests at Society of Medical Consultants to Armed Forces. Afternoon appointments with S. Adams; General Goodpaster; C. A. Case and C. A. Case, Jr.; General Goodpaster; J. C. Jordan, Harlan Hobbs, and B. N. Harlow; Secretary McElroy, D. A. Quarles, and General Goodpaster.

12 Washington. Morning appointments with Vice-President Nixon, Secretaries Dulles and Anderson, Budget Director Brundage, C. D. Dillon, C. A. Herter, S. Adams, and General Goodpaster; National Security Council session; Vice-President Nixon, Secretaries McElroy and Dulles, G. Gray, L. A. Hoegh, J. E. Hoover, Generals Thomas, Goodpaster, Twining, and Cutler, Admiral Strauss, A. W. Dulles, J. W. Yeagley, and J. S. Lay; Secretary Dulles and J. C. Hagerty; S. Adams; Secretary Dulles, R. Murphy, W. M. Rountree, and C. B. Elbrick; Billy G. Byars (owner, Byars Royal Oaks Farm) and G. E. Allen (off the record). Hosts Crusade for Freedom luncheon. Afternoon appointments with General Smith (off

the record); Aneurin Bevan (Head, British Labor Party), Viscount Hood (Minister, British Embassy), and C. B. Elbrick; S. Adams; W. J. Hopkins. Practices golf. Appointment with Secretary Anderson, W. M. Martin, R. J. Saulnier, and G. M. Hauge.

13 Washington. Appointments with General Goodpaster; J. C. Hagerty; A. Larson; S. Adams; Attorney General Rogers, S. Adams, M. M. Rabb, General Persons, and G. D. Morgan about civil rights (off the record); W. J. Hopkins; A. Larson; S. Adams; J. C. Hagerty and General Goodpaster; Secretary Dulles, Ambassador Richards, W. M. Rountree, C. B. Elbrick, and R. Murphy; General Goodpaster. Airborne for Oklahoma City. Meets with Oklahoma Republicans; Republican Finance Group; Flemming Award Winners; D. Kennedy, S. Flynn, and W. K. Warren; Congressman Belcher, T. J. Cuzalina, and Mr. and Mrs. Victor Harlow. Addresses audience at Municipal Auditorium. Airborne for Washington.

14 Washington. Appointments with S. Adams; National Security Council session; Secretary Dulles, G. Frederick Reinhardt, and J. C. Hagerty; General Goodpaster; S. Adams; Stanley Reed (Chairman, Civil Rights Commission) and S. Adams; General Goodpaster. Delivers address at National Defense Executive Reserve Conference. Appointments with General Goodpaster and J. C. Hagerty; Dr. M. S. Eisenhower (off the record).

15 Washington. Appointments with Budget Director Brundage, C. B. Randall, and S. Adams; G. E. Allen and S. Adams. Witnesses swearing-in of G. V. Allen as Director of United States Information Agency and J. R. Killian as Special Assistant to the President. Appointments with Secretary Dulles and S. Adams; Cabinet meeting; Secretary McElroy; G. D. Morgan; W. J. Hopkins; S. Adams. Airborne for Augusta. To Augusta National Golf Club for golf with E. B. Dudley and C. Roberts. Appointments with W. E. Robinson; W. E. Robinson, E. D. Slater, and C. Roberts.

16 Augusta, Georgia. To Augusta National Golf Club for golf with E. D. Slater, W. E. Robinson, and E. B. Dudley. Hosts dinner for Mr. and Mrs. G. M.

Humphrey, General Snyder, C. Roberts, and W. E. Robinson.

17 Augusta, Georgia. Attends services at Reid Memorial Presbyterian Church. To Augusta National Golf Club for golf with J. D. Ames, E. B. Dudley, and C. Roberts.

18 Augusta, Georgia. To Augusta National Golf Club for golf with E. B. Dudley, S. S. Larmon, and D. Casey.

19 Augusta, Georgia. Appointment with Secretary McElroy, W. J. McNeil, C. B. Randall, General Goodpaster, J. C. Hagerty, and Colonel Draper. To Augusta National Golf Club for golf with E. D. Slater, C. Roberts, and E. B. Dudley.

20 Augusta, Georgia. To Augusta National Golf Club for golf with E. B. Dudley, B. T. Leithead, and F. Willard.

21 Augusta, Georgia. To Augusta National Golf Club for golf with E. B. Dudley, W. E. Robinson, and L. Stockard. Airborne for Washington. Appointments with R. K. Gray; A. Larson; R. K. Gray; S. Adams; R. K. Gray; W. J. Hopkins; Secretary Anderson; Postmaster General Summerfield; G. D. Morgan. Attends dinner in honor of Attorney General and Mrs. Brownell.

22 Washington. Appointments with J. C. Hagerty and General Goodpaster; Cabinet meeting; Secretary McElroy, D. A. Quarles, J. R. Killian, and General Goodpaster; General Goodpaster; Secretary Dulles, J. Palmer, and General Goodpaster; General Persons; G. D. Morgan; S. Adams and R. K. Gray. Lunch. Afternoon appointments with S. Adams; National Security Council session; Secretary Anderson; R. K. Gray; Secretary McElroy; Dr. Rabi; Secretary Dulles; H. G. Cushing; P. G. Hoffman (off the record).

23 Washington. Appointments with General Persons; General Goodpaster; F. J. Donohue, W. A. Ruschmeyer, and Captain Crittenberger (off the record); Attorney General Rogers; Congressman Cole and General Persons; W. J. Hopkins; A. Larson; R. K.

Gray and General Goodpaster; General Cutler and J. S. Lay.

24 Washington. No official appointments.

25 Washington. Morning appointments with General Goodpaster; A. Larson; General Goodpaster; B. M. Shanley; General Goodpaster. Greets King Mohamed V (Morocco). Holds state dinner in honor of King Mohamed V.

26 Washington. No official appointments due to illness.

27 Washington. Receives King Mohamed V, Prince Moulay Abdallah (King's son), and Abderrahman Nagai (interpreter).

28 Washington. Attends Thanksgiving Day services at National Presbyterian Church.

29 Washington. To Gettysburg. Inspects farm.

30 Gettysburg. Visits with C. Roberts. Inspects farm. Dinner at home of Major J. S. D. Eisenhower.

December 1 Gettysburg. Visits country store. Visits with G. E. Allen.

2 Gettysburg. Returns to Washington. Appointments with S. Adams; General Goodpaster; Cabinet meeting. Practices golf. Appointments with Secretary Dulles; S. Adams; S. Adams and C. D. Dillon; Secretary Dulles; Secretary McElroy.

3 Washington. Appointments with General Goodpaster; J. C. Hagerty; General Persons; S. Adams; S. Adams and R. J. Saulnier (off the record); Secretary Dulles and Adlai E. Stevenson; bipartisan Legislative Leaders; Generals Persons and Goodpaster; General Persons; S. Adams; J. R. Killian; S. Adams; J. C. Hagerty; Vice-President Nixon; J. C. Hagerty; General Goodpaster; General Persons; S. Adams.

4 Washington. Appointments with General Goodpaster; General Cutler; J. C. Hagerty; General Persons; Attorney General Rogers and Judge Lawrence E. Walsh (off the record); Attorney General Rogers; Legislative Leaders; S. Adams; T. E. Stephens; Legislative Leaders; J. R. Killian.

5   Washington. Appointments with J. C. Hagerty; General Goodpaster; Secretary Dulles, U.S. Ambassador Heath (to Saudi Arabia), and J. C. Hagerty; National Security Council session; Secretary McElroy and General Goodpaster; J. C. Hagerty; General Goodpaster. To Gettysburg.

6   Gettysburg. Inspects farm with G. E. Allen. Dinner with Mr. and Mrs. G. E. Allen.

7   Gettysburg. Visits country store with General Snyder and G. E. Allen. Shoots crows. Dinner with Mr. and Mrs. G. E. Allen.

8   Gettysburg. Inspects farm with Chief West.

9   Gettysburg. Returns to Washington. Appointments with General Goodpaster and J. C. Hagerty.

10   Washington. Appointments with General Goodpaster; T. E. Stephens; J. C. Hagerty and General Goodpaster; Nuri Pasha al-Said (former Prime Minister, Iraq), W. M. Rountree, and Saleh Mahdi (Iraqi Embassy); General Goodpaster; Colonel Draper; General Goodpaster. Physical examination. Appointments with R. J. Saulnier; G. D. Morgan; Major J. S. D. Eisenhower; General Persons and J. C. Hagerty; General Goodpaster.

11   Washington. Appointments with Secretary Mitchell and S. Adams; S. Adams; Budget Director Brundage and M. H. Stans; W. J. Hopkins; S. Adams; Secretary Dulles, G. F. Reinhardt, G. Smith, C. B. Elbrick, and Generals Goodpaster and Cutler; Secretary Dulles; S. Adams; M. Kellogg (off the record); K. B. McCann and General Goodpaster; K. B. McCann.

12   Washington. Appointments with J. R. Killian, R. B. Perkins, L. G. Derthick, E. L. Richardson, Budget Director Brundage, S. Adams, and General Persons; National Security Council session; Secretary Dulles; Dr. M. S. Eisenhower; General Cutler; Secretary Weeks; J. H. Smith; S. Adams; G. D. Morgan; General Goodpaster. Lunch. Afternoon appointments with Dr. M. S. Eisenhower and K. B. McCann; K. B. McCann; S. Adams; Colonel Carruth, H. Wilkinson III, and G. M. Hauge; Major J. S. D. Eisenhower and K. B. McCann; K. B. McCann. Practices golf.

13   Washington. Appointments with General Good-
      paster; R. J. Saulnier; Ambassador Chapman (from
      Ghana) and W. T. Buchanan. Records Christmas
      message for Armed Forces. Appointments with
      General Goodpaster; S. Adams; J. R. Killian and
      S. Adams; General Goodpaster, Captain Aurand,
      and H. R. McPhee; S. Adams; General Goodpaster;
      S. Adams and General Goodpaster; General Good-
      paster; W. J. Hopkins. Airborne for Loring Air Force
      Base, Maine. Tours base. Hears speech by General
      Martin on Strategic Air Command. Airborne for
      Paris, France.

14   Paris, France. Attends Color and Honor Guard cer-
      emonies at Orly Airport. Dinner at U.S. Embassy.

15   Paris, France. Attends services at American Cathe-
      dral with U.S. Ambassador and Mrs. Houghton, Ma-
      jor J. S. D. Eisenhower, and Secretary and Mrs.
      Dulles. Lunch with U.S. Ambassador and Mrs.
      Houghton, General and Mrs. Norstad, General and
      Mrs. Schuyler, General and Mrs. Burgess, and Gen-
      eral Goodpaster. Visits Secretary and Mrs. McElroy.
      Appointment with Secretary Anderson. Dinner with
      Major J. S. D. Eisenhower, Secretary and Mrs. McEl-
      roy, and U.S. Ambassador and Mrs. Houghton.

16   Paris, France. Appointment with Prime Minister
      Macmillan. Attends opening session of Heads of
      Government meeting. Lunch at Embassy Resi-
      dence. Attends plenary session. Dinner with U.S.
      Ambassador and Mrs. Houghton, Mrs. J. F. Dulles,
      and Major J. S. D. Eisenhower.

17   Paris, France. Appointments with Adone Zoli (For-
      eign Minister, Italy); Chancellor Adenauer. Visits
      SHAPE. Lunch at Embassy Residence. Attends ple-
      nary session. Attends dinner hosted by President
      Coty (France).

18   Paris, France. Appointments with President Con-
      stantin Karamanlis (Greece); President Adnan
      Menderes (Turkey). Attends luncheon hosted by
      President Coty. Appointment with Ambassador And-
      vord (from Norway). Attends plenary session. Dinner
      with Secretary and Mrs. Dulles, Ambassador and Mrs.
      Houghton, and Generals Snyder and Goodpaster.

19   Paris, France. Meets with Agricultural Society of France. Attends final session of meeting. Airborne for Washington.

20   Washington. Appointment with S. Adams. Witnesses swearing-in of Sumner G. Whittier as Administrator of Veterans Affairs. Appointments with Vice-President Nixon; R. K. Gray; Secretary Anderson, F. C. Scribner, Budget Director Brundage, M. H. Stans, and S. Adams.

21   Washington. Appointments with General Goodpaster; S. Adams; R. K. Gray; S. Adams; G. E. Allen. Practices golf. Appointments with General Goodpaster; S. Adams; J. C. Hagerty.

22   Washington. Attends services with Mrs. Eisenhower at National Presbyterian Church. Visits homes of Colonel and Mrs. Moore and General and Mrs. Gruenther.

23   Washington. Appointments with General Goodpaster; W. J. Hopkins; J. C. Hagerty; R. J. Saulnier; President U. Win Maung (Burma), Ambassador Win (from Burma), and W. T. Buchanan; General Goodpaster; Secretary Dulles; General Goodpaster; Secretary Anderson, Budget Director Brundage, R. J. Saulnier, and General Goodpaster; National Security Council session; J. C. Hagerty. Participates in Christmas Pageant of Peace with Mrs. Eisenhower. Makes television and radio report on NATO with Secretary Dulles.

24   Washington. Appointments with B. N. Harlow and Generals Persons and Goodpaster; G. D. Morgan; General Cutler and J. S. Lay. Dental appointment with Colonel Fairchild.

25   Washington. [Page missing.]

26   Washington. Appointments with General Goodpaster; J. C. Hagerty; W. A. Ruschmeyer and F. J. Donohue (off the record); C. Roberts; Secretary Dulles; General Persons; C. Roberts; General Persons; A. Larson; General Goodpaster; J. C. Hagerty, I. J. Martin, and E. A. McCabe; W. J. Hopkins.

27   Washington. Appointments with T. E. Stephens; L. A. Minnich; General Persons; J. C. Hagerty;

G. D. Morgan and E. A. McCabe; Ambassador Morgenstierne (from Norway, retiring). To Gettysburg. Hunts with D. D. Eisenhower II. Inspects grounds with Chief West.

28   Gettysburg. Inspects farm with General Nevins. Skeet shooting with Major J. S. D. Eisenhower and D. D. Eisenhower II.

29   Gettysburg. Attends services with Mrs. Eisenhower at Presbyterian Church of Gettysburg. Visits Major J. S. D. Eisenhower. Skeet shooting with Major J. S. D. Eisenhower, D. D. Eisenhower II, and Captain Trefry.

30   Gettysburg. Meets with Secretary Folsom. Visits Major J. S. D. Eisenhower. Practices golf with Major J. S. D. Eisenhower and D. D. Eisenhower II. Skeet shooting with Major J. S. D. Eisenhower, D. D. Eisenhower II, and Sergeant Moaney.

31   Gettysburg. Appointment with Budget Director Brundage, J. R. Killian, and M. H. Stans. Inspects Feaster farm. Tours grounds with Boris Timshenko. Hosts New Year's Eve party with Mrs. Eisenhower for General and Mrs. Nevins, Mr. and Mrs. G. E. Allen, M. Allen, Mrs. M. Keane, and H. Brewer.

1958

January   1   Gettysburg. Visits with Major J. S. D. Eisenhower and family, Colonel and Mrs. Tkach, and J. Tkach.

2   Gettysburg. Returns to Washington. Appointments with S. Adams; J. C. Hagerty and A. Larson; G. D. Morgan; Secretary McElroy, D. A. Quarles, General Persons, and A. Larson; J. C. Hagerty; Secretary Dulles; Dr. M. S. Eisenhower and J. R. Killian.

3   Washington. Morning appointments with G. D. Morgan; General Goodpaster; Cabinet meeting; Attorney General Rogers, S. Adams, and J. C. Hagerty. Witnesses swearing-in of Civil Rights Commission members, followed by appointments with A. S. Flemming and R. C. Siciliano; A. S. Flemming; S. Adams and T. E. Stephens. To Gettysburg. Inspects farm. Tours Feaster farm with General Gruenther and Colonel Moore.

4   Gettysburg. Visits Major J. S. D. Eisenhower. Visits with B. T. Leithead, C. Roberts, and Ambassador Whitney; H. H. Gruenther; Pearl Mesta; Major and Mrs. J. S. D. Eisenhower and family and Colonel and Mrs. Fletcher.

5   Gettysburg. Visits with General and Mrs. Gruenther, Ambassador Whitney, B. T. Leithead, C. Roberts, and Major and Mrs. J. S. D. Eisenhower.

6   Gettysburg. Returns to Washington. Appointments with Ambassador Lodge; R. K. Gray; National Security Council session; Ambassador Lodge; Mrs. Eisenhower; W. J. Hopkins. Listens to Atlanta Boys Choir. Lunch. Afternoon appointments with S. Adams; Ambassador Lodge, A. Larson, and J. C. Hagerty about State of the Union Address; General Goodpaster.

7   Washington. Attends Service of Intercession and Holy Communion at National Presbyterian Church for opening of Congress. Appointments with General Persons and I. J. Martin; A. Larson; General Persons; Legislative Leaders; General Persons; S. Adams; J. R. Killian, S. Adams, Generals Persons, Cutler, and Goodpaster, and B. N. Harlow; H. Darby and General Persons (off the record). Lunch. Afternoon appointments with A. Larson; C. E. Wilson and S. Adams; General Goodpaster; S. Adams.

8   Washington. Morning appointments with S. Adams; J. C. Hagerty; A. Larson; S. Adams; General Persons; A. Larson; S. Adams. Lunch. Afternoon appointments with A. Larson; General Persons; S. Adams. Practices golf.

9   Washington. Delivers State of the Union Address. Afternoon appointments with General Goodpaster; President's Advisory Committee on Government Organization (off the record); N. A. Rockefeller, A. S. Flemming, S. Adams, and General Persons; S. Adams and General Persons; General Persons; S. Adams; General Goodpaster; T. E. Stephens. Practices golf.

10   Washington. Morning appointments with General Goodpaster; S. Adams and T. E. Stephens; M. J. McCaffree; Vice-President Nixon (off the record);

Cabinet meeting; Secretary Anderson, J. B. Baird (Under Secretary, Treasury), and J. C. Hagerty; Reverends Robert R. Brown and William H. Marmion and S. Adams; Colonel Schulz; R. J. Saulnier; U.S. Ambassador Wilson Clark Flake (to Ghana) and R. K. Gray; R. K. Gray; H. M. Alcorn; S. Adams and J. Rowley; J. Rowley. Lunch. Afternoon appointments with W. J. Hopkins; Captain Aurand; J. C. Hagerty; General Goodpaster; S. Adams. Views movie.

11 Washington. Morning appointments with Captain Harry C. Butcher (off the record); General Persons; D. A. Quarles and Generals Twining, Loper, Persons, and Goodpaster (off the record); General Goodpaster; General Goodpaster and W. J. Hopkins; Colonel Schulz and J. Rowley; B. M. Shanley; S. Adams; General Persons. Swims.

12 Washington. Attends services at National Presbyterian Church.

13 Washington. Morning appointments with General Persons; General Goodpaster; J. C. Hagerty; G. D. Morgan and E. A. McCabe; R. K. Gray; Senator Smathers, J. O'Keefe, and E. A. McCabe; Ambassador Houghton; A. Nielsen; S. Adams. Lunch. Afternoon appointments with General Persons; General Quesada, S. Adams, and G. D. Morgan; G. D. Morgan; General Persons; G. D. Morgan; P. D. Reed and S. S. Larmon. Evening appointment with Secretary Anderson, W. M. Martin, R. J. Saulnier, and G. M. Hauge.

14 Washington. Morning appointments with S. Adams and General Goodpaster; General Goodpaster; General Persons and I. J. Martin; Legislative Leaders; Prime Minister Souvanna Phouma (Laos), Laotian officials, W. S. Robertson, W. T. Buchanan, U.S. Ambassador J. Graham Parsons (to Laos), and Charles Sedgwick (interpreter); Secretary Dulles. Off-the-record lunch with R. W. Howard. Afternoon appointments with J. C. Hagerty; General Cutler and A. Larson; A. Larson and J. C. Hagerty; S. Adams; Secretaries Weeks, McElroy, Brucker, and Anderson, D. A. Quarles, Budget Director Brundage, B. N. Harlow, S. Adams, G. D. Morgan, and Generals Persons and Goodpaster; Secretary McElroy;

J. C. Hagerty; General Persons; R. K. Gray. Visits General Snyder.

15 Washington. Morning appointments with R. K. Gray; W. J. Hopkins; S. Adams; U.S. Ambassador Walter C. Dowling (to Korea) and R. K. Gray; General Persons; General Goodpaster; J. C. Hagerty; General Goodpaster; pre-news briefing; news conference; J. C. Hagerty and A. Wheaton; J. C. Hagerty; General Persons; G. D. Morgan. Lunch. Afternoon appointments with T. E. Stephens; S. Adams and G. D. Morgan; General Goodpaster; R. K. Gray. Practices golf.

16 Washington. Morning appointments with G. D. Morgan; General Goodpaster and W. J. Hopkins; General Persons; Congressman Rees, General Persons, R. C. Siciliano, and J. Z. Anderson (off the record); National Security Council session; General Cutler, A. W. Dulles, J. R. Killian, and Generals Twining and Goodpaster (off the record); General Twining; N. A. Rockefeller and General Goodpaster; N. A. Rockefeller. Lunch. Afternoon appointments with G. D. Morgan; G. S. Clinton, Congressman Williams, and S. Adams; T. E. Stephens; S. Adams; General Persons; General Goodpaster. Hosts dinner with Mrs. Eisenhower for Vice-President Nixon and Cabinet members.

17 Washington. Morning appointments with R. K. Gray; General Goodpaster. Views movie. Appointments with Secretary Dulles; Cabinet meeting; Secretary McElroy; J. R. Killian. Off-the-record appointments with Vice-President Nixon and E. Johnston; Admiral Radford. Lunch. Afternoon appointments with J. C. Hagerty; A. Larson; S. Adams. Practices golf with G. E. Allen.

18 Washington. Morning appointments with F. C. Akers (off the record); U.S. Ambassador Whitney; Judge John Minor Wisdom (New Orleans, Louisiana); T. E. Stephens; General Goodpaster; J. C. Hagerty. Swims and practices golf with G. E. Allen.

19 Washington. Attends services at National Presbyterian Church with D. D. Eisenhower II. Tours Tidal Basin and Haines Point.

20   Washington. Morning appointments with W. J. Hopkins; J. C. Hagerty and General Goodpaster; General Persons; A. Larson; T. E. Stephens; General Goodpaster; General Bradley (off the record); Generals Persons and Goodpaster. To MATS terminal en route to Chicago. Addresses guests at United Republican Fund of Illinois Presidential Dinner. To Stock Yard Inn.

21   Chicago. Returns to Washington. Afternoon appointments with S. Adams; R. K. Gray; General Goodpaster; General Cutler and J. S. Lay; Secretary McElroy, J. R. Killian, Generals Cutler and Goodpaster, and J. S. Lay; Secretary McElroy; J. R. Killian; General Goodpaster; G. D. Morgan.

22   Washington. Morning appointments with J. C. Hagerty; G. D. Morgan; General Goodpaster; National Security Council session; Secretary Dulles; Admiral Strauss and General Goodpaster. Lunch. Afternoon appointments with W. J. Hopkins; S. Adams and G. D. Morgan; J. C. Hagerty; Secretary Weeks, James R. Durfee (Chairman, Civil Aeronautics Board), and G. D. Morgan (off the record); Joseph Fitzgerald (Director, Bureau of Air Operations) (off the record); Secretary Weeks; G. Gray; General Cutler; G. D. Morgan; A. Larson. Practices golf.

23   Washington. Morning appointments with G. D. Morgan; J. C. Hagerty and General Goodpaster; General Goodpaster; Ambassador Percy Spender (from Australia) and W. T. Buchanan; S. Adams; W. E. Robinson; R. K. Gray; General Goodpaster; Senator Knowland (off the record); A. Nielsen. Lunch. Afternoon appointments with G. M. Humphrey; General Goodpaster. Practices golf on south lawn. Appointment with G. E. Allen and J. C. Hagerty. Swims. Hosts dinner and musical entertainment with Mrs. Eisenhower in honor of Congressman Rayburn.

24   Washington. Morning appointments with R. K. Gray and Colonel Schulz; General Goodpaster; General Cutler; Cabinet meeting; G. D. Morgan; General Goodpaster; A. F. Burns (off the record). Off-the-record lunch with Dr. M. S. Eisenhower. Afternoon

appointments with J. C. Hagerty; General Goodpaster; Secretary Weeks; G. D. Morgan. Swims.

25   Washington. Morning appointments with J. C. Hagerty; G. D. Morgan; W. J. Hopkins; J. C. Hagerty; B. N. Harlow, General Goodpaster, and R. K. Gray. To Pentagon for meeting with Secretary McElroy and Department of Defense officials. Returns to White House for appointment with General Goodpaster.

26   Washington. No official appointments.

27   Washington. Morning appointments with Colonel Schulz; J. C. Hagerty; Budget Director Brundage and Admiral Strauss; S. Adams; Secretary Anderson, Samuel C. Waugh (President, Export-Import Bank of Washington), Tom B. Coughran (Assistant Secretary, Treasury), and G. M. Hauge; Secretary Anderson. Attends ceremony in honor of Smith-Mundt Act 10th anniversary, followed by appointments with J. C. Hagerty; A. S. Nevins, W. A. Ruschmeyer, F. J. Donohue, and Colonel Schulz (off the record); A. S. Nevins; W. J. Hopkins. Attends luncheon on economic development and security problems. Presents gold medals to first recipients of President's Award for Distinguished Federal Civilian Service. Afternoon appointments with Secretary Mitchell and J. C. Hagerty; Secretary Mitchell, Attorney General Rogers, and J. C. Hagerty; Budget Director Brundage, R. E. Merriam, and I. J. Martin; J. M. Ashbrook and Michael Gill. Practices golf on south lawn. Appointment with General Goodpaster.

28   Washington. Morning appointments with J. C. Hagerty; W. J. Hopkins; General Goodpaster; General Persons and R. C. Siciliano; Senator Dirksen and General Persons (off the record); Legislative Leaders; Senator Knowland; G. D. Morgan; J. C. Hagerty; R. K. Gray; U.S. Ambassador Krekeler, W. T. Buchanan, and R. K. Gray; C. A. Herter; Secretary Weeks; S. Adams and R. K. Gray. Lunch. Afternoon appointments with S. Adams and General Goodpaster; Secretary McElroy; W. J. Hopkins; S. Adams; J. B. Baird; General Goodpaster. Practices golf. Dentist appointment.

29   Washington. To MATS terminal en route to Kansas City, Kansas. Attends funeral services for Arthur B. Eisenhower. Returns to Washington.

30   Washington. Morning appointments with General Goodpaster; G. D. Morgan; S. Adams; National Security Council session; Secretary McElroy, D. A. Quarles, Generals Persons, Twining, and Goodpaster, and B. N. Harlow (off the record); General Goodpaster; General Persons; R. J. Saulnier; K. B. McCann; S. Adams. Lunch. Afternoon appointments with J. R. Killian, J. C. Hagerty, and General Goodpaster; J. C. Hagerty; General Persons; Captain Aurand; General Snyder; S. Adams, A. Larson, and G. M. Hauge.

31   Washington. Attends Republican National Committee breakfast at Statler Hotel. Morning appointments with General Goodpaster; Secretary Weeks; H. E. Stassen (off the record); W. J. Hopkins; S. Adams and J. Z. Anderson; Senator Thye, S. Adams, and J. Z. Anderson; S. Adams; Jean Monnet (Head, French Financial Mission); General Goodpaster; G. D. Morgan. To MATS terminal en route to Augusta, Georgia. Receives Boy Scout handbook and 1957 Scout Report from Explorer Scout Mac Hanna. To Augusta National Golf Club for golf with C. Roberts and B. T. Leithead.

February 1   Augusta, Georgia. To Augusta National Golf Club for golf with C. Roberts, J. Gould, and F. Willard.

2   Augusta, Georgia. To Augusta National Golf Club to practice golf with C. Roberts and B. T. Leithead. Boards *Columbine* en route to Washington.

3   Washington. Morning appointments with J. C. Hagerty and General Goodpaster; J. C. Hagerty; R. K. Gray; S. Adams; R. K. Gray. Listens to Augsburg College Choir (Minneapolis, Minnesota). Late morning appointments with Secretary Benson; J. Z. Anderson; Attorney General Rogers. Lunch.

4   Washington. Morning appointments with General Goodpaster; S. Adams, General Persons, B. N. Harlow, I. J. Martin, and J. Z. Anderson; Legislative Leaders; J. R. Killian, Dr. George B. Kistiakowsky

(Science Advisory Committee), General Goodpaster, and Dr. Herbert York (Director, Livermore Laboratory) (off the record); M. J. McCaffree; General Goodpaster. Lunch. Afternoon appointments with S. Adams; H. R. McPhee; General Persons. Hosts dinner with Mrs. Eisenhower for military and science officials.

5   Washington. Morning appointments with General Persons; J. C. Hagerty; Congressmen Carnahan and Merrow; General Persons and J. C. Hagerty; pre-news briefing; news conference; J. C. Hagerty; R. L. Biggers (off the record); W. J. Hopkins. Lunch. Afternoon appointments with General Goodpaster; Secretary Dulles and Ambassador Thompson; Secretary Dulles; General Goodpaster; General Goodpaster and R. K. Gray.

6   Washington. Morning appointments with General Goodpaster; National Security Council session; Vice-President Nixon; S. Adams; P. G. Hoffman (off the record); H. R. McPhee. Lunch. Receives cap and gown from American College of Surgeons. Evening appointment with General Cutler.

7   Washington. Morning appointments with W. J. Hopkins; J. C. Hagerty; General Goodpaster; Attorney General Rogers and Secretary Mitchell; S. Adams; Attorney General Rogers; John K. Dole (Plain Dealing, Louisiana); J. R. Killian, Dr. E. N. Land (Science Advisory Committee), and General Goodpaster (off the record); J. C. Hagerty. Receives Boy Scouts and scouting officials, followed by appointments with H. E. Stassen; J. C. Hagerty; General Goodpaster; S. Adams.

8   Washington. Morning appointments with General Goodpaster; Vice-President Nixon and Attorney General Rogers; S. Adams; J. C. Hagerty.

9   Washington. No official appointments.

10   Washington. Morning appointments with R. K. Gray; J. C. Hagerty; Ambassador Luc Fouche (from Haiti) and W. T. Buchanan; J. C. Hagerty; Secretary Dulles. Receives Baker Report (off the record), followed by appointment with Ambassador Nadim Dimechkie (from Lebanon) and W. T. Buchanan.

Lunch. Afternoon appointments with General Goodpaster; U.S. Ambassador Parker T. Hart (to Jordan); W. J. Hopkins; A. Larson; Secretary Anderson, W. M. Martin, G. M. Hauge, and R. J. Saulnier. Hosts dinner with Mrs. Eisenhower for Diplomatic Corps, followed by musical entertainment.

11 Washington. Breakfast meeting with Vice-President Nixon, Secretaries Weeks and Mitchell, Postmaster General Summerfield, M. H. Stans, G. M. Hauge, J. C. Hagerty, General Persons, and R. J. Saulnier. Morning appointment with Postmaster General Summerfield and Secretary Weeks. Records broadcast for Red Cross, followed by appointments with J. C. Hagerty; Ambassador Mikhail A. Menshikov (from U.S.S.R.) and W. T. Buchanan; R. K. Gray; G. D. Morgan and General Goodpaster; J. C. Hagerty; Willy Brandt (Governing Mayor, Berlin), Albrecht von Kessel (Charge d'Affaires, German Embassy), Raymond E. Lisle (Acting Director, Office of German Affairs), and R. K. Gray; R. K. Gray; U.S. Ambassador Riddleberger (to Greece); General Goodpaster. Lunch. Hosts dinner with Mrs. Eisenhower for Diplomatic Corps, followed by musical entertainment.

12 Washington. Off-the-record breakfast meeting with N. A. Rockefeller. Morning appointments with General Goodpaster; J. C. Hagerty; General Goodpaster; Secretary McElroy; S. Adams; General Goodpaster; General Persons and B. N. Harlow. Records economic message. Lunch. Afternoon appointments with Captain Aurand; G. D. Morgan; R. K. Gray; W. J. Hopkins; S. Adams; Governor Underwood and S. Adams; General Goodpaster; General Cutler and J. S. Lay; S. Adams.

13 Washington. Morning appointments with General Goodpaster, Captain Aurand, and H. R. McPhee; General Goodpaster; W. J. Hopkins; C. A. Herter, A. W. Dulles, and General Cutler (off the record); J. R. Killian; Secretary McElroy; R. K. Gray. To MATS terminal en route to Thomasville, Georgia, with Mrs. Eisenhower. Visits Milestone Plantation.

14 Thomasville. Visits with W. E. Robinson and Mr. and Mrs. E. D. Slater.

15   Thomasville. Visits with W. E. Robinson, E. D. Slater, and R. W. Woodruff.

16   Thomasville. No official appointments.

17   Thomasville. Lunch at Ichauway Plantation with R. W. Woodruff, General Snyder, Mr. and Mrs. G. M. Humphrey, Mr. and Mrs. E. D. Slater, and W. E. Robinson. Visits Blue Springs Plantation.

18   Thomasville. No official appointments.

19   Thomasville. To Holly Hill Farm with G. M. Humphrey, General Snyder, W. E. Robinson, and E. D. Slater.

20   Thomasville. Hunts with G. M. Humphrey.

21   Thomasville. Hunts with G. M. Humphrey, E. D. Slater, W. E. Robinson, and General Snyder.

22   Thomasville. Visits Swift Plantation. Hunts with G. M. Humphrey.

23   Thomasville. Breakfast meeting with G. M. Humphrey and W. E. Robinson. To Spence Air Force Base en route to Phoenix, Arizona. To Paradise Valley Country Club for golf with Eldred Zimmerman (golf pro), E. C. Pulliam, and J. C. Hagerty. To Sky Harbor Airport en route to Washington.

24   Washington. Morning appointments with S. Adams; J. C. Hagerty; S. Adams; R. K. Gray; Vice-President Nixon; General Goodpaster; Secretary Benson. Addresses guests at National Food Conference at Statler Hotel. Lunch. Afternoon appointments with S. Adams; Congressman Williams. Attends meeting of President's Committee on Fund-Raising, followed by appointments with S. Adams; General Goodpaster; R. K. Gray; Colonel Schulz; Secretary Dulles; General Goodpaster; Dr. M. S. Eisenhower. Practices golf on south lawn. Evening appointment with General Goodpaster and Captain Aurand.

25   Washington. Hosts breakfast for General Ydigoras Fuentes (President-elect, Guatemala). Morning appointments with General Persons, I. J. Martin, and Secretary Seaton; Legislative Leaders; R. K. Gray; Admiral Strauss, D. A. Quarles, J. R. Killian, M. H. Stans, Generals Goodpaster, Loper, and Persons,

and Dr. R. Bacher (off the record); Admiral Strauss, J. R. Killian, and General Goodpaster. Lunch. Afternoon appointments with J. B. Baird and Assistants to Treasury Secretary; R. K. Gray; S. Adams; Dr. M. S. Eisenhower; J. C. Hagerty. Practices golf on south lawn. Delivers address at Conference on Foreign Aspects of United States National Security.

26   Washington. [Page missing.]

27   Washington. [Page missing.] Afternoon appointment with G. M. Hauge. Swims. Practices golf. Hosts stag dinner.

28   Washington. Morning appointments with S. Adams; G. D. Morgan; Attorney General Rogers; Vice-President Nixon; Cabinet meeting; General Goodpaster; W. J. Hopkins. Has molar extracted and neurological examination at Walter Reed Hospital. Visits General Paul at hospital.

March   1   Washington. Undergoes complete neurological examination at Walter Reed Hospital. Afternoon appointment with Secretary Dulles and C. B. Elbrick.

2   Washington. Attends services at National Presbyterian Church with Major J. S. D. Eisenhower and grandchildren.

3   Washington. Morning appointments with S. Adams; R. K. Gray; J. C. Hagerty; Vice-President Nixon, Attorney General Rogers, and J. C. Hagerty; B. S. Adkins and R. K. Gray; Ambassador Wilhelm Grewe (from Germany) and W. T. Buchanan; General Goodpaster; Benjamin McKelway (Editor, *Washington Evening Star*) and J. C. Hagerty (off the record); J. C. Hagerty; General Cutler and J. S. Lay; Virginius Dabney (Editor, *Richmond Times Dispatch*), Paul Black (Publisher, *Toledo Blade*), John Cline (Editorial Staff, *Washington Evening Star*), and J. C. Hagerty (off the record); Secretary Dulles; Ambassador Menshikov and Secretary Dulles; Secretary Dulles; J. C. Hagerty; S. Adams. Lunch. Afternoon appointments with General Goodpaster; General Goodpaster and G. Gray; P. E. Areeda and G. M. Hauge (off the record); J. C. Hagerty; R. K. Gray; General Bragdon; Secretary Anderson, L. S. Rothschild, Budget Director Brundage, B. D. Tallamy,

S. Adams, General Persons, and I. J. Martin about the highway program (off the record); R. K. Gray; Secretaries Anderson and Weeks, G. Gray, A. Shivers, Jake Hamon, Andrew Howsley, W. A. Moncrief, G. D. Morgan, and S. Adams (off the record); S. Adams and G. D. Morgan; G. D. Morgan.

4   Washington. Morning appointments with S. Adams; Secretary Mitchell; W. J. Hopkins; J. C. Hagerty; Jack Sutherland (photographer) and Thomas O'Halloran; G. D. Morgan; General Persons and I. J. Martin; R. K. Gray; J. Z. Anderson; Vice-President Nixon; Legislative Leaders; Congressman Arends and B. N. Harlow; K. B. McCann; J. C. Hagerty. Receives 4-H Club Winners of Achievement, Leadership, and Citizenship awards. Lunch. Afternoon appointments with R. K. Gray; Secretary Dulles and Ambassador Wadsworth; R. K. Gray; S. Adams; General Goodpaster. Attends off-the-record meeting.

5   Washington. Morning appointments with Charles R. Yates (personal friend); R. K. Gray. Receives 1958 Eisenhower Exchange Fellows, followed by appointments with M. M. Anderson (off the record); General Goodpaster; pre-news briefing; news conference; J. C. Hagerty; N. A. Rockefeller, J. R. Killian, Budget Director Brundage, A. Kimball, B. N. Harlow, W. Finan, and Generals Persons and Goodpaster; N. A. Rockefeller; General Goodpaster; S. Adams. Dentist appointment. Lunch. Afternoon appointments with J. C. Hagerty, General Goodpaster, and Colonel Schulz; J. C. Hagerty; R. K. Gray; General Goodpaster; R. K. Gray; H. Pyle. Practices golf on south lawn. Late afternoon appointments with General Goodpaster; W. J. Hopkins.

6   Washington. Breakfast meeting with U.S. Ambassador Lodge. Morning appointments with U.S. Ambassador Lodge; General Goodpaster; National Security Council session; J. C. Hagerty; Secretary Seaton, S. Adams, General Persons, J. C. Hagerty, Budget Director Brundage, and M. H. Stans; Reverend Graham; General Goodpaster; S. Adams. Lunch. Afternoon appointments with A. Larson; General Goodpaster; R. K. Gray; J. R. Killian, Dr. York, and General Goodpaster; General Good-

paster; J. C. Hagerty. Practices golf on south lawn. Late afternoon appointments with R. K. Gray; G. D. Morgan; Secretary Anderson; Secretary Anderson, W. M. Martin, R. J. Saulnier, and G. M. Hauge.

7   Washington. Morning appointments with J. C. Hagerty; General Goodpaster; J. C. Hagerty; Secretary Weeks; Cabinet meeting; Secretaries Dulles and Anderson, Attorney General Rogers, Budget Director Brundage, General Persons, and G. D. Morgan to discuss German vested assets (off the record); Secretary Dulles; General Goodpaster; R. K. Gray; General Goodpaster; Attorney General Rogers to discuss judgeships. Makes film for Regional Conferences on Highway Traffic Safety. Lunch. Afternoon appointments with General Goodpaster; Budget Director Brundage; General Persons. Practices golf on south lawn. Late afternoon appointments with General Persons, R. J. Saulnier, G. M. Hauge, B. N. Harlow, and J. C. Hagerty; Postmaster General Summerfield.

8   Washington. Breakfast meeting with Senator Knowland. Morning appointments with C. A. Herter and General Cutler; General Cutler; J. C. Hagerty; J. Black (off the record); Secretaries Anderson and Mitchell and General Persons; General Persons; Secretary Mitchell; G. D. Morgan; Budget Director Brundage; A. Larson; General Persons.

9   Washington. Attends services at National Presbyterian Church with Major J. S. D. Eisenhower and grandchildren.

10   Washington. Morning appointments with General Goodpaster; J. C. Hagerty; General Persons; W. J. Hopkins; John Cross and G. D. Morgan (off the record); General Goodpaster; Ambassador Don Celeo Davila (from Honduras) and W. T. Buchanan; General Goodpaster; Secretary Weeks, C. B. Randall, C. D. Dillon, and G. M. Hauge; J. R. Killian, Dr. Kistiakowsky, and General Goodpaster; General Goodpaster and R. K. Gray; Captain Beach; General Ronald Weeks (British Army); General Goodpaster and W. J. Hopkins. Lunch. Practices golf on south lawn. Afternoon appointments with J. C. Hagerty; General Persons; Senator Potter and Gen-

eral Persons. Hosts dinner for Reciprocal Trade Group.

11 Washington. Morning appointments with General Persons and I. J. Martin; Legislative Leaders; Ralph D. Pittman (off the record). Dentist appointment. Greets Mrs. Eisenhower upon her return from Phoenix at MATS terminal with Mrs. J. S. D. Eisenhower and S. E. Eisenhower.

12 Washington. Morning appointments with General Goodpaster; B. N. Harlow; J. C. Hagerty; R. K. Gray; General Persons; Secretary Anderson, Budget Director Brundage, R. J. Saulnier, James T. O'Connell, M. H. Stans, General Persons, G. D. Morgan, G. M. Hauge, and J. C. Hagerty; G. M. Hauge and P. E. Areeda; W. J. Hopkins; Karl G. Harr (Deputy Assistant, Defense Secretary) and General Cutler (off the record); General Cutler; Secretary McElroy, C. A. Coolidge, C. B. Randall, B. N. Harlow, and Generals Persons and Goodpaster; R. K. Gray. Receives Teacher of the Year, Jean Listebarger (Iowa), and education officials. Lunch. Afternoon appointments with R. K. Gray; Mayor Nicholson; General Goodpaster; J. C. Hagerty; L. F. McCollum (off the record).

13 Washington. Morning appointments with General Goodpaster; S. Adams and General Persons; J. C. Hagerty; W. J. Hopkins; General Goodpaster; C. A. Herter; General Cutler; National Security Council session; Secretary Mitchell; AFL-CIO Executive Committee; Secretary Mitchell, J. C. Hagerty, and G. M. Hauge; J. C. Hagerty. Lunch. Afternoon appointments with J. C. Hagerty; H. M. Alcorn; Secretaries Weeks, Anderson, and Mitchell, S. Adams, and General Persons; J. C. Hagerty; S. Adams; General Goodpaster and W. J. Hopkins; General Goodpaster. Swims. Meets with Business Advisory Council.

14 Washington. Morning appointments with Cabinet meeting; A. Larson; I. J. Martin; Senator H. A. Smith (off the record); C. A. Herter; J. C. Hagerty. Lunch. Afternoon appointments with General Goodpaster; J. C. Hagerty.

15 Washington. Morning appointments with General Cutler; General Sun Yup Paik (Chief of Staff, Ko-

rea) and Colonel Schulz (off the record); General Goodpaster; Secretary Seaton, S. Adams, and General Persons; G. D. Morgan; J. C. Hagerty; R. M. Kyes. Lunch.

16 Washington. Attends services with Mrs. Eisenhower at National Presbyterian Church.

17 Washington. Morning appointments with Colonel Schulz; General Persons; J. C. Hagerty and General Goodpaster; S. Adams; S. Adams; General Goodpaster; J. C. Hagerty; J. F. Shields; J. C. Hagerty; Postmaster General Summerfield; S. Adams; A. S. Flemming. Hosts luncheon for Foreign Service Institute Advisory Committee. Afternoon appointments with Secretary Anderson, J. T. O'Connell, S. Adams, G. D. Morgan, Newell Brown (Assistant Secretary of Labor), H. Pyle, J. C. Hagerty, and F. Bane to discuss reemployment compensation; Secretary Anderson; G. D. Morgan; W. J. Hopkins; S. Adams and J. C. Hagerty; J. C. Hagerty; S. Adams. Practices golf on south lawn. Evening appointments with General Goodpaster and J. C. Hagerty; R. K. Gray; A. Larson.

18 Washington. Morning appointments with Secretary Folsom; J. R. Killian, General Persons, G. D. Morgan, and I. J. Martin; Secretary Anderson; Senators Knowland, Bridges, Dirksen, and Saltonstall, General Persons, G. D. Morgan, and I. J. Martin; Legislative Leaders; Vice-President Nixon and S. Adams. Witnesses swearing-in ceremony for Budget Director Stans. Appointment with J. C. Hagerty. Addresses guests at Republican Women's National Conference. Late afternoon appointments with General Persons; General Goodpaster; Disabled American Veterans leaders and E. D. Chesney.

19 Washington. Morning appointments with S. Adams and R. E. Merriam; J. C. Hagerty; T. E. Stephens; W. J. Hopkins; General Goodpaster; R. J. Saulnier; S. Adams; Secretaries Weeks, Anderson, and Mitchell, S. Adams, Budget Director Stans, General Persons, G. D. Morgan, G. M. Hauge, R. J. Saulnier, and H. Pyle; Secretary Dulles; S. Adams; Dr. Sarvepalli Radhakrishnan (Vice-President, India), Ambassador Mehta, D. Kennedy, and Clement E. Conger (Act-

ing Chief of Protocol); General Persons, G. M. Hauge, and J. Z. Anderson; Congressmen Martin and Hill, Secretary Benson, G. M. Hauge, and J. Z. Anderson; Secretary Benson and G. M. Hauge; G. M. Hauge. Lunch. Afternoon appointments with G. D. Morgan and H. Pyle; S. Adams. Meeting to discuss unemployment and general economic situation, followed by appointments with Secretaries Anderson and Mitchell; S. Adams; J. C. Hagerty; R. K. Gray.

20 Washington. Morning appointments with General Goodpaster; General Persons; National Security Council session. Witnesses swearing-in ceremony for K. G. Harr as Special Assistant for Security Operations. Appointments with AMVETS representatives; R. K. Gray. Lunch. Afternoon appointments with J. R. Killian and General Goodpaster; G. M. Hauge; W. J. Hopkins; Secretary McElroy, D. A. Quarles, J. R. Killian, Budget Director Stans, and Generals Goodpaster, Twining, and Persons; General Persons; General Goodpaster. Swims. Evening off-the-record appointment with General Cutler, C. A. Herter, Admiral Strauss, M. D. Sprague, General Goodpaster, and J. R. Killian.

21 Washington. Morning appointments with General Goodpaster; Cabinet meeting; Secretaries Anderson and Weeks, R. J. Saulnier, and Budget Director Stans; Secretary Anderson; G. Gray; S. Adams; J. C. Hagerty. Lunch.

22 Washington. Appointment with General Goodpaster. To MATS terminal en route to Augusta, Georgia. To Augusta National Golf Club for golf with Major J. S. D. Eisenhower, C. Roberts, and W. E. Robinson.

23 Augusta, Georgia. To Augusta National Golf Club for golf with Major J. S. D. Eisenhower, C. Roberts, and W. E. Robinson. Returns to Washington.

24 Washington. Morning appointments with T. E. Stephens; General Goodpaster; S. Adams, T. E. Stephens, and J. C. Hagerty; W. J. Hopkins; Vice Chancellor Ludwig Erhard (Germany), C. B. Elbrick, Grasse Schaare (interpreter), and N. M.

Lejins; Mr. and Mrs. P. F. Brundage; Secretaries Weeks and Anderson, F. H. Mueller, S. Adams, and General Goodpaster; G. D. Morgan; W. J. Hopkins. Lunch. Attends off-the-record appointment to discuss advanced military planning, followed by afternoon appointments with T. E. Stephens; Secretaries McElroy and Dulles, D. A. Quarles, A. W. Dulles, Admiral Strauss, and Generals Twining and Cutler; Secretary Dulles.

25 Washington. Morning appointments with T. E. Stephens; Secretaries Mitchell, Weeks, and Anderson, S. Adams, General Persons, G. D. Morgan, and I. J. Martin; Legislative Leaders; S. Adams and General Persons; S. Adams; British Parliament members, W. T. Buchanan, General Gerald Schwab, and Nils Olsson; General Goodpaster. Delivers address at President's Conference on Occupational Safety. Lunch. Afternoon appointments with G. D. Morgan; J. C. Hagerty and Generals Cutler and Goodpaster; J. C. Hagerty; T. E. Stephens; Budget Director Stans; T. E. Stephens; Richard L. Roudebush (Commander, Veterans of Foreign Wars), O. B. Ketchum, and John Smith (Public Relations Officer); S. Adams; S. Adams and G. M. Hauge; T. E. Stephens; Secretary Anderson, Laurence B. Robbins (Assistant Secretary, Treasury), R. J. Saulnier, and Wendell B. Barnes to discuss small business equity financing. Swims. Practices golf. Meets with General Norstad.

26 Washington. Morning appointments with W. J. Hopkins; G. D. Morgan; J. C. Hagerty; General Cutler; T. E. Stephens; S. Adams; pre-news briefing; news conference; Ambassador Yadarola and William P. Snow (Assistant Secretary of State, Acting); Claude A. Barnett (Director, Associated Negro Press, Inc.), E. F. Morrow, and T. E. Stephens; Ambassador Hector Santaella (from Venezuela) and C. E. Conger; J. C. Hagerty. Lunch. Afternoon appointments with J. C. Hagerty; H. M. Alcorn and S. Adams; A. Larson; General Goodpaster; J. C. Hagerty. Records remarks on book *Outer Space.*

27 Washington. Morning appointments with W. J. Hopkins; T. E. Stephens; General Goodpaster; G. D.

Morgan; J. C. Hagerty and General Goodpaster; M. J. McCaffree; National Security Council session; Ambassador Paul G. Koht (from Norway) and W. T. Buchanan; Ambassador Howard Beale (from Australia) and W. T. Buchanan; T. E. Stephens. Hosts luncheon in honor of President-elect Mario Echandi Jimenez (Costa Rica). Afternoon appointments with Dr. M. S. Eisenhower (off the record); J. C. Hagerty; General Van Fleet; J. C. Hagerty and General Goodpaster; S. Adams and J. Z. Anderson. Delivers address at National Conference of Organizations on International Trade Policy dinner at Sheraton Park Hotel.

28 Washington. Off-the-record breakfast with Secretary McElroy, Congressmen Arends, Kilday, and Vinson, and B. N. Harlow. Morning appointments with Ambassador Lodge; Cabinet meeting; S. Adams and G. M. Hauge; Senators Aiken, Allott, Carlson, Mundt, and Young and J. Z. Anderson to discuss agricultural situation; G. D. Morgan, J. Z. Anderson, G. M. Hauge, S. Adams, J. C. Hagerty, and Secretary Benson; C. S. Thomas and RNC Finance Committee Vice-Chairmen; U.S. Ambassador Allison (to Czechoslovakia). Lunch. Afternoon appointments with J. C. Hagerty; Secretary Dulles; General Cutler and J. S. Lay; General Goodpaster. To Gettysburg farm.

29 Gettysburg. Tours farm with A. S. Nevins. Shoots skeet with D. D. Eisenhower II. Visits residence of Major J. S. D. Eisenhower with Mrs. Eisenhower.

30 Gettysburg. Attends services at Presbyterian Church of Gettysburg with Mrs. Eisenhower. Visits with Major and Mrs. J. S. D. Eisenhower and family and General and Mrs. Nevins.

31 Gettysburg. Attends birthday party for D. D. Eisenhower II. Returns to Washington for afternoon appointments with T. E. Stephens; General Persons; B. N. Harlow, J. Z. Anderson, and G. M. Hauge. Records agriculture message. Receives White House Press Photographers Association Contest winners. Appointments with W. J. Hopkins; General Goodpaster; Secretary Dulles; Senators Russell and Saltonstall, Secretary McElroy, General Persons, and B. N. Harlow (off the record).

April   1   Washington. Morning appointments with S. Adams; J. C. Hagerty; General Persons; B. N. Harlow, I. J. Martin, and General Goodpaster; Legislative Leaders; General Persons and B. N. Harlow; General Persons; Secretary McElroy, D. A. Quarles, Budget Director Stans, W. F. Schaub, J. R. Killian, and General Persons (off the record); Polish Legion of American Veterans; Colonel Tkach; S. Adams; J. C. Hagerty and G. D. Morgan; J. C. Hagerty; R. J. Saulnier and G. M. Hauge; General Goodpaster; Secretary Weeks, Charles H. Percy (President, Bell and Howell), and General Persons; Secretary Dulles. Practices golf on south lawn.

         2   Washington. Morning appointments with T. E. Stephens; W. J. Hopkins; G. D. Morgan; S. Adams; Dr. M. S. Eisenhower (off the record); G. D. Morgan; Ward M. Canaday (President, Overland Corporation); pre-news briefing; news conference. Receives son of S. Adams and friends; General Goodpaster; General Cutler and J. S. Lay; T. E. Stephens; A. B. Mason (off the record). Receives film "Ambassadors with Wings" from Ex-Cello Corporation executives, Senator Potter, and T. E. Stephens, followed by appointments with J. R. Killian and General Goodpaster; B. M. Baruch and Secretary Anderson. Lunch meeting with C. W. Jones, T. E. Stephens, J. C. Hagerty, A. F. Burns, and Captain Aurand. Afternoon appointments with C. W. Jones and A. F. Burns; Vice-President Nixon. Practices golf on south lawn. Evening appointment with General Goodpaster.

         3   Washington. Morning appointments with General Goodpaster; S. Adams; National Security Council session; Secretary Dulles; General Goodpaster; T. E. Stephens; group to discuss redevelopment of Southwest Washington, D.C.; A. S. Flemming, Budget Director Stans, and A. Kimball (off the record); A. S. Flemming (off the record). Receives baseball passes from W. S. Robertson, Joseph Haynes, T. E. Stephens, and J. C. Hagerty. Lunch. Afternoon appointments with W. J. Hopkins; J. C. Hagerty; M. J. McCaffree; U.S. Ambassador James S. Moose (to Sudan); G. D. Morgan; S. Adams. Visits Captain Hazlett at U.S. Naval Hospital. To Gettysburg farm.

4   Gettysburg. Visits residence of Major J. S. D. Eisenhower. Attends Good Friday services at Presbyterian
Church of Gettysburg with Mrs. Eisenhower. To Gettysburg Country Club for golf with General Nevins.
Shoots skeet with D. D. Eisenhower II.

5   Gettysburg. Visits residence of Major J. S. D. Eisenhower. To Gettysburg Country Club for golf with
Major J. S. D. Eisenhower and General Nevins.

6   Gettysburg. Attends Easter Sunday services at Presbyterian Church of Gettysburg with Mrs. Eisenhower and Major and Mrs. J. S. D. Eisenhower and
children. Returns to Washington.

7   Washington. Morning appointments with T. E.
Stephens; J. C. Hagerty; General Goodpaster; Secretary Dulles and P. J. Farley; T. E. Stephens; G. D.
Morgan; W. J. Hopkins; S. Adams. Lunch. Afternoon appointments with J. C. Hagerty; S. Adams;
Ambassador Young; Admiral Strauss; R. J. Saulnier;
General Cutler; W. J. Hopkins; General Goodpaster; T. E. Stephens; Generals Schuyler and Gruenther.

8   Washington. Morning appointments with J. C.
Hagerty; S. Adams; T. E. Stephens; R. K. Gray; Secretary McElroy and S. Adams; Secretary McElroy;
Secretary Anderson, W. M. Martin, R. J. Saulnier,
and G. M. Hauge; S. Adams and T. E. Stephens;
General   Goodpaster;   International   Economic
Growth Executive Committee. Lunch. Afternoon
appointments with General Goodpaster; B. N. Harlow; Captain Aurand; T. E. Stephens. Practices golf
on south lawn. Swims. Off-the-record appointment
with Secretary Gates and Admiral Burke.

9   Washington. Morning appointments with T. E.
Stephens; U.S. Ambassador Robert Newbegin (to
Honduras); General Goodpaster; pre-news briefing;
news conference; B. N. Harlow and General Good-
paster; T. E. Stephens; Irving Geist and Colonel
Schulz. Greets Federation Aeronautique Interna-
tionale delegates, followed by appointments with
J. C. Hagerty; S. Adams and B. N. Harlow. Lunch.
Afternoon appointments with T. E. Stephens; Gen-
eral Goodpaster; J. Z. Anderson; T. E. Stephens and

G. D. Morgan; B. N. Harlow. Practices golf on south lawn. Swims.

10 Washington. Morning appointments with Senator Cooper and S. Adams; Baroness Marguerita Stiernstedt (Swedish representative, People-to-People) and C. E. Wilson; S. Adams; General Bragdon, R. E. Merriam, and S. Adams; Secretary Weeks; G. D. Morgan; Secretary Weeks, B. D. Tallamy, R. E. Merriam, L. S. Rothschild, S. Adams, General Bragdon, and G. D. Morgan; Secretary Dulles. Lunch. Afternoon appointments with W. J. Hopkins; B. N. Harlow; S. Adams; S. Adams, G. D. Morgan, General Bragdon, and R. W. Jones; S. Adams and B. N. Harlow; S. Adams; General Goodpaster. Swims.

11 Washington. Morning appointments with T. E. Stephens; S. Adams; G. D. Morgan; General Goodpaster; G. D. Morgan; Secretary Dulles and J. C. Hagerty; S. Adams. To MATS terminal en route to Augusta, Georgia. To Augusta National Golf Club for golf with B. T. Leithead, J. Franklin, and C. Roberts.

12 Augusta, Georgia. Takes walk with B. T. Leithead, W. A. Jones, and General Snyder. Practices golf. Plays golf with W. A. Jones, W. E. Robinson, and F. Edwards. Dinner with W. A. Jones, R. W. Woodruff, W. E. Robinson, B. T. Leithead, C. Roberts, and C. J. Schoo.

13 Augusta, Georgia. Practices golf. Plays golf with W. A. Jones, R. W. Woodruff, and J. Roberts. Returns to Washington.

14 Washington. Morning appointments with T. E. Stephens; Vice-President Nixon; General Snyder; General Goodpaster; Budget Director Stans; J. R. Killian; National Security Council session; General Goodpaster. Attends opening baseball game at Griffith Stadium.

15 Washington. Off-the-record breakfast meeting with F. J. Donohue, W. A. Ruschmeyer, and Colonel Schulz. Morning appointments with J. C. Hagerty; S. Adams, I. J. Martin, and H. R. McPhee; Legislative Leaders; Dr. Elliott; D. A. Quarles, Budget Director Stans, S. Adams, B. N. Harlow, General Good-

paster, H. R. McPhee, and R. E. Merriam to discuss military pay bill (off the record); S. Adams, Budget Director Stans, and H. R. McPhee (off the record); R. J. Saulnier, Budget Director Stans, L. S. Rothschild, S. Adams, R. E. Merriam, General Bragdon, and I. J. Martin; T. E. Stephens; S. Adams; H. R. McPhee. Lunch. Afternoon appointments with Secretary Weeks and S. Adams; B. N. Harlow; Captain Aurand; S. Adams and Secretary Seaton; S. Adams. Practices golf on south lawn.

16   Washington. Morning appointments with S. Adams; J. C. Hagerty; T. E. Stephens; S. Adams and H. R. McPhee; Attorney General Rogers; General Goodpaster; pre-news briefing; news conference; General Goodpaster; S. Adams and T. E. Stephens; Ambassador Nicolas Arroyo y Marquez (from Cuba); James Copley (President, Copley Press), Robert Richards (Copley Washington Bureau Chief), Bill Boyd (San Diego Union), and J. C. Hagerty (off the record); S. Adams; B. N. Harlow; S. Adams. Lunch. Afternoon appointments with S. Adams and H. R. McPhee; J. C. Hagerty; S. Adams. Practices golf on south lawn.

17   Washington. Morning appointments with B. N. Harlow; T. E. Stephens; B. N. Harlow and General Goodpaster; General Goodpaster; Secretary Weeks and grandson; Secretary Benson, G. Gray, T. D. Morse, General Goodpaster, and S. Adams to discuss emergency food agency (off the record); S. Adams, Budget Director Stans, and General Goodpaster; S. Adams; General Goodpaster, S. Adams, Budget Director Stans, and R. J. Saulnier; R. J. Saulnier; J. R. Killian and General Goodpaster; General Goodpaster; S. Adams; Jack Foster (Editor, *Rocky Mountain News*) (off the record). Addresses guests at American Society of Newspaper Editors and International Press Institute luncheon. To Burning Tree Country Club for golf with Colonel Belshe.

18   Washington. Morning appointments with S. Adams and T. E. Stephens; Ambassador Wilfried Platzer (from Austria) and W. T. Buchanan; General Clark (off the record); General Goodpaster; Ambassador

Lodge; Cabinet meeting; Vice-President Nixon; General Goodpaster and W. J. Hopkins. To Camp David, Maryland, with General Goodpaster and Captain Aurand. Fishes at Little Hunting Creek with G. E. Allen. Views movie "Decision at Sundown" with Mrs. Eisenhower.

19 Camp David, Maryland. To Gettysburg farm. To Gettysburg Country Club for golf with G. E. Allen. Returns to Camp David for lunch with G. E. Allen and W. A. Jones. To Gettysburg. Inspects farm with G. E. Allen and W. A. Jones. Inspects Allen farm. Returns to Camp David.

20 Camp David, Maryland. Returns to Washington.

21 Washington. Morning appointments with General Goodpaster; T. E. Stephens; S. Adams and H. R. McPhee; S. Adams; J. C. Hagerty; General Cutler and J. S. Lay; Scandinavian Fraternity of America members, Senator Saltonstall, and Congressman Wigglesworth. Lunch. Afternoon appointments with General Goodpaster; Secretary McElroy and General Goodpaster; H. Brownell; S. Adams; L. S. Rothschild, F. C. Nash, R. E. Merriam, and H. R. McPhee. Practices golf on south lawn.

22 Washington. Morning appointments with General Goodpaster; S. Adams; General Persons, I. J. Martin, B. N. Harlow, and J. Z. Anderson; Legislative Leaders; Secretary Weeks (off the record); Dr. Rabi and General Goodpaster. Presents Young American Medal for Bravery to Harold T. Murray, Jr. Appointments with Generals Biddle and Goodpaster (off the record); H. M. Alcorn and S. Adams; Postmaster General Summerfield and J. Z. Anderson. Lunch. Afternoon appointments with J. C. Hagerty; General Persons; M. J. McCaffree; T. E. Stephens; General Goodpaster; S. Adams and T. E. Stephens. Practices golf on south lawn. Swims. Off-the-record appointment with Congressman Rayburn. Attends Republican senatorial dinner with Mrs. Eisenhower.

23 Washington. Breakfast meeting with Admiral Radford (off the record). Morning appointments with Admiral Radford (off the record); H. R. McPhee; W. J. Hopkins; S. Adams; General Persons; General

Goodpaster; Leo J. Conway, David Blauschild, Congresswoman Bolton, and T. E. Stephens to discuss "Buy Now and End Recession" campaign; pre-news briefing; news conference; United Service Organization leaders and T. E. Stephens; A. C. Jacobs; T. E. Stephens. Lunch. Afternoon appointments with T. E. Stephens; W. J. Hopkins; S. Adams; Secretary Dulles and T. E. Stephens; General Goodpaster. Practices golf on south lawn. Late afternoon appointments with General Persons; T. E. Stephens.

24 Washington. Breakfast meeting with Senator Knowland. Appointments with S. Adams; General Persons; A. E. Summerfield, Jr.; Secretary Anderson; National Security Council session; General Goodpaster; Secretaries Dulles and Seaton and S. Adams; Secretary Seaton and S. Adams; S. Adams; H. R. McPhee; U.S. Ambassador Sheldon T. Mills (to Afghanistan); T. E. Stephens; Lloyd F. MacMahon (Chairman, National Citizens for Eisenhower-Nixon, 1958), Michael Horan, L. W. Douglas, and Mildred Babino; G. M. Hauge and father; General Goodpaster; S. Adams. Lunch. Afternoon appointments with D. Thornton, J. E. Manning, Congressman Scott, Robert Fellows, and T. E. Stephens to discuss Air Force Academy; S. Adams; Governor McKeldin, Richard Weigle (President, St. John's College), and S. Adams; American Retail Federation representatives; Postmaster General Summerfield, General Persons, and J. Z. Anderson; W. J. Hopkins; General Goodpaster; Colonel Schulz; J. C. Hagerty; S. Adams. Attends private showing of Churchill's paintings at the Smithsonian Institution with Mrs. Eisenhower. Practices golf.

25 Washington. Breakfast meeting with Joint Chiefs of Staff. Morning appointments with Vice-President Nixon; M. J. McCaffree; Secretary Weeks and S. Adams; Cabinet meeting; Secretary Dulles; S. Adams and General Bragdon; R. J. Saulnier; I. J. Martin; H. R. McPhee; G. M. Hauge; W. J. Hopkins; General Persons, B. N. Harlow, and General Goodpaster; Junior Chamber of Commerce officers; Ambassador Alphand, Ferges Groussard (Editor, *Figaro*), and C. B. Elbrick (off the record); S. Adams.

To MATS terminal en route to Augusta, Georgia. To Augusta National Golf Club for golf with B. T. Leithead, W. E. Robinson, and C. Roberts.

26   Augusta, Georgia. To Augusta National Golf Club for golf with G. Stout, T. Butler, and R. McConnell. Inspects new golf course site with C. Roberts, General Snyder, and Johnny Graves (gardener).

27   Augusta, Georgia. Attends services at Reid Memorial Presbyterian Church with J. C. Hagerty and J. Rowley. To Augusta National Golf Club for golf with C. Roberts, W. E. Robinson, and C. MacAdams.

28   Augusta, Georgia. To Augusta National Golf Club. Practices golf with G. Stout. Golf with B. T. Leithead, W. E. Robinson, and T. Butler. Returns to Washington. Records Law Day message. Afternoon appointments with Secretary McElroy and B. N. Harlow (off the record); T. E. Stephens.

29   Washington. Breakfast meeting with Congressman Martin. Morning appointments with I. J. Martin and Generals Persons and Goodpaster; Secretary Mitchell; Legislative Leaders; Web Maddox and T. E. Stephens; J. C. Hagerty; R. J. Saulnier; B. G. Byars and G. E. Allen (off the record). Lunch. Afternoon appointments with General Cutler, J. S. Lay, and K. G. Harr; T. E. Stephens; Admiral Strauss; Advisory Committee on Government Organization (off the record).

30   Washington. Morning appointments with T. E. Stephens; B. N. Harlow; General Persons; T. E. Stephens; Attorney General Rogers; T. E. Stephens; B. M. Shanley; General Ira G. Eaker (Air Force, retired); pre-news briefing; news conference; G. D. Morgan; W. J. Hopkins; Congressman Canfield, Walter Kennedy (Administrative Assistant to Canfield), and T. E. Stephens; T. E. Stephens; B. N. Harlow; Senator Malone and I. J. Martin; General Tom Campbell; General Goodpaster. Lunch. To Burning Tree Country Club for golf with Colonel Belshe, F. Akers, and J. C. Bryant. Appointment with J. C. Hagerty and B. N. Harlow. Addresses guests at United States Chamber of Commerce dinner at Sheraton Park Hotel.

May   1   Washington. Breakfast meeting with White House staff (off the record). Morning appointments with J. Z. Anderson; General Goodpaster; Secretary Weeks and T. E. Stephens; National Security Council session; Secretaries Dulles and McElroy, D. A. Quarles, J. R. Killian, Admiral Strauss, G. C. Smith, and Generals Loper, Cutler, and Goodpaster (off the record); T. E. Stephens; Mayor and Mrs. Eugene Lambert (Duluth, Minnesota), Senator Thye, and General Persons; General Persons; Richard Flohr (Secret Service). Afternoon appointments with Auguste R. Lindt (High Commissioner for Refugees, United Nations) and J. W. Hanes; G. D. Morgan; B. N. Harlow and J. C. Hagerty. Practices golf on south lawn.

2   Washington. Morning appointments with General Persons; Secretary Weeks; Senator Knowland; Cabinet meeting; Secretary Dulles and C. A. Herter; Ambassador Mehta and W. T. Buchanan (off the record); J. C. Hagerty; J. D. Ames and T. E. Stephens; World Amateur Golf Team Championship organizers; General Goodpaster. Lunch. Afternoon appointments with T. E. Stephens; W. J. Hopkins; G. D. Morgan; B. N. Harlow; T. E. Stephens. Practices golf on south lawn.

3   Washington. Appointment with T. E. Stephens. To Burning Tree Country Club.

4   Washington. To Stratford, Virginia, with Mrs. Eisenhower for ceremony honoring Robert E. Lee. Tours grounds of Stratford Hall and addresses guests. Returns to Washington.

5   Washington. Morning appointments with General Goodpaster; General Persons; G. D. Morgan; General Cutler and J. S. Lay (off the record); T. E. Stephens; Secretary Anderson, D. T. Smith, and General Persons (off the record); Secretary Anderson; H. Conwell Snoke (Vice-President, Goodwill Industries). Greets Karl J. Fink, National Goodwill Worker of 1957. Appointments with National Citizens for Eisenhower-Nixon 1958 Committee; B. N. Harlow; Mrs. Frank Hanna and Mrs. George Vaughan (Junior Leagues of America). Greets Ju-

nior League conference delegates. Lunch. Afternoon appointments with B. N. Harlow; A. S. Flemming; B. N. Harlow; Milton C. Lightner and S. F. Dunn (National Association for Manufacturers); General Persons; B. N. Harlow.

6   Washington. Morning appointments with T. E. Stephens; B. N. Harlow; General Persons and I. J. Martin; G. M. Hauge; Legislative Leaders. Participates in Operation Alert exercises. Delivers address at Advertising Council conference. Hosts luncheon with Mrs. Eisenhower for Princess Astrid (Norway) and Prince Bertil (Sweden). Afternoon appointment with B. N. Harlow. Attends Republican National Committee dinner. Delivers nationwide television broadcast.

7   Washington. Morning appointments with General Goodpaster; U.S. Ambassador Walter Howe (to Chile); W. S. Robertson; Sarit Thanarat (Supreme Commander, Thailand), Chalermchal Charuvastr (Secretary to Thanarat), Ambassador Khoman, and W. S. Robertson; J. C. Hagerty; General Goodpaster; G. V. Allen and General Goodpaster; R. J. Saulnier; J. Z. Anderson; T. E. Stephens; General Persons. Lunch. Afternoon appointments with S. Adams, Attorney General Rogers, Secretary Brucker, and Colonel Seignious; Attorney General Rogers; W. J. Hopkins. Practices golf on south lawn.

8   Washington. Morning appointments with J. C. Hagerty; Secretary McElroy, C. A. Herter, and Generals Twining and Goodpaster; National Security Council session; Dr. Katz; T. E. Stephens; R. K. Gray. Addresses members of President's Committee on Employment of the Physically Handicapped. Presents awards to national essay contest winners George Kessler, Wayne S. Garner, and Rosalie D. Carson. Presents President's trophy to Mrs. Louise Lake, Handicapped American of the Year. Appointments with Secretary Weeks and H. Kearns; S. Adams and I. J. Martin; T. E. Stephens and J. C. Hagerty. Lunch. Plants oak tree to celebrate Theodore Roosevelt Centennial, followed by appointments with Dr. M. S. Eisenhower (off the

record); L. W. Hall. Practices golf on south lawn. Hosts dinner with Mrs. Eisenhower for Supreme Court Justices, followed by musical entertainment.

9   Washington. Morning appointments with T. E. Stephens; J. Z. Anderson; H. R. McPhee; J. C. Hagerty; G. Gray and General Cutler; J. C. Hagerty; Secretary Anderson; Congressman Corbett and J. Z. Anderson to discuss Postal Pay and Rate bill; S. Adams and T. E. Stephens; T. E. Stephens. To Burning Tree Country Club for golf with Congressmen Halleck and Arends and Colonel Belshe. Accompanies Mrs. Eisenhower to Union Station with grandchildren for her trip to Denver, Colorado.

10   Washington. Morning appointments with Generals Goodpaster and Persons and S. Adams; General Goodpaster; Major J. S. D. Eisenhower. To Burning Tree Country Club for golf with Colonel Belshe, Major J. S. D. Eisenhower, and J. E. McClure.

11   Washington. Attends services at National Presbyterian Church with grandchildren.

12   Washington. Morning appointments with W. J. Hopkins; J. C. Hagerty; S. Adams; General Persons; Senator Wiley and family (off the record); J. C. Hagerty; General Persons; G. D. Morgan; Generals Twining and Goodpaster; General Goodpaster; S. Adams and T. E. Stephens; S. Adams; Inter-American Board of Defense representatives; Postmaster General Summerfield; Mr. and Mrs. John Hertz, Jr., Frank Odlum, and G. E. Allen (off the record); T. E. Stephens. Lunch. Afternoon appointments with J. C. Hagerty; J. C. Hagerty and E. F. Morrow. Addresses guests at National Newspaper Publishers Association dinner at Presidential Arms Hotel, followed by appointments with General Goodpaster; Secretary Dulles; J. C. Hagerty; Secretary McElroy and B. N. Harlow; General Goodpaster. Practices golf on south lawn.

13   Washington. Morning appointments with M. J. McCaffree; General Persons, G. D. Morgan, and I. J. Martin; General Goodpaster; Legislative Leaders; Senator Knowland; Attorney General Rogers and

S. Adams; Edward G. Barry (President, Lions International), Congressman Martin, and T. E. Stephens; J. C. Hagerty; S. P. Skouras, Edmund Reek (Vice-President, Movietone Newsreels), and T. E. Stephens; G. D. Morgan; Secretary Anderson, S. Adams, and General Persons. Hosts luncheon in honor of Prime Ministers of Denmark, Finland, and Norway. Afternoon appointments with J. C. Hagerty and General Goodpaster; T. E. Stephens; J. C. Hagerty and General Goodpaster; Spencer Olin and T. E. Stephens (off the record); General Goodpaster; J. C. Hagerty; General Persons; Secretary Dulles. Practices golf.

14   Washington. Morning appointments with General Goodpaster; Admiral Strauss and General Goodpaster; W. J. Hopkins; pre-news briefing; news conference; Mrs. Simon B. Buckner (personal friend) and T. E. Stephens; General Goodpaster. Greets joint meeting of English-speaking Orthopaedic Associations. To Burning Tree Country Club for golf with Generals Twining and Norstad and Colonel Belshe. Appointments with Secretary McElroy, B. N. Harlow, and S. Adams (off the record); G. D. Morgan.

15   Washington. Breakfast meeting with Senator Knowland. Morning appointments with B. N. Harlow; G. M. Hauge. Receives first volume of *Public Papers of the Presidents*, followed by appointments with Secretary Anderson, W. M. Martin, R. J. Saulnier, and G. M. Hauge; R. J. Saulnier; W. J. Hopkins; General Goodpaster; J. S. Lay; T. E. Stephens; Congressman Becker and J. Z. Anderson; Secretary Dulles, A. Dean, and L. Becker; Secretary Dulles. To MATS terminal to greet Vice-President Nixon. Lunch with Vice-President Nixon and Secretary Dulles. Afternoon appointments with S. Adams; General Goodpaster. Practices golf on south lawn. Hosts off-the-record stag dinner.

16   Washington. Morning appointments with B. N. Harlow; G. D. Morgan; General Goodpaster; Secretary McElroy and General Goodpaster; Cabinet meeting; Secretary Dulles. Witnesses swearing-in ceremony for R. K. Gray as Secretary to the Cabinet. Ap-

pointments with Secretary Weeks; T. E. Stephens; Attorney General Rogers and L. E. Walsh; S. Adams; T. E. Stephens; Catholic War Veterans leaders; F. J. Donohue, John Jackson, Jr., and Colonel Schulz (off the record); S. Adams. Lunch. To Burning Tree Country Club for golf with Congressman Westland, Colonel Belshe, and F. Akers. Off-the-record meeting with Secretary Dulles, A. W. Dulles, and Generals Twining and Curtis E. LeMay.

17   Washington. Morning appointments with B. N. Harlow; Del E. Webb; S. Adams; General Persons; General Goodpaster; A. Larson and G. M. Hauge. To Union Station to meet Mrs. Eisenhower.

18   Washington. Attends services at National Presbyterian Church with Mrs. Eisenhower and D. D. Eisenhower II. To Gettysburg farm. Inspects cattle with G. E. Allen. Visits residence of Major J. S. D. Eisenhower. Returns to Washington.

19   Washington. Morning appointments with General Persons, B. N. Harlow, and I. J. Martin; Legislative Leaders; T. E. Stephens; G. D. Morgan; W. J. Hopkins; Mrs. J. S. D. Eisenhower and daughter; J. C. Hagerty; Prince Bernhard. Hosts luncheon in honor of Chancellor Julius Raab (Austria). Afternoon appointments with Chancellor Raab and Secretary Dulles; Chancellor Raab, Secretary Dulles, Ambassador Platzer, Paul Zedtwitz (Austrian Embassy), Frederick W. Jandrey (Acting Assistant, Secretary of State), Dr. Erick Haider (Special Assistant to Raab), and Carl Charlick (interpreter); T. E. Stephens; G. M. Hauge; General Goodpaster. Practices golf on south lawn. Late afternoon appointments with J. C. Hagerty; B. N. Harlow; T. E. Stephens; J. C. Hagerty; General Persons, R. J. Saulnier, and R. E. Merriam.

20   Washington. Morning appointments with S. Adams and T. E. Stephens; S. Adams and General Persons; General Persons; G. D. Morgan; W. J. Hopkins; Congressmen Carnahan and Morrow, and General Persons; Attorney General Rogers and General Persons; General Persons. Airborne for Barlow, Pennsylvania. Votes. Boards *Columbine* en route to New York City. Lunch with Stephen Kennedy (Po-

lice Commissioner, New York City), U. E. Baughman, J. C. Hagerty, R. Montgomery, and General Snyder. Meets with Citizens for Eisenhower-Nixon 1958 Campaign. Afternoon appointments with Finance Group; Helen Weaver; T. E. Stephens and G. M. Hauge; L. Appleby and T. E. Stephens; Field Marshal Montgomery, T. E. Stephens, and David Marx; Kurt Smith and Mrs. Ludwig Furch and daughter. Addresses guests at American Management Association Economic Mobilization Conference dinner. Addresses guests at Newspaper Reporters Association Annual Installation dinner. Returns to Washington.

21 Washington. Breakfast meeting with Field Marshal Montgomery. Morning appointments with General Goodpaster; D. A. Quarles and Generals Twining and Goodpaster; J. C. Hagerty; T. E. Stephens; W. J. Hopkins; G. Gray and Captain Aurand; Secretary Seaton, General Persons, and J. Z. Anderson; American Bar Association officers; Mrs. Oswald B. Lord (Commission on Human Rights, United Nations); Budget Director Stans and R. E. Merriam; General Goodpaster. To Burning Tree Country Club for golf with E. B. Dudley and Colonel Belshe.

22 Washington. Morning appointments with General Goodpaster; J. R. Killian; G. D. Morgan; Secretary Dulles (off the record); J. R. Killian (off the record); National Security Council session; Secretary Dulles; S. Adams, General Quesada, J. Z. Anderson, and J. C. Hagerty; General Curtis; Congressman Judd and S. Adams (off the record); Ambassador Ali Gholi Ardalan (from Iran); T. E. Stephens; General Goodpaster; J. C. Hagerty. Dedicates new NBC color television studio. Appointments with J. C. Hagerty; R. Montgomery; J. C. Hagerty, Marvin Arrowsmith (Associated Press), and Francis Stephenson (*New York Daily News*); Congressmen Preston and Clevenger, General Quesada, J. Z. Anderson, and J. C. Hagerty. Practices golf on south lawn. Hosts dinner with Mrs. Eisenhower in honor of Field Marshal Montgomery.

23 Washington. Morning appointments with T. E. Stephens; S. Adams; General Joyce and Captain

Aurand; Cabinet meeting; B. N. Harlow; D. A. Quarles, G. Gray, William H. Francis, and John Clear (off the record); J. C. Hagerty. Greets winner of Moscow International Concert Pianist Competition, Harvey Lavan Cliburn, followed by appointments with Ambassador Mohammed H. Maiwandwal (from Afghanistan) and W. T. Buchanan; J. B. Fisk (Science Advisory Committee) and J. R. Killian (off the record); G. D. Morgan; General Goodpaster; W. J. Hopkins; S. Adams. Airborne for Gettysburg farm with General Snyder. To Gettysburg Country Club for golf with G. E. Allen.

24   Gettysburg. To Gettysburg Country Club for golf with G. E. Allen and General Nevins. Inspects cattle with G. E. Allen, General Nevins, and W. E. Robinson.

25   Gettysburg. Visits with W. E. Robinson, F. Ladd, General and Mrs. Nevins, and Mr. and Mrs. G. E. Allen. Returns to Washington.

26   Washington. Morning appointments with T. E. Stephens; General Twining; S. Adams; Secretary Dulles; Secretary Mitchell and S. Adams. Delivers address at opening ceremony for atomic energy plant in Shippingport, Pennsylvania. Appointments with S. Goldwyn; G. D. Morgan; S. Adams; T. E. Stephens; Secretary McElroy and B. N. Harlow; R. J. Saulnier; W. J. Hopkins; L. A. Minnich; Secretary Anderson, General Persons, and J. C. Hagerty. Practices golf on south lawn. Views film on defense modernization with S. P. Skouras (off the record). Evening appointment with Captain Aurand.

27   Washington. Morning appointments with General Persons, B. N. Harlow, and I. J. Martin; J. Z. Anderson; Legislative Leaders; T. E. Stephens; B. N. Harlow; Congressman Taber and B. N. Harlow; Lester Markel and J. C. Hagerty (off the record); Admiral Strauss; AMVETS Memorial Scholarship winners; Secretary Dulles, C. A. Herter, and J. C. Hagerty. Lunch. Afternoon appointments with A. S. Flemming; G. D. Morgan; Congressman McCormack (off the record); J. C. Hagerty. Signs Postal Pay and Rate bill. Practices golf.

28 Washington. Morning appointments with B. Patterson; G. D. Morgan; West Point cadets, U.S. Naval Academy midshipmen, T. E. Stephens, Colonel Schulz, and Captain Aurand; S. Adams and T. E. Stephens; S. Adams; J. R. Killian and J. C. Hagerty; General Goodpaster; pre-news briefing; news conference; Secretary McElroy; Benjamin H. Chasin (National Commander, Jewish War Veterans), Bernard Weitzer (National Legislative Director), and E. D. Chesney; B. N. Harlow; J. C. Hagerty; T. E. Stephens, J. C. Hagerty, Captains Aurand and Crittenberger, and Colonels Schulz and Draper. To Burning Tree Country Club for golf with G. P. Nye, F. Akers, and Colonel Belshe. Evening appointment with Attorney General Rogers.

29 Washington. Morning appointments with General Goodpaster; M. J. McCaffree; J. R. Killian, General Persons, and G. D. Morgan; C. A. Herter and General Goodpaster; National Security Council session; A. W. Dulles, J. R. Killian, Generals Cutler and Goodpaster, R. Amory, J. Beard, and J. S. Lay; Dr. M. S. Eisenhower; General Goodpaster; W. J. Hopkins; G. D. Morgan; B. N. Harlow; T. E. Stephens; General Goodpaster; Francis E. Townsend (Los Angeles, California), R. C. Townsend (son), and T. E. Stephens. Lunch. Afternoon appointments with T. E. Stephens; General Goodpaster; S. Adams; Secretary Weeks, C. D. Dillon, and G. Gray (off the record); G. D. Morgan; D. Anderson; Secretary Anderson, W. M. Martin, and J. B. Baird; G. M. Hauge; S. Adams; General Goodpaster. Practices golf on south lawn.

30 Washington. Receives Congressional Medal of Honor winners. Attends ceremonies for unknown soldiers from World War II and Korean War at Arlington National Cemetery. Presents Medals of Honor to unknown soldiers and places wreath on Tomb of the Unknown Soldier. Airborne for Gettysburg. To Gettysburg Country Club for golf with General Nevins.

31 Gettysburg. To Gettysburg Country Club for golf with General Nevins and Major J. S. D. Eisenhower. Inspects cattle. To Little Hunting Creek, Thurmont,

Maryland. Fishes with General Snyder. Cook-out with Mrs. Eisenhower, Major and Mrs. J. S. D. Eisenhower and family, and General and Mrs. Snyder.

June 1 Gettysburg. Attends services at Presbyterian Church of Gettysburg with Mrs. Eisenhower. To Gettysburg Country Club for golf with General Nevins. Dinner with Major J. S. D. Eisenhower and family.

2 Gettysburg. Inspects farm with Chief West. To Emmitsburg, Maryland. Delivers commencement address and receives honorary degree from Mount St. Mary's College. Returns to Washington. Lunch. Afternoon appointments with Secretary Dulles and C. A. Herter; R. R. Rubottom; J. C. Hagerty; S. Adams; T. E. Stephens. Practices golf. Off-the-record appointment with Congressman Mahon.

3 Washington. Morning appointments with W. J. Hopkins; S. Adams; General Goodpaster; Generals Twining and Goodpaster; National Security Council session; C. A. Herter, Secretary McElroy, A. W. Dulles, G. Gray, G. V. Allen, and General Goodpaster to discuss radio broadcasting facilities abroad; Secretary McElroy; T. E. Stephens; R. J. Saulnier; J. A. McCone and S. Adams; representatives of youth political organizations; Secretary Weeks, General Quesada, D. A. Quarles, R. E. Merriam, General Persons, and G. D. Morgan. Lunch. To Burning Tree Country Club for golf with S. Adams, J. A. McCone, and F. Akers.

4 Washington. Morning appointments with G. D. Morgan; Secretary Weeks and F. H. Mueller; General Goodpaster. Airborne for Annapolis. Delivers address at Naval Academy graduation exercises. Returns to Washington. Greets President Theodor Heuss (Germany). Afternoon appointments with S. Adams and R. W. Jones; J. B. Hollister; Secretary Dulles; T. E. Stephens; General Goodpaster. Practices golf on south lawn. Hosts dinner with Mrs. Eisenhower in honor of President Heuss, followed by musical entertainment.

5 Washington. Morning appointments with G. V. Allen, C. D. Dillon, General Persons, I. J. Martin, and S. Adams; Legislative Leaders; General Persons;

Congresswoman Bolton, Mrs. Albert Harkness (Regent, Mt. Vernon Ladies Association), and T. E. Stephens; J. P. Martin; General Persons and J. C. Hagerty; Ambassador Ernani do Amaral Peixoto (from Brazil) and R. R. Rubottom; H. M. Alcorn and T. E. Stephens; T. D. Morse, Dr. Reed, G. M. Hauge, and J. Z. Anderson; M. J. McCaffree. Lunch. Afternoon appointments with W. J. Hopkins; U.S. Ambassador Whitney. To Burning Tree Country Club for golf with U.S. Ambassador Whitney and Colonel Belshe.

6   Washington. Breakfast meeting with Republican congressmen. Cabinet meeting; D. A. Quarles and Attorney General Rogers; Attorney General Rogers; Secretary Folsom, J. R. Killian, R. E. Merriam, S. Adams, General Persons, and E. A. McCabe; General Persons; G. D. Morgan; Sixto Duran Ballen (Minster of Public Works and Communications, Ecuador), Ambassador Jose R. Chiriboga, and W. P. Snow; Catholic University speech and drama students; General Goodpaster; General Persons; W. J. Hopkins. Lunch. Afternoon appointments with S. Adams; G. M. Hauge. Practices golf on south lawn. Attends dinner hosted by President Heuss with Mrs. Eisenhower.

7   Washington. Morning appointments with T. E. Stephens; General Persons; General Goodpaster. To Burning Tree Country Club for golf with General Goodpaster and Congressman Arends and Halleck.

8   Washington. Attends services at National Presbyterian Church. To Burning Tree Country Club for golf with Colonel Belshe, J. E. Shea, and L. J. Bernard.

9   Washington. Morning appointments with J. C. Hagerty, T. E. Stephens, Postmaster General Summerfield, and J. Z. Anderson; Postmaster General Summerfield and T. E. Stephens; Secretary Folsom, General Persons, and I. J. Martin; General Persons and I. J. Martin; B. N. Harlow; T. E. Stephens; General Goodpaster; Admiral Strauss and General Goodpaster; Secretary Dulles, C. B. Elbrick, and G. F. Reinhardt to discuss Macmillan meetings; General Goodpaster. Lunch. Witnesses swearing-in ceremony for Gordon M. Tiffany as Civil Rights

Commission Staff Director. Appointments with J. C. Hagerty; Prime Minister Macmillan; Secretary Dulles; Prime Minister Macmillan and British and U.S. officials.

10 Washington. Morning appointments with General Persons; Secretary Seaton, General Persons, I. J. Martin, E. A. McCabe, and J. Z. Anderson; Legislative Leaders. To Baltimore with Prime Minister Macmillan for commencement exercises at Johns Hopkins University. Receives honorary degree. Returns to Washington. Appointment with Prime Minister Macmillan and Ambassador Caccia. Lunch. To Burning Tree Country Club for golf with G. E. Allen and Colonel Belshe. Hosts off-the-record stag dinner.

11 Washington. Morning appointments with W. J. Hopkins; B. N. Harlow; Dr. Elson; J. C. Hagerty. Lunch. Afternoon appointments with General Goodpaster; R. L. Biggers; G. D. Morgan; J. C. Hagerty; Secretary Dulles and U.S. Ambassador Whitney; Prime Minister Macmillan, Ambassador Caccia, Secretary Dulles, and U.S. Ambassador Whitney; General Goodpaster; Secretary Dulles, U.S. Ambassador Whitney, and J. C. Hagerty; Colonel Schulz; General Goodpaster. Practices golf on south lawn. Appointments with General Goodpaster; General Persons.

12 Washington. Greets School Safety Patrol from Gainesville, Florida, followed by morning appointments with Colonel and Mrs. Russell Louden and grandson, Lillian Van Santen, and T. E. Stephens; M. J. McCaffree; W. J. Hopkins; S. Adams; Generals Jacob L. Devers and Goodpaster; L. Little and T. E. Stephens; Walker Stone (off the record); General Goodpaster; Ohio school officials, Secretary Folsom, and G. M. Hauge. Lunch. Afternoon appointments with Secretary Weeks, R. Anderson, and L. B. Robbins (off the record); General Persons; General Quesada; J. C. Hagerty. Practices golf on south grounds. Appointment with General Persons.

13 Washington. Morning appointments with General Goodpaster; Admiral Strauss and General Goodpaster; Cabinet meeting; Secretaries McElroy and Mitchell and J. C. Hagerty; Secretary McElroy and General Goodpaster; Secretary McElroy; Ambas-

sador Houghton; B. R. Sen (Director-General, Food and Agriculture Organization) and J. W. Hanes; Mrs. O. R. Reid (off the record); G. D. Morgan; W. J. Hopkins; General Goodpaster; General Gruenther. To Gettysburg farm. To Gettysburg Country Club for golf with G. E. Allen.

14   Gettysburg. To Gettysburg Country Club for golf with G. E. Allen and General Nevins. Visits with Major and Mrs. J. S. D. Eisenhower and family and Mrs. M. Keane.

15   Gettysburg. Attends services at Presbyterian Church of Gettysburg. To Gettysburg Country Club for golf with Major J. S. D. Eisenhower, G. E. Allen, and General Nevins. Returns to Washington.

16   Washington. Morning appointments with J. C. Hagerty; T. E. Stephens; General Persons and J. C. Hagerty; Budget Director Stans, R. C. Siciliano, and T. E. Stephens; W. J. Hopkins; S. Adams; General Twining; S. Adams and J. C. Hagerty; General Burgess; 1958 Honorary Science Award winners; Ambassador Carlos S. Antillon-Hernandez (from Guatemala) and C. E. Conger. Lunch. Afternoon appointments with D. C. Gainey; Congressman Chenoweth; Boy Scouts and leaders; J. C. Hagerty; Secretary Dulles; Secretary Dulles, W. S. Robertson, and U.S. Ambassador Bohlen; J. C. Hagerty; S. Adams; S. Adams and J. C. Hagerty; G. M. Humphrey. Practices golf on south lawn.

17   Washington. Breakfast meeting with Senator Knowland (off the record). Morning appointments with Legislative Leaders; M. J. McCaffree; Mrs. F. M. Dearborn and sons and General Cutler; T. E. Stephens and Captain Aurand; Dr. and Mrs. Ronald Meredith (Pastor, Kansas), Sandra Meredith (daughter), David Baker (Secretary to Meredith), and T. E. Stephens; J. C. Hagerty. Greets President and Mrs. Carlos P. Garcia (Philippines). Lunch. Afternoon appointments with G. D. Morgan; A. W. Dulles, Dr. Scoville, B. N. Harlow, and General Goodpaster (off the record); General Persons; T. E. Stephens; Congressman Hill and grandson and T. E. Stephens (off the record); T. E. Stephens; General Goodpaster and H. R. McPhee; J. C. Hagerty;

A. Nielsen and J. C. Hagerty; S. Adams. Practices golf on south lawn. Hosts dinner with Mrs. Eisenhower in honor of President and Mrs. Garcia, followed by a musical program.

18 Washington. Morning appointments with J. C. Hagerty; pre-news briefing; news conference; Secretary Dulles, G. D. Morgan, and T. E. Stephens; President Garcia, Ambassador Carlos P. Romulo (from Philippines), Secretary Dulles, W. S. Robertson, U.S. Ambassador Bohlen, J. Gordon Mein (Director, Office of Southwest Pacific Affairs), and G. D. Morgan; T. E. Stephens and General Goodpaster; Science Advisory Committee. Lunch. To Burning Tree Country Club for golf with Colonel Belshe and F. Akers. Appointment with T. E. Stephens and J. C. Hagerty.

19 Washington. Attends breakfast for Republican state chairmen. National Security Council session. Morning appointments with Secretary Dulles; Secretary Anderson, W. S. Robertson, and T. B. Coughran; T. E. Stephens; S. Adams and General Goodpaster; Congressman Curtis and J. Z. Anderson; Secretary Benson and T. E. Stephens; 4-H conference delegates; Secretary Benson. Lunch. Afternoon appointments with A. Wheaton; R. J. Saulnier; Fred Blumenthal (*Parade* magazine), Larry Freed (*Parade* magazine), Glenn Bayless, Jr., T. E. Stephens, and A. Wheaton; J. R. Killian, Budget Director Stans, General Persons, and E. A. McCabe. Practices golf on south lawn. Attends dinner hosted by President and Mrs. Garcia with Mrs. Eisenhower.

20 Washington. Morning appointments with R. L. Biggers (off the record); General Goodpaster; G. D. Morgan; W. J. Hopkins; S. Adams; T. E. Stephens. To Quantico, Virginia, to address attendees at Secretary of Defense conference. Visits Mount Vernon. Late afternoon appointments with S. Adams, T. E. Stephens, General Goodpaster, Captain Aurand, and Lieutenant Butts; General Goodpaster; H. R. McPhee.

21 Washington. Appointment with General Goodpaster. To Burning Tree Country Club for golf with G. E. Allen, J. Black, and Colonel Belshe.

22   Washington. No official appointments.

23   Washington. Morning appointments with T. E. Stephens; Attorney General Rogers, R. C. Siciliano, and E. F. Morrow; J. C. Hagerty; Ambassador Mansour El-Kekhia (from Lybia) and J. Palmer; Ambassador Don Cesar Barros Hurtado (from Argentina) and R. R. Rubottom; Generals Twining and Goodpaster; S. Adams; Lester B. Granger (Executive Secretary, National Urban League), Dr. Martin Luther King, Jr., Asa P. Randolph (Vice-President, Brotherhood of Sleeping Car Porters), Roy Wilkins (Executive Secretary, NAACP), Attorney General Rogers, R. C. Siciliano, and E. F. Morrow; General Gruenther and T. E. Stephens; American Junior Red Cross. Lunch. Afternoon appointments with Senator H. A. Smith; General Goodpaster; G. M. Hauge; T. E. Stephens; S. Adams and General Persons; Verelda Moran (Social Office, retiring); Secretary Weeks. Practices golf on south lawn.

24   Washington. Morning appointments with M. J. McCaffree; Generals Persons and Goodpaster, Secretary McElroy, D. A. Quarles, Budget Director Stans, B. N. Harlow, I. J. Martin, and W. J. McNeil; Legislative Leaders; Senator Knowland; General Persons; Attorney General Rogers; General Persons; Budget Director Stans; Secretary Brucker and T. E. Stephens; G. V. Allen and General Goodpaster. Hosts stag luncheon in honor of Prime Minister Sardar M. Daud (Afghanistan). Afternoon appointments with General Persons and J. C. Hagerty; B. N. Harlow; T. E. Stephens. Practices golf on south lawn.

25   Washington. Breakfast meeting with P. G. Hoffman (off the record). Morning appointments with Ambassador Leo Mates (from Yugoslavia) and C. B. Elbrick; T. E. Stephens; J. C. Hagerty; General Cutler; S. Adams; Secretary Seaton; W. J. Hopkins; G. D. Morgan; Secretary Dulles, D. A. Quarles, A. W. Dulles, J. R. Killian, and General Goodpaster (off the record); A. C. Jacobs and S. Adams; General Goodpaster; S. Adams; B. N. Harlow. To Burning Tree Country Club for golf with Colonel Belshe, J. E. Shea, and L. J. Bernard. Evening appointments

with General Goodpaster; J. C. Hagerty; Secretary Dulles and J. C. Hagerty.

26 Washington. Breakfast meeting with Senator Bridges (off the record). Appointments with B. N. Harlow; T. E. Stephens and J. C. Hagerty; General Persons; National Security Council session; Secretary Dulles, W. M. Rountree, U.S. Ambassador Mills, and Fred Bartlett (State Department, South Asian Affairs); J. Z. Anderson; Rabbi Judah Nadich and family (off the record); General Goodpaster and W. J. Hopkins; U.S. Ambassador Young; J. Z. Anderson; B. N. Harlow. Lunch. Afternoon appointments with General Goodpaster; Mr. and Mrs. J. E. Shea and children (off the record); Secretary Dulles; Prime Minister Daud, Ambassador Maiwandwal, Adbur R. Pazhwak (U.N. representative, Afghanistan), Secretary Dulles, W. M. Rountree, U.S. Ambassador Mills, F. Bartlett, Muhammed Yusuf, and Edwin Wright (interpreter); T. E. Stephens; G. M. Hauge; General Goodpaster; T. E. Stephens and General Snyder; General Gruenther.

27 Washington. Breakfast meeting with U.S. Ambassador Lodge (off the record). Morning appointments with J. Z. Anderson; T. E. Stephens; W. J. Hopkins; General Goodpaster; Secretary Anderson and D. T. Smith (off the record); Cabinet meeting; Secretaries McElroy and Dulles, Admiral Strauss, C. A. Herter, and General Cutler (off the record); Secretaries Dulles and McElroy, D. A. Quarles, Generals Loper, Twining, and Cutler, R. Murphy, P. J. Farley, K. G. Harr, and Admiral Parker (off the record); Admiral Strauss; T. E. Stephens and W. J. Hopkins. Lunch. To Burning Tree Country Club for golf with J. E. McClure. Appointment with J. C. Hagerty.

28 Washington. Morning appointments with H. R. McPhee; J. C. Hagerty; G. Gray, L. A. Hoegh, and General Goodpaster; General Goodpaster; General Persons. To Admiral Strauss's farm at Brandy Station, Virginia, with General Snyder and G. E. Allen. Inspects bulls. Returns to Washington.

29 Washington. Attends services at National Presbyterian Church.

30   Washington. Morning appointments with Postmaster General Summerfield; T. E. Stephens; J. C. Hagerty; T. E. Stephens; Ambassador Erik C. Boheman (from Sweden) and F. W. Jandrey; M. J. McCaffree; J. R. Killian and General Persons; Governor McKeldin and S. Adams. Starts presses to open newspaper printing plant. Appointments with General Cutler; G. D. Morgan; W. J. Hopkins. Hosts stag luncheon for the Shah of Iran. Afternoon appointments with the Shah and Captain Aurand; T. E. Stephens; W. J. Hopkins. Practices golf on south lawn. Evening appointments with G. D. Morgan; B. N. Harlow.

July   1   Washington. Morning appointments with General Persons, I. J. Martin, B. N. Harlow, and R. C. Siciliano; J. C. Hagerty; Legislative Leaders; Senator Dirksen and J. Z. Anderson; S. Adams and T. E. Stephens; T. E. Stephens; Mrs. P. Gibson and T. E. Stephens; J. Z. Anderson and J. C. Hagerty; J. A. McCone; nuns from France, Maryland, and Washington, D.C.; General Persons. Lunch. Afternoon appointments with L. A. Minnich; G. D. Morgan; Governor Stepovich and Secretary Seaton; General Van Fleet; Secretary Dulles; Shah of Iran, Secretary Dulles, W. M. Rountree, and Ambassador Ardalan; J. C. Hagerty. Boards *Barbara Anne* with Mrs. Eisenhower and sails around Potomac River.

       2   Washington. Morning appointments with General Persons; J. Z. Anderson; W. J. Hopkins; J. C. Hagerty; pre-news briefing; news conference; J. C. Hagerty; General Persons; group to discuss Education Bill; A. Larson. Lunch. Afternoon appointments with Budget Director Stans; General Persons; G. D. Morgan and H. R. McPhee; J. C. Hagerty; S. Adams; G. M. Hauge; General Goodpaster; S. Adams, General Persons, and G. D. Morgan; General Persons. Practices golf on south lawn.

       3   Washington. Morning appointments with General Goodpaster; General Persons and I. J. Martin; A. Larson; Secretary Anderson and Nelson P. Rose (Assistant General Counsel, Treasury Department); National Security Council session; Secretary McElroy; General Goodpaster and G. D. Morgan;

S. Adams and General Twining; Secretary Dulles, C. B. Elbrick, P. J. Farley, A. W. Dulles, D. A. Quarles, G. C. Smith, and General Goodpaster to discuss Secretary Dulles's trip to Paris; T. E. Stephens; B. N. Harlow; Governor Gary, Mr. Hamill (Legal Aid, Governor Gary), and B. N. Harlow to discuss Oklahoma problems. Lunch. Afternoon appointments with General Goodpaster; W. J. Hopkins; J. C. Hagerty; Captain Aurand; R. J. Saulnier; Captain Aurand; J. C. Hagerty; G. D. Morgan; M. J. McCaffree; General Goodpaster. To Gettysburg farm with grandchildren.

4   Gettysburg. To Gettysburg Country Club for golf with D. D. Eisenhower II and General Nevins. Skeet shooting with General Gruenther and grandchildren. Watches grandchildren ride horses.

5   Gettysburg. To Gettysburg Country Club for golf with General Nevins, D. D. Eisenhower II, and General Gruenther. Visits Feaster farm with Generals Snyder, Gruenther, and Nevins.

6   Gettysburg. Returns to Washington with grandchildren.

7   Washington. Morning appointments with General Persons; S. Adams; General Goodpaster; S. Adams and L. A. Hoegh; Cabinet meeting; Secretary McElroy; Secretary Dulles, Gerry Green, and C. B. Elbrick; World Wars Tank Corps Association; I. J. Martin; Senator Williams and I. J. Martin (off the record). Lunch. Afternoon appointments with W. J. Hopkins; J. R. Killian, General Persons, and E. A. McCabe; C. B. Randall, E. L. Ryerson, J. Stephens, and S. Adams (off the record); General Goodpaster; T. E. Stephens and G. D. Morgan; Senator Martin and General Persons; Colonel Walters; General Persons; W. J. Hopkins; S. Adams, General Persons, B. N. Harlow, R. E. Merriam, and E. A. McCabe; Senator Johnson (off the record).

8   Washington. Breakfast meeting with Senator Byrd (off the record). Airborne for Ottawa, Canada, with Mrs. Eisenhower. Lunch with Governor General Vincent Massey, Secretary and Mrs. Dulles, and General Snyder. Afternoon appointments with Prime

Minister Diefenbaker, Secretary Dulles, L. T. Merchant, and Sidney Smith (Secretary of State, External Affairs, Canada). Attends dinner hosted by Governor General Massey with Mrs. Eisenhower.

9   Ottawa. Attends wreath-laying ceremony at National War Memorial. Addresses members of Parliament. Morning appointment with Secretary Dulles, L. T. Merchant, and Cabinet members. Visits United States embassy. Attends luncheon in his honor hosted by Prime Minister Diefenbaker. To Lake Champlain Lookout to view Ottawa Valley. Attends reception at United States embassy, hosted by Mr. and Mrs. L. T. Merchant. Dinner with Mr. and Mrs. L. T. Merchant and Secretary and Mrs. Dulles.

10   Ottawa. Greets embassy staff at American Chancery. Attends private luncheon at U.S. embassy. To Ottawa Hunt Golf Club for golf with L. T. Merchant. Receives honorary club membership. Hosts dinner with Mrs. Eisenhower in honor of Governor General Massey.

11   Ottawa. Airborne for Massena, New York. Inspects St. Lawrence Seaway Development. Returns to Washington. Late afternoon appointments with Colonel Schulz; General Persons, B. N. Harlow, and I. J. Martin; General Persons; Dr. M. S. Eisenhower; W. J. Hopkins; General Goodpaster; General Persons; G. D. Morgan; Senator Russell (off the record).

12   Washington. Morning appointments with L. A. Hoegh and General Goodpaster; J. R. Killian and General Goodpaster; Dr. M. S. Eisenhower and R. E. Eisenhower; General Persons; S. Adams. To Burning Tree Country Club for golf with Congressman Halleck, Colonel Belshe, and J. E. Shea.

13   Washington. Attends services with Mrs. Eisenhower at National Presbyterian Church.

14   Washington. Morning appointments with General Goodpaster; T. E. Stephens; General Persons. Witnesses swearing-in ceremony for J. A. McCone as Chairman, Atomic Energy Commission. Appointments with Vice-President Nixon; National Security Council session; Secretary Dulles, A. W. Dulles,

D. A. Quarles, M. D. Sprague, G. F. Reinhardt, W. Macomber, James L. Berry, Stuart Rockwell (State Department, Near Eastern and South Asian Affairs), and Generals Twining and Goodpaster. Awards Medal of Freedom to Admiral Strauss. Lunch. Afternoon appointments with S. Adams, Secretary Weeks, G. D. Morgan, Budget Director Stans, and General Persons; bipartisan Legislative Leaders; Secretary Dulles, A. W. Dulles, D. A. Quarles, and Generals Twining and Goodpaster; Major J. S. D. Eisenhower; Secretary Dulles; J. C. Hagerty; T. E. Stephens.

15   Washington. Breakfast meeting with Vice-President Nixon (off the record). Appointments with J. C. Hagerty and General Goodpaster; Captain Aurand; R. C. Siciliano; J. C. Hagerty and General Goodpaster; J. C. Hagerty; Vice-President Nixon and General Persons; General Goodpaster; G. D. Morgan; S. Adams; J. C. Hagerty; General Cutler; Generals Twining and Goodpaster; American Field Service leaders and students; E. D. Slater. Attends luncheon in honor of Madame Chiang Kai-shek. Afternoon appointments with J. C. Hagerty; W. J. Hopkins; Secretary Dulles; General Persons; W. Macomber; General Persons and B. N. Harlow; J. C. Hagerty; G. D. Morgan; General Goodpaster and W. J. Hopkins; S. Adams. Records speech on Middle East situation. Practices golf on south lawn.

16   Washington. Morning appointments with J. C. Hagerty; S. Adams and T. E. Stephens; General Goodpaster; General Persons, I. J. Martin, and B. N. Harlow; Senators Knowland, Bridges, and Dirksen; Legislative Leaders; General Goodpaster; T. E. Stephens; General Goodpaster; J. C. Hagerty; T. E. Stephens; Ambassador Manuel G. Escalante Duran (from Costa Rica) and W. T. Buchanan; Ambassador Jose Serrano Palma (from Chile) and W. T. Buchanan; J. C. Hagerty; General Persons. Witnesses swearing-in ceremony for L. A. Hoegh as Director, Office of Defense and Civilian Mobilization), followed by appointments with Secretaries Dulles and McElroy, C. D. Dillon, M. D. Sprague, Admiral Charles K. Bergin (International Security Affairs), R. Murphy, A. W. Dulles, W. Macomber, and Gen-

erals Persons, Twining, and Goodpaster; General Goodpaster. Lunch. Afternoon appointments with D. A. Quarles, Budget Director Stans, B. N. Harlow, General Goodpaster, Charles Finucane, and Judge Stephen Jackson (off the record); B. N. Harlow; Attorney General Rogers and S. Adams; General Persons; Commander Ralph Williams and Captain Aurand; A. S. Flemming. Dentist appointment. Practices golf.

17   Washington. Morning appointments with General Goodpaster; General Persons; J. C. Hagerty; J. R. Killian and General Goodpaster; T. E. Stephens and G. D. Morgan; Senator Javits, Louis J. Lefkowitz (Attorney General, New York State), T. E. Stephens, and G. D. Morgan; John Jackson (personal friend) and Captain Crittenberger (off the record); U.S. Ambassador Heath; F. W. Jandrey and General Goodpaster; Ambassador Gunnar V. Jarring (from Sweden), W. T. Buchanan, and F. W. Jandrey; S. Adams; R. J. Saulnier; General Goodpaster. Lunch. Afternoon appointments with A. S. Flemming; Justice Harold H. Burton and Attorney General Rogers (off the record); Secretary Anderson, W. M. Martin, and J. B. Baird; General Goodpaster; S. Lloyd, Secretary Dulles, Lord Hood, and G. F. Reinhardt; J. C. Hagerty; U.S. Ambassador Warren. Practices golf on south lawn.

18   Washington. Breakfast meeting with Senator Bridges (off the record). Appointments with General Persons; General Goodpaster; Cabinet meeting; Secretary Weeks; James Murphy; T. E. Stephens; Admiral Strauss; H. Pyle; General Goodpaster; G. D. Morgan; W. J. Hopkins. Lunch. Afternoon appointments with General Goodpaster and Captain Aurand; General Persons; A. Larson; J. C. Hagerty; W. J. Hopkins; S. Adams; Generals Goodpaster and Twining; J. C. Hagerty; General Goodpaster; General Persons; J. C. Hagerty; Republican senators, Secretary Dulles, C. D. Dillon, General Persons, and B. N. Harlow.

19   Washington. Morning appointments with J. C. Hagerty; General Goodpaster; General Persons and C. D. Dillon; General Goodpaster. Airborne for Get-

tysburg farm. Visits Major J. S. D. Eisenhower's farm. Hosts birthday party for General Nevins with Mrs. Eisenhower.

20 Gettysburg. Returns to Washington. Morning appointment with Vice-President Nixon, Secretary Dulles, C. A. Herter, W. M. Rountree, G. F. Reinhardt, G. V. Allen, A. W. Dulles, Secretary McElroy, Generals Twining and Goodpaster, and John N. Irwin (Deputy Assistant Secretary of Defense) to discuss Near East situation.

21 Washington. Breakfast meeting with Congressman Cannon (off the record). Morning appointments with J. C. Hagerty; W. J. Hopkins; J. C. Hagerty; General Goodpaster; B. N. Harlow; J. C. Hagerty; T. E. Stephens; W. J. Hopkins; members of Emergency Board to Investigate Disputes at Eastern Airlines, G. D. Morgan, and Frank O'Neill (National Mediation Board); T. E. Stephens; Secretary Anderson, W. M. Martin, R. J. Saulnier, and G. M. Hauge; General Goodpaster. Lunch. Afternoon appointments with General Cutler; General Goodpaster. Practices golf on south lawn. Appointments with Secretary Dulles and G. F. Reinhardt; General Goodpaster; General Persons; General Goodpaster. Attends farewell stag dinner for General Cutler.

22 Washington. Morning appointments with General Persons, J. R. Killian, and B. N. Harlow; I. J. Martin; General Goodpaster; I. J. Martin; Legislative Leaders; John A. Hannah and S. Adams to discuss Civil Right Commission; Mr. and Mrs. O. Preston Robinson (Salt Lake City, Utah), D. O. McKay, and Secretary and Mrs. Benson; General Goodpaster; T. E. Stephens; G. M. Hauge; T. E. Stephens; General Goodpaster; General Persons; G. D. Morgan; J. C. Hagerty; Secretary Dulles, J. C. Hagerty, and J. N. Greene (Special Assistant, Secretary of State); General Goodpaster. Practices golf.

23 Washington. Morning appointments with J. C. Hagerty; General Goodpaster; M. J. McCaffree; Secretary Seaton and Governor Quinn; M. J. McCaffree; General Goodpaster; National Citizens for Eisenhower-Nixon, 1958, leaders; G. V. Allen, S. Adams, and General Goodpaster; S. Adams and

General Goodpaster. Receives "Handbook for Emergencies" from Boy Scout Robert J. New. Appointments with T. E. Stephens; G. Gray. Witnesses swearing-in ceremony for G. Gray as Special Assistant to the President, Naval Affairs. Hosts stag luncheon in honor of Prime Minister Kwame Nkrumah (Ghana). Appointments with J. C. Hagerty; W. J. Hopkins; Secretary Dulles, G. F. Reinhardt, W. M. Rountree, D. A. Quarles, A. W. Dulles, Generals Twining and Goodpaster; Secretary Dulles; General Goodpaster; J. C. Hagerty; S. Adams. Practices golf on south lawn.

24 Washington. Morning appointments with General Persons; General Goodpaster; Secretary Anderson, General Persons, and J. B. Baird; G. Gray; National Security Council session; Secretary Dulles, D. A. Quarles, G. V. Allen, J. A. McCone, Admiral Strauss, G. Gray, K. G. Harr, G. Smith, and General Goodpaster; Secretary Dulles and G. Smith; Prime Minister Nkrumah, U.S. Ambassador Chapman, C. A. Herter, and J. Palmer; S. Adams and B. N. Harlow; B. N. Harlow; Reserve Officers Association. Lunch. Afternoon appointments with J. C. Hagerty; J. C. Hagerty and General Goodpaster; Secretary Dulles, J. C. Hagerty, and General Goodpaster; W. J. Hopkins; J. C. Hagerty and General Goodpaster; General Persons. Practices golf.

25 Washington. Morning appointments with General Persons; Admiral Strauss; J. R. Killian and General Goodpaster; S. Adams; Cabinet meeting; Secretary Dulles, C. A. Herter, General Goodpaster, G. F. Reinhardt, and J. C. Hagerty; S. Adams; H. M. Alcorn and T. E. Stephens (off the record); U.S. Ambassador Charles W. Yost (to Morocco); J. R. Killian; A. Larson and J. C. Hagerty; General Goodpaster. Lunch. Afternoon appointment with G. D. Morgan; B. N. Harlow and General Goodpaster; General Goodpaster. Airborne for Gettysburg farm. Practices golf with Major J. S. D. Eisenhower.

26 Gettysburg. To Gettysburg Country Club for golf with Major J. S. D. Eisenhower. Visits with Major J. S. D. Eisenhower and children and General and Mrs. Snyder.

27   Gettysburg. Attends services at Presbyterian Church of Gettysburg with General Snyder and J. Rowley. Returns to Washington.

28   Washington. Morning appointments with T. E. Stephens; M. J. McCaffree; J. C. Hagerty; G. D. Morgan; T. E. Stephens; G. Gray and J. S. Lay; General Goodpaster; H. E. Stassen; Secretary McElroy; Secretary Folsom; G. D. Morgan. Lunch. Afternoon appointments with J. R. Killian and S. Adams; J. C. Hagerty and General Goodpaster; General Goodpaster; K. B. McCann. Practices golf on south lawn. Attends reception for retiring Republican senators at Burning Tree Country Club.

29   Washington. Morning appointments with Secretary Seaton, C. D. Dillon, G. V. Allen, General Persons, B. N. Harlow, I. J. Martin, and General Goodpaster; Legislative Leaders; M. J. McCaffree; Ambassador Don Juan Plate (from Paraguay); J. C. Hagerty; S. Adams; J. R. Killian and Dr. T. Keith Glennan (President, Case Institute of Technology) (off the record); General Goodpaster; Secretary Dulles. Hosts stag luncheon in honor of Foreign Minister Amintore Fanfani (Italy). Afternoon appointments with K. B. McCann; General Persons; Admiral Strauss and J. C. Hagerty; Budget Director Stans, R. E. Merriam, S. Adams, and G. D. Morgan; G. D. Morgan. Attends reception at Cosmos Club in honor of M. B. Folsom's retirement.

30   Washington. Morning appointments with J. C. Hagerty; G. M. Humphrey; R. J. Saulnier; Secretary Dulles and C. D. Jackson; General Goodpaster; Foreign Minister Fanfani, Secretary Dulles, and Raimonde Manzini (Chief of Cabinet, Italian Foreign Office); Foreign Minister Fanfani, R. Manzini, Ambassador Brosio, Secretary Dulles, F. W. Jandrey, Robert Corrigan (Protocol, State Department), and Edward C. Fenimore (interpreter); J. C. Hagerty; G. E. Allen and S. Bradford. Lunch. Afternoon appointments with General Goodpaster; W. J. Hopkins; J. C. Hagerty. Practices golf on south lawn.

31   Washington. Morning appointments with General Goodpaster; J. C. Hagerty; Budget Director Stans, J. A. McCone, S. Adams, and B. N. Harlow to discuss

Atomic Energy Commission authorization bill; General Persons; J. R. Killian, G. Gray, and General Goodpaster; National Security Council session; Secretary Dulles, Admiral Strauss, G. V. Allen, and Captain Gardner to discuss second International Conference on Peaceful Uses of Atomic Energy. Unveils model of U.S. exhibit for atomic energy conference. Appointments with Secretary Dulles; Captain Crittenberger; T. E. Stephens; General Goodpaster. Lunch. Afternoon appointments with Captain Crittenberger; S. Adams; C. A. Herter and S. Adams; General Persons and J. C. Hagerty; General Goodpaster; G. D. Morgan; Secretary Dulles and C. D. Jackson. Practices golf on south lawn. Hosts off-the-record dinner in honor of J. A. McCone. Views movie with Mrs. Eisenhower.

August   1   Washington. Morning appointments with Ambassador Lodge; Cabinet meeting; Jorge Gonzalez-Rubio Vargas (newspaper reporter, Ecuador), J. C. Hagerty, and Abbe Rowe. Witnesses swearing-in ceremony of A. S. Flemming as Secretary of Health, Education, and Welfare. Appointments with Senator H. A. Smith; G. D. Morgan and General Goodpaster; Secretary Flemming and family and friends; General Goodpaster; B. N. Harlow; W. J. Hopkins; General Persons; J. C. Hagerty; General Persons. Lunch. Afternoon appointments with General Persons; A. Larson; J. C. Hagerty; General Goodpaster; G. D. Morgan; W. J. Hopkins. Practices golf on south lawn. Greets Dr. M. S. Eisenhower on his return from Central America.

          2   Washington. Morning appointment with General Goodpaster. To Burning Tree Country Club for golf with Major J. S. D. Eisenhower. Appointment with General Goodpaster.

          3   Washington. No official appointments.

          4   Washington. Morning appointments with General Persons; G. D. Morgan; S. Adams and Budget Director Stans; General Persons; Congressmen Hale and Morrow, General Persons, and G. D. Morgan; G. D. Morgan; J. C. Hagerty; T. E. Stephens; General Quesada and S. Adams; R. J. Saulnier; G. Gray; G. D. Morgan; J. R. Killian and General Goodpaster;

General Goodpaster; S. Adams and T. E. Stephens; C. D. Dillon and General Persons. Lunch. Afternoon appointments with J. C. Hagerty; S. Adams, G. D. Morgan, and J. Sutherland; T. E. Stephens; General Goodpaster. Practices golf with G. E. Allen on south lawn. Late afternoon appointments with General Goodpaster; Secretary Flemming, S. Adams, and E. A. McCabe; C. D. Dillon, General Persons, and B. N. Harlow; G. D. Morgan.

5   Washington. Morning appointments with C. D. Dillon, General Persons, and B. N. Harlow; I. J. Martin; Secretary Flemming and E. A. McCabe; Legislative Leaders; General Persons; Congressman Halleck; W. J. Hopkins; General Persons; S. Adams; T. E. Stephens; J. Ernest Wilkins (Civil Rights Commission) and S. Adams; T. E. Stephens; Postmaster General Summerfield and Ormond E. Hunt (Post Office Advisory Board) (off the record); J. C. Hagerty; Barbara Gunderson (Co-chair, Citizens for Eisenhower Congressional Committee); S. Adams. To Burning Tree Country Club for golf with Vice-President Nixon, Attorney General Rogers, and J. E. McClure. Evening appointment with C. A. Herter, C. D. Jackson, F. O. Wilcox, Dr. M. S. Eisenhower, J. C. Hagerty, and General Goodpaster.

6   Washington. Morning appointments with T. E. Stephens and J. Z. Anderson; W. J. Hopkins; T. E. Stephens; General Goodpaster and Colonel Schulz; C. D. Jackson and J. C. Hagerty; General Goodpaster; pre-news briefing; news conference; T. E. Stephens; Secretary Weeks; George Sullivan and family (former guard of President); General Goodpaster. Lunch. Afternoon appointments with General Goodpaster; J. C. Hagerty; General Persons and General Goodpaster; G. D. Morgan; General Persons; W. J. Hopkins; General Persons; General Goodpaster. Practices golf on south lawn.

7   Washington. Morning appointments with General Goodpaster; J. C. Hagerty; L. A. Hoegh, General Goodpaster, and H. R. McPhee; National Security Council session; I. J. Martin; Noble J. Johnson (Judge, resigning); J. R. Killian and Dr. Glennan; Colonel Draper; General Spaatz and Colonel

Draper. Receives 1958 International Air Cadet Exchange Group, followed by appointments with J. Z. Anderson and family; Secretary Anderson, Budget Director Stans, Secretary Flemming, S. Adams, and General Persons. Lunch. Afternoon appointments with T. E. Stephens; S. Adams; J. C. Hagerty; G. M. Hauge; Drs. Glennan and Dryden; T. E. Stephens; General Goodpaster; Admiral Strauss; T. E. Stephens; Secretary Dulles and C. A. Herter; General Goodpaster; Foreign Minister Louis Mars (Haiti), Secretary Dulles, C. A. Herter, and Mr. Wieland (interpreter); J. C. Hagerty; General Persons.

8 Washington. Breakfast meeting with Senator Knowland. Appointments with S. Adams; Cabinet meeting; Secretary Dulles and General Persons; Postmaster General Summerfield, Secretaries Mitchell and Weeks, S. Adams, R. J. Saulnier, General Goodpaster, and Attorney General Rogers (off the record); Secretary Mitchell and S. Adams; P. G. Hoffman; U.S. Ambassador Folger (to Belgium); J. C. Hagerty. Lunch. Presents Legion of Merit to Commander Anderson. Afternoon appointments with General Goodpaster, G. D. Morgan; S. Adams; W. J. Hopkins. To Gettysburg farm. To Gettysburg Country Club for golf with G. E. Allen.

9 Gettysburg. To Gettysburg Country Club for golf with General Nevins and G. E. Allen. Tours show barn with G. E. Allen and Generals Nevins and Gruenther. Visits Mr. and Mrs. C. Willard.

10 Gettysburg. Visits with Mr. and Mrs. G. E. Allen and General and Mrs. Gruenther. Returns to Washington.

11 Washington. Morning appointments with T. E. Stephens; J. C. Hagerty; G. Gray; Generals Twining and Goodpaster; T. E. Stephens; Ambassador Moustafa Kamel (from United Arab Republic) and R. Corrigan; Secretaries Dulles and Anderson, C. D. Jackson, W. M. Rountree, C. D. Dillon, and General Goodpaster; Oswald C. J. Hoffmann (Lutheran Laymen's League), J. W. Boehns (former Congressman, Indiana), and G. M. Hauge; Congressmen Schwengel and Nimtz, David C. Mearns (Library of Con-

gress), Victor Birely, and T. E. Stephens. Lunch. Afternoon appointments with T. E. Stephens; Secretary Flemming, Budget Director Stans, S. Adams, General Persons, and G. D. Morgan to discuss school bill; General Persons; H. Pyle; G. M. Hauge; General Goodpaster. Practices golf on south lawn.

12   Washington. Morning appointments with Secretary Flemming, S. Adams, General Persons, and I. J. Martin; Legislative Leaders; Secretary Dulles, C. D. Jackson, and General Goodpaster; J. C. Hagerty and General Goodpaster; Secretaries McElroy and Gates and G. D. Morgan; Secretary Anderson, W. M. Martin, R. J. Saulnier, J. B. Baird, and G. M. Hauge; J. A. McCone, Admiral Paul F. Foster (Atomic Energy Commission), Dr. Norris E. Bradbury (Director, Los Alamos Laboratory), Dr. Teller, G. Gray, and General Goodpaster (off the record); G. D. Morgan; General Goodpaster; W. J. Hopkins; G. D. Morgan. Practices golf on south lawn. Airborne for New York City. Evening appointments with U.S. Ambassador Lodge; Secretary General Dag Hammarskjold (United Nations) and U.S. Ambassador Wadsworth; Secretary Dulles and J. N. Greene; C. Roberts, L. M. Stockard, J. Gould, and S. S. Larmon; S. Kennedy; Secretary Dulles and R. Murphy; C. D. Jackson, T. E. Stephens, General Goodpaster, J. C. Hagerty, A. Whitman, and M. J. McCaffree.

13   New York City. Appointments with E. D. Slater; Alan James (State Department); S. Kennedy; Ambassador Lodge and Pete Thacker; Secretary Dulles. Addresses U.N. General Assembly. Returns to Washington. Morning appointments with S. Adams; W. J. Hopkins; Colonel Schulz. To Burning Tree Country Club for golf with Colonel Belshe and Major J. S. D. Eisenhower.

14   Washington. Morning appointments with General Persons; T. E. Stephens; G. Gray and General Goodpaster; G. Gray; National Security Council session; Vice-President Nixon, Secretaries Anderson and McElroy, D. A. Quarles, A. W. Dulles, C. A. Herter, G. Smith, L. A. Hoegh, G. Gray, J. S. Lay, and Generals Twining and Goodpaster; G. V. Allen and J. C. Hagerty; L. E. Walsh; Ambassador Marcos

Falcon Briceno (from Venezuela) and W. T. Buchanan; H. M. Alcorn, Eileen Alcorn (daughter), and Elizabeth Gebhart; H. M. Alcorn; G. D. Morgan. Lunch. Afternoon appointments with W. J. Hopkins; General Persons. Practices golf on south lawn.

15   Washington. Morning appointments with General Goodpaster; T. E. Stephens; J. C. Hagerty; General Goodpaster; General Persons; Cabinet meeting; Vice-President Nixon; General Goodpaster; J. C. Hagerty; S. Adams; General Persons, C. D. Dillon, J. Z. Anderson, and B. N. Harlow; Secretary Flemming; General Goodpaster; General Persons. Airborne for Gettysburg farm. To Gettysburg Country Club for golf with General Nevins and G. E. Allen. Dinner and bridge with C. Roberts, W. E. Robinson, and G. E. Allen.

16   Gettysburg. To Gettysburg Country Club for golf with C. Roberts, Major J. S. D. Eisenhower, W. E. Robinson, G. E. Allen, and General Nevins. Visits Feaster farm and residence of Major J. S. D. Eisenhower. Hosts dinner with Mrs. Eisenhower for wedding anniversary of General and Mrs. Nevins.

17   Gettysburg. Attends services at Presbyterian Church of Gettysburg with B. A. Eisenhower and C. Roberts. Visits with G. E. Allen, C. Roberts, and W. E. Robinson. Returns to Washington.

18   Washington. Morning appointments with T. E. Stephens; G. Gray; G. D. Morgan and General Goodpaster; J. C. Hagerty; W. J. Hopkins; General Goodpaster; General Persons; A. F. Burns; Attorney General Rogers and General Persons. Lunch. Afternoon appointments with Dr. M. S. Eisenhower; General Persons; S. Adams; T. E. Stephens; C. A. Herter, D. A. Quarles, J. R. Killian, J. A. McCone, A. W. Dulles, G. Gray, P. J. Farley, General Clovis Byers, Ambassador Wadsworth, and Spurgeon Keeney (off the record); H. Pyle; W. J. Hopkins. Practices golf.

19   Washington. Morning appointments with Secretaries Anderson and Flemming, S. Adams, General Persons, and I. J. Martin; C. D. Dillon, S. Adams,

General Persons, and I. J. Martin; T. E. Stephens; C. D. Dillon; Legislative Leaders; T. E. Stephens; J. C. Hagerty; General Persons and J. Z. Anderson; H. M. Alcorn, S. Olin, and H. Pyle; T. E. Stephens; H. M. Alcorn; General Goodpaster. Witnesses swearing-in ceremony for Dr. Glennan as Administrator, National Aeronautics and Space Council, and Dr. Dryden as Deputy Administrator, National Aeronautics and Space Council. Appointments with G. D. Morgan; General Goodpaster; G. Gray and J. A. McCone; General Persons; H. R. McPhee. Lunch. To Burning Tree Country Club for golf with General Clark, J. E. McClure, and Congressman Belcher. Evening appointment with bipartisan group to discuss mutual security appropriations (off the record).

20   Washington. Morning appointments with J. R. Killian and S. Adams; pre-news briefing; news conference; J. C. Hagerty; C. A. Herter, J. R. Killian, and Generals Persons and Goodpaster; J. C. Hagerty; Congressman Belcher and Mr. and Mrs. P. C. Ferguson (Gubernatorial candidate, Oklahoma) (off the record); General Goodpaster; T. E. Stephens; G. D. Morgan; T. E. Stephens. Lunch. Afternoon appointments with W. J. Hopkins; Admiral Strauss; S. Adams; Colonel Charles C. Herrick (former classmate, West Point); W. J. Hopkins; General Goodpaster; S. Adams; T. E. Stephens; General Persons; General Goodpaster; Secretary Dulles and C. A. Herter; Secretary Dulles, C. A. Herter, J. A. McCone, D. A. Quarles, Ambassador Wadsworth, A. W. Dulles, J. R. Killian, and Generals Persons and Goodpaster; Secretary Dulles, A. W. Dulles, and Ambassador Wadsworth; Secretary Dulles.

21   Washington. Morning appointments with T. E. Stephens; S. Adams; T. E. Stephens; J. C. Hagerty; Attorney General Rogers; National Security Council session; Secretary McElroy; Willard F. Libby (Acting Chair, Atomic Energy Commission) and General Goodpaster; S. Adams; G. Gray, R. E. Merriam, L. A. Hoegh, J. R. Killian, and S. Adams (off the record); S. Adams and Generals Persons and Goodpaster; Captain Aurand and General Goodpaster; G. D. Morgan. Records message for United Community Campaigns. Lunch. Afternoon appoint-

ments with W. J. Hopkins; R. J. Saulnier; Charlie Moore (*Time* magazine, *Life* magazine) and J. C. Hagerty. Practices golf on south lawn. Appointments with General Goodpaster; Foreign Minister Maurice C. de Murville (France), Ambassador Alphand, C. A. Herter, and C. B. Elbrick.

22 Washington. Morning appointments with Secretary Flemming, J. R. Killian, R. E. Merriam, E. L. Richardson, General Persons, and E. A. McCabe; General Persons; Clare B. Williams (Assistant Chair, RNC) and H. M. Alcorn; J. C. Hagerty and General Goodpaster; T. E. Stephens; T. E. Stephens and E. F. Morrow; delegation of Improved Benevolent and Protective Order of Elks; General Persons. Records message on cessation of nuclear tests. Appointments with General Goodpaster; T. E. Stephens; J. A. McCone and General Persons. Lunch. To Burning Tree Country Club for golf with J. C. Hagerty. Appointments with G. D. Morgan; Secretary Dulles and C. A. Herter; General Goodpaster.

23 Washington. Morning appointments with General Persons; G. D. Morgan; T. E. Stephens; General Goodpaster; Senator Beall, Congressman Quie, and E. D. Chesney to discuss Bainbridge Naval Training Center; Senator Watkins, H. Pyle, and General Persons; family of Senator Watkins; General Persons. To Burning Tree Country Club for golf with F. Akers. Lunch.

24 Washington. Attends services at National Presbyterian Church. To Hillsboro, Virginia, with Mrs. Eisenhower to visit farm of Colonel and Mrs. Moore. Visits farm of General and Mrs. Howard. Returns to Washington.

25 Washington. Morning appointments with H. Pyle; J. C. Hagerty; S. Adams; T. E. Stephens; General Goodpaster; J. Z. Anderson; S. Adams and Malcolm C. Moos; General Persons; T. E. Stephens; W. J. Hopkins; Colonel Schulz; General Goodpaster; General Persons; Senator H. A. Smith. Lunch. Afternoon appointments with Ambassador Henrik de Kauffmann (from Denmark, retiring) and W. T. Buchanan; E. A. McCabe; Congressman O'Hara (retiring) and E. A. McCabe; General Goodpaster;

G. Gray; General Goodpaster; D. A. Quarles, Admiral Burke, C. A. Herter, Ambassador Parsons, and Generals Twining and Goodpaster (off the record).

26 Washington. Morning appointments with T. E. Stephens; General Persons and J. C. Hagerty; I. J. Martin; Senator Barrett, General Persons, and A. Scott (off the record); General Goodpaster; G. D. Morgan; Congressman Williams; General Persons; G. Gray and S. E. Gleason; Vice-President Nixon; Secretary Anderson; General Devers; S. Adams; General Goodpaster. To Burning Tree Country Club for golf with Vice-President Nixon, Congressman Arends, and Colonel Belshe. Appointment with Dr. M. S. Eisenhower. Meets with Business Advisory Council.

27 Washington. Morning appointments with H. Hoover, Jr.; General Persons; Secretary Anderson, S. Adams, Budget Director Stans, R. J. Saulnier, and A. M. Cole (off the record); Secretary Anderson; T. E. Stephens; L. E. Walsh, J. L. Rankin, Secretary Anderson, S. Adams, General Persons, G. D. Morgan, J. C. Hagerty, I. J. Martin, A. Wheaton, and General Goodpaster; pre-news briefing; news conference; Harry A. Bullis (Chairman, International Development Advisory Board) and C. D. Dillon; E. D. Chesney; Republican congressional candidates (off the record); K. B. McCann. Telephones Republican National Committee meeting. Lunch. Afternoon appointments with T. E. Stephens and General Goodpaster; National Security Council session; Secretary McElroy, D. A. Quarles, J. A. McCone, G. Gray, Colonels Harbour and Foster, and Generals Twining, Loper, Goodpaster, and White (off the record); S. Adams and General Goodpaster; L. E. Walsh, J. L. Rankin, Secretary Anderson, S. Adams, and G. D. Morgan; G. D. Morgan. Practices golf on south lawn.

28 Washington. Morning appointments with W. J. Hopkins; G. D. Morgan; General Goodpaster; S. Adams; Cabinet meeting; Secretary McElroy, D. A. Quarles, and Generals Twining and Goodpaster (off the record); A. W. Dulles and Generals Cabell, Twining, and Goodpaster (off the record); Secretary Ander-

son and Russell C. Harrington (Commissioner, Internal Revenue) (off the record); Admiral Strauss and Postmaster General Summerfield; T. E. Stephens; H. M. Alcorn. To Burning Tree Country Club for golf with Colonel Belshe. Evening appointment with G. D. Morgan.

29 Washington. Morning appointments with S. Adams, Budget Director Stans, and General Persons; Senator Symington and General Goodpaster (off the record); C. A. Herter, A. W. Dulles, D. A. Quarles, John N. Irving, Generals Twining and Goodpaster, and Admiral Burke (off the record); S. Adams and Budget Director Stans; General Persons. To Burning Tree Country Club for golf with G. E. Allen and Colonel Belshe. Afternoon appointments with S. Adams; General Goodpaster; S. Adams and General Persons. Airborne for Quonset Point Naval Air Station, Rhode Island. Reviews honor guard. Airborne for Fort Adams. Views movie "Van Heflin" with G. E. Allen, General Snyder, and Colonel Tkach.

30 Newport, Rhode Island. To Newport Country Club for golf with H. G. Cushing, G. E. Allen, and N. Palmer. Fishes with General Snyder, G. E. Allen, and Captain Aurand.

31 Newport, Rhode Island. Attends services at Chapel by the Sea, U.S. Naval Hospital. To Newport Country Club for golf with G. E. Allen, H. G. Cushing, and N. Palmer.

September 1 Newport, Rhode Island. To Newport Country Club for golf with G. E. Allen, H. G. Cushing, and N. Palmer. Deep sea fishing with G. E. Allen, General Snyder, Colonel Tkach, and Captain Aurand.

2 Newport, Rhode Island. To Newport Country Club for golf with G. E. Allen, H. G. Cushing, and N. Palmer. Afternoon appointments with G. D. Morgan; W. Hawks; J. C. Hagerty; G. D. Morgan; T. E. Stephens. Walks around waterfront and views movie "From Hell to Texas" with G. E. Allen.

3 Newport, Rhode Island. To Block Island. Fishes with G. E. Allen, Captain Aurand, Sergeant Moaney, and Colonel Sheenan. Returns to Fort Adams.

4   Newport, Rhode Island. Morning appointments with W. W. Aldrich; J. C. Hagerty; Secretary Dulles, J. N. Greene, General Goodpaster, and J. C. Hagerty to discuss Quemoy and Formosa; General Goodpaster. To Newport Country Club for golf with G. E. Allen, W. E. Robinson, and U.S. Ambassador Whitney.

5   Newport, Rhode Island. To Newport Country Club for golf with U.S. Ambassador Whitney, W. E. Robinson, and G. E. Allen.

6   Newport, Rhode Island. Returns to Washington. Morning appointments with Secretaries Mitchell and Weeks, J. Allen Overton (Deputy General Counsel, Commerce Department), S. Adams, and G. D. Morgan; Budget Director Stans; J. C. Hagerty; Mr. and Mrs. G. M. Hauge and children; Attorney General Rogers and S. Adams; Attorney General Rogers; Secretary McElroy, General Quesada, S. Adams, and B. N. Harlow; William B. Franke (Under Secretary, Navy), Secretary McElroy, Admiral Mumma, B. N. Harlow, and General Goodpaster; G. D. Morgan. Attends luncheon to discuss Taiwan Straits situation. Hosts reception for American and British Commonwealth university educators. Airborne for Newport, Rhode Island with grandchildren.

7   Newport, Rhode Island. Attends services at Chapel by the Sea, U.S. Naval Hospital, with Mrs. Eisenhower and grandchildren.

8   Newport, Rhode Island. To Newport Country Club for golf with Colonel Belshe, H. G. Cushing, and N. Palmer. Practices golf with D. D. Eisenhower II. Greets C. Roberts, B. T. Leithead, and W. A. Jones. Watches U.S. Marine Drill team.

9   Newport, Rhode Island. To Newport Country Club for golf with B. T. Leithead, W. A. Jones, and C. Roberts.

10   Newport, Rhode Island. Morning appointment with G. Gray and General Goodpaster. To Newport Country Club for golf with N. Palmer and G. E. Allen.

11   Newport, Rhode Island. To Newport Country Club for golf with G. E. Allen and N. Palmer. Returns to

Washington. Morning appointments with General Goodpaster; Secretary McElroy; Secretary Dulles, J. N. Greene, J. C. Hagerty, General Goodpaster, and R. Montgomery; Secretary Dulles and J. N. Greene. Delivers radio and television address on Taiwan Straits situation.

12   Washington. Airborne for Newport, Rhode Island. To Newport Country Club for golf with G. E. Allen, H. G. Cushing, and N. Palmer. Tours residence grounds and poses for photographs.

13   Newport, Rhode Island. Airborne for West Greenwich, Rhode Island. Visits farm of Mr. and Mrs. W. A. Jones. Fishes with Mrs. W. A. Jones. Plays bridge. Fishes with G. E. Allen. Attends barbecue luncheon. Shoots skeet and ducks. Inspects livestock. Fishes with W. A. Jones. Airborne for Newport, Rhode Island.

14   Newport, Rhode Island. Attends services at U.S. Naval School Officer Candidate Chapel. Visits Lieutenant Weyrauch at U.S. Naval Base Hospital. To Newport Country Club for golf with G. E. Allen, W. E. Robinson, and N. Palmer.

15   Newport, Rhode Island. Morning appointments with delegates from Sister Kenny Foundation; Rhode Island Republican candidates. To Newport Country Club for golf with G. E. Allen, W. A. Jones, and N. Palmer. Visits Trinity Church and Touro Synagogue. Visits Mayor Wilkinson and family.

16   Newport, Rhode Island. To Newport Country Club for golf with H. G. Cushing, John N. Stearns, and N. Palmer. Appointments with Attorney General Rogers and G. D. Morgan; foreign officers attending Navy War College.

17   Newport, Rhode Island. Appointments with J. C. Hagerty; Captain Aurand. To Sakonnet Point. Walks with G. E. Allen.

18   Newport, Rhode Island. To Newport Country Club for golf with G. E. Allen, W. A. Jones, and W. E. Robinson.

19   Newport, Rhode Island. Airborne for West Greenwich, Rhode Island. Visits farm of Mr. and Mrs.

W. A. Jones. Fishes with Mrs. W. A. Jones. Fishes with J. C. Hagerty and George Wheatley (farm superintendent). Fishes with Captain Aurand and G. Wheatley. Airborne for Newport, Rhode Island.

20 Newport, Rhode Island. Watches International Yacht Races. To Newport Country Club for golf with W. A. Jones, G. E. Allen, and W. E. Robinson.

21 Newport, Rhode Island. To Newport Country Club for golf with G. E. Allen, W. E. Robinson, and W. A. Jones.

22 Newport, Rhode Island. Appointments with T. E. Stephens; S. Adams and J. C. Hagerty; General Goodpaster; S. Adams and General Goodpaster; General Goodpaster; J. C. Hagerty; S. Adams and J. C. Hagerty. To Newport Country Club for golf with H. G. Cushing, N. Palmer, and C. W. Jones. Tours Newport with C. W. Jones.

23 Newport, Rhode Island. Returns to Washington. Morning appointments with General Goodpaster; T. E. Stephens. Attends luncheon in honor of Latin American foreign ministers. Records statement for Congressman Scott's reelection campaign. Afternoon appointments with Attorney General Rogers; J. R. Killian, Dr. Glennan, and G. Gray; G. Gray; General Goodpaster; J. C. Hagerty.

24 Washington. Morning appointments with Colonel Schulz; General Persons; J. C. Hagerty; M. J. McCaffree; R. C. Siciliano; Secretary McElroy and General Persons; J. R. Killian and General Goodpaster; National Aeronautics and Space Council; Secretary McElroy; General Persons; J. C. Hagerty; S. Adams. Witnesses swearing-in ceremony of M. C. Moos as Administrative Assistant to President. Appointments with S. Adams; R. C. Siciliano; D. Paarlberg and G. M. Hauge; General Goodpaster. To Burning Tree Country Club for golf with Colonel Belshe. Evening appointments with General Persons; General Goodpaster; T. E. Stephens.

25 Washington. Morning appointments with S. Adams; W. J. Hopkins; General Goodpaster; General Persons; J. C. Hagerty; G. D. Morgan; National Security Council session; Secretary McElroy; T. E. Stephens;

Secretary Anderson, J. B. Baird, and W. M. Martin. Witnesses swearing-in ceremonies for Outdoor Recreation Resources Review Commission, followed by appointments with H. M. Alcorn, S. Adams, and T. E. Stephens; H. M. Alcorn. Lunch. Afternoon appointments with G. Gray; General Smith (off the record); Mr. and Mrs. A. S. E. Barnett; General Goodpaster; Secretary Benson; General Persons; P. G. Hoffman (off the record).

26 Washington. Morning appointments with Colonel Schulz; Cabinet meeting; T. E. Stephens; General Persons; W. J. Hopkins; Ambassador Melas and W. T. Buchanan. Receives National Symphony Orchestra tickets, followed by appointments with I. Geist; Generals Quesada and Persons; Generals Persons and Goodpaster; G. D. Morgan, W. J. Hopkins, and General Goodpaster; G. D. Morgan and W. J. Hopkins. Airborne for Johnstown, Pennsylvania. Addresses guests at bicentennial celebration of Fort Ligonier. Attends reception at Mellon Estate. Returns to Washington.

27 Washington. Morning appointments with General Goodpaster; J. Dart (off the record); G. M. Hauge and D. Paarlberg (off the record); M. C. Moos, T. E. Stephens, and S. Adams (off the record); S. Adams. To Burning Tree Country Club for golf with J. E. Lemon, G. E. Allen, and General Norstad.

28 Washington. Attends services at National Presbyterian Church. Fishes at Little Hunting Creek with G. E. Allen and General Snyder.

29 Washington. Morning appointments with General Norstad; R. J. Saulnier; Generals Twining and Goodpaster; Secretary Dulles; T. C. Mann; J. C. Hagerty; M. C. Moos. Lunch. Afternoon appointments with T. E. Stephens; H. M. Alcorn; G. Gray; Secretary Seaton; General Persons; W. J. Hopkins; General Goodpaster; J. C. Hagerty. Practices golf on south lawn.

30 Washington. Breakfast meeting with G. M. Hauge. Morning appointments with M. J. McCaffree; General Persons; S. Adams; G. M. Hauge; General Quesada and J. C. Hagerty; General Goodpaster; J. R.

Killian and General Goodpaster; General Goodpaster; Ambassador Zaude G. Heywot (from Ethiopia) and W. T. Buchanan; Ambassador George Kungchao Yeh (from China) and W. T. Buchanan; M. C. Moos; General Persons. Lunch. Afternoon appointments with Prime Minister Norodom Sihanouk (Cambodia), Ambassador Nong Kimny (Cambodia), W. S. Robertson, and W. T. Buchanan. Attends luncheon in honor of Prime Minister Sihanouk. To Burning Tree Country Club for golf with Generals Twining and Norstad and Colonel Belshe.

October 1 Washington. Morning appointments with General Persons; S. Adams; General Persons; J. C. Hagerty; General Goodpaster; Attorney General Rogers, General Persons, and J. C. Hagerty; pre-news briefing; news conference; General Goodpaster; W. J. Hopkins; H. R. McPhee and General Goodpaster; General Goodpaster. Attends Prayers for Peace services for National Day of Prayer at National Presbyterian Church with Mrs. Eisenhower. Views movie.

2 Washington. Morning appointments with H. Pyle; General Persons; J. C. Hagerty; National Security Council session; Secretary Dulles and A. W. Dulles; Secretary Dulles; Secretary Dulles and J. C. Hagerty; Secretary Dulles; U.S. Ambassador Young, Joseph M. A. H. Luns (Minister of Foreign Affairs, Netherlands), and General Goodpaster (off the record); T. E. Stephens; B. N. Harlow. Records Christmas message to armed forces. Lunch. To White House Library. To Burning Tree Country Club for golf with Colonel Belshe.

3 Washington. Morning appointments with General Persons, B. N. Harlow, and General Goodpaster; B. N. Harlow, General Goodpaster, and J. C. Hagerty; W. J. Hopkins; Secretary Flemming; General Persons. Poses for photographs with congressional candidates (off the record), followed by appointments with H. Pyle; General Snyder; G. V. Allen; J. C. Hagerty; S. Adams and Bob Hampton; Anthony D'Alessandro (congressional candidate) and E. D. Chesney (off the record); Wesley Powell (gubernatorial candidate), T. E. Stephens, and General Persons; H. M. Alcorn; T. E. Stephens and Colonel Wal-

ters; M. C. Moos; B. N. Harlow; T. E. Stephens. Greets and listens to Little Singers of Paris. To Walter Reed Hospital for physical examination. Remains overnight.

4   Washington. To Burning Tree Country Club for golf with Colonel Belshe.

5   Washington. No official appointments.

6   Washington. Morning appointments with M. J. McCaffree; M. C. Moos; Ambassador Brosio, C. A. Herter, and F. W. Jandrey (off the record); Attorney General Rogers; General Persons; U. E. Baughman; C. A. Herter and General Goodpaster; D. C. Gainey; Congressman Keating and T. E. Stephens. Hosts luncheon for Republican politicians. Afternoon appointments with T. E. Stephens; M. C. Moos; D. W. Kendall and General Persons; General Bragdon. Hosts off-the-record stag dinner.

7   Washington. Morning appointments with W. J. Hopkins; J. C. Hagerty; Attorney General Rogers and Judge Potter Stewart to discuss Supreme Court Justices (off the record); General Goodpaster; J. A. McCone and General Goodpaster; General Persons; H. R. McPhee; G. Gray; J. C. Hagerty; General William H. Abendroth (President, Washington International Horse Show), F. C. Akers, and T. E. Stephens; T. E. Stephens. Witnesses swearing-in ceremony for General Persons as Assistant to President, followed by appointments with T. E. Stephens; H. M. Alcorn and T. E. Stephens; James K. Vardaman (Board of Governors, Federal Reserve System, retiring); T. E. Stephens. Lunch. To Burning Tree Country Club for golf with R. W. Woodruff, Colonel Belshe, and F. C. Akers.

8   Washington. Morning appointments with T. E. Stephens; T. E. Stephens and R. K. Gray; H. Pyle; M. C. Moos (off the record); T. E. Stephens and J. C. Hagerty; Ambassador Richard Rafael Seppala (from Finland) and W. T. Buchanan; General Goodpaster; D. A. Quarles and General Goodpaster. Witnesses swearing-in ceremony for D. Paarlberg as Special Assistant to the President, followed by appointments with General Persons and R. E. Mer-

riam; H. M. Alcorn and H. Pyle; Secretary Weeks; M. C. Moos. Lunch. Afternoon appointments with T. E. Stephens; M. C. Moos; U.S. Ambassador Young; General Goodpaster; J. C. Hagerty; General Persons. Practices golf on south lawn.

9 Washington. Morning appointments with J. C. Hagerty and General Goodpaster; General Goodpaster; General Persons; H. Pyle; M. J. McCaffree; W. J. Hopkins; General Goodpaster; Cabinet meeting; Secretaries Mitchell and Dulles, R. Murphy, and General Persons; Secretary Dulles; Secretary Mitchell; Postmaster General Summerfield; H. R. McPhee; T. E. Stephens. Airborne for Camp David, Maryland. Fishes at Little Hunting Creek with General Snyder.

10 Camp David, Maryland. Inspects Nerve Center with Captain Aurand and J. Rowley. To Gettysburg Country Club for golf with G. E. Allen, General Nevins, W. A. Jones, C. Roberts, and R. Sleichter. Inspects cattle.

11 Camp David, Maryland. Inspects Gettysburg farm. To Gettysburg Country Club for golf with G. E. Allen, C. Roberts, and General Nevins.

12 Camp David, Maryland. Airborne for Harrisburg, Pennsylvania. Airborne for New York City. Poses for photographs with Republican candidates. Delivers address at Columbus Circle ceremony. Attends luncheon. Afternoon appointment with Edmund F. Wagner (President, Interchurch Center) and Grayson Kirk (President, Columbia University). Delivers address at Interchurch Center cornerstone-laying ceremony. Returns to Washington.

13 Washington. Morning appointments with T. E. Stephens; General Persons; Generals Twining and Goodpaster; General Persons and B. N. Harlow. Delivers address at cornerstone-laying ceremony at Georgetown University for Foreign Service School and receives honorary degree. Appointments with Lions International representatives; Charles R. Hook (Chairman, Armco Steel) (off the record). Lunch. Afternoon appointments with G. Gray and General Goodpaster; National Security Council ses-

sion; Secretary Dulles and T. E. Stephens; B. N. Harlow.

14   Washington. To Statler Hotel with Mrs. Eisenhower for Republican breakfast in honor of the President's birthday. Morning appointments with T. E. Stephens; General Goodpaster; J. C. Hagerty. Receives recording of 1953 Presidential Inaugural Prayer set to music, followed by J. C. Hagerty; T. E. Stephens; Thai parliamentarians. Attends requiem mass for Pope Pius XII at St. Matthews Cathedral. Lunch. To Burning Tree Country Club for golf with Colonel Belshe. Evening appointments with Secretary Dulles; Richard Gill; M. C. Moos and B. N. Harlow.

15   Washington. Morning appointments with John Cowles (President, *Minneapolis Star* and *Tribune*) (off the record); M. C. Moos and B. N. Harlow; Generals Persons and Goodpaster and J. C. Hagerty; pre-news briefing; news conference; T. E. Stephens; Washington International Horse Show participants; W. J. Hopkins; Secretary Mitchell and R. J. Saulnier; R. J. Saulnier; General Goodpaster. To Burning Tree Country Club for golf with Colonel Belshe and G. E. Allen. Attends Washington International Horse Show.

16   Washington. Morning appointments with M. C. Moos and B. N. Harlow; G. Gray; National Security Council session; G. Gray. Presents 40 millionth copy of *Infant Care* for publication, followed by appointments with Postmaster General Summerfield; M. J. McCaffree; T. E. Stephens and J. C. Hagerty; General Goodpaster. Lunch with James F. Gault. Appointments with T. E. Stephens; M. C. Moos and B. N. Harlow; Douglas Black (President, Doubleday and Co.). Practices golf. Hosts stag dinner for Lord Mountbatten.

17   Washington. Morning appointments with W. J. Hopkins; H. R. McPhee; S. Adams. Airborne for Cedar Rapids, Iowa. Delivers address at National Cornpicking Contest. Poses for photographs. Airborne for Salina, Kansas. To Abilene, Kansas, with Mrs. Eisenhower. Tours Eisenhower home and museum. Attends cocktail party hosted by Eisenhower Foundation with T. E. Stephens.

18   Abilene, Kansas. Visits parents' graves in Abilene
      Cemetery. Visits Mrs. Arthur Hurd (personal
      friend). Poses for photographs at Abilene High
      School. To Salina, Kansas. Airborne for Denver, Col-
      orado. To residence of E. Doud. To Littleton, Col-
      orado, to inspect missile plant of Martin Co. Tours
      Cherry Hills Country Club. Views housing devel-
      opment in Bloomfield, Colorado. To Brown Palace
      Hotel.

19   Denver, Colorado. Attends services with Mrs. Eisen-
      hower at Corona Presbyterian Church.

20   Denver, Colorado. Airborne for Los Angeles. At-
      tends off-the-record luncheon hosted by J. Dart.
      Poses for photographs with Republican congres-
      sional candidates. Appointments with L. Wright;
      Margaret M. Brock; General Hill; General and Mrs.
      LeRoy Watson (personal friend). Addresses audi-
      ence at Shrine Auditorium. Visits with Jacqueline
      Cochran.

21   Los Angeles. Airborne for San Francisco. Greets
      fund-raising leaders at Civic Auditorium. Partici-
      pates in television question-and-answer program.
      Addresses audience at Civic Auditorium. Lunch
      with Republican finance committee members. Air-
      borne for Chicago.

22   Chicago. Attends coffee hour with Mrs. Eisenhower
      at Blackstone Hotel. Lunch with E. D. Eisenhower.
      Meets with Republican activists. Appointment with
      Congressman Halleck. Addresses guests at Republi-
      can activists and candidates dinner. Addresses
      guests at National Safety Council dinner.

23   Chicago. Returns to Washington. Morning ap-
      pointments with General Persons and H. M. Alcorn;
      Major J. S. D. Eisenhower. Hosts luncheon with Mrs.
      Eisenhower for Queen Frederika (Greece). Ap-
      pointments with General Persons; General Good-
      paster and Major J. S. D. Eisenhower; T. E.
      Stephens; General Goodpaster and Captain Au-
      rand; Major J. S. D. Eisenhower. Practices golf on
      south lawn.

24   Washington. Morning appointments with T. E.
      Stephens; General Persons; W. J. Hopkins; T. E.

Stephens; L. S. Rothschild; Vincent J. Celeste (Republican senatorial candidate) and E. D. Chesney; G. Gray and General Goodpaster; Admiral Strauss; J. C. Hagerty; Dr. Glennan and J. R. Killian; Secretary Dulles and General Persons. To Burning Tree Country Club for golf with Reverend C. Pardee Erdman, J. E. McClure, and General Goodpaster.

25   Washington. Morning appointments with General Persons and H. Pyle; B. N. Harlow and M. C. Moos. Witnesses swearing-in ceremony for B. N. Harlow as Deputy Assistant for Congressional Affairs. Appointments with Mr. and Mrs. Chester Gish (cousin); J. C. Hagerty; T. E. Stephens; Ambassador Wadsworth, C. A. Herter, and G. Gray; R. K. Gray; General Goodpaster. To Burning Tree Country Club for golf with R. D. Pittman, Admiral Carney, and R. C. Simmons.

26   Washington. Attends services at National Presbyterian Church.

27   Washington. Morning appointments with W. J. Hopkins; Ambassador Rishikesh Shah (from Nepal); Ambassador Marke Nikezic (from Yugoslavia); General Twining and Major J. S. D. Eisenhower; Major J. S. D. Eisenhower; B. N. Harlow and M. C. Moos; General Persons and J. C. Hagerty; M. C. Moos; T. E. Stephens; General Persons, J. C. Hagerty, General Goodpaster, and Major J. S. D. Eisenhower; Major J. S. D. Eisenhower; T. E. Stephens. Lunch. Afternoon appointments with T. E. Stephens; M. C. Moos; General Persons; T. E. Stephens; H. Pyle; Major J. S. D. Eisenhower. Airborne for Charleston, West Virginia. Addresses assembly at Kanawha Airport. Airborne for Pittsburgh, Pennsylvania. Delivers televised address at Syrian Mosque. Airborne for New York City. To Astor Hotel.

28   New York City. Appointments with Emanuel Goldman and M. Snyder; D. Marx; B. T. Leithead. Lunch with C. Roberts, W. A. Jones, W. E. Robinson, S. S. Larmon, J. Gould, E. D. Slater, G. E. Allen, G. Keehn, and G. Murphy. Addresses Republican campaign workers and members of Citizens for Eisenhower. Addresses guests at Football Hall of Fame dinner. Returns to Washington.

29 Washington. Morning appointments with Generals Persons and Goodpaster; Major J. S. D. Eisenhower; General Persons; J. C. Hagerty; W. J. Hopkins; B. N. Harlow and M. C. Moos; T. E. Stephens; D. A. Quarles, Dr. Glennan, J. R. Killian, and General Goodpaster (off the record); National Aeronautics and Space Council; T. E. Stephens. To Burning Tree Country Club for golf with Colonel Belshe.

30 Washington. Morning appointments with General Persons; Ambassador Briggs; National Security Council session; Secretary Dulles and General Twining; T. E. Stephens; B. N. Harlow and M. C. Moos. Lunch with Sidney Weinberg (off the record). To Burning Tree Country Club for golf with Colonel Belshe.

31 Washington. Morning appointments with T. E. Stephens; Ambassador Alexis S. Liatis (from Greece) and W. T. Buchanan; Ambassador Georges Helsbourg (from Luxembourg) and W. T. Buchanan; Ambassador Manuel Barrau Pelaez (from Bolivia) and W. T. Buchanan; Ambassador Kield Gustav Knuth-Winterfeldt (from Denmark) and W. T. Buchanan; General Goodpaster and W. J. Hopkins; General Goodpaster; John Campion; Major J. S. D. Eisenhower; General Persons, M. C. Moos, and J. C. Hagerty. Lunch. Afternoon appointments with T. E. Stephens; M. C. Moos and J. C. Hagerty. Practices golf on south lawn. To Baltimore, Maryland. Addresses audience at televised Republican rally. Returns to Washington.

November 1 Washington. Morning appointments with General Persons; H. R. McPhee; W. J. Hopkins; General Persons and H. M. Alcorn; T. E. Stephens. To Burning Tree Country Club for golf with W. E. Robinson, J. E. Shea, and J. C. Hagerty.

2 Washington. To Gettysburg with W. E. Robinson, G. E. Allen, and General Snyder. Inspects Gettysburg farm and Feaster farm. Returns to Washington.

3 Washington. Morning appointments with General Persons; T. E. Stephens and J. C. Hagerty; Major J. S. D. Eisenhower; G. Gray and S. E. Gleason; Am-

bassador Berry (to Ceylon); Budget Director Stans, Secretary Anderson, R. E. Merriam, General Persons, and G. D. Morgan. Witnesses swearing-in ceremony for G. D. Morgan as Deputy Assistant to the President and D. W. Kendall as Special Counsel to the President. Appointments with Secretary Anderson, M. Moncrief, J. Hamon, A. Howsley, and General Persons (off the record); Secretary Anderson and General Persons; Secretary Dulles and A. W. Dulles; J. C. Hagerty; T. E. Stephens; Captain Aurand; General Goodpaster and Major J. S. D. Eisenhower. Lunch. Afternoon appointments with T. E. Stephens; Senator Eulogio Rodriguez (Philippines), Ambassador Romulo, and W. S. Robertson; General Persons and T. E. Stephens; Secretary Anderson, General Persons, Budget Director Stans, R. E. Merriam, D. W. Kendall, B. N. Harlow, G. D. Morgan, General Goodpaster, and D. Paarlberg. Practices golf on south lawn. Late afternoon appointments with T. E. Stephens and J. C. Hagerty; General Goodpaster and Major J. S. D. Eisenhower.

4   Washington. Morning appointments with Major J. S. D. Eisenhower; Secretary Dulles. Airborne for Gettysburg. Votes at Barlow Township Fire House. Returns to Washington. Morning appointments with Secretary Anderson; General Persons and G. D. Morgan. Lunch. To Burning Tree Country Club for golf with Major J. S. D. Eisenhower, Colonel Belshe, and F. Ewing. Inspects new offices of General Goodpaster and G. D. Morgan with A. Whitman.

5   Washington. Morning appointments with General Persons and J. C. Hagerty; Secretary Anderson and Dana Latham (Commissioner, IRS); Ambassador Houghton (off the record); pre-news briefing; news conference; General Goodpaster and Major J. S. D. Eisenhower; Major J. S. D. Eisenhower; Senator Cooper and General Persons; W. J. Hopkins; General Persons. Attends funeral of Captain Hazlett. Late morning appointment with William C. Foster (Chairman, U.S. Experts, Safeguards Against Surprise Attack), Dr. Kistiakowsky, General Otto F. Wayland (Commander, Tactical Air Command, USAF), and G. Gray to discuss upcoming Geneva talks. Witnesses swearing-in ceremony for General Quesada

as Administrator, Federal Aviation Agency. Lunch. Afternoon appointments with General Persons and G. D. Morgan; Captain Aurand; General Goodpaster, H. R. McPhee, and Captain Aurand; General Goodpaster; R. J. Saulnier and Dr. Karl Brandt; H. M. Alcorn and T. E. Stephens; Secretary Weeks and General Quesada; T. E. Stephens; General Persons, J. R. Killian, Budget Director Stans, G. Gray, General Goodpaster, G. D. Morgan, and B. N. Harlow; Vice-President Nixon (off the record); General Goodpaster. Attends reception in honor of Secretary and Mrs. Weeks hosted by Admiral and Mrs. Strauss.

6   Washington. Morning appointments with Secretary Anderson and General Persons; T. E. Stephens; Cabinet meeting; Secretary Weeks; National Security Council session; General Goodpaster and Major J. S. D. Eisenhower; W. J. Hopkins; D. W. Kendall; General Persons; General Persons and Colonel Draper; T. E. Stephens. Lunch. Afternoon appointments with T. E. Stephens; General Persons; Captain Crittenberger. Practices golf on south lawn. Appointments with Secretary Dulles, D. A. Quarles, Admiral Foster, P. J. Farley, and J. C. Hagerty to discuss developments at Geneva; Dr. M. S. Eisenhower and family (off the record).

7   Washington. Morning appointments with Captain Aurand; L. A. Minnich; General Persons and R. E. Merriam; veterans group; B. N. Harlow and R. E. Merriam; Alberto Philippe (President, International Junior Chamber of Commerce) and T. E. Stephens; Captain Crittenberger; Secretary Flemming and General Persons; T. E. Stephens; G. D. Morgan and W. J. Hopkins. To MATS terminal en route to Toledo, Ohio. To Cedar Point Club for hunting with G. M. Humphrey and Cornelius Mominee (caretaker, Cedar Point Club).

8   Toledo, Ohio. To Cedar Point Club for duck hunting with G. M. Humphrey. Boards *Columbine* en route to Tacoma, Washington. Visits residence of E. N. Eisenhower.

9   Tacoma, Washington. Visits with E. N. Eisenhower. Evening appointment with Secretary Dulles.

10   Tacoma, Washington. Boards *Columbine* en route to Seattle, Washington. To Olympic Hotel. Delivers address at Colombo Plan Conference. Started machine to countdown for Century 21 Electronic Exposition, 1961. Returns to Washington.

11   Washington. Morning appointments with Secretary McElroy; J. C. Hagerty; G. D. Morgan. Lunch. Afternoon appointment with R. E. Merriam.

12   Washington. Morning appointments with T. E. Stephens; Postmaster General Summerfield; Frederic J. Donner (Chairman of Board, General Motors Corporation) (off the record); J. C. Hagerty; J. A. McCone; H. E. Stassen; B. N. Harlow; Retired Officers Association leaders and B. N. Harlow to discuss retirement pay for officers; W. J. Hopkins; Congressman and Mrs. Williams (off the record). Presents Harmon International Trophy to General LeMay and Commander Jack R. Hunt. Late morning appointment with G. Gray. Lunch. To Burning Tree Country Club for golf with Congressman Arends and Colonel Belshe. Receives Supreme Court members and officers.

13   Washington. Morning appointments with R. E. Merriam; National Security Council session; Secretary Anderson; G. Gray; G. V. Allen; G. V. Allen, H. C. McClellan, and K. G. Harr; J. C. Hagerty; T. E. Stephens; J. C. Hagerty. Witnesses swearing-in ceremony for Admiral Strauss as Secretary of Commerce. Appointments with A. W. Dulles; Rajkumari A. Kaur (Chairman, Red Cross, India) and General Gruenther; M. J. McCaffree. To Burning Tree Country Club for golf with Colonel Belshe, L. J. Bernard, and J. E. McClure.

14   Washington. Morning appointments with L. A. Minnich; J. C. Hagerty; D. W. Kendall; W. J. Hopkins; E. Johnston; R. J. Saulnier; G. D. Morgan; G. Gray; Ambassador Lodge; Ambassador James D. Zellerbach (to Italy); T. E. Stephens. Lunch. To Burning Tree Country Club for golf with Colonel Belshe. Afternoon appointment with D. W. Kendall. Attends birthday dinner for Mrs. Eisenhower at residence of Major J. S. D. and Mrs. Eisenhower.

15 Washington. Morning appointments with G. D. Morgan; J. C. Hagerty; G. D. Morgan and B. N. Harlow.

16 Washington. Attends services with Mrs. Eisenhower at National Presbyterian Church.

17 Washington. Off-the-record morning appointments with A. Nielsen; Secretary Anderson, Budget Director Stans, and G. D. Morgan; A. Nielsen. Other appointments with J. C. Hagerty; Dr. Glennan; Ambassador Bruce and F. W. Jandrey; Dr. Raymond B. Allen (Chancellor, University of California) to discuss People-to-People program; J. A. McCone and B. N. Harlow; Senator Gore and B. N. Harlow to discuss Geneva meetings and suspending nuclear tests; T. E. Stephens; B. N. Harlow. Lunch. Afternoon appointments with T. E. Stephens; J. M. Dodge; Secretary Anderson, J. B. Baird, and Charles Gable (Treasury Department); Secretary Anderson; R. J. Saulnier; G. D. Morgan. Views movie with G. E. Allen.

18 Washington. Off-the-record breakfast meeting with G. Keith Funston (President, New York Stock Exchange). Appointments with Ambassador Midhat Juma (from Jordan) and R. Corrigan; J. C. Hagerty; Budget Director Stans; National Urban League; Mrs. Iven C. Kincheloe (widow), J. C. Hagerty, and Colonel Draper; Colonel Draper; W. J. Hopkins; Secretary Dulles; P. G. Hoffman (off the record). Lunch. Afternoon appointments with T. E. Stephens and Colonel Draper; J. C. Hagerty. Practices golf on south lawn. Evening appointment with Senator Johnson and Secretary Anderson (off the record).

19 Washington. Breakfast meeting with Congressman Martin and B. N. Harlow. Morning appointments with Lieutenant General Jean M. Piatte and Colonel Walters; Senator Goldwater and E. A. McCabe (off the record); Secretary Mitchell; Attorney General Rogers, Secretary Mitchell, M. B. Folsom, G. D. Morgan, and R. C. Siciliano (off the record); Major J. S. D. Eisenhower; T. E. Stephens; J. R. Killian; R. E. Merriam; United States flag design group. Lunch. Afternoon appointments with U.S. Ambassador Wigglesworth (to Canada); Secretary Ander-

son, W. M. Martin, R. J. Saulnier, and D. Paarlberg to discuss economic situation; Major J. S. D. Eisenhower; G. Gray. Practices golf. Appointment with G. D. Morgan and J. C. Hagerty.

20   Washington. Morning appointments with R. C. Siciliano; T. E. Stephens; D. W. Kendall; General Goodpaster and Major J. S. D. Eisenhower; G. D. Morgan; Cabinet meeting; G. D. Morgan; Major J. S. D. Eisenhower; National Security Council session; G. D. Morgan and Major J. S. D. Eisenhower; W. J. Hopkins; George Champion (President, Chase Manhattan Bank). Airborne for Augusta, Georgia. To Augusta National Golf Club for golf with G. Champion, J. Franklin, and E. Peabody.

21   Augusta, Georgia. To August National Golf Club. To train station to meet Mrs. Eisenhower. Lunch. To Augusta National Golf Club for golf with B. T. Leithead, A. S. Flemming, and C. Roberts.

22   Augusta, Georgia. Practices golf at Augusta National Golf Club. Golf with C. Roberts, E. D. Slater, and J. Roberts.

23   Augusta, Georgia. Attends services with Mrs. Eisenhower at Reid Memorial Presbyterian Church. To Augusta National Golf Club for golf with C. Roberts, G. Stout, and F. E. Townsend.

24   Augusta, Georgia. Morning appointment with General Draper, T. E. Stephens, R. E. Merriam, and Colonel Draper. To Augusta National Golf Club for golf with W. E. Robinson, L. M. Stockard, and E. D. Slater.

25   Augusta, Georgia. To Augusta National Golf Club for golf with W. E. Robinson, E. D. Slater, and L. M. Stockard. Lunch.

26   Augusta, Georgia. To Augusta National Golf Club for golf with E. D. Slater, W. E. Robinson, and C. R. Yates. Visits with Major and Mrs. J. S. D. Eisenhower and family.

27   Augusta, Georgia. Watches D. D. Eisenhower II practice golf. Practices golf. Lunch. To Augusta National Golf Club for golf with Major J. S. D. Eisenhower, W. E. Robinson, and George Schooie.

Thanksgiving dinner with Mrs. Eisenhower and Major and Mrs. J. S. D. Eisenhower and family. Visits Club House with Mrs. Eisenhower and friends.

28   Augusta, Georgia. Morning appointment with Secretary McElroy, D. A. Quarles, W. J. McNeil, Budget Director Stans, G. Gray, B. N. Harlow, W. M. Holaday, Major J. S. D. Eisenhower, and Generals Goodpaster, Randall, and Twining. To Augusta National Golf Club for golf with Major J. S. D. Eisenhower, W. E. Robinson, and R. W. Woodruff. Visits with R. W. Jones and W. E. Robinson.

29   Augusta, Georgia. To Augusta National Golf Club for golf with Major J. S. D. Eisenhower, Billy J. Patton, and William Zimmerman. Lunch.

30   Augusta, Georgia. Practices golf. Morning appointment with Secretary Dulles, L. T. Merchant, Dr. M. S. Eisenhower, J. N. Greene, General LeMay, and Colonel E. Q. Steffes. Poses for photographs. Lunch. To Augusta National Golf Club for golf with C. Roberts, W. E. Robinson, and J. Franklin.

December 1   Augusta, Georgia. To Augusta National Golf Club for golf with C. Roberts, W. E. Robinson, and G. Stout.

2   Augusta, Georgia. To Augusta National Golf Club for golf with Major J. S. D. Eisenhower, W. E. Robinson, and G. Stout. Returns to Washington.

3   Washington. Morning appointments with General Persons, G. D. Morgan, and General Goodpaster; Secretary McElroy, D. A. Quarles, J. R. Killian, Dr. Glennan, and Generals Persons and Goodpaster; National Aeronautics and Space Council; Vice-President Nixon; Major J. S. D. Eisenhower; D. W. Kendall; R. J. Saulnier; Secretary Benson and D. Paarlberg (off the record); Secretary Anderson, Budget Director Stans, and General Persons; Postmaster General Summerfield to discuss upcoming speech. Lunch. Afternoon appointments with T. E. Stephens and Major J. S. D. Eisenhower; J. C. Hagerty; T. E. Stephens; National Security Council session; G. Gray; General Persons; General Goodpaster and Major J. S. D. Eisenhower. Hosts stag dinner (off the record).

4   Washington. Breakfast meeting with Senator Knowland. Morning appointments with Senator Knowland; Major J. S. D. Eisenhower; K. G. Harr (off the record); Secretary Strauss (off the record); R. J. Saulnier (off the record); T. E. Stephens and Major J. S. D. Eisenhower; H. S. Cullman; T. E. Stephens, General Goodpaster, and Major J. S. D. Eisenhower; General Persons; General Goodpaster. Lunch. Greets newspaper subscription contest winners. Afternoon appointments with E. D. Eisenhower; T. E. Stephens; General Goodpaster and Major J. S. D. Eisenhower; Major J. S. D. Eisenhower. Practices golf on south lawn.

5   Washington. Morning appointments with T. E. Stephens; J. R. Killian (off the record); Cabinet meeting; General Bradley; J. A. Hannah; General Persons; Major J. S. D. Eisenhower. Lunch. Afternoon appointments with T. E. Stephens; General Goodpaster; H. M. Alcorn, General Persons, and T. E. Stephens; Secretaries McElroy and Gates and Admiral Burke; Major J. S. D. Eisenhower.

6   Washington. Breakfast meeting with U.S. Ambassador Lodge. Appointments with General Goodpaster; Colonel Draper; National Security Council session; General Goodpaster and Major J. S. D. Eisenhower; C. A. Herter; General Persons and R. E. Merriam; R. J. Saulnier and R. K. Gray (off the record). Lunch. Afternoon appointments with N. A. Rockefeller (off the record); Advisory Committee on Government Organization.

7   Washington. Attends services with Mrs. Eisenhower at National Presbyterian Church.

8   Washington. Morning appointments with T. E. Stephens; M. C. Moos; R. C. Siciliano; Amleto G. Cicognani (Cardinal-designate) and R. C. Siciliano; J. C. Hagerty; J. Z. Anderson; Telecommunications Committee, Office of Civil and Defense Mobilization; G. Gray; Ross L. Malone (President, American Bar Association) and Attorney General Rogers. Lunch. Afternoon appointments with J. C. Hagerty; A. Larson; Ambassador Ernest Bonhomme (from Haiti) and W. T. Buchanan; Ambassador Mo-

hammed Ali Currim Chagla (from India) and W. T. Buchanan; Major J. S. D. Eisenhower. To Walter Reed Hospital with General Snyder to visit Secretary Dulles, Generals Heaton and Parks, and Colonel Inez Haynes. Late afternoon appointment with Major J. S. D. Eisenhower. Swims.

9   Washington. Morning appointments with General Goodpaster and Major J. S. D. Eisenhower; General Persons; Senator Humphrey and General Persons; Hamilton Fish, T. E. Stephens, and Colonel Schulz; Freedoms Foundation at Valley Forge leaders; W. J. Hopkins; General Persons and T. E. Stephens; J. R. Killian. Lunch. Afternoon appointments with T. E. Stephens; General Persons. Practices golf on south lawn. Late afternoon appointments with General Goodpaster; Major J. S. D. Eisenhower; H. Darby; Secretary Anderson.

10   Washington. Morning appointments with M. J. McCaffree; Colonel Schulz; D. W. Kendall; Senator H. A. Smith (off the record); J. C. Hagerty; General Persons; pre-news briefing; news conference; J. C. Hagerty; E. J. Hughes (off the record); General Persons. Lunch. Off-the-record appointments with Secretary Mitchell; Secretary Anderson, D. A. Quarles, C. D. Dillon, Budget Director Stans, and General Persons; Secretary Anderson, C. D. Dillon, and General Persons; F. J. Donohue, W. A. Ruschmeyer, Colonel Schulz, and Major J. S. D. Eisenhower, followed by appointments with B. N. Harlow; W. J. Hopkins; Major J. S. D. Eisenhower; General Goodpaster; Major J. S. D. Eisenhower; General Goodpaster.

11   Washington. Morning appointments with Colonel Schulz; W. J. Hopkins; T. E. Stephens; D. W. Kendall; J. C. Hagerty; Vice-President Nixon; A. W. Dulles; National Security Council session; Secretary Anderson, Generals Taylor and Goodpaster, G. Gray, C. A. Herter, L. T. Merchant, Major J. S. D. Eisenhower, Vice-President Nixon, D. A. Quarles, A. W. Dulles, and J. S. Lay; Vice-President Nixon. Off-the-record appointments with Congressman Brownson and J. Z. Anderson; Congressman Morano and J. Z. Anderson; J. C. Hagerty; P. Hotchkis. Lunch. Afternoon appointments with General Persons and G. D.

Morgan; R. E. Merriam; General Goodpaster. Practices golf on south lawn. Swims. Hosts Supreme Court Dinner, followed by musical entertainment.

12 Washington. Morning appointments with Congressman Pelly, Congresswoman-elect Catherine May, and J. Z. Anderson; Cabinet meeting. Views model of new New York City Post Office, followed by appointments with Ambassador James C. Bonbright (to Sweden); Secretary Flemming; Senator Case and E. A. McCabe; Major J. S. D. Eisenhower. Lunch. Afternoon appointments with J. C. Hagerty; General Goodpaster, Major J. S. D. Eisenhower, Secretary Dulles, C. A. Herter, J. N. Greene, and J. C. Hagerty; Secretary Dulles, Major J. S. D. Eisenhower, and General Goodpaster; G. Gray; R. J. Saulnier; Major J. S. D. Eisenhower. Swims.

13 Washington. Morning appointments with T. E. Stephens; General Bragdon (off the record); G. D. Morgan, D. W. Kendall, General Persons, Budget Director Stans, B. N. Harlow, and R. E. Merriam; W. J. Hopkins; D. W. Kendall; M. C. Moos; General Goodpaster; General Persons; Major J. S. D. Eisenhower.

14 Washington. Attends services at National Presbyterian Church.

15 Washington. Morning appointments with Senator Dirksen; Secretary Anderson and General Persons; Secretary Anderson; Legislative Leaders. Attends Crusade for Freedom luncheon. Legislative Leaders, followed by afternoon appointments with Senator Bridges; T. E. Stephens; General Persons; H. M. Alcorn.

16 Washington. Breakfast meeting with members of National Agricultural Advisory Commission. Morning appointments with General Goodpaster; Board of Consultants on Foreign Intelligence Activities (off the record); Secretary Anderson, W. M. Martin, Budget Director Stans, R. J. Saulnier, General Persons, D. Paarlberg, and D. Smith (off the record); General Persons; Secretary Flemming and M. C. Moos; Secretary Flemming, M. C. Moos, B. S. Adkins, Mrs. Rolin Brown, and Katherine Oet-

tinger; National Committee for the 1960 White House Conference on Children and Youth. Presents 1958 Collier Trophy to General Curtis. Late morning appointments with J. Cochran and Mr. and Mrs. Tom Lanphier. Lunch. Afternoon appointments with General Persons; Generals Persons and Goodpaster; Cabinet meeting; G. Gray and General Goodpaster; Major J. S. D. Eisenhower; M. C. Moos; General Persons; General Cutler (off the record).

17   Washington. Breakfast meeting with Senator Bridges (off the record). Appointments with M. J. McCaffree; General Goodpaster; Congresswoman Rogers and David Williams (National Commander, Disabled American Veterans); W. J. Hopkins; General Persons; General Goodpaster; W. F. Libby; Senator Dirksen and Lindley Ruddick (1958 Boy of the Year); General Persons; J. R. Killian, A. W. Dulles, R. Bissell, Dr. Edward M. Purcell, Dr. Land, D. A. Quarles, R. Horner, and General Goodpaster (off the record); Attorney General Rogers; Secretary Mitchell and R. J. Saulnier; Major J. S. D. Eisenhower. Lunch. Afternoon appointments with P. E. Areeda; H. M. Alcorn and T. E. Stephens; Major J. S. D. Eisenhower; General Persons; Major J. S. D. Eisenhower. Swims. Hosts dinner with Mrs. Eisenhower for diplomatic corps members, followed by musical entertainment.

18   Washington. Morning appointments with General Goodpaster; General Persons; T. E. Stephens; Vice-President Nixon, H. M. Alcorn, General Persons, and D. W. Kendall (off the record); National Security Council session; Vice-President Nixon; U.S. Ambassador John D. Jernegan (to Iraq); T. E. Stephens; Senator Potter and E. A. McCabe; J. R. Killian, General Goodpaster, and Dr. Glennan; T. E. Stephens and J. C. Hagerty; Major J. S. D. Eisenhower. Lunch. Afternoon appointments with D. W. Kendall; Major J. S. D. Eisenhower; T. E. Stephens; Major J. S. D. Eisenhower. Hosts dinner with Mrs. Eisenhower for diplomatic corps members, followed by musical entertainment.

19   Washington. Morning appointments with Generals Persons and Goodpaster; J. C. Hagerty; Cabinet

meeting; U.S. Ambassador Lodge; Vice-President Nixon; Major J. S. D. Eisenhower; Paul Bagwell (Republican gubernatorial candidate), Postmaster General Summerfield, and D. W. Kendall (off the record); L. W. Douglas. Lunch. Afternoon appointments with C. A. Herter, D. A. Quarles, J. A. McCone, G. Gray, R. Murphy, Major J. S. D. Eisenhower, Admiral Parker, Colonel Schinz, J. S. Lay, and Generals Twining, Loper, and Goodpaster (off the record); General Goodpaster and Major J. S. D. Eisenhower; W. J. Hopkins; Major J. S. D. Eisenhower; J. C. Hagerty; Major J. S. D. Eisenhower. Dinner at home of Vice-President and Mrs. Nixon.

20   Washington. Morning appointments with General Joyce and Captain Aurand (off the record); J. C. Hagerty; Major J. S. D. Eisenhower; Captain Aurand; J. C. Hagerty; General Persons; D. W. Kendall.

21   Washington. Attends services with Mrs. Eisenhower at National Presbyterian Church. Visits residence of Major J. S. D. Eisenhower with Mrs. Eisenhower and W. E. Robinson.

22   Washington. Off-the-record breakfast meeting with Secretary Flemming, N. A. Rockefeller, and Dr. M. S. Eisenhower. Morning appointments with Secretary Flemming and General Persons; Ambassador Elbrick (to Portugal); General Goodpaster and Major J. S. D. Eisenhower; J. C. Hagerty; Generals Twining, Taylor, LeMay, Pate, and Goodpaster, Admiral Burke, Secretary McElroy, D. A. Quarles, G. Gray, B. N. Harlow, and Major J. S. D. Eisenhower; General Goodpaster; J. R. Killian; Dr. Katz. Hosts White House staff Christmas party with Mrs. Eisenhower. Lunch. Afternoon appointments with T. E. Stephens; G. D. Morgan; Secretary Strauss; M. C. Moos and Dr. M. S. Eisenhower (off the record); Major J. S. D. Eisenhower; General Spaatz (off the record).

23   Washington. Morning appointments with General Persons; General Goodpaster and Major J. S. D. Eisenhower; General Persons, D. A. Quarles, and Dr. York; National Security Council session; Vice-President Nixon, W. M. Rountree, General Goodpaster, and Major J. S. D. Eisenhower; Vice-President Nixon; D. A. Quarles; C. B. Williams and T. E.

Stephens; Senator Javits, Congressman Keating, and E. A. McCabe. Lunch. Afternoon appointments with Major J. S. D. Eisenhower; T. E. Stephens; General Goodpaster; General Persons; General Persons and M. C. Moos; General Persons. Practices golf on south lawn. Swims. Delivers televised Christmas message to nation. Lights Christmas Tree. Dinner with General and Mrs. Clay.

24 Washington. Morning appointments with D. W. Kendall; Major J. S. D. Eisenhower and W. J. Hopkins; Major J. S. D. Eisenhower; B. N. Harlow; J. C. Hagerty; General Goodpaster; G. Gray; M. M. Rabb; T. E. Stephens and D. W. Kendall; T. E. Stephens; W. J. Hopkins. Lunch. Afternoon appointments with W. J. Hopkins; B. N. Harlow; R. E. Merriam; R. J. Saulnier. Practices golf on south lawn.

25 Washington. [Page missing.]

26 Washington. Morning appointments with Major J. S. D. Eisenhower; G. Gray, A. W. Dulles, General Goodpaster, and Major J. S. D. Eisenhower; J. C. Hagerty; General Persons; General Goodpaster; General Persons. To Gettysburg farm with Mrs. Eisenhower and D. D. Eisenhower II.

27 Gettysburg. Shops with D. D. Eisenhower II. Inspects cattle with General Nevins. Hunts with D. D. Eisenhower II.

28 Gettysburg. Visits with W. E. Robinson and General Gruenther.

29 Gettysburg. Shops with D. D. Eisenhower II.

30 Gettysburg. Hunts rabbit and quail with D. D. Eisenhower II. Visits with General and Mrs. Paul.

31 Gettysburg. Appointment with General Persons and M. C. Moos to discuss State of the Union Address.

1959

January 1 Gettysburg. Spends day with Mrs. Eisenhower and Major and Mrs. J. S. D. Eisenhower and children.

2	Gettysburg. Morning appointment with U.S. Flag Commission. Shoots skeet with Major J. S. D. Eisenhower and D. D. Eisenhower II. Hunts rabbits. Visits residence of Major J. S. D. Eisenhower.

3	Gettysburg. Returns to Washington. Morning appointments with T. E. Stephens; G. Gray and General Goodpaster; General Persons; General Goodpaster and Major J. S. D. Eisenhower; J. R. Killian, Dr. Glennan, and J. C. Hagerty; G. D. Morgan, Budget Director Stans, R. W. Jones, and R. E. Merriam; General Persons. Signs proclamation admitting Alaska as 49th state and Executive Order for new U.S. Flag design. Off-the-record lunch with Senator Russell. To Gettysburg farm. Practices golf. Shoots skeet with Major J. S. D. Eisenhower and D. D. Eisenhower II.

4	Gettysburg. Attends services with Mrs. Eisenhower and D. D. Eisenhower II at Presbyterian Church of Gettysburg. Returns to Washington.

5	Washington. Morning appointments with Dr. M. S. Eisenhower; J. R. Killian, Dr. Glennan, and General Persons; General Persons; Secretary Dulles; Bipartisan Legislative Leaders; Secretary McElroy; Major J. S. D. Eisenhower; Senator Malone and E. A. McCabe (off the record); J. B. Fisk, J. R. Killian, and General Goodpaster. Lunch. Afternoon appointments with A. Larson (off the record); General Persons and M. C. Moos; T. E. Stephens; Major J. S. D. Eisenhower. Evening off-the-record appointment with Vice-President Nixon, H. M. Alcorn, L. W. Hall, C. B. Williams, Mrs. P. Gibson; J. M. Ashbrook, S. Olin, J. Dart, D. C. Gainey, C. H. Percy, J. Bachelder, C. Robinson, General Persons, T. E. Stephens, D. W. Kendall, and F. C. Scribner (off the record).

6	Washington. Breakfast meeting with C. H. Percy (off the record). Morning appointments with C. H. Percy (off the record); Secretary Flemming and General Persons (off the record); T. E. Stephens; Major J. S. D. Eisenhower; J. C. Hagerty; General Persons and B. N. Harlow; F. L. Pace; R. L. Biggers (off the record); S. P. Skouras; T. E. Stephens. Lunch. Afternoon appointments with T. E. Stephens; Postmaster General Summerfield; General Persons;

T. E. Stephens; Major J. S. D. Eisenhower; M. C. Moos; J. C. Hagerty; C. H. Percy; J. C. Hagerty; General Persons, J. C. Hagerty, and B. N. Harlow.

7   Washington. Attends Service of Intercession and Holy Communion on reconvention of Congress at National Presbyterian Church. Morning appointments with General Persons and J. C. Hagerty; M. J. McCaffree; U.S. Ambassador G. Lewis Jones (to Tunisia); H. M. Alcorn, General Persons, and D. W. Kendall; Secretary Mitchell to discuss Federal Civilian Employee awards; J. R. Durfee and D. W. Kendall (off the record); G. V. Allen, E. Johnston, and J. C. Hagerty; G. V. Allen; national Presbyterian leaders; General Persons and J. C. Hagerty; General Bragdon. Lunch. Afternoon appointments with General Goodpaster and Major J. S. D. Eisenhower; R. J. Saulnier; W. J. Hopkins; Major J. S. D. Eisenhower; General Persons; J. C. Hagerty; Major J. S. D. Eisenhower; M. C. Moos and Major J. S. D. Eisenhower; M. C. Moos; M. C. Moos, General Goodpaster, and Major J. S. D. Eisenhower.

8   Washington. Morning appointments with Ambassador Whitney; U.S. Ambassador Hill, R. R. Rubottom, and Major J. S. D. Eisenhower; J. C. Hagerty; Secretary McElroy, D. A. Quarles, and General Goodpaster; General Goodpaster; M. C. Moos; Major J. S. D. Eisenhower; T. E. Stephens. Lunch.

9   Washington. Morning appointments with W. J. Hopkins; J. R. Killian; T. B. McCabe and T. E. Stephens (off the record). Greets Canadian Parliament members, followed by appointments with R. J. Saulnier; J. R. Killian and General Goodpaster. Delivers State of the Union Address. Lunch. Afternoon appointments with W. J. Hopkins; Major J. S. D. Eisenhower. To Camp David, Maryland. Visits with Mr. and Mrs. G. E. Allen.

10 Camp David, Maryland. To Gettysburg farm with G. E. Allen and Colonel Tkach. Inspects cattle. Visits Allen farm. To Camp David.

11 Camp David, Maryland. Returns to Washington with Mrs. Eisenhower.

12   Washington. Morning appointments with T. E.
Stephens; Major J. S. D. Eisenhower; General Persons; Secretary Dulles, C. A. Herter, G. Gray, P. J.
Farley, J. Erwin, Major J. S. D. Eisenhower, J. A. McCone, and Generals Twining, Loper, and Goodpaster (off the record); Secretaries Dulles and McElroy, Generals G. H. Davidson, Twining, and
Goodpaster, and Major J. S. D. Eisenhower; Secretary Dulles; Boone Grose and Generals Goodpaster
and Davidson; General Davidson; J. R. Killian and
Dr. Kistiakowsky; H. R. Luce and Dr. Elson (off the
record). Attends luncheon for West Point Class of
1915 at Army Navy Club. Appointments with D. W.
Kendall; J. C. Hagerty; General Persons and T. E.
Stephens; General Goodpaster; T. E. Stephens and
Major J. S. D. Eisenhower; Major J. S. D. Eisenhower; General Goodpaster.

13   Washington. Morning appointments with General
Persons; General Persons and Senator Saltonstall;
Legislative Leaders; T. E. Stephens; Generals Twining and Goodpaster; Congressman Halleck and
B. N. Harlow; J. C. Hagerty; American Farm Bureau
Board of Directors; G. Gray; B. N. Harlow; Colonel
Thomas; Major J. S. D. Eisenhower. Lunch. Practices golf. Afternoon appointments with T. E.
Stephens; J. C. Hagerty; M. C. Moos; General Goodpaster; General Persons and R. E. Merriam.

14   Washington. Morning appointments with W. J. Hopkins; General Persons; Major J. S. D. Eisenhower;
General Clark (off the record); National Association of Manufacturers representatives and General
Goodpaster; Ernest Marples (Postmaster General,
Great Britain), Ambassador Caccia, and Postmaster
General Summerfield; General Persons, J. C.
Hagerty, L. T. Merchant, J. R. Killian, R. E. Merriam,
General Goodpaster, and A. Wheaton; General
Goodpaster. Attends luncheon at National Press
Club. Televised question-and-answer session. Afternoon appointments with T. E. Stephens; General
Goodpaster; W. J. Hopkins; Major J. S. D. Eisenhower. Practices golf on south lawn. Addresses
guests at dinner for Association of State Planning
and Development Agencies.

15 Washington. Morning appointments with T. E. Stephens; A. M. Cole and D. W. Kendall; National Security Council session; Secretary Dulles, C. A. Herter, and T. E. Stephens; Congressman Judd, H. A. Bullis, P. Heffelfinger, and T. E. Stephens (off the record); General Persons. Off-the-record lunch with Hadley Cantril, General Goodpaster, and Major J. S. D. Eisenhower. Afternoon appointments with Major J. S. D. Eisenhower; D. W. Kendall. Practices golf on south lawn, followed by appointments with J. C. Hagerty; General Goodpaster and Major J. S. D. Eisenhower; H. M. Alcorn, General Persons, D. W. Kendall, and R. E. Merriam; Secretaries Anderson and Flemming and General Persons; General Smith (off the record).

16 Washington. Morning appointments with J. C. Hagerty; Cabinet meeting; General Persons; Variety Clubs International members; J. A. McCone and General Goodpaster; Atomic Energy Commission, J. A. McCone, and General Goodpaster; Budget Director Stans and R. W. Jones. Lunch. Afternoon appointments with T. E. Stephens; General Snyder; U.S. Ambassador Walter C. Ploeser (to Paraguay); Major J. S. D. Eisenhower; General Goodpaster; W. J. Hopkins; Legislative Leaders (off the record).

17 Washington. Morning appointments with Major J. S. D. Eisenhower; General Goodpaster; Secretary Dulles, L. T. Merchant, Ambassador Thompson, and J. C. Hagerty; Deputy Premier Anastas Mikoyan (USSR), Ambassador Menshikov, Oleg A. Troyanovski (interpreter), Secretary Dulles, L. T. Merchant, and Ambassador Thompson; Major J. S. D. Eisenhower; C. H. Percy and R. E. Merriam (off the record); General Goodpaster and W. J. Hopkins; General Goodpaster; Major J. S. D. Eisenhower.

18 Washington. Attends services at National Presbyterian Church with D. D. Eisenhower II.

19 Washington. Morning appointments with General Persons and D. W. Kendall; J. C. Hagerty; G. Gray (off the record); Secretary Flemming and Major J. S. D. Eisenhower; Attorney General Rogers; Walter W. Goeepinger (President, National Corn Growers Association) and D. Paarlberg; Major J. S. D. Eisen-

hower. Records budget statement for Congress. Lunch. Afternoon appointments with J. C. Hagerty; E. N. Eisenhower, E. D. Eisenhower, and Dr. M. S. Eisenhower; General Persons and B. N. Harlow; T. E. Stephens; Major J. S. D. Eisenhower. Attends family dinner in honor of E. N. Eisenhower's birthday.

20   Washington. Breakfast meeting with Senator Dirksen and Congressman Halleck. Appointments with Legislative Leaders; W. J. Hopkins; T. E. Stephens. Presents medals to recipients of President's Award for Distinguished Federal Civilian Service. Returns to Legislative Leaders, followed by appointment with Secretary Dulles. Greets President Arturo Frondizi (Argentina). Lunch. Afternoon appointments with E. D. Eisenhower; Dr. M. S. Eisenhower; T. E. Stephens; G. D. Morgan; J. R. Killian; General Persons and G. D. Morgan; General Goodpaster and Major J. S. D. Eisenhower. Hosts dinner with Mrs. Eisenhower in honor of President and Señora Frondizi, followed by musical entertainment.

21   Washington. Morning appointments with D. W. Kendall; W. J. Hopkins; General Persons and J. C. Hagerty; pre-news briefing; news conference; J. C. Hagerty; General J. M. Swing (Commissioner, Immigration and Naturalization Service) (off the record); President's Committee for Traffic Safety. Lunch. Afternoon appointments with T. E. Stephens; B. N. Harlow; M. C. Moos; T. E. Stephens; Generals Frederick W. Boye and Bragdon; Mrs. O. R. Reid (off the record); Colonel Draper; General Goodpaster; General Persons; Major J. S. D. Eisenhower. Practices golf on south lawn.

22   Washington. Morning appointments with General Persons; J. C. Hagerty; Harold Boeschenstein, Stephen Bechtel, and Major J. S. D. Eisenhower (off the record); Secretaries Dulles and McElroy; National Security Council session; Secretary Dulles and R. R. Rubottom; General Persons; General Goodpaster. Lunch. Off-the-record appointments with C. Roberts; C. E. Wilson; J. M. Budinger; C. Roberts. Afternoon appointments with T. E. Stephens; G. M. Hauge; General Persons, D. W. Kendall, and B. N. Harlow. Attends dinner hosted

by President and Señora Frondizi with Mrs. Eisenhower.

23   Washington. Morning appointments with T. E. Stephens; General Persons; D. W. Kendall; Ambassador Dowling and W. S. Robertson; Cabinet meeting; Major J. S. D. Eisenhower; General Persons; W. J. Hopkins; R. E. Merriam; Ralph Cake; General Persons; T. E. Stephens. Attends luncheon for U.S. Exhibition, Moscow, Advisory Committee. Appointments with W. J. Hopkins; G. D. Morgan; J. C. Hagerty and General Goodpaster; General Goodpaster. To Camp David, Maryland.

24   Camp David, Maryland. To Gettysburg farm with G. E. Allen and General Snyder. Inspects Eisenhower and Allen farms. To Camp David.

25   Camp David, Maryland. Returns to Washington.

26   Washington. Morning appointments with T. E. Stephens; Paul McCracken (Council of Economic Affairs) and R. J. Saulnier; M. J. McCaffree; Major J. S. D. Eisenhower; General Cutler; Ambassador Mohieddin Fekini (from Libya) and R. Corrigan; Major J. S. D. Eisenhower; Secretary Strauss; General Persons; Major J. S. D. Eisenhower; Maurice Sexton (President, International Junior Chamber of Commerce), T. E. Stephens, and Virginia Junior Chamber of Commerce leaders; J. C. Hagerty, T. E. Stephens, Captain Aurand, and Major J. S. D. Eisenhower; W. J. Hopkins; Major J. S. D. Eisenhower. Records Red Cross message and tribute to Leonard Bernstein. Lunch. Afternoon appointments with T. E. Stephens and J. C. Hagerty; Secretary Dulles; U.S. Ambassador Smith (off the record); B. N. Harlow; J. C. Hagerty; General Persons. Hosts dinner with Mrs. Eisenhower for Vice-President Nixon and Cabinet, followed by musical entertainment.

27   Washington. Off-the-record breakfast with Senator Bridges, Congressman Byrnes, and B. N. Harlow (off the record). Appointments with Legislative Leaders; P. Sarasin (Secretary General, SEATO) and W. S. Robertson; Mayor W. F. Nicholson and R. E. Merriam; Ambassador Antonio C. Flores (from Mexico) and R. Corrigan; W. J. Hopkins and Major

J. S. D. Eisenhower; General Goodpaster. Lunch. Afternoon appointments with K. C. Royall (off the record); W. J. Hopkins; G. Gray; General Goodpaster; General Goodpaster and Major J. S. D. Eisenhower; D. W. Kendall. Hosts dinner with Mrs. Eisenhower in honor of Congressman Rayburn, followed by musical entertainment.

28 Washington. Morning appointments with G. D. Morgan; Senator Bennett, D. W. Kendall, and General Persons (off the record). Greets American Mother of the Year, Mrs. David R. Coker, followed by appointments with J. C. Hagerty; General Persons; pre-news briefing; news conference; J. C. Hagerty; Dr. Katz; American Legion leaders and E. D. Chesney. Lunch. Afternoon appointments with General Persons and B. N. Harlow; H. M. Alcorn, General Persons, D. W. Kendall, and T. E. Stephens; Major J. S. D. Eisenhower; C. D. Jackson; Secretary Anderson, Senator Johnson, Congressman Rayburn, and B. N. Harlow (off the record).

29 Washington. Breakfast meeting with senators and White House staff. Appointments with National Security Council; Secretary Dulles; J. A. McCone, Harold Price (Director, Division of Licensing and Regulation), Clifford K. Beck, Dwight Ink, General Goodpaster, and Major J. S. D. Eisenhower (off the record); Jewish War Veterans leaders and E. D. Chesney; J. C. Hagerty and General Goodpaster; General Persons. Lunch. Afternoon appointments with General Persons and B. N. Harlow; W. J. Hopkins; Major J. S. D. Eisenhower; Secretary Anderson and J. B. Baird (off the record); Secretaries Dulles and McElroy, G. Gray, R. Murphy, L. T. Merchant, C. A. Herter, D. A. Quarles, Major J. S. D. Eisenhower, and Generals Twining and Goodpaster to discuss Berlin; W. J. Hopkins; General Goodpaster, Captain Aurand, H. R. McPhee, and Major J. S. D. Eisenhower; M. C. Moos; B. N. Harlow; General Goodpaster; General Persons; General Swing (off the record).

30 Washington. Breakfast meeting with Republican congressmen and White House staff. Morning appointments with Postmaster General Summerfield;

Cabinet meeting; General Persons; Secretary Anderson, D. W. Kendall, and H. King, Jr. (off the record); B. N. Harlow; U.S. Chamber of Commerce representatives; General Persons; Kenneth Holland (President, Institute of International Education). Delivers address at National Conference on Exchange of Persons at Mayflower Hotel. Lunch. Afternoon appointments with Major J. S. D. Eisenhower; Budget Director Stans; Secretaries Anderson and Flemming, Attorney General Rogers, General Persons, G. D. Morgan, and B. N. Harlow; Attorney General Rogers; T. E. Stephens and General Goodpaster; General Goodpaster. Practices golf on south lawn. Late afternoon appointments with D. W. Kendall; W. J. Hopkins.

31 Washington. Morning appointments with General Persons; General Persons and R. E. Merriam; R. Flohr; T. E. Stephens; Colonel Schulz. Practices golf.

February 1 Washington. Attends services with Mrs. Eisenhower at National Presbyterian Church.

2 Washington. Morning appointments with D. W. Kendall; General Persons; Major J. S. D. Eisenhower; G. E. Allen, A. M. Washburn, and H. C. McClellan to discuss Moscow fair; General Goodpaster and Major J. S. D. Eisenhower; U.S. Veterans of Foreign Wars; Secretary Anderson, General Persons, and B. N. Harlow. Presents Heart-of-the-Year Award to Senator Johnson. Late morning appointments with Senator Johnson; General Persons; Secretary Flemming and General Persons. Lunch. Afternoon appointments with Major J. S. D. Eisenhower; General Goodpaster; General Persons and B. N. Harlow; Major J. S. D. Eisenhower and General Goodpaster; J. C. Hagerty, T. E. Stephens, and General Goodpaster; T. E. Stephens; General Persons and D. W. Kendall; General Persons; D. W. Kendall; Major J. S. D. Eisenhower.

3 Washington. Hosts breakfast for Republican congressmen. Morning appointments with General Persons; Legislative Leaders; G. Gray; E. Johnston. Lunch. Afternoon appointments with J. C. Hagerty; Secretary Dulles and L. T. Merchant; J. N. Greene; C. D. Dillon; General Persons; Dr. Elliott; Major

J. S. D. Eisenhower; W. J. Hopkins; Attorney General Rogers and General Persons; D. W. Kendall; General Persons; Major J. S. D. Eisenhower; Republican senators and congressmen, Secretary Flemming, Attorney General Rogers, General Persons, B. N. Harlow, J. Z. Anderson, and E. A. McCabe (off the record).

4   Washington. Morning appointments with D. W. Kendall; Melville B. Grosvenor (President, National Geographic Society) and General Goodpaster. Presents National Geographic Society's Hubbard Medal to Vivian Fuchs and Admiral George Dufek, followed by appointments with General Goodpaster; G. D. Morgan; pre-news briefing; news conference; W. J. Hopkins; Attorney General Rogers and General Persons; Attorney General Rogers, Secretaries Anderson and Flemming, and General Persons; Senator Johnson, Secretaries Flemming and Anderson, Attorney General Rogers, General Persons, and B. N. Harlow (off the record); General Goodpaster. Airborne for Thomasville, Georgia. To Milestone Plantation.

5   Thomasville, Georgia. Hunts quail with B. T. Leithead, W. E. Robinson, and G. M. Humphrey. Evening appointment with R. W. Woodruff and J. C. Hagerty. Plays bridge.

6   Thomasville, Georgia. Hunts quail at Whitney plantation with General Snyder, B. T. Leithead, W. E. Robinson, and G. M. Humphrey. Plays bridge.

7   Thomasville, Georgia. Hunts quail with G. M. Humphrey, B. T. Leithead, W. E. Robinson, and General Snyder at Firman plantation. Plays bridge.

8   Thomasville, Georgia. Inspects stable and dog kennels. To Spence Air Force Base en route to Washington.

9   Washington. Morning appointments with T. E. Stephens and J. C. Hagerty; General Persons; M. C. Moos; R. J. Saulnier; T. E. Stephens and J. C. Hagerty; General Twining and Major J. S. D. Eisenhower; Major J. S. D. Eisenhower; T. E. Stephens, J. C. Hagerty, and Captain Aurand to discuss St. Lawrence Seaway; R. E. Merriam; Attorney General

Rogers. Lunch. Afternoon appointments with W. J. Hopkins; T. E. Stephens; Major J. S. D. Eisenhower; C. D. Dillon, General Persons, and D. W. Kendall; General Persons and D. W. Kendall; T. E. Stephens; General Persons.

10   Washington. Morning appointments with General Persons; General Persons and G. D. Morgan; T. E. Stephens; Senators Cooper and Morton and G. D. Morgan; D. W. Kendall; J. C. Hagerty; General Goodpaster; pre-news briefing; news conference; J. C. Hagerty; G. V. Allen. Greets plastics industry officials. Appointments with Vice-Chancellor Bruno Pitterman (Austria), Ambassador Platzer, F. D. Kohler, and N. M. Lejins; General Goodpaster. Lunch. Afternoon appointments with T. E. Stephens; M. C. Moos. Practices golf on south lawn. Late afternoon appointments with J. R. Killian, General Goodpaster, and Drs. Edwin H. Land and Edward M. Purcell (off the record); Major J. S. D. Eisenhower; G. D. Morgan and General Goodpaster.

11   Washington. Morning appointments with J. C. Hagerty; G. D. Morgan; R. E. Merriam; T. E. Stephens; W. Brandt, Ambassador Grewe (Germany), and L. T. Merchant; M. C. Moos; J. A. McCone, Budget Director Stans, and General Goodpaster; U.S. Ambassador Bohlen; Colonel and Mrs. Logan Serles (off the record); R. E. Merriam; W. J. Hopkins; M. C. Moos. Greets Boy Scouts. Lunch. Addresses National Rural Electric Cooperative Association. Practices golf on south lawn. Afternoon appointments with J. C. Hagerty and Major J. S. D. Eisenhower; T. E. Stephens; G. D. Morgan; Major J. S. D. Eisenhower. Delivers address at National Lincoln Sesquicentennial dinner.

12   Washington. Morning appointments with D. W. Kendall; Attorney General Rogers; C. D. Dillon; National Security Council session; Secretary McElroy, D. A. Quarles, Generals Twining and Goodpaster, and Major J. S. D. Eisenhower; Secretary McElroy. Presents Big Brother of the Year Award to Secretary McElroy. Receives St. Ann's Infant Home group, followed by appointments with M. C. Moos; Major J. S. D. Eisenhower. Lunch. Practices golf. Attends

twenty-fifth anniversary celebration of Import-Export Bank. Late afternoon appointment with T. E. Stephens.

13 Washington. Appointments with General Persons; W. J. Hopkins; Secretary Anderson, W. M. Martin, R. J. Saulnier, and D. Paarlberg to discuss inflation and economic situation; L. E. Walsh and General Persons (off the record); Generals Harmon and Persons; General Snyder; U.S. Ambassador Lodge (off the record); J. C. Hagerty; General Goodpaster; Ambassador Walter Muller (from Chile) and W. T. Buchanan; Secretary McElroy and General Goodpaster; Major J. S. D. Eisenhower. Lunch. Practices golf on south lawn.

14 Washington. Morning appointments with C. D. Dillon, Major J. S. D. Eisenhower, General Persons, and General Goodpaster; Generals Persons and Goodpaster. Visits Secretary Dulles and General Parks at Walter Reed Hospital.

15 Washington. Attends services at National Presbyterian Church with Major J. S. D. Eisenhower and D. D. Eisenhower II.

16 Washington. Morning appointments with W. J. Hopkins; J. C. Hagerty; Major J. S. D. Eisenhower; G. Gray; U.S. Ambassador Philip W. Bonsal (to Cuba); Secretary Flemming; T. E. Stephens and B. N. Harlow; Governor Furcolo, Secretary Flemming, and R. E. Merriam to discuss educational accreditation; T. E. Stephens; Major J. S. D. Eisenhower. Lunch. Afternoon appointments with R. E. Merriam; General Persons; J. B. Conant and R. E. Merriam (off the record); T. E. Stephens. Practices golf on south lawn. Appointments with General Goodpaster and H. R. McPhee; R. E. Merriam; General Persons; H. Pyle and General Persons.

17 Washington. Breakfast meeting with Senator Saltonstall, Congressman Hoeven, and B. N. Harlow (off the record). Morning appointments with Legislative Leaders; General Persons; L. E. Walsh; R. E. Merriam; C. A. Herter and General Goodpaster. Receives White House Press Photographers' Association Photo Contest winners. Greets Eisenhower

Exchange fellows, followed by appointments with Senator Allott and T. E. Stephens; W. J. Hopkins. Lunch. Afternoon appointments with General Goodpaster; T. E. Stephens; D. W. Kendall; H. Pyle; General Goodpaster; General Persons. Visits Secretary Dulles at Walter Reed Hospital. Practices golf on south lawn. Late afternoon appointments with General Goodpaster; Major J. S. D. Eisenhower; General Goodpaster; Major J. S. D. Eisenhower. Attends National Symphony Orchestra with Major and Mrs. J. S. D. Eisenhower and Captain and Mrs. Aurand.

18   Washington. Off-the-record breakfast meeting with Lawrence Kimpton (Chancellor, University of Chicago) and R. E. Merriam. Appointments with Major J. S. D. Eisenhower; D. W. Kendall and H. R. McPhee; M. J. McCaffree; Major J. S. D. Eisenhower; General Persons, T. E. Stephens, and B. N. Harlow; J. C. Hagerty; pre-news briefing; news conference; T. E. Stephens; L. E. Walsh; Drs. Glennan and Dryden, J. R. Killian, Secretary Anderson, Budget Director Stans, and Generals Goodpaster and Persons; General Persons and Budget Director Stans; General Persons; W. J. Hopkins. Lunch. Boards *Columbine* en route to Austin, Texas.

19   Austin, Texas. Airborne for Acapulco, Mexico. Meets President Adolfo Lopez Mateos at Federal Palace. Attends luncheon aboard presidential yacht. Cruises around Acapulco Harbor. Attends dinner in his honor, followed by entertainment.

20   Acapulco, Mexico. Attends luncheon. Attends dinner in his honor, followed by entertainment. Returns to Washington.

21   Washington. Morning appointments with General Persons; Major J. S. D. Eisenhower; General Goodpaster. Visits Secretary Dulles and General Parks at Walter Reed Hospital. Late morning appointment with General Goodpaster.

22   Washington. To Gettysburg farm. Inspects farm with Major J. S. D. Eisenhower and S. Eisenhower. Lunch at residence of Major J. S. D. Eisenhower. Returns to Washington.

23 Washington. Morning appointments with J. C. Hagerty; General Goodpaster; C. A. Herter and General Goodpaster; General Goodpaster; G. D. Morgan. Visits Secretary Dulles at Walter Reed Hospital. Hosts off-the-record stag dinner for West Point Class of 1915 classmates.

24 Washington. Morning appointments with Secretary Strauss, D. Paarlberg, and B. N. Harlow; Legislative Leaders; General Goodpaster; U.S. Ambassador Byroade (to Afghanistan); E. A. McCabe; National Association of Real Estate Boards representatives and E. A. McCabe; Dr. Glennan and General Persons. Lunch. Afternoon appointments with T. E. Stephens; W. J. Hopkins; M. C. Moos and Major J. S. D. Eisenhower; A. W. Dulles and General Goodpaster (off the record); Major J. S. D. Eisenhower. Practices golf on south lawn. Late afternoon appointment with T. E. Stephens.

25 Washington. Morning appointments with General Persons; Cambodian legislators; General Goodpaster; J. R. Killian; pre-news briefing; news conference; North Dakota delegation; Clarence Francis and T. E. Stephens (off the record). Delivers address at U.S. Savings Bonds Conference. Lunch. Afternoon appointments with D. W. Kendall; H. M. Alcorn, General Persons, and D. W. Kendall; General Persons and D. Paarlberg; J. R. Killian and General Goodpaster; Generals Persons and Goodpaster. Practices golf on south lawn. Appointments with Major J. S. D. Eisenhower; General Goodpaster; J. C. Hagerty; Major J. S. D. Eisenhower. Swims.

26 Washington. Breakfast meeting with Senators Keating, Scott, and Prouty, General Persons, B. N. Harlow, and E. A. McCabe. Morning appointments with General Persons; National Security Council session; Secretary McElroy; G. Gray; Cumberland Gap National Historical Park Dedication Committee; Senator Byrd; W. J. Hopkins; General Persons and B. N. Harlow; A. C. Jacobs; Major J. S. D. Eisenhower. Lunch. Afternoon appointments with Major J. S. D. Eisenhower; Secretary Anderson, General Persons, and D. W. Kendall; General Persons. Practices golf on south lawn. Appointments with General Good-

paster; B. N. Harlow; Major J. S. D. Eisenhower. Holds off-the-record meeting with Republican senators and congressmen.

27 Washington. Breakfast meeting with Marshall Field, Jr. (off the record). Appointments with J. C. Hagerty; Cabinet meeting; Secretary Strauss (off the record); Major J. S. D. Eisenhower; G. D. Morgan; T. E. Stephens. Attends presentation of Simon Bolivar statue. Lunch. Afternoon appointments with P. G. Hoffman. Visits Secretary Dulles at Walter Reed Hospital. Appointments with D. W. Kendall; R. E. Merriam and General Persons; L. A. Hoegh and G. D. Morgan; T. E. Stephens; General Persons.

28 Washington. Morning appointments with R. J. Saulnier and G. D. Morgan; J. C. Hagerty; G. D. Morgan; T. E. Stephens; W. J. Hopkins; Postmaster General Summerfield; General Persons; Major J. S. D. Eisenhower. Practices golf.

March 1 Washington. Attends services at National Presbyterian Church with G. E. Allen and D. D. Eisenhower II.

2 Washington. Morning appointments with Major J. S. D. Eisenhower; T. E. Stephens; Major J. S. D. Eisenhower; G. Gray and General Goodpaster; Major J. S. D. Eisenhower. Receives 18th Annual Science Talent Search winners, followed by appointments with General Goodpaster; Ambassador Heeney (Canada); Generals Persons and Goodpaster and J. C. Hagerty; Optimist International leaders, Governor McKeldin, and T. E. Stephens; Dr. Glennan and General Goodpaster. Hosts stag luncheon in honor of Edwin Plowden (Chairman, Atomic Energy Authority, Great Britain). Afternoon appointments with National Aeronautics and Space Council; Vice-President Nixon; R. E. Merriam; T. E. Stephens; General Goodpaster; General and Mrs. Schuyler.

3 Washington. Morning appointments with General Goodpaster and Major J. S. D. Eisenhower; General Persons; Legislative Leaders; Senators Saltonstall and Dirksen and E. A. McCabe; G. D. Morgan; T. E.

Stephens; J. C. Hagerty; G. Gray and General Goodpaster; E. A. McCabe; T. E. Stephens; U.S. Junior
Chamber of Commerce leaders and T. E. Stephens;
General Goodpaster. Starts machinery in modern-
ized Washington Post Office. Receives 4-H Club
representatives, followed by appointments with Secretary Benson; General Goodpaster; Major J. S. D.
Eisenhower. Lunch. Afternoon appointments with
Major J. S. D. Eisenhower; G. D. Morgan; General
Persons; T. E. Stephens. Practices golf on south
lawn. Off-the-record appointment with S. S. Larmon
and P. Reed.

4   Washington. Morning appointments with Major
J. S. D. Eisenhower; W. D. Kerr (off the record); U.S.
Ambassador Philip K. Crowe (to South Africa); Gen-
eral Goodpaster and Major J. S. D. Eisenhower;
General Goodpaster; General Persons and D. Paarl-
berg; General Persons and J. C. Hagerty; J. C.
Hagerty; pre-news briefing; news conference; Gen-
eral Persons and J. C. Hagerty; General Goodpaster;
Prince Constantine (Greece), Ambassador Liatis,
Major Joseph Lepczyk (Military escort, Greece), and
W. T. Buchanan; Secretary Benson; American Meat
Institute board members; General Persons; Major
J. S. D. Eisenhower. Lunch. Afternoon appointments
with D. W. Kendall; J. R. Killian, Drs. Kistiakowsky
and Brockway McMillan, D. A. Quarles, Admiral
John H. Sides, G. Gray, Major J. S. D. Eisenhower,
and Generals Twining, Goodpaster, and Persons
(off the record); General Twining. Practices golf on
south lawn. Appointment with General Goodpaster.

5   Washington. Morning appointments with J. Z. An-
derson; W. J. Hopkins; General Persons and D. W.
Kendall; Major J. S. D. Eisenhower; Investment
Bankers Association of America; General Good-
paster; Major J. S. D. Eisenhower; National Security
Council session (off the record); Secretary McElroy;
G. Gray and J. C. Hagerty; J. C. Hagerty; General
Goodpaster. Lunch. Afternoon appointments with
Major J. S. D. Eisenhower; General Persons and
J. C. Hagerty; Secretary Anderson, C. D. Dillon,
Budget Director Stans, T. Grayson Upton (Assistant
Secretary of Treasury), George Willis (Treasury),
and D. Paarlberg (off the record); Budget Director

Stans; T. E. Stephens; Major J. S. D. Eisenhower; General Persons. Practices golf on south lawn. Off-the-record evening appointment with Senators Dirksen and Bridges, Congressmen Halleck and Taber, General Persons, J. Z. Anderson, and E. A. McCabe.

6 Washington. Morning appointments with J. C. Hagerty and Major J. S. D. Eisenhower; Major J. S. D. Eisenhower; Generals Persons and Goodpaster and Major J. S. D. Eisenhower; National Capital Flower and Garden Show leaders; Cabinet meeting; C. A. Herter, General Goodpaster, and Secretary McElroy; C. A. Herter and General Goodpaster; Legislative Leaders; J. C. Hagerty and General Goodpaster; C. A. Herter and General Goodpaster; Ambassador Lodge; Major J. S. D. Eisenhower. Lunch. Afternoon appointments with Major J. S. D. Eisenhower and S. Eisenhower; W. J. Hopkins; T. E. Stephens. Practices golf on south lawn. Visits Secretary Dulles at Walter Reed Hospital. Off-the-record appointment with Vice-President Nixon, Secretary McElroy, C. A. Herter, A. W. Dulles, B. N. Harlow, Major J. S. D. Eisenhower, General Persons and Republican senators and congressmen.

7 Washington. Morning appointments with T. E. Stephens; J. C. Hagerty; G. D. Morgan and D. W. Kendall; Secretary Mitchell, Budget Director Stans, and G. D. Morgan; Budget Director Stans and G. D. Morgan; G. D. Morgan; T. E. Stephens; Secretary Flemming, Budget Director Stans, and R. E. Merriam; Secretary Flemming; Major J. S. D. Eisenhower; W. J. Hopkins; Major J. S. D. Eisenhower; M. C. Moos; T. E. Stephens; Major J. S. D. Eisenhower. Lunch.

8 Washington. Attends services at National Presbyterian Church with D. D. Eisenhower II. Visits residence of R. Flohr.

9 Washington. Morning appointments with General Persons; G. Gray; Major J. S. D. Eisenhower; Congressman Auchincloss and J. Z. Anderson; General Goodpaster and Major J. S. D. Eisenhower. Witnesses swearing-in ceremony for R. W. Jones as Civil Service Commissioner, followed by appointments with General Persons, J. C. Hagerty, and M. C. Moos;

J. C. Hagerty; Generals Twining and Goodpaster and Major J. S. D. Eisenhower; General Twining and Major J. S. D. Eisenhower; General Goodpaster. Visits Secretary Dulles at Walter Reed Hospital. Late morning appointments with T. E. Stephens and General Goodpaster; General Goodpaster. Lunch. Afternoon appointments with General Persons and J. C. Hagerty; D. A. Quarles, Secretary McElroy, R. Murphy, H. Vance, Colonels Jack R. Brown and Benjamin A. Mead, Generals Persons, Twining, Loper, LeMay, and Goodpaster, and Major J. S. D. Eisenhower (off the record); Secretary McElroy and General Goodpaster; T. E. Stephens; General Persons. Practices golf on south lawn. Appointment with W. J. Hopkins.

10   Washington. Breakfast meeting with Congressmen Allen and Arends and B. N. Harlow (off the record). Appointments with General Persons and R. C. Siciliano; Legislative Leaders; General Goodpaster; T. E. Stephens. Greets President Jose M. Lemus (El Salvador). Off-the-record lunch with General Saylor. Appointments with G. D. Morgan and D. W. Kendall; General Goodpaster; Secretaries Anderson and Flemming and General Persons; Major J. S. D. Eisenhower. Practices golf. Late afternoon appointments with Major J. S. D. Eisenhower; Congressmen Halleck and McCormack, C. A. Herter, and B. N. Harlow (off the record). Hosts dinner with Mrs. Eisenhower in honor of President and Mrs. Lemus, followed by musical entertainment.

11   Washington. Morning appointments with Major J. S. D. Eisenhower and W. J. Hopkins; General Persons and G. D. Morgan; G. D. Morgan; J. C. Hagerty; Ambassador Dato N. A. Kamil (from Malaya) and W. T. Buchanan; T. E. Stephens; General Goodpaster; pre-news briefing; news conference; J. C. Hagerty; President Lemus, El Salvador officials, C. A. Herter, R. R. Rubottom, W. T. Buchanan, Ambassador Thorsten V. Kalijarvi (to El Salvador), Secretary Anderson, Colonel Walters, and Major J. S. D. Eisenhower. Lunch. Afternoon appointments with T. E. Stephens; Secretary Mitchell; General Persons and J. C. Hagerty; General Goodpaster; General Persons; General Goodpaster.

12 Washington. Morning appointments with M. C. Moos; General Goodpaster; D. A. Quarles, Generals Twining and Goodpaster, Admiral O'Beirne, Colonels Mason, Selden, and Durezzo, Captains Schneider and Aurand, and Major J. S. D. Eisenhower; National Security Council session; T. E. Stephens; W. J. Hopkins; J. C. Hagerty; General Persons; G. D. Morgan and D. W. Kendall; H. M. Alcorn and T. E. Stephens. Greets United Christian Youth Movement. Greets Republican precinct workers. Lunch. Afternoon appointments with Major J. S. D. Eisenhower; J. C. Hagerty; T. E. Stephens; M. C. Moos; Commissioner David Karrick and D. W. Kendall; Dr. M. S. Eisenhower, Secretaries Anderson and Flemming, C. H. Percy, G. M. Hauge, and R. E. Merriam (off the record); C. H. Percy and G. M. Hauge (off the record); General Goodpaster; D. W. Kendall. Attends dinner hosted by President and Mrs. Lemus.

13 Washington. Morning appointments with R. C. Siciliano and Major J. S. D. Eisenhower; Major J. S. D. Eisenhower; M. J. McCaffree; T. E. Stephens; G. D. Morgan; J. C. Hagerty, T. E. Stephens, and E. A. McCabe; Ambassador Ali (from Pakistan) and C. E. Conger; W. J. Hopkins; Cabinet meeting; Vice-President Nixon; Vice-President Nixon and Allen W. Wallis (Dean, University of Chicago School of Business); T. E. Stephens; J. R. Killian, D. W. Kendall, and Robert N. Kreidler (technical assistant) (off the record). Signs Executive Order on Federal Council for Science and Technology. Late morning appointments with J. R. Killian; General Goodpaster; J. R. Killian and General Goodpaster; General Goodpaster. Hosts luncheon for Republican Committee on Program and Progress. Visits Secretary Dulles at Walter Reed Hospital. Practices golf on south lawn. Afternoon appointments with J. C. Hagerty and J. N. Irwin; General Persons, G. D. Morgan, and B. N. Harlow; R. J. Saulnier; D. Paarlberg and P. E. Areeda; Major J. S. D. Eisenhower; T. E. Stephens.

14 Washington. Morning appointments with Major J. S. D. Eisenhower; G. D. Morgan; Governor Quinn, Secretary Seaton, and J. C. Hagerty; M. C. Moos (off

the record); C. A. Herter and General Goodpaster; M. C. Moos; Governor Hatfield and R. E. Merriam. To Saint Joseph College, Emmitsburg, Maryland. Mrs. Eisenhower receives honorary degree. To Sharpsburg, Maryland, to visit Antietam Battlefield. Returns to Washington.

15   Washington. No official appointments.

16   Washington. Morning appointments with Major J. S. D. Eisenhower; Ambassador Ernesto Dihigo Trigo (from Cuba) and C. E. Conger; L. Markel (off the record); M. C. Moos and General Goodpaster. Lunch. Practices golf on south lawn. Works on speech. Addresses nation via television and radio regarding Berlin situation and security position of United States and its allies.

17   Washington. Morning appointments with General Goodpaster; M. J. McCaffree; Committee to study U.S. Military Assistance Program; Prime Minister Amadou Ahidjo (Cameroun), Ambassador Alphand, Joseph C. Satterthwaite (Assistant Secretary of State, Africa), Colonel Walters, and Major J. S. D. Eisenhower; C. A. Herter, L. T. Merchant, G. F. Reinhardt, R. Murphy, J. C. Hagerty, General Goodpaster, and Major J. S. D. Eisenhower; T. E. Stephens; Major J. S. D. Eisenhower. Greets President Sean T. O'Kelly (Ireland). Lunch. Afternoon appointments with T. E. Stephens and J. C. Hagerty; G. Gray and General Goodpaster; C. A. Herter, Secretary McElroy, G. Gray, D. A. Quarles, J. N. Irwin, R. Murphy, L. T. Merchant, J. S. Lay, G. Smith, Generals Persons, Twining, and Goodpaster, and Major J. S. D. Eisenhower (off the record); Secretary McElroy and C. A. Herter; T. E. Stephens; D. W. Kendall, T. E. Stephens, and General Persons; T. E. Stephens; General Goodpaster; E. J. Hughes, Major J. S. D. Eisenhower; Vice-President Nixon (off the record). Attends ceremonies of Friendly Sons of Ireland and Ancient Order of Hibernians. Hosts dinner with Mrs. Eisenhower in honor of President and Mrs. O'Kelly, followed by musical entertainment.

18   Washington. Morning appointments with W. J. Hopkins; General Persons; Frank H. Higgins (Assistant Secretary of Army, resigning) (off the record); Am-

bassador Platzer and W. T. Buchanan; J. C. Hagerty; W. J. Hopkins. Witnesses swearing-in ceremony for A. W. Wallis as Executive Vice-Chairman, Cabinet Committee on Price Stability for Economic Growth. Appointments with H. M. Alcorn and General Persons; J. C. Hagerty and H. R. McPhee; T. E. Stephens and Major J. S. D. Eisenhower; Senator Morton and General Persons (off the record); Major J. S. D. Eisenhower. Witnesses swearing-in ceremony for C. A. Wheeler as Staff Assistant. Appointments with General Persons, T. E. Stephens, and R. E. Merriam; R. E. Merriam; Major J. S. D. Eisenhower; L. Kimpton, F. L. Pace, Secretary Anderson, General Persons, and R. E. Merriam (off the record); C. B. Williams and T. E. Stephens (off the record); General Goodpaster. Lunch. Afternoon appointments with T. E. Stephens; General Persons and J. C. Hagerty; J. C. Hagerty. Practices golf.

19 Washington. Morning appointments with H. R. McPhee; General Goodpaster; T. E. Stephens; C. A. Herter, R. Murphy, L. T. Merchant, G. F. Reinhardt, Ambassador Whitney, J. C. Hagerty, General Goodpaster, and Major J. S. D. Eisenhower; Ambassador Ricardo Arias (Panama) and W. T. Buchanan; G. Gray; J. R. Killian and General Goodpaster; Secretary Anderson and J. B. Baird (off the record). Attends luncheon hosted by President O'Kelly with Mrs. Eisenhower at Mayflower Hotel. Afternoon appointments with T. E. Stephens; D. Paarlberg, P. E. Areeda, and Major J. S. D. Eisenhower; General Goodpaster; Major J. S. D. Eisenhower. Practices golf on south lawn. Late afternoon appointments with Major J. S. D. Eisenhower; General Persons and R. E. Merriam; Major J. S. D. Eisenhower. Visits Secretary Dulles at Walter Reed Hospital.

20 Washington. Morning appointments with T. E. Stephens and General Goodpaster; T. E. Stephens; General Goodpaster; Major J. S. D. Eisenhower; Prime Minister Macmillan and S. Lloyd. Visits Secretary Dulles at Walter Reed Hospital with Prime Minister Macmillan, S. Lloyd, and Captain Aurand. Airborne for Camp David, Maryland. To Gettysburg farm with Prime Minister Macmillan. Inspects farm. Returns to Camp David.

21   Camp David, Maryland. Remains at Camp David with Prime Minister Macmillan and party.

22   Camp David, Maryland. To Thurmont, Maryland, with Prime Minister Macmillan. Attends services at Trinity United Church of Christ. Tours summer residence of F. Akers. Returns to Washington. Visits residence of Secretary Dulles. To British Embassy.

23   Washington. Morning appointments with T. E. Stephens; General Persons and R. E. Merriam; General Persons; J. C. Hagerty; General Persons and G. D. Morgan; Major J. S. D. Eisenhower; W. J. Hopkins; Governors' Conference Executive Committee; R. E. Merriam and Major J. S. D. Eisenhower; G. V. Allen; Ambassador Aziz Ahmed (Pakistan) and R. Corrigan; D. W. Kendall. Lunch. Practices golf on south lawn, followed by afternoon appointments with M. C. Moos; Prime Minister Macmillan and British and U.S. officials; General Goodpaster.

24   Washington. Morning appointments with General Persons and B. N. Harlow; Legislative Leaders; G. Gray; Prime Minister Hans Christian Hansen (Denmark), Ambassador Knuth-Winterfeldt, and L. T. Merchant; General Goodpaster and Major J. S. D. Eisenhower; J. C. Hagerty and Major J. S. D. Eisenhower; Major J. S. D. Eisenhower; T. E. Stephens. Hosts stag luncheon for King Hussein (Jordan). Afternoon appointment with T. E. Stephens. Practices golf on south lawn.

25   Washington. Morning appointments with G. Gray; U.S. Ambassador William C. Trimble (to Cambodia); W. J. Hopkins; pre-news briefing; news conference; J. C. Hagerty; King Hussein, Prime Minister Samir Rifa'i (Jordan), Ambassador Juma, C. A. Herter, W. M. Rountree, U.S. Ambassador Mills, W. T. Buchanan, and Major J. S. D. Eisenhower; Major J. S. D. Eisenhower; General Goodpaster. Lunch. Afternoon appointments with T. E. Stephens; G. D. Morgan and D. W. Kendall. Practices golf on south lawn. Off-the-record evening appointment with Dr. M. S. Eisenhower.

26   Washington. Appointment with T. E. Stephens; J. N. Greene (off the record); W. J. Hopkins; General

Persons; T. E. Stephens; Vice-President Nixon, C. A. Herter, D. A. Quarles, J. A. McCone, A. W. Dulles, G. Gray, L. T. Merchant, Martin Hillenbrand, Generals Twining and Goodpaster, and Major J. S. D. Eisenhower (off the record); J. C. Hagerty; Vice-President Nixon; National Security Council session; C. A. Herter, F. C. Scribner, and General Goodpaster; G. D. Morgan; General Goodpaster; Major J. S. D. Eisenhower. Greets Edna Donley, National Teacher of the Year. Makes film on NATO Defense College. Airborne for Gettysburg farm. To Gettysburg Country Club for golf with General Nevins.

27 Gettysburg. Tours farm with General Nevins. Attends Good Friday services with Mrs. Eisenhower and Mrs. E. J. Hughes at Methodist Church of Gettysburg.

28 Gettysburg. To Gettysburg Country Club for golf with Major J. S. D. Eisenhower and General Nevins.

29 Gettysburg. Walks around grounds with Chief West. Attends Easter Sunday services with Mrs. Eisenhower and Mrs. E. J. Hughes at Presbyterian Church of Gettysburg. Lunch with Major and Mrs. J. S. D. Eisenhower and family.

30 Gettysburg. Returns to Washington. Lunch. Afternoon appointments with T. E. Stephens; R. J. Saulnier; G. Gray; J. C. Hagerty; Major J. S. D. Eisenhower; General Persons; General Goodpaster.

31 Washington. Morning appointments with Major J. S. D. Eisenhower; D. W. Kendall and General Goodpaster; D. W. Kendall; Secretary Flemming and General Persons; T. E. Stephens; Captain Crittenberger; T. E. Stephens and Captain Crittenberger. Army, Navy, and Air Force chaplains present new hymnal. Off-the-record appointments with C. A. Herter, C. D. Dillon, and General Goodpaster; C. A. Herter and General Goodpaster; General Persons and D. W. Kendall; Olympic Committee leaders; Dr. Earl D. Emery and son (personal friend). Lunch. Afternoon appointments with Major J. S. D. Eisenhower; T. E. Stephens; U.S. Ambassador Bruce; M. C. Moos and Major J. S. D. Eisenhower. Practices golf on south lawn.

April 1 Washington. Morning appointments with T. E. Stephens; D. W. Kendall. Receives 1959 baseball pass from W. S. Robertson and American League representatives. Off-the-record appointments with H. M. Alcorn, T. E. Stephens, and General Persons; H. M. Alcorn; General Clark; Dr. James L. Morrill (University of Minnesota) and R. E. Merriam, followed by appointments with Secretary Mitchell; Dr. Glennan and General Persons; T. E. Stephens; General Goodpaster; R. E. Merriam; Mr. and Mrs. Walker Buckner.

2 Washington. Morning appointments with Major J. S. D. Eisenhower; General Goodpaster; National Security Council session. Delivers address at tenth anniversary NATO Spring Ministerial Meeting. Hosts stag luncheon for NATO group. Afternoon appointments with General Goodpaster; Generals Persons and Goodpaster, J. R. Killian, J. A. McCone, E. Staats, David Z. Beckler, and Drs. Waterman, York, E. R. Piore, and Edwin M. McMillan (off the record); J. A. McCone and General Goodpaster (off the record); J. A. McCone (off the record); G. Gray and General Goodpaster; G. Gray; General Goodpaster; M. C. Moos.

3 Washington. Morning appointments with Major J. S. D. Eisenhower; D. W. Kendall; W. J. Hopkins; J. C. Hagerty; D. Anderson (off the record); A. W. Dulles, Secretary McElroy, D. A. Quarles, R. Murphy, J. R. Killian, R. Bissell, Generals Twining and Goodpaster, and Major J. S. D. Eisenhower (off the record); Secretary Seaton and Wilbur A. Dexheimer (Commissioner, Bureau of Reclamation); General Goodpaster; W. A. Ruschmeyer, F. J. Donohue, and Colonel Schulz (off the record); National Association of Evangelicals; National Cherry Blossom Festival organizers. Airborne for Gettysburg farm. Inspects barn and Allen farm with G. E. Allen.

4 Gettysburg. To Gettysburg College with Mrs. Eisenhower. Delivers address at Founder's Day ceremony. Visits with G. E. Allen, W. E. Robinson, General and Mrs. Nevins, and Mrs. E. J. Hughes.

5 Gettysburg. Walks around farm. To Hartley farm, duck pond, and residence of Major J. S. D. Eisen-

hower with G. E. Allen. Visits with General and Mrs. Nevins. Returns to Washington.

6   Washington. Off-the-record breakfast meeting with J. R. Killian and Dr. York. Morning appointments with General Persons and J. R. Killian (off the record); General Norstad (off the record); T. E. Stephens; Secretary Mitchell, General Persons, and J. C. Hagerty; J. C. Hagerty; W. S. Robertson; U Law Yone (Special Emissary, Prime Minister of Burma) and W. S. Robertson (off the record); C. A. Herter, U.S. Ambassador Wadsworth, and General Goodpaster; C. A. Herter and General Goodpaster; T. E. Stephens; M. C. Moos; T. E. Stephens; General Persons. Lunch. Afternoon appointments with J. C. Hagerty and R. E. Merriam; General Persons; Postmaster General Summerfield and General Persons (off the record); Vice-President Nixon. Practices golf on south lawn. Evening appointments with General Goodpaster; G. E. Allen.

7   Washington. Morning appointments with General Goodpaster; D. W. Kendall; T. E. Stephens; General Goodpaster; Secretary McElroy, R. Bissell, and General Goodpaster (off the record); General Goodpaster; General Persons. Airborne for Augusta, Georgia. To Augusta National Golf Club for golf with C. Roberts, W. E. Robinson, and B. Nelson. Tours Augusta National Golf Club with Mrs. Eisenhower. Visits Mr. and Mrs. R. W. Jones, Mr. and Mrs. R. W. Woodruff, and Mrs. C. J. Schoo at Jones Cottage.

8   Augusta, Georgia. To Augusta National Golf Club for golf with R. W. Woodruff, E. D. Slater, and C. J. Schoo.

9   Augusta, Georgia. To Augusta National Golf Club for golf with T. R. Garlington, W. E. Robinson, and B. T. Leithead.

10   Augusta, Georgia. To Augusta National Golf Club for golf with R. W. Woodruff, E. D. Slater, and W. E. Robinson. Afternoon appointment with Republican Nominating Committee. Poses for photographs.

11   Augusta, Georgia. To Augusta National Golf Club for golf with A. Bradley, W. A. Jones, and S. S. Lar-

mon. Evening appointment with A. W. Dulles and J. N. Greene.

12   Augusta, Georgia. Attends services with Mrs. Eisenhower at Reid Memorial Presbyterian Church. To Augusta National Golf Club for golf with C. Roberts, W. E. Robinson, W. A. Jones, B. J. Patton, and A. Bradley.

13   Augusta, Georgia. Returns to Washington. Visits Secretary Dulles at Walter Reed Hospital. Afternoon appointments with Major J. S. D. Eisenhower; General Persons; T. E. Stephens; W. J. Hopkins; General Persons, D. W. Kendall, and R. E. Merriam; Secretary Anderson and D. W. Kendall; R. J. Saulnier; General Goodpaster. To Red Cross building with Mrs. Eisenhower. Delivers address at Advertising Council conference. Appointments with General Goodpaster; T. E. Stephens; C. A. Herter (off the record); Major J. S. D. Eisenhower. To Mayflower Hotel. Delivers address at Republican Women's National Conference dinner.

14   Washington. Morning appointments with General Persons and B. N. Harlow; Legislative Leaders; General Persons, G. D. Morgan, R. E. Merriam, Budget Director Stans, and R. C. Siciliano; D. W. Kendall; T. E. Stephens; Major J. S. D. Eisenhower. Delivers address at dedication of Senator Robert A. Taft Memorial. Receives Council of Bishops, Methodist Church. Boards *Columbine* en route to Augusta, Georgia. To Augusta National Golf Club for golf with C. Roberts, J. Roberts, and J. Franklin.

15   Augusta, Georgia. News conference to announce retirement of Secretary Dulles. Practices golf. To Augusta National Golf Club for golf with C. Roberts, W. E. Robinson, and G. Stout.

16   Augusta, Georgia. To Augusta National Golf Club for golf with General Goodpaster and G. Gray. Afternoon golf with C. Roberts, E. D. Slater, and G. Stout.

17   Augusta, Georgia. Practices golf. To Augusta National Golf Club for golf with Major J. S. D. Eisenhower, C. Roberts, and L. M. Stockard. Visits with General Gruenther.

18   Augusta, Georgia. Appointment with C. A. Herter (new Secretary of State). Practices golf. To Augusta National Golf Club for golf with Major J. S. D. Eisenhower, W. E. Robinson, and F. Willard. Visits with G. E. Allen.

19   Augusta, Georgia. Visits Pro Shop with G. E. Allen. To Augusta National Golf Club for golf with G. E. Allen, W. E. Robinson, and J. O. Chiles. Plays bridge with G. E. Allen, W. E. Robinson, and C. Roberts.

20   Augusta, Georgia. To Augusta National Golf Club for golf with W. E. Robinson, G. E. Allen, and J. O. Chiles. Practices golf.

21   Augusta, Georgia. To Augusta National Golf Club for golf with G. E. Allen, W. E. Robinson, and C. Roberts. Returns to Washington. Late afternoon appointments with T. E. Stephens, General Goodpaster, and W. J. Hopkins; B. N. Harlow, General Goodpaster, R. E. Merriam, and Major J. S. D. Eisenhower; G. E. Allen; Major J. S. D. Eisenhower.

22   Washington. Breakfast meeting with Senator Dirksen, Congressman Halleck, and B. N. Harlow (off the record). Morning appointments with Legislative Leaders; T. E. Stephens; B. N. Harlow; T. E. Stephens; T. E. Stephens, J. C. Hagerty, and General Goodpaster; G. Gray; Florida Presbyterian College representatives; Dr. Vittorino Veronese (Director General, UNESCO), A. Berding, and Major J. S. D. Eisenhower; Senator Case (off the record); Mr. and Mrs. C. A. Herter, Secretary Dulles, and T. E. Stephens. Witnesses swearing-in ceremony for C. A. Herter as Secretary of State. Lunch. Afternoon appointments with Major J. S. D. Eisenhower; W. J. Hopkins; American Battle Monuments Commission; A. F. Burns and R. E. Merriam (off the record); Major J. S. D. Eisenhower; H. R. McPhee. Practices golf on south lawn.

23   Washington. Off-the-record breakfast meeting with Dr. M. S. Eisenhower and Secretary Flemming. Morning appointments with Vice-President Nixon; National Security Council session; General Goodpaster; Generals Draper, Gruenther, and Goodpaster, J. J. McCloy, T. S. Voorhees, and R. E. Mer-

riam. To Walter Reed Hospital for swearing-in of J. F. Dulles as Special Consultant to the President. To Sheraton Carlton Hotel. Delivers address to Board of Directors of National Association of Manufacturers. Lunch. Afternoon appointments with General Goodpaster; Major J. S. D. Eisenhower. To Sheraton Park Hotel. Delivers address to guests of International Chamber of Commerce. Late afternoon appointments with T. E. Stephens; Secretary Herter, C. D. Dillon, L. T. Merchant, and General Goodpaster; G. D. Morgan; R. E. Merriam and General Goodpaster; R. E. Merriam; R. E. Merriam and General Goodpaster; T. E. Stephens, R. E. Merriam, and General Goodpaster; M. C. Moos; Major J. S. D. Eisenhower.

24   Washington. Breakfast meeting with P. H. Spaak, Secretary Herter, and L. T. Merchant. Morning appointments with P. H. Spaak, Secretary Herter, and L. T. Merchant; L. A. Hoegh; Cabinet meeting; Secretaries Flemming and Anderson, Budget Director Stans, and G. D. Morgan; Governors Del Sesto, Furcolo, and Powell, Seymour Harris (Chairman, New England Governor's Committee on Textiles), D. Paarlberg, E. Staats, and D. Price to discuss textile situation; General Goodpaster and Major J. S. D. Eisenhower; T. E. Stephens and A. Rowe. Lunch. Afternoon appointments with T. E. Stephens; M. J. McCaffree; Secretary Anderson, J. B. Baird, W. M. Martin, R. J. Saulnier, and D. Paarlberg; R. J. Saulnier. Practices golf on south lawn. Appointment with General Goodpaster.

25   Washington. Morning appointments with Major J. S. D. Eisenhower; General Goodpaster. To Burning Tree Country Club for golf with Colonel Belshe, General Estes, and M. E. Parkinson.

26   Washington. Attends services at National Presbyterian Church. To Gettysburg. Lunch with G. E. Allen, Colonel Tkach, and General Nevins. Inspects skeet range and barn. Returns to Washington.

27   Washington. Morning appointments with Ambassador Telli B. Diallo (from Guinea), W. T. Buchanan, and C. Sedgwick; Secretary Anderson, C. D. Dillon, L. A. Hoegh, Secretary Seaton, G. D. Morgan, and

D. Paarlberg to discuss easing restriction on Canadian oil; C. D. Dillon; J. C. Hagerty; Secretary Herter, C. D. Dillon, and General Goodpaster. To Constitution Hall to address annual meeting of U.S. Chamber of Commerce. Appointments with General Melvin J. Maas (Chairman, President's Committee on Employment of Physically Handicapped); D. W. Kendall and H. R. McPhee; Dr. Glennan, J. R. Killian, Franklyn W. Phillips (NASA), and General Goodpaster; J. R. Killian and General Goodpaster. Lunch. Afternoon appointments with National Aeronautics and Space Council; Secretary Anderson, Budget Director Stans, G. D. Morgan, B. N. Harlow, and General Goodpaster. Visits J. F. Dulles at Walter Reed Hospital. Practices golf on south lawn. Evening appointment with General Goodpaster.

28   Washington. Off-the-record breakfast meeting with Senator Bridges, Congressman Byrnes, and B. N. Harlow. Morning appointments with Legislative Leaders; G. Gray; Archbishop Iakovos, T. Pappas, and S. P. Skouras; T. Pappas and T. E. Stephens; General Goodpaster; J. C. Hagerty and G. D. Morgan. Lunch. Afternoon appointments with C. D. Jackson; General Goodpaster; G. D. Morgan.

29   Washington. Morning appointments with J. C. Hagerty; Dr. Edgar B. Brossard (Chairman, U.S. Tariff Commission) and D. W. Kendall; D. W. Kendall; R. J. Saulnier; General Goodpaster; J. C. Hagerty, J. R. Killian, and Major J. S. D. Eisenhower; pre-news briefing; news conference; J. C. Hagerty; T. E. Stephens; S. C. Waugh (off the record); Attorney General Rogers (off the record); General Goodpaster; G. D. Morgan and B. N. Harlow; B. N. Harlow; Rene Jeanneret (Geneva, Switzerland) and Colonel Schulz (off the record); T. E. Stephens; W. J. Hopkins. Lunch. To Burning Tree Country Club for golf with Colonel Belshe. Appointment with B. N. Harlow.

30   Washington. Morning appointments with Major J. S. D. Eisenhower; General Goodpaster; Carl E. Haymond (personal friend) and son and T. E. Stephens (off the record); R. K. Gray; National Security

Council session (off the record); National Security Council session; Vice-President Nixon and C. D. Dillon; Defense presentation; Irving S. Olds (Chairman of Trustees, Cooper Union) and Arthur A. Houghton; Attorney General Rogers, D. W. Kendall, and J. C. Hagerty; D. W. Kendall and J. C. Hagerty; J. C. Hagerty and W. J. Hopkins; J. C. Hagerty. Lunch. Practices golf on south lawn. Afternoon appointments with G. D. Morgan; General Goodpaster; W. J. Hopkins. Attends reception for children of former Presidents.

May   1   Washington. Morning appointments with J. C. Hagerty; T. E. Stephens; D. W. Kendall; Maurice Chevalier and Ambassador Alphand (off the record); Postmaster General Summerfield (off the record); Secretary Benson (off the record); Cabinet meeting; General Goodpaster; J. C. Hagerty; U.S. Ambassador Luce and J. C. Hagerty; T. E. Stephens. Receives AMVETS Peace Award. Airborne for Gettysburg farm. To residence of F. Akers in Thurmont, Maryland. Fishes. To Gettysburg farm. Walks with S. Eisenhower.

2   Gettysburg. To Newman farm and residence of Major J. S. D. Eisenhower. Morning appointment with Secretary Herter, J. C. Hagerty, and Major J. S. D. Eisenhower. To Gettysburg Country Club for golf with G. E. Allen and General Nevins. Dinner with General and Mrs. Nevins, Mr. and Mrs. G. E. Allen, and General and Mrs. Snyder.

3   Gettysburg. Attends services at Presbyterian Church of Gettysburg with General Nevins. To Bendersville, Pennsylvania, with G. E. Allen. Views apple blossoms. To Gettysburg farm. Inspects cattle with G. E. Allen and General Nevins. Shoots skeet with D. D. Eisenhower II. Returns to Washington.

4   Washington. Morning appointments with Major J. S. D. Eisenhower; T. E. Stephens and J. C. Hagerty; D. Paarlberg; D. W. Kendall; M. C. Moos; T. E. Stephens; Major J. S. D. Eisenhower; K. G. Harr and General Goodpaster; General Goodpaster; G. Gray; T. E. Stephens; Secretary Herter and General Goodpaster. Lunch. To Burning Tree Country Club for

golf with Colonel Belshe. Late afternoon appointments with D. W. Kendall and General Goodpaster; D. W. Kendall. Greets Winston S. Churchill.

5 Washington. Morning appointments with General Goodpaster; Secretary Herter, A. W. Dulles, D. A. Quarles, J. A. McCone, G. Gray, J. R. Killian, P. J. Farley, K. G. Harr, and General Goodpaster; Congressman Martin and H. H. Gruenther; Secretary Flemming (off the record); pre-news briefing; news conference; J. C. Hagerty; W. J. Hopkins; B. N. Harlow; T. E. Stephens; J. R. Killian and M. C. Moos (off the record); J. R. Killian (off the record); D. W. Kendall and General Goodpaster; Congressman and Mrs. Nelson, Mr. and Mrs. Helmuth Kurth, and B. N. Harlow; Major J. S. D. Eisenhower. Receives William Junker, Goodwill Worker of 1959. Lunch. To Natural Arboretum with W. S. Churchill. To Walter Reed Hospital with W. S. Churchill to visit J. F. Dulles and General Marshall. Afternoon appointments with Colonel Draper; Major J. S. D. Eisenhower; T. E. Stephens. Hosts stag dinner in honor of W. S. Churchill.

6 Washington. Morning appointments with T. E. Stephens; J. C. Hagerty; General Persons and B. N. Harlow; Legislative Leaders; General Persons, Senator Dirksen, Congressman Halleck, and B. N. Harlow; D. Paarlberg; Food for Peace Conference participants; J. R. Killian, Dr. Kistiakowsky, and General Persons. Lunch. Airborne for Gettysburg farm with W. S. Churchill. Tours farm and Gettysburg Battlefield. Returns to Washington. Afternoon appointments with T. E. Stephens; General Goodpaster; General Persons; W. J. Hopkins. Practices golf on south lawn. Hosts stag dinner in honor of W. S. Churchill.

7 Washington. Off-the-record breakfast meeting with Congressman Williams. Morning appointments with Budget Director Stans, General Persons, G. D. Morgan, and B. N. Harlow; Attorney General Rogers (off the record); G. Gray; National Security Council session; Marian Huff and Mrs. R. L. Bowman (off the record); G. D. Morgan; Secretary Herter; W. W. Aldrich (off the record); Dr. Elson

(off the record); B. M. Baruch; General Persons. Lunch. Afternoon appointments with T. E. Stephens; J. C. Hagerty; Major J. S. D. Eisenhower; T. E. Stephens; W. J. Hopkins; R. W. Woodruff. Practices golf on south lawn. To British Embassy with Major J. S. D. Eisenhower for dinner hosted by W. S. Churchill.

8 Washington. Morning appointments with Major J. S. D. Eisenhower; H. R. McPhee; General Goodpaster; J. C. Hagerty. Presents Young American Medal for Bravery to William J. Steury. Appointments with General Persons, J. C. Hagerty, and Major J. S. D. Eisenhower; General Persons; Secretary Herter and Generals Goodpaster and Persons; Major J. S. D. Eisenhower; R. J. Saulnier (off the record); G. D. Morgan. Lunch. To Walter Reed Hospital for chest x-ray. Visits J. F. Dulles. To Camp David, Maryland. To Gettysburg Country Club for golf with General Snyder and G. E. Allen. To residence of F. C. Akers. Fishes. To Camp David, Maryland.

9 Camp David, Maryland. To Gettysburg with General Snyder and G. E. Allen. To Gettysburg Country Club for golf with G. E. Allen and General Nevins. Tours farm. To Camp David. Inspects Laurel Cottage with Lieutenant Weyrauch. Dinner with General Gruenther and W. E. Robinson.

10 [Page missing.]

11 Washington. Morning appointments with Major J. S. D. Eisenhower; M. J. McCaffree; General Persons; T. E. Stephens; General Persons; G. D. Morgan; W. J. Hopkins; Secretary McElroy; G. Gray; John W. Wheeler-Bennett (Garsington Manor, England) (off the record); General Persons and T. E. Stephens. Greets King Baudouin (Belgium). Lunch. Afternoon appointments with T. E. Stephens; F. Gurley (off the record); T. E. Stephens; M. C. Moos; T. E. Stephens; T. E. Stephens and J. C. Hagerty. Practices golf. Hosts dinner with Mrs. Eisenhower in honor of King Baudouin, followed by a piano recital by Leon Fleisher.

12 Washington. Morning appointments with General Persons and B. N. Harlow; Legislative Leaders; Rev-

erend John P. Markoe (personal friend) (off the record); M. C. Moos; J. C. Hagerty; T. E. Stephens and J. C. Hagerty; W. J. Hopkins. Lunch. Attends funeral of D. A. Quarles. Late afternoon appointments with T. E. Stephens; General Goodpaster.

13   Washington. Morning appointments with G. D. Morgan and H. R. McPhee; C. D. Dillon and General Goodpaster; National Security Council session; Secretary McElroy and General Goodpaster; H. R. McPhee; T. E. Stephens; J. C. Hagerty; pre-news briefing; news conference; General Persons; L. A. Hoegh; Civil Defense Directors; Colonel Arthur Sheets (Director, Oregon Civil Defense Agency); J. C. Hagerty; Lindholm family (off the record); General Persons and G. D. Morgan. Lunch. Afternoon appointments with Major J. S. D. Eisenhower; T. E. Stephens; M. C. Moos; W. J. Hopkins. Visits J. F. Dulles at Walter Reed Hospital. Late afternoon appointments with T. E. Stephens; General Persons and H. R. McPhee; Secretary McElroy (off the record); General Persons. Attends dinner in his honor at Belgian Embassy hosted by King Baudouin.

14   Washington. Morning appointments with T. E. Stephens; General Goodpaster; Major J. S. D. Eisenhower; General Persons; T. E. Stephens; General Goodpaster. Airborne for Newark, New Jersey. To New York City. Participates in ground-breaking ceremonies for Lincoln Center for Performing Arts. Attends U.S. World Trade Fair. Appointments with Herman Tritz and E. Goldman; T. E. Stephens; M. Hahn; David McDonald (President, United Steelworkers of America); J. R. Killian; Mr. and Mrs. G. G. Kalmanson (Johannesburg, Africa); Leslie Nicholls; Leon Michael; Dr. Katz; Dr. Barnaby Keeney (President, Brown University) and W. W. Aldrich; S. Kennedy, W. W. Aldrich, and Walter Arn (Police Commissioner); S. S. Larmon; W. E. Robinson; B. T. Leithead; G. M. Hauge; G. E. Allen; C. Roberts; D. Marx. Addresses guests at Science Symposium dinner. Returns to Washington.

15   Washington. Morning appointments with General Persons; Major J. S. D. Eisenhower; H. R. McPhee;

General Goodpaster; U.S. Ambassador Lodge and General Goodpaster (off the record); Secretary McElroy and General Goodpaster; W. J. Hopkins; Cabinet meeting; Secretary Benson; Secretary McElroy, C. D. Dillon, R. Murphy, A. W. Dulles, G. Gray, and General Taylor (off the record); R. J. Saulnier; J. Z. Anderson; Ambassador Abba Eban (from Israel) and R. Corrigan; General Goodpaster; Major J. S. D. Eisenhower. Receives petitions from 'Alerted Americans' in support of a balanced budget. Lunch. To Burning Tree Country Club for golf with G. E. Allen and Colonel Belshe. Evening appointment with Secretary Mitchell.

16   Washington. Airborne for Colorado Springs, Colorado. Tours Air Force Academy. Receives Academy diploma and addresses cadets. Airborne for Denver, Colorado. Visits home of E. Doud.

17   Denver, Colorado. Tours Broomfield Heights, Columbine Country Club, and Greenwood Lake. Visits home of E. Doud. Returns to Washington.

18   Washington. Morning appointments with Major J. S. D. Eisenhower; General Persons; G. Gray; Secretary Flemming; T. E. Stephens; General Goodpaster. Presents International Solomon Guggenheim Award to Joan Miro. Late morning appointments with J. C. Hagerty; D. Paarlberg; Ambassador Flores and R. R. Rubottom; Secretary Strauss (off the record); J. C. Hagerty; American Committee on Italian Migration Symposium delegates; G. D. Morgan; General Goodpaster; J. Z. Anderson and family. Visits Secretary Dulles, Generals Twining and Marshall, and Mrs. Persons at Walter Reed Hospital. Lunch. Afternoon appointments with J. C. Hagerty; W. J. Hopkins. Practices golf on south lawn.

19   Washington. Morning appointments with Generals Persons and Goodpaster and B. N. Harlow; H. R. McPhee; Secretaries McElroy and Gates; Legislative Leaders; General Persons; W. J. Hopkins; Major J. S. D. Eisenhower; General Goodpaster; Science Advisory Committee (off the record). Presents scholastic achievement awards to blind students. Lunch. Afternoon appointments with General Persons; Secretary Mitchell, R. J. Saulnier, General Per-

sons, G. D. Morgan, and H. R. McPhee. Dentist appointment. To Burning Tree Country Club for golf with Colonel Belshe. Hosts off-the-record stag dinner.

20   Washington. Morning appointments with H. R. McPhee; Major J. S. D. Eisenhower; Senator H. A. Smith and Major J. S. D. Eisenhower (off the record); Judge Phillips (off the record); General Persons, J. C. Hagerty, and Major J. S. D. Eisenhower; General Persons; Ambassador Miloslav Rusek (from Czechoslovakia) and R. Corrigan; M. C. Moos; T. E. Stephens; R. J. Saulnier; Attorney General Rogers; General Persons and J. C. Hagerty; Attorney General Rogers; American Bar Association Board of Governors; Major J. S. D. Eisenhower. Lunch. Afternoon appointments with T. E. Stephens; G. D. Morgan; T. E. Stephens and M. C. Moos; General Goodpaster. Practices golf on south lawn.

21   Washington. Off-the-record breakfast meeting with Vice-President Nixon. Appointments with Vice-President Nixon; National Security Council session; C. D. Dillon and General Goodpaster; Major J. S. D. Eisenhower; W. J. Hopkins; General Persons; Secretary Anderson, J. B. Baird, R. Mayo, R. J. Saulnier, and General Persons; Secretary Anderson; National League of Insured Savings Associations; H. Brownell; T. E. Stephens and B. N. Harlow; J. C. Hagerty. Lunch. Afternoon appointments with Major J. S. D. Eisenhower; T. E. Stephens. To Burning Tree Country Club for golf with G. E. Allen and Major J. S. D. Eisenhower.

22   Washington. Breakfast meeting with Secretary General Hammarskjold, U.S. Ambassador Lodge, and C. D. Dillon. Appointments with Secretary General Hammarskjold and U.S. Ambassador Lodge; General Persons; Cabinet meeting; Antoine Pinay (Foreign Minister of Finance, France), Ambassador Alphand, R. Murphy, and Raymond Arasse (Staff Assistant to Pinay); General Goodpaster, Major J. S. D. Eisenhower, and H. R. McPhee. Airborne for Annapolis, Maryland. To St. John's College. Addresses guests at dedication ceremonies for Francis Scott Key Memorial Hall and Mellon Hall. Airborne for

Gettysburg farm. To Gettysburg Country Club for golf with G. E. Allen.

23 Gettysburg. To Gettysburg Country Club for golf with G. E. Allen. Visits cattle barn and Allen farm with G. E. Allen and Major J. S. D. Eisenhower and S. Eisenhower. Tours Newman farm and skeet range with Mr. and Mrs. H. Titus and General Nevins. Visits with General and Mrs. Nevins.

24 Gettysburg. Walks around residence with Chief West. Returns to Washington. To Dulles residence with Mrs. Eisenhower to express condolences to Mrs. Dulles.

25 Washington. Morning appointments with Colonel Schulz; General Persons; J. Z. Anderson; T. E. Stephens; M. C. Moos; J. C. Hagerty; General Persons; General Goodpaster; G. Gray; Senator Morton and D. W. Kendall. Lunch. Afternoon appointments with T. E. Stephens; Major J. S. D. Eisenhower; T. E. Stephens. Practices golf on south lawn. Late afternoon appointment with M. C. Moos.

26 Washington. Morning appointments with Colonel Schulz; General Goodpaster; General Persons and B. N. Harlow; J. C. Hagerty; Legislative Leaders; Senator Dirksen and Congressman Halleck; G. D. Morgan; D. W. Kendall; General Persons; T. E. Stephens; J. C. Hagerty; General Goodpaster; Senator Allott and G. D. Morgan; C. D. Dillon and General Goodpaster; J. R. Killian; Sloan Fellows; J. R. Killian; Major J. S. D. Eisenhower. Off-the-record meeting to discuss new Navy Department Building. Records personal message in Broadcast Room. Dentist appointment. Late afternoon appointment with J. C. Hagerty. Practices golf on south lawn.

27 Washington. Morning appointments with Colonel Schulz; Major J. S. D. Eisenhower; Generals Persons and Goodpaster; D. Paarlberg and J. Z. Anderson (off the record); M. C. Moos; Prime Minister Robert Menzies (Australia), Ambassador Beale (from Australia), W. S. Robertson, and J. G. Mein; Secretary Herter, C. D. Dillon, and General Goodpaster; U.S. Ambassador Houghton and General Goodpaster; Chancellor Adenauer, Henrich von Brentano (For-

eign Minister, Germany), Ambassador Grewe, Secretary Herter, and H. Weber; Secretary Herter. To Washington National Cathedral with Mrs. Eisenhower for funeral of J. F. Dulles. To Arlington National Cemetery for graveside committal services. Dentist appointment.

28 Washington. Morning appointments with Major J. S. D. Eisenhower and J. C. Hagerty; C. D. Dillon, J. A. McCone, Admiral Foster, and General Goodpaster; National Security Council session; Secretary Herter and L. T. Merchant; Secretary Herter, Andrei A. Gromyko (Minister of Foreign Affairs, USSR), S. Lloyd, and M. C. de Murville; J. C. Hagerty; Secretary Herter; General Goodpaster and W. J. Hopkins. Receives Military Academy yearbooks from cadets and midshipmen. Hosts luncheon for Ministers of Foreign Affairs. To Burning Tree Country Club for golf with Major J. S. D. Eisenhower, G. E. Allen, and Colonel Belshe.

29 Washington. Morning appointments with General Persons; General Cress (off the record); G. V. Allen; Major J. S. D. Eisenhower; G. D. Morgan, L. A. Hoegh, D. Paarlberg, and P. E. Areeda (off the record); Herschel D. Newsom (Master, National Grange), Joseph Parker (Legislative Counsel, National Grange), J. Z. Anderson, and D. Paarlberg; D. Paarlberg; Dr. Allen (off the record); A. F. Burns, F. L. Pace, R. E. Merriam, and General Persons (off the record); D. W. Kendall and Major J. S. D. Eisenhower; General Goodpaster. Lunch. Attends baseball game at Griffith Stadium. Evening appointment with General Goodpaster and Major J. S. D. Eisenhower.

30 Washington. To Burning Tree Country Club for golf with W. E. Robinson, E. D. Slater, and G. E. Allen.

31 Washington. Attends services at National Presbyterian Church.

June 1 Washington. Morning appointments with General Persons; J. C. Hagerty; G. Gray; W. J. Hopkins; B. N. Harlow; Dr. Glennan and General Persons; Ambassador Visutr Arthayukti (from Thailand) and W. T. Buchanan; T. E. Stephens; Judge Thomas Yager (Superior Court, Los Angeles) and T. E. Stephens; J. C. Hagerty; General Persons. Lunch. Afternoon appointments with G. Gray; D. W. Kendall; M. C. Moos; D. Paarlberg; T. E. Stephens. Practices golf on south lawn. Off-the-record appointment with Republican senators and congressmen.

2   Washington. Morning appointments with General Persons and B. N. Harlow; W. J. Hopkins; General Persons; R. E. Merriam; Legislative Leaders; R. J. Saulnier; Dr. J. A. Kessler (Massachusetts Institute of Technology), J. R. Killian, and J. C. Hagerty; J. R. Killian; W. J. Hopkins; T. E. Stephens and M. C. Moos; Ambassador Robert Silvercruys (from Belgium) and W. T. Buchanan; D. Thomas; J. C. Hagerty.

3   Washington. Morning appointments with T. E. Stephens; B. S. Adkins; U.S. Ambassador Briggs; pre-news briefing; news conference; J. C. Hagerty; J. R. Killian and Dr. Jerome B. Wiesner (off the record); J. C. Hagerty. Lunch. To Burning Tree Country Club for golf with Colonel Belshe, General Musgrave, and J. Shay. Evening appointment with T. E. Stephens.

4   Washington. [Page missing.] Receives business magazine editors, followed by late morning appointments with D. W. Kendall; M. C. Moos; Major J. S. D. Eisenhower. Off-the-record lunch with Francis de Guingand (former Chief of Staff for Field Marshal Montgomery) (off the record). Afternoon appointments with General Persons; J. C. Hagerty and Major J. S. D. Eisenhower. Visits General Twining and D. McKay at Walter Reed Hospital. Practices golf on south lawn.

5   Washington. Morning appointments with General Persons; D. W. Kendall; General Goodpaster; Dr. M. S. Eisenhower; Cabinet meeting; General Persons, Secretary Anderson, and Budget Director Stans; C. D. Dillon and Major J. S. D. Eisenhower; M. C. Moos; T. E. Stephens; Major J. S. D. Eisenhower; W. J. Hopkins; R. E. Merriam; General Goodpaster and Major J. S. D. Eisenhower; L. Erhard (Minister of Economics, Germany), Franz Krapf (Charge d'affaires), G. Schaare, R. Murphy, and Major J. S. D.

Eisenhower; G. D. Morgan and General Good-paster; G. D. Morgan. Lunch. Airborne for Gettysburg farm. To Gettysburg Country Club for golf with General Nevins.

6   Gettysburg. To Gettysburg Country Club for golf with General Nevins. Tours Brannum farm with General Nevins and R. S. Hartley. To skeet range. Hosts picnic with Mrs. Eisenhower for White House Mansion employees and Secret Service personnel.

7   Gettysburg. Attends services at Presbyterian Church of Gettysburg. To Harpers Ferry and Charlestown, West Virginia, with Mrs. Eisenhower. To Purcellville, Virginia, with Mrs. Eisenhower. Visits Holiday Hill Farm, residence of Colonel and Mrs. Moore. Returns to Washington.

8   Washington. Morning appointments with M. C. Moos; General Persons; T. E. Stephens; General Goodpaster; Major J. S. D. Eisenhower; General Goodpaster and Major J. S. D. Eisenhower; G. Gray, J. R. Killian, General Goodpaster, and Major J. S. D. Eisenhower (off the record); C. D. Dillon, A. W. Dulles, Secretary Gates, J. R. Killian, J. A. McCone, G. Gray, P. J. Farley, Generals Persons and Goodpaster, and Major J. S. D. Eisenhower (off the record); General Persons; Secretary Benson and D. Paarlberg; Generals Bragdon and Persons. Witnesses swearing-in of T. S. Gates as Deputy Secretary of Defense, followed by late morning appointments with T. S. Gates, Fred A. Bantz, and Cecil Milne; Generals Bragdon and Persons; G. Gray; M. C. Moos; T. E. Stephens; Major J. S. D. Eisenhower. Lunch. Afternoon appointments with T. E. Stephens; General Persons; Secretary Mitchell, General Persons, G. D. Morgan, and E. A. McCabe; M. C. Moos; T. E. Stephens; Major J. S. D. Eisenhower. Practices golf on south lawn. Addresses testimonial dinner honoring congressional Republicans.

9   Washington. Morning appointments with R. K. Gray; W. J. Hopkins; General Persons, B. N. Harlow, R. E. Merriam, and J. Z. Anderson; Legislative Leaders. Witnesses swearing-in ceremony for George M. Johnson as Civil Rights Commissioner. Appoint-

ments with J. A. McCone and General Persons; M. C. Moos and General Goodpaster; General Goodpaster. Addresses delegates of Civil Rights State Advisory Committee. Lunch. Receives first letter sent by missile mail from Noble Upperman (mail carrier). Afternoon appointments with General Norstad and Major J. S. D. Eisenhower (off the record); C. D. Dillon and Generals Persons and Goodpaster; Major J. S. D. Eisenhower; Vice-President Nixon, C. D. Dillon, Secretaries McElroy and Gates, G. Gray, J. R. Killian, Generals Lemnitzer, Goodpaster, Persons, and White, Admiral Burke, W. M. Holaday, Budget Director Stans, A. G. Waggoner, and J. W. Klotz; Secretaries McElroy and Gates, Admiral Burke, and Generals Lemnitzer, White, and Persons; Secretaries McElroy and Gates; General Persons. Airborne for Atlantic City, New Jersey. Attends reception hosted by Dr. Louis Orr. Greets American Medical Association Science Award Winners. Addresses American Medical Association convention. Returns to Washington.

10   Washington. Morning appointments with General Persons and G. D. Morgan; G. D. Morgan; D. W. Kendall; T. E. Stephens; Major J. S. D. Eisenhower; General Goodpaster; M. C. Moos; T. E. Stephens; J. C. Hagerty; General Goodpaster; C. D. Dillon and General Goodpaster; European Economic Community leaders, C. D. Dillon, U.S. Ambassador Butterworth, W. T. Buchanan, and General Goodpaster; D. W. Kendall; Major J. S. D. Eisenhower. Lunch. Afternoon appointments with barber; T. E. Stephens; B. N. Harlow; W. J. Hopkins; General Persons; Budget Director Stans, General Persons, B. N. Harlow, and R. C. Siciliano. To Burning Tree Country Club for golf with J. E. Shea and J. E. McClure.

11   Washington. Breakfast meeting with Vice-President Nixon. Morning appointments with Vice-President Nixon; General Persons; Major J. S. D. Eisenhower; Congressman Wainwright and B. N. Harlow (off the record); General Goodpaster; Secretary Flemming; Ambassador Ali H. Sulaiman (from Iraq) and W. T. Buchanan; T. E. Stephens; Major J. S. D. Eisenhower; General Goodpaster. Records Fourth of July message for Armed Forces and Voice of America.

Lunch. Afternoon appointments with J. Z. Anderson; General Persons; H. R. McPhee; General Persons and R. E. Merriam; M. C. Moos.

12   Washington. Breakfast meeting with F. J. Donohue, W. A. Ruschmeyer, and Colonel Schulz (off the record). Morning appointments with R. C. Siciliano; General Persons; Governor Rockefeller; G. Gray, B. N. Harlow, and Generals Persons and Goodpaster; General Persons. Witnesses swearing-in of C. D. Dillon as Under Secretary of State, followed by appointments with M. C. Moos, J. C. Hagerty, and General Persons; R. E. Merriam; C. D. Dillon, L. A. Hoegh, General Persons, D. Paarlberg, and P. E. Areeda (off the record); C. D. Dillon (off the record); C. D. Dillon, Secretary Flemming, A. Kimball, Budget Director Stans, and R. E. Merriam (off the record); R. E. Merriam; M. C. Moos; General Goodpaster; W. J. Hopkins. Addresses Foreign Service Institute Senior Officers graduation. Lunch. Afternoon appointment with Major J. S. D. Eisenhower. Airborne for Gettysburg farm. To Gettysburg Country Club for golf with General Nevins.

13   Gettysburg. To Gettysburg Country Club for golf with General Nevins and R. Sleichter. Inspects cattle with R. S. Hartley. Walks to duck pond. Shoots skeet with General Nevins.

14   Gettysburg. Attends services with Mrs. Eisenhower at Presbyterian Church of Gettysburg. To Gettysburg Country Club for golf with General Nevins and R. Sleichter. Returns to Washington.

15   Washington. Morning appointments with T. E. Stephens; Major J. S. D. Eisenhower; Major J. S. D. Eisenhower and G. V. Allen. Receives American Guides to American Exposition in Moscow, followed by appointments with Senator Morton, General Persons, and D. W. Kendall; Clark Kerr (President, University of California) and R. E. Merriam (off the record); Congressman Cederberg, Arnold T. Olson (President, Evangelical Free Church), and J. Z. Anderson; B. N. Harlow, D. W. Kendall, and General Persons; L. A. Minnich; Fulbright Scholarships board; C. D. Dillon and General Goodpaster (off the record); C. D. Dillon, W. Macomber, B. N. Har-

low, and Generals Persons and Goodpaster (off the record); C. D. Dillon, Budget Director Stans, and T. G. Upton (off the record). Lunch. Afternoon appointments with T. E. Stephens. Practices golf on south lawn. Appointments with D. W. Kendall and B. N. Harlow; General Goodpaster; Major J. S. D. Eisenhower. Visits residence of Major J. S. D. Eisenhower with Mrs. Eisenhower.

16   Washington. Morning appointments with General Persons and B. N. Harlow; General Goodpaster; Legislative Leaders; T. E. Stephens; General Persons; R. E. Merriam; Dr. Murphy; Federico Bigi (Secretary of State, San Marino), Pietro Giancecchi (Minister of Public Works, San Marino), Ivan B. White (Assistant Secretary of State, San Marino), and Wells Stabler (interpreter); General Goodpaster; T. E. Stephens; General Goodpaster. Addresses opening of National 4-H Club Center. Lunch. To Burning Tree Country Club for golf with Senators Lausche and Bush and Colonel Belshe.

17   Washington. Breakfast meeting with Eugene Black (President, International Bank for Reconstruction and Development). Morning appointments with C. D. Dillon, Secretary McElroy, General Goodpaster, and G. Gray; C. D. Dillon; J. C. Hagerty and General Goodpaster; pre-news briefing; news conference; J. C. Hagerty and General Goodpaster; Franz C. Koenig (Archbishop, Vienna), Ambassador Platzer, Leopold Ungar, and W. T. Buchanan; U. E. Baughman; T. E. Stephens; Governor Muñoz-Marin and G. D. Morgan; General Goodpaster; Reverend Good and family (Honolulu), Paul F. Schench, and J. Z. Anderson; General Goodpaster. Lunch. Afternoon appointments with Captain Aurand; W. J. Hopkins; D. W. Kendall; Major J. S. D. Eisenhower; General Persons; T. E. Stephens; Major J. S. D. Eisenhower; T. E. Stephens; General Persons. Practices golf on south lawn.

18   Washington. Morning appointments with A. Nielsen; General Goodpaster; U.S. Ambassador Ellsworth Bunker (to India and Nepal); T. E. Stephens; National Security Council session; C. D. Dillon and General Goodpaster; G. Gray; Pinin Farina (Turin,

Italy), R. C. Siciliano, and Carlo Piccoli (interpreter) (off the record); J. R. Killian, G. Gray, Dr. H. Brooks, and Major J. S. D. Eisenhower. Off-the-record lunch with K. C. Royall. Afternoon appointments with K. C. Royall (off the record); T. E. Stephens; J. C. Hagerty; M. C. Moos; Walter Nelson (President, Mortgage Bankers Association), A. Nielsen, and Sam Neal. To Burning Tree Country Club for golf with Colonel Belshe. Addresses dinner celebrating Federal Housing Administration twenty-fifth anniversary.

19   Washington. Morning appointments with General Persons; J. C. Hagerty; G. D. Morgan; D. W. Kendall; General Goodpaster; General Persons; J. C. Hagerty; Major J. S. D. Eisenhower; Secretary Strauss; General Persons; General Goodpaster. Airborne for Gettysburg farm. Tours farm with A. Nielsen and General Nevins. To Gettysburg Country Club for golf with G. E. Allen and General Nevins.

20   Gettysburg. To Gettysburg Country Club for golf with G. E. Allen and General Nevins. To Thurmont, Maryland, with G. E. Allen to visit residence of F. Akers. Fishes. Dinner with Mrs. Eisenhower, G. E. Allen, General and Mrs. Nevins, Major and Mrs. J. S. D. Eisenhower, B. A. Eisenhower, and M. J. Eisenhower.

21   Gettysburg. Attends services with General Nevins and G. E. Allen at Presbyterian Church of Gettysburg. To Gettysburg Country Club for golf with G. E. Allen, General Nevins, and R. Sleichter. Visits residence of Major J. S. D. Eisenhower. Returns to Washington.

22   Washington. Breakfast meeting with Secretary Herter and C. D. Dillon. Morning appointments with Cabinet Committee on Price Stability; General Persons; G. Gray; W. J. Hopkins; D. Anderson, Hamilton F. Armstrong (Editor, *Foreign Affairs*), A. F. Burns, General Cutler, Dr. Colgate Darden (President, University of Virginia), Colonel Draper, G. McGhee, Admiral Radford, Richard Sentner (Executive Vice-President, U.S. Steel), Dr. Arthur Smithies (Harvard University), and John Vorys (off the record); A. F. Burns; T. E. Stephens; General

Persons and G. D. Morgan; group of governors; T. E. Stephens. Lunch. Afternoon appointments with Cabinet committee; U.S. Ambassador Lodge. Practices golf on south lawn. Evening appointments with Generals Goodpaster; General Cutler.

23   Washington. Morning appointments with General Persons; T. E. Stephens; General Persons and G. D. Morgan; D. W. Kendall; General Persons, R. E. Merriam, and General Goodpaster; R. E. Merriam and General Goodpaster; D. Paarlberg and P. E. Areeda; W. J. Hopkins; W. M. Canaday; M. C. Moos; Secretary Gates, J. A. McCone, J. R. Killian, G. Gray, Drs. York and Kistiakowsky, and General Goodpaster (off the record); M. C. Moos and Major J. S. D. Eisenhower; Major J. S. D. Eisenhower; AMVETS leaders, E. D. Chesney, and Major J. S. D. Eisenhower. Receives AMVETS Memorial Scholarship Winners. Lunch. To Burning Tree Country Club for golf with Colonel Belshe. Off-the-record appointment with Colonel and Mrs. Stack.

24   Washington. Morning appointments with Major J. S. D. Eisenhower; R. E. Merriam; General Persons; G. Gray, Secretary McElroy, General Loper, and J. A. McCone (off the record); J. A. McCone; U.S. Ambassador Cabot; T. E. Stephens and J. Rowley; Colonel Draper; General Goodpaster; General Persons and D. W. Kendall; General Persons, D. W. Kendall, B. N. Harlow, and General Goodpaster; Generals Goodpaster and Persons and B. N. Harlow; General Persons; T. E. Stephens; Congressman Robison and son and J. Z. Anderson; H. M. Alcorn; Zelma George, Congresswoman Bolton, and J. Z. Anderson; Major J. S. D. Eisenhower; General Persons and G. D. Morgan. Lunch. Afternoon appointments with M. C. Moos; T. E. Stephens; General Persons; Secretary Anderson, J. B. Baird, and General Persons; General Persons; General Goodpaster; T. E. Stephens. Practices golf on south lawn. Off-the-record evening appointment with B. N. Harlow and Senators Johnson, Fulbright, Russell, and Gray.

25   Washington. Morning appointments with General Persons; General Goodpaster; Secretary Herter; Na-

tional Security Council session; G. Gray, Secretaries Herter, McElroy, and Gates, Admiral Burke, A. W. Dulles, Generals Lemnitzer, White, Pate, and Goodpaster, and J. Critchfield (off the record); W. J. Hopkins; General Persons. Awards Major's Oak Leaf Cluster to Captain Crittenberger, followed by appointments with General Persons, G. D. Morgan, and H. R. McPhee; H. R. McPhee; D. W. Kendall; U. S. Ambassador Reid (to Israel); General Persons; Major J. S. D. Eisenhower. Lunch. To Burning Tree Country Club for golf with Congressmen Budge and Westland and Colonel Belshe.

26 Washington. To MATS terminal en route to Saint Hubert, Canada. Greeted by Queen Elizabeth, Prince Philip, and Prime Minister and Mrs. Diefenbaker. Addresses dedication ceremony for Saint Lawrence Seaway. Hosts luncheon aboard British royal yacht. Returns to Washington.

27 Washington. To Burning Tree Country Club for golf with G. E. Allen, Colonel Belshe, and J. E. Lemon.

28 Washington. Attends services with Mrs. Eisenhower at National Presbyterian Church. To Burning Tree Country Club for bridge with G. E. Allen, J. E. Lemon, and Colonel Belshe. Practices golf.

29 Washington. Morning appointments with T. E. Stephens; Major J. S. D. Eisenhower; M. J. McCaffree; General Persons and T. E. Stephens; D. W. Kendall; General Persons; T. E. Stephens; General Goodpaster; J. R. Killian; W. S. Robertson; R. W. Woodruff; Secretary Flemming; W. J. Hopkins; Mr. and Mrs. H. A. Mark and niece and T. E. Stephens. Receives elephant tusk. Airborne for New York City. Attends Soviet Exhibition of Science, Technology, and Culture. Returns to Washington. Hosts off-the-record dinner with Mrs. Eisenhower.

30 Washington. Morning appointments with General Persons and B. N. Harlow; General Persons; Legislative Leaders; General Persons; General Goodpaster; Dr. Glennan, J. R. Killian, F. W. Phillips, and General Goodpaster; Mrs. Eisenhower; T. E. Stephens. Awards Distinguished Service Medal to General Taylor, followed by appointments with

D. W. Kendall and H. R. McPhee; J. J. Jackson, Mrs. Eisenhower, and Colonel Schulz to sign personal papers (off the record). Witnesses swearing-in ceremony for Dr. J. T. Rettaliato and Dr. W. Burden as National Aeronautics Space Council members. Appointments with Secretary McElroy and General Goodpaster. Lunch. Afternoon appointments with Major J. S. D. Eisenhower; T. E. Stephens; S. P. Skouras (off the record); National Aeronautics and Space Council; D. W. Kendall; General Persons and R. E. Merriam; General Persons; M. C. Moos.

July 1   Washington. Morning appointments with Major J. S. D. Eisenhower; G. Gray; Secretary Mitchell and General Persons; pre-news briefing; news conference; Congressman Becker and family; Governor Ahmed Bargach (Casablanca), Ambassador Mehdi Ben Aboud (from Morocco), J. C. Satterthwaite, and C. Nowfel; Budget Director Stans, General Bragdon, and G. D. Morgan; T. E. Stephens; Secretary Herter; Frol R. Kozlov (First Deputy Premier, U.S.S.R.), Ambassador Menshikov, A. A. Soldatov (Ministry of Foreign Affairs, U.S.S.R.), V. N. Sukhadrov (interpreter), Secretary Herter, John McSweeney (Acting Director of Soviet Union Affairs, State Department), and Alexander Akalovsky (interpreter); Secretary Herter. Lunch. To Burning Tree Country Club for golf with J. E. McClure. Evening appointments with D. W. Kendall; Major J. S. D. Eisenhower. Hosts reception with Mrs. Eisenhower for White House officials to celebrate 43rd wedding anniversary.

2   Washington. Morning appointments with T. E. Stephens; Major J. S. D. Eisenhower; General Goodpaster; U.S. Ambassador Bernard A. Gufler (to Ceylon); Secretaries Herter, McElroy, and Gates, Admiral Radford, G. Gray, G. Smith, and General Goodpaster; Secretary Herter and General Goodpaster; L. Wright and D. W. Kendall; General Persons; Senator Javits and E. A. McCabe; Congressman Scott, Secretary Seaton, General McNamara (Quartermaster General), Colonel J. S. Cook, Eugene S. Cowen, E. A. McCabe, General Persons, and T. E. Stephens; General Persons; Congressman Mason, Budget Di-

rector Stans, R. J. Saulnier, D. W. Kendall, and General Persons to discuss housing; Major J. S. D. Eisenhower; G. D. Morgan; Major J. S. D. Eisenhower. Lunch. Afternoon appointments with U. E. Baughman; W. J. Hopkins; Major J. S. D. Eisenhower. Airborne for Camp David, Maryland. To Gettysburg Country Club for golf with Major J. S. D. Eisenhower. Visits residence of Major J. S. D. Eisenhower.

3   Camp David, Maryland. Airborne for Gettysburg. To Gettysburg Country Club for golf with G. E. Allen, W. E. Robinson, General Snyder, and R. Sleichter. Tours farm. Airborne for Camp David.

4   Camp David, Maryland. Returns to Washington. Addresses ceremonies at United States Capitol. Airborne for Gettysburg. To Gettysburg Country Club for golf with W. E. Robinson, Major J. S. D. Eisenhower, and R. Sleichter. Airborne for Camp David.

5   Camp David, Maryland. Airborne for Gettysburg. To Gettysburg Country Club for golf with G. E. Allen. Airborne for Camp David. Views movie "These Thousand Hills" with Mrs. Eisenhower.

6   Camp David, Maryland. Returns to Washington. Morning appointments with W. J. Hopkins; General Persons; Attorney General Rogers and General Persons; J. C. Hagerty; R. K. Gray; General Persons and D. W. Kendall; G. Gray; T. E. Stephens; U.S. Ambassador John H. Morrow (to New Guinea); General Goodpaster; D. W. Kendall and H. R. McPhee; D. W. Kendall. Lunch. Afternoon appointments with Major J. S. D. Eisenhower; Dr. M. S. Eisenhower; Major J. S. D. Eisenhower. Practices golf on south lawn.

7   Washington. Morning appointments with General Persons and B. N. Harlow; Legislative Leaders; General Persons, G. D. Morgan, D. W. Kendall, R. J. Saulnier, and H. R. McPhee; A. W. Dulles, R. Bissell, and General Goodpaster (off the record); A. W. Dulles (off the record); Governor Quinn and Secretary Seaton; J. A. McCone, Secretary Gates, G. D. Morgan, B. N. Harlow, and Generals Loper, Starbird, and Goodpaster; J. A. McCone and Generals

Starbird and Goodpaster; G. Gray and B. N. Harlow; Major J. S. D. Eisenhower. Lunch. Afternoon appointments with Generals Swing, Heaton, and Snyder, and D. W. Kendall; General Swing. To Burning Tree Country Club for golf with J. Black, F. C. Akers, and J. E. Shea.

8   Washington. Morning appointments with General Persons; General Goodpaster; W. J. Hopkins; Secretary Herter, A. W. Dulles, R. Bissell, and General Goodpaster (off the record); Secretary Herter; Congressmen Utt and Wilson; Major J. S. D. Eisenhower; T. E. Stephens; General Persons and J. C. Hagerty; pre-news briefing; news conference; J. C. Hagerty; D. W. Kendall; Rotary Club leaders and T. E. Stephens; L. D. Das (President, Newspaper Editors of India) and J. C. Hagerty (off the record); Major J. S. D. Eisenhower; E. Hastings and Colonel Schulz. Lunch. Afternoon appointments with General Goodpaster. Makes recording for Boy Scouts, followed by appointments with General Persons and T. E. Stephens; T. E. Stephens; D. W. Kendall and R. E. Merriam. Practices golf on south lawn.

9   Washington. Morning appointments with General Persons; National Security Council session; Secretary Herter and D. W. Kendall; Secretary Herter and General Goodpaster; T. E. Stephens; General Goodpaster; Mr. and Mrs. L. Russell McKee. Receives Mass Transportation Survey Report. Lunch. To Burning Tree Country Club for golf with Congressmen Budge and Halleck and Colonel Belshe.

10   Washington. Morning appointments with General Persons; Senator Morton, General Persons, and D. W. Kendall; D. W. Kendall; J. C. Hagerty; T. E. Stephens; Colonel Schulz; Secretary Benson (off the record); D. W. Kendall; Young Republican National Federation leaders and D. W. Kendall; General Gruenther; Junior Red Cross Delegates; T. E. Stephens; Congressman Roosevelt and children; General Goodpaster and H. R. McPhee; Major J. S. D. Eisenhower; General Goodpaster. Lunch. Evening appointment with Secretary Herter, C. D. Dillon, L. T. Merchant, R. Murphy, and General Goodpaster.

11   Washington. To Burning Tree Country Club for golf with Congressmen Halleck and Budge and Colonel Belshe.

12   Washington. Attends services at National Presbyterian Church. To Burning Tree Country Club for golf with Major J. S. D. Eisenhower and Colonel Belshe.

13   Washington. Morning appointments with General Persons; Secretary Mitchell, General Persons, D. Paarlberg, D. W. Kendall, and J. C. Hagerty; General Goodpaster; Vice-President Nixon; Vice-President Nixon and General Persons; Vice-President Nixon; J. C. Hagerty; Vice-President Nixon and J. C. Hagerty; Secretary Gates, J. A. McCone, J. R. Killian, Dr. Kistiakowsky, Generals Luedecke, Loper, Starbird, and Goodpaster, and Admirals Burke and Parker (off the record); Major J. S. D. Eisenhower; General Goodpaster; G. Gray and T. E. Stephens; G. Gray; Secretary Anderson, W. M. Martin, J. B. Baird, R. J. Saulnier, and D. Paarlberg; J. C. Hagerty; G. D. Morgan; Ambassador Arturo Ramirez Pinto (from Guatemala) and W. T. Buchanan; General Persons and R. E. Merriam; Major J. S. D. Eisenhower. Lunch. Afternoon appointments with D. W. Kendall; W. J. Hopkins; T. E. Stephens; J. C. Hagerty; Generals Persons and Goodpaster; General Goodpaster; T. E. Stephens; Major J. S. D. Eisenhower; M. C. Moos; T. E. Stephens. Practices golf.

14   Washington. Morning appointments with General Persons, B. N. Harlow, and Budget Director Stans; Senator Dirksen; Legislative Leaders; J. R. Killian; Secretary Flemming and R. C. Siciliano (off the record); R. C. Siciliano (off the record); Admiral Radford and General Goodpaster; Major J. S. D. Eisenhower. Lunch. Afternoon appointments with General Persons; T. E. Stephens; G. D. Morgan and J. C. Hagerty; G. D. Morgan and J. C. Hagerty; Generals Persons and Goodpaster; General Goodpaster.

15   Washington. Morning appointments with T. E. Stephens; General Goodpaster; General Persons; Secretary Mitchell, R. J. Saulnier, and G. D. Morgan; Admiral Strauss (off the record); D. W. Kendall; J. C.

Hagerty; pre-news briefing; news conference; J. C. Hagerty. Witnesses swearing-in ceremony for Dr. Kistiakowsky as Special Assistant to the President. Appointments with G. Gray; G. Gray and General Goodpaster; R. E. Merriam and General Goodpaster; R. E. Merriam; Colonel Draper; Drs. Glennan and Dryden and General Goodpaster. Lunch. Afternoon appointments with T. E. Stephens; Major J. S. D. Eisenhower; D. W. Kendall and H. R. McPhee. Practices golf on south lawn.

16   Washington. Morning appointments with General Persons; T. E. Stephens; C. D. Dillon and General Goodpaster; National Security Council session; Attorney General Rogers to discuss Lincoln papers; C. D. Dillon; E. D. Slater and J. C. Hagerty. Addresses American Field Service International Scholarship Students. Appointments with E. D. Slater and J. C. Hagerty; E. D. Slater; Secretary Anderson. Lunch. To Burning Tree Country Club for golf with E. D. Slater, J. E. McClure, and Congressman Arends. Evening appointments with E. D. Slater; Major J. S. D. Eisenhower; D. W. Kendall; Major J. S. D. Eisenhower.

17   Washington. Morning appointments with Major J. S. D. Eisenhower; General Persons; U.S. Ambassador Lodge (off the record); Cabinet meeting; C. D. Dillon, Secretary McElroy, and General Goodpaster (off the record); C. D. Dillon and General Goodpaster (off the record); Secretary Mitchell, General Persons, G. D. Morgan; J. A. McCone and General Goodpaster; D. W. Kendall; F. G. Jameson and B. N. Harlow; Major J. S. D. Eisenhower; T. E. Stephens; General Persons. To Burning Tree Country Club for golf with Congressman Arends, J. E. McClure, and J. E. Shea. Late afternoon appointments with General Persons; J. C. Hagerty; General Persons.

18   Washington. Morning appointments with General Goodpaster; W. J. Hopkins; Major J. S. D. Eisenhower; D. W. Kendall. Practices golf on south lawn.

19   Washington. Visits residence of Dr. M. S. Eisenhower in Baltimore, Maryland.

20   Washington. Morning appointments with General Persons; Major J. S. D. Eisenhower; General Goodpaster; G. Gray; A. W. Dulles, J. R. Killian, Secretary McElroy, Dr. Kistiakowsky, R. Bissell, and Generals White, Cabell, and Goodpaster (off the record); R. J. Saulnier, Secretary Mitchell, D. Paarlberg, and General Persons; Ambassador Luis F. Thomen (from Dominican Republic) and W. T. Buchanan; Generals Boye and Bragdon (off the record); General Goodpaster; General Persons. Lunch. Practices golf on south lawn. Afternoon appointments with Major J. S. D. Eisenhower; General Snyder. Views movie. Hosts off-the-record stag dinner.

21   Washington. Morning appointments with General Persons, G. D. Morgan, B. N. Harlow, E. A. McCabe, Budget Director Stans, and R. E. Merriam; General Persons; F. H. Mueller and General Persons; Legislative Leaders; Secretary Mitchell; W. J. Hopkins; D. W. Kendall; T. E. Stephens; General Goodpaster; State Winners of "My True Security-The American Way" program; A. B. Kline and D. Paarlberg; G. Gray and General Goodpaster; G. Gray; Ambassador Osman El Hadari (from Sudan) and W. T. Buchanan; General Persons and R. E. Merriam. Lunch. Afternoon appointments with C. D. Dillon and General Goodpaster (off the record). To Burning Tree Country Club for golf with F. Ewing, J. E. Lemon, and Colonel Belshe. Appointments with Ambassador Menshikov, C. D. Dillon, and R. Murphy (off the record); C. D. Dillon and General Goodpaster (off the record).

22   Washington. Morning appointments with T. E. Stephens; J. C. Hagerty; General Persons; Postmaster General Summerfield; J. C. Hagerty; pre-news briefing; news conference; J. C. Hagerty; Edward F. Wilson (Assistant Secretary, Health, Education, and Welfare) and Adin Hister (President, Future Farmers of America); Future Farmers of America conference delegates; Major J. S. D. Eisenhower; Vice-President Nixon, C. D. Dillon, and Major J. S. D. Eisenhower. Lunch. Afternoon appointments with J. C. Hagerty; D. Paarlberg and P. E. Areeda to discuss tuna imports; General Goodpaster; Captain Aurand; General Persons. Practices golf on south lawn.

Appointments with Major J. S. D. Eisenhower; C. D. Dillon, R. Murphy, and General Goodpaster (off the record); General Goodpaster.

23 Washington. Morning appointments with R. E. Merriam; General Goodpaster and Major J. S. D. Eisenhower; Postmaster General Summerfield; General Goodpaster; Generals Persons and Goodpaster; National Security Council session; G. Gray and S. E. Gleason; C. D. Dillon, Secretary Gates, J. A. McCone, A. W. Dulles, Dr. Kistiakowsky, G. Gray, P. J. Farley, S. Keeney, Major J. S. D. Eisenhower, and Generals Starbird, Loper, and Goodpaster (off the record); T. E. Stephens and B. N. Harlow; T. E. Stephens; D. W. Kendall; Ambassador Walther M. Salles (from Brazil) and W. T. Buchanan; U.S. Ambassador Rountree (to Pakistan); R. E. Merriam. Lunch. Afternoon appointments with General Cutler; T. E. Stephens; J. C. Hagerty. To Burning Tree Country Club for golf with G. E. Allen and Colonel Belshe.

24 Washington. Morning appointments with Colonels V. D. Olson and V. A. Armstrong (off the record); General Goodpaster; General Persons and D. W. Kendall; Major J. S. D. Eisenhower; J. C. Hagerty; General Persons and B. N. Harlow; General Goodpaster. To Gettysburg farm. To Gettysburg Country Club for golf with G. E. Allen.

25 Gettysburg. To Gettysburg Country Club for golf with G. E. Allen. Tours barn and inspects cattle with General Nevins. Views movie "It Happened to Jane" with Mrs. Eisenhower, Mr. and Mrs. G. E. Allen, and General and Mrs. Snyder.

26 Gettysburg. Attends services at Presbyterian Church of Gettysburg with G. E. Allen. To Gettysburg Country Club for golf with G. E. Allen and R. Sleichter. Visits with Colonel and Mrs. Thompson.

27 Gettysburg. Returns to Washington. Morning appointments with J. C. Hagerty; General Persons; General Goodpaster; Secretary Mitchell, General Persons, and G. D. Morgan; G. Gray and R. K. Gray; G. Gray, C. Haskins, and E. A. McCabe; Secretary Flemming, E. L. Richardson, Budget Director Stans,

G. D. Morgan, B. N. Harlow, and R. E. Merriam (off the record); Generals Twining and Goodpaster; R. J. Saulnier. Lunch. Afternoon appointments with C. D. Dillon and General Goodpaster; Budget Director Stans, E. Staats, General Persons, and R. E. Merriam; J. C. Hagerty; T. E. Stephens. Practices golf on south lawn. Hosts off-the-record stag dinner.

28 Washington. Morning appointments with General Persons; General Persons, Secretary Flemming, E. L. Richardson, B. N. Harlow, E. A. McCabe, R. E. Merriam, and G. D. Morgan; Legislative Leaders; C. D. Dillon; G. D. Morgan; E. Johnston; M. C. Moos; General Goodpaster. Lunch. Afternoon appointments with T. E. Stephens; General Goodpaster; T. E. Stephens; General Goodpaster; D. W. Kendall; G. D. Morgan and H. R. McPhee; C. Vardaman and T. E. Stephens; W. J. Hopkins; Major J. S. D. Eisenhower; B. N. Harlow. Practices golf on south lawn.

29 Washington. Breakfast meeting with SOS Club. Morning appointments with Secretary Mitchell, R. J. Saulnier, and General Persons; J. C. Hagerty; G. D. Morgan and J. C. Hagerty; pre-news briefing; news conference; J. C. Hagerty and B. N. Harlow; General Persons, G. D. Morgan, and R. E. Merriam; Tennessee Valley Authority directors, General Persons, G. D. Morgan, and R. E. Merriam. Presents Robert L. Hague Maritime Award to Malcolm P. McLean. Late morning appointments with C. D. Dillon, C. A. Coolidge, and General Goodpaster; C. D. Dillon and General Goodpaster. Lunch. Afternoon appointments with General Persons; General Goodpaster; General Persons; General Goodpaster; T. E. Stephens; General Goodpaster; General Persons; M. C. Moos. Practices golf on south lawn.

30 Washington. Morning appointments with General Goodpaster; Major J. S. D. Eisenhower; D. Paarlberg; Senator Cooper, Congressmen Baker and Reece, and R. E. Merriam; T. E. Stephens; National Security Council session; C. D. Dillon and Major J. S. D. Eisenhower; C. D. Dillon, Secretary Flemming, Budget Director Stans, General Persons, and R. E. Merriam to discuss State Department reorganization (off the record); General Persons; Secretary

Flemming and General Persons; D. W. Kendall; National Tire Dealers and Retreaders Association leaders and D. W. Kendall; D. W. Kendall; Jacques de Dixmude (Chairman, Belgian Chiefs of Staff) and Colonel Schulz (off the record); Major Crittenberger and family (off the record); General Goodpaster; General Persons; Major J. S. D. Eisenhower. Lunch. Afternoon appointments with W. J. Hopkins; J. C. Hagerty; General Goodpaster; General Persons, B. N. Harlow, and D. Paarlberg; T. E. Stephens; General Persons. Practices golf on south lawn.

31 Washington. Off-the-record breakfast meeting with Senator Bridges. Morning appointments with Colonel Draper; G. D. Morgan, D. W. Kendall, and R. E. Merriam; D. W. Kendall; Cabinet meeting; Secretary Anderson, R. J. Saulnier, Budget Director Stans, G. D. Morgan, and R. E. Merriam (off the record); C. D. Dillon, Major J. S. D. Eisenhower, and D. W. Kendall; Governor Collins and Congressmen Cramer and Sikes; governors returning from trip to USSR; W. J. Hopkins; Utah Young Republican Club representatives; Secretary Benson; K. G. Harr. Makes film on Traffic Safety and Law Day. Lunch. Appointment with General Goodpaster and Major J. S. D. Eisenhower. Airborne for Gettysburg farm. To Gettysburg Country Club for golf with G. E. Allen.

August 1 Gettysburg. To Gettysburg Country Club for golf with G. E. Allen. Visits with J. E. Lemon. Late afternoon appointment with C. D. Dillon, R. Murphy, and J. C. Hagerty.

2 Gettysburg. Visits with General and Mrs. Gruenther. Returns to Washington.

3 Washington. Morning appointments with General Persons, B. N. Harlow, T. E. Stephens, and J. C. Hagerty; J. C. Hagerty; T. E. Stephens; Major J. S. D. Eisenhower; J. C. Hagerty; Major J. S. D. Eisenhower; R. Murphy, U.S. Ambassador Whitney, General Persons, and J. C. Hagerty; R. Murphy and U.S. Ambassador Whitney. Holds special news conference regarding exchange of visits with Chairman Nikita Khrushchev (U.S.S.R.); Attorney General

Rogers and General Persons; G. Gray; B. N. Harlow; General Persons. To Burning Tree Country Club for golf with U.S. Ambassador Whitney, C. V. McAdam, Sr., and C. V. McAdam, Jr. Evening appointments with T. E. Stephens; B. N. Harlow; Senator Johnson, Congressman Rayburn, Secretary Anderson, and B. N. Harlow (off the record).

4   Washington. Breakfast meeting with Senator Dirksen, Congressman Halleck, General Persons, and B. N. Harlow. Morning appointments with General Persons; Major J. S. D. Eisenhower; General Persons, J. C. Hagerty, and T. E. Stephens; T. E. Stephens and J. C. Hagerty; J. C. Hagerty; Secretaries McElroy and Franke and Major J. S. D. Eisenhower; Secretaries McElroy and Franke, General Persons, and Major J. S. D. Eisenhower; Secretary McElroy, General Persons, and Major J. S. D. Eisenhower; Secretary McElroy and Major J. S. D. Eisenhower; Dr. Kistiakowsky and Major J. S. D. Eisenhower; Ambassador Bonhomme and R. R. Rubottom; R. K. Gray; W. J. Hopkins; General Persons and J. C. Hagerty; Secretary Anderson and General Persons. Lunch. Afternoon appointments with Major J. S. D. Eisenhower; J. C. Hagerty; Lillian Dennison (retiring); General Persons and E. A. McCabe; D. W. Kendall; G. E. Allen. Practices golf on south lawn. Evening appointments with J. C. Hagerty; General Persons and B. N. Harlow; Congressmen Ford and Mahon and B. N. Harlow (off the record).

5   Washington. Hosts breakfast for Republican congressmen. Morning appointments with G. D. Morgan; Major J. S. D. Eisenhower; J. C. Hagerty; C. D. Dillon and Major J. S. D. Eisenhower; Secretary McElroy, R. Murphy, Generals Quesada and Twining, Admiral O'Beirne, Colonel Martin, G. Gray, and Major J. S. D. Eisenhower (off the record); J. C. Hagerty; Senator Allott and T. E. Stephens; T. E. Stephens. To Burning Tree Country Club for golf with Congressman Arends. Appointments with General Persons; Major J. S. D. Eisenhower; Vice-President Nixon, Dr. M. S. Eisenhower, General Persons, G. D. Morgan, T. E. Stephens, B. N. Harlow, D. W. Kendall, C. D. Dillon, Major J. S. D. Eisenhower, and J. C. Hagerty; General Persons and B. N. Harlow;

General Persons; Major J. S. D. Eisenhower; T. E. Stephens.

6 Washington. Morning appointments with B. N. Harlow; G. D. Morgan; G. D. Morgan, E. A. McCabe, and Colonel Schulz; General Persons; N. Cousins and Major J. S. D. Eisenhower (off the record); National Security Council; Secretary McElroy, General Twining, and Major J. S. D. Eisenhower; G. Gray, A. W. Dulles, R. Murphy, and Major J. S. D. Eisenhower; Secretary Mitchell and General Persons; Attorney General Rogers and General Persons; General Persons; General Persons and B. N. Harlow. Lunch. Afternoon appointments with Congressmen Mack, Cramer, Scherer, Baldwin, and Halleck, Attorney General Rogers, G. D. Morgan, B. N. Harlow, and R. E. Merriam to discuss TVA bill; Secretary Mitchell, General Persons, and E. A. McCabe. Practices golf on south lawn. Appointment with Secretary Herter and C. D. Dillon. Delivers radio and television address regarding labor unions and labor reform bill. Hosts off-the-record stag dinner.

7 Washington. Morning appointments with General Persons; W. J. Hopkins; General Persons; R. E. Merriam; U.S. Ambassador Lodge (off the record); Cabinet meeting; D. W. Kendall; Major J. S. D. Eisenhower; U.S. Ambassador Folger; Secretary Herter, C. D. Dillon, and Major J. S. D. Eisenhower; Secretary Flemming, General Persons, Budget Director Stans, E. L. Richardson, G. D. Morgan, D. W. Kendall, and R. E. Merriam (off the record); Governor and Mrs. Quinn and Secretary Seaton; Governor Quinn's assistants; W. J. Hopkins. Lunch. To Gettysburg farm. Inspects building with Chief West. To Gettysburg Country Club for golf with R. Sleichter.

8 Gettysburg. Visits residence of Major J. S. D. Eisenhower. Inspects show barn. Visits with W. E. Robinson, General and Mrs. Gruenther, G. E. and Mrs. Allen, and General and Mrs. Snyder.

9 Gettysburg. Tours farm with Mrs. G. E. Allen.

10 Gettysburg. To Gettysburg Country Club for golf with W. E. Robinson. Returns to Washington. Af-

ternoon appointments with General Persons; Major J. S. D. Eisenhower; C. D. Dillon and Major J. S. D. Eisenhower; Dennis Smeby (Annual Teenage Safe Driving Road-e-o contestant), Congressman Westland, and T. E. Stephens; Colonel Schulz and Captain Aurand. Witnesses swearing-in ceremony of F. H. Mueller as Secretary of Commerce. Afternoon appointment with J. C. Hagerty. Greets Annual Teenage Safe Driving Road-e-o contestants. Poses for photographs, followed by appointments with J. C. Hagerty; Lions Club International leaders, Congressman Laird, and Senator Dirksen. Hosts off-the-record stag dinner.

11 Washington. Morning appointments with General Persons and B. N. Harlow; Legislative Leaders; G. Gray; Secretary Flemming, General Persons, Budget Director Stans, E. L. Richardson, G. D. Morgan, B. N. Harlow, R. E. Merriam, and D. W. Kendall; D. W. Kendall; G. Gray; General Persons; C. D. Dillon and Major J. S. D. Eisenhower; U.S. Ambassador Langley and C. D. Dillon; General Decker and Major J. S. D. Eisenhower (off the record); W. J. Hopkins; T. E. Stephens; Postmaster General Summerfield; C. R. Larson, Postmaster General Summerfield, and J. C. Hagerty. Receives National Rural Letter Carriers Association members. Lunch. Afternoon appointments with General Persons and T. E. Stephens. Airborne for Gettysburg farm. To Gettysburg Country Club for golf with W. E. Robinson and General Nevins. Visits Nevins farm.

12 Gettysburg. Holds special news conference regarding upcoming visits with Chairman Khrushchev and Laos situation. To Gettysburg Country Club for golf with W. E. Robinson, W. A. Jones, and General Nevins.

13 Gettysburg. To Gettysburg Country Club for golf with W. E. Robinson, W. A. Jones, and R. Sleichter.

14 Gettysburg. To Gettysburg Country Club for golf with W. E. Robinson, W. A. Jones, C. Roberts, and General Nevins.

15 Gettysburg. Tours farm with A. Wyeth. Visits with W. E. Robinson, C. Roberts, and W. A. Jones.

16   Gettysburg. Attends services at Presbyterian Church of Gettysburg. Visits with A. Wyeth, General and Mrs. Nevins, C. Roberts, and W. E. Robinson.

17   Gettysburg. To Gettysburg Country Club for golf with D. D. Eisenhower II. Visits with U.S. Ambassador Whitney.

18   Gettysburg. Returns to Washington. Morning appointments with General Persons; P. G. Hoffman; Secretary Mitchell, General Persons, G. D. Morgan, and J. C. Hagerty; National Security Council session; General Persons; Governor Rockefeller and R. E. Merriam to discuss civil defense; Governor Rockefeller. Records message for United Community Campaigns of America. Lunch. Afternoon appointments with W. J. Hopkins; D. W. Kendall. Airborne for Gettysburg farm. To Gettysburg Country Club for golf with G. E. Allen and D. D. Eisenhower II.

19   Gettysburg. To Gettysburg Country Club for golf with G. E. Allen and D. D. Eisenhower II. Fishes at Akers farm.

20   Gettysburg. Surveys farm. Picks vegetables. To Gettysburg Country Club for golf with G. E. Allen.

21   Gettysburg. To Gettysburg Country Club for golf with G. E. Allen. Returns to Washington. Morning appointments with G. Gray; Secretary Herter, R. Murphy, L. T. Merchant, I. B. White, General Goodpaster, and Major J. S. D. Eisenhower; Ambassador Louis Scheyven (from Belgium) and R. Corrigan; Budget Director Stans, G. D. Morgan, R. J. Saulnier, R. E. Merriam, and D. W. Kendall (off the record); G. D. Morgan and D. W. Kendall (off the record); General Goodpaster; Ambassador George Macovescu (from Rumania) and C. E. Conger; D. W. Kendall. Signs proclamation admitting Hawaii into the Union. Appointments with Vice-President Nixon; Ambassador On Sein (from Burma) and R. Corrigan; Senator Wiley and E. A. McCabe; General Goodpaster. Airborne for Gettysburg farm. Visits residence of Major J. S. D. Eisenhower with Mrs. Eisenhower.

22   Gettysburg. To Gettysburg Country Club for golf with G. E. Allen. Shops in York, Pennsylvania. Tours with G. E. Allen and Generals Nevins and Snyder.

23   Gettysburg. To Gettysburg Country Club for golf with G. E. Allen. Attends services with Mrs. Eisenhower at Presbyterian Church of Gettysburg. Returns to Washington.

24   Washington. Morning appointments with General Persons; General Goodpaster; R. J. Saulnier; J. C. Hagerty; Major J. S. D. Eisenhower; Secretary Anderson, General Persons, and G. D. Morgan; General Persons; Generals Norstad and Goodpaster; Major J. S. D. Eisenhower; Secretary Flemming; D. W. Kendall; General Goodpaster. Lunch. Afternoon appointments with Secretary Herter and General Goodpaster; Secretary Herter, R. Murphy, L. T. Merchant, J. N. Irwin, U.S. Ambassador Lodge, C. D. Dillon, and General Goodpaster; General Goodpaster; Vice-President Nixon (off the record); General Goodpaster. Practices golf on south lawn. Appointment with Major J. S. D. Eisenhower.

25   Washington. Morning appointments with Major J. S. D. Eisenhower; General Persons and G. D. Morgan; C. D. Dillon, General Persons, G. D. Morgan, B. N. Harlow, and R. C. Siciliano; General Persons, C. D. Dillon, and B. N. Harlow; Legislative Leaders; General Persons; Attorney General Rogers; Admiral Strauss; pre-news briefing; news conference; General Persons, G. D. Morgan, and P. E. Areeda; General Persons and G. D. Morgan. Lunch. Afternoon appointments with Major J. S. D. Eisenhower; D. W. Kendall; Major J. S. D. Eisenhower; General Persons; General Persons and D. W. Kendall; Secretary Anderson and Generals Cutler and Persons; R. E. Merriam; R. E. Merriam and General Goodpaster; R. E. Merriam, D. W. Kendall, and General Goodpaster; R. E. Merriam and D. W. Kendall; R. E. Merriam. Practices golf on south lawn. Evening appointments with D. W. Kendall; Major J. S. D. Eisenhower.

26   Washington. To Andrews Air Force base en route to Bonn, Germany. Makes stopover in Newfoundland. Visits Officers Club. Receives coat of arms from city of Troisdorf.

27   Bonn, Germany. Morning appointments with German officials; Chancellor Adenauer. News confer-

ence. Attends luncheon in his honor, hosted by Chancellor Adenauer. Meets with Chancellor Adenauer. Airborne for London, England. Attends dinner at residence of U.S. Ambassador Whitney.

28 London, England. Airborne for Aberdeen, Scotland. Lunch at Balmoral Castle with Queen Elizabeth, Prince Philip, and royal family. Visits with royal family. Dinner at Balmoral Castle.

29 Aberdeen, Scotland. Airborne for Oxfordshire, England. Lunch at home of Prime Minister Macmillan. Appointment with Prime Minister Macmillan, Secretary Herter, and S. Lloyd.

30 Oxfordshire, England. Appointment with Prime Minister Macmillan, Secretary Herter, and S. Lloyd. Attends services at Ellesborough Church with Prime Minister Macmillan, U.S. Ambassador Whitney, and S. Lloyd. Meets with Prime Minister Macmillan, Secretary Herter, and S. Lloyd.

31 Oxfordshire, England. To London. Visits St. Paul's Cathedral. Attends luncheon at American Embassy Residence. Meets with Fernando M. Castiella (Foreign Minister, Spain), Secretary Herter, and U.S. Ambassador Lodge. Visits 10 Downing Street. Participates in informal television report with Prime Minister Macmillan. Attends dinner hosted by Prime Minister Macmillan.

September 1 London, England. Works at American Embassy. Hosts stag dinner for wartime associates.

2 London, England. Airborne for Paris, France. Lunch at Elysee Palace. Afternoon appointment with President de Gaulle (France) and French and U.S. officials. Meets Chiefs of Diplomatic Mission. Places wreath at Tomb of Unknown Soldier. Delivers address. Attends dinner in his honor hosted by President de Gaulle at Elysee Palace.

3 Paris, France. Morning appointment with P. H. Spaak, J. M. A. H. Luns, Secretary Herter, General Burgess, L. T. Merchant, Mr. Nolting, and Colonel Walters. Addresses General Council of NATO. Meets with Prime Minister Antonio Segni (Italy) and Italian and U.S. officials. Hosts luncheon in

honor of President de Gaulle. Receives Medal of the Republic of France. Addresses members of SHAPE. To Rambouillet. Attends dinner at Chateau de Rambouillet.

4   Rambouillet, France. Airborne for Prestwick, Scotland. To Culzean Castle. To Turnberry Hotel golf course. Visits with Brigadier Steel; Mr. and Mrs. D. Kennedy.

5   Maybole, Scotland. To Turnberry Hotel golf course for golf. Tours castle gardens with Mr. and Mrs. D. Kennedy, Marques of Ailsa and children, and W. Blair. Hosts dinner for White House staff.

6   Maybole, Scotland. Attends services at Kirkoswald Presbyterian Church with U.S. Ambassador Whitney, Major J. S. D. Eisenhower, and J. F. Gault. To Turnberry Hotel golf course.

7   Maybole, Scotland. Tours home of Robert Burns. To Prestwick. Returns to Washington.

8   Washington. Morning appointments with General Persons, B. N. Harlow, and R. E. Merriam; Legislative Leaders; Senator Dirksen; M. C. Moos; Secretary Mitchell, General Persons, and G. D. Morgan; General Persons; Civil Rights Commission; D. W. Kendall. Lunch. Afternoon appointments with Dr. M. S. Eisenhower; C. D. Dillon and General Goodpaster. Practices golf on south lawn. Late afternoon appointments with Secretary Flemming and T. E. Stephens; Secretary Seaton, Budget Director Stans, General Persons, B. N. Harlow, and R. E. Merriam; G. D. Morgan.

9   Washington. Breakfast meeting with U.S. Ambassador Lodge. Morning appointments with U.S. Ambassador Lodge; General Goodpaster; General Persons; U.S. Ambassador Elbert G. Mathews (to Liberia); M. C. Moos; R. J. Saulnier; Drs. Glennan and Dryden and General Goodpaster; T. E. Stephens, General Goodpaster, Captain Aurand, and J. Rowley; Secretary Flemming, Dr. E. T. Dahlberg, and T. E. Stephens; National Council of Churches of Christ delegation; G. D. Morgan and D. W. Kendall; T. E. Stephens. Lunch. Afternoon appointments

with T. E. Stephens; D. W. Kendall; R. E. Merriam; M. C. Moos; General Persons.

10 Washington. Morning appointments with M. C. Moos; National Security Council session; Attorney General Rogers; C. D. Dillon and General Goodpaster; G. V. Allen; Generals Persons and Goodpaster; General Goodpaster; Attorney General Rogers and J. E. Hoover; M. C. Moos and General Goodpaster; M. C. Moos and R. Montgomery. Lunch. Afternoon appointments with W. J. Hopkins; H. R. McPhee. Swims. Practices golf on south lawn. Addresses nation via television and radio on recent European trip. Hosts off-the-record stag dinner.

11 Washington. Morning appointments with Major J. S. D. Eisenhower; General Persons; J. C. Hagerty; General Persons; General Goodpaster; Cabinet meeting; Postmaster General Summerfield; Attorney General Rogers; Secretary McElroy, C. D. Dillon, G. Gray, A. W. Dulles, R. Murphy, U.S. Ambassador Parsons, and Generals Twining and Goodpaster (off the record); Major J. S. D. Eisenhower; General Goodpaster; U.S. Ambassador Walter N. Walmsley (to Tunisia); T. E. Stephens. Lunch. To Burning Tree Country Club for golf with G. E. Allen and Colonel Belshe. Airborne for Gettysburg farm. Visits residence of Major J. S. D. Eisenhower. Returns to Washington.

12 Washington. Airborne for Gettysburg farm. To Gettysburg Country Club for golf with Major J. S. D. Eisenhower, G. E. Allen, and General Nevins. Views horse show in Arendtsville, Maryland. Returns to Washington.

13 Washington. Attends services at National Presbyterian Church with G. E. Allen. To Burning Tree Country Club for golf with G. E. Allen and Colonel Belshe.

14 Washington. Morning appointments with J. C. Hagerty; General Goodpaster; D. W. Kendall; Budget Director Stans, General Persons, E. Staats, and R. E. Merriam; Secretaries Herter and Anderson, C. D. Dillon, L. T. Merchant, R. Murphy, U.S. Ambassador Thompson, General Persons, and F. D.

Kohler; G. Gray and General Goodpaster (off the record); Ambassador Avraham Harman (from Israel) and R. Corrigan; T. E. Stephens; Congressmen Griffin and Landrum and J. Z. Anderson; Secretary Flemming; Secretary Mitchell, General Persons, and G. D. Morgan. Hosts luncheon with Mrs. Eisenhower for Princess Beatrix of the Netherlands. Afternoon appointments with W. J. Hopkins; General Goodpaster; Drs. Kistiakowsky and Dryden and J. C. Hagerty; D. W. Kendall; B. N. Harlow; General Goodpaster; Senators Bridges, Dirksen, Kuchel, Morton, and Saltonstall, Congressmen Byrnes, Halleck, Arends, Hoeven, and Allen, General Persons, B. N. Harlow, E. A. McCabe, and J. Z. Anderson.

15 Washington. Morning appointments with J. C. Hagerty; General Persons; J. C. Hagerty; General Swing (off the record); General Persons and J. C. Hagerty; T. E. Stephens; Major J. S. D. Eisenhower; General Goodpaster. Welcomes Chairman Khrushchev. Afternoon appointments with Major J. S. D. Eisenhower; Captain Aurand; Vice-President Nixon, Secretary Herter, U.S. Ambassador Thompson, F. D. Kohler, and General Goodpaster; Chairman Khrushchev and Soviet and U.S. officials; Chairman Khrushchev and interpreter. Takes helicopter trip over Washington with Chairman Khrushchev. Hosts dinner with Mrs. Eisenhower in honor of Chairman and Mrs. Khrushchev, followed by musical entertainment.

16 Washington. Morning appointments with General Persons; D. W. Kendall; National Conference on Citizenship leaders and T. E. Stephens; J. C. Hagerty; Secretary Anderson, Budget Director Stans, R. J. Saulnier, General Persons, G. D. Morgan, and J. B. Baird (off the record); M. C. Moos and General Goodpaster; Secretary McElroy and General Goodpaster; M. C. Moos; Dr. Arthur A. Hauck (Director, Washington International Center), Robert H. Thayer (Assistant to Secretary of State, Coordination of International Educational and Cultural Relations), and T. E. Stephens; International Teacher Development Program participants; T. E. Stephens, General Goodpaster, and W. J. Hopkins; T. E. Stephens; General Goodpaster. Lunch. To Burning

Tree Country Club for golf with Colonel Belshe. Attends dinner hosted by President and Mrs. Khrushchev with Mrs. Eisenhower.

17 Washington. Breakfast meeting with A. Nielsen. Morning appointments with General Goodpaster; General Persons and B. N. Harlow; National Security Council session; T. E. Stephens; R. J. Saulnier; General Persons, J. C. Hagerty, and Major J. S. D. Eisenhower; pre-news briefing; news conference; M. J. McCaffree; General Persons; Major J. S. D. Eisenhower; General Persons and Major J. S. D. Eisenhower. Airborne for Gettysburg farm. To Gettysburg Country Club for golf with G. E. Allen and Major J. S. D. Eisenhower.

18 Gettysburg. To Gettysburg Country Club for golf with G. E. Allen. Inspects farm with General Snyder and Major J. S. D. Eisenhower.

19 Gettysburg. To Gettysburg Country Club for golf with G. E. Allen and Major J. S. D. Eisenhower. Appointment with B. N. Harlow and R. E. Merriam. To Carlisle, Pennsylvania, with G. E. Allen and General Snyder to visit Congressman Cannon.

20 Gettysburg. Attends services with Mrs. Eisenhower at Presbyterian Church of Gettysburg. Attends ceremony inaugurating UPI teletype system. To Gettysburg Country Club for golf with G. E. Allen and General Nevins. Visits with Mr. and Mrs. Brewer. Returns to Washington.

21 Washington. Morning appointments with T. E. Stephens; General Goodpaster; General Persons; J. C. Hagerty; Dr. Glennan and Generals Persons and Goodpaster; General Goodpaster; Prime Minister Rashid Karame (Lebanon), Ambassador Nadim Dimechkie (from Lebanon), R. Murphy, Ambassador Hart, and Colonel Walters. Lunch. Afternoon appointments with W. J. Hopkins; D. W. Kendall; G. D. Morgan and P. E. Areeda; D. W. Kendall; R. E. Merriam; General Goodpaster; General Persons. Practices golf.

22 Washington. Breakfast meeting with Senator Morton, General Persons, and D. W. Kendall. Appointments with Secretary Anderson, D. W. Kendall, U.S.

Savings Bonds directors, and J. C. Hagerty to discuss new government savings bonds. Reads statement on bond interest. Late morning appointments with H. C. McClellan to discuss U.S. Exhibit at Moscow Fair; briefing for Khrushchev meetings (off the record); Secretary Mueller and General Persons; D. W. Kendall; R. C. Siciliano; T. E. Stephens; General Goodpaster. Lunch. Afternoon appointments with T. E. Stephens; Admiral Strauss; General Persons; General Cutler; General Goodpaster; J. C. Hagerty.

23   Washington. Morning appointments with M. J. Mc-Caffree; Erwin D. Canham (President, Chamber of Commerce), Arch N. Booth (Executive Vice-President, Chamber of Commerce), C. B. Randall, and D. Paarlberg; General Persons; W. J. Hopkins; Secretaries Mitchell and Mueller, R. J. Saulnier, General Persons, and G. D. Morgan; J. E. Hoover (off the record); General Goodpaster and H. R. McPhee; H. R. McPhee; Label A. Katz (President, B'nai B'rith), Maurice Bisgyer (Executive Vice-President, B'nai B'rith), and Mrs. Charles D. Solovich (President, B'nai B'rith Women); R. E. Merriam, H. R. McPhee, and E. Staats; H. R. McPhee and General Goodpaster; General Goodpaster and Captain Aurand. Lunch. Afternoon appointments with Vice-President Nixon (off the record); T. E. Stephens; General Persons and T. E. Stephens; Vice-President Nixon, General Persons, and A. W. Wallis; J. C. Hagerty; Dr. M. S. Eisenhower; Captain Aurand. Dinner with Dr. M. S. Eisenhower.

24   Washington. Morning appointments with G. D. Morgan; J. C. Hagerty; Budget Director Stans; General Goodpaster; briefing on Khrushchev appointments; D. W. Kendall; Dr. M. S. Eisenhower. Lunch. Afternoon appointments with General Goodpaster; General Persons; General Goodpaster.

25   Washington. Morning appointments with D. W. Kendall; G. Gray; General Goodpaster and Captain Aurand; Secretary Herter, U.S. Ambassadors Lodge and Thompson, L. T. Merchant, and General Goodpaster; Captain Aurand; General Goodpaster; General Persons. Airborne for Camp David, Maryland, with Chairman Khrushchev.

26   Camp David, Maryland. Morning appointment with Chairman Khrushchev, Secretary Herter, Vice-President Nixon, Ambassadors Menshikov, Lodge, and Thompson, F. D. Kohler, General Goodpaster, Major J. S. D. Eisenhower, A. A. Gromyko, A. A. Soldatov, and O. A. Troyanovsky (interpreter). Tours Camp David with Chairman Khrushchev, O. A. Troyanovsky, and Captain Aurand. Meets with Chairman Khrushchev, A. Akalovsky, and O. A. Troyanovsky. Airborne for Gettysburg farm. Tours farm with Chairman Khrushchev. Airborne for Camp David. Meets with Chairman Khrushchev, Secretary Herter, L. T. Merchant, U.S. Ambassador Thompson, F. D. Kohler, A. Akalovsky, A. A. Gromyko, A. A. Soldatov, and O. A. Troyanovsky.

27   Camp David, Maryland. Attends services at Presbyterian Church of Gettysburg with General Goodpaster and Major J. S. D. Eisenhower. Meets with Chairman Khrushchev; Secretary Herter, C. D. Dillon, L. T. Merchant, Secretary Gates, F. D. Kohler, J. C. Hagerty, General Goodpaster, and A. Berding; Chairman Khrushchev. Returns to Washington.

28   Washington. Morning appointments with General Persons; General Persons, Secretaries Mitchell, Mueller, and Anderson, R. J. Saulnier, Attorney General Rogers, D. W. Kendall, J. F. Finnegan, and J. C. Hagerty; General Persons; T. E. Stephens. Delivers address at annual meeting on International Bank and International Monetary Fund. Pre-news briefing; news conference. Appointments with R. C. Siciliano; Archbishop Egidio Vagnozzi and R. C. Siciliano; J. C. Hagerty; Generals Twining and Goodpaster; General Persons and Harold Boechenstein; Secretaries Anderson, Mitchell, and Mueller, D. W. Kendall, H. Boechenstein, and General Persons; J. C. Hagerty; D. W. Kendall; T. E. Stephens; G. E. Allen; General Persons; General Goodpaster; T. E. Stephens. Practices golf on south lawn.

29   Washington. Morning appointments with General Persons; J. C. Hagerty; T. E. Stephens; Attorney General Rogers (off the record). Receives ticket to Rodeo World Series, followed by appointments with General Persons; J. C. Hagerty and Colonel Draper;

T. E. Stephens; Dr. Kistiakowsky and General Good-paster (off the record); Joseph J. Woolfson ("Know Your America" Week Committee) and Harold P. Nutter; T. Khoman (Minister, Foreign Affairs, Thailand) and Ambassadors Arthayukti and Parsons; A. F. Burns; General Goodpaster. Lunch. Afternoon appointments with General Persons; J. C. Hagerty; General Goodpaster; J. C. Hagerty; T. E. Stephens; Secretary Mitchell, D. W. Kendall, General Persons, and J. C. Hagerty. Practices golf on south lawn. Appointment with General Goodpaster.

30   Washington. Morning appointments with General Persons, D. W. Kendall, and B. N. Harlow; Secretary Mitchell; General Persons and J. C. Hagerty; T. E. Stephens; steel industry representatives to discuss steel strike; General Persons and D. W. Kendall; D. W. Kendall; W. J. Hopkins; steel industry labor representatives; General Persons and D. W. Kendall; G. Gray; U.S. Ambassador William A. M. Burden (to Belgium); U.S. Ambassador Henry E. Stebbins (to Nepal); T. E. Stephens; General Goodpaster; T. E. Stephens; Prime Minister Segni and Italian and U.S. officials. Hosts luncheon with Mrs. Eisenhower in honor of Prime Minister Segni. Airborne for Palm Springs, California. To residence of G. E. Allen.

October   1   Palm Springs, California. To Eldorado Country Club for golf with G. E. Allen, F. F. Gosden, and W. E. Robinson.

2   Palm Springs, California. To Eldorado Country Club for golf with G. E. Allen, F. F. Gosden, and J. C. Hagerty.

3   Palm Springs, California. To Eldorado Country Club for golf with G. E. Allen, F. F. Gosden, and W. E. Robinson.

4   Palm Springs, California. To Indio, California. Tours ranch of F. Odlum. Hosts outdoor barbeque. Views movie "Cattle Empire" with guests.

5   Palm Springs, California. To Eldorado Country Club for golf with G. E. Allen, F. F. Gosden, and W. E. Robinson. Views movie with W. E. Robinson, F. F. Gosden, General Snyder, Colonel Draper, and G. M. Murphy.

6   Palm Springs, California. To Eldorado Country Club for golf with G. E. Allen, W. E. Robinson, and F. F. Gosden. Dinner with W. E. Robinson, Congressman Dawson, J. Hines, and Colonel Draper. Views movie "Last Hunt" with guests.

7   Palm Springs, California. To Eldorado Country Club for golf with G. E. Allen, W. E. Robinson, and J. C. Hagerty. Tours La Quinta Hotel. Dinner with W. E. Robinson, F. F. Gosden, and General Snyder.

8   Palm Springs, California. Returns to Washington. Hosts dinner in honor of Lord Mountbatten.

9   Washington. Morning appointments with Generals Persons and Goodpaster; General Persons, D. W. Kendall, Secretaries Anderson, Mueller, and Mitchell, R. J. Saulnier, Attorney General Rogers, and J. C. Hagerty; Secretary Herter and General Goodpaster; Major J. S. D. Eisenhower; General Persons; Major J. S. D. Eisenhower; T. E. Stephens; Pan American Medical Congress representatives; R. E. Merriam; General Goodpaster. Greets President Mateos. Lunch. Afternoon appointments with Prime Minister Menderes, Secretary Herter, and Ambassadors Urguplu, Warren, and Jones; Prime Minister Manucher Eqbal (Iran), Secretary Herter, U.S. Ambassador Jones, and C. Sedgwick; Manzur Qadir (Minister of Foreign Affairs, Pakistan), Ambassador Ahmed, Secretary Herter, and U.S. Ambassador Jones; M. C. Moos and Major J. S. D. Eisenhower; Secretary Mitchell, General Persons, D. W. Kendall, J. C. Hagerty, and E. A. McCabe. Practices golf on south lawn. Hosts dinner with Mrs. Eisenhower in honor of President and Mrs. Mateos, followed by musical entertainment.

10 Washington. Morning appointments with General Goodpaster; T. E. Stephens; President Mateos, Ambassador Manuel Tello (from Mexico), and Frederico Mariscal (Chief of Protocol, Mexico). Airborne for Camp David, Maryland, with President Mateos. To Gettysburg farm. Tours farm and residence of Major J. S. D. Eisenhower with President Mateos. Airborne for Camp David, Maryland. Views movie "Horse Soldiers" with guests.

11   Camp David, Maryland. Returns to Washington. Attends services at National Presbyterian Church. Dinner at Mexican Embassy.

12   Washington. Morning appointments with K. B. McCann; General Persons and D. W. Kendall; General Goodpaster; Secretary Herter, C. D. Dillon, R. R. Rubottom, Secretary Brucker, G. M. Roderick, S. C. Waugh, E. Staats, V. Brand, and General Goodpaster (off the record); G. Gray; Ambassador Arias and W. T. Buchanan; J. C. Hagerty; Prince Sardar M. Naim (Foreign Minister, Afghanistan), Ambassador Maiwandwal, A. R. Pazhwak, and U.S. Ambassador Jones. Receives elephant from Prime Minister Abbe F. Youlou (Congo). Lunch. To Burning Tree Country Club for golf with Congressman Arends and Colonel Belshe. Addresses guests at White House Correspondents Association dinner.

13   Washington. Morning appointments with Major J. S. D. Eisenhower; General Persons; D. W. Kendall and W. J. Hopkins; W. J. Hopkins; R. E. Merriam; General Goodpaster. Receives birthday cake and oak trees. Airborne for Abilene, Kansas. Addresses guests at groundbreaking ceremonies for Eisenhower Library. Greets Nettie S. Jackson, Wes Jackson, and Florence Etherington. Luncheon with Governors National Fund Raising Committee, Eisenhower Presidential Library. Appointments with Mr. and Mrs. Ralph Wareham and son (personal friends); C. R. Yates; C. Roberts, B. T. Leithead, E. D. Slater, and J. Campbell. Visits family plot. Attends reception. Meets with Mr. and Mrs. Joyce C. Hall. Dinner with Dr. M. S. Eisenhower and Major J. S. D. Eisenhower.

14   Abilene, Kansas. Receives birthday cake from Abilene High School Student Council. Returns to Washington. Receives serenade from U.S. Army Chorus. Lunch. Afternoon appointments with Secretary Anderson, W. M. Martin, R. J. Saulnier, and D. Paarlberg; Secretary Mitchell, D. W. Kendall, and J. C. Hagerty; J. C. Hagerty; General Goodpaster.

15   Washington. Morning appointments with A. Nielsen; Major J. S. D. Eisenhower; Ambassador Emilion Donato del Carril (from Argentina), C. E. Conger, and

Colonel Walters; National Security Council session; Vice-President Nixon; Prime Minister Abdullah Ibrahim (Morocco), Ambassador Aboud, J. C. Satterthwaite, and Colonel Walters; Secretary Anderson and R. E. Merriam; General Goodpaster and R. E. Merriam; General Goodpaster. To Burning Tree Country Club for golf with J. E. Shea, G. Bunker, and Colonel Belshe.

16 Washington. Morning appointments with Secretary Herter, L. T. Merchant, G. F. Reinhardt, F. D. Kohler, and General Goodpaster; Prince Asfa Wossen H. Selassie (Ethiopia), Ambassador Otto E. Abraham (Ethiopia to U.K.), Ambassador Heywot, and W. T. Buchanan; General Goodpaster; U.S. Ambassador Thompson; Dr. Marcolino Candau (Director General, World Health Organization); R. P. Burroughs (off the record); T. E. Stephens. Lunch. To Burning Tree Country Club for golf with G. E. Allen, U.S. Ambassador Whitney, and J. E. Lemon. Signs Proclamation of Mourning for General Marshall.

17 Washington. Appointment with Major J. S. D. Eisenhower. To Burning Tree Country Club for golf with J. E. Lemon and Colonel Belshe.

18 Washington. Attends services at National Presbyterian Church. To Burning Tree Country Club for golf with G. E. Allen.

19 Washington. Morning appointments with General Persons, D. W. Kendall, and J. C. Hagerty; General Persons; A. W. Dulles and Major J. S. D. Eisenhower (off the record); A. F. Burns, F. L. Pace, J. R. Killian, J. Brownlee, General Persons, and R. E. Merriam (off the record); Board of Inquiry on Steel Strike; National Bible Week Committee; G. V. Allen; People-to-People Program Committee; Secretary Mitchell, L. E. Walsh, G. C. Doub, R. J. Dodds, R. J. Saulnier, General Persons, D. W. Kendall, and J. C. Hagerty; R. J. Saulnier and R. J. Dodds; J. C. Hagerty. Lunch. Afternoon appointments with General Persons; T. E. Stephens. Practices golf.

20 Washington. Morning appointments with W. J. Hopkins; Major J. S. D. Eisenhower; General Persons;

Senator Cooper and General Persons (off the record); Gwen Rowan; General Goodpaster and Major J. S. D. Eisenhower; General Goodpaster; Ambassador Yusuf Haikal (from Jordan), R. Corrigan, and Colonel Draper; Secretary Flemming and General Goodpaster; General Bragdon. Receives 1959 Award of Merit from American Institute of Consulting Engineers. Appointments with Major J. S. D. Eisenhower; General Persons; D. Paarlberg and H. R. McPhee to discuss tariffs; General Persons; Major J. S. D. Eisenhower. Lunch. Attends funeral of General Marshall. Afternoon appointments with General Persons; Major J. S. D. Eisenhower; J. C. Hagerty; General Persons. Practices golf on south lawn.

21   Washington. Morning appointments with J. C. Hagerty; T. E. Stephens; General Goodpaster; Secretary Herter, J. C. Hagerty, and Generals Persons and Goodpaster; NASA officials; Generals Persons and Goodpaster; Secretary Brucker and General Persons. Airborne for Augusta, Georgia. To Augusta National Golf Club.

22   Augusta, Georgia. News conference on space administration, steel strike, and upcoming summit. To Augusta National Golf Club for golf with E. D. Slater, B. T. Leithead, and Major J. S. D. Eisenhower.

23   Augusta, Georgia. To Augusta National Golf Club for golf with E. D. Slater, B. T. Leithead, Major J. S. D. Eisenhower, and C. R. Yates.

24   Augusta, Georgia. To Augusta National Golf Club for golf with E. D. Slater, B. T. Leithead, and C. R. Yates.

25   Augusta, Georgia. To Augusta National Golf Club for golf with E. D. Slater, B. T. Leithead, and C. R. Yates. Returns to Washington.

26   Washington. Morning appointments with General Goodpaster; G. D. Morgan and J. Z. Anderson; General Goodpaster; A. W. Dulles and General Goodpaster (off the record); Attorney General Rogers; P. J. Farley; J. C. Hagerty; Major J. S. D. Eisenhower. Greets President and Mrs. Sekou Toure (Republic of Guinea). Lunch. Afternoon appointments with T. E. Stephens; Drs. Glennan and Kistiakowsky, F. W.

Phillips, and General Goodpaster (off the record); J. C. Hagerty; National Aeronautics and Space Council. Hosts state dinner with Mrs. Eisenhower in honor of President and Mrs. Toure, followed by musical entertainment.

27 Washington. Morning appointments with U.S. Ambassador Young; Ambassador W. M. Q. Halm (from Ghana) and W. T. Buchanan; President Toure and Guinea and U.S. officials; R. Murphy; J. A. McCone and General Goodpaster; M. C. Moos. Addresses National Association of Postmasters annual meeting. Appointments with Postmaster General Summerfield and J. C. Hagerty; Postmaster General Summerfield and T. E. Stephens; Postmaster General Summerfield. Lunch. Afternoon appointments with T. E. Stephens; Secretary Herter, L. T. Merchant, and Major J. S. D. Eisenhower; Major J. S. D. Eisenhower. Practices golf on south lawn.

28 Washington. Morning appointments with T. E. Stephens; W. J. Hopkins; Prime Minister Nash (New Zealand), G. D. L. White, and U.S. Ambassador Parsons; pre-news briefing; news conference; J. C. Hagerty; T. E. Stephens; Senator Flanders (off the record); General Goodpaster. Attends luncheon hosted by President and Mrs. Toure with Mrs. Eisenhower. Afternoon appointments with G. D. Morgan; Governor Rockefeller. Practices golf.

29 Washington. Morning appointments with J. B. Baird (off the record); G. Gray; National Security Council session; T. E. Stephens. Records message for USIA. Appointments with General Goodpaster; D. Paarlberg; H. R. McPhee; B. N. Harlow; Major J. S. D. Eisenhower. Lunch. To Burning Tree Country Club for golf with Colonel Belshe. Physical exam at Walter Reed Hospital. Dinner with General Heaton and General Snyder.

30 Washington. Physical exam at Walter Reed Hospital.

31 Washington. Morning appointments with J. C. Hagerty; Secretary Herter, J. C. Hagerty, and Captain Aurand; Secretary Herter and Captain Aurand; J. C. Hagerty; W. J. Hopkins.

November 1   Washington. To Gettysburg farm. Inspects farm with Chief West and General Nevins. Lunch at residence of Major J. S. D. Eisenhower with Mrs. Eisenhower. Returns to Washington.

2   Washington. Addresses Cabinet Committee on Price Stability for Economic Growth. Appointments with Colonel Schulz; V. Stouffer, T. Pappas, and T. E. Stephens to discuss Republican dinners in January; H. Strode and L. A. Minnich (off the record); Secretary Herter, J. C. Hagerty, and General Goodpaster; General Goodpaster and Major J. S. D. Eisenhower. To Burning Tree Country Club for golf with Colonel Belshe.

3   Washington. Morning appointments with Major J. S. D. Eisenhower; J. C. Hagerty and General Goodpaster; G. D. Morgan and General Goodpaster; General Goodpaster; U.S. Ambassador Houghton; T. E. Stephens; B. N. Harlow; Reserve Officers Association representatives; General Goodpaster; Secretary McElroy and General Goodpaster. Participates in ribbon-cutting ceremony for extension of George Washington Memorial Parkway. To Langley, Virginia. Delivers address at cornerstone-laying ceremony for new CIA building. Airborne for Gettysburg. Votes in Pennsylvania elections. Returns to Washington. Lunch. Afternoon appointments with Major J. S. D. Eisenhower; Captain Aurand; T. E. Stephens; Colonel Draper. Practices golf on south lawn.

4   Washington. Morning appointments with Major J. S. D. Eisenhower; Generals Norstad and Goodpaster (off the record); pre-news briefing; news conference; G. Gray; Dr. Kistiakowsky and General Goodpaster; W. B. Barnes; Major J. S. D. Eisenhower; General Goodpaster. Lunch. To Burning Tree Country Club for golf with Colonel Belshe, Senator Lausche, and C. D. Smith. Evening appointment with T. E. Stephens.

5   Washington. Morning appointments with Secretary Mitchell; J. C. Hagerty; G. V. Allen and Major J. S. D. Eisenhower; National Security Council session; Secretary McElroy and Major J. S. D. Eisenhower; Secretary Herter, J. A. McCone, and Dr. Kistiakowsky;

Secretary Herter; T. E. Stephens; Ferdinand Graf (Defense Minister, Austria), Ambassador Platzer (from Austria), W. T. Buchanan, and Colonel Walters; R. R. Rubottom; President Pedro Aramburu (Argentina, provisional), Ambassador del Carril, R. R. Rubottom, Dr. E. L. Tinker, and Colonel Walters; General Goodpaster and Major J. S. D. Eisenhower; General Goodpaster. Lunch. Practices golf. Afternoon appointments with Mrs. Saylor and friends; Admiral Charles E. Lambe (Chief of Naval Staff, Great Britain); General Goodpaster; Secretary Mitchell and D. McDonald (off the record); T. E. Stephens; H. R. McPhee and W. J. Hopkins; General Goodpaster.

6 Washington. Morning appointments with J. C. Hagerty; U.S. Ambassador Lodge; General Goodpaster and R. E. Merriam; U.S. Ambassador Sessions (to Finland); Cabinet meeting; Secretary Mitchell; General Goodpaster; President's Advisory Committee on Government Organization (off the record); General Quesada; K. B. McCann (off the record). Lunch. To Burning Tree Country Club for golf with Colonel Belshe. Views movie.

7 Washington. Morning appointments with J. C. Hagerty; T. E. Stephens; G. D. Morgan; Captain Aurand; G. D. Morgan; Colonel Schulz; T. E. Stephens; K. B. McCann; Major J. S. D. Eisenhower; W. J. Hopkins; T. E. Stephens, J. C. Hagerty, Colonel Schulz, and Captain Aurand.

8 Washington. Attends services with Mrs. Eisenhower at National Presbyterian Church.

9 Washington. Morning appointments with K. B. McCann; Major J. S. D. Eisenhower; J. C. Hagerty. Lunch. Afternoon appointments with Colonel Schulz. Practices golf on south lawn. Appointments with T. E. Stephens and J. C. Hagerty; J. C. Hagerty; General Goodpaster. Hosts reception for Supreme Court members.

10 Washington. Morning appointments with J. C. Hagerty; T. E. Stephens and J. C. Hagerty; Major J. S. D. Eisenhower; General Goodpaster and Major J. S. D. Eisenhower; General Goodpaster and H. R.

McPhee; General Goodpaster; G. Gray; T. E. Stephens; Major J. S. D. Eisenhower; M. Kestnbaum (off the record); G. D. Morgan and D. Paarlberg (off the record); R. J. Saulnier; Secretary Weeks; R. E. Merriam. Records message for R. W. Woodruff. Lunch. Afternoon appointments with Secretary Benson and D. Paarlberg; Major J. S. D. Eisenhower; Secretary Anderson. Views movie.

11   Washington. Morning appointments with Major Streiff; J. C. Hagerty; H. R. McPhee; W. J. Hopkins; General Goodpaster; Major J. S. D. Eisenhower; National Security Council session; Cabinet meeting; Secretary Herter; J. A. McCone (off the record); U.S. Ambassador William P. Snow (to Burma); U.S. Ambassador Dowling; B. Gunderson. Lunch. Afternoon appointments with Colonels Schulz and Tkach; Budget Director Stans, G. D. Morgan, R. J. Saulnier, E. Staats, and R. E. Merriam; M. C. Moos; J. C. Hagerty.

12   Washington. Morning appointments with E. Plowden, J. A. McCone, and General Goodpaster; Prime Minister Felix Houphoust-Boigny (Ivory Coast), Ambassador Alphand, J. C. Satterthwaite, and Marcel von Essen (interpreter); G. D. Morgan and General Goodpaster; General Campbell; Budget Director Stans and General Goodpaster. Airborne for Augusta, Georgia. To Augusta National Golf Club for golf with G. E. Allen, W. E. Robinson, and G. Stout.

13   Augusta, Georgia. Greets Mrs. Eisenhower. Practices golf with Mrs. C. W. Jones. To Augusta National Golf Club for golf with W. A. Jones, C. W. Jones, and G. E. Allen.

14   Augusta, Georgia. To Augusta National Golf Club for golf with C. Roberts, B. T. Leithead, and R. E. Larson.

15   Augusta, Georgia. Works in office. To Augusta National Golf Club for golf with G. E. Allen, W. E. Robinson, and E. D. Slater. Works in office.

16   Augusta, Georgia. Morning appointment with Secretaries McElroy and Gates, M. D. Sprague, Generals Persons, Randall, Twining, and Goodpaster, G. Gray, Dr. Kistiakowsky, Budget Director Stans,

and W. F. Schaub. To Augusta National Golf Club for golf with C. Roberts and S. S. Larmon. Practices golf.

17   Augusta, Georgia. Works in office. To Augusta National Golf Club for golf with C. J. Schoo, W. A. Jones, and S. S. Larmon. Visits with C. Roberts.

18   Augusta, Georgia. Morning appointment with Generals Twining, White, Lemnitzer, Pate, and Goodpaster and Admiral Burke. To Augusta National Golf Club for golf with W. E. Robinson, G. Stout, E. Peabody, and C. Roberts.

19   Augusta, Georgia. Works in office. To Augusta National Golf Club for golf with J. Franklin, C. Roberts, and W. E. Robinson.

20   Augusta, Georgia. Works in office. To Augusta National Golf Club for golf with G. Stout, C. R. Yates, C. Roberts, and W. E. Robinson.

21   Augusta, Georgia. Works in office. Morning appointment with Secretaries Gates, Brucker, Douglas, and Franke, Dr. York, Generals Brown and Goodpaster, and H. R. Logan. To Augusta National Golf Club for golf with W. E. Robinson, C. Roberts, and C. R. Yates.

22   Augusta, Georgia. Attends services with Mrs. Eisenhower at Reid Memorial Presbyterian Church. To Augusta National Golf Club for golf with J. Roberts, C. Roberts, and W. E. Robinson. With Mrs. Eisenhower, visits with General and Mrs. Gruenther, Mr. and Mrs. C. Roberts, and W. E. Robinson.

23   Augusta, Georgia. Works in office. To Augusta National Golf Club for golf with W. E. Robinson, C. Roberts, and B. J. Patton. Returns to Washington. Evening appointments with General Goodpaster; T. E. Stephens, J. C. Hagerty, General Goodpaster, and Major J. S. D. Eisenhower.

24   Washington. Morning appointments with T. E. Stephens; S. Martini; General Persons; P. H. Spaak, Secretary Herter, General Burgess, and C. Sedgwick; Secretary Anderson, Budget Director Stans, and General Persons; General Persons and Major J. S. D. Eisenhower; Professor Vasily S. Emelyanov

(Director, Atomic Energy, U.S.S.R.), J. A. McCone, Raymond Garthoff (interpreter), and Major J. S. D. Eisenhower; U.S. Ambassador McConaughy (to Korea); R. C. Siciliano; General Persons. Lunch. Afternoon appointments with K. B. McCann (off the record); General Bradley; K. B. McCann; T. E. Stephens; General Goodpaster; T. E. Stephens; R. C. Siciliano; Major J. S. D. Eisenhower; T. E. Stephens.

25   Washington. Morning appointments with General Persons and G. D. Morgan; Budget Director Stans and General Goodpaster; Vice-President Nixon; National Security Council session; General Persons; Secretaries Herter, Anderson, McElroy, and Gates, Budget Director Stans, C. D. Dillon, J. N. Irwin, C. H. Shuff, J. O. Bell, L. J. Saccio, and Generals Palmer, Twining, Persons, and Goodpaster (off the record); U.S. Ambassador Dowling; A. Larson and D. W. Kendall. Lunch. Afternoon appointments with Major J. S. D. Eisenhower; General Goodpaster; D. W. Kendall; General Persons and M. C. Moos; General Snyder.

26   Washington. No official appointments.

27   Washington. Cabinet meeting. Morning appointments with General Persons; T. E. Stephens; L. T. Merchant and Major J. S. D. Eisenhower; M. C. Moos; C. D. Dillon; D. W. Kendall; W. J. Hopkins; General Persons; General Goodpaster. Lunch. Afternoon appointments with T. E. Stephens; J. C. Hagerty. Practices golf on south lawn.

28   Washington. Morning appointments with Senator Case and F. C. Wilkinson; General Goodpaster; B. N. Harlow and K. B. McCann; T. E. Stephens; General Goodpaster; Major J. S. D. Eisenhower; T. E. Stephens; J. C. Hagerty and B. N. Harlow; B. N. Harlow.

29   Washington. Attends services at National Presbyterian Church.

30   Washington. Breakfast meeting with Vice-President Nixon, Senators Johnson, Fulbright, Dirksen, and Wiley, Congressmen Rayburn, Chiperfield, and Morgan, Secretary Herter, R. Murphy, General Persons, J. C. Hagerty, and B. N. Harlow. Morning ap-

pointments with T. E. Stephens; Major J. S. D. Eisenhower; T. E. Stephens; G. Gray; T. E. Stephens; General Bragdon (off the record); Ambassador Koht (from Norway) and General Goodpaster; T. E. Stephens; J. C. Hagerty; R. K. Gray; General Persons. Lunch. Afternoon appointments with Major J. S. D. Eisenhower; K. B. McCann; B. N. Harlow and Major J. S. D. Eisenhower; General Persons; W. J. Hopkins; General Goodpaster.

December 1 Washington. Morning appointments with General Goodpaster; Secretary Herter, General Goodpaster, and Major J. S. D. Eisenhower; National Security Council session. Presents Medal of Freedom to Secretary McElroy (retiring). Appointments with General Goodpaster; Joint Chiefs of Staff (off the record); W. J. Hopkins; Major J. S. D. Eisenhower; Ambassador Nouphat Chounramany (from Laos), W. T. Buchanan, and C. Sedgwick; Lieutenant Weyrauch (off the record); K. B. McCann. Lunch. Afternoon appointments with T. E. Stephens, J. C. Hagerty, and Major J. S. D. Eisenhower. Practices golf on south lawn. Late afternoon appointments with P. G. Hoffman; Major J. S. D. Eisenhower; General Goodpaster.

2 Washington. Breakfast meeting with Senator Morton, General Persons, and D. W. Kendall. Morning appointments with Major J. S. D. Eisenhower and R. E. Merriam; Major J. S. D. Eisenhower; Senator Morton, V. B. Stouffer, T. Pappas, G. Murphy, and S. Olin (off the record); General Persons; pre-news briefing; news conference; J. C. Hagerty; K. B. McCann; B. N. Harlow; Major J. S. D. Eisenhower. Witnesses swearing-in ceremony for T. S. Gates as Defense Secretary. Practices golf on south lawn. Visits General Smith at Walter Reed Hospital and General Horkan at home with Major J. S. D. Eisenhower. Late afternoon appointment with Major J. S. D. Eisenhower. Hosts reception for members of the press who will accompany him on goodwill mission abroad.

3 Washington. Morning appointments with General Persons, G. D. Morgan, and D. W. Kendall; U.S. Ambassador John D. Hickerson (to Philippines);

G. Gray (off the record); National Security Council session; Vice-President Nixon; Secretary Herter, F. Eaton, and General Goodpaster; R. F. Courtney, General Goodpaster, and Major J. S. D. Eisenhower; Members of Advisory Committee on Inter-American Affairs; J. C. Hagerty and B. N. Harlow. Lunch. Afternoon appointments with General Persons, Secretary Anderson, R. E. Merriam, and Budget Director Stans; Secretary Mitchell; W. J. Hopkins; General Goodpaster; General Goodpaster and Major J. S. D. Eisenhower; B. N. Harlow; Major J. S. D. Eisenhower; Secretary Mitchell; J. C. Hagerty; K. B. McCann; J. C. Hagerty; Major J. S. D. Eisenhower. Makes television and radio report to nation about goodwill mission. Airborne for Rome.

4   Rome, Italy. Meets with President Giovanni Gronchi (Italy), R. Murphy, U.S. Ambassador Zellerbach (to Italy), General Goodpaster, Colonel Walters, Major J. S. D. Eisenhower, O. Horsey, Prime Minister Segni, Ambassador Grazzi, and T. A. Cippico. Attends dinner and reception hosted by President Gronchi.

5   Rome, Italy. Visits Tomb of the Unknown Soldier. Visits American Embassy. Appointment with Prime Minister Segni and Italian and U.S. officials. Attends stag luncheon hosted by Prime Minister Segni in his honor. Meets with President Gronchi, Prime Minister Segni, and Italian and U.S. officials. Hosts dinner in honor of President Gronchi.

6   Rome, Italy. Attends services at St. Paul's Episcopal Church with Colonel Schulz and Major and Mrs. J. S. D. Eisenhower. Has audience with Pope John XXIII. Airborne for Ankara, Turkey. Places wreath at tomb of Ataturk. Appointment with President Celal Bayar (Turkey) and Turkish and U.S. officials. Receives honorary doctorate from University of Ankara. Attends dinner hosted by President Bayar in his honor.

7   Ankara, Turkey. Airborne for Karachi, Pakistan. Attends dinner hosted by President Mohammed Ayub Khan (Pakistan) in his honor, followed by entertainment.

8   Karachi, Pakistan. Greets members of American community. Meets with President Ayub Kahn and Pakistani and U.S. officials. Views horse show. Places wreath on tomb of Quaid-i-azam Mohammed Ali Jinnah. Views cricket match. Attends luncheon hosted by President Ayub Khan in his honor. Delivers address. Tours Karachi and Korangi via helicopter with President Ayub Khan. Hosts dinner in honor of President Ayub Khan.

9   Karachi, Pakistan. Airborne for Kabul, Afghanistan. Meets with King Mohammed Zahir (Afghanistan) and Afghanistan and U.S. officials. Attends luncheon hosted by King Zahir in his honor. Addresses American community of Kabul. Airborne for New Delhi, India.

10   New Delhi, India. Places wreath on tomb of Mahatma Gandhi. Plants tree. Meets with President Rajendra Prasad (India), E. Bunker, and Captain Aurand. Visits with Prime Minister Shri Jawaharlal Nehru (India). Meets with Prime Minister Nehru and Indian and U.S. officials. Attends luncheon hosted by Prime Minister Nehru and Indira Gandhi in his honor. Addresses joint session of Indian Parliament. Attends banquet hosted by President Prasad in his honor, followed by Indian dance and music.

11   New Delhi, India. Tours American Embassy. Receives honorary degree from the University of Delhi. Hosts luncheon in honor of President Prasad. Visits World Agriculture Fair.

12   New Delhi, India. Attends reception. Hosts dinner in honor of Prime Minister Nehru.

13   New Delhi, India. Attends services at the Protestant Church of India Cathedral with President Prasad. Airborne for Agra, India. Visits Taj Mahal. Tours Rural Institute and village of Laraonda. Airborne for New Delhi. Delivers address at civic reception. Dinner with Prime Minister Nehru.

14   New Delhi, India. Airborne for Tehran, Iran. Meets with Shah Mohammad Reza Pahlavi, U.S. Ambassador Edward T. Wailes (to Iran), R. Murphy, Major

J. S. D. Eisenhower, and Generals Snyder and Goodpaster. Addresses Iranian Parliament. Attends luncheon hosted by Shah Pahlavi in his honor. Airborne for Athens, Greece. Greets Greek people at airport. Places wreath on Tomb of the Unknown Soldier. Attends dinner hosted by King Paul in his honor.

15 Athens, Greece. Breakfast meeting with U.S. Ambassador Briggs, R. Murphy, and General Goodpaster. Addresses Greek Parliament. Meets with Prime Minister Caramanlis and Greek and U.S. officials. Presents decoration to General Constantinos Dovas. Receives honorary membership in Academy of Athens. Attends luncheon hosted by King Paul and Queen Frederika in his honor. Airborne for U.S.S. *Des Moines.*

16 Aboard U.S.S. *Des Moines.* No official appointments.

17 Aboard U.S.S. *Des Moines.* Airborne for Tunis, Tunisia. Breakfast meeting and talks with President Habib Bourguiba (Tunisia) and Tunisian and U.S. officials. Returns to U.S.S. *Des Moines.*

18 Aboard U.S.S. *Des Moines.* Disembarks at Toulon, France. Entrains for Paris.

19 Paris, France. Attends Four Power Meeting. Meets with President de Gaulle. Attends Four Power Meeting.

20 Paris, France. To Rambouillet, France. Meets with President de Gaulle, Prime Minister Macmillan, Prime Minister M. Michel Debre (France), and Colonel Walters. Meets with President de Gaulle, Prime Minister Macmillan, and Chancellor Adenauer. To Paris. Meets with Chancellor Adenauer and M. Hillenbrand.

21 Paris, France. Meets with Prime Minister Debre and Colonel Walters. Addresses employees of American Chancellery. Meets with President de Gaulle, Secretary Herter, L. T. Merchant, F. D. Kohler, General Goodpaster, Colonel Walters, Prime Minister Macmillan, and Chancellor Adenauer. Airborne for Madrid. Meets with General Francisco Franco. Attends dinner hosted by General Franco.

22 Madrid, Spain. Meets with General Franco and Spanish and U.S. officials. Airborne for Casablanca, Morocco. Attends luncheon hosted by King Mohamed V (Morocco) in his honor. Meets with King Mohamed V, Crown Prince, C. Nowfel, and Major J. S. D. Eisenhower. Returns to Washington.

23 Washington. Morning appointments with General Persons; General Goodpaster and Major J. S. D. Eisenhower; Vice-President Nixon; C. D. Dillon, A. W. Dulles, U.S. Ambassador Parsons, and Generals Persons and Goodpaster (off the record); C. D. Dillon and General Goodpaster (off the record); J. C. Hagerty; Secretary Mitchell; Secretaries Mitchell and Mueller, Attorney General Rogers, P. A. Ray, General Persons, J. C. Hagerty, G. D. Morgan, D. W. Kendall, and R. J. Saulnier; K. B. McCann. Lunch. Afternoon appointments with K. B. McCann and R. Montgomery; W. J. Hopkins; General Persons; G. Gray. Attends Christmas Pageant of Peace with Mrs. Eisenhower.

24 Washington. Morning appointments with General Persons, J. C. Hagerty, and B. Patterson; General Persons and J. C. Hagerty; General Persons; R. E. Merriam; W. J. Hopkins; J. W. Marriott (off the record); R. J. Saulnier and General Persons (off the record); General Goodpaster. Lunch. Attends Christmas Eve services with Mrs. Eisenhower at National Presbyterian Church.

25 Washington. No official appointments.

26 Washington. To Gettysburg farm. Visits skeet range with Chief West. Visits residence of Major J. S. D. Eisenhower. Returns to Washington.

27 Washington. Airborne for Augusta, Georgia. To Augusta National Golf Club for golf with G. E. Allen, W. E. Robinson, and W. A. Jones.

28 Augusta, Georgia. [Page missing.]

29 Augusta, Georgia. [Page missing.]

30 Augusta, Georgia. Meets with General Persons and M. C. Moos. To Augusta National Golf Club for golf with G. E. Allen, R. W. Woodruff, and E. D. Slater.

31 Augusta, Georgia. Works in office. To Augusta National Golf Club for golf with B. T. Leithead, G. E.
Allen, and E. D. Slater.

1960

January 1 Augusta, Georgia. Works in office. Visits W. E.
Robinson and B. T. Leithead.

2 Augusta, Georgia. Meets with G. D. Morgan, Bud-
et Director Stans, E. Staats, and R. E. Merriam. To
Augusta National Golf Club for golf with S. S. Larmon, D. Keene, and E. D. Slater.

3 Augusta, Georgia. Works in office. To Augusta National Golf Club for golf with G. Stout, W. E. Robinson, and J. Roberts.

4 Augusta, Georgia. Works in office. Hunts quail. To
Augusta National Golf Club for golf with W. E.
Robinson, G. Stout, and J. Roberts.

5 Augusta, Georgia. Works in office. To Augusta National Golf Club for golf with J. Franklin, W. E.
Robinson, and J. Roberts. Returns to Washington.

6 Washington. Attends service of Intercession and Holy
Communion for opening of Congress at National
Presbyterian Church with General Persons, J. C.
Hagerty, and T. E. Stephens. Morning appointments
with T. E. Stephens; General Goodpaster; M. C.
Moos; C. D. Dillon; General Goodpaster; Cabinet
meeting; Vice-President Nixon; General Goodpaster;
General Persons; R. J. Saulnier; Major J. S. D. Eisen-
hower. Lunch. Afternoon appointments with M. C.
Moos; Major J. S. D. Eisenhower; General Cutler
(off the record). Attends birthday celebration for
Senator Dirksen.

7 Washington. Morning appointments with General
Goodpaster; J. C. Hagerty; G. D. Morgan; T. E. Ste-
phens; J. C. Hall; Major J. S. D. Eisenhower; G. Gray;
M. C. Moos; General Goodpaster; J. C. Hagerty;
General Persons; M. C. Moos. Delivers State of the
Union Address to Congress. Appointments with Na-
tional Security Council session; General Good-
paster.

8   Washington. Morning appointments with R. E. Merriam; J. C. Hagerty; B. N. Harlow; Drs. Glennan, Dryden, and Kistiakowsky, B. N. Harlow, G. D. Morgan, and Generals Persons and Goodpaster (off the record); Attorney General Rogers; General Goodpaster, Major J. S. D. Eisenhower, and W. J. Hopkins; General Goodpaster and Major J. S. D. Eisenhower; General Goodpaster. To Gettysburg farm. Inspects farm.

9   Gettysburg. Hunts. Visits skeet range and duck pond with G. E. Allen and General Nevins. Visits skeet range with Chief West, G. E. Allen, Major and Mrs. J. S. D. Eisenhower, and D. D. Eisenhower II.

10   Gettysburg. Visits Allen farm and Country Kitchen with G. E. Allen. Returns to Washington.

11   Washington. Morning appointments with T. E. Stephens; Postmaster General Summerfield; General Persons; Vice-President Nixon, Secretary Anderson, A. W. Dulles, and General Persons (off the record); Vice-President Nixon (off the record); T. E. Stephens; G. D. Morgan; Dr. Glennan and Generals Persons and Goodpaster (off the record); G. D. Morgan; General Goodpaster; Ambassador Menshikov and R. Davis; T. E. Stephens; W. J. Hopkins; J. C. Hagerty. Lunch. Practices golf on south lawn. Views gifts received on goodwill mission. Bipartisan Legislative Leaders.

12   Washington. Breakfast meeting with Senator Dirksen, Congressman Halleck, General Persons, and B. N. Harlow (off the record). Appointments with Legislative Leaders; Ambassador Julio A. Lacarte (from Uruguay) and W. T. Buchanan; T. E. Stephens and General Goodpaster; Generals Persons and Goodpaster, Secretary Anderson, Budget Director Stans, E. Staats, and Drs. Glennan and Dryden. Lunch. Afternoon appointments with Major J. S. D. Eisenhower; National Aeronautics and Space Council; J. H. Douglas; General Persons; J. C. Hagerty.

13   Washington. Breakfast meeting with U.S. Ambassador Lodge. Appointments with U.S. Ambassador Lodge; General Persons; G. Gray; T. E. Ste-

phens; General Persons and J. C. Hagerty; pre-news briefing; news conference; F. J. Donohue, W. A. Ruschmeyer, and Colonel Schulz (off the record); W. J. Hopkins; General Persons. Lunch. Afternoon appointments with T. E. Stephens; B. N. Harlow; D. W. Kendall and H. R. McPhee; R. E. Merriam; General Persons. Practices golf on south lawn. Appointments with M. C. Moos; General Goodpaster; Senators Johnson and Bridges, Dr. Glennan, and B. N. Harlow (off the record).

14   Washington. Breakfast meeting with Congressmen Martin, Brooks, and McCormack, Dr. Glennan, and B. N. Harlow (off the record). National Security Council session. Appointments with G. D. Morgan; M. C. Moos; Vice-President Nixon; Dr. Kistiakowsky and General Goodpaster (off the record); R. B. Robertson and B. N. Harlow (off the record); General Goodpaster. Lunch. Afternoon appointments with R. E. Merriam; General Persons; D. W. Kendall; General Goodpaster; Cabinet meeting; Ambassador Menshikov and R. Davis; Mrs. J. S. D. Eisenhower; Senator Morton.

15   Washington. Morning appointments with General Persons; General Goodpaster; General Persons; B. N. Harlow; Dr. Peter G. Voutov (Minister, Bulgaria) and C. E. Conger; W. J. Hopkins. Airborne for Albany, Georgia. To Blue Springs Plantation. Hunts with Mr. and Mrs. W. A. Jones, G. E. Allen, Mr. and Mrs. S. Murphy, and General Snyder. Attends reception hosted by Mr. And Mrs. W. A. Jones.

16   Albany, Georgia. Hunts with W. A. Jones, C. W. Jones, and General Snyder. Lunch. Hunts with W. A. Jones, G. M. Humphrey, U.S. Ambassador Whitney, G. E. Allen, and S. Murphy. Attends reception.

17   Albany, Georgia. Returns to Washington.

18   Washington. Morning appointments with General Persons; General Goodpaster; Budget Director Stans, E. Staats, and D. W. Kendall; Secretary Herter, D. MacArthur, U.S. Ambassador Parsons, and General Goodpaster. Attends funeral of General Joyce with Mrs. Eisenhower. Appointments with R. K. Gray; General Persons; M. C. Moos. Lunch.

Afternoon appointments with R. J. Saulnier; General Persons; R. K. Gray; M. J. McCaffree; General Goodpaster.

19   Washington. Morning appointments with G. D. Morgan; G. Gray; General Goodpaster; M. C. Moos; Prime Minister Kishi and Japanese and U.S. officials. Hosts luncheon in honor of Prime Minister Kishi. Signs Treaty of Mutual Cooperation and Security with Japan. Swims. Off-the-record appointment with Dr. and Lady Elliott.

20   Washington. Morning appointments with General Persons; General Goodpaster; G. D. Morgan; D. W. Kendall; Attorney General Rogers and J. D. Randall; Senator Morton, Congressman Brownson, General Persons, D. W. Kendall, R. E. Merriam, and Douglas Price (off the record); General Persons and R. E. Merriam; General Goodpaster; D. W. Kendall; General Goodpaster; W. J. Hopkins; M. C. Moos; Senators Javits and Cooper and E. A. McCabe (off the record). Addresses Young Republican Federation National Leadership Training School. Lunch. Afternoon appointments with General Persons; Prime Minister Kishi and Japanese and U.S. officials; General Goodpaster; R. K. Gray.

21   Washington. Breakfast meeting with Republican members of Congress. National Security Council session. Appointments with Secretary Herter, G. Gray, J. H. Douglas, P. J. Farley, and Generals Goodpaster, White, and Loper (off the record); National Association of Manufacturers representatives and R. E. Merriam; President's Committee on Traffic Safety; Dr. Katz (off the record). Lunch. Afternoon appointments with General Goodpaster; M. C. Moos.

22   Washington. Morning appointments with General Persons; G. D. Morgan; General Persons; U.S. Ambassador Lodge; Cabinet meeting; Secretary Flemming; Admiral Strauss (off the record). Lunch. Afternoon appointments with M. C. Moos; W. J. Hopkins; General Goodpaster.

23   Washington. Morning appointments with General Goodpaster; Secretary Herter and General Goodpaster. To Gettysburg farm. Inspects barns. Lunch

with G. E. Allen at home of Major J. S. D. Eisenhower. Returns to Washington.

24 Washington. Attends services with Mrs. Eisenhower at National Presbyterian Church.

25 Washington. Addresses National Association of Real Estate Boards breakfast. Morning appointments with T. E. Stephens; General Persons and R. E. Merriam; Governors' Conference Civil Defense meeting; T. E. Stephens; General Bragdon; J. C. Hagerty; General Persons; General Twining. Receives books for Abilene Library from American Jewish Committee. Appointments with General Goodpaster; Secretary Herter, U.S. Ambassador Bonsal (to Cuba), R. R. Rubottom, and Generals Persons and Goodpaster; Governor Rockefeller, Secretaries Anderson and Flemming, Robert MacCrate (Counsel, Governor Rockefeller), J. A. Kieffer, and R. E. Merriam (off the record). Hosts luncheon for Civil Defense meeting members. Afternoon appointments with Generals Goodpaster and Nelson and Colonels Sampson, McNally, and Schulz; General Persons; R. E. Merriam; General Persons.

26 Washington. Morning appointments with Attorney General Rogers, General Persons, and G. D. Morgan (off the record); General Persons; General Goodpaster; G. Gray; W. J. Hopkins; General Persons and J. C. Hagerty; pre-news briefing; news conference; J. C. Hagerty; Dr. Glennan, G. D. Morgan, and H. R. McPhee (off the record); U.S. Ambassador John J. Muccio (to Guatemala). Lunch. Practices golf. Afternoon appointments with T. E. Stephens; S. P. Skouras; T. E. Stephens, General Goodpaster, and Major J. S. D. Eisenhower; General Goodpaster. Dinner with U.S. Ambassador and Mrs. Whitney (off the record).

27 Washington. Morning appointments with Major J. S. D. Eisenhower; T. E. Stephens; Akinremi Akapo (Nigeria) and ICA officials; General Goodpaster; General Persons; W. J. Hopkins. Airborne for Denver, Colorado. Meets Republican state legislators. Visits with Mr. and Mrs. A. Nielsen and Mr. and Mrs. W. Nicholson. Airborne for Los Angeles. Addresses Republican dinner. Receives gold medal

commemorating contribution to peace and freedom.

28   Los Angeles. Breakfast meeting with California Republican leaders. Airborne for La Quinta, California. To Eldorado Country Club for golf with G. E. Allen, F. F. Gosden, W. E. Robinson, and C. W. Jones.

29   La Quinta, California. To Eldorado Country Club for golf with G. E. Allen, F. F. Gosden, and W. E. Robinson. Views movie "Sage of Hemp Brown" with guests.

30   La Quinta, California. To Eldorado Country Club for golf with C. W. Jones, G. E. Allen, and W. E. Robinson. Hosts luncheon.

31   LaQuinta, California. To Eldorado Country Club for golf with G. E. Allen and F. F. Gosden. Tours La Quinta Country Club.

February 1   La Quinta, California. Airborne for Denver, Colorado. Visits home of E. Doud. Returns to Washington. Late afternoon appointments with T. E. Stephens; General Persons, G. D. Morgan, Secretary Benson, B. N. Harlow, D. W. Kendall, and R. E. Merriam; Colonel Schulz; General Persons.

2   Washington. Witnesses swearing-in of General Cutler as U.S. Director, Inter-American Development Bank. Morning appointments with General Persons; General Persons and B. N. Harlow; Legislative Leaders; Vice-President Nixon; General Goodpaster; Board of Consultants on Foreign Intelligence Activities; Rabbi Israel Goldstein, Senator Javits, and General Goodpaster; Generals Persons and Goodpaster and Major J. S. D. Eisenhower; General Goodpaster and Major J. S. D. Eisenhower. Lunch. Afternoon appointments with General Persons; General Goodpaster; J. B. Baird (off the record); Secretary Herter and General Goodpaster; B. N. Harlow; T. S. Gates, J. H. Douglas, and General Goodpaster; R. E. Merriam; General Goodpaster; S. Adams (off the record).

3   Washington. Morning appointments with Colonel Schulz; W. J. Hopkins; G. Gray; J. A. McCone and General Goodpaster; General Persons and J. C.

Hagerty; pre-news briefing; news conference; General Goodpaster; C. D. Dillon, U.S. Ambassador Riddleberger (to Greece), J. Bell, J. N. Irwin, W. Palmer, E. Staats, V. Brand, General Persons, G. D. Morgan, and R. E. Merriam; General Goodpaster; Major J. S. D. Eisenhower; R. E. Merriam. Lunch. Practices golf. Afternoon appointments with T. E. Stephens; M. C. Moos; General Goodpaster; J. C. Hagerty.

4 Washington. Morning appointments with General Goodpaster; General Persons, D. Paarlberg, B. N. Harlow, and G. D. Morgan. Presents awards to divers. Appointments with G. Gray, Secretary Herter, L. T. Merchant, Secretary Gates, J. H. Douglas, Generals Cabell and Twining, J. N. Irwin, A. W. Dulles, and D. Fitzgerald; National Security Council session; Disabled American Veterans leaders and E. D. Chesney; Jewish Theological Seminary of America; Admiral Strauss; Generals Goodpaster and Persons and J. C. Hagerty. Lunch. Afternoon appointments with W. J. Hopkins; T. E. Stephens; B. N. Harlow. Practices golf.

5 Washington. Morning appointments with R. E. Merriam; D. W. Kendall; D. Paarlberg and P. E. Areeda to discuss tariffs; Secretary Herter, J. H. Douglas, Drs. Kistiakowsky and York, G. Gray, J. V. Charyk, and Generals Twining, Cabell, and Goodpaster; Secretary Herter and General Goodpaster; J. A. Hannah and D. W. Kendall (off the record); R. E. Merriam; General Persons. To Gettysburg farm. Walks around grounds.

6 Gettysburg. Visits residence of Major J. S. D. Eisenhower. Afternoon appointment with B. N. Harlow and D. Paarlberg.

7 Gettysburg. Attends services with Mrs. Eisenhower at Presbyterian Church of Gettysburg. Returns to Washington.

8 Washington. Morning appointments with General Persons; C. H. Percy and Senator Morton; R. J. Saulnier; Secretary Herter and General Goodpaster; General Persons, T. E. Stephens. Addresses dedication ceremonies for Veterans of Foreign Wars building. Lunch. Afternoon appointments with Gen-

eral Persons; General Lemnitzer (off the record); General Persons and Captain Aurand; T. E. Stephens; B. N. Harlow; W. J. Hopkins; General Goodpaster; General Persons and Captain Aurand.

9   Washington. Off-the-record breakfast meeting with Republican congressmen. Appointments with Legislative Leaders; General Persons and B. N. Harlow; Gridiron Club Executive Committee; General Persons and J. C. Hagerty; C. R. Griffith and T. E. Stephens; G. Gray; Major J. S. D. Eisenhower. Records Red Cross and Boy Scout messages. Appointments with J. C. Hagerty; General Goodpaster; General Persons. Airborne for Gettysburg farm.

10 Gettysburg. To Andrews Air Force base en route to Cape Canaveral, Florida. Receives briefings. Tours base. Returns to Washington. Appointment with General Goodpaster. Practices golf on south lawn. Appointment with General Goodpaster.

11 Washington. Off-the-record breakfast meeting with P. G. Hoffman. Appointments with U.S. Ambassador Reinhardt (to United Arab Republic); General Goodpaster; General Persons; W. J. Hopkins; J. C. Hagerty; pre-news briefing; news conference; J. C. Hagerty and T. E. Stephens; U.S. Ambassador Tyler Thompson (to Iceland); General Goodpaster; Robert V. Hatcher and son (off the record); Major J. S. D. Eisenhower. Lunch. Practices golf. Afternoon appointments with D. W. Kendall; Generals Devers, North, and Persons; Major Streiff.

12 Washington. Off-the-record breakfast meeting with Dr. M. S. Eisenhower. Works on South American speeches with Dr. M. S. Eisenhower. Appointments with G. Gray, R. E. Merriam, and General Goodpaster; National Security Council session; Vice-President Nixon; General Twining; General Goodpaster; J. C. Hagerty; T. E. Stephens; Major J. S. D. Eisenhower. To Gettysburg farm. Tours farm with R. L. Biggers. Visits residence of Major J. S. D. Eisenhower with Mrs. Eisenhower and R. Wood.

13 Gettysburg. Attends grandson's basketball game at Gettysburg High School.

14　Gettysburg. Visits with Major J. S. D. Eisenhower and family. Returns to Washington.

15　Washington. Morning appointments with Ambassador Victor Andrade (from Bolivia) and W. T. Buchanan; Senator H. A. Smith (off the record); W. D. Pawley; Secretary Herter and General Goodpaster; Secretary Flemming and General Persons; General Persons; T. E. Stephens; Republican congressional candidate; W. D. Pawley; T. E. Stephens. Lunch. Afternoon appointments with General Persons and T. E. Stephens; General Persons, B. N. Harlow, and M. C. Moos; A. Nielsen; Secretaries Mitchell and Mueller, R. J. Saulnier, General Persons, and G. D. Morgan; A. Nielsen; Republican congressmen and senators (off the record).

16　Washington. Morning appointments with General Persons and B. N. Harlow; J. C. Hagerty; Legislative Leaders; General Goodpaster; Crusade for Freedom members; Ambassador Carlos A. Clulow (from Uruguay), W. T. Buchanan, and D. Barnes; R. P. Burroughs (off the record); D. W. Kendall; E. Johnston (off the record); D. W. Kendall. Lunch. Visits General Smith and Mrs. M. Clark at Walter Reed Hospital. Afternoon appointments with T. E. Stephens; General Persons; General Goodpaster; T. E. Stephens.

17　Washington. Morning appointments with W. J. Hopkins; General Persons; University of Uruguay law students; pre-news briefing; news conference; D. C. Power, Admiral Bell, and T. E. Stephens (off the record); E. A. McCabe; Senator Beall, Congressman Miller, and E. A. McCabe; General Persons and J. C. Hagerty; U.S. Ambassador Moose (to Sudan); Attorney General Rogers (off the record). Lunch. Afternoon appointments with G. Gray and General Goodpaster; General Persons; T. E. Stephens.

18　Washington. Attends Annual Prayer Breakfast of International Council for Christian Leadership. Morning appointments with Secretaries Gates and Herter, L. A. Hoegh, J. A. McCone, F. M. Eaton, C. D. Dillon, P. J. Farley, Generals Twining, Lemnitzer, White, Goodpaster, Persons, and Loper, Admiral Burke, A. W. Dulles, Dr. Kistiakowsky, G. Gray,

J. N. Irwin, G. Smith, and J. S. Lay (off the record); National Security Council session; General Goodpaster; Admiral Wright; Soviet officials; D. W. Kendall. Lunch. Afternoon appointments with T. E. Stephens; General Goodpaster; Senator Smathers and B. N. Harlow (off the record).

19 Washington. Morning appointments with D. W. Kendall and Generals Goodpaster and Persons; General Persons; M. J. McCaffree; General Persons; Governor Reed, General Persons, D. W. Kendall, and R. E. Merriam; General Goodpaster and W. J. Hopkins; General Goodpaster; J. C. Hagerty. Presents Big Brother of the Year Award to Cardinal Spellman. Receives 17th Annual Photo Contest winners. Lunch. Afternoon appointments with General Persons and B. N. Harlow. Practices golf on south lawn.

20 Washington. Morning appointments with Secretary Flemming, D. W. Kendall, and H. R. McPhee; D. W. Kendall and H. R. McPhee; D. W. Kendall and P. E. Areeda; D. W. Kendall, General Goodpaster, and W. J. Hopkins; D. W. Kendall; General Mark Clark; J. C. Hagerty; B. N. Harlow; W. E. Robinson; T. E. Stephens; B. N. Harlow and General Goodpaster.

21 Washington. Attends services at National Presbyterian Church.

22 Washington. Airborne for San Juan, Puerto Rico. Meets with Governor Muñoz-Marin and Cabinet. Airborne for Ramey Air Force Base, Puerto Rico. To Borinquen golf course for golf with J. C. Hagerty, General Preston, and Colonel Draper. Attends reception in his honor.

23 Ramey Air Force Base, Puerto Rico. Airborne for Brasilia, Brazil. Visits Eisenhower Commemorative Monument. Participates in cornerstone-laying ceremony at U.S. Embassy site with Dr. Kubitschek. Attends reception and dinner.

24 Brasilia, Brazil. Airborne for Rio de Janeiro, Brazil. Addresses Joint Session of National Congress. Meets Supreme Court justices of Brazil. Receives Ambassadors. Attends dinner hosted by Dr. Kubitschek in his honor.

| 25 | Rio de Janeiro, Brazil. Airborne for Sao Paulo, Brazil. Places wreath on Brazilian Expeditionary Forces of World War II Monument. Attends luncheon in his honor. Airborne for Rio de Janeiro. Visits plane crash survivors. Hosts dinner in honor of Dr. Kubitschek. |

25 Rio de Janeiro, Brazil. Airborne for Sao Paulo, Brazil. Places wreath on Brazilian Expeditionary Forces of World War II Monument. Attends luncheon in his honor. Airborne for Rio de Janeiro. Visits plane crash survivors. Hosts dinner in honor of Dr. Kubitschek.

26 Rio de Janeiro, Brazil. Airborne for Buenos Aires, Argentina. Lunch with Secretary Herter, U.S. Ambassador Beaulac (to Argentina) and Mrs. Beaulac, Dr. M. S. Eisenhower, Generals Goodpaster and Snyder, and Major J. S. D. Eisenhower. Meets with President Frondizi (Argentina). Addresses National Congress of Argentina. Attends American Embassy diplomatic reception. Attends dinner hosted by President and Señora Frondizi in his honor.

27 Buenos Aires, Argentina. Airborne for Mar del Plata, Argentina. Meets mayors. Airborne for San Carlos de Bariloche, Argentina. To Llao-Llao Hotel for golf with Major J. S. D. Eisenhower and J. C. Hagerty. Hosts dinner in honor of President Frondizi.

28 San Carlos de Bariloche, Argentina. Fishes in Lake Traful. Lunch at Lariviere residence. Attends conference at residence of Mrs. Leonora H. de Ortis Basualdo. Signs Declaration of Bariloche with President Frondizi.

29 San Carlos de Bariloche, Argentina. Airborne for Santiago, Chile. Lunch with U.S. Ambassador Howe, Secretary Herter, Dr. M. S. Eisenhower, and General Snyder. Meets with President Alessandri (Chile). Attends dinner hosted by President Alessandri in his honor.

March 1 Santiago, Chile. Addresses National Congress of Chile. Views San Gregorio housing development. Hosts dinner in honor of President Alessandri.

2 Santiago, Chile. Airborne for Montevideo, Uruguay. Makes official call on National Council of Government. Meets with President Nardone and Uruguay and U.S. officials. Addresses special session of Uruguayan Congress. Attends banquet hosted by President and Mrs. Nardone in his honor.

3   Montevideo, Uruguay. Airborne for Buenos Aires, Argentina. Airborne for Paramaribo, Surinam. Meets with Governor Jan van Tilburg and Surinam and U.S. officials. Airborne for Ramey Air Force Base, Puerto Rico.

4   Ramey Air Force Base, Puerto Rico. Addresses guests at American Assembly luncheon. To Dorado Beach Hotel golf course for golf with Major J. S. D. Eisenhower, E. B. Dudley, and R. Gilbert.

5   Ramey Air Force Base, Puerto Rico. To Borinquen golf course for golf with J. C. Hagerty, Colonel Draper, and General Preston. Attends dinner at home of General Preston. Visits entertainment at Officers' Club.

6   Ramey Air Force Base, Puerto Rico. To Dorado Beach Hotel golf course for golf with J. C. Hagerty, E. B. Dudley, and R. Gilbert.

7   Ramey Air Force Base, Puerto Rico. To Borinquen golf course for golf with General Preston, Colonel Draper, and J. C. Hagerty. Returns to Washington. Afternoon appointments with Vice-President Nixon; J. C. Hagerty; General Goodpaster; General Persons.

8   Washington. Morning appointments with T. E. Stephens; General Persons and B. N. Harlow; Legislative Leaders; Norman A. Erbe (Attorney General, Iowa) and T. E. Stephens. Presents Awards for Distinguished Federal Civilian Service. Lunch. Afternoon appointments with General Goodpaster; Ambassador Menshikov and R. Davis; General Goodpaster; Secretary Herter, L. T. Merchant, F. D. Kohler, Secretary Gates, Ambassador Bohlen, J. H. Douglas, J. N. Irwin, and Generals White and Goodpaster. Broadcasts national television and radio message on trip to South America.

9   Washington. Morning appointments with D. W. Kendall; T. E. Stephens, General Goodpaster, and G. D. Morgan; General Goodpaster; R. J. Saulnier; G. Gray; M. J. McCaffree; Major J. S. D. Eisenhower; Postmaster General Summerfield; General Goodpaster; Mr. and Mrs. A. Rowe and T. E. Stephens;

Malina Savedra (Chile) and Colonel Walters; General Persons, J. C. Hagerty, and D. W. Kendall; General Persons and D. W. Kendall; General Persons, D. W. Kendall, and J. Doefer (off the record); General Persons; General Persons and D. W. Kendall; D. W. Kendall; R. E. Merriam; J. C. Hagerty. Hosts stag luncheon for American Republics Mission Chiefs. Morning appointments with T. E. Stephens; General Persons; M. C. Moos; G. D. Morgan and H. R. McPhee.

10 Washington. Morning appointments with General Persons; B. N. Harlow; J. A. McCone, C. D. Dillon, and Major J. S. D. Eisenhower (off the record); National Security Council session; Prime Minister David Ben Gurion (Israel), U.S. Ambassadors Harman and Jones, C. D. Dillon, and J. C. Hagerty; J. C. Hagerty. Lunch. Afternoon appointments with W. J. Hopkins; General Persons, G. D. Morgan, and H. R. McPhee; General Persons; H. R. McPhee; T. E. Stephens. Practices golf. Attends Indiana State Society meeting in honor of Congressman Halleck.

11 Washington. [Page missing.] Cabinet meeting, followed by morning appointments with G. D. Morgan; Secretary Anderson and C. D. Dillon (off the record); C. D. Dillon, D. W. Kendall, H. R. McPhee, and P. E. Areeda (off the record); General Goodpaster; M. C. Moos; J. C. Hagerty; R. E. Merriam; General Persons. Lunch.

12 Washington. [Page missing.] Attends Gridiron dinner at Statler Hotel.

13 Washington. [Page missing.]

14 Washington. [Page missing.]

15 Washington. [Page missing.] Late morning appointments with Mrs. Marshall, Dr. Glennan, General Persons, and D. W. Kendall; T. E. Stephens. Hosts stag luncheon in honor of Chancellor Adenauer. Afternoon appointments with T. E. Stephens; Major J. S. D. Eisenhower. Practices golf on south lawn. Late afternoon appointments with Major J. S. D. Eisenhower; D. W. Kendall; General Goodpaster.

16 Washington. Off-the-record breakfast meeting with W. S. Paley. Morning appointments with Secretary Benson; General Persons; J. C. Hagerty; pre-news briefing; news conference. Addresses Washington Conference of the Advertising Council. Receives USO Annual Award from USO National Council. Lunch. Afternoon appointments with G. D. Morgan; Secretary Anderson, Budget Director Stans, and General Persons; Secretary Anderson; T. E. Stephens; A. Nielsen and son-in-law; Major J. S. D. Eisenhower; General Goodpaster and J. C. Hagerty.

17 Washington. Breakfast meeting with G. M. Humphrey (off the record). Appointments with General Persons and R. E. Merriam; Secretaries Herter and Gates, Budget Director Stans, L. T. Merchant, Admiral Burke, A. W. Dulles, R. Bissell, J. N. Irwin, G. Gray, K. G. Harr, Generals Cabell and Goodpaster, J. S. Lay, C. D. Dillon, R. Helms, and G. Smith (off the record); National Security Council session; Secretary Herter; R. E. Merriam. Presents President's Cup to winners of 1958 and 1959 Cup Regatta Speed Boat Races. Appointments with General Goodpaster; H. Guggenheim (off the record). Lunch with W. E. Robinson and B. T. Leithead (off the record). Off-the-record afternoon appointments with Vice-President Nixon, Secretaries Anderson and Herter, L. T. Merchant, R. R. Rubottom, A. W. Dulles, Admiral Burke, J. N. Irwin, R. Bissell, Colonel King, G. Gray, General Goodpaster, and Major J. S. D. Eisenhower; Vice-President Nixon and Secretary Anderson; Vice-President Nixon; K. C. Royall.

18 Washington. Morning appointments with Major J. S. D. Eisenhower; General Goodpaster; Vice-President Nixon, General Persons, and R. E. Merriam; General Persons; T. E. Stephens; Major J. S. D. Eisenhower; T. E. Stephens; Secretary Anderson, W. M. Martin, J. B. Baird, R. J. Saulnier, D. Paarlberg, and General Persons; C. D. Dillon, D. W. Kendall, and H. R. McPhee; Budget Director Stans, D. W. Kendall, H. R. McPhee, and P. E. Areeda; D. W. Kendall; Secretary Gates and General Goodpaster; T. E. Stephens. Lunch. Afternoon appointments with J. C. Hagerty; Major J. S. D. Eisenhower; Hoa-

cio Lafer (Foreign Minister, Brazil), Ambassador Salles, and R. R. Rubottom; T. E. Stephens and General Goodpaster; W. J. Hopkins; General Persons, B. N. Harlow, and R. E. Merriam. Off-the-record legislative meeting. To Camp David, Maryland.

19　Camp David, Maryland. To residence of Major J. S. D. Eisenhower in Gettysburg. Inspects cattle with G. E. Allen. To Camp David. Shoots skeet with G. E. Allen and Captain Aurand. Views movie "Four Fast Guns" with G. E. Allen, B. A. Eisenhower, and General Snyder.

20　Camp David, Maryland. Shoots skeet with G. E. Allen and Captain Aurand. Visits with Major J. S. D. Eisenhower and family.

21　Camp David, Maryland. Returns to Washington. Morning appointments with General Persons; General Goodpaster; J. C. Hagerty; J. C. Hagerty and General Goodpaster; Secretaries Brucker and Herter, G. Roderick, R. R. Rubottom, L. T. Merchant, and Generals Persons and Goodpaster; Secretaries Herter and Brucker; Secretary Herter and General Goodpaster; G. Gray; T. E. Stephens and R. E. Merriam; R. E. Merriam; General Clark (off the record); C. D. Dillon and U.S. Ambassador Briggs; D. W. Kendall, H. R. McPhee, and P. E. Areeda; D. W. Kendall; General Persons. Lunch. Afternoon appointments with General Goodpaster; T. E. Stephens; D. Black (off the record); J. C. Hagerty and General Goodpaster; General Persons; Secretary Flemming, Senator Morton, and General Persons; Major J. S. D. Eisenhower; W. J. Hopkins; Major J. S. D. Eisenhower.

22　Washington. Morning appointments with General Persons, B. N. Harlow, R. E. Merriam, and Secretary Flemming; Legislative Leaders; Secretary Flemming, B. N. Harlow, and R. E. Merriam; Mr. and Mrs. H. Ford and son, R. Markley, and T. E. Stephens; Eisenhower Exchange Fellows; T. B. McCabe and T. E. Stephens; T. E. Stephens; M. C. Moos. Lunch. Afternoon appointments with General Snyder; J. C. Hagerty; General Persons; General Persons and R. E. Merriam; General Goodpaster; Major J. S. D. Eisenhower.

23   Washington. Morning appointments with General Persons; D. W. Kendall; Secretary Herter, C. D. Dillon, and General Goodpaster; T. E. Stephens; J. A. McCone, Budget Director Stans, Dr. Kistiakowsky, and Generals Persons and Goodpaster; Governor Hatfield, Judge and Mrs. Hall Lusk, and J. Frank; Mrs. W. Reid and children and J. C. Hagerty (off the record); Ambassador Aboud and J. C. Satterthwaite; General Goodpaster; Colonel Walters and General Goodpaster; F. M. Castiella, Ambassador Jose M. de Areilza (from Spain), Jaime de Pinies, Secretary Herter, U.S. Ambassador Lodge, I. B. White, and Colonel Walters; Ambassador Ardeshir Zahedi (from Iran) and W. T. Buchanan. Lunch. Afternoon appointments with W. J. Hopkins; Generals Goodpaster and Persons and B. N. Harlow. Practices golf on south lawn. Late afternoon appointments with T. E. Stephens; General Goodpaster; Major J. S. D. Eisenhower; General Goodpaster.

24   Washington. Morning appointments with General Goodpaster; J. C. Hagerty; T. E. Stephens; Secretary Herter, A. W. Dulles, and General Goodpaster (off the record); National Security Council session; Secretary Herter, J. H. Douglas, J. A. McCone, C. D. Dillon, and Dr. Kistiakowsky; G. Gray, J. N. Irwin, and General Goodpaster; General Persons; Investment Bankers Association of America representatives; J. E. Lemon; S. High. Lunch. Afternoon appointments with R. E. Merriam; J. C. Hagerty; W. J. Hopkins. Practices golf.

25   Washington. Morning appointments with T. E. Stephens; General Persons; U.S. Ambassador Lodge; Vice-President Nixon and General Persons; General Goodpaster; Cabinet meeting; General Goodpaster; Vice-President Nixon; J. C. Hagerty; T. E. Stephens and D. W. Kendall; Piotr Jaroszewicz (Deputy Prime Minister, Poland), Ambassador Rouald Spasowski (Poland), Bohdan Lewandowski (Foreign Ministry, Poland), R. Davis, and E. S. Glenn; General Goodpaster; Colonel Draper. Lunch. Afternoon appointments with Colonel Draper; Colonel Schulz; Major J. S. D. Eisenhower; Colonel Schulz and Major J. S. D. Eisenhower; P. E. Areeda; General Goodpaster; J. C. Hagerty and Colonels

Draper and Schulz; Generals Persons and Good-paster.

26 Washington. Morning appointments with J. C. Hagerty; Senator Hickenlooper and B. N. Harlow; General Bragdon; General Goodpaster; Major J. S. D. Eisenhower; B. N. Harlow and General Good-paster; Major J. S. D. Eisenhower.

27 Washington. Attends services with Mrs. Eisenhower at National Presbyterian Church. To University of Maryland. Delivers address at Golden Anniversary White House Conference on Children and Youth.

28 Washington. Off-the-record breakfast meeting with Congressmen Ford and Laird, General Persons, and B. N. Harlow. Morning appointments with J. C. Hagerty; T. E. Stephens; General Goodpaster; D. W. Kendall; General Persons; J. C. Hagerty; Captain Au-rand; General Goodpaster and Major J. S. D. Eisen-hower; T. E. Stephens; Prime Minister Macmillan. Airborne for Camp David, Maryland, with Prime Minister Macmillan. Reads statement to press. Nu-clear test negotiations. Airborne for Gettysburg farm with Prime Minister Macmillan. Visits residence of Major J. S. D. Eisenhower and tours farm with Prime Minister Macmillan. To Camp David, Maryland.

29 Camp David, Maryland. Nuclear test negotiations. Tours Waynesboro, Gettysburg, and Gettysburg bat-tlefields with Prime Minister Macmillan.

30 Camp David, Maryland. Returns to Washington. Pre-news briefing; news conference. Morning ap-pointments with Senator Javits and Auschwitz sur-vivors; D. Paarlberg and General Persons; National Coal Association leaders and R. E. Merriam; Major J. S. D. Eisenhower. Lunch. Afternoon appoint-ments with General Persons and D. W. Kendall; AFL-CIO leaders and D. W. Kendall; Dr. Kistia-kowsky and Generals Persons and Goodpaster; Gen-eral Persons and D. W. Kendall; General Good-paster; P. E. Areeda; Major J. S. D. Eisenhower; J. C. Hagerty; General Persons; B. A. Eisenhower; Prime Minister Macmillan and Philip de Zulueta.

31 Washington. Morning appointments with W. J. Hop-kins; D. W. Kendall; General Goodpaster; Vice-Pres-

ident Nixon and General Persons; G. Gray; General Persons, J. C. Hagerty, and D. W. Kendall; Caroline K. Simon (Secretary of State, New York), Irving Halpern (husband) and T. E. Stephens (off the record); American Legion leaders and E. D. Chesney; Secretary Anderson and J. B. Baird; Reverend Graham; D. W. Kendall. Lunch. Afternoon appointments with General Goodpaster; J. C. Hagerty; T. E. Stephens; General Persons. Practices golf. Hosts reception for Little Cabinet and Independent Agencies Group.

April 1 Washington. Morning appointments with H. H. Gruenther; J. C. Hagerty; General Burgess and L. J. Alexis; Vice-President Nixon, Secretary Herter, J. H. Douglas, L. A. Hoegh, Admirals Burke and Blackburn, Generals Lemnitzer, LeMay, Goodpaster, and Shoup, Budget Director Stans, C. D. Dillon, A. W. Dulles, G. Gray, Dr. Kistiakowsky, Major J. S. D. Eisenhower, J. S. Lay, C. D. Fonvielle, and Jack Fresh (off the record); National Security Council session; R. E. Horner and Drs. Glennan, Tepper, Silverstein, and Dryden; J. C. Hagerty; Ambassador Carlos S. de Santamaria (from Colombia) and W. T. Buchanan; General Persons; T. E. Stephens; J. Z. Anderson; D. W. Kendall; General Goodpaster. Lunch. Afternoon appointments with General Goodpaster; General Persons; M. C. Moos. Practices golf on south lawn. Late afternoon appointments with M. C. Moos; Dr. Glennan and J. C. Hagerty.

2 Washington. Morning appointment with General Goodpaster. To Burning Tree Country Club for golf with J. E. Lemon.

3 Washington. Attends services at National Presbyterian Church.

4 Washington. Morning appointments with D. W. Kendall; J. C. Hagerty; Congressman Becker, B. N. Harlow, and General Goodpaster; D. W. Kendall; Senator Allott, D. W. Kendall, and E. A. McCabe; B. N. Harlow; Export Expansion Committee; 1960 Boy of the Year, Nicholas Beck; General Goodpaster. Lunch. Afternoon appointments with General Goodpaster; Attorney General Rogers; W. J. Hopkins. Practices golf on south lawn. Delivers address

at National Republican Party Women's Conference, Jumbo Jamboree.

5   Washington. Morning appointments with General Goodpaster; General Goodpaster and G. D. Morgan; B. N. Harlow and General Goodpaster; Legislative Leaders; General Goodpaster; Secretaries Mitchell and Mueller and G. D. Morgan; R. E. Merriam; Major J. S. D. Eisenhower. Greets President and Mrs. Alberto Lleras (Colombia). Lunch. Afternoon appointments with Secretary Herter and General Goodpaster; General Goodpaster; Colonel Schulz; D. W. Kendall. Swims. Hosts dinner with Mrs. Eisenhower in honor of President and Mrs. Lleras, followed by entertainment.

6   Washington. Morning appointments with Major J. S. D. Eisenhower; G. D. Morgan; W. J. Hopkins; General Goodpaster and B. N. Harlow; General Clark (off the record); D. W. Kendall; E. Michie, Eric Gebsen, and D. W. Kendall (off the record); G. Gray and General Goodpaster; Secretary Gates, J. H. Douglas, Franklin B. Lincoln, Generals Twining and Goodpaster, and B. N. Harlow; Douglas Fairbanks, Jr.; R. E. Merriam; Secretary Mueller, B. D. Tallamy, General Bragdon, R. E. Merriam, and Colonel John A. Meek (off the record); President Lleras, Ambassador de Santamaria, Secretary Herter, U.S. Ambassador Dempster McIntosh (to Colombia), and R. R. Rubottom. Lunch. Afternoon appointments with G. D. Morgan; Herbert Feis (Institute of Advanced Studies, Princeton University) and General Goodpaster (off the record); G. D. Morgan and Colonel Schulz; R. E. Merriam; A. Krock (off the record); Major J. S. D. Eisenhower and Colonel Schulz; W. Marriott (off the record).

7   Washington. Hosts breakfast for Republican Policy Committee. Morning appointments with W. J. Hopkins; General Goodpaster; National Security Council session; Vice-President Nixon; G. D. Morgan and D. W. Kendall; J. A. McCone and General Goodpaster (off the record); B. N. Harlow; J. Z. Anderson; Mayor Thomas T. Taber, Senator Case, Congressman Frelinghuysen and J. Z. Anderson. Practices golf on south lawn. Airborne for Camp

David, Maryland. Visits Gettysburg farm and residence of Major J. S. D. Eisenhower with President Lleras. Returns to Washington. Attends dinner with Mrs. Eisenhower in their honor, hosted by President and Mrs. Lleras.

8   Washington. Morning appointments with D. W. Kendall; W. A. Ruschmeyer, F. J. Donohue, and Colonel Schulz (off the record); Vice-President Nixon; Cabinet meeting; Major J. S. D. Eisenhower; Attorney General Rogers; Dr. Glennan, Major J. S. D. Eisenhower, and General Goodpaster; Oliver Leese (off the record); Ambassador Erasmo de la Guardia (from Panama) and C. E. Conger; U.S. Ambassador Selden Chapin (to Peru); Edgar W. Garbisch (New York); Major J. S. D. Eisenhower; R. J. Saulnier; D. W. Kendall; General Goodpaster; Congressman Byrnes, D. W. Kendall, and G. D. Morgan (off the record). Practices golf on south lawn.

9   Washington. Morning appointments with Major J. S. D. Eisenhower; General Goodpaster; Major J. S. D. Eisenhower; R. E. Merriam; G. Gray; W. J. Hopkins; D. W. Kendall and G. D. Morgan; Colonel Schulz; Major J. S. D. Eisenhower; M. J. McCaffree. Airborne for Gettysburg farm. Visits home of General Willard S. Paul. Returns to Washington.

10 Washington. No official appointments.

11 Washington. Morning appointments with S. Martini; R. E. Merriam and General Bragdon; Major J. S. D. Eisenhower; General Goodpaster and Major J. S. D. Eisenhower; General Goodpaster; Secretary Flemming; G. D. Morgan, B. N. Harlow, and R. E. Merriam; General Goodpaster; M. C. Moos; Major J. S. D. Eisenhower. To MATS terminal en route to Augusta, Georgia. To Augusta National Golf Club for golf with C. Roberts, L. S. Heaton, and A. Palmer.

12 Augusta, Georgia. Works in office. To Augusta National Golf Club for golf with L. S. Heaton, G. Stout, E. D. Slater, and A. Bradley. Visits with Mr. and Mrs. R. W. Woodruff.

13 Augusta, Georgia. To Augusta National Golf Club for golf with W. A. Jones, R. W. Woodruff, and General Goodpaster.

14 Augusta, Georgia. Morning appointment with H. R. McPhee and P. E. Areeda. To Augusta National Golf Club for golf with W. E. Robinson and L. S. Heaton.

15 Augusta, Georgia. Works at office. Fishes. To Augusta National Golf Club for golf with W. E. Robinson and Major and Mrs. J. S. D. Eisenhower.

16 Augusta, Georgia. Works at office. To Augusta National Golf Club for golf with Major J. S. D. Eisenhower, R. W. Woodruff, and W. E. Robinson. Fishes with D. D. Eisenhower II.

17 Augusta, Georgia. Rides in golf cart with grandchildren. Visits C. Roberts. Attends services at Reid Memorial Presbyterian Church. To Augusta National Golf Club for golf with C. Roberts, J. Roberts, and C. J. Schoo.

18 Augusta, Georgia. Returns to Washington. Appointment with H. R. McPhee. Attends opening Senators game and throws out first baseball. Airborne for Augusta, Georgia. To Augusta National Golf Club.

19 Augusta, Georgia. Appointment with Dr. C. R. Holton. To Augusta National Golf Club for golf with G. E. Allen, W. E. Robinson, and Colonel Belshe.

20 Augusta, Georgia. Works in office. To Augusta National Golf Club for golf with Major J. S. D. Eisenhower, G. E. Allen, W. E. Robinson, and J. E. Lemon. Dinner with Mrs. Eisenhower, Major J. S. D. Eisenhower, G. E. Allen, W. E. Robinson, and J. E. Lemon.

21 Augusta, Georgia. Works in office. To Augusta National Golf Club for golf with Major J. S. D. Eisenhower, Colonel Belshe, and G. E. Allen. Returns to Washington. Evening appointments with T. E. Stephens; J. J. McCloy.

22 Washington. Morning appointments with General Goodpaster; D. A. Paarlberg to discuss wheat problem in India; Mrs. H. Wallace, Mrs. T. M. Scott, Marty G. Scott, Mona Scott, Michelle Scott, and Tommy Ashton (off the record); Ambassador Melih Esenbel (from Turkey) and C. E. Conger; Major J. S. D. Eisenhower; W. J. Hopkins; Secretary Herter, C. D. Dillon, U.S. Ambassador Houghton, General

Goodpaster, and Major J. S. D. Eisenhower; J. A. Mc-
Cone and General Goodpaster; Dr. M. S. Eisenhower. Receives Air Force Academy yearbook.
Greets President de Gaulle. Lunch. Afternoon appointments with H. R. McPhee; Major J. S. D. Eisenhower; T. E. Stephens and General Goodpaster;
F. F. Gosden; General Goodpaster; President de
Gaulle; T. E. Stephens; J. C. Hagerty; General Goodpaster. Hosts dinner with Mrs. Eisenhower in honor
of President and Mrs. de Gaulle, followed by musical entertainment.

23   Washington. Morning appointments with G. D.
Morgan, B. N. Harlow, and R. E. Merriam; B. N.
Harlow; U.S. Ambassador Byroade; G. Gray; J. C.
Hagerty; General Goodpaster. Attends wreath-lay-
ing ceremony with President de Gualle. To Burning
Tree Country Club for golf with J. E. Lemon,
Colonel Belshe, and G. Cornell.

24   Washington. Attends services at National Presbyterian Church. Airborne for Gettysburg farm. Tours
farm and visits residence of Major J. S. D. Eisenhower with President de Gaulle. Airborne for Camp
David, Maryland. Returns to Washington.

25   Washington. Morning appointments with Colonel
Schulz; U.S. Ambassador Ellsworth Bunker (to India); U.S. Ambassador Rountree; W. D. Pawley (off
the record); General Clark and Secretary Herter
(off the record); President de Gaulle, Prime Minister de Murville, and French and U.S. officials; Secretary Herter and General Goodpaster. Promotes
Colonel Walters, followed by appointments with
J. C. Hagerty; Major J. S. D. Eisenhower; T. E.
Stephens; Secretary Benson. Greets National 4-H
Club members. Lunch. Afternoon appointments
with General Goodpaster and B. N. Harlow; G. D.
Morgan, R. E. Merriam, and Secretary Flemming;
Major J. S. D. Eisenhower. Practices golf on south
lawn. Attends dinner in their honor with Mrs. Eisen-
hower, hosted by President and Mrs. de Gaulle.

26   Washington. Morning appointments with President
and Mrs. de Gaulle; B. N. Harlow; Legislative Leaders; Mrs. Eisenhower and cousins; Secretary
Mitchell; Secretary Mitchell and G. D. Morgan;

George Meany (President, AFL-CIO) and Secretary Mitchell; D. W. Kendall. Lunch. To Burning Tree Country Club for golf with Colonel Belshe, R. Dunn, and J. E. Lemon.

27 Washington. Morning appointments with M. J. Mc-Caffree; General Goodpaster; Secretary Flemming, Dr. Kistiakowsky, and General Goodpaster. Witnesses swearing-in ceremony for D. Paarlberg as Food-for-Peace Coordinator. Pre-news briefing; news conference. Late morning appointments with H. D. Newsom and G. D. Morgan; R. Cake (off the record); T. E. Stephens; Major J. S. D. Eisenhower. Greets King Mehandra and Queen Ratna (Nepal). Lunch. Afternoon appointments with G. D. Morgan; Major J. S. D. Eisenhower; J. C. Hagerty and General Goodpaster; W. J. Hopkins. Practices golf. Hosts dinner with Mrs. Eisenhower in honor of King Mehandra and Queen Ratna.

28 Washington. Morning appointments with B. N. Harlow and R. E. Merriam; G. Gray; National Security Council session; G. Gray and T. E. Stephens; King Mehandra; King Mehandra, Subarna S. J. B. Rana (Deputy Prime Minister, Nepal), Ambassador Rishikesh Shaha (Nepal), L. W. Henderson, and U.S. Ambassadors Stebbins and Hart; General Goodpaster and R. E. Merriam; Major J. S. D. Eisenhower; Secretary Anderson, J. B. Baird, and C. Walker (off the record); Major J. S. D. Eisenhower. Lunch. To Burning Tree Country Club for golf with Colonel Belshe, F. C. Akers, and J. E. McClure.

29 Washington. Breakfast meeting with Republican senators. Cabinet meeting. Appointments with U.S. Ambassador Lodge; T. E. Stephens; Inter-American Development Bank directors; Dr. Jonas E. Salk, Secretary Flemming, and Dr. Abraham Horowitz (Regional Director, World Health Organization); Major J. S. D. Eisenhower; NSC Net Evaluation Subcommittee, Vice-President Nixon, Secretary Gates, G. Gray, and Generals Twining and Goodpaster; Vice-President Nixon. Lunch. Afternoon appointments with Major J. S. D. Eisenhower; C. B. Randall; General Goodpaster; Colonel Schulz; D. W. Kendall; W. J. Hopkins; Major J. S. D. Eisenhower. Practices

golf on south lawn. Attends dinner with Mrs. Eisenhower in their honor, hosted by King Mehandra and Queen Ratna.

30   Washington. Appointment with General Goodpaster. Airborne for Gettysburg farm. To Gettysburg Country Club for golf with Major J. S. D. Eisenhower, G. E. Allen, General Nevins, and D. D. Eisenhower II. To Camp David, Maryland. Visits residence of F. C. Akers with G. E. Allen. Views movie.

May   1   Camp David, Maryland. Bowls with G. E. Allen and M. J. Eisenhower. Visits Gettysburg farm with G. E. Allen. Practices golf. Shoots skeet. Returns to Washington.

2   Washington. Morning appointments with T. E. Stephens; B. N. Harlow; T. E. Stephens; B. N. Harlow; W. J. Hopkins; General Goodpaster; S. P. Skouras. Addresses U.S. Chamber of Commerce annual meeting. Appointments with B. N. Harlow; G. Gray; Captain Aurand; Rudolph F. Bannow (President, National Association of Manufacturers) and Secretary Mueller. Lunch. Afternoon appointments with Colonel Norris, Major J. S. D. Eisenhower, and Major Streiff. Attends dedication services at National Cathedral for windows in memory of Samuel Gompers, William Green, and Philip Murray. Receives life membership at Ligonier Golf Club. Late afternoon appointments with Secretaries Anderson and Flemming, D. Lindsey, Budget Director Stans, E. Staats, General Persons, G. D. Morgan, and R. E. Merriam (off the record); General Persons. Practices golf on south lawn. Addresses guests at dinner for Committee for International Economic Growth and Committee to Strengthen Frontiers of Freedom.

3   Washington. Airborne for Fort Benning, Georgia. Attends demonstration of Army equipment; delivers speech. Returns to Washington.

4   Washington. Breakfast meeting with 82nd Club. Appointments with Congressman Gubser and J. Z. Anderson; General Persons; J. C. Hagerty and D. Paarlberg; Attorney General Rogers and General Persons. Signs U.S.-India Wheat Agreement, followed by appointments with R. E. Merriam; Sena-

tors Cooper and Scott, Governor Underwood, and E. A. McCabe; General Persons; Drs. Kistiakowsky and Long and Generals Persons and Goodpaster; T. E. Stephens. To Burning Tree Country Club for golf with A. Shivers, J. E. Lemon, and Colonel Belshe.

5   Washington. Airborne for High Point, Civil Defense Relocation Site. Tours site. National Security Council session. Speaks over closed-circuit television. Returns to Washington. Late morning appointments with General Goodpaster; T. E. Stephens; G. Gray; J. C. Hagerty and General Goodpaster; General Goodpaster; Generals Twining and Goodpaster; General Persons and R. E. Merriam. Lunch. Afternoon appointments with K. B. McCann; Secretary Flemming; G. D. Morgan. Dentist appointment. Late afternoon appointments with T. E. Stephens and General Goodpaster; H. R. McPhee; W. J. Hopkins; General Persons. Practices golf on south lawn.

6   Washington. Morning appointments with G. Gray; General Goodpaster; General Caffey (off the record); General Persons, Attorney General Rogers, and D. W. Kendall; M. C. Moos (off the record); U.S. Ambassador Howard P. Jones (to Indonesia); C. D. Dillon and General Goodpaster; B. N. Harlow. Signs Civil Rights Bill. Appointments with General Persons and D. W. Kendall; Committee to Coordinate Federal Urban Area Assistance Programs (off the record); General Goodpaster; Reverends Blake and Smith and T. E. Stephens; General Persons. Addresses AFL-CIO Union Industries Show. Airborne for Gettysburg farm. To Gettysburg Country Club for golf with G. E. Allen. Plays baseball with D. D. Eisenhower II.

7   Gettysburg. To Gettysburg Country Club for golf with G. E. Allen and General Nevins. Fishes with F. C. Akers. Dinner at residence of Major J. S. D. Eisenhower with Mrs. Eisenhower, G. E. and Mrs. Allen, General and Mrs. Nevins, and Colonel Tkach.

8   Gettysburg. Attends services at Presbyterian Church of Gettysburg. Returns to Washington.

9   Washington. Hosts breakfast for Republican congressmen. Appointments with General Persons and

B. N. Harlow; General Persons; W. J. Hopkins; G. Gray; E. A. McCabe; General Persons; J. C. Hagerty; R. J. Saulnier; National Association of Savings Banks officers; Senator Case and E. A. McCabe (off the record); General Goodpaster; Dr. Kistiakowsky and D. Paarlberg; B. N. Harlow; General Foulkes (Chairman, Chiefs of Staff, Canada) and Major J. S. D. Eisenhower; D. W. Kendall. Attends 1915 West Point Class reunion luncheon. Afternoon appointments with General Goodpaster; General Persons; G. Gray and General Goodpaster; G. Gray; National Security Council session; Vice-President Nixon; Congressman Rayburn and B. N. Harlow (off the record).

10   Washington. Morning appointments with W. J. Hopkins; General Goodpaster; B. N. Harlow and General Persons; Legislative Leaders; General Goodpaster; D. W. Kendall; General Persons; Sam Witwer (Senatorial candidate) and R. E. Merriam; J. C. Hagerty; R. J. Saulnier. Presents Legion of Merit to Captain Beach, followed by appointments with P. E. Areeda; General Goodpaster; Attorney General Rogers. Presents Scholastic Achievement Awards to blind students. Lunch. Afternoon appointments with Secretary Herter, L. T. Merchant, F. D. Kohler, and General Goodpaster; Vice-President Nixon; T. E. Stephens; General Goodpaster; General Persons; General Goodpaster; General Persons; Major J. S. D. Eisenhower; T. E. Stephens. Practices golf.

11   Washington. Breakfast meeting with Republican senators. Morning appointments with Dr. C. G. King (Executive Director, Nutrition Foundation) and D. Paarlberg; General Persons; J. C. Hagerty and General Goodpaster; J. C. Hagerty; pre-news briefing; news conference; T. E. Stephens; National League of Insured Savings Associations officers; T. E. Stephens. Receives Mr. Travel Award. Lunch. To Burning Tree Country Club for golf with Colonel Belshe, T. Webb, and J. E. Shea. Appointments with T. E. Stephens; B. N. Harlow.

12   Washington. Hosts breakfast for Republican congressmen. Cabinet meeting. Late morning appointments with Secretary Herter; R. Montgomery

and J. Cagney; Vice-President Nixon; Admiral Strauss; J. L. Peters and G. V. Allen; G. V. Allen; Postmaster General Summerfield. Presents Young American Medals for Bravery to Sharon L. Beoro and Neil W. Lomenson. Lunch. Afternoon appointments with Dr. M. S. Eisenhower; T. E. Stephens; W. J. Hopkins; General Goodpaster and Major J. S. D. Eisenhower; K. B. McCann; General Goodpaster; Major J. S. D. Eisenhower. Practices golf on south lawn. Delivers address at American Helicopter Society meeting.

13   Washington. Morning appointments with General Persons, D. W. Kendall, and H. R. McPhee; Secretary Flemming, Dr. Kistiakowsky, and Generals Persons and Goodpaster; General Goodpaster; U.S. Ambassador Leland Barrows (to Cameroun); General Twining, Colonels Ennis, Blankman, Moore, and Stern, and Captain Lowe (off the record); Generals Twining and Goodpaster and Major J. S. D. Eisenhower; Senator Smathers, W. D. Pawley, and General Persons; W. Flenniken and T. E. Stephens (off the record); G. Gray; H. R. McPhee; G. C. Lodge (off the record); Major J. S. D. Eisenhower. Lunch. Afternoon appointments with C. D. Dillon, R. R. Rubottom, U.S. Ambassador Farland (to Dominican Republic), and Generals Persons and Goodpaster; C. D. Dillon and General Goodpaster; J. B. Baird and D. W. Kendall; General Goodpaster, D. W. Kendall, and H. R. McPhee; W. J. Hopkins; General Goodpaster. Practices golf on south lawn.

14   Washington. Morning appointments with S. Martini; General Goodpaster; D. W. Kendall, P. E. Areeda, and H. R. McPhee; General Goodpaster; W. J. Hopkins; General Goodpaster and G. D. Morgan. Views golf tournament at Burning Tree Country Club with W. E. Robinson. Airborne for Paris.

15   Paris, France. Meets with President de Gaulle, Chancellor Adenauer, Prime Minister Macmillan, Secretary Herter, L. T. Merchant, General Goodpaster, and Colonel Walters; President de Gaulle, Chancellor Adenauer, and Prime Minister Macmillan.

16   Paris, France. Meets with Prime Minister Macmillan, Chancellor Adenauer, President de Gaulle, and Chairman Khrushchev.

17   Paris, France. Meets with President de Gaulle, Chancellor Adenauer, and Prime Minister Macmillan. To Marnes la Coquette, France with Prime Minister Macmillan. To Paris. Meets with Prime Minister Macmillan, President de Gaulle, and Chancellor Adenauer.

18   Paris, France. Tours Notre Dame Cathedral and St. Chapelle. Attends luncheon hosted by President de Gaulle. Meets with Prime Minister Macmillan; Prime Minister Macmillan, President de Gaulle, and Chancellor Adenauer.

19   Paris, France. Airborne for Lisbon. Meets with President Americo Deus R. Thomaz (Portugal); American Embassy staff and spouses. Attends luncheon in his honor, hosted by President Thomaz. Receives chiefs of diplomatic missions. Tours gardens of Queluz Palace. Meets with Dr. A. Salazar. Hosts dinner in honor of President and Mrs. Thomaz.

20   Lisbon, Portugal. Airborne for Terceira Island, Azores. Tours Lajes Field. Returns to Washington. Afternoon appointments with D. W. Kendall; Generals Persons and Goodpaster; U.S. Ambassador Lodge.

21   Washington. To Gettysburg farm. To Gettysburg Country Club for golf with G. E. Allen, W. E. Robinson, D. D. Eisenhower II, and General Nevins. Visits with General Gruenther.

22   Gettysburg. Attends services at Presbyterian Church of Gettysburg. Visits with Captain Butcher and family and Major Streiff and son.

23   Gettysburg. Returns to Washington. Morning appointments with Major J. S. D. Eisenhower; T. E. Stephens; General Persons; General Goodpaster; General Persons; Secretary Herter; General Persons, G. D. Morgan, and D. W. Kendall; General Goodpaster. Lunch. Afternoon appointments with M. C. Moos, B. N. Harlow, and General Persons; General Goodpaster; Major J. S. D. Eisenhower; T. E. Stephens; C. W. Jones.

24 Washington. Morning appointments with W. J. Hopkins; T. E. Stephens; G. Gray and Major J. S. D. Eisenhower (off the record); General Goodpaster; National Security Council session; Secretary Herter; General Goodpaster; M. C. Moos; General Persons; D. W. Kendall. Lunch. Afternoon appointments with General Persons; M. C. Moos, B. N. Harlow, J. C. Hagerty, and General Persons; General Goodpaster; Major J. S. D. Eisenhower; General Persons. Practices golf.

25 Washington. Morning appointments with Major J. S. D. Eisenhower; General Persons and B. N. Harlow; General Goodpaster and Major J. S. D. Eisenhower; General Persons; General Goodpaster; General Persons; General Persons and Vice-President Nixon; W. J. Hopkins; J. C. Hagerty; General Persons; T. E. Stephens; General Persons. Lunch. Afternoon appointments with General Goodpaster, M. C. Moos, and B. N. Harlow. Works on speech. Dentist appointment. Practices golf. Addresses nation via radio and television.

26 Washington. Breakfast meeting with bipartisan legislative leaders. Morning appointments with General Persons and B. N. Harlow; General Goodpaster; Budget Director Stans; R. E. Merriam; Governor Smylie and R. E. Merriam; Dr. Kistiakowsky, G. Gray, and General Goodpaster (off the record); General Persons; G. Gray; Shigeru Yoshida (former Prime Minister, Japan), Ambassadors Asakai and Parsons, and T. Shimanouchi; General Persons. Receives Benjamin Franklin papers. Lunch. Afternoon appointments with Colonel Schulz; General Goodpaster; D. W. Kendall; Cabinet meeting; W. J. Hopkins; T. E. Stephens; Major J. S. D. Eisenhower. Airborne for Gettysburg farm. Tours grounds with Chief West. Practices golf.

27 Gettysburg. To Gettysburg Country Club for golf with W. E. Robinson and Generals Nevins and Snyder. Appointment with T. E. Stephens, J. C. Hagerty, General Goodpaster, and Major J. S. D. Eisenhower. Shoots skeet with Mrs. W. E. Robinson. Visits duck pond with W. E. Robinson.

28   Gettysburg. Shops in Biglersville, Pennsylvania, with
      W. E. Robinson. To residence of F. C. Akers with
      W. E. Robinson.

29   Gettysburg. Attends services with Mrs. Eisenhower
      at Presbyterian Church of Gettysburg.

30   Gettysburg. Walks around grounds with Chief West.
      Tours Fort Ritchie, Maryland, with Major J. S. D.
      Eisenhower. To Gettysburg. Returns to Washington.

31   Washington. Morning appointments with T. E.
      Stephens and General Goodpaster; General Good-
      paster; J. C. Hagerty and G. Gray; M. C. Moos; Gen-
      eral Persons; Dr. Glennan and General Goodpaster;
      P. Sarasin and U.S. Ambassador Parsons. Hosts stag
      luncheon for SEATO. National Security Council ses-
      sion. Appointments with Secretary Anderson and
      C. D. Dillon; General Persons; General Goodpaster;
      Colonel Schulz; W. J. Hopkins; T. E. Stephens; G. D.
      Morgan; Lt. Colonel J. S. D. Eisenhower; T. E.
      Stephens. Practices golf.

June   1   Washington. Morning appointments with T. E.
      Stephens; General Persons; T. E. Stephens; Atlantic
      Conference of Young Political Leaders delegates; J.
      C. Hagerty; General Goodpaster; Prime Minister
      Nash and U.S. Ambassador Parsons; Congressman
      Younger and J. Z. Anderson; D. W. Kendall and P.
      E. Areeda; General Persons; D. W. Kendall; Budget
      Director Stans, Secretary Anderson, R. J. Saulnier,
      and General Persons. Receives West Point and Naval
      Academy yearbooks. Lunch. Visits General St. John,
      Colonel Higdon, and Mrs. Eisenhower at Walter
      Reed Hospital with Lt. Colonel J. S. D. Eisenhower.
      To Burning Tree Country Club for golf with
      Colonel Belshe. Afternoon appointments with M. C.
      Moos; Lt. Colonel J. S. D. Eisenhower. Delivers ad-
      dress at dinner for Boy Scouts of America.

        2   Washington. Breakfast meeting with Senator Dirk-
      sen, Congressman Halleck, General Persons, and
      B. N. Harlow. Morning appointments with Secretary
      Flemming and B. N. Harlow; Legislative Leaders;
      Secretary Mitchell, G. D. Morgan, and E. A. Mc-
      Cabe; Committee on Chilean Relief; Committee on

Government Employment Policy; T. E. Stephens and General Goodpaster. Lunch. To Burning Tree Country Club for golf with Colonel Belshe, J. E. Lemon, and W. W. Rapley. Visits Mrs. Eisenhower at Walter Reed Hospital.

3   Washington. Morning appointment with General Persons. Receives commemorative stamp album honoring "The American Woman." Cabinet meeting. Appointments with D. W. Kendall and H. R. McPhee; Secretary Benson; Secretaries Gates and Herter, L. T. Merchant, J. H. Douglas, General Goodpaster, and Lt. Colonel J. S. D. Eisenhower; General Goodpaster and Lt. Colonel J. S. D. Eisenhower; M. J. McCaffree. Lunch. Afternoon appointments with Colonel Schulz; Lt. Colonel J. S. D. Eisenhower; General Goodpaster; Prime Minister Diefenbaker; Prime Minister Diefenbaker and Canadian and U.S. officials; L. R. Merchant, General Goodpaster and Lt. Colonel J. S. D. Eisenhower; General Goodpaster. Hosts dinner with Mrs. Eisenhower in honor of Prime Minister and Mrs. Diefenbaker, followed by musical entertainment.

4   Washington. Morning appointments with W. Cowles and R. E. Merriam; G. Gray; D. W. Kendall; W. J. Hopkins; Priscilla Woodruff and Mary Ann Bieniek; Stellakis Parthenopolous (5 year old, Greece); General Goodpaster. Visits Mrs. Eisenhower at Walter Reed Hospital. Appointment with General Goodpaster. Airborne for West Point, New York. Visits Evelyn K. LaDue. Attends Class of 1915 Reunion Dinner.

5   West Point, New York. Airborne for South Bend, Indiana. Receives ROTC detachment. Attends luncheon. Addresses commencement exercises of University of Notre Dame and receives honorary degree. Airborne for West Point, New York. Attends Class of 1915 picnic.

6   West Point, New York. Tours Thayer Museum and New East Barracks. Places wreath on Thayer statue. Plants tree. Lunch with Class of 1915. Receives 1960 class ring. Attends Class of 1915 alumni meeting. Attends Class of 1915 dinner.

7   West Point, New York. Returns to Washington. Morning appointments with General Persons and R. E. Merriam; General Goodpaster; General Persons; Jewish War Veterans officers and E. D. Chesney; Colonel Schulz; G. Gray, Secretaries Gates and Anderson, C. D. Dillon, and General Persons (off the record); National Small Businessmen's Association; Colonel Schulz. Lunch. Afternoon appointments with K. B. McCann; General Persons. Visits Mrs. Eisenhower at Walter Reed Hospital. Late afternoon appointments with General Goodpaster; Lt. Colonel J. S. D. Eisenhower. Practices golf.

8   Washington. Breakfast meeting with Governor Rockefeller. Appointments with Ambassador Mikael Imru (from Ethiopia) and W. T. Buchanan; Ambassador Reid; Ambassador Alejos (from Guatemala) and C. E. Conger; General Persons; D. W. Kendall and W. J. Hopkins; Ambassador Chon Il-Kwon (Korea) and W. T. Buchanan; E. A. McCabe and B. N. Harlow. Visits Mrs. Eisenhower at Walter Reed Hospital. Lunch. Afternoon appointments with Drs. Rabi and Kistiakowsky (off the record); National Security Council session; Vice-President Nixon, C. D. Dillon, and General Persons; B. N. Harlow and R. W. Woodruff (off the record); U.S. Ambassador Whitney (off the record); Dr. T. Dooley. Practices golf.

9   Washington. Morning appointments with Generals Persons and Goodpaster; Legislative Leaders; Prime Minister Pedro G. Beltram (Peru), R. R. Rubottom, and T. C. Achilles; General Persons and K. B. McCann. Makes films "Salute to Senator Saltonstall" and "Republican Workshop." To Burning Tree Country Club for golf with W. E. Robinson, J. E. Lemon, and C. B. Monroe. Late afternoon appointment with Senator Johnson, Congressman Rayburn, and B. N. Harlow.

10   Washington. Morning appointments with Generals Persons and Goodpaster; General Goodpaster; General Goodpaster and Lt. Colonel J. S. D. Eisenhower; General Goodpaster; AMVETS officials and E. D. Chesney; Secretary Herter, C. D. Dillon, Generals Persons and Goodpaster; Colonel Draper;

J. Cochran; Attorney General Rogers and B. N. Harlow; R. E. Merriam; Ambassador Muller, Mr. Schneider, W. Coerr, and R. E. Merriam; General Persons. Lunch. To Burning Tree Country Club for golf with J. E. Shea, W. E. Robinson, and Colonel Belshe. Visits Mrs. Eisenhower at Walter Reed Hospital with W. E. Robinson. Evening appointments with Governor Davis, J. Underhill, and R. E. Merriam; General Goodpaster.

11   Washington. Morning appointments with B. N. Harlow, R. E. Merriam, and General Goodpaster; Colonel Schulz; D. W. Kendall and W. J. Hopkins; General Goodpaster; Postmaster General Summerfield; P. E. Areeda; G. Gray; B. N. Harlow; General Goodpaster. To Burning Tree Country Club for golf with G. E. Allen, W. E. Robinson, and Colonel Belshe. Visits Mrs. Eisenhower at Walter Reed Hospital with grandchildren.

12   Washington. Airborne for Anchorage, Alaska. Receives briefing. Poses for photographs. Attends reception.

13   Anchorage, Alaska. Airborne for Manila, Philippines.

14   Manila, Philippines. Arrives and remains at Malacanang Palace.

15   Manila, Philippines. Breakfast meeting with President and Mrs. Garcia, Mr. and Mrs. F. Campos, and Lt. Colonel and Mrs. J. S. D. Eisenhower. Meets with President Garcia. Lays wreath on Rizal Monument. Attends luncheon in his honor, hosted by President Garcia. Addresses joint session of Philippine Congress. Greets American community. Attends state dinner and reception in his honor, hosted by President and Mrs. Garcia.

16   Manila, Philippines. Airborne for University of Philippines. Receives honorary degree. Lays wreaths at U.S. Military Cemetery. Attends luncheon in his honor, hosted by Philippine and American Chambers of Commerce. Delivers address at public rally. Hosts reception and dinner in honor of President and Mrs. Garcia. Cruises to Taipei, Taiwan.

17   Aboard U.S.S. *St. Paul.*

18 Taipei, Taiwan. Attends private lunch. Lays wreath at Martyrs' Shrine. Meets with President Chiang Kai-shek. Delivers address. Attends reception and state dinner hosted by President and Mrs. Chiang Kai-shek in his honor.

19 Taipei, Taiwan. Attends services at Shihlin Chapel. Meets with President Chiang Kai-shek and Taiwan and U.S. officials. Airborne for Okinawa. Delivers brief address. Meets with Chief Executive Ota. Airborne for Seoul, Korea. Receives group of Korean school children.

20 Seoul, Korea. Breakfast meeting with U.S. Ambassador and Mrs. McConaughy. Greets American community. Attends luncheon. Meets with Prime Minister Huh. Addresses National Assembly. Receives L. D. Knox and J. B. Vaughan. Reviews troops. Lays wreath at Unknown Soldiers' Monument. Delivers address. Attends reception. Airborne for Honolulu, Hawaii.

21 Honolulu, Hawaii. To Kaneohe Marine Golf Club for golf with Lt. Colonel J. S. D. Eisenhower, General Goodpaster, and J. C. Hagerty.

22 Honolulu, Hawaii. To Kaneohe Marine Golf Club for golf with J. C. Hagerty, General Goodpaster, and Lt. Colonel J. S. D. Eisenhower. Hosts cocktail party.

23 Honolulu, Hawaii. To Kaneohe Marine Golf Club for golf with J. C. Hagerty, General Goodpaster, and Lt. Colonel J. S. D. Eisenhower. Views movie "Please Don't Eat the Daisies" with Lt. Colonel and Mrs. J. S. D. Eisenhower and Captain Aurand.

24 Honolulu, Hawaii. To Kaneohe Marine Golf Club for golf with General Goodpaster, J. C. Hagerty, and Lt. Colonel J. S. D. Eisenhower. Cruises on launch. Attends reception hosted by Governor and Mrs. Quinn in his honor. Visits with Governor and Mrs. Quinn, Mr. and Mrs. Harry D. Felt, Major and Mrs. Gannon, and Lieutenant and Mrs. Keliher.

25 Honolulu, Hawaii. To Kaneohe Marine Golf Club for golf with Lt. Colonel J. S. D. Eisenhower, R. C. Weede, and M. M. Magruder. Returns to Washington.

26   Washington. No official appointments.

27   Washington. Morning appointments with W. J. Hopkins; Lt. Colonel J. S. D. Eisenhower; T. E. Stephens; General Persons; D. W. Kendall; W. J. Hopkins; Vice-President Nixon; J. C. Hagerty; Secretary Herter, C. D. Dillon, and General Goodpaster; J. A. McCone and General Goodpaster; General Goodpaster; J. C. Hagerty; General Goodpaster. Lunch. Addresses nation on trip.

28   Washington. Morning appointments with General Persons and B. N. Harlow; H. R. McPhee; General Goodpaster; Legislative Leaders; T. E. Stephens; B. N. Harlow; J. C. Hagerty; General Persons; General Goodpaster; General Persons. Greets National Elks Youth Leadership Contest winner, Steven K. Smith. Witnesses swearing-in ceremony of General Bragdon as Civil Aeronautics Board member. Greets King Bhumibol Adulyadeh and Queen Sirikit (Thailand). Lunch. Afternoon appointments with W. J. Hopkins; J. C. Hagerty; H. R. Luce (off the record); Secretary Anderson, Senators Dirksen and Williams, and D. Lindsay; Senator Dirksen and B. N. Harlow; B. N. Harlow; D. W. Kendall and H. R. McPhee; J. C. Hagerty. Presents Legion of Merit to King Bhumibol. Hosts dinner with Mrs. Eisenhower in honor of King Bhumibol and Queen Sirikit, followed by entertainment.

29   Washington. Morning appointments with D. W. Kendall and H. R. McPhee; Secretary Mitchell and General Persons; T. E. Stephens; G. Gray; Mrs. Duane Duke (cousin) and T. E. Stephens; American Heritage Tour high school students; Generals Westmoreland and Goodpaster; General Persons; King Bhumibol; King Bhubimol and Thai and U.S. officials; Secretary Herter; T. E. Stephens. Delivers address at dedication ceremony for National Grange building. Lunch. Afternoon appointments with General Persons; Lt. Colonel J. S. D. Eisenhower; T. E. Stephens. Practices golf. Visits dinner in honor of Secretary Mitchell. Attends off-the-record dinner hosted by the Advisory Council of the Chamber of Commerce.

30   Washington. Off-the-record breakfast meeting with Dr. M. S. Eisenhower. Morning appointments with General Persons and H. R. McPhee; National Security Council session; Lt. Colonel J. S. D. Eisenhower; T. E. Stephens and Captain Aurand; General Goodpaster; Senator Morton, General Persons, T. E. Stephens, J. C. Hagerty, and R. E. Merriam; R. J. Saulnier; Lt. Colonel J. S. D. Eisenhower; General Persons. Lunch. Afternoon appointments with D. W. Kendall; General Goodpaster; General Persons; T. E. Stephens; General Cutler. Attends reception and dinner with Mrs. Eisenhower in their honor hosted by King Bhumibol and Queen Sirikit.

July   1   Washington. Breakfast meeting with Republican senators. Morning appointments with Cabinet; Secretary Benson; Secretary Herter; J. C. Hagerty; L. E. Walsh; D. W. Kendall; T. E. Stephens. Presents 50-star flag to Senator Scott for July 4, followed by appointments with General Persons; General Goodpaster; Ambassador Flores and R. R. Rubottom; L. T. Merchant, E. R. Hardin, Generals Twining and Goodpaster, H. L. Wood, and Lt. Colonel J. S. D. Eisenhower; General Goodpaster; T. E. Stephens; General Goodpaster. Lunch. To Gettysburg farm with Mrs. Eisenhower. Visits with W. E. Robinson.

        2   Gettysburg. To Gettysburg Country Club for golf with W. E. Robinson, General Nevins, and R. Sleichter. Appointment with D. W. Kendall. Inspects fitting barn with G. E. Allen, W. E. Robinson, and General Nevins. To Gettysburg Country Club for golf with G. E. Allen and W. E. Robinson.

        3   Gettysburg. Attends services at Presbyterian Church of Gettysburg. Visits residence of Lt. Colonel J. S. D. Eisenhower. To Gettysburg Country Club for golf with G. E. Allen, W. E. Robinson, and B. T. Leithead.

        4   Gettysburg. To Gettysburg Country Club for golf with G. E. Allen, B. T. Leithead, and W. E. Robinson. Returns to Washington.

        5   Washington. Off-the-record breakfast meeting with Senator Morton, U.S. Ambassador Folger, L. W.

Hall, General Persons, and T. E. Stephens. Morning appointments with J. C. Hagerty; Vice-President Nixon, Secretary Anderson, U.S. Ambassador Lodge, General Persons, C. D. Dillon, and J. C. Hagerty (off the record); Vice-President Nixon (off the record); General Persons; Secretary Benson (off the record); P. E. Areeda; Lt. Colonel J. S. D. Eisenhower. Lunch. Afternoon appointments with T. E. Stephens; D. W. Kendall; General Persons; J. C. Hagerty; M. C. Moos; Lt. Colonel J. S. D. Eisenhower; General Persons. Practices golf.

6   Washington. Morning appointments with G. Gray; W. J. Hopkins; General Persons; Congressman Ford, Meinard Van Ens, and J. Z. Anderson; pre-news briefing; news conference; C. D. Dillon, Secretary Anderson, R. R. Rubottom, T. D. Morse, T. C. Mann, General Persons, J. C. Hagerty, and Lt. Colonel J. S. D. Eisenhower (off the record); Secretary Gates and Lt. Colonel J. S. D. Eisenhower. Lunch. Afternoon appointments with General Persons, D. Paarlberg, J. C. Hagerty, and G. D. Morgan; D. W. Kendall; H. R. McPhee; Lt. Colonel J. S. D. Eisenhower.

7   Washington. Morning appointments with T. E. Stephens; National Security Council session; C. D. Dillon, G. Gray, General Persons, Dr. Kistiakowsky, and Lt. Colonel J. S. D. Eisenhower (off the record); Dr. A. C. B. Lovell, Viscount Hood, E. S. Hiscocks, and Drs. Glennan, Dryden, and Kistiakowsky; J. G. Powers, R. Ash, and G. D. Morgan (off the record); D. W. Kendall and H. R. McPhee. Lunch. Airborne for Newport, Rhode Island. To Newport Country Club for golf with H. G. Cushing, G. E. Allen, and J. Farrell.

8   Newport, Rhode Island. To Newport Country Club for golf with H. G. Cushing, G. E. Allen, and J. C. Hagerty. Fishes with G. E. Allen.

9   Newport, Rhode Island. Visits Hianloland Farms, home of W. A. Jones. Fishes with W. A. Jones. Lunch with W. A. Jones, C. W. Jones, G. E. Allen, and B. T. Leithead. Shoots skeet with W. A. Jones and C. W. Jones. Fishes with G. E. Allen.

10   Newport, Rhode Island. Attends services at U.S. Naval School Officer Candidate Chapel with B. T. Leithead, G. E. Allen, and Captain Aurand. To Newport Country Club for golf with H. G. Cushing, B. T. Leithead, and G. E. Allen. Meets with Secretary Herter, R. R. Rubottom, General Goodpaster, and J. C. Hagerty.

11   Newport, Rhode Island. Appointments with Secretary Herter and R. R. Buttom to discuss Soviet downing of American RB47; news conference. To Newport Country Club for golf with H. G. Cushing, G. E. Allen, and J. Farrell. Cruises around Newport.

12   Newport, Rhode Island. To Newport Country Club for golf with H. G. Cushing, G. E. Allen, and J. Farrell. Afternoon appointments with Science Advisory Committee; G. Gray, D. W. Kendall, and M. C. Moos.

13   Newport, Rhode Island. Works in office. To Newport Country Club for golf with H. G. Cushing, J. C. Hagerty, J. Farrell, and W. E. Robinson.

14   Newport, Rhode Island. Appointments with J. C. Hagerty; Captain Aurand; W. E. Robinson; Lt. Colonel J. S. D. Eisenhower, D. W. Kendall, and H. R. McPhee.

15   Newport, Rhode Island. Appointments with J. C. Hagerty; T. E. Stephens. To Newport Country Club for golf with G. E. Allen, W. E. Robinson, and H. G. Cushing. Attends reception for White House staff with Captain Aurand, hosted by Admiral Moore. Visits with B. T. Leithead.

16   Newport, Rhode Island. To Newport Country Club for golf with B. T. Leithead, G. E. Allen, and W. E. Robinson. Fishes at Hianloland Farms.

17   Newport, Rhode Island. Attends services at U.S. Naval Officer Candidates Chapel with Captain Aurand. To Newport Country Club for golf with G. E. Allen, B. T. Leithead, and W. E. Robinson. Afternoon appointment with Secretary Anderson and Attorney General Rogers.

18   Newport, Rhode Island. To Newport Country Club for golf with G. E. Allen, B. T. Leithead, and H. G.

Cushing. Appointments with T. E. Stephens; G. D. Morgan; Captain Aurand; U.S. Ambassador Arthur L. Richards (to Ethiopia); C. E. Wilson; T. E. Stephens; S. Adams (off the record); Governor and Mrs. Del Sesto and Mayor and Mrs. Maher.

19   Newport, Rhode Island. To Newport Country Club for golf with J. C. Hagerty, H. G. Cushing, and J. Farrell. Morning appointments with J. C. Hagerty and T. E. Stephens; U.S. Ambassador Trimble; Ambassador de Areilza and F. D. Kohler; Secretary Herter, F. O. Wilcox, F. D. Kohler, U.S. Ambassador Bohlen, General Goodpaster, and J. C. Hagerty; General Goodpaster; G. Gray; J. C. Hagerty; Dr. M. S. Eisenhower and M. C. Moos.

20   Newport, Rhode Island. Appointment with Dr. M. S. Eisenhower, M. C. Moos, and K. Spaulding. To Newport Country Club for golf with G. E. Allen, W. E. Robinson, and B. T. Leithead.

21   Newport, Rhode Island. To Newport Country Club for golf with G. E. Allen, W. E. Robinson, and B. T. Leithead.

22   Newport, Rhode Island. To Newport Country Club for golf with B. T. Leithead, G. E. Allen, and W. E. Robinson. Accompanied by Mrs. Eisenhower delivers address at ceremony naming Washington Square Eisenhower Park. Afternoon appointments with Dr. Wriston, F. L. Pace, and J. C. Hagerty; Barbara Wriston; T. C. Mann and P. E. Areeda to discuss civil aviation agreements with Mexico and Philippines; Lt. Colonel J. S. D. Eisenhower and M. C. Moos; T. E. Stephens; Lt. Colonel J. S. D. Eisenhower and M. C. Moos.

23   Newport, Rhode Island. To Newport Country Club for golf with G. E. Allen, W. E. Robinson, and B. T. Leithead. Views movie with Mr. and Mrs. G. E. Allen, Mrs. Snyder, W. E. Robinson, and B. T. Leithead.

24   Newport, Rhode Island. To Newport Country Club for golf with G. E. Allen, W. E. Robinson, and B. T. Leithead. Works in office. Cooks steak dinner with Mrs. Eisenhower.

25   Newport, Rhode Island. To Newport Country Club for golf with W. E. Robinson and H. G. Cushing. In-

spects submarine. National Security Council session. Appointments with Secretary Herter, C. D. Dillon, A. W. Dulles, G. C. Smith, Secretary Gates, H. Pattison, and E. Staats.

26   Newport, Rhode Island. Morning appointments with T. E. Stephens; J. C. Hagerty; Captain Aurand. With Mrs. Eisenhower airborne for Chicago for Republican National Convention. Meets with Vice-President Nixon and family; D. C. Gainey. Meets Republican National Convention delegates. Addresses convention. Attends dinner in honor of Senators Dirksen, Bridges, Saltonstall, and Kuchel.

27   Chicago. Attends breakfast hosted by National Republican Finance Committee. Makes address. Appointments with L. W. Hall; E. D. Eisenhower and family, J. E. Starem, and Colonel and Mrs. Carter. Lunch with Vice-President Nixon, W. A. Jones, C. W. Jones, S. S. Larmon, C. Roberts, Dr. M. S. Eisenhower, W. E. Robinson, L. W. Hall, and C. H. Percy. Airborne for Denver, Colorado.

28   Denver, Colorado. Attends National Boy Scout Jamboree. Visits home of E. Doud. Lunch at Cherry Hills Country Club. Tours Denver. Visits home of E. Doud.

29   Denver, Colorado. Fishes at ranch of B. F. Swan. Lunch with A. Nielsen and C. Roberts. Visits with E. Doud with Mrs. Eisenhower.

30   Denver, Colorado. Tours Denver with A. Nielsen. Visits E. Doud with Mrs. Eisenhower.

31   Denver, Colorado. Airborne for Newport, Rhode Island.

August   1   Newport, Rhode Island. To Newport Country Club for golf with W. A. Jones, C. W. Jones, and S. S. Larmon. Lunch aboard *Barbara Anne*. Appointments with Dr. J. Stein, Dr. S. Farber, and General Snyder; General Goodpaster; National Security Council session. Airborne for Kingston, Rhode Island. Receives honorary degree from University of Rhode Island. Airborne for Newport, Rhode Island. Evening appointment with Vice-President Nixon, J. Shepley, J. C. Hagerty, and U.S. Ambassador Lodge, H. Klein, and R. Finch.

2 Newport, Rhode Island. To Newport Country Club for golf with W. A. Jones, C. W. Jones, and S. S. Larmon. Works in office.

3 Newport, Rhode Island. To Newport Country Club for golf with W. A. Jones, S. S. Larmon, and H. G. Cushing. Afternoon appointments with Robert E. O'Neill (President, Newport Chamber of Commerce) and Frank Nunes (Vice-President, Newport Chamber of Commerce); Ambassadors Maiwandwal and Jones; Generals Norstad and Goodpaster; G. Gray, K. G. Harr, and M. D. Sprague; Mr. and Mrs. M. D. Sprague and family; G. Gray; General Goodpaster; J. C. Hagerty; Admiral Bernard L. Austin.

4 Newport, Rhode Island. To Newport Country Club for golf with W. A. Jones, C. W. Jones, and S. S. Larmon.

5 Newport, Rhode Island. To Newport Country Club for golf with W. A. Jones, C. W. Jones, and S. S. Larmon. To Constellation Pier with grandchildren. Entertains Admiral and Mrs. Weakley, Admiral Moore, Admiral and Mrs. Austin, and Captain and Mrs. James with Mrs. Eisenhower.

6 Newport, Rhode Island. To Newport Country Club for golf with Lt. Colonel J. S. D. Eisenhower, E. D. Slater, and C. Roberts.

7 Newport, Rhode Island. Attends services at U.S. Naval Officers Candidate Chapel with grandchildren. Greets winners of All Navy Tennis Tournament. To Newport Country Club for golf with C. Roberts, E. D. Slater, and H. G. Cushing. Returns to Washington.

8 Washington. Morning appointments with Colonel Schulz; W. J. Hopkins; General Persons, J. C. Hagerty, and B. N. Harlow; Lt. Colonel J. S. D. Eisenhower. Records message to Congress. Lunch. Afternoon appointments with Lt. Colonel J. S. D. Eisenhower; General Persons; T. E. Stephens; Lt. Colonel J. S. D. Eisenhower; B. N. Harlow; General Goodpaster; G. D. Morgan and D. W. Kendall; G. D. Morgan; T. E. Stephens. Makes recording for National Association of County Officials.

9   Washington. Breakfast meeting with Republican senators. Appointments with Vice-President Nixon; General Goodpaster; General Persons; W. J. Hopkins; A. W. Dulles, L. T. Merchant, Lt. Colonel J. S. D. Eisenhower, and Generals Robert A. Breitweiser, Twining, Persons, and Goodpaster; T. E. Stephens; Generals Twining, Persons, and Goodpaster; U.S. Ambassador Farland; General Persons; T. E. Stephens. To Burning Tree Country Club for golf with J. E. Lemon and Colonel Belshe.

10   Washington. Morning appointments with T. E. Stephens; General Persons; L. W. Hall and General Persons; G. Gray and General Goodpaster; G. Gray; R. J. Saulnier; W. J. Hopkins; J. C. Hagerty; pre-news briefing; news conference; Colonel Walters (off the record); T. E. Stephens; Secretary Seaton (off the record); General Curtis (off the record); T. E. Stephens; General Persons; General Goodpaster. Lunch. Afternoon appointments with Colonel Draper and Captain Aurand; Lt. Colonel J. S. D. Eisenhower; T. E. Stephens; J. C. Hagerty; W. J. Hopkins.

11   Washington. Morning appointments with General Persons; General Speidel and Lieutenant Colonel Moore (off the record); General Swing; A. B. Mason (off the record); General Persons; General Baker (off the record); J. C. Hagerty; General Goodpaster; Secretary Gates, Generals Goodpaster and Twining, Admiral Burke, J. H. Douglas, and Lt. Colonel J. S. D. Eisenhower; D. W. Kendall; Generals Persons and Goodpaster, J. C. Hagerty, and D. W. Kendall; Secretary Gates, J. C. Hagerty, and Generals Twining, Persons, and Goodpaster; W. J. Hopkins; Lt. Colonel J. S. D. Eisenhower. Makes "Republican Congressional Committee" and "Republican Roundup and Refresher Committee Workshop" films. Lunch. Afternoon appointments with J. C. Hagerty; Secretary Anderson and J. B. Baird (off the record); Lt. Colonel J. S. D. Eisenhower; P. E. Areeda; Lt. Colonel J. S. D. Eisenhower. Practices golf on south lawn. Attends reception of Army Distaff Foundation.

12   Washington. Morning appointments with General Goodpaster; Lt. Colonel J. S. D. Eisenhower; Na-

tional Security Council session; Secretary Herter; T. E. Stephens and Lt. Colonel J. S. D. Eisenhower; W. J. Hopkins. Airborne for Camp David, Maryland. Fishes at residence of F. C. Akers. To Gettysburg Country Club for golf with G. E. Allen and General Nevins.

13   Camp David, Maryland. To Gettysburg with G. E. Allen, W. E. Robinson, and General Snyder. Inspects farm. To Gettysburg Country Club for golf with G. E. Allen, W. E. Robinson, and General Nevins. Visits residence of G. E. Allen. To Camp David, Maryland.

14   Camp David, Maryland. Attends services at Presbyterian Church of Gettysburg with G. E. Allen. Visits farm. Practices golf with Captain Aurand.

15   Camp David, Maryland. Returns to Washington. Morning appointments with W. E. Robinson; General Persons; Vice-President Nixon, U.S. Ambassador Lodge, Senator Morton, General Persons, and J. C. Hagerty; Cabinet meeting; U.S. Ambassador Lodge, Secretary Herter, and General Persons; Secretary Herter, G. Gray, and Generals Persons and Goodpaster; General Persons; Secretary Gates, D. C. Sharp, General White, J. C. Hagerty, and Colonel Draper. Views capsule retrieved from satellite Discoverer XIII. Lunch. Afternoon appointments with J. C. Hagerty; J. A. McCone and General Goodpaster; Generals Persons and Goodpaster and B. N. Harlow; B. N. Harlow; W. J. Hopkins; A. Larson; General Goodpaster; J. Rowley; Lt. Colonel J. S. D. Eisenhower. Practices golf. Attends baseball game at Griffith Stadium.

16   Washington. Morning appointments with General Goodpaster; General Persons and B. N. Harlow; Vice-President Nixon; Legislative Leaders; Secretary Flemming and General Persons; General Persons; Dr. Edward H. Litchfield (Chancellor, University of Pittsburgh); J. C. Hagerty; W. J. Hopkins; R. Bowie and General Goodpaster. Lunch. To Burning Tree Country Club for golf with T. Webb and Colonel Belshe. Watches grandchildren play baseball.

17   Washington. Morning appointments with General Persons and D. W. Kendall; General Persons;

G. Gray; U.S. Ambassador Christian M. Ravndal (to Czechoslovak Socialist Republic); U.S. Ambassador Karl L. Rankin (to Yugoslavia); General Goodpaster; J. C. Hagerty and General Goodpaster; J. C. Hagerty; pre-news briefing; news conference; Dr. Glennan and General Persons (off the record); Postmaster General Summerfield; Secretaries Anderson and Flemming, Budget Director Stans, General Persons, G. D. Morgan, and B. N. Harlow; General Goodpaster, Lt. Colonel J. S. D. Eisenhower, and Captain Aurand; Commander Williams; Lt. Colonel J. S. D. Eisenhower. Lunch. Afternoon appointments with General Goodpaster; T. E. Stephens and Lt. Colonel J. S. D. Eisenhower. Visits S. Eisenhower at Walter Reed Hospital with Lt. Colonel J. S. D. Eisenhower. Appointment with Lt. Colonel J. S. D. Eisenhower.

18   Washington. Appointment with Secretary Mitchell; National Security Council session; G. Gray, Secretaries Anderson and Gates, Generals Lemnitzer, Goodpaster, and Persons, A. W. Dulles, and R. Bissell (off the record); C. D. Dillon and General Goodpaster; Lt. Colonel J. S. D. Eisenhower; General Persons; Ambassador Chiriboga (from Spain) and L. D. Mallory; General Persons; Lt. Colonel J. S. D. Eisenhower. Lunch. To Burning Tree Country Club for golf with R. W. Woodruff, Lt. Colonel J. S. D. Eisenhower, and D. D. Eisenhower II.

19   Washington. Morning appointments with Generals Persons and Goodpaster; General Goodpaster; Secretary Benson (off the record); J. A. McCone, L. T. Merchant, and General Goodpaster; General Goodpaster; Senator Carlson, William H. Fribley (National Commander, Disabled American Veterans), and T. E. Stephens; T. E. Stephens; Senator Morton, G. Murphy, and Generals Persons and Goodpaster (off the record); Ambassador Mariano de Y. Orbegoso (from Spain) and W. T. Buchanan; J. C. Hagerty; U.S. Ambassador Folger, L. W. Hall, and General Persons; L. W. Hall and U.S. Ambassador Folger; D. W. Kendall and General Goodpaster; General Goodpaster; D. W. Kendall; General Goodpaster. Lunch. Afternoon appointments with Captain Aurand, General Goodpaster, and Lt. Colonel

J. S. D. Eisenhower; D. Wilson and J. C. Hagerty (off the record); Lt. Colonel J. S. D. Eisenhower. Cruises to Mount Vernon, Virginia, and back to Washington.

20 Washington. Morning appointment with Lt. Colonel J. S. D. Eisenhower. To Burning Tree Country Club for golf with J. E. McClure, General Bradley, and Colonel Belshe.

21 Washington. Attends services with Mrs. Eisenhower at National Presbyterian Church.

22 Washington. Morning appointments with General Persons; P. E. Areeda; T. E. Stephens; Wheeler family; T. E. Stephens; Lt. Colonel J. S. D. Eisenhower; F. E. Davis, J. Hank, and T. E. Stephens; Secretary Brucker, General Lemnitzer, C. K. Gailey, R. Lee, Lt. Colonel J. S. D. Eisenhower, and J. F. Ladd; Lt. Colonel J. S. D. Eisenhower; 1959 Physician's award winner Dr. John H. Aldes (off the record). Lunch. Afternoon appointments with General Persons and R. E. Merriam; D. W. Kendall; Lt. Colonel J. S. D. Eisenhower; T. Nichols; General Goodpaster; G. D. Morgan. Practices golf on south lawn.

23 Washington. Morning appointments with D. W. Kendall; General Persons and B. N. Harlow; B. N. Harlow; Vice-President Nixon; Legislative Leaders; G. D. Morgan; W. J. Hopkins; Vice-President Nixon and General Persons; Oliver Willets and T. E. Stephens. Makes film for United Community Campaigns. Appointments with T. E. Stephens; M. C. Moos; J. C. Hagerty. Lunch. To Burning Tree Country Club for golf with Lt. Colonel J. S. D. Eisenhower and G. E. Allen.

24 Washington. Morning appointments with G. D. Morgan and D. W. Kendall; G. Gray and General Goodpaster; G. Gray and Generals Persons and Goodpaster; Secretary Gates, J. H. Douglas, Drs. Kistiakowsky and Robertson, G. Gray, and General Persons (off the record); General Goodpaster; Ambassador Mukrato Notowidigdo (from Indonesia) and U.S. Ambassador Parsons; D. W. Kendall; General Goodpaster; J. C. Hagerty; pre-news briefing; news conference; Lt. Colonel J. S. D. Eisenhower. Golf and lunch at Burning Tree Country Club with G. E.

Allen. Afternoon appointment with Lt. Colonel J. S. D. Eisenhower. Attends dinner hosted by Senator and Mrs. Dirksen.

25   Washington. Morning appointments with Lt. Colonel J. S. D. Eisenhower; Dr. Kistiakowsky, J. Charyk, Dr. Land, A. W. Dulles, G. Gray, and General Goodpaster (off the record); National Security Council session; Secretary Anderson; Vietnamese parliamentarians; General Persons, T. E. Stephens, J. C. Hagerty, and Colonel Thomas; T. E. Stephens. Lunch. Afternoon appointments with General Goodpaster; General Persons; Lt. Colonel J. S. D. Eisenhower; Generals Persons and Goodpaster; General Persons and B. N. Harlow; General Persons. Practices golf on south lawn. Meets with Senators Dirksen and Johnson, Congressmen Halleck and Rayburn, General Persons, and B. N. Harlow (off the record).

26   Washington. Morning appointments with Lt. Colonel J. S. D. Eisenhower; D. W. Kendall; General Goodpaster; W. J. Hopkins; G. D. Morgan. Presents Distinguished Service Award to Sumner G. Whittier. Cabinet meeting, followed by appointments with Attorney General Rogers; Crawford H. Greenewalt (President, E. I. DuPont, deNemours, and Co.), Secretary Anderson, D. Lindsay, and Attorney General Rogers (off the record); C. D. Dillon, J. C. Hagerty, and B. N. Harlow; J. Z. Anderson, J. Pierson, and T. E. Stephens; B. N. Harlow and General Goodpaster; General Persons, D. W. Kendall, R. E. Merriam, and Lt. Colonel J. S. D. Eisenhower; D. W. Kendall, R. E. Merriam, and Lt. Colonel J. S. D. Eisenhower; Lt. Colonel J. S. D. Eisenhower; B. N. Harlow. Airborne for Gettysburg. Visits residence of Lt. Colonel J. S. D. Eisenhower. Inspects farm. Airborne for Camp David, Maryland. Tours Camp David. Returns to Washington.

27   Washington. To Burning Tree Country Club for golf with E. N. Eisenhower, General Bradley, J. E. McClure, and Judge Landis.

28   Washington. Attends services at National Presbyterian Church. To Gettysburg farm with Mrs. Eisenhower. Returns to Washington.

29 Washington. Morning appointments with General Persons; B. N. Harlow; General Persons; R. J. Saulnier; T. E. Stephens; Dr. J. B. Smith; M. C. Moos; General Goodpaster; Generals Twining and Goodpaster; General Goodpaster; Lt. Colonel J. S. D. Eisenhower; D. Black and Lt. Colonel J. S. D. Eisenhower (off the record); M. C. Moos; T. E. Stephens. Delivers address at American Bar Association annual convention. Afternoon appointments with Lt. Colonel J. S. D. Eisenhower; T. E. Stephens; General Goodpaster; B. N. Harlow. Greets British and American Bar associations members.

30 Washington. Breakfast meeting with Republican leaders. Appointments with General Persons; W. J. Hopkins; M. C. Moos; Republican senators and congressmen; T. E. Stephens; J. C. Hagerty; General Persons and R. E. Merriam; M. C. Moos; General Goodpaster; Senator Allott; General Clark (off the record); General Cutler; T. E. Stephens; General Persons and son. Lunch. Afternoon appointments with Colonel Schulz, Major Streiff, and Lt. Colonel J. S. D. Eisenhower; Secretary Herter and General Goodpaster; T. E. Stephens. Visits Vice-President Nixon, Dr. York, and General Dahlquist at Walter Reed Hospital.

31 Washington. Morning appointments with General Persons; J. C. Hagerty; Lt. Colonel J. S. D. Eisenhower; M. C. Moos; congressional candidates; Senator Mundt, R. Berry, and E. A. McCabe; T. E. Stephens and R. E. Merriam; Secretary Anderson, Budget Director Stans, General Persons, and R. J. Saulnier; Secretary Anderson; Dr. K. Wells; Freedoms Foundation at Valley Forge representatives; Admiral Strauss; C. E. Wilson; H. R. McPhee; W. J. Hopkins. Lunch. Afternoon appointments with Lt. Colonel J. S. D. Eisenhower; W. J. Hopkins; M. C. Moos; R. E. Merriam; T. E. Stephens. Practices golf on south lawn.

September 1 Washington. Morning appointments with General Persons; congressional candidates; Secretaries Herter and Brucker, L. T. Merchant, G. Roderick, General Persons, and Lt. Colonel J. S. D. Eisenhower; Secretary Herter, L. T. Merchant, and Lt.

Colonel J. S. D. Eisenhower; R. E. Merriam. Addresses Fifth International Congress on Nutrition. Late morning appointments with Ambassador Alejos, C. Higdon, and Lt. Colonel J. S. D. Eisenhower; General Goodpaster; General Persons. Lunch. Afternoon appointments with Lt. Colonel J. S. D. Eisenhower; G. D. Morgan; General Goodpaster; General Persons; Lt. Colonel J. S. D. Eisenhower; General Goodpaster; R. E. Merriam; General Goodpaster.

2 Washington. To Burning Tree Country Club for golf with Lt. Colonel J. S. D. Eisenhower and J. E. Lemon. Appointments with J. C. Hagerty; General Goodpaster. Lunch. Afternoon appointments with General Persons; Joint Chiefs of Staff and Service Secretaries; General Goodpaster; Ambassador Muller, R. M. Phillips, and Lt. Colonel J. S. D. Eisenhower; W. J. Hopkins; D. W. Kendall, H. R. McPhee, and P. E. Areeda; R. E. Merriam; G. D. Morgan; Lt. Colonel J. S. D. Eisenhower; M. C. Moos. Airborne for Dahlgreen, Virginia. Cruises to Breton Bay, Maryland. Views movie.

3 Aboard *Barbara Anne*. Lands at Leonardtown, Maryland. To Cedar Point Golf Club for golf with Lt. Colonel J. S. D. Eisenhower and D. D. Eisenhower II. To Piney Point, Maryland. Cruises on Potomac. Fishes in Herring Creek.

4 Aboard *Barbara Anne*. Dinner with Lt. Colonel J. S. D. Eisenhower and family.

5 Aboard *Barbara Anne*. Shoots trap with Captain Aurand. To White House.

6 Washington. Morning appointments with T. E. Stephens; J. C. Hagerty, B. N. Harlow, and R. E. Merriam; B. N. Harlow; General Persons, J. C. Hagerty, and General Goodpaster; W. J. Hopkins. Presents citation to John Bowles for leadership in "Let's All Register, Let's All Vote" campaign. To Fort Leslie J. McNair. Delivers address at dedication of new academic building of Industrial College of the Armed Forces. Tours college. Returns to Washington. Late morning appointments with General Goodpaster; M. C. Moos; T. E. Stephens and H. R. McPhee; B. N. Harlow. Lunch. To Burning Tree Country Club

for golf with Colonel Belshe. Evening appointments with General Goodpaster; Secretary Herter and H. R. McPhee; Secretary Herter, General Goodpaster, and B. N. Harlow.

7   Washington. Morning appointments with T. E. Stephens; General Persons; T. E. Stephens; J. B. Baird and Secretary Anderson; Ambassador Jones; pre-news briefing; news conference; T. E. Stephens and R. E. Merriam; National Science Foundation Executive Committee; U.S. Ambassador Lodge; T. E. Stephens. Witnesses swearing-in ceremony for Ambassador Wadsworth as U.S. United Nations Representative. Lunch. Afternoon appointments with Secretary Herter and General Goodpaster; Congressman Short; National Security Council session; Secretary Herter and H. R. McPhee; General Goodpaster; T. E. Stephens; Major Streiff; D. Black, K. McCormick, and Lt. Colonel J. S. D. Eisenhower (off the record); R. E. Merriam. Hosts stag dinner for Republican dinners chairmen.

8   Washington. Morning appointment with General Goodpaster. Airborne for Huntsville, Alabama. Delivers address at dedication of Marshall Space Flight Center. Tours airfield. Returns to Washington. Afternoon appointments with T. E. Stephens; G. D. Morgan; M. C. Moos; Fannie T. de Newbery (Argentina) and son and T. E. Stephens; H. R. McPhee and P. E. Areeda; G. M. Hauge; Colonel Draper, Lt. Colonel J. S. D. Eisenhower, and W. J. Hopkins; W. J. Hopkins; H. R. McPhee. Dinner with C. V. McAdam (off the record).

9   Washington. Airborne for Gettysburg farm. To Gettysburg Country Club for golf with G. E. Allen, Colonel Belshe, and A. Palmer. Attends South Mountain Fair. To Gettysburg Country Club for golf with G. E. Allen.

10 Gettysburg. To Gettysburg Country Club for golf with G. E. Allen. To Hagerstown, Maryland. To Gettysburg.

11 Gettysburg. Attends services with Mrs. Eisenhower at Presbyterian Church of Gettysburg. Returns to Washington.

12   Washington. Morning appointments with T. E. Stephens; T. E. Stephens and R. E. Merriam. To Baltimore, Maryland. Addresses Kick-Off Campaign. Returns to Washington for appointments with Ambassador Esenbel and C. E. Conger; Generals Norstad and Goodpaster and R. Bowie (off the record); General Goodpaster. Lunch. Afternoon appointments with General Goodpaster; W. J. Hopkins; J. A. McCone and General Goodpaster; Secretary Herter and General Goodpaster; J. C. Hagerty and K. G. Harr. Practices golf on south lawn. Attends SHAPE Reunion Dinner.

13   Washington. Morning appointments with Major Streiff; G. D. Morgan, D. W. Kendall, and H. R. McPhee; T. E. Stephens; F. W. Pershing and Major Streiff. Airborne for Fort Myer, Virginia. Places wreath on grave of General Pershing. Returns to Washington. Appointments with General Snyder; G. Gray; Rotary Club officials and T. E. Stephens; Senator Hickenlooper and E. A. McCabe; T. E. Stephens and R. E. Merriam; T. E. Stephens; General Goodpaster. Lunch. To Burning Tree Country Club for golf with Colonel Belshe. Afternoon appointments with Lt. Colonel J. S. D. Eisenhower and J. C. Hagerty; M. C. Moos. Views movie with Lt. Colonel J. S. D. Eisenhower.

14   Washington. Morning appointments with Lt. Colonel J. S. D. Eisenhower; G. D. Morgan and D. W. Kendall; W. J. Hopkins; U.S. Ambassador McConaughy and Lt. Colonel J. S. D. Eisenhower; T. E. Stephens; William B. Walsh (President, Project HOPE), R. E. Merriam, and General Snyder; H. R. McPhee; Lt. Colonel J. S. D. Eisenhower; General T. B. Larkin; Lt. Colonel J. S. D. Eisenhower; National Association of Life Underwriters officials; Secretary Anderson (off the record); Secretary Flemming, D. W. Kendall, and H. R. McPhee (off the record). Lunch. To Burning Tree Country Club for golf with J. E. Lemon, R. W. Woodruff, and Colonel Belshe. Visits with R. W. Woodruff.

15   Washington. Morning appointments with J. C. Hagerty; C. D. Dillon, L. T. Merchant, A. W. Dulles, G. Gray, R. Bissell, and J. H. Douglas (off the

record); National Security Council session; G. D. Morgan; Forest Products Industries representatives; Senator Aiken; T. E. Stephens and R. E. Merriam; G. D. Morgan, D. W. Kendall, and H. R. McPhee; P. E. Areeda, G. D. Morgan, D. W. Kendall, H. R. McPhee, and M. C. Moos; G. D. Morgan, H. R. McPhee, and M. C. Moos; M. C. Moos and H. R. McPhee; M. C. Moos; A. Kimball; Lt. Colonel J. S. D. Eisenhower; T. E. Stephens and General Goodpaster. Lunch. To Burning Tree Country Club for golf with Colonel Belshe. Annual physical examination at Walter Reed Hospital.

16 Washington. Morning appointment with D. W. Kendall, H. R. McPhee, and M. C. Moos. To Camp David, Maryland with Mrs. Eisenhower. To Gettysburg farm with E. D. Eisenhower. Inspects farm. Visits residence of Lt. Colonel J. S. D. Eisenhower. Airborne for Camp David, Maryland. Shoots skeet with E. D. Eisenhower and Captain Aurand.

17 Camp David, Maryland. To Gettysburg Country Club. Golf with C. V. McAdam, Sr., C. V. McAdam, Jr., and Lt. Colonel J. S. D. Eisenhower. Airborne for Camp David, Maryland. Cooks steaks.

18 Camp David, Maryland. Returns to Washington.

19 Washington. Morning appointments with T. E. Stephens; U.S. Ambassador Whitney; Earl of Home (Foreign Secretary, Great Britain), Ambassadors Whitney, Caccia, and Bohlen, Secretary Herter, F. D. Kohler, R. A. Hare, Woodruff Wallner, and Lt. Colonel J. S. D. Eisenhower; Secretary Herter and Lt. Colonel J. S. D. Eisenhower; Secretary Herter, F. D. Kohler, U.S. Ambassador Bohlen, R. A. Hare, W. Wallner, M. C. Moos, and General Twining; American Nationalities for Nixon-Lodge Committee; General Twining and Lt. Colonel J. S. D. Eisenhower; M. J. McCaffree; Lt. Colonel J. S. D. Eisenhower and J. Rowley; Army Distaff Foundation representatives; J. C. Hagerty. Lunch. Afternoon appointments with Mr. and Mrs. Miguel Vilaro (Uruguay) and Lt. Colonel J. S. D. Eisenhower; J. C. Hagerty; Vice-President Nixon; B. Hibbs (off the record); U.S. Ambassador Taylor. Practices golf. Hosts White House dinner.

20   Washington. Morning appointments with Lt. Colonel J. S. D. Eisenhower; G. D. Morgan; U.S. Ambassador MacArthur (to Japan) and Lt. Colonel J. S. D. Eisenhower; Lt. Colonel J. S. D. Eisenhower; T. E. Stephens; Conference of Major National Jewish Organizations representatives; Secretary Anderson, J. B. Baird, W. M. Martin, R. J. Saulnier, and D. Paarlberg; Eduardo V. Haedo (National Councilor, Uruguay), Ambassador Clulow, U.S. Ambassador Robert Woodward (to Uruguay), Fernando Van Reigersberg (interpreter), and Clarence Boonstra (State Department); congressional candidates; R. L. Biggers; R. E. Merriam; C. D. Dillon and T. E. Stephens. To Burning Tree Country Club for golf with T. R. Garlington, J. E. Lemon, and Colonel Belshe.

21   Washington. Morning appointments with T. E. Stephens; G. Gray; National Security Council session; C. D. Dillon, G. D. Morgan, and M. C. Moos; General Hurley; T. E. Stephens; J. C. Hagerty; M. C. Moos; Colonel Draper and J. Rowley; Captain Aurand and C. Langello. Lunch. Afternoon appointments with T. E. Stephens; General Goodpaster; Lt. Colonel J. S. D. Eisenhower; T. E. Stephens. Airborne for Fort Myer, Virginia. Reviews troops. Returns to Washington. Practices golf on south lawn.

22   Washington. Airborne for New York City. Addresses U.N. General Assembly. Hosts luncheon in honor of representatives of Latin American countries. Appointments with Prime Minister Nkrumah, Ambassador Halm, Secretary Herter, J. C. Satterthwaite, and General Goodpaster; Prime Minister Koirala (Nepal), Ambassador Shada (from Nepal), Secretary Herter, U.S. Ambassador Jones, and Lt. Colonel J. S. D. Eisenhower; Prime Minister Saeb Salaam (Lebanon), Fuad Ammoun, Ambassador George Hakim (from Lebanon), Ambassador Nadim Dimechkie (from Lebanon), Secretary Herter, U.S. Ambassador Jones, and Lt. Colonel J. S. D. Eisenhower; President Josef B. Tito (Yugoslavia), Ambassador Mates, General Koca Popovic (Foreign Minister, Yugoslavia), Ambassador Nikezic, Secretary Herter, F. D. Kohler, U.S. Ambassador Bohlen, General Goodpaster, and Lt. Colonel J. S. D. Eisen-

hower; G. E. Allen, W. A. Jones, B. T. Leithead, U.S. Ambassador Whitney, and C. Roberts; Mr. and Mrs. B. Cerf; W. E. Robinson.

23 New York City. Breakfast meeting with W. E. Robinson, Generals Goodpaster and Snyder, M. C. Moos, A. C. Whitman, Colonel Schulz, and Lt. Colonel J. S. D. Eisenhower. Morning appointments with President Sylvanus E. Olympio (Togo), Paulin Freitas (Foreign Minister, Togo), Secretary Herter, J. C. Satterthwaite, and Lt. Colonel J. S. D. Eisenhower; Prince Naim, Ambassador Maiwandwal, Secretary Herter, U.S. Ambassador Jones, and General Goodpaster. Returns to Washington. Afternoon appointments with T. E. Stephens; Secretary Anderson, Budget Director Stans, and R. J. Saulnier to discuss mid-year budget figures; Secretary Anderson; Secretary Benson; R. E. Merriam; D. W. Kendall and M. C. Moos; M. C. Moos; General Goodpaster; T. E. Stephens; J. C. Hagerty. Practices golf on south lawn.

24 Washington. Morning appointment with General Goodpaster. To Burning Tree Country Club for golf with G. E. Allen. Airborne for Annapolis, Maryland. Views Navy-Villanova football game. Returns to Washington.

25 Washington. Attends services at National Presbyterian Church.

26 Washington. Airborne for Philadelphia, Pennsylvania. Addresses Association of Certified Accountants annual meeting. Addresses Eisenhower Exchange Fellowships. Airborne for New York City. Lunch with Governor Rockefeller. Afternoon appointments with Prime Minister Nehru, Subimal Dutt (Foreign Secretary, India), Secretary Herter, U.S. Ambassador Jones, and Lt. Colonel J. S. D. Eisenhower; Gamel Abdul Nasser (President, United Arab Republic) and United Arab Republic and U.S. officials; W. E. Robinson and W. A. Jones. Attends reception at Statler Hilton Hotel. Addresses National Conference of Catholic Charities dinner. Visits with W. E. Robinson, W. A. Jones, R. Montgomery, S. Kennedy, E. Wynn, U.S. Ambassador Whitney, and R. W. Woodruff.

27   New York City. Returns to Washington. Hosts dinner with Mrs. Eisenhower in honor of Prince Akihito and Princess Michiko (Japan) followed by a musical program.

28   Washington. Morning appointments with G. D. Morgan and Lt. Colonel J. S. D. Eisenhower; T. E. Stephens; U.S. Ambassador Rubottom (to Argentina); G. Gray; General Goodpaster; General Goodpaster; Dr. Kistiakowsky; T. E. Stephens; U.S. Ambassador Young; Dr. Elson; U.S. Ambassador Thomas J. Kiernan (to Ireland) and W. T. Buchanan; D. W. Kendall; G. D. Morgan; General Goodpaster; Crown Prince of Norway, Ambassador Koht, Jan Arner (Aide to Prince), and W. T. Buchanan; Lt. Colonel J. S. D. Eisenhower; R. E. Merriam; M. C. Moos. Lunch. Afternoon appointments with F. C. Scribner, General Persons, and R. E. Merriam; R. E. Merriam. Practices golf on south lawn.

29   Washington. Morning appointments with Lt. Colonel J. S. D. Eisenhower; J. C. Hagerty; G. Gray and General Goodpaster; National Security Council session. Presents Distinguished Service Medal to General Twining. Appointments with Lt. Colonel J. S. D. Eisenhower; Colonel Schulz; General Goodpaster. Airborne for Chicago. Meets with E. D. Eisenhower and John F. Kubik. Delivers address at Republican fund-raising dinner. Meets with F. Gurley, E. L. Ryerson, D. Stuart, T. E. Stephens, and R. Montgomery.

30   Chicago, Illinois. Delivers address at convention of Polish American Congress. Airborne for Denver, Colorado. Attends funeral services for E. Doud.

October   1   Denver, Colorado. Returns to Washington.

2   Washington. [Page missing.]

3   Washington. Morning appointments with General Persons; P. R. Bass and Colonel Schulz (off the record); W. E. Robinson; General Persons; Vice-President Nixon and General Persons; W. J. Hopkins; Colonel Draper; J. D. Ames. Presents Harmon International Trophies to Captains Joe B. Jordan

and Joseph W. Kittinger. Receives 1960 World Amateur Golf Team Championship winners. Records message for satellite. Late morning appointments with T. E. Stephens; Ambassador Habib Bourguiba, Jr. (from Tunisia to France), Ambassador Mondi Slim (from Tunisia), and J. C. Satterthwaite; Secretary Gates, L. T. Merchant, J. N. Irwin, J. H. Douglas, F. D. Kohler, and General Goodpaster. Lunch. To Burning Tree Country Club for golf with J. E. Lemon.

4   Washington. Breakfast meeting with P. H. Spaak, C. D. Dillon, L. T. Merchant, General Burgess, F. D. Kohler, and E. S. Glenn. Morning appointments with T. E. Stephens; General Goodpaster; General Persons, J. C. Hagerty, and R. E. Merriam; E. D. Chesney. Presents AMVETS Scholarship Awards, followed by appointments with M. C. Moos; C. D. Dillon, Secretaries Anderson and Gates, Budget Director Stans, J. H. Douglas, J. B. Baird, and General Persons (off the record); C. D. Dillon, Secretary Gates, J. H. Douglas, and J. C. Hagerty (off the record); J. C. Hagerty. Addresses International Chiefs of Police Association conference. Lunch. Afternoon appointments with J. C. Hagerty; General Goodpaster; P. G. Hoffman (off the record); T. E. Stephens and General Goodpaster; Lt. Colonel J. S. D. Eisenhower. Practices golf on south lawn.

5   Washington. Attends services for National Day of Prayer with General Persons. Morning appointments with General Persons; General Leroy Lutes; General Persons; G. Gray; U.S. Ambassador Charles R. Burrows (to Honduras); Admiral Radford (off the record); Admiral Radford and General Persons (off the record); J. C. Hagerty and R. Montgomery; M. C. Moos; C. D. Dillon and Lt. Colonel J. S. D. Eisenhower; U.S. Ambassador Riddleberger and S. N. Chatterjee (Indian Embassy); engineers from India; General Goodpaster; D. W. Kendall. Lunch. To Burning Tree Country Club for golf with G. E. Allen.

6   Washington. Morning appointments with General Goodpaster; Ambassador William C. Naude (from South Africa) and C. E. Conger; Secretary Gates, A. W. Dulles, G. Gray, L. T. Merchant, K. G. Harr,

and General Goodpaster (off the record); National Security Council session; President Sukarno (Indonesia), Dr. Subandrio (Foreign Minister, Indonesia), C. D. Dillon and J. M. Steeves; Indonesian officials; C. D. Dillon, J. C. Hagerty, and General Goodpaster; General Goodpaster; Lt. Colonel J. S. D. Eisenhower; M. C. Moos.

7   Washington. Morning appointments with T. E. Stephens and Lt. Colonel J. S. D. Eisenhower; General Goodpaster; Dr. Kistiakowsky and General Persons; Cabinet meeting; Secretary Anderson and C. D. Dillon; King Hussein and Jordanian and U.S. officials; J. M. A. H. Luns, Dr. J. H. van Roijen, U.S. Ambassador Young, F. D. Kohler, and General Goodpaster (off the record); T. E. Stephens. Hosts luncheon for Prince Albert and Princess Paola (Belgium). To Burning Tree Country Club for golf with Lt. Colonel J. S. D. Eisenhower and G. E. Allen.

8   Washington. Morning appointments with S. G. Whittier and R. E. Merriam; Veterans Administration managers; R. E. Merriam; Prime Minister Abubakar T. Balewa (Nigeria) and Nigerian and U.S. officials; C. D. Dillon and Lt. Colonel J. S. D. Eisenhower; General Goodpaster and Lt. Colonel J. S. D. Eisenhower; Lt. Colonel J. S. D. Eisenhower; General Goodpaster; P. E. Areeda; R. E. Merriam and R. Montgomery; W. J. Hopkins; R. E. Merriam; General Goodpaster. Lunch. Attends Fall Party dinner at Burning Tree Country Club.

9   Washington. Attends services with Mrs. Eisenhower at National Presbyterian Church.

10   Washington. Morning appointments with General Persons and R. E. Merriam; General Persons, J. C. Hagerty, R. E. Merriam and General Goodpaster; R. Montgomery; M. C. Moos; T. E. Stephens; Generals Lemnitzer and Goodpaster; T. E. Stephens; B. S. Adkins; National Committee for White House Conference on Children and Youth. Lunch. Afternoon appointments with Generals Goodpaster and Persons, Dr. Kistiakowsky, and R. E. Merriam; M. J. McCaffree; General Goodpaster. Practices golf. Participates in Question and Answer television broadcast.

11 Washington. Breakfast meeting with J. R. Killian and Drs. Kistiakowsky and York. Appointments with General Goodpaster; A. M. Washburn and Colonel and Mrs. Edward P. F. Eagan (Chairman, People-to-People Sports Committee); International Field Hockey Festival participants; W. A. Ruschmeyer, John Queenan, Thomas Hogan, and Lt. Colonel J. S. D. Eisenhower (off the record); C. D. Dillon, L. T. Merchant, J. M. Steeves, Secretary Gates, Generals Lemnitzer and Goodpaster, and A. W. Dulles (off the record); D. A. Morse, Secretary Mitchell, and T. E. Stephens; General Goodpaster. Greets King Frederik IX and Queen Ingrid (Denmark). Lunch. Afternoon appointments with T. E. Stephens; J. C. Hagerty; General Persons; M. C. Moos; T. E. Stephens and D. W. Kendall; T. E. Stephens; G. D. Morgan; General Persons; T. E. Stephens. Practices golf. Hosts dinner with Mrs. Eisenhower in honor of the King and Queen of Denmark, followed by musical entertainment.

12 Washington. Morning appointments with E. F. Bennett and R. E. Merriam; R. J. Saulnier; T. E. Stephens; King Frederik, C. D. Dillon, U.S. Ambassador Peterson, J. Krag, and Ambassador Knuth-Winterfeldt; Prime Minister Segni, Ambassador Brosio, F. D. Kohler, C. A. Straneo, and General Goodpaster. To Burning Tree Country Club for luncheon. Plays golf with C. Roberts, W. A. Jones, and B. T. Leithead. Hosts off-the-record stag dinner.

13 Washington. Morning appointments with T. E. Stephens; Vote Getters for Nixon and Lodge (off the record); M. C. Moos; Secretaries Herter, Gates, and Anderson, L. A. Hoegh, Budget Director Stans, C. D. Dillon, J. R. Rubel, A. W. Dulles, Dr. Kistiakowsky, K. G. Harr, W. P. Ennis, Dr. Scoville, A. R. Ash, Generals Persons, Lemnitzer, and Goodpaster, Lt. Colonel J. S. D. Eisenhower, M. W. Boggs, G. C. Smith, J. Daniel, and C. Ahearn (off the record); Attorney General Rogers; National Security Council session; C. D. Dillon, Secretary Mueller, and Generals Persons and Goodpaster; Diosdado P. Macapagal (Vice-President, Philippines), Ambassador Romulo, and J. M. Steeves. Attends off-the-record

luncheon for Republican Finance Group. Afternoon appointments with R. E. Merriam; General Persons, T. E. Stephens, and Colonel Draper; T. E. Stephens; Dr. Glennan and Lt. Colonel J. S. D. Eisenhower; W. J. Hopkins; T. E. Stephens. Attends dinner with Mrs. Eisenhower in their honor, hosted by King and Queen of Denmark. Attends Royal Danish Ballet.

14 Washington. Receives White House Police honorary membership plaque for birthday. Morning appointments with P. E. Areeda; Republican National Committee; U.S. Ambassador Newbegin (to Haiti); news reporters; Harry Oppenheimer and Maurice Tempelsman (off the record); General Maxwell and W. J. Monaghan; R. J. Saulnier and General Persons; General Goodpaster; U.N. delegations from Africa. Lunch. Airborne for Gettysburg farm. To Gettysburg Country Club for golf with General Nevins.

15 Gettysburg. To Gettysburg Country Club for golf with General Nevins and R. Sleichter. Examines barns with General Nevins and R. S. Hartley. Visits with General and Mrs. Nevins.

16 Gettysburg. Visits with Lt. Colonel J. S. D. Eisenhower and family. Returns to Washington.

17 Washington. Morning appointments with C. D. Dillon, T. C. Mann, and Generals Persons and Goodpaster; G. Gray, K. G. Harr, and General Goodpaster; General Goodpaster; Secretary Herter and General Goodpaster. Airborne for Detroit, Michigan. Addresses Women of Michigan Committee. Meets with P. Bagwell, Congressman Bentley, J. B. Martin, A. S. Loeze, L. Lindemer, and W. C. Greany. Addresses National Automobile Show Industry dinner.

18 Detroit, Michigan. Airborne for Richfield, Minnesota. Makes address. Airborne for Red Wing, Minnesota. Addresses dedication of New Hiawatha Bridge. Airborne for Abilene, Kansas. Tours Eisenhower Library and Museum. Visits family home. Airborne for Palm Springs, California. Dinner at Eldorado Country Club with W. A. Jones, C. S. Jones,

F. F. Gosden, General Snyder, and R. Montgomery. Plays bridge.

19   Palm Springs, California. Breakfast meeting with W. A. Jones, Helen Dettweiler, F. F. Gosden, and J. C. Hagerty. Golf with W. A. Jones, C. S. Jones, F. F. Gosden, and H. Dettweiler. Works on speeches. Dinner with G. E. Allen, F. F. Gosden, W. A. Jones, C. S. Jones, R. Montgomery, and General Snyder. Plays bridge.

20   Palm Springs, California. Airborne for San Francisco. Records television address. Attends reception at St. Francis Hotel. Addresses Commonwealth Club of California dinner.

21   San Francisco, California. Airborne for San Diego, California. Tours Naval Air Station. Airborne for Chula Vista, California. Addresses Inter-American Municipal Organization luncheon. Airborne for Palm Springs, California. To Eldorado Country Club for golf with S. S. Larmon, F. F. Gosden, and G. E. Allen. Dinner at G. E. Allen residence with C. S. Jones, W. A. Jones, S. S. Larmon, R. Montgomery, and General Snyder.

22   Palm Springs, California. To Eldorado Country Club for golf with W. A. Jones, C. S. Jones, and S. S. Larmon. Dinner with G. E. Allen, W. A. Jones, C. S. Jones, R. Montgomery, F. F. Gosden, S. S. Larmon, and Colonel Draper. Views movies "Blue Springs, Albany, Georgia" and "Angels in the Outfield."

23   Palm Springs, California. Attends services at Community Church with G. E. Allen and J. C. Hagerty. To Eldorado Country Club for golf with G. E. Allen, F. F. Gosden, and L. Firestone. Dinner with G. E. Allen, S. S. Larmon, Colonel Draper, R. Montgomery, C. S. Jones, and W. A. Jones. Views movie "Colt 45."

24   Palm Springs, California. Airborne for Del Rio, Texas. To Ciudad Acuna, Mexico. Meets with President Lopez Mateos, Secretary Herter, T. Mann, U.S. Ambassador Hill, M. Osborne, and Colonel Walters. Attends luncheon. Signs official declaration on Amistad Dam construction. Airborne for

Del Rio, Texas. Airborne for Houston, Texas. Addresses convocation at Rice University.

25   Houston, Texas. Attends breakfast hosted by O. C. Hobby. Returns to Washington. Afternoon appointments with Secretary Anderson, W. M. Martin, J. B. Baird, and F. Von Klemperer; Generals Persons and Goodpaster; General Goodpaster; T. E. Stephens; General Persons, J. C. Hagerty, M. C. Moos, B. N. Harlow, R. E. Merriam, and K. B. McCann; General Persons; T. E. Stephens.

26   Washington. Morning appointments with American Retail Federation representatives; General Persons; General Goodpaster; W. D. Pawley (off the record); Secretary Herter; Prime Minister Tunku A. R. P. al-Haj (Malaya), Ambassador Kamil, Enche Z. I. B. Ahmed (Ministry of External Affairs, Malaya), Secretary Herter, J. M. Steeves, and U.S. Ambassador Byington; Generals Goodpaster and Persons, G. D. Morgan, J. C. Hagerty, and G. Gray; G. D. Morgan; G. Gray; M. J. McCaffree; B. N. Harlow, K. B. McCann, and M. C. Moos. Hosts stag luncheon in honor of Prime Minister al-Haj. Afternoon appointments with W. E. Robinson; Generals Persons and Goodpaster; T. E. Stephens and Major Streiff; General Persons; M. C. Moos; B. N. Harlow and K. B. McCann. Practices golf on south lawn.

27   Washington. Morning appointments with General Persons, B. N. Harlow, and K. B. McCann; Secretary Anderson and J. B. Baird (off the record); P. E. Areeda; K. B. McCann, B. N. Harlow, and M. C. Moos; General Goodpaster. Airborne for Staunton, Virginia. Visits mother's birthplace. Plants Liberty Tree. Visits birthplace of Woodrow Wilson. Gives address at Mary Baldwin College. Attends luncheon at college. Returns to Washington.

28   Washington. Morning appointments with General Persons, B. N. Harlow, K. B. McCann, and J. C. Hagerty; General Persons, J. C. Hagerty, and B. N. Harlow; General Persons and J. C. Hagerty; M. C. Moos; T. E. Stephens; General Persons and B. N. Harlow. Lunch. Afternoon appointments with J. C. Hagerty and General Goodpaster; General Good-

paster. Airborne for Philadelphia, Pennsylvania. Attends reception at Hotel Bellevue Stratford. Addresses Nixon for President Club dinner. Returns to Washington.

29   Washington. Records speech introduction. Morning appointments with W. J. Hopkins; T. E. Stephens and J. C. Hagerty; J. C. Hagerty; General Goodpaster. To Burning Tree Country Club for golf with Colonel Belshe, W. McElvoy, and V. Johnson.

30   Washington. Attends services at National Presbyterian Church. To Gettysburg farm with Mrs. Eisenhower. Tours farm. Returns to Washington.

31   Washington. Morning appointments with General Persons; National Security Council session. Receives award from Campfire Girls National Council. Appointments with family of Sergeant Moaney; Ambassador Zenon Roseides (from Cyprus), C. Spruks, and Mr. King. Lunch with Vice-President Nixon, General Persons, R. E. Merriam, L. W. Hall, Secretary Seaton, F. C. Scribner, T. E. Stephens, J. C. Hagerty, K. B. McCann, and B. N. Harlow. Afternoon appointments with Vice-President Nixon; General Persons; General Goodpaster; Generals Persons and Goodpaster; General Persons; speech writers; R. E. Merriam.

November 1   Washington. Morning appointments with General Persons and D. W. Kendall; T. E. Stephens; J. McCrary and T. E. Stephens; Secretary Mitchell; L. W. Hall, General Persons, T. E. Stephens, and R. E. Merriam; M. C. Moos; Admiral Strauss; C. D. Dillon; Budget Director Stans, R. Reid, U.S. Ambassador Riddleberger, J. C. Satterthwaite, J. Bell, and General Goodpaster (off the record); General Persons; J. C. Hagerty. To Burning Tree Country Club for golf with J. E. Lemon.

2   Washington. Airborne for New York City. Addresses Republican rally at Roosevelt Field Shopping Center. Airborne for Westchester County, New York. Addresses Republican rally at Westchester County Airport. Airborne for New York City. Addresses rally at Herald Square. Appointment with Major M. G. Remo. Records speech. Addresses rally at New York Coliseum.

3   New York City. Views General Motors Motorama. Returns to Washington. Morning appointments with General Persons; General Goodpaster; Ambassador Michel Douathe (from Central African Republic), C. Spruks, and C. Sedgwick; Ambassador Andre Alakpo (from Togo), C. Spruks, and C. Sedgwick; Ambassador Alejos and T. C. Mann; Ambassador Briceno, T. C. Mann, and E. J. Sparks; T. C. Mann; D. W. Kendall. Lunch. Afternoon appointments with K. B. McCann; General Persons, R. E. Merriam, and M. C. Moos; General Persons; T. E. Stephens and General Goodpaster; K. B. McCann; T. E. Stephens. Practices golf on south lawn. Views movies.

4   Washington. Morning appointments with General Persons; General Bradley; General Goodpaster; Lt. Colonel J. S. D. Eisenhower; General Persons. Airborne for Cleveland, Ohio. Addresses rally. Meets with Rabbi A. H. Silver; Cleveland newspaper editors. Delivers address at luncheon for Republican Men. Delivers address to Republican Women. Airborne for Pittsburgh, Pennsylvania. Addresses guests at dinner for Allegheny County Republican Executive Committee. Views campaign movie. Returns to Washington.

5   Washington. Morning appointments with D. W. Kendall and General Goodpaster; General Goodpaster; T. E. Stephens; J. C. Hagerty; Lt. Colonel J. S. D. Eisenhower; R. E. Merriam and M. C. Moos; Lt. Colonel J. S. D. Eisenhower. Airborne for Camp David, Maryland. Airborne for Gettysburg farm. Hunts quail and pheasant with G. E. Allen. Airborne for Camp David, Maryland.

6   Camp David, Maryland. Attends services with G. E. Allen at Presbyterian Church of Gettysburg. To Gettysburg farm. Inspects cattle. To Camp David, Maryland. Returns to Washington.

7   Washington. Morning appointments with General Persons; National Security Council session; Secretary Gates, T. C. Mann, G. Gray, K. G. Harr, L. T. Merchant, and General Lemnitzer; Generals Lemnitzer and Goodpaster; U.S. Ambassador Houghton; K. B. McCann; General Persons; Admiral Dennison

and General Goodpaster. Lunch. Afternoon appointments with K. B. McCann; General Persons; R. Montgomery and Elizabeth M. Young; T. E. Stephens. Delivers televised address to nation.

8   Washington. Airborne for Gettysburg. Votes. Returns to Washington. Morning appointments with T. E. Stephens; Lt. Colonel J. S. D. Eisenhower; G. Gray, L. T. Merchant, J. H. Douglas, General Cabell, and D. Fitzgerald (off the record); R. Bissell and E. A. Stanalis (off the record); General Goodpaster; G. Gray; General Goodpaster; Secretary Benson; P. E. Areeda and D. W. Kendall; J. A. McCone and Lt. Colonel J. S. D. Eisenhower (off the record); General Persons, J. C. Hagerty, R. E. Merriam, and General Goodpaster; Lt. Colonel J. S. D. Eisenhower; General Goodpaster; J. C. Hagerty. Visits with Republican party workers, staff, and Cabinet members. Delivers televised Election Night address.

9   Washington. Morning appointments with Colonel Schulz and Lt. Colonel J. S. D. Eisenhower; Generals Persons and Goodpaster, Colonel Schulz, and Lt. Colonel J. S. D. Eisenhower; General Persons; Lt. Colonel J. S. D. Eisenhower; U.S. Ambassador Elbrick (to Portugal); J. C. Hagerty; Secretaries Gates and Anderson, C. D. Dillon, Generals Lemnitzer, Goodpaster, and Persons, Budget Director Stans, W. M. Martin, J. B. Baird, D. Paarlberg, J. H. Douglas, and D. W. Kendall; Generals Persons and Goodpaster, Colonel Schulz, and Lt. Colonel J. S. D. Eisenhower; Captain Aurand; General Persons; Cabinet meeting; Secretary Herter and General Goodpaster; Secretary Gates and J. A. McCone; Senator Morton and General Persons. Airborne for Augusta, Georgia. To Augusta National Golf Club for golf with E. D. Slater and C. Roberts. Dinner with C. Roberts and E. D. Slater.

10 Augusta, Georgia. Works in office. Practices golf. To Augusta National Golf Club for golf with W. E. Robinson, J. Gould, and G. Stout.

11 Augusta, Georgia. Works in office. To Augusta National Golf Club for golf with C. Roberts, J. Roberts, and E. D. Slater.

12   Augusta, Georgia. Works in office. To Augusta National Golf Club for golf with W. E. Robinson, W. D. Kerr, and F. Willard. Dinner with W. E. Robinson, E. D. Slater, and C. Roberts.

13   Augusta, Georgia. Works in office. To Augusta National Golf Club for golf with S. S. Larmon, E. D. Slater, and G. Stout.

14   Augusta, Georgia. Works in office. Practices golf with G. Stout. To Augusta National Golf Club for golf with G. Stout, E. D. Slater, and Lt. Colonel J. S. D. Eisenhower. Attends birthday party for Mrs. Eisenhower.

15   Augusta, Georgia. Meets with F. Floete, R. Daly, B. N. Harlow, W. J. Hopkins, K. B. McCann, Colonel Schultz, and Major Strieff. To Augusta National Golf Club for golf with G. Stout. Meets with Secretaries Anderson and Gates and General Goodpaster.

16   Augusta, Georgia. Works in office. To Augusta National Golf Club for golf with W. Thayer, W. E. Robinson, and R. W. Woodruff. News conference. Fishes. Golfs with C. Roberts, W. M. Fulcher, and J. Franklin.

17   Augusta, Georgia. Meets with National Security Council session. Lunch at Club House with National Security Council. Watches General Goodpaster, Lt. Colonel J. S. D. Eisenhower, G. Gray, and G. Stout play golf. Meets with T. E. Stephens and W. A. Jones. Visits C. Roberts.

18   Augusta, Georgia. To Augusta National Golf Club for golf with C. Roberts, W. A. Jones, and G. Stout.

19   Augusta, Georgia. Works in office. To Augusta National Golf Club for golf with W. E. Robinson, W. A. Jones, and G. E. Allen.

20   Augusta, Georgia. Works in office. Attends services at Reid Memorial Presbyterian Church with J. C. Hagerty. To Augusta National Golf Club for golf with G. E. Allen and General Gruenther. Attends party hosted by White House press and photographers in honor of J. C. Hagerty.

21   Augusta, Georgia. Works in office. To Augusta National Golf Club for golf with G. E. Allen and

G. Stout. To Aiken, South Carolina, and back with G. E. Allen.

22 Augusta, Georgia. Airborne for Albany, Georgia. Airborne for Blue Spring Plantation. Hunts quail with W. A. Jones, G. E. Allen, General Snyder, J. C. Hagerty, and L. Alwell.

23 Albany, Georgia. Visits stable. Hunts quail. Picnic. Returns to Washington.

24 Washington. No official appointments.

25 Washington. Morning appointments with General Goodpaster; D. W. Kendall; Drs. Kistiakowsky and Rathjens and General Goodpaster; W. J. Hopkins; D. W. Kendall; General Goodpaster; Congressman and Mrs. Byrd and children and E. D. Chesney (off the record); G. Gray and A. W. Dulles; A. W. Dulles; G. Gray; Generals Devers, McAuliffe, and Goodpaster. Lunch. Afternoon appointments with Lt. Colonel J. S. D. Eisenhower; A. Nielsen; Lt. Colonel J. S. D. Eisenhower; Mrs. J. S. D. Eisenhower.

26 Washington. Morning appointments with Colonel Schulz; General Goodpaster; R. J. Saulnier; Lt. Colonel J. S. D. Eisenhower; W. J. Hopkins. Lunch. Watches movie with G. E. Allen.

27 Washington. Attends services at National Presbyterian Church. To Burning Tree Country Club for golf with G. E. Allen and Colonel Belshe.

28 Washington. Morning appointments with J. C. Hagerty; Mexican officials; General Persons; Secretary Flemming and R. E. Merriam; U.S. Ambassador Lodge; Secretary Anderson, C. D. Dillon, J. C. Hagerty, and Generals Persons and Goodpaster; T. E. Stephens. Addresses guests at Republican Appointees luncheon. Afternoon appointments with T. E. Stephens; General Persons. Practices golf.

29 Washington. Morning appointments with General Persons and J. C. Hagerty; D. W. Kendall; W. D. Pawley (off the record); F. H. Higgins (off the record); General Goodpaster; Generals Lemnitzer and Goodpaster; Secretary Anderson, C. D. Dillon, Secretary Gates, A. W. Dulles, G. Gray, J. H. Douglas, R. Bissell, and General Persons; G. Gray; T. E.

Stephens; General Goodpaster; T. E. Stephens. Lunch. To Burning Tree Country Club for golf with Lt. Colonel J. S. D. Eisenhower and Colonel Belshe.

30 Washington. Morning appointments with W. J. Hopkins; Secretary Anderson, C. D. Dillon, Budget Director Stans, General Persons, and Lt. Colonel J. S. D. Eisenhower; Lt. Colonel J. S. D. Eisenhower; D. Black and Lt. Colonel J. S. D. Eisenhower (off the record); J. A. Volpe (Governor-elect) and R. E. Merriam; General Clark (off the record); Japanese officials (off the record); Postmaster General Summerfield; General Persons; R. V. Fleming. Participates in dedication of Presbyterian Home for elderly. Lunch with Dr. M. S. Eisenhower and E. N. Eisenhower. Afternoon appointments with D. Black, B. Hibbs, K. McCormick, and Lt. Colonel J. S. D. Eisenhower (off the record); General Goodpaster. Attends White House dinner, followed by dancing.

December 1 Washington. Morning appointments with T. E. Stephens; National Security Council session; C. D. Dillon, J. N. Irwin, and General Goodpaster; R. Montgomery; General Goodpaster; Lewis Rosenstiel (President, Schenley Industries) (off the record); J. C. Hall; General Goodpaster; General Strong. Lunch. Afternoon appointments with Budget Director Stans; W. S. Paley and R. Montgomery; General Persons; Governor Rockefeller; T. E. Stephens and Colonel Schulz; Lt. Colonel J. S. D. Eisenhower; Colonel Schulz and Lt. Colonel J. S. D. Eisenhower. Hosts White House dinner with Mrs. Eisenhower, followed by dancing.

2 Washington. Morning appointments with D. W. Kendall and H. R. McPhee; General Persons; Secretary Anderson, Budget Director Stans, R. J. Saulnier, E. Staats, R. E. Merriam, and Generals Persons and Goodpaster; R. E. Merriam and Generals Persons and Goodpaster; U.S. Ambassador Lodge; Secretary Mitchell; W. J. Hopkins; T. S. Voorhees and R. E. Merriam; T. E. Stephens; J. C. Hagerty. Lunch.

3 Washington. Airborne for Gettysburg farm. Hunts with Lt. Colonel J. S. D. Eisenhower. Airborne for Camp David, Maryland. Returns to Washington.

4   Washington. No official appointments.

5   Washington. Off-the-record breakfast meeting with Congressman Halleck, General Persons, and B. N. Harlow. Appointments with General Persons and J. C. Hagerty; C. D. Dillon, D. W. Kendall, H. R. McPhee, and P. E. Areeda; Ambassador Louis Rakotomalala (from Malaya), W. T. Buchanan, and E. S. Glenn; Ambassador Lee-Wook Chang (Korea) and W. T. Buchanan. Receives tiger from India. Presents Collier Trophy to U.S. Air Force, Convair Division (General Dynamics Corporation), and Space Technology Laboratories. Appointments with General Goodpaster; R. E. Merriam. Lunch with Commission on National Goals. Afternoon appointments with Budget Director Stans, Secretary Gates, J. H. Douglas, F. B. Lincoln, R. E. Merriam, and Generals Lemnitzer, Persons, and Goodpaster to discuss defense budget; R. E. Merriam; Senator Dirksen (off the record); B. N. Harlow and Lt. Colonel J. S. D. Eisenhower; General Goodpaster.

6   Washington. Morning appointments with Lt. Colonel J. S. D. Eisenhower; General Persons and J. C. Hagerty; General Persons; Lt. Colonel J. S. D. Eisenhower; Captain Aurand and General Persons; President-elect Kennedy; General Goodpaster; President-elect Kennedy and Cabinet members; National Agricultural Advisory Commission; Civil War Centennial Commission; General Goodpaster. Lunch. To Burning Tree Country Club for golf with Colonel Belshe and J. E. Lemon. Meets with Lt. Colonel J. S. D. Eisenhower.

7   Washington. Morning appointments with G. D. Morgan; T. E. Stephens; Generals Persons and Goodpaster; G. Gray; Ambassador Bulent Usakligil (from Turkey) and W. T. Buchanan; Ambassador Augusto A. Arango (from Panama) and W. T. Buchanan; Senator Johnson (off the record). Records Christmas message to armed forces. Late morning appointments with General Goodpaster; Budget Director Stans, E. Staats, R. J. Saulnier, D. Paarlberg, Secretary Anderson, C. Walker, R. E. Merriam, and Generals Persons and Goodpaster; W. Cisler, C. Weed, H. Hoover, Jr., and T. E. Ste-

phens; H. Hoover, Jr.; General Persons. Addresses guests at American Red Cross luncheon. Afternoon appointments with T. E. Stephens; B. N. Harlow; Lt. Colonel J. S. D. Eisenhower; W. J. Hopkins; General Persons; Harold Boeschenstein and son (off the record). Addresses guests at dinner for Business Advisory Council.

8   Washington. Morning appointments with T. E. Stephens; National Security Council session; T. E. Stephens; Dr. Elliott; Congressman Curtis, D. Brown, and R. Briggs; James I. McCord (President, Princeton Theological Seminary); Lt. Colonel J. S. D. Eisenhower; T. E. Stephens. Lunch. Afternoon appointments with Generals Goodpaster and Persons and J. C. Hagerty; Colonel Schulz; Attorney General Rogers; General Goodpaster.

9   Washington. Morning appointments with General Persons; T. E. Stephens and General Goodpaster; H. R. McPhee; Ambassador Lindt (from Switzerland) and W. T. Buchanan; Lt. Colonel J. S. D. Eisenhower; Prime Minister Mamadou Dia (Senegal), Ambassador Ousmane Soce Diop (from Senegal), J. C. Satterthwaite, W. T. Buchanan, and E. S. Glenn; Ambassador Alakpo; Secretary Anderson, C. D. Dillon, General Persons, G. D. Morgan, and General Goodpaster (off the record); W. J. Hopkins, H. R. McPhee, and General Goodpaster; General Goodpaster and H. R. McPhee; General Goodpaster; T. E. Stephens; H. R. McPhee. Airborne for Augusta, Georgia. To Augusta National Golf Club for golf with C. Roberts and J. Roberts. Dinner with J. Gould, C. Roberts, W. E. Robinson, and E. D. Slater.

10   Augusta, Georgia. Attends Augusta National Golf Club Board of Directors meeting. Golf with Secretary Flemming, T. B. Butler, and B. T. Leithead.

11   Augusta, Georgia. To Augusta National Golf Club for golf with O. R. Reid, J. Frank, and B. J. Patton. Dinner in club house.

12   Augusta, Georgia. Returns to Washington. Morning appointments with T. E. Stephens; U.S. Ambassador Zellerbach; G. Gray and General Goodpaster; M. D.

Sprague and General Goodpaster (off the record); R. E. Merriam, General Byers, and A. Wallace; Prime Minister Ould Daddah (Mauritania), J. C. Satterthwaite, C. E. Conger, and E. S. Glenn; T. E. Stephens and J. C. Hagerty. Lunch. Afternoon appointments with T. E. Stephens; Secretary Anderson, Budget Director Stans, W. M. Martin, J. B. Baird, C. Walker, General Persons, and D. Paarlberg (off the record); General Goodpaster; H. R. McPhee; T. E. Stephens.

13 Washington. Morning appointments with Lt. Colonel J. S. D. Eisenhower; General Persons; J. C. Hagerty; Robert Meckler (Chairman, American Golf Classic), Loren Tibbals (Sports Editor, *Knight* Newspapers), Congressman Ayres, Charles Idan (Campaign Director, Congressman Ayres), A. E. Brubaker, and J. Z. Anderson; J. C. Hagerty; Admiral Strauss (off the record); G. Cooper; T. E. Stephens. Receives records of Lincoln Sesquicentennial Commission. Receives Coatesville Declaration. Lunch. Afternoon appointments with B. N. Harlow; M. C. Moos; Lt. Colonel J. S. D. Eisenhower; General Persons, G. D. Morgan, J. C. Hagerty, and H. R. McPhee; T. E. Stephens. Hosts reception for Supreme Court members. To Walter Reed Hospital for physical examination.

14 Washington. Undergoes tests and x-rays at Walter Reed Hospital.

15 Washington. Completes physical examination. Appointments with J. C. Hagerty; D. C. Gainey; G. Gray. Lunch. Afternoon appointments with B. N. Harlow; General Persons; General Goodpaster; Vice-President Nixon, Senator Morton, General Persons, and B. N. Harlow (off the record); Vice-President Nixon and Senator Morton (off the record); Vice-President Nixon (off the record); R. E. Merriam and General Goodpaster; Lt. Colonel J. S. D. Eisenhower.

16 Washington. Morning appointments with Colonel Schulz; General Persons; C. D. Dillon; W. R. Burke, W. F. Hauck, T. E. Stephens, and E. D. Chesney. Receives Judaism and World Peace Award from Synagogue Council of America. Receives woodcut art.

Late morning appointments with R. J. Saulnier; P. G. Hoffman; D. Latham and F. C. Scribner; G. D. Morgan and General Goodpaster; U.S. Ambassador Whitney and Lt. Colonel J. S. D. Eisenhower; General Persons. Attends West Point Class of 1915 reunion luncheon.

17 Washington. Morning appointments with General Goodpaster; J. A. McCone, Secretary Franke, and General Goodpaster (off the record); J. A. McCone and General Goodpaster (off the record); B. N. Harlow; Congressman and Mrs. Byrnes and children; Congressman Byrnes and B. N. Harlow; Ben Guill and sons and B. N. Harlow; B. Gunderson; G. Gray; J. C. Hagerty; W. J. Hopkins; H. R. McPhee.

18 Washington. Attends services with Mrs. Eisenhower at National Presbyterian Church.

19 Washington. Morning appointments with General Persons; G. D. Morgan; Reverend Graham; Drs. Glennan, Dryden, and Slomans, and General Goodpaster (off the record); T. E. Stephens; Science Advisory Committee; Dewitt Wallace (*Reader's Digest*) and Lt. Colonel J. S. D. Eisenhower (off the record); General Persons and M. C. Moos. Lunch. Afternoon appointments with Generals Persons and Quesada, W. Gillilland, G. D. Morgan, J. C. Hagerty, and D. W. Kendall; T. E. Stephens and General Goodpaster; Secretaries Gates, Herter, and Anderson, J. A. McCone, A. W. Dulles, Dr. Kistiakowsky, A. Berding, K. G. Harr, G. Gray, R. Murphy, P. J. Farley, J. C. Hagerty, and Generals Lemnitzer and Goodpaster (off the record); General Goodpaster; Lt. Colonel J. S. D. Eisenhower; T. E. Stephens. Presents National Security Medal to R. Murphy.

20 Washington. Morning appointments with Colonel Schulz; R. E. Merriam; G. D. Morgan; General Goodpaster; Cabinet meeting; Secretary Flemming, G. D. Morgan, and J. C. Hagerty; Antoine W. Yameogo (Director of Treasury, Upper Volta), J. Penfield, C. Sedgwick, and Lt. Colonel J. S. D. Eisenhower. Lunch. Afternoon appointments with Lt. Colonel J. S. D. Eisenhower; National Security Council session; D. Black and Lt. Colonel J. S. D. Eisenhower (off the record); P. E. Areeda. Swims.

21   Washington. Morning appointments with General
      Goodpaster; J. C. Hagerty; Secretary Anderson,
      Budget Director Stans, C. Walker, R. J. Saulnier, G. D.
      Morgan, R. E. Merriam, D. Paarlberg, and General
      Goodpaster; Secretary Anderson; General Good-
      paster; Budget Director Stans, D. W. Kendall, and
      P. E. Areeda (off the record); D. W. Kendall; Gen-
      eral Goodpaster; Secretary Franke, J. C. Hagerty,
      and Captain Aurand to discuss Carrier fire in Brook-
      lyn; Mrs. J. F. Brownlee, General and Mrs. Clark,
      Secretary Flemming, and Lt. Colonel J. S. D. Eisen-
      hower; E. Johnston (off the record). Lunch with
      B. T. Leithead and C. R. Palmer (off the record).
      Afternoon appointments with D. W. Kendall, P. E.
      Areeda, and G. D. Morgan; G. D. Morgan; Secretary
      Brucker, G. H. Roderick, Admiral Wilson, D. W.
      Kendall, P. E. Areeda, and J. F. Ladd (off the
      record); General Goodpaster; P. E. Areeda; G. D.
      Morgan; Lt. Colonel J. S. D. Eisenhower. Hosts off-
      the-record reception with Mrs. Eisenhower for
      White House social aides.

22   Washington. Morning appointments with Secretary
      Mitchell and J. C. Hagerty; Commission on railroad
      industry labor problems; National Security Council;
      Mr. and Mrs. J. P. O' Connell and children, Mr. and
      Mrs. G. C. Lodge and children, and Mrs. N. Brown
      and children (off the record). Hosts Christmas re-
      ception with Mrs. Eisenhower. Lunch. Afternoon
      appointments with Lt. Colonel J. S. D. Eisenhower;
      Senator Hickenlooper; General Goodpaster; Gen-
      eral Persons.

23   Washington. Morning appointments with Secretary
      Seaton, E. F. Bennett, T. C. Mann, General Persons,
      G. D. Morgan, and D. Paarlberg (off the record);
      General Persons; Secretary Seaton; T. E. Stephens;
      Mr. and Mrs. V. Robinson (personal friend) (off the
      record). Visits Sergeant Moaney at Walter Reed Hos-
      pital. Appointments with General Bradley; Colonel
      A. S. Williams and son and Lt. Colonel J. S. D. Eisen-
      hower (off the record); General Goodpaster; S. S.
      Larmon and family, B. T. Leithead and family, Gen-
      eral and Mrs. Gruenther and family, and E. D. Slater
      and family. Hosts party for friends' grandchildren
      with Mrs. Eisenhower (off the record). Lunch. Af-

ternoon appointments with R. Montgomery; J. C. Hagerty and R. Montgomery; T. E. Stephens; H. R. McPhee; W. J. Hopkins. Swims. Delivers address at Christmas Pageant of Peace.

24 Washington. Morning appointments with Colonel Schulz; G. D. Morgan and D. W. Kendall; General Goodpaster; General Persons.

25 Washington. Attends services at National Presbyterian Church with Mrs. Eisenhower.

26 Washington. Morning appointments with G. Gray; Congressman Wilson and children (off the record); Senator Kuchel (off the record); G. Craig and daughter (off the record); General Nevins and Lt. Colonel J. S. D. Eisenhower. Lunch.

27 Washington. Morning appointments with Lt. Colonel J. S. D. Eisenhower; T. E. Stephens; Colonel Schulz; Lt. Colonel J. S. D. Eisenhower; Secretary Mitchell. Visits Sergeant Moaney at Walter Reed Hospital. Appointments with Ambassador Abdoulaye Maiga (from Mali), W. T. Buchanan, and E. S. Glenn; S. P. Skouras (off the record); C. D. Jackson (off the record). Lunch. Airborne for Gettysburg farm. Tours new president's office at Gettysburg College. Returns to Washington.

28 Washington. Morning appointments with Colonel Schulz; General Persons; Colonel Schulz; D. W. Kendall; T. E. Stephens; Mr. and Mrs. Eugene Lyons and daughter (off the record); W. D. Pawley (off the record); M. D. Sprague, General Goodpaster, and G. Gray (off the record); T. E. Stephens and General Persons; Captain Butcher (off the record); M. C. Moos; General Goodpaster; W. J. Hopkins. Lunch. Afternoon appointments with Lt. Colonel J. S. D. Eisenhower; W. J. Hopkins; R. E. Merriam; Lt. Colonel J. S. D. Eisenhower.

29 Washington. Dentist appointment. Morning appointments with Colonel Schulz; G. Gray; National Security Council session; L. T. Merchant; T. E. Stephens; Native American schoolchildren; R. E. Merriam and General Goodpaster; General Goodpaster; T. E. Stephens. Lunch. Afternoon appointments with T. E. Stephens; M. C. Moos; Lt. Colonel

J. S. D. Eisenhower; General Goodpaster; R. E. Merriam, General Goodpaster, H. R. McPhee, and P. E. Areeda.

30   Washington. Morning appointments with General Persons; Secretary Mitchell; W. J. Hopkins; Budget Director Stans, E. Staats, General Persons, G. D. Morgan, R. E. Merriam, and General Goodpaster; M. C. Moos; Mr. and Mrs. Lewis Parsons, Ben Fluchus, and T. E. Stephens (off the record); R. Carroll, Mrs. P. Carroll, and D. Carroll (off the record); T. E. Stephens; former White House aides John Hollowell and Roy Colvin; Lt. Colonel J. S. D. Eisenhower; R. E. Merriam. Lunch.

31   Washington. Morning appointments with General Goodpaster and Lt. Colonel J. S. D. Eisenhower; D. W. Kendall; General Goodpaster; Colonel Schulz; B. N. Harlow; R. Flohr; J. C. Hagerty and Generals Persons and Goodpaster; General Persons; Senator Bush and B. N. Harlow; General Goodpaster; A. W. Dulles, L. T. Merchant, U.S. Ambassador Parsons, J. M. Steeves, J. H. Douglas, G. Gray, J. C. Hagerty, Lt. Colonel J. S. D. Eisenhower, and Generals Persons, Cabell, Lemnitzer, and Goodpaster to discuss situation in Laos (off the record); Generals Persons and Goodpaster. Lunch.

1961

January   1   Washington. Attends services at National Presbyterian Church.

2   Washington. Off-the-record appointment with Secretary Herter, L. T. Merchant, J. H. Douglas, A. W. Dulles, J. C. Hagerty, and Generals Lemnitzer and Goodpaster to discuss situation in Laos.

3   Washington. Attends Service of Intercession and Holy Communion at National Presbyterian Church with J. C. Hagerty. Morning appointments with Secretaries Herter, Anderson, and Gates, J. H. Douglas, Generals Lemnitzer and Goodpaster, L. T. Merchant, A. W. Dulles, R. Bissell, C. T. Barnes, G. Gray, T. C. Mann, and Congressman Williams (off the record); General Lemnitzer; General Persons; U.S.

Ambassador Maurice M. Bernbaum (to Ecuador); General Persons and B. N. Harlow. Lunch. Afternoon appointments with G. Gray and General Goodpaster; General Goodpaster; Lt. Colonel J. S. D. Eisenhower.

4   Washington. Breakfast meeting with Senator Dirksen, Congressman Halleck, General Persons, and B. N. Harlow (off the record). Legislative Leaders. Airborne for Gettysburg. Inspects offices at Gettysburg College. Returns to Washington. Afternoon appointments with General Persons; R. E. Merriam; R. J. Saulnier; T. E. Stephens; General Goodpaster; D. Black and Lt. Colonel J. S. D. Eisenhower; A. Krock, R. Drummond, R. Richards, L. Wilson, J. Hightower, and J. C. Hagerty (off the record).

5   Washington. Breakfast meeting with Senator Bridges and B. N. Harlow. Morning appointments with General Persons; National Security Council session; Secretary Gates and General Goodpaster; General Goodpaster; foreign intelligence activities board of consultants; L. W. Douglas; Mr. and Mrs. Jacques Brazy and family (off the record). Lunch with Vice-President Nixon and B. N. Harlow. Afternoon appointments with Lt. Colonel J. S. D. Eisenhower; D. W. Kendall; T. E. Stephens; Postmaster General Summerfield. Attends dinner hosted by Senators Bridges and Dirksen and families.

6   Washington. Morning appointments with R. E. Merriam; T. E. Stephens; Generals Goodpaster, Lemnitzer, and Decker, Lt. Colonel J. S. D. Eisenhower, and W. E. Robinson (off the record); Ambassador Julius M. Udochi (from Nigeria) and W. T. Buchanan; General Goodpaster; D. Anderson; Mrs. J. B. Parks, Mrs. P. Gibson, and T. E. Stephens; Reba Miller (off the record); Mrs. Lord; T. E. Stephens. Attends Republican National Committee luncheon. Afternoon appointments with Dr. M. S. Eisenhower and M. C. Moos; Dr. M. S. Eisenhower; J. C. Hagerty and Colonel Draper; T. E. Stephens; R. E. Merriam; General Goodpaster; Lt. Colonel J. S. D. Eisenhower. Swims. Late afternoon appointments with W. J. Hopkins; D. Paarlberg and P. E. Areeda; Lt. Colonel J. S. D. Eisenhower; G. D. Morgan; Dr. M. S. Eisenhower.

7　Washington. Airborne for Fort Gordon, Georgia. Reviews troops. Airborne for Augusta National Golf Club for golf with E. D. Slater, C. Roberts, and J. E. Lemon.

8　Augusta, Georgia. To Augusta National Golf Club for golf with C. Roberts, E. D. Slater, and J. E. Lemon. Returns to Washington.

9　Washington. Breakfast meeting with Senator Goldwater and B. N. Harlow. Appointments with T. E. Stephens and J. C. Hagerty; G. Meany; Generals Lemnitzer and Goodpaster; R. E. Merriam. Opens White House Conference on Aging. Appointments with J. J. McCloy (off the record); General Goodpaster; T. E. Stephens. Lunch at Pentagon with Secretary Gates and Defense Department officials. Afternoon appointments with General Persons; D. W. Kendall; G. D. Morgan, D. W. Kendall, H. R. McPhee, and P. E. Areeda; Generals Persons and Goodpaster; General Goodpaster and H. R. McPhee; General Persons. Attends birthday party for Vice-President Nixon.

10　Washington. Morning appointments with Colonel Schulz; General Goodpaster; General Persons and B. N. Harlow; Legislative Leaders; R. E. Merriam, M. C. Moos, and H. R. McPhee; E. F. Morrow (off the record); J. J. Nance (Chairman, Central National Bank, Cleveland, Ohio) (off the record); M. C. Moos. Presents Certificates of Merit to White House retirees. Receives Big Brother of the Year Award. Lunch. Afternoon appointments with R. L. Biggers, Colonel Schulz, and Lt. Colonel J. S. D. Eisenhower (off the record); R. E. Merriam; Secretary Gates, G. Gray, A. W. Dulles, J. H. Douglas, L. T. Merchant, T. C. Mann, and W. Willauer (off the record); G. Gray; General Persons; G. D. Morgan. Attends American Society of Chemical Engineers dinner. Receives Hoover Medal to commemorate civic and humanitarian achievement.

11　Washington. Breakfast meeting with congressional leaders. Appointments with General Persons and A. Wheaton; D. W. Kendall and General Goodpaster; House of Freedom group; U.S. Ambassador Crowe; A. Wheaton; T. E. Stephens. Presents President's Awards for Distinguished Federal Civilian Service. Lunch at home of General Lemnitzer. Afternoon appointments with R. E. Merriam; President's Committee on Government Contracts; Mrs. O. R. Reid; General Goodpaster. Swims. Attends dinner hosted by Cabinet members with Mrs. Eisenhower.

12 Washington. Morning appointments with General Persons and A. Wheaton; Colonel Schulz; General Goodpaster; National Security Council session; General Goodpaster; T. E. Stephens; General Goodpaster; Yasujiro Tsutsumi and family, Ambassador Asakai, General Lemnitzer, and T. Hageya (interpreter). Lunch. Afternoon appointments with Lt. Colonel J. S. D. Eisenhower; E. D. Eisenhower (off the record); T. E. Stephens; J. B. Baird, D. Lindsay, R. J. Saulnier, Budget Director Stans, D. W. Kendall, C. B. Randall, Secretary Mueller, P. A. Ray, and General Persons; M. Pickford and Mr. Hirtley (off the record); E. D. Eisenhower.

13 Washington. Breakfast meeting with Senators and Congressmen. Morning appointments with Mr. and Mrs. S. P. Skouras, F. Leslie, and Mr. McDonald (off the record); Cabinet meeting; J. A. McCone, Secretary Gates, Generals Lemnitzer and Loper, H. P. Van Ormer, A. L. Burgess, and Lt. Colonel J. S. D. Eisenhower (off the record); J. A. McCone; Secretary Herter and General Goodpaster; W. R. Hearst, Jr., H. Pyle, and J. W. Bethea (off the record); Senator H. A. Smith and T. E. Stephens (off the record); General Goodpaster and H. R. McPhee. Lunch. Afternoon appointments with Dr. M. S. Eisenhower, E. D. Eisenhower, and Bud Eisenhower; R. Gros; T. E. Stephens; H. R. McPhee; D. W. Kendall; Lt. Colonel J. S. D. Eisenhower; Captain Aurand; General Persons. Airborne for Camp David, Maryland.

14 Camp David, Maryland. No official appointments.

15 Camp David, Maryland. Returns to Washington.

16 Washington. Morning appointments with R. J. Saulnier; Colonel Schulz; T. E. Stephens; Congresswoman St. George (off the record); General Per-

sons; W. J. Hopkins; Secretary Mitchell; General Persons; T. E. Stephens; Lt. Colonel J. S. D. Eisenhower; Ambassador Jose A. M. Gova (from Venezuela) and W. T. Buchanan; P. Grimm (off the record); Generals Lemnitzer and Goodpaster; Congressman Conte and children (off the record); J. N. Irwin and family (off the record); Ambassador Aime Raymond N'Thepe (from Cameroun), W. T. Buchanan, and E. S. Glenn; Budget Director Stans; M. J. McCaffree; J. C. Hagerty. Lunch. Dentist appointment. Afternoon appointments with General Goodpaster; D. W. Kendall, G. D. Morgan, P. E. Areeda, and H. R. McPhee; General Goodpaster; Lt. Colonel J. S. D. Eisenhower. Hosts stag dinner for news reporters.

17 Washington. Morning appointments with W. J. Hopkins; T. E. Stephens; Senator Javits and B. N. Harlow (off the record); Mr. and Mrs. R. A. Forsythe and children (off the record); D. W. Kendall; Ambassador Konan Bedie (from Ivory Coast), C. E. Conger, and E. S. Glenn; Shigeko Kodera, Dr. Turo Kosaka, U.S. Ambassador Parsons, Mr. and Mrs. B. O'Connor, J. Sakamoto, V. Roberts, and Ambassador Asakai; S. E. Graham and W. Bryan (off the record); W. T. Buchanan; Prime Minister Diefenbaker, Ambassador Heeney, E. D. Fulton, Secretary Herter, E. F. Bennett, and W. T. Buchanan. Signs Columbia River Treaty. Appointments with Prime Minister Diefenbaker; E. Black (off the record); Secretary Benson (off the record); Admiral Strauss (off the record); U.S. Ambassador Whitney (off the record); M. J. McCaffree; R. J. Saulnier; A. Leopold (off the record). Hosts luncheon in connection with Columbia River Treaty. Appointments with G. D. Morgan, D. W. Kendall, and H. R. McPhee; W. E. Robinson, W. A. Jones, and A. Nielsen. Delivers farewell address via television and radio.

18 Washington. Morning appointments with R. D. Barnard and family; J. C. Hagerty; H. R. McPhee; P. E. Areeda; Lt. Colonel J. S. D. Eisenhower; G. D. Morgan, J. C. Hagerty, B. N. Harlow, and General Goodpaster; News conference; S. C. Waugh; D. W. Kendall; Vice-President Nixon; W. T. Faricy; General Goodpaster; U.S. Ambassador Young. Lunch. Af-

ternoon appointments with Lt. Colonel J. S. D. Eisenhower; General Goodpaster; R. E. Merriam; Dr. Glennan; G. Gray, A. W. Dulles, and General Goodpaster (off the record); Attorney General Rogers. Presents Medal of Freedom to Secretaries Herter and Gates, J. H. Douglas, G. Gray, General Goodpaster, and Dr. Kistiakowsky. Appointments with J. C. Hagerty; J. Campbell; General Goodpaster; General Persons; H. R. McPhee. Hosts party for staff and secretaries.

19   Washington. Morning appointments with General Goodpaster; General Persons; General Persons and J. C. Hagerty; General Goodpaster; H. R. McPhee; President-elect Kennedy; President-elect Kennedy, Secretaries Herter, Anderson, and Gates, and designated Secretaries Dean Rusk and Robert McNamara; General Persons; W. J. Hopkins; M. C. Moos; General Goodpaster; Secretary Flemming; D. W. Kendall. Lunch. Afternoon appointments with Lt. Colonel J. S. D. Eisenhower; Colonel Schulz; B. N. Harlow. Tours offices.

Index

elections, 1089–91, 1100; and minerals stabilization plan, 889–90; and Mitchell's memo on budget, economy, 621–22; and Mitchell's plan on human resources, 85–86; on 1960 election, 2136; and Nixon as congressional foreign policy liaison, 410–12; and oil import quotas, 758–59; on People-to-People program, 364–66, 684–85; Persons succeeds, 2189–95; on post for Hendrickson, 357; on post for Jackson, 695–96; on presidential disability, 711–14; on publicity for young Republicans, 524–25; publishes memoir, 1239–40, 1256–58, 2225–26; questions for E., 1256–58; Republicans add fuel to flame, 957; and Republican spirit of hopelessness, 1089–91; resigns, 1116–17, 1127, 1128–29, 1239–40, 1563–64; sends birthday wishes, 2136; and Simpson, 518; and skiing, 1239–40, 2225–26; on Strauss's rejection, 1563–64; on Thye and dairy situation in Minnesota, 693–94; on Trade Agreements Extension bill, 661–62; and vacancy on SEC, 109–10; on wheat disposal program, 40–42; on White House appointments, 396–99; and wool tariff issue, 265–67; writes memoir, 1253–54

Aden, (British) Colony of, British difficulties in, 102, 104

Adenauer, Konrad: background, 125; on balance of payments, 2172–73; and Berlin crisis, 1476–77, 1676–77; on Communist menace, 1496, 1817–18, 2121–23; on Communist propaganda, 1893–94; dines with Herter, 1852–54; on disarmament discussions, 242, 1015; and discussions with Dulles, 666–67, 1015; and Dulles's death, 1491–92; on E.'s letter to Bulganin, 727; on E.'s talks with Khrushchev, 1676–77, 1686–87, 1852–54; on European trade policies, 1799–1800; on exchange visits with Khrushchev, 1615–16; favors heads of government meeting, 2172–73; fears "British weakness," 1496; on financial and economic issues, 2121–23; on gold outflow, 2121–23; illness of, 2189; on institute to study Soviet ideology, 1893–94; irritates E., 1620–21; leadership of, 180–81; and Marshall Plan, 2121–23; meets with Anderson, Dillon, 2141–42, 2172–73; meets with Herter, 1476–77; meets with Norstad, 125; and memo on E.-Khrushchev talks, 1685–86; mental health of, 1852–54; message from, to Khrushchev, 1817–18; on Mideast problems, 1015; on Nasser's political ambitions, 1020–22; opposes demilitarization of Germany, 632–36; on reduction of British forces in Germany, 147–50; on reelection, 125, 170–71; and reunification of Ger-

many, 242, 1496; on rights in Berlin, 1852–54; and Soviet note on atomic weaponry, 191–94; on "Spiritual Power of Communism," 1893–94; on tank procurement for West Germany, 206, 242, 265–67, 389–90; on tenth anniversary as chancellor, 1658; and West German defense forces, 242. *See also* Germany, Federal Republic of

—France: and de Gaulle's tripartite philosophy, 1159–62, 2068–73; and de Gaulle on U.S. withdrawal from NATO, 1767–68; on discussions with Debré and Couve de Murville, 2115–18, 2141–42; on European integration, 2115–18; on France under de Gaulle, 1015; on French intentions in nuclear field, 1020–22; and NATO's nuclear weapons policy, 2115–18, 2141–42

—NATO: and France, 1767–68, 2115–18; and ministerial meeting (December 1960), 2172–73, 2189; nuclear weapons policy, 2141–42, 2172–73, 2189; and weaponry capabilities of NATO, 242

—Summit Conference (May 1960): and *modus vivendi* with Soviets, 1697–1700; planning for, 1601–3, 1615–16, 1676–77, 1817–18; timing consultations regarding, 1691–92, 1697–1700

—United States: Adenauer attends Dulles funeral, 1496; Adenauer visits U.S., 150, 170–71, 215–16, 242, 1796–97, 1817–18, 1852–54; on costs of U.S. force in Germany, 147–50; E. briefs Kennedy on Adenauer, 2189–95; E. meets with Adenauer, 1496, 1620–21, 1623–25, 1648–50, 1658, 1659, 1686–87, 1852–54; and exchange visits with Khrushchev, 1614–15, 1615–16; on friendship with U.S., 125, 242; on 1960 election, 1852–54; on return of vested German assets, 170–71, 242, 1796–97; University of California honors Adenauer, 1817–18, 1852–54

—Western Summit Conference: Adenauer agrees to attend, 1718–19; de Gaulle opposes, 1706–8; discussions on, 1614–15, 1615–16

Adler, Herbert L., 1040

Advanced Research Projects Agency. *See* ARPA

Advertising Council: and budget fight, 1452–53; E. addresses, 1452–53

Advisory Board of Economic Growth and Stability, Burns proposes reconstruction of, 813–14

Advisory Committee on Government Organization. *See* President's Advisory Committee on Government Organization

Advisory Committee on Transport Policy and Organization, 777–82

Adzhubei, Alexis I., 1684

Aerodynamic missiles. *See* Missiles

Ahmed, Aziz, 2209–10
Aid to Dependent Children, 1361–62
Aiken, George David: background, 396; and
farm bill tactics, 1045–46; opposes AEC
legislation, 395–96
Aircraft: Aero–Commander, 558–60; and ANP,
752–53; on atomic weaponry for Canberras, 107–9; and B-52H, 2149–50; on B-70
bomber program, 1810, 2149–50; on C-
130B transport for Republic of China,
2244–45; on DC-3s as feeder aircraft, 547;
on downing of C-130 Hercules, 1687–88;
on downing of RB-47 airplane, 2008–9,
2012–13, 2015, 2111–13; Draper's duties,
558–60; drops leaflets over Havana, 1731–
32; E. flies Stearman Trainer, 1736; on E.'s
safety in helicopters, 553, 558–60; on F-
104s for Pakistan, 1919–23; on Globemas-
ters for POL supplies to Jordan, 1013–15;
on hazardous cargoes, 935; jet aircraft, observations on, 1589–91, 1783–84; on jet
aircraft and trans-Pacific routes, 2252–54;
on jet aircraft for Yugoslavia, 376–77; on
jet transport planes, 1466–67; on nuclear-
powered aircraft, 752–53; pre-inaugural,
for Kennedy, 2206; on subsidies for feeder
airlines, 547; and Super-Constellation,
558–60; on transport aircraft for Paraguay,
1725–26; on U.S. flights over Arctic, 843;
on U.S. flights over U.K., 872–73; on U.S.-
U.K. air operations, 935, 936–37; on violations by, at Soviet border, 1031–32. See also
U-2 flights
Aircraft carriers: and intraservice rivalry, 735;
nuclear carriers v. nuclear submarines,
735, 738; obsolescence of, 735
Aircraft Nuclear Propulsion Project (ANP):
Kennedy terminates, 753; Price's support
of, 752–53
Air defense: and alert measures plan with
Canada, 267; and coordination in NATO,
1785–87, 1819–20; and Sky Hawk exercise,
1647, 1661–62. See also France, Republic
of; NATO
Air Force, Department of, awards procurement
contracts in labor surplus areas, 760–65
Air Force, Secretary of. See Douglas, James
Henderson, Jr.; Quarles, Donald Aubrey
Airlines: in Alaska, 405; on BOAC routes to
Hong Kong–San Francisco via Tokyo,
1599–1601; on certification of Alaska,
Northwest, and Pacific Northern Airlines,
405; on KLM airlines route, 2256–57;
Northwest v. Pan American, 406–7; and
Pacific Great Circle routes, 406–7; and
trans-Pacific air routes, 2252–54; and
Trans-Pacific Renewal Case, 720; on
U.S.-U.K. Pacific air route changes,
1599–1601. See also KLM Royal Dutch

Airlines; Northwest Orient Airlines; Pacific
Northern Airlines; Pan American World
Airways; South Pacific Airlines; Trans
World Airlines
Airports: on airport facilities bill, 1422–23;
Burke Airport, 369–72; Chantilly Airport,
369–72; Dulles International Airport, 369–
72; Friendship Airport, 369–72; improve-
ment of, 1330; National Airport, 369–72;
in Washington, D.C., 369–72
Air power. See also Aircraft; New Look; Nike-
Ajax; Nike/Talos; Strategic Air Command;
United States Air Force
Air routes. See Airlines; Civil Aeronautics
Board
Airways Modernization Act of 1957, 1081–82
Airways Modernization Board, 369–72, 1081–
82
Akers, Floyd DeSoto, 675
Akihito, Crown Prince of Japan, 1978–79,
2090–91. See also Japan
Alabama: and Alabama–Coosa River develop-
ment, 1665–67; and Millers Ferry lock/
dam, 1665–67; and school integration,
1134–35, 1375–78; and tidelands litigation,
550–51, 893–95
Alabama Power Company, 1665–67
Alam, Zafar, 2198
Alanbrooke, Viscount of Brookeborough. See
Brooke, Alan Francis
Alaska: on airline subsidies in, 405; and Alaska
Defense Command, 1977–78; on certifica-
tion of airlines in, 405; E.'s goodwill trip to
Ankara (December 1959), 1761–62, 1762–
63; on E.'s goodwill tour to Far East, 1976–
77, 1977–78; E. visits Fort Richardson,
1977–78; on Great Circle air routes, 288,
406–7; and midterm election, 1193–94;
statehood for, 1153–56; on Willis's appreciation, 405
Albertini, Germaine, 1969–70
Albert Schweitzer Education Foundation,
1404–6
ALCOA. See Aluminum Company of America;
Raw materials; Strategic materials
Alcorn, Hugh Meade, Jr.: and Adams's resignation, 1089–91; addresses Cabinet, 69–70;
background, 36; on critics of DOD in
midterm campaign, 1141–42; on critics of
fiscal program in midterm campaign,
1143–44; E.'s esteem for, 1235–36, 1259–
61, 1436; on E.'s post-midterm election intentions, 1205–6; and GOP apathy, 1118;
on GOP conservatives and liberals, 396–
99; and GOP head as member of Cabinet,
258–59; on GOP political philosophy,
396–99, 801–3; on governor's race in California, 1081; heads RNC, 36; meets with
E., 69–70; meets with finance committee,

1259–61; on midterm campaign reports, 1186–87, 1205–6; on Modern Republicanism, 396–99; on need to "sell" GOP, 1216–17, 1309–10; on need for young Republicans, 751–52, 1436; and new GOP plan, 69–70; and Percy as GOP head, 1236–39; on rebuilding GOP, 1205–6, 1236–39, 1239–40, 1259–61; and Republican Party Committee, 1305; resigns, 1235–36, 1436, 1862–63; on right-to-work issue, 1165–67; Roberts scores, 1235–36; on timing of E.'s campaign speeches, 1186–87

Alejos, Carlos, 2086, 2087

Alessandri Rodríguez, Jorge, 1859–60. *See also* Chile, Republic of

Alexander, Harold Rupert Leofric George ("Alex"): background, 949–50; on Dulles's death, 1508–9; E.'s esteem for, 1295–98, 1508–9, 2181, 2187; illness of, 1271–73, 1508–9; and summit site, 1508–9; and World War II reunion, 1271–73, 1508–9, 1558–59, 1620–21

Alexander, Henry Clay, 1311–13

Alexander, Holmes Moss, 1545–46

Algeria: Ayub Khan's concern, 2209–10; Bourguiba's concern, 1113–15; de Gaulle's declaration on, 1654–57, 1667–69, 1673–75, 1681–82, 1740–42; and de Gaulle's leadership, 917, 2223–25; de Gaulle's view, 1654–57, 1931–33; E., Macmillan serve in, World War II, 1852–54; E., Murphy serve in, World War II, 1715–16; and French-Algerian conflict, 46–47, 746, 827–29, 831–34, 1654–57, 1673–75, 1931–33; and French colonialism, 952–60; French settler insurgency in, 1811; insurrection in, 917; and Loi-Cadre legislation, 563–67; and Moslem nationalists, 831–34; and refugees at Tunisia-Algeria border, 766–67; and relations with France, 831–34, 1931–33; Schweitzer's view, 46–47, 88; seeks independence, 1250–51; and Soviet vote in U.N., 1708; U.N. debate regarding, 1250–51, 2223–25. *See also* De Gaulle, Charles André Joseph Marie; France, Republic of; Tunisia, Republic of

al-Khayyal, Sheikh Abdullah: and aide-memoire on Gulf of Aqaba dispute, 297–99; background, 53–55; and Egyptian-Israeli dispute, 53–55; and Israeli-Saudi Arabian dispute, 194–96, 197–98

Allen, George Edward: and Allen-Byars partnership, 89–90, 682–84, 885–86, 1016–17; on Allen's leap year birthdays, 733; article by, on friendship with E., 1945–46, 1949–50; attends Es.' New Year's Eve party, 632; attends stag weekend at Camp David, 1338–39; background, 13–14; and "Banned," 202–3, 219, 248, 249; bridge

with E., 137–38, 660–61, 1106–7, 1452–53; "Brilliant Speed" loses, 1106–7; on butchering beef, 609–11; on calorie and cholesterol values, 1874–75; and campaign for National Presbyterian Church, 363; on delivering butchered beef, 609–11; on disposal of inferior livestock, 16–17; on Edgar E.'s health, 109–10; and Eisenhower Farms name, 89–90; E. offers ham to, 1345; on Emanuel's death, 2173–74; E. reports on trip to Milestone, 1338–39; and golf, 1106–7, 1439–40, 1792–93, 1812–13; and "horse deal," 137–38, 164–65, 202–3, 248, 249; invites E. to California, 1345, 1792–93, 1859; joins Es. at Milestone Plantation, 13–14; on Knowland's gubernatorial candidacy, 1064–68; on La Quinta Country Club offer, 1859; and Marx's Hoop-Zing, 1099–1100; and Meyner's meeting with E., 631–32, 754–55; Nevins as farm manager for, 16–17; and Nielsen's investment advice, 1365–66; on office for E. at Gettysburg College, 1822; as partner in Gettysburg farms, 16–17; on purchasing a horse, 164–65; and Robinson, 1264–65; vacations in California, 1345, 1365–66; and "Very Speedy," 1704–5; visits E. at Augusta, 1439–40, 1452–53; visits E. at Gettysburg farm, 631–32; visits E. at Newport, 1106–7; visits E. at White House, 660–61; on weight problems, 1106–7, 1338–39, 1345, 1874–75

Allen, George Venable: accompanies Nixon to USSR, 1594; attends NSC meeting, 1250; background, 269–70, 963; on communication with Arab states, 1027–31; on functions of VOA, 1250; heads USIA, 1027–31; on Makarios and British public opinion, 269–70; and NSC membership, 743–45; and People-to-People fundraising and structure, 684–85; on political warfare, 1568–69; and psychological warfare study, 1611–13; reports on Brussels World's Fair, 963–64; sends speech draft, 1026

Allen, Leo Elwood: attends White House luncheon, 1142; background, 1046

Allen, Mary (Keane), 733; background, 13–14; on delivering butchered beef, 610; on E.'s trip to Western Europe, 1638; joins Es. at Milestone Plantation, 13–14; visits at Gettysburg farm, 1638

Allen, Raymond Bernard, 1229–30

Allen, William M., 1165–67

Allied Laboratories, Inc., 891

Allott, Gordon Llewellyn: background, 751–52; returns to Senate, 2161–62

Allyn, Stanley Charles ("Chick"), 1350–52

Alphand, Hervé: on arms for Tunisia, 563–67; background, 188–91; on dinner for Coty,

188–91; on French naval forces in Mediterranean, 1313–14, 1412–15; meets with de Gaulle, 1919–23; reports on Berlin crisis, 1424–26; and tripartite talks, 1159–62, 2028–30; and U.S. commitments, 1740–42; and Western Summit Conference, 1697–1700, 1712–13
Alphand, Merenda Nicole, 188–91
al-Quwatli (Quwaitli, Quwatly, Kuwatly), Shukri: attends Cairo Conference, 100; as president of Syria, 26. *See also* Syria
Alsogaray, Alvaro Carlos, 2081, 2082
Alsop, Joseph Wright, Jr.: attacks Wilson, 1043–44; background, 1043; E.'s opinion of, 866–67, 1043–44; on Gavin, 1043–44; as irresponsible journalist, 1935–41, 2168–70; Wilson's opinion of, 1043–44
Altschul, Frank: analyzes world situation, 512–16; background, 516; on cold war, 512–16; on Congress, 512–16; on foreign aid, 512–16; on sputnik, 512–16
Aluminum Company of America (ALCOA), and antitrust suit against, 208–9
Aluminum industry: stockpiles, as anti-strike weapon, 1737–39; strikes, 1519–20; on U.S. consumption, 1519–20; and Volta River Project, 637–39, 2037–38. *See also* Raw materials; Strategic materials
Amberg, Richard Hiller, 1063–64
American Armed Forces Institute, 27
American Assembly. *See* Columbia University: American Assembly
American Bank, and U.S. aid to Latin America, 2211–13
American Bar Association (ABA): and appointments to federal judiciary, 110–11; on Cokes for ABA-BBA party, 2077–78; and Dethmers, 1721; E.'s address to (1949), 1535; E. proclaims Law Day, 996–97; promotes peace through law, 996–97
American Broadcasting System, 1842–43
American College of Surgeons: awards E. honorary fellowship, 203–4; invites E. to speak, 55–56, 203–4
American Economic Association, 640–41
American Express Company, 1914–15
American Farm Bureau Federation (AFBF), proposes plan to fight inflation, 1290–91
American Farm School, 362–63
American Federation of Labor (AFL), supports U.S. stand in Berlin crisis, 1576–77
American Federation of Labor–Congress of Industrial Organizations (AFL-CIO): and CBS inflation programs, 1417; supports U.S. stand in Berlin crisis, 1576–77
American Heart Association: Clark seeks E.'s support, 37–38; and federal *v.* private fundraising projects, 37–38
American Home Products Corporation, 891
American Indians. *See* Native Americans

American Latvian Association, and painting for E., 153–54
American Legion: Clark addresses, 457–58; Gruenther addresses, 457–58; Lewis denounces Status of Forces Agreements, 457–58; McElroy addresses, 1141–42; and McKneally's visit to USSR, 1886–87; and Status of Forces Agreements, 457–58
American Library Association, 668–69
American Management Association, 897–98, 929–30
American Medical Association (AMA): E. addresses, 1521; invites E. to address, 55–56
American National Exhibition. *See* American National Exposition
American National Exposition (Sokolniki Park, USSR), 1466–67, 1589–91; Nixon opens, 1585–86, 1594; return of E.'s painting from, 1597–98
American National Red Cross, Gruenther heads, 13–14, 145, 457–58. *See also* International Red Cross
American Publications Bureau, 696–97
American Red Cross: and European Red Cross Study Centers, 1152–53; and federal disaster relief programs, 1129–30; international role of, 1152–53; and Junior Red Cross, 1152–53; on proposal by Buxton and Hobbs, 1152–53; and United Givers Fund, 1129–30; White's petition, 1152–53
American Republics. *See* Latin America
Americans for Democratic Action (ADA): philosophy of, in California, 1064–68; school of thinking, 1135–36
American Society of Newspaper Editors (ASNE): E.'s addresses to, 296, 774, 789–91, 797–99, 817–18, 865, 1935–41; hosts Castro, 1456
American Telephone and Telegraph Company (AT&T): and antitrust consent decrees, 251–53; role of, in budget fight, 1416–17, 1430–31
Ames, John Dawes: background, 173; on dinner for Coty, 188–91
Ames, Mrs. John Dawes, 188–91
Amherst College, 2146
Amistad Dam, 1373
Amman (capital of Jordan), and POL supplies for Jordan, 1013–15
Amos 'n Andy show, 939–40
Anderson, Clayton and Company, 1230
Anderson, Clinton Presba, 1581–82
Anderson, Dillon: angers E., 594–96; background, 340–42; as campaign speaker on foreign affairs, defense, 1793–96; on DOD reorganization, 878–79; on Japanese economy and foreign trade, 1445–46; on Mideast oil imports, 340–42; opposes tax cuts, 878–79; replies to Johnson, 878–79; on State of the Union Address, 663–64; as

successor to McElroy, 1477–79; on Texas offshore oil rights (tidelands), 594–96; visits Southeast Asia, 1445–46

Anderson, Jack Z.: background, 693; and Cotton's newsletter, 1865

Anderson, Robert Bernerd, 1228; and antitrust suits against oil, gas producers, 570–71; attends NSC meeting, 593–94; attends stag dinner, 334–35; background, 187–88, 222–23; and balance of payments, 2172–73, 2189–95; briefs Kennedy on budget matters, 2189–95; and British economic problems, 644–45; on budgetary refinancing, 1233–34; and Burns's talk on recession, 793–95; as campaign speaker on presidency, foreign affairs, treasury, 1793–96; on causes of gold outflow, 2199–2200; on certificates of indebtedness, 1023–24; Coblentz scores, 2168–70; and Committee on Economic Development, 777–82; and Committee on World Economic Practices, 1311–13; confers with E. on recession recovery, 719, 769–71; confers with Kyes on recession recovery, 777–82; on customs post for Sayler, 477; and Declaration of Common Purpose, 544–45; Dillon succeeds, 2233–34; drafts speech for E., 1675–76; on E.'s address to Assembly of World's Religions, 1249; and economic aid to Turkey, 1051; E. recommends Gould for tax court judgeship, 818; E. recommends Rouse for treasury post, 380–81; on federal bond issues, 450–51; on fiscal program and midterm campaign, 1141–42, 1143–44; on foreign exchange and economic welfare, 859–61; on German economic issues, 2121–23; and Goldwater's speech, 2199–2200; heads Cabinet committee on tax reform, 1042–43; and Humphrey's advice on federal budget, 589–91; and Johnson's view on economy, 878–79; on long-term interest rates, 902; on Lubell's findings, 950–51; on maritime labor union fears, 1394–95; and media exposure on budget fight, 1369–71; meets with Adenauer, 2141–42, 2172–73; meets with E., 685–86, 1143–44; meets with foreign ministers abroad, 1143–44; and mission to Bonn on balance of payments, 2168–70; and Mitchell's memo on budget, economy, 621–22; on monetary and credit systems, 450–51, 2059–60; and most-favored nation status for Poland, 2160; on national debt reduction, 1007–13, 1867–68; as 1960 presidential nominee, 1201–2; on NSC membership, 743–45; and oil import quotas, 385–87, 758–59; and postattack economic plans, 444–46; on post for Goodpaster, 2189–95; as Secretary of the Treasury, 187–88, 222–23, 334–35, 339–

40, 385–87; and security leak on redeployment, 2204; sends Lincoln pennies, 1304–5; on situation in Cuba, 1990–91; as successor to Dulles, 2215; on support for budget-inflation measures, 1184–85; and tax auditing procedures, 586–87; on tax breaks for teachers, 905–6; and taxes on musical instruments, 1915; on tax reductions, 975–76; as Texas "favorite son" candidate, 1942; on U.S. foreign aid policies, 2199–2200; and U.S. policy in Latin America, 1218–19; as vice-presidential candidate, 2018–19; as vice-presidential nominee, 1870–71; visits New Delhi, 1143–44; and *Wall Street Journal,* 902

Andrew, Albert Christian Edward, The Prince, 1816, 1830

Andvord, Rolf Otto, 628–29

Ankony Farms, cattle sale by, 16–17, 29–30

Antarctica, 823

Antitrust legislation: against drug companies, 891; against oil, gas producers, 570–71; and ALCOA, 208–9; and antitrust law, 929–30; and AT&T, 251–53; in budget fight, 1430–31; and Clayton Antitrust Act, 251–53, 741–43; and Department of Justice, 208–9, 251–53; and DuPont, 741–43; and IBM, 251–53; and RCA, 251–53; and Salk vaccine, 891; and Sherman Antitrust Act, 741–43; and Winn case, 1788–89. *See also* Brownell, Herbert, Jr.; Justice, Department of; Rogers, William Pierce

ANVIL, political *v.* military objectives of, 2181, 2187

ANZUS Treaty, 728–29; and Australia-New Zealand-U.K.-U.S. military plans, 844–46

Apartheid. *See* Civil rights

Appleton, Arthur I., 1206

Aqaba, and POL supplies for Jordan, 1013–15. *See also* Gulf of Aqaba

AQUATONE, background, 107–9, 575, 579, 1943. *See also* U-2 flights

Arabi Island, dispute regarding, 22–23, 26

Arab-Israeli conflict. *See* Arab States; Egypt; Israel, State of; Saudi Arabia

Arab-Israeli War (1949). *See* Arab States; Israel, State of

Arab League, 2098

Arab Socialist Resurrection (Baath) Party, and elections in Syria, 166, 168

Arab States: and Arab-Israeli conflict, 19–27, 293–95, 512–16, 607–8, 1027–31; and Arab Union, 705–8; on Bourguiba as friend of West, 574–79; concern of, on Communist influence in Syria, 383–85; and conference at Beirut, 2097, 2098; E.'s plan to aid, 1055–56; and Lahoud Plan, 293–95; in Mideast talks, Khrushchev's view, 1017–19; and Nasser's anti-Western propaganda, 1007–13, 1027–31; Nasser as

Armstrong, J. Sinclair, 110
Armstrong Cork Company, 1416–17
Army, Department of: and active duty policy for National Guard, 32–33; on appropriations for Corps of Engineers, 760–65; on appropriations for rivers, harbors, and flood control, 760–65; awards procurement contracts in labor surplus areas, 760–65; and Caffey's disability status, 1946–47; on land compensation for Ryukyuans, 1049–51; on motorization of military funerals, 51–52; and Saturn project, 1798–99; and U.S.-Panamanian relations, 2088–89. *See also* United States Army
Army Command and General Staff College (Fort Leavenworth), John E. as candidate for, 12–13
Army Distaff Foundation: and Distaff Hall, 2093–94, 2198–99; E. supports charity benefit for, 2093–94; on Jones's gift to, 2198–99; Mamie E. as honorary president of women's advisory committee, 2198–99
Army-Navy football game, 1804–5
Army of Northern Virginia, 240
Army Nurse Corps. *See* United States Army Nurse Corps
Arn, Edward F.: background, 110–11; seeks federal judicial appointment, 110–11, 382
ARPA (Advanced Research Projects Agency): to fund inflatable satellite project, 1000–1001; transfers specific projects to NASA, 1000–1001
Ascot (England), 1001
Asia: and Afro-Asian resolution on colonialism, 2200–2201, 2219–21; Champion visits, 1900; Communist expansion in, 2227–30; effective use of propaganda in, 1250; on need to develop purchasing power, 319–25; and SEATO, 453–54; Soviet aggression in, 493–94; and U.S. economic aid to Japan, 1517–19; U.S. policy in, 86–87, 1215–16. *See also* Far East; Goodwill tour to Europe, Asia, Mediterranean, Near East, and North Africa (December 1959); SEATO; Southeast Asia
Assembly of World's Religions, address to, 1248–49
Assistant to the President, holds Cabinet rank, 2189–95. *See also* Adams, Sherman; Persons, Wilton Burton
Associated Press (AP), 1935–41
Association of American Universities (AAU), 714–15, 1105–6; and loyalty oath requirements, 1505–7
Association of Universities of the British Commonwealth, 1105–6
Astrid, Princess of Norway, visits U.S., 708–9
Aswan Dam. *See* Egypt
Athletics. *See* Sports

Atlanta Constitution, 834–35, 1087–88. *See also* McGill, Ralph Emerson
Atlantic Alliance, 1159–62. *See also* Cold war; NATO
Atlantic Community. *See* Cold war; NATO
Atlantic Monthly, reports on Brussels World's Fair, 963–64
Atlas: and Air Force's satellite reconnaissance project, 498; on funding for guided missile program, 162–63, 496–97; and missile gap, 1342
Atlas-Titan, an overlapping missile program, 292–93
Atomic energy, 103; appropriations for, 1188–90; on concepts in reactor development, 1311; and federal role in construction, 385–87, 395–96; international controls of, 848–49; peaceful uses of, 256–57, 721–27, 1153–56, 1682–83, 1844–48, 1887–90; and Plowshare Project, 2019–20; and U.S.S. *Savannah*, 376; and U.S.S. *Seawolf*, 487–88. *See also* Atomic Energy Commission; Atomic weaponry; Disarmament
Atomic Energy Act of 1946, 2189–95
Atomic Energy Act of 1954: amendments to, 642–44, 804–6, 906–7, 936–37, 1024–25, 2189–95; on controlling circle of nuclear powers, 1844–48; and exchange of restricted data, 39–40, 804–6, 906–7, 936–37, 1654–57; and executive powers for regulatory commissions, 2214–15; Macmillan's view, 521–22, 632–36, 936–37; and suspension of tests, 804–6; on transfer of atomic weapons to allies, 1844–48
Atomic Energy Commission (AEC): and ANP, 752–53; on atomic reactor concepts, 1311; and atomic weaponry storage sites, 1031–32; and atomic weaponry tests, 216–18, 618–20, 632–36; and construction authorization, 385–87; and Dutch nuclear submarine, 2102; E. briefs Kennedy on, 2189–95; establishes Fermi Award, 795–96; and executive powers for regulatory commissions, 2214–15; and HARDTACK, 455–56, 819–22; increased spending in, 589–91; on legislative success in Congress, 395–96; Meyer scores, 1787–88; and national security, 446–49; on nuclear-powered aircraft, 752–53; on nuclear weapons test moratorium, 1068–69; on research and development laboratories, 1068–69; and scientific achievements of, 503–5; and Senate hearings on Strauss, 1484, 1543–45; and Soviet veto controversy, 1359–60; Strauss resigns, 921; on test suspension negotiations, 1058–59, 1060–63, 1399–1402; on U.S.-U.K. cooperation in inspections, 920–21; and U.S.-U.K. exchange of atomic data, 1060–63. *See also* Joint Committee on

and OECD, 1968–69; pledges to protect Laos via SEATO, 2223–25; and Sihanouk's letter, 1390; site of SEATO meeting (March 1957), 81–82, 86–87; and trans-Pacific air routes to, 2252–54

Australia-New Zealand-U.S. Conference. *See* ANZUS

Austria, Republic of: and Austrian Peace Treaty, 263–64, 797–99; and Hungarian refugees, 207–8

Automobile Dealer Franchise Act of 1956, 209

Automobile industry: on collective bargaining with UAW, 741–43; and excise taxes, 824–25; and franchise rights for dealers, 208–9; role of, in economic recovery, 824–25, 952–60, 1561–62; splurge by, 786

Averoff-Tossizza, Evangelos, 943

Ayres, William Hanes, 751–52

Ayub Khan, Mohammed (also Muhammad, Mohammad): on Algeria, 2209–10; background, 1147, 1768–69; on Communist threat in North Africa, 2209–10; on de Gaulle, 2209–10; E. meets with, 1778; on French–Pakistani relations, 2209–10; on golf greens grass for Pakistan, 2197–98; on Indo–Pakistani relations, 1774–76, 1791–92, 1919–23; leadership of, 1768–69; on martial law in Pakistan, 1147; on modernizing Pakistan's army, 1778; and Pushtunistan, 1919–23; on U.S. military aircraft for Pakistan, 1919–23. *See also* Pakistan, Islamic Republic of

Azzam Pasha, Abdul Rahman: background, 198; and Gulf of Aqaba dispute, 297–99; meets with Dulles, 198, 297–99

Baath Party. *See* Arab Socialist Resurrection Party

Baghdad Pact: British view, 102, 104; and coup d'état in Iraq, 998–1000; and crisis in Jordan, 158–60; Dulles attends meetings of, 631, 642–44, 695–96, 696–97, 705–8, 1015, 1020–22; Iran's concern, 1321–25; and London Declaration, 1323, 1324; and MAP, 998–1000; on substitute for, 1020–22; and United Arab Republic, 705–8; U.S. agrees to join Military Committee, 104; and U.S. collective security planning, 998–1000; on U.S. support for Iran, Pakistan, Turkey, 998–1000

Baghdad Pact Ministerial Council, 1324

Bahama Islands, and waivers of nonimmigrant visas, 1333–34

Baird, Julian Braden: on attrition rates, 1023–24; background, 381; as campaign speaker on treasury, 1793–96; on DOD payment policies, 523; on monetary system reforms, 2059–60; as Under Secretary of Treasury for Monetary Affairs, 419; wager with E. on debt refinancing, 1023–24

Baker, Howard Henry, 268–69

Baker, Milton Grafly, 2146

Baker, Robert G., 360–61

Baker, Ruth, 360–61

Baldwin, Dr., 66

Ball, George Wildman, 2232

Ballistic missiles. *See* Missiles

Balmoral Castle, E. visits, 1616–17, 1620–21, 1623–25, 1641

Baltimore Colts, 246

Baltimore Orioles, 2092

Baltimore Sun, and article on budget cut, 133, 135–36

Bandaranaike, Solomon West Ridgway Dias, 961–62. *See also* Ceylon, State of

Bandung Conference, 1662–63

"Banned." *See* Allen, George Edward; Whitney, John Hay

Bantz, William B.: background, 1254–55; as candidate for federal judgeship, 1254–55, 1403

Barbados: and Federation of British West Indies, 317–19; and U.S. naval base at Chaguaramas, Trinidad, 317–19

Barbara Anne, 977

Barnes, C. Tracy, 2197

Barnes, J. Hampton, 153–54

Barnes, Stanley Nelson, 1793–96

Barrett, Frank A., 812

Barrientos, César, 1725–26

Barron's Financial Weekly, 2211

Barton, Bill, 156

Baruch, Bernard Mannes ("Bernie"): as adviser to E., 1383; on Aswan Dam project, 408–10; background, 48, 2051; and Baruch Plan, 249–50; birthday greetings to, 2051; on Churchill's health, 950–51; disagrees with Coit, 48; and E.'s "indisposition," 264–65; on E. as Socialist, 1383; and German question, 1360–61; on Lubell's findings, 950–51; and Lubell memo on Syria, 408–10; on monetary system reforms, 2059–60; on NSC membership, 743–45; publishes autobiography, 48, 408–10; and Soviet opportunism, 1360–61; suggests E. speak on Mideast issues, 408–10; on U.S.-Soviet relations, 1360–61. *See also* Baruch Plan

Baruch Plan, Soviets reject, 249–50, 618–20, 656, 659

Bataan Day, and anniversary of fall of Bataan, 825

Batista y Zaldívar, Fulgencio: background, 1876; and Castro, 1456, 2039–42

Bator, Francis Michel, 2125–26

Battle of the Bulge, 1731–32

Battle of Lexington, 157

Baudouin I, King of Belgians, 1484–85. *See also* Belgium, Kingdom of

Baughman, Urbanus Edmund: background,

156; on Barton's civil service status, 156; E. commends, on protection for Nixon, 899–900; E.'s esteem for, 2217

Bauxite, 1542–43, 2037–38

Bayar, Celal: background, 944–45; on economic aid for Turkey, 944–45, 1051; on IMF aid for Turkey, 944–45, 1051; on OEEC aid for Turkey, 944–45, 1051; and Paris talks on aid to Turkey, 1051; on U.S. force in Lebanon, 998–1000. *See also* Turkey, Republic of

Bayeux, 1295–98

Beall, James Glenn, 372

Beane, Carol, 418

Bech, Joseph, 617

Bechtel, Stephen Davison: background, 783; as campaign speaker on commerce, 1793–96; and report by Committee on World Economic Practices, 1311–13; urges E. meet with BAC, 783–84

Bedard, Philip, 188–91

Bedard, Mrs., 188–91

Bedouins, on poverty of, Saud's view, 22

Beef. *See* Livestock

Beeley, Harold, 833

Belchem, Ronald Frederick King, 1558–59

Belgian Congo. *See* Congo, Republic of

Belgium, Kingdom of: and Antwerp in World War II, 1653–54; Benson visits, 2056–58; and Brussels World's Fair, 1104–5; deploys forces in Congo, 2170–71; on E.'s appreciation for gifts, 1484–85; and law of the sea, 1911–12; on strengthening NATO, 1767–68; on troops in Katanga, 2030–32, 2048–49; Tunisia seeks arms from, 563–67. *See also* Baudouin I

Belle Springs Cemetery, 1571

Belshe, Thomas M., 474–75

Bendetsen, Karl Robin, 904–5

Ben Gurion, David: background, 34–36; on developments in Gaza, 94–95; on POL supplies for Jordan, 1013–15; seeks delay on withdrawal of forces, 74–75; seeks postponement of U.N. discussions, 57–59; stern messages to, 34–36, 57–59; suffers pneumonia, 34–36; visits U.S., 2065–66; on withdrawal of Israeli force from Egypt, 34–36, 57–59, 74–75, 94–95. *See also* Israel, State of

Bennett, Wallace Foster, attends luncheon at White House, 1142

Benson, Ezra Taft: on budget and farm programs, 1200–1201; campaigns in Arizona, 1172; campaigns in Indiana, 1172; as campaign speaker on agriculture, 1793–96; campaigns in Wisconsin, 1172; on Conger's proposals, 1895–98; congressmen score, on farm subsidies, 735; and controls on loans, 1200–1201; and cotton subsidies, 1355–57,

1357–58; cuts dairy price supports, 693–94, 787–89; cutting acreage supports, 1200–1201; and dairy situation in Minnesota, 693–94; E. declines book foreword for, 1802–3; E.'s esteem for, 734, 1172; on E.'s REA speech, 1349; on farm bill tactics, 1045–46; on farm program, 786; on federal role in agriculture, 1200–1201; on federal role in education, 1307–9; on federal spending, 1123; and Fifth World Forestry Congress, 1917; on foreign trade policies, 1622; hears Mormon Tabernacle Choir, 1172; and Humphrey's advice on federal budget, 589–91; illness of, 1116–17; on interagency cooperation, 1622; and legislative program in 1960, 2056–58; livestock growers support, 812; on making millionaires with federal subsidies, 1200–1201; meets with E., 1200–1201; and message to Congress on surplus wheat crisis, 1598–99; and minerals stabilization plan, 889–90; and necessary concessions, 787–89; and old German aphorism, 787, 788; opposes price-freeze bill, 787–89; on Paarlberg's transfer, 1116–17; and Phillips's concerns, 461–62; proposes invitation to Nasser, 2058, 2065–66; on replacing Hauge, 1058; reports on Indiana and Arizona politics, 1172; reports on trade trip, 2056–58; Republicans score, as campaign speaker, 1793–96; scores Dillon, 1622; seeks E.'s support on farm program, 1739–40; and soil bank program, 461–62; supports Goldwater, 1172; undergoes gall bladder surgery, 1739–40; visits Egypt, 2056–58, 2058; visits Europe and Middle East, 2056–58; to visit Latin America, 2080–82; and wheat disposal program, 40–42, 1739–40. *See also* Agriculture, Department of

Berlin. *See* Germany

Bermingham, Edward John: appreciation to, 1162–63; attends stag dinner, 538; background, 152–53; death of, 538; gives elephant to E., 538; illness of, 538; on restoration of Abilene home, 1162–63; on U.S. loans to Pemex, 152–53; on U.S.-Mexican relations, 152–53

Bermingham, Katherine (Carpenter) ("K"): background, 538; at Brown Palace, 1162–63; E.'s esteem for late husband, 1162–63; entertains Stuarts, 1326–27; and restoration of E.'s boyhood home, 1162–63

Bermuda Conference (1953), E.'s recollections of, 112–13

Bermuda Conference (1957), 111–12, 112–13; on atomic tests, 216–18, 819, 822; and Buraimi, 102, 104; closing declaration, 216–18, 819; and Cyprus, 103, 104, 118–19; discusses strengthening WEU, 128–29; Dulles

1860–61, 1997–99, 2066–67; guided missiles tracking station in, 104–5; on inter-American economic cooperation, 1242–44, 1997–99; Kubitschek's view on Pan American issues, 924–25, 925–26, 1997–99; López Mateos visits, 1784–85; Luce, as U.S. ambassador to, 850; on Operation Pan America, 1242–44, 1997–99; on Pan American action in cold war, 925–26; on reply to Kubitschek, 924–25, 925–26; and report on Brasilia, 2066–67; Rubottom recommends Dulles visit, 631. *See also* Kubitschek de Oliveira, Juscelino

Breech, Ernest R.: background, 659; on government role in satellite production, 659–60; meets with E., 659–60; member, BAC, 783–84

Brennan, William Joseph, Jr., 39

Brentano, Heinrich von: attacks on, as homosexual, 1509–10; background, 149–50; Dulles meets with, 1020–22; on German support for U.S. military force in FRG, 147–50; meets with E., 1496; and negotiations on Berlin crisis, 1487–88, 1540–41

Brier pipes, 1110–11

Bricker, John William, 60–61

Bricker amendment: E.'s exasperation with, 60–61; E. opposes, 60–61; further revisions to, 60–61

Bridge: with Allen, 137–38, 660–61; with Ames, 173; at Augusta, 707–8; an award for "Pete" Jones, 854; with Bobby Jones, 874–75; with Casey, 173; E.'s game "suffers," 145; on E.-Gruenther system, 1609–10; with John E., 1651–52; with "Pete" Jones, 164, 543, 660–61, 854, 1630–31, 1651–52; with Roberts, 173, 1001–2, 1262–63, 1630–31; with Robinson, 1630–31, 1651–52; on Solomon's winning game, 1609–10; with Tkach, 137–38; with Whitney, 137–38; Yarborough defined, 181; with Yates, 1812–13. *See also* Gruenther, Alfred Maximilian

Bridges, Henry Styles: background, 255; on Bohlen's transfer, 1577–79; on Brussels World's Fair, 963–64; favors bipartisan conference on Formosa, 1120–21; Howard's view, 255; recommends Smith for Civil Service Commission, 1036–37; as "right-wing" senator, 396–99; scores reciprocal trade bill, 952–60; supports DOD reorganization and space bills, 1016

Briggs, Charles William, 2118–19

Briggs, James Elbert, 890

British Bar Association (BBA): attends convention in Washington, D.C., 2035–36; Cokes for, from Robinson, 2077–78

British Broadcasting Corporation (BBC): and Hungarian uprising, 232–33; and tribute

to Montgomery, 948–50; and Voice of America, 232–33

British Commonwealth of Nations, and Gold Coast Independence Ceremonies, 17–18

British Fighter Command, 1819–20

British Overseas Airways Corporation (BOAC): and air routes to Hong Kong–San Francisco via Tokyo, 1599–1601; U.S.-U.K. air route changes, 1599–1601

British West Indies, and Chaguaramas as new capital, 317–19

British West Indies Federation: chooses Trinidad as capital site, 317–19; U.S.-U.K. discussions with, 332–34

Brooke, Alan Francis (Alanbrooke, the Viscount of Brookeborough), ("Brookie"): background, 689–91; Bryant's books on, 689–91; on crossing the Rhine, 689–91; and *Crusade in Europe*, 2153–55; E.'s wartime recollections of, 689–91, 1295–98, 2153–55, 2184, 2185–86; meets E. in Algiers, 2185; scores Churchill, 689–91; scores E., 689–91, 1731–32; wartime diaries by, 689–91, 1295–98, 1731–32; and World War II reunions, 1558–59, 1620–21

Brown, Clarence J., 255–56

Brown, Edmund Gerald ("Pat"): background, 1081; as gubernatorial candidate in California, 1081; Hearst papers support, 1081; wins gubernatorial midterm, 1193–94

Brown, Park Larmon, 49

Brown, Robert Raymond, 465–66

Brownell, Doris A. (McCarter), 188–91

Brownell, Herbert, Jr.: on Adams's questions, 1256–58; advises against meeting with Faubus, 425–26; on antitrust consent decrees, 251–53; on antitrust suit against ALCOA, 208–9; on appointments to federal judiciary, 110–11; on automobile dealers' franchise rights, 208–9; background, 38–39; and Bricker amendment, 60–61; Byrnes scores, 328–31; as campaign speaker on judiciary, 1793–96; on civil air agreement with KLM, 81–82; and civil rights legislation, 328–31; on crisis in Little Rock, 460–61, 465–66; on dinner for Coty, 188–91; on E.'s Cabinet appointments, 1256–58; encourages E.'s candidacy, 1746–56; on exchange of restricted data, 39–40; and FBI report on Mason, 507; Forbes's protest, 482–83; meets with E., Faubus, 481–82; and Nixon as congressional foreign policy liaison, 410–12; Nixons entertain, 597–98; and offshore oil rights (tidelands) litigation, 594–96, 893–95; on question of presidential disability, 76–77, 138–40; recalls 1952 presidential nomination, 1253–54; returns to private practice, 39, 382, 597–98; and submerged lands legislation, 550–51, 893–95; as Supreme Court appointee, 38–39, 1108–10

Brownie, 1339–40

Browning, Frederick Arthur Montague ("Boy"): background, 1248; on Monty's memoir, 1247–48; on U.S.-U.K. spirit in World War II, 1247–48; and World War II reunion, 1271–73

Brown University: E. declines invitation, 1523–24; speech draft for, 1492–94, 1629–30

Brown v. Board of Education: and constitutional duty, 482–83; and crisis in Little Rock, 482–83, 506; on governors' pledge to defy, 538–39. *See also* Civil rights; Supreme Court of the United States

Bruce, David Kirkpatrick Este, 1021

Brucker, Wilber Marion, 1141–42; and Army Distaff benefit show, 2093–94; background, 141; on Cabinet invitation protocol, 499–500; as campaign speaker on defense, 1141–42, 1793–96; on closing Fort Polk, 1347–48; and Declaration of Common Purpose, 544–45; and governor of Panama Canal Zone, 2088–89; honors Heaton, 251; investigates Hoiles's death, 1962–63; on John E.'s promotion, 1965; on McNamara as Quartermaster General, 141, 143–44; and medical training for Latin American doctors, 1840–41; meets with E., 1840–41; on Panamanian grievances, 1827–28; on reassignment for Heaton, 251; on U.S. diplomatic mission chief, Panama, 2088–89; on U.S.-Panamanian relations, 1840–41, 2088–89. *See also* Army, Department of

Brundage, Howard Denton, 1310–11

Brundage, Percival Flack, 200; attends dinner honoring Elizabeth II, 499–500; background, 9–10; on Cabinet invitation protocol, 499–500; disapproves Bragdon's plan, 9–10; on FCDA conversion, 11–12; and foreign aid Development Loan Fund, 183–84; on foreign aid, an exception to budget limits, 400; heads Budget Bureau, 9–10; and Humphrey's advice on federal budget, 589–91; on NSC membership, 743–45; on plan for American Armed Forces Institute, 27–29; on post-attack economic plans, 444–46; resigns, 771. *See also* Budget, Bureau of

Brundrett, Frederick, 1024, 1025

Bruson. *See* Gruson, Sydney

Brussels World's Fair (Brussels Universal and International Exhibition 1958): on abstract art at, 963–64; Allen's report on, 963–64; appropriations for, 517; and *Atlantic Monthly* article on, 963–64; Cherne's letter on, 1104–5; Circarama exhibit, 963–64; Cullman's concern, 517; favorable press on, 1104–5; and industrial progress in

Hungary, 1564–65; on "The Unfinished Work," 963–64

Bryant, Sir Arthur, 689–91

Bryngelson, Miriam D., 2158

Buchanan, Ruth Elizabeth (Hale), 188–91

Buchanan, Wiley Thomas, 188–91

Buddhism. *See* Religion

Budget, Bureau of (BOB): and Advertising Council, 1452–53; and appropriations for medical research, 1594–97; approves funds for federal prison, 923–24; AT&T role on budget fight, 1430–31; on balancing budget, 434–37, 446–49, 621–22, 1198–1200, 1252–53, 1326–27, 1329–31, 1334–35, 1361–62, 1391, 1415–16, 1422–23, 1877–78; and *Baltimore Sun* article, 133; bedtime story on budget deficits, 1566–67; Brundage heads, 9–10; on budgetary refinancing, 1233–34; on budget surplus, 2015–16, 2018; Burns's memo on budget and U.S. economy, 621–22; on Cabinet/congressional relations, 549; and Chamber of Commerce, 1430–31; and Cordiner Committee recommendations, 93–94; and deficit spending in recession, 813–14; director of, holds Cabinet rank, 2189–95; divergence of views on, 1282–83; and Draper Committee Report, 1515–16; E. briefs Kennedy on, 2189–95; and Fairless Committee Report, 95–96, 97–98; for farm program, 1200–1201; on federal spending, 1184–85, 1663–65; on fiscal integrity, 1361–62; on foreign aid, 400; on foreign service academy, 1069–70; on funding national memorials, 1094–95; on FY 1958 budget, 531–32; on FY 1959 budget, 1233–34, 1239–40; on FY 1960 budget, 1233–34, 1252–53, 1325–26, 1329–31, 1416–17, 1560–61; on FY 1961 budget, 1545, 1665–67; Goldwater scores E. on budget, 157–58; Hauge's view, 1252–53; and Hoover Commission, 199–200; and H.R. 1466, 923; Humphrey's address on, 176–77; Humphrey's advice on federal budget, 589–91; on influencing votes in Congress, 1428–29; and Interior Department, 1545; Marsh's view, 44, 45; and media exposure on budget fight, 1369–71; on military base closings, 1742–43; and military defense budget, 561, 593–94; and military pay bill, 910–11; and Millers Ferry lock/dam, 1665–67; Mills supports debt limit, 1047; Mitchell's memo on budget and U.S. economy, 621–22; mutual security and budget, 154–55, 174–76, 446–49, 493–94, 537, 1329–31, 1331–32; and National Planning Association recommendations, 512–16; and national security, 44, 45, 1415–16; obligations of federal budget, 419–23; opposes Development Loan Fund, 183–85; and police protection at U.N. meeting, 2125; on proficiency and responsibility pay programs, 910–11; and public works planning, 9–10, 760–65; on reducing national debt, Lazarus's plan, 1867–68; and retired officers' military pay, 1560–61; Rockefeller's view on *New York Times* article, 531–32; selection of 1960 campaign speakers, 1793–96; Slater's recommendations, 196; and special interest groups, 583, 1560–61; and sound monetary policies, 415–17; and State of the Union Address, 1282–83; and "tight money," 275–76. *See also* Defense, Department of; Monetary policy; Taxation

Budinger, John Michael ("Jack"): and antitrust law, 929–30; background, 608, 686; on E. as honorary member of Blind Brook, 685–86; on management-labor problems, 929–30; on meeting with business leaders, 608; as president of Blind Brook, 685–86; proposes economic high command, 685–86

Buenos Aires, 1489

Bulganin, Nikolai Aleksandrovich: advice to, 191–94; background, 15; on broadening scientific, cultural, athletic ties, 649–59, 726, 727; and Cairo Afro-Asian Conference, 726, 727; and cold war, 649–59, 721–27; on collective security, 649–59; on conventional weapons production, 649–59; on correspondence with E., 757–58, 801; on dangers of war, 649–59; decries NATO policies, 636–37; and Eastern Europe, 649–59; E. offers to meet, 657; E. replies to, 636–37, 642–44, 644–45, 649–59, 721–27; on friendship and peaceful cooperation, 649–59, 721–27; and Geneva Summit Conference, 649–59; Italian ambassador's view, 740–41; on Khrushchev's speech, 721, 727; on letters from, 632–36, 636–37, 667–68; on letter-writing tactics of, 696–97; Macmillan replies to, 206, 231, 234–35, 644–45, 696–97, 728–29; meets with E., 659; and Moscow Manifesto, 726, 727; on NATO, 649–59; on pact of non-aggression, 636–37, 649–59; and Pact of Paris, 724, 727; on peoples of Eastern Europe, 721–27; proposals by, on Germany, 649–59; proposes cultural exchange with U.K., 191–94; proposes "personal contact" between statesmen, 649–59; proposes summit meeting, 649–59, 667–68, 696–97, 757–58; and reunification of Germany, 721–27; scores U.S. policy, 792–93; on strengthening U.N., 649–59, 721–27; supports Open Skies proposal, 1670–71; and surprise attacks, 649–59; on trade with U.K., 191–94; on trade with U.S., 649–59, 981–82; on U.K. force levels in FRG, 191–94; on U.N. Charter, 649–59, 721–27; on uses of outer space, 649–59, 721–27, 819–22; on U.S.-

USSR summit, 721–27, 792–93; visits London with Khrushchev, 192, 194; and Warsaw Pact, 636–37, 649–59; writes to Macmillan, 191–94, 231. *See also* Soviet Union

—atomic weaponry: on banning, in Germany, Poland, Czechoslovakia, 649–59; on halting production of fissionable material, 1844–48; and nuclear disarmament proposals, 632–36, 649–59, 721–27; on nuclear weapons production, 649–59, 721–27; proposal of ground inspection plan, 14–15; proposal of nuclear tests suspension, 636–37, 649–59; warning to Denmark, FRG, Norway on NATO atomic weaponry, 191–94

Bullis, Harry Amos: background, 490; on budget surplus, 2015–16; on Cooper's support of mutual security program, 1985–86; on Crabtree's release, 490; on golf, 2015–16; on E.'s goodwill trip to Far East, 1985–86; on Taipei, 1985–86; on Wilson's column, 490

Bundy, McGeorge: background, 2194–95; as Kennedy's national security adviser, 2189–95

Bunker, Ellsworth: background, 885; and collapse of ten-nation disarmament talks, 1993–95; and Indo-Pakistani dispute, 884–85, 1774–76, 1919–23; as U.S. ambassador to India, 885; and U.S.-Indian relations, 1919–23; and U.S. position on law of the sea, 1818–19

Buraimi Oasis: and British, 21, 26, 102, 104; dispute in, with Saudi Arabia, 21, 26, 102, 104; and Muscat/Oman dispute, 332–34

Bureau of Far Eastern Affairs, 2244–45

Burger, Warren Earl, 1108–10

Burgess, Carter L., 2044–45

Burgess, Warren Randolph: background, 997–98; on E.'s differences with de Gaulle, 2115–18

Burke, Arleigh Albert: and alcohol policy on Navy ships, 1764; background, 1302; Khrushchev scores, 1453–56; and Naval Observatory as church site, 1301–2; opposes interservice coordination in strategic planning, 2099–2100; sends E. scotch whiskey, 1764; on staff organization at SAC HQ, 2099–2100; and Vanguard program, 1764

Burke, Jack, 137–38

Burke Airport. *See* Airports

Burma, Union of: and communism, 512–16; and trans-Pacific air routes to, 2252–54

Burnett, William Riley, 767

Burning Tree Country Club. *See* Golf

Burns, Arthur Frank: addresses Management Conference, 793–95; advises E. on investments, 512; on Advisory Board on Economic Growth and Stability, 813–14; on aid to railroads, 813–14; on Arthur E.'s death, 706–7; on automobile industry, 786; background, 277; on bond market, 277–78; on budget and U.S. economy, 621–22; and bureaucratic red tape, 813–14; on business leaders' role in economy, 793–95; on capital gains tax reform, 886–87, 928–29; on consumer price controls, 813–14; death of father, 731; on economic gloom, 640–41; on economic growth, 1716–17; on E.'s indigestion and stock market, 264–65; on E.'s leadership, 540–41; E. scores union leaders, 1144; and E.'s speech on "Science and Security," 540–41; on E.'s vacation, 540–41; on excessive federal spending, 1123, 1144; on FY 1959 budget, 621–22; and Goals Committee, 1722–25; and Gruenther's service on Goals Committee, 1507–8; on Highway Act of 1956, 813–14; on Jewkes's proposal, 706–7; on "long term holdings," 886–87; and media exposure on budget fight, 1369–71; meets Russian economists, 1716–17; on political reality, 928–29; and "Prosperity Without Inflation," 813–14; on public works programs, 769–71; on recession, 731, 769–71, 786, 813–14; on reducing defense spending, 1716–17; reports on Soviet speakers, 640–41; resigns as chair, Council of Economic Advisors, 540–41; sends book, 640–41; speaks on current recession, 731, 786, 793–95; on stimulating economic recovery, 813–14, 872, 886–87; on tax reform, 793–95, 813–14, 872, 886–87, 928–29; on unemployment insurance, 813–14, 1407–8; as valued adviser, 540–41, 1144; writes on inflation, 277–78

Burns, Robert, 202

Burroughs, Robert Phillips: on American films for Africa, 1828; background, 1702–3

Burrows, Albert Collins, 1572–73

Burton, Harold Hitz, 1108–10

Bush, Prescott Sheldon: attends White House luncheon, 1142; background, 751–52; as vice-presidential nominee, 1870–71

Bush, Vannevar: background, 519; on concept and function of JCS, 518–19; on Rockefeller Committee, 518–19; on Sputnik, 518–19

Business. *See* Economy, U.S.

Business Advisory Committee. *See* Business Advisory Council

Business Advisory Council (BAC): briefings by, on national defense, 572–73; E. meets with, 783–84; E. speaks to, on spiritual values, 624–25; investigates ICA, 1800–1801; on Mueller as member, 1589; and satellite production, 659–60; supports MSA, 174–76

Business Week, 209

Butcher, Harry Cecil ("Butch"): background, 562; on death of Pew's stepson, 1410–11; diary by, irritates E., 1410–11; on E.'s current problems, 562; Monty publishes E.'s letter to, 1410–11; on suffering by association with E., 1444; on TORCH anniversary, 562

Butler, Estelle K., 535–36

Butler, John Marshall, 372

Butterworth, W. Walton, 2103

Buxton, Frank W., 1152–53

Buy American Act, and oil imports quotas, 774–76, 895–96

Byars, Billy G.: and Allen-Byars partnership, 89–90, 682–84, 1016–17; background, 89–90; on curing steer meat, 597; E. gives painting to, 1477; on E.'s health, 597; and Eisenhower Farms name, 89–90; on preparing hamburger meat, 597; visits E., 597

Byington, Homer Morrison, Jr., 2237–38

Byrd, Harry Flood: background, 161; and civil rights, 1375–78; and media exposure on budget fight, 1369–71; opposes Burke Airport site, 372; proposes Senate inquiry on financial structure, 160–61, 163; supports AEC legislation, 395–96

Byrd, Robert Carlyle, 1392

Byrnes, James Francis: background, 330; civil rights legislation, 328–31; on E.'s postwar wish to retire, 1746–56; on jury trials, 328–31; Marshall succeeds, 1498–99; scores Brownell, 328–31; as Secretary of State, 1498–99

Byrnes, John William, 1764–65

Byroade, Henry Alfred, 1918

Cabell, Charles Pearre: background, 368, 1119; briefs Truman on Far East, 1119; on oil reserves in Indonesia, 368

Cabinet, U.S., 1198–1200: Alcorn addresses, 69–70; attends dinner for Nixons, 1315–16; attends stag dinner for Humphrey, 334–35; Brundage reports on spending, 589–91; on Cabinet invitation protocol, 499–500; Carman's invitation to, 49–50; on congressional relations with, 549; discusses domestic matters, 1582–83; discusses federal aid to education, 1307–9; discusses federal subsidies of feeder airlines, 547; discusses oil import quotas, 758–59; discusses union abuses, 674; discusses wheat disposal program, 40–42; Dulles reports on SEATO meeting, 791–92; on E.'s appointments to, 1256–58; on FCDA head as member of, 11–12; and First Secretary of Government, 1700–1702; on GOP head as member of, 258–59; and High's memo on foreign policy, 2049–50; on inevitable compromises, 1281–82; on

discussions at, with de Gaulle, 1919–23; discussions at, with Khrushchev, 1482, 1676–77, 1670–71, 1678–81, 1687–88, 1691–92, 1718–19, 1757–58, 1844–48, 1878–79; discussions at, with Macmillan, 1397–98, 1438–39, 1440–42, 1481–82, 1981–82, 1989–90; and discussions on Polaris bases in Scotland, 2009–11; and discussions on seismic research program, 1999–2001; discussions at, on Skybolt and Polaris programs, 2147; E. briefs Kennedy on, 2189–95; Macmillan visits, 1424–26, 1431–32, 1511, 1512; as site for World War II reunion, 1271–73, 1531–32, 1558–59, 1820–21; stag weekend at, 1338–39

Camp Meade, Maryland, 711

Camp Polk, Louisiana. *See* Fort Polk, Louisiana

Canada: on aid to Ceylon, 961–62; and Atlantic salmon treaty, 1057; on atomic test suspension negotiations, 1058–59; and Bermuda Conference security leak, 113–14; and collapse of Summit Conference (May 1960), 1960–61; and crude oil imports, 1403–4, 1457–59; Dulles visits, 336–37; E. addresses Parliament, 909–10; and E.'s goodwill tour to Far East (June 1960), 1976–77; Elizabeth II visits, 1130; E.'s thoughts on peaceful air passage, 1976–77; and European trade policies, 1799–1800; E. visits, 883, 1111–13; on exchange of restricted data, 39–40; on free trade with U.S., 883; and ICC in Laos, 2219–21, 2227–30; and law of the sea, 1652–53, 1911–12; on lead/zinc import quotas, 1111–13; and London disarmament talks, 278–79, 618–20; Macmillan visits, 936–37; Mountbattens visit, 1059–60; Mount Eisenhower, dedication of, 1079–80; and NORAD, 1661–62; and nuclear disarmament, 473–74, 618–20; and OECD, 1799–1800, 1968–69; and plans for alert measures, 107–9, 267; on Quebec as site for summit, 1541–42, 1591–93, 1601–3; St. Lawrence Seaway, dedication of, 1130, 1393–94, 1541–42; and security safeguards with U.S., U.K., 128–29; on sharing defense burden, 2189–95; and Sky Hawk air defense exercise, 1647, 1661–62; and Sky Shield air defense exercise, 1661–62; and Stassen's gaffe on disarmament, 236–38; and three-mile limit on territorial seas, 749–50, 776–77; and tripartite consultations, 1967–68; on U.S.-Canadian citizenship, 772–73; on U.S.-Canadian military relations, 1661–62; on U.S. foreign trade policies, 909–10, 1799–1800; and Venezuelan oil market, 1457–59; and Volta River project, 552–53; on waivers of non-immigrant visas, 1333–34; on wheat disposal program, 40–42, 909–10; Wigglesworth, as

U.S. ambassador to, 850; and World War II reunion, 1523, 1531–32

Canada-United States Ministerial Committee on Joint Defense, 1403–4, 1661–62

Canada-United States Permanent Joint Board on Defense, 1661–62

Canaday, Ward Murphey: background, 609; on engineering and science scholarships, 609; on Hungarian industrial progress, 1564–65; and leaks on Discoverer XIV launch, 2067; on recession and automobile excise tax, 824–25; on State Department policies, 1564–65

Canham, Erwin Dain: background, 1671–72; and Goals Commission, 1812–13; and U.S. Chamber of Commerce, 1671–72; and U.S. foreign trade expansion, 1671–72

Capehart, Homer Earl, 396–99

Capehart Housing Act, 400–401; and omnibus housing bill, 1007–13

Capitalism: and communism, 2039–42; self-discipline and, 1277–79

Caracas Conference. *See* Tenth Inter-American Conference

Caribbean Sea, 317–19; Castro's aggression in, 1601–3; explosive situation in, 1601–3; and OAS meeting, 1601–3

Carlson, Carolyn, 718

Carlson, Joel E.: background, 718; joins E. at Augusta, 2161–62; sends condolences on Arthur E.'s death, 718

Carlyle, Thomas, 427

Carman, Harry James, 49–50

Carnahan, A.S.J., 336

Carnegie Corporation of New York, 946

Carnegie Endowment for International Peace, 1279–81

Carnegie Institute, 527

Carpenters' unions, investigation of, 1153–56

Carroll, Lewis, 711

Carter, W. Beverly, Jr., 511

Carter, William Arnold, 2088–89

Case, Charles Augustine ("Charley"): background, 110–11; on E.'s family gravesite, 1479; E. visits, in Abilene, 1167–68; recommends Arn for federal judiciary, 110–11

Case, Francis Higbee, 585–86

Casey, Douglas, 173

Caspian Sea, 1032

Castiella y Maiz, Fernando Maria: background, 1861–62; on Latin American economic and political goals, 1872–74; meets with E., 1872–74; on religious freedom for Protestants in Spain, 1861–62

Castillo, Odilia Paloma de, 338–39

Castillo Armas, Carlos Enrique, 338–39

CASTLE, on fallout from, 216–18. *See also* Atomic weaponry: tests of

Castro Ruz, Fidel: addresses National Press Club, 1456; addresses newspaper editors,

1456; aggression of, in Caribbean, 1601–3, 1710–12; appears on "Meet the Press," 1456; attends U.N. session, 2126; background, 1456; chooses Agrarian Reform Law, 2001–7; commits to Soviet bloc, 2001–7, 2039–42; and Cuban sugar quota, 2001–7; E.'s view, 1875–76, 1995–96, 2001–7, 2039–42; expropriates American properties, 2001–7, 2039–42; and Guatemala, 2086–88; Kraft's esteem for, 1875–76; a "little Hitler," 1995–96; ousts Batista, 1456; Pawley's view, 1919–23; political leadership of, 1456, 1875–76, 2039–42; revolutionary regime of, 1456, 2039–42; and U.S. position on Guantanamo, 2142–43; visits U.S., 1456, 2001–7, 2104–5. *See also* Cuba, Republic of

Catania Plain (Province of Italy), 1295–98

Catholic Charities, National Conference of, E. addresses, 2120–21

Catholics. *See* Religion

Cattle. *See* Livestock

Causin, Janis (Eisenhower) (niece), 1254–55; attends Inauguration ceremonies, 7, 8; background, 8

Causin, William Oliver, 1254–55; attends Inauguration ceremonies, 7, 8; background, 8

Celebrities Committee for Nixon-Lodge, 2165–66

Celler, Emanuel, 252

"Cemetery" (Willie Frank Parteet), 134–35

CENTO. *See* Central Treaty Organization

Central African Republic, 2160–61

Central America, Milton E.'s trip to, 631, 645–46, 1230–32. *See also* Eisenhower, Milton Stover; Latin America

Central Europe. *See* Europe: Central Europe

Central Intelligence Agency (CIA): on civil war in Laos, 2219–21, 2223–25; on communism in Cuba, 2244–45; and Declaration of Common Purpose, 544–45; and discussions on atomic weaponry, 1396–97; E. briefs Kennedy on, 2189–95; and 5412 Group on Cuba, 2196–97; and foreign aid determination, 1331–32; and foreign trade expansion, 1671–72; informs E. on Communist activities, 1935–41; and insurrection in Indonesia, 844–46; and Kerala, 829; and psychological warfare study, 1611–13; on reducing overseas staffs, 2195–96; and U.S. program in Cuba, 2196–97; and security breaches, 1692–93; on unified bipartisan foreign policy, 396–99; and U-2 incident, 1943; and waivers of non-immigrant visas, 1334; warns Nixon on Latin American unrest, 899–900. *See also* Dulles, Allen Welsh

Central Treaty Organization (CENTO): Herter attends meeting of, 1915–17; Herter's report on, 1931; on Iran's role in defense of,

2095–98; on Shah's attitude, 1931; on Turkish ties with, 1974–75

Ceylon, State of: Development Loan Fund authorizes aid to, 961–62; de Zoysa visits U.S., 961–62; economic problems in, 961–62; floods in, 961–62; and Gluck as U.S. ambassador to, 338–39; Gunewardene transmits message, 961–62; seeks U.S. aid, 961–62. *See also* Bandaranaike, Solomon West Ridgway Dias

Chaguaramas (British West Indies), 317–19

Chamber of Commerce of the United States: and budget fight, 1430–31; and Canham's proposal on foreign trade expansion, 1671–72; E. addresses, 1393–94; Litchfield's address to, 1956–59

Chamberlain, Charles Ernest, 863

Chambers, William E., 2182, 2187

Chamoun, Camille Nimr: background, 47; on Communist influence in Jordan, 158–60; meets with Hammarskjöld, 984–86; on NATO meeting, 607–8; as president of Lebanon, 159, 869–70, 984–86; requests U.S. force in Lebanon, 952–60, 984–86; seeks second term, 952–60; seen as indecisive, 952–60; supports U.S. policies in Near East, 47; on U.S. aid to Lebanon, 869–70, 952–60. *See also* Lebanon, Republic of

Champion, George: accompanies E. to Augusta, 1212–13; background, 1212–13; on Conant, 1352–53; on E.'s goodwill trip to Pakistan and India, 1868–69; on High's illness, 1212–13; on Philippines, 1868–69; on Rahman Putra, 1868–69, 1900; visits Asia, 1900

Chandler, Norman, 1066, 1068

Chantilly Airport. *See* Airports

Chapman, Daniel Ahmling, 2037–38

Charlotte Observer, 506

Cheatham, Owen Robertson: background, 312; dedicates church window to E., 312; on inflation, 1554; memorializes inaugural prayer, 312; on national debt, 1554; supports housing bill, 1554

Chehab, Fuad: background, 953, 957–58; election of, 1036, 1183–84; plays politics in Lebanon, 953, 957–58. *See also* Lebanon, Republic of

Chemical warfare, and *Denver Post* article on nerve gas, 134

Chequers (Buckinghamshire), as site for talks with Macmillan, 1620–21, 1641, 1654–57

Cherne, Leo M., 1104

Cherry Hills Country Club. *See* Golf

Chewning, Caroline Cupler (Mosher), 188–91

Chewning, Edmund Taylor, 188–91

Chiang Kai-shek: background, 1085–86; on Communist distortion of joint communiqué, 1197–98; on crisis in Taiwan Straits, 1085–86; as defiant rebel, 1678–81, 1681–

82; discussions with, 2244–45; E. sends C-130B aircraft, 2244–45; esteem of, for E., 2244–45; E. visits, 1985–86; irritates E., 1085–86; issues joint statement with E., 1985–86; Khrushchev's view, 1101–2, 1678–81; on mainland liberation policy, 1168–70; meets with Dulles, 1144–45, 1168–70; on solidarity with U.S., 1168–70, 2244–45; temperament of, 1085–86, 1092–93; on troop withdrawal by amphibious lift, 1139–41; on U.S. aid to China, 1085–86, 1103–4, 2244–45. *See also* China, Republic of

ChiComs. *See* China, People's Republic of

Chief Justice of the United States. *See* Supreme Court of the United States; Warren, Earl

Chief of Naval Operations (CNO). *See* Burke, Arleigh Albert

Childs, Marquis William, 1935–41

Chile, Republic of: and Castro's aggression, 1601–3; on Chilean students' letter, 1884–85; on Chile–Argentine border dispute, 1859–60; and E.'s goodwill trip (December 1959), 1762–63; E. visits, 631, 1762–63, 1784–85, 1842–43, 1860–61; López Mateos visits, 1784–85; and minerals stabilization plan, 889–90; and proposed copper tariff, 708–9, 889–90; Rubottom recommends Dulles visit, 631. *See also* Alessandri, Rodríguez Jorge

Chiles, John O., 188–91

Chiles, Mrs. John O., 188–91

China, Imperial Government of, 263–64

China, People's Republic of (PRC, Communist China, Red China, ChiComs), 103; and ambassadorial talks at Geneva, 1092–93, 1101–2; on border incursions in India, 1648–50, 1662–63; British recognition of, 279–80, 844–46; Chiang Kai-shek's policy toward, 1168–70; Chinese as followers of Genghis Khan, 1188–90; and Chinese People's Liberation Army, 1101–2; on commitment of, to Castro, 2001–7, 2039–42; communization of, 512–16; distorts joint communiqué, 1197–98; Dulles speaks on communism in, 279–80; on force of arms by, 1678–81; and "Great Leap Forward," 1188–90; high morale in, 1188–90; India competes with, 59–60; interest of, in Latin America, 1872–74; and Jordan, 158–60; Khrushchev's view, 1101–2, 1678–81, 1681–82, 1685–86; Khrushchev visits, 1101–2; and nuclear aspirations, 1631–32; on nuclear disarmament, Wallace's view, 242–43; and People's Communes, 1188–90; and Russian-Chinese trade differential, 204–5, 211–12, 234–35; and use of atomic weaponry, 1092–93; U.S. policy toward, 86–87, 1215–16, 1223–24; and U.S. prisoners in, 930–31; Wallace's view, 1631–32;

and Warsaw negotiations, 1139–41; White requests travel to, 976–77. *See also* China, Republic of; Communism; Communists
—Formosa, as conquest of Red China, 1119, 1131–33
—Korean War, 1101–2
—Laos, invasion of, 1670–71, 2219–21, 2227–30
—Peiping, Khrushchev visits, 1101–2
—Penghu (Pescadores) Islands: as conquest of Red China, 1131–33; defense of, 1101–2
—Quemoy and Matsu: bombardment of, 1085–86; 1101–2, 1139–41; as conquests of Red China, 1131–33; suspension of bombardment, 1139–41, 1168–70
—Taiwan Straits: crisis in, 1085–86, 1119; suspends bombardment of, 1197–98

China, Republic of (Nationalist China, Formosa, Chinats): Chiang Kai-shek's policy on mainland liberation, 1168–70; high morale in, 1139–41; an international question, 1678–81; issues joint communiqué, 1197–98; Khrushchev's view, 1678–81, 1681–82, 1685–86; receives U.S. C-130B transport aircraft, 2244–45; resists Communist aggression, 2244–45; Soviet relations with, 1322; and Treaty of Mutual Security, 1131–33, 1678–81; on use of atomic weaponry, 1092–93, 1103–4; on U.S. military support for, 1085–86; U.S. policy on, 86–87, 1085–86, 1092–93, 1131–33, 1151–52, 2244–45. *See also* Chiang Kai-shek; China, People's Republic of
—Formosa, 1027–31, 1127; on bipartisan conference regarding, 1120–21; and goodwill tour to Far East (June 1960), 1941–42, 2244–45; Green's concern, 1131–33; and Joint Resolution of Congress, 1131–33; and Red China attacks on, 1101–2
—Formosa Straits: crisis in, affects E.'s golf game, 1104–5; E.'s concern, 1106–7, 1131–33; on troop withdrawal by amphibious lift, 1139–41
—Matsu: bombardment of, 1101–2; Chiang's forces on, 1085–86, 1197–98; defense of, 1085–86, 1092–93, 1103–4, 1151–52; Green's concern, 1131–33; Red China suspends bombardment, 1139–41, 1168–70; Truman's statement on, 1119
—Pescadores: defense of, 1101–2, 1131–33; Khrushchev, on use of force, 1678–81
—Quemoy: bombardment of, 1101–2; Chiang's forces on, 1085–86, 1197–98; defense of, 1085–86, 1092–93, 1103–4, 1151–52; E.'s concern, 1106–7; Green's concern, 1131–33; Red China suspends bombardment, 1139–41, 1168–70; Truman's statement on, 1119
—Taipei: E. visits, 1980–81, 1982–83; impressions of, 1985–86

—Taiwan: crisis in straits, 1085–86, 1092–93, 1103–4, 1197–98; Defense Command moves supplies, 1139–41; Kennedy's view, 1141–42; and Khrushchev, on use of force, 1678–81; Khrushchev's protest, 1101–2; Red China suspends bombardment, 1197–98; and support for mutual security program, 1947–49; and trans-Pacific air routes to, 2252–54

China Committee of the Paris Consultative Group (CHINCOM): British oppose U.S. on China trade, 204–5; on embargo items to Communist China, 204–5; French oppose controls on China trade, 204–5; meets in Paris, 204–5, 234–35; and Soviet-China trade differential, 234–35

Chinats. See China, Republic of

CHINCOM. See China Committee of the Paris Consultative Group

Chou En-lai, 1092–93

Christian Life Commission, of Southern Baptist Convention, 1146

Christmas Island (Gilbert and Ellice Islands, Pacific), as nuclear test site, 872–73

Chrysler Corporation, to raise prices, 522–23

Chundrigar, Ismail Ibrahim, 555–56. See also Pakistan, Islamic Republic of

Churchill, Clementine ("Clemmie") (Hozier): background, 558; cancels U.S. visit, 1208–9; suffers influenza, 715–16, 1208–9

Churchill, Sarah, Lady Audley: background, 111–12; takes role in play, 1171–72; on U.S. exhibit of Churchill's paintings, 111–12

Churchill, Winston Spencer: Alanbrooke scores, 689–91; and Bermuda Conference (1953), 112–13; birthday greetings to, 2164; on British domination of India, 952–60; on British ground commander for OVERLORD, 2181–82; on Churchill College at Cambridge University, 880–81; on colonialism, 952–60; and Cyprus, 952–60; on diplomatic recognition, 279–80; discusses DRAGOON with Roosevelt, 2181, 2187; on Dulles's death, 1495; E.'s esteem for, 689–91, 1303, 1495, 1505, 2180, 2186–87; enjoys daughter's role as actress, 1171–72; on E.'s relationship with Monty, 1547–49; exhibits at Royal Academy, 1208–9; Hall visits, 1535–36, 2179–80; health of, 950–51, 1171–72; illness of, 715–16, 852–53; on India, 952–60; and Ismay's memoir, 2164, 2171–72, 2180–88; Ismay's view of, 1295–98; meets with E. in Algiers, 2185; Murphy visits, 1535–36; on overlord, 1746–56, 2180–88; receives Order of Liberation of France, 1192–93; sends book, 557–58; suffers accident, 2164, 2179–80; vacations in France, 715–16; welcomes E. to Europe, 620–21; and World War II reminiscences,

1307; and World War II reunion, 1620–21; writes from Marrakech, 1307; writes *Second World War*, 1780

—United States: cancels visit to, 715–16, 1171–72, 1208–9; E. chooses scene of Ourika River and Atlas Mountains, 1171–72, 1208–9, 1495; on 1960 election loss, 2179–80; on papers of, to Library of Congress, 1535–36; papers of, on microfilm, 1535–36; plans visit to U.S., 715–16, 1208–9; promises painting to E., 283, 715–16; and U.S. exhibition of paintings by, 111–12, 283, 525, 526–27, 531–32, 557–58, 620–21, 715–16, 852–53, 1171–72, 1208–9; visits E., 557–58, 1295–98, 1307, 1471, 1495, 1505, 1535–36; visits Gettysburg, 1495

Churchill College at Cambridge University, 880–81

Cincinnati Art Museum, 527

Cisler, Walker Lee: background, 289; as Secretary of Defense, 289; as successor to McElroy, 1477–79

Citadel, The, 739–40

Cities Service Companies, 1136

Citizens Committee for the Hoover Report: completes mission, 1095–97; E. commends, 1095–97

Citizens for Eisenhower: Baker's view, 360–61; E.'s view, 360–61; Hoffman's role in, 2243–44; Mattingly's plan for grassroots action, 106. See also Citizens for Eisenhower-Nixon 1958 Committee

Citizens for Eisenhower-Nixon 1958 Committee, 866–67; and Alcorn's plan to strengthen GOP, 69–70; and Crabtree, 490; E.'s advice to, in Southern California, 1217–18; and Knowland's gubernatorial candidacy, 1070–71; on pledges for, 897–98

Citizens Union of the City of New York: background, 49–50; E. declines invitation from, 49–50

Civil Aeronautics Act, and airline certification, 405

Civil Aeronautics Administration (CAA), and Washington, D.C. airport sites, 369–72

Civil Aeronautics Board (CAB): and Airways Modernization Board, 1081–82; and BOAC air routes to Hong Kong-San Francisco via Tokyo, 1599–1601; E. disapproves Trans-Pacific Route Case, 2252–54; and foreign policy issues, 2252–54; and Northwest Orient Airlines, 288, 406–7, 1599–1601, 2252–54; and Pacific Great Circle route awards, 288, 406–7, 720; and Pan American World Airways, 288, 406–7, 2252–54; and South Pacific Airlines, 2252–54; and Trans-Pacific Renewal Case, 720; and Trans World Airlines, 2252–54

Civil defense: E.'s view, 1865–66; and fallout

shelter program, 584–85, 1865–66, 1991–93; and federal-state responsibility for, 584–85; and Gaither Report recommendations, 584–85; governors adopt civil defense plan, 1617–18; New York State's plan, 1605–6, 1865–66; and radioactive fallout report, 1605–6, 1617–18

Civil Defense Act of 1950, Cabinet approves modifications to, 11–12

Civil Defense Administration. *See* Federal Civil Defense Administration

Civil liberties. *See* Civil rights

Civil rights, 957; and age discrimination, 1863–64; on apartheid, 2074–76; Beane's view, 418; Carter's view, 511; and Cotton's newsletter, 1865; and discrimination against Gbedemah, 552–53; divergence of views on, 1282–83; E.'s position, 415–17, 1087–88, 2052–53; and equality in education, 255–56, 506, 1146; and GOP, 396–99; Hannah's view, 1007–13; and high school closings, 1106–7, 1134–35, 1146; and Johnson, 1375–78, 2052–53; Lodge's view, 464; Lucille E.'s view, 1079–80; McGill's view on, 486, 1087–88, 1826–27; on moderates and extremists, 1375–78; on Morrow as U.S. ambassador to Guinea, 1503–4; on patience and progress in, 921–22; Phelps's view, 446–49; and *Plessy* v. *Ferguson*, 506; proposed legislation on, 1337; and racial incident in Maryland, 2160–61; on respect for law, 465–66, 479, 486–87, 921–22, 1375–78; Rogers's view, 1337; and school integration, 540–41; and school segregation, 319–25, 328–31; on sit-ins in the South, 1935–41; in the South, 319–25, 328–31, 1935–41; and State of the Union Address, 1282–83; and Supreme Court, 319–25, 328–31, 1077–78, 1079–80; and "undesirable social mingling," 1935–41; and voting rights abuses in South, 1924–25. *See also* Civil Rights Acts of 1957, 1960; Supreme Court of the United States

—Little Rock, Arkansas, 441–42, 562, 597, 1106–7, 1127; an appeal for calm in, 476; and Arkansas National Guard, 425–26, 460–61, 462–64; as blow to U.S. prestige, 530–31, 551–52; and Bonus March, 479–80; and Brussels World's Fair, 963–64; call to spiritual leaders, 524; and Central High School, 425–26, 462–64, 465–66, 466–67, 479, 481–82, 483–84, 486–87, 511, 1087–88, 1134–35; on church leaders' support in, 465–66; civic leaders advise Faubus, 476; courts delay integration, 1077–78, 1079–80; crisis in, 413, 425–26, 441–42, 460–61, 462–64, 1088–89; E.'s "magnificent decision," 464; Engstrom commends E., 466–67; Faubus meets with E., 425–26, 481–82; and Forbes's protest, 482–83; and

Golden Rule, 490; Hoyt's view, 475–76; Lawrence's view, 875–78; McGill's view, 486, 538–39, 834–35; Mann's call for help, 460–61; on Mason's embarrassment, 530–31; and meeting with governors, 466–67, 474–75; message to King on, 479; Miller's view, 538–39; and Mothers' League of Little Rock, 425–26; need for domestic stability, 525; and Newport "vacation," 457–58; on Poole's view, 483–84; on removal of federal troops, 466–67, 474–75, 481–82; on respect for law, 486–87; Robinson's view, 921–22; Russell compares E. to Hitler, 462–64; on sending federal troops, 1865; and sense of duty, 480–81, 482–83, 532; on "stupidity and duplicity" of Faubus, 474–75; Wilson's view, 490; Wyche's view, 506

Civil Rights, Commission on: E.'s recommendations, 392–94; establishment of, 392–94; Hannah's view, 1007–13; proposed legislation regarding, 1337, 1375–78

Civil Rights, National Conference on, 1521

Civil Rights Act of 1957, 274–75; Beane's view, 418; Byrnes's view, 328–31; and Cotton's newsletter, 1865; E. signs, 392–94, 448; GOP role in passage of, 1924–25; on jury trial section, 328–31, 346, 354–56, 375

Civil Rights Act of 1960, 1924–25

Civil service, 1153–56; and benefits for federal workers, 261–62, 446–49; E. approves civil service pay raise, 1007–13; E. vetoes increase for classified workers, 444; E. vetoes increases for judicial and legislative workers, 444; and loyalty oath requirements, 1505–7; and pay raise legislation, 740–41; and postal workers' salaries, 319–25, 444. *See also* Civil Service Commission; Post Office Department

Civil Service Commission: on appointment to, for Smith, 1036–37; E. appoints Gunderson to, 1036–37; E. briefs Kennedy on, 2189–95; Ellsworth heads, 200; E.'s view, 52; and Hoover Commission recommendations, 199–200; Young resigns as head, 52, 200

Civil War: ("Jeb") Stuart's role in, 240; Monty's view, at Gettysburg, 1203–4; and Wiley-Milhollen's *They Who Fought Here*, 1826–27

Civil War Centennial Commission, appointments to, 587–88

Clark, Edwin Norman: background, 1856; on Dominican Republic's problems, 1919–23; on ousting Trujillo, 1919–23; proposes aid to Trujillo, 1855–56

Clark, Mark Wayne: background, 37; heads Heart Association campaign, 37; opposes Status of Forces Agreement, 457–58; seeks support in heart campaign, 37

Clark, Thomas Campbell, 1580–81

and Soviet preemptive buying, 491–93; on
Soviet propaganda in third-world nations,
1893–94; on spiritual values in, 1210–11,
1248–49, 1801–2; and Sulzberger's article,
666–67, 667–68; Sulzberger's editorial on,
1319–21; and talks with Khrushchev, 1678;
as theme in Brown, Harvard speeches,
1629–30; and U.S. nuclear power, 303–7;
and U.S. policy in, 2242–43; and U.S. policy in Southeast Asia, 86–87; and U.S.-Thai
relations, 2151–53; and U-2 flights, 107–9,
1950–51; and Western Summit Conference, 1706–8; and Western world's need
for oil, 986–87. See also Disarmament; Free
world; Soviet Union; United Nations;
United States: foreign policy
Cole, William Sterling ("Stub"): on atomic
weapons tests, 216–18, 295–96; background, 217; and weapon production,
295–96
Coley, Chief, 1983–84
Colgate University, 554
Collective security: and Baghdad Pact, 998–
1000, 1322–25; Bulganin's view, 649–59;
and Cambodia's relations with Thailand
and Vietnam, 1432–35; concept of, in U.S.
foreign policy, 142–43, 2242–43; Dulles addresses U.N., 442–43; E. accepts NATO assignment, 1746–56; E.'s view, 649–59,
1872–74; and economic aid to Third
World, 918; Fairless Committee reports on,
95–96, 97–98; Randall's view, 95–96; and
Republican principles, 801–3; and Soviet
attempts to create friction, 191–94; and
Soviet relations with Iran, 1321–25; and
third-world nationalism, 115–17; Turkey's
commitment to, 1974–75; and unified air
defense system, 1785–87; and U.S. aid to
Iranian forces, 998–1000; and U.S. nuclear
power, 303–7; Wriston's view, 1965–67. See
also Cold war, Free world; NATO; United
Nations
Collier, Henry DeWard, 1066, 1068
Colombia, Republic of: and collapse of Summit Conference (May 1960), 1953–54; and
Indo-Pakistani dispute, 555–56; Nixon visits, 841, 899–900; and proposed trans-
isthmus canal, 2019–20
Colombo Plan for Cooperative Economic Development in Southeast Asia (Colombo Nations; Colombo Pact Nations), E. addresses
conference of, 1138–39, 1163–64, 1220–
21
Colonialism: advice to Churchill on, 952–60;
de Gaulle's view, 1654–57; and French
colonialism in Africa, 1654–57; and French
policy in Vietnam, 952–60; and U.N. anti-
colonialism resolution, 2200–2201, 2219–
21
Colorado: Allott returns to Senate, 2161–62;

Black campaigns in, 1100; Dominick wins
election to House, 2161–62; E. campaigns
in, 1138–39; and midterm elections, 1100;
and 1960 election results, 2161–62; and
real estate holdings in, 394–95, 783–84;
Republicans favor Lodge, Anderson as candidates, 2018–19
—Denver: affection for, 1097–98, 1105–6; log
house near, 1487; urban development in,
1487. See also Eisenhower, Dwight David: vacations
Colt, Samuel Sloan, 380–81
Columbia Broadcasting System (CBS), 1842–
43; and censorship, 1417; and inflation
programs, 1417; and media exposure on
budget fight, 1369–71
Columbia University: and Conservation of Human Resources Project, 68–69; E. addresses students at, 1965–67; and E.'s candidacy, 1746–56; E. as president of, 308,
434–37, 714–15, 1746–56; on E. as trustee
emeritus, 2178–79; recommendation of
Hacker, 747
—American Assembly, 508–9; background,
218–19; E.'s role in founding, 2178–79;
and Goals Commission, 1812–13; Humphrey joins board of, 218–19; supports
MSA, 174–76
—Bicentennial celebration, and commemorative stamp honoring, 349–50
—Institute of War and Peace Studies, 1279–
81, 2178–79
—New York School of Social Work, 2178–79;
E. as honorary trustee of, 489; honors
Rockefellers, 488–89
Columbine (airplane): on flights to/from Mile-
stone, 1338–39, 1339–40, 1349–50;
Roberts, Robinson accompany E. on, 1228;
Strauss accompanies E. on, 598–99; to take
Dulles to Bermuda Conference 1957, 86–
87; takes E., Champion to Augusta, 1212–
13; and travel plans from Bermuda, 106–7,
109
Columbine Country Club, 1365–66, 2161–62
Combined Chiefs of Staff, World War II,
1852–54
Commander in Chief, Caribbean (CINCARIB),
2088–89
Commander in Chief, Pacific Fleet (CINCPAC).
See Hopwood, Herbert Gladstone
Commander in Chief, Strategic Air Command
(CINSAC), 2099–2100
Commerce, Department of, 675–76; and area
redevelopment legislation, 1329–31; and
domestic economy, 1426–27; on economic
recession recovery, 718–19; on economic
stabilization measures in Iran, 2095–98;
and FAA, 1081–82; and Fairless Committee
Report, 95–96; and First Secretary of Government, 695–96, 1700–1702; and foreign

trade expansion, 1671–72; recommends disapproval of airline bill, 547; and selection of 1960 campaign speakers on, 1793–96; on Strauss as Secretary, 920–21, 1446–47; on subsidies for feeder airlines, 547; and surplus corn for Mexico, 152; and Trade Agreements Extension bill, 661–62; and Washington, D.C., airport sites, 369–72. *See also* Mueller, Frederick Henry; Strauss, Lewis Lichtenstein; Weeks, Sinclair

Commission on Foreign Economic Policy. *See* Randall Commission

Commission on Intergovernmental Relations. *See* Hoover Commission

Commission on National Goals: and American Assembly, 1812–13; and Burns, 1352–53, 1722–25; Burns, Pace cochair, 1507–8; and Canham, 1812–13; and Conant, 1352–53, 1812–13; contributions to, 1812–13; and Darden, 1812–13; E.'s philosophy, 1722–25; establishment of, 1812–13; and federal aid to education, 1284; and Ford, 1812–13; funding for, 1507–8; and Greenewalt, 1812–13; and Gruenther, 1507–8; and Jones, 1812–13; and Kerr, 1812–13; and Killian, 1812–13; and Meany, 1812–13; members of, 1812–13; and Pace, 1352–53, 1722–25; and Sloan, 1812–13; and Wood, 1812–13; and Wriston, 1812–13

Commission on Organization of the Executive Branch of the Government. *See* Hoover Commission

Commission on Veterans' Pensions (Bradley Commission): Bradley chairs, 458–60; mission of, 458–60; recommendations by, 451–52

Committee for Economic Development (CED): establishment of, 777–82; supports MSA, 174–76

Committee on Education Beyond the High School, 458–60

Committee on Energy Supplies and Resources Policy. *See* Cabinet, U.S.; Natural gas; Oil industry

Committee for International Economic Growth, 1919–23, 1947–49

Committee of Nine, 1997–99

Committee on Program and Progress, 1259–61

Committee for Public Education, 1134–35, 1146

Committee to Strengthen the Frontiers of Freedom, 1947–49

Committee of Ten on Disarmament. *See* Ten-Nation Committee on Disarmament

Committee of Twenty-one: at Bogotá, 1997–99, 2086–88; and Inter-American Development Bank, 1442–43; passes Act of Bogotá, 2086–88; promotes economic growth in Latin America, 1488–91; studies underde-

velopment in Pan American states, 1242–44

Committee on World Economic Practices (also Committee on World Trade Practices), 1311–13, 1350–52

Committee on World Trade Practices. *See* Committee on World Economic Practices

Commodity Credit Corporation (CCC): and barter contracts, 1542–43; and cotton exports, 1398–99

Commodore Hotel, 1256

Common Market: Budinger proposes "economic high command," 685–86; development of, in Western Europe, 952–60; Dillon reports on talks, 1799–1800; and Japan, 1799–1800; and reciprocal trade legislation, 952–60. *See also* European Economic Community; Organization for European Economic Cooperation

Commonwealth of Pennsylvania v. *Steve Nelson,* 875–78

Communism: Adenauer's view, 1496; in Africa, 2011–12; and atheistic ideology, 465–66; in Ceylon, 961–62; in China, 279–80, 512–16; in Cuba, 1731–32, 2039–42, 2244–45; differences with free world, 88–89, 1277–79; as doctrine of socialism, 671–72; Dulles as bulwark against, 1450–51; and ecumenicalism, 1319–21, 1325–26; and Eisenhower Doctrine, 83–85; and financial burdens on U.S., 434–37; free world's fight against, 6, 43–46, 78–81, 381, 465–66, 666–67, 831–34, 918, 2121–23; in Germany, 2121–23; Globke on ideology of, 1893–94; GOP opposes, 396–99, 801–3; growing threat of, 1188–90; in Guatemala, 2086–88; in Haiti, 1048–49; in Hungary, 1564–65; Hussein opposes, 2114–15; and impact of, on Soviet policy, 1893–94; and imperialistic communism, 1188–90; in Indonesia, 952–60; in Iran, 2095–98; in Ivory Coast, 2011–12; in Jordan, 158–60, 194–96; in Korea, 1514; Lane's view, 424–25; in Laos, 2227–30, 2248–50; in Mideast, 191–94, 607–8; Morris's proposal, 2166–68; and Moscow Manifesto, 726, 727; and mutual security program, 319–25, 385–87, 1188–90; and nationalism, 179–80; and new type of cold war, 385–87; in North Africa, 2209–10; Overstreets' book on, 1360–61; and Pan American solidarity, 924–25, 925–26; and reduction of British NATO forces, 166, 168; in Saudi Arabia, 20, 197–98; in South Korea, 1263–64; and Soviet ideology and policy institute, 1893–94; on spirituality and atheism in Mideast, 1027–31; in third world, 115–17, 1893–94; on threat of Communist subversion, 1901–2; and U.S. policy in Southeast Asia, 86–87; in Vietnam, 898–99. *See also* China, People's Republic of; Cold war; Communist Party of the Soviet Union; Communists; Soviet Union

Communist bloc: balloon incursions over, 1031–32; impact of propaganda on third-world nations, 1893–94; intervenes in Laos, 2227–30; and recognition of North Vietnam, 1902–4. *See also* Sino-Soviet bloc; Soviet bloc

Communist Party of the Soviet Union: declaration by, promotes communism, 649–59; Overstreets' book on, 1360–61; slanders U.S., 649–59; 20th Congress of, meets in Moscow, 191–94; in United Arab Republic, 1322. *See also* Communism; Communists

Communists, 134; aggression by, in Formosa Straits, 1131–33; aggression by, in ROK, 387–88; aggression by, in Thailand, 2151–53; attack Adenauer, 1817–18; and Berlin crisis, 1352–53, 1487–88; Butler's view, 535–36; in Cuba, 2001–7; on dangers of Communist imperialism, 427–31; demonstrate in Japan, 1982–83; distort U.S.-Nationalist China communiqué, 1197–98; in Dominican Republic, 1855–56; and E.'s goodwill trip to Far East (June 1960), 1985–86; in Egypt, 293–95; in France, 622–23; in Indonesia, 625–26, 844–46; 952–60, 1331–32; and intelligence regarding activities of, 1935–41; on invitation to Soviet students, 789–91, 791–92, 797–99; in Iraq, 1481–82; and *Jencks* v. *U.S.*, 272; in Kerala, 829; Kraft's interest in, 1877; in Laos, 2219–21, 2223–25, 2227–30; in Latin America, 1872–74; Nehru's influence on, 1213–15, 1215–16; in Okinawa, 827–29; Parker's view, 1635–36; and Pathet Lao, 2219–21; policies of, and SEATO, 453–54; prosecution of, 875–78; and Sihanouk, 1390; in Southeast Asia, 1432–35; and state bar admissions, 875–78; on student exchange programs, 692–93, 789–91, 797–99; in Syria, 383–85, 389–90; and terrorist attack in Ankara, 696–97; thwart E.'s visit to Japan, 1978–79, 1985–86; on trade with China, 204–5; and United Arab Republic, 705–8; on U.S. policy in cold war, 2242–43; on violations of Korean Armistice Agreement, 314–16; wage economic warfare, 415–17; and Western collective security, 303–7, 415–17, 1872–74. *See also* China, People's Republic of; Communism; Communist Party of the Soviet Union; Soviet Union

Community Chest: and federal disaster relief programs, 1129–30; and United Givers Fund, 1129–30

Community Facilities Bill of 1958, 840; fails to pass, 1007–13

Company of Cutlers of Hallamshire, 215–16

Conant, James Bryant: background, 946; and Berlin crisis, 1352–53; as candidate for USMA Thayer Award, 968–69; Champion's view, 1352–53; E.'s esteem for, 1352–53; and Goals Commission, 1812–13; on industry's aid to education, 945–47

Confederacy, Army of, 240

Conference of Agricultural Workers, Byelorussian Soviet Socialist Republic, 727

Conference of Governors: address to, 275–76, 282; adopts civil defense plan, 1617–18; authorizes Joint Federal-State Action Committee, 419–23, 2035–36; E. meets with (1954), 754–55. *See also* Southern Governors' Conference

Conger, Mary, 1895–98

Congo, Republic of: on crisis in Katanga, 2030–32, 2048–49; de Gaulle's view, 2046–47, 2068–73, 2084; education in, 2166–68; Khrushchev's view, 2015; Touré's view, 2048–49, 2170–71; U.N. support in, 2030–32, 2048–49, 2170–71; U.S. policy in, 2170–71; U.S. support in, 2030–32, 2048–49, 2170–71; on withdrawal of Belgian troops, 2048–49. *See also* Africa; Kasavubu, Joseph

Congress, U.S.: acts on E.'s rank and salary, 2060–62; on congressional immunity question, 1209; control of, on declaration of war, 649–59; on dispositions and tempers, 1941–42; and Draper Committee Report, 1515–16; E.'s relationship with, 2043–44; E. testifies on aid to Germany, 2121–23; and executive powers for regulatory commissions, 2214–15; and executive privilege, 1733–35; faith of, in NATO, 2068–73; and Farm Bureau concerns, 1290–91; and "Fortress America" concept, 354–56; on funding national memorials, 1094–95; on handling congressional mail, 408; and influence of public opinion, 1039–40; on judicial legislation, 875–78; Lincoln's service in, 1332–33; and loyalty oath requirements, 1505–7; on members of, and appointive posts, 268–69; on members of, as self-serving, 319–25, 886–87, 1007–13; and President's Advisory Committee on Government Organization, 2159; and question of presidential disability, 138–40; on railroad insurance laws, 1496–98; on relations of, with Cabinet, 549; on television-radio station licenses, 1209; and water resources program, 1665–67. *See also* House of Representatives, U.S.; Legislative leaders; Senate, U.S.

—Eighty-fourth (January 3, 1955–January 3, 1957): fails to act on question of presidential disability, 76–77; and pay raises for classified government workers, 261–62

—Eighty-fifth (January 3, 1957–January 3,

and security leak following Bermuda Conference (1957), 120; and self-interest of, on farm subsidies, 735; and Sixteenth Amendment, 1188–90; and Small Business Administration, 760–65; and special interest groups, 238–39, 583, 886–87; Suhrawardy addresses, 350–51; on support for IAEA, 220–21; supports Nationalist China, 1103–4; on support for U.S. force in FRG, 147–50; on support for USIA, 220–21; and Supreme Court, 272, 875–78, 925–26; and tariffs on lead/zinc imports, 759–60; and tax relief for small business, 760–65; and tax reform, 928–29; and tidelands oil issue, 893–95; Trade Agreements Extension Act, 661–62, 1016; and trade with China, 204–5, 211–12; on transportation policy, 484–85; and unification of armed forces, 509–10, 811; on U.S. aid to free world economy, 1073–76; on waivers of non-immigrant visas, 1333–34; and Washington, D.C., airport sites, 369–72; and White House appointments, 396–99

—Eighty-sixth (January 3, 1959–January 3, 1961): address to, on NATO, 1746–56; adjourns, 1569–70, 1616–17, 1941–42; and airport facilities bill, 1422–23; and appointment of federal judges, 1343–45; approves appropriations for Labor, HEW, 2034–35; authorizes Fermi Award, 795–96; and Berlin crisis, 1378–79; and bill signing, 1941–42; and B-70 program, 1810; and civil rights legislation, 1924–25; and Connally reservation, 1823–24, 1851–52; convenes, 1283; on defense-budget controversy, 1415–16; on disappointing legislation, 1569–70; divided, at cross purposes, 1340–43; and DOD reorganization, 2189–95; and Draper Committee report, 1515–16; and duration of Summit Conference (May 1960), 1894–95; and E.'s goodwill trip to Europe, 1616–17; extends unemployment insurance benefits, 1407–8; fails to pass farm legislation, 1802–3; and federal expenditures, 1329–31; and five-point farm program, 1739–40; and food stamp plan, 1688–89; and foreign aid, 1329–31; on German assets in U.S., 1796–97; and health insurance legislation, 1919–23; holds hearings on ANP, 752–53; increases defense estimates, 1991–93; and Inter-American Development Bank, 1488–91; on Korea as ally in free world, 1514; and Landrum-Griffin bill, 1630–31; and long-term federal debt legislation, 1233–34; and medical care for elderly, 1702–3; messages to, 1281–82, 1598–99; and Millers Ferry lock/dam, 1665–67; and moderation on race question, 1375–78; and mutual secu-

rity program, 1329–31, 1468–70, 1733–35, 1828–30, 1947–49; and national debt reduction, 1867–68; and NSC, 1538–40; on opening of, 1801–2; on Philippine sugar import quotas, 1881–82; and police protection at U.N. meeting, 2125; on postal rate increases, 1839, 1944–45; and preemption in federal/state legislation, 1480; and proposed Nasser visit, 2065–66; on protection from disruptive strikes, 1737–39; on retired military officers' pay, 1560–61; reduces defense estimates, 1991–93; and right-to-work legislation, 1165–67; and Saturn project, 1798–99; Second Session opens, 1783–84; on security breaches, 1692–93; and seismic research program, 1999–2001; on service academy boards of visitors/trustees, 1672–73; and Social Progress Trust Fund, 2211–13; and special interest groups, 1583–84, 1995–96; steel strike legislation, 1737–39; on surplus wheat crisis, 1598–99; on troop deployment for NATO, 1746–56; and TVA expansion, 1764–65; and TVA legislation, 1583–84, 1608–9; on unemployment insurance, 1407–8; on unemployment legislation, 1381–82; and U.S. Citizens Commission on NATO, 2083–84; on withholding ICA funds, 2214–15

—Eighty-seventh (January 3, 1961–January 3, 1963): and farm program guidelines, 2056–58

—Joint Committee on Atomic Energy (JCAE): Agreements for Cooperation Subcommittee approves amendments to Atomic Energy Act of 1954, 906–7; on construction of Dutch nuclear submarine, 2102; Durham chairs, 40; E. briefs Kennedy on, 2189–95; E. favors discontinuance of, 2189–95; Lawrence, Mills, Teller testify before, 287; opposes exchange of restricted data, 39–40; on Strauss in conflict with, 920–21

Congress of European American Associations, 364–66

Congress of Industrial Organizations (CIO): philosophy of, in California, 1064–68; school of thinking, 1135–36

Congressional Joint Economic Committee, 1832–33

Congressional Medal of Honor, 933–34

Connally Amendment; Connally reservation, 1823–24, 1851–52. See International Court of Justice

Conservation. See Natural resources: conservation; Water resources

Conservation of human resources. See Columbia University

Conservatism, 2123–24

Considine, Robert Bernard, 1964–65
Constantinople Convention of 1888. *See* Convention of 1888
Constitution of the United States, 419–23; and civil rights, 319–25, 346, 415–17, 506, 921–22; and crisis at Little Rock, 462–64, 465–66, 482–83, 506; on duty to uphold, 482–83, 577, 1079–80; on executive powers for regulatory commissions, 2214–15; and executive privilege, 1733–35; and federal role in education, 1307–9; and "lame duck" presidency, 245; and loyalty oath requirements, 1505–7; and national election process, 2158; and National Historical Publications Commission, 937–38; and presidency, 1290–91; on presidential approval of bills, 923; and question of presidential disability, 76–77, 138–40, 711–14; respect for, 319–25; and Sixteenth Amendment, 1188–90, 1195–96; and Supreme Court, Hutton's view, 299–300; and Twenty-fifth Amendment, 711–14; and Twenty-second Amendment, 245; and U.S. Citizens Commission on NATO, 2083–84; and *Watkins* v. *United States*, 875–78; on withholding ICA funds, 2214–15. *See also* Civil rights
Construction: and home loans to veterans, 449–50; and projects for economic recovery, 952–60. *See also* Education; Highways
Consultation of American Foreign Ministers, 2087–88
Consumer Bankers Association, 2166–68
Convention of 1888, and Suez Canal crisis, 24–25, 27, 129–31. *See also* Egypt
Cook, Don, 1955–56
Cooper, John Sherman: on appointment of federal judges, 1344; background, 268–69; discusses DOD reorganization, 830; opposes AEC legislation, 395–96; recommends Baker for TVA post, 268–69; supports mutual security program, 1985–86
Cooper, Richard Conrad, 1728
Cooper Union for the Advancement of Science and Art, 1826–27
Copper industry: purchase plan for, 889–90; stockpiles, as anti-strike weapon, 1737–39; and tariff on, in Chile, 708–9, 889–90. *See also* Minerals; Raw materials; Strategic materials
Cordiner, Ralph Jarron: background, 94; and Cordiner Committee recommendations, 93–94; on DOD reorganization, 838–39; on letter to business community, 838–39; letter by, on machinery imports, 1449–50; member, BAC, 783–84
Cordiner Committee on Modernization of Pay Structure for Members of the Armed Services, 93–94; Congress approves Cordiner Plan, 1007–13; Hazlett's view, 735–36, 738;

and military pay bill, 709–10, 910–11; Tower's concern, 709–10
Cordiner Plan. *See* Cordiner Committee on Modernization of Pay Structure for Members of the Armed Services
Corn industry, record harvest, 1958, 1201
Corporal, DOD plans phase-out for, 292–93. *See also* Missiles
Corps of Engineers. *See* United States Army Corps of Engineers
Corsica, insurrection in, 917
COSSAC. *See* Cossack Plan
Cossack Plan (COSSAC): E.'s view, 2182; and Ismay's memoir, 2187
Costa Rica, Republic of: Edgar E. plans trip to, 1809; and E.'s goodwill trip (December 1959), 1762–63; Milton E. visits, 1218–19; Nielsen visits, 896–97
Cotton, Norris, 1865
Cotton industry, 461–62; and Agricultural Act of 1956, 1398–99; and cotton export program, 1398–99; subsidies for, and Mexico, 1355–57, 1357–58, 1483–84, 1485–86, 1488–91
Coty, René: background, 188–91; and French Cabinet crisis, 188–91; guest list for State dinner honoring, 188–91; on invitations to, 708–9; postpones visit to U.S., 188–91, 648–49. *See also* France, Republic of
Council of Economic Advisors (CEA): and airline subsidies, 547; Burns resigns, 540–41; E. briefs Kennedy on, 2189–95; and economic recession recovery, 718–19; and foreign trade expansion, 1671–72; Saulnier meets with E., 685–86; supports mutual aid, 96
Council on Foreign Economic Policy: and Committee on World Economic Practices, 1311–13; Dodge's role in creation of, 1700–1702; and interagency cooperation, 1622; scores administration policies, 1700–1702; supports Fairless Committee recommendations, 97–98; and wheat disposal program, 40–42
Council of Foreign Ministers, meets at San José, Costa Rica, August 1959, 2039–42
Council on Foreign Relations (CFR): E. schedules speech to, 1492–94; publishes Kissinger's book, 343–44
Council on Youth Fitness. *See* President's Council on Youth Fitness
Counterpart funds: for Brussels World's Fair, 517; misuse of, by congressmen, 407–8
Cousins, Norman: on atomic testing and fallout, 270–71, 287, 295–96; background, 46–47; on disarmament and world peace, 580, 1504; and National Committee for Sane Nuclear Policy, 584–85; and Rule of Law, 1504; and Schweitzer's letter, 46–47,

88; and Sprague's recommendations, 584–85

Couto, Ruth Ann, 1901–2

Couve de Murville, Maurice: Adenauer talks with, 2115–18, 2141–42; attends Istanbul meetings, 1927–28; background, 978; and Dulles's death, 1491–92, 1499–1500; meets with de Gaulle, 1919–23; meets with Dulles, 978–79, 1412–15; on negotiations regarding summit, 1610; on procedures at Summit Conference, 1909, 1927–28; on rights in Berlin, 1610; and Summit Conference interpretation procedures, 1927–28; on tripartite consultations, 1967–68. *See also* France, Republic of

Cowles, Gardner ("Mike"), 1899

Cowles, John: background, 1215; on Dulles, 1899; on editorial criticisms of E., 1899; on errors in Far East policy, 1215–16, 1899; on Nehru's influence at Geneva talks, 1215–16; on U.S. seen as warmongering, 1215–16

Cox, Robert Vinsant, 1393–94

Cox, Willard R., 301

Crabtree, Nate L., 490

Crawford, J. H., 426–27

Crerar, Henry Duncan Graham: background, 1273; and World War II reunion, 1271–73, 1523

Crime, increase in, 2098

Crittenberger, Dale Jackson, 276

Cross, Nancy J., 437–38

Crosthwaite, Ponsonby Moore, 378–79

Crusade in Europe, 308, 2222–23; and Allen's "style," 1945–46; E.'s philosophy in writing, 1295–98, 2153–55; on foreword by Ismay, 1730–31; and menace of communism, 512–16; new edition of, 1730–31

Crusade for Freedom, 530–31, 580–81

Cuba, Republic of: aggression of, in Caribbean, 1601–3, 2001–7, 2039–42; and apathy of *campesinos,* 2039–42; arms stockpile in, 2001–7; on Castro's political leadership, 1875–76, 2001–7, 2039–42; Castro visits U.S., 1456; and Chilean students' view, 1884–85; commits to Soviet bloc, 2001–7; communism in, 1731–32, 2039–42, 2244–45; Communists seize University of Havana, 2039–42; concerns regarding, 1990–91, 1995–96, 2001–7, 2039–42; and Council of Foreign Ministers meeting, 2039–42; E. briefs Kennedy on, 2189–95; expropriates U.S. businesses, 2051–52; Habana Cathedral protests communism, 2039–42; invades Haiti, 1710–12; Macmillan supports U.S. policy on, 2001–7, 2009–11; and National Agrarian Reform Institute, 1731–32; and Nationalization Law of July 6, 1960, 2039–42; needs tankers to carry Soviet oil, 2001–7, 2039–42; and OAS, 2001–7; Pawley's view, 1919–23; on reorganization of U.S. program in, 2196–97; revolution in, 1456; and Shell Oil property, 2039–42; on Sino-Soviet interests in, 1872–74, 2001–7, 2039–42; and Sugar Act amendments, 1995–96, 2001–7; and sugar industry, 1731–32; and sugar quota, 1881–82, 2001–7; takes over U.S.-U.K. oil refineries, 2001–7, 2039–42; trade and aid agreement with Soviets, 2001–7; and U.N., 2001–7; on U.S. arms policy, 2001–7; and U.S. covert operations, 2001–7; on U.S.-Cuban relations, 1456, 1919–23, 2001–7, 2027–28, 2039–42, 2196–97, 2244–45; U.S. ends relations with, 2196–97; on U.S. plans to invade, 2196–97; and U.S. position on Guantanamo, 2142–43; and waivers of non-immigrant visas, 1334; Wickersham's concern, 1731–32. *See also* Castro Ruz, Fidel

Cullen, Hugh Roy, 63–64

Cullman, Howard Stix: on abstract art at Brussels World's Fair, 963–64; Allen's report on Brussels World's Fair, 963–64; *Atlantic Monthly* on Brussels World's Fair, 963–64; background, 517; and Cherne's letter on Brussels World's Fair, 1104–5; counterpart funds for Brussels World's Fair, 517; injures finger, 1104–5

Cultural Exchange Program, and Communist influence in Syria, 383–85

Culzean Castle: background, 74; E. urges Whitneys to visit, 866–67; E. visits, 200–201, 1650–51, 1651–52, 1660; Purdy visits, 74; Whitneys postpone visit, 313–14; Whitneys visit, 200–201, 202–3

Cunningham, Andrew Browne: background, 949; illness of, 1271–73; and World War II reunion, 1271–73

Cunningham, Bill, 187

Currency: on balance of payments, 2189–95; conversion of, for Ryukyu Islands, 919–20, 1049–51; on Democrats' debasement of, 1935–41; E. briefs Kennedy on, 2189–95; and gold outflow, 2189–95, 2199–2200; on strength of, in world economy, 1073–76, 2189–95. *See also* Federal Reserve System; Gold; Monetary policy

Curtice, Harlow Herbert, 742

Customs, Bureau of, on post for Sayler, 477

Cutler, Robert ("Bobby"): on Adams's resignation, 1128–29; and Altschul's letter, 512–16; on armed forces seminars, 508–9; asks aid for Harvard, 714–15; background, 55–56; on Churchill College at Cambridge University, 880–81; on defense briefings, 508–9, 572–73; delivers E.'s address to American College of Surgeons, 203–4;

drafts reply to Hotchkis, 572–73; drafts reply to Knowland, 865–66; drafts reply to Potter, 503–5; on E. as young officer, 647; and Harlow, 1128–29; and Hauge, 1128–29; and Jackson's role as adviser, 768–69; and Morgan's appointment, 1128–29; on Ravdin's invitations to E., 55–56; on Republicans who score Adams, 1128–29; resigns as special assistant, 1077–78; returns to Old Colony, 1128–29; on Science Advisory Committee conclusions, 519–20; as Special Assistant, NSC, 743–45; suffers eye problems, 1128–29; suffers sleep problems, 1128–29; on Turkey and NATO expenditures, 303–7; visits Europe, 1128–29; visits grandniece, 1077–78; visits Yugoslavia, 1077–78

Cypress Point Club, Es. vacation at, 90–91

Cyprus, Republic of: advice to Churchill on, 952–60; and British colonialism, 827–29, 952–60; conflict regarding, 118–19, 612–13; discussions on, at Bermuda Conference 1957, 118–19; Greece rejects conference on, 1174–75; independence for, 2009–11; and Macmillan's talks with E., Dulles, 936–37; Macmillan's view, 103, 104, 118, 1127–28; and Makarios, 103, 104, 118, 118–19, 167, 168–69, 269–70, 302; mob violence in, 940–42; Monty's concern, 612–13; NAC considers conflict regarding, 940–42, 942–44; and NATO alliance, 118–19, 612–13, 1125–26; Paul I protests British plan for, 1125–26; and POL supplies to Jordan, 1013–15; on resettlement of Turks, 940–42; resolution of conflict, 2009–11; and Turkish-Greek settlement on, 1346, 1358–59; U.N. debate on, 612–13; U.S. view on, 612–13, 1125–26. See also Greece; Turkey, Republic of

Czechoslovakia, Republic of, 1076–77, 1164–65; and ambassadorial talks at Geneva, 1092–93; attends disarmament talks at Geneva, 932–33, 1058–59; de Gaulle's view, 1412–15; on downing of U.S. helicopter, 930–31; on nuclear weaponry in, Bulganin's view, 649–59; and Rapacki Plan, 632–36; Soviets propose Foreign Ministers' Meeting on Berlin crisis, 1424–26; surveillance of U.S. embassy, 1076–77; U.S. relations with, 1076–77

D-Day, 1271–73; Churchill's forebodings on, 1746–56, 2184–85; and Ismay's memoir, 2180–88; no universal confidence in, 1746–56. See also OVERLORD; World War II

Daily Worker, 641–42

Dallas Council on World Affairs, 1248–49

Dalton, Ted, 486–87

Daniel, Price Marion: background, 550–51,

596; on Diablo/Dos Amigos/Amistad Dam, 1373; on offshore oil rights (tidelands), 594–96; on promotion for Lee, 1300–1301

Darby, Edith Marie (Cubbison), 1157–58

Darby, Harry: background, 1157–58; on E.'s family gravesite, 1479, 1547; on Eisenhower Library and Museum, 1157–58; on E.'s visit to Abilene, 1157–58

Darden, Colgate, 1812–13

Dart, Justin Whitlock: background, 327; on E.'s Los Angeles campaign trip, 1181–82; on GOP finances, 1181–82; on "Labor Monopoly," 1181–82; meets with E., 1305; on rebuilding GOP, 1236–39, 1259–61, 1305; receives painting from E., 1305; on Salk vaccine for Air Force recruits, 1145–46; on son's illness, 327, 1124–25, 1145–46

Dart, Peter Walgreen: background, 327; illness of, 327, 1124–25, 1145–46

Daud, Sardar Mohammed (also Daoud, Sarder Mohammed), 708–9

Davidson, Garrison Holt ("Gar"): background, 543; on E.'s gift to West Point Museum, 1996–97; on placing E.'s official papers, 1970–71; as superintendent, West Point, 543, 554, 1850–51, 1970–71; takes new assignment, 1970–71; on USMA reunion, 1970–71

Davidson, Verone M. (Gruenther), 543, 554

Davis, Abraham N., 110

Davis, John Edward, 1975

Davis, Nina (Eristova-Shervashitze), 1247

Davis, Thomas Jefferson ("Tommy," "T.J."): on armed forces pay rates, 1245–47; background, 1246; on retired officers' pay rates, 1245–47, 1560–61

Davis, Virginia Stuart (Waller), 240

Dawson, Howard D., 588–89

Dean, Arthur Hobson: background, 750, 857; and Conference on Law of the Sea, 749–50; on U.S. relations with Latin America, 857

Dean, John Gunther, 2101, 2102

Dearborn, Frederick M., Jr.: background, 273; on defense and education programs, 583; on foreign public opinion reports, 273; on special interest groups, 583

Debré, Michel: Adenauer talks with, 2115–18, 2141–42; background, 1785–87; on French participation in NATO, 1785–87, 1819–20; talks with Norstad, de Gaulle, 1819–20

Decker, George Henry: background, 388, 2195; as C in C, U.N. Command, 388; on post for Goodpaster, 2189–95, 2205–6; on reduction of force in ROK, 387–88

Declaration of Common Purpose, 522, 544–45

Declaration of Independence, 419–23; Beane's

view, 418; concepts of, in Little Rock crisis, 465–66

Declaration of San José, 2088

Defense, Department of (DOD), 376–77, 675–76; on aid to Iran, 1848–50; on appropriations for, 512–16, 561, 593–94, 1007–13, 1188–90, 1828–30, 1991–93; and atomic test suspension negotiations, 1058–59, 1060–63; and Bolte Committee Report, 2234–35; and B-70 bomber program, 2149–50; on budget for military assistance, 410–12; on cause of Korean War, 1991–93; on civil war in Laos, 2219–21, 2223–25, 2248–50; on closing Fort Polk, 1347–48; and construction of Dutch nuclear submarine, 2102; and Cordiner Committee, 93–94, 289–90, 709–10; and crisis in Lebanon, 952–60; on critics of, 1141–42; on currency conversion in Ryukyus, 919–20, 1049–51; on cuts in research/development, 496–97; on defense economies, 1347–48; on defense spending, Soviet view, 1716–17; and disarmament-atomic tests linkage, 1288–89, 1359–60; on discipline/responsibility in armed forces, 1031–32; on domestic economy, 1426–27; and Draper Committee Report, 1515–16; on economic recession recovery, 718–19; on economy in foreign aid, 121–22, 493–94; on E.'s defense policies, 2211; and exchange of restricted data, 936–37; on expenditures as insurance against war, 424–25; and Fairless Committee Report, 95–96, 97–98; and First Secretary of Government, 1700–1702; and funds for procurement and construction, 760–65; and Gaither Report recommendations, 584–85; on GAO access to information, 1194–95; Gates resigns, 2238–39; and guided missile program, 162–63, 292–93, 347–49, 498, 503–5, 561; and Hoover Commission recommendations, 199–200; on increased spending in, 589–91; on inflatable satellite project, 1000–1001; on land holdings in Puerto Rico, 346–47; and McElroy, 735, 737, 1477–79; Meyer scores, 1787–88; and Mideast crisis, 1003–7; and military aid program, 97–98, 354–56; and military pay bill, 910–11; on military spending/public works projects, 817–18; and missiles tracking station site in Brazil, 104–5; and mutual security program, 154–55, 446–49, 1828–30; and NATO strike force using Polaris missiles, 2115–18; and naval forces command structure in Mediterranean, 1313–14; and New Look, 545–47; on nuclear-powered aircraft, 752–53; on offensive weapons for Jordan, 359–60; on payment policies of, 523; on pay for proficiency flying, 1421–22; and pay rates for retired officers, 1245–47,

1560–61; and Percy's Task Force, 1719–20; on POL supplies for Jordan, 1013–15; on Quarles's death/successor, 1475–76, 1477–79; on reducing overseas staffs, 2195–96; rejects Knowland's proposal, 865–66; on resumption of nuclear tests, 1627–28; on Salk vaccine for Air Force recruits, 1145–46; and security breaches, 843, 1692–93; and selection of 1960 campaign speakers, 1793–96; on sending missile mail, 1520; on service academy boards of visitors/trustees, 1672–73; on Skybolt program, 2139–41, 2147, 2149–50; and trade with Communist China, 204–5; and unified bipartisan foreign policy, 396–99; and U.S. force in FRG, 147–50; and U.S.-Panamanian relations, 1744–46; and U.S. policy toward Ryukyus, 827–29, 1049–51; on U.S.-U.K. atomic cooperation, 920–21, 1024–25; and U.S.-U.K. staff planning, 1481–82; on weapons systems procurement program, 1284–85; White's blunder, 347–49

—reorganization of, 509–10, 667–68, 677–78, 1153–56; address to editors on, 797–99, 817–18; Anderson's view, 878–79; on assurances to atomic lab personnel, 965; and Bendetsen's support, 904–5; as bipartisan issue, 843–44; and business principles, 838–39, 863–65; Case's proposal, 585–86; and changing technology in cold war, 863–65; and Congress, 878–79, 1007–13; Congress passes reorganization bill, 1037–38; continuing concerns, 952–60; Dillon's support of, 1037–38; on flexible response to technology, 838–39; and German general staff system, 735, 738; and interservice rivalries, 677–78, 811, 873–74, 952–60; Krock's view, 908–9; and legislative revisions, 888; on Leithead's support, 1039–40; and letter to business community, 838–39, 863–65; and Navy League, 836–37; and New Look, 545–47; Nielsen supports, 896–97; opposition to, 811, 878–79; and plan for, 807–8, 811; and procurement contracts from business community, 836–37; and procurement services legislation, 1054–55; on Robertson's support, 904–5; and role of public affairs officers, 1289–90; and Spaatz, 836–37; and State of the Union Address, 663–64; and Symington Committee report, 2189–95

Defense, Secretary of: on announcements of scientific achievement, 686–87; on authority of, 863–65; and DOD reorganization plan, 807–8, 863–65, 888; and selection of chiefs of MAAGs, 131–32. See also Gates, Thomas Sovereign, Jr.; McElroy, Neil Hosler; Wilson, Charles Erwin

Defense Advisory Committee on Professional and Technical Compensation. See Cordiner

conspiracy, 1740–42; de Gaulle scores U.S. on Algeria, Guinea, 1250–51; de Gaulle scores U.S. on Congo, 2068–73; and Dulles's "unsatisfactory" meeting with de Gaulle, 1250–51; E. briefs Kennedy on de Gaulle, 2189–95; E. suggests U.S. visit, 978–79; E.'s talks with de Gaulle, 1616–17, 1620–21, 1648–50, 1654–57, 1659, 1667–69, 1681–82, 1926–27, 1927–28; and Khrushchev's U.S. visit, 1614–15, 1654–57; on U.S. nuclear "selfishness," 2046–47

—Western Summit Conference, 1614–15, 1615–16; de Gaulle agrees to attend, 1712–13, 1718–19; de Gaulle opposes, 1614–15, 1706–8; E. agrees to, 1529–30; timing for, 1706–8

De Gaullists, in France, 622–23

de Guingand, Francis Wilfred ("Freddie"): background, 1519; and Ismay's memoir, 2180–88; meets with E., 1519–20, 1531–32; and Monty, 1547–49, 1634–35, 2182; on U.S. aluminum consumption, 1519–20; on World War II reunions, 1519, 1523, 1531–32, 1547–49, 1558–59, 1620–21, 1634–35, 1820–21

de la Guardia, Ernesto, Jr.: background, 1713–15; and U.S.-Panamanian relations, 1744–46. *See also* Panama, Republic of

de Lattre de Tassigny, Jean, 954, 959

Delhi University. *See* University of Delhi

Democratic National Committee (DNC): on E.'s domestic and foreign policies, 213–15, 1150–51; and E.'s fiscal policy, 213–15

Democratic National Convention, 1746–56

Democratic party: on "demagogues," Douglas's view, 975–76; and E.'s goodwill trip abroad, 1743–44; encourages E.'s candidacy, 1746–56; E. scores radical wing of, 1163–64, 1164–65; favors public works programs, 769–71; fiscal policies of, 432–34; Freeman's view, 1746–56; and 1960 presidential election, 2052–53; political factionalism in, 622–23; political philosophy of, 432–34, 1935–41; and recession recovery, 769–71; and Reuther, 1961–62. *See also* Democrats

Democratic Policy Committee, Johnson heads, 70

Democrats: on appointments of, to Civil Rights Commission, 392–94; and appointments of, to Supreme Court, 38–39, 1108–10; and bipartisan conference on Formosa, 1120–21; and budget fight, 1430–31; and Colorado midterm election, 1100; and delegation to U.N. General Assembly, 335–36; on differences with Republicans, 812, 2043–44; Earl E. scores foreign policy of, 1164–65; on mutual aid programs committee, 661–62; and natural gas legislation,

213–15; north/south, marriage of convenience, 1375–78; Proxmire wins Wisconsin special election, 396–99; score medical research funds, 1663–65; sponsor food stamp plan, 1688–89; sponsor health care for elderly, 1702–3; sweep 1958 midterm elections, 69–70, 1193–94, 1217–18, 2018. *See also* Democratic National Committee

Dempsey, Miles Christopher: background, 1558–59; and World War II reunions, 1558–59, 1620–21. *See also* World War II

Denmark, Kingdom of, 2184; Bulganin's warning on atomic weaponry, 191–94; and law of the sea, 1652–53; and NATO alliance, 882; royals visit U.S., 2099, 2130–31; and World War II shipping case, 414–15. *See also* Frederik IX, King of Denmark; Ingrid, Queen of Denmark

Denver Post, suppresses article on nerve gas, 134

De Pauw University, Macmillan speaks at, 333, 739–40, 936–37

Depressed Areas Bill, 1007–13, 1329–31

Depression. *See* Economy, U.S.

de Quay, Jan Eduard, 2256–57

Derthick, Lawrence Gridley, 946

De Saint-Phalle, Andre, 1557–58

Desegregation. *See* Civil rights; Supreme Court of the United States

Dethmers, John R., 1721

Development Loan Fund (DLF), 97–98, 183–85; delegation of, visits Turkey, 1823; and economic aid to Guatemala, 2087, 2088; and foreign aid appropriations, 220–21, 1041; on foreign trade and domestic economy, 859–61; and gold outflow, 2199–2200; and Mutual Security Act of 1957, 354–56; Nixon's role in, 410–12; on role of, in free world economy, 1073–76; Sibley's view, 391; on transferring capital to Inter-American Bank, 1943–44; and U.S. aid to Ceylon, 961–62; and U.S. aid to Ghana, 552–53, 637–39; and U.S. aid to Haiti, 1710–12; and U.S. aid to Latin America, 2211–13; and Volta River Project, 2037–38

Devers, Jacob Loucks ("Jake"), 968–69

Dewey, Frances E. (Hutt), 188–91

Dewey, John, 800, 801

Dewey, Thomas Edmund: background, 188–91, 393; as campaign speaker on judiciary, 1793–96; commends E.'s speeches, 1170–71; on dinner for Coty, 188–91; E. recommends, to Civil Rights Commission, 392–94; on GOP "lackluster attitude," 1170–71; on GOP principles, 1170–71; as governor of New York, 1335–37; as gubernatorial candidate for reelection, 1746–56; loses to Truman, 1746–56; on midterm election,

Dominick, Peter Hoyt, 2161–62
Donohue, Frank J., 627–28
Donovan, Robert John, 358
Donovan, William Joseph, 1611–13
Dooley, Malcolm W., 1973
Dooley, Thomas Anthony, III, 1971–73
Dos Amigos Dam. *See* Diablo/DosAmigos/
Amistad Dam
Doubleday and Company, Inc.: and Kornitzer,
830–31; on post-presidency memoirs, 2085,
2092–93, 2159, 2207, 2222–23; publishes
Crusade in Europe, 2085; publishes Jones's
book, 2060–62
Doud, Elivera (Carlson) ("Min"): background,
106–7; on daughters' diagnosis of, 783–84;
David E. visits, 1569–70; death of, 1637–
38, 2062–63; and E.'s goodwill trip to Europe, 1637–38; E. sends vase to, 616–17;
Es. visit, 1162–63, 1637–38, 2021–22; with
family at Gettysburg, 106–7; on grandchildren, 1569–70; Gruenther reports on,
783–84; health of, 616–17, 1138–39,
1637–38; invitation to Washington, 1138–
39; on John E.'s family at Gettysburg,
1569–70; Mamie E. visits, 1637–38, 1770–
72, 1792–93; and Mrs. Bonebrake, 1637–
38; and Nielsen as adviser to, 413–14,
783–84; revises will, 413–14; visits Es. in
Paris, 617
Douglas, Helen Gahagan, 1870
Douglas, James Henderson, Jr., 1142; background, 499, 558–60; on Cabinet invitation
protocol, 499–500; as campaign speaker
on defense, 1141–42; on closing Ethan
Allen Air Force Base, 1742–43; and Declaration of Common Purpose, 544–45; and
Draper's efficiency report, 558–60; and
Eisenhower Golf Course at U.S. Air Force
Academy, 890; on flight training for Air
Force cadets, 1255; on recommendations
by Academy board, 1255; as Secretary of
Air Force, 558–60
Douglas, Lewis Williams: background, 860; on
Democratic "demagogues," 975–76; on for-
eign aid, 859–61; illness of, 859–61; on
public works expenditures, 859–61; on re-
cession recovery, 859–61; on reciprocal
trade bill, 859–61; on tariff reduction and
free trade, 859–61; on tax reductions,
975–76
Douglas-Home, Alexander Frederick (Lord
Home), 2094–95
Dow-Jones industrial average, 783–84
Dowling, Walter C.: on Adenauer's talks with
French, 2141–42; background, 315, 316;
meets with Adenauer, 2115–18; negotiates
with Rhee on ROK force reduction, 314–
16, 387–88
DRAGOON, political *v.* military objectives of,
2181, 2187

Draper, William Grafton, 1736; advises E. on
flight conditions, 185–86; background,
185; efficiency report for, 558–60; as E.'s
personal pilot, 558–60; on E.'s safety in helicopters, 553; on Parker's retirement, 1736
Draper, William Henry, Jr., and Draper Committee report, 1515–16
Draper Committee: and Five Year Military Assistance Plan, 1515–16; on reports from,
1515–16
Drees, Willem, 81–82
Drennan, Walter R., 1875–76
Drew, Gerald Augustin, 1048–49
Drummond, Roscoe: background, 1045; E.'s
esteem for, 1044–45; meets with E., 1995–
96; on responsible journalism, 1502–3,
1935–41
Drumright, Everett Francis: background, 1086;
on Chiang's attitude, 1085–86; and crisis
in Taiwan Straits, 1085–86; on U.S. support of Nationalist China, 1085–86, 2244–
45
Dry, Leonard D., Jr., 826, 827
Dudley, Edward Bishop, Jr.: advises E. on golf,
352; applauds Humphrey's golf game, 173;
background, 173; E. sends "Spectacle of
Sport," 623–24; leaves Augusta for Puerto
Rican club, 352, 354–56, 475–76, 623–24;
as pro at Broadmoor, 352; sends new golf
clubs, 623–24; suffers heart condition,
1079; on swing weights for E.'s clubs, 623–
24, 699
Dudley, Ruth, 352
Duffus, Robert Luther, 603–4
Duke University, and Rule of Law for Peace
Center, 996–97, 1038–39, 1279–81
Dulles, Allen Welsh, 1119; background, 159;
briefs Kennedy on Berlin, Far East, Cuba,
2189–95; on crisis in Taiwan Straits, 1085–
86; death of brother, 1508–9; and Declaration of Common Purpose, 544–45; discussions with Macmillan on atomic weaponry,
1396–97; on Egyptian dissatisfaction with
Nasser, 180–81; on funding for People-to-
-People program, 487–88; and Kerala, 829;
and letter on communism in Cuba, 2244–
45; and Macaulay's view on democracy,
1556–57; and NSC, 743–45; and oil reserves in Indonesia, 368; on opposition to
Trujillo, 1855–56; on plot to assassinate
Hussein, 988–90; on political warfare,
1568–69; on POL supplies for Jordan,
1013–15; on presidential succession in
Lebanon, 869–70; and psychological warfare study, 1611–13; reports to NSC on Indonesia, 844–46; on situation in Jordan,
158–60; on Soviet-Iranian relations, 1321–
25; on takeover of Pakistani government,
1147; testifies on economy, 1832–33; on
U.S. aid to Lebanon, 869–70, 952–60; on

U.S.-Iranian relations, 1321–25; visits Brussels World's Fair, 1104–5; on world opinion in Little Rock crisis, 475–76. *See also* Central Intelligence Agency

Dulles, Eleanor Lansing, 1804

Dulles, Janet Pomeroy (Avery): background, 188–91; husband's death, 1508–9

Dulles, John Foster, 33, 823; addresses National Council of Churches, 1210–11; addresses Veterans of Foreign Wars, 1055–56; on ambassadors-at-large, 2103–4; and *America the Vincible*, 1976; and apathy among U.S. ambassadors, 903–4; on appointment for Luce, 850; on appointment for Morrow, 70, 82–83; on appointment for Wigglesworth, 850; approves reconnaissance balloon project, 1031–32; on assurances to atomic lab personnel, 965; attacks on, 640; attends dinner honoring Elizabeth II, 499–500; attends NAC ministerial meeting, 180, 181, 871, 1248–49, 1258; attends Peace Conference at The Hague, 263–64; attends Pope Pius XII's funeral, 1144–45; attends SEATO meetings, 81–82, 86–87, 631, 782, 784–85, 791–92, 844–46; background, 263–64; and Baghdad Pact, 102, 104, 642–44, 695–96, 998–1000, 1015, 1020–22; as bulwark against Imperialistic Communism, 1450–51, 1457; on Cabinet/congressional relations, 549; and Cabinet invitation protocol, 499–500; and Churchill's painting exhibit in U.S., 526–27; on cold war rhetoric, 535–36, 843; and Committee on World Economic Practices, 1311–13; Cowles's view, 1899; and Development Loan Fund, 183–85; on diplomatic recognition, 279–80; East scores, 434–37; and Eden's surgery, 167, 169; E.'s esteem for, 263–64, 434–37, 630, 640, 666–67, 734, 1450–51, 1804; and Eisenhower Doctrine, 83–85, 263–64; on Elson's visit to Mideast, 273–74; esteem of, for E., 1450–51; European opinion of, 1505; on expenses for personal representatives, 358–59; on fifty years of foreign service, 263–64; on First Secretary of Government, 664–65, 695–96, 1700–1702; and foreign aid determination, 1331–32; foreign policy statement by, 1150–51, 1151–52; on foreign service academy, 1069–70; on foreign service appointments, 1537–38; on foreword for book about, 1804; on funds for Brussels World's Fair, 517; and Gaither Report, 584–85; and HARDTACK, 455–56; Herter as successor to, 1364–65, 1368–69, 1452, 2215, 2242–43; for Hobbs, banking introductions, 717–18; on Hoffman's speech, 671–72; on Hotchkis's suggestions, 508–9; Hughes declines return to government, 171–72; and Jackson's role on for-

eign aid, 768–69; Jackson suggests new post for, 664–65; kind words for, 640–41; and Kissinger's book, 358; on Kyes's proposals, 777–82; and Lawrence's proposal, 592–93; on loose talk from DOD, 843; on Macmillan, E., at Johns Hopkins commencement, 835–36; and media reports on Muscat/Oman dispute, 332–34; on message to Hays, 556–57; and mutual security, 1331–32; news conferences by, 293–95, 784–85; and National Planning Board study, 493–94; on Nixon as congressional foreign policy liaison, 410–12; on objectives of foreign policy, 478; on Persian Gulf islands issue, 22–23, 26; on photos for ambassadors, 114–15; on political ambassadorial appointments, 325–26; portrait of, by E., 1107–8; on post for Whitney, 1049; prepares for second congressional session, 604–5; on process for foreign affairs speech drafts, 1026; on question of presidential disability, 711–14; receives USMA Thayer Award, 968–69; recommends against meeting with Thomas, 331–32; on reply to Altschul, 512–16; on resettlement/repatriation of Palestinian refugees, 293–95; and Rule of Law, 1038–39, 1158–59; on Schuyler as Norstad's successor, 1298–99; and SEATO, 453–54; as Secretary of State, 2211–13; sees draft of speech, 561; sees Jackson's memorandums, 1098–99; sees Luce's speech, 1158–59; and Sibley/Lanham letters on mutual security, 391; and spiritual values in cold war, 1210–11, 1249; and Sprague's proposal, 584–85; statement by, on policy of containment, 1314–15; and State of the Union Address, 667–68; on successor to, 1364–65, 1368–69, 2215; Sulzberger scores, 666–67, 667–68; on support for MSA, 154–55, 174–76; and Trade Agreements Extension bill, 661–62; travels to Europe, 1248–49, 1333–34; on tripartite relationship with U.S., U.K., France, 1159–62, 1412–15; on U.S. foreign policy successes, 789–91, 797–99; on USIA in Far East, 453–54; and USIA as State Department agency, 220–21; and U.S. private investments abroad, 2051–52; vacations on Duck Island, 231, 362–63, 378–79, 1211–12; vacations in Jamaica, 1258, 1276–77; and Voice of America, 232–33; on waivers of non-immigrant visas, 1333–34. *See also* State, Department of

—Africa, and French-Algerian question at U.N., 46–47

—Arctic: on atomic attack via, 898; on inspection system in, 898; Sobolev's protest on flights, 843

—Argentina, Rubottom recommends Dulles visit, 631

791–92, 797–99; on E.'s speech to U.N., 591–92; E.'s suggestions on statement by Dulles, 918
—Summit Conference (May 1960): on conditions for meeting, 728–29, 739–40, 748–49, 782, 804–6; draft reply to Khrushchev regarding, 961
—Sweden, protests U.S. intervention in Lebanon, 988–90
—Syria: on Communist influence in, 383–85, 389–90, 427–31; and discussions with Caccia on internal problems, 166, 167–68
—Trieste, 2211–13
—Tunisia: on arms for, 563–67, 574–79; on relations with France, 746, 766–67
—Turkey: and Baghdad Pact, 998–1000; economic aid to, 944–45; 1051; on NATO and military expenditures, 303–7; terrorists attack, in Ankara, 696–97; on U.S. military aid to, 998–1000
—United Kingdom: on bilateral atomic cooperation agreement, 1024–25; and British economic problems, 644–45; and British nuclear arms program, 278–79; and Bulganin's letter to Macmillan, 191–94, 642–44, 644–45; on Communist influence in Syria, 389–90; on conditions for summit meeting, 748–49; on coordination with U.S. policies, 696–97; and Declaration of Common Purpose, 544–45; on disarmament talks with USSR, 231, 642–44; on exchange of restricted data with, 39–40, 642–44, 906–7, 1060–63; on Greer's Ferry Dam project, 1316–17; on Lloyd's concerns, 181; and Macmillan's cable on disarmament, 632–36; and Macmillan's visit to U.S., 739–40, 936–37; and Oman/Muscat dispute, 378–79, 379–80; and Queen's invitation, 541–42; on Queen's visit, 1130; on pact of non-aggression, 642–44; and reduction of British NATO forces, 75–76, 997–98; on tank procurement for West Germany, 206; on talks with Macmillan, 1399–1402; trade with China, 204–5; and withdrawal of forces from Jordan, Lebanon, 1183–84; and withdrawal of Israeli force from Egypt, 63–64; and wool tariff issue, 265–67. See also Macmillan, Maurice Harold
—United Nations: on delegation to General Assembly, 335–36; Lodge's view on promoting U.N. policies, 636–37; role of, on Mideast issues, 1034–36
—Uruguay, Rubottom recommends Dulles visit, 631
—Vietnam: Geneva Accords on, 2211–13; U.S. position in, 86–87
Dulles, John Watson Foster, 1358
Dulles International Airport. See Airports
du Maurier, Daphne (Lady Browning), 1248

Duncan, David Douglas, 1916
Dunne, Irene, 336
Duplessis, Joseph-Siffred, 1623
Du Pont, E. I. de Nemours & Company, and divestiture of GM stock, 741–43
Durbrow, Elbridge: and allegations on aid to Vietnam, 1639–40; background, 899; delivers message to Diem, 898–99, 1640; delivers vase to Diem, 1474–75; supports Diem, 2138–39; as U.S. ambassador to Vietnam, 898–99
Durfee, James R.: background, 288; chairs CAB, 288; and Trans-Pacific Renewal Case, 720
Durham, Carl Thomas, 40
Duruz, Willis P., 1019–20
Duvalier, François: background, 1048; on Haitian coup attempt, 1048–49; offers U.S. military facilities in Haiti, 1710–12; as president of Haiti, 1048–49; proposes Haitian bauxite barter for U.S. wheat, 1542–43; seeks U.S. aid, 1048–49, 1710–12. See also Haiti, Republic of
Dwight D. Eisenhower Library. See Eisenhower Library
Dwight D. Eisenhower Museum. See Eisenhower Museum
Dworshak, Henry Clarence, 396

Eaker, Ira Clarence, 836–37
Eakin, LeRoy, 301
East, Bion Rose, 434–37
East, Norma (Schmidt), 437
East Asia. See Far East
East Berlin. See German Democratic Republic
Eastern Europe. See Europe: Eastern Europe
East Germany. See German Democratic Republic
Eastland, James Oliver, 1375–78
East-West tensions. See Cold war
Eaton, Frederick McCurdy, 1995
Eban, Abba Solomon: background, 57–59; on overflights of POL supplies for Jordan, 1013–15; on withdrawal of Israeli force from Egypt, 57–59, 72–73, 94–95
Echo I, launch of, 2216–17. See also Satellites
Economic Club of New York, 1276–77, 1277–79
Economic Conference of American States, 1488–91
Economic Development Fund, and U.S. aid to Greece, 362–63
Economic Mobilization Conference, American Management Association: E. addresses, 858–59, 861, 880, 897–98; Nixon addresses, 880; Weeks addresses, 880
Economy, foreign: and balance of payments, 2168–70, 2189–95, 2195–96; and capital expenditures for exports, 1350–52; on coal industry and oil imports, 1392–93; and

Committee on World Economic Practices, 1311–13; and communism, 512–16; on crude oil imports regulation, 1403–4; on financial and economic issues in Germany, 2121–23; Haiti's barter proposal, 1542–43; and importance of foreign trade, 319–25, 981–82, 1622, 1671–72; on imports and trade restrictions, 1426–27, 1881–82; Kyes's proposal, 777–82; on Philippine sugar import quotas, 1881–82; and Sino-Soviet bloc economic offensive, 1311–13; Soviets request trade credits, 1468–70; U.S. aid to, and gold outflow, 2199–2200; on U.S. economic aid to Japan, 1517–19; on U.S. resources to free world, 1073–76, 1350–52; on USSR trade with Finland, Yugoslavia, 1322, 1324; on U.S.-USSR trade agreements, 1482. *See also* Trade, international; United States: foreign trade

Economy, U.S., 667–68, 1153–56; Allyn's memo on, 1350–52; annual report on, 629–30; on balancing budget, 1198–1200, 1233–34, 1334–35; Bator's view on government spending, 2125–26; bedtime story on national debt, 1566–67; Black's view, 1088–89; on budgetary refinancing, 1233–34; Budinger proposes economic high command, 685–86; Burns's observations, 277–78, 540–41, 621–22, 640–41, 731, 813–14, 1144; and capital expenditures, 1350–52; and centralization of federal power, 1500–1502; and Coca-Cola prices in White House, 1877–78; on confidence in U.S. dollar, 1198–1200, 2189–95; on controlling federal expenditures, 1123, 1188–90; and Dow-Jones industrial average, 783–84; on economic incentives, 1198–1200; and farm program, 446–49, 461–62; favorable view of, 310; on federal interference in, 1534–35, 1935–41; and federal pay bill vetoes, 444; and federal role in recession recovery, 760–65, 777–82, 813–14; and foreign markets, 1350–52, 1671–72; on GNP and personal income, 1531; Goldwater's view, 157–58; and GOP conservatism, 801–3; growth of, Soviet view, 1716–17; Hacker's view, 2125–26; Hauge's view, 982–84; Hobby's view, 1402–3; on imports and trade restrictions, 1426–27, 1881–82; on investment in capital goods and jobs, 1353–54; on labor-management issues, 1144, 1165–67; and limits to defense expenditures, 292–93, 774; on long-term interest rates, 902; Lubell's findings, 950–51; Luce's editorial on, 2043–44; Marsh's view, 43–46; McGill's view, 2123–24; Mitchell's view, 621–22; on national debt limit, 1047, 1500–1502, 1554; Nielsen's view, 783–84; on postattack economic plans, 444–46;

and private enterprise, 61–62, 1350–52; on protection from disruptive strikes, 1737–39; and relationship to foreign programs, 410–12; report on, 1228–30; on rise in interest rates, 1663–65; and role of business leaders, 793–95; Saulnier advises Stassen on, 1561–62; Saulnier's report on, 629–30; on self-discipline and capitalism, 1277–79; and self-reliance, 1935–41; on special taxes, 1198–1200; Stassen's view, 1561–62; statements on, 777–82, 879–80; and state's responsibility, 1198–1200; Summerfield's view, 858–59, 1391; as topic, in E.'s speeches, 1492–94; on U.S. economic system, 1277–79. *See also* Budget, Bureau of; Council of Economic Advisors; Taxation; United States: domestic policy

—big business: and antitrust legislation, 251–53; and DOD reorganization, 836–37, 838–39, 863–65, 1039–40; E. meets with leaders of, 1135–36, 1137–38, 1141–42, 1143–44; and influence of, on Congress, 1039–40; Kraft scores U.S. businessmen, 1875–76; in Latin America, 1875–76; on leadership in defeating inflation, 1007–13; and letters to, on combating inflation, 1184–85; students score U.S. businessmen, 1856–57

—depression: on depression of 1930s, 1663–65; Humphrey's view on, 133; Little's view, 432–34

—employment, 1153–56; and age discrimination, 1863–64; and job specialization, 1935–41; and life expectancy, 1935–41; opportunities for, 736; students' views, 1856–57

—inflation, 1153–56; Ackers commends E., 1553; and automobile industry's splurge, 786; and budget fight, 1452–53; Burns's view, 277–78; and Cabinet Committee on Wages and Prices, 1042–43; causes of, 319–25, 419–23; CBS schedules programs on, 1417; on controlling, 310, 316, 396–99, 415–17, 419–23, 444, 1428–29; Crawford's analogy, 426–27; on dangers of, 432–34, 1326–27; and deficit spending, 813–14, 1007–13, 1135–36, 1153–56, 1228–30, 1329–31; as "economic hari-kiri," 1422–23; E.'s view, 6, 78–81, 1383; farmers plan to fight, 1290–91; and federal controls, 61–62; on GM's auto price raise, 522–23; Hasley's concern, 440–41; Hobby's view, 1402–3; and home loans to veterans, 449–50; Jacoby's view, 1228–30; Little's view, 432–34; Luce's editorial on, 2043–44; Marsh's view, 45; and media exposure on budget fight, 1369–71; Moley's view, 1334–35; and postal pay raise bill, 423–24; on postwar inflation, 419–23, 423–24, 440–41;

Stassen's concern, 1561–62; and State of
the Union Address, 1228–30; and support
letters on combating, 1184–85; as "thief
and robber," 1554
—National debt, 434–37, 446–49, 1007–13,
1023–24, 1047, 1233–34, 1500–1502, 1554,
1566–67, 1867–68
—recession: Adler takes action, 1039–40; on
aid to railroads, 777–82; and automobile
industry's role, 786, 952–60; and budget
deficits, 813–14, 1007–13, 1033, 1195–96;
and bureaucratic red tape, 813–14; Burns's
views on, 731, 769–71, 786, 793–95, 813–
14, 886–87; and capital gains, 886–87; on
consumer price controls, 813–14; on coordination in recovery, 718–19; on costs of
federal programs, 793–95; Douglas's view,
859–61; E.'s view, 512, 736, 786, 813–14,
861; and excise tax on automobiles, 824–
25; favorable indices on recovery, 952–60;
and federal role in recovery, 731, 760–65,
777–82, 801–3, 813–14, 859–61, 861, 952–
60; and Fed policies, 952–60; gloom and
doom boys on, 740–41; on highway construction program, 813–14; on increasing
consumer buying, 863; and labor's wage
demands, 803–4; on measures to stimulate
economy, 777–82, 813–14, 886–87; and
midterm election, 1143–44; and partisanship, 731, 734; and possible tax cut, 736,
738, 813–14, 872; and "President's Sale,"
863; and price-freeze bill, 787–89; and
public construction projects, 952–60; and
railroad regulations, 813–14; and Rockefeller Brothers Fund report, 846–47; and
unemployment insurance, 813–14
—small business: on attitudes in, 812; Cabinet
Committee on, 886–87; Phelps's view,
446–49; President's Conference on, 446–
49; and Small Business Tax Revision Act of
1958, 760–65; on tax relief for, 760–65
—unemployment: and disappearance of free
lands, 434–37; in economic recession,
760–65; and employment opportunities,
736, 1185–86; and Federal Council on Employment Security, 1381–82; Furcolo's proposal, 1381–82; and railroad insurance
laws, 1496–98; Senate considers aid for,
760–65; and Temporary Unemployment
Compensation Act of 1958, 760–65; and
unemployment compensation, 1361–62,
1381–82; and unemployment insurance
system, 813–14, 1407–8
Ecuador, Republic of: and crisis in Lebanon,
952–60; and E.'s goodwill trip (December
1959), 1762–63; Nixon visits, 841
Eden, Robert Anthony: assurances to, (1953),
2139–41; background, 169; on demilitarization of Central Europe, 632–36; on

diplomatic recognition, 279–80; health of,
1359; undergoes surgery, 167, 169; and
U.S. tanks for FRG, 150–51, 389–90; and
U-2 flights, 107–9; writes memoirs, 1359
Edstrom, Ed, 1807
Education: and "baby boom" demands for,
458–60; and ban on U.S. textbooks in
Egypt, 1251–52; on benefits for service
personnel, 458–60; and Bradley Commission, 458–60; and Churchill College at
Cambridge University, 880–81; on college
tuitions, 419–23; on cultural, technical, education exchange with Soviets, 673, 692–
93, 726, 727, 774, 789–91, 791–92, 797–
99, 1685–86; on curriculum for Marx god-
children, 1115–16; on engineering and science scholarships, 560–61, 609; on equality in public schools, 1146; federal aid for,
233–34, 255–56, 282, 417–18, 431–32,
527–29, 645–46, 1307–9; for gifted children, 534–35; on Guinean students visit in
U.S., 1902–4; for handicapped children,
534–35; Hopkins's analogy, 905–6; importance of, in collective security, 115–17,
417–18; on industry's aid to, 527–29, 945–
47; on invitation to Soviet students, 789–
91, 791–92, 797–99, 822–23; and Life editorial on, 799–801; and military spending,
817–18; and national defense education
scholarships, 980–81; on national goals in,
1284; on need for, in civil rights, 506,
1375–78; on need for scientists, 503–5,
534–35, 560–61, 609, 645–46, 880–81,
1007–13; in Panama, 1744–46, 1827–28;
on relating foreign affairs to local affairs,
1492–94; on relating foreign affairs to U.S.
economy, 1492–94; and Russian language
instruction in Egypt, 1251–52; and school
construction, 255–56, 282, 417–18, 431–
32; and segregation, 328–31; and State of
the Union Address, 663–64; and status of
teachers, 905–6; as strategy in cold war,
2166–68; on tax breaks for teachers, 905–
6; and taxes on musical instruments, 1915;
in third world nations, 2166–68; on value
of reiteration, 799–801; in Vietnam, 2138–
39. See also Civil rights; Supreme Court of
the United States
Education, Office of. See Office of Education
Egiziano, Stephen J. See Martini, Steve E.
Egypt: and Afro-Asian Conference, Cairo, 726,
727; and Anglo-French invasion of, 34–36;
and arms purchases from U.S., 98–100;
and Aswan Dam project, 408–10, 532–34,
2211–13; attends Cairo Conference, 27,
72–73, 100; and Baghdad Pact, 998–1000;
Benson visits, 2056–58, 2058; concern regarding dispute, 135–36; and Fedayeen,
24, 27, 94–95; Finder's view, 53; and free

passage through Straits of Tiran and Gulf of Aqaba, 129–31, 281; and General Armistice line, 34–36, 72–73, 91–93; and Hare's consultations, 194–96; and Informational Media Guaranty program, 1251–52; and internationalization of Gaza Strip, 25; Israeli invasion of, 34–36; and maritime traffic in Mideast, 53–55, 98–100; and maritime traffic in Straits of Tiran, 94–95; and military governor at Gaza, 94–95; and 1949 Armistice Agreement, 34–36; occupies Tiran and Sanafir islands, 53–55; rejects U.S. arms offer, 427–31; and United Arab Republic, 705–8, 1003–7; and U.N. Resolution on conflict with Israel, 34–36, 72–73, 74–75, 129–31

—France: Mollet's view on conflict with Israel, 91–93; withdraws force from, 34–36

—Israel: Ben Gurion's terms of withdrawal, 34–36; forces of, at Gaza and Sharm el Sheikh, 34–36, 53–55, 91–93; forces of, at Straits of Aqaba, 53–55; on problems at Gaza, 94–95, 98–100; and Soviet Union, 129–31; withdraws forces, 72–73, 74–75, 98–100

—Jordan: and Egypt, U.S. view, 158–60; Egypt's influence on, 293–95; and plot to assassinate Hussein, 988–90; and reclamation of Jordan River Valley, 293–95

—Lebanon: on Muslim opposition to Chamoun, 869–70; on smuggling arms from Egypt, 952–60

—Soviet Union: and Russian language instruction in Egypt, 1251–52; sells arms to Egypt, 408–10; and Syria, 562–63

—Suez Canal, 539–40, 551–52, 814–15; and British oil possessions, 332–34; British view, 100–104, 180–81; Chamoun supports U.S. policies in crisis at, 47; as channel for trade, 129–31; closing of, 24, 25, 34–36, 80; discussions on, at Bermuda Conference 1957, 100–104, 166; and Dulles, 1261–62; Egypt's declaration on administration of, 129–31; Elson's view, 1027–31; E.'s view, 100–104, 166, 168, 574–79; and free passage through Straits of Tiran and Gulf of Aqaba, 281; invasion of, 297–99; and Israeli shipping, 24, 63–64; Jones's view, 532–34; nationalization of, 297–99; and oil for Europe, 18–19; Saud's view, 24–25, 129–31, 194–96; threatens Mideast security, 98–100; UNEF force enters, 34–36; and U.S.-Egyptian relations, 1251–52; on U.S. intervention in crisis, 988–90; and U.S.-U.K. tensions, 526–27; and withdrawal of Israeli force, 34–36, 63–64. See also Middle East; Nasser, Gamal Abdul

—Syria, and Soviet Union, 562–63

—Tunisia, Egypt offers arms to, as gift, 567–70

—United Kingdom: British difficulties in

Egypt, 100–104; Macmillan's view, 63–64; withdraws force from, 34–36

—United States: and ban on U.S. textbooks, 1251–52; and relations with Nasser, 562–63

Egyptian-Israeli dispute. See Egypt; Israel, State of; Saudi Arabia

Eisenhower, Alida B., 6, 8

Eisenhower, Amanda. See Eisenhower, Hannah Amanda

Eisenhower, Arthur Bradford (brother): attends Inauguration ceremonies (1957), 5–6; background, 8; birthday greetings to, 551–52; on burial at Abilene Museum, 938–39; death of, 698–99, 706–7, 718, 830–31, 938–39; E.'s concern for, 5–7, 10–11; Edgar's E.'s view, 8; enjoys bridge at Mission Hills Club, 6; enters Johns Hopkins Hospital, 11; finances of, 6; health of, 5–8, 10–11; and Kornitzer, 830–31; marriages of, 6, 8; suffers arterial sclerosis, 11; suffers eye ailment, 11; suffers heart condition, 11. See also Eisenhower, Louise Sondra (Grieb)

Eisenhower, Barbara Anne ("Anne") (granddaughter), 1097–98; birth of, 532–34; on E.'s investments for, 1306; moves to Gettysburg, 1569–70; visits friend, 1569–70; at White House, 1569–70

Eisenhower, Barbara Jean (Thompson) (daughter-in-law): accompanies E. on goodwill tour (December 1959), 1768–69, 1770–72; accompanies E. on goodwill tour to Far East (June 1960), 1980–81, 1983–84; to accompany E.'? to USSR, 1806–7; in Alexandria, 156; attends Edgar E.'s birthday dinner, 1334–35; background, 109; celebrates Es.' wedding anniversary, 977–78; celebrates John E.'s birthday at White House, 327–28; E.'s investments for, 1306; enjoys Honolulu, 1983–84; at Gettysburg farm with family, 109, 127; moves family to Gettysburg, 1569–70; Secret Service protection for, 2217; "skin dives" in Honolulu, 1983–84; visits parents in Florida, 2165; at White House with family, 772–73

Eisenhower, Catherine (wife of Earl). See Eisenhower, Kathryn (McIntyre)

Eisenhower, David Jacob (father), 1156–57; on gravesite of, 1156–57, 1173–74, 1479, 1547; guidance by, 603–4; and Hardendorf, 812

Eisenhower, Doud Dwight ("Icky") (son), death of, 328

Eisenhower, Dwight David ("Ike"): on Adams, 1128–29; on administrators, 308; on admirals, laymen as science experts, 598–99; Alanbrooke scores, 689–91; on American apathy, 795–96; on Anglo-Saxon male affection, 1683–84; on attacking motives, 251–53; attends Arthur E.'s funeral, 698–

Rally, 1746–56; media interest in, 1746–56; on meeting with Taft, 1746–56; on middle-of-the-road philosophy, 1746–56; and national groundswell, 1746–56; negative reaction (1943), 1746–56; on persuasive visitors, 1746–56; on pressure at Columbia, 1746–56; pressure from Democrats, 1746–56; on pressure at NATO, 1746–56; on pressure in 1947, 1746–56; pressure from Republicans, 1746–56; resigns NATO post, 1746–56; and Robinson, 1746–56; and sense of duty, 1746–56; and Wadsworth, 1746–56; and Winchell, 1746–56
—health of: appreciation to Snyder, 2226; campaigning strains E.'s endurance, 2143–45; contracts chronic bronchitis, 59, 67, 68, 86, 87, 109–10, 135–36; feels well, 814–15; fights cough and cold, 144, 718; gains weight, 1336, 1338–39, 1339–40; suffers bursitis attack, 2168–70; suffers ear infection, 106–7, 173; suffers intestinal upset, 247, 248, 257, 264–65, 271; suffers tracheitis, 106–7, 173; on tooth extraction, 743; undergoes annual physical, 1722, 2202–4; undergoes neurological exam, 743, 814–15. *See also* heart attack; ileitis; stroke *below*
  —heart attack, 66–68, 1286–87, 1500–1502; on avoiding stress, 554, 2150; on controlling anger, 7, 8, 127–28, 2150; and heart fund drive, 37–38; on introspection following, 327; Knox writes, 373–74, 1783–84; Koger stays in touch, 1097–98; and question of presidential disability, 76–77; on rest and diet regimen following, 66–68; Turner stays in touch, 144, 1105–6; on value of naps, 1225–26, 1286–87, 1317–18; Williams stays in touch, 367–68. *See also* Fitzsimons Army Hospital
  —ileitis (ileotransverse colostomy), 345, 1127; and Heaton as E.'s surgeon, 251
  —stroke (cerebral occlusion), 598–99, 608; attends NATO meeting, in spite of, 604–5, 616–17, 646–47, 734, 737; cancels speech plans, 572–73, 591–92; Clement's view, 622–23; on Duffus's view, 603–4; needs rest, 604–5; plays hooky at NATO meeting, 620; questions on, from press, 667–68; suffers aphasia, 604–5, 734; Whitney's advice, 662–63
—honors: Collar of the Supreme Order of the Chrysanthemum, 2090–91; Croix de la Libération (1945), 1192–93; and Eisenhower State Park dedication, 853–54; honorary degree, Brown University, 1523–24; honorary degree, Johns Hopkins University, 815–16; honorary degree, University of Delhi, 1770–72; honorary degree, University of Notre Dame, 1825–26, 1839–40, 1971–73; honorary degree, University of Richmond (1946), 240; honorary fellowship, American College of Surgeons, 203–4, 858; and Wilbur's Medal of Honor story, 933–34
—Inauguration: attends inaugural balls, 9; Clay declines, 43; dreads viewing parade, 6; family attends, 5–8; Hughes assists with Inaugural Address, 171–72; and Inaugural Prayer, 312; on public and private ceremonies, 8, 9; and Second Inaugural Address, 154–55; Turner attends, 144
—political philosophy: in Administration policies, 446–49; on aggression in name of "civil war," 986–87; on American middle class, 2127–28; on "Bible for Republicans," 396–99; brothers support middle-of-road GOP philosophy, 1163–64, 1164–65, 1961–62; on civil rights and the South, 1087–88, 1375–78; on congressmen *v.* governors, 1407–8; on development of foreign economies, 21–22, 78–81, 1517–19; and differences between Democrats and Republicans, 812; on "difficult period" for Congress, 385–87; on duty in civil rights crisis, 480–81, 482–83, 532; on fiscal responsibility in government, 1064–68, 1137–38, 1153–56; on foreign aid, 115–17, 354–56, 868; on "Fortress America" concept, 354–56; on freedom and self-restraint, 2016–18; and Goals Committee, 1722–25; on goals of government, 1340–43; on GOP head as member of Cabinet, 258–59; on GOP "hopelessness," 1088–89, 1089–91; on greatest challenge, 2254–56; Gruenther scores E.'s French, 615–16; on Kennedy-Nixon debates, 2145–46; and Macaulay's view on democracy, 1556–57; on middle way, 1534–35, 1746–56, 1934–35, 1935–41, 2123–24, 2221; and moderation on race question, 1375–78; on "modern republicanism," 132–33, 157–58, 253–55, 396–99, 434–37, 467–68; on moral truths, 1934–35; on mutual security program, 174–76, 389–90; and National Planning Association recommendations, 512–16; on national purpose, 2254–56; on need for GOP unity, 396–99, 432–34; on optimism, 797–99, 1852–54; on personalities *v.* policies, 1201–2, 1217–18; on pessimism, 797–99; on polarization of world power, 376–77; on political paternalism, 1935–41, 2118–19; on political responsibility, 1135–36, 1137–38; on politics and politicians, 1193–94; on power of public opinion, 1027–31; on pressure groups, 1556–57; on prosperity, poverty, and good fortune, 275–76; on reciprocal trade, 868; rejects "welfare state," 1153–56, 1361–62; reply to Bul-

1392–93; considers aid to Greece, 362–63; considers student exchange with Soviets, 673, 726, 727; and construction of atomic power plants, 385–87, 395–96; on controlling inflation, 61–62, 310, 316, 319–25, 419–23, 423–24, 440–41, 444, 1228–30; and Cowles brothers' criticisms, 1899; and crisis in Little Rock, 482–83; Democrats charge pro-business, 213–15; and Development Loan Fund, 184–85; and differences in operations and policies, 1151–52; differs with Fed, 1206; E. cites record of, 446–49; on economy in foreign aid, 121–22; Edgar E. criticizes federal spending in, 152–53; favors states' right to prosecute Communists, 875–78; and foreign economic aid, 78–81; on functions of, at close of, 2119–20; Goldwater's attack on, 157–58; and High's memo on foreign policy, 2049–50; and Indian land claims, 875–78; and inevitable compromises, 1281–82; and Inter-American Development Bank, 1442–43; on international air routes, 288; Johnson scores, 878–79; on Jordan's instability, 158–60; and Knowland, 376–77; Lawrence's view on foreign aid, 155–56; likened to New Deal–Fair Deal Administration, 213–15; McGill scores, 2230–32; and Minerals Stabilization Plan, 991–92; Mitchell's support of, 1332–33; and monetary policy, 187–88, 277–78, 2189–95; Monty scores, 1463; and national spirit of hopelessness, 1089–91; on need for Republican teamwork, 253–55; official duties in, 172–73; personnel changes in, 52; policy of, on ambassadorial appointments, 338–39; and policy of moderate government, 1100; on political balance in Supreme Court appointees, 38–39; on public support for policies of, 1628–29; and public works programs, 769–71; and REA legislation, 1349; on recession recovery, 769–71, 777–82; and recommendations by Citizens Committee for Hoover Report, 1095–97; reducing federal expenditures, 261–62, 289–90, 583, 589–91, 1064–68; rejects food stamp plan, 1688–89; on return of vested German assets, 170–71, 1796–97; and school integration, 834–35; on science in national security, 609; and small business, 446–49; on sound fiscal policy, 1100, 1153–56; and Stassen's gaffe on disarmament, 236–38, 247–49; and State of the Union Address, 1282–83; Summerfield's view on recession, 858–59; Supplee's view, 415–17; on support for programs of, 707–8; supports commodity study groups, 1488–91; supports multilateral trade, 265–67, 1230–32; on tax and spend policies of, Hoffman's view, 78–81;

on transferring control to Kennedy, 2189–95; waning days of, 2244–45
—legislative program: and antitrust legislation, 251–53; on balancing budget, 1326–27; and civil rights legislation, 346, 354–56; disappointment in, 1569–70; and DOD reorganization bill, 863–65; and Eisenhower Doctrine, 83–85; and farm bill tactics, 1045–46; and foreign aid appropriations, 1041, 1329–31; and FY 1958 budget, 531–32; and GOP support in Congress, 813–14; and Hoover Commission, 199–200; and Housing Act, 319–25; leaders discuss current issues, 1007–13; message to Congress on, 1919–23; and mutual security program, 385–87, 389–90, 536–37; and natural gas legislation, 63–64, 213–15; on Nixon as congressional foreign policy liaison, 410–12; and political individualism, 787–89; and race question, 1375–78; and school construction program, 1307–9; and secret ballots in labor law, 674; to stimulate economy, 760–65, 1228–30; on support for U.S. force in FRG, 147–50; and timing of proposals, 410–12; on transportation policy, 484–85; and unwarranted federal spending, 1007–13, 1135–36; and voting rights abuses in South, 1924–25. *See also* Congress, U.S.; House of Representatives, U.S.; Senate, U.S.
Eisenhower Birthplace Foundation, Inc., Earl E. visits, 853–54
Eisenhower boyhood home: Bermingham's contributions to, 1162–63; E. visits, 1162–63, 1479
Eisenhower brothers: on Arthur E.'s burial at Abilene Museum, 938–39; on family gravesite, 1156–57, 1173–74, 1479, 1547; and Kornitzer, 830–31; meet for Wisconsin fishing vacation, 2155; on moving Paul E.'s remains to Abilene, 1571; support middle-of-road Republican philosophy, 1163–64, 1164–65
Eisenhower Doctrine, 1020–22, 1848–50, 2211–13; and communism in Syria, 383–85; and crisis in Jordan, 158–60; Dulles's role, 2211–13; Finder's view, 53; and Israel, 158–60; and Joint Resolution of Congress, 83–85, 142–43; Knowland's view, 71–72; and Richards's mission to Mideast, 83–85, 383–85; Russell's view, 71–72; Senate passes resolution on, 71–72, 263–64; Truman's view, 56–57
Eisenhower Exchange Fellowships, Inc.: on art for headquarters of, 153–54; E. addresses trustees of, 2036
Eisenhower Farms, 29–30, 74, 89–90, 931–32; on conflicts of interest, 682–84; herdsire for, 885–86. *See also* Gettysburg farm
Eisenhower Foundation for the Promotion of

on E. as Socialist, 1383; and GOP convention, 1253–54; on Hoffman's salesmanship,
2243–44; recollections of, 1212–13;
Stassen's recollection, 1253–54; and Texas
tidelands, 893–95; Thye's recollection,
1253–54
—presidential 1956: and civil rights/integra-
tion platform, 486–87; and modern Republicanism, 396–99, 434–37, 467–68;
platform in, 396–99. *See also* Eisenhower,
Dwight David: presidency; Nixon, Richard
Milhous
—presidential 1960: Adams's view of candidates, 2136; on antagonism between Rockefeller and Nixon, 1632–34; and blunder
regarding Blum, 2091–92; on campaign
fundraising, 1990–91, 2068; on closed circuit television dinner, 1990–91, 2062–63;
in Colorado, 2161–62; and defense question, 1828–30; Democrat voters for, 2157;
E. campaigns in Chicago, 2062–63; E. campaigns in New York, 2143–45; E. campaigns in New York with Nixon, 2145–46;
E. campaigns in Philadelphia, 2145–46; E.
campaigns in West, 2131–32, 2136, 2143–
45; E. contributes to, 2068; E. declines
South Dakota campaign stop, 1925; on E.
as Nixon's sponsor, 1925; E. speaks in
Boston, 2062–63; E. speaks to Republican
National Convention, 2018, 2036; E. speaks
to Republican women, 2127–28, 2128,
2130–31; E. votes for Nixon-Lodge, 2151;
frenzy of, 1690; on GOP in Illinois, 2109–
11; GOP preparation for, 1181–82, 1182–
83; on Hauge's tree analogy, 2089–90; and
High's memo on foreign policy, 2049–50;
on Independents and switch-voting Democrats, 1975, 2157; on Kennedy as Catholic
candidate, 1963–64; on Kennedy-Johnson
ticket, 2052–53; and Kennedy-Nixon debates, 2130–31, 2145–46; and legislative
program on agriculture, 1802–3; on
Lodge, Anderson as candidates, 2018–19;
Lodge as vice-presidential candidate, 2056;
and Mamie E.'s campaign speech, 2062–
63; and medical care for elderly, 1702–3;
and National Citizens for Nixon, 2044–45;
on national election process, 2158; on
need for continuous work in GOP, 1309–
10; on need for personable candidates,
1207–8; on 1960 election loss, 2156, 2157,
2157–58, 2165, 2165–66, 2258–59; on
Nixon, 1553, 1870–71, 2128, 2258–59;
Nixon accepts nomination, 2018–19;
Nixon campaigns in Cincinnati, 2145–46;
on Nixon and Jewish vote, 1869–70, 1870–
71; on Nixon and NAACP, 2052–53; no
room for disunity in, 1195–96; on politics
and religion, 1963–64; problems in New
York State, 2143–45; and Quemoy-Matsu issue, 2130–31; and Republican Party Committee, 1305; on Roberts as fundraiser for
Volunteers for Nixon, 2068; on Rockefeller,
1553; on selections for Speakers' Bureau,
1793–96; on Southern Democrats' disaffection, 2036, 2052–53; and strains on E.'s endurance, 2143–45; on Stratton's problems,
2109–11; support from Morgans, 2128–29;
in Texas, 1975; and U.S. policy in Iran,
2095–98; on vice-presidential nominees,
1870–71; on Victory Fund dinners, 1990–
91; on victory in 1960 elections, 1862–63.
See also Johnson, Lyndon Baines; Kennedy,
John Fitzgerald; Lodge, Henry Cabot;
Nixon, Richard Milhous
—presidential 1964: E.'s optimism regarding,
2165–66; Goldwater loses, 2165–66; Johnson wins, 2165–66
Electoral College, 2158
Eli Lilly & Company, 891
Elizabeth, Queen Mother of Great Britain,
1816
Elizabeth II, Queen of Great Britain: announces pregnancy, 1616–17, 1620–21,
1623–25, 1641; attends St. Lawrence Seaway dedication, 1541–42; attends Whitney's
dinner, 1241–42; background, 181; and
birth of Prince Andrew, 1828–30; and
Chile-Argentine border dispute, 1859–60;
E. visits, at Balmoral, 1616–17, 1620–21,
1623–25, 1641; on letters of appreciation,
502–3; on message from, 1241–42; Rockefeller attends dinner honoring, 488–89;
sends scones recipe, 1816; on state dinner
honoring, 261, 499–500; visits U.S., 181,
212, 243–44, 342, 495–96, 502–3, 526–27,
1130
Elkin, Daniel Collier, 203–4
Ellender, Allen Joseph, 580–81
Ellis, Clyde Taylor, 1349
Ellison, Newell Windom, 1415–16
Ellsworth, Harris, 200
Elmendorf Air Force Base, Alaska, 1977–78
El Salvador, Republic of: and E.'s goodwill trip
(December 1959), 1762–63; and Hemispheric Producer's Agreement, 1488–91;
and Inter-American Cotton Conference,
1488–91; Milton E. visits, 1218–19
Elson, Edward Lee Roy: on Arabs, 1027–31;
background, 182; and brochure on Arab-
Israeli dispute, 1027–31; and campaign for
National Presbyterian Church, 363; on E.'s
gift to building fund, 1536–37; invites Es.
to church service, 182–83; on Israel, 1027–
31; on Nasser, 1027–31; on Naval Observatory as church site, 1301–2; on Palestine,
1027–31; requests E.'s photograph, 182–
83; sermon by, on cold war, 535–36; visits

economic recession recovery, 718–19, 760–65; and Emergency Housing Bill, 760–65; and Housing Act of 1957, 449–50; and omnibus housing bill, 1007–13; and residential loan rates, 783–84. *See also* Housing

Federalism, E.'s view, 282, 1340–43

Federal Maritime Board, and construction of superliners, 987–88, 1007–13

Federal National Mortgage Association: and Emergency Housing Bill, 760–65; on funds to stimulate home construction, 760–65; and Housing Act of 1957, 449–50

Federal Power Commission (FPC): and natural gas legislation, 213–15; and natural gas pipeline rates, 765–66; and regulations on natural gas sales, 63–64; and water resources program, 1665–67

Federal Preemptive Doctrine, 878

Federal Property and Administrative Services Act of 1949: and presidential library, 1904–8; and presidential papers collection, 1904–8

Federal Reserve System (Fed): and adjustment of interest rates, 760–65; and certificates of indebtedness, 1023–24; and Crawford's analogy, 426–27; on credit controls, 1206; and DOD payment policies, 523; and economic recession recovery, 718–19, 760–65, 769–71, 777–82, 952–60; Martin meets regularly with E., 685–86; and monetary policy, 187–88, 277–78, 450–51; on rise in interest rates, 1663–65; Summerfield's view, 858–59; and tax payments in federal bonds, 588–89. *See also* Currency; Fiscal policy; Gold; Martin, William McChesney, Jr.; Monetary policy

Federal-State Commission. *See* Joint Federal-State Action Committee

Federal Trade Commission (FTC): House investigates Adams-Goldfine relationship, 952–60; investigates quiz show scandals, 1729

F-86 Sidewinder weapons system, 2096, 2098

Ferguson, Sarah A., 1863–64

Fermi, Enrico, 795–96

Fernández, Patricio, 1884–85

Fernando de Noronha Island (Brazil), 105

Fifth World Forestry Congress, E. as patron of, 1917

Finder, Leonard V.: background, 53; on Egypt, Jewish view, 53; on Eisenhower Doctrine, 53; encourages E.'s candidacy, 1746–56, 2123–24

Finland, Republic of: and NATO alliance, 882; Soviet relations with, 1322, 1324

Finley, David Edward, 27, 28

Finsterwald, Dow, 353–54

Finucane, Charles Cecil: Assistant Secretary of Defense for Manpower, Personnel, and Re-

serve, 2234–35; background, 1479; and Bolte Committee Report, 2234–35; as successor to McElroy, 1477–79

Firestone Tire & Rubber Company, 1136

First International Conference on American States, 1442–43

First Secretary of the Government, 664–65, 675–76, 695–96; Senate rejects proposal, 1700–1702

First Supplemental Appropriations Act of 1959, and Danish shipping case, 414–15

Fiscal policy: and ADA-CIO philosophy, 1064–68; Anderson's pessimism, 1233–34; on balancing budget, 1233–34; Dawson's recommendation, 588–89; and Democratic party, 432–34, 1935–41; and DNC, 213–15; Hauge's view, 1195–96; Humphrey testifies on, 277–78; and midterm election, 1153–56; and national debt, 434–37, 446–49, 1047, 1554, 1867–68; and post-attack economic plans, 444–46; on refinancing bond issues, 1233–34; and Republicans, 396–99, 432–34, 801–3, 1064–68, 1100, 1935–41; Saulnier's optimism, 1233–34; and Senate, 277–78. *See* Currency; Economy, U.S.; Federal Reserve System; Gold; Monetary policy

Fisher, Lawrence Peter, 716–17

Fishing: on Atlantic salmon treaty with Canada, 1057; on California tuna fishers, 1562–63; E. longs for, 268; E. prefers, to skiing, 2225–26; on Fisher's invitation, 716–17; on fishery jurisdiction, 1652–53; and fishery zones for coastal states, 749–50; on flies from Nielsen, 977–78; and Iceland, 871, 1652–53; in Latin and South American waters, 776–77; and law of the sea, 749–50, 776–77, 1652–53, 1818–19, 1911–12; on making fishing gear, 1500–1502; Milton E. reports on, 300–302; with Nielsen, 2021–22. *See also* Geneva Conferences on Law of the Sea

Fitzsimons Army Hospital, 76–77, 144, 373–74; and Hering, 1500–1502; and Knox, 1783–84. *See also* Eisenhower, Dwight David: heart attack

Flake, Wilson Clark, 639

Flanigan, Aimee (Magnus), 523

Flanigan, Horace C. ("Hap"), 523

Fleeson, Doris, 1940

Fleming, Lamar, Jr.: Anderson, Clayton view on Latin America, 1230–32; background, 1231; and cotton export program, 1398–99; on "hostile nationalism," 1230–32; and Milton E.'s report on Latin America, 1230–32; on reciprocal trade issues, 1230–32; on U.S. tariffs, 1230–32

Fleming, Robert Vedder, 380–81

Flemming, Arthur Sherwood: background, 624, 968–69; as campaign speaker on HEW, 1793–96; as candidate for USMA

consultations, 1967–68, 1987–88, 2028–30

Foreign Operations Administration (FOA), and Stassen, 1256–58

Foreign policy. *See* United States: foreign policy

Foreign relations. *See* United States: foreign policy

Foreign Service Academy, 1537–38

Foreign Service Act Amendments of 1960, 1537–38

Foreign Service Buildings Committee, 1874

Foreign Service Institute, E. addresses, 1537–38

Foreign Service of the United States: and Administration policy on briefings for appointees, 338–39; on ambassadorial expenses and U.S. taxes, 1651–52; on apathy among U.S. ambassadors, 903–4; on attitudes among officers of, 1315–16, 2103–4; on diplomatic relations with Panama Canal Zone, 2088–89; federal support for, 1188–90; and foreign service academy, 1069–70, 1537–38; and Gluck's appointment, 338–39; Morrow's interest in, 70, 82–83; Nielsen's esteem for, 896–97; on performance evaluations, 2103–4; and political ambassadorial appointments, 325–26, 1537–38; on question of Bohlen's transfer, 1574–76, 1577–79; on representation allowances, 1537–38; on requests for photos for ambassadors, 114–15

Formosa. *See* China, Republic of: Formosa

Formosa Resolution, 263–64, 1131–33, 2211–13. *See also* China, Republic of: Formosa

Formosa Straits. *See* China, Republic of: Formosa

Forrest, Nathan, 28, 29

Forrestal, James Vincent, 145

Forrestal, Josephine (Ogden), 145

Fort, Deborah Fredericks, 1217–18

Fort Belvoir, Virginia, John E. takes post at, 156, 543–44

Fort Benning, Georgia, 427; E.'s service at, 1962–63; on high morale at, 1962–63; and Hoiles's death, 1962–63. *See also* Eisenhower, John Sheldon Doud

Fort Bragg, North Carolina, 1097–98

Fort Leavenworth, Kansas, 1876; on E. as young officer, 647. *See also* Army Command and General Staff College

Fort Ligonier, Pennsylvania: bicentennial celebration at, 951, 1117, 1118, 1119–20, 1382–83; E. speaks at, 1117, 1119–20, 1135–36, 1137–38

Fort Polk, Louisiana, 400–401; closing of, 1347–48; reopens, 1347–48

Fort Richardson, Alaska, E. visits, 1977–78

Fort Ritchie, Maryland, E. visits, 1965

Fort Sam Houston, Texas, 1321

"Fortress America," 354–56

Fortune magazine, publishes Gulf Oil letter, 1135–36

Fosburg, James Whitney, 202

Foster, Jack, 818

Foster, John Watson, 264, 1369

4-H Clubs, National Conference of, meets E. in Rose Garden, 1919–23

Four-Power Working Group, and Germany, 1424–26

Fourteenth Amendment. *See* Constitution of the United States

Fourth Extraordinary Meeting of the Inter-American Economic and Social Council. *See* Rio Treaty

Four Wise Men, 1799–1800

Fox, Frederic Ewing, 1804

France, Republic of: and Bermuda Conference security leak, 113–14; blindness of, toward colonialism, 952–60; Cabinet crisis in, 188–91, 648–49; on cold war defenses, 1159–62; de Gaulle's patriotism, 1785–87; de Gaulle as president of, 917, 1285–86; economic situation in, 574–79, 952–60; E.'s goodwill trip to Paris (December 1959), 1761–62, 1762–63; and English as universal language, 548; E. visits, 1620–21, 1659; on Foreign Ministers' Meeting negotiations, 1541–42; and French West Africa, 2011–12; nd Good Offices mission, 831–34; government of, falls, 567–70, 574–79, 831–34; governments of, irritate E., 2223–25; Houghton, as U.S. ambassador to, 125; and Ismay's memoir, 2180–88; Jackson, on E.-de Gaulle relations, 1588; liberation of, 978–79; like a "spoiled child," 574–79; on moral, political, military deterioration of, 952–60; on Norstad's talks with de Gaulle, Debré, 1819–20; and Palestine Conciliation Commission, 1098–99; political factionalism in, 622–23; prestige of, Salazar's view, 125; and pre–World War II appeasement, 1017–19; and tripartite consultations, 1159–62, 1250–51, 1673–75, 1967–68, 1987–88, 2028–30, 2046–47, 2068–73; and World War II reunion, 1523, 1531–32. *See also* de Gaulle, Charles André Joseph Marie; Summit Conference (May 1960); Western Summit Conference

—Africa: communism in, 1654–57; French colonialism in, 1654–57; and Guinea, 1654–57; sets up consulates at Bamako, Mali, 2100–2102

—Algeria: and African-Asian resolution in U.N., 46–47; border fighting in, 738; Bourguiba's concern, 766–67, 1113–15; de Gaulle's declaration on, 1667–69, 1681–82; and de Gaulle's plan, 1654–57, 1673–

Frederik IX, King of Denmark: attends ballet with E., 2130–31; visits U.S., 2099
Frederika, Queen of the Hellenes, 119
Freedoms Foundation, 511
Free enterprise. *See* Private enterprise
Freeman, Douglas Southall: background, 240; on biographies by, 691–92; hosts luncheon for E., Nimitz, 240; prays for E.'s candidacy, 1746–56; scores Democratic party, 1746–56
Freeman, Orville Lothrop, 2232
Free world: on Adenauer's leadership, 1658; and African nations, 831–34; and American isolationism, 2068–73; appraisal of, by National Planning Association, 493–94, 512–16; and Bourguiba, 1113–15, 2133–35; and British economy, 80; and Cambodia's relations with Thailand and Vietnam, 1432–35; and collapse of Summit Conference (May 1960), 1960–61; and Committee on World Economic Practices, 1311–13; and crisis in Formosa Straits, 1131–33; and Cuba's need for Soviet oil, 2001–7; defenses of, de Gaulle's concern, 1159–62; and disarmament policy, 442–43, 456; on economic growth in, 1073–76; on E.'s goodwill trips, 1761–62, 1762–63; and fight against communism, 78–81, 88–89, 191–94, 194–96, 381, 898–99, 918, 1168–70, 1901–2; and foreign aid, 43–46, 142–43, 155–56, 537, 561; and free trade, 265–67, 859–61, 1449–50; and friendship among nations of, 21; on Indo-Pakistani relations, 1774–76; and Iran's vulnerability, 1321–25; Jackson's speech draft on, 1670–71; and Korea, 1514; and Krushchev's rudeness, 1374; and law of the sea, 1911–12; and meaning of freedom, 592–93; military strength of, 545–47; and missiles tracking in Brazil, 104–5; munitions supply to, 206; and mutual security program, 319–25, 385–87, 389–90, 1329–31, 1947–49; and national self-interest, 1675–76; and NATO, 625–26, 2115–18; and oil imports for, 340–42; and Operation Pan America, 1242–44, 1997–99; on ordnance supply to, 211–12; and polarization of world power, 376–77; and promise to Myklebost, 2054–55; and psychological warfare, 1611–13; and reply to Bulganin, 649–59; and Russian-Chinese trade differential, 211–12, 234–35; on sources for material replacement, 389–90; and sovereignty of free world nations, 918; and Soviet economic offensive, 1424–26; Soviet threat to, in Near East and North Africa, 1113–15; and spirit of solidarity, 1406–7, 1500–1502, 1878–79, 1953–54; on spiritual values in, 1210–11, 1248–49, 1801–2; and Stassen's

gaffe on disarmament, 236–38; supports Iran, 2095–98; tensions in, 574–79; on testing nuclear weaponry, 473–74, 618–20; and three-mile limit in territorial seas, 749–50; and tripartite consultations, 1159–62, 1967–68, 2068–73; Turkey's role in, 1974–75; U.S. as principal banker to, 2123–24; and U.S. policy in cold war, 2242–43; on U.S. relations with Cuba, 2001–7; on U.S. role in economy of, 1073–76; and U.S. role in Korea, 314–16; and U.S.-Thai relations, 2151–53; and U.S.-U.K. ties, 491–93, 521–22; and U.S.-Vietnam relations, 1639–40. *See also* Cold war; Communism
Frelinghuysen, Peter, Jr., 751–52
French Equatorial Africa, and French colonialism, 952–60
French Territorial Air Defense (DAT), 1819–20, 1926–27
French West Africa, 2011–12
Friedel, Samuel Nathaniel, 2092
Friendship Airport. *See* Airports
Frondizi, Arturo: background, 359, 841; and Benson's visit, 2081, 2082; and Bogotá meeting of Committee of 21, 2080–82; on Chile-Argentine border dispute, 1859–60; inauguration of, 326, 359, 841; Nixon attends inauguration of, 841; seeks U.S. economic aid, 2080–82; on trade relations with Europe, 1968–69; on U.S.-Argentine relations, 841, 2080–82; visits U.S., 1265–66, 1307. *See also* Argentina, Republic of
Frost, Robert Lee, 881–82
F Street Club, 1746–56
Fulbright, James William, 1375–78
Funerals, on motorization of military funerals, 51–52
Funston, George Keith, 2018
Furcolo, Foster, 1381–82

Gabes, 569
Gable, Clark, 2150
Gadsby, Edward Northrup, 110
Gaillard, Félix: on arms for Tunisia, 563–67, 567–70; background, 565; Dulles's view, 831–34; E.'s view, 563–67, 736, 738; on French relations with Atlantic Community, 831–34; on French relations with North Africa, 831–34; on Good Offices mission, 831–34; meets with E., 563–67; recalls French ambassador, 736, 738; speaks at NATO meeting, 617–18. *See also* France, Republic of
Gainey, Daniel Charles: background, 241; on Dulles's illness, 1368–69; on Dulles's successor, 1368–69; on E.'s foreign policy, 1368–69; gives E. Arabian filly, 241
Gainsford, Miss, 1651–52

Gainza Paz, Alberto, 151–52
Gaither, H. Rowan: background, 502; illness of, 584–85. *See also* Gaither Report
Gaither Report, 668–69; background, 584–85; E.'s view, 584–85; recommendations of, 584–85; Sprague's recommendations, 584–85; warns of inadequate defenses, 545–47
Gale, Humfrey Myddelton: background, 1654; and Monty, on rush to Berlin, 1653–54, 2182, 2187. *See also* World War II
Gall, John Christian: on Ankonian 3551, 186; attends stag dinner, 186; background, 186; on dinner for Coty, 188–91; on E.'s heifer from press women, 186
Gall, Mrs. John Christian, 188–91
Gallin-Douathe, Michel, 2160–61
Gallup poll, on budget, 1326–27
Galvin, Robert W., 751–52
Ganong, Carey K., 772–73
Garcia, Carlos Polestico: addresses U.S. Congress, 771–72; Akers attends inauguration of, 675; on anniversary of Bataan's fall, 825; background, 675, 772; on Philippine sugar quota, 1881–82; visits U.S., 675, 771–72, 825. *See also* Philippines, Republic of
Gareloch, Scotland, 2009–11
Garfield, James Abram: background, 139, 140, 711–14; death of, 140, 711–14; and question of presidential disability, 138–40, 711–14
Garlington, Mrs. Thomas Richard, 188–91
Garlington, Thomas Richard, 188–91
Gascoyne-Cecil, Robert Arthur James. *See* Salisbury, fifth marquess of
Gates, Natalie Brush, 1804–5
Gates, Thomas Sovereign, Jr., 1142; to accompany E. to Summit Conference, 1850; appreciation to, 2238–39; approves message to de Gaulle, 2028–30; background, 499, 1479; and Bolte Committee Report, 2234–35; and B-70 bomber program, 1810, 2149–50; on Cabinet invitation protocol, 499–500; as campaign speaker on defense, 1141–42, 1793–96; and coordination in strategic planning, 2099–2100; and Declaration of Common Purpose, 544–45; and defense policies, 2211; on Goodpaster as aide to Kennedy, 2189–95, 2205–6; on Polaris MRBMs, 1989–90; on Presbyterian church site, 1301–2; on rank for service academy heads, 1850–51; resigns, 2238–39; as Secretary of Defense, 1477–79, 1810; on Skybolt bomber-missile program, 1981–82, 1989–90, 2147; and Strategic Target Planning Staff study, 2135–36; as successor to McElroy, 1477–79, 1810; and U.S. position on Guantanamo, 2142–43. *See also* Defense, Department of
Gault, James Frederick ("Jimmy"): on Argyll and Sutherland regimental insignia, 1220–

21, 1281–82; background, 201; on ceremonies at St. Paul's Cathedral, 1220–21, 1281–82; on golf, 200, 1220–21; and guests at Culzean, 200–201, 202–3, 313–14; marital problems of, 313–14; visits Canada, U.S., 1220–21
Gault, Margaret Ella (Campbell), 313–14
Gavin, James Maurice, 1043–44
Gaza Strip: and Arab refugees at, 92–93; and Armistice Agreement, 91–93; internationalization of, 24–25; Israeli forces at, 34–36; on military governor for, 94–95; UNEF controls border at, 98–100, 102, 104; and U.N.'s order of urgency, 57–59; on withdrawal of Israeli forces at, 24–25, 53–55, 63–64, 72–73, 91–93, 94–95. *See also* Egypt; Israel, State of
Gbedemah, Komla Agbeli: background, 552–53; discrimination against, 552–53; meets with E., 552–53; visits U.S., 552–53; and Volta River Project, 2037–38
Gelée, Max, 2029–30
Geneen, Harold Sydney, 2051–52
General Accounting Office (GAO), and access to Inspectors General reports, 1194–95
General Agreement on Tariffs and Trade (GATT): conference of, 1562–63; investigates Japanese tuna fishers, 1562–63
General Agreement for Technical Cooperation, 151–52
General Electric Company, 1136; and imports of heavy power equipment, 1449–50
General Motors Company: on collective bargaining with UAW, 741–43; Curtice's view, 742; and Du Pont's divestiture of GM stock, 741–43; raises auto prices, 522–23
General Services Administration (GSA): E. briefs Kennedy on, 2189–95; Floete heads, 952; Mansure seeks post with, 952; and presidential papers collection, 1904–8, 1970–71
Geneva Accords (1954): and Cambodia, 2248–50; and Dulles, 2211–13; and Laos, 2219–21; and Vietnam, 2211–13
Geneva Agreements, and recognition of North Vietnam, 1902–4
Geneva Conference on the Discontinuance of Nuclear Tests (October 31, 1958). *See* Geneva Nuclear Test Conference
Geneva Conference on the Discontinuance of Nuclear Tests and the Draft of a Test Ban Treaty (October 31, 1958). *See* Geneva Nuclear Test Conference
Geneva Conference of Experts on Surprise Attack (November 10–December 18, 1958): and Cowles, 1215–16; and Dulles, 1213–15; and Nehru, 1223–24; and Soviets, 1412–15; stalls, 1213–15
Geneva Conference on Law of the Sea (February–April 1958): and Canadian compro-

mise proposal, 776–77, 1652–53; and fishery zones for coastal states, 749–50, 776–77; India's support, 1818–19; and law of the sea, 749–50, 776–77; U.K., U.S. positions on three-mile limit, 749–50, 776–77; U.N. calls for conference, 749–50

Geneva Conference on Law of the Sea (Spring 1960): E. seeks international support, 1911–12; and fishery jurisdiction, 1652–53; on fishing rights, 1911–12; on India's position, 1818–19; on six-mile territorial sea, 1911–12; U.S.-Canada differences, 1652–53; on U.S.-Canada proposal, 1911–12; on U.S. position, 1818–19

Geneva Conference on Law of the Sea (December 10, 1982), 1911–12

Geneva Conference on Law of the Sea (November 16, 1994), 1911–12

Geneva Conference of Technical Experts on Detecting Nuclear Tests (July 1–August 21, 1958): and data exchange with U.K., 1058–59, 1060–63; and Khrushchev, 1463–66; and protocol on cessation of atomic testing, 1058–59; on seismic signals, 1399–1402

Geneva Nuclear Test Conference (adjourns October 31, 1958; resumes April 13, 1959; recesses August 27, 1959; resumes October 27, 1959): on atmospheric pollution, 1440–42, 1447–48, 1463–66, 1797–98; on atomic test suspension negotiations, 1399–1402, 1438–39, 1463–66, 1627–28, 1694–96, 1787–88, 1797–98, 1828–30; British view, 1213–15; and communiqué from E., Macmillan, 1887–90; on dangers of radioactivity, 1447–48; deadlocks, 1213–15; and disarmament-atomic testing linkage, 1276, 1288–89; and Dulles's death, 1486, 1499–1500; E. ends voluntary moratorium, 1787–88; E.'s impression of Gromyko, 1499–1500; E. recalls "Spirit of Geneva," 1453–56; and impasse on disarmament, 1223–24; and impasse on testing, 1813–14; JCS view, 1627–28; and message to Khrushchev, 1438–39, 1844–48; and message to Nehru, 1213–15, 1215–16, 1223–24; on numbers of inspection trips, 1367–68, 1374, 1467–68; on predetermined test inspections, 1463–66, 1887–90; on procedures for onsite inspections, 1447–48; on progress regarding, 1510–12; recess of, 1409–10, 2064–65; on seismic research program, 1999–2001, 2064–65; and Soviet veto, 1359–60, 1438–39, 1440–42, 1447–48, 1463–66, 1467–68; and status of Berlin, 1510–12; and technical working group II, 1887–90; and tripartite talks, 1828–30; on unacceptable Soviet proposals, 1412–15; on underground tests, 1444–45, 1447–48, 1787–88, 1828–30, 1887–90,

2064–65; on unilateral moratorium, 1440–42, 1797–98; Wadsworth recommends recess, 1399–1402. *See also* Ten-Nation Committee on Disarmament

Geneva Nuclear Test Negotiations. *See* Geneva Nuclear Test Conference

Geneva Summit Conference (July 1955): and ambassadorial talks, 1092–93, 1101–2; considers student exchange with Soviets, 673; disappointment follows "Spirit of Geneva," 1453–56; and Eastern European states, 649–59; and E.'s disarmament proposal, 14–15, 249–50; E.'s view on, 247–49; and Formosa crisis, 1101–2; and media exchange with Soviets, 249–50; and national interests, 1691–92; and Open Skies proposal, 249–50, 820; and proposed summit (May 1960), 804–6; on U.S.-Soviet scientific, cultural, athletic ties, 649–59; on U.S.-Soviet trade, 981–82

Geneva Surprise Attack Conference (November 10–December 18, 1958). *See* Geneva Conference of Experts on Surprise Attack

Geneva Technical Conference on Nuclear Testing (July 1–August 21, 1958). *See* Geneva Conference of Technical Experts on Detecting Nuclear Tests

Genghis Khan, 1189

George, Walter Franklin, 354–56

George Washington University, 2146

Georgia: and ad photo error, 1858; E. hunts at Blue Springs Plantation, 2166–68, 2168–70; fine turkey country in, 662–63; and Georgians for Nixon, 2128–29; and Isenhour family, 438; on red ants in, 1033, 1053–54; and school integration, 1134–35, 1375–78; and sit-ins in South, 1935–41; and Warm Springs Foundation, 37–38. *See also* Eisenhower, Dwight David: vacations; Golf: Augusta National Golf Club

Gerhardsen, Einar: attends NATO meeting, 629; background, 882; E., Rayburn meet with, 882; visits Washington, D.C., 628–29

German Democratic Republic (GDR, East Germany), 1164–65; and Berlin crisis, 1261–62; de Gaulle's view, 1412–15; on downed helicopter in, 930–31; and Gromyko's charge on propaganda, 1509–10; Gromyko proposes all-German negotiators, 1585–86; and Guinean foreign policy, 1902–4; Khrushchev speaks on conditions in, 721–27; on participation of, at summit, 1697–1700; and principle of self-determination, 1878–79; and radio attacks on Gromyko, 1509–10; and Rapacki Plan, 632–36; and Soviet conditions for summit, 792–93; and USSR, 2115–18

Germany: and Berlin crisis, 1319–21, 1378–79, 1389, 1406–7, 1412–15, 1417–18, 1418–19, 1424–26, 1430–31, 1487–88, 1540–41,

1574–76, 1587–88, 1676–77, 2068–73; Bulganin would ban nuclear weaponry in, 649–59; and Communist menace, 1496; and conditions for summit meeting, 748–49, 961, 1510–12, 1574–76, 1591–93, 1654–57, 1676–77, 1689–90; on E. as military governor, U.S. Zone, 1746–56; folk song of, 598–99; and Foreign Ministers' Meeting negotiations, 1540–41, 1541–42, 1585–86, 1607–8; and France, 1250–51, 1419–21; on free elections in, 649–59; and German General Staff (1914), 735, 738; Gromyko's proposal, 1585–86; and Ismay's memoir, 2180–88; and Ministry of War (1914), 735; Monty proposes rush to Berlin, 1653–54, 2184, 2188; peace treaty with, 1533, 1540–41; reunification of, 180–81, 191–94, 632–36, 649–59, 721–27, 973–75, 1412–15, 1540–41, 1676–77; surrenders, World War II, 1746–56. *See also* Adenauer, Konrad; German Democratic Republic; Germany, Federal Republic of; Summit Conference (May 1960); Western Summit Conference; World War II

Germany, Federal Republic of (FRG, West Germany): on Adenauer's tenth anniversary as chancellor, 1658; on aid to third-world nations, 2121–23; Baruch's view, 1360–61; Benson visits, 2056–58; Bruce's view, 1020–22; on build-up of military force in, 147–50, 242; on civilian as military governor, 1746–56; and Contingency Planning Group, 1424–26; de Gaulle's view, 1412–15; and demilitarization of, 632–36; and discussions on disarmament, 242; on economic aid to Turkey, 944–45; and EDC, 1658; elections in, 148, 1852–54; and European integration, 242, 2115–18; fights inflation, 310; on financial and economic issues, 2121–23; and force levels in, 1610; and gold outflow, 2121–23; Gromyko's concessions, 1509–10; on June 16th statement, 1601–3; and Marshall Plan, 2121–23; and NATO, 1658; on neutralization of, 632–36; Norstad visits, 125; not to manufacture atomic weaponry, 1887–90; production per man in, 577; and Rapacki Plan, 632–36; restoration of sovereignty in, 147–50; and reunification of, 242, 1496, 1591–93, 1676–77; on selection of MAAGs chiefs, 131–32; as sovereign state, 1658; and Summit Conference (May 1960), 1817–18; and tripartite talks, 1159–62; on Western rights in Berlin, 1520–22, 1540–41, 1585–86; and WEU, 1658. *See also* Adenauer, Konrad; Germany

—Bonn (Capital): E. visits, 1620–21; hosts NAC ministerial meeting, 180, 181

—France: Adenauer's influence on French, 2141–42; de Gaulle promotes ties with

FRG, 1785–87; and de Gaulle's attitude on Berlin, 1250–51; and de Gaulle on tripartite alliance, 2068–73, 2115–18

—Indonesia, military aid to, 1331–32

—NATO: and Blankenhorn, 1437–38; and Italy's jealousy, 181; and ministerial meeting (December 1960), 2172–73; and NATO alliance, 125; and nuclear weapons policy, 2141–42; role of, in FRG, 1419–21; and stockpile system, 2115–18; on strengthening, 1767–68; weaponry capabilities of, 242

—United Kingdom: on purchase of Centurion tanks, 150–51, 206; and reduction of British force in, 147–50, 191–94, 997–98

—United States: and agreement on support for U.S. force, 147–50, 242; Anderson's visit, on balance of payments, 2168–70; on costs of U.S. force in, 147–50, 242; Dulles meets with Adenauer, 1015; E. meets with Adenauer, 1620–21, 1659; and 1960 U.S. elections, 1852–54; purchases U.S. M-48 tanks, 211–12, 242, 265–67, 389–90; and return of vested German assets, 170–71, 242, 1796–97; and Stassen's gaffe on disarmament, 236–38, 247–49; on U.S. support for FRG, 1817–18, 2121–23

—USSR: Khrushchev's view on postwar state, 1844–48, 1887–90; Soviet attitude, 1879–80; and Soviet conditions for summit, 792–93; and Soviet note on atomic weaponry, 191–94

—West Berlin: Adenauer's fear, 1476–77, 2115–18; AFL-CIO supports U.S. stand in, 1576–77; crisis in, 1261–62, 1352–53, 1371–73, 1378–79, 1395–96, 1406–7, 1607–8, 1670–71; as demilitarized free city, 1261–62; E. briefs Kennedy on, 2189–95; Edgar E.'s concern, 1923–24, 1935–41; and Foreign Ministers' Meeting negotiations, 1533, 1540–41, 1541–42, 1607–8, 1610; as "free city," 1817–18; Gromyko's charge on propaganda, 1509–10; Khrushchev's "ultimatum," 1955–56; on *modus vivendi* with Soviets, 1706–8; Soviet threat regarding, 1325–26, 1412–15; and summit negotiations, 1525–27, 1601–3, 1691–92, 1697–1700; and talks with Khrushchev regarding, 1676–77, 1681–82, 1685–86, 1686–87; and time limit on negotiations, 1676–77, 1681–82, 1694–96, 1706–8; troop levels in, 1607–8, 1610; weak tactical position in, 1541–42; on Western rights in, 1591–93, 1601–3, 1676–77, 1852–54

Gerow, Leonard Townsend ("Gee"), 1203–4

Gerow, Mary Louise (Kennedy), 1204

Gettysburg, Pennsylvania: Es. attend Presbyterian church in, 1225; E., Monty visit battlefield, 182–83, 185–86, 240, 1203–4; John E.'s family moves to, 1569–70; on postpresidency welcome, 2073–74; Stuart's role

Gray, Elisha II, 1479
Gray, Gordon: appreciation to, and esteem for, 2246–47; on attendance at OCB, NSC meetings, 2119–20; attends dinner honoring Elizabeth II, 499–500; background, 341–42, 484–85; on Cabinet invitation protocol, 499–500; on deterioration of national railways, 484–85; and effect of oil imports on national security, 340–42, 774–76, 895–96; heads ODM, 341–42, 895–96; heads study of transportation policy, 484–85; on Hotchkis's suggestions, 508–9; and NSC investigation, 1538–40; and NSC meeting on Berlin crisis, 1378–79; and NSC membership, 743–45; and NSC operations, 2189–95, 2246–47; on oil import quotas, 758–59; to plan NSC meetings, 1995–96; on political warfare, 1568–69; and postattack economic plans, 444–46; resigns, 2246–47; on Science Advisory Committee conclusions, 519–20
Gray, James T.: background, 200, 202; on Whitneys' visit to Culzean, 200–201, 202–3, 313–14
Great Britain. See United Kingdom
Great Circle. See Airlines; Civil Aeronautics Board
Great Northern Paper Company, 1148
Greece (Hellenic Republic), 88–89, 1424–26; on cattle for American Farm School, 362–63; E.'s goodwill trip to Athens (December 1959), 1718–19, 1761–62, 1762–63, 1778; and Makarios, 103, 104, 118, 118–19, 167, 168–69; on Makarios and British public opinion, 269–70, 302; on NATO force assignments to SACEUR, 1313–14; on postwar aid to, 179–80, 303–7; seeks U.S. aid, 362–63, 400; on stationing IRBMs in Greece, 1512–13; on Summit collapse, 1953–54; and Truman (1947), 1027–31
—Cyprus, 103, 104, 118, 118–19; and British plan for, 1125–26, 1127–28; considers withdrawing from NATO, 942–44; Greece rejects conference on, 1174–75; independence for, 2009–11; Monty's view, 612–13; NAC considers conflict, 940–42, 942–44; and NATO alliance, 118–19, 612–13, 952–60, 1125–26; and Turkish-Greek settlement on, 1346, 1358–59, 2009–11; and U.N. debate on, 612–13; U.S. attitude regarding, 1174–75; and violence of EOKA, 612–13
Green, Theodore Francis, 1131–33
Greene, Nathanael, 28, 29
Greenewalt, Crawford Hallock, 1813
Greenland (Denmark), role of, in World War II, 414–15
Greentree Stables, 164–65
Greenwood Plantation. See Whitney, John Hay
Greer's Ferry Dam, Arkansas, 1316–17, 1426–27

Grewe, Wilhelm C.: background, 1700; on German assets in U.S., 1796–97; and Western Summit Conference, 1697–1700, 1712–13
Griffin, Charles Donald, 1983–84
Grim, Clair M.: background, 610; on butchering beef, 609–11, 826
Gromyko, Andrei Andreevich: attacks on, as homosexual, 1509–10; background, 248, 249; on Berlin crisis, 1509–10, 1607–8; on conditions for summit meeting, 792–93, 1499–1500, 1509–10, 1520–22, 1525–27, 1585–86, 1610; delivers invitation to summit, 1779; and Dulles's death, 1499–1500; E.'s favorable impression, 1499–1500; Herter's difficulties with, 1585–86; and June 16th statement, 1601–3; and Moscow talks, 1367–68; on pact of non-aggression, 1685–86; on proposals regarding summit, 973–75, 1529–30, 1601–3; proposes all-German committee, 1585–86, 1607–8; on recess of Foreign Ministers' Meeting, 1533; on rights in Berlin, 1601–3; role of, as foreign minister, 248; on West Berlin propaganda, 1509–10
Gronchi, Giovanni, 1769
Gross National Product (GNP), 1198–1200; and foreign trade, 1350–52; Strauss reports on, 1451, 1531
Grover, Wayne Clayton, 938
Gruber, Helen L. (Drennan), 1875–76
Gruber, William Rudolph, background, 1875–76
Gruenther, Alfred Maximilian: addresses SAE convention, 667–68; attends League of Red Cross Societies, 1106–7; attends Red Cross conference in India, 532–34, 543; background, 13–14; birthday greetings to, 743; call me Ike!, 2213–14; as campaign speaker on presidency, 1793–96; on cold war, 707–8; on dinner for Coty, 188–91; E. apologizes to, 13–14; and E.'s Newport "vacation," 457–58; on E.'s news conference, 1303; E. recalls World War II, 1303; esteem of, for Schuyler, 680–81; and fundraising for Dr. Dooley, 1971–73; and Goals Commission, 1507–8, 1722–25, 1812–13; heads American Red Cross, 14, 145, 1152–53; on international role of American Red Cross, 1152–53; on Ismay's health, 2131–32; and Ismay's letter, 1303; on Knowland's gubernatorial candidacy, 1064–68; on Little Rock crisis, 457–58; on Mark Clark, 457–58; meets with E., 215–16; on "Min's" condition, 783–84; on Red Cross post, Lewis's view, 457–58; reports on tennis game, 1106–7; scores E.'s French, 615–16; on speaking tour abroad, 1106–7, 1152–53, 1325–26; on Status of Forces Treaties, 457–58; on Sulzberger's article, 666–67, 667–68; as vice-presidential nominee, 1871;

visits E. at Augusta, 1452–53; visits E. at Gettysburg, 49; and Walker's letter, 707–8; in Wichita, Kansas, 688–89; work schedule of, 1303
—bridge, 532–34, 543; on E.-Gruenther system, 1609–10; on games with E., 137–38, 145, 543, 743, 1452–53; on Jones's game, 854; on Solomon's game, 1609–10; solves a "problem," 49; as undisputed champions, 1325–26
Gruenther, Grace Elizabeth (Crum), 188–91; background, 14
Gruson, Sydney, 1767–68
Guantanamo Bay Naval Base: and Castro, 1456; U.S. position regarding, 2142–43. *See also* Cuba, Republic of
Guaranty Trust Company, and merger with J. P. Morgan and Company, 1252–53, 1311–13
Guatemala, Republic of, 1027–31; and assassination of Castillo Armas, 338–39; coffee prices in, 1292–93, 2086–88; and communism, 512–16, 2086–88; and Development Loan Fund, 1292–93, 2087, 2088; and Dulles, 2211–13; and E.'s goodwill trip (December 1959), 1762–63; and Export-Import Bank, 2087; on Gonzales Lopez as president, 338–39; Milton E. visits, 1218–19; on reply to Ydígoras Fuentes, 1292–93; U.S. aid to, 2086–88; and U.S.-Guatemalan relations, 338–39, 2001–7, 2086–88. *See also* Ydígoras Fuentes, Miguel
Guaymas, Mexico, 1484
Guerra, Manuel, 697–98
Guggenheim, Harry Frank, 1919–23
Guggenheim Foundation, John Simon, 747
Guided missiles. *See* Missiles
Guinea, Republic of: announces Soviet aid to, 1902–4; communism in, 1654–57; declares independence, 1654–57; and East Germany, 1902–4; on foreign policy of, 1902–4; and France, 1250–51; on Morrow as U.S. ambassador to, 1503–4; and North Vietnam, 1902–4; on recognition of Communist regimes, 1902–4; and situation in Congo, 2048–49; and United Nations, 1250–51. *See also* Touré, Sékou
Gulf of Aqaba: discussions on, at Bermuda Conference (1957), 102, 104; as international pathway for pilgrims, 53–55, 296–97, 297–99, 427–31; international waters at, 24, 27, 53–55, 63–64, 98–100, 281, 297–99, 427–31; Israeli forces at, 24, 34–36, 53–55; on Israeli warships at, 194–96, 197–98, 296–97, 297–99; on POL supplies for Jordan, 1013–15; on Saudi Arabia's sovereignty at, 194–96, 197–98, 297–99; U.N. control of, 104, 197–98; U.S. endorses right of free passage, 57–59, 197–98, 281,

297–99, 427–31. *See also* Aqaba; Egypt; Israel, State of; Straits of Aqaba
Gulf of Mexico, and submerged lands claims, 550–51; and Texas offshore oil rights (tidelands), 550–51, 594–96, 893–95
Gulf Oil Corporation, 208–9; and political responsibility, 1135–36
Gulf of Parla, 317–19
Gunderson, Barbara (Bates), 1037
Gunewardene, R. S. S., 962
Gurley, Fred G., 1496–98
Gursel, Cemal, 1974–75. *See also* Turkey, Republic of

Hacker, Louis Morton: on American steel industry, 747; background, 747; E.'s recommendation of, 747; as Guggenheim fellow, 747; reviews Bator's book, 2125–26
Hagerty, James Campbell, 1027, 2226–27; advises E. on National Library Week endorsement, 668–69; advises Stassen on GOP nominees, 1201–2; on announcing scientific achievements, 686–87; apologizes to Dulles on leak, 264; appreciation to, esteem for, 2240–41; assists on State of the Union draft, 663–64; to attend stag dinner, 1568–69, 1612; background, 61–62; on Berlin crisis, 1406–7; on economic recession recovery, 719, 769–71; E. plays hooky at NATO meeting, 620; on E. as teacher, 2240–41; on E.'s tribute to Monty, 948–50; on E.'s visit to Japan, 1978–79; forwards McGill's letter, 538–39; and governor's race in California, 1081; and Hesburgh's invitation, 1825–26; and Krock's view on inflation, 61–62; and *Life* article on E.'s letters, 1423; and McGill's letter on civil rights, 1134–35; and media exposure on budget fight, 1369–71; meets with Markel, 1871–72; on miscommunication with Norwegians, 628–29; and national days of prayer, 1052–53; on 1960 campaign fundraising, 1990–91; on Nixon-Dulles foreign policy statements, 1150–51; notes by, on E.'s talk, 1801–2; on peace-oriented publicity, 686–87; on presidential speech agenda, 1492–94; on question of Bohlen's transfer, 1574–76; on reply to Bulganin, 721–27; resigns, 2240–41; on rumor regarding Khrushchev, 1007–13; on statistics for news conference, 1924–25; on Wilbur's Medal of Honor story, 933–34
Hagerty, Marjorie (Lucas), 2240–41
Haiti, Republic of: on bauxite barter for U.S. wheat, 1542–43; and Castro's aggression, 1601–3, 1710–12; Communist influence in, 1048–49; coup attempt in, 1048–49; on democratic and economic progress in, 1710–12; Duvalier seeks U.S. aid, 1048–49,

Harsco Corporation, 1153–56

Hartley, Robert S.: advises on purchase of heifers, 74; background, 16–17; on breeding Brockmere 10, 885–86; on butchering steers, 825–27; on disposal of inferior livestock, 16–17; Erica heifer wins at Ohio State Fair, 1086; as herdsman on Eisenhower-Allen farms, 16–17; and Pennsylvania Livestock Exposition, 391–92; on Synovex as steer feed, 678–79; takes course on artificial insemination, 126–27; on visiting Strauss's farm, 931–32

Harvard University, 606–7; draft for speech at, 1492–94, 1629–30; and Military-Scientific Dinner, 785; seeks E.'s support for funds, 714–15

Harvey, I. J., Jr., 686

Hasley, Anne S. (Mrs. Raymond G.), 440–41

Hassan, Moulay: background, 1884; on U.S.-Moroccan relations, 1931–33; visits U.S., 1931–33

Hastie, William Henry, 393

Hastings, Kester Lovejoy, 141

Hasty, Mr. and Mrs. Gordon, 1339–40

Hatfield, Mark Odom: background, 1207; as campaign speaker on interior, 1793–96; as governor of Oregon, 1207–8; meets with E., 1861–62; on rebuilding GOP, 1236–39; wins in midterm election, 1236–39, 1239–40

Hatta, Mohammed, 845

Hauge, Gabriel ("Gabe"): addresses Economic Club of New York, 1276–77, 1277–79; and Adler-Leithead exchange, 1039–40; background, 142–43; on budget fight, 1195–96, 1430–31; and Burns's talk on recession, 793–95; and Byrd investigation of financial system, 163; as campaign speaker on treasury, commerce, HEW, 1793–96; cautions on federal budget, 1252–53; commends E.'s economic policy, 982–84; confers with E. on recession recovery, 719, 769–71; on congressional appropriations, 1195–96; defines "monetary policy," 187–88; on domestic and foreign issues, 1329–31; drafts message on U.S. foreign policy, 142–43; E.'s esteem for, 982–84, 1110–11; on E.'s eyeglasses, 1430–31; epigrams by, 1110–11; E. rejects tree analogy, 2089–90; on E.'s speeches, 909–10, 1430–31; on fiscal policy, 1195–96; investments advice for E., 1252–53; on letter by, to *New York Times,* 1195–96; to meet Mikoyan, 1276–77, 1277–79; meets regularly with E., 685–86; and modern Republicanism, 1110–11; on 1958, 1960 elections, 1188–90, 1195–96; on recession recovery, 859–61; on refinancing national debt, 1007–13; resigns, 982–84, 1001–2, 1039–40, 1058, 1110–11,

1116–17, 1128–29, 1195–96; on Rockefeller's governorship, 1430–31; on successor to, 1058; on tax payments in federal bonds, 588–89

Havens, Mrs., 1800–1801

Hawaii, 144, 1105–6; and CAB on trans-Pacific air routes, 2252–54; on election results in, 1606–7; E. plans rest stop in, 1941–42; E. visits Honolulu, 1980–81, 1983–84; and goodwill tour to Far East (June 1960), 1941–42, 1980–81, 1983–84; and Great Circle air routes, 288; statehood for, 1606–7

Hayden, Carl Trumbell, 188–91

Hayden, Nan (Downing), 188–91

Hayes, Rutherford Birchard, inauguration of, 9

Hays, Brooks: background, 426; as intermediary in Little Rock crisis, 426; joins E., Faubus, at Newport, 481–82

Hays, Wayne Levere, 556–57

Hazlett, Edward Everett, Jr. ("Swede"): on arms for Tunisia, 574–79, 736, 738; and Bermuda Conference 1957, 135–36; birthday greetings to, 736; and Bourguiba, 736, 738; on budget cuts, 135–36; on civil rights, 319–25; on Congress, 319–25; and Cordiner Report on retired personnel, 735–36, 738; on crisis in Little Rock, 577–78, 579; death of, 1187; on DOD reorganization, 1167–68; E. attends funeral of, 1187; on economy and recession, 736, 738; E.'s correspondence with, 1187; and E.'s esteem for Adams, 734; and E.'s esteem for Benson, 734; and E.'s esteem for Dulles, 734; E.'s esteem for Macmillan, 135–36; and E.'s esteem for McElroy, 734; on E.'s schedule, 135–36; E. sends flowers to, 59, 276, 797, 1187; and E.'s skeet range at farm, 135–36; on E.'s speeches agenda, 577; E. visits, in hospital, 319–25; and farm subsidies, 735; final letter from, 1167–68; on foreign aid and trade, 319–25; and Gaillard, 736, 738; on German General Staff system, 735, 738; on Girard case, 319–25; on hostile Congress, 1167–68; illness of, 59, 135–36, 275–76, 319–25, 574–79, 733–38, 797, 1167–68; on inflation, 319–25; on interservice rivalries, 735, 738; on intraservice rivalries, 735, 738; on isolationism, 319–25; on loss of temper, 578; on "the louse in Arkansas," 1167–68; on Menshikov, 734, 737; and Mideast crisis, 135–36; on Montgomery's blunder, 734, 737; on mutual security program, 319–25; on Navy football, 736; on "Neanderthal Republicans," 276; on 1958 congressional elections, 735; on nuclear aircraft carriers and submarines, 735, 738; and obsolescence of Navy aircraft carriers, 735, 738; and Pearson's prophecy, 735, 738; on politicians, 734; on postal workers' salaries, 319–25; on recession and partisanship, 735, 736; sitting for sculptors, 135–36; on Soviet arms developments, 574–79; on Suez crisis, 574–79; on Summit Conference, 736, 738; on third-world countries, 319–25; on troublesome French, 574–79, 736, 738; undergoes lung surgery, 827; and unification of services, 735, 738; on U.S. landings in Lebanon, 1167–68; and U-2 overflights, 579

Hazlett, Elizabeth ("Ibby"): background, 135–36; E.'s note on Swede's death, 1187; on E.'s visit to Abilene, 1167–68; on Swede's illness, 827, 1167–68

Heads of Government meetings, 248, 249, 307, 525, 544–45, 556–57, 563–67, 591–92, 617–18, 620, 627–28, 649–59, 721–27, 734, 737, 739–40, 831–34; E. proposes, 1034–36; Khrushchev proposes, 973–75, 1034–36, 1667–69. See also NATO: NATO meetings; Summit Conference (May 1960); Western Summit Conference

Health, Education, and Welfare, Department of (HEW): appropriations for, 1594–97, 1663–65, 2034–35; on education, E.'s appeal, 645–46; on English as universal language, 548; on federal v. private fundraising projects, 37–38; Flemming's budget proposals, 1198–1200; Flemming to head, 968–69; Folsom heads, 37–38; and health care for elderly, 1702–3; and Hobby, 1256–58; on loyalty oath requirements, 1505–7; and Milton E., 645–46, 2148–49; and National Defense Education Act, 1505–7; and OASI, 1064–68; on scientific achievements of, 503–5; and selection of 1960 campaign speakers, 1793–96

Hearst, William Randolph, Jr., 1964–65

Hearst Consolidated Publishing Corporation, and governor's race in California, 1081

Heath, Donald R., 160

Heaton, Leonard Dudley: background, 251; declines Surgeon General post, 251; E.'s esteem for, 251; E. sends Gillette blades to, 1722; and question of presidential disability, 711–14; on reassignment of, 251; receives DSM, 251

Heaton, Sara Hill (Richardson), 1722

Heckett, Eric Harlow: attends stag dinner, 185–86; background, 185–86; on dinner for Coty, 188–91; on entries at Ohio State Fair, 1086; on fiscal responsibility, 1153–56; on labor racketeering, 1153–56; on midterm elections, 1153–56; need for Republican congress, 1153–56; proposes foreign service academy, 1069–70; visits Get-

tysburg farm, 185–86; on welfare state, 1153–56

Heckett, Greta Shield: background, 185–86; on dinner for Coty, 188–91; visits Gettysburg farm, 185–86

Heeney, Arnold D. P., 41

Heffelfinger, F. Peavey, 1949–50

Heidi (the dog), 694

Helicopters: Draper's duties, 558–60; E.'s safety in, 553, 558–60; E.'s use of, for golf, 127–28, 134–35

Heller, Sam Raymond: background, 77–78; and E.'s restored 1942 Cadillac, 77–78; supports Arn for judicial post, 110–11

Hell's Canyon, as campaign issue, 1256–58

Helm, Harold, 196

Henderson, Leon, 494

Henderson, Loy Wesley: background, 390; and Communist influence in Syria, 389–90, 427–31; and foreign service academy, 1069–70; meets with Turks and Iraquis, 429–30; and waivers of non-immigrant visas, 1334

Hendrickson, Dan, 357

Hendrickson, Robert Clymer: background, 357; seeks government post, 357

Hennig, William Henry, 903

Henning, W. L., 74

Herald-Tribune. See *New York Herald-Tribune*

Hering, Earl Lee ("Ig"), 1500–1502

Hering, Lucy, 1501

Herter, Christian Archibald, 273, 1744; as Acting Secretary of State, 1261–62; on ambassadorial appointments, 338–39; attends CENTO meeting, 1915–17; attends OAS meeting, 2051–52, 2058, 2068–73; to attend stag dinner, 1568–69; authority of, at Foreign Ministers' Meeting, 1525–27; background, 42, 82; on balance of payments, 2189–95; on banking introductions for Hobbs, 717–18; on Big Bend recreation area, 1356, 1357; birthday greetings to, 801; on Cabinet invitation protocol, 499–500; on cold war strategies, 1568–69; on communications from Dillon, 1529–30; and Connally reservation, 1823–24, 1851–52; and data on independent nations, 2211–13; and Development Loan Fund, 183–84; and downing of RB-47 airplane, 2008–9; on Dulles's attendance at London talks, 336–37; and Dulles-Chiang-Kai-shek joint communiqué, 1197–98; on Dulles's death, 1486, 1491–92; on Dulles's funeral, 1491–92; E.'s esteem for, and appreciation to, 2242–43; and E.'s goodwill tour (December 1959), 1769–70, 1778; E.'s hope for cold war resolution, 1499–1500; E. nominates, as Secretary of State, 1452; frustrations of, at Foreign Ministers' Meet-

Adenauer, 1476–77, 1852–54, 2172–73;
and note to Soviets on Berlin access, 1261–
62; and NSC meeting on Berlin, 1378–79;
on rights in Berlin, 1591–93, 1601–3,
1610, 1676–77; and tank procurement for
West Germany, 206; on West Berlin propaganda, 1509–10

—Ghana, and Volta River Project, 2037–38,
2162–63

—Haiti, and draft reply to Duvalier, 1048–49

—Hungary, on seating Kadar delegation at
U.N., 1232–33

—Iceland, crisis in, 871

—India: on Indo-Pakistani dispute, 555–56,
1774–76; message to Nehru on Laos,
2227–30; on Nehru's birthday, 1735

—Iran, and Baghdad Pact, 1323–25

—Japan: cancels invitation, 2090–91; invites E.
to visit, 1757–58; and Treaty of Mutual Cooperation and Security, 1959–60

—Jordan, Herter meets with Hussein, 2114–15

—Kashmir, State Department memo on, 146–
47

—Laos: civil war in, 2223–25, 2227–30; and Sihanouk's concern, 2248–50

—Latin America: on cotton subsidies for Mexico, 1355–57, 1357–58; data on aid to,
2211–13; on Diablo/Dos Amigos/Amistad
Dam, 1373; on Garcia's U.S. visit, 771–72;
on Gonzales Lopez in Guatemala, 338–39;
on letter of esteem for Ruiz Cortines,
1211–12; on López Mateos, 1355–57,
1357–58; and Milton E.'s report on Central America, 1244; and OAS meeting,
1601–3; Panamanian grievances, 1827–28;
on Rio Grande dam, 1356, 1357; on Under
Secretary for Latin American Affairs,
1919–23; and U.S.-Argentine relations,
151–52; on U.S.-Panamanian relations,
1744–46, 1827–28

—Malaya, on Rahman's U.S. visit, 1900

—Mexico: on E.'s goodwill tour of Latin
America, 1860–61; and Plowshare Project,
2019–20

—Morocco, U.S. bases and forces in, 1882–84

—Muscat/Oman, dispute regarding, 378–79

—NATO: and Gruson story, 1767–68; Herter
addresses meeting of, 1437–38; Herter attends ministerial meeting, 1769–70, 2189,
2204; on message to Hays, 556–57; and security leak on redeployment, 2204; on U.S.
troop withdrawal, 1769–70

—Netherlands: on civil air agreement with
KLM, 81–82; on Luns's U.S. visit, 1555

—Pakistan: and Baghdad Pact, 1324; on Indo-
Pakistani dispute, 555–56, 1774–76

—Panama Canal Zone: and de la Guardia's
concerns, 1713–15; diplomatic relations
with, 1744–46, 2088–89

—Paraguay, U.S. aid to, 1725–26

—Philippines, and sugar imports quota, 1881–
82

—Poland, most-favored nation status for, 2160

—Scotland, on Polaris facilities in, 2032

—Soviet Union: on cultural, technical, educational exchange, 692–93; on delegation to
accompany E. to, 1850; on E.'s message to
Khrushchev, 1529–30; on E.'s visit to
USSR, 1806–7, 1850; on follow-up talks
with Khrushchev, 1682–83; on Gromyko,
1585–86, 1607–8; Khrushchev misinter-
prets U.S. policy, 1844–48; on Khrushchev's reply, 1533, 1585–86; on Khrushchev's U.S. visit, 1567–68, 1585–86,
1591–93; on McKneally's plans to visit,
1886–87; on meeting with Khrushchev,
1567–68; on missing USAF airmen, 1687–
88; on rebuttal to Gromyko, 1509–10; on
Soviet ideology and policy institute, 1893–
94; on Soviet preemptive buying and economic warfare, 491–93; on Soviet proposals on outer space, 784–85; U.K.-USSR relations, 231

—Summit Conference (May 1960): on Adenauer and Steering Committee, 1817–18;
collapses, 1955–56, 1960; on Geneva as site
for, 1491–92; Gromyko's view, 1607–8;
Herter leaves for Paris, 1915–17; on an informal summit, 1527–29; and interpretation procedures at, 1927–28; Macmillan's
impatience for, 1591–93; on prerequisites
for, 1509–10, 1574–76, 1591–93; on procedures at, 1909, 1927–28; on Quebec as site
for, 1591–93; and reports of allied disunity,
1955–56; on timing and site for, 1591–93,
1593–94; U.S. delegation to, 1850, 1910;
on Western position at Foreign Ministers'
Meeting, 1540–41, 1585–86, 1593–94,
1610

—Syria, on Communist influence in, 383–85

—Thailand, and Cambodia, 1390

—Tunisia, and Bourguiba's letter, 1113–15

—Turkey, and Baghdad Pact, 1323–25

—United Kingdom: Adenauer's view, 1496; on
coordination in U.S.-U.K. policies, 696–97;
Herter attends dinner honoring Elizabeth
II, 499–500; on Lloyd's problem, 1509–10;
on Macmillan/Bulganin correspondence,
231, 234–35; on Macmillan's message from
Moscow, 1359–60; on Skybolt and Polaris
programs, 2139–41, 2147; on tripartite
consultations, 1967–68; U.K.-USSR relations, 231; on U.S. bases in U.K., 2012–13;
on U.S. flights over U.K., 872–73; on U.S.-
U.K. atomic cooperation, 920–21

—United Nations: on address to U.N. Correspondents Association, 1673–75; and delegation to U.N. General Assembly, 335–36;
on Khrushchev's behavior at, 2094–95; on
seating Kadar delegation at U.N., 1232–33

—Vietnam: and Cambodia, 1390; supports Diem, 2138–39
—Western Summit Conference: on arrangements for, 1697–1700, 1712–13; and de Gaulle, 1706–8; Dillon proposes, 1529–30
—Yugoslavia, on military aid to, 376–77
Herter, Mary Caroline (Pratt), 188–91
Hesburgh, Theodore Martin: background, 1825–26; on Notre Dame commencement address, 1839–40; on Notre Dame invitation leak, 1825–26
Hess, Elmer, 2045–46
Heuss, Theodor: background, 181; dinner honoring, 188–91; illness of, 181; visits U.S., 181, 708–9, 739–40. *See also* Germany, Federal Republic of
Hibbs, Ben: background, 2062; on post-presidency writing, 2060–62, 2207, 2222–23
Hickenlooper, Bourke Blakemore: background, 396–99; on Bohlen's transfer, 1577–79
Hickey, E. James, 691–92
High, Dorothy Brown (Cutler), 1213
High, Stanley Hoflund: background, 524; on crisis in Little Rock, 524; E. recalls 1952 campaign, 1212–13; on foreign policy, 2049–50; illness of, 1212–13, 1429–30; on moral and spiritual values, 524; and *Reader's Digest* article on E., 1429–30
Highways, 1153–56; and federal aid for construction of, 760–65; and highway fuel taxes, 1198–1200; and highway trust fund, 1198–1200; and military spending, 817–18; and states' responsibility for regulations on, 282
Hill, Jim Dan, 1203–4
Hill, Robert Charles: background, 83; esteem for, in Mexico, 1356, 1357; on imports of lead/zinc, 992; as U.S. ambassador to Mexico, 83, 1356, 1357, 1380–81
Hill, William Silas: background, 789; and farm bill tactics, 1045–46; and farm program, 787–89; and inflexible price supports, 787–89
Hills, Lee: background, 948; on managing *New York Herald-Tribune*, 947–48, 966–68; and Whitney, 1053–54
Hill School, 2146
Hilton, Conrad Nicholson, 1153–56
Hindus, migration of, to Moslem India, 146–47
Hirohito, Emperor of Japan, 1978–79
Hitler, Adolf, 689, 2181, 2183, 2185, 2186; and German General Staff, 737–38; Russell compares E. to, 462–64
HMS *Britannia,* 1130
Hobbs, Conrad, 1152–53
Hobbs, Leland Stanford, 717–18
Hobby, Oveta Culp: background, 1257–58,

1402–3; as campaign speaker on HEW, 1793–96; as "favorite son" candidate, 1942; as Federal Security Agency head, 1257; as HEW head, 1257–58; on Nixon's North Dakota speech, 1975; supports balanced budget, 1402–3; and Texas election, 1975
Hobby, William Pettus: background, 1402–3; illness of, 1942
Hodgson, Paul Alfred ("P.A."), 1804–5
Hoegh, Leo Arthur: background, 445; heads Office of Civil and Defense Mobilization, 1394–95, 2189–95; on imports of heavy power machinery, 1449–50; on imports and trade restrictions, 1426–27; on maritime labor union fears, 1394–95; on NSC membership, 743–45; and postattack economic plans, 444–46
Hoeven, Charles Bernard: background, 1599; as campaign speaker on agriculture, 1793–96; and message to Congress on surplus wheat crisis, 1598–99
Hoffer, Eric, 1342, 1343
Hoffman, Clare Eugene, 1194–95
Hoffman, Dorothy (Brown), 672
Hoffman, Paul Gray: on Adams's mistakes, 957, 960; addresses New School for Social Research, 671–72; administers Marshall Plan, 436, 437, 661–62, 2243–44; background, 80; and Citizens for Eisenhower, 2243–44; as controversial Republican, 436; and Cyprus, 952–60; and de Gaulle, 952–60; and DOD reorganization, 952–60; East scores, 436; E. comments on speech by, 671–72; and economic recovery from recession, 952–60; E.'s esteem for, 2243–44; E.'s view, 434–37; and France, 952–60; Humphrey protests Hoffman's plan, 115–17; and Indonesia, 952–60; and Lebanon, 952–60; meets with E., 952–60; and mutual aid appropriations, 952–60; and mutual trade renewal, 952–60; on peace prospects, 671–72; proposes foreign aid plan, 78–81; on rebuilding GOP, 1236–39; reciprocal trade, 952–60; sends article, 78–81, 115–17; as spokesman for trade agreements extension and mutual security program, 661–62; suggests message to Nehru, 1213–15, 1215–16; and U.N. Special Fund, 2243–44; urges E. to address U.N., 952–60; urges E.'s candidacy for president, 2243–44; and Vietnam, 952–60; visits Brussels World's Fair, 1104–5; visits E., 952–60; visits Nehru, 1213–15
Hogan, Ben, 137–38
Hoiles, Walter, 1962–63
Holaday, William Marion: background, 292–93, 502; on duplication in guided missile programs, 292–93; as Guided Missiles Director, 502, 545–47
Holland. *See* Netherlands, The

Holland, Sidney George, 846
Holland, Spessard Lindsey: background, 369–72; and civil rights, 1375–78; on Washington, D.C., airport site, 369–72
Hollings, Ernest Frederick, 1858
Hollingsworth, Leon S., 438
Hollister, John Baker, 98. *See also* International Cooperation Administration
Holman, Eugene, 783
Holmes, Julius Cecil, 266
Holy Places of Islam, 98–100, 129–31, 197–98, 296–97, 383–85, 427–31. *See also* Religion; Saud, ibn Abd al-Aziz; Saudi Arabia
Home, Lord. *See* Douglas-Home, Alexander Frederick
Honduras, Republic of: and E.'s goodwill trip (December 1959), 1762–63; Guatemala's protest, 2001–7; Milton E. visits, 1218–19
Honest John, DOD plans phase-out for, 292–93
Hong Kong (British Crown Colony), trans-Pacific air routes to, 2252–54
Hood, Viscount Samuel, 1927–28
Hook, Charles Ruffin: background, 1260; as campaign speaker on postal service, 1793–96; commends Alcorn, 1259–61
Hoover, Herbert Clark: attends stag dinner (1953), 1535; background, 200; and Civil Service Commission, 199–200; on federal interference in economy, 1534–35; meets with E., 200; on middle way, 1534–35; supports National Library Week, 668–69; visits E. (1953), 1535; White House mail load for, 1619. *See also* Hoover Commission
Hoover, J. Edgar: appreciation to, 2257; background, 792; and invitation to Soviet students, 791–92; on Kraft's sermon, 1877; on waivers of non-immigrant visas, 1333–34
Hoover Commission: background, 199–200; Citizens Committee concludes mission, 1095–97; and government appropriations, 199–200; Hoover's complaints, 199–200; recommendations of, 1700–1702; on waivers of non-immigrant visas, 1333–34. *See also* Government Reorganization Plan; President's Advisory Committee on Government Organization; United States Commission on Organization of Executive Branch of Government
HOPE (Health Opportunity for People Everywhere), 2091
Hopkins, Mark, 905–6
Hopkins, William J., 1619; and U.S. Citizens Commission on NATO, 2083–84
Hopwood, Herbert Gladstone, 1983–84
Hopwood, Jean (Fulton), 1984
Horkan, George Anthony, 2033
Hospitals: federal aid to, 823–24, 1663–65, 2034–35; and military spending, 817–18
Hotchkis, Preston: background, 508–9; meets

with E., 572–73; suggests armed forces seminars, 508–9; suggests defense briefings, 508–9, 572–73
Houdon, Jean Antoine, 135–36
Houghton, Amory: to accompany E. to Summit Conference, 1850; on ambassadorial expenses and U.S. taxes, 1651–52; on arms for Tunisia, 563–67; background, 125; and de Gaulle on U.S. withdrawal from NATO, 1767–68; dines with E. at U.S. embassy, 620; on dinner for Coty, 188–91; E.'s esteem for, 125; and fall of French government, 831–34; on French-Tunisian relations, 831–34; meets with de Gaulle, 1919–23; as U.S. ambassador to France, 125
Houghton, Laura DeKay (Richardson): background, 188–91; dines with E. at U.S. embassy, 620; a "grand gal," 1590
Houphouët-Boigny, Félix, 2011–12
House Omnibus Bill of 1958, 1007–13
Houser, Theodore V., 783
House of Representatives, U.S.: and airport facilities bill, 1422–23; on amendments to Atomic Energy Act of 1954, 906–7; cuts funding for Development Loan Fund, 354–56, 1041; defeats farm bill, 1045–46; defeats federal aid for school construction, 417–18, 1307–9; defeats Minerals Stabilization Plan, 991–92, 1111–13; and DOD procurement services legislation, 1054–55; and DOD reorganization, 863–65, 904–5; E. opposes NSC investigation, 1538–40; and farm bill tactics, 1045–46; holds Goldfine in contempt, 1089–91; and Hoover Commission recommendations, 199–200; and House Omnibus Bill, 1007–13; investigates Doerfer, 1841–42; and medical care for elderly, 1702–3; and midterm election, 1193–94; and mutual security appropriations, 1904; and mutual security legislation, 400, 1002, 1041; and natural gas legislation, 213–15; passes civil rights legislation, 274–75, 319–25; passes federal preemption doctrine bill, 925–26; passes foreign aid authorization, 882; passes Landrum-Griffin bill, 1630–31; passes military pay bill, 910–11, 2053–54; passes reciprocal trade bill, 952–60, 1047; passes revised farm bill, 1045–46; passes tax reform bill, 928–29; and Reorganization Act of 1949, 1700–1702; on retired officers pay, 1560–61; sustains E.'s veto, 1054–55; and TVA bond issues, 1583–84; and Washington, D.C., airport sites, 369–72
—Appropriations Committee: and additions to defense budget, 1007–13; and appropriations for medical research, 1594–97; and mutual security appropriation, 354–56, 389–90; Passman blocks mutual aid fund-

53; E. declines visit to Milestone, 1792–93; and Educational Bill, 1007–13; E.'s esteem for, 222–23, 339–40; on E.'s upcoming travels, 1792–93; farewell stag dinner for, 334–35; on federal expenditures, 589–91, 593–94, 1007–13; on financial structure inquiry, 160–61, 163; on flights to/from Milestone, 1338–39, 1339–40, 1349–50; and game laws, 1295; gives cracker barrel to Augusta National Golf Shop, 334–35, 345, 582–83; on GM auto prices, 522–23; on Goals Commission, 1722–25; on grandson's golf game, 394; and Hoffman's foreign aid plan, 78–81, 115–17; and Housing Bill, 1007–13; on Humphrey's golf game, 394; on hunting, 732, 1138–39, 1148–49, 1364–65; on inflation, 310, 522–23; invites E. to Ohio, 1138–39; joins American Assembly board, 218–19; and Lubell's findings, 950–51; and Maritime Bill, 1007–13; may visit Brazil, 1148–49; meets with E., 165, 176–77, 522–23; on midterm campaign fundraising, 1148–49; at Milestone Plantation, 13–14, 43, 49–50, 137–38, 632, 732, 1138–39, 1148–49, 1336, 1338–39, 1339–40, 1349–50, 1364–65; and Mortgage Reinsurance Bill, 1007–13; on mutual security program, 187, 1007–13; on national budget, view of, 44–46, 176–77; and national debt refinancing, 1007–13; and negotiations with Soviets, 1007–13; and Omnibus Farm Bill, 1007–13; plays golf with E., 165, 172–73; portrait of, by E., 1107–8; and Postal Bill, 1007–13; on post for Rouse, 380–81; and problems in Mideast, 1007–13; and Public Works Bill, 1007–13; receives invitation to join Augusta National, 532; recommends Cisler, 289; on red ants in Georgia, 1033; resignation of, 187–88, 218–19, 223–25, 289, 334–35, 339–40, 394; and SEC vacancy, 109–10; sends speech, 522–23; and Simpson, 518; and steel strike, 1626–27; testifies on fiscal and monetary policies, 277–78; on Thomasville, 1138–39, 1148–49; as Treasury Secretary, 1256–58; and U.S. intervention in Lebanon, 1007–13; to visit Brazil, 1148–49; visits Es. at Augusta, 161–62, 165, 176–77; and Wideners, 419

Humphrey, George Magoffin (grandson), 394

Humphrey, Hubert Horatio, Jr., 268

Humphrey, Pamela (Stark): on accident at Milestone Plantation, 1339–40; attends church with Es., 161–62; background, 13–14; on dinner for Coty, 188–91; Es. visit, 13–14, 732; visits Es. at Augusta, 161–62, 165, 172–73

Humphreys, Harry Elmer, Jr., 79, 81

Hungarian Refugee Relief, President's Committee for, 207–8

Hungary, Republic of, 1076–77, 1164–65; on an American window in, 1190–91; E. creates relief committee for, 207–8; on industrial progress in, 1564–65; Khrushchev speaks on conditions in, 721–27; and principle of self-determination, 1878–79; refugees from, flee to Austria, 207–8; on refugees from, in U.S., 529; on seating Kadar delegation at U.N., 1098–99, 1190–91, 1191–92, 1232–33; U.S. relations with, 1076–77. *See also* Kadar, Janos

—revolt in: and Mindszenty, 1190–91; and Nagy's execution, 981–82, 1190–91; and policy for disengagement, 632–36; and Soviet Union, 191–94, 207–8, 1576–77; and U.N. action, 649–59; and Voice of America, 232–33

Hunting: birds, at Blue Springs Plantation, 2166–68, 2168–70, 2174; birds, at Greenwood Plantation, 1364–65; birds, at Milestone Plantation, 732, 740–41, 1033, 1338–39, 1349–50, 1364–65, 1792–93, 2073–74; and "Code of the Shooter," 1831; at Culzean, 200–201, 202–3; on dove shoot at Greenwood Plantation, 662–63; duck hunting with Humphrey, 1148–49; ducks, pheasants, with Jones, 1106–7; on E.'s 1873 sporting rifle, 1800–1801; and game laws at Greenwood Plantation, 1295; in Georgia, 2239–40; Stuarts hunt quail, 1326–27; on turkey and quail hunts, 1033, 2168–70, 2174, 2230–32

Hurd, Maud Rogers: background, 111; E. visits, in Abilene, 1167–68

HUSKY, 1295–98

Hussein ibn Talal, King of Jordan: attacks Nasser, 2114–15; attends Cairo Conference, 100; background, 100; Chamoun's concern on Communist influence in Jordan, 158–60; on Communist influence in Syria, 383–85; E.'s respect for, 173; imposes martial law, 159; Iraqi forces to aid Jordan, 158–60; meets with Herter, 2114–15; and Nasser, 180–81; plot against, 988–90, 1003–7; receives M-47 tanks from U.S., 359–60; Saud's support for, 158–60, 180–81, 194–96; seeks U.S. support, 158–60, 1395–96; speaks at U.N., 2114–15; takes anti-Communist stand, 158–60, 166; visits E., 1395–96, 2114–15. *See also* Jordan, Kingdom of

Hutchison, Harriet Sidney (Thompson), 188–91

Hutchison, Ralph Cooper, 188–91

Hutton, Edward F., 299–300

Hydrogen bomb: on banning, Soviet view, 721–27; and China, 242–43; and federal civil defense, 11–12; Khrushchev's boast, 721–27; and redwing, 216–18; and Science Advisory Committee conclusions, 519–20;

and scientific antagonists, 519–20; and security leaks, 843; Soviets protest frontier flights, 848–49; on suspension of tests, 1060–63; and Teller, 598–99; Wallace's fear, 242–43. *See also* Atomic weaponry; castle; redwing

Ibáñez del Campo, Carlos: background, 709; cancels visit to U.S., 889; and invitation to visit U.S., 708–9; and proposed copper tariff, 708–9, 889–90

Ibn Saud, Abdul Aziz, King of Saudi Arabia until November 1953. *See also* Saud, ibn Abd al-Aziz; Saud Ibn Abdul Aziz Al-Feisal

Ibrahim, Moulay Abdallah, 1884

Iceland, Republic of, 1424–26; crisis in, 871; and Denmark's role in World War II, 414–15; and law of the sea, 749–50, 871, 1652–53

Ichuaway Plantation. *See* Woodruff, Robert Winship

Ickes, Harold Le Clair, 1256, 1257

Idlewild Airport, 137–38

Idris I, King of United Kingdom of Libya, 767. *See also* Libya, United Kingdom of

Ikeda, Hayato, 2090–91

Illinois: and Chicago GOP dinner, 751–52; E. campaigns in, 1138–39, 1170–71, 2062–63; and Great Circle air routes, 406–7; and racketeering in Chicago's restaurant industry, 1153–56; as site for U.S. Penitentiary in Marion, 923–24; Stratton's problems, 2109–11

Immigration: Hungarian refugees protest U.S. policy, 207–8; and visas for Emanuel's servants, 697–98. *See also* Refugees

Immigration and Nationality Act of 1952, 207–8, 1333

Immigration and Naturalization Service (INS): on pre-flight inspections, 1333–34; on Public Law 414, 1333–34; and visas for Emanuel's servants, 697–98; on waivers for non-immigrant visas, 1333–34

Inaugural Day, 1339–40

Inauguration. *See* Eisenhower, Dwight David: Inauguration

Independent nations, E. requests statistical data on, 2211–13

India, Republic of: and Agriculture Fair at New Delhi, 1582–83, 1718–19; border incursions by Red Chinese (Bhutan and Sikkim), 1648–50, 1662–63; Communist influence in, 829; Communists lose in Kerala elections, 829; competes with Red China, 59–60; and crisis in Laos, 2227–30; and crisis in Lebanon, 952–60; Diem visits, 898–99; and division of Indus River waters, 839–40; E. dines with Nehru, 1769–70; and E.'s goodwill trip to New Delhi (De-

cember 1959), 884–85, 1662–63, 1735, 1761–62, 1762–63, 1769–70, 1770–72, 1778, 1976; E. visits, 1648–50, 1662–63, 1718–19, 1735, 1735; and Geneva Conference on Law of the Sea, 1818–19; and ICC in Laos, 2219–21, 2227–30; and Indo-Pakistani dispute, 146–47, 512–16, 555–56, 839–40, 851–52, 884–85, 1791–92; and Jarring report, 555–56; and Kashmir issue, 146–47, 555–56, 839–40, 1774–76, 1919–23; and Kerala, 829; and Khrushchev's endorsement of Cuban Revolution, 2001–7; Khrushchev recommends, at Mideast talks, 1003–7; Krishnamachari visits U.S., 596; and law of the sea, 776–77; Lodge proposes loan to, 464; and messages to Nehru, 1213–15, 1215–16, 1662–63; on Nehru's influence for peace, 1223–24, 1735; Nehru visits U.S., 59–60, 146–47; neutrality of, in cold war, 1223–24; on refugees from Pakistan, 146–47; and Second Five Year Plan, Bowles's view, 59–60; and Summit collapse, 1953–54; surplus agricultural commodities for, 59–60; and Tibet, 1648–50; and trans-Pacific air routes, 2252–54; University of Delhi honors E., 1770–72; U.S. aid to, 59–60; and U.S.-Japan iron ore project in, 1517–19. *See also* Kashmir; Nehru, Jawaharlal; Pakistan, Islamic Republic of

Indiana, on politics in, 1172

Indian Affairs, Bureau of, and funds for building and maintenance, 760–65

Indian Claims Commission Act of 1946, 875–78

Indochina: de Lattre's role in, 952–60; and French colonialism, 952–60; and repatriation of Guinean nationals, 1902–4. *See also* France, Republic of; Vietnam, Democratic Republic of; Vietnam, Republic of

Indonesia, Republic of: A. Dulles reports to NSC on, 844–46; anti-Communist forces in, 844–46; claims West New Guinea, 625–26, 2237–38; Communist influence in, 844–46, 952–60; Communist shipments to, 1331–32; on covert aid to, 844–46; and dispute with Netherlands, 625–26, 801, 844–46; military aid to, 1331–32; on oil reserves in, 368; on rebellion in the Celebes, 1331–32; on rebellion in Sumatra, 844–46, 952–60, 1331–32; receives jet aircraft from Sino-Soviet bloc, 1331–32; and Sukarno's ambitions, 952–60; and trans-Pacific air routes to Java, 2252–54; U.S. aid to, 952–60; U.S. concerns regarding, 952–60. *See also* Sukarno, Achmed

Industry: aid to education by, 527–29, 945–47; and breakdown of "laissez-faire," 1935–41; in Hungary, 1564–65; and industrialization in third-world nations, 85–86; and industrialization in U.S., 434–37; in USSR, 264–65; and volunteerism, 879–80. *See also* Automobile industry; Coal industry; Manufacturers; Maritime industry; Oil industry; Steel industry

Inflation. *See* Economy, U.S.

Informational Media Guaranty program (IMG), and Egypt, 1251–52

Ingrid, Queen of Denmark: attends ballet with E., 2130–31; visits U.S., 2099

Inspectors General: on access to reports by, 1194–95; and weapons procurement, 1284–85

Institute for International Social Research, 1072

Institute of War and Peace Studies. *See* Columbia University

Insurance: on FHA mortgages, 760–65; on health care for elderly, 1702–3, 1919–23; and medical benefits, 1935–41; and Mortgage Reinsurance bill, 1007–13; on national unemployment insurance system, 813–14, 1153–56, 1407–8; and OASI, 1064–68; and railroad unemployment laws, 1496–98

Integration. *See* Civil rights

Intelligence: and political warfare, 1568–69; and security leak following Bermuda Conference 1957, 120; and Soviet technological competence, 1991–93. *See also* Central Intelligence Agency; Dulles, Allen Welsh; Federal Bureau of Investigation

Intemann, Eugenie, 1925–26

Interagency Committee on Agricultural Surplus Disposal, 1622

Inter-American Defense Board, and U.S. naval base at Chaguaramas, Trinidad, 317–19

Inter-American Development Bank: charter for, 1244, 1442–43; E.'s support of, 1442–43; 1488–91; and Export-Import Bank, 1488–91; and International Bank for Reconstruction and Development, 1488–91; to locate in Washington, D.C., 1442–43; and outflow of gold, 2199–2200; structural organization of, 1997–99; on transferring capital to, 1943–44

Inter-American Peace Committee, 2087–88

Inter-American Press Association, E. addresses, 500

Inter-American Treaty of Reciprocal Assistance of 1947 (Rio Treaty), and Cuba, 2001–7

Intercontinental Ballistic Missile program (ICBM): on funding for, 162–63; and Manhattan District missile program, 498; and missile gap, 1342; and progress of research and development, 292–93; on Soviet development of, 519–20, 1141–42; testing of, 104–5, 519–20. *See also* Intermediate

Range Ballistic Missile program; Missiles; Submarines

Interior, Department of: and appropriations for Bureau of Reclamation, 760–65; and appropriations for small reclamation projects, 760–65; on budget and bureaucracy issues, 1545; on oil import quotas, 1457–59; on Oil Imports Appeals Board, 1403–4; and Secretary of the Interior, 1256–58; and selection of 1960 campaign speakers on, 1793–96; and tariffs on lead/zinc imports, 759–60; and uranium mining in U.S. Southwest, 812. *See also* McKay, Douglas; Seaton, Frederick Andrew

Intermediate Range Ballistic Missile program (IRBM): E. calls conference regarding, 347–49; on funding for, 162–63; on manning missiles by U.S. personnel, 729–30; progress of research and development, 292–93, 545–47; on stationing IRBMs in Greece, 1512–13; and U.S.-U.K. agreement on, 729–30; Wilson halts production of Jupiter-Thor missiles, 496–97. *See also* Intercontinental Range Ballistic Missile program; Missiles; Submarines

Internal Revenue, Bureau of, and ambassadorial expenses, 1651–52

Internal Revenue Code, and long-term investments, 886–87

Internal Revenue Service (IRS): on changes to Form 1040, 586–87; and tax auditing procedures, 586–87; and Truman Administration scandals, 1089–91. *See also* Taxation

International Association of Machinists: *IAM* v. *Gonzales*, 925–26; on preemptive legislation, 925–26; and Taft-Hartley Act, 925–26. *See also* Labor unions

International Atomic Energy Agency (IAEA): Johnson supports funding for, 220–21; Republicans oppose, 220–21; as U.S. policy success, 797–99; on U.S.-USSR support of safeguard procedures, 1844–48, 1887–90. *See also* Atomic energy; Atomic Energy Commission

International Bank for Reconstruction and Development (IBRD), 1442–43; Black heads, 95–96; E. addresses, 1675–76; and economic aid for Argentina, 2080–82; and economic aid to free world, 1073–76; and economic aid for Paraguay, 1725–26; and Inter-American Development Bank, 1488–91; meets in New Delhi, 1143–44; on U.S. aid to Japan, 1517–19; and Volta River Project, 637–39, 2037–38. *See also* World Bank

International Boundary and Water Commission, 1373

International Business Machines (IBM), 1136; and antitrust consent decrees, 251–53

International Commission for the Supervision and Control of the Armistice in Laos (ICC), 2219–21, 2248–50
International Commodity Association, 2056–58
International Control Commission (ICC): and civil war in Laos, 2219–21, 2227–30; and Soviet aid to Pathet Lao, 2227–30; and tactics of Polish members, 2227–30
International Cooperation Administration (ICA), 376–77, 675–76; on aid to Ceylon, 961–62; on aid for Haiti, 1710–12; BAC investigates, 1800–1801; background, 97–98; on Cabinet/congressional relations, 549; on constitutionality of withholding funds from, 2214–15; and Fairless Committee recommendations, 97–98; and First Secretary of Government, 695–96, 1700–1702; and French West Africa, 2011–12; Hollister heads, 98; integration of, with State Department, 97–98, 1700–1702; in Kerala, 829; and Milton E., 2148–49; on need for technical personnel, 1918–19; offers support to Dooley, 1971–73; on operations of, in Bolivia, 1019–20; opposes Development Loan Fund, 183–84; and Overseas Missions Program, 1800–1801; on reducing overseas staffs, 2195–96; report by, on Vietnam program, 1733–35; size of, 1800–1801; Slater's view, 196; on strength of, Nielsen's view, 1800–1801; and U.S. aid to Latin America, 2211–13. *See also* Smith, James Hopkins, Jr.
International Cotton Advisory Committee/ Council: and cotton export program, 1357–58, 1398–99; and Mexico, 1485–86
International Court of Justice, 197–98; and Chile-Argentine border dispute, 1859–60; and Connally reservation, 1823–24, 1851–52; and Egyptian-Israeli dispute, 53–55; E.'s view, 2077–78; and Panama, 1713–15; and waterway at Gulf of Aqaba, 296–97, 297–99, 427–31
International Development Association (IDA): and Committee on World Economic Practices, 1311–13; E. supports, 1675–76; as U.S. aid to free world economy, 1073–76
International Development Fund, and Anglo-American alliance, 507–8
International Finance Corporation (IFC), E. addresses, 1675–76
International Geophysical Year, 686–87
International Industrial Development Conference, 342, 439
International Labor Organization (ILO), 1635–36
International Monetary Fund (IMF), 1442–43; E. addresses, 1675–76; on economic aid for Argentina, 2080–82; on economic aid to free world, 1073–76; and economic aid for Turkey, 944–45, 1051; Gbedemah

meets with, 552–53; meets in New Delhi, 1073–76, 1143–44; and U.S. aid for India, 59–60; and U.S. aid to Latin America, 2211–13
International Press Institute, E. addresses, 817–18, 1935–41
International Red Cross: Gruenther attends conference of, 543; and release of downed U.S. airmen, 930–31; and repatriation of Guinean nationals, 1902–4. *See also* American National Red Cross
International Telephone and Telegraph Corporation (ITT), and U.S. private investments abroad, 2051–52
International Village, 1696–97
Interstate Commerce Commission (ICC), 507; on aid to railroads, in recession, 777–82; and national railways, 484–85; and Transportation Act of 1958, 777–82
Investments, 1204–5, 2021–22; and B-A-W Company, 1365–66; and Broomfield Company, 1365–66; in capital goods and jobs, 1353–54; and Columbine Country Club, 2161–62; on cost of foreign investments, 2199–2200; and Dutch Creek Investment Company, 1365–66; by E., for family, 1306; Hauge's advice on, 1252–53; on investors' market, 1500–1502; and Lake View Investment Company, 1365–66; and Middlefield Development Company, 1365–66; on municipal *v.* commercial bonds, 1228; Nielsen's role, 1487; and Turnpike Land Company, 1365–66; and Wynetka Investment Company, 1365–66. *See also* Hauge, Gabriel; Nielsen, Aksel; Roberts, Charles de Clifford
Iowa: and Cowles brothers' criticisms, 1899; E. campaigns in, 1138–39, 1170–71; Khrushchev visits, 1670–71
Iran, Islamic Republic of, 1027–31, 1492–94; Afghanistan threatens, 1773–74; aggression by, in Saudi Arabia, 21–23, 26; and agreement with Standard Oil of Indiana, 1007–13; on Arabi and Farsi islands dispute, 22, 26; and Baghdad Pact, 102, 104, 998–1000, 1323–25; and CENTO defense, 1931, 2096, 2098; and communism, 512–16, 1321–25, 2095–98; and coup d'état in Iraq, 998–1000; and Dulles, 2211–13; on economic aid from U.S., 2095–98; E.'s goodwill trip to (December 1959), 1718–19, 1761–62, 1762–63, 1773–74, 1778, 1781–82; on Eurasian forces threat, 1773–74; on Irani-Afghanistani relations, 2095–98; on Irani-Iraqui relations, 2095–98; on Irani-Israeli relations, 2095–98; Iraq threatens, 1773–74; land reform in, 1772–73; and law of the sea negotiations, 1911–12; and Mikoyan's threat to collective security, 1322; in need of U.S. support, 993–96,

and Straits of Aqaba, 24–25, 53–55, 63–64, 98–100; on withdrawal of Israeli forces, 34–36, 63–64, 72–73, 74–75, 91–93, 98–100
—France, and Mollet's view on conflict with Egypt, 91–93
—Jordan: crisis in, 158–60; and POL supplies for, 1013–15; and reclamation of Jordan River Valley, 293–95; and U.S. aid to, 359–60
—Saudi Arabia: on free passage through Straits of Tiran and Gulf of Aqaba, 281; on Israeli warships at Gulf of Aqaba, 194–96, 197–98, 296–97, 297–99; raids on, by Israelis, 24, 27; Saud proposes destruction of Israel, 603; on sovereignty of, 194–96, 197–98, 297–99, 427–31
—Syria: Communist influence in, 383–85; and overflights to Jordan, 1013–15
Italy, Republic of: Brooke's view, in World War II, 2185–86; and construction of Dutch nuclear submarine, 2102; E.'s goodwill trip to Rome (December 1959), 1718–19, 1761–62, 1762–63, 1768–69, 1769–70, 1778; and English as universal language, 548; and German reunification, 180–81; Italian ambassador of, on Bulganin, 740–41; and jealousy of Germany, 181; Luce resigns as U.S. ambassador to, 518; and NATO force assignments to SACEUR, 1313–14; on selection of MAAGs chiefs, 131–32; Soviets propose attendance of, at summit, 804–6; and tripartite consultations, 1159–62, 1967–68; Tunisia seeks arms from, 563–67. See also Trieste; Yugoslavia, Federal People's Republic of
Ivory Coast. See Africa

Jackson, Charles Douglas ("C. D."): on Anglo-American alliance, 507–8; attends stag dinner, 1612; background, 112, 393; on Berlin crisis speech, 1430–31; birthday greetings from E., 1423; on birthday tribute, 495; on budget battle, 174–76; on cold war strategies, 1568–69; on controlling atomic weaponry, 507–8; declines disarmament post, 695–96; on DOD reorganization, 677–78; drafts disarmament speech for E., 837–38; on Dulles and rule of law, 1158–59; on E.'s address to U.N., 1098–99; on Eastern European satellite nations, 1098–99; and E.'s correspondence with Luce, 1976; on E.'s goodwill tour (December 1959), 1777–78; and E.'s reaction to article, 1423; E. recommends, to Civil Rights Commission, 392–94; on E.'s speech at Orly Airport, 613–14; as favored adviser, 507–8, 613–14, 1098–99; on foreign aid presentation to Congress, 769; on foreign policy speech drafts, 1158–59; on International

Development Fund, 507–8; on "lame duck" presidency, 245; and Life editorial on education, 799–801; on Macmillan's meeting with E., 507–8; meets with E., 677–78; on Mideast development plan, 1098–99; on Mutual Security Program, 154–55, 174–76; on Palestine Conciliation Commission, 1098–99; and party platforms, 245; and Patterson's ideas on Summit Conference, 1915–17; on post-presidency writing, 2222–23; proposes disarmament plan, 837–38; proposes political warfare meeting, 1568–69; proposes speech on Khrushchev's visit, 1670–71; and psychological warfare, 1611–13; as publisher, Life magazine, 1915–17, 2222–23; recalls E. at Algiers, 495; resigns from Radio Free Europe, 1232–33; on return trip from Bermuda Conference (1957), 112–13; on seating Kadar delegation at U.N., 1190–91, 1191–92, 1232–33; sends book on de Gaulle, 1588; sends book on Kremlin, 1915–17; sends Life series on religion, 112–13; on speech drafts for E., 837–38, 1055–56, 1098–99; on State of the Union Address, 663–64, 677–78; and strategies on de Gaulle, 1588; suggests new post for Dulles, 664–65, 695–96; as Under Secretary of State, 695–96
Jackson, Grace (Bristed), 1778
Jackson, Henry Martin: background, 1539; and cold war strategy, 1991–93; criticizes NSC, 1538–40
Jacob, Edward Ian Claud, 948–50
Jacoby, Neil Herman, 1228–30
Jamaica: Dulles visit, 1258; and Federation of British West Indies, 317–19
Jameson, Frank Gard, 1582
Jameson, Henry B.: background, 924; on federal facility in Abilene, 923–24; on second-class postal rates, 1944–45
Japan, 1492–94; and air freight system, 1445–46; on BOAC air routes via Tokyo, 1599–1601; cancels E.'s visit, 1978–79, 1980–81, 1982–83, 2090–91; Communist disorders in, 1985–86; competes with U.S. tuna fishers, 1562–63; concerns of, on nuclear testing, 473–74; on currency conversion for Ryukyu Islands, 919–20, 1049–51; Diet adjourns, 919–20; Diet approves treaty, 1959–60; and E.'s goodwill tour to Far East (June 1960), 1941–42, 1978–79, 1982–83; and foreign trade policies, 1445–46, 1799–1800; on Girard case, 259–61, 319–25, 435, 437; gives E. vase, 616–17; on Great Circle air routes to, 288, 406–7; on fishing rights in Sea of Japan, 512–16; and inflation, 310; invites E. to visit, 1757–58, 1766–67, 1790–91, 1806–7, 1900; and Japanese Import-Export Bank, 1517–19; Korea's hatred of, 512–16; and Kurile Islands,

857; on land compensation question, 1049–51; living standards in, 319–25; and mob influence on Kishi, 1995–96; and Okinawa base, 827–29, 857, 1049–51; prime minister of, visits E., 268; proposes suspension of nuclear testing, 473–74; and trans-Pacific air routes to, 2252–54; on Treaty of Mutual Cooperation and Security, 1959–60, 1985–86; on underwriting Japanese Export-Import Bank, 1517–19; on U.S.-Japanese relations, 1982–83, 2090–91; and U.S. policy toward Ryukyus, 827–29, 1049–51; and USSR, 857; on U.S.-USSR talks, 2111–13; and U-2 flights, 1959–60. *See also* Ikeda, Hayato; Kishi, Nobusuke

Jarring, Gunnar Valfrid: background, 555–56, 989–90; protests U.S. intervention in Lebanon, 988–90; reports on Indo-Pakistani dispute, 555–56

Java. *See* Indonesia, Republic of

Javits, Jacob Koppel ("Jack"): background, 745; on Connally reservation repeal, 1851–52; proposes labor-management conference, 1832–33; and public membership on NSC, 743–45

Jefferson, Thomas, 2124

Jefferson National Expansion Memorial, 1094–95

Jenner, William Ezra, 878

Jessup, John Knox, 800

Jewkes, John, 706–7

Jews: and Arab-Israeli conflict, 19–27; Finder's view, 53; and 1960 election, 1869–70; voters in U.S., 26. *See also* Israel, State of; Religion: Jews

Jodl, Alfred Gustav, 2185, 2188

Johns Hopkins University: awards honorary degrees to E., Macmillan, 815–16, 835–36, 1404–6; on E. as trustee of, 2178–79; Macmillan speaks at commencement, 815–16, 835–36; Milton E. as president of, 714–15, 815–16, 1780–81, 2148–49

Johnson, Claudia (Taylor) ("Lady Bird"), 188–91

Johnson, Douglas Valentine, 1988

Johnson, Joseph Blaine, 583

Johnson, Lyndon Baines: Anderson replies to, 878–79; background, 70; and Big Bend recreation area, 1356, 1357, 1380–81; and delegation to U.N. General Assembly, 335–36; on dinner for Coty, 188–91; E. congratulates, 2156; on foreign aid appropriations, 1041; introduces civil rights legislation, 1375–78; and López Mateos, 1380–81; and missile gap investigation, 1342; on Morrow's appointment, 70; and NSC investigation, 1538–40; on oil import quotas, 774–76; proposes "Open Curtain," 249–50; protests USIA funding, 220–21; and question of presidential disability, 711–14;

scores E. Administration, 878–79; seen as betraying South, 2052–53; as Senate Majority Leader, 70; supports E. on U-2 incident, 1943; supports IAEA, 220–21; supports Mutual Security Program, 220–21; supports space bill, 1016; supports Trade Agreements Extension Act, 1016; on Texas submerged lands, 550–51, 594–96; and Tidelands Act, 550–51; and U.S. relations with Mexico, 1380–81; wins 1964 election, 2165–66

Johnson, U. Alexis, 1102

Johnston, Eric A.: and American films for Africa, 1828; background, 293–95; meets with E., 1828; plan by, for reclamation of Jordan River Valley, 293–95, 408–10; role of, in Trade Agreements Extension and mutual security programs, 661–62; seeks bipartisan support for mutual security program, 740–41, 1027–31, 1039–40

Johnston, Lemon and Company, 1536–37

Johnston, Marjorie C., 548

Johnston, Olin Dewitt, 1375–78

Joint Chiefs of Staff (JCS): and civil war in Laos, 1670–71, 2223–25; on concept and function of, 518–19; and coordination in strategic planning, 2099–2100; on crisis in Taiwan Straits, 1085–86; and DOD reorganization plan, 807–8, 888, 904–5; on force levels in Turkey, 303–7; on force reductions in ROK, 387–88; and guided missile programs, 347–49; Kissinger proposes reorganization of, 343–44; and Navy League, 836–37; and political crisis in Laos, 2219–21; on Quemoy and Matsu, 1139–41; receive Mills's letter, 862; on resumption of nuclear testing, 1627–28; on U.S.-U.K. nuclear cooperation, 936–37; and U-2 incident, 1943; White's blunder, 347–49; on withdrawal of U.S. forces from Lebanon, 1034–36. *See also* Lemnitzer, Lyman L.; Radford, Arthur William; Twining, Nathan Farragut

Joint Committee on Atomic Energy. *See* Congress, U.S.: Joint Committee on Atomic Energy

Joint Federal-State Action Committee, 419–23, 2035–36

Joint Policy Declaration, and Republic of Korea, 314–16

Joint Resolution of Congress (January 29, 1955), and defense of Formosa, 263–64, 1131–33; Promote Peace and Stability in the Middle East (March 7, 1957). *See* Eisenhower Doctrine

Joint Strategic Target Planning Staff (JSTPS): investigation of, 2135–36; and national strategic target list, 2099–2100; and single integrated operational plan, 2099–2100

Jones, Arnold R., 269

Jones, Charles S.: and ADA-CIO philosophy, 1064–68; attends birthday dinner, 157; background, 157; in California with E., 1812–13; on California gubernatorial race, 1064–68, 1089–91; on domestic and foreign issues, 1330; E.'s appreciation to, 1181; and E.'s esteem for Knowland, 1064–68; forwards Loker's letter, 1361–62; as fundraiser in midterm elections, 1181; and Gosden story, 1630–31; on Knowland's gubernatorial candidacy, 1064–68, 1070–71, 1089–91; on OASI, 1064–68; on Republican principles, 1064–68; and RNC Committee on Program and Progress, 1259–61; supports labor bill, 1630–31

Jones, Genevieve ("Jenny"), 1181

Jones, Mary (Malone), 670

Jones, Nettie Marie (Marvin): background, 164; hospitality of, 2174; visits Es. at Augusta, 164

Jones, Robert ("Bobby") Tyre, Jr.: background, 670–71; on bridge with E., 874–75; on Calamity Jane putter, 1709–10; and E.'s painting of Augusta's 16th hole, 1107–8; on exploding number five wood, 874–75; on gift book for E., 670–71; and heavy greens at Augusta, 1709–10; and Masters tournament, 1709–10; on painting for Golf House, 670–71; portrait of, by E., 670–71; sends Spalding clubs, 699, 874–75

Jones, Sam Houston, 1347–48

Jones, William Alton ("Pete"): on Aswan Dam negotiations, 532–34; at Augusta National Golf Shop, 334–35; background, 13–14; and bedtime story on national debt, 1566–67; at Blue Springs Plantation, 2166–68, 2168–70, 2174; on bridge with E., 164, 543, 660–61, 854, 1651–52; on bridge with Gruenther, 532–34; on congressmen, 383; at Culzean with E., 1650–51, 1660; Es. celebrate birthday of, 157; as E.'s confidant, 1089–91; and E.'s faith in economy, 512; E. leaves pistol at Blue Springs Plantation, 2174; entertains E. at West Greenwich, R.I., 1106–7; on E.'s portrait of, 382–83; on E.'s visitors from Indian School, 2218–19; on gift to Army Distaff Foundation, 2198–99; gives money to David, 532–34; on Goals Commission, 1812–13; golfs with E., 164, 1812–13; hunts birds with E., 732, 2166–68, 2168–70; joins E. at Culzean, 1651–52; on Knowland's gubernatorial candidacy, 1070–71; on locating show barn, 126–27; meets with Nasser, 532–34; on Petroleum Advisory Council, 660–61; and Pitzer schoolhouse, 126–27, 177–78, 178–79; purchases Brandon and Redding farms, 126–27; suffers dental problems, 164, 178–79; supports Citizens for Eisenhower-Nixon, 1070–71; as teacher of bridge, 854;

visits Es. at Augusta, 164, 178–79; visits E. at White House, 532–34, 660–61, 2174; visits Gettysburg farm, 126–27, 137–38

Jordan, Kingdom of: and Anglo-Jordanian mutual defense treaty, 158–60; and Arab nationalists, 158–60; attends Cairo Conference, 23, 27, 72–73, 100; and Baghdad Pact, 159; Benson reports on trade trip to, 2056–58; British difficulties in, 102; Chamoun's concern on Communist influence in, 158–60, 2056–58; and Communist influence in Syria, 383–85; disarmament efforts in, 275–76; on economic and military instability in, 158–60; Egypt's influence on, 293–95; and Eisenhower Doctrine, 158–60; E.'s view, 173; fears Soviet power, 408–10; fights Communist influences, 166; forms Arab Union, 705–8; and Nasser, 180–81, 293–95; in need of U.S. support, 988–90, 993–96, 1007–13; and plot against Hussein, 988–90, 1003–7; on POL for, 1013–15; political uncertainty in, 293–95; receives M-47 tanks from U.S., 359–60; and reclamation of Jordan River Valley, 293–95; riots in, 158–60; Saud's support for Hussein, 158–60, 180–81, 194–96; seeks wheat for seeding, 2056–58; on U.K. forces in, 993–96, 1013–15; and United Arab Republic, 705–8; U.S. offers economic aid to, 158–60; U.S. policy regarding, 158–60, 194–96; U.S. sends arms to, 427–31; on withdrawal of forces from, 1034–36, 1183–84. See also Hussein ibn Talal

Jordan River Project (Eric Johnston Plan), 293–95, 408–10

Josephs, Devereux Colt, 783–84

Joyce, Kenyon Ashe, 28

Joxe, Louis, 1988

J. P. Morgan and Company, and merger with Guaranty Trust Company, 1311–13

Judd, Walter Henry: background, 336; defends Dulles, 640; as delegate to U.N. General Assembly, 335–36, 640

Judea, 88–89

Judiciary: on appointment for Arn, 110–11, 382; on appointment for Bantz, 1254–55, 1403; on appointment of federal judges, 756, 1292, 1343–45; on appointment for Gould, 818; on appointment for Mason, 507; on appointment for Watkins, 1273–74; and civil rights legislation, 354–56, 375, 530–31; and Court of Claims, 1273–74, 1292, 1581–82; and crisis at Little Rock, 462–64, 482–83; Hutton's view, 299–300; and selection of 1960 campaign speakers on, 1793–96. See also Justice, Department of; Supreme Court of the United States; United States Government: judicial branch

Junior Chamber of Commerce, 1393–94

Jupiter missile program, 347–49; Army postpones Jupiter-C rocket launch, 686–87; and Army's satellite reconnaissance project, 498; on funding for guided missile program, 162–63. *See also* Missiles

Jupiter-Thor: an overlapping missile program, 292–93; Wilson halts production of, 496–97. *See also* Missiles

Justice, Department of: announces pipeline investigation, 570–71; and antitrust legislation, 208–9, 251–53; on appointment for Dethmers, 1721; on appointment of federal judges, 756, 1343–45; and automobile dealers' franchise rights, 208–9; and Bricker amendment, 60–61; and civil rights legislation, 328–31, 1337, 1375–78; and crisis at Little Rock, 425–26; and Danish shipping case, 414–15; favors states' right to prosecute Communists, 875–78; federal support for, 1188–90; on increase in juvenile crimes, 2098; and Indian land claims, 875–78; investigates Du Pont on antitrust violation, 741–43; investigates quiz show scandals, 1729; and issuance of visas, 1333–34; and management-labor problems, 929–30; on question of presidential disability, 76–77; and selection of 1960 campaign speakers, 1793–96; Shuman's view, 1290–91; and Strauss nomination hearings, 1446–47; and suit against ALCOA, 208–9; and tidelands litigation, 550–51, 594–96, 893–95; on Witt's retirement, 1720–21. *See also* Judiciary; United States Government: judicial branch

Juvenile delinquency: E. schedules speech on, 1492–94; E.'s view, 2020–21; on increases in, 2098

Kadar, Janos: background, 1191; regime of, in Hungary, 1190–91; on seating delegation of, at U.N., 1190–91, 1191–92, 1232–33. *See also* Hungary, Republic of

Kaiser Engineering Company, 2037–38

Kaiser International, 2162–63

Kamp, Joseph P., 1106–7

Kaneohe Marine Corps Air Station, 1983–84

Kansas, 382; E. campaigns in, 1138–39, 2136; and Eisenhower Presidential Library Commission, 1904–8; exhibits Churchill paintings, 715–16

—Abilene: E.'s campaigns in, 1746–56; and family burial site, 1156–57, 1173–74, 1571; and high school yearbook prophecies, 574; on moving Paul E.'s remains to, 1571; seeks federal facility, 923–24. *See also* Eisenhower, Dwight David: trips; Eisenhower Foundation; Eisenhower Museum

Kant, Immanuel, 799

Kappel, Frederick Russell, 1417

Karamanlis, Constantine: background, 119; on

Cypriot and NATO alliance, 118–19, 613; E. urges restraint, 940–42; seeks U.S. aid to Greece, 362–63; seeks U.S. intervention on Cypriot question, 613, 940–42; and Turkish-Greek settlement on Cyprus, 1346. *See also* Greece

Kasavubu, Joseph, 2170–71. *See also* Congo, Republic of

Kashmir: E. reports to Macmillan on, 146–47; and Indo-Pakistani dispute, 146–47, 512–16, 555–56, 839–40, 884–85, 1774–76, 1791–92, 1919–23; Nehru's view, 146–47; on plebiscite, 146–47; U.N. role regarding, 146–47, 555–56. *See also* India, Republic of; Pakistan, Islamic Republic of

Kass, Garfield, 1304

Katz, Milton, 138–40

Kean, Robert Winthrop, 680

Keating, Kenneth Barnard: background, 1171; and Rockefeller-Keating slate, 1170–71; wins New York midterm election, 1239–40

Keefer, Cornelia (Mrs. Frank R.), 710

Keefer, Frank, 710

Keeney, Barnaby Conrad, 1523–24

Kefauver, Carey Estes: and antitrust legislation, 251–53; background, 252; protests Strauss nomination, 1446–47

Keita, Modibo, 2100–2102. *See also* Mali, Republic of; Senegal, Republic of

Keller, William S., 2045–46

Kellogg, Marion Knight, 694

Kellogg-Briand Pact. *See* Pact of Paris

Kemper, James Scott, 2110

Kendall, Charles H., 214

Kendall, David Walbridge: background, 1395; on Doerfer investigation, 1841–42; on post for Reed, 1914–15

Kennedy, Donald Sipe, 570–71

Kennedy, Jacqueline Lee (Bouvier), 2063

Kennedy, John Fitzgerald: on Adenauer, 2189–95; A. Dulles briefs, on foreign issues, 2189–95; advice to, on reorganization, 2189–95; Anderson briefs, on budgetary issues, 2189–95; announces candidacy, 1886; and Assistant to the President, 2189–95; on Atomic Energy Commission, 2189–95; on atomic tests moratorium, 1886; on atomic weaponry, 2189–95; background, 1886; on balance of payments, 2189–95; on balancing budgets, 2189–95; on ballistic missile proposal, 2189–95; and Benson, 2056–58; on Berlin, 2189–95; on Bureau of Budget, 2189–95; on Cabinet, 2189–95; on Camp David, 2189–95; on Canada's role in free world defense, 2189–95; carries New York, 2157–58; as Catholic candidate, 1963–64; on Central Intelligence Agency, 2189–95; on Civil Service Commission, 2189–95; on civil war in Laos, 2248–50; on Congress, 2189–95; on Council of Economic Advi-

1591–93, 1601–3, 1604–5, 1614–15, 1615–16, 1618, 1628–29, 1631–32, 1635–36, 1647, 1659, 1662–63, 1669–70, 1670–71, 1673–75, 1678, 1683–84, 1757–58, 1766–67; on meeting with American governors, 1567–68; meets with Rockefeller, 1632–34; and memorandum on talks with Khrushchev, 1685–86, 1686–87; on missing USAF airmen, 1687–88; on political influence of U.S. workers, 1576–77; and U.S. economic challenge, 843–44, 1415–16; on U.S. labor and Berlin crisis, 1576–77; on U.S. recognition of United Arab Republic, 1003–7; on U.S.-USSR arms and space race, 1901–2; on U.S.-USSR trade relations, 1482; and U-2 incident, 1943, 1950–51; "We will bury you," 1415–16, 1953–54

—Western Summit Conference: E. keeps Khrushchev informed, 1718–19; on need for, 1718–19; on timing of summit, 1757–58

Khrushchev, Nina (Petrovna), 1684

Khrushchev, Rada (Mrs. A. I. Adzhubei), 1684

Khrushchev, Sergei N., 1684

Khrushchev, Yuliya N. (Mrs. Gontar), 1684

Killian, Elizabeth (Parks), 1580

Killian, James Rhine, Jr.: on atomic test inspections, 1374; attends NATO meeting, 618; background, 545–47; as candidate for USMA Thayer Award, 968–69; E.'s esteem for, 1579–80; on engineering and science scholarships, 609; on federal role in satellite production, 659–60; and Goals Commission, 1812–13; and Humphrey's advice on federal budget, 589–91; Krock's esteem for, 1502–3; on Macmillan's test ban proposal, 1444–45; medallion for, 1579–80; and NASA, 1502–3; on NSC membership, 743–45; on Price and ANP, 752–53; resigns, 1502–3, 1579–80; and seismic research program, 1399–1402; as Special Assistant, NSC, 743–45; as Special Assistant on Science and Technology, 503–5, 545–47, 560–61, 574, 598–99, 609; on technical experts as disarmament inspectors, 901–2; on U.S. educational needs, 645–46; and yearbook prophecy, 574

Killian Committee. See Office of Defense Mobilization: Science Advisory Committee

Kim, Daeyung, 2016–18

Kimbrough, James Claude, 2045–46

Kimpton, Lawrence A., 1725

King, Martin Luther, Jr., 479

Kirk, Alan Goodrich, 1271–73

Kishi, Nobusuke: on atomic testing, 473–74; background, 473; on currency conversion for Ryukyu Islands, 919–20, 1049–51; Japan cancels E.'s visit, 1978–79; and Japan's sensitivity to nuclear weaponry, 473–74; and land compensation question, 1049–51;

mob influence on, 1995–96; receives golf clubs from E., 1693; on Treaty of Mutual Cooperation and Security, 1959–60; on U.S. force in Lebanon, 988–90; visits U.S., 919–20. See also Japan

Kissinger, Henry Alfred: background, 343–44; book by, on atomic weaponry, 343–44, 358

Kistiakowsky, George Bogdan: to attend stag dinner, 1612; background, 1628; and Joint Strategic Target Planning Staff study, 2135–36; and resumption of nuclear testing, 1627–28; on Richter scale, 1813–14; and threshold concept, 1813–14; and underwater atomic tests, 1627–28

Klein, Herbert G.: background, 1594; and Nixon's nomination, 2018–19

Kline, Allan Blair, 1793–96

KLM Royal Dutch Airlines, and civil air agreement with U.S., 81–82

Klutznick, Philip M., 336

Knight, Goodwin Jess: background, 1067, 1202; and "Big Switch," 1064–68; as California candidate for Senate, 1064–68; as governor of California, 1064–68, 1201–2; loses Senate race in midterm election, 1193–94; promises Nixon support, 1201–2; and Stassen's view on midterm election, 1201–2

Knowland, Helen Davis (Herrick): background, 188–91; and Kamp's pamphlet, 1106–7

Knowland, William Fife: background, 71; and "Big Switch," 1064–68; breakfasts with E., 376–77, 399; and California politics, 1064–68, 1089–91; as candidate for California governor, 1064–68, 1070–71, 1089–91, 1106–7; and civil rights legislation, 346; Dart's fundraiser for, 1181–82; and delegation to U.N. General Assembly, 335–36; on dinner for Coty, 188–91; disappoints E. in foreign relations, 952–60; and E. Administration, 376–77, 396–99; E.'s esteem for, 346, 396–99, 1064–68; and farm program, 787–89; on First Secretary of Government, 675–76; Howard's view, 255; irritates Jones, 1064–68; on links with Kamp, 1106–7; loses midterm election, 1193–94, 1236–39; proposes National Freedom Board, 675–76, 865–66; and right-to-work issue, 1123–24; scores reciprocal trade bill, 952–60; seen as conservative, 396–99; seen as moderate, 1070–71; as Senate Minority Leader, 71–72; on Stassen's charges, 1201–2; supports E. on Mideast aid resolution, 71–72; on U.S. relations with Yugoslavia, 376–77

Knox, Lorraine P.: attends E. at Fitzsimons Hospital, 373–74; background, 373–74; birthday greetings to, 814–15; on E.'s goodwill tour to Europe, Asia, Mediterranean, Near East, and North Africa (December 1959), 1783–84; on jet travel, 1783–84; on People-to-People program, 1783–84

Knuckles, Mason K., 1815–16

Knudsen, Thorkild R., 1071

Knudsen, Valley (Filtzer), 1071

Koenig, Pierre Joseph: background, 1273; and World War II reunion, 1271–73, 1523, 1558–59

Koger, Carline E.: attends E. at Fitzsimons Hospital, 373–74; background, 373–74; transfers to Fort Bragg, 1097–98

Kohler, Foy David, 1594

Kohler, Walter Jodok, Jr.: background, 399; loses Wisconsin special election, 399, 433

Komarek, Ed, 1364–65

Konigsberg v. State Bar of California et al., 875–78

Korea, Democratic People's Republic of (North Korea): and Chinese Communists, 1101–2; on downing of U.S. plane, 930–31. *See also* Korean War

Korea, Republic of (South Korea) (ROK): as ally in free world, 1514; civil unrest in, 1933; on Communist infiltration in, 1263–64; and Democratic party, 1263–64; Diem visits, 898–99; E. visits Seoul, 1980–81, 1982–83; on freedom and self-restraint, 2016–18; and "Grandfather Ike," 2016–18; and hatred of Japan, 512–16; and Liberal party, 1263–64; overthrow of Rhee, 1995–96; Rhee retires, 1933; on Security Law revision, 1263–64; and support for mutual security program, 1947–49; on suppression of political opposition, 1263–64; and trans-Pacific air routes to, 2252–54; Truman sends U.S. force to, 993; on U.S. role in military aid, 314–16, 1514; on U.S. role in military force reduction, 314–16, 387–88. *See also* Korean War; Rhee, Syngman

Korean War, 512–16, 1153–56; contributory cause of, 1991–93; and GI bill, 458–60; and Truman, 1027–31; and Unknown Soldier, 892

—Armistice Agreement: Dulles's role in, 2211–13; and modernization of ROK weaponry, 314–16; as U.S. policy success, 797–99; violations of, by Communists, 314–16

Kornitzer, Bela, 830–31

Kosaka, Zantaro, 2090–91

Koslov, Frol R. *See* Kozlov, Frol R.

Kostelanetz, Andre, 188–91

Kozlov, Frol R.: background, 1529; E. proposes meeting with Khrushchev, 1567–68; and Khrushchev-E. correspondence, 1585–86, 1604–5; and Soviet exhibit in New York, 1529

Kraft, Joseph, 1871

Kraft, Virgil A.: admires Castro, 1875–76; background, 1876; condemns the "military mind," 1875–76; FBI investigates, 1877; scores American businessmen, 1875–76; sermon by, 1875–76, 1877

Kremlin. *See* Soviet Union

Krishamachari, Tiruvallur Thattai, 596

Krock, Arthur: background, 61–62; on DOD reorganization, 908–9; editorial by, on foreign aid, 121–22; E.'s esteem for, 1044–45, 1502–3; on E. as socialist, 1383; on Freeman's biographies of Washington and Lee, 691–92; on Hickey's esteem for E., 691–92; and responsible journalism, 1935–41; writes column, "In the Nation," 1045; writes on inflation, 61–62; writes on Killian, Strauss, 1502–3

Kubitschek de Oliveira, Juscelino: background, 104–5; E. replies to, 924–25, 1997–99; E. visits, 1997–99; and guided missiles tracking station in Brazil, 104–5; and Inter-American Development Bank, 1997–99; on inter-American economic cooperation, 1242–44, 1997–99; on Operation Pan America, 1242–44, 1997–99; on Pan American action in cold war, 925–26. *See also* Brazil, Federative Republic of

Kuchel, Thomas Henry, 361–62

Ku Klux Klan, 1108–10

Kurile Islands (Kuriles), and Soviet-Japanese relations, 857

Kurtz, L. A., 292–93

Kuwait: on Arabi and Farsi islands dispute, 22, 26; Communist threat to, 1481–82; oil production in, 102, 104; threats to, from UAR, Iraq, 1481–82

Kyes, Roger M., 777–82. *See also* Defense, Department of

Labor: and age discrimination, 1863–64; and Blough's speech, 1824–25; and collective bargaining, 741–43; divergence of views on, 1282–83; and federal pay bills vetoes, 444; Javits proposes conference, 1832–33; Jones supports labor bill, 1630–31; on labor costs and economic security, 1181–82; on leadership by, to defeat inflation, 1007–13; and McClellan Committee investigation, 1153–56; on management-labor problems, 929–30, 1144, 1165–67, 1727–28; and midterm elections, 1100; opposes DOD reorganization, 878–79; on racketeering investigation, 1153–56; and right-to-work issues, 1070–71, 1123–24, 1165–67, 1193–94; and State of the Union Address, 1282–83; supports U.S. stand in Berlin crisis, 1576–77; on wage demands and recession, 803–4. *See also* Economy, U.S.; Labor unions; Management; Steel industry; Taft-Hartley Labor Relations Act of 1947

Labor, Department of: appropriations for,

1663–65, 2034–35; and economic recession recovery, 718–19; and Federal Advisory Council on Employment Security, 1381–82; and First Secretary of Government, 695–96, 1700–1702; and foreign trade expansion, 1671–72; and 1960 campaign speakers on, 1793–96; on problems with management, 929–30. *See also* Labor; Labor unions

Labor, Secretary of. *See* Goldberg, Arthur Joseph; Mitchell, James Paul

Labor unions: and collective bargaining, 741–43; on congressional investigation of featherbedding, 777–82; E. scores leaders of, 1144; on farmers' unions, 1895–98; fight Taft's bid for reelection, 1950, 1070–71; on labor-management issues, 1144; on maritime labor union fears, 1394–95; oppose Knowland's bid for governor of California, 1070–71; and right-to-work issues, 1070–71, 1106–7, 1165–67; on secret ballots in labor law, 674; and steel strike, 1582–83, 1626–27; and Teamsters racketeering activities, 587, 1153–56; on "work rules," 1727–28. *See also* American Federation of Labor; Congress of Industrial Organizations; Labor; Steel industry; Taft-Hartley Labor Relations Act of 1947; Teamsters, International Brotherhood of; United Mine Workers

Lachner, Marshall Smith, 1185–86

Ladgham, M. Bahi, 746

Laher, F. J., 361–62

Lahoud, Salim, 293–95

Laird, Melvin Robert ("Mel"), 1594–97

Lamaseries (a monastery of lamas), 799, 801

Lambert, Marion L. J. ("Mickey"), 301

Lampe, Erwin J., 1217–18

Landes, George, 431–32

Landrum-Griffin Labor Reform Bill, 674, 1153–56, 1630–31

Lane, Jack F., Jr., 424–25

Lange, Halvard Manthey, 628–29

Langer, William, 396

Langley, James McLellan: background, 885; on Indo-Pakistani dispute, 884–85, 1774–76; on takeover of Pakistani government, 1147; as U.S. ambassador to Pakistan, 885

Lanham, Henderson Lovelace, 391

Laniel, Joseph, 113

Lansing, Robert, 1369

Laos, Kingdom of: and Boun Oum, 2219–21, 2248–50; civil war in, 1670–71, 2219–21, 2223–25, 2226–27, 2227–30, 2248–50; and communism, 512–16, 2219–21, 2223–25, 2227–30, 2248–50; on Dooley's hospital, 1971–73; and ICC, 2219–21, 2227–30; Macmillan's concern, 2219–21; and Neo Lao Hak Zat, 2227–30; and Pathet Lao, 1670–71, 2219–21, 2223–25, 2227–30; on

refugees from, in Cambodia, 2248–50; SEATO pledges protection to, 2223–25; and Sihanouk's concern, 2248–50; and Souvanna Phouma, 2219–21, 2227–30; Soviet air drops in, 2227–30; and U.N. anticolonialism resolution, 2219–21; U.S. aid to, 1670–71; U.S. policy in, 2227–30; and Vientiane accords of 1957, 2227–30; and Vietminh, 2219–21, 2223–25, 2227–30. *See also* Savang Vatthana

La Quinta Country Club, 1859

Lardner, John, 670–71

Larmon, Sigurd Stanton ("Sig"): accompanies E. on vacations, 49; background, 49; and bridge hand "problem," 49; on remedies for GOP, 1216–17; on State of the Union Address, 663–64; visits Jamaica, 49

Larson, Arthur: argues for USIA funding, 220–21; background, 545–47, 561; and bipartisan issues, 843–44; on credibility for VOA, 232–33; and Declaration of Common Purpose, 544–45; and documentary publications, 937–38; drafts speech on defense, scientific achievements, 545–47, 561; E.'s appreciation to, 663–64; edits E.'s speech, 774; on E.'s speech to editors, 797–99; on E.'s speech to GOP congressmen, 843–44; on foreign aid appropriations, 537; on law over force project, 996–97; and People-to-People program, 364–66; resigns, 1039, 1116–17; and rule of law for peace project, 1038–39; on speech ideas from Mencken, 671; as USIA director, 232–33

Latin America: and Act of Bogotá, 2088; and anti-Nixon demonstrations, 899–900; Benson visits, 2080–82; Castro's aggression in, 1601–3, 2244–45; on Chilean students' letter, 1884–85; and Chile-Argentine border dispute, 1859–60; and collapse of Summit Conference (May 1960), 1953–54; and Committee for Inter-American Affairs, 1242–44, 1244; and cotton exports, 1398–99; and Cuban living standards, 2039–42; on developing purchasing power, 319–25; on Dulles and E.'s visit to, 631; E. entertains foreign ministers of, 1108–10; on E.'s goodwill tour (December 1959), 1761–62, 1762–63; on E.'s goodwill tour to (February/March 1960), 1780–81, 1784–85, 1827–28, 1842–43, 1852–54, 1860–61, 1882–84, 1953–54; E., Milton E. visit Mexico, 1354–55, 1355–57, 1357–58, 1363, 1375, 1380–81; on hemispheric solidarity, 1457–59; on hostile nationalism, 1230–32; and Inter-American Development Bank, 1442–43, 1488–91, 1943–44, 1997–99; on inter-American economic cooperation, 1242–44, 1875–76; Kubitschek's view on Pan American issues, 924–25; López Mateos tours, 1784–85, 1860–61; Macmillan

Lee, William Lecel: background, 1300–1301; as E.'s flight instructor, 1300–1301, 1736; on promotion for, 1300–1301

Lee, William Myers ("Billy"), 1866–67

Leeward Islands, and Federation of British West Indies, 317–19

Leffler, Ross Lillie, 1057

Legislative leaders: and antitrust suits against drug companies, 891; and Army Distaff show, 2093–94; on bipartisan support, 1164–65; and cold war issues, 512–16; and concern on federal spending, 1007–13; on Congress and preemption doctrine, 925–26; and Connolly Amendment, 1851–52; cooperation by, in security matters, 1538–40; Democrat, decline meeting with E., 1239–40; Democrat, and natural gas legislation, 213–15; discuss appropriations for medical research, 1594–97; discuss Cowles brothers' criticisms, 1899; discuss current issues, 1007–13; discuss farm bill tactics, 1045–46; discuss farm problem, 787–89; discuss U.S. trade with Communist China, 204–5; discuss White House appointments, 396–99; E. meets with, 604–5, 1520–22; E. proposes business manager post, 1700–1702; E. proposes First Secretary of Government, 1700–1702; E. proposes predeparture discussions with, 1743–44; and flexible price supports, 787–89; and foreign aid program, 220–21; and foreign policy, 1150–51; hear E. on foreign aid, 220–21; hear E. on midterm elections, 1135–36, 1137–38, 1141–42, 1143–44; hear report on Bermuda Conference 1957, 113–14; hear Slater on foreign aid operations, 196; and Hoover Commission recommendations, 1095–97; on lead/zinc imports, 759–60; and meetings with, 578; and message to Congress on surplus wheat crisis, 1598–99; and National Defense Education Act, 1007–13; on pay rates for retired officers, 1245–47; and preemptive legislation, 925–26; and proposed summit, 728–29; on public works expenditures, 760–65; and Salk vaccine, 891; and tax reform, 886–87; on U.S. support of Baghdad Pact, 998–1000

—Republican: and compulsory health insurance, 1919–23; on French-Tunisian conflict, 746; on funding mutual security program, 769; and GOP apathy, 1137–38, 1143–44; and GOP solidarity, 253–55; to meet with E., 1239–40; receive new Lincoln pennies, 1304–5; score Stratton, 2109–11; on support for Baghdad Pact nations, 998–1000

Leithead, Barry T.: on Adler's complaint, 1039–40; background, 867; on cooking steaks, 868–69; develops cataract, 1364–65; on foreign aid legislation, 1039–40; on Hauge at Manufacturers Trust, 1039–40; joins E. at Milestone Plantation, 1336, 1349–50, 1364–65; on Milton E. as Father of the Year, 892–93; on "Muskateers" in Europe, 939–40, 964–65, 1001–2; on 1960 election problems in New York, 2143–45; plays golf with E. at Augusta, 866–67, 868–69; sends steaks, 868–69; supports DOD reorganization bill, 1039–40; to take shotgun lessons, 1364–65

Lemieux, Albert Arby, S.J., 1963–64

Lemnitzer, Lyman L.: background, 314, 315; leaves U.N. command, 388; negotiates with Rhee on ROK force reduction, 314–16, 387–88. See also Joint Chiefs of Staff

Lemon, James Hanson: background, 1205; E.'s esteem for, 1204–5; E. recommends to Tkach, 1204–5; and gift to church building fund, 1536–37; on Washington Mutual Investors Fund, 1204–5

Lewis, Fulton, Jr., 457–58

Lewis, John Llewellyn, 1393

Liberalism: in California, 1064–68; and centralization of power, 2123–24; E.'s view, 2123–24; and GOP liberals, 396–99, 1193–94; and Nixon, 1935–41; and press, 483–84; and Taft, 233–34

Liberia, Republic of, Nixon visits, 168

Liberts, Ludolfs, 153–54

Library of Congress, and Churchill's papers, 1535–36

Libya, United Kingdom of, 869–70; combats Nasserism, 168; on effective use of propaganda in, 993–96, 1250; and law of the sea, 1911–12; Nasser's influence in, 1250; Nixon visits, 168; and refugees at Tunisia-Algeria border, 766–67; on U.S.-U.K. aid to, 869–70. See also Idris I

Life magazine: and article on E.'s letters, 1423; E. commends editorial on education, 799–801; endorses E. Administration, 1991–93; on Jackson as publisher, 1915–17; and Luce, 1976; on post-presidency writing, 1808, 2222–23; publishes Churchill's *Second World War*, 1780; and series on religion, 112–13; and Wilbur's Medal of Honor story, 933–34

Lincoln, Abraham, 133; addresses House, 1328; bronze of, gift from Whitney, 137–38; busts of, 135–36; as congressman, 1332–33; E.'s esteem for, 691–92; E.'s portrait of, 710; E. schedules speech on, 1492–94; failures of, 1332–33; and GOP, 1961–62; on government of, by, for people, 1341; and Lincoln pennies, 1304–5; as master of expressive prose, 799–801; and middle-of-the-road philosophy, 1961–62;

on role of government, 1153–56, 1328,
1935–41
Lincoln Day, and GOP, 751–52
Lincoln Sesquicentennial Commission: appointments to, 587–88; E. speaks at annual
dinner, 1338–39; E. speaks at inauguration
of, 587–88
Lindbergh, Anne Spencer (Morrow), 188–91
Lindbergh, Charles Augustus, 188–91
Lindsay, John Vliet: background, 1207; on rebuilding GOP, 1236–39; wins in midterm
election, 1207–8, 1236–39
Lippmann, Walter: background, 867; E.'s view,
866–67; as irresponsible journalist, 1935–
41, 2168–70
Liquor industry, 2177–78
Litchfield, Edward Harold: addresses Chamber
of Commerce, 1956–59; background, 393;
on corporate voluntary action, 1956–59; E.
declines University of Pittsburgh post,
2178–79; E. recommends, to Civil Rights
Commission, 392–94; on foreign markets
and tariffs, 1956–59; on life expectancy,
1956–59; on management-labor statesmanship, 1956–59; on meaning of knowledge,
1956–59; on medical achievements, 1956–
59; on personal responsibility, 1956–59; on
retirement ages, 1956–59
Litchfield, Joan M., 439–50
Lithuania, 1164–65; Soviet relations with, 1322
Little, William L., 432–34
Littlejohn, Robert McGowan, 2033
Little Rock, Arkansas. See Civil rights: Little
Rock, Arkansas
Livestock, growers support Benson, 812. See
also Agriculture, Department of; Gettysburg
farm
—beef: on Black Angus for American Farm
School in Greece, 362–63; on breeding
Scottish bulls, 326; on butchering steers,
825–27; on cattle for Khrushchev from E.,
Strauss, 1766–67, 1790–91; on curing steer
meat, 597, 1226–27; on disposal of inferior
Angus, 16–17; import-export regulations
on, 185–86; on preparing hamburger
meat, 597; on steer sale prices, 817; on
Stratford Hall herd, 868; on Synovex as
steer feed, 678–79
Lleras Camargo, Alberto, 1953–54
Lloyd, John Selwyn Brooke, 1241–42; on Aden
as "Free World outpost," 104; and Allen,
1704–5; attends Bermuda Conference
(1953), 101, 103; attends NAC ministerial
meeting, 180, 181; background, 103; and
Baghdad Pact, 104; on British economic
problems, 644–45; on Buraimi Oasis conflict, 102, 104; on Communist influence in
Syria, 389–90; on conditions for summit
meeting, 782, 1591–93, 1601–3; on coordi-

nation in U.S.-U.K. policies, 696–97; on
crisis in Cyprus, 1127–28; on crisis in Iceland, 871; and Cuba's aggression in
Caribbean, 2001–7; on de Gaulle and
NATO, 1250–51; delivers tirade on Nasser,
101; Douglas-Home succeeds, 2094–95; on
Dulles-Chiang Kai-shek talks, 1197–98; and
Dulles's death, 1491–92, 1499–1500; on
E.'s draft reply to Bulganin, 642–44; E.'s
esteem for, 1509–10, 1510–12; on E.'s visit
with Elizabeth II, 1616–17; on foreign ministers' negotiations, 1541–42, 1601–3; on
FRG purchase of U.S. tanks, 389–90; and
Geneva Nuclear Test Conference, 1058–
59, 1438–39; on invitation to Camp David,
1397–98; Khrushchev proposes meeting on
Mideast, 1020–22; and Khrushchev's reply,
1533; on Lebanon's demands, 869–70; on
Libya, 869–70; London press reports on,
1509–10; on Mideast problems, 993–96;
on Muscat/Oman dispute, 378–79; on
procedures at Summit Conference, 1909,
1927–28; role of, as foreign minister, 248;
on seating Kadar delegation at U.N., 1232–
33; on Suez Canal crisis, 101–2, 180, 181;
trade with China, 204–5; on tripartite consultations, 1967–68, 1987–88, 2027–28;
urges Dulles attend Baghdad Pact meeting,
642–44; on U.S.-Cuban relations, 2001–7;
on U.S.-U.K. aid to Libya, 869–70; on
world opinion regarding atomic testing,
1060–63. See also United Kingdom
Loch Linnhe, Scotland, 1989–90, 2009–11
Lodge, Emily (Sears), 1684
Lodge, Henry Cabot, Jr. ("Cabot"), 1744; on
Adenauer, 1852–54; applauds Meany's appointment, 464; assists in Khrushchev's
visit, 1683–84; assists on State of the Union
draft, 663–64; background, 336; on Cabi-
net/congressional relations, 549; as campaign speaker on presidency, foreign affairs, 1793–96; commends E. in Little Rock
crisis, 464; on defense of Lebanon, 984–
86, 1003–7; as delegate to U.N. General
Assembly, 335–36; and DOD reorganization plan, 811; and Dulles's speech at U.N.,
442–43; E.'s appreciation to, 2056; encourages E.'s candidacy, 1746–56; on Khrushchev's speech at U.N., 2078–79; on letter
from, 636–37; on loose talk from DOD,
843; on Menshikov, 1682–83; and Mideast
development plan, 1098–99; on Muscat/
Oman dispute, 378–79; and 1960 election
problems in New York, 2143–45; on opposition to unification of armed services, 811;
on promoting U.N. policies, 636–37; on
rebuilding GOP, 1236–39; recommends
Kissinger's book, 343–44; recommends
loan to India, 464; on seating Kadar dele-

Luke, Marion I., 611
Lumumba, Patrice, 2031. *See also* Congo, Republic of
Luns, Joseph Marie Antoine Hubert: attends NATO meeting at White House, 1437–38; background, 1437; as Dutch foreign minister, 1437; on KLM airlines route, 2256–57; meets with E., 1555; as NAC president, 1437–38; to visit U.S., 1555. *See also* Netherlands, The
Lusk, Hall Stoner, 1861–62
Lutz, William C., 518–19

McAdam, Charles Vincent, Sr.: and Alexander's columns on E., 1545–46; background, 1546; golf with, 1545–46, 2050; and post-presidency writing, 1802, 2050, 2092–93
McAdam, Marguerite (Wimby) ("Peg"), 2050
MacArthur, Douglas: background, 479–80; birthday greetings to, 1315; and Bonus March, 479–80; E. opposes Medal of Honor for, 933–34
MacArthur, Douglas II: background, 920; on cancellation of E.'s Japan visit, 1982–83; on currency conversion for Ryukyu Islands, 919–20, 1049–51; Japanese attacks on, 1982–83; and land compensation question, 1049–51; on U.S. policy toward Okinawa, 827–29, 1049–51
MacArthur, Laura Louise (Barkley) ("Wahwee"), background, 1983
McCabe, Edward Aeneas: background, 863; drafts reply to Hoffman, 1195; on national defense education bill, 980–81; on right-to-work issue, 1165–67
McCabe, Thomas Bayard, 153–54
McCaffree, Mary Jane: background, 188–91; Cabinet rank and invitation protocol, 499–500; on dinner for Coty, 188–91; on entertainment for Elizabeth II's visit, 261
McCallum, John, 1949–50
McCann, Kevin Coyle: assists with Catholic Charities speech, 2120–21; background, 68–69; birthday greetings to, 2120–21; on foreign aid, nationalism, 179–80; returns to Defiance College, 673; on student exchange with Soviets, 673
McCann, Ruth (Potter), 2121
McCann-Erickson, Incorporated, 795–96
McCarthy, Frank, 1705–6
McCarthy, Joseph Raymond: background, 399; death of, 399; East's view, 434–37; and special election for Senate seat of, 433–34
Macaulay, Thomas Babington, 1556–57
McChesney, Donald S., 509–10
McChord Air Force Base (Tacoma, Washington), 1163–64
McClellan, Harold Chadick, 1597–98
McClellan, John Little: background, 1155; and

McClellan Committee labor racketeering investigation, 1153–56, 1165–67
McClellan Committee. *See* McClellan, John Little
McClendon, Sarah Newcomb: apologizes, 840; background, 187–88; on E.'s golf, 840; on monetary policy, 187–88; on public works, 840
McCloy, John Jay ("Jack"): addresses MIT, 873–74; addresses War College, 873–74; as adviser to missile program, 501–2; background, 502; on DOD reorganization, 863–65, 873–74, 878–79; interservice rivalries, 873–74; and unification of services, 873–74
McCone, John Alex: and atomic reactor concepts, 1311; on atomic test moratorium, 1068–69; attends Pope Pius XII's funeral, 1144–45; background, 393; chairs AEC, 1064–68; on construction of Dutch nuclear submarine, 2102; E. recommends, to Civil Rights Commission, 392–94; on E.'s speech, 560–61; on Geneva Nuclear Test Conference, 2064–65; holds news conference, 1311; on Macmillan's test ban proposal, 1444–45; reports on Norstad's health, 1952–53; on White House swimming pool privileges, 1056
McCone, Rosemary (Cooper): background, 561; on White House swimming pool privileges, 1056
McConnaughey, George Carlton, 280
McConnell, Joseph Howard, 2251–52
McConnell, Robert Earl, 1216–17
McCormack, John William: background, 188–91; on dinner for Coty, 188–91; favors bipartisan conference on Formosa crisis, 1120–21; on report of E.'s sleeping, 1283
McCormack, M. Harriet (Joyce), 188–91
McCormick, Kenneth Dale, 2077
McCormick, R. L., 946
McCrary, John Reagan, Jr. ("Tex"): background, 489; on New York politics, 488–89; on Nixon's candidacy in 1960, 1870–71; sends *Esquire* article on Nixon, 1870–71; supports Rockefeller for New York governor, 488–89; on vice-presidential nominees in 1960, 1870–71
McCrum, Marie, 614
McDonald, David John: background, 1728; on Blough's speech, 1824–25; scores Cooper, 1727–28; on steel strike negotiations, 1727–28, 1824–25
McDonnell, James Smith, Jr., 1430–31
McDonnell, William Archie, 1430–31
McDonough, Gordon Leo, 1016
McElroy, Mary Camilla (Fry), 1478
McElroy, Neil Hosler: addresses American Legion, 1141–42; on advisers for missile program, 501–2; on appreciation of scientists,

785; on atomic test policy, 1627–28; on authority for IRBMs in Greece, 1512–13; background, 478; on balloon incursions, 1031–32; and Cabinet committee on wages and prices, 1042–43; calls ANP "disgrace," 753; as campaign speaker on presidency, defense, 1141–42, 1793–96; on closing Fort Polk, 1347–48; and Contingency Planning Group, 1424–26; on critics of DOD in midterm campaign, 1141–42; on currency conversion in Ryukyu Islands, 919–20; and Declaration of Common Purpose, 544–45; on Defense Orientation briefings, 572–73; and defense policies, 2211; on discipline and responsibility in armed forces, 1031–32; on disclosure of atomic weapons storage sites, 1031–32; and DOD reorganization, 585–86, 677–78, 735, 737, 904–5; E.'s esteem for, 593–94, 735; on federal role in satellite production, 659–60; Gates succeeds, 1810; on Hotchkis's suggestions, 508–9, 572–73; and Humphrey's advice on federal budget, 589–91; on inflatable satellite project, 1000–1001; Khrushchev scores, 1453–56; and Larson's speech, 545–47; on loose talk and leaks, 843; on maritime labor union fears, 1394–95; and military pay bill, 910–11; and Military-Scientific Dinner, 785; on missile development programs, 496–97; on overtime work in missile production, 496–97; on pay for proficiency flying, 1421–22; on political warfare, 1568–69; on publicity for young Republicans, 524–25; on Quarles as successor to, 1475–76; on Quemoy and Matsu, 1139–41; on recommendations for Air Force Academy, 1255; on role of DOD public affairs officers, 1289–90; on Schuyler as Norstad's successor, 1298–99; as Secretary of Defense, 477–78, 501–2, 593–94, 1477–79; and service academy student exchange, 688–89; and service integration, 735, 737; on Soviet border violations, 1031–32; on Soviet nuclear tests suspension, 819–22; and Sputnik, 593–94; on successor to, 1477–79; on successor to Quarles, 1477–79; on technical experts at disarmament inspectors, 901–2; and U.S. flights over Arctic, 843; on U.S. flights over U.K., 872–73; on U.S. naval forces command structure in Mediterranean, 1313–14; and U.S. policy toward Ryukyus, 827–29; on U.S.-U.K. atomic cooperation, 544–45, 920–21; as vice-presidential nominee, 1871; visits Japan, Korea, 1141–42; on weapons systems procurement program, 1284–85. *See also* Defense, Department of

McElvain, Joseph E., 1222–23

McGill, Ralph Emerson: article by, on conservatism, 2123–24; background, 538–39;

on civil rights and integration, 1087–88, 1134–35; on Conference of Southern Governors, 538–39; on conservatives and liberals, 2123–24; and Cooper Union speech, 1826–27; on crisis in Little Rock, 486; E. scores writings of, 2230–32; and Goldwater, 2123–24; on Kennedy's appointments, 2230–32; on middle way, E.'s view, 2123–24; on Miller's editorial, 538–39; on post–Little Rock crisis, 538–39, 834–35; on school closings, 1134–35; and states' rights, 2123–24; on Wiley-Milhollen Civil War book, 1826–27; writes on cracker barrel mentality, 582–83; writes on Killian's appointment, 574; on yearbook prophecies, 574

McGonigle, Arthur T., 757

Machiavelli, Niccolo di Bernardo, 799

McKay, David O., 1116–17

McKay, Douglas, 1256, 1257. *See also* Interior, Department of

McKinley, William, 399

McKinney, R. L., Jr., 853–54

McKneally, Martin Boswell, 1886–87

McLaren, Norman Loyall ("Blackie"): background, 350–51, 1066, 1068; and Knowland's gubernatorial candidacy, 1064–68; on Suhrawardy's visit to Bohemian Grove, 350–51

McLeod, R. W. Scott, 145

McMahon, James O'Brien (Brien), 1754, 1756

MacMahon, Lloyd F.: background, 897; on funds for Knowland's gubernatorial candidacy, 1070–71; on pledges for Citizens for Eisenhower-Nixon 1958, 897–98

Macmillan, Dorothy Evelyn (Cavendish), 390

Macmillan, Helen Artie (Belles), 1648

Macmillan, Maurice Harold, 1241–42, 1877–78; addresses House of Commons, 739–40, 2012–13; appreciation to, 1648, 1650–51; and AQUATONE, 107–9; attends Bermuda Conference (1957), 87, 100, 112–13, 120, 128–29, 146–47, 150, 247, 248; background, 63–64; and Baghdad Pact, 102–4; and Bermuda Conference security leak, 113–14; birthday greetings from, 495–96, 2129–30; on BOAC air routes, 1599–1601; and British economy, 75–76, 150–51, 166, 168, 644–45, 1496; on British elections, 1691–92; and British oil possessions, 332–34; as British Prime Minister, 63–64; broadcast by, 642–44, 662–63; on Buraimi dispute, 102, 104, 332–34; on Chaguaramas as British West Indian capital, 317–19, 332–34; on Churchill's visit with E., 1471; on Commonwealth tour, 662–63, 728–29; considers trip to Latin America, 1973; discusses Kashmir with E., 146–47; on discussions with A. Dulles on atomic weaponry, 1396–97; and discussions on Africa, 1424–

Churchill's paintings, 111–12; on U.S. flights over U.K, 872–73; and U.S. intervention in Lebanon, 984–86; and U.S. mutual aid program, 389–90; on U.S.-U.K. air operations, 935, 936–37; on U.S.-U.K. military atomic cooperation, 936–37, 1024–25, 1060–63; on U.S.-U.K. staff planning, 1481–82; on U.S.-U.K. ties, 491–93, 507–8, 521–22, 526–27, 544–45

—Western Summit Conference, 1614–15, 1615–16, 1691–92, 1697–1700; de Gaulle opposes, 1706–8, 1708; Western powers agree to meet, 1718–19

McNamara, Andrew Thomas: background, 141; as Quartermaster General, 141, 143–44, 2033; on rank and retirement of, 2033

McNamara, Robert Strange, 2211

McNaught Syndicate, and post-presidency writing, 1802, 2050, 2092–93

McNeil, Wilfred James, 199–200

McPherson, Leo A., 2127–28

McRae, James Wilson, 1068

Madagascar, and French colonialism, 952–60

Madison, James, publication of papers of, 937–38

Madison Square Garden: and Billy Graham's crusade, 363–64; and rally for E.'s candidacy, 1746–56

Magliore, Paul Eugene, 1712

Magnuson, Warren Grant, 1447

Magruder, Lloyd Burns, 2053–54

Maharbal, 2188

Mahendra Bir Bikram Shah Deva, King of Nepal: dissolves government, 2250–51; to visit U.S., 1779. *See also* Nepal, Kingdom of

Maine: and food stamp plan, 1688–89; midterm election in, 1106–7

Maine Chance Farm, 733, 1293–94, 1339–40

Maiwandwal, Mohammad Hashim, 2136–38

Makarios III, Archbishop and Ethnarch of Cyprus: arrest of, by British, 103, 104; background, 104; on Cypriot independence, 169; Macmillan's view, 118, 168; opposes conference on Cypriot dispute, 1174–75; release of, 103, 104, 118, 167, 168–69; Skouras, and British public opinion, 269–70, 302; speaks before U.N., 169; visits New York City, 169. *See also* Cyprus

Malaya, Independent Federation of: boycotts South African goods, 2074–76; Champion visits, 1900; and Rahman, 1868–69, 1900, 2074–76; and trans-Pacific air routes to, 2252–54; U.N. position on apartheid, 2074–76; U.S. position on apartheid, 2074–76; and West New Guinea, 2237–38. *See also* Rahman Putra al-Haj, Tunku Abdul

Mali, Republic of: background, 2100–2102; Dean as charge d'affaires ad interim, 2100–2102; on Mali-Senegal split, 2100–

2102; U.S. aid to, 2100–2102; U.S. recognition of, 2100–2102; U.S. sets up consulate at Bamako, 2100–2102. *See also* Keita, Modibo

Malik, Charles, 47

Mallory v. *United States,* 875–78

Mamie's Cottage; Mamie's Cabin: background, 157; and David E.'s portrait, 670–71; on donors to, 2251–52; Es. entertain at, 157. *See also* Eisenhower, Mamie Geneva Doud

Management: and Blough's speech, 1824–25; Burns speaks on, 793–95; E. speaks on, 858–59, 861, 879–80; Javits proposes productivity conference, 1832–33; and management-labor problems, 929–30, 1144, 1727–28; opposes DOD reorganization, 878–79; and right-to-work laws, 1165–67; and Taft-Hartley Act, 1737–39; and Teamsters Union tactics, 587; on "work rules," 1727–28. *See also* Labor; Steel industry

Manhattan Engineer District. *See* United States Army Corps of Engineers

Manhattan Project, 498

Manila Pact. *See* SEATO

Mann, Thomas Clifton, 1244

Mann, Woodrow Wilson, 460–61

Mannheim (Germany), 2183, 2188

Manning, Fred M., Sr., 239

Manning, Hazel, 239

Manning, J. E. ("Jack"), 890

Manpower: on need for scientific, 527–29, 534–35, 560–61, 645–46, 945–47, 980–81; on reduction of military manpower, 649–59. *See also* Human resources

Mansfield, Maureen (Hayes), 188–91

Mansfield, Michael Joseph ("Mike"): background, 188–91; on dinner for Coty, 188–91; on downing of RB-47 airplane, 2008–9; and executive privilege, 1733–35; requests ICA report on Vietnam, 1733–35

Mansure, Edmund F., 952

Manufacturers: and automobile dealers' franchise rights, 208–9; and illicit liquor manufacturing, 2177–78. *See also* Industry

Manufacturers Trust Company, 1039–40; and budget fight, 1416–17

Mao Tse-tung, 2004

Marcel, Gabriel-Honoré, 801

March of Dimes, Roosevelt's role in founding, 37

Margaret Rose, The Princess, 1816

Maritime industry: E. vetoes Maritime Bill, 1007–13; and labor union fears, 1394–95; on law of the sea, 749–50, 776–77; and merchant marine, 987–88; tanker shortages in, 18–19. *See also* Egypt: Suez Canal; Geneva Conferences on Law of the Sea; Oil industry; United States: foreign trade

Markel, Lester, 1871–72

irresponsibility of, 641–42, 1935–41; and *Kansas City Star,* 1935–41; on liberal press, 483–84; on McGill's views, 2230–32; on "new" E., 1545–46; on *New York Herald-Tribune,* 2168–70; on Pearson as "housefly," 1546–47; pessimistic predictions by, on OVERLORD, 1746–56; and *Philadelphia Bulletin,* 1935–41; and *Philadelphia Inquirer,* 1935–41; quotes E. on Civil War generals, 240; reacts to Sputnik launch, 641–42; *Rocky Mountain News* on U.S. businessmen, 1856–57; scores E. on Gettysburg farm supports, 676–77; on the "silly season for reporters," 134–35; on Strauss as Secretary of Commerce, 1446–47; supports de Gaulle on Algeria, 1673–75; on U.S.-U.K. libel laws, 1935–41; and U-2 incident, 1943; *Washington Post* and CBS inflation programs, 1417; Wilson writes on civil rights, 490; as World War II armchair strategists, 2182. *See also New York Herald-Tribune; New York Times; U.S. News & World Report*
—radio: E. speaks on spiritual values, 1249; and E.'s speeches on defense posture, 572–73; and Farewell Address, 2205; on jamming VOA broadcasts, 1682–83. *See also* Eisenhower, Dwight David: speeches
—television: Benson seeks support on farm program, 1739–40; Castro appears on "Meet the Press," 1456; and CBS inflation programs, 1417; and closed circuit fundraising dinner, 2062–63; and Council on Youth Fitness, 452–53; E. exceeds TV time limit, 1842–43; and E.'s midterm election speeches, 1182–83; E. reports on European tour (August 1959), 1653–54; E. reports on Latin American tour, 1842–43; E. speaks on Berlin crisis, 1406–7, 1418–19; E. speaks on 1960 election issues, 2127–28; E. speaks on spiritual values, 1249; and E.'s speeches on defense posture, 572–73; E.'s use of, in budget fight, 1326–27; and Farewell Address, 2205; "Fight to Win" speech in Chicago, 1158–59; Mitchell speaks on "Face the Nation," 1332–33; and Nixon-Kennedy debates, 2130–31; opens new moral era, 1726–27; Percy debates on "The Big Issue," 879–80; and quiz-show scandals, 1726–27, 1729; on television programming responsibilities, 1729; on United Press as objective, 1935–41. *See also* Eisenhower, Dwight David: speeches
Medical International Corporation (MEDICO), 1971–73
Medical profession, and work of Dr. Tom Dooley, 1971–73
—medical benefits: for elderly, 1702–3; and insurance for, 1935–41; and rising costs of medical care, 1935–41

—medical research: on appropriations for HEW, NIH, and PHS, 1594–97, 2034–35; on federal support for, 1663–65; and heart fund campaign, 37–38; and prevention of blindness, 2034–35; private funding for, 1594–97
—medical schools, federal aid to, 823–24, 1663–65
—physicians: advice to E. from, 5–8, 554, 1225–26; E. denies White's visit to China, 976–77; and funding for medical research, 1594–97; and Luce's illness, 518; and medical research, 238–39; and Saud's son, 195, 196. *See also* Snyder, Howard McCrum, Sr.
Mediterranean: and command structure in, under NATO, 1313–14, 1419–21, 1667–69; and cotton exports, 1398–99; E.'s goodwill trip to (December 1959), 1761–62, 1762–63; and Egypt's monopoly over maritime traffic, 53–55; on French naval forces in, 1313–14, 1412–15, 1419–21, 1667–69, 1785–87; and operations in World War II, 2185; on U.S. naval forces in, 1313–14
Meir, Golda, 75. *See also* Israel, State of
Melas, George V., 362–63
Mellon, Constance (Prosser), 1383
Mellon, Paul, 1382–83
Mellon, Richard King, 2146; and ADA-CIO thinking, 1135–36; on antitrust suit against ALCOA, 208–9; background, 210; on domestic and foreign issues, 1330; E. apologizes to, 1382–83; E.'s appreciation to, 1119–20, 1135–36; on federal spending, 1135–36; as GOP supporter, 1118, 1135–36; on Gulf Oil Corporation, 1135–36; invites E. to Fort Ligonier bicentennial, 951, 1119–20, 1135–36; on midterm elections, 1135–36; supports Scott, 1119–20, 1135–36
Mellot, Art, 382
Memorial Day, 892
"Memphis Case," 765–66
Mencken, Henry Louis ("H. L."), 671
Menderes, Adnan: background, 307; on conflict regarding Cyprus, 613, 940–42; and Dulles, 666–67, 1020–22; E. urges restraint, 940–42, 942–44; execution of, 1823; meets with Development Loan Fund delegation, 1823; meets with E., 613; overthrow of, 1995–96; and Turkish-Greek settlement on Cyprus, 1346; on U.S. aid to Turkey, 303–7. *See also* Turkey, Republic of
Mennonites. *See* Religion: Mennonites
Menshikov, Mikhail Alekseevich: background, 734, 737; on conditions for summit meeting, 748–49, 792–93, 1585–86; delivers Khrushchev's letter to Dulles, 821; E.'s view, 734, 1682–83; on E.'s visit to USSR, 1806–7; on Khrushchev's interest in U.S. visit, 1585–86; on proposed meeting with

2254–56; and Muscat/Oman dispute, 332–34; NATO's role in, 303–7; need of, to develop purchasing power, 319–25; on oil imports from, and U.S. national security, 340–42; on refugees, Reid's concern, 293–95; Richards's mission to, 83–85, 194–96; Russell's view on aid to, 71–72; Salazar's view on U.S. action in, 125; Saud's concerns on NATO meeting, 607–8; Saud proposes destruction of Israel, 603; Soviet proposal condemning force, 234–35; Soviet role in, 191–94, 408–10, 493–94; and spirit of nationalism, 993–96; on substitute for Baghdad Pact, 1020–22; and Suez Canal dispute, 98–100, 166, 168, 194–96; and Syria, 173; threats to free world in, 1159–62; and Tunisia's appeal for arms, 574–79; and United Arab Republic, 705–8; U.S. economic aid in, 408–10; U.S. policies in, 47, 72–73, 98–100, 194–96, 801; and U.S. relations with Nasser, 562–63; on Western world's need for oil, 986–87

Middle East Resolution (March 7, 1957). See Eisenhower Doctrine

Middleton, Drew: on allied disunity, 1955–56; article by, embarrasses E., 113–14, 120; background, 114

Middle way. See Eisenhower, Dwight David: political philosophy

Mid East, Mideast. See Middle East

Mid-range ballistic missiles (MRBM), 1989–90; as British contribution to NATO, 2009–11; and NATO, 2139–41, 2189. See also Intermediate Range Ballistic Missile Program; Missiles

Mikoyan, Anastas Ivanovich, 1305; addresses Economic Club of New York, 1276–77; background, 1277; endorses Castro, 2001–7; meets with Dulles, 1276–77, 1277–79; meets with E., 1277–79; to meet Hauge, 1276–77, 1277–79; and Moscow talks, 1367–68, 1396–97; threatens collective security, 1322; on U.S. economic system, 1277–79; visits Cuba, 2001–7; visits U.S., 1276–77, 1277–79, 1304–5, 1314–15, 1321, 1322. See also Soviet Union

Miles, Henry M., 946

Milestone Plantation. See Humphrey, George Magoffin

Milhollen, Hirst Dillon, 1826–27

Military Air Transport Service, 1466–67

Military Assistance Advisory Group (MAAG). See United States Military Assistance Advisory Group

Military Assistance Program, President's Committee to Study, 1515–16

Military Assistance Program of 1958 (MAP): and Baghdad Pact, 998–1000; and new equipment for ROK, 387–88

Military-industrial complex, 2205

Military Pay Bill, 1984–85. See Armed Services; Congress, U.S.; Defense, Department of

Military Retirement Bill of 1958 (Pay Equalization Bill), 1984–85, 2053–54

Military-Scientific Dinner, 785

Mill, Edward K., Jr., 1842

Millar, Frederick Hoyer, 1987

Miller, A. C., 1146

Miller, Arthur Lemoine, 1727

Miller, Lorene, 1105–6

Miller, William Edward, 2241–42

Miller, William Johnson, 538–39

Mills, Ann, 862

Mills, Mark John, 862

Mills, Mark Muir: background, 287; death of, 862; E.'s esteem for, 862; meets with E. on radioactive fallout, 287, 295–96; testifies before JCAE, 287, 295–96

Mills, Pauline ("Polly") (Riedeburg), 862

Mills, Wilbur Daigh, 1047

Milwaukee Journal, 433

Minaud, Jean, 1952–53

Mindszenty, Jozsef Cardinal, 1191

Minerals, and Minerals Stabilization Plan, 889–90, 991–92, 1111–13. See also Raw materials; Strategic materials

Minerals Stabilization Plan. See Domestic Minerals Stabilization Plan

Minneapolis Tribune, 490

Minnesota: and dairy situation in, 693–94; E. campaigns in, 2136; E. recalls presidential nomination, 1746–56; Stassen recalls 1952 presidential nomination, 1253–54; State Centennial in, 709; Thye recalls 1952 presidential nomination, 1253–54

Minorities. See also African Americans; Jews; Native Americans

Mirza, Iskander: background, 709; on Indo-Pakistani dispute, 839–40, 884–85; on invitation to visit U.S., 708–9; on martial law in Pakistan, 1147; overthrows Pakistani government, 1147; on U.S. force in Lebanon, 998–1000. See also Pakistan, Islamic Republic of

Missiles, 562: on advisers for program, 501–2; ALBM, 1981–82; Blue Streak rocket program, 1981–82, 2139–41; Case's proposal, 585–86; discussions on, with Macmillan, 1396–97; on duplication in programs, 292–93, 496–97, 561; funding for, and interservice rivalry, 162–63, 292–93, 347–49, 498, 686–87; on guided missile mail, 1520; guided missiles tracking station in Brazil, 104–5; and IRBM agreement with U.K., 729–30; Lawrence's spoof on "gap," 1843; and Manhattan District missile program, 498; and missile gap, 1342; Mitchell supports program, 1332–33; national defense and production of, 1406–7; and NATO strike force using Polaris, 2115–18; on

Strait, 1295–98; and Murrow, 1410–11; and OVERLORD, 1295–98, 2180–88; proposes rush to Berlin, 1653–54, 2182–83, 2184, 2188; publishes E.'s letter to Butcher, 1410–11; scores NATO, 1463; seeks E.'s support on Cypriot question, 612–13; and Sicily campaign, 1295–98; a "small magpie," 1463; visits Gettysburg farm, battlefield, 182–83, 185–86, 240, 1203–4; visits Moscow, 1463; wager with, 2186, 2188; wishes to make amends, 1547–49; and World War II, 1203–4, 1295–98, 2180–88; would have sacked both Lee and Meade, 1203–4. *See also* World War II

Montgomery, Robert: as adviser to E., 737, 2232–33; background, 737; gives E. bad advice, 734, 737; on publication rights to E.'s life story, 979, 2232–33

Montgomery, Ruth Shick, 272

Moore, Ernest, 935

Moore, George Gordon, Jr.: background, 31–32; Es. visit, 1477; and Michael Gill, 31–32; on painting for Byars, 1477

Moore, James Edward, 1298

Moore, Mable Frances Doud ("Mike"), 2114; background, 783–84; on "Min's" health, 783–84, 1637–38; on visits with "Min," 1637–38

Moore, Mamie Eisenhower: to attend Mary Washington College, 2114; background, 2020–21; on "beatniks," 2020–21; on family affection, 2020–21; on juvenile delinquency, 2020–21; on younger generation, 2020–21

Moos, Malcolm Charles: background, 671; on Berlin crisis speech, 1406–7; on Brown and Harvard speeches, 1629–30; drafts Fort Ligonier speech, 1117; edits Mencken's book, 671; on E.'s mutual security speech, 1919–23; on E.'s speech agenda, 1492–94

Morgan, Dale (Mrs. G. Philip), 2128–29

Morgan, Frederick Edgworth, 2182, 2187

Morgan, Gerald Demuth, 1009, 1013, 1765; on appointment of federal judges, 1344; background, 63–64, 406–7; as Deputy Assistant to the President, 1128–29; on Dethmers as candidate for Circuit Court of Appeals, 1721; drafts message to Goldwater, 157; drafts reply to Furcolo, 1381–82; on economic recession recovery, 769–71; and oil import quotas, 758–59, 895–96; on Pacific routes for Northwest and Pan American airlines, 406–7; and question of presidential disability, 711–14; and Trans-Pacific Renewal Case, 720

Morgan, G. Philip, 2129

Morgan, J. P. & Company, and merger with Guaranty Trust Company of New York, 1252–53, 1311–13

Mormon Tabernacle Choir, 1172

Morocco, Kingdom of, 801; on Agadir earthquake, 1882–84; combats Nasserism, 168; and de Gaulle's leadership, 917; E.'s goodwill trip to (December 1959), 1718–19, 1761–62, 1762–63, 1778, 1882–84, 1931–33; and French-Algerian conflict, 746, 1931–33; and French colonialism, 952–60; Gruenther visits, 1106–7; and law of the sea, 1911–12; on Moroccan-American relations, 1882–84, 1931–33; Nixon visits, 168; on Summit collapse, 1953–54; tripartite talks on, 1673–75; on U.S. bases in, 1882–84, 1931–33; on withdrawal at Ben Slimane, 1882–84. *See also* Mohamed V

Morrill, James Lewis, 1725

Morris, Arthur J., 2166–68

Morrow, E. Frederic, 1503–4

Morrow, John Howard, 1503–4

Morrow, Wright Francis: applauds speech on Berlin crisis, 1418–19; background, 70; on foreign service appointment for, 70, 82–83; on Khrushchev, 1418–19; on lawsuit in Mexico, 1418–19; supports E., 70

Mortgage Reinsurance Bill, 1007–13

Mortimer, Charles G., 905–6

Morton, Sterling, 2195–96

Morton, Thruston Ballard: on appointment of federal judges, 1344; background, 751–52; as campaign speaker on presidency, 1793–96; on conduct of national campaign, 1793–96; heads RNC, 1793–96, 1862–63, 1990–91; on Mamie E.'s campaign speech, 2062–63; on 1960 campaign fundraising, 1990–91; on Stratton's problems, 2109–11; as vice-presidential nominee, 1871

Moscow. *See* Soviet Union

Moscow Manifesto, 652, 658, 726, 727

Moslems. *See* Religion

Mossadeq, Mohammed; Mossadegh, Mohammed, and Dulles, 2211–13

Mothers' League of Little Rock. *See* Civil rights: Little Rock

Motor News Analysis, 208–9

Mountbatten, Edwina Cynthia Annette (Ashley): background, 1060; on Dickie's proposal to, 1770–72; Es. host dinner party for, 1059–60; illness of, 1059–60; visits Canada and U.S., 1059–60

Mountbatten, Louis Francis Albert ("Dickie"): background, 319; on coincidence at Delhi University, 1770–72; Es. host dinner party for, 1059–60, 1692–93; E. hosts stag dinner for, 1059–60, 1770–72; proposes to Edwina, 1770–72; on security breaches, 1692–93; sends socks, 1770–72; visits Canada, 1059–60; visits E., 1770–72

Mount Eisenhower, Edgar E. represents E. at ceremonies, 1079–80

Mueller, Frederick Henry ("Fritz"): to attend stag dinner, 1568–69, 1612; and BAC, 1589; background, 1589; as campaign speaker on commerce, 1793–96; on conflict of interest, 1874; on Mueller Metals Corporation, 1874; report by, on New York World's Fair, 2163–64; as Secretary of Commerce, 1589; on son's business ethics, 1874; and U.S. Chamber of Commerce, 1671–72; on U.S. foreign trade expansion, 1671–72. *See also* Commerce, Department of

Mullen, Robert Rodolf, 1517–19

Mundt, Karl Earl, 1925

Munõz Marin, Luis, 373

Murphy, 1339–40

Murphy, Bernard A., 697–98

Murphy, Franklin David: background, 393; as candidate for USMA Thayer Award, 968–69; on Churchill's papers, 1535–36; E. recommends, to Civil Rights Commission, 392–94; visits Churchill, 1535–36; visits E., 1535–36

Murphy, George Lloyd: background, 1066, 1068; and Knowland's gubernatorial candidacy, 1064–68; on 1960 election loss, 2165–66; on Nixon-Kennedy debates, 2165–66; suffers flu, 2165–66

Murphy, Juliette (Henkel), 2165–66

Murphy, Mildred Claire (Taylor), 1716

Murphy, Robert Daniel, 1604–5; accompanies E. on goodwill tour (December 1959), 1715–16, 1768–69, 1777–78; on Algeria in World War II, 1715–16; background, 378; on Bohlen's transfer, 1576; and fall of French government, 831–34; on French-Tunisian relations, 746, 766–67; on good offices mission, 831–34; on Korea's National Security Law, 1263–64; on meeting with Khrushchev, 1567–68; meets with Ladgham and Mokaddem, 746; Menshikov contacts, 1585–86; and message protocol, 1509–10; and Muscat/Oman dispute, 378–79; and Parker's concern on Khrushchev's visit, 1635–36; on proposed meeting with Khrushchev, 1567–68; on refugees at Tunisia-Algeria border, 766–67; on Republican victory in 1960 election, 1862–63; resigns as chair, OCB, 1715–16; resigns as Under Secretary of State for Political Affairs, 1715–16; retires, 1744–46; and rumor of U.S. troop withdrawal, 1769–70; and tripartite consultation in Africa, 1987–88

Murray, Thomas ("Tom") Jefferson: background, 262; opposes pay increases for postal workers, 261–62; on partisan politics in Post Office, 1839

Murrow, Edward R., 1410–11

Muscat: and Agreement of Al-Sib, 379–80; and Buraimi, 332–34; and dispute with Saud, 332–34; E.'s view, 332–34, 378–79; Macmillan's view, 378–79, 379–80

Muslims. *See* Religion: Moslems

Musser, Beulah, 1156–57

Musser, Christian O., 1156–57

Musser, Hannah Amanda (Eisenhower), 1156–57

Mussolini, Benito, 1590; on Nasser as a "second Mussolini," 101, 104

Mutual aid: on appropriations for, 512–16, 952–60; as bipartisan issue, 843–44; Boeschenstein's support on, 536–37; economy in, 121–22; E.'s view, 43–46; importance of, 400, 1188–90; and need for unified bipartisan foreign policy, 396–99; and State of the Union Address, 663–64. *See also* Mutual Security Program; United States: foreign aid

Mutual Broadcasting System, 1842–43

Mutual Defense Treaty, and Republic of Korea, 314–16

Mutual security: addresses on, 171–72, 179–80, 478, 537, 1437–38; as America's best investment, 319–25, 446–49, 537; on cuts in funding, 975–76, 1828–30; and personal sacrifice, 1500–1502; and Republican principles, 801–3; and Sibley/Lanham letters on, 391; on U.S. as arsenal for material supply, 389–90. *See also* Collective security; Mutual Security Acts; Mutual security Administration; United States: foreign aid

—Mutual Security Program, 379–80; appropriations for, 400, 882, 1041, 1329–31, 1430–31, 1904, 1947–49; on bipartisan support for, 740–41, 843–44, 1027–31; and congressional debates, 207–8, 1007–13; Cooper supports, 1985–86; and Development Loan Fund, 183–85, 220–21, 354–56, 1041; and Draper Committee Report, 1515–16; E.'s disappointment in cuts, 1002; E. seeks support for, 882, 1947–49; E.'s view, 142–43, 154–55, 174–76, 207–8; and executive powers in regulatory commissions, 2214–15; and executive privilege, 1733–35; and Fairless Committee Report, 95–96, 97–98; and "Fortress America" concept, 354–56; and FY 1958 budget, 176–77; Hoffman's role in support for, 661–62; importance of, 415–17; and Indo-Pakistani dispute, 1774–76; Jackson's role on, 154–55, 768–69; Johnson supports funding for, 220–21; lacks favorable public opinion, 1039–40; and maritime labor union fears, 1394–95; on need to educate Americans regarding, 381; Nixon's role in, 410–12; and political individualism, 787–89; purposes of, 179–80; Randall's view, 95–96,

National Bituminous Coal Advisory Council, 1392–93

National Book Committee, 668–69

National Broadcasting Company (NBC): E. exceeds TV time limit, 1842–43; elects Strauss to board, 1789–90

National Cardiac Research Foundation, 976–77

National Catholic Welfare Conference, sends food shipments to Morocco, 207–8

National Citizens for Eisenhower-Nixon 1958 Committee. *See* Citizens for Eisenhower-Nixon 1958 Committee

National Citizens for Nixon, 2044–45

National Committee for a Sane Nuclear Policy, recommendations of, 584–85

National Council of Churches of Christ of America, 465–66; address to, 1249; Dulles addresses, 1210–11

National Council of Negro Women, Inc., E.'s greeting to, 530–31

National Day of Prayer, 1052–53

National Day of Prayer for Permanent Peace, 1052–53

National debt. *See* Economy, U.S.

National defense. *See* Defense, Department of; United States: national security

National Defense Education Act of 1958, 980–81, 1007–13; and loyalty oath requirements, 1505–7

National Education Association, E. addresses, 431–32

National Football Foundation, E. addresses, 1163–64, 1185–86

National Foundation to Honor General Dwight D. Eisenhower and the United States Armed Forces, Inc. *See* Eisenhower Foundation

National Foundation for Infantile Paralysis: and President's Birthday Ball, 37–38; Roosevelt's role in founding, 37; and Salk vaccine, 891

National Freedom Board, 675–76, 865–66

National Fund for Medical Education, E.'s address to, 342, 512, 523, 527–29

National Goals Committee. *See* Goals Commission

National Golfer, 623–24

National Guard: active duty policy for, 32–33; E.'s view, 32–33; Wilson scores, 32–33. *See also* Arkansas; Civil rights: Little Rock

National Historical Publications Commission (NHPC), E. commends, 937–38

National Industrial Recovery Act, 760–65

National Institutes of Health (NIH), appropriations for, 1594–97, 1663–65, 2034–35

Nationalism: and foreign aid, 121–22; and "hostile nationalism," 1230–32; Nasser's use of, in Pan-Arab States, 993–96, 1027–

31; spirit of, 179–80, 993–96; in Third World, 115–17

Nationalist China. *See* China, Republic of

National Labor Relations Board, 1630–31

National Library Week, 668–69

National Organization of Cyprus Fighters (EOKA), 612–13

National Park Service, and funds for roads and facilities, 760–65

National Petroleum Council (NPC), background, 660–61

National Plan for Civil Defense and Defense Mobilization, 1605–6

National Planning Association, Committee on International Policy: on cold war concerns, 493–94; recommendations by, 512–16

National Presbyterian Church: Es. attend, 1052–53, 1225; E. unveils cornerstone at, 1580–81; on Richardson's contribution, 1580–81; service at, on Opening of Congress, 1801–2; site, 1459–60. *See also* Luce, Henry Robinson; Religion: Presbyterians

National Press Club: Castro addresses, 1456; E. addresses, 1295–98, 1302–3, 1321, 1342, 1935–41; Edstrom heads, 1807; Lawrence heads, 1294–95

National Rural Electric Cooperative Association, E. addresses, 1338–39, 1349

National Science Foundation: achievements of, 503–5; E. asks increase in funding for, 645–46, 980–81

National security. *See* United States: national security

National Security Council (NSC): and Actions No. 1653, 1690, and 1733, 292–93; Anderson attends, 593–94; on attendance at meetings of, 2119–20; briefings by, on national defense posture, 572–73; on costs of space program, 593–94; on crisis in Laos, 2219–21; discusses ballistic missile program, 2172–73; discusses democracy in third world, 1556–57; discusses Dominican Republic, 1855–56; discusses failed reconnaissance balloon project, 1031–32; discusses military force reductions, 1736–37; discusses nuclear weapons policy for NATO, 2141–42, 2172–73; discusses Polaris submarine project, 2172–73; and Draper Committee Report, 1515–16; E. briefs Kennedy on, 2189–95; E. opposes congressional investigation of, 1538–40; establishes Security Resources Panel, ODM Science Advisory Committee, 584–85; and European trade policies, 1799–1800; and 5412 Group on Cuba, 2196–97; and First Secretary of Government, 675–76, 1700–1702; on function of, 743–45; on functions of VOA, 1250; Gray to plan meetings of, 1995–96; Gray's recommendations, 2246–

1365–66, 1487; on DOD reorganization, 896–97; and Dominick, 2161–62; and Dutch Creek Investment Company, 1365–66; E.'s appreciation to, 2021–22; E. declines United Air Lines board, 2079–80; E. meets with, in Denver, 1487; on E.'s sporting rifle, 1800–1801; on fishing, 268, 2021–22; and Fraser post office on Eisenhower Drive, 413–14; on golf scores at Pebble Beach, 1726–27; on Helen's illness, 1225–26, 1226–27; illness of, 1286–87, 1317–18; invites E. to Fraser ranch, 268; and John E.'s investments, 394–95; and Lake View Investment Company, 1365–66; on log house history, 1487; meets with E. on Denver real estate holdings, 394–95; to meet Rhyne, 2099; and Middlefield Development Company, 1365–66; and "Min's" condition, 783–84; "Min" revises her will, 413–14; on 1960 election results, 2161–62; and package for Mamie, 1365–66; postpones visit with E., 1286–87; recommends Gould for tax court judgeship, 818; represents E. in Costa Rica, 896–97; and residential loan rates, 783–84; sends fishing flies, 977–78; on site for New York World's Fair, 1726–27; on steer sale prices, 817; and Stouffer's frozen foods, 50–51; on strength of ICA, 1800–1801; and Turnpike Land Company, 1365–66; on University Hills Shopping Center, 394–95, 783–84; visits Mrs. Havens, 1800–1801; visits White House, 413–14, 896–97; on work and leisure, 1365–66; Wynetka Investment Company, 1365–66. *See also* Investments

Nielsen, Helen (Maurer), background, 977; health of, 1487; illness of, 1225–26, 1226–27, 1286–87, 1317–18

Nielsen, N. Chris, 1915

Nietzche, Friedrich Wilhelm, 799

Nike-Ajax, DOD plans phase-out for, 292–93. *See also* Missiles

Nike/Talos, an overlapping missile program, 292–93. *See also* Missiles

Nimitz, Chester William: background, 240, 688; on service academy student exchange, 688–89; University of Richmond honors, 240

Nittany Farms, 74

Nixon, Julie, 2156

Nixon, Patricia, 2156

Nixon, Richard Milhous: accepts Republican nomination, 2018–19; on Acheson's foreign policy, 1150–51; to act for E. at Summit Conference (May 1960), 1909, 1910–11; as "acting president," 711–14; and Adams's resignation, 1089–91; addresses Economic Mobilization Conference, 858–59; on Anderson as vice-presidential candidate, 2018–19; appreciation to, 646–47; on appreciation to Republican women, 1925–26; attends dedication at St. Paul's Cathedral, 1241–42; attends Frondizi's inauguration, 841; attends Gold Coast (Ghana) Independence Ceremonies, 17–18, 100, 168, 552–53, 637–39; attends Kennedy's inauguration, 2258–59; to attend stag dinner, 1568–69, 1612; on attitudes among foreign service officers, 1315–16; and Benson's report on trade trip, 2056–58; birthday wishes to, 646–47; on Cabinet/congressional relations, 549; and California politics, 1201–2; campaigns in midterm elections, 1181; as congressional foreign policy liaison, 410–12; declines Carman's invitation, 49–50; declines Saud's invitation, 99; defends administration leaders, 213–15; on Dillon as Treasury Secretary, 2202–4; dinner honoring, 1315–16; E. commends campaign efforts of, 1150–51; E. commends, following Latin American riots, 899–900; on economic recession recovery, 719; E.'s esteem for, 1201–2, 1594, 2128, 2258–59; on E.'s goodwill tour (December 1959), 1743–44, 1768–69; on E. as mentor-sponsor, 1925; Fairless hosts luncheon for, 1137–38; on Faubus, 474–75; on federal *v.* states' rights issues, 2035–36; Forbes's protest, 482–83; foreign policy statement by, 1150–51, 1151–52; gives party for Brownells, 597–98; on golf with E., Belshe, 474–75; on Green's letter, 1131–33; joins California law firm, 2258–59; Kubitschek's view on Pan American issues, 924–25; and Lawrence's proposal, 592–93; on "liberalism" of, 1935–41; on Lodge as vice-presidential candidate, 2018–19; loses California gubernatorial race, 2258–59; on Macmillan's invitation to London, 1466–67; and media exposure on budget fight, 1369–71; on missing USAF airmen, 1687–88; names Burger Chief Justice, 1108–10; and *New York Times* interview, 1871–72; at odds with Rockefeller on Khrushchev invitation, 1632–34; opens American National Exposition (Moscow), 1585–86, 1594; and People-to-People fundraising and structure, 684–85; and question of presidential disability, 76–77, 711–14; on rebuilding GOP, 1236–39, 1259–61, 1277–79; resigns presidency, 2258–59; on right-to-work legislation, 1123–24; riots against, in Latin America, 899–900, 924–25; on Secret Service protection for, 899–900; and Southern California Citizens for Eisenhower-Nixon, 1217–18; and Stassen's charges, 1201–2; supports Alcorn as RNC head, 1235–36; on travel time to Moscow, 1589–91; on trip to Latin America, 631, 841, 899–900, 924–25; un-

derstands need for GOP unity, 396–99; and U.S. monetary system reforms, 2059–60; vacations in West Virginia, 410–12; visits African nations, 17–18, 100, 167, 168; visits Moscow, 1466–67, 1585–86, 1587–88, 1591–93, 1593–94, 1594, 1632–34; visits U.K., 1207–8, 1241–42, 1281–82; wins presidency in 1968, 1972, 2258–59
—candidacy (1960): Adams's view of, as candidate, 2136; attends Boston fundraiser, 2109–11; attends launching of S.S. *Hope*, 2091; and Benson, 2056–58; on Burgess's support, 2044–45; campaigns with Lodge, E., 2145–46; campaigns in Los Angelos, 2145–46; campaigns in New York with E., 2145–46; campaigns in San Francisco, 2091; on campaign speakers in support of, 1793–96; on civil rights, 1975, 2052–53; debates with Kennedy, 2130–31, 2136, 2145–46, E.'s advice to, 2130–31; on E.'s campaign contribution, 2068; E. commends, 2091, 2128, 2130–31; election advice to, 2109–11; on election loss, 2156, 2157, 2258–59; and *Esquire* article on, 1870–71; as E.'s successor, 1201–2; E. votes for, 2151; on GOP in Illinois, 2109–11; and Hauge's tree analogy, 2089–90; Hobby's concern, 1975; on Independents and switch-voting Democrats, 1975; and Jewish vote, 1869–70, 1870–71; Knight promises support, 1201–2; loses election, 2157, 2157–58, 2165–66; and Mamie E.'s campaign speech, 2062–63; and NAACP affiliation, 2052–53; and National Citizens for Nixon, 2044–45; on 1960 campaign fundraising, 1990–91; and 1960 presidential election, 1201–2, 1553, 2052–53; presidential abilities of, 2258–59; problems in New York, 2143–45; on question of appeal to Independents, Democrats, 2136; radio broadcasts by, 2145–46; schedules TV talks, 2145–46; on speech by, in Cincinnati, 2145–46; on speech by, in North Dakota, 1975; and Stratton's problems, 2109–11; in Texas, 1975; and vice-presidential nominees, 1870–71; and Volunteers for Nixon, 2068; wins Colorado's electoral votes, 2161–62

Nixon, Thelma Catherine Patricia (Ryan) ("Pat"): accompanies Nixon to USSR, 1594; on attitudes among foreign service officers, 1315–16; background, 597–98; E. commends, 2130–31; gives party for Brownells, 597–98; and Mamie E.'s campaign speech, 2062–63; on 1960 election loss, 2156; visits U.K., 1241–42, 1281–82

Nixon for President Club, 2146

Nkrumah, Kwame: background, 552–53; on Belgian troop deployment, 2030–32; on E.-

Khrushchev meeting, 2111–13; on Ghanian transmission system, 2162–63; and Hammarskjöld, 2030–32; on Katanga question, 2030–32; on report of Preparatory Commission, 552–53; seeks U.S. aid, 552–53, 637–39; on situation in Congo, 2030–32; and Timberlake, 2030–32; on U.N. support in Congo, 2030–32; on U.S. support in Congo, 2030–32; visits U.S., 637–39, 708–9, 2162–63; on Volta River project, 552–53, 637–39, 2037–38, 2162–63. *See also* Ghana, Republic of

Nobel Prize, 46–47, 503–5, 795–96

Noble, Allan Herbert Percy, 278–79

Nong Kimny, 2250

NORAD (North American Air Defense Command), and cancellation of Sky Hawk air defense exercise, 1661–62

Norell, James Alden, 1854–55

Norgren, Carl August, 1856–57

Norland, Donald Richard, 2012

Normandy, 503, 1653–54, 1746–56

Norstad, Isabelle Helen (Jenkins), 125

Norstad, Lauris ("Larry"): on atomic disarmament, 1926–27; background, 75–76; and Berlin crisis, 1378–79; on discussions with de Gaulle, Debré, 1819–20; on E.'s discussions with de Gaulle, 1785–87, 1926–27; and E.'s esteem for Houghton, 125; and E.'s visit to Marnes-la-Coquette, 1952–53; and E.'s visit to Villa St. Pierre, 1952–53; on fishing, 1952–53; and French fleet in Mediterranean, 1419–21, 1785–87, 1819–20; on French "obstructive tactics," 1250–51; illness of, 1952–53; on inspection zones, 1926–27; meets with Adenauer, 125, 2115–18; to meet de Gaulle, 1785–87; meets with Dulles, 1250–51; meets with Salazar, 125; on NATO air defense coordination, 1785–87, 1819–20, 1926–27; and NATO alliance, 125; and naval problems in allied command, 1819–20; proposes economies within NATO, 303–7; protests reduction of Turkish force levels, 303–7; and reduction of British NATO forces, 75–76, 125; retires, 1298–99; as SACEUR, 75–76; on Schuyler's successor, 1298–99; on Turkey and NATO defense expenditures, 303–7; and U.K. force levels in Germany, 997–98; on Walters as interpreter, 1819–20. *See also* NATO

North Africa: Communist threat in, 2209–10; and de Gaulle's leadership, 917; and European–North African cooperation, 831–34; and France's role in arms for Tunisia, 563–67, 567–70; invasion of, 933–34; Murphy's service in, 1715–16; on relations with France, 801, 831–34, 952–60; Soviet influence in, 1113–15; and TORCH, 562, 2181, 2187. *See also* Africa; Goodwill tour to Europe, Asia, Mediterranean, Near East, and North Africa (December 1959)

North American Air Defense Command. *See* NORAD

North Atlantic Alliance. *See* Atlantic Alliance; NATO

North Atlantic Council (NAC): and air defense issues, 2115–18; celebrates tenth anniversary, 1437–38; and conditions for summit meeting, 728–29; considers conflict regarding Cyprus, 940–42, 942–44, 1125–26, 1174–75; discusses atomic weapons policy, 181, 2189; discusses German, Italian NATO roles, 181; discusses unified air defense system, 1785–87; E. addresses, 1654–57; France withdraws fleet from NATO control, 1412–15, 1419–21; Luns as president of, 1437–38; ministers meet in Bonn (May 1957), 180, 181; ministers meet in Copenhagen (May 1958), 871; ministers meet in Paris (December 1956), 147, 149, 544–45; ministers meet in Paris (December 1958), 1248–49, 1250–51, 1258; ministers meet in Paris (December 1959), 1691–92, 1767–68; ministers meet in Paris (December 1960), 2189; ministers meet in Washington (April 1959), 1424–26; and NATO force assignments to SACEUR, 1313–14; on nuclear and conventional forces, 303–7; reviews reply to Bulganin, 642–44; role of, in free world defenses, 1159–62; and U.K. force levels in Germany, 997–98; and U.S. concern regarding Cyprus, 940–42, 1127–28

North Atlantic Treaty Organization. *See* NATO

North Carolina, E. meets with governor of, 466–67, 474–75

North Dakota: Hobby's recommendation, 1975; and Interior Cabinet post, 1256–58; Nixon speaks in, 1975

North Korea. *See* Korea, Democratic People's Republic of

North Vietnam. *See* Vietnam, Socialist Republic of

Northwest Orient Airlines: certification of, 405; E. approves CAB recommendations, 2252–54; and Pacific Great Circle route, 288, 406–7; Redpath's view on CAB awards, 288

Norway, Kingdom of: Brooke's view, in World War II, 2186; and Bulganin's warning on atomic weaponry, 191–94; and crisis in Lebanon, 952–60; and downing of RB-47 airplane, 2008–9; on Gerhardsen's visit, 882; and law of the sea, 749–50, 1652–53; on miscommunication with Norwegians, 628–29; and reply to Myklebost, 2054–55; royals of, visit U.S., 708–9. *See also* Astrid, Princess of Norway; Bertel, Prince of Norway

Nott, Frank Harold, 1052–53

Nuclear energy. *See* Atomic energy

Nuclear Ship (NS) U.S.S. *Savannah:* background, 376; E. proposes name, 376

Nuclear weaponry. *See* Atomic weaponry; Disarmament; Geneva Nuclear Test Conference

OASI (Old Age and Survivors Insurance): background, 1064–68; and increase in benefits of, 1064–68; and medical care for the elderly, 1702–3

Ochs, Adolph Shelby, 349–50

O'Connell, James Timothy, 769–71

O'Connell, Michael D., 90–91

O'Connor, Roderic Ladew, 697–98

Odlum, Floyd Bostwick, 211

Odlum, Jacqueline (Cochran). *See* Cochran, Jacqueline

O'Donnell, John Parsons, 1189

Office of Civil and Defense Mobilization (OCDM): and civil defense program, 1605–6; and crude oil imports regulation, 1403–4; director of, holds Cabinet rank, 2189–95; E. briefs Kennedy on, 2189–95; on imports and trade restrictions, 1426–27, 1449–50; on oil imports from Canada, 1403–4. *See also* Office of Defense Mobilization

Office of Comptroller General, 2214–15

Office of Defense Mobilization (ODM), 213–15; on Cabinet/congressional relations, 549; and Cabinet report on railways, 484–85; and effect of oil imports on national security, 340–42, 895–96, 1403–4, 1426–27. *See also* Flemming, Arthur Sherwood; Gray, Gordon; Office of Civil and Defense Mobilization

—Science Advisory Committee, 501–2; conclusions of, on nuclear testing, 519–20; cooperates with NSC, 743–45; discusses federal role in scientific projects, 503–5; and Gaither Report, 584–85; on need for scientific training, 534–35; Rabi heads, 503–5, 519–20; and Security Resources Panel, 584–85; separates satellite program from missile development, 498; Sprague's recommendations, 584–85

Office of Education, strengthening of, 980–81

Office of Inspector General, 2214–15

Office of Private Cooperation, 364–66

Office of Strategic Services (OSS), and psychological warfare, 1611–13

Officer Personnel Act of 1947, and Bolte Committee Report, 2234–35

Officers' Reserve Corps, 400–401

Ohio: Erica heifer wins at State Fair, 1086; on GOP fundraising in, 1148–49; and Huron schools project, 945–47

Oil Import Control Board, 1555–56

Oil industry: and Buraimi dispute, 332–34; and Buy American Act, 774–76, 895–96; and Canadian market, 1457–59; and coal industry, 1392–93; and crude oil imports regulation, 1403–4; Cuba seeks tankers to transport Soviet oil, 2001–7, 2039–42; Cuba takes over U.S.-U.K. refineries, 2001–7, 2039–42; and destruction of Syrian pipelines, 80; and Egypt's monopoly on maritime traffic in Mideast, 53–55; E. orders cuts in imports, 774–76; E.'s proclamation on imports, 1403–4; excise taxes on, 928–29; exploration of, in Persian Gulf, 1007–13; on import quotas, 758–59, 774–76, 895–96, 1555–56; Iran's agreement with Standard Oil of Indiana, 1007–13; Kuwait, as great producer of, 102, 104, 1481–82; on limiting imports of, 385–87, 1392–93; and Muscat/Oman dispute, 378–79; and national security, 340–42, 774–76, 895–96; and natural gas bill scandal, 63–64; need for, in Western Europe, 44, 986–87; and offshore oil rights litigation (tidelands), 893–95; and Oil Imports Appeals Board, 1403–4; producers of, and antitrust suits, 570–71; producers of, and pipeline interests, 570–71; production of, in Iran, 102, 104; production of, in Iraq, 102, 104; production of, in Mideast, 102, 104; production of, in Saudi Arabia, 102, 104; reserves of, in Indonesia, 368; and Special Cabinet Committee to Investigate Crude Oil Imports, 340–42, 895–96; and U.S. oil for Western Europe, 18–19; and Venezuelan imports regulations, 1457–59; and Voluntary Oil Import Program, 1403–4. See also Iran; Mexico; Submerged Lands Act of 1953; United Kingdom

O'Kelly, Sean Thomas, 1395–96. See also Ireland, Republic of

Okinawa: E. visits, 1980–81, 1985–86; and land compensation question, 919–20, 1049–51; on Okinawa base, 827–29; and trans-Pacific air routes to, 2252–54; and U.S. relations with Japan, 827–29, 857, 1049–51

Old Age and Survivors Insurance. See OASI

Oleta O'Connor Yates et al. v. United States, 875–78

Olin, John Merrill: advises E. on guns, 368–69; advises E. on skeet and trap shoots, 310–11, 368–69; advises Leithead on guns, 1364–65; on Atlantic salmon treaty with Canada, 1057; background, 311; on communism, 1188–90; on developments in Red China, 1188–90; on extremists, 1188–90; on federal budget obligations, 1188–90; on federal spending, 1188–90; gives E. shotgun, 310–11; and Lee's proposal on taxation, 1188–90; on mutual aid, 1188–

90; on socialism, 1188–90; supports GOP, 1188–90

Oliver, James Churchill, 1688–89

O'Mahoney, Joseph Christopher, 252–53

Oman, 389–90; and Agreement of Al-Sib, 379–80; and dispute with Sultan of Muscat, 332–34; Macmillan's view, 378–79, 379–80; U.S. view, 378–79, 379–80

Oman, Imam of. See Oman

Omnibus Farm Bill, 1007–13

101st Airborne Division, and crisis at Little Rock, 460–61, 462–64. See also Civil rights

Open Curtain Proposal, 249–50

Open Skies Proposal, 249–50, 820, 848–49; Bulganin favors, 1670–71; Khrushchev opposes, 1670–71. See also Eisenhower, Dwight David: speeches

Operation Alert 1957, and postattack economic plans, 444–46. See also Civil Defense Administration

Operation Pan America: and Committee of Twenty-One, 1242–44, 1997–99; and inter-American economic cooperation, 1242–44, 1997–99; and Special Committee to Study the Formulation of New Measures for Economic Cooperation, 1242–44, 1997–99

Operations Coordinating Board (OCB): on attendance at meetings of, 2119–20; E. briefs Kennedy on, 2189–95; on functions of VOA, 1250; Gray reports on, 2246–47; Knowland's proposal, 865–66; Murphy resigns as chair, 1715–16; and psychological warfare, 1611–13; and U.S. policy toward Yugoslavia, 376–77. See also National Security Council

Oppenheimer, J. Robert, 1544

Ordnance: as measure of international friendship, 427–31; and modernization of weaponry in ROK, 314–16, 387–88; on offensive weaponry for Jordan, 359–60; on reduction of conventional weapons, 649–59; on weapons systems procurement program, 1284–85. See also Atomic weaponry; Missiles

Oregon: and ADA-CIO philosophy, 1064–68; Hatfield wins midterm election in, 1236–39; and Interior Cabinet post, 1256–58; and Pacific Great Circle air routes, 288, 406–7

Organizational Study Committee, and First Secretary of Government, 1700–1702. See also President's Advisory Committee on Government Organization

Organization of American States (OAS), 1488–91; and Cuba, 1601–3, 2001–7, 2039–42; on E.'s goodwill trip (December 1959), 1762–63; fears Castro's excesses, 1875–76; Herter attends meetings of, 1601–3, 1607–8, 2051–52, 2068–73; and Inter-American Development Bank, 1442–43; on ousting

Trujillo, 1919–23; and situation in Caribbean, 1601–3

Organization for Economic Cooperation and Development (OECD), 1799–1800

Organization for European Economic Cooperation (OEEC): on economic aid for Turkey, 944–45; and European trade policies, 1799–1800; and Four Wise Men, 1799–1800; and reciprocal trade legislation, 952–60. *See also* Common Market

Orient. *See* Far East

Orly International Airport, 613–14

O'Sullivan, Clifford, 1721

Ouimet, Francis D., 670–71

Outer Seven. *See* European Free Trade Association

Outer space: and ARPA, 1000–1001; on Dulles's embarrassment, 784–85; and establishment of NASA, 1000–1001, 1153–56; and Explorer I, 727; for man's exploration, 649–59; for peaceful purposes, 649–59, 721–27, 819–22; and Soviet proposals, 784–85. *See also* Explorer I; Mercury; Missiles; NASA; Satellites; Vanguard

OVERLORD, 1295–98; Churchill's foreboding, 1746–56, 2184–85; E.'s pride in outcome, 1746–56; E. proposes plan for, 2180–88; and Ismay's memoir, 2180–88; Monty's role, 1653–54; on U.S.-U.K. preparations for, 2180–88. *See also* World War II

Overstreet, Bonaro W., 1360–61

Overstreet, Harry A., 1360–61

Owens-Corning Fiberglas Corporation, 1136

Oxnam, Garfield Bromley, 210

Paarlberg, Don: background, 1117; and Canham's proposal, 1671–72; and cotton exports program, 1398–99; drafts reply to Mullen, 1519; on farm legislation, 1739–40; on imports and trade restrictions, 1426–27; joins White House staff, 1116–17; on Philippine sugar quota, 1881–82; on retiring national debt, 1867–68

Pace, Frank, Jr.: background, 1508; and Goals Commission, 1722–25; as Goals Commission vice-chair, 1812–13; and Gruenther's service on National Goals Committee, 1507–8

Pacelli, Eugene. *See* Pope Pius XII

Pacific Northern Airlines, certification of, 405. *See also* Airlines

Pacific Ocean: and Pacific Great Circle air routes, 288, 406–7, 1599–1601; South Pacific islands and French colonialism, 952–60

Pacific Proving Ground, atomic tests at, 216–18

Pact of Mutual Cooperation. *See* Baghdad Pact

Pact of non-aggression. *See* Bulganin, Nikolai Aleksandrovich; Dulles, John Foster;

Macmillan, Maurice Harold; NATO; Soviet Union; United Nations

Pact of Paris (Kellogg-Briand Pact), and renunciation of war, 724, 727

Pahlavi, Mohammed Reza (Shah of Iran): on Afghanistani threat to Iran, 1848–50, 2095–98; and Arabi and Farsi islands dispute, 22, 26; on Baghdad Pact, 998–1000, 1323–25; and CENTO defense, 2096, 2098; and CENTO meeting, 1931; on coup d'état in Iraq, 998–1000; and E.'s goodwill trip to Iran (December 1959), 1772–73, 1773–74, 1781–82; on Eurasian forces threat, 1773–74; on goals for Iranian forces, 1848–50; on Iranian-Israeli relations, 2095–98; on Iran-USSR treaty, 1321–25; on Iraqi-Iranian relations, 2095–98; on Iraqi threat to Iran, 1848–50; and Joint Resolution to Promote Peace and Stability in Middle East, 1848–50; on land reform in Iran, 1772–73; and law of the sea negotiations, 1911–12; meets with E., 709; on new weaponry from U.S., 2095–98; resists pressure from USSR, 2095–98; Saud's view, 23; on Soviet threat to Iran, 1773–74, 1781–82, 1782–83, 2095–98; on U.S. aid to Iranian armed forces, 998–1000, 1773–74, 1781–82, 1848–50, 2095–98; on U.S. economic aid to Iran, 2095–98; on U.S.-Iranian relations, 1321–25, 2095–98; and U.S. presidential election (1960), 2095; visits U.S., 709, 998–1000, 1323. *See also* Iran, Islamic Republic of

Paine, Thomas, 799

Painting: of Bavarian church, 2225–26; for Byars, 1477; by Churchill, for E., 283, 715–16, 1171–72, 1208–9; Churchill exhibits at Royal Academy, 1208–9; on "Deserted Barn," 1305, 1318–19; for Eisenhower Exchange Fellowships headquarters, 153–54; on E.'s painting, Fosburgh's view, 202; of Franciscan Mission San Carlos Borromeo, 90–91; of Franklin, for Fairless, 1623; gift of, from López Mateos, 1762–63; for Golf House, 670–71; on interest in color, 1318–19; of Jones, 382–83, 670–71; of Ourika River and Atlas Mountains, 1171–72, 1208–9, 1495; paintings for Pennsylvania exhibit, 1107–8; portrait of David E., 670–71, 1107–8; reproductions of Washington, Lincoln, 709–10; on return of painting from USSR, 1597–98; on Russell's works, 668–69; and sculptors, 135–36; of 16th hole at Augusta, 1107–8; and snow scene in Rockies, 1107–8; and Stephens's portrait of Ouimet, 670–71; for Strauss, 1549–50; on three heads, Dulles, Humphrey, Wilson, 1107–8; and U.S. exhibition of Churchill's paintings, 111–12, 283, 525, 526–27, 531–32, 620–21, 715–16, 852–53,

1171–72; and U.S. exhibition in Moscow, 1557–58; for Whitneys, 202; on Wyeth's portrait of E., 1780

Pakistan, Islamic Republic of: and Afghanistani-Pakistani relations, 1919–23; and Algeria, 2209–10; and Baghdad Pact, 1323–25; and CENTO, 1931; on Communist threat in North Africa, 2209–10; E.'s goodwill trip to (December 1959), 884–85, 1718–19, 1761–62, 1762–63, 1768–69, 1769–70, 1778; on French-Pakistani relations, 2209–10; on golf greens grass for, 2197–98; and Indo-Pakistani dispute, 146–47, 512–16, 555–56, 839–40, 851–52, 884–85, 1774–76, 1791–92, 1919–23; and Inter-College Exchange Program, 2197–98; and Jarring report, 555–56; and Kashmir, 1919–23; martial law in, 1147; migration of Hindus from, to India, 146–47; on modernizing army, 1778; and Pathans, 1919–23; and Pushtunistan issue, 1919–23, 2136–38; signs Baghdad Pact, 104; Soviet threat to collective security, 1321–25; and substitute for Baghdad Pact, 1020–22; Suhrawardy visits Bohemian Grove, 350–51; Suhrawardy visits E., 301; and support for mutual security program, 1947–49; on takeover of government, 1147; U.S. military aid for, 1774–76; on U.S. military aircraft for, 1919–23; U.S. military support for, 993–96, 998–1000. *See also* Ayub Khan, Mohammed; India, Republic of; Kashmir; Mirza, Iskander

Palestine: and Anglo-American Committee of Inquiry, 1152–53; Elson's view, 1027–31; Palestine Conciliation Commission, 1098–99; resettlement of refugees from, 293–95; as threat to Mideast security, 98–100

Paley, William Samuel, 1864–65

Palmer, Arnold Daniel, 1137. *See also* Golf

Palmer, Norman, 475–76

Panama, Republic of, 991–92; and Castro's aggression, 1601–3; de la Guardia's concerns, 1713–15; on education in, 1744–46; and E.'s goodwill trip (December 1959), 1762–63; grievances of, against U.S., 1827–28; housing in, 1840–41; on medical training for Latin American doctors, 1840–41; and Memorandum of Understanding, 1713–15; Merchant visits, 1744–46; Milton E. visits, 645–46, 1218–19; and proposed trans-isthmus canal, 2019–20; student riots in Panama City, Colon, 1713–15, 1744–46; on U.S.-Panamanian relations, 1713–15, 1744–46, 1809, 1827–28, 1840–41, 2088–89. *See also* de la Guardia, Ernesto, Jr.

—Canal Zone: governor of, and U.S. diplomatic mission, 1744–46, 2088–89; and operating policies in, 1713–15; problems in,

1840–41; on raising the Panamanian flag, 1744–46, 1809, 2088–89; titular sovereignty of, 1744–46

Panama Canal Company. *See also* Panama, Republic of: Canal Zone

Panama Canal Treaty of 1955, 1713–15

Pan America: and Paraguay, 1725–26; on U.S.-Pan American action in cold war, 925–26. *See also* Latin America

Pan American World Airways: and CAB, 406–7; certification of, 405; E. approves CAB recommendations, 2252–54; and Pacific Great Circle air route, 288, 406–7; and Redpath's view on CAB route awards, 288. *See also* Airlines

Pandit, Vijaya Lakshmi, 1649, 1650

Papers of Thomas Jefferson, 349–50

Parade magazine, 1033

Paraguay, Republic of: Amberg as special representative to, 1063–64; economic development in, 1725–26; and E.'s goodwill trip (December 1959), 1762–63; and IBRD, 1725–26; Nixon visits, 841, 899–900; requests transport aircraft, 1725–26; Rubottom recommends Dulles visit to, 631; and Treaty of Friendship, Commerce, and Navigation, 1725–26; on U.S.-Paraguayan relations, 1725–26. *See also* Stroessner, Alfredo

Paris: liberation of, 613–14, 1588, 1614–15, 1615–16, 1969–70; Pact of Paris, 724, 727; Parisians welcome E., 1654–57; on talks with de Gaulle, 1667–69. *See also* Goodwill tours; NATO: NATO meeting (December 1957); Summit Conference (May 1960); Western Summit Conference (December 1959)

Park, Samuel Culver, Jr., 1310–11

Parke Davis & Company, 891

Parker, Cola Godden, 1635–36

Parker, Edwin Lynch, 874–75

Parker, Hugh Arthur ("Lefty"), 1736

Parker, Janet L. (Baker), 1736

Parmachenee Lake (Maine), 413

Parsons, C. A. and Company, 1317

Parsons, Lewis Morgan, 1108

Parteet, Willie Frank. *See* "Cemetery"

Partial disagreement proposals, 632–36

Partial disarmament proposal, 632–36

Passman, Otto Ernest: background, 959; and mutual security appropriation, 1947–49

Pathet Lao: and civil war in Laos, 1670–71, 2219–21, 2223–25; Soviet support of, 2227–30; on support by North Vietnam, 1670–71, 2223–25. *See also* Laos, Kingdom of

Patronage, E.'s view, 268–69

Patten, Gilbert, 751–52

Patterson, Morehead, 1915, 1916

Patterson, Mrs. Percy R., background, 1222–23; on Thanksgiving gift to, 1223

logical warfare study, 1611–13; on reappointing Emanuel to Air Force Academy Board, 1923; on rebuilding GOP, 1259–61; and Republican Party Committee, 1305; and TVA bill, 1583–84; on water resource program, 1665–67; and Wyeth's portrait of E., 1780

Peru, Republic of: and anti-Nixon demonstrations at San Marcos University, 899–900; and Castro's aggression, 1601–3; and E.'s goodwill trip (December 1959), 1762–63; and lead/zinc import quotas, 1111–13; López Mateos visits, 1784–85; and minerals stabilization plan, 889–90; Nixon visits, 841, 899–900; takes anti-Castro stand, 2244–45

Pescadores (Penghu Islands). See China, Republic of: Pescadores

Petersen, Theodore Scarborough: background, 784, 1066, 1068; and Knowland's gubernatorial candidacy, 1064–68; member, BAC, 783–84

Peterson, Frederick Valdemar Erastus ("Val"), 11–12

Petroleum Advisory Council, 660–61

Petroleum Week, on natural gas legislation, 214

Pew, Arthur E., Jr., 1410–11

Pew, Joseph Newton, Jr., 1135–36

Phelps, George E.: and Atomic Energy Commission, 446–49; background, 446–49; on balancing the budget, 446–49; on decentralization of federal power, 446–49; on "Fair Deal-ism," 446–49; on farm program, 446–49; on farm surpluses, 446–49; on federal *v.* state responsibilities, 446–49; on flexible price supports, 446–49; on mutual security, 446–49; on national debt, 446–49; on national security, 446–49; on postal workers pay raise, 446–49; on Republicans, 446–49; on small business, 446–49; on social security program, 446–49; on taxation, 446–49; on tidelands legislation, 446–49; on U.S. economy, 446–49; on veterans programs, 446–49

Philadelphia Bulletin. See Media: press

Philip, The Prince, Duke of Edinburgh: attends St. Lawrence Seaway dedication, 1541–42; background, 181; E. visits Balmoral, 1616–17, 1620–21, 1623–25, 1641; visits U.S., 181, 243–44, 342, 495–96, 502–3, 526–27, 1130

Philippines, Republic of: Akers reports on, 675; on anniversary of Bataan's fall, 825; Bohlen's mission in, 1577–79; Diem visits, 898–99; and E.'s goodwill trip to (June 1960), 1868–69, 1941–42, 1982–83, 1983–84, 1985–86; E. serves in, 1736; and Garcia's inauguration, 675; on Garcia's U.S. visit, 675, 771–72, 825; and Huk Rebellion, 512–16; on increasing sugar imports quota,

1881–82; on "independencia," as watchword in, 115; and Indo-Pakistani dispute, 555–56; and Military Bases Agreement of 1947, 1577–79; pledges to protect Laos via SEATO, 2223–25; and trans-Pacific air routes to, 2252–54; U.S. aid to, 115

Phillips, J. E., Sr., 461–62

Phillips, Orie Leon, background, 60–61; and Bricker amendment, 60–61; on Gould, 818

Phillips Exeter Academy, 2146

Phillips Petroleum Company, and natural gas legislation, 213–15

Phillips Petroleum Company v. State of Wisconsin, and Supreme Court ruling, 213–15

Phoumi Nosavan, 2219–21

Phumiphol Aduldet. *See* Bhumibol Adulyadej

Phumiphon Adundet. *See* Bhumibol Adulyadej

Physical fitness, 452–53. *See also* Sports

Physicians. *See* Medical profession

Pierrot, A. Ogden, Jr., 2197–98

Pike, Thomas Potter, 719

Pineau, Christian: on arms for Tunisia, 563–67; background, 249, 565; on conditions for summit meeting, 782; on fall of French government, 831–34; protests U.S. arms for Tunisia, 567–70; role of, as foreign minister, 248

Pinkley, Virgil, 1755

Pittsburgh Courier, 511

Pittsburgh Plate Glass Company, 208–9

Pitzer schoolhouse: E.'s interest in, 177–78; John E. purchases, 126–27; Mamie E.'s view, 126–27; restoration of, 126–27. *See also* Gettysburg farm

Plato, 799

Platte, Lieutenant General and Mme., 188–91

Plessy v. Ferguson, 506. *See also* Civil rights

Plowden, Edwin Noel, 1659; on atomic tests inspections, 906–7; background, 907; reports on atomic inspections, 920–21; reports on U.S.-U.K. military atomic cooperation agreement, 920–21, 1024–25

Plowshare Project. *See* Mexico

Poetry Society of America, honors Frost, 881–82

P.O.L. (Petroleum, Oil, Lubricants), and supplies for Jordan, 1013–15

Poland, People's Republic of: and ambassadorial talks at Geneva, 1092–93, 1139–41; attends disarmament talks at Geneva, 932–33, 1058–59; de Gaulle's view, 1412–15; and ICC role in Laos, 2219–21, 2227–30; Khrushchev speaks on conditions in, 721–27; most-favored-nation status for, 2160; in need of U.S. aid, 1098–99; on nuclear weaponry in, Bulganin's view, 649–59; presents Rapacki Plan, 632–36; reconnaissance balloon descends in, 1031–32; Soviet relations with, 1076–77, 1322; Soviets propose Foreign Ministers' Meeting on Berlin

Revolutionary War, 157, 425
Rexall Drug Company, 1136
Reynolds, 1338
Reynolds Metals Company, 1542–43
Rhee, Syngman: agrees to reduce ROK forces, 387–88; background, 314–16; fears Communists, 314–16; on fear of Japanese expansion, 512–16; goes into exile in Hawaii, 1933; on Korea as ally in free world, 1514; on National Security Law revision, 1263–64; overthrow of, 1995–96; retires from political life, 1933; on suppression of political opposition, 1263–64; on U.S. role in ROK military force reduction, 314–16, 387–88; on U.S. role in ROK weaponry, 314–16. See also Korea, Republic of
Rheims, 423–24
Rhine River: crossing, in World War II, 689–91, 1295–98, 2182–83; and Monty, 1653–54, 2182–83. See also World War II
Rhode Island. See Eisenhower, Dwight David: vacations
Rhyne, Charles Sylvanus, 2099
Rice, John Stanley: background, 1574; offers office, 1822
Rice, Lester, 623–24
Rice, Stephen Ewing, 818
Richards, James Prioleau: background, 84–85; and Eisenhower Doctrine, 83–85, 383–85; meets with Saud, 383–85; travels to Mideast, 83–85; visits Saudi Arabia, 194–96
Richardson, Sidney Williams ("Sid"): on AEC construction legislation, 385–87; background, 18–19; on difficult Congress, E.'s view, 385–87; illness of, 1580–81; on limiting oil imports, 385–87; on mutual security program, 385–87; and National Presbyterian Church campaign, 18–19, 363, 1580–81; on natural gas legislation, 213–15; on new type of cold war, 385–87; regards to, 1345; sends flowers to Mamie E., 385; writes regarding oil industry, 368
Richfield Oil Corporation, 1136
Richter scale, 1813–14, 1890; and seismic research program, 1999–2001
Rickover, Hyman George, 1594
Riddleberger, James W.: background, 943; meets with Averoff-Tossizza, 942–44; reports on Cypriot question, 942–44
Ridgway, Matthew Bunker: background, 1756; Monty declines help from, 2184
Rio Treaty; Rio Conference. See Inter-American Treaty of Reciprocal Assistance of 1947
River Brethren. See Religion: River Brethren
River Clyde, Scotland, and Polaris, 1981–82, 1989–90, 2009–11, 2032, 2139–41
River and Harbor Act of 1945, 1665–67
Rivers and Harbors, Flood Control and Water Supply Acts of 1958, 1007–13

Rivers and harbors programs, 878–79. See also Water resources
Roberts, Charles de Clifford ("Cliff"): accompanies E. on Columbine, 1228; achieves winning golf scores, 1428; on Adams's "mistake," 1089–91; appreciation to, on midterm campaign support, 1182–83; on assessment for Augusta National Golf Club, 842–43; attends Augusta Jamboree, Masters, 1428; background, 127–28; on Dillon as Treasury Secretary, 2233–34; on donors to Mamie's Cabin, 2251–52; Dudley resigns from Augusta, 352, 353–54; as E.'s confidant, 1089–91; E. contributes to 1960 election campaign, 2068; as E.'s investment adviser, 512, 1228; on E.'s investments for family, 1306; E. recommends Sleichter as pro, 353–54; on E.'s upset stomach, 257; favors Percy to head RNC, 1235–36; as fundraiser for 1960 election, 2068; on hedge shoots for Gettysburg farm, 611; on "hopelessness" in GOP, 1088–89, 1089–91; and Humphrey's cracker barrel for Augusta, 334–35, 345, 582–83; on jet planes, 1589–91; joins Es. at Augusta Thanksgiving, 1228, 1235–36; on Knowland's gubernatorial candidacy, 1064–68, 1070–71, 1089–91; on Laura Houghton, 1590; on Little Rock crisis, 532; marriage of, 1262–63, 1306, 1428, 1584, 1589–91; meets with E. at Augusta, 1235–36; and Mellon's views on Gulf Oil, 1135–36; on "Muskateers" in Europe, 939–40, 964–65, 1001–2; on Nixon's trip to Moscow, 1589–91; and painting of Augusta's 16th hole, 1107–8; plays bridge with E., 173; plays golf with E. at Augusta, 795–96, 801–3, 866–67; on pledges for Citizens for Eisenhower-Nixon 1958, 897–98; on remedies for GOP, 1216–17, 1235–36, 1259–61; on Republican party fundraising, 1089–91; on Republican party principles, 801–3; on Roberts as "Tulips," 1001–2; scores Alcorn, 1235–36, 1259–61; sends French bread, 1589–91; sends golf plaque, 127–28; sends Spectacle of Sport, 611; on Stouffer food products, 257; on Trade Mart in Rome, 1589–91; visits Europe, 1584, 1589–91; on Volunteers for Nixon, 2068; on woodcarving of "Ike the Golfer," 1494
Roberts, Frank Kenyon, 997–98
Roberts, Kenneth Allison, 1665–67
Roberts, Letitia: background, 1263, 1428; in Europe with Roberts, 1584, 1589–91
Robertson, A. Willis: background, 396; and civil rights, 1375–78; opposes Burke Airport site, 372; supports AEC legislation, 395–96
Robertson, Reuben Buck, Jr.: background, 42,

for federal facility, 923–24; addresses Fordham University law alumni, 1337; on antitrust suits against drug companies, 891; on antitrust suits against oil and gas producers, 570–71; on appointment of federal judges, 756, 1292, 1343–45; on Arn's nomination for judgeship, 382; and Atomic Energy Act, 2214–15; as Attorney General, 382, 570–71; background, 382; and Bantz as federal judge, 1254–55, 1403; as campaign speaker on presidency, judiciary, 1793–96; on congressional immunity question, 1209; and Connally reservation, 1823–24, 1851–52; on constitutionality of withholding ICA funds, 2214–15; on crime, 2098; on Dethmers as candidate for Court of Appeals, 1721; and Du Pont's divestiture of GM stock, 741–43; E. sends talk by, to Woodruff, 1337; on executive powers for regulatory commissions, 2214–15; and federal disaster relief programs, 1129–30; and Frost, 881–82; on functions of Supreme Court, 875–78; and high school closings, 1134–35; on immigration visas for Emanuel's servants, 697–98; on juvenile delinquency, 2098; and Lawrence's proposal, 592–93; and McGill's editorial on civil rights, 834–35; on maritime labor union fears, 1394–95; meets with E., 1108–10; and NSC meeting on Berlin crisis, 1378–79; on NSC membership, 743–45; opposes Jenner bill, 875–78; on Petroleum Advisory Council, 660–61; on preemption in federal/state legislation, 925–26, 1480; on publicity for young Republicans, 524–25; and question of presidential disability, 711–14; on Rosentiel's proposal, 2177–78; and Salk vaccine, 891; and security breaches, 1692–93; on self-discipline, 1524; speaks at St. Lawrence University, 1524; succeeds Brownell, 382; supports Connally reservation repeal, 1851–52; on Supreme Court appointments, 1108–10; and Supreme Court decisions on labor unions, 925–26; on tidelands oil issue, 550–51, 594–96, 893–95; and TV-radio immunity issue, 1209; on United Givers Fund, 1129–30; as vice-presidential nominee, 1871; on Winn antitrust case, 1788–89. *See also* Attorneys General
Romania, 1164–65; attends atomic test suspension negotiations at Geneva, 1058–59
Rome treaties, 2115–18
Roncalli, Angelo Giuseppe. *See* Pope John XXIII
Rood, Rodney, 1181
Roosevelt, Anna Eleanor: background, 207–8; on Hungarian refugees, 207–8; on starvation in Morocco, 207–8; visits Brussels World's Fair, 1104

Roosevelt, Franklin Delano: establishes PWA, 764; Lowry scores, 1029–30; and Moley, 1334–35; role of, in founding March of Dimes, 37; role of, in World War II, 1027–31, 2181, 2187
Rosentiel, Lewis S., 2177–78
Rountree, William Manning: on Afghanistani-Pakistani relations, 1919–23; background, 297; on difficulties in relations with Saudi Arabia, 297–99; on Greek-Cypriot dispute, 1174–75; on Indo-Pakistani relations, 1774–76, 1919–23; meets with Azzam Pasha, 297–99; on pilgrim routes through Gulf of Aqaba, 296–97
Rouse, Robert G.: background, 381; and E.'s recommendation, 380–81; Woodruff's recommendation, 380–81
Rowley, James J.: background, 553; E.'s appreciation to, 2217; on E.'s safety in helicopters, 553
Royal Academy, Robertses visit, 1584
Royal Air Force (RAF): and AQUATONE, 107–9; equips Canberras with atomic weaponry, 107–9
Royall, Kenneth Claiborne, 1108–10, 1914
Rub al Khali. *See* Empty Quarter
Rubber, stockpiles, as anti-strike weapon, 1737–39
Rubottom, Roy Richard, Jr.: attends meetings in Mexico, 1356, 1357; background, 151–52; and Clark's plan to aid Trujillo, 1855–56; and Kubitschek, 924–25; and Milton E.'s report on Central America, 1244; recommends Dulles visit South America, 631; and U.S.-Argentine relations, 151–52
Ruffner, Clark L., 2030
Ruhr Valley (Germany), 2182–84, 2188
Ruiz Cortines, Adolfo: background, 70; gift for, 246–47; on lead/zinc tariffs, 759–60, 991–92, 1230–32; letter of esteem for, 1211–12; Milton E. visits, 246–47, 366–67; and Minerals Stabilization Plan, 991–92; sends gifts, 366–67; on surplus corn sale to Mexico, 152–53. *See also* Mexico
Ruiz Cortines, Señora, 366–67
Rule of Law for Peace, commission on, 996–97, 1038–39, 1158–59, 1279–81; Cousins drafts speech on, 1504
Rural Electrification Administration (REA): E.'s address on, 1349; and "pipsqueak" lobbyist, 1349
Ruschmeyer, Walter, 627–28
Rusk, Dean: background, 2208–9; E.'s view, 2230–32; to meet with Herter, 2208–9; as Secretary of State, 2208–9, 2230–32
Russell, Charles Marion, 669
Russell, Fred, 670–71
Russell, Richard Brevard: alleges troop misdeeds at Little Rock, 462–64; background, 71; compares E. to Hitler in Little Rock

Power memorandum, 98–100; on Suez Canal crisis, 24–25, 27, 98–100, 129–31, 194–96; supports Hussein in Jordanian crisis, 158–60, 180–81, 194–96; on treatment for Prince Mashur, 196; on United Arab Republic, 705–8; urges E. to entertain Nasser and al-Quwatly, 26; on U.S.-Arab relations, 98–100; on U.S.-Saudi relations, 98–100, 427–31; visits U.S., 19–27, 53–55, 72–73, 98–100, 129–31, 194–96, 1027–31. *See also* Saudi Arabia

Saudi Arabia: and Aden, 102; as anti-communistic, 20; and Arab-Israeli conflict, 19–27, 603; attends Cairo Conference, 23, 27, 72–73, 100; on British-Saudi relations, 20–21, 100–104, 332–34; and Buraimi controversy, 21, 26, 102, 104, 332–34; and Communist influence in Syria, 383–85; and Elson's visit, 273–74; and Empty Quarter, 21–26; forces of, to aid Jordan, 158–60; and free passage through Straits of Tiran and Gulf of Aqaba, 281, 297–99, 427–31; importance of Suez Canal to, 129–31; and Israeli withdrawal from Egypt, 53–55, 72–73, 98–100; and Muscat/Oman dispute, 332–34, 378–79; oil production in, 102, 104; rejects U.S. aide-memoire, 427–31; Saud proposes destruction of Israel, 603; seeks arms, 21, 26; and Soviet-Saudi relations, 19–27; and United Arab Republic, 705–8; on U.S. aid for, 19–27; and U.S. military aid program, 42–43, 427–31; on U.S.-Saudi relations, 98–100, 197–98, 297–99, 427–31. *See also* Egypt; Israel, State of; Saud, ibn Abd al-Aziz

Saud Ibn Abdul Aziz Al-Feisal, as Crown Prince of Saudi Arabia, until November 1953; thereafter King. *See* Saud, ibn Abd al-Aziz

Saulnier, Raymond J. ("Steve"), 1228; advises E. on speech draft, 861; advises Stassen on economy, 1561–62; background, 265; on Brussels World's Fair, 963–64; on budgetary refinancing, 1233–34; and Burns's report on Soviet industries, 264–65; and Burns's talk on recession, 793–95; and Cabinet committee on wages and prices, 1042–43; on Cabinet invitation protocol, 499–500; on Chamberlain's proposal, 863; and Committee on Economic Development, 777–82; on conference on productivity, 1832–33; confers with E. on recession recovery, 769–71; on coordination in economic recession recovery, 718–19; on domestic economy, 1426–27; economic report by, 629–30; and Humphrey's advice on federal budget, 589–91; meets with E., 629–30, 685–86, 1924–25; and Mitchell's memo on budget and U.S. economy, 621–

22; and postattack economic plans, 444–46; on public works expenditures, 859–61; on refinancing national debt, 1007–13; on retiring national debt, 1867–68; and right-to-work issue, 1165–67; skeptical of Summerfield's plan, 858–59; on tax reduction in recession recovery, 859–61

Savang Vatthana, King of Laos: background, 2219–21; and civil war in Laos, 2223–25. *See also* Laos, Kingdom of; Souvanna Phouma

Savannah. See Nuclear Ship *Savannah;* U.S.S. *Savannah*

Saybrook Banner of Arms, 606

Sayler, Jessie Dale (Dixon), 477

Sayler, Henry Benton, 477; background, 376; on naming U.S.S. *Savannah*, 376; supports Georgians for Nixon, 2128–29

Scandinavia, and NATO alliance, 882

Scatena, Robin and Terrill, 419–23

Schaefer, Julius Earl, 688–89

Schenley Industries, Inc., 2177–78

Scherer, Gordon Harry, 1608–9

Schmutz, Ivan, 529

Schoeppel, Andrew Frank: attends White House luncheon, 1142; background, 789; irritates E., 787–89; on political individualism, 787–89

Schoo, Clarence John ("Schooey"), 874–75

Schoo, Grace (Harwood), 1281–82

Schools. *See* Education

Schulz, Robert Ludwig ("Bob"): accompanies E. on midterm campaign trip, 1162–63; on Arthur E.'s burial at Abilene Museum, 938–39; background, 310–11; on Bermingham's illness, 538; catalogs E.'s books, 1266–67; and E. as candidate (1952), 1746–56; and E.'s golf clubs, 2035–36; and Goldman, 847–48; on Irvin's gift, 1266–67; on package for Mamie E., 1365–66

Schuyler, Cortlandt van Rensselaer ("Cort"): attends luncheon for E., 680–81; background, 681; E.'s esteem for, 680–81; retirement of, 680–81, 1298–99; as SACEUR, 1298–99

Schuyler, Wynona (Coykendall) ("Wy"), 681

Schware v. *Board of Bar Examiners of New Mexico*, 875–78

Schwartz, General, 1105–6

Schwarz, Hamilton D., 539–40

Schweitzer, Albert: background, 46–47; Princeton's invitation to, 1404–6; scores Dulles, 1404–6; scores U.S. atomic testing, 1404–6; writes E. on French-Algerian question, 46–47, 88

Schweizer, John M., Jr., 1484–85

Science Advisory Committee. *See* Office of Defense Mobilization: Science Advisory Committee

Scientific Advisory Committee. *See* Office of Defense Mobilization: Science Advisory Committee

Scientists: on announcing achievements of, 686–87; appreciation of, 785; on awards for achievement, 795–96; on Churchill College at Cambridge University, 880–81; on scientific manpower in U.S., 503–5, 534–35, 560–61, 609, 645–46, 1007–13; on U.S.-USSR achievements, 1901–2

Scotland: and Black Brutus of E.F., 291, 326; on breeding Scottish bulls, 326; on cattle imports from, 29–30; E. visits, 1650–51; golf at Maybole, with Gault, 1220–21; golf at Prestwick, 202; on locating sub tender in Gareloch, 2009–11; on Polaris facilities in Clyde area, 2032, 2139–41; on sub base at Holy Loch, 2139–41; on sub base at Loch Linnhe, 1989–90, 2009–11; on sub base at River Clyde, 1989–90, 2009–11. *See also* Balmoral Castle; Culzean Castle

Scott, Hugh Doggett, Jr.: background, 1120; Mellon's support for, 1119–20, 1136; as vice-presidential nominee, 1871; wins Senate seat, 1138, 1153–56

Scott, Randolph, 890

Scribner, Fred Clark, Jr.: background, 589; as campaign speaker on treasury, 1793–96; on tax payments in federal bonds, 588–89

Sculptors, sittings for, E.'s dislike of, 135–36

Sea of Japan, 512–16

Sears, Roebuck and Company, 1136

SEATO (Southeast Asia Treaty Organization) (Manila Pact): on Australia-New Zealand-U.K.-U.S. military plans, 844–46; and civil war in Laos, 2223–25; discusses Berlin crisis, 1694–96; discusses summit negotiations, 771–72; Dulles attends meetings of, 81–82, 86–87, 631, 771–72, 782, 784–85, 789–91; on exchange of military data, 771–72; meets in Washington, D.C., 1878–79; and Pakistan, 2209–10; pledges protection to Laos, 2223–25; and relations with NATO, 771–72; role of, in cold war defenses, 1159–62; and role of Thailand, 2151–53; on Sarasin as Secretary General, 453–54; and support for mutual security program, 1947–49; and U.S. policy in Laos, 2227–30; and U.S. policy in Southeast Asia, 86–87, 263–64. *See also* Far East; Southeast Asia

Seaton, Frederick Andrew: on Atlantic salmon treaty with Canada, 1057; background, 1094–95; as campaign speaker on defense, interior, 1793–96; on diplomacy in Cambodia, 1606–7; on election results in Hawaii, 1606–7; on funding national memorials, 1094–95; hosts dinner honoring Hauge,

1110–11; Interior Department budget and bureaucracy issues, 1545; and Jefferson National Expansion Memorial, 1094–95; as 1960 presidential nominee, 1201–2; on oil import quotas, 1555–56; supports statehood for Hawaii, 1606–7; as vice-presidential nominee, 1871. *See also* Interior, Department of

Seattle University, E. declines invitation from, 1963–64

Secretary of Agriculture, and government reorganization, 1700–1702. *See* Agriculture, Department of; Benson, Ezra Taft; Freeman, Orville Lothrop

Secretary of the Air Force, and Declaration of Common Purpose, 544–45. *See also* Douglas, James Henderson, Jr.; Quarles, Donald Aubrey; Talbott, Harold Elsner; United States Air Force

Secretary of the Army, and Declaration of Common Purpose, 544–45. *See also* Army, Department of; Brucker, Wilber Marion; Stevens, Robert Ten Broeck

Secretary of Commerce. *See* Commerce, Department of; Mueller, Frederick Henry; Strauss, Lewis Lichtenstein; Weeks, Sinclair

Secretary of Defense, and line of command in DOD reorganization, 904–5. *See* Defense, Department of; Gates, Thomas Sovereign, Jr.; McElroy, Neil Hosler; McNamara, Robert Strange; Wilson, Charles Erwin

Secretary of the Interior: and government reorganization, 1700–1702; and Ickes, 1256–58; and McKay, 1256–58. *See also* Interior, Department of; McKay, Douglas; Seaton, Frederick Andrew

Secretary of the Navy. *See* Anderson, Robert Bernerd; Franke, William Birrell; Gates, Thomas Sovereign, Jr.; Thomas, Charles Sparks; United States Navy

Secretary of State: on Byrnes as, 1498–99; and E.'s esteem for Dulles, 436, 437; and executive powers in regulatory commissions, 2214–15; and First Secretary of Government, 1700–1702; on Marshall as, 1498–99; Milton E. as advisor to, 2148–49; on new role for Dulles, 664–65, 695–96; not an errand boy, 1521; on question of presidential disability, 711–14. *See also* Dulles, John Foster; Herter, Christian Archibald; Rusk, Dean; State, Department of

Secretary of the Treasury, and executive powers in regulatory commissions, 2214–15. *See* Anderson, Robert Bernerd; Dillon, Clarence Douglas; Humphrey, George Magoffin; Treasury, Department of

Secret Service. *See* United States Secret Service

Securities and Exchange Commission (SEC): Edgar recommends Davis to, 109–10;

Gadsby heads, 109–10; House investigates Adams-Goldfine relationship, 952–60

Segregation. *See* Civil rights

Seifert, Charles W., 400–401

Senate, U.S., 187–88; acts on Weeks Committee proposals, 484–85; and aid to education, 255–56; and airport facilities bill, 1422–23; amends civil rights bill, 328–31, 346, 354–56; approves Minerals Stabilization Plan, 1111–13; confirms delegates to U.N. General Assembly, 335–36; confirms Gluck as U.S. ambassador to Ceylon, 338–39; confirms Herter as Secretary of State, 1452; confirms McElroy as Secretary of Defense, 477–78; confirms Morrow as U.S. ambassador to Guinea, 1503–4; confirms Mueller as Secretary of Commerce, 1589; and Connally Amendment, 1851–52; considers aid to unemployed, 760–65; and Cordiner Committee recommendations, 93–94, 289–90; and Danish shipping case, 414–15; debates civil rights measure, 274–75; debates reciprocal trade legislation, 1016; Democratic majority in, 1193–94, 1984–85; and DOD reorganization, 904–5; E. opposes NSC investigation, 1538–40; extends Trade Agreements Act, 1047; Goldwater scores E. in speech to, 157–58; and Harris-Fulbright natural gas bill, 63–64; and Hoover Commission recommendations, 199–200; and Housing legislation, 1007–13, 1329–31; introduces price-freeze bill, 787–89; Knowland, Bridges score reciprocal trade bill, 952–60; labor racketeering measure fails, 1153–56; and loyalty oath requirements, 1505–7; and medical care for elderly, 1702–3; and military retirement bill, 1984–85, 2053–54; and mutual security appropriations, 354–56, 389–90, 400, 1002, 1041; overrides E.'s veto, 1054–55; passes Military Pay Bill, 910–11; passes Minerals Stabilization Plan, 991–92; passes resolution on Mideast aid, 71–72, 142–43; passes revised farm bill, 1045–46; and Pay Equalization Bill, 1984–85; on reciprocal trade legislation, 952–60; rejects Strauss's nomination, 920–21, 1543–45, 1553–54, 1581–82; and Reorganization Act of 1949, 1700–1702; on residential loan rates, 783–84; on retired officers pay, 1560–61; on "right-wing" senators, 396–99; on southern senators and civil rights, 1375–78; stalls school construction legislation, 1307–9; on subsidies of feeder airlines (S. 2229), 547; and Supreme Court jurisdictions, 875–78; tables Jenner bill, 875–78; Teller testifies before investigating committee, 598–99; and TVA bond issues, 1583–84, 1608–9; and Washington, D.C., airport sites, 369–72

—Appropriations Committee: and appropriations for Labor, HEW, 2034–35; and appropriations for medical research, 1594–97; and Development Loan Fund, 184–85, 220–21, 354–56; Humphrey testifies on Coast Guard aircraft funds, 133; and IAEA, 220–21; increases mutual security funds, 1041; and Mutual Security Program, 220–21, 1002; recommends defense increases, 1007–13; and USIA, 220–21

—Armed Services Committee: and NSC membership, 743–45; and pay rates for retired officers, 1245–47

—Banking Committee, approves housing bill appropriations, 1334–35

—Commerce Committee, approves Mueller as Secretary of Commerce, 1589

—Finance Committee: Byrd proposes financial system inquiry, 160–61, 163; Humphrey testifies on fiscal and monetary policies, 277–78

—Foreign Relations Committee: and Connally reservation, 1823–24, 1851–52; Dulles's statement before, 918, 1314–15; and foreign service academy, 1069–70; Gluck testifies before, 338–39; Johnson supports foreign aid program, 220–21; McLeod testifies before, 145; and mutual security, 1331–32; questions wisdom of pact of non-aggression, 642–44; subcommittee on State Department Organization and Public Affairs investigates Vietnam aid program, 1639–40, 1733–35; and Treaty of Mutual Cooperation and Security with Japan, 1959–60

—Government Operations Committee: establishes Subcommittee on National Policy Machinery, 1538–40, 1991–93; on First Secretary of Government, 1700–1702; Luce testifies before, 1991–93

—Interstate and Foreign Commerce Committee, and Strauss nomination hearings, 1446–47, 1484, 1502–3, 1543–45; and Surface Transportation Subcommittee, 777–82

—Judiciary Committee: Antitrust and Monopoly Subcommittee of, 252–53; and Equal Rights Amendment, 437–38; kills federal preemption doctrine bill, 925–26; and Trading with the Enemy Subcommittee on disposal of foreign assets, 170–71

—Labor and Public Welfare Committee, members of, as campaign speakers on labor, 1793–96

—Select Committee on Improper Activities in Labor or Management Field: hears testimony on Teamsters Union tactics, 587; McClellan chairs, 1153–56; recommendations by, 1153–56

Senegal, Republic of, and Mali-Senegal split,

2100–2102; U.S. recognition of, 2100–
2102. *See also* Keita, Modibo
Servicemen's Readjustment Act of 1944 (GI
bill), 458–60
Service Pipe Line of Tulsa, Oklahoma, 570–71
Sessions, Edson O., 1793–96
Seychelles, and Makarios, 104, 118, 118–19,
269–70
Sfax, 569
Shah of Iran. *See* Pahlavi, Mohammed Reza
Shanley, Bernard Michael: background, 188–
91; campaigns for New Jersey Senate seat,
679–80; on dinner for Coty, 188–91; on
invitation to Presbyterian Convention,
344–45; loses in New Jersey primary, 679–
80; seeks campaign funds, 679–80
Shanley, Maureen Virginia (Smith), 188–91
SHAPE (Supreme Headquarters Allied Powers,
Europe): and British Fighter Command,
1819–20; E. addresses, 1654–57; E. refrains
from visit, 1952–53; E. visits, 604–5, 616–
17, 734, 737; and French Territorial Air
Defense, 1926–27; on integrated commands at, 1667–69, 1819–20
Sharm el Sheikh: Israeli forces at, 34–36; role
of U.N. at, 72–73, 91–93; and UNEF, 91–
93; UNEF remains at, 104
Shell Oil Company, 2007, 2039–42
Shepherd, Joshua K., 476
Shepherd, William M., 476
Sheraton Park Hotel, 609–11
Sherman Antitrust Act, 741–43; and antitrust
suits against drug companies, 891; and
Winn case, 1788–89
Sherwood, Jack, 900
Shipping: E. vetoes maritime bill, 1007–13;
and international law at Gulf of Aqaba, 24,
27, 53–55, 98–100, 129–31, 194–96, 197–
98, 281, 297–99, 427–31; in Straits of
Tiran, 94–95, 197–98, 281; and U.S.S. *Sa-
vannah*, 376. *See also* Egypt: Suez Canal;
Maritime industry
Shivers, Allan: background, 393; E. recom-
mends, to Civil Rights Commission, 392–
94; on tidelands oil issue, 893–95
Shivers, Marialice (Shary), 895
Shoda, Michiko, Crown Princess of Japan,
1978–79
Shuman, Charles B., 1290–91
Siberia: and E.'s trip to Japan via, 1766–67,
1790–91, 1806–7; on "Hunting in Siberia,"
1790–91; on Vladivostok, 1766–67
Sibley, John Adams, 391
Siciliano, Rocco Carmine: background, 1793–
96; as campaign speaker on labor, 1793–
96; commends Reid, 1149
Sides, John H., 292–93
Sidewinder, 2096, 2098
Sihanouk Upayvareach, Samdech Preah
Norodom: background, 1390, 1472–74; on

Cambodia's relations with Thailand, 1390,
1432–35, 1472–74; on Cambodia's relations with U.S., 1390, 1432–35, 1472–74,
2013–14; on Cambodia's relations with
Vietnam, 1390, 1432–35, 1472–74; as Chief
of State, 2013–14; concern of, on Laos,
2248–50; on father's illness, 1432–35;
health of, 1472–74; invites E. to visit,
2013–14; on Lao refugees in Cambodia,
2248–50; on neutralization of Cambodia
and Laos, 2248–50; proposes international
conference on Laos, 2248–50; on release
of letter by, 1390; and SEATO, 1432–35.
See also Cambodia, Kingdom of
Simmons, Gene, 1364–65
Simmons, Gordon: background, 732; and bird
shoot at Greenwood Plantation, 1364–65
Simpson, Richard Murray: attends White
House luncheon, 1142; background, 518;
and dispute with RNC, 518; scores administration policies, 518
Simpson, William Hood, 1271–73
Singapore, Republic of, and trans-Pacific air
routes to, 2252–54
Single Integrated Operations Plan (SIOP),
2135–36
Sino-Soviet bloc, 649–59; aggression by, and
U.S. policy, 1131–33; and civil war in Laos,
2223–25, 2227–30; and Committee on
World Economic Practices, 1311–13; eco-
nomic offensive by, 1311–13, 1671–72; of-
fers aid to Algerian nationalists, 2209–10;
sends jet aircraft to Indonesia, 1331–32;
and Sihanouk, 2013–14
Sirikit Kitiyakara, Queen of Thailand: back-
ground, 2011; on protocol in Europe,
2011; visits U.S., 2011, 2151–53. *See also*
Thailand, Kingdom of
Sixteenth Amendment. *See* Constitution of the
United States
Skaff, Woody, 587
Skeet shooting, 135–36, 310–11, 368–69,
2218–19
Skinner, Moretta Hinkle, 36
Skouras, Spyros Panagiotes: background, 269–
70; on Makarios and British public opin-
ion, 269–70, 302; on movie room at Gettys-
burg farm, 2207–8; on publicity for young
Republicans, 524–25
Skybolt bomber-missile program, 1981–82,
1989–90, 2147; E.'s concern, 2149–50;
Macmillan's letter regarding, 2139–41; and
Polaris missile program, 1981–82, 2147. *See
also* Missiles
Sky Hawk air defense exercise, cancellation of,
1647, 1661–62
Sky Shield air defense exercise, 1661–62
Slater, Ellis Dwinnell ("Slats"): and Adams's
memoir, 1239–40; attends birthday dinner,
157; background, 138; on dinner for Coty,

drafts speech for NATO meeting, 617–18; and security leak on redeployment, 2204; and Stevenson's role at NATO meeting, 571–72, 605–6; strike force using Polaris missiles, 2115–18; and U.S. Citizens Commission on NATO, 2083–84; and U.S. naval forces in Mediterranean, 1313–14; and WEU, 128–29
—Netherlands: and civil air agreement with KLM, 81–82; and U.S. Embassy at the Hague, 1555
—Norway, on miscommunication with Norwegians, 628–29
—Pakistan: and draft message to Chundrigar, 555–56; and draft message to Mirza, 1147; and Indo-Pakistani dispute, 1774–76, 1919–23
—Palestine, and issue of Palestinian refugees, 293–95
—Panama: Cake's idea, 1840–41; on U.S. relations with, 1827–28, 2088–89
—Paraguay, and draft message to Stroessner, 1725–26; on U.S. aid to, 1725–26
—Philippines: and draft messages to Garcia, 825, 1881–82; on Garcia's U.S. visit, 771–72, 825
—Poland: and most-favored-nation status for, 2160; on seating Kadar delegation at U.N., 1190–91, 1191–92, 1232–33
—Ryukyu Islands, on currency conversion in, 919–20, 1049–51; and U.S. policy toward, 827–29, 1049–51
—Saudi Arabia: and draft messages to Saud, 53–55, 72–73, 98–100, 129–31, 194–96, 427–31, 607–8, 705–8; and meeting with Saud, 19–27; and travelers to Holy Places, 197–98, 296–97
—Soviet Union: Baruch's view, 1360–61; and draft messages to Bulganin, 191–94, 649–59, 721–27; and draft messages to Khrushchev, 819–22, 848–49, 901–2, 932–33, 981–82, 1101–2, 1447–48, 1463–66, 1718–19, 1757–58, 1806–7, 1844–48, 1887–90, 1910–11; drafts message to Parker, 1635–36; on friendship teams exchange with, 1076–77; investigation of overflight at Soviet border, 1031–32; and invitation to Soviet students, 791–92; on missing USAF airmen, 1687–88; on Nixon's visit to Moscow, 1594; on Soviet ideology and policy institute, 1893–94; and Soviet proposals on outer space, 784–85; and translation of Khrushchev's reply, 1585–86; and U.S.-Soviet exchange projects, 1076–77; and U.S.-Soviet trade, 981–82
—Summit Conference, drafts letters to international leaders, 1953–54
—Thailand, on relations with Cambodia, Vietnam, 1432–35, 2013–14

—Tunisia, and draft messages to Bourguiba, 1113–15, 2133–35
—Turkey: and draft message to Bayar, 1051; and draft message to Gursel, 1974–75; on economic aid for, 944–45
—United Kingdom: and draft message to Churchill, 1192–93; and draft messages to Macmillan, 128–29, 278–79, 544–45, 729–30, 906–7, 936–37, 993–96, 1367–68, 1399–1402, 1438–39, 1440–42, 1444–45, 1527–29, 1541–42, 1967–68, 1981–82, 1999–2001, 2001–7, 2012–13, 2015, 2027–28, 2032, 2039–42, 2046–47, 2094–95, 2139–41, 2147, 2219–21; and draft message to Monty, 612–13; on retirement tribute to Monty, 948–50; and tripartite consultations, 2046–47; on U.S.-U.K. atomic cooperation, 920–21; and U.S.-U.K. staff planning, 1481–82
—United Nations: and delegation to General Assembly, 335–36; on Khrushchev's address to, 2078–79; and law of the sea, 1911–12; and police protection for meeting of, 2104–5
—Venezuela: and oil import quotas, 1457–59; as site for Inter-American Development Bank, 1442–43
—Vietnam: on aid program for, 1733–35; and civil war in Laos, 2219–21; drafts message to Diem, 1639–40, 2138–39; on gift vase for Diem, 1474–75; on relations with Cambodia, Thailand, 1432–35, 2013–14
—Yugoslavia, on military aid to, 376–77
States' rights, 1153–56; and crisis at Little Rock, 462–64, 1079–80; Edgar E.'s view, 2035–36; in education, 527–29, 1307–9; E.'s view, 446–49, 2123–24; Goldwater's view, 2123–24; and preemptive legislation, 925–26; to prosecute Communists, 875–78; on standards for Bar admission, 875–78; and states' responsibilities, 275–76, 282, 431–32; and three-mile limit on territorial seas, 550–51, 749–50, 776–77, 893–95. See also Supreme Court of the United States; United States: federal-state issues
State of the Union Address. See Eisenhower, Dwight David: speeches
Status of Forces Agreement and Headquarters Protocol: Clark opposes, 457–58; E. supports, 319–25, 434–37; and Girard case, 319–25; Gruenther supports, 457–58; Lewis scores, 457–58
Steel industry: and Blough's speech, 1824–25; on E. as mediator, 1626–27, 1727–28; and featherbedding, 1626–27, 1727–28; government role in, 1626–27; and "Memphis Case," 765–66; and "Robber Barons," 747; and settlement of strike, 1737–39; speculation on strike legislation, 1737–39; and

steel strike, 1582–83, 1626–27, 1737–39, 1824–25; Supreme Court approves injunction, 1727–28; and Taft-Hartley Act, 1737–39; and union view on "work rules," 1727–28

Stein, Jules, 2034

Steinberg, Jill Robin, 454–55

Steinmetz, Charles Proteus, 534–35

Stengel, Casey, 254

Stennis, John Cornelius: background, 1377; and Military Pay Bill, 1984–85

Stephens, Thomas Edgar, 670–71

Stephens, Thomas Edwin, 924, 1136, 1411, 1524, 1659, 1789–90, 1840–41, 1956–59, 2207–8; to advise Rockefeller, 488–89; background, 43, 106; on E.'s speech at Gettysburg College, 1279–81; and E.'s visit to Fort Ligonier, 951; and Gettysburg office for E., 1573–74; on presidential speech agenda, 1492–94; and Republican party politics, 106; returns to White House, 106; talks with Earl E., 614–15

Stevens, Stanley Smith, 785

Stevenson, Adlai Ewing: as ambassador to U.N., 2232; background, 313–14; declines NATO meeting, 605–6; and Hell's Canyon Dam, 1256–58; to meet with Dulles on NATO meeting, 571–72; memo by, on NATO meeting, 605–6; receives honorary degree from Oxford, 313–14; and right-to-work issue, 1123–24; Whitney entertains, 313–14

Stevenson, Jordan & Harrison, "Monthly Digest of Business Conditions and Probabilities," 1189

Stewart, Potter, 1108–10

Stillman, Charles, 196

Stimson, Henry Lewis, 115, 117

Stock market: decline in, 1226–27; effect of economy on, 783–84; and E.'s indigestion, 264–65; and home building industry, 783–84

Stouffer, Vernon Bigelow: background, 50–51; E. declines Stouffer Corporation board, 2079–80; on electric oven repair, 1022–23; installs electric oven at Gettysburg farm, 50–51; sends frozen foods, 50–51, 257

Stout, Gene, 354

Straits of Aqaba: on international waters at, 98–100, 194–96, 197–98; and safe passage for religious pilgrims, 53–55; withdrawal of Israeli force at, 53–55. See also Egypt; Gulf of Aqaba; Israel, State of

Straits of Tiran, 34–36; international character of, 91–93; and maritime traffic in, 94–95, 197–98, 281

Strategic Air Command (SAC): Gaither Report recommendations, 584–85; and Joint Strategic Target Planning Staff study,

2135–36; staff organization at, 2099–2100; and U-2 flights, 107–9; on vulnerability of, in nuclear attack, 584–85

Strategic materials: inventories of, as anti-strike weapons, 1737–39; and plutonium production in atomic power reactors, 1024–25; and Volta River project, 552–53, 637–39. See also Minerals; Raw materials

Strategic Target Planning Staff. See Joint Strategic Target Planning Staff

Stratton, William Grant, 2109–11

Strauss, Alice (Hanauer), 188–91, 1549–50

Strauss, Franz-Josef, 147, 149

Strauss, Lewis Lichtenstein, 289; on admirals and laymen as science experts, 598–99; on AEC success in Congress, 395–96; on Amandale Eileenmere 492-8, 1789–90; on assurances to atomic lab personnel, 965; and "Atoms for Peace" speech (1953), 113; on AT&T and budget fight, 1416–17; attends dinner honoring Elizabeth II, 499–500; attends NATO meeting, 598–99, 618; background, 39–40; on Bulganin-Eisenhower correspondence, 649–59; on Cabinet invitation protocol, 499–500; on cattle for Khrushchev, 1766–67; on CBS inflation programs, 1417; and Committee on World Economic Practices, 1311–13; and conference on peaceful uses of atomic energy, 256–57; and Cordiner's letter on machinery imports, 1449–50; and course on artificial insemination, 126–27; Court of Claims negates Anderson's charge, 1581–82; on dinner for Coty, 188–91; and "Doktor Eisenbart," 598; drafts statement on nuclear testing, 456; E.'s disdain for attackers of, 1484; Es. entertain, 1549–50; E.'s esteem for, 1543–45, 1549–50; E. sends painting to, 1549–50; esteem of, for E., 1543–45; on exchange of restricted data, 39–40, 906–7; and fallout radiation, 270–71, 287; and "free" communications, 1417; on free trade and national security, 1449–50; Krock's esteem for, 1502–3; on Maryland livestock show, 1659; medallion for, from E., 1549–50; and media exposure on budget fight, 1369–71; meets with E., 1659, 1789–90; as member, NBC, RCA boards, 1789–90; and NSC membership, 743–45; opposes Dulles on Soviet test ban, 819–22; and People-to-People exchange program, 256–57; on performance of hay machine, 931–32; proposes E. address U.N., post-Khrushchev visit, 1669–70; proposes Swiss role in atomic test inspections, 1880–81; on Rabi and Teller, 519–20; reports on GNP, 1451, 1531; reports on U.S.-U.K. military atomic cooperation agreement, 1024–25; resigns, 920–21, 1543–45; and Science Advisory Committee recommendations,

519–20; as Secretary of Commerce, 920–21, 1369–71, 1446–47, 1502–3; Senate rejects nomination, 920–21, 1484, 1502–3, 1543–45, 1563–64, 1581–82; on Soviet nuclear tests suspension, 819–22; on technical experts as disarmament inspectors, 901–2; Teller's testimony on behalf of, 1553–54; on testing atomic weaponry, 216–18, 270–71, 455–56, 519–20; transfers interest in Brockmere 10, 885–86, 931–32, 1789–90; travels in *Columbine* with E., 598–99; on U.S.-U.K. cooperation in atomic inspections, 920–21. *See also* Atomic Energy Commission; Commerce, Department of

Strecker, Frances, 2205

Strecker, George O., 2205

Stroessner, Alfredo: background, 1725–26; inauguration of, 1063–64; on transport aircraft for Paraguay, 1725–26; on U.S.-Paraguayan relations, 1725–26. *See also* Paraguay, Republic of

Strong, Kenneth William Dobson, 1274–76. *See also* World War II

Stuart, James Ewell Brown ("Jeb"), 240

Stuart, Robert Douglas ("Doug"): background, 1326–27; on dangers of inflation, 1326–27; and E.'s use of television, 1326–27; on Kemper as National Committeeman, 2110; shoots quail in Alabama, 1326–27; supports budget program, 1326–27

Studebaker Corporation, E. declines gift automobile, 2235–36

Students: address to, at Columbia, 1965–67; commend E., 439–50; exchanges, 692–93, 726, 727, 774, 789–91, 791–92, 797–99, 822–23; from Guinea visit, 1902–4; letter to, in Chile, 1884–85; letter to, in Korea, 2016–18; letter to, in U.S., 2016–18; riots by, in Panama, 1713–15, 1744–46; riots by, in Turkey, 1931; score U.S. businessmen, 1856–57; service academy exchange, 688–89

Submarines: and construction of Dutch nuclear submarine, 2102; and intraservice rivalry, 735, 738; on naming ballistic missile submarines, 1613; Polaris facilities in Scotland, 2032, 2139–41; and Polaris sub bases in U.K., 1981–82, 1989–90, 2009–11; on U.S.S. *John Marshall*, 1613; on U.S.S. *Nathan Hale*, 1613; on U.S.S. *Sam Houston*, 1613; on U.S.S. *Thomas A. Edison*, 1613; v. nuclear aircraft carriers, 735, 738

Submerged Lands Act of 1953: Johnson's protest, 550–51; and Supreme Court, 893–95. *See also* Natural resources; Oil industry; Tidelands legislation

Suchner, R. W., 223–25

Sudan: and effective use of propaganda in, 993–96; with Ethiopia, combats Nasserism, 168; Nixon visits, 167, 168

Suez Canal. *See* Egypt: Suez Canal

Sugar Act Amendments, and Cuba's sugar quota, 1995–96, 2001–7

Sugar Act of 1948, 1881–82

Sugar Act of 1956, 1881–82, 1995–96

Sugar industry: in Cuba, 1731–32, 2001–7; on increasing Philippine imports quota, 1881–82; and 1956 Sugar Act, 1995–96

Sugarman, Mrs. Harry, 451–52

Suhrawardy, Huseyn Shaheed: addresses Congress, 350–51; background, 301; discusses U.S.-Pakistan relations, 301; visits Bohemian Grove, 350–51; visits E., 301

Sukarno, Achmed: ambitions of, 955; background, 959; declares Indonesian independence, 845; on E.-Khrushchev meeting, 2111–13; leftist leanings of, 845, 955; on U.S. political support, 1332. *See* Indonesia, Republic of

Sulzberger, Arthur Hays: background, 349–50; on C. L. Sulzberger's column, 1319–21, 1325–26; on commemorative stamp for Ochs, 349–50; and Duffus's editorial, 603–4; E. recommends, to Civil Rights Commission, 392–94; on *New York Times* editorial, 1319–21

Sulzberger, Cyrus Leo ("C.L.," "Cy"): article by, on nuclear disarmament, 242–43; background, 667; column by, on ecumenical movement, 1319–21, 1325–26; E. scores article by, 666–67, 667–68; Gruenther scores, 667–68; on Pope John XXIII, 1319–21, 1325–26; scores Dulles, 666–67

Sulzberger, Marina Tatiana (Lada), 1325–26

Sumatra: rebellion in, 844–46; and trans-Pacific air routes to, 2252–54. *See also* Indonesia, Republic of

Summerfield, Arthur Ellsworth, Sr.: background, 188–91; and Cabinet committee on wages and prices, 1042–43; as campaign speaker on postal service, 1793–96; on commemorative stamp for Ochs, 349–50; condolences, on Arthur E.'s death, 698–99; on dinner for Coty, 188–91; on economic recession recovery, 719; on Fed policies, 858–59; and GOP head as member of Cabinet, 258–59; on IRS tax auditing procedures, 586–87; on partisan politics in Post Office, 1839; on promoting American optimism, 858–59; and *Reader's Digest*, 1636–37; on rebuilding GOP, 1236–39; as RNC head, 1236–39; on second class postal rates, 1944–45; sends missile mail, 1520; on Suchner's concerns, 223–25; supports Postal Rate Bill, 1007–13; and talk by, on U.S. economy, 1391; on teamster union racketeering, 587; on U.S. private investments abroad, 2051–52

Summerfield, Arthur ("Bud") Ellsworth, Jr.: appreciation to, for Heidi the dog, 694; attends stag dinner, 258–59; on automobile dealers' franchise rights, 208–9; background, 208–9, 259; on GOP head as member of Cabinet, 258–59; writes E. on GOP speech, 694

Summerfield, Miriam W.(Graim): background, 188–91; condolences, on Arthur E.'s death, 698–99

Summit Conference (May 1960), 1761–62, 1900; Adenauer participates in organization for, 1817–18; Adenauer's view, 1697–1700; agreement on date, 1779; announcement of, 1689–90; on atomic disarmament and inspection zones, 1926–27; and Berlin crisis, 1487–88, 1510–12, 1520–22, 1525–27, 1574–76, 1587–88, 1591–93, 1685–86, 1955–56; Bulganin's view, 667–68, 696–97, 792–93; collapses, 1950–51, 1952, 1953–54, 1969–70, 2111–13; on conditions for, 728–29, 736, 738, 739–40, 748–49, 782, 804–6, 1604–5; on de Gaulle as host, 1919–23, 1894–95; de Gaulle's view, 1697–1700, 1740–42, 1927–28; Diefenbaker speaks on collapse, 1960–61; to discuss FRG-USSR issues, 1817–18; on draft agenda for, 973–75; draft reply to Khrushchev regarding, 961; on duration of meeting, 1894–95, 1910–11; E. considers Moscow visit, 1601–3, 1604–5, 1691–92; E. keeps Khrushchev informed, 1718–19; E. prefers four-power basis, 1697–1700; E.'s reservations regarding, 632–36, 696–97, 1424–26, 1499–1500; E. speaks on collapse, 1960; and foreign ministers in preparation, 768–69, 1591–93; Geneva as site for, 1491–92; Gromyko's role, 973–75, 1499–1500, 1601–3; and interpretation, 1927–28; on Italy's participation, 804–6; Jackson's role as adviser on, 768–69, 1915–17; on June 16th statement, 1591–93, 1601–3; Khrushchev's attitude, 973–75, 1499–1500, 1691–92, 1740–42; Khrushchev endorses Cuban Revolution, 2001–7; Khrushchev's U.S. visit, 1585–86, 1591–93, 1601–3, 1604–5, 1614–15, 1615–16; Macmillan counter-attacks Khrushchev, 2015; on Macmillan's impatience for, 1591–93; meetings on, in Turkey, 1931; and *modus vivendi* with Soviets, 1697–1700; on Nash's talks with Khrushchev, 1878–79; Nixon to act for E. at, 1909, 1910–11; on participation of other countries, 1697–1700; Patterson's proposals, 1915–17; on preliminary discussions with de Gaulle, 1516–17; prerequisites for, 1509–10; on procedures at, 1909, 1927–28; and progress at Foreign Ministers' Meeting, 1520–22, 1525–27, 1574–76, 1585–86, 1587–88, 1601–3, 1604–5; and progress at Geneva Nuclear Test Conference, 1510–12,

1844–48; on reports of allied disunity, 1955–56; and rights in Berlin, 1697–1700; Robinson's view, on collapse, 1960; on role of foreign ministers, 1927–28; on role of Secretary of State, 1521; and SEATO, 771–72; security leakage regarding, 1601–3; Soviets break off discussions regarding, 1003–7; and Soviet vote on Algeria in U.N., 1708–7; and Steering Committee, 1817–18; on timing and site for, 1591–93, 1593–94, 1601–3, 1685–86, 1689–90, 1691–92, 1757–58; on U.S. advisers to, 1910; on U.S. delegation to, 1850, 1910; Western position regarding, 782, 1691–92; on Western rights as condition for, 1487–88; Working Group recommendations, 1424–26. *See also* Foreign Ministers' Meetings: Geneva (May–August 1959); Western Summit Conference —U-2 overflight: as Khrushchev's "device," 1953–54; and Khrushchev's ultimatum, 1950–51, 1969–70

Summit Meeting of Negro Leaders, 921–22

Summit meetings. *See* Geneva Summit Meeting (July 1955); Summit Conference (May 1960); Western Summit Conference

SUNFED (Special United Nations Fund for Economic Development). *See* United Nations

Supplee, Cochran Bryant, 415–17

Supreme Commander of Allied Powers in Europe. *See* SACEUR

Supreme Court of the United States: on appointments to, 38–39, 1108–10; Brennan's appointment to, 39; Brownell declines appointment to, 38–39; and *Brown* v. *Board of Education*, 482–83, 506, 538–39; Burger as Chief Justice, 1108–10; calls special session, 1077–78; on charges of "legislating," 875–78; on confessions of accused, 875–78; on Congress and Supreme Court appellate jurisdiction, 875–78; and Constitution, 299–300, 1079–80, 1290–91; and crisis in Little Rock, 465–66, 482–83, 577–78, 579, 1079–80, 1087–88; decisions by, on labor unions, 925–26; on E.'s criticism of, 272; and Eighth Circuit Court of Appeals, 1077–78, 1079–80, 1087–88; and Farm Bureau concerns, 1290–91; and Federal Preemptive Doctrine, 875–78; on functions of, 875–78; Harlan's appointment to, 39; on Indian claims, 875–78; on interpretations under Smith Act, 272; and *Jencks* v. *United States*, 272; and Jenner bill, 875–78; judicial legislation, 875–78; *Konigsberg* v. *State Bar of California*, 875–78; on Lawrence's column, 875–78; on legislative investigations, 875–78; on limiting jurisdiction of, 875–78; Little Rock school board seeks review, 1079–80, 1134–35; *Mallory* v. *United States*, 875–78; and "Memphis Case," 765–

66; and offshore oil rights litigation (tide-lands), 550–51, 594–96, 893–95; and *Oleta O'Connor Yates et al. v. United States*, 875–78; orders of, must be upheld, 577; *Pennsylvania v. Nelson*, 875–78; and Phillips Petroleum case, 213–15; and *Plessy v. Ferguson*, 506; on political balance of, 38–39, 1108–10; on preemption in federal/state legislation, 925–26, 1480; and presidency, 1290–91; and question of presidential disability, 138–40; requires Du Pont divestiture of GM stock, 741–43; rules on natural gas pipeline rates, 765–66; rules on steel strike, 1727–28; on school integration, 1077–78, 1079–80; on *Schware v. Board of Bar Examiners of New Mexico*, 875–78; on states' right to prosecute Communists, 875–78; and states' standards on Bar admission, 875–78; and Submerged Lands Act, 550–51; and *Sweezy v. New Hampshire*, 875–78; Warren's appointment to, 39; and *Watkins v. United States*, 875–78. *See also* Civil rights; Judiciary; Justice, Department of; United States Government: Judiciary; Warren, Earl

Suramarit, Norodom: background, 1434–35; death of, 2013–14

Sverdrup, Leif John, 291

Swan, Bal F., 2241

Sweden: on European trade policies, 1799–1800; on lessons from, 2118–19; protests U.S. force in Lebanon, 988–90; socialization in, 1856–57

Swenson, Stanley Prescott, 2198

Sweezy v. New Hampshire, 875–78

Swing, Joseph May, 1333–34

Swinson, Clara, 417–18

Switzerland: and Chile-Argentina border dispute, 1859–60; on European trade policies, 1799–1800; Gruenther visits, 1106–7; to host disarmament talks at Geneva, 901–2, 932–33; on Swiss role in atomic test inspections, 1880–81; Tunisia seeks arms from, 563–67. *See also* Foreign Ministers' Meetings; Geneva Accords; Geneva Agreements; Geneva Conferences; Geneva Conventions

Symington, Stuart: background, 1142, 2195; and defense spending, 1991–93; reports on DOD reorganization, 2189–95; scores DOD, 1142

Synovex, 678–79

Syria, 562, 597: attends Cairo Conference, 23, 27, 72–73; and Baath Party, 169; British difficulties in, 102; Communist influence in, 383–85, 389–90, 427–31, 512–16; destruction of pipelines in, 80; and Eisenhower Doctrine, 383–85; E.'s view, 173; expels U.S. embassy officials, 383–85; and Johnston Plan, 408–10; and Jordan, U.S.

view, 158–60; on Muslim opposition to Chamoun, 869–70; pro-Soviet trends in, 293–95; and reclamation of Jordan River Valley, 293–95; rejects U.S. arms offer, 427–31; on smuggling arms for Lebanon, 952–60; Soviet influence in, 166, 168, 383–85, 427–31, 562–63; and Soviets, Saud's view, 23; and United Arab Republic, 705–8, 1003–7. *See also* al-Quwatli, Shukri

Taft, Charles Phelps, 467–68

Taft, Robert Alphonso: death of, 233–34; declines commitment to Western European security, 1746–56; E.'s esteem for, 233–34; and election of 1950, 1070–71; E. meets with, on collective security, 1746–56; on federal aid to education, 255–56; Williams's view, 233–34

Taft, William Howard, 467–68

Taft-Hartley Labor Relations Act of 1947: injunctive process of, 1737–39; and labor reform legislation, 1630–31; and preemptive legislation, 925–26; and right-to-work laws, 1070–71, 1165–67; and steel strike, 1727–28, 1737–39

Taipei, 1980–81. *See also* China, Republic of

Tait, Don, 699

Taiwan. *See* China, Republic of: Taiwan

Talmadge, Herman Eugene, 1375–78

Talos, 292–93

Tanks: Centurions from U.K. for FRG, 150–51, 206; U.S. M-47s for Jordan, 359–60; U.S. M-47 and M-48s for FRG, 150–51, 206, 211–12, 265–67, 389–90; on the Patton tank (M-47), 581

Tapp, Jesse Washington, 1058

Tariff Act of 1930, 991–92

Tariff Commission. *See* United States Tariff Commission

Tariffs: and importance of free world trade, 1449–50; on lead/zinc tariffs, 759–60, 991–92, 1111–13, 1121–22, 1230–32, 1488–91; and Minerals Stabilization Plan, 991–92; reduction of, as federal anti-strike weapon, 1737–39; reduction of, in recession, 859–61; on U.S.-Soviet trade, 981–82; on wool imports, 265–67. *See also* General Agreement on Tariffs and Trade; United States: foreign trade; United States Tariff Commission

Tartar, 292–93

Taxation, 1153–56; and appropriations for medical research, 1594–97; and Cabinet Committee on Small Business, 886–87; and costs of government programs, 793–95; and economic cold war, 1415–16, 1417–18; and effects of deficits, 793–95, 813–14; and excise tax on automobiles, 824–25; and excise taxes on musical instruments, 1915; and federal *v.* states' rights is-

sues, 2035–36; and FY 1958 budget, 531–32; and government spending, 78–81, 1007–13; and Hauge's advice, 1252–53; and Humphrey's view, 133; importance of incentive, 1198–1200; on investment strategies, 1228; on IRS tax auditing procedures, 586–87; Lee's proposal, 1188–90, 1195–96; level of, contributes to inflation, 415–17; Nielsen's view, 783–84; Phelps's view, 446–49, 451–52; and ratio of expenditures to GNP, 1198–1200; and recovery in economic recession, 769–71, 777–82, 824–25, 872, 886–87, 1007–13; reduction of, 261–62, 736, 738, 777–82, 793–95, 813–14, 872; on reductions, 859–61, 861, 975–76; on reforms, 872, 886–87, 928–29, 1198–1200, 1200–1201, 1991–93; and retirement plans, 1935–41; Robie's view, 187, 446–49; and Rockefeller Brothers Fund recommendations, 846–47; Swan's concern, 2241; on tax-free liquor imports, 2177–78; and tax relief for small businesses, 760–65. See also Economy, U.S.
—capital gains, and tax reform, 886–87, 928–29
—corporate tax: extension of rates, 928–29; renewals on, 928–29
—excise tax: and Kyes's proposal, 777–82; renewals on, 928–29; repeal of, 928–29; revision of provisions, 928–29
—income tax: Kyes's proposal, 777–82; Lee's proposal, 1188–90, 1198–1200; on payments in federal bonds, 588–89. See also Investments

Taylor, Henry Junior ("Harry"), 1422–23
Taylor, Maxwell Davenport: as Army Chief of Staff, 12–13; background, 12–13; evaluates John E.'s performance, 12–13; and guided missile program, 347–49; and McNamara as Quartermaster General, 141, 143–44; suffers back ailment, 12–13
Taylor, Olivia Fay (Kimbro), 1423
Teamsters, International Brotherhood of: racketeering activities of, 587; Senate investigation of, 1153–56. See also Labor unions
Technical Amendments Act of 1958, 760–65, 905–6
Technical Survey Group, and Volta River Project, 637–39
Technology, and Churchill College at Cambridge University, 880–81
Tedder, Arthur William: background, 949; and invitation to visit U.S., 1625; and Monty, on rush to Berlin, 1653–54, 2182, 2188; on Monty as author, 1625, 1820–21; suffers stroke, 1908–9; visits U.S., 1820–21, 1908–9; on world tour, 1820–21; and World War II reunion, 1620–21, 1625, 1820–21. See also World War II
Tedder, Marie de Seton (Black) ("Toppy"):

background, 1821; and Tedder's illness, 1908–9
Tedder, Richard Seton: background, 1625; as E.'s godson, 1908–9
Television. See Media
Teller, Edward H.: advocates openness on nuclear data, 2055; article by, on nuclear secrecy, 2055; background, 287; favors metric system, 1553–54; meets with E. on radioactive fallout, 287, 295–96; on nuclear weapons test moratorium, 1068–69; on Rabi's antagonism, 519–20; testifies before Senate committee, 287, 295–96, 598–99; testifies on behalf of Strauss, 1553–54. See also Atomic weaponry
Tello Baurraud, Manuel, 1357
Temporary Unemployment Compensation Act of 1958, extends unemployment benefits, 760–65, 1381–82
Ten-Nation Committee on Disarmament (Geneva, March 1960): on collapse of talks, 1993–95, 2111–13; and Khrushchev's proposal, 1694–96; and participation of other nations at summit, 1697–1700; on U.S. role in disarmament negotiations, 1993–95. See also Geneva Nuclear Test Conference; United Nations Disarmament Commission
Tennessee, E. meets with governor of, 466–67, 474–75. See also Tennessee Valley Authority
Tennessee Valley Authority (TVA): awards turbo-generator contract to British firm, 1316–17; and Dixon-Yates controversy, 1543–45, 1581–82, 1582–83; expansion of, in Kentucky, 1764–65; on H.R. 3460, 1608–9; Jones heads, 269; on private v. public power, 1608–9; and Strauss nomination hearings, 1446–47; and TVA bill, 1583–84, 1608–9
Tennessee Valley Authority Act of 1933, and H.R. 3460, 1608–9
Tenth Inter-American Conference (Caracas Conference) (March 1954), 263–64, 925–26
Tenure of Office Act: and President Andrew Johnson, 138–40; and question of presidential disability, 138–40
Terrier/Tartar, an overlapping missile program, 292–93. See also Missiles
Texaco Oil Company, 2007
Texas: on Anderson, Hobby as "favorite son" candidates, 1942; and Eisenhower State Park, Denison, 853–54; and E.'s midterm election agenda, 1186–87; and Morrow's view on foreign service post, 82–83; and Republican State Committee, 214; and San Antonio auto accident, 1321; on submerged lands claims, 550–51; and Texas offshore oil rights litigation (tidelands), 550–51, 594–96, 893–95

Thailand, Kingdom of: Boye attends dinner for royals, 1984–85; Diem visits, 898–99; pledges to protect Laos via SEATO, 2223–25; on relations with Cambodia, 1390, 1432–35, 1472–74, 2013–14; on release of Sihanouk's letter, 1390; royals of, visit U.S., 2011, 2151–53; and Sarasin as prime minister of, 453–54; and SEATO, 1432–35, 2151–53; and trans-Pacific air routes to, 2252–54; on U.S. aid to, 2151–53; and U.S.-Thai relations, 2151–53. *See also* Bhumibol Adulyadej; Sirikit Kitiyakara

Thayer, Edward C., 647

Thayer, Robert Helyer, 1697

Thayer, Sylvanus, 968–69

Thayer, Walter Nelson, 2168–70

Thebaud, Fritz St. Firmin, 1711

Thermonuclear weaponry. *See also* Atomic weaponry; Hydrogen bomb

Third world: on aid to, from Germany, 2121–23; on aid to, by world powers, 1878–79; on education as cold war strategy, 2166–68; effective use of propaganda in, 1027–31; on impact of Soviet propaganda on, 1893–94; and international morality, 1890–92; Macaulay's view, 1555–56; and Mutual Security Program, 1002, 1027–31; need of, to develop purchasing power, 319–25; and religious philosophy, 1890–92; and Soviet ideology and policy institute, 1893–94; on U.S. relations with, 1027–31; U.S. role in economic growth programs, 1073–76

Thomas, Charles Allen, 784

Thomas, Norman Mattoon, 331–32

Thompson, Beatrice (Birchfield) ("Bee," "Bea"), 543–44, 2052–53

Thompson, Llewellyn E., Jr.: accompanies Khrushchev on U.S. tour, 1682–83; to accompany E. to Summit Conference, 1850; background, 793; on cattle for Khrushchev, 1766–67; on conditions for summit meeting, 748–49, 792–93; on E.'s itinerary in USSR, 1806–7; on E.'s reply to Khrushchev, 1585–86; on E.'s USSR exit via Siberia, 1790–91; to keep Khrushchev informed, 1718–19; protests Soviet riot on Lebanon, 1034–36; on reply to Bulganin, 726; on return of E.'s painting from USSR, 1597–98; on timing and site for summit, 1593–94; as U.S. ambassador to USSR, 793

Thompson, Percy Walter ("Perc"): background, 543–44; Barbara E. visits, 2165; birthday greetings to, 543–44; as candidate for Florida Secretary of State, 2052–53, 2165; on Kennedy-Johnson ticket, 2052–53; loses in Florida election, 2165; on 1960 election loss, 2165; on Nixon and NAACP, 2052–53; on politics in South, 2052–53; on U.S.-Canadian citizenship, 772–73

Thomson, Edwin Keith, 812

Thor, on funding for guided missile program, 162–63. *See also* Missiles

Thoreau, Henry David, 799

Thorneycroft, George Edward Peter, 316

Thornton, Daniel I. J., 890

Thurmond, James Strom: background, 1016, 1375–78; as civil rights extremist, 1375–78; introduces amendments to reciprocal trade bill, 1016

Thye, Edward John: background, 693, 1253–54; on dairy situation in Minnesota, 693–94; loses in midterm election, 1253–54; protests dairy price supports, 693–94; recalls 1952 presidential nomination, 1253–54

Tibet, 1648–50, 1662–63

Tidelands legislation, 446–49; E. supports, 594–96, 893–95; Johnson's protest, 550–51; and Texas offshore oil rights litigation, 594–96, 893–95; Truman vetoes, 594–96. *See also* Louisiana; Submerged Lands Act of 1953; Supreme Court of the United States; Texas

Timberlake, Clare Hayes, 2031

Time-Life Corporation, and post-presidency writing, 1802

Time magazine, 731; and Wyeth's portrait of E., 1780

Tin industry. *See* Raw materials; Strategic materials

Tiros I and II, launch of, 2216–17. *See also* Satellites

Titan: on funding for guided missile program, 162–63; and missile gap, 1342; Wilson lowers priority of, 496–97. *See also* Missiles

Titanium industry. *See* Raw materials; Strategic materials

Tito, Josip Broz: background, 377; on E.-Khrushchev meeting, 2111–13; seeks military aid to Yugoslavia, 376–77. *See also* Yugoslavia, Federal People's Republic of

Tkach, Walter Robert: background, 137; on bridge with E., 137; on Lemon as investment adviser, 1204–5

TORCH: anniversary of, 562; E.'s view, 2181, 2187; and Ismay's memoir, 2180–88; and Murphy's role, 1715–16. *See also* World War II

Totalitarianism, E.'s view, 85–86

Touré, Sékou: announces Soviet aid to Guinea, 1902–4; background, 1655, 1656; de Gaulle's view, 1654–57; and Geneva Agreements, 1902–4; on Guinea's foreign policy, 1902–4; on Guinean recognition of East Germany, 1902–4; on repatriation of Guinean nationals, 1902–4; on U.N. support in Congo, 2048–49, 2170–71; on U.S. policy in Congo, 2170–71; on U.S. recognition of North Vietnam, 1902–4; on U.S.

recognition of Republic of Vietnam, 1902–4; visits U.S., 1902–4. *See also* Guinea, Republic of

Tower, Anna Cleave, 709–10

Trade, international: aids foreign economies, 319–25; Benson's concerns, 1622; between Japan and Southeast Asia, 1445–46; between Soviet Union and U.K., 191–94, 649–59; and conditions for summit meeting, 748–49; and European trade policies, 1799–1800; E.'s view, 265–67, 319–25; on imports and trade restrictions, 1426–27, 1431–32, 1881–82; Johnson supports Trade Agreements Extension Act, 661–62, 1016; Kyes's proposal, 777–82; with Latin America, 1230–32; on lead/zinc tariffs, 759–60, 991–92, 1111–13, 1121–22, 1230–32, 1488–91; Lodge's view, 661–62; and Minerals Stabilization Plan, 991–92; Percy speaks on importance of, 879–80; on Philippine sugar import quotas, 1881–82; and Sino-Soviet trade differential, 234–35; on Soviet economic warfare, 491–93; on Soviet preemptive buying, 491–93; and State of the Union Address, 663–64; on U.S. economic aid to Japan, 1517–19; on U.S. role in free world, 1073–76, 1230–32; on U.S.-Soviet trade, 981–82, 1468–70, 1481–82, 1482, 1685–86. *See also* Economy, foreign; Reciprocal Trade Agreements Act; United States: foreign trade

Trade Agreements Committee, 1622

Trade Agreements Extension Act of 1958: four-year extension of, 1047; Johnson supports, 661–62, 1016; and lead/zinc import quotas, 1111–13; Lodge's recommendations on, 661–62; and State of the Union Address, 663–64

Trade Policy Committee, 1622

Transportation Act of 1958, 777–82

Transportation Study Group, report by, 777–82. *See also* Railroads

Trans World Airlines, E. approves CAB recommendations for, 2252–54. *See also* Airlines

Trap shooting, 310–11, 368–69. *See also* Hunting

Treasury, Department of the: Anderson meets with E., 685–86; Anderson as Secretary, 187–88, 339–40; and area redevelopment legislation, 1329–31; and budget cut, 133; and Byrd investigation of financial system, 163; on certificates of indebtedness, 1023–24; on Dillon as Secretary, 2202–4, 2233–34; and economic aid to Turkey, 944–45; and economic recession recovery, 718–19, 777–82; on expenditures in, 589–91; and Fairless Committee Report, 95–96; and First Secretary of Government, 695–96, 1700–1702; on fiscal program in midterm campaign, 1143–44; Humphrey resigns,

187–88, 339–40; increased spending in, 589–91; issues new Lincoln pennies, 1304–5; opposes Development Loan Fund, 183–85; and public offering of federal bonds, 450–51; reports on gold drain, 2199–2200; and selection of 1960 campaign speakers on, 1793–96; and tax payments in federal bonds, 588–89; on treasury financing, 902, 1233–34; unwarranted drains on, 1007–13; on U.S. monetary system reforms, 2059–60; and *Wall Street Journal*, 902. *See also* Anderson, Robert Bernerd; Humphrey, George Magoffin

Treaty of Friendship, Commerce, and Navigation (1859), and Paraguay, 1725–26

Treaty of Friendship, Commerce, and Navigation (1953), and Danish shipping case, 414–15

Treaty of Mutual Cooperation and Security with Japan, 1959–60

Treaty of Mutual Security with Republic of China, 1131–33, 1678–81

Treaty of Rome. *See* European Economic Community

Treaty of St. Petersburg, 857

Trees. *See also* Gettysburg farm: trees and shrubs

Trendex Public Opinion Poll, 1581–82

Trieste: and communism, 512–16; and Dulles, 2211–13; on U.S. role in settlement, 884–85. *See also* Italy, Republic of; Yugoslavia, Federal People's Republic of

Trimble, William Cattell: background, 1434; on Lao refugees in Cambodia, 2248–50; as U.S. ambassador to Cambodia, 1432–35, 2013–14

Trinidad, Republic of: and British West Indies Federation, 317–19, 332–34; and U.S. naval base at Chaguaramas, 317–19

Tripartite consultations: on Africa, 1967–68, 1987–88, 2028–30; on alert procedure, 107–9; de Gaulle's view, 1159–62, 1250–51, 1412–15, 1654–57, 1673–75, 1979–80, 2027–28, 2046–47, 2068–73; on improvements in, 1987–88; Macmillan's view, 1967–68; on Morocco and Tunisia, 1673–75

Trujillo y Molina, Hector Bienvenido: background, 317; inauguration of, 317. *See also* Dominican Republic

Trujillo y Molina, Rafael Leonidas: on asylum for, 1855–56; background, 1856; Clark's plan to aid Dominican Republic, 1855–56; on ousting, 1919–23. *See also* Dominican Republic

Truman, Bess (Wallace), 892

Truman, Harry S.: asks E. to head NATO forces, 1746–56; on bipartisan foreign policy, 56–57; bust of, 135–36; on Byrnes as Secretary of State, 1498–99; Cabell briefs, on Far East, 1119; and Coit, 48; and corruption scandals, 1089–91; declines Memorial Day invitation, 892; defeats Dewey, 1746–56; on E. as courier for, 1498–99; and Eisenhower Doctrine, 56–57; E.'s postwar wish to retire, 1746–56; and E. as presidential candidate, 1746–56; establishes National Petroleum Council, 660–61; and Iran (1946), 1027–31; Khrushchev's charge, 1453–56; and Korea, 993, 1027–31; Lowry scores, 1029–30; and Marshall Plan, 434–37; on Marshall as Secretary of State, 1498–99; meets E. aboard U.S.S. *Williamsburg*, 1302–3, 1498–99; and Pauley, 1089–91; and Pendergast machine, 754–55; on relationship with E., Meyner's view, 754–55; and report on American Armed Forces Institute, 27–29; statement by, on Quemoy and Matsu, 1119; supports National Library Week, 668–69; supports U.S. force in Lebanon, 993; travels to Europe, 892; and Turkey and Greece (1947), 1027–31; vetoes tidelands bill, 594–96

Tsarapkin, Semen K.: background, 1465; on treaty for cessation of nuclear weapons tests, 1887–90

Tungsten industry, price support program for, 889–90. *See also* Raw Materials; Strategic Materials; Tariffs

Tunisia, Republic of: and attack on French patrol, 736, 738; on Bourguiba as Chief of State, 563–67; Bourguiba's concerns, 1113–15, 2133–35; combats Nasserism, 168; Constituent Assembly abolishes monarchy, 563–67; and de Gaulle's leadership, 917; and Development Loan Fund, 2133–35; E.'s goodwill trip to (December 1959), 1718–19, 1761–62, 1762–63, 1778; and France, 563–67, 567–70, 574–79, 736, 738, 746; French air attack on, 736, 738, 746; and French airbase at Bizerte, 766–67; and French colonialism, 952–60; and Good Offices mission, 746, 831–34; and law of the sea, 1911–12; and Moslems in Algeria, 831–34; Nasser offers arms to, 567–70, 574–79; Nixon visits, 168; petitions U.N. Security Council, 746; receives wheat from U.S., 2133–35; on refugees at Tunisia-Algeria border, 766–67; seeks arms from West, 563–67, 567–70, 574–79; seeks U.S. aid, 2133–35; and Summit collapse 1953–54; tripartite talks on, 1673–75. *See also* Algeria; Bourguiba, Habib; France, Republic of

Turkey, Republic of: and Baghdad Pact, 1323–25; Bayar seeks economic aid for, 944–45; and CENTO, 1931, 1974–75; and Communist influence in Syria, 383–85, 389–90; and Cyprus, 103, 104, 118–19, 302, 612–13, 940–42, 1127–28, 1174–75; on Cyprus

and NATO alliance, 940–42, 952–60; and Development Loan Fund delegation, 1823; discussions on, at Bermuda Conference 1957, 103, 104; on economic aid for, from IMF, 944–45; on economic aid for, from OEEC, 944–45; on E.'s goodwill trip to (December 1959), 1718–19, 1768–69, 1769–70, 1778, 1974–75; elections in, 1974–75; fears Soviet power, 408–10; on Gursel as president, 1974–75; and independence for Cyprus, 2009–11; and Makarios, 302; military coup in, 1823, 1931, 1974–75; Monty's view on Cyprus, 612–13; NAC considers conflict regarding Cyprus, 940–42, 942–44; and NATO alliance, 118–19, 612–13, 1974–75; and NATO defense expenditures, 303–7; and NATO force levels, 303–7; in need of U.S. support, 993–96, 1823; and overthrow of Menderes, 1974–75, 1995–96; and Palestine Conciliation Commission, 1098–99; Paris talks on aid to, 1051; on postwar aid to, 179–80, 303–7; receives U.S. military aid, 998–1000; signs Baghdad Pact, 104; on Soviet threat to collective security, 1322; Spaak proposes settlement on Cypriot dispute, 612–13; student-led riots in, 1931; and substitute for Baghdad Pact, 1020–22; and Summit collapse, 1953–54; Summit and NATO partners meet in, 1931; and support for mutual security program, 1947–49; terrorists attack in Ankara, 696–97; on ties with NATO and CENTO, 1974–75; and Truman (1947), 1027–31; and Turkish-Greek settlement on, 1346, 1358–59. *See also* Bayar, Celal; Gursel, Cemal

Turner, Courtney S., 1859

Turner, Edythe P.: attends E. at Fitzsimmons, 144; attends Inauguration, 144; background, 144; as chief nurse, Tripler Hospital, Hawaii, 144, 373–74, 1105–6

Tuttle, Elbert Parr, 1108–10

Twenty-fifth Amendment. *See* Constitution of the United States

Twenty-second Amendment. *See* Constitution of the United States

Twining, Nathan Farragut: background, 744; and coordination in strategic planning, 2099–2100; and DOD reorganization, 677–78; on Formosa crisis, 1168–70; and NSC, 743–45; on POL supplies for Jordan, 1013–15; on Schuyler's successor, 1298–99; on Soviet nuclear tests suspension, 819–22; on staff organization at SAC HQ, 2099–2100; on U.S. flights over U.K., 872–73; on withdrawal of U.S. forces from Lebanon, 1034–36. *See also* Joint Chiefs of Staff

Uganda, Republic of, Nixon visits, 168
Underdeveloped nations. *See* Third world

forces in Mediterranean, 1419–21; Pineau protests U.S.-U.K. arms for Tunisia, 567–70
—Germany: and Berlin crisis, 1261–62; on "British weakness," Adenauer's view, 1496; on FRG purchase of Centurion tanks, 150–51, 206, 211–12, 265–67; reunification of, 180–81; Soviets propose Foreign Ministers' Meeting regarding, 1424–26; and support for British forces in Federal Republic, 147–50
—Ghana (Gold Coast): Independence Ceremonies for, 17–18; and Volta River project, 552–53
—Greece: and Cyprus, 103, 104, 612–13, 940–42, 952–60; Makarios and British public opinion, 269–70, 302; Monty's concern, 612–13; release of Makarios, 118, 118–19, 167, 168–69
—Iceland, British oppose territorial sea policy, 871
—India, and Indo-Pakistani dispute, 555–56, 839–40
—Indonesia, military aid to, 1331–32
—Israel: and Egyptian-Israeli dispute, 34–36, 63–64; and withdrawal of force from Egypt, 63–64
—Japan, on BOAC air routes via Tokyo, 1599–1601
—Jordan: British forces stabilize, 993–96, 1013–15; receives military aid from U.K., 359–60; seeks support from U.K., 988–90; on withdrawal of British force from, 1183–84
—Kuwait, U.K. buys oil from, 1481–82
—Laos, U.K. pledges to protect, via SEATO, 2223–25
—Lebanon, withdrawal of U.S.-U.K. force from, 1183–84
—Libya, on U.S.-U.K. aid to, 869–70
—NATO: command structure of, 1419–21; on force assignments to SACEUR, 1313–14; and reduction of NATO force, 75–76, 125, 166, 167–68, 191–94; 997–98; on strengthening NATO, 1767–68
—Pakistan, and Indo-Pakistani dispute, 555–56, 839–40
—Red China, U.K.-U.S. trade with, 204–5, 211–12
—Saudi Arabia: British relations with, 20, 21; and Muscat/Oman dispute, 332–34, 378–79
—Soviet Union: Bulganin's letter to Macmillan, 191–94; and E.'s message to Khrushchev, 848–49; as "formidable people," 491–93; and Hungarian revolt, 191–94; requests trade credits, 1468–70, 1481–82; and Soviet proposal on Mideast, 234–35; on testing atomic weaponry, 649–59, 804–6
—Summit Conference: British dislike Geneva

as site, 1491–92; collapse of, 2111–13; on conditions for, 782, 804–6; on draft agenda for, 973–75. *See* Summit Conference (May 1960)
—Syria, Communist influence in, 389–90, 427–31
—Tunisia, on arms for, 563–67, 567–70, 574–79
—Turkey: and Cyprus, 103, 104, 612–13, 940–42, 952–60; economic aid to, 944–45; Monty's concern, 612–13
—United Nations, and anti-colonialism resolution, 2200–2201
—United States: and Anglo-American relations, 100–104, 204–5, 243–44, 313–14, 378–79, 379–80, 491–93, 502–3, 507–8, 521–22, 526–27, 544–45, 1316–17, 1648, 1691–92, 1704–5, 2012–13; and AQUATONE, 107–9; on bilateral meetings with U.S., 521–22, 920–21; on British pressure to join Baghdad Pact, 102, 104; and Bulganin's letter to Macmillan, 191–94; on controlling atomic weaponry, 507–8; and cooperation on atomic tests inspections, 906–7, 1374; on coordination in U.S.-U.K. policies, 696–97, 1020–22; and downing of RB-47 airplane, 2012–13, 2015; and Egyptian-Israeli dispute, 63–64; on FRG purchase of U.S. tanks, 389–90; and Greer's Ferry Dam turbine contract, 1316–17, 1426–27; and imports of heavy power machinery, 1449–50; on imports and trade restrictions, 1426–27; Macmillan discusses atomic weaponry, 1396–97; and nuclear weapons for RAF bombers, 107–9; and security safeguards, 128–29; and trade with China, 204–5, 211–12; and tripartite alert procedure, 107–9; on U.S. flights over U.K., 872–73; on U.S.-U.K. air operations, 935; on U.S.-U.K. cooperation on atomic issues, 920–21, 1024–25, 1060–63, 1844–48; on U.S.-U.K. cooperation in World War II, 1247–48, 2180–88; on Whitney as ambassador, 2168–70; and wool tariff issue, 265–67; and world opinion regarding atomic tests, 1060–63
United Nations (U.N.), 44; and anti-colonialism resolution, 2200–2201; and "Atoms for Peace" speech (1953), 113, 591–92, 819–22; and Bermuda Conference (1957), 100–104, 216–18, 819, 822; on Charter of, 649–59, 671–72, 721–27, 1003–7, 1017–19, 1034–36, 1215–16; and collective security measures, 649–59; and Connally reservation, 1823–24; and Declaration of January 1, 1942, 1003–7; and discussions on lead/zinc production, 1111–13, 1488–91; en-

Gaulle differences on NATO, 2115–18; and Egyptian-Israeli dispute, 34–36, 72–73, 91–93; and Eisenhower Doctrine, 71–72, 158–60; E. opposes NSC investigation, 1538–40; E.'s responsibility, 1717–18; on errors in Far East policy, 1215–16; and exchange of restricted data, 906–7; and Fairless Committee recommendations, 97–98; Finder's view, 53; and First Secretary of Government, 1700–1702; and Formosa situation, 1092–93, 1131–33; and Franco--American relations, 952–60, 1285–86, 1424–26, 2046–47; and French-Tunisian question, 746; and German reunification, 180–81; on global unrest, 1995–96; Goldwyn scores *Time* on, 1869–70; and Gulf of Aqaba, 194–96, 197–98, 297–99, 427–31; on "guns *and* butter," 512–16; on "guns or butter," 493–94; High's memo on, 2049–50; on importance of, to U.S. economy, 1492–94; on improving tripartite consultations, 1967–68, 1979–80, 1987–88, 2068–73; and Indonesia, 952–60; on Indo-Pakistani dispute, 146–47, 555–56, 884–85, 1774–76; on insurgency in Algiers, 1811, 1931–33; and Iran, 1321–25; and IRBM agreement with U.K., 729–30; and Johnston Plan, 408–10; and Jordan, 158–60; in Latin America, 1218–19, 1872–74; and law of the sea, 1911–12; on Lebanon, 47, 952–60, 984–86, 1003–7; and Mali-Senegal split, 2100–2102; and message to Khrushchev, 819–22; and Mexico, 1355–57, 1357–58, 1363, 1483–84; and Monty's concern on Cypriot question, 612–13; and mutual aid programs, 536–37; on Nixon as congressional foreign policy liaison, 410–12; on nuclear disarmament, 473–74, 618–20, 632–36, 1694–96; on objectives of, 478, 1953–54; on Operation Pan America, 1242–44, 1997–99; on ousting Trujillo, 1919–23; and Pakistan-Pushtunistan-Afghanistan controversy, 2136–38; and Palestine Conciliation Commission, 1098–99; and Panama Canal Zone, 1713–15, 2088–89; and Paraguay, 1725–26; pledges to protect Laos via SEATO, 2223–25; on promoting Chinese-Russian disunity, 242–43; and relations with Cambodia, 2013–14; and relations with Japan, 827–29; and repatriation of Palestinian refugees, 293–95; and reply to Bulganin, 649–59; and return of vested German assets, 170–71; Rockefeller scores, 1918–19; and role of economic aid in, 142–43, 408–10, 561; and rule of law over force, 996–97; security safeguards with Canada, U.K., 128–29; and seismic research program, 1999–2001, 2064–65; and selection of 1960 campaign speakers on, 1793–96; and situation in

Congo, 2030–32, 2084; and Soviet-Iranian relations, 1321–25; and Soviet proposal on Mideast, 234–35; and Stassen's gaffe on disarmament, 236–38, 247–49; and Suez crisis, 574–79; on talks with Khrushchev, 1685–86, 1694–96; and three-mile limit on territorial seas, 749–50, 776–77; on transfer of atomic weapons to allies, 1844–48, 1887–90; on travel to Red China, 976–77; and tripartite alert procedure, 107–9; on Turkey, 303–7; and U.S. aid to Iranian armed forces, 998–1000; on U.S.-Arab relations, 98–100, 1027–31; on U.S. as "interventorial," 1919–23; U.S.-Panamanian relations, 1744–46; on U.S. policy in cold war, 2242–43; on U.S. relations with Cuba, 1456, 1919–23, 2001–7, 2039–42; on U.S. relations with third-world nations, 1027–31; on U.S. resources and NATO, 303–7; on U.S.-Saudi relations, 98–100; and U.S.-Thai relations, 2151–53; on U.S.-U.K. air operations, 935; on U.S.-U.K. cooperation in atomic inspections, 906–7, 920–21, 1374; on U.S.-U.K. relations with Saud, 332–34; on U.S.-U.K. solidarity, 521–22, 920–21; on U.S.-Vietnam relations, 898–99, 1639–40; and WEU, 128–29. *See also* Atomic weaponry; Bermuda Conferences (1953), (1957); Cold war; Disarmament; *individual nations;* Middle East; State, Department of; Summit (May 1960); Tripartite talks

—foreign trade, 103, 536–37; and balance of payments, 2168–70, 2189–95, 2195–96; and capital expenditures for exports, 1350–52; coal industry and oil imports, 1392–93; and crude oil import regulation, 1403–4; on expansion of, 1671–72; on European trade policies, 1799–1800; on financial and economic issues in Germany, 2121–23; on Haiti's barter proposal, 1542–43; on imports of heavy electrical machinery, 1449–50; on imports and trade restrictions, 1426–27, 1431–32, 1881–82; on industrial progress in Hungary, 1564–65; and interagency cooperation, 1622; and Japanese economy, 1445–46; Johnson supports Trade Agreements Extension Act, 1016; Kyes's proposal, 777–82; with Latin America, 1230–32; on lead/zinc tariffs, 759–60, 991–92, 1111–13, 1121–22, 1230–32, 1488–91; and Minerals Stabilization Plan, 991–92; and most-favored-nation status for Poland, 2160; and mutual trade renewal, 952–60; and oil import quotas, 895–96; and oil supply for Europe, 18–19; Percy speaks on importance of, 879–80; and Russian-Chinese trade differential, 204–5, 211–12, 234–35; talks on, with world leaders, 1682–83; on U.S.-Canada trade, 883, 909–10; on U.S. role in free world economy, 1073–76, 1449–50; on U.S.-Soviet trade, 981–82, 1482; USSR requests trade credits, 1468–70; and wool tariff issue, 265–67. *See also* Economy, foreign; Trade, international; United States Tariff Commission

—national security: as bipartisan issue, 843–44; and budget, 1415–16, 1417–18; and Cordiner Committee recommendations, 93–94; and crude oil import regulation, 1403–4; and effects of oil imports on, 340–42, 774–76, 895–96; E. opposes NSC investigation, 1538–40; E. speaks on, 493–94; and FCDA, 11–12; and funding for missile program, 162–63, 292–93; Gray's recommendations on NSC, 2246–47; Gruenther's view, 707–8; and importance of foreign aid, 78–81, 537; and importance of testing nuclear weaponry, 473–74, 618–20; and imports of heavy power machinery, 1449–50; on imports and trade restrictions, 1426–27, 1449–50; John E. joins White House staff, 156; national budget for, 43–46, 446–49; and national defense education scholarships, 980–81; and Nixon as congressional liaison on, 410–12; and public membership on NSC, 743–45; and Republican principles, 801–3; Rockefeller's concern, 531–32. *See also* Defense, Department of

United States Air Force (USAF): and ANP, 752–53; Case proposes reorganization in, 585–86; on closing Ethan Allen Air Force Base, 1742–43; deploys aircraft to Turkey, 427–31; develops guided missile program, 162–63, 593–94; and DOD reorganization plan, 888; errs in reconnaissance balloon project, 1031–32; and GAO access to Inspector General's report, 1194–95; and guided missiles tracking station in Brazil, 104–5; and leaks on Discoverer XIV satellite launch, 2067; on military base closings, 1742–43; and missile gap, 1342; on missing USAF airmen, 1687–88; Parker retires, 1736, 1736–37; on reappointing Emanuel to Board of Visitors, 1923; and reconnaissance satellite project, 498; on Salk vaccine for recruits, 1145–46; Soviets hold U.S. fliers, 2111–13; on staff organization at SAC HQ, 2099–2100; White's blunder, 347–49; withdraws from Lebanon, 1034–36. *See also* Aircraft; Air power; New Look; Strategic Air Command

United States Air Force Academy (USAFA): on airfield construction at, 1255; on boards of visitors/trustees, 1672–73; and Eisenhower Golf Course, 890; establishment of, 688–89; on flight training at, 1255; Second As-

sembly scores U.S. businessmen, 1856–57; on student exchange with USMA, USNA, 688–89; on two-star rank for head, 1850–51

United States Army: on army forms of address, 1854–55; on army rank insignia, 1854–55; auctions E.'s old 1942 Cadillac, 77–78; on Bradley as Chief of Staff, 1746–56; Case proposes reorganization in, 585–86; on dedication in service, 1962–63; and *Denver Post* article on nerve gas, 134; develops guided missile program, 162–63; and DOD reorganization plan, 888; on Draper as E.'s liaison officer, 558–60; on E. as Chief of Staff, 1746–56; E.'s farewell to, 2218–19; on forms of address, 1854–55; and Fort Polk, 1347–48; and Girard trial, 259–61, 319–25, 434–37; on Hoiles's death, 1962–63; influence of, on E., 603–4; on maneuvers in Louisiana, 1347–48; on medical care for dependents, 400–401; on morale in, 400–401; and Panamanian grievances, 1827–28; and pay raise legislation, 400–401, 735–36, 738; and reconnaissance satellite project, 498; Regular Army officers in, 400–401; Seifert's complaints, 400–401; supports Status of Forces Agreement, 457–58; on survivorship benefits, 400–401; Wilson scores missile plan, 347–49. *See also* Armed forces; Armed services

United States Army Corps of Engineers: and civil works projects, 760–65, 769–71; and ICA construction contracts, 1918–19; and Manhattan Engineer District, 498

United States Army Nurse Corps, and Williams's resignation, 367–68

United States Army Reserve, Seifert's complaints, 400–401

United States Chamber of Commerce. *See* Chamber of Commerce of the United States

United States Coast Guard, and appropriation for aircraft, 133

United States Commission on Organization of Executive Branch of Government. *See* Hoover Commission

United States Disarmament Administration, 1708–9

United States Government: and automobile dealers' franchise rights, 208–9; and breakdown of "laissez-faire" in industry, 1935–41; on civil rights and respect for law, 465–66; and Connolly Amendment, 1823–24; on decentralization of power in, 446–49; and economies in administration of, 43–46; financial obligations of, 1188–90; and fiscal responsibility, 1935–41; and Girard trial, 259–61, 434–37; goals of, 1340–43; on government spending, 78–81, 589–91,

1135–36, 1153–56, 1663–65; importance of public debate, 1340–43; on loyalty of associates, subordinates, 2043–44; must live within its means, 1184–85, 1354–55; and need for "good husbandry," 1663–65; on protection from disruptive strikes, 1737–39; on quality of dignity in, 2043–44; role of, in economic recession, 760–65, 769–71; role of, in management-labor problems, 929–30, 1144, 1165–67; role of, in scientific projects, 503–5; on self-reliance, 1935–41; on spending and wage-price spiral, 1153–56; and State of the Union Address, 663–64; and television programming, 1726–27, 1729; on transferring control to Kennedy, 2189–95. *See also* United States: domestic policy; United States: foreign policy
—Executive Branch: and business manager post, 1700–1702; and civil rights legislation, 328–31, 354–56; on congressional partisan antagonism toward, 2043–44; and crisis in Little Rock, 462–64; and executive powers in independent regulatory commissions, 2214–15; and executive privilege, 1733–35; on FCDA conversion to, 11–12; and ICA report on Vietnam program, 1733–35; on interagency cooperation, 1622; and "lame duck" presidency, 245; and monetary policy, 187–88; and mutual security program, 1733–35; on Nixon as congressional foreign policy liaison, 410–12; and NSC investigation, 1538–40; on permanent disarmament agency in State Department, 1708–9; reviews natural gas legislation, 63–64; and Supreme Court, 1290–91; and U.S. Citizens Commission on NATO, 2083–84. *See also* Hoover Commission
—federal-state issues: E.'s view, 446–49, 1328, 1340–43, 1935–41, 2035–36; and federal budget limits, 419–23; on federal role in education, 458–60, 527–29, 1307–9; on governors' responsibilities, 2035–36; and highway regulations, 282; and medical care for elderly, 1702–3; on national unemployment insurance system, 1407–8; and needs of hospitals and medical schools, 823–24; and preemptive legislation, 925–26; and public works planning, 9–10, 760–65; and right-to-work legislation, 1123–24, 1165–67; and school construction, 282, 417–18, 431–32; Shuman's view, 1290–91; and state responsibilities in labor matters, 1165–67; and tidelands oil litigation, 550–51, 893–95; and urban renewal, 282; and water resource program, 1665–67
—Judicial Branch: and crisis in Little Rock, 482–83; and selection of 1960 campaign

speakers on, 1793–96. *See also* Civil rights; Judiciary; Justice, Department of; Supreme Court of the United States
—Legislative Branch, and "lame duck" presidency, 245; and NSC investigation, 1538–40; and U.S. Citizens Commission on NATO, 2083–84. *See also* Congress, U.S.; House of Representatives, U.S.; Senate, U.S.
United States Information Agency (USIA), 675–76; Allen heads, 1027–31; and American National Exposition, 1597–98; appropriations for, 173, 512–16; and assistant secretaries of state, 453–54; and congressional debate on 1958 budget, 232–33; continues foreign public opinion reports, 273; and Declaration of Common Purpose, 544–45; E. briefs Kennedy on, 2189–95; effective use of propaganda, in Mideast, 1027–31, 1250; and First Secretary of Government, 695–96, 1700–1702; on functions of VOA, 1250; Johnson protests funding for, 220–21; in Kerala, 829; Larson argues for funding, 220–21; and Milton E., 2148–49; and NHPC documentary publications, 937–38; on Nixon at Moscow exhibit, 1466–67; and People-to-People program, 364–66, 453–54; and psychological warfare study, 1611–13; reports on Cuba, 2001–7; on return of E.'s painting from USSR, 1597–98; rioters burn library in Tripoli, 952–60; and SEATO, 453–54; Slater's view, 196; sponsors "Asian Artists in Crystal," 1474–75; as State Department agency, 220–21, 1700–1702; and Voice of America, 232–33. *See also* Larson, Arthur
United States Intelligence Board, 1692–93
United States Marine Corps: awards procurement contracts in labor surplus areas, 760–65; and DOD reorganization plan, 888; E. visits, at Kaneohe, 1983–84; helps reorganize Haiti's military forces, 1048–49; and Lebanon landings, 984–86; with Sixth Fleet, move into eastern Mediterranean, 158; withdraws from Lebanon, 1034–36
United States merchant marine, E.'s view, 987–88
United States Military Academy (West Point; USMA): on Blaik's retirement, 1299–1300; on boards of visitors/trustees, 1672–73; E. attends class of 1915 reunion, 543, 554, 1970–71; E. gives car flags to West Point Museum, 1996–97; and E.'s official papers, 1970–71; on E. as shy correspondent, 1804–5; and federal role in education, 1307–9; on football at, 554, 1299–1300; and 42d anniversary of E.'s graduation, 179–80; influence of, on E., 603–4; and Mason, 507; on plans for class reunion,

Volta River Project. *See* Ghana, Republic of

Voluntary Oil Import Program, 1403–4

Volunteerism: and charity, 2120–21; on corporate action, 1956–59; and crude oil imports, 895–96; E.'s view, 203–4; by industry, 879–80

Volunteers for Nixon-Lodge: Rhyne heads, 2099; Roberts raises funds for, 2068

Voting: Earl E.'s view, 614; and Jewish voters in U.S., 26; and national election process, 2158; rights in civil rights legislation, 328–31, 354–56, 415–17; on secret ballots in labor law, 674; turnout, in 1956, 2118–19; in U.S., Saud's view, 26; and voting referees, 1924–25; on voting rights abuses in the South, 1924–25. *See also* Elections

Wadsworth, George E., 194, 195

Wadsworth, James J.: to accompany E. to Summit, 1850; as alternate delegate to U.N. General Assembly, 336; on atomic test suspension agreement, 1447–48; on miscommunication with Norwegians, 628–29; recommends recess at Geneva talks, 1399–1402; reviews Jarring report on Indo-Pakistani dispute, 555–56; on U.N. anticolonialism resolution, 2200–2201; as U.S. ambassador to U.N., 2189–95

Wadsworth, James Wolcott, Jr., 1755

Wages: and Cabinet committee regarding, 1042–43; and DOD procurement services, 1054–55; and federal pay bill vetoes, 444; on federal spending and wage-price spiral, 1153–56; on restraint in demands for, 432–34, 1165–67. *See also* Economy, U.S.

Wailes, Edward Thompson: background, 1324–25; on resistance to USSR pressures, 2097; as U.S. ambassador to Iran, 998–1000; on U.S.-Iranian relations, 1321–25, 2095–98

Wainwright, Charles W., 1452

Wainwright, Stuyvesant II ("Stuyve"): background, 980; on national defense education scholarships, 980–81; on service academy boards of visitors/trustees, 1672–73

Walker, Paul, 707–8

Wallace, DeWitt: and article in *Reader's Digest*, 1429–30; background, 1430; on *"Republican Digest,"* 1429–30, 1636–37; and Stans's article in *Reader's Digest*, 1636–37; Summerfield's goal, 1636–37

Wallace, Henry Agard: background, 62–63; compares Washington and E., 62–63; on Khrushchev's visit, 1631–32; on nuclear disarmament, 242–43; on Sino-Soviet disunity, 242–43, 1631–32

Wall Street Journal: a "bunch of babies!" 902; on housing industry, 1554; questions treasury financing, 902; Wriston's article pleases E., 1965–67. *See also* Media: press

Walmsley, Walter Newbold, Jr., 2135

Walsh, Lawrence Edward: background, 1721; as campaign speaker on judiciary, 1793–96; as Deputy Attorney General, 1721; and Dethmers, 1721

Walsh, William B., 2091

Walter, Francis Eugene, 1333

Walter Reed Army Hospital: Dulles as patient at, 359–60, 1349–50, 1437–38, 1450–51, 1451; and Edgar E.'s health problems, 66–68; E. undergoes annual physical, 1722, 2202–4; E. undergoes neurological exam, 743, 814–15; Mamie E. undergoes surgery, 374–75; Mamie E. visits for checkup, 66–68; Marshall's death, 1703–4

Walter Reed Medical Center, Prince Mashur visits, for treatment, 196

Walters, Vernon A. ("Dick"): background, 618; as interpreter for Norstad, 1819–20; translates E.'s Orly Airport speech, 617–18

Wang Ping-nan, 1102

War: British fear of nuclear, 1704–5; and civil defense program, 11–12, 1605–6; on constitutional control over, in U.S., 649–59; and crisis in Formosa Straits, 1131–33; on dangers of, 1003–7; and defense expenditures as insurance against, 424–25; effect of, on education and career plans, 458–60; and foreign aid as insurance against, 419–23; Lowry's view, 1027–31; and Pact of Paris, 726, 727; as "preposterously and mutually annihilative," 927–28; and rule of law over force, 996–97; and U.S. policy in cold war, 2242–43; U.S. seen as warmongering, 1215–16. *See also* Civil War; Cold war; Eisenhower, Dwight David; Korean War; Revolutionary War; World War I; World War II; World War III

War Claims Act of 1948, and return of vested German assets, 170–71

War College. *See* National War College

War Department: E.'s postwar wish to retire, 1746–56; military intelligence division reports by, 1220

Warren, Earl: background, 29; Burger succeeds, 1108–10; on criticism of Supreme Court decisions, 272; on dinner for Coty, 188–91; heads European museums study, 29; Lucille E.'s view, 1079–80; and right-to-work issue, 1123–24. *See also* Supreme Court of the United States

Warren, Nina P. (Myers), 188–91

Warren, William Kelly, 570–71

Warren Petroleum Corporation, 208–9

Warsaw Pact, 632–36; and conditions for summit meeting, 748–49, 804–6; and pact of non-aggression, 636–37, 649–59; on transfer of atomic weapons to Soviet allies, 1844–48

Waseda University (Japan), 1517

Washburn, Abbott McConnell: background, 685, 1103; on People-to-People program, 684–85; protests U.S. policy on Formosa crisis, 1103–4; on return of E.'s painting from USSR, 1597–98

Washington, D.C. *See* District of Columbia

Washington, Genoa S., 336

Washington, George, 106, 133; bust of, 135–36; E.'s esteem for, 62–63; on entangling alliances, 62–63; E.'s portrait of, 710; Farewell Address by, 62–63; on Freeman's biography of, 691–92; Hickey compares, to E., 691–92; Newburgh Address by, 62–63; presidential papers of, 1904–8; religious faith of, 62–63; Wallace compares with E., 62–63

Washington Senators, 2256

Washington State: and ADE-CIO philosophy, 1064–68; on Bantz for District Court post, 1403; defeats right-to-work referendum, 1165–67; and Interior Cabinet post, 1256–58; and Pacific Great Circle air routes, 288, 406–7

Water resources: and Alabama River/Montgomery channel, 1665–67; on appropriations for Bureau of Reclamation, 760–65; on appropriations for rivers, harbors, and flood control, 760–65; on appropriations for watershed protection and flood prevention, 760–65, 1665–67; and Claiborne lock and dam, 1665–67; and Jones Bluff dam, 1665–67; and Millers Ferry lock/dam, 1665–67; and River and Harbor Act of 1945, 1665–67. *See also* Natural resources; Tennessee Valley Authority

Waters, George Patton, 581

Waters, John Knight, 581

Watkins, Arthur Vivian, 1273–74

Watkinson, Harold Arthur: background, 1982; on Polaris submarine bases, 1989–90; and Skybolt missile program, 2147

Watkins v. *United States*, 875–78

Watson, Arthur Kittredge ("Dick"), 1076–77

Watson, Thomas John, 415–17

Watson, Thomas John, Jr., 1947–49

Weaponry. *See* Atomic weaponry; Missiles; Ordnance

Weaver, Dick, 310–11

Weeks, Sinclair: accompanies E. to BAC meeting, 783–84; addresses Economic Mobilization Conference, 858–59; background, 215; and Cabinet committee on wages and prices, 1042–43; on CAB and Pacific Great Circle air routes, 288; defends E., 215; on economic recession recovery, 719; and effect of oil imports on national security, 340–42, 895–96; favors Burke Airport site, 369–72; on financing superliners, 988; heads Cabinet committee on transport policy, 484–85, 777–82; and Humphrey's ad-

vice on federal budget, 589–91; on maritime labor union fears, 1394–95; on naming U.S.S. *Savannah*, 376; and oil import quotas, 758–59, 774–76; recommends veto on airline subsidies bill, 547; on secret ballots in labor law, 674; on trade relations with Europe, 1968–69; and Trans-Pacific Renewal Case, 720. *See also* Commerce, Department of

Weick, Paul Charles, 1345

Weinberg, Sidney James: background, 393; E. recommends, to Civil Rights Commission, 392–94; on job prospects for Adams, 1239–40

Welfare and Pension Plans Disclosure Act of 1958, 1153–56

Wells, Herman B., 336

Wells, Kenneth Dale, 511

West, J. Bernard, 693, 1056

West (U.S.): E.'s midterm campaign trips to, 1064–68, 1138–39, 1148–49, 1162–63, 1170–71, 1171–72; E.'s 1960 campaign trips to, 2131–32, 2143–45; and support for mutual security programs, 624–25; water rights in, 1256–58

West, Walter A. (Chief): background, 610, 611; on delivering butchered beef, 609–11; and electric oven at Gettysburg farm, 1022–23; on hedge shoots for Gettysburg farm, 611

West Berlin. *See* Germany, Federal Republic of

Western Alliance. *See* Western powers

Western Electric Corporation, 251–53

Western Europe. *See* Europe: Western Europe

Western European Union (WEU): and FRG, 1658; Macmillan's view, 128–29; and NATO, 128–29; security safeguards in, 128–29; on strengthening of, 128–29; studies NATO force levels, 125; on troop strength in West Germany, 147–50. *See also* Europe: Western Europe

Western powers; Western world: and Arab-Israeli conflict, 512–16; on Berlin crisis, 1261–62, 1371–73, 1540–41; and cold war, 1319–21; and communization of China, 512–16; and conditions for summit, 1574–76; dangers to, in North Africa, 831–34; de Gaulle's view, 2046–47, 2223–25; fail to neutralize Nasser, 993–96; and four-power partial disarmament proposal, 632–36; need effective propaganda in Mideast, 993–96; on need for oil, 986–87; and pact of non-aggression, 642–44; and Tunisia's appeal for arms, 563–67, 567–70, 574–79. *See also* Cold war; Free world; Summit Conference (May 1960); Western Summit Conference

Western Summit Conference (Paris, December 19, 1959), 1667–69; de Gaulle agrees to attend, 1712–13; de Gaulle opposes, 1614–15, 1706–8, 1708; Dillon proposes, 1529–

30; and E.'s goodwill trip (December 1959), 1762–63, 1766–67; E. keeps Khrushchev informed, 1718–19; E. offers to host, 1691–92; E. proposes, 1614–15, 1691–92; Macmillan favors, 1615–16; on timing and site for, 1697–1700, 1706–8; on timing of Summit Conference (May 1960), 1757–58; on U.S. role in NATO defense, 1767–68. *See also* Heads of Government meetings; Summit Conference (May 1960)

West Germany. *See* Germany, Federal Republic of

West Indies. *See* British West Indies Federation

Westinghouse Electric Corporation, on construction of generators in U.S., 580–81

Westmoreland, William Childs: background, 1996–97; on car flags for West Point Museum, 1996–97; as USMA head, 1850–51

West Point. *See* United States Military Academy

West Point Museum: receives E.'s car flags, 1996–97; receives Napoleon's sword, 1996–97

West Virginia, E. campaigns in, 1138–39, 1163–64, 1170–71

Wheat industry: on barter of Haitian bauxite for, 1542–43; E. vetoes wheat bill, 1598–99; Jordan's need for, 2056–58; and message to Congress on surplus, 1598–99; and price support program, 1290–91; and record harvest, 1958, 1200–1201; shipments of, to Tunisia, 2133–35; on surpluses of, 1895–98; on U.S. disposal program, 40–42, 909–10, 1739–40. *See also* Agriculture, Department of; Benson, Ezra Taft

Whelan, Maybell (Stewart), 211

Whelan, Thomas E., 211

Whipple, Jay Northam, 1788–89

White, Charles McElroy, 134

White, Francis, 82–83

White, Paul Dudley: background, 976–77, 1152–53; on international role of American Red Cross, 1152–53; requests travel to Red China, 976–77; visits New Zealand and Australia, 976–77

White, Robert M., II, 1311

White, Thomas Dresser: as Air Force Chief of Staff, 347–49; background, 349; blunder by, 347–49; on coordination in strategic planning, 2099–2100; on Parker's retirement, 1736–37

White, William Smith, 1031

White House: on appointment of federal judges, 1343–45; bell ringers at, 1282–83; Christmas tree lighting at, 1258; Churchill visits, 557–58; on Coca-Cola prices in, 1877–78; dinner for O'Kelly at, 1395–96; Es. celebrate Thanksgiving at, 2174; and Edgar E.'s birthday celebration, 1265–66; E. entertains staff of, at Gettysburg, 1394;

Elizabeth II visits, 495–96, 502–3, 1130; E. practices golf at, 1709–10; and E.'s restored 1942 Cadillac, 77–78; and E.'s use of helicopters from, 553; evacuation activities, 2189–95; freezes butchered beef, 609–11; on functions of, 2189–95; and Heidi the dog, 694; hosts Mormon Tabernacle Choir, 1172; and Humphrey's cracker barrel for Augusta Golf Shop, 334–35; Javits proposes labor-management conference, 1832–33; John E.'s birthday celebration at, 327–28; John E.'s family stays at, 772–73; John E. joins staff at, 156; Jones visits, 532–34; Kennedy meets with E. at, 2189–95; League of Women Voters visits, 143; at Newport, on Little Rock crisis, 457–58, 460–61; Nielsen visits, 413–14; Paarlberg joins staff, 1116–17; on peace-oriented statements by, 686–87; on presidential mail loads at, 1619; and records section, 2189–95; rejects heart fund drive link with E., 37–38; releases Green's letter, 1131–33; resignations deplete staff, 1116–17; restoration of, 334–35; and role of civilian staff, 2189–95; and role of military aides, 2189–95; and Secret Service protection for E., 2217; and Signal Corps, 2189–95; staff of, supports Alcorn, 1235–36; staff of, works on E.'s speeches, 1919–23; Stephens returns to, 106; swimming pool privileges at, 1056; transportation functions, 2189–95

White House Conference on Youth, 1492–94

Whiteley, John Francis Martin ("Jock"), background, 1274–76. *See also* World War II

White Sulphur Springs (W. Va.), 991–92

Whitman, Ann Cook, 11–12, 105, 375, 512, 826, 897, 1107–8, 1394, 1546, 1659, 1736, 2207–8, 2226–27; accompanies E. to Newport, 1100; on aid to Indian girls, 2218–19; on Allen's ham, 1338–39, 1345; on Allen's invitation, 1345; and Allen's race horse, 248, 249; on Allen and right-to-work issue, 1165–67; on Anderson's letter, 594–96; and Anderson's speech draft, 1675–76; on appointment of federal judges, 1344; on appointment for Thye, 693–94; on art for Eisenhower Exchange Fellowships headquarters, 153–54; and assessment for Augusta National Golf Club, 842–43; assists E. on speech draft, 879–80; and "Atoms for Peace" speech (1953), 113; attends NATO meeting, 618; on attitudes in foreign service, 1315–16; and Berlin crisis, 1406–7; on Bohlen's transfer, 1574–76; and Budinger's proposal, 608; and Butcher's letter, 1410–11; on Cake's idea, 1840–41; on Champion's view of Conant, 1352–53; on Churchill at Gettysburg, 1495; on Churchill's painting exhibit in U.S., 526–

27; commends U.N. speech, 1055–56; contributes to MEDICO, 1971–73; on correspondence with Hanes, 2132–33; on correspondence with Presbyterians, 344–45; and Cotton's newsletter, 1865; creates file on columnists, 1044–45; and crisis in Little Rock, 465–66; on Dart's postscript, 1305; and Dawson's proposal, 588–89; on delivering butchered beef, 611; and Dethmers, 1721; on Discoverer XIV launch leaks, 2067; on Doerfer, 1841–42; drafts letter to McAdam, 1545–46; drafts letter to Nielsen, 413–14; drafts letter to Tedder, 1625; and Dulles's death, 1486; on E.'s attendance at NATO meeting, 604–5; and E.'s correspondence, 1637–38; on E.'s correspondence with Hazlett, 1187; on Edgar E.'s criticisms, 152–53; and E.'s disposition, 578; on E.'s friendly gesture to Macmillan, 378–79; on E.'s golf wager with Allen, 1439–40; on Eisenhower Park dedication, 853–54; on election problems in New York State, 2143–45; and electric golf car for E., 361–62; on E.'s letter to Lowry, 1027–31; on E.'s letter to Vinson, 888; and E.'s meeting with Faubus at Newport, 481–82; and E.'s memo on oil, 986–87; on E.'s message to Thomas, 331–32; on E.'s mutual security speech, 1919–23; and E.'s post-presidency writing, 2092–93; on E.'s state of mind, 952–60; E.'s view on de Gaulle, 917; E.'s view on steel strike, 1737–39; on E.'s visit with Edgar E., 1163–64; has "fancy machine," 394–95; on flights to/from Milestone, 1338–39, 1339–40; and Fort Ligonier speech, 1117; forwards Butcher's message, 562; forwards Finder's letter to Dulles, 53; forwards Goodson's letter, 491; forwards Jackson's message, 507–8; forwards message to Goldwater, 1209; forwards message to Herter, 238; forwards message to Rood, 1181; forwards political party differences to Hardendorf, 812; forwards speech draft to Moos, 1629–30; and Gainey's message on Dulles, 1368–69; and gift Studebaker for E., 2235–36; on Gruenther's work schedule, 1303; and Hauge's investments advice, 1252–53; and Hauge's tree analogy, 2089–90; and health care for elderly, 1702–3; and hedge shoots for Gettysburg farm, 611; and High's memo on foreign policy, 2049–50; on Hobbs, Gruenther's view, 1152–53; on Jackson's proposal, 664–65; on Jackson's role as adviser, 768–69, 1915–17; and Knowland's candidacy, 1070–71; on Larson as speechwriter, 774; on legislative leaders meeting, 787–89; on Lincoln pennies from Anderson, 1304–5; and Loker's letter, 1361–62; loses sweater, 1651–52; on McElvain's "bureau-

cratic language," 1222–23; and McGill's editorial, 834–35; on Macmillan at Johns Hopkins commencement, 835–36, 867; on Macmillan's U.S. visit, 739–40; on meeting with Meyner, 631–32; and message to Benson, 1172; on messages to Macmillan, 336–37, 993–96, 1955–56; on message protocol, 1509–10; on message to Strauss, 1449–50; on message to Truman, 56–57; and Milton E.'s report on Latin America, 1218–19; and Milton E.'s speeches, 88–89; on Milton E. at White House dinner, 2155; misdirects letter to Brownell, 81–82; on Morgan's correspondence, 2128–29; on Nielsen's schedule, 2099; on Nixon's debating style, 2130–31; on Nixon and NAACP, 2052–53; and Parker's retirement, 1736; and Pay Equalization Bill, 1984–85; praises E.'s speech, 1418–19; on problems in Mideast, 1020–22; and procedures for handling congressional mail, 408; on Ravdin's invitations, 55–56; reacts to published article, 1423; on Reid's appointment with E., 947–48; on replacing E.'s golf clubs, 874–75; replies to Howard, 253–55; replies to Lowe, 1138; on reply to Biggs, 1340–43; on reply to Bulganin, 721–27; on reply to McCloy, 863–65; and report on juvenile crime, 2098; reports on Williams's illness, 1474; and Roberts as fundraiser for Nixon, 2068; and Rockefeller, 65–66, 488–89, 1354–55, 1632–34; on Ruth E.'s visit to Mexico, 309; sends check to Patterson, 1223; sends Cousins's letter to Strauss, 271; sends note to Gruenther, 2213–14; and Sibley/Lanham letters on mutual security, 391; on stag dinners, 196, 1568–69; telephones message for Macmillan, 644–45; and toys from Marx, 1099–1100; tracks down Koger, 1097–98; tracks down Turner, 1105–6; and Trendex poll on Strauss hearings, 1581–82; and U.S. flights over U.K., 872–73; on USMA class reunion, 1293–94; on *Wall Street Journal*, 902; and Whitney's letter, 1364–65; and Whitney's visit, 1690; and Williams's view on Pearson, 1546–47; and Witt's retirement, 1720–21; on Woodruff's health, 354–56

Whitney, Betsey Cushing (Roosevelt), 137–38; accompanies Es. to Milestone Plantation, 13–14; background, 13–14; chats with Mamie E., 313–14; on E.'s painting, 202; health of, 1063–64, 1148; on sweaters for Mamie E., 1651–52; vacations at Fishers Island, 313–14; visits Culzean, 200–201, 202–3; visits White House, 662–63

Whitney, George: background, 1049; on monetary system reforms, 2059–60; on post for, 1049

Whitney, John Hay ("Jock"), 1603; accompa-

Saud, 32–33; on E.'s "rebuke" of, in National Guard dispute, 32–33; on exchange of restricted data, 39–40; and force reductions in ROK, 387–88; and Gavin, 1043–44; and IRBM agreement with U.K., 729–30; on IRBM/ICBM programs, 162–63, 292–93, 347–49; and land use on military bases in Puerto Rico, 372–73; McElroy succeeds, 477–78; on McNamara, 211; and modernization of weaponry in ROK, 314–16; and overtime work in missile production, 496–97; portrait of, 1107–8; on reducing duplication in missile program, 496–97; retires, 477–78; scores Army missile plan, 347–49; scores National Guard, 32–33; on selecting chiefs of MAAGs, 131–32; visits Bohemian Grove, 350–51; visits E. at Augusta, 32–33; works to reduce military budget, 589–91. *See also* Defense, Department of

Wilson, Donald Malcolm, 933–34
Wilson, Jessie Ann (Curtis), 32–33
Wilson, John, 2128
Wilson, Priscilla, 2128
Wilson, Richard Lawson, 490
Wilson, Robert Carleton, 1562–63
Wilson, Thomas Woodrow, 1369; background, 139, 140; and difficulties following Mexican Revolution, 279–80; inauguration of, 9; Lawrence's article on, 1619; and question of presidential disability, 138–40, 711–14; suffers stroke, 140, 711–14

Winchell, Walter, 1755
Wind, Herbert Warren, 611
Windward Islands, and Federation of British West Indies, 317–19
Winn, F. Bliss, 1788–89
Wisconsin, 274–75; fishing in, 716–17; special election in, 396–99, 432–34
Witt, Edgar E., 1720–21
Witwer, Samuel W., 2110
Womack Army Hospital, 1097–98
Women, 467–68; and appointees to Civil Service Commission, 1036–37; as appointees to federal posts, 1036–37; E. on appreciation to Republican women, 1925–26; as Cabinet appointees, 1256–58; on conference of women's groups, 530–31; equal rights for, 437–38; on heifer from press women, 186; and League of Women Voters, 142–43; and political candidates, 1942; and Trendex Poll on Strauss hearings, 1581–82; and TV panel with GOP women, 1182–83, 2127–28, 2128, 2130–31

Woodruff, George W., 1913
Woodruff, Nell (Hodgson), 2231, 2232
Woodruff, Robert Winship: background, 219; on civil rights legislation, 354–56; on Cokes for ABA-BBA party, 2077–78; on Cokes for Newport staff, 2077–78; on Dud-

ley, 354–56; on E.'s Coca-Cola drinking style, 1776–77; E. recommends, to Civil Rights Commission, 392–94; on foreign aid, E.'s view, 354–56; on George's death, 354–56; and Goals Commission, 1812–13; health of, 354–56, 381; and Humphrey's cracker barrel for Augusta, 582–83; at Ichuaway Plantation, 1349–50; joins E. at Milestone Plantation, 1349–50; on Kennedy's appointments, E.'s view, 2230–32; on McGill's writings, E.'s view, 2230–32; meets with E., 381; on Mueller and BAC, 1589; on Mueller as Secretary of Commerce, 1589; on mutual security, E.'s view, 381; and painting for Fairless, 1623; recommends Rouse for treasury post, 380–81; on Rogers's talk, 1337; sends "What is a Quail Hunter?" 2230–32; and Sibley/Lanham letters on mutual security, 391; on special interest groups, 1583–84; on TVA legislation, 1583–84

Woods, Rose Mary: background, 1151; on Nixon and NAACP, 2052–53; and Nixon's nomination, 2018–19; and Rockefeller-Nixon antagonism, 1632–34
Wool industry, on wool tariff issue with Great Britain, 265–67. *See also* Raw materials
Work Projects Administration (WPA), mission of, 760–65
Works Progress Administration (WPA). *See* Work Projects Administration
World Bank: and Aswan Dam project, 408–10; and economic aid to Ghana, 637–39; and International Development Association, 1073–76; meets in New Delhi, 1143–44; and U.S. aid to free world economy, 1073–76; and U.S. aid to Latin America, 1488–91, 2211–13; and Volta River Project, 2162–63. *See also* International Bank for Reconstruction and Development
World peace: Bulganin's proposals on, 649–59; and Carnegie Foundation for International Peace, 1279–81; E.'s commitment to, 1787–88; an end in itself, 797–99; on E., Nehru as leaders for, 596; Hoffman speaks on, 671–72; and Institute of War and Peace Studies, 1279–81; López Mateos commends E., 1784–85; Moore's view, 2020–21; not in arms alone, 1875–76; Paul proposes "Institute of Peace," 1279–81; and peace/disarmament letter to world leaders, 579–80; on peaceful air passage, 1976–77; on peace-oriented publicity, 686–87; and role of American Red Cross, 1152–53; on rule of law for peace project, 1038–39, 1279–81; and spiritual values, 1248–49; Sulzberger's editorial on, 1319–21; on U.S.-Soviet cooperation for, 1003–7; waging of, in U.S., 649–59; Wallace's view, 1631–32. *See also* Cold war; Free world

World's Fair of 1964, 1726–27

World War I: and Argonne battle, 951; and Pact of Paris, 726, 727; and Passchendaele, 1747; and public opinion, 1572; and Verdun, 1747; and Vimy Ridge, 1747

World War II, 933–34; on aggressions in 1930s, 988–90, 1003–7; on air defense coordination in, 1785–87; and Alanbrooke's diary, 689–91, 1295–98, 1731–32; and Alexander, 2180–88; and anniversary of fall of Bataan, 825; and ANVIL, 2180–88; Branch recalls day in Rheims, 423–24; on British-American history of, 1820–21, 2180–88; and Chambers, 2180–88; and Churchill, 2180–88; and Combined Chiefs of Staff, 1852–54; and communist subjugation of satellite states, 512–16; and conservation of human resources, 68–69; and Cossack Plan (COSSAC), 2180–88; and creation of U.N., 1034–36; on crossing the Rhine, 689–91, 1295–98, 1653–54, 2180–88; and Danish shipping case, 414–15; and D-Day, 2180–88; and de Gaulle, 917; and de Guingand, 2180–88; on distorted history of, 1271–73, 1295–98; and Dodecanese plan, 2180–88; and DRAGOON, 2180–88; and drive to Berlin, 1220, 1295–98, 1653–54, 2180–88; on E., Murphy's service in Algeria, 1715–16; on E.'s postwar tour, 1746–56; on E. as presidential candidate, 1746–56; E.'s pride in success, 1746–56; E. recalls Macmillan in Algiers, 1852–54; E.'s recollections of, 1303, 1307, 2180–88; and E.'s recollections of Alanbrooke, 689–91, 2180–88; and E.'s restored 1942 Cadillac, 77–78; France honors Churchill, 1192–93; and French deterioration following, 952–60; and Gale, 2180–88; and German surrender, 1746–56; and human suffering inflicted by Nazism, 1887–90; on inflation following, 419–23, 423–24, 440–41; and Ismay's memoir, 2180–88; and liberation of Paris, 978–79, 1969–70; and lingering fear of Japan, 1517–19; and map table for E., 502–3; and Mannheim, 2180–88; and MARKET-GARDEN, 2180–88; and Marshall, 2180–88; and Mediterranean operations, 2180–88; on Memorial Chapel at St. Paul's Cathedral, 1220–21; and Monty's memoir, 303–7, 1203–4, 1220, 1247–48, 1295–98, 1820–21; and Monty's preposterous proposal, 1653–54, 2180–88; and Morgan, 2180–88; on narrow v. broad front, 2180–88; and Ninth U.S. Army, 2180–88; occupation, following, 1746–56; and overlord, 1295–98, 2180–88; and "pencil thrust," 2180–88; and postwar issues, 649–59; on prewar appeasement, 1003–7, 1017–19; and Remagen, 2180–88; and re-

turn of vested German assets, 170–71; on reunions with comrades, 1271–73, 1274–76, 1295–98, 1303, 1508–9, 1519, 1523, 1547–49, 1558–59, 1620–21, 1623–25, 1625, 1634–35, 1820–21; and Ruhr envelopment, 2180–88; and Ridgway's Airborne Corps, 2180–88; and Roosevelt, 1027–31, 2180–88; and SLEDGEHAMMER, 2180–88; and Smith, 2180–88; and Soviet domination of satellite countries, 1164–65; and Tedder, 2180–88; and TORCH, 562, 1715–16, 2180–88; and Unknown Soldier, 892; on U.S.-U.K. cooperation, 1247–48, 2180–88; Victory Order of the Day, 1730–31, 1731–32. See also Montgomery, Bernard Law

World War III: prevention of, through mutual security program, 415–17; prospects of, 1901–2; and use of atomic weaponry, 1092–93

Wormser, Felix Edgar: background, 883; on U.S.-Canada free trade, 883; on U.S. monetary system reforms, 2059–60

Wright, Clement Hale, 479–80

Wright, Loyd, 1333

Wright Report, and waivers of non-immigrant visas, 1333–34

Wriston, Henry Merritt: article by, pleases E., 1965–67; background, 218–19; chairs Goals Commission, 1812–13; on freedom v. security, 1965–67; heads American Assembly, 218–19; on Hotchkis's suggestion, 508–9; invites Humphrey on American Assembly board, 218–19; lectures at Bowdoin College, 1965–67; and patronage appointments, 1537–38; proposes foreign service training, 1537–38; on representation allowances, 1537–38; visits E., 218–19

Wyche, Ira Thomas ("Bill"), 506

Wyeth, Andrew, 1780

Yalta Conference, and Eastern European states, 649–59

Yasin, Yusuf Sheikh, 53–55

Yates, Charles R. ("Charlie"): background, 1087; on bridge with E., 1812–13; Democrat supports GOP fundraiser, 1684–85; on E.'s busy agenda, 1582–83; as E.'s golf partner at Augusta, 1709–10; longs for golf at Augusta, 1582–83

Yale University, 606–7

Ydígoras Fuentes, Miguel: background, 1292–93; on U.S. aid for Guatemala, 1292–93, 2086–88. See also Guatemala, Republic of

Yeh, George Kung-chao, 1139–41

Yemen, Republic of: and Aden, 104; Soviet assistance to, 104

Yost, Charles Woodruff: background, 93; and Egyptian-Israeli dispute, 91–93; and